THE OXFORD HANDBOOK OF

EMPIRICAL AESTHETICS

OXFORD LIBRARY OF PSYCHOLOGY

The Oxford Handbook of Parenting and Moral Development
Edited by Deborah J. Laible, Gustavo Carlo, Laura M. Padilla Walker

The Oxford Handbook of Stigma, Discrimination, and Health
Edited by Brenda Major, John F. Dovidio, and Bruce G. Link

The Oxford Handbook of Deaf Studies in Learning and Cognition
Edited by Marc Marschark and Harry Knoors

The Oxford Handbook of Empirical Aesthetics
Edited by Marcos Nadal and Oshin Vartanian

The Oxford Handbook of 4E Cognition
Edited by Albert Newen, Leon De Bruin, and Shaun Gallagher

The Oxford Handbook of Attention
Edited by Anna C. Nobre and Sabine Kastner

The Oxford Handbook of Clinical Child and Adolescent Psychology
Edited by Thomas H. Ollendick, Susan W. White, and Bradley A. White

The Oxford Handbook of Group Creativity and Innovation
Edited by Paul B. Paulus and Bernard A. Nijstad

The Oxford Handbook of Organizational Citizenship Behavior
Edited by Philip M. Podsakoff, Scott B. MacKenzie, and Nathan P. Podsakoff

The Oxford Handbook of Digital Technologies and Mental Health
Edited by Marc N. Potenza, Kyle Faust, David Faust

The Oxford Handbook of Sexual and Gender Minority Mental Health
Edited by Esther D. Rothblum

The Oxford Handbook of Psychological Situations
Edited by John F. Rauthmann, Ryne Sherman, and David C. Funder

The Oxford Handbook of Human Motivation, 2e
Edited by Richard Ryan

The Oxford Handbook of Integrative Health Science
Edited by Carol D. Ryff and Robert F. Krueger

The Oxford Handbook of Positive Psychology, 3e
Edited by C.R. Snyder, Shane J. Lopez, Lisa M. Edwards, and Susana C. Marques

The Oxford Handbook of Dialectical Behaviour Therapy
Edited by Michaela A. Swales

The Oxford Handbook of Music and the Brain
Edited by Michael H. Thaut and Donald A. Hodges

The Oxford Handbook of Expertise
Edited by Paul Ward, Jan Maarten Schraagen, Julie Gore, and Emilie M. Roth

The Oxford Handbook of Singing
Edited by Graham F. Welch, David M. Howard, and John Nix

The Oxford Handbook of Evolutionary Psychology and Behavioral Endocrinology
Edited by Lisa L. M. Welling and Todd K. Shackelford

The Oxford Handbook of Autism and Co-Occurring Psychiatric Conditions
Edited by Susan W. White, Brenna B. Maddox, and Carla A. Mazefsky

The Oxford Handbook of Adolescent Substance Abuse
Edited by Robert A. Zucker and Sandra A. Brown

THE OXFORD HANDBOOK OF

EMPIRICAL AESTHETICS

Edited by

MARCOS NADAL

OSHIN VARTANIAN

OXFORD

UNIVERSITY PRESS

OXFORD
UNIVERSITY PRESS

Great Clarendon Street, Oxford, OX2 6DP,
United Kingdom

Oxford University Press is a department of the University of Oxford.
It furthers the University's objective of excellence in research, scholarship,
and education by publishing worldwide. Oxford is a registered trade mark of
Oxford University Press in the UK and in certain other countries

© Oxford University Press 2022

The moral rights of the authors have been asserted

First Edition published in 2022

Impression: 1

Published in the United States of America by Oxford University Press
198 Madison Avenue, New York, NY 10016, United States of America

British Library Cataloguing in Publication Data

Data available

Library of Congress Control Number: 2022935324

ISBN 978–0–19–882435–0

DOI: 10.1093/oxfordhb/9780198824350.001.0001

Printed and bound by
CPI Group (UK) Ltd, Croydon, CR0 4YY

ADVANCE PRAISE

A must-have for those interested in the psychology of aesthetics, the arts, and subjective experiences that in the past have defied empirical investigation.

ROBERT J. Sternberg,
Professor of Psychology,
Cornell University, USA

How do we respond to and evaluate works of art? How is our response shaped by biology, culture, and/or personality? What methods are used to answer such questions empirically? For all researchers in the field of empirical aesthetics, and for readers outside the field interested in art and the mind, this handbook is an essential resource.

Ellen Winner
Professor Emerita of Psychology, Boston College, USA
Senior Research Associate, Project Zero, Harvard Graduate School of Education, USA
Author of *How Art Works: A Psychological Exploration* (OUP, 2019)

In 1871 Gustav Theodor Fechner conceived of an experimental aesthetics, studying art from below rather than above, using empirical not philosophical methods, studying what *is* liked rather than what *should* be liked. *The Oxford Handbook of Empirical Aesthetics* comprehensively summarises progress in realising Fechner's vision.

Chris McManus,
Professor of Psychology,
University College London, UK

Filled to the brim with chapters on every imaginable aspect of the exciting and expanding field of empirical aesthetics. Overseen by masterful editors, this book is required reading for any scholar of the arts.

James C. Kaufman,
Professor of Educational Psychology,
University of Connecticut, USA

Preface

MARCOS NADAL AND OSHIN VARTANIAN

The *Madonna des Bürgermeisters Jacob Meyer zum Hasen*, painted by Hans Holbein the Younger in 1526, sold for about $75 million on July 12, 2011, becoming Germany's most expensive artwork at the time (Gropp, 2011). Not only is it regarded among the greatest German Renaissance paintings, the *Madonna* sparked one of the fiercest and most consequential controversies in art history, and motivated Gustav Theodor Fechner to use empirical methods to study the appreciation of art. In doing so, he founded empirical aesthetics.

In 1743, the Dresden Gemäldegalerie acquired Hans Holbein's *Madonna des Bürgermeisters Jacob Meyer zum Hasen*. This was no small addition to its collection for, at the time, it was considered the greatest painting in German art, equal to Raphael's *Sistine Madonna*. It must have come as a shock when, in 1821, a second version surfaced in a private collection in Darmstadt. The question of which version was the authentic Holbein, and which the copy, quickly became a national controversy. What began as a dispute among academics soon flared into a full-blown political affair, entangled with ideological passions (Bader, 2018b). Artists and academic art historians competed for the authority to decide on the works' authenticity. Each side rolled out countless essays and pamphlets, printed and distributed reproductions of the paintings accompanied by analyses, arguments, and counterarguments, and spoke at conferences and exhibitions.

Fechner had been interested in the Holbein *Madonna* controversy at least since shortly after publishing his *Elements of Psychophysics* (Fechner, 1860). He compiled, presented, and discussed the history of the conflict and the two sides to it (Fechner, 1871a), and he plunged into it himself with several iconographic analyses (Fechner, 1866a-b, 1868, 1870a-b). In his opinion, both were authentic paintings by Holbein, but they expressed two different meanings. He thought that Holbein painted the Darmstadt version first, and intended it for a chapel, and the Dresden version later, and intended it for the family home (Fechner, 1870a). Fechner concluded that the Dresden version was a votive work, and that the sick-looking infant was an amalgamation of the Christ Child and the donor's ill child (Fechner, 1866b). Later, he speculated that the oldest woman in the painting was Meyer's deceased first wife, and that the figure of the Madonna was the portrait of one of Meyer's deceased daughters carrying her sick son (Fechner, 1868).

The way to settle the conflict, it was finally agreed, was to exhibit the two paintings together. So, in 1869, the plans began for a Holbein retrospective exhibition that would feature, for the first time ever, both versions of the *Madonna* side by side. The exhibition had to be postponed, however, because of the Franco-Prussian war (July 19, 1870 – January 28, 1871). The exhibition had been on Fechner's mind while writing his monograph *On Experimental Aesthetics*, published in early 1871. Fechner (1871b) devoted much of it to arguing for the use of empirical methods in the study of aesthetics. He made his point mainly in reference to the pleasure of simple forms. But he also believed that the methods of empirical aesthetics could be used to study art, especially in the case of comparable artworks that have led to unresolved disputes among connoisseurs. He explicitly mentioned the two versions of Holbein's *Madonna* as the sort of case to which his new methods could be applied. He expected that the joint exhibition would add fuel to the conflict about authenticity without necessarily settling it. His experimental aesthetics, however, could answer a different, more fertile, question: which of the two versions is more preferred aesthetically by people in general, or by experts vs. laypeople, or by men vs. women? (Fechner, 1871b).

Finally, the peace treaty was signed in May 1871, and the plans for the exhibition moved forward. It took place from August 15 to October 15, 1871, in Dresden's recently built Prinzen Pavillion. By the time's standards, it was massive. On display were over 500 items, including paintings, woodcuts, drawings, and photographs, lent from over 60 museums, galleries, and private collections from over 40 European cities. It was the first time masterpieces had been transported across frontiers for an exhibition on such a scale; the first time an art exhibition had been promoted by art history academics, and not aristocrats, nobility, governments, or artist associations (Haskell, 2000); and the first time the paintings were seen side by side. Alfred Richard Diether, artist and teacher at the School of Arts and Crafts, captured the interest of the exhibition's visitors for the *Madonnas* in the pencil and watercolor image on the cover of this book. The exhibition catalogue included a bibliography of over 70 publications on the controversy compiled by Fechner (Bader, 2018b), showing just how absorbed in the controversy he had become.

The exhibition committee allowed Fechner to conduct the research on the visitors' preferences he had been planning for a year. In the hall where the two paintings were exhibited, he placed an announcement of his study, a table and necessary writing materials, the instructions for participants, and a booklet with space for the visitors to write their answers. The scene, sketched by the renowned German painter Adolph Menzel in his pocketbook, as "Plebiscite table" (Figure 1), was certainly an unusual one to see at a museum. The art historians at the exhibition dismissed Fechner's study, for the issue of aesthetic value could only confound the issue of authenticity (Bätschmann, 1996). In an analysis of the role that the Holbein exhibition at Dresden played in the forging of art history as an academic discipline, Bader (2018a) recounts the skeptical remarks of one of the most eminent Holbein scholars: "Off to one side, on a writing desk, can be found a pen, a large book, and a placard above it. Professor Fechner, the highly-regarded physicist in Leipzig (...) intends to enable a decision between the two pictures on the basis of universal suffrage" (Bader, 2018a, p. 7).

The instructions asked the visitors to state which of the two *Madonnas* made such an appealing and positive impression as to grant it a place in their room for constant or repeated contemplation. Fechner asked them to disregard the artworks' deterioration caused by the darkening varnish and other conservation defects. The visitors were also asked to write their name, title, position, and place of residence, and had space to make open remarks about the comparison and the reasons for their responses (Fechner, 1872).

Fechner's analysis of the responses showed that the visitors generally preferred the Darmstadt *Madonna*. But he was, nevertheless, disappointed with the outcome of the study. Of the 11,842 visitors to the exhibition, only 113 answered his survey, and many of them clearly did not understand the goal of the study or the instructions. He devoted much of his report to outlining the improvements to the methods and instructions that were required for similar studies in the future (Fechner, 1872). On top of this, art-historical research on the two paintings later proved that Fechner's iconographic analyses were wrong. The Darmstadt *Madonna* was the only authentic Holbein and the Dresden *Madonna* was a copy of the original, painted over a century after the original (1635/1637) by Bartholomäus Sarburgh (Bader, 2018b).

Fechner's disappointing experiment and his incorrect iconographic analyses of the *Madonnas* should not overshadow the magnitude of his achievements in 1871. First, by finding value in the public's reception and appreciation of art, he broke with the tradition that considered that the only legitimate value of art could be set by experts and academics. Second, he showed that understanding the way laypeople appreciate art was worthy of scientific study, and that such a study should and could be pursued with empirical methods. Third, he was the first to collect data on the aesthetic appreciation of art from over 100 people, to use statistical techniques to determine the aesthetic value of artworks for the whole sample, to study the impact of individual variables, such as sex and expertise, and to study aesthetic appreciation in a public space (Leder, 2005). So, it was at the greatest art exhibition of his time, absorbed in the most resounding and long-lasting dispute on an artwork's authenticity, in the presence of a masterpiece of German art, and amid skepticism, misunderstanding, and disappointment, that Fechner sowed the seeds of the new field of empirical aesthetics.

One hundred and fifty years have passed since the Dresden exhibition, and empirical aesthetics has come a long way. The first steps were uncertain and, early on, the prospects were not very encouraging at all. Titchener (1910) saw very little progress in empirical aesthetics in his survey of the major advances in psychology between 1900 and 1910, and wrote that "No doubt, the time is still distant, if indeed it is fated to arrive at all, when experimental aesthetics shall bear to a *System der Aesthetik* the relation that experimental now sustains to systematic psychology" (Titchener, 1910, p. 419). In contrast, he reported a resurgence and extension of psychophysics during the very same period (Titchener, 1910). Psychologists were still conducting all manner of experiments to probe the effects of differential increments on sensation 50 years after Fechner's (1860) *Psychophysics*, but they had only conducted a handful of studies on aesthetic appreciation, mostly on the effects of the proportions of simple geometrical forms, 34 years after Fechner's (1876) *Aesthetics*. Psychologists' interest in the two fields founded by Fechner could hardly have been more unalike. But why?

The reason, in Santayana's (1896) words, was that:

> The moderns, also, even within the field of psychology, have studied first the function of perception and the theory of knowledge, by which we seem to be informed about external things; they have in comparison neglected the exclusively subjective and human department of imagination and emotion. We have still to recognize in practice the truth that from these despised feelings of ours the great world of perception derives all its value, if not also its existence.
>
> (Santayana, 1896, p. 3)

So, psychologists preferred to study the *scaling* of sensation (psychophysics) because they believed it reflected objective facts about the world, rather than the *value* of sensation (aesthetics) because they believed it reflected only the feelings of the observer.

However, with functionalist psychology, the focus of inquiry began shifting from the mechanisms of sensation to the functions of sensation. From the point of view of functionalism, psychophysics' study of valueless sensation made little sense. Organisms do not sense the world for the mere point of determining the intensity of stimulation. They sense it to value the options it offers, and to determine the most advantageous course of action. There is no sensing for the sake of sensing. Psychologists, and also neuroscientists, became more interested in sensory values, in the role that pleasantness and unpleasantness play in the adaptation of individuals and species to their environment, and began studying things like reward value and motivation.

Following the trail of new findings and new methods of psychology and neuroscience, in the past century empirical aesthetics has amassed a wealth of knowledge on the psychological and neurobiological process involved in aesthetic valuation: liking, beauty, preference, attractiveness, and so on. Most research has traditionally focused on the visual aesthetics of figures, shapes, and paintings, or on the auditory aesthetics of music. But the past 20 years have witnessed a surge in empirical studies on the aesthetics of language and poetry, of movement and dance, of interior and exterior architecture, of design and consumer products, and of the presentation of food on dishes.

Empirical aesthetics is thriving like never before, expanding at a fast pace and diversifying in many directions. We felt the time was right for a comprehensive and balanced handbook. We believe the field will benefit greatly from a single source that takes stock of the field; that brings together and organizes current knowledge on a diversity of topics, and uses it as a springboard for imagining its future. Our intention was to produce a handbook that can be used both as an aid for teaching the next generation of empirical aestheticians and as a tool for research.

We have grouped the chapters into seven broad sections. The reason is purely organizational, not because we believe that these represent separate issues. In fact, they reflect the inseparable components of empirical aesthetics: an object that is valued, a person that does the valuing, and a context in which the valuation takes place. The eight chapters in Section 1 provide the historical, conceptual, biological, and evolutionary foundations of empirical aesthetics. Section 2 includes nine chapters on the basic methods of empirical aesthetics, from the historiometric to noninvasive brain stimulation. The seven chapters in Section 3 focus on the object features that have traditionally been the main focus of empirical aesthetics. Section 4 includes eight chapters on the aesthetic appreciation of different art forms, including music, dance, architecture, film, poetry, and narrative. The six chapters in Section 5 turn inwards to the person, and examine the role of cognition, personality, age, expertise, aesthetic sensitivity, and cultural background in aesthetic appreciation. Section 6 includes five chapters that focus on the context of aesthetic experience, from laboratories to everyday situations, and to museums. Finally, Section 7 incudes three chapters on the application of empirical aesthetics to design, consumer products, and dining.

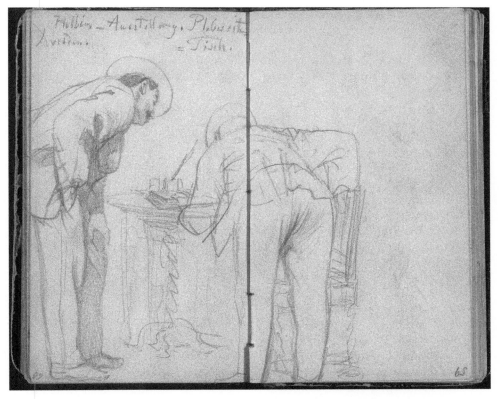

FIGURE 1. Adolph Menzel, Holbein-Ausstellung, Plebiscit-Tisch, Dresden. Ident. Nr. SZ Menzel Skb.36, S.59/60 © Photo: Kupferstichkabinett der Staatlichen Museen zu Berlin – Preußischer Kulturbesitz. Fotograf/in: Wolfram Büttner. Reproduced with permission.

The editors of this volume would like to express their deepest gratitude to the authors for the time, diligence, and care they have put into each of the chapters that make up this book. Contributions to handbooks are not valued nearly enough by academic performance metrics. We would also like to thank Charlotte Holloway, Laura Heston, and Martin Baum at Oxford University Press, whose commitment, guidance, and support from beginning to end made this handbook a reality.

References

Bader, L. (2018a). Artists versus art historians? Conflicting interpretations in the Holbein controversy. *Journal of Art Historiography, 19*, 1–23.

Bader, L. (2018b). The Holbein exhibition of 1871—an iconic turning point for art history. In M. W. Gahtan & D. Pegazzano (Eds.), *Monographic exhibitions and the history of art* (pp. 129–142). New York, NY: Routledge.

Bätschmann, O. (1996). Der Holbein-Streit: eine Krise der Kunstgeschichte. *Jahrbuch Der Berliner Museen, 38*, 87–100.

Fechner, G. T. (1860). *Elemente der Psychophysik.* Leipzig: Breitkopf und Härtel.

Fechner, G. T. (1866a). Die historischen Quellen und Verhandlungen über die Holbein'sche Madonna: Monographisch zusammengestellt und discutirt. *Archiv Für Die Zeichnenden Künste, 12*, 193–266.

Fechner, G. T. (1866b). Vorbesprechung über die Dentungsfrage der Holbein'schen Madonna mit Rücksicht auf die Handzeiclmung Nr. 65 des Baseler Museum. *Archiv Für Die Zeichnenden Künste, 12*, 1–30.

Fechner, G. T. (1868). Nachtrag zu den drei Abhandlungen über die Holbein'sche (Meier'sche) Madonna. *Archiv Für Die Zeichnenden Künste, 14*, 149–187.

Fechner, G. T. (1870a). Der Streit um die beiden Madonnen von Holbein. *Die Grenzboten. Zeitschrift Fur Politik Und Literatur, 2*, 1–18.

Fechner, G. T. (1870b). Ueber das Holbein'sche Votivbild mit dem Bürgermeister Schwartz in Augsburg. *Archiv Für Die Zeichnenden Künste, 16*, 1–39.

Fechner, G. T. (1871a). *Ueber die Aechtheitsfrage der Holbein'schen Madonna. Discussion un Acten.* Leipzig: Breitkopf und Härtel.

Fechner, G. T. (1871b). *Zur experimentalen Aesthetik.* Leipzig: Hirzel.

Fechner, G. T. (1872). *Bericht über das auf der Dresdner Holbein-ausstellung ausgelegte Album.* Leipzig: Breitkopf und Härtel.

Fechner, G. T. (1876). *Vorschule der Ästhetik.* Leipzig: Breitkopf und Härtel.

Gropp, R.-M. (2011, July 14). Holbein—Madonna. Deutschlands teuerstes Kunstwerk. *Frankfurter Allgemeine Zeitung.*

Haskell, F. (2000). *The Ephemeral Museum: Old Master Paintings and the Rise of the Art Exhibition.* New Haven, CT: Yale University Press.

Leder, H. (2005). Zur Psychologie der Rezeption moderner Kunst. In B. Graf & A. B. Müller (Eds.), *Sichtweisen. Zur veränderten Wahrnehmung von Objekten in Museen* (pp. 79–90). Berlin: VS Verlag für Sozialwissenschaften.

Santayana, G. (1896). *The sense of beauty. Being the outline of aesthetic theory.* New York: Charles Scribner's Sons.

Titchener, E. B. (1910). The past decade in experimental psychology. *The American Journal of Psychology, 21*, 404–421.

Contents

List of Contributors   xvii

SECTION 1. FOUNDATIONS

1. Empirical Aesthetics: An Overview   3
   MARCOS NADAL AND OSHIN VARTANIAN

2. One Hundred Years of Empirical Aesthetics:
   Fechner to Berlyne (1876–1976)   39
   MARCOS NADAL AND ESTHER UREÑA

3. Revisiting Fechner's Methods   83
   GESCHE WESTPHAL-FITCH

4. The Link Between Empirical Aesthetics and Philosophy   99
   WILLIAM P. SEELEY

5. Appreciation Modes in Empirical Aesthetics   116
   ROLF REBER

6. Exploring the Landscape of Emotion in Aesthetic Experience   136
   GERALD C. CUPCHIK

7. The Neurobiology of Sensory Valuation   150
   MARTIN SKOV

8. The Evolution of Aesthetics and Beauty   183
   DAHLIA W. ZAIDEL

SECTION 2. METHODS

9. Historiometric Methods   199
   DEAN KEITH SIMONTON

10. Observation Method in Empirical Aesthetics   219
    PABLO P. L. TINIO AND EVA SPECKER

11. Observational Drawing Research Methods   235
    JUSTIN OSTROFSKY

12. Implicit Measures in the Aesthetic Domain   256
    LETIZIA PALUMBO

13. The Study of Eye Movements in Empirical Aesthetics   273
    PAUL LOCHER

14. Electrophysiology   291
    THOMAS JACOBSEN AND STINA KLEIN

15. Functional Neuroimaging in Empirical Aesthetics and
    Neuroaesthetics   308
    TOMOHIRO ISHIZU

16. Noninvasive Brain Stimulation: Contribution to Research in
    Neuroaesthetics   339
    ZAIRA CATTANEO

17. Integrated Methods: A Call for Integrative and Interdisciplinary
    Aesthetics Research   359
    MARTIN TRÖNDLE, STEVEN GREENWOOD, CHANDRASEKHAR
    RAMAKRISHNAN, FOLKERT UHDE, HAUKE EGERMANN, AND WOLFGANG
    TSCHACHER

SECTION 3. OBJECT FEATURES

18. The Role of Collative Variables in Aesthetic Experiences   385
    MANUELA M. MARIN

19. Processing Fluency   430
    MICHAEL FORSTER

20. The Use of Visual Statistical Features in Empirical Aesthetics   447
    DANIEL GRAHAM

21. Color   475
    OSHIN VARTANIAN

22. The Study of Symmetry in Empirical Aesthetics   488
    MARCO BERTAMINI AND GIULIA RAMPONE

23. The Curvature Effect   510
    GUIDO CORRADI AND ENRIC MUNAR

24. Facial Attractiveness   533
    ALEKSANDRA MITROVIC AND JÜRGEN GOLLER

SECTION 4. ARTFORMS

25. The Empirical Aesthetics of Music   573
    ELVIRA BRATTICO

26. The Aesthetics of Action and Movement   605
    EMILY S. CROSS AND ANDREA ORLANDI

27. Aesthetics of Dance   623
    BEATRIZ CALVO-MERINO

28. The Audio-Visual Aesthetics of Music and Dance   638
    GUIDO ORGS AND CLAIRE HOWLIN

29. Aesthetic Responses to Architecture   660
    ALEXANDER COBURN AND ANJAN CHATTERJEE

30. Aesthetics, Technology, and Popular Movies   682
    JAMES E. CUTTING

31. Empirical Aesthetics of Poetry   704
    WINFRIED MENNINGHAUS AND STEFAN BLOHM

32. Aesthetic Responses to the Characters, Plots, Worlds, and Style of
    Stories   721
    MARTA M. MASLEJ, JOSHUA A. QUINLAN, AND RAYMOND A. MAR

SECTION 5. THE PERSON

33. The Role of Attention, Executive Processes, and Memory in
    Aesthetic Experience   751
    JOHN W. MULLENNIX

34. Children's Appreciation of Art   770
    THALIA R. GOLDSTEIN

35. The Influence of Expertise on Aesthetics   787
    AARON KOZBELT

36. The Influence of Personality on Aesthetic Preferences   820
    VIREN SWAMI AND ADRIAN FURNHAM

37. Aesthetic Sensitivity   834
    NILS MYSZKOWSKI

38. Cross-Cultural Empirical Aesthetics   853
    XIAOLEI SUN AND JIAJIA CHE

SECTION 6. THE CONTEXT

39. The General Impact of Context on Aesthetic Experience   885
    MATTHEW PELOWSKI AND EVA SPECKER

40. Empirical Aesthetics: Context, Extra Information, and Framing   921
    HELMUT LEDER AND MATTHEW PELOWSKI

41. Studying Empirical Aesthetics in Museum Contexts   943
    JEFFREY K. SMITH AND LISA F. SMITH

42. Aesthetic Experience in Everyday Environments   960
    PAUL J. SILVIA AND KATHERINE N. COTTER

43. The Impact of the Social Context on Aesthetic Experience   973
    STEFANO MASTANDREA

SECTION 7. APPLICATIONS

44. Design and Aesthetics   993
    PAUL HEKKERT

45. The Role of Empirical Aesthetics in Consumer Behavior   1010
    VANESSA M. PATRICK AND HENRIK HAGTVEDT

46. On the Empirical Aesthetics of Plating   1027
    CHARLES SPENCE

Index   1053

List of Contributors

Marco Bertamini, Università di Padova, Italy

Stefan Blohm, Radboud University, Netherlands

Elvira Brattico, Aarhus University, Denmark

Zaira Cattaneo, University of Bergamo, Italy

Anjan Chatterjee, University of Pennsylvania, USA

Jiajia Che, University of the Balearic Islands, Spain

Alex Coburn, University of Cambridge, UK

Guido Corradi, University of the Balearic Islands, Spain

Katherine N. Cotter, University of Pennsylvania, USA

Emily S. Cross, Macquarie University, Australia and University of Glasgow, UK

Gerald C. Cupchik, University of Toronto, Canada

James E. Cutting, Cornell University, USA

Hauke Egermann, Zeppelin University, Germany

Michael Forster, University of Vienna, Austria

Adrian Furnham, Norwegian Business School, Norway

Thalia R. Goldstein, George Mason University, USA

Jürgen Goller, University of Vienna, Austria

Daniel Graham, Hobart and William Smith Colleges, USA

Steven Greenwood, Zeppelin University, Germany

Henrik Hagtvedt, Boston College, USA

Paul Hekkert, Delft University of Technology, The Netherlands

Claire Howlin, Trinity College Dublin, Ireland

Tomohiro Ishizu, Kansai University, Japan

Thomas Jacobsen, Helmut Schmidt University/University of the Federal Armed Forces Hamburg, Germany

Stina Klein, Helmut Schmidt University/University of the Federal Armed Forces Hamburg, Germany

Aaron Kozbelt, Brooklyn College, City University of New York, USA

Helmut Leder, University of Vienna, Austria

Paul Locher, Montclair State University, USA

Raymond A. Mar, York University, Canada

Manuela M. Marin, University of Vienna, Austria

Stefano Mastandrea, Roma Tre University, Italy

Marta M. Maslej, The Centre for Addiction and Mental Health, Canada

Winfried Menninghaus, Max Planck Institute for Empirical Aesthetics, Germany

Beatriz Calvo-Merino, City University of London, UK

Aleksandra Mitrovic, University of Vienna, Austria

John W. Mullennix, University of Pittsburgh, USA

Enric Munar, University of the Balearic Islands, Spain

Marcos Nadal, University of the Balearic Islands, Spain

Guido Orgs, Goldsmiths, University of London, UK

Andrea Orlandi, Sapienza University of Rome, Italy

Justin Ostrofsky, Stockton University, USA

Letizia Palumbo, Liverpool Hope University, UK

Vanessa M. Patrick, University of Houston, USA

Matthew Pelowski, University of Vienna, Austria

Joshua A. Quinlan, York University, Canada

Chandrasekhar Ramakrishnan, Zeppelin University, Germany

Giulia Rampone, University of Liverpool, UK

Rolf Reber, University of Oslo, Norway

William P. Seeley, University of Southern Maine

Paul J. Silvia, University of North Carolina at Greensboro, USA

Dean Keith Simonton, University of California, Davis, USA

Martin Skov, Copenhagen University Hospital Hvidovre, Denmark

Jeffrey K. Smith, University of Otago, New Zealand

Lisa F. Smith, University of Otago, New Zealand

Eva Specker, University of Vienna, Faculty of Psychology, Austria

Charles Spence, University of Oxford, UK

Xiaolei Sun, University of the Balearic Islands, Spain

Viren Swami, Anglia Ruskin University, UK, and Perdana University, Malaysia

Pablo P. L. Tinio, Montclair State University, USA

Martin Tröndle, Zeppelin University, Germany

Wolfgang Tschacher, University Bern, Switzerland

Folkert Uhde, Radialsystem V, Germany

Esther Ureña, University of the Balearic Islands, Spain

Oshin Vartanian, University of Toronto, Canada

Gesche Westphal-Fitch, University of Vienna, Austria

Dahlia W. Zaidel, University of California at Los Angeles, USA

SECTION 1

FOUNDATIONS

CHAPTER 1

EMPIRICAL AESTHETICS

An Overview

MARCOS NADAL AND OSHIN VARTANIAN

WHAT IS EMPIRICAL AESTHETICS?

GUSTAV T. Fechner (1871, 1876) had high hopes for empirical aesthetics. He expected it to evolve into a unified system of general principles of beauty and art. Fechner's empirical aesthetics, thus, had the same goals as philosophy, but it progressed in the opposite direction. Whereas philosophical aesthetics began "from above," with general principles that could then be applied to specific cases, empirical aesthetics began "from below." Aesthetics from below meant dealing first with the most basic elements and facts of aesthetics. It meant, specifically, explaining the reasons for liking and disliking particular cases, and why objects give pleasure or displeasure. From these explanations, a series of principles could then be deduced, which would eventually coalesce into a comprehensive system of beauty and the arts. Fechner, thus, conceived *empirical aesthetics as the scientific investigation of beauty and art that begins by collecting specific facts that can later be used to build up general principles and, eventually, a general system of aesthetics.*

A century later, this general system of aesthetics was still not in sight. Empirical aesthetics had not even made much progress moving from the particular cases to the general principles (see Section 2, and Nadal & Ureña, this volume). Daniel E. Berlyne summarized the achievements of a century-worth of research in empirical aesthetics as "relatively sparse and, on the whole, not profoundly enlightening" (Berlyne, 1974, p. 5). Berlyne (1971, 1974) attributed the lack of meaningful progress to unfounded assumptions, outdated theories, and obsolete methods. So, he set out to place empirical aesthetics within a general information theory and motivational framework and to develop a new suite of methods. Berlyne's (1974) "new experimental aesthetics" differed from Fechner's "old experimental aesthetics" in that it focused on properties that modified arousal levels, its explanations were grounded in motivational mechanisms, it studied nonverbal behavior as well as verbal judgments, and it did not aspire to produce an autonomous aesthetic system, but to show how aesthetic phenomena were the result of common psychological processes. As such, Berlyne (1972) conceived *empirical aesthetics as the scientific study of the motivational effects of collative properties of stimulus patterns*. More specifically, empirical aesthetics was the study of how and why structural features make stimuli appear surprising, novel, complex, or ambiguous; how they modulate arousal levels and, consequently, the stimuli's hedonic value, that is to say, their pleasurableness, reward value, and incentive value (Berlyne, 1974).

In the 50 years that have passed since Berlyne (1971) reformulated empirical aesthetics via his new experimental aesthetics, the field has grown substantially and has benefited from the addition of many new methods. Berlyne's focus on arousal-related motivational mechanisms turned out to be overly restrictive and simplistic. We now know that liking something, or finding it pleasing, beautiful, or attractive, is not merely a matter of responding to its features. We know that liking, pleasingness, beauty, and attractiveness are influenced by momentary personal factors, such as expectations, available information (Pelowski & Specker, this volume and Leder & Pelowski, this volume), attention, and memory (Mullennix, this volume), and by stable personal attributes, such as personality (Swami & Furnham, this volume), age, (Goldstein, this volume), expertise (Kozbelt, this volume), aesthetic sensitivity (Myszkowski, this volume), and cultural background (Che & Sun, this volume), among others. Even the physical context (Smith & Smith, this volume and Silvia & Cotter, this volume) and the social context (Mastandrea, this volume) can modulate assessments of liking, pleasingness, beauty, and attractiveness. Indeed, aesthetic appreciation is a good example of the contextual permeability of perception, cognition, and emotion (Bar, 2004; Mesquita, Barrett, & Smith, 2010). We also know now that aesthetic appreciation cannot be reduced to arousal-boosting or -reducing motivational mechanisms. We know it involves complex interactions between several perceptual, cognitive, and affective processes—realized in the form of top-down and bottom-up processes (Chatterjee & Vartanian, 2014; Leder, Belke, Oeberst, & Augustin, 2004; Skov, 2019). Berlyne was right when he argued that the phenomena we consider aesthetic rely on general neural and psychological mechanisms, although the data and methods available to him could not reveal the diversity and complexity of those mechanisms.

Clearly, the knowledge we have gained and the methods we have added since Berlyne (1971, 1974) refashioned empirical aesthetics, and certainly since Fechner (1871, 1876) created the domain, require broadening the definition of empirical aesthetics. The most inclusive definition would conceive *empirical aesthetics as the scientific field that uses empirical methods to study aesthetics*. Although tautological, this definition specifies the features of the knowledge empirical aesthetics seeks and generates (scientific knowledge), the kinds of methods it uses (empirical methods), and what the knowledge it seeks and generates is about (aesthetics). It avoids Fechner's promise of a general system of art and aesthetics, and Berlyne's reduction of all explanation to a single major mechanism. The scientific and empirical aspects of this definition are probably quite uncontroversial, but there will surely be disagreement among empirical aestheticians today about what aesthetics is. So, let us first see what it means that empirical aesthetics is a scientific field, and why it is that it uses empirical methods. We can then turn to the contentious issue of what aesthetics is or is not about.

Empirical aesthetics is a scientific field

Science relies on a system of procedures that generate a particular kind of knowledge about some natural (as opposed to supernatural) phenomenon. The kind of knowledge science produces is descriptive and explanatory, testable, replicable, revisable, incremental, and collective. Thus, empirical aesthetics seeks and produces a different kind of knowledge than the one philosophical aesthetics does (Seeley, this volume). What, specifically, does it entail that empirical aesthetics is a scientific domain?

- First, that, as with research in biology, medicine, and other scientific disciplines, research in empirical aesthetics occurs with the understanding that its focus of study is coextensive with the natural world. As such, research findings and inferences emerging in empirical aesthetics must be informed by and can potentially contribute to knowledge in other domains of natural science.
- Second, that empirical aesthetics generates *descriptive* knowledge by recording data as they are observed, as with surveys and questionnaires, natural observation, and central tendency and dispersion summary statistics. It also generates *explanatory* knowledge when it uses experimental methods. Experiments involve the manipulation of one or several factors and the observation of the effects on one or several outcomes under controlled conditions. Experimental control is indispensable for explanations in terms of causes and effects, and the associated ability to draw causal inferences.
- Third, it means that knowledge in empirical aesthetics is not disjointed, but assembled into scientific theories. Empirical aesthetics formulates scientific theories based on the descriptive and explanatory knowledge it generates. It uses those theories to make predictions about future results, in the form of hypotheses, and to interpret those results. Thus, the theories of empirical aesthetics should make clear and falsifiable predictions, be consistent with existing results, and make accurate predictions of new results. A good scientific theory is able to accurately describe (what), identify the underlying mechanisms (how), and interpret (why) observations in its domain (Dayan & Abbott, 2001, p. xiii).
- Fourth, it means that these descriptive and explanatory results can be—and should be—*tested* again in *replication* studies. Many tenets in empirical aesthetics, and psychology and neuroscience in general, rest only on single experiments, even though some are taught and presented in handbooks as established facts. The knowledge generated by empirical aesthetics should be reliable, but reliability is difficult to measure unless experiments are repeated and replicated. Some of these replications might confirm previous results, and support their conclusions, while others might not. Reiterated failures to replicate should lead to the rejection of

those tenets, and to new alternative explanations. In this sense, attempts at falsification must be central to the practice of the science.

- Fifth, it means that the findings in empirical aesthetics are *revisable*. It is not a weakness of scientific knowledge that it is revisable and provisional; it is one of its fundamental strengths. With revision comes progress, so the more a scientific field revises it knowledge, the faster it progresses. A scientific domain is alive when there is room for major improvements to current knowledge, but lifeless when there is little room for improvement, if that is possible at all. The revisability of scientific knowledge is what distinguishes it from dogma. Scientific dogmatism—resistance to revise ideas held on to as truths despite challenging results—has more in common with faith than with science.

- Sixth, it means that empirical aesthetics commonly progresses through the piece-meal accretion of results produced by different teams of researchers. New findings, or a reinterpretation of old ones, might occasionally make a field leap forward, and some individuals have a pivotal impact on progress, as Fechner and Berlyne undoubtedly had on empirical aesthetics. But these are the exceptions. As a rule, science is an *incremental* and *collective* endeavor.

Empirical aesthetics uses empirical methods

Empirical methods are those that produce data through observation and measurement. Empirical data are fundamental to the testability, replicability, and revisability of scientific knowledge. Some of the early methods of empirical aesthetics were derived from psychophysics, and they continue to be prominent today. They involve the measurement of people's responses to controlled variations in stimulus features, such as proportion, symmetry, complexity, or predictability. As neighboring fields advanced, empirical aesthetics also borrowed methods from behavioral psychology, cognitive psychology and, more recently, cognitive neuroscience. The methods now available to empirical aesthetics allow recording verbal judgments, choices and preferences, exploratory time and movements, implicit measures, eye movements, psychophysiological measures, temporal and spatial patterns of brain activity, and the effects of brain stimulation, among others. In addition, technological innovations have made it possible to use several of these methods simultaneously, enhancing greatly our knowledge of various phenomena across multiple levels of measurement (see the chapters in Section 2).

Collecting, analyzing, and systematically organizing observations are essential to the goals of empirical aesthetics. However, this does not mean that there is no theorizing or conceptual work to be done by researchers. Observations are valuable and meaningful to the extent that they have implications for theory. In science, a theory is a formal explanation of a substantial set of observations. The goal of scientific theories is usually to reveal the mechanisms whereby a set of observed or hypothetical causes leads to a set of observed or hypothetical consequences. For instance, Berlyne's (1971) theory mentioned above was intended to explain how certain stimulus properties (i.e., observed causes) induced certain arousal dynamics (i.e., hypothesized consequences) that, in turn, lead to (i.e., hypothesized causes) pleasure or displeasure (i.e., observed consequences). Theories are the source of the interpretation of patterns of collected observations, and the source of predictions about future observations. Indeed, it is debatable whether atheoretical observation is even possible, given that our decisions regarding what to observe are influenced heavily by expectations. Thus, empirical aesthetics does not collect observations for the sake of it, but rather to improve its explanations and predictions.

Empirical aesthetics studies aesthetics

Aesthetics is a concept that means different things to different people (Anglada-Tort & Skov, 2020). In the Western tradition of thinking, aesthetics has had two main foci: making and appreciating art, and the appreciation of the value of certain perceptual features (Levinson, 2003; Sparshott, 1963). This dual focus made sense to, and was adopted by, Fechner and others when they applied empirical methods to aesthetics in the late 19th century. Külpe (1897), for instance, wrote that

> The objects investigated by the science are on the one hand judgments of aesthetic pleasure and displeasure, and on the other works of art. The separation of the two groups shows that there was truth in the old distinction between a philosophy of beauty and a philosophy of art. The aesthetic judgment extends beyond works of art, since there is a beauty of nature as well as of art; and works of art give us more than the aesthetic judgment, since when we have decided as to the pleasingness or displeasingness of their impression we can go on to discuss the conditions of their origination, the relation between portrayal and portrayed, between the form and contents, copy and model, etc. etc.
>
> (Külpe, 1897, p. 88)

Berlyne (1972) agreed that empirical aesthetics should study art *and* aesthetic appreciation, but he was wary of grounding the definition of the field on either aspect. Such a definition, he believed, would misleadingly suggest that aesthetics was a separate domain of human life, and would cut empirical aesthetics off from the rest of the behavioral and brain sciences: "The essentially superstitious view that the aesthetic realm is sharply distinct from the rest of life and governed by principles peculiar to itself has long been a bugbear" (Berlyne, 1972, p. 304).

Today, empirical aesthetics continues to be divided about what makes art and aesthetic experiences unique and different to other kinds of objects and experiences, respectively. The various positions on this topic lie along a continuum. At one pole of the continuum we find researchers who argue that art and aesthetic experience involve unique forms of pleasure or emotion, and that it is therefore important to distinguish aesthetic pleasure, aesthetic emotions or art emotions from nonaesthetic or non-art-based pleasure and emotion (Christensen, 2017; Fingerhut & Prinz, 2020; Makin, 2017;

Menninghaus et al., 2019). At the other pole of the continuum we find researchers who argue that art and aesthetic experience involve the same kind of pleasure and emotions as any other kind of object and experience and that, therefore, the notions of aesthetic pleasure, aesthetic or art emotions are unnecessary and misleading (Berlyne, 1972; Nadal & Skov, 2018; Skov & Nadal, 2019, 2020). Somewhere between both of these poles we find the views of researchers who have argued that aesthetic experiences arise from a unique combination of general cognitive and affective processes (Leder et al., 2004; Pelowski, Markey, Forster, Gerger, & Leder, 2017), and those who have argued that aesthetic emotion is ordinary emotion lacking its motivational component (Chatterjee, 2014; Chatterjee & Vartanian, 2014).

A Brief History of Empirical Aesthetics

Founding empirical aesthetics

If psychophysics is considered as the oldest domain of experimental psychology, then empirical aesthetics is rightly considered as the second oldest (Berlyne, 1972; Seeley, 2014a). Both were founded by Gustav Theodor Fechner: in 1860 he published his *Elements of Psychophysics* (Fechner, 1860), and in 1876, *Preschool of Aesthetics* (Fechner, 1876). His approach to aesthetics was shaped by the priority he gave to empirical knowledge, and his view that striving for pleasure was a major force driving human behavior. As we saw in the previous section, Fechner advocated an aesthetics from below, that is to say, starting with individuals' likes and dislikes, choices and preferences. Pooling together and averaging the results from many people would level out individual peculiarities and reveal the laws that explain how certain sensory features, and their combinations, give rise to pleasure or displeasure and, therefore liking or disliking. To achieve this goal, he developed three methods (Westphal-Fitch, this volume): the method of choice, which requires participants to select among several alternatives the one they find most pleasing; the method of production, which requires them to produce pleasing examples of simple shapes or figures; and the method of use, which measures (nonpurposeful) features in objects that are manufactured, bought, and used, under the assumption that the most common ones are the most pleasing ones. He also deduced a number of principles that underlie aesthetic pleasure: that sensory impressions must occur above a certain threshold of pleasure, that objects that give rise to aesthetic pleasure are often composite and manifold, that the features should be aligned toward the same end and be harmonious, and so on.

Fechner had a monumental impact on psychology, but he had no school or students to follow his program. It came to Wundt's students to set empirical aesthetics into motion (see Nadal and Ureña, this volume). Among their most influential works were Witmer's (1894) study of the effects of the proportion of linear figures on pleasingness judgments; Martin's (1906) systematic examination of Fechner's principles of aesthetics using the methods of psychophysics and simple figures consisting of lines that differed in orientation, length, curvature, and thickness; and Külpe's (1907, 1921) refinement, systematization, and extension of Fechner's methods and principles.

Empirical aesthetics during the decades of behaviorism

Whereas German psychology in the late 19th and early 20th centuries focused on the *what* and *how* of consciousness, that is to say, on what takes place in conscious sensation, feeling and thinking, and how it takes place, American psychology focused on the *why*. Its goal was to understand how the mind enabled humans to adapt to their environment. Adaptation implies the competition among individuals with different traits or capacities that confer them greater or lesser advantages in a given context. So, when the American psychologists turned their attention to empirical aesthetics, in the early decades of the 20th century, it was with a focus on individual differences (H. Clark, Quackenbush, & Washburn, 1913; Thorndike, 1917).

During the behaviorist decades it became paramount to understand why some stimuli are more rewarding. Many studies were conducted in the musical domain on the affective value of single tones, simultaneous pairs of tones, simple tone sequences, different cadences, major and minor modes, consonance and dissonance, variations in rhythm, and repeated exposure (Edmonds & Smith, 1923; Farnsworth, 1925, 1926a, 1926b, Guernsey, 1928; Heinlein, 1925, 1928; Hevner, 1935b, 1936; Ortmann, 1928, 1926). In the visual domain, researchers studied people's affective responses and associations elicited by simple lines and forms, the consistency and variability in people's responses to paintings, the effects of different kinds of information on the appreciation of paintings, and the effect of age and development on aesthetic preference, among other topics (Barnhart, 1940; Brighouse, 1939a, 1939b; Cahalan, 1939; Clair, 1939; Davis, 1933; Farnsworth, 1932; Hevner, 1935a; Hevner & Mueller, 1939; Israeli, 1928; Lundholm, 1921; Poffenberger & Barrows, 1924; Voss, 1939; Weber, 1931; Yokoyama, 1921). But there was no matching the torrent of studies on preferences for colors and color combinations, on the expressiveness of colors, and on the influence of personality, age, and culture on those phenomena (e.g., Allesch, 1925; Garth, 1924; Garth & Collado, 1929; Geissler, 1917; Katz & Breed, 1922; Michaels, 1924; Staples, 1931; Stratton, 1923; Washburn, Haight, & Regensburg, 1921).

Psychometric empirical aesthetics

The decades of behaviorist hegemony were also the golden age of testing all kinds of psychological processes involved in aesthetics: sensitivity to visual balance and complexity;

discrimination and memory for pitch, intensity, consonance, and rhythm; aptitude in design; and the appreciation of visual art, literature, and music (Adler, 1929; Barron & Welsh, 1952; Carroll, 1933; Farnsworth, 1931; Graves, 1948; Guilford & Guilford, 1931; Heinlein, 1925; Logasa & Wright, 1930; Madison, 1942; McAdory, 1933; McCarthy, 1930; Meier, 1926, 1942; Meier & Seashore, 1929; Stanton, 1928; Welsh & Barron, 1949; Williams, Winter, & Woods, 1938; Wing, 1941).

Two of the most influential efforts to develop valid and reliable measures of mental abilities for art and aesthetics were those of Seashore and Meier in Iowa, and those of Hans J. Eysenck in London. Carl E. Seashore published the *Seashore Measures of Musical Talents*, which provided a relatively good index of the receptive side of musical talent. Norman C. Meier and Seashore later applied similar principles to the visual domain, and developed the *Meier-Seashore Art Judgment Test* (Meier & Seashore, 1929). A new version followed, the *Meier Art Tests: I. Art Judgment* (Meier, 1940), and later a new test, the *Meier Art Tests: II. Aesthetic Perception* (Meier, 1963).

Hans J. Eysenck identified a general objective factor of aesthetic appreciation that distinguished people who were better at identifying beauty in objects and designs from those who were worse at doing so. A second bipolar factor distinguished participants according to the style of art they preferred (Eysenck, 1941c). Eysenck believed that this factor was universal and innate (Eysenck, 1941a, 1941b, 1942, 1981). Later in his life, he developed the Visual Aesthetic Sensitivity Test (VAST) in collaboration with the German artist and designer Karl Otto Götz to measure individual differences in good taste (Chan, Eysenck, & Götz, 1980; Götz, Borisy, Lynn, & Eysenck, 1979; Iwawaki, Eysenck, & Götz, 1979).

The Gestalt school of psychology

Gestalt's most significant contribution to psychology was the school's conception of perception and understanding as emergent processes that go beyond the mere recording of the elements in the stimulus. They suggested a number of grouping principles, such as proximity, continuation, similarity, or closure, which organized parts of the visual scene into wholes, such as objects, clusters, and overall scenes. These and other Gestalt principles were applied to art and aesthetics by Rudolf Arnheim (1964, 1966, 1969). He explained many traditional aspects of training in "Beaux Arts" schools in terms of Gestalt's principles of organization: balance, symmetry, composition, and dynamical complexity, by which he meant an optimal trade-off between order and complexity. Even more importantly, Arnheim argued that aesthetic experiences arise not from the mere automatic and passive recording of aspects of the visual field, but from the awareness of dynamic forces inherent to the stimuli. This awareness is attained by the integration of two sources of information: the structured configurations received from the image and the patterns toward which the individual is oriented by virtue of his experience and disposition. The overall configuration of these dynamical visual forces constitutes what Arnheim (1974) referred to as the structural skeleton of the design. To Arnheim, the essence of an artwork is to create a dynamic whole by integrating this structural skeleton with the depicted subject matter.

Berlyne's new experimental aesthetics

Daniel Berlyne is responsible for revitalizing the scientific study of art and aesthetics during the 1960s and 1970s. His research program, known as psychobiological aesthetics, became the starting point for contemporary empirical aesthetics. Its main objective was to detail a set of motivational laws that could explain people's preference for certain kinds of stimuli. From this point of view, the hedonic tone induced by a stimulus—the power to reward an operant response and to generate preference or pleasure expressed through verbal assessments (Berlyne, 1971)—depended on the level of arousal that it was capable of eliciting in relation to the organism's current arousal level. Given that organisms tend to search for the optimal hedonic value, they would tend to expose themselves to different stimuli as a function of their arousal potential.

Berlyne (1971) noted three classes of variables that determine a given stimulus' arousal potential, mainly through the amount of information transmitted to the organism. These were: (a) psychophysical variables, such as brightness, saturation, predominant wavelength, and so on; (b) ecological variables, including those elements that might have acquired associations with biologically relevant events or activities; and (c) collative properties, such as novelty, surprise, complexity, ambiguity, or asymmetry. Collative properties refer to aspects of the object that have the potential to increase or reduce arousal because of the way and extent to which they compare with previously experienced objects. In relation to aesthetics and art, Berlyne suggested that interest and preference for an image depend primarily on how complex such a stimulus appears to the viewer (Berlyne, 1963; Berlyne, Ogilvie, & Parham, 1968). Perceived complexity, in turn, is related to such factors as the regularity of the pattern, the number of elements that form the scene, their heterogeneity, or the irregularity of the forms (Berlyne, 1970). Thus, under normal conditions, that is to say, with an intermediate level of arousal, people were expected to prefer intermediately complex artworks over highly complex or very simple ones, regardless of modality and medium. Depending on the current arousal level, such preferences could shift toward more complex or simpler objects.

Martindale's connectionist prototype model

If Berlyne's work is the first step toward a cognitive approach to empirical aesthetics, Colin Martindale's is its consolidation. Martindale developed a connectionist model that explained the effects of prototypicality on aesthetic preference as a result of basic cognitive functioning (Martindale, 1984, 1988). He modeled cognition as a large network of interconnected cognitive units (i.e., nodes), segregated into a number of analyzers. The output of these sensory analyzers constitutes the input for a number of perceptual or gnostic analyzers. These perceptual analyzers include a series of cognitive units at the lower levels that code the distinctive features. Specific excitement patterns of feature units define units in the next level, and so on up the hierarchy in the perceptual analyzers. Hence, a reduced number of feature units are able to define a vast number of unitary percepts. The output from perceptual analyzers enters the semantic analyzer, which includes one cognitive unit for each concept a person has. Activity from here is passed on to the episodic analyzer, which contains memories. This analyzer produces outputs that correspond to events coded propositionally.

This architecture could model aesthetic experience:

> Apprehension of a work of art of any sort will involve activation of cognitive units in sensory, gnostic, semantic, and episodic analyzers. (...) the pleasure engendered by a work of art will be a positive monotonic function of how activated this entire ensemble of cognitive units is. The more activated the ensemble of units, the more pleasurable an observer will find the stimulus to be.
>
> (Martindale, 1988, p. 26)

Martindale (1984, 1988) hypothesized that prototypical stimuli are encoded by stronger cognitive units, and given that aesthetic pleasure is a function of the activation level of cognitive units, prototypical and meaningful stimuli are predicted to be associated with higher levels of aesthetic preference than stimuli that are atypical.

Martindale's experiments confirmed this prediction. They proved that prototypicality accounted for close to five times more variance in aesthetic preference than collative variables (Martindale, Moore, & Borkum, 1990; Martindale, Moore, & West, 1988). Moreover, Martindale and colleagues (1990) showed that some of the aesthetic effects Berlyne had attributed to complexity actually owed to meaningfulness. Thus, the key determinant of aesthetic appreciation was not collative variables, but prototypicality, which facilitates meaningfulness (Rosch & Mervis, 1975; Rosch, Mervis, Gray, Johnson, & Boyes-Braem, 1976).

CONTEMPORARY ACCOUNTS OF AESTHETIC APPRECIATION

Processing fluency

The world is not an easy place to live in. It is complex and often unpredictable. Our cognitive systems must deal with the barrage of varied kinds of sensations we constantly receive, to create representations of objects and events in the present and to assess their relevance in light of our goals and motivations, to regulate our many homeostatic systems, and to plan for the future based on our past experiences. Not surprisingly, natural selection has endowed cognitive systems with a taste for efficiency and with several means to simplify their tasks. For instance, sorting reality into discrete categories, and abstracting prototypes to represent those categories, saves us much time and effort in navigating the physical and social world. From this point of view, it makes sense, as Martindale (1988) argued, that we should prefer typical exemplars, because they give us more for less: prototypical exemplars convey more information about the category than less prototypical exemplars. There are many other examples of cognition's taste for ease and efficiency: we tend to prefer the familiar to the unfamiliar, the clear to the unclear, the symmetrical to the asymmetrical, and so on.

Reber, Schwarz, and Winkielman (2004) noticed that there are many domains in which ease of processing is experienced as pleasant, and several factors that contribute to ease of processing. They suggested that ease of processing might be a general principle of aesthetic appreciation: "The more fluently perceivers can process an object, the more positive their aesthetic response" (Reber et al., 2004, p. 364). This processing fluency model of aesthetic appreciation (see Forster, this volume) is based on the premises that some stimuli are easier to process than others, and that ease of processing has hedonic consequences: easy processing is experienced as a pleasant feeling of fluency, whereas difficult processing is experienced as an unpleasant feeling of disfluency. Because we commonly rely on feelings when evaluating objects, we tend to consider objects we subjectively feel as more fluent as also more beautiful, likable, and attractive (Forster, Leder, & Ansorge, 2013, 2016). The processing fluency account is appealing because it provides a simple explanation for many scattered findings in empirical aesthetics, and because it is grounded on a general principle of cognition (Jacoby, Kelley, & Dywan, 1989).

The Pleasure–Interest Model of Aesthetic Liking

We seem to have a mystery on our hands. Berlyne's (1971) arousal account of aesthetic appreciation predicts people will generally prefer objects that are relatively complex, novel, and ambiguous, and there are results that confirm people prefer a moderately arousing challenge (Marin, Lampatz, Wandl, & Leder, 2016). In contrast, Reber and colleagues' (2004) fluency account predicts people generally prefer objects that are experienced as easily processed, and there are results that confirm this too (Forster et al., 2013). How can we reconcile this discrepancy?

Graf & Landwehr (2015; 2017) developed a dual-processing model, called the Pleasure–Interest Model of Aesthetic Liking, to explain why under some circumstances people prefer a degree of challenge, and why under other circumstances they prefer ease of processing. Their model is based on the distinction between two forms of processing: automatic processing, which is stimulus driven, and controlled processing, which is perceiver driven. In some cases, aesthetic judgments are fast and automatic, and will be based primarily on pleasure or displeasure responses to stimuli. In other cases, when the motivation is sufficient, the controlled processing mode becomes engaged, eliciting aesthetic interest. These two processing modes lead to two different forms of liking. Automatic processing leads to pleasure-based liking, which is greatest for easily processed stimuli, and controlled processing leads to interest-based liking owing to the reduction in disfluency, which is greatest for challenging stimuli. From this perspective, the arousal and fluency accounts each captures only half of a dual-processing liking system. This model has found support in studies on musical (Omigie et al., 2019) and visual (Miller & Hübner, 2019; Van Geert & Wagemans, 2019) preferences.

Information-processing model of aesthetic appreciation

Leder and colleagues introduced an information-processing model to account for the interaction of various component processes in the computation of aesthetic experience (Leder et al., 2004). Leder and colleagues' (2004) model comprises of five information-processing stages that are connected in sequence, as well as through several feedback loops. Information flow is unidirectional in some parts of the model and bidirectional in others, such that certain phases involve bottom-up as well as top-down processing. In addition, there is an affective evaluation stream that runs parallel to this sequential stream and receives its output.

The input into the system is an artwork, or an object of aesthetic interest. Then, at each stage, a particular operation is performed on the artwork, therefore extracting various characteristics from it. The first stage involves *perceptual analyses*. At this stage features such as complexity or symmetry are distilled. For example, there is much research demonstrating that people prefer more to less symmetrical design. According to this model, this information is processed rather early in the stream. This stage is not under the influence of top-down processes, and is stimulus driven. The second stage involves *implicit memory integration*, where the perceptual information is related to past experience. For example, we know that people prefer colors that are more prototypical. However, we also know that what is deemed prototypical depends in part on personal experience. At this stage people compare what they see to what they know, and this affects their responses to it. This stage is presumed to be under the indirect influence of top-down processes. The third stage involves *explicit classification*, and this is where expertise comes into play. At this point, the person analyzes content information, and also explicit information about the style of the artwork. There is much evidence demonstrating that expertise affects the way in which artworks are processed, and this is one of the stages where the difference between experts and novices would be apparent.

The penultimate stage is referred to as *cognitive mastering*, the moment at which interpretation or meaning is imposed on the artwork. Thus, having already distilled its perceptual properties and placed it within self-referential (implicit memory integration) and explicit (explicit classification) contexts, we make sense of what it is that we see. Of course, what one observes is also influenced by expertise in the visual arts, so that different cues become more or less important in giving meaning to the artwork. In the final stage, referred to as *evaluation*, we appraise the meaning or interpretation that was placed on the artwork during mastering. This evaluative stage generates two outputs: aesthetic judgment and aesthetic emotion, which are the endpoints of the aesthetic experience. If cognitive mastering is successful and the subject has successfully interpreted the artwork, it will be evaluated as either a good or a poor work of art. Those aesthetic judgments will in turn be accompanied by positive and negative aesthetic emotions, respectively. On the other hand, if cognitive mastering is unsuccessful, then the artwork will likely be evaluated as a poor work of art, and be accompanied by negative aesthetic emotion.

Since its original introduction in 2004, the model has been updated. Leder and Nadal (2014) revised the model to include recent findings on the way emotions (see Cupchik, this volume) and the physical and social context (see the chapters in Section 6) shape aesthetic appreciation, and to place the framework into an evolutionary context. Later, Pelowski and colleagues (2017) substantially expanded the scope of the model to account for bottom-up and top-down processes related to the appreciation of art including transformative aesthetic experience, as well as to connect the model's processing stages with activity in brain regions.

Neuroaesthetics

For most of its history, empirical aesthetics has relied on the study of patients with brain lesions or neurodegenerative diseases for knowledge about the neural systems underlying aesthetics (Chatterjee, 2004, 2006; Zaidel, 2005). The brain imaging methods developed in the 1990s were added to the methodological stock of empirical aesthetics in the 2000s (Nadal, Munar, Capó, Rosselló, & Cela-Conde, 2008), and have had a transformative effect on the field (Skov, 2019). Researchers can now infer, from observed changes in different indices of neural activity, the brain mechanisms that transform information about the stimulus and other external and internal factors, such as task goals, expertise, or verbal primes, into different degrees of liking and disliking. Neuroimaging studies have shown that even the apparently simple judgment of something as likable involves orchestrating activity in many different networks of brain regions (Skov, 2019).

The results of neurophysiology (Jacobsen and Klein, this volume), neuroimaging (Ishizu, this volume), and brain stimulation (Cattaneo, this volume) studies have shown that aesthetic appreciation involves coordinated activity in three networks of brain regions: prefrontal, parietal, and temporal cortical regions related to evaluative judgment, attentional processing, and memory retrieval; the reward circuit, including cortical and subcortical regions, as well as some of the regulators of this circuit; and a network of low-, mid-, and high-level cortical sensory regions (Nadal, 2013; Nadal & Pearce, 2011). Meta-analyses confirm that the brain regions most commonly activated in studies of aesthetic appreciation are related to perception and representation of affective value (Brown, Gao, Tisdelle, Eickhoff, & Liotti, 2011; Chuan-Peng, Huang, Eickhoff, Peng, & Sui, 2020; Vartanian & Skov, 2014).

These results have inspired new ways of thinking about aesthetic appreciation (Skov, this volume). Some researchers see in the neuroscientific results the indicators of neural activity that is specific to aesthetics (Ishizu & Zeki, 2013; Kawabata & Zeki, 2004). Conversely, others have argued that aesthetic appreciation does not involve specific brain regions or neural activity patterns, but the same networks as general sensory valuation (Skov, 2019; Skov & Nadal, 2018). Somewhere in-between lie the positions of Vessel and colleagues (2012) and Chatterjee and Vartanian (2014). To Vessel and colleagues (2012), the key to aesthetic experiences is the integration of sensory and emotional brain signals through inward contemplation and self-referential processes, reflected in the increased activation of brain regions that integrate the default-mode network during intense aesthetic experiences. Chatterjee and Vartanian (2014) conceived aesthetic experiences as emergent states that arise from the interaction between neural systems involved in sensory-motor processes, emotion and valuation, and meaning and knowledge. They argued that, although the interactions between these systems are the same as in aesthetic and nonaesthetic interactions with objects, aesthetic experiences differ from nonaesthetic experiences in that the cognitive appraisals focus on the context in which the interaction takes place (like a museum or a concert hall) and the object and its features, rather than on the outcomes.

Factors that influence aesthetics

As noted above, the basic strategy for the generation of knowledge in empirical aesthetics is the empirical method. Studies of this kind begin with one or a few theory-driven hypotheses that specify the expected correlative or causal relation between one or more causal factors, and one or more outcome variables. Depending on the goals and the nature of the study (e.g., observational, quasi-experimental, experimental), and on the causal factors and outcome variables specified by the hypotheses, researchers will use one or several methods to observe and measure responses. This section examines some of the basic causal factors that are commonly studied in empirical aesthetics, whereas the next section examines some of the most common measurement methods.

The basic factors that influence aesthetic appreciation can be grouped into three broad categories: those that have to do with the features of the object that is appreciated (see the chapters in Sections 3 and 4), those that have to do with the person who is doing the appreciating (see the chapters in Section 5), and those that have to do with the context in which the appreciation is taking place (see the chapters in Section 6) (see also Jacobsen, 2006). As it takes place in everyday life, aesthetic appreciation is brought about by interactions among factors of the three sorts. However, most studies in empirical aesthetics will study the effects of one of these factors, while exerting some kind and measure of control on the others.

Object features

The object features that influence aesthetic appreciation vary from one sensory modality to another, and from one art form to the next. A comprehensive treatment of these is given in the chapters included in Sections 3 and 4. Still, some general principles apply across sensory modalities and art forms. As we saw above, Berlyne (1971, 1974) showed that collative properties have a strong effect on aesthetic appreciation. According to Berlyne (1971), certain features of sound and visual patterns that vary in space and time contribute to the complexity, novelty, and surprisingness of musical compositions, landscapes, paintings, choreographies, poems, movies, and so on. He expected that people would generally prefer intermediate levels of complexity, in any of its visual and auditory forms (Marin, this volume).

Fluency theory (Forster et al., 2013; Reber et al., 2004) is another example of a general principle that applies across modalities and media. As we saw above, the theory posits that certain features of visual or auditory objects makes them easier or more difficult to process, and that people will prefer those that are experienced as easier (Forster, this volume). Fluency theory encompasses Martindale's (Martindale, 1984; Martindale & Moore, 1988) prototype theory because one of the features that makes objects easier to process is their typicality.

The features that contribute to complexity, novelty, surprise, variability, and fluency are attributes of objects, such as the number of elements in a display or the figure–ground contrast. However, collative properties and fluency are actually subjective, that is to say, they are attributes of people's experience of those objects (Berlyne, 1971, 1974; Forster et al., 2013). Nevertheless, the chapters on collative properties and fluency are included in Section 3, which focuses on object features, for the practical reason that they are usually manipulated experimentally by adjusting object properties.

Personal features

The main goal of empirical aesthetics has been to provide general explanations for the way features of objects shape the way people value them (Berlyne, 1971; Martindale, 1990; McManus & Wu, 2013). Such explanations often rely on general perceptual, cognitive, and affective processes to account for regular and predictable responses to complexity, symmetry, balance, contour, and so on (Leder & Nadal, 2014; Pelowski et al., 2017).

However, people differ substantially in what they like and prefer (Jacobsen, 2004; Jacobsen & Höfel, 2002). Aesthetic appreciation, thus, is not merely a response to object features. Fechner (1866) believed that aesthetic appreciation was the result of the interaction and interweaving of two factors. One, the direct factor, referred to object properties; and the other, the association factor, referred to each person's knowledge, memories, and past experiences. Segal (1905, 1906) confirmed that object features alone could not account for aesthetic appreciation. He argued that aesthetic appreciation was not a response to object features, but people's thoughts and feelings about those features, and that these depended to a large extent on their personalities, moods, and dispositions.

Since those early experiments, a vast amount of evidence has accumulated on differences among people in their aesthetic preferences, especially for cultural products, such as art and architecture (Vessel, Maurer, Denker, & Starr, 2018). Such differences have been attributed to the effects of momentary deployments of cognitive resources, such as attention or working memory (Mullennix, this volume); factors that change slowly throughout life, such as age (Goldstein, this volume) and expertise (Kozbelt, this volume); and factors that remain relatively stable throughout life, such as personality (Swami & Furnham, this volume), aesthetic sensitivity (Myszkowski, this volume), and cultural background (Che & Su, this volume).

This extensive knowledge of the effects of personal attributes shows how wrong it is to conceive aesthetic appreciation (liking, beauty, or attractiveness) as a direct and passive effect of object features. Aesthetic appreciation is an active process that is modulated by many personal attributes. However, this feature is not just true of aesthetic appreciation, but rather true of all human experience. Our experience of the world is not the result of passive reactions to events. We construct our experience of the world through active processes of perception ("Whether beautiful or ugly or just conveniently at hand, the world of experience is produced by the [person] who experiences it" [Neisser, 1967, p. 3]), memory ("remembering appears to be far more decisively an affair of construction rather than one of mere reproduction" [Bartlett, 1932, p. 205]), and emotion ("each emotional episode is constructed rather than triggered" [Barrett & Russell, 2015, p. 4]). The main goal of cognitive psychology was to "discover and to describe formally the meanings that human beings created out of their encounters with the world, and then to propose hypotheses about what meaning-making processes were implicated" (Bruner, 1990, p. 2).

Context features

Human cognition does not take place in the void. Recent developments in cognitive psychology and neuroscience have shown that it relies to a considerable extent on the organizing resources present in the surrounding environment (Hutchins, 1995). These developments emphasize the situatedness of cognition, and the role of contextual constraints and affordances in perception, memory, and action (Barsalou, 2008; Clark, 1997; Hutchins, 1995; Smith & Vela, 2001). From this perspective, "Mental events and human behaviors can be thought of as states that emerge from moment-by-moment interaction with the environment rather than proceeding in autonomous, invariant, context-free fashion from preformed predispositions or causes. Inherently, a mind exists in context" (Barrett, Mesquita, & Smith, 2010, p. 5).

Despite this reality, empirical aesthetics has traditionally conducted its studies in psychological or neuroimaging laboratories. These laboratories are designed intentionally to minimize the sort of contextual elements that contribute to shaping experiences in everyday environments, such as other people, sounds and smells, decorations, design furniture, and art (Mastandrea, Bartoli, & Bove, 2009; Tschacher et al., 2012). In *Art as Experience*, Dewey (1934) highlighted the fundamental role of context in the experience of art: "Experience is a matter of the interaction of organism with its environment, an environment that is human as well as physical, that includes the materials of tradition and institutions as well as local surroundings" (Dewey, 1934, p. 256). But it was not until the 1990s that empirical aesthetics began systematically studying the effects of different contextual aspects on aesthetic experience (Section 6). Some of these studies examined the impact of art exhibition arrangement, artwork presentation, and the amount and kind of information on the behavior of museum visitors (Bitgood & Patterson, 1993; Falk, 1993; Temme, 1992). Other studies examined the effects of information about the artworks, their titles, and the artists on aesthetic appreciation, looking time, and eye movement patterns (Belke, Leder, & Augustin, 2006; Franklin, Becklen, & Doyle, 1993; Hristova, Georgieva, & Grinberg, 2011; Millis, 2001). Others attempted to determine whether presentation format has an impact on the evaluation of formal features of artworks and their appreciation (Locher, Smith, & Smith, 2001; Locher, Smith, & Smith, 1999). Only in the past decade have studies tested the effects of the actual physical context (laboratory, museum, or street) in which aesthetic appreciation takes place on outcome measures of interest (Brieber, Leder, & Nadal, 2015; Brieber, Nadal, Leder, & Rosenberg, 2014; Gartus & Leder, 2014; Grüner, Specker, & Leder, 2019). Together, these studies demonstrate that if "human cognition is always situated in a complex sociocultural world and cannot be unaffected by it" (Hutchins, 1995, p. xiii), then art is certainly no exception.

Measurement Methods

As noted above, the goals of each particular study determine the set of factors that are expected to cause or be associated with the set of outcomes, and the most suitable methods to measure these outcomes. These methods fall into four groups, depending on whether they measure historical data, verbal responses, nonverbal responses, or psychophysiological changes.

Historiometric methods

These methods allow researchers to analyze quantitatively historical data on samples of historical individuals, such as artists, or of historical objects, such as artworks, and their social and cultural environment (Simonton, 1990). The goal of these methods is to test hypotheses about factors surrounding individuals, objects, or movements that have become of historical relevance (Simonton, this volume). The basic units of analysis range from specific creations to individuals and to entire movements and periods. Simonton

(2018), for instance, used historiometric methods to study the circumstances that favor the alternations of golden ages, formed by clusters of highly creative individuals, and periods of relatively little creativity. Martindale (1990) analyzed different sorts of historical data, and showed that across many art forms and periods, a common pressure to attain novelty drives artists and movements to break with the rules.

Verbal ratings and judgments

This is, by far, the most commonly used method to analyze the outcomes of aesthetic appreciation (Berlyne, 1972, 1974). It requires participants to express verbally some aspect of the way they experience a stimulus. The most common aspects participants are asked to inform us about are descriptive aspects of the stimuli (such as their complexity, regularity, or novelty), evaluative aspects of the hedonic value (such as interestingness, pleasingness, liking, beauty, or attractiveness), and internal states (such as evoked emotions or meanings). There are many other different ways to collect verbal ratings and judgments. The most common ones are giving participants the choice between two possible alternatives (e.g., simple or complex, like or do not like), giving participants graded scales divided into several points that represent discrete degrees of their response (e.g., more or less complex, like more or less), or using continuous scales that represent all possible gradations of their response. These verbal measures are usually accompanied by measures of response times, under the assumption that they reflect something about the processing of the responses, such as task difficulty, response elaboration, or indecision. The particular aspect that is measured and the way it is measured are determined by, and should be in consonance with, each study's goals and hypotheses, especially when measures differ in their degree of sensitivity to the effects of certain factors (e.g., Palumbo & Bertamini, 2016).

Verbal ratings and judgments are among the easiest measures of aesthetic appreciation to collect and analyze, but, for several reasons, they are also among the most problematic. Verbal measurements have several weaknesses, especially when not combined with other forms of measurement. First, the vast majority of studies in empirical aesthetics have measured participants' verbal responses using Fechner's method of choice (Westphal-Fitch, this volume). Thus, most of the knowledge in the field rests on variations upon a single method. Second, they are the result of introspection. Psychology rejected introspective methods early in the 20th century for good reasons: it is unclear how accurate people are when they access their own psychological processes and states, and their responses are easily and unwillingly influenced by undesired factors, such as expectations, social desirability, and other demand characteristics of the study. Third, participants' verbal responses will reflect their understanding of the instructions and scales. Descriptive terms such as complex or simple, and descriptive terms such as liking, beauty, and attractiveness, can mean different things to different participants, and participants differ in the way they use them in reference to the rated or judged objects.

One way to avoid these problems would be to dispense with measuring verbal responses entirely. But, for several reasons, this might be an excessively radical and undesirable solution. First, verbal ratings and judgments are a rich source of information about aesthetic appreciation. Second, they often produce results that correlate with those of nonverbal measurements (Berlyne, 1972). For instance, verbal measures of preference for curvature (i.e., people generally rate curved shapes as more pleasing and likable than angular shapes) are supported by several forms of nonverbal measures that indicate that people find curved shapes more approachable (Bertamini, Palumbo, Gheorghes, & Galatsidas, 2016). Third, not all verbal measures require participants to introspect about their responses. There are several kinds of tasks that measure participants' implicit attitudes toward or associations between objects, situations or values (Palumbo, this volume). For instance, Palumbo and colleagues (2015) used implicit measures to show that participants associated curved shapes with positive and safe concepts, and angular shapes with negative and threatening concepts. Fourth, several valid and reliable methods exist for the analysis and interpretation of declarative self-report data that can shed light on the mechanics of thought, such as think-aloud protocols. Thus, rather than discarding verbal measures, it is better to design experiments that control for the kinds of extraneous influences they are sensitive to, and to combine them with nonverbal, implicit, or physiological measures.

Measurement of nonverbal behavior

Berlyne (1972, 1974) classified behavioral measures into measures of exploration choice and measure of exploration time. Measures of exploration choice quantify the frequency with which participants choose to expose themselves to different alternative objects (Tinio & Specker, this volume). In the laboratory, this procedure usually involves initially presenting the alternatives to participants, giving them the chance of choosing among the alternatives for additional presentations, and measuring the frequency of choices. In the field, such as in museums or in parks, this procedure usually requires researchers to record the objects, among all the alternatives, visitors choose to engage with (Mitschke, Goller, & Leder, 2017). Measures of exploration time quantify the time participants choose to spend engaged with different alternative objects. Brieber and colleagues (2014), for instance, measured the time participants chose to view artworks in the laboratory and in a museum, and found a relation between the chosen viewing time and how much participants liked the artworks. Hayden and colleagues (2007) measured the relation between attractiveness, viewing time, and cost, and found that people are willing to pay more and work harder to spend time viewing images of attractive people of the opposite sex than of less attractive people.

Eye movements constitute an especially interesting form of exploratory behavior for empirical aesthetics. Eye tracking methods allow the simultaneous measurement of exploratory behavior, in the form of the regions of an image that participants choose to explore in more or less detail, and of exploratory time, in the form of the duration of fixations at a given location. Many studies have shown that the factors that influence aesthetic appreciation also influence the locations participants focus on, the time they spend at each location, and the path from one location to another (Locher, this volume).

Psychophysiological measures

Empirical aesthetics has benefited greatly from improvements to the precision and reliability of the instruments to measure psychophysiological parameters, advances in the computer software for analyzing psychophysiological data, reductions in the expense of these systems, and the development of mobile devices that can be used outside of the laboratory. Studies that make use of these measures, most often in combination with verbal or nonverbal behavioral measures, are becoming more and more common. Researchers have studied the physiological components of aesthetic appreciation using peripheral measurements, such as skin conductance, facial muscle contractions, pupillary dilation, and measurements or transient alterations of brain activity using electroencephalography, magnetoencephalography, functional resonance magnetic imaging, and brain stimulation (Jacobsen & Klein, this volume; Ishizu, this volume; and Cattaneo, this volume). The field is also on the verge of incorporating interoceptive measures into its methodological stock, which will show the relation between aesthetic appreciation and signals from different organs of our respiratory, cardiac, and digestive systems.

SUBDOMAINS OF EMPIRICAL AESTHETICS

Although, as we have seen, empirical aesthetics began as a branch of experimental psychology, in its 150 years of history it has been enriched by the addition of different perspectives (Seeley, 2014a). Today, empirical aesthetics is multidisciplinary endeavor, and can be regarded as the intersection of the empirical facets of different scientific approaches to aesthetics: psychological aesthetics, neuroaesthetics, evolutionary aesthetics, environmental aesthetics, psychometric aesthetics, computational aesthetics, and medical aesthetics (Figure 1.1).

- Psychological aesthetics is the oldest of these domains, as it corresponds with Fechner's (1871, 1876) notion of experimental aesthetics. Its main goal is to understand the psychological processes involved in aesthetic appreciation and creation, as well as its psychological consequences. Arnheim's Gestalt perspective and Leder and colleagues' (2004) information-processing model were crucial contributions to psychological aesthetics. An example of empirical research in this domain is Brielman and Pelli's (2017)'s use of cognitive load manipulations to demonstrate that appreciating beauty entails the participation of executive functions.

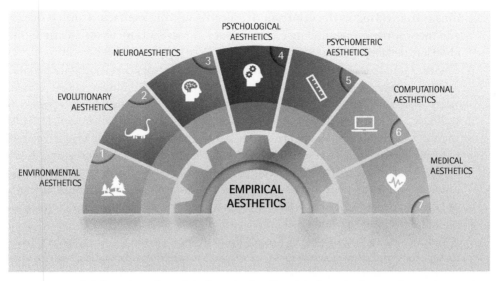

FIGURE 1.1. Subdomains of empirical aesthetics. Empirical aesthetics can be understood as the intersection of the empirical facets of environmental aesthetics, evolutionary aesthetics, neuroaesthetics, psychological aesthetics, psychometric aesthetics, computational aesthetics, and medical aesthetics.

- Neuroaesthetics is one of the most recent additions to the domains of empirical aesthetics. Zeki (1999) coined the term and argued that knowledge about visual processing in the brain could explain how the different features of artworks, such as color or movement, achieved their appealing effects. The first empirical studies on the neural underpinnings of aesthetic appreciation soon followed (Cela-Conde et al., 2004; Jacobsen & Höfel, 2001; Kawabata & Zeki, 2004; Vartanian & Goel, 2004). Urgesi and colleagues (2007) and Calvo-Merino and colleagues' (2010) studies showing that the aesthetic appreciation of dance engages brain systems related to the representation of movement illustrate the sort of work in this domain.
- Evolutionary aesthetics applies the principles and methods of evolutionary biology to the problems of aesthetics. Its goal is to explain the origins and evolution of aesthetic appreciation and creation as the result of natural and sexual selection (Gangestad & Scheyd, 2005; Prum, 2017; Voland & Grammer, 2003; Zaidel, Nadal, Flexas, & Enric, 2013). Given that most work in this domain assumes that art and aesthetics constitute adaptations, that is to say, traits that increased the chances for survival and reproduction to their possessors, one of the fundamental questions concerns the adaptive advantages conferred by art and aesthetics. There are many examples of empirical work in this domain that show a close relation between aesthetics and signals of health, social, and sexual status (Fink, Grammer, & Matts, 2006; Skamel, 2003). Although these studies have traditionally focused on the signals and the signaler, the interest is currently shifting toward the complex

processes involved in the valuation of those signals (Achorn & Rosenthal, 2020), and the way these valuation mechanisms exploit pre-existing sensory biases in the choosers' sensory system (Ryan, 2018).

- Environmental aesthetics seeks to understand the factors that modulate people's aesthetic responses to natural and urban environments (Kaplan, 1992; Ulrich, 1977). Some of the most striking work has been conducted on the effects on wellness and stress reduction of certain features of natural environments (Ulrich, 1991; Ulrich et al., 1991) and interior architectural spaces (Fich et al., 2014). A classic example of the kind of research conducted in this domain is Balling and Falk's (1982) study showing that children prefer savannah-type landscapes over other kinds of landscapes, but that as people grow up they tend to prefer familiar kinds of landscapes just as much, which they interpreted as evidence for an innate preparedness to prefer savannah-like environments.

- Psychometric aesthetics is a broad domain that aims to develop adequate instruments for the measurement of art and aesthetic appreciation, talent, and knowledge. The domain grew out of early interest in quantifying group norms and variations (Thorndike, 1916, 1917), and of the early visual art and music aptitude tests (Meier & Seashore, 1929). Myszkowski and colleagues' (2017, 2018) recent studies on the Visual Aesthetic Sensitivity Test are good illustrations of the kind of empirical work conducted in this domain.

- Computational aesthetics develops mathematical models of choices in aesthetic appreciation and creation based on the principles that underlie aesthetic forms (Emch, 1900; Greenfield & Machado, 2012; Hoenig, 2005). Schmidhuber (2006) developed artificial agents that simulate scientists and artists in their curiosity and creativity. The agents incorporate two learning systems: a model of the agent's history of interaction with the environment; and a reinforcement learner, which selects new actions. This reinforcement learner is motivated to invent new and interesting things, and it does so by choosing increasingly complex and unpredictable patterns. Other fully automated systems have been developed to combine an automatic art critic architecture and a genetic programming engine. These combinations used evolutionary computation to generate images that a neural network can discriminate and classify. The iterative process leads to the refinement of the network's function and drives the evolutionary algorithm to explore new paths (Machado, Romero, Cardoso, & Santos, 2005; Machado, Romero, & Manaris, 2008). Some of the most recent developments in computational aesthetics involve neural networks that are able to predict humans' aesthetic judgments, suggest enhancements to the aesthetic quality of images, and even imitate art styles (Schwarz, Wieschollek, & Lensch, 2018; Talebi & Milanfar, 2018).

- Medical aesthetics is mostly concerned with the relation between physical appearance and its health and wellbeing consequences. Its interventions usually involve reconstructive surgery due to traumatic injury or skin diseases, cosmetic surgery, and dental implants. Studies on the psychological causes and consequences of satisfaction with cosmetic surgery are illustrative examples of empirical work in this domain (Brunton et al., 2014; Herruer, Prins, van Heerbeek, Verhage-Damen, & Ingels, 2015; von Soest, Kvalem, Roald, & Skolleborg, 2009).

Some of the future challenges facing empirical aesthetics concern its constituting domains. Anglada-Tort and Skov (2020) have shown that whereas some of these domains share a common understanding of important concepts and that knowledge generated in one is used in the other, as is the case with neuroaesthetics and psychological aesthetics, other domains seem to have their own understanding of central concepts and share little knowledge with the rest of the domains, as is the case with computational aesthetics and medical aesthetics, for instance. There is still much to be done in the way of integration, and much to be gained too. Another challenge for the future of empirical aesthetics is adding further domains. Empirical aesthetics would benefit enormously from a domain on comparative aesthetics (Westphal-Fitch & Fitch, 2015) and a domain on genetic aesthetics. Although the literature on animal visual and auditory preferences is vast, it is largely unconsidered by empirical aesthetics, and very few studies have directly compared aesthetic preferences of humans and nonhuman animals (Mühlenbeck, Jacobsen, Pritsch, & Liebal, 2017; Mühlenbeck, Liebal, Pritsch, & Jacobsen, 2015, 2016; Munar, Gomez-Puerto, Call, & Nadal, 2015). Genetic aesthetics is one of the most promising and unexplored possibilities for empirical aesthetics. It is therefore encouraging to see the first steps in this direction, with a study that shows that variation in the intensity of aesthetic experience is due partly to genetic factors (Bignardi, Ticini, Smit, & Polderman, 2020).

Ties with Neighboring Fields, Past and Future

Empirical aesthetics feeds from and contributes to other fields in the behavioral and brain sciences that provide concepts and methods to study cognition and its neural underpinnings, and other fields in the humanities and biology that study different aspects of art and aesthetics.

Empirical aesthetics is tied to other fields of the behavioral and brain sciences because the appreciation and creation of art and aesthetics is the product of fundamental features of brain structure and function. As such, they are governed by the same psychological and neurobiological principles as any other human activity (Berlyne, 1971; Skov & Nadal, 2018). The importance of these general principles for empirical aesthetics cannot be overstated: "There can be no understanding of art without bringing art into relation with non-artistic forms of behavior" (Berlyne, 1971, p. 26). Transformative progress in empirical aesthetics has always been the result of strengthening the ties with other domains of psychology and neuroscience: Fechner (1871) founded the domain by using psychophysical methods to establish it, Arnheim (1974) applied the Gestalt principles to the appreciation of art, Berlyne (1971) used general motivational and information theory principles applied to aesthetic appreciation, and neuroaesthetics emerged when the methods and concepts of neuroscience were used to ask questions about neuroaesthetics (Chatterjee, 2011; Nadal & Pearce, 2011).

Among the domains of the behavioral and brain sciences, empirical aesthetics has intersected most often with personality psychology, social psychology, consumer psychology, affective neuroscience, neuroeconomics, and social neuroscience. In the future, this list could be expanded to include other fields, such as cognitive engineering, to study how aesthetic features can improve the design of human–machine interfaces; physiology, to study the role of interoceptive signals participate in aesthetic appreciation; neurogenomics, to study the relation between genetic expression in neural tissue and aesthetic appreciation; and neuroethics, to better understand the moral and societal implications of facial and aesthetic deformities on judgment.

Part of what makes aesthetics such a fascinating topic is the many angles from which it can be approached. No single approach—empirical aesthetics included—can hope to provide a complete picture of the many facets of art and aesthetics. George Santayana (1904) realized this when discussing the place of aesthetics in relation to psychology:

> the question whether aesthetics is a part of psychology or a separate discipline is (. . .) an insoluble question, because it creates a dilemma which does not exist in the facts. A part of psychology deals with aesthetic matters, but cannot exhaust them; parts of other sciences also deal with the same. A single and complete aesthetic science, natural or ideal, is an idol of the cave and a scholastic chimera.
>
> (Santayana, 1904, p. 327)

This is just as true today as it was a century ago.

A comprehensive understanding of aesthetics can only emerge from the dialogue between neighboring fields that approach it from different angles. For instance, for several decades, empirical aesthetics has had a very fruitful relation with the field of design (Erk, Spitzer, Wunderlich, Galley, & Walter, 2002; Ho, Lu, & Chen, 2016; Schaefer & Rotte, 2007), and we are currently witnessing the beginning of what it seems will be a fascinating interaction between empirical aesthetics and architecture (Eberhard, 2009; Goldstein, 2006; Graham, Gosling, & Travis, 2015; Sternberg & Wilson, 2006).

The relation between empirical aesthetics and some of the humanities, however, has not always been as fruitful as could be hoped for (Seeley, this volume and Reber, this volume). Nevertheless, despite important conceptual and methodological differences between empirical and philosophical aesthetics, it has been shown that there are plenty of reasons and grounds for rapprochement between philosophical and empirical aesthetics (Hayn-Leichsenring & Chatterjee, 2019; Seeley, 2006, 2011, 2014b). The same is true for the interaction between empirical aesthetics and art theory and art history (Bullot & Reber, 2013; Kozbelt & Seeley, 2007), a collaboration that has already proved to be extremely fruitful when common goals are set (Brinkmann, Commare, Leder, & Rosenberg, 2014; Leder et al., 2019). There is great potential in the future for empirical aesthetics if it can establish significant links with the fields of human evolution and sexual selection, to study the geometric patterns and decorations created by our evolutionary ancestors and the similarities between human preferences and animal displays and mate choice (Skov, 2020).

ACKNOWLEDGMENTS

We would like to thank Aenne Brielmann and Giacomo Bignardi for helpful comments that substantially improved this chapter.

REFERENCES

Achorn, A. M., & Rosenthal, G. G. (2020). It's not about him: Mismeasuring "good genes" in sexual selection. *Trends in Ecology & Evolution, 35*(3), 206–219. https://doi.org/10.1016/j.tree.2019.11.007

Adler, M. J. (1929). Music appreciation: An experimental approach to its measurement. *Archives of Psychology, 110*, 1–102.

Allesch, G. J. v. (1925). Die ästhetische Erscheinungsweise der Farben. *Psychologische Forschung, 6*(1), 1–91.https://doi.org/10.1007/BF00444162

Anglada-Tort, M., & Skov, M. (2020). *What counts as aesthetics in science? A bibliometric analysis and visualization of the scientific literature from 1970 to 2018. Psychology of Aesthetics, Creativity, and the Arts.* Advance online publication. https://doi.org/10.1037/aca0000350

Arnheim, R. (1964). *Art and visual perception.* Berkeley, CA: University of California Press.

Arnheim, R. (1966). *Toward a psychology of art.* Berkeley, CA: University of California Press.

Arnheim, R. (1969). *Visual thinking.* Berkeley, CA: University of California Press.

Arnheim, R. (1974). *Art and visual perception. A psychology of the creative eye. The new version.* Berkeley, CA: University of California Press.

Balling, J. D., & Falk, J. H. (1982). Development of visual preference for natural environments. *Environment and Behavior, 14*, 5–28.

Bar, M. (2004). Visual objects in context. *Nature Reviews Neuroscience, 5*, 617–629.

Barnhart, E. N. (1940). The criteria used in preferential judgments of geometrical forms. *American Journal of Psychology, 53*, 354–370.

Barrett, L. F., Mesquita, B., & Smith, E. R. (2010). The context principle. In B. Mesquita, L. F. Barrett, & E. R. Smith (Eds.), *The mind in context* (pp. 1–22). New York, NY: Guilford Press.

Barrett, L. F., & Russell, J. A. (2015). *The psychological construction of emotion.* New York, NY: The Guilford Press.

Barron, F., & Welsh, G. S. (1952). Artistic perception as a possible factor in personality style: Its measurement by a figure preference test. *Journal of Psychology, 33*, 199–203.

Barsalou, L. W. (2008). Grounded cognition. *Annual Review of Psychology, 59*, 617–645.

Bartlett, F. C. (1932). *Remembering. A study in experimental and social psychology.* Cambridge: Cambridge University Press.

Belke, B., Leder, H., & Augustin, D. (2006). Mastering style—Effects of explicit style-related information, art knowledge and affective state on appreciation of abstract paintings. *Psychology Science, 48*, 115–134.

Berlyne, D. E. (1963). Complexity and incongruity variables as determinants of exploratory choice and evaluative ratings. *Canadian Journal of Psychology, 17,* 274–290.

Berlyne, D. E. (1970). Novelty, complexity, and hedonic value. *Perception & Psychophysics, 8,* 279–286.

Berlyne, D. E. (1971). *Aesthetics and psychobiology.* New York, NY: Appleton-Century-Crofts.

Berlyne, D. E. (1972). Ends and means of experimental aesthetics. *Canadian Journal of Psychology, 26,* 303–325).

Berlyne, D. E. (1974). The new experimental aesthetics. In D. E. Berlyne (Ed.), *Studies in the new experimental aesthetics: Steps toward an objective psychology of aesthetic appreciation* (pp. 1–26). Washington, DC: Hemisphere Publishing Corporation.

Berlyne, D. E., Ogilvie, J. C., & Parham, L. C. C. (1968). The dimensionality of visual complexity, interestingness, and pleasingness. *Canadian Journal of Psychology, 22,* 376–387.

Bertamini, M., Palumbo, L., Gheorghes, T. N., & Galatsidas, M. (2016). Do observers like curvature or do they dislike angularity? *British Journal of Psychology, 107,* 154–178.

Bignardi, G., Ticini, L. F., Smit, D., & Polderman, T. J. (2020). Domain-specific and domain-general genetic and environmental effects on the intensity of visual aesthetic appraisal. *PsyArXiv,* February 7. https://doi.org/10.31234/osf.io/79nbq

Bitgood, S., & Patterson, D. D. (1993). The effects of gallery changes on visitor reading and object viewing time. *Environment and Behavior, 25,* 761–781.

Brieber, D., Leder, H., & Nadal, M. (2015). The experience of art in museums: An attempt to dissociate the role of physical context and genuineness. *Empirical Studies of the Arts, 33,* 95–105. https://doi.org/10.1177/0276237415570000

Brieber, D., Nadal, M., Leder, H., & Rosenberg, R. (2014). Art in time and space: Context modulates the relation between art experience and viewing time. *PLoS ONE, 9*(6), e99019. https://doi.org/10.1371/journal.pone.0099019

Brielmann, A. A., & Pelli, D. G. (2017). Beauty requires thought. *Current Biology, 27,* 1506–1513.

Brighouse, G. (1939a). A study of aesthetic apperception. *Psychological Monographs, 51,* 1–22.

Brighouse, G. (1939b). Variability in preference for simple forms. *Psychological Monographs, 51,* 68–74.

Brinkmann, H., Commare, L., Leder, H., & Rosenberg, R. (2014). Abstract art as a universal language? *Leonardo, 47,* 256–257.

Brown, S., Gao, X., Tisdelle, L., Eickhoff, & Liotti, M. (2011). Naturalizing aesthetics: Brain areas for aesthetic appraisal across sensory modalities. *NeuroImage, 58,* 250–258.

Bruner, J. (1990). *Acts of meaning.* Cambridge, MA: Harvard University Press.

Brunton, G., Paraskeva, N., Caird, J., Bird, K. S., Kavanagh, J., Kwan, I., . . . Thomas, J. (2014). Psychosocial predictors, assessment, and outcomes of cosmetic procedures: A systematic rapid evidence assessment. *Aesthetic Plastic Surgery, 38*(5), 1030–1040. https://doi.org/10.1007/s00266-014-0369-4

Bullot, N. J., & Reber, R. (2013). The artful mind meets art history: Toward a psycho-historical framework for the science of art appreciation. *Behavioral and Brain Sciences, 36,* 123–137.

Cahalan, E. J. (1939). The consistency of aesthetic judgment. *Psychological Monographs, 51,* 75–87. https://doi.org/10.1037/h0093478

Calvo-Merino, B., Urgesi, C., Orgs, G., Aglioti, S. M., & Haggard, P. (2010). Extrastriate body area underlies aesthetic evaluation of body stimuli. *Experimental Brain Research, 204,* 447–456.

Carroll, H. A. (1933). What do the Meier-Seashore and the McAdory Art Tests measure? *Journal of Educational Research, 26,* 661–665.

Cela-Conde, C. J., Marty, G., Maestú, F., Ortiz, T., Munar, E., Fernández, A., . . . Quesney, F. (2004). Activation of the prefrontal cortex in the human visual aesthetic perception. *Proceedings of the National Academy of Sciences USA*, *101*, 6321–6325.

Chan, J., Eysenck, H. J., & Götz, K. O. (1980). A new visual aesthetic sensitivity test: III Cross-cultural comparison between Hong Kong children and adults, and English and Japanese samples. *Perceptual and Motor Skills*, *50*, 1325–1326.

Chatterjee, A. (2004). The neuropsychology of visual artistic production. *Neuropsychologia*, *42*, 1568–1583.

Chatterjee, A. (2006). The neuropsychology of visual art: Conferring capacity. *International Review of Neurobiology*, *74*, 39–49.

Chatterjee, A. (2011). Neuroaesthetics: A coming of age story. *Journal of Cognitive Neuroscience*, *23*, 53–62.

Chatterjee, A. (2014). Scientific aesthetics: Three steps forward. *British Journal of Psychology*, *105*, 465–467.

Chatterjee, A., & Vartanian, O. (2014). Neuroaesthetics. *Trends in Cognitive Sciences*, *18*, 370–375.

Christensen, J. F. (2017). Pleasure junkies all around! Why it matters and why 'the arts' might be the answer: a biopsychological perspective. *Proceedings of the Royal Society B: Biological Sciences*, *284*(1854), 20162837. https://doi.org/10.1098/rspb.2016.2837

Chuan-Peng, H., Huang, Y., Eickhoff, S. B., Peng, K., & Sui, J. (2020). Seeking the "beauty center" in the brain: A meta-analysis of fMRI studies of beautiful human faces and visual art. *Cognitive, Affective, & Behavioral Neuroscience*, *20*, 1200–1215. https://doi.org/10.3758/s13415-020-00827-z

Clair, M. B. (1939). Variation in the perception of aesthetic qualities in paintings. *Psychological Monographs*, *51*(5), 52–67.

Clark, A. (1997). *Being there. Putting brain, body, and world together again*. Cambridge, MA: MIT Press.

Clark, H., Quackenbush, N., & Washburn, M. F. (1913). A suggested coefficient of affective sensitiveness. *American Journal of Psychology*, *24*, 583–585.

Davis, F. C. (1933). Aesthetic proportion. *American Journal of Psychology*, *45*, 298–302.

Dayan, P., & Abbott, L. F. (2001). *Theoretical neuroscience. computational and mathematical modeling of neural systems*. Cambridge, MA: MIT Press.

Dewey, J. (1934). *Art as experience*. New York, NY: Minton, Balch & Company.

Eberhard, J. P. (2009). Applying neuroscience to architecture. *Neuron*, *62*, 753–756.

Edmonds, E. M., & Smith, M. E. (1923). The phenomenological description of musical intervals. *American Journal of Psychology*, *34*, 287–291. https://doi.org/10.2307/1413583

Emch, A. (1900). Mathematical principles of esthetic forms. *The Monist*, *11*, 50–64.

Erk, S., Spitzer, M., Wunderlich, A. P., Galley, L., & Walter, H. (2002). Cultural objects modulate reward circuitry. *NeuroReport*, *13*, 2499–2503.

Eysenck, H. J. (1941a). A critical and experimental study of colour preferences. *American Journal of Psychology*, *54*, 385–394.

Eysenck, H. J. (1941b). The empirical determination of an aesthetic formula. *Psychological Review*, *48*, 83–92.

Eysenck, H. J. (1941c). 'Type'-Factors in aesthetic judgments. *British Journal of Psychology*, *31*, 262–270.

Eysenck, H. J. (1942). The experimental study of the "Good Gestalt"—A new approach. *Psychological Review*, *49*, 344–363.

Eysenck, H. J. (1981). Aesthetic preferences and individual differences. In D. O'Hare (Ed.), *Psychology and the arts* (pp. 76–101). Brighton: The Harvester Press.

Falk, J. H. (1993). Assessing the impact of exhibit arrangement on visitor behavior and learning. *Curator, 36*, 133–146.

Farnsworth, P. R. (1925). Atonic endings in melodies. *American Journal of Psychology, 36*, 394–400. https://doi.org/10.2307/1414163

Farnsworth, P. R. (1926a). Ending preferences among the three positions of the tonic chord. *Journal of Comparative Psychology, 6*, 95–102. https://doi.org/10.1037/h0072802

Farnsworth, P. R. (1926b). The effect of repetition on ending preferences in melodies. *American Journal of Psychology, 37*, 116–122.

Farnsworth, P. R. (1931). An historical, critical and experimental study of the Seashore-Kwalwasser test battery. *Genetic Psychology Monographs, 9*, 291–393.

Farnsworth, P. R. (1932). Preferences for rectangles. *Journal of General Psychology, 7*, 479–481. https://doi.org/10.1080/00221309.1932.9918480

Fechner, G. T. (1860). *Elemente der Psychophysik*. Leipzig, Germany: Breitkopf und Härtel.

Fechner, G. T. (1866). Das Associationsprincip in der Aesthetik. *Zeitschrift Für Bildende Kunst, 1*, 179–191.

Fechner, G. T. (1871). *Zur experimentalen Aesthetik*. Leipzig, Germany: Hirzel.

Fechner, G. T. (1876). *Vorschule der Ästhetik*. Leipzig, Germany: Breitkopf und Härtel.

Fich, L. B., Jönsson, P., Kirkegaard, P. H., Wallergård, M., Garde, A. H., & Hansen, A. (2014). Can architectural design alter the physiological reaction to psychosocial stress? A virtual TSST experiment. *Physiology & Behavior, 135*, 91–97.

Fingerhut, J., & Prinz, J. J. (2020). Aesthetic emotions reconsidered. *The Monist, 103*, 223–239.

Fink, B., Grammer, K., & Matts, P. J. (2006). Visible skin color distribution plays a role in the perception of age, attractiveness, and health in female faces. *Evolution and Human Behavior, 27*, 433–442.

Forster, M., Leder, H., & Ansorge, U. (2013). It felt fluent, and I liked it: Subjective feeling of fluency rather than objective fluency determines liking. *Emotion, 13*, 280–289. https://doi.org/10.1037/a0030115

Forster, M., Leder, H., & Ansorge, U. (2016). Exploring the subjective feeling of fluency. *Experimental Psychology, 63*, 45–58. https://doi.org/10.1027/1618-3169/a000311

Franklin, M. B., Becklen, R. C., & Doyle, C. L. (1993). The influence of titles on how paintings are seen. *Leonardo, 26*, 103–108.

Gangestad, S. W., & Scheyd, G. J. (2005). The evolution of human physical attractiveness. *Annual Review of Anthropology, 34*(1), 523–548. https://doi.org/10.1146/annurev.anthro.33.070203.143733

Garth, T. R. (1924). A color preference scale for one thousand white children. *Journal of Experimental Psychology, 7*, 233–241.

Garth, T. R., & Collado, I. R. (1929). The color preferences of Filipino children. *Journal of Comparative Psychology, 9*, 397–404.

Gartus, A., & Leder, H. (2014). The white cube of the museum versus the gray cube of the street: The role of context in aesthetic evaluations. *Psychology of Aesthetics, Creativity, and the Arts, 8*, 311–320.

Geissler, L. R. (1917). The affective tone of color-combinations. In *Studies in Psychology* (pp. 150–174). Worcester, MA: Louis N. Wilson.

Goldstein, R. N. (2006). Architectural design and the collaborative research environment. *Cell, 127*, 243–246.

Götz, K. O., Borisy, A. R., Lynn, R., & Eysenck, H. J. (1979). A new visual aesthetic sensitivity test: I Construction and psychometric properties. *Perceptual and Motor Skills, 49,* 795–802.

Graf, L. K., & Landwehr, J. R. (2015). A dual-process perspective on fluency-based aesthetics: The pleasure-interest model of aesthetic liking. *Personality and Social Psychology Review, 19,* 395–410.

Graf, L. K. M., & Landwehr, J. R. (2017). Aesthetic pleasure versus aesthetic interest: The two routes to aesthetic liking. *Frontiers in Psychology, 8,* 15. https://doi.org/10.3389/fpsyg.2017.00015

Graham, L. T., Gosling, S. D., & Travis, C. K. (2015). The psychology of home environments: A call for research on residential space. *Perspectives on Psychological Science, 10,* 346–356.

Graves, M. (1948). *Design judgement test.* San Antonio, TX: Psychological Corporation.

Greenfield, G., & Machado, P. (2012). Guest editors' introduction. *Journal of Mathematics and the Arts, 6,* 59–64.

Grüner, S., Specker, E., & Leder, H. (2019). Effects of context and genuineness in the experience of art. *Empirical Studies of the Arts, 37,* 138–152. https://doi.org/10.1177/0276237418822896

Guernsey, M. (1928). The rôle of consonance and dissonance in music. *American Journal of Psychology, 40,* 173–204.

Guilford, J. P., & Guilford, R. B. (1931). A prognostic test for students in design. *Journal of Applied Psychology, 15,* 335–345. https://doi.org/10.1037/h0069952

Hayden, B. Y., Parikh, P. C., Deaner, R. O., & Platt, M. L. (2007). Economic principles motivating social attention in humans. *Proceedings of the Royal Society B: Biological Sciences, 274*(1619), 1751–1756. https://doi.org/10.1098/rspb.2007.0368

Hayn-Leichsenring, G. U., & Chatterjee, A. (2019). Colliding terminological systems—Immanuel Kant and contemporary empirical aesthetics. *Empirical Studies of the Arts, 37,* 197–219. https://doi.org/https://doi.org/10.1177/0276237418818635

Heinlein, C. P. (1925). An experimental study of the Seashore Consonance Test. *Journal of Experimental Psychology, 8,* 408–433.

Heinlein, C. P. (1928). The affective characters of the major and minor modes in music. *Journal of Comparative Psychology, 8,* 101–142.

Herruer, J. M., Prins, J. B., van Heerbeek, N., Verhage-Damen, G. W. J. A., & Ingels, K. J. A. O. (2015). Negative predictors for satisfaction in patients seeking facial cosmetic surgery: A systematic review. *Plastic and Reconstructive Surgery, 135*(6), 1596–1605.

Hevner, K. (1935a). Experimental studies of the affective value of colors and lines. *Journal of Applied Psychology, 19,* 385–398.

Hevner, K. (1935b). The affective character of the major and minor modes in music. *American Journal of Psychology, 47,* 103–118.

Hevner, K. (1936). Experimental studies of the elements of expression in music. *American Journal of Psychology, 48,* 246–268.

Hevner, K., & Mueller, J. H. (1939). The effectiveness of various types of art appreciation aids. *Journal of Abnormal and Social Psychology, 34,* 63–72. https://doi.org/10.1037/h0059214

Ho, C.-H., Lu, Y.-N., & Chen, C.-H. (2016). Influence of curvature and expertise on aesthetic preferences for mobile device designs. *International Journal of Design, 10,* 17–25.

Hoenig, F. (2005). Defining computational aesthetics. In L. Neumann, M. Sbert, B. Gooch, & W. Purgathofer (Eds.), *Proceedings of the First Eurographics Conference on Computational Aesthetics in Graphics, Visualization and Imaging* (pp. 13–18). Aire-la-Ville, Switzerland: The Eurographics Association.

Hristova, E., Georgieva, S., & Grinberg, M. (2011). Top-down influences on eye-movements during painting perception: The effect of task and titles. In A. Esposito, A. M. Esposito, R. Martone, V. Müller, & G. Scarpetta (Eds.), *Toward autonomous, adaptive, and context-aware multimodal interfaces. Theoretical and practical issues* (pp. 104–115). Berlin: Springer-Verlag.

Hutchins, E. (1995). *Cognition in the wild*. Cambridge, MA: MIT Press.

Ishizu, T., & Zeki, S. (2013). The brain's specialized systems for aesthetic and perceptual judgment. *European Journal of Neuroscience, 37,* 1413–1420.

Israeli, N. (1928). Affective reactions to painting reproductions. A study in the psychology of aesthetics. *Journal of Applied Psychology, 12,* 125–139.

Iwawaki, S., Eysenck, H. J., & Götz, K. O. (1979). A new visual aesthetic sensitivity test (VAST): II. Cross-cultural comparison between England and Japan. *Perceptual and Motor Skills, 49,* 859–862.

Jacobsen, T. (2004). Individual and group modelling of aesthetic judgment strategies. *British Journal of Psychology, 95,* 41–56.

Jacobsen, T. (2006). Bridging the arts and sciences: A framework for the psychology of aesthetics. *Leonardo, 39,* 155–162.

Jacobsen, T., & Höfel, L. (2001). Aesthetics electrified: An analysis of descriptive symmetry and evaluative aesthetic judgment processes using event-related brain potentials. *Empirical Studies of the Arts, 19,* 177–190.

Jacobsen, T., & Höfel, L. (2002). Aesthetic judgments of novel graphic patterns: Analyses of individual judgments. *Perceptual and Motor Skills, 95,* 755–766.

Jacoby, L. L., Kelley, C. M., & Dywan, J. (1989). Memory attributions. In H. L. Roediger III & F. I. M. Craik (Eds.), *Varieties of memory and consciousness: Essays in honour of Endel Tulving* (pp. 391–422). Hillsdale, NJ: Lawrence Erlbaum.

Kaplan, S. (1992). Environmental preference in a knowledge-seeking, knowledge-using organism. In J. H. Barkow, L. Cosmides, & J. Tooby (Eds.), *The adapted mind: Evolutionary psychology and the generation of culture* (pp. 581–598). New York, NY: Oxford University Press.

Katz, S. E., & Breed, F. S. (1922). Color preferences of children. *Journal of Applied Psychology, 6,* 255–266.

Kawabata, H., & Zeki, S. (2004). Neural correlates of beauty. *Journal of Neurophysiology, 91,* 1699–1705.

Kozbelt, A., & Seeley, W. P. (2007). Integrating art historical, psychological, and neuroscientific explanations of artists' advantages in drawing and perception. *Psychology of Aesthetics, Creativity, and the Arts, 1,* 80–90.

Külpe, O. (1897). *Introduction to philosophy*. London: Swan Sonnenschein & Co.

Külpe, O. (1907). Der gegenwärtige Stand der experimentellen Ästhetik. In F. Schumann (Ed.), *Bericht über den II. Kongreß für experimentelle Psychologie in Würzburg vom 18. bis 21. April 1906* (pp. 1–57). Leipzig, Germany: Barth.

Külpe, O. (1921). *Grundlagen der Ästhetik*. Leipzig, Germany: S. Hirzel.

Leder, H., Belke, B., Oeberst, A., & Augustin, D. (2004). A model of aesthetic appreciation and aesthetic judgments. *British Journal of Psychology, 95,* 489–508.

Leder, H., & Nadal, M. (2014). Ten years of a model of aesthetic appreciation and aesthetic judgments: The aesthetic episode—Developments and challenges in empirical aesthetics. *British Journal of Psychology, 105*(4), 443–464. https://doi.org/10.1111/bjop.12084

Leder, H., Tinio, P. P. L., Brieber, D., Kröner, T., Jacobsen, T., & Rosenberg, R. (2019). Symmetry is not a universal law of beauty. *Empirical Studies of the Arts, 37,* 104–114.

Levinson, J. (2003). Philosophical aesthetics: An overview. In J. Levinson (Ed.), *The Oxford handbook of aesthetics* (pp. 3–24). Oxford: Oxford University Press.

Locher, P. J., Smith, K. S., & Smith, L. F. (2001). The influence of presentation format and viewer training in the visual arts on the perception of pictorial and aesthetic qualities of paintings. *Perception, 30,* 449–465.

Locher, P., Smith, L., & Smith, J. (1999). Original paintings versus slide and computer reproductions: A comparison of viewer responses. *Empirical Studies of the Arts, 17,* 121–129.

Logasa, H. A., & Wright, M. M. (1930). *Tests for the appreciation of literature.* Bloomington, IN: Public School Publishing Co.

Lundholm, H. (1921). The affective tone of lines: Experimental researches. *Psychological Review, 28,* 43–60.

Machado, P., Romero, J., Cardoso, A., & Santos, A. (2005). Partially interactive evolutionary artists. *New Generation Computing, 23,* 143–155.

Machado, P., Romero, J., & Manaris, B. (2008). Experiments in computational aesthetics. An iterative approach to stylistic change in evolutionary art. In J. Romero & P. Machado (Eds.), *The art of artificial evolution. Natural computing series* (pp. 381–415). Berlin: Springer.

Madison, T. H. (1942). Interval discrimination as a measure of musical aptitude. *Archives of Psychology, 268,* 5–99.

Makin, A. D. J. (2017). The gap between aesthetic science and aesthetic experience. *Journal of Consciousness Studies, 24,* 184–213.

Marin, M. M., Lampatz, A., Wandl, M., & Leder, H. (2016). Berlyne revisited: Evidence for the multifaceted nature of hedonic tone in the appreciation of paintings and music. *Frontiers in Human Neuroscience, 10,* 536. https://doi.org/10.3389/fnhum.2016.00536

Martin, L. J. (1906). An experimental study of Fechner's principles of aesthetics. *Psychological Review, 13,* 142–219.

Martindale, C. (1984). The pleasures of thought: A theory of cognitive hedonics. *Journal of Mind and Behavior, 5,* 49–80.

Martindale, C. (1988). Aesthetics, psychobiology, and cognition. In F. Farley & R. Neperud (Eds.), *The foundations of aesthetics, art, and art education* (pp. 7–42). New York, NY: Praeger.

Martindale, C. (1990). *The clockwork muse: The predictability of artistic styles.* New York, NY: Basic Books.

Martindale, C., & Moore, K. (1988). Priming, prototypicality, and preference. *Journal of Experimental Psychology: Human Perception and Performance, 14,* 661–670.

Martindale, C., Moore, K., & Borkum, J. (1990). Aesthetic preference: Anomalous findings for Berlyne's Psychobiological Theory. *American Journal of Psychology, 103,* 53–80.

Martindale, C., Moore, K., & West, A. (1988). Relationship of preference judgments to typicality, novelty, and mere exposure. *Empirical Studies of the Arts, 6,* 79–96.

Mastandrea, S., Bartoli, G., & Bove, G. (2009). Preferences for ancient and modern art museums: Visitor experiences and personality characteristics. *Psychology of Aesthetics, Creativity, and the Arts, 3,* 164–173.

McAdory, M. (1933). *The construction and validation of an art test.* New York, NY: Columbia University Press.

McCarthy, D. (1930). A study of the Seashore measures of musical talent. *Journal of Applied Psychology, 14,* 437–455. https://doi.org/10.1037/h0073360

McManus, I. C., & Wu, W. (2013). "The square is … bulky, heavy, contented, plain, good-natured, stupid …": A cross-cultural study of the aesthetics and meanings of rectangles. *Psychology of Aesthetics, Creativity, and the Arts, 7,* 130–139. https://doi.org/10.1037/a0030469

Meier, N. C. (1926). Aesthetic judgment as a measure of art talent. *University of Iowa studies. Series on aims and progress of research* (Vol. 1). Iowa City, IA: University of Iowa.

Meier, N. C. (1940). *Meier art tests. I. Art judgment.* Iowa City, IA: State University of Iowa, Bureau of Educational Research and Service.

Meier, N. C. (1942). *The Meier art judgment test.* Iowa City, IA: Bureau of Educational Research and Service, University of Iowa.

Meier, N. C. (1963). *Meier art tests. II. Aesthetic perception.* Iowa City, IA: Bureau of Educational Research and Service, University of Iowa.

Meier, N. C., & Seashore, C. E. (1929). *The Meier-Seashore art judgment test.* Iowa City, IA: Bureau of Educational Research, University of Iowa.

Menninghaus, W., Wagner, V., Wassiliwizky, E., Schindler, I., Hanich, J., Jacobsen, T., & Koelsch, S. (2019). What are aesthetic emotions? *Psychological Review, 126,* 171–195.

Mesquita, B., Barrett, L. F., & Smith, E. R. (2010). *The mind in context.* New York, NY: Guilford Press.

Michaels, G. M. (1924). Color preferences according to age. *American Journal of Psychology, 35,* 79–87.

Miller, C. A., & Hübner, R. (2019). Two routes to aesthetic preference, one route to aesthetic inference. *Psychology of Aesthetics, Creativity, and the Arts, 14*(2), 237–249 https://doi.org/10.1037/aca0000241

Millis, K. (2001). Making meaning brings pleasure: The influence of titles on aesthetic experiences. *Emotion, 1,* 320–329.

Mitschke, V., Goller, J., & Leder, H. (2017). Exploring everyday encounters with street art using a multimethod design. *Psychology of Aesthetics, Creativity, and the Arts, 11,* 276–283.

Mühlenbeck, C. A., Liebal, K., Pritsch, C., & Jacobsen, T. (2015). Gaze duration biases for colours in combination with dissonant and consonant sounds: A comparative eye-tracking study with orangutans. *PLoS ONE, 10*(10), e0139894.

Mühlenbeck, C., Jacobsen, T., Pritsch, C., & Liebal, K. (2017). Cultural and species differences in gazing patterns for marked and decorated objects: A comparative eye-tracking study. *Frontiers in Psychology, 8,* 6.

Mühlenbeck, C., Liebal, K., Pritsch, C., & Jacobsen, T. (2016). Differences in the visual perception of symmetric patterns in orangutans (*Pongo pygmaeus abelii*) and two human cultural groups: A comparative eye-tracking study. *Frontiers in Psychology, 7,* 408. https://doi.org/10.3389/fpsyg.2016.00408

Munar, E., Gomez-Puerto, G., Call, J., & Nadal, M. (2015). Common visual preference for curved contours in humans and great apes. *PLoS ONE, 10*(11). https://doi.org/10.1371/journal.pone.0141106

Myszkowski, N., Çelik, P., & Storme, M. (2018). A meta-analysis of the relationship between intelligence and visual "taste" measures. *Psychology of Aesthetics, Creativity, and the Arts, 12,* 24–33.

Myszkowski, N., & Storme, M. (2017). Measuring "good taste" with the Visual Aesthetic Sensitivity Test-Revised (VAST-R). *Personality and Individual Differences, 117,* 91–100.

Nadal, M. (2013). The experience of art. Insights from neuroimaging. *Progress in Brain Research, 204,* 135–158. https://doi.org/10.1016/B978-0-444-63287-6.00007-5

Nadal, M., Munar, E., Capó, M. À., Rosselló, J., & Cela-Conde, C. J. (2008). Towards a framework for the study of the neural correlates of aesthetic preference. *Spatial Vision, 21,* 379–396. https://doi.org/10.1163/156856808784532653

Nadal, M., & Pearce, M. T. (2011). The Copenhagen Neuroaesthetics Conference: Prospects and pitfalls for an emerging field. *Brain and Cognition, 76*(1), 172–183. https://doi.org/10.1016/j.bandc.2011.01.009

Nadal, M., & Skov, M. (2018). The pleasure of art as a matter of fact. *Proceedings of the Royal Society B: Biological Sciences, 285*(1875), 20172252. https://doi.org/10.1098/rspb.2017.2252

Neisser, U. (1967). *Cognitive psychology.* Englewood Cliffs, NJ: Prentice Hall.

Omigie, D., Frieler, K., Bär, C., Muralikrishnan, R., Wald-Fuhrmann, M., & Fischinger, T. (2019). Experiencing musical beauty: Emotional subtypes and their physiological and musico-acoustic correlates. *Psychology of Aesthetics, Creativity, and the Arts, 15*(2), 197–215. https://doi.org/10.1037/aca0000271

Ortmann, O. (1926). On the melodic relativity of tones. *Psychological Monographs, 35,* i–47.

Ortmann, O. (1928). Tonal intensity as an aesthetic determinant. *The Musical Quarterly, 14,* 178–191.

Palumbo, L., & Bertamini, M. (2016). The curvature effect: A comparison between preference tasks. *Empirical Studies of the Arts, 34,* 35–52.

Palumbo, L., Ruta, N., & Bertamini, M. (2015). Comparing angular and curved shapes in terms of implicit associations and approach/avoidance responses. *PLoS ONE, 10,* e0140043. https://doi.org/10.1371/journal.pone.0140043

Pelowski, M., Markey, P. S., Forster, M., Gerger, G., & Leder, H. (2017). Move me, astonish me ... delight my eyes and brain: The Vienna Integrated Model of top-down and bottom-up processes in Art Perception (VIMAP) and corresponding affective, evaluative, and neuro-physiological correlates. *Physics of Life Reviews, 21,* 80–125.

Poffenberger, A. T., & Barrows, B. E. (1924). The feeling value of lines. *Journal of Applied Psychology, 8,* 187–205.

Prum, R. O. (2017). *The evolution of beauty: How Darwin's Forgotten theory of mate choice shapes the animal world—And us.* New York, NY: Doubleday.

Reber, R., Schwarz, N., & Winkielman, P. (2004). Processing fluency and aesthetic pleasure: Is beauty in the perceiver's processing experience? *Personality and Social Psychology Review, 8,* 364–382.

Rosch, E., & Mervis, C. B. (1975). Family resemblances: Studies in the internal structure of categories. *Cognitive Psychology, 7,* 573–605. https://doi.org/10.1016/0010-0285(75)90024-9

Rosch, E., Mervis, C. B., Gray, W. D., Johnson, D. M., & Boyes-Braem, P. (1976). Basic objects in natural categories. *Cognitive Psychology, 8,* 382–439.

Ryan, M. J. (2018). *A taste for the beautiful. The evolution of attraction.* Princeton, NJ: Princeton University Press.

Santayana, G. (1904). What is aesthetics? *The Philosophical Review, 13,* 320–327.

Schaefer, M., & Rotte, M. (2007). Favorite brands as cultural objects modulate reward circuit. *NeuroReport, 18,* 141–145.

Schmidhuber, J. (2006). Developmental robotics, optimal artificial curiosity, creativity, music, and the fine arts. *Connection Science, 18,* 173–187.

Schwarz, K., Wieschollek, P., & Lensch, H. P. A. (2018). Will people like your image? Learning the aesthetic space. *2018 IEEE Winter Conference on Applications of Computer Vision (WACV),* 2048–2057. https://doi.org/10.1109/WACV.2018.00226

Seeley, W. P. (2006). Naturalizing aesthetics: art and the cognitive neuroscience of vision. *Journal of Visual Art Practice, 5,* 195–213.

Seeley, W. P. (2011). What is the cognitive neuroscience of art ... and why should we care? *American Society for Aesthetics Newsletter, 31,* 1–4.

Seeley, W. P. (2014a). Empirical aesthetics. In M. Kelly (Ed.), *Oxford encyclopedia of aesthetics* (2nd ed.). New York, NY: Oxford University Press.

Seeley, W. P. (2014b). Philosophy of art and empirical aesthetics: resistance and rapprochement. In P. P. L. Tinio & J. K. Smith (Eds.), *The Cambridge handbook of the psychology of aesthetics and the arts* (pp. 35–59). Cambridge: Cambridge University Press.

Segal, J. (1905). Die bewußte Selbsttäuschung als Kern des ästhetischen Genießen. *Archiv Für Die Gesamte Psychologie, 6,* 254–270.

Segal, J. (1906). Über die Wohlgefälligkeit einfacher räumlicher Formen: Eine psychologische-ästhetische Untersuchung. *Archiv Für Die Gesamte Psychologie, 7,* 55–124.

Simonton, D. K. (1990). *Psychology, science, and history: An introduction to historiometry.* New Haven, CT: Yale University Press.

Simonton, D. K. (2018). Intellectual genius in the Islamic Golden Age: Cross-civilization replications, extensions, and modifications. *Psychology of Aesthetics, Creativity, and the Arts, 12,* 125–135.

Skamel, U. (2003). Beauty and sex appeal: Sexual selection of aesthetic preferences. In E. Voland & K. Grammer (Eds.), *Evolutionary Aesthetics* (pp. 173–200). Berlin: Springer-Verlag.

Skov, M. (2019). Aesthetic appreciation: The view from neuroimaging. *Empirical Studies of the Arts, 37,* 220–248. https://doi.org/https://doi.org/10.1177/0276237419839257

Skov, M. (2020). Animal Preferences: Implications of sexual selection research for empirical aesthetics. *Psychology of Aesthetics, Creativity, and the Arts,* Advance online publication. https://doi.org/10.13140/RG.2.2.21110.75847

Skov, M., & Nadal, M. (2018). Art is not special: An assault on the last lines of defense against the naturalization of the human mind. *Reviews in the Neurosciences, 29,* 699–702. https://doi.org/10.1515/revneuro-2017-0085

Skov, M., & Nadal, M. (2019). The nature of perception and emotion in aesthetic appreciation: A response to Makin's challenge to empirical aesthetics. *Psychology of Aesthetics, Creativity, and the Arts, 15,* 470–483. https://doi.org/10.1037/aca0000278

Skov, M., & Nadal, M. (2020). There are no aesthetic emotions: Comment on Menninghaus et al. (2019). *Psychological Review, 127,* 640–649.

Smith, S. M., & Vela, E. (2001). Environmental context-dependent memory: A review and meta-analysis. *Psychonomic Bulletin & Review, 8,* 203–220.

Sparshott, F. E. (1963). *The structure of aesthetics.* Toronto: Toronto University Press.

Stanton, H. M. (1928). Seashore measures of musical talent. *Psychological Monographs, 2,* 135–144. https://doi.org/10.1037/h0093342

Staples, R. (1931). Color vision and color preference in infancy and childhood. *Psychological Bulletin, 28,* 297–308.

Sternberg, E. M., & Wilson, M. A. (2006). Neuroscience and architecture: Seeking common ground. *Cell, 127,* 239–242.

Stratton, G. M. (1923). The color red, and the anger of cattle. *Psychological Review, 30,* 321–325.

Talebi, H., & Milanfar, P. (2018). NIMA: Neural image assessment. *IEEE Transactions on Image Processing, 27*(8), 3998–4011. https://doi.org/10.1109/TIP.2018.2831899

Temme, J. E. V. (1992). Amount and kind of information in museums: Its effects on visitors satisfaction and appreciation of art. *Visual Arts Research, 2,* 28–36.

Thorndike, E. L. (1916). Tests of esthetic appreciation. *Journal of Educational Psychology, 7,* 509–522.

Thorndike, E. L. (1917). Individual differences in judgments of the beauty of simple forms. *Psychological Review, 24,* 147–153.

Tschacher, W., Greenwood, S., Kirchberg, V., Wintzerith, S., van den Berg, K., & Tröndle, M. (2012). Physiological correlates of aesthetic perception of artworks in a museum. *Psychology of Aesthetics, Creativity, and the Arts, 6,* 96–103.

Ulrich, R. S. (1977). Visual landscape preference: A model and applications. *Man–Environment Systems, 7,* 279–293.

Ulrich, R. S. (1991). Effects of interior design on wellness: Theory and recent scientific research. *Journal of Health Care Interior Design, 3,* 97–109.

Ulrich, R. S., Simons, R. F., Losito, B. D., Fiorito, E., Miles, M. A., & Zelson, M. (1991). Stress recovery during exposure to natural and urban environments. *Journal of Environmental Psychology, 11,* 201–230.

Urgesi, C., Calvo-Merino, B., Haggard, P., & Aglioti, S. M. (2007). Transcranial magnetic stimulation reveals two cortical pathways for visual body processing. *Journal of Neuroscience, 27,* 8023–8030.

Van Geert, E., & Wagemans, J. (2019). Order, complexity, and aesthetic preferences for neatly organized compositions. *Psychology of Aesthetics, Creativity, and the Arts, 15*(3), 484–504. https://doi.org/10.1037/aca0000276

Vartanian, O., & Goel, V. (2004). Neuroanatomical correlates of aesthetic preference for paintings. *NeuroReport, 15,* 893–897.

Vartanian, O., & Skov, M. (2014). Neural correlates of viewing paintings: Evidence from a quantitative meta-analysis of functional magnetic resonance imaging data. *Brain and Cognition, 87,* 52–56.

Vessel, E A, Starr, G. G., & Rubin, N. (2012). The brain on art: Intense aesthetic experience activates the default mode network. *Frontiers in Human Neuroscience, 6,* 66. https://doi.org/10.3389/fnhum.2012.00066

Vessel, E. A., Maurer, N., Denker, A. H., & Starr, G. G. (2018). Stronger shared taste for natural aesthetic domains than for artifacts of human culture. *Cognition, 179,* 121–131. https://doi.org/10.1016/j.cognition.2018.06.009

Voland, E., & Grammer, K. (2003). *Evolutionary aesthetics.* Berlin: Springer.

von Soest, T., Kvalem, I. L., Roald, H. E., & Skolleborg, K. C. (2009). The effects of cosmetic surgery on body image, self-esteem, and psychological problems. *Journal of Plastic, Reconstructive & Aesthetic Surgery, 62*(10), 1238–1244. https://doi.org/https://doi.org/10.1016/j.bjps.2007.12.093

Voss, M. D. (1939). A study of conditions affecting the functioning of the art appreciation process at the child-level. *Psychological Monographs, 48,* 1–39.

Washburn, M. F., Haight, D., & Regensburg, J. (1921). The relation of the pleasantness of color combinations to that of the colors seen singly. *American Journal of Psychology, 32,* 145–146.

Weber, C. O. (1931). The aesthetics of rectangles and theories of affection. *Journal of Applied Psychology, 31,* 310–318.

Welsh, G. S., & Barron, F. (1949). *Barron-Welsh art scale.* Palo Alto, CA: Consulting Psychology Press.

Westphal-Fitch, G., & Fitch, W. T. (2015). Towards a comparative approach to empirical aesthetics. In J. P. Huston, M. Nadal, F. Mora, A. Agnati, & C. J. Cela-Conde (Eds.), *Art, aesthetics and the brain* (pp. 386–407). Oxford: Oxford University Press.

Williams, E. D., Winter, L., & Woods, J. M. (1938). Tests of literary appreciation. *British Journal of Educational Psychology, 8,* 265–284.

Wing, H. D. (1941). A factorial study of musical tests. *British Journal of Psychology, 31,* 341–355.

Witmer, L. (1894). Zur experimentellen Aesthetik einfacher räumlicher Formverhältnisse. *Philosophische Studien, 9,* 96–144.

Yokoyama, M. (1921). Affective tendency as conditioned by color and form. *American Journal of Psychology, 32,* 81–107.

Zaidel, D. W. (2005). *Neuropsychology of art: Neurological, cognitive, and evolutionary perspectives.* Hove: Psychology Press.

Zaidel, D. W., Nadal, M., Flexas, A., & Enric, M. (2013). An evolutionary approach to art and aesthetic experience. *Psychology of Aesthetics, Creativity, and the Arts, 7,* 100–109. https://doi.org/10.1037/a0028797

Zeki, S. (1999). *Inner vision. An exploration of art and the brain.* Oxford: Oxford University Press.

CHAPTER 2

ONE HUNDRED YEARS OF EMPIRICAL AESTHETICS

Fechner to Berlyne (1876–1976)

MARCOS NADAL AND ESTHER UREÑA

FECHNER: THE QUEST FOR THE MATHEMATICAL RELATION BETWEEN MIND AND MATTER

GUSTAV Theodor Fechner (1801–1887) was born in Lusatia when it was still part of the Holy Roman Empire. Steam locomotives, bicycles, working telegraphs, zippers, photography, and phonographic recording had not yet been invented, and Antarctica had not been discovered. Fechner lived through the dissolution of the old Empire, the establishment of the German Confederation, the revolutions of 1848, the Seven Weeks' War of 1866 between Prussia and Austria, and the founding of the German Empire in 1871. It was the time of the German Romantic composers Ludwig van Beethoven, Franz Schubert, and Richard Wagner; the Romantic painters Caspar David Friedrich and Philipp Otto Runge; and the Naturalist painters Adolph Menzel and Karl von Piloty.

Fechner studied medicine but never practiced, turning instead to physics. He began translating French chemistry and physics books into German, and later conducted experiments on electricity and magnetism, earning him a professorship of physics at the University of Leipzig. He went on to study subjective color experiences, and eventually physiology and psychology (Boring, 1950; Heidelberger, 2004). In psychology, Fechner is known as the founder of psychophysics and empirical aesthetics. However, the foundational texts of psychophysics and empirical aesthetics amount only to just over 5% of the pages he ever wrote (Scheerer, 1987). He founded psychophysics and empirical aesthetics in the service of his philosophy, and as a means to reconcile his dual loyalty: he had become skilled in, and relied upon, the methods of materialistic science, but he was also a passionate idealist, deeply influenced by the natural philosophies of Lorenz Oken and Friedrich W. J. Schelling (Boring, 1950; Flugel, 1933). His way through this contradiction between materialism and idealism was to affirm the identity of mind and matter, to argue that they are different aspects of reality, and to seek the laws that govern their relation. To him, the physical and psychical were two manifestations of one and the same: all consciousness had a material correspondent, and all matter—plants, the Earth, and the universe included—was conscious (Hall, 1912; Heidelberger, 2004).

Fechner was convinced that the relation between the material and conscious aspects of reality could be formulated in exact mathematical terms. But first, he needed to understand the quantitative relation between stimulation and sensation, so he began measuring how relative increases in simulation led to changes in sensation. Fechner realized that a geometric series of stimulations corresponded to an arithmetic series of sensations: an increase in sensation depended on the ratio of the increase in stimulation to the total stimulation. Thus, the greater the first stimulus, the greater the difference between it and the second in order for them to be discriminated (Boring, 1950; Hall, 1912). For a decade he worked on developing appropriate psychophysical methods and performing experiments on sensory thresholds, culminating in his *Elements of Psychophysics* (Fechner, 1860).

THE FOUNDING OF EMPIRICAL AESTHETICS

Fechner began his investigations into aesthetics around 1840 (C. G. Allesch, 2018; Meischner-Metge, 2010). Between 1865 and 1876, he published several papers and the foundational text of empirical aesthetics, *Vorschule der Aesthetik* (Fechner, 1876), translated as *Preschool of Aesthetics* or *Propaedeutics of Aesthetics* (Berlyne, 1971; Jacobsen, 2006; Ortlieb, Kügel, & Carbon, 2020; Vartanian, 2014). Fechner's goal was to lay the foundations for a fully fledged system of aesthetics that would eventually unify and articulate general principles of beauty and art. Reflecting the value he placed on empirical knowledge and his conviction that the purpose of thought and action was to attain the greatest possible pleasure, Fechner conceived empirical aesthetics as part of general hedonics (Arnheim, 1992): the study of what arouses pleasure and how.

Empirical aesthetics was to begin "from below," with the most basic elements and facts of aesthetics, in contrast with philosophical aesthetics, which began "from above," with general principles that could then be applied to specific cases. Empirical aesthetics, therefore, should begin with the reasons for liking and disliking particular cases, and explain why specific objects give pleasure or displeasure. These explanations could later be integrated into a set of principles, which would, in turn, coalesce into the comprehensive system of beauty and the arts that Fechner had envisioned.

To achieve this goal, he developed three methods that required collecting and averaging the responses of groups of people (see Westphal-Fitch, this volume). The *method of choice* required participants to select the most pleasing among a number of alternatives. Using this method, he found that when people were asked to choose among 10 rectangles with different ratios, most chose rectangles close to the golden section. The *method of production* required participants to produce pleasing examples of simple shapes or figures. He found, for instance, that when people were asked to move crossbars of different lengths up and down a vertical bar until they found the most pleasing position, most favored the crossbars that were placed two thirds of the way up the vertical and four sevenths or five ninths of the vertical's length. The *method of use* consisted of measuring nonpurposeful features of commonplace objects, under the assumption that the most common ones were the most pleasing ones. He found, among other things, that the height–width proportions of game cards, visiting cards, picture frames, and the printed area of book pages were frequently very close to the golden section.

The results of experiments and observations using those methods led Fechner (1876) to a fundamental conclusion: liking and disliking were determined by the interaction of a *direct* factor and an *associative* factor. The direct factor was the pleasingness or displeasingness produced by the structural object features and their arrangements (e.g., organization, complexity, proportion). The associative factor referred to the knowledge, memories, and past experiences each person brought to the encounter with the object. Liking or disliking was, therefore, not an automatic response to arrangements of object features. To Fechner, they were the result of the meaning or value those features and their arrangements have for each person, depending on their knowledge and past experiences.

Fechner (1876) proposed several principles of aesthetic pleasure. The most basic was that sensory impressions must occur above a certain *threshold* of pleasure. An object cannot be aesthetically pleasing if its features do not reach this threshold. This threshold can be reached and surpassed by the additive effect of several sensory features acting in concert, each of which might not be strong enough alone. This led him to conclude that objects that give rise to aesthetic pleasure are often composite and manifold and, therefore, to formulate the principle of the *union of diverse elements*. If the many features of an object are to pass the pleasure threshold, they should be aligned toward the same end and be harmonious. This line of reasoning led him to formulate additional principles, such as those of *clearness*, *contrast*, or *sequence*.

With the *Vorschule*, Fechner concluded his work in empirical aesthetics. He wrote about the topic only once again, to address some criticisms and clarify his principle of association (Fechner, 1878). He devoted the last decade of his life to rounding off his philosophy and to the research and criticism that had grown around his *Psychophysics*.

The Pioneers of Empirical Aesthetics

Fechner had no school or students of his own to pursue his vision for empirical aesthetics. Psychophysics and empirical aesthetics were developed in Wundt and G. E.

Müller's laboratories, though severed from their ultimate philosophical purpose, and made to fit the standards of the nascent scientific psychology (Arnheim, 1992). Psychophysics and empirical aesthetics were no longer meant to reveal the material and conscious duality of the universe. They became fields of experimental psychology and, therefore, meant to reveal the basic elements of the conscious mind. Wilhelm Wundt (1832–1920) founded the first psychological research laboratory in Leipzig in 1879. Wundt's goal was to turn psychology into an independent science, developing general explanatory laws based on experiment and observation. The task of psychology, in Wundt's view, was to analyze conscious processes in terms of their basic elements, and to explain how they interact. Georg Elias Müller (1850–1934) became the leading figure in psychophysics after Fechner's death. He undertook a revision and extension of the methods of psychophysics, and placed the Göttingen psychology laboratory almost on a par with Wundt's (Boring, 1950). After Fechner, empirical aesthetics was pioneered by Wundt and G. E. Müller's students (Figure 2.1), including Witmer, Stratton, Meumann, Müsterberg, Martin, and Külpe, and later by their own students.

Lightner Witmer (1867–1956) is known mainly for founding clinical psychology. He was the first to use the principles of scientific psychology to diagnose and treat behavioral problems in children, he coined the term *clinical psychology* to name a new profession, and he established the world's first psychological clinic in 1896, where he supervised the first generation of clinical psychologists (McReynolds, 1987). He is less known as one of Wundt's first PhD students to continue Fechner's empirical aesthetics. Witmer had worked on individual differences in reaction times as James McKeen Cattell's assistant at the University of Pennsylvania, and had hoped to continue his PhD research on that topic. Wundt, however, persuaded him to examine the effects of the proportion of linear figures (crosses, vertical lines divided by dots) and simple forms (triangles, rectangles, and ellipses) on pleasingness judgments. Witmer found that rectangles conforming close to the golden section were the most pleasing. He argued that preferences for rectangles were driven by the balance between *unity* and *diversity*: whereas squares represent the maximum degree of unity but lack diversity, and very slender rectangles represent the maximum degree of diversity but lack unity, rectangles close to the golden section represent an optimal balance between unity and diversity (Witmer, 1894a, 1894b).

Witmer (1892) conjectured that the pleasing or displeasing effects of proportion owe to the ease or unease of eye movements as they follow the figures' forms. However, George Malcom Stratton's (1865–1957) early photographic recordings of eye movements showed that this could not be the case. Stratton had also studied with Wundt at Leipzig and had conducted on himself the famous experiments on visual experiences in the absence of retinal image inversion by wearing up–down and left–right inverting glasses for several consecutive days (Stratton, 1897a, 1897b). Stratton's (1902) pioneering eye tracking studies showed that the eyes never moved smoothly, no matter how smooth the line that was followed. Eye movements were jerky, with darting movements (saccades) followed by instants of rest (fixations), creating irregular, dithering, and angular paths. Symmetrical figures did not lead to symmetrical eye movements, and there was no

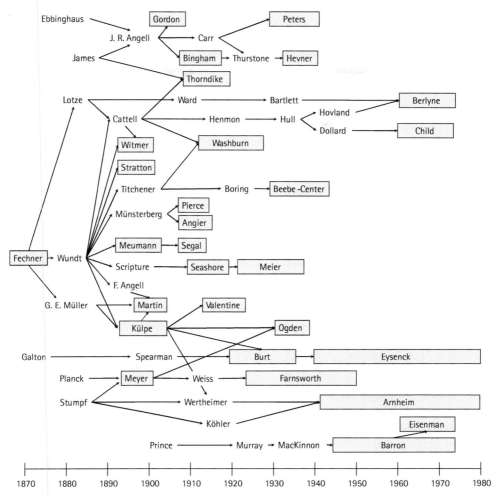

FIGURE 2.1. Major figures in the history of empirical aesthetics. Shaded boxes indicate authors whose work is covered in the chapter. Arrows indicate a major influence, such as teacher–student or mentor–mentee. Boxes are placed chronologically, and cover approximately the period in which each author conducted research on empirical aesthetics.

appreciable difference between the eyes' path when looking at beautiful or ugly forms (Stratton, 1906). He concluded that "Since the eye's movement during the observation of a line or figure is so unlike the form which we perceive and enjoy, it seems illogical to ascribe this enjoyment to the character of the eye's movements to the sensations which arise in this way" (Stratton, 1902, p. 350).

Hugo Münsterberg (1863–1916), founder of applied psychology (Boring, 1950), also studied under Wundt at Leipzig. Later, as head of the Harvard psychological laboratory, he supervised several experiments on the aesthetic appreciation of rhythm in music and poetry (MacDougall, 1903; Stetson, 1903), and symmetry and proportion in visual designs (Angier, 1903; Pfuffer, 1903). Under Münsterberg's supervision, Edgar Pierce (1870–1929) completed his PhD thesis on the relation between symmetry and liking. He presented his participants with three lines, two fixed at the extremes and one movable along the horizontal axis in between, and asked them to place the movable one in the most agreeable position. Participants tended to place the line in a position approximately consistent with the golden section. But when the test figure included more fixed lines, participants placed the movable one almost midway between the two closest fixed ones, resulting in symmetrical divisions. Regardless of the number of fixed lines, participants said they were striving for stability, which seemed more pleasing to them (Pierce, 1894). After his thesis, Pierce abandoned psychology to manage a hotel. His success allowed him to leave a bequest of over $800,000 to Harvard's psychology department. Those funds have sponsored the William James lectures, the first of which was given by John Dewey, and published as *Art as Experience* (Dewey, 1934).

Hugo Münsterberg also supervised Roswell Parker Angier's (1874–1946) thesis, which built upon Witmer's findings on the golden section. He was critical of the assumption that group averages approximating the golden section corresponded to a norm of aesthetic pleasingness, while deviations from it were treated as errors. He asked participants to divide horizontal lines at the place they found most pleasing. The proportion averaged across participants was close to the golden section, but only two of the nine participants regularly produced line divisions that corresponded to the golden section (Angier, 1903). This confirmed that the golden section is not a universal aesthetic norm, but rather a mathematical abstraction that results from averaging across participants (Green, 1995). Angier continued to conduct research on the psychology of vision, and was appointed Professor of Psychology at Yale University and Chairman of the Board of the Institute of Psychology, which housed, among others, Robert M. Yerkes' Primate Laboratory.

The founder of experimental education, Ernst Meumann (1862–1915), also began his career at Wundt's laboratory studying empirical aesthetics (Boring, 1950; Stoerring, 1923). Meumann had a broad understanding of empirical aesthetics: it should provide psychological explanations for aesthetic production and appreciation, it should establish aesthetic norms, and award art a key place in the history of human civilization (Meumann, 1908, 1919; Stoerring, 1923). One of Meumann's students, Jakub Segal (1880–1943), combined introspective and psychophysical methods to study aesthetic appreciation in a series of experiments. He presented participants with straight lines in different orientations, zigzag lines with different periods, and rectangles and triangles of different proportions. Participants were asked to choose the figures that they liked the most, the ones they found moderately pleasing, those that were displeasing, and those that were found indifferent, and to explain the impression that each figure had made on them. Segal found that the figures elicited a broad range of feelings and thoughts in participants. When these thoughts and feelings were clear, the figure pleased, but when they were unclear, the figure displeased (Segal, 1906). The source of pleasingness was not, therefore, the figures' features, but the suggested thoughts and feelings (Segal, 1905, 1907). The two main classes of personal factors that contributed to shaping these thoughts were people's different personalities, and their moods and dispositions when encountering the object. Segal (1905, 1906) conceived these as "pre-aesthetic" factors, common to all sorts of experiences, and not specific to aesthetic experiences. Segal continued writing and teaching psychological aesthetics as Professor of Experimental Pedagogy at the Free University of Warsaw. However, a disease progressively deprived him of movement and eventually forced him to give up his work and his professorship. Ill, and almost unable to move, Segal was murdered in August 1943 at the Gestapo headquarters on Aleja Szucha, in the Warsaw ghetto (Rieser, 1962; Tatarkiewicz, 1946; Woleński, 2011).

None of Wundt and Müller's students had such a fundamental role and lasting effect on empirical aesthetics as Oswald Külpe (1862–1915). After he arrived at Würzburg in 1894, he began studying, teaching, and publishing on empirical aesthetics. Külpe saw psychology as the science of the facts of experience (Külpe, 1895), and empirical aesthetics, therefore, as the science of aesthetic experience. He conceived aesthetic experience as a special sort of receptive state elicited when encountering certain objects (mainly artworks), and aesthetics as the science that studies those objects, the effects, and the value of that receptive state. Aesthetic experiences, however, were not merely due to sensory stimulation, they were the result of the way combinations of sensory elements in space and time lead to perception, judgment, and memory. He proposed three factors that foster aesthetic experiences from sensation (Külpe, 1895): (1) The determinateness of the mental representation of a sensation: the more definitive the effect, the greater the pleasingness. (2) The degree of ease with which a sensation is represented: too easy does not elicit feeling, moderately easy excites pleasure, and too difficult excites unpleasantness. (3) The relation between the overall representation and that of its constituents: the greater the agreement, the more pleasing. The first of these factors anticipated *fluency theory* (Reber, Schwarz, & Winkielman, 2004), the second anticipated Berlyne's *motivational theory* (Berlyne, 1971), and the third anticipated the *Gestalt theory* (Arnheim, 1964). In addition to his refinement, systematization, and extension of Fechner's methods and principles (Külpe, 1907, 1921), Külpe had a lasting influence on empirical aesthetics through his students, especially those from the United States—Lillien J. Martin and Robert M. Ogden—and in the United Kingdom—Charles W. Valentine and Cyril Burt.

Lillien Jane Martin (1851–1943) spent 4 years at Göttingen (1894–1898), even though at that time Göttingen University did not accept women as regular students. She became G. E. Müller's assistant, and they worked together on studies on the psychophysics of lifted weights. The resulting monograph she and Müller published (Martin & Müller, 1899) became a classic in psychophysics (Boring, 1950; Stevens & Gardner, 1982). In 1898, Martin obtained a position at Stanford University with Frank Angell to form a two-person department. She was in charge of equipping and running the psychological laboratory and acted as chair during Angell's sabbatical leaves (Stevens & Gardner, 1982). In 1915 she became the first woman to head a Stanford department. She returned to Germany several summers to continue her studies and research with Külpe, at Würzburg (1907), Bonn (1908 and 1912), and Munich (1914). At Külpe's request, she was awarded an honorary PhD by the University of Bonn in 1913 for her contributions to psychology. The award's citation mentioned, in addition to her contributions to psychophysics, her experimental studies of theories of aesthetics and of Fechner's aesthetic laws (Stevens & Gardner, 1982). She used a combination of introspection and several psychophysical methods to investigate people's responses to comical images taken from newspapers and magazines (Martin, 1905), and, in a thorough examination of Fechner's principles of aesthetics, to investigate people's liking for paintings and simple figures consisting of lines that differed in orientation, length, curvature, and thickness (Martin, 1906). She found support for some of Fechner's aesthetic principles and for some of his conjectures, such as that information about artist and title increases liking for paintings (Martin, 1906, p. 204). But she also found evidence against some of Fechner's principles, such as the principle of contrast: when a liked and disliked figure are presented simultaneously, instead of liking the liked one more, participants liked it less (Martin, 1906, p. 212). In all the experiments she conducted, she found remarkable differences among participants in the extent to which their responses agreed or disagreed with Fechner's principles.

Robert Morris Ogden (1877–1959) graduated from Cornell with a major in psychology and a minor in aesthetics. Titchener, his psychology teacher, encouraged him to study at Würzburg with Külpe, who supervised his PhD on the influence of the rate of reading meaningful and meaningless materials aloud on learning and memory (Dallenbach, 1959; Ogden, 1938). He took up several positions after returning to the United States, including at the University of Missouri as Max Meyer's assistant, until he was hired by Cornell in 1916, where he spent the rest of his life. Two of Ogden's contributions to empirical aesthetics stand out. First, he was the first and main proponent of Gestalt psychology in the United States, translating Gestalt books into English, and inviting Gestalt psychologists (Koffka, Köhler, and Lewin) as visiting professors. Second, in his *Psychology of Art*, he rendered in psychological terms the basic concepts of aesthetics, and the fundamental elements of music, poetry, and visual art (Ogden, 1938).

After graduating in psychology from Cambridge, Charles Wilfred Valentine (1879–1964) spent 1908 at Würzburg studying Külpe's psychological methods (Burt, 1964). Upon his return to the United Kingdom, he used some of Fechner's methods he had learnt with Külpe to study the features underlying children and adults' aesthetic appreciation of musical tones and intervals. He found, for instance, that most people feel that the apparent pitch of an interval corresponds to the higher note, that the order in which people prefer intervals does not match the order of the degree of consonance, that, before the age of 9, children show no preference for concords over discords, that children over 12 prefer musical intervals in a similar order to adults, and that intelligence has no impact on preference for musical intervals (Myers & Valentine, 1914; Valentine, 1913a, 1914). His most significant contribution to empirical aesthetics was perhaps his *Introduction to the Experimental Psychology of Beauty* (Valentine, 1913b), which covered virtually every experiment conducted on preferences for color, shape, symmetry, and complex images to that date, and also on preferences for music in the second edition

(Valentine, 1919). He updated and rewrote the whole book, and included two chapters on the appreciation of poetry shortly before dying (Valentine, 1962).

AMERICAN FUNCTIONAL
EMPIRICAL AESTHETICS

Wundt's structural psychological tradition focused on the *what* and *how* of consciousness: on what takes place in conscious sensation, feeling and thinking, and how it takes place. American psychology, in contrast, focused on the *why* of conscious processes, their function. Led by John Dewey and James Rowland Angell at the University of Chicago, American functional psychology aimed to understand the causes of conscious phenomena, and more specifically, to understand how the mind enables the adaptation of humans to their environment. At Columbia, James McKeen Cattell's functional psychology focused on the traits or capacities that confer people greater or lesser advantages in their adaptation to their environment. Cattell was convinced that a practical psychology required understanding individual differences in these capacities. He invented the term *mental test*, and promoted mental testing (Boring, 1950).

Cattell offered Edward Lee Thorndike (1874–1949) a position at Columbia to study associative processes in animals. Thorndike is renowned for his puzzle boxes for cats, dogs, and chicks. The animals were confined in the boxes but could escape by operating certain mechanisms in the box. He observed that the animals learnt by trial and error and accidental success. The success of a correct movement caused such a movement to be learnt. From these experiments he derived his principles of *effect* and *exercise*. Cattel encouraged Thorndike to apply to children and adolescents the techniques he had developed for animals, paving the way for his contributions to educational psychology and mental testing. As part of his work on mental tests, Thorndike developed a means of measuring the merit of children's drawings based on psychophysical rules of scaling (Thorndike, 1913, 1924). He also developed a measure of aesthetic appreciation, the goal of which was to produce standardized measurement instruments that could be used to test people's ability for aesthetic appreciation in the context of instruction and vocational guidance (Thorndike, 1916, 1917). He published measures of agreement (Thorndike, 1916) and disagreement (Thorndike, 1917) of people's liking for simple figures, such as rectangles, crosses, and triangles of different proportions, differently spaced lines, and couplet endings. The measure of agreement could be used to establish degrees of aesthetic merit, and the deviations from this consensus could be understood as the measure of people's ability for aesthetic appreciation.

Although, at the time, Columbia did not admit women to graduate studies, Margaret Floy Washburn (1871–1939) was given permission to register in Cattell's classes as a listener (Washburn, 1932). Cattell, a lifelong supporter of equal opportunities, treated her as a regular student and demanded from her the same as from the men (Dallenbach,

1940; Washburn, 1932). In 1892, he encouraged her to pursue her PhD studies at Cornell, where Titchener had just arrived to take over the psychological laboratory, becoming the first woman ever to be awarded a doctorate in psychology. That same year, she was elected to the America Psychological Association, and became the president in 1921 (Dallenbach, 1940; Pillsbury, 1940). Her book on comparative psychology *The Animal Mind*, initially published in 1908 and kept up to date through the fourth edition of 1936, was considered the most thorough text on the topic for decades (Boring, 1950; Pillsbury, 1940).

Her contributions to empirical aesthetics included studies on the conditions that influenced the pleasingness of colors, on individual differences in the strength of aesthetic pleasure, and a test of aesthetic judgment. Her work on color preferences showed that judgments of saturated colors were more extreme than the judgments of tints, and that these were more extreme than the shades, but that her participants found the tints generally more pleasing than the shades, and these more pleasing than the saturated colors (Washburn, 1911); that fatigue reduced the pleasingness judgments, especially in the case of highly saturated colors (Norris, Twiss, & Washburn, 1911); that smaller areas were more pleasing than larger areas in the case of saturated colors, and that larger areas were more pleasing than smaller areas in the case of tints and shades (D. Clark, Goodell, & Washburn, 1911); that over the course of a minute of looking at saturated colors they became less pleasing but tints and shades became more pleasing (Crawford & Washburn, 1911); and that spoken negative adjectives about colors (e.g., "faded," "crude") reduced the judged pleasingness of those colors, and positive adjectives (e.g., "warm," "delicate") increased their judged pleasingness (Powelson & Washburn, 1913).

Washburn also studied individual differences in the strength of pleasingness or un-pleasantness reactions. She introduced the concept of *affective sensitiveness* to distinguish between people who strongly tended to like and dislike materials of different sorts, including tones, colors, and speech sounds, from people who were relatively indifferent to those materials (Babbitt, Woods, & Washburn, 1915; H. Clark, Quackenbush, & Washburn, 1913). Affective sensitiveness was not fixed; it depended on certain circumstances and conditions, such as fatigue, which tends to reduce affective sensitiveness (Robbins, Smith, & Washburn, 1915). Poets were more affectively sensitive than science students, suggesting that affective sensitiveness was related to experience and expertise in art and aesthetics (Washburn, Hatt, & Holt, 1923).

Finally, Washburn also produced one of the first tests of aesthetic judgment of pictures. Cattell and colleagues (1918) selected 36 reproductions of artworks that ranged from technically excellent to the popular and sentimental, and asked three experts to rank the images in the order they would like to own the originals (leaving financial value aside). They calculated the average rank for each of the 36 artworks to form a composite expert rank. They then asked 144 participants to perform the same ranking, and to answer whether they had studied drawing or painting, whether they had studied art history, whether they had visited many galleries, and whether they were especially interested in images. The average correlation between experts' ranking and participants with artistic training was .49, participants who were artistically naïve was −.11, and untrained participants but interested in images was .43. Cattell and colleagues (1918) concluded that even an interest in pictures was enough to lead participants to approximate the experts' ranking.

Kate Gordon (1878–1963) enrolled at the University of Chicago in 1896, where she obtained her PhD with a dissertation on *The Psychology of Meaning*, which provided a unified psychological account of economic, logical, ethical, and aesthetic value. The common denominator of value across these domains was, she argued, agreeableness, which she conceived as pure sensuous pleasure. The psychological measure of value, she proposed, was the intensity of this pleasant feeling and the complexity and relations of the valued content (Gordon, 1903). Gordon was awarded an Association of Collegiate Alumnae (ACA) European fellowship to study at Würzburg with Külpe during the winter of 1903–1904. After returning to the United States, she began her studies in empirical aesthetics on the topic of color. Her study of the aesthetics of color aimed to understand the reason for placing some colors toward the center of an area and others toward the outside (Gordon, 1912). She created two basic designs that enabled some colors to be arranged closer to the center and others closer to the edge, while at the same time being appealing to the participants. Figure 2.2 shows the variations of these designs. She only combined two colors at a time: blue and yellow, red and green, blue and red, green and yellow, blue and green, and red and yellow. For all the color combinations, the preferred figure was the one that had the brighter color in the center and the darker color at the edges (Figure 2.2 III). Moreover, the greater the disparity in brightness between the colors in each pair, the greater the preference for the arrangement in Figure 2.2 III (Gordon, 1912).

Gordon continued her studies of color combinations using 50 colored plates of oriental rugs. She asked three people to arrange the cards in order of aesthetic merit, and she averaged their scores. She then alternatively placed each of the plates in two series, creating approximately similar ranges of aesthetic merit. She asked 207 participants to arrange each set in order of their beauty. The results clearly indicated a vast variation in the arrangements. Without exception, every rug was placed close to the top by some participants and close to the bottom by others. She retested 38 of the participants 3 or more weeks later, and found an extraordinary consistency in judgments. Thus, participants were highly consistent with their own beauty rankings, but inconsistent with the group rankings (Gordon, 1923).

Later, she examined the impact of pleasantness and unpleasantness on memory. Her goal was to ascertain whether pleasant or unpleasant sensations are more likely to be recalled. She selected 10 odors that ranged widely in affective quality, and asked her participants to smell the contents while she told them their names. She also prepared 10 similar bottles that contained only water, but she also said the name of one of the odors while participants smelled these. Two hundred participants were asked to remember the names of the odors because they would subsequently be asked to point to them, and then to arrange the bottles in order of their agreeableness. She found that participants recalled 49% of the names of the odors they had ranked as pleasant, 56% of the names of the odors they ranked as indifferent, and 50% of the names of the odors they ranked as unpleasant. However, their recall was 31% better when the bottles actually contained the odor than when they did not. The correlation between the rank order of agreeableness

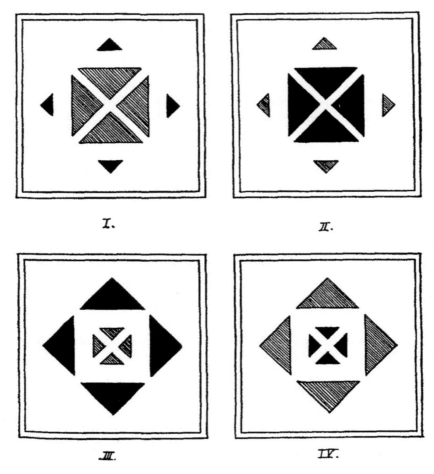

FIGURE 2.2. Color arrangements in Gordon's (1912) study. Black triangles indicate darker colors and lined triangles indicate brighter colors.

Reproduced from Gordon, K. (1912). Esthetics of simple color arrangements. *Psychological Review, 19,* 352–363. The content is in the public domain.

and the order of successful recall was −.07; that is to say, the likelihood of recalling an odor is not related to its affective value (Gordon, 1925).

EMPIRICAL AESTHETICS IN THE AGE OF BEHAVIORISM

American functionalism, comparative psychology, and the possibilities of an objective psychology in the image of Russian reflexology came together in 1913 when John

Broadus Watson initiated his quest against introspection (Watson, 1913). Interest in empirical aesthetics did not wane during the age of behaviorism. Quite the contrary, empirical studies on aesthetics multiplied between 1920 and 1950. Under the stimulus–response scheme of behaviorism, a crucial issue was understanding the factors that modulate the affective value of stimuli. The study of the pleasingness of colors, shapes, musical tones, and intervals became a crucial part of understanding why some stimuli were more rewarding than others.

Empirical aesthetics of music

A remarkable number of studies during the 1920s and 1930s examined the affective value of musical tones, simultaneous pairs of tones, simple tone sequences, various kinds of resolutions, major and minor modes, consonance and dissonance, and variations in rhythm, the effects of repetition, and the formal elements of music that modulate its expressiveness (Edmonds & Smith, 1923; Farnsworth, 1925, 1926a, 1926c; Guernsey, 1928; Heinlein, 1925; 1928; Hevner, 1935c, 1936; Ortmann, 1928, 1926).

The empirical aesthetics of music has its roots in the thought and work of Carl Stumpf. Stumpf had studied with Lotze at Göttingen and had befriended Fechner in Leipzig (Woodward, 2015), where he served as a participant in some of Fechner's experiments on the golden section (Boring, 1950). Stumpf wrote over 50 papers and books on acoustics and several aspects of music, including its evolution, its variations across cultures, the perception of tones, consonance, and dissonance (C. G. Allesch, 2018). Stumpf's work on music was continued by Max Friedrich Meyer (1873–1967), who obtained his PhD in Berlin under Stumpf and the physicist Max Planck's supervision (Esper, 1966). Later, at the University of Missouri, he produced the first completely behaviorist version of psychology (Meyer, 1911), two years before Watson's (Pillsbury, 1929). At Missouri, he continued his work on music (Meyer, 1900, 1901), studying the aesthetic effects of final tones, the intonation of musical intervals, and *quartertone* music (Esper, 1966). Meyer's behaviorism had a profound influence on Albert P. Weiss, one of his students and assistants, who later headed the psychological laboratory at Ohio. It was there, under Weiss' supervision, that Paul Randolph Farnsworth (1899–1978) earned his PhD. He would go on to conduct more than 40 studies on preference for music between 1925 and 1950, and to be the first president of Division 10 of the American Psychological Association (APA), The Society for the Psychology of Aesthetics, Creativity, and the Arts.

Farnsworth's (1958) research on music was a blend of the Stumpf–Meyer approach to music and Weiss's social behaviorism: musical preference was acquired through exposure to the music of the time and culture in which people develop, and should therefore be considered an eminently social phenomenon. Social factors, such as peer pressure and conformity, were the key to understanding musical preferences.

Meyer's (1903) work on preferences for endings had shown that people generally prefer musical endings on the tonic, as they are experienced as complete and reposed.

Farnsworth (1925) showed that there is an order of preference for endings on other notes. For instance, when the tonic of a melody is C, people generally prefer endings on G to endings on E, and they generally prefer endings on E to endings on B flat. But, if exposure to music was a key determinant of preference, as Farnsworth believed, then familiarization and training should have important effects. Indeed, Farnsworth (1926c) showed that preferences for musical endings could be changed in the direction of the least preferred. Familiarization with a particular ending through repetition during the experimental trials increased the sense of completion and repose, even for the endings that initially were least likely to be experienced as reposed and complete: the more often a person hears musical sequences ending in a certain interval from the tonic, the more that person will prefer those endings.

Farnsworth (1926a) also examined whether long-term familiarization through training had an effect on the appreciation of music. He tested whether the root position and first inversion of chords create a sense of repose and completeness, whether the second inversion creates a sense of instability, and whether the relation between the tone arrangement and aesthetic appreciation is modulated by training. He found that participants who had no musical training did not express a substantial difference in their experience of repose and completeness for the three arrangements, although they tended to favor the root position and second inversion. For participants with musical training, the more training they had, the more complete and reposed they found the first inversion, and the less complete and reposed they found the second, with the root position occupying an intermediate position. He concluded from these and other studies that habit, experience, and training were the fundamental determinants of musical preferences (Farnsworth, 1926b).

Kate Hevner (1898–1984) published more than a dozen papers on preferences for musical, visual, and speech stimuli between 1930 and 1940. Her academic background was very different to Farnsworth's. Hevner obtained her Master's in Psychology at Columbia, and earned her PhD at Chicago on different methods for constructing psychological scales under the supervision of Louis Leon Thurstone (Hevner, 1930a). At Chicago, J. R. Angell had been a prolific PhD supervisor. Among his students, besides the behaviorist J. B. Watson, were Harvey A. Carr and Walter V. Bingham. Carr succeeded J. R. Angell as Professor of Psychology and became the major representative of functional psychology (Boring, 1950). Bingham conducted several experiments on the generation of the experience of melody from discrete tones and proposed a motor theory of melody (Bingham, 1910), and reviewed studies on the comparison of music across cultures (Bingham, 1914). He established the first department of applied psychology in the United States, the Division of Applied Psychology at Carnegie Institute of Technology in Pittsburg, where he hired Thurstone, who had been assistant to Thomas Edison and later also studied with J. R. Angell at Chicago (Horst, 1955). Thurstone returned to Chicago in 1924 as an Associate Professor with Carr, and began teaching and researching attitude scaling, psychological measurement, and their applications to different situations (Gulliksen, 1968).

Thus, Kate Hevner had joined America's foremost functional psychology department with an emphasis in developing systems for psychological measurement. She studied the appreciation of painting—testing, for instance, the effects of different kinds of information on the pleasantness of paintings (Hevner & Mueller, 1939)—and of poetry—examining, for instance, the contributions of vowel sounds, consonant sounds, meter, and voice inflection on the affective responses to poems (Hevner, 1937a). But it is to our understanding of the appreciation of music that she contributed most. Her first studies aimed to develop a test of music appreciation that included actual musical compositions as items, and not merely simple tones or tone sequences. The initial version of the test (Hevner, 1930b) included 25 items. Each item consisted of a fragment of classical music played in its original and three altered forms: eliminated, which omitted many of the tones creating a bare version; elaborated, which introduced additional tones; and changed, which altered the phrasing or melody. Participants had to say which version of each item they had liked best or found most pleasing, and which the second best. Two points were given when the original was liked best, and one when it was liked second best. She found that several of the items lacked diagnostic value, and that having to listen to four versions for each item meant that performance relied excessively on memory. A simpler version of the test that included only two alternatives for each item proved to be easier for participants, to have psychometric properties as good as the version with four alternatives, and to produce results in agreement with tests for basic musical abilities, such as consonance discrimination or memory for tones (Hevner, 1931).

She later turned to studying the elements of music that contribute to its expressiveness. Some of those elements suggest motion, such as tempo and rhythm, while other elements suggest tension, such as melody (pitch rises and falls, and variations around the tonic), harmony (consonance and dissonance, smoothness and harshness, position, degree, successions of harmony), and mode (Hevner, 1935b). In her studies on musical expressiveness she manipulated each of these elements in isolation, while controlling the rest. Hevner (1935c), for instance, presented participants with two identical versions of each composition, except for the fact that one was written in the major and the other in minor mode. She found that the pieces in major mode were considered happier, brighter, lighter, more triumphant, more exalting, and more satisfying than the pieces in minor mode, which were considered darker, sadder, gloomier, more frustrating, more melancholic, and more depressing, and that participants who had more musical training and ability discriminated the modes better.

In a later series of studies, she built on this method, and developed stimuli that varied solely in mode, rhythm, consonance, or direction of melody (Hevner, 1936). Her results confirmed that the major mode is experienced as happy, graceful, and playful, whereas the minor mode is experienced as sad, sentimental, and dreamy. She also found that firm rhythms are experienced as vigorous and dignified, compared with flowing rhythms, which are experienced as happy, graceful, and tender; that complex and dissonant harmonies are experienced as exciting and agitating, while simple and consonant harmonies are experienced as happy, serene, and lyrical; and that rising or falling melodies do not lead to notable differences in the expressiveness of music.

Empirical aesthetics of visual forms, color, and art

During this period, researchers also conducted many studies on preferences for simple lines and forms, on the consistency and variability in people's responses to paintings, on the effects of different kinds of information on the appreciation of paintings, and on the effect of age and development, among other issues (Barnhart, 1940; Brighouse, 1939a, 1939b; Cahalan, 1939; Clair, 1939; Davis, 1933; Farnsworth, 1932; Hevner, 1935a; Hevner & Mueller, 1939; Israeli, 1928; Lundholm, 1921; Poffenberger & Barrows, 1924; Voss, 1939; Weber, 1931; Yokoyama, 1921).

Preference for color was an especially prolific research area. Dozens of studies investigated general patterns in color preferences, individual differences in color preferences and their relation to personality, the effects of age and development, and cross-cultural agreement, among other topics (e.g., G. J. v. Allesch, 1925; Garth, 1924; Garth & Collado, 1929; Geissler, 1917; Katz & Breed, 1922; Michaels, 1924; Staples, 1931; Stratton, 1923; Washburn, Haight, & Regensburg, 1921). Chandler's (1934) review of the literature on color preferences highlighted the enormous differences among people. He concluded that "the human organism is not so constituted as to react in a definitive way to each color or each combination of colors. No color is invariably and unconditionally pleasant or unpleasant, exciting or soothing, dignified or tawdry. Such effects depend on a multitude of factors that vary with individual observers and changing circumstances" (Chandler, 1934, pp. 114–115). Eysenck (1941b), however, found considerable agreement between participants in their color preferences. People preferred, in descending order: blue, red, green, violet, yellow, and orange (orange and yellow, in the case of men). Eysenck (1941b) attributed the discrepancies among the different studies that had struck Chandler (1934) to the differences in the materials that had been used (some had used colored papers, others dyed textiles, others colored lights, and others colored crayons). However, he observed that many studies had included among their colors some similar to the ones he had used (highly saturated blue, red, green, violet, orange, and yellow). He averaged the rank for each of these colors in 16 studies that had studied color preferences in Caucasians and in 10 that had studied color preferences in people from other ethnic backgrounds. The average correlation for the preference order was .82 in the first case, and .72 in the latter, and .96 together. These results led Eysenck (1941b) to conclude that the agreement among people in color preferences was, in actual fact, extremely high.

The psychology of pleasantness and unpleasantness

A major goal during the period of behaviorism was to understand the affective value of stimuli: why and how do organisms experience some stimuli as pleasant and others as unpleasant? This was the question John Gilbert Beebe-Center (1897–1958) set out to answer. Beebe-Center began studying psychology at Harvard in 1915, but he left for Europe during World War I to join the American Ambulance Service. Later, he served with the French army at Verdun and Aisne, and as a civilian French interpreter for the Intelligence Section of the Chief of Staff of the American Expeditionary Forces (Boring, 1959). After the war, he returned to Harvard, where he graduated in psychology, and obtained his PhD in 1926, with a thesis showing that the affective value of odors depended on the pleasantness and unpleasantness of preceding odors (Beebe-Center, 1929b). He spent a year as a postdoctoral fellow in the psychology department of the University of Berlin, where the Gestalt movement was thriving under the leadership of Max Wertheimer and Wolfgang Köhler, as we will see in the section on "The Gestalt School of Psychology."

Beebe-Center (1932) conceived pleasantness and unpleasantness as the positive and negative values of the hedonic tone of experience. He distinguished three classes of variables that have an influence on hedonic tone: features of the primary stimuli (the object that is experienced as pleasant or unpleasant), features of secondary stimuli (other present and past stimuli), and variables that characterize the person's physiological and affective states, experience, goals, and mindset. Thus, the pleasantness or unpleasantness we experience from an object is a function of the object's sensory qualities, of the spatial and temporal context surrounding the experienced object, and of our past, current, and desired states. The first class of variables explains why there is a certain degree of agreement among people in what they find pleasant and unpleasant, whereas the second and third classes of variables explain why there is a certain degree of disagreement among people, and even within people at different times.

His studies on the first class of variables led him to the conviction that certain features confer upon objects a general hedonic value: stimuli have the potential to influence hedonic tone in the same way in all people. In practice, the influence of general hedonic value on hedonic tone can be masked by the effects of the other two classes of variables. However, by applying the same mathematical treatment that enabled separating a general factor of intelligence from specific factors, Beebe-Center (1929a) believed that the general hedonic values of stimuli could be isolated from the influence of contextual and personal influences. Such statistical procedures led to a measure of the extent to which stimuli please people, that is to say, their general hedonic value, and a measure of agreement between each person's judgments and the objects' general hedonic value, that is to say, each person's aesthetic sensitivity.

His studies on secondary stimuli were greatly influenced by the principles of Gestalt he had learnt in Berlin, and focused mainly on the effects of hedonic contrast. Beebe-Center (1929b) examined how the affective value of a set of stimuli changed as a result of the repeated presentation of extreme cases in the set. He showed that the affective value of odors in a set was greater after repeated presentations of the 10 most unpleasant ones than after repeated presentations of the 10 most pleasant ones. From these and similar results, he deduced the law of *mass contrast*: "The hedonic tone corresponding to a present stimulus varies conversely with the sum of hedonic tone corresponding to those past stimuli whose phenomenal correlates constitute with the phenomenal correlate of the present stimulus a unitary temporal group" (Beebe-Center, 1932, p. 229).

How is the experience of hedonic tone produced? Beebe-Center (1930) believed there was evidence that the experience of pleasantness and unpleasantness owed to specific processes that took place in the sensory organs. He argued that hedonic tone was a result of sensory processes because of the many parallels in the processes underlying sensory experience and hedonic tone. Both, for instance, are influenced by contrast and expectation. Moreover, he believed that the sensory processes that gave rise to hedonic tone were of a special class because they could produce, under certain circumstances, a specific class of bodily correlates not common to the experience of sensory qualities: pleasure was experienced as a bright pressure in the upper part of the body, and unpleasantness as a dull pressure in the abdomen.

These parallels that Beebe-Center (1930, 1932) drew between hedonic tone and sensation, together with the general premises of Carr's (1925) functional psychology, became the starting point for Henry N. Peters' (1908–1963) work on the psychology of pleasantness and unpleasantness. Peters obtained his PhD at Chicago under the supervision of Harvey A. Carr, and became a supporter of functional psychology. To Carr, psychology was the study of "the acquisition, fixation, retention, organization, and evaluation of experiences, and their subsequent utilization in the guidance of conduct" (Carr, 1925, p. 1). Central to his approach was the *adaptive act*, which consisted of a motive, a setting, and a response that satisfied the motive. Adaptive acts enable learning and the adaptation of the organism to its environment: the successful responses are repeated whenever the motive arises in that setting.

From this functional perspective, Peters (1935) understood pleasantness and unpleasantness as attributes that organisms, humans included, assign to objects based on their tendencies to react to them. An object is labeled as pleasant when the organism normally has a positive reaction to it, such as when it approaches it or prolongs its experience of it, and unpleasant if it normally has a negative reaction to it, such as when it avoids or cuts the experience short. Although the reaction is elicited by the object, the nature of the reaction (to approach/remain or avoid/withdraw) is determined by the organism's motives. Thus, people—organisms in general—make value judgments about objects, that is to say, judgments of pleasantness and unpleasantness, but also of good or bad, attractive or repulsive, and so on, based on what they have learnt about their own tendencies to react toward them depending on their motives. Even the meaning of pleasant and unpleasant is gained fundamentally through experience and learning. Even though some reaction tendencies are inherited or instinctual (Peters, 1955), it is mostly through approaching or avoiding certain objects that organisms learn that some are pleasant and others unpleasant because they are congruent or incongruent with their motives.

Peters tested his theory in a series of experiments in which he asked participants to judge the pleasantness or unpleasantness of several kinds of stimuli, including colors, pictures, and Japanese words phonetically written in English (Peters, 1938a, 1938b, 1939a, 1939b, 1943a, 1943b; Peters & Rodgers, 1947). In a series of trials, participants were then presented with the stimuli, one at a time, and had to implicitly learn, using certain cues, to react positively to some of them by naming the colors, reaching for the pictures, or pronouncing the words, and negatively to others by doing nothing. After the learning phase, participants were asked to judge the pleasantness or unpleasantness of all the stimuli again. His results showed that the stimuli the participants had learnt to respond positively to were now judged as more pleasant than on the first occasion, whereas the stimuli the participants had learnt to respond negatively to were judged as less pleasant. He also found that these effects were still present after a week, though weaker, and that the pleasantness effect of approach was stronger than the unpleasantness effect of avoidance.

His theoretical and empirical work on value judgments served as the foundation for his views on aesthetic experience (Peters, 1942). To him, aesthetic experience was the affective state that is operationalized in terms of value judgments. To Peters, these affective states were responses and, therefore, the product of the same determinants that produce any kind of response: inherited predisposition, motivational selection, and association. Peters believed that people responded not to the physical aspects of objects but their psychological or conceptual meaning. Consequently, he believed that it was wrong to conceive of unity, complexity, simplicity, balance, symmetry, and other qualities as attributes of the physical stimulus, because they are meaningless except in terms of human reactions. The aesthetic experience was the product of three elements: attitudes (personality, motives, and sets), perception, and experience. He conceived of aesthetic experiences as a form of perceptual experience, one in which people's set is to observe and judge value rather than other perceptual qualities. In addition, experience included the effects of repeated presentations and learning.

PSYCHOMETRIC EMPIRICAL AESTHETICS

The decades of behaviorist hegemony were also the golden age of tests for all kinds of mental processes involved in aesthetics, such as sensitivity to visual balance and complexity, discrimination and memory for musical pitch, intensity, consonance, and rhythm, aptitude in design, and the appreciation of visual art, literature, and music (Adler, 1929; F. X. Barron & Welsh, 1952; Carroll, 1933; Farnsworth, 1931; Graves, 1948; Guilford & Guilford, 1931; Heinlein, 1925; Logasa & Wright, 1930; Madison, 1942; McAdory, 1933; McCarthy, 1930; Meier, 1926; 1942; Meier & Seashore, 1929; Stanton, 1928; Welsh & Barron, 1949; Williams, Winter, & Woods, 1938; Wing, 1941).

Work on developing these sorts of tests was so abundant and varied during the decades of behaviorism that it deserves its own section. Chandler and Barnhart's (1938) bibliography provides more than 70 papers published between 1910 and 1937 on tests of visual aesthetics alone. The tests measure general art talent, drawing ability, talent for design, discrimination of composition, harmony, and balance, art appreciation, and aesthetic sensitivity. Lehman's (1969) selected bibliography on musical testing alone is 15 pages long. It includes more than 50 different tests, most of which were developed and published before 1950, and more than 100 papers and unpublished materials analyzing different aspects of those tests. They include measures of general music appreciation, such as Hevner's (1930b, 1931) noted on the section on "Empirical Aesthetics in the Age of Behaviorism," preference, and taste, of general musical talent, singing talent, musical performance, musical expressiveness, auditory imagination, musical memory, sensitivity to cadence and phrasing, discrimination of tones, of intervals, and consonance and dissonance, and rhythmic performance and discrimination. Among the most influential and sustained programs to develop valid and reliable measures of abilities for art and aesthetics, and to understand the nature of individual differences, were those of Seashore and Meier, Burt, Eysenck, and Child, and Barron and Eisenman.

The measurement of musical and artistic talent

Carl Emil Seashore (1866–1949) graduated from Yale under the guidance of George Trumbull Ladd, and received his doctorate in 1895 under the supervision of Edward Wheeler Scripture. Scripture had studied with Wundt at his Leipzig laboratory at the same time as Külpe, Meumann, Frank Angell, and Titchener. In 1897, Seashore arrived at the University of Iowa and stayed there until his retirement (Metfessel, 1950). In 1910, he began his lifelong project on music, which led to the Seashore Measures of Musical Talents in 1919, two books on the psychology of music, and more than 100 papers on several aspects of music production and appreciation (Bathurst & Sinclair, 1928). He believed that several aspects of music made it possible to develop valid and reliable measurements: (1) The formal idiom of music enabled an exhaustive identification of the factors contributing to musical talent. (2) All aspects of production were carried through sound waves, enabling the faithful recording of all relevant aspects of the stimuli. (3) Musical beauty emerges from artistic deviations from rigidness, and ugliness from unartistic deviations, enabling tangible means for the expression of beauty. (4) Music enabled the classification of psychological factors that are responsible for musical performance and appreciation. (5) Measures of abilities make it possible to identify impediments in certain capacities, and to determine whether they are remediable. (6) Musical education could be improved, because training was conceived as the acquisition of a series of skills, and because students could become aware of their skills and work on them (Seashore, 1930). He recorded six fundamental measures of music, standardized the procedure, and published group measurements. The Seashore Measures of Musical Talents provided a good index of the receptive side of musical talent. Such measures were understood as specific and as a sample of a broader set of musical factors.

Seashore continued this line of work with Norman Meier, one of his PhD students. Together they developed the Meier–Seashore Art Judgment Test (Meier & Seashore, 1929), based on some of the same principles that had guided the development of his earlier musical talent measures. Norman C. Meier (1893–1967) began his professional life as a draftsman in Pittsburg, eventually working for the United States Geological Survey. During World War I, he served at the American Expeditionary Forces head-quarters in Chaumont, France. After returning to the United States, he resumed his work as a draftsman and enrolled at the University of Chicago. He earned his PhD at the University of Iowa with a thesis on the use of aesthetic judgments as a measure of art talent (Meier, 1926).

Meier (1939) believed that artistic aptitude rested on six factors: manual skill or craftsman ability, energy output and perseverance in its discharge, general and aesthetic intelligence, perceptual facility, creative imagination, and aesthetic judgment. The first three he believed were largely innate, and the last three largely acquired. Of these six, he argued that aesthetic judgment, or the ability to recognize the aesthetic quality in the relation among elements of an organization, had the greatest potential for success as the grounds for a measure of artistic talent (Meier, 1927, 1928). He selected 200 artistic etchings, mezzotints, and dry-point images, and produced pairs of faithful and altered versions of each (G. Clark, 1987). He discarded the pairs that were least discriminant, ending up with 50 items consisting of pairs of faithful and altered versions and 10 items consisting of one faithful and three altered versions. Participants' task was to choose the best version in each item. The result was the Meier–Seashore Art Judgment Test (Meier & Seashore, 1929).

He later issued a new version, known as the *Meier Art Tests: I. Art Judgment* (Meier, 1940). This test is premised upon the notions that the aesthetic character of art resides in the organization of parts according to universal principles common to all good art, and that the function of aesthetic judgment is to detect these relations. It contains 100 items, of which 94 are based on artworks and six on designs for vases. Each item contains a pair of similar black and white images, one of which has been altered to deteriorate its composition. Participants have to select the better version. Meier later published the second part of the test, the *Meier Art Tests: II. Aesthetic Perception* (Meier, 1963). It was conceived and designed to measure the perceptual facility factor of artistic talent, that is to say, the ability to detect subtle aspects that have aesthetic significance. This test has 50 items, each consisting of four versions of the same artwork. One of these is the original, while the other three resemble the original but their form, design, or composition has been altered, sometimes quite subtly. Participants are asked to compare the composition and design of each of the four sets, noting how the versions differ, what makes one aes-thetically better, and to rank them in descending order.

The measurement of aesthetic sensitivity

In the United Kingdom, interest in individual differences in aesthetic judgment and their measurement grew out of Cyril Burt's (1883–1971) studies of children's artistic competence in London, during the 1920s and 1930s. Burt had spent a year studying with Külpe at Würzburg, at the same time as Valentine. Burt was strongly influenced by Francis Galton's interest in individual differences, mental testing, correlations, and eugenics (Boring, 1950; Burt, 1962; MacKenzie, 1976). To Burt, it was incontrovertible that intelligence and mental abilities were genetically based, that they were the main determinants of social position within the hierarchy of occupational classes, and that they could be measured objectively and accurately using mental tests (Norton, 1981). He introduced mental tests and psychometrics into the education system and systematically studied the distribution of intelligence, mental abilities, and achievements of the London school population. He determined averages and normal ranges; he developed standardized measures and compiled test batteries. And he used children's performance on such tests to set them along the vocational path fitted to their natural aptitudes.

The battery that Burt devised to measure children's abilities included several tasks of literary, musical, and visual appreciation and creation, consisting of ranking fragments and images, paired and triple comparisons, composition, and drawing. He believed— following Spearman's approach to intelligence—that there existed a unitary aesthetic ability, inherited and unalterable, that could be measured by means of responses to simple tests. Burt referred to this as the *general factor for artistic ability*, and believed it underlay the ability to appreciate relations among elements in art, combinations of lines and colors, sounds, or words (Burt, 1933, 1949). Burt's main interest shifted from educational psychology to statistical theory after 1932, when he succeeded Spearman as Professor of Psychology at the University College London (Wooldrige, 1994).

Burt's PhD student, Hans Jürgen Eysenck (1916–1997), continued this psychometric approach to aesthetics. Eysenck assembled 18 sets of pictures, including portraits, photographs of statues of Roman emperors, pencil drawings by Claude Lorrain, photographs of vases, Malayan masks, Japanese paintings, reproductions of colored embroidery, and curves of mathematical functions. He then asked 18 participants to rank the materials in each set in order of liking. Eysenck's (1940) factor analysis of participants' rankings revealed a factor accounting for 20.6% of the variance across sets, which he called the *general objective factor of aesthetic appreciation*. Faithful to Galton and Burt, he asserted that this factor was responsible for performance on virtually any conceivable test of aesthetic appreciation, that it was common to all humans, determined largely by biological factors, and innate (Eysenck, 1941b. 1941c, 1942, 1981).

Eysenck believed this factor, T, corresponded to the ability to appreciate objective beauty, that is, people's *taste*, or *aesthetic sensitivity* (Eysenck, 1941c, 1942). In Eysenck's view, aesthetic sensitivity was a distinct, general, and stable ability. It was distinct because it was unrelated to other personal traits ("[this ability], independently of intelligence and personality, determines the degree of good or bad taste," Eysenck, 1983, p. 213), general because it explained performance on virtually all measures of artistic ability ("it covers a large number of, probably all, pictorial tests," Eysenck, 1940, p. 100), stable because it was biologically determined and innate ("[it] presumably [has] a genetic foundation in the structure of the nervous system," Götz, Borisy, Lynn, & Eysenck, 1979, p. 801), and insensitive to experience ("[it] is independent of teaching, tradition, and other irrelevant associations," Eysenck, 1940, p. 102).

Eysenck identified a second factor when the influence of T was minimized. This factor, K, was bipolar and distinguished "those who like modern art, bright, sunny photographs, and Kolbe statues, from those who like the older masters, cloudy, fore-boding photographs, and the statues of Maillol and Barlach" (Eysenck, 1941a, p. 266). The main characteristic of the *K* factor is "one of brightness or intensity as opposed to darkness or lack of intensity" (Eysenck, 1983, p. 91).

In Eysenck's (1941a, 1942) view, aesthetic sensitivity scaled as the degree to which liking approximated *true aesthetic value*. True aesthetic value could be estimated by averaging people's preference or by resorting to experts' opinion. Aesthetic sensitivity could thus be calculated by simply subtracting people's average liking ratings from group averages or from experts' judgments. Eysenck used different kinds of materials to measure aesthetic sensitivity. He first correlated liking ranks of artworks (e.g., portraits, drawings, landscapes, statues) and objects (e.g., vases, mathematical functions, flowers, clocks) with the average rankings (Eysenck, 1940). He later used simple geometric designs (Eysenck, 1972; Eysenck & Castle, 1971) taken from Birkhoff (1933) and the *Barron–Welsh Figure Preference Test* (F. X. Barron & Welsh, 1952; Welsh & Barron, 1949). Finally, he developed the Visual Aesthetic Sensitivity Test (VAST) in collaboration with the German artist and designer Karl Otto Götz (Chan, Eysenck, & Götz, 1980; Götz et al., 1979; Iwawaki, Eysenck, & Götz, 1979).

Eysenck's notion of the general, independent, and biologically determined factor of aesthetic appreciation rested on the assumptions that the average ranking of images in a set represented their aesthetic value, and that the extent to which people's prefer-ence agreed with the average constituted a valid measure of their aesthetic sensitivity. Irvin Long Child (1915–2000) was skeptical of these assumptions and set out to test them experimentally. Child's perspective on aesthetic sensitivity was very different to Eysenck's. He looked at it through the lens of learning theory, humanistic psychology, and anthropology. Child earned his PhD at Yale in 1939 (Machotka, 2002), where Clark Hull awoke his interest in learning theory, and where O. Hobart Mowrer, Neal E. Miller, John Dollard, and others were using animal learning paradigms to study the roles of drive, cue, response, and reward in the sort of phenomena that were crucial to Freud's psychoanalyses, such as conflict, frustration, and repression (Coons, 2002; Myers, 1973). From his analysis under John Dollard, he learnt about personality theory, and through his research collaboration with the anthropologist—and brother-in-law—John W. M. Whiting, he became sensitive to the role of culture in structuring cognition and person-ality (Whiting & Child, 1953).

Child (1962) assembled 12 sets of 60 reproductions of artworks depicting groups of people, landscapes, abstract art, still lives, religious content, and so on. He asked 14 art or art history students to divide each of the sets into 10 piles of approximately six pictures each according to their aesthetic merit. He then asked two different groups of 22 students with little or no artistic training to distribute each of the sets into 10 piles of approximately six pictures each, from those they liked least to those they liked most. His results revealed only very small correlations between aesthetic merit rank and prefer-ence rank, and no clear relation between individuals' agreement with group preferences and their agreement with the external criterion of aesthetic value. From these results he concluded that it was wrong to equate, as Eysenck had, group averages of preference with aesthetic value, and similarity to average preferences with aesthetic sensitivity. Aesthetic sensitivity, Child (1962) concluded, is properly measured in relation to an external standard set by experts, not in relation to group averages. Individual differences in aesthetic sensitivity reflect differences in familiarity with and acceptance of the tradition of aesthetic evaluation. In Child's (1962, 1965) view, aesthetic sensitivity is cultivated with practice and is the result not of a specific ability, but of general cognitive style and personality. High aesthetic sensitivity is the manifestation of an

> actively inquiring mind, seeking out experience that may be challenging because of complexity or novelty, even alert to the potential experience offered by stimuli not already in the focus of attention, interested in understanding each experience thoroughly and for its own sake rather than contemplating it superficially and promptly filing it away in a category, and able to do all this with respect to the world inside himself as well as the world outside.
>
> (Child, 1965, p. 508)

Child subsequently conducted one of the most extensive cross-cultural research programs on aesthetic sensitivity (Che, Sun, Gallardo, & Nadal, 2018). In a series of studies, he showed that people from different parts of the world who are interested in art tend to show agreement as to what constitutes good artworks. He attributed this high agreement in aesthetic valuation among experts from different cultures to the commonalities among the traditions of aesthetic assessment around the world, and to the openness of art experts to the aesthetic features of other cultures (Child & Siroto, 1965; Ford, Prothro, & Child, 1966; Iwao & Child, 1966; Iwao, Child, & García, 1969). Moreover, he found that despite cultural differences, people who have an interest in aesthetic values and art around the world show similar personality trends that lead them to develop interest in art: tolerance for complexity, independence of judgment, regression in the service of the ego, and preference for autonomy, variety, and intellectual and perceptual challenges (Anwar & Child, 1972; Child & Iwao, 1968; Haritos-Fatouros & Child, 1977).

Simplicity–complexity as a factor of perceptual preference

Frank Barron (Francis Xavier Barron, 1922–2002), president of APA's Division 10, The Society for Psychology of Aesthetics, Creativity, and the Arts (1971–1972), and Division 32, Humanistic Psychology (1989–1990) (Arons, 2003), arrived at the study of aesthetic preferences through his lifelong interest in creativity. Barron obtained his bachelor degree at the University of Minnesota, after serving as army medic in Europe during World War II (Montuori, 2003). With his PhD in 1950 from the University of California, Berkeley, he began his seminal research on creativity (F. X. Barron, 1963, 1969) at the Institute of Personality Assessment and Research, University of California, Berkeley, under the direction of Donald W. MacKinnon. The Institute had its roots in Harvard's

Psychological Clinic, where MacKinnon had been supervised by Henry A. Murray, and in the personnel assessment centers of the Office of Strategic Services (Handler, 2001; Smith & Anderson, 1989), the forerunner of the Central Intelligence Agency, where MacKinnon and Murray worked together during World War II (Murray & Mackinnon, 1946). The Harvard Psychological Clinic had been established in 1926 by the Harvard physician Morton Prince (Triplet, 1992; White, 1992). The Clinic was part of Prince's endeavors to separate the field of psychopathology from psychiatry (he had founded the *Journal of Abnormal Psychology* in 1906 with the same goal). If psychopathology were taught only in medical schools, Prince believed, then scientific research would become secondary to the practical issues involved in running a psychiatric ward (White, 1992). In 1926, Henry Murray was hired as Prince's assistant and, when Prince retired in 1928, he took over the Clinic (Smith & Anderson, 1989; Triplet, 1992). At the Clinic, he introduced psychopathology and European personality and clinical theories into American academic psychology, systematized the study of personality, and developed research and assessment methods, such as the Thematic Apperception Test (Morgan & Murray, 1935; Smith & Anderson, 1989; Triplet, 1992).

At the Institute of Personality Assessment and Research, and influenced by the humanistic perspectives of Murray and MacKinnon, Barron focused on understanding creativity and the characteristics of creative people in different domains, including science, philosophy, art, religion, and entrepreneurship. What made creative people distinct was their disposition to originality, independence of judgment, ego-strength, psychological health, aesthetic sensitivity, and their preference for complexity (F. X. Barron, 1963, 1969; Montuori, 2003).

Barron saw a correspondence between his views on the relation between creativity and complexity and Welsh's approach to the assessment of psychological disorders. Welsh (1949) had constructed a test consisting of 200 drawings and administered it to large groups of psychiatric patients and healthy controls. The Welsh Figure Preference Test required participants to indicate whether they liked each of the drawings. The factor analysis revealed a general *acceptance factor*, related to the general tendency of the participant to either like or dislike the drawings, and a *bipolar factor*, orthogonal to the previous one, related to the preference for simple–symmetrical figures or for complex–asymmetrical figures. Healthy participants tended to form two distinct groups with markedly different personality traits. Those who preferred simple and symmetrical figures were conservative and conventional, while those who preferred the other kind of stimuli were eccentric, cynical, and radical (Barron, 1952). Welsh and Barron (1949) enlarged the test to 400 stimuli and included a specific scale that could discriminate between the preference of artists and nonartists and be used independently.

Using the Barron–Welsh (1952) Art Scale, Barron (1952) found that people who prefer simple–symmetrical drawings also prefer paintings portraying etiquette, religious motifs, and scenes reflecting a certain degree of authority, and rejected paintings with esoteric, unnatural and openly sensual contents. Conversely, people who prefer more complex drawings also prefer modern, experimental paintings, those with primitive or sensual content, and disliked those related to religion, aristocracy, tradition, and emotional control. Barron (1952) suggested that these differences might be explained by the different views both groups of participants have of themselves and the world. The analysis of their responses on a checklist of adjectives they used to describe themselves revealed that they had different attitudes toward the perception of stability, predictability, balance, symmetry, and the use of simple general principles, as well as toward tradition, religion, authority, and sensuality. The group that preferred simple–symmetric figures described themselves as contented, gentle, conservative, unaffected, patient, and peaceable, while the group who preferred complex–asymmetric figures described themselves as unstable, dissatisfied, pessimistic, emotional, pleasure-seeking, and irritable. These results add to the increasing consistency of the suggestion that the extroversion–introversion and conservatism–radicalism dimensions contribute to the preference for visual stimuli varying in complexity.

In sum, Barron (1953) showed that people differ according to whether they prefer perceiving and dealing with simplicity or with complexity, and that this factor predicts differences in originality and intellectual independence, interpersonal relationships, social conformity, and views on politics, economics, religion, authority, and tradition. What is the origin of these differences in preference for complexity? Barron (1972, 1976) began exploring the genetics behind this factor in two pioneering studies on monozygotic (MZ) and dizygotic (DZ) twins. MZ twins are genetically identical, and DZ twins are on average 50% identical. Comparing the degree of similarity in the performance of MZ and DZ pairs on tests of a certain capacity allows estimating the impact of genetics on that capacity: if the performance of MZ twins is more similar than the performance of DZ, it can be assumed that genetics has a strong influence on that capacity (Bignardi, Ticini, Smit, & Polderman, 2020). Barron (1972) tested 59 pairs of Italian twins, 30 MZ and 29 DZ, and 57 pairs of American twins, 29 MZ and 28 DZ, on several measures of creative thinking and aesthetic appreciation, including the Barron–Welsh Art Scale as a measure of preference for complexity (F. X. Barron & Welsh, 1952). Barron (1972) reported an intraclass correlation of .58 among the Italian MZ twins' preference for complexity, and of .66 for the American MZ twins preference for complexity. In contrast, the intraclass correlation was close to zero for DZ twins from both countries. Barron's (1972) results would, therefore, suggest an important genetic influence on preference for complexity. In a similar study, Barron and Parisi (1976) tested 61 pairs of Italian twins, 36 MZ and 25 DZ, on several measures of creativity and two measures of aesthetic judgment: The Barron–Welsh Arts Scale and Irvin Child's Test of Esthetic Judgment, consisting of 100 pairs of similar pictures, one of which is superior to the other. Barron and Parisi (1976) reported similar intraclass correlations for MZ and DZ twins: for the Barron–Welsh Arts Scale, the MZ correlation was .16 and the DZ correlation was .29. For Child's Test of Esthetic Judgment, the MZ correlation was .57 and the DZ correlation was .69. Barron and Parisi's (1976) results, therefore, questioned Barron's (1972) earlier results, and suggested that genetics has little impact on both of these measures of aesthetic judgment. Despite this contradiction in results, these studies showed promise for a behavioral genetics of aesthetic appreciation (Bignardi et al., 2020).

Russell Eisenman (1940–) corroborated and extended these conclusions in a series of experiments: high school and college students who are more creative prefer more complex polygonal figures and find them more meaningful than less creative peers (R. Eisenman & Robinson, 1967; R. E. Taylor & Eisenman, 1964). However, subsequent studies showed that the relation between preference for complexity and creativity is not straightforward. First, preference for complexity–simplicity seems to be modulated by mental health: Eisenman (1965) showed that schizophrenic patients preferred less complex polygons and less novel poems than healthy control participants. Second, the relation between preference for complexity and creativity is modulated by sex and personality traits linked to birth order. Eisenman's (1965) results showed that first-born participants were more anxious and more likely to prefer simpler polygons than later-born participants. Subsequent studies showed that the effect of birth order interacted with sex: later-born women generally preferred highly complex polygons, whereas later-born men generally preferred the simplest polygons. First-born men and women preferred polygons of intermediate complexity (R. Eisenman, 1967a). Eisenman (1967; Taylor & Eisenman, 1968) postulated that these results might have to do with the impact of socialization patterns on people's personality. Finally, Eisenman's (1967b) results questioned Barron's (1963) treatment of complexity and asymmetry as part of the same dimension: preferences for complexity and symmetry are not necessarily the same. In fact, there was evidence that even complexity was not a singular dimension: different forms of complexity have different effects on preference (R. Eisenman & Rappaport, 1967; Grove & Eisenman, 1970).

THE GESTALT SCHOOL OF PSYCHOLOGY

Almost at the same time as when behaviorism was developing in the United States (Watson, 1913), the Gestalt school of psychology began taking shape in Germany. Gestalt rejected Wundt's division of conscious experience into elements: the key to understanding the mind was in the study of organized and dynamic wholes, or fields, in which each part interacts with all the others. The movement grew out of the work of Wertheimer, Köhler, and Koffka. Max Wertheimer was one of Stumpf's students in Berlin and, after graduating, he earned his PhD in 1904 at Würzburg, under Külpe's supervision. Köhler and Koffka earned their PhDs in Berlin under Stumpf's supervision in 1909. The three of them were in Frankfurt by 1910. After World War I, word arrived at the United States of the new school. As noted in the section on "The Pioneers of Empirical Aesthetics," Ogden, one of Külpe's students, did much to promote Gestalt psychology in the United States, especially with the rise of the Nazi party in Germany during the 1930s. Koffka visited the United States in 1924 and, in 1927, he earned a position at Smith College. Köhler visited in 1925 and 1927 and, in 1935, he earned a position at Swarthmore. In 1933, Wertheimer earned a position at the New School for Social Research in New York.

One of Gestalt's most significant contributions was their explanation of perception and understanding of objects and scenes as emergent processes that go beyond the mere recording of the elements in the stimulus. From the Gestalt perspective, perceiving was not about passively receiving sensations, it was about actively exploring and organizing perception. They suggested a number of grouping principles, such as proximity, continuation, similarity, or closure, which organized parts of the visual scene into wholes, such as objects, clusters, and overall scenes. These principles were subordinate to, or specific manifestations of, the general principle of *Prägnanz*: we tend to perceive the most concise and structured configuration consistent with the information presented.

Although art and aesthetics were never a primary concern for Wertheimer or Köhler, Koffka (1940) explored Gestalt's implications for the appreciation of art and beauty. Koffka (1940) openly rejected the psychophysical approach whereby beauty is defined in terms of the physical properties of the stimulus. From the Gestalt point of view, appreciation of beauty and art emerges from the interaction of the viewer's psychological processes and the artwork's features. Koffka (1940) considered works of art to be special kinds of good Gestalts, in that their constituents are placed by the demand of the whole and that the dynamic forces are particularly well balanced. An artwork is appealing as a structure, not as a collection of parts, but as a consistent entirety where each constituent requires the others. This structure is in close dynamic interaction with the viewer, who is actively organizing the artwork in one direction, and being affected by it in the other.

Rudolf Arnheim (1904–2007) was responsible for the most thorough application of the Gestalt principles to artworks and aesthetics. Arnheim had been Max Wertheimer's assistant and PhD student. He too moved away from Germany, where the Nazi party had seized power. He first went to Rome, then London and, finally, the United States, where he joined Wertheimer at the New School for Social Research in 1940 (Verstegen, 1996). In 1968, he became Professor of Art Psychology at Harvard University's Carpenter Center for the Visual Arts, and from 1974 to 1984, he taught art psychology at the Art History Institute of the University of Michigan at Ann Arbor (Verstegen, 1996).

Arnheim's fundamental thesis, developed in detail in his book *Visual Thinking* (Arnheim, 1969), was that perceptual processes are analogous to the processes of productive thinking: "The elementary processes of perception, far from being mere passive registration, [are] creative acts of grasping structure even beyond the mere grouping and selecting of parts. What happens in perception [is] similar to what at a higher psychological level is described as understanding or insight" (Arnheim, 1947, p. 70). The resulting percepts have several attributes, two of which are the most important to Arnheim's approach because to him they are what art is about. The first is *directed tension*, or *expression*: the upward striving of a tree, or the rise and fall of a musical scale. The second attribute is *intensity*: the strength or weakness of that directed tension (Arnheim, 1961). The overall configuration of these dynamical visual forces constitutes what Arnheim (1964) referred to as the structural skeleton of the design. The essence of an artwork is to create a dynamic whole by integrating this structural skeleton with the depicted subject matter. Viewers spontaneously balance parts and wholes in search for the integrated structure of the artwork.

Apprehending artistic expression is not about perceiving such measurable features as shape, size, hue, or pitch, but about perceiving the directed tensions conveyed in the stimuli. The perception of directed tensions, Arnheim (1961) argued, is essential to aesthetic appreciation, but not specific to it: apprehending artistic expression is achieved through general perceptual processes. In addition to the apprehension of directed tensions, appreciating art involves two other processes. First, it involves the ability to evaluate balance, rhythm, and unity to judge the goodness of compositional structure. Again, these abilities are not specific to art, but general abilities involved in the perception of directed tensions. Second, because artistic expression has a semantic function, appreciating art involves evaluating the meaning, relevance, and truth of the artwork's message. This second kind of evaluation relies on the spectators' life experiences, memories, values, and preferences.

Thus, to Arnheim (1964, 1966, 1969), aesthetic appreciation arises essentially from dynamic perceptual processes. Perception is not the mere automatic and passive recording of aspects of the visual field. Rather, perceiving means becoming aware of dynamic forces inherent to the stimuli. This awareness is attained by the integration of two sources of information: the structured configurations received from the image and the patterns toward which individuals are oriented by virtue of their own experience and disposition.

The New Experimental Aesthetics

The work of Daniel Ellis Berlyne (1924–1976) during the 1960s and 1970s had a substantial impact on contemporary empirical aesthetics (Cupchik, 1986, 2020; Day, 1977). He provided the field with a new explanatory framework based on motivational theory and grounded on neuroscience, he introduced new experimental designs and analytical procedures, and he prompted a host of new questions. Berlyne began studying modern languages at Trinity College, Cambridge, but then switched to psychology, where Fredric Bartlett was Professor of Experimental Psychology. After serving in World War II in the Intelligence Corps, he graduated in psychology in 1947 (Myers, 1973). Berlyne became more interested in the research of the American neobehaviorists at Yale than in the research being conducted at Cambridge. He was especially fascinated by Hull, Mowrer, and Miller's research on motivation. In 1951 he managed to obtain a fellowship at Yale, where he earned his PhD in 1953 under the supervision of Carl I. Hovland (Barnes, 2012; Myers, 1973), a decade and a half after Irvin Child. Like Child earlier, Berlyne underwent psychotherapy with Dollard, which also influenced his views on human motivation (Myers, 1973). After Yale, Berlyne held positions at Aberdeen, Center for Advanced Study in the Behavioral Sciences at Palo Alto, California, the University of California, Berkeley, Piaget's *Centre International d'Épistémologie Génétique* in Geneva, and Boston. He finally accepted a permanent position at the University of Toronto in 1962, where he stayed until his death in 1976.

Berlyne focused on motivation for most of his career. In his book *Conflict, Arousal, and Curiosity* (Berlyne, 1960) he presented his motivational theory of exploration, intended to explain the motivation of perceptual and intellectual activities: curiosity, interest, directed thinking, and aesthetics. From this perspective, curiosity and exploration are organisms' responses to the arousal caused by the uncertainty and conflict about selecting behaviors. Curiosity prompts organisms to explore their surroundings in different manners, resolving the conflict, and returning arousal to an optimal level. During exploratory behavior, the organism compares and contrasts various aspects and properties of the stimuli it encounters, collating information. The collative variables are the properties of the stimuli that are compared, such as novelty, incongruity, surprisingness, uncertainty, and complexity. Exposure to stimuli varying in such features changes organisms' arousal levels, producing pleasant or unpleasant feelings.

As he worked on his *Conflict, Arousal, and Curiosity*, and influenced by Hebb's (1949) *The Organization of Behavior*, he came to realize how important it was for psychological models to take neuroscientific findings into account (Myers, 1973). This realization, together with his continuing research on curiosity and the time he spent as Visiting Professor at the *Institut d'Esthétique et des Sciences de l'Art* at the University of Paris, coalesced into his landmark book on empirical aesthetics: *Aesthetics and Psychobiology* (Berlyne, 1971). This was followed in 1974 by *Studies in the New Experimental Aesthetics* (Berlyne, 1974), a collection of studies carried out by himself and his colleagues that explored different possible applications of motivation theory to aesthetics.

Berlyne (1971) argued that aesthetic appreciation, liking and disliking, are the result of general motivational and hedonic processes and that, therefore, the enjoyment of art and aesthetics can be explained in terms of those motivational and hedonic processes. Neuroscience had shown that the motivational state of an organism is the product of the activity of three neural systems: a primary reward system, an aversion system, and a secondary reward system, whose activity inhibits the aversion system (Berlyne, 1971). The activity of the three systems depends on the organism's degree of arousal, which in turn depends, among other factors, on the configuration of stimuli from the environment. Given that the primary reward system is the most sensitive to the organism's arousal, moderate increases of arousal during a relatively low arousal state are usually pleasant. The aversion system's threshold is somewhat higher, such that if arousal continues to grow it becomes active, counteracting the effects of the primary reward system. If the arousal becomes very high, the activity of the aversion system can exceed that of the primary reward system. For each degree of arousal, the resultant hedonic tone can be calculated by means of the algebraic sum of the activity curves of the primary reward and aversion systems. Hence, moderate increases of arousal in a resting organism increase its positive hedonic tone up to a given point, beyond which additional increases in arousal potential do not modify the activity of the primary reward system. At a certain point, and because of the initiation of the activity of the aversion system, higher arousal decreases the overall hedonic tone. This can even lead to a negative hedonic state if arousal pushes the activity of the aversion system beyond a given threshold that corresponds to the maximum level of activity of the primary reward system.

The hedonic tone induced by a stimulus, defined as the capacity to reward an operant response and to generate preference or pleasure expressed through verbal assessments (Berlyne, 1971), depends on the level of arousal that it is capable of eliciting and the organism's current arousal level. Given that organisms tend to search for the optimal hedonic value, they will tend to expose themselves to different stimuli as a function of their arousal potential. Berlyne (1971) noted three classes of variables that determine a given stimulus's arousal potential, mainly through the amount of information transmitted to the organism. These are: *psychophysical* variables, such as brightness, saturation, predominant wavelength, and so on; *ecological* variables, including those elements that might have acquired associations with biologically relevant events or activities; and *collative* variables, such as novelty, surprise, complexity, ambiguity, or asymmetry.

These general motivational and hedonic principles explain people's aesthetic preferences, and their liking or disliking for art. People's interest in and curiosity for art are the product of arousal-regulating behaviors. In Berlyne's view, works of art are composed of assemblages of elements that possess a specific structure. Experiencing an artwork involves judging similarities and differences among the artworks' elements, their regularity and irregularity, their predictability or unpredictability, and so on; and between the artworks' elements and those experienced previously or anticipated, in terms of novelty, expectedness, or surprisingness. Thus, aesthetic interest and preference, like all sorts of interest and preference, depend on how novel, complex, or unexpected an object appears to the viewer (Berlyne, 1963; Berlyne, Ogilvie, & Parham, 1968). In normal conditions, that is to say, with an intermediate level of arousal, people are expected to prefer intermediately novel, complex, or unexpected artworks over excessively or insufficiently novel, complex, or unexpected ones. When arousal level is high people will tend to prefer less novel, complex, or unexpected artworks, and when arousal level is low, they will tend to prefer more novel, complex, or unexpected artworks.

Berlyne's work has had a lasting influence on contemporary research in empirical aesthetics and the psychology of art (Jacobsen, 2006): "Modern research on experimental aesthetics still takes inspiration from Berlyne's ideas about how collative variables affect arousal, interest, and preference. The influence of the Berlyne tradition may be best seen in the intensity of debates about alternative theories of aesthetic response" (Silvia, 2005, p. 119).

Concluding Remarks

The year Daniel Berlyne died, 1976, was the centennial of Fechner's *Vorschule der Ästhetik* (Fechner, 1876). Those 100 years saw the foundation of empirical aesthetics and its structural, functional, behaviorist, differential, Gestalt, and motivational incarnations, as we have summarized in this chapter. A comprehensive account of this rich history is well beyond the scope of a single chapter. This chapter, therefore, is necessarily selective, aiming only to provide the basic historical context for the rest of the chapters in this handbook. Given that most of them cover theories and results published since the late 1970s, we have concentrated on the first 100 years of empirical aesthetics (for recent trends see Cupchik, Arnheim, & Martindale, 1999; Greb, Elvers, & Fischinger, 2017; Martindale, 2007a, 2007b). We have focused on strictly empirical work, in the sense that it not only advocated for a fact-based or materialist approach to aesthetics, but actually produced and interpreted empirical observations. For this reason, we did not cover the influential writings of, for instance, Vischer and Lipps on empathy, or Bullough on "psychical distance" (C. G. Allesch, 1987; 1988; Cupchik, 2020).

Psychophysics and empirical aesthetics were both developed by Fechner. Psychophysics thrived and eventually merged into experimental psychology, whereas empirical aesthetics became a sort of specialty field. Even as early as 1910, it was apparent to Titchener (1910) that while psychophysics was progressing in leaps and bounds, empirical aesthetics was almost where Fechner had left off. The reason for the slower progress of empirical aesthetics is that it attracted fewer researchers than other areas of experimental psychology. During its first century it did not draw the critical mass of researchers that other areas of psychology did. *Aesthetics* means different things to different people (Anglada-Tort & Skov, 2020). As conceived by Fechner, empirical aesthetics sought to understand sensory pleasure, generally speaking. As conceived by Berlyne, it sought to understand the regulation of hedonic tone. But the field's name lent itself to being seen by others as dealing strictly with particular issues related to beauty and art. In fact, even some of the major figures in empirical aesthetics portrayed the field as concerned specifically with beautiful objects (Hevner, 1937b), or with art (Külpe, 1895). Experimental psychologists saw this as a very narrow window into the human mind, and one plagued by imprecise concepts, such as *beauty* and *art*. Such areas as perception, learning, emotion, or motivation seemed better suited to reveal the general principles of the human mind. Berlyne (1971) believed that limiting aesthetics to special objects, like artworks, special qualities, like beauty, and special emotions, like awe, was the greatest impediment for progress in empirical aesthetics.

Although empirical aesthetics ebbed and flowed, there was never a period in which it dried out completely. Looking back on its history, we can see that all major psychological schools of thought, from Wundt's late-19th-century structuralism to the 1960s' neobehaviorism, made important contributions to empirical aesthetics. Moreover, some of these contributions were made by, or under the supervision of, prominent psychologists whose names can be found in any psychology textbook: Wilhelm Wundt, the founder of the first psychological research laboratory; Lightner Witmer, the founder of clinical psychology; Hugo Münsterberg, the founder of applied psychology; Ernst Meumann, the founder of experimental education; Oswald Külpe, the founder of the Würzburg school of psychology; James McKeen Cattell, pioneer in mental testing; Edward L. Thorndike, known for his learning principles of effect and exercise; Lillien Martin, pioneer in psychophysics; Margaret Washburn, pioneer in comparative psychology and first woman to earn a PhD in psychology; Louis L. Thurstone, pioneer in psychometrics and intelligence testing; Hans J. Eysenck, proponent of the neuroticism–extraversion–psychoticism model of personality; and Daniel E. Berlyne, the neobehaviorist motivational theorist.

As practitioners of empirical aesthetics today, it behooves us to be aware of the history of our field. What Edwin G. Boring wrote about historical knowledge in experimental psychology is equally true about empirical aesthetics: "The experimental psychologist (. . .) needs historical sophistication within his own sphere of expertness. Without such knowledge he sees the present in distorted perspective, he mistakes old facts and old views for new, and he remains unable to evaluate the significance of new movements and methods" (Boring, 1950, p. ix).

Acknowledgments

We are grateful to Ana Clemente, Giacomo Bignardi, and Oshin Vartanian for helpful comments on an earlier version of this chapter.

References

Adler, M. J. (1929). Music appreciation: An experimental approach to its measurement. *Archives of Psychology, 110*, 1–102.

Allesch, C. G. (1987). *Geschichte der psychologischen ästhetik*. Göttingen: Hogrefe.

Allesch, C. G. (1988). 100 Jahre »Ästhetik von unten«. In K.-E. Behne, G. Kleinen, & H. de la Motte-Haber (Eds.), *Musikpsychologie. Jahrbuch der Deutschen Gesellschaft für Musikpsychologie. Band 5: Empirische Forschungen—Ästhetische Experimente* (pp. 11–31). Wilhelmshaven: Noetzel.

Allesch, C. G. (2018). Psychology in emerging aesthetics. In L. Tateo (Ed.), *An old melody in a new song. Theory and history in the human and social sciences* (pp. 33–50). Berlin: Springer.

Allesch, G. J. v. (1925). Die ästhetische Erscheinungsweise der Farben. *Psychologische Forschung, 6*(1), 1–91. https://doi.org/10.1007/BF00444162

Angier, R. P. (1903). The aesthetics of unequal division. In H. Münsterberg (Ed.), *Harvard psychological studies* (Vol. 1, pp. 541–561). Boston, MA: Houghton, Mifflin and Company.

Anglada-Tort, M., & Skov, M. (2020). What counts as aesthetics in science? A bibliometric analysis and visualization of the scientific literature from 1970 to 2018. Psychology of Aesthetics, Creativity, and the Arts. Advance online publication. https://doi.org/10.1037/aca0000350

Anwar, M. P., & Child, I. L. (1972). Personality and esthetic sensitivity in an Islamic culture. *The Journal of Social Psychology, 87*, 21–28.

Arnheim, R. (1947). Perceptual abstraction and art. *Psychological Review, 54*, 66–82.

Arnheim, R. (1961). Emotion and feeling in psychology and art. In M. Henle (Ed.), *Documents of Gestalt psychology* (pp. 334–352). Berkeley and Los Angeles, CA: University of California Press.

Arnheim, R. (1964). *Art and visual perception*. Berkeley, CA: University of California Press.

Arnheim, R. (1966). *Toward a psychology of art*. Berkeley, CA: University of California Press.

Arnheim, R. (1969). *Visual thinking*. Berkeley, CA: University of California Press.

Arnheim, R. (1992). The other Gustav Theodor Fechner. In S. Koch & D. E. Leary (Eds.), *A century of psychology as science* (pp. 856–865). Washington, DC: American Psychological Association.

Arons, M. (2003). A tribute to Frank Barron: He helped bend a century. *Journal of Humanistic Psychology, 43,* 26–33. https://doi.org/10.1177/0022167802250105

Babbitt, M., Woods, M., & Washburn, M. F. (1915). Affective sensitiveness to colors, tone intervals, and articulate sounds. *The American Journal of Psychology, 26,* 289–291.

Barnes, M. E. (2012). Berlyne, Daniel E. In R. W. Rieber (Ed.), *Encyclopedia of the History of Psychological Theories* (pp. 115–119). New York, NY: Springer.

Barnhart, E. N. (1940). The criteria used in preferential judgments of geometrical forms. *The American Journal of Psychology, 53,* 354–370.

Barron, F. (1972). Twin resemblances in creative thinking and aesthetic judgment. In F. Barron (Ed.), *Artists in the making* (pp. 174–181). New York, NY: Seminar Press.

Barron, F., & Parisi, P. (1976). Twin resemblances in creativity and in esthetic and emotional expression. *Acta Geneticae Medicae et Gemellologiae: Twin Research, 25,* 213–217.

Barron, F. X. (1952). Personality style and perceptual choice. *Journal of Personality, 20,* 385–401.

Barron, F. X. (1953). Complexity-simplicity as a personality dimension. *Journal of Abnormal and Social Psychology, 48,* 163–172. https://doi.org/10.1037/h0054907

Barron, F. X. (1963). *Creativity and psychological health.* Princeton, NJ: Van Nostrand.

Barron, F. X. (1969). *Creative person, creative process.* New York, NY: Holt, Rinehart & Winston.

Barron, F. X., & Welsh, G. S. (1952). Artistic perception as a possible factor in personality style: Its measurement by a figure preference test. *The Journal of Psychology, 33,* 199–203.

Bathurst, J. E., & Sinclair, R. D. (1928). A complete annotated bibliography of the writings of Carl Emil Seashore. *Psychological Monographs, 39,* 3–22.

Beebe-Center, J. G. (1929a). General affective value. *Psychological Review, 36,* 472–480. https://doi.org/10.1037/h0072281

Beebe-Center, J. G. (1929b). The law of affective equilibrium. *The American Journal of Psychology, 1,* 54–69. https://doi.org/10.2307/1415108

Beebe-Center, J. G. (1930). The relation between affectivity and specific processes in sense-organs. *Psychological Review, 37,* 327–333. https://doi.org/10.1037/h0070687

Beebe-Center, J. G. (1932). *The psychology of pleasantness and unpleasantness.* New York, NY: D. Van Nostrand Company.

Berlyne, D. E. (1960). *Conflict, arousal and curiosity.* New York, NY: McGraw-Hill.

Berlyne, D. E. (1963). Complexity and incongruity variables as determinants of exploratory choice and evaluative ratings. *Canadian Journal of Psychology, 17,* 274–290.

Berlyne, D. E. (1971). *Aesthetics and psychobiology.* New York, NY: Appleton-Century-Crofts.

Berlyne, D. E. (1974). *Studies in the new experimental aesthetics: Steps toward an objective psychology of aesthetic appreciation.* Washington, DC: Hemisphere Publishing Corporation.

Berlyne, D. E., Ogilvie, J. C., & Parham, L. C. C. (1968). The dimensionality of visual complexity, interestingness, and pleasingness. *Canadian Journal of Psychology, 22,* 376–387.

Bignardi, G., Ticini, L. F., Smit, D., & Polderman, T. J. (2020). Domain-specific and domain-general genetic and environmental effects on the intensity of visual aesthetic appraisal. *PsyArXiv.* https://doi.org/10.31234/osf.io/79nbq

Bingham, W. V. (1910). Studies in melody. *The Psychological Review: Monograph Supplements, 12,* i–89.

Bingham, W. V. (1914). Five years of progress in comparative musical science. *Psychological Bulletin, 11,* 421–433. https://doi.org/10.1037/h0075722

Birkhoff, G. D. (1933). *Aesthetic measure*. Cambridge, MA: Harvard University Press.

Boring, E. G. (1950). *A history of experimental psychology* (2nd ed.). New York, NY: Appleton-Century-Crofts.

Boring, E. G. (1959). John Gilbert Beebe-Center: 1897–1958. *The American Journal of Psychology, 72*, 311–315.

Brighouse, G. (1939a). A study of aesthetic apperception. *Psychological Monographs, 51*, 1–22.

Brighouse, G. (1939b). Variability in preference for simple forms. *Psychological Monographs, 51*, 68–74.

Burt, C. (1933). *How the mind works*. London: Allen and Unwin.

Burt, C. (1949). The structure of the mind. A review of the results of factor analysis. *British Journal of Educational Psychology, 19*, 176–199.

Burt, C. (1962). Francis Galton and his contributions to psychology. *The British Journal of Statistical Psychology, 15*, 1–49.

Burt, C. (1964). Charles Wilfrid Valentine (1879–1964). *British Journal of Educational Psychology, 34*, 219–222.

Cahalan, E. J. (1939). The consistency of aesthetic judgment. *Psychological Monographs, 51*, 75–87. https://doi.org/10.1037/h0093478

Carr, H. A. (1925). *Psychology: A study of mental activity*. New York, NY: Longmans, Green & Co.

Carroll, H. A. (1933). What do the Meier-Seashore and the McAdory art tests measure? *The Journal of Educational Research, 26*, 661–665.

Cattell, J., Glascock, J., & Washburn, M. F. (1918). Experiments on a possible test of aesthetic judgment of pictures. *The American Journal of Psychology, 29*, 333–336.

Chan, J., Eysenck, H. J., & Götz, K. O. (1980). A new visual aesthetic sensitivity test: III Cross-cultural comparison between Hong Kong children and adults, and English and Japanese samples. *Perceptual and Motor Skills, 50*, 1325–1326.

Chandler, A. R. (1934). *Beauty and human nature. Elements of psychological aesthetics*. New York, NY: Appelton-Century.

Chandler, A. R., & Barnhart, E. N. (1938). *Bibliography of psychological and experimental aesthetics 1864–1937*. Berkeley, CA: University of California Press.

Che, J., Sun, X., Gallardo, V., & Nadal, M. (2018). Cross-cultural empirical aesthetics. *Progress in Brain Research, 237*. https://doi.org/10.1016/bs.pbr.2018.03.002

Child, I. L. (1962). Personal preferences as an expression of aesthetic sensitivity. *Journal of Personality, 30*, 496–512.

Child, I. L. (1965). Personality correlates of esthetic judgment in college students. *Journal of Personality, 33*, 476–511.

Child, I. L., & Iwao, S. (1968). Personality and esthetic sensitivity: Extension of findings to younger age and to different culture. *Journal of Personality and Social Psychology, 8*, 308–312.

Child, I. L., & Siroto, L. (1965). BaKwele and American esthetic evaluations compared. *Ethnology, 4*, 349–360.

Clair, M. B. (1939). Variation in the perception of aesthetic qualities in paintings. *Psychological Monographs, 51*(5), 52–67.

Clark, D., Goodell, M. S., & Washburn, M. F. (1911). The effect of area on the pleasantness of colors. *The American Journal of Psychology, 22*, 578–579.

Clark, G. (1987). Norman C. Meier: A critique of his tests and research. In G. Clark, E. Zimmermann, & M. Zurmuehlen (Eds.), *Understanding art testing: Past influences, Norman*

C. Meier's contributions, present concerns, and future possibilities (pp. 46–59). Reston, VA: National Art Education Association.

Clark, H., Quackenbush, N., & Washburn, M. F. (1913). A suggested coefficient of affective sensitiveness. *The American Journal of Psychology, 24*, 583–585.

Coons, E. E. (2002). Neal Elgar Miller (1909–2002). *American Psychologist, 57*, 784–786.

Crawford, D., & Washburn, M. F. (1911). Fluctuations in the affective value of colors during fixation for one minute. *The American Journal of Psychology, 22*, 579–582.

Cupchik, G. C. (1986). A decade after Berlyne. New directions in experimental aesthetics. *Poetics, 15*, 345–369.

Cupchik, G. C. (2020). One hundred and fifty years after Fechner: A view from the "middle of the storm." *Psychology of Aesthetics, Creativity, and the Arts.* https://doi.org/10.1037/aca0000352

Cupchik, G. C., Arnheim, R., & Martindale, C. (1999). A history of Division 10 (Psychology and the Arts): Through the eyes of past presidents. In D. A. Dewsbury (Ed.), *Unification through division: Histories of the divisions of the American Psychological Association. Vol IV* (pp. 9–34). Washington, DC: American Psychological Association.

Dallenbach, K. M. (1940). Margaret Floy Washburn (1871–1939). *The American Journal of Psychology, 53*, 1–5.

Dallenbach, K. M. (1959). Robert Morris Ogden: 1877–1959. *The American Journal of Psychology, 72*, 472–477.

Davis, F. C. (1933). Aesthetic proportion. *The American Journal of Psychology, 45*, 298–302.

Day, H. I. (1977). Daniel Ellis Berlyne (1924–1976). *Motivation and Emotion, 4*, 377–383. https://doi.org/10.1007/bf00992542

Dewey, J. (1934). *Art as experience.* New York, NY: Minton, Balch & Company.

Edmonds, E. M., & Smith, M. E. (1923). The phenomenological description of musical intervals. *The American Journal of Psychology, 34*, 287–291. https://doi.org/10.2307/1413583

Eisenman, R. (1965). Birth order, aesthetic preference, and volunteering for an electric shock experiment. *Psychonomic Science, 3*, 151–152. https://doi.org/10.3758/bf03343068

Eisenman, R. (1967). Complexity-simplicity: II. Birth order and sex differences. *Psychonomic Science, 8*, 171–172.

Eisenman, R., & Robinson, N. (1967). Complexity-simplicity, creativity, intelligence, and other correlates. *Journal of Psychology: Interdisciplinary and Applied, 67*, 331–334. https://doi.org/10.1080/00223980.1967.10544937

Eisenman, R. (1965). Aesthetic preferences of schizophrenics. *Perceptual and Motor Skills, 20*, 601–604.

Eisenman, R. (1967a). Birth-order and sex differences in aesthetic preference for complexity-simplicity. *The Journal of General Psychology, 77*, 121–126.

Eisenman, R. (1967b). Complexity-simplicity: I. Preference for symmetry and rejection of complexity. *Psychonomic Science, 8*(4), 169–170.

Eisenman, R., & Rappaport, J. (1967). Complexity preference and semantic differential ratings of complexity-simplicity and symmetry-asymmetry. *Psychonomic Science, 7*, 147–148. https://doi.org/10.3758/BF03328508

Esper, E. (1966). Max Meyer and the psychology of music. *Journal of Music Theory, 10*, 182–199. https://doi.org/10.2307/843241

Eysenck, H. J. (1940). The "general factor" in aesthetic judgements. *British Journal of Psychology, 31*, 94–102.

Eysenck, H. J. (1941a). "Type"-Factors in aesthetic judgments. *British Journal of Psychology*, *31*, 262–270.

Eysenck, H. J. (1941b). A critical and experimental study of colour preferences. *American Journal of Psychology*, *54*, 385–394.

Eysenck, H. J. (1941c). The empirical determination of an aesthetic formula. *Psychological Review*, *48*, 83–92.

Eysenck, H. J. (1942). The experimental study of the "Good Gestalt"—A new approach. *Psychological Review*, *49*, 344–363.

Eysenck, H. J. (1972). Preference judgments for polygons, designs and drawings. *Perceptual and Motor Skills*, *34*, 396–398.

Eysenck, H. J. (1981). Aesthetic preferences and individual differences. In D. O'Hare (Ed.), *Psychology and the arts* (pp. 76–101). Brighton: The Harvester Press.

Eysenck, H. J. (1983). A new measure of "good taste" in visual art. *Leonardo*, *16*, 229–231.

Eysenck, H. J., & Castle, M. (1971). Comparative study of artists and nonartists on the Maitland Graves Design Judgment Test. *Journal of Applied Psychology*, *55*, 389–392.

Farnsworth, P. R. (1925). Atonic endings in melodies. *The American Journal of Psychology*, *36*, 394–400. https://doi.org/10.2307/1414163

Farnsworth, P. R. (1926a). Ending preferences among the three positions of the tonic chord. *Journal of Comparative Psychology*, *6*, 95–102. https://doi.org/10.1037/h0072802

Farnsworth, P. R. (1926b). Ending preferences in two musical situations. *The American Journal of Psychology*, *37*, 237–240. https://doi.org/10.2307/1413691

Farnsworth, P. R. (1926c). The effect of repetition on ending preferences in melodies. *The American Journal of Psychology*, *37*, 116–122.

Farnsworth, P. R. (1931). An historical, critical and experimental study of the Seashore-Kwalwasser test battery. *Genetic Psychology Monographs*, 291–393.

Farnsworth, P. R. (1932). Preferences for rectangles. *Journal of General Psychology*, *7*, 479–481. https://doi.org/10.1080/00221309.1932.9918480

Farnsworth, P. R. (1958). *The social psychology of music*. New York, NY: The Dryden Press.

Fechner, G. T. (1860). *Elemente der Psychophysik*. Leipzig: Breitkopf und Härtel.

Fechner, G. T. (1871). *Zur experimentalen Aesthetik*. Leipzig: Hirzel.

Fechner, G. T. (1876). *Vorschule der Ästhetik*. Leipzig: Breitkopf und Härtel.

Fechner, G. T. (1878). Wie es der experimentalen Aesthetik seither ergangen ist. *Im Neuen Reich*, *8*, 41–51, 81–96.

Flugel, J. C. (1933). *A hundred years of psychology*. Andover: Duckworth.

Ford, C. S., Prothro, E. T., & Child, I. L. (1966). Some transcultural comparisons of esthetic judgment. *Journal of Social Psychology*, *68*, 19–26.

Garth, T. R. (1924). A color preference scale for one thousand white children. *Journal of Experimental Psychology*, *7*, 233–241.

Garth, T. R., & Collado, I. R. (1929). The color preferences of Filipino children. *Journal of Comparative Psychology*, *9*, 397–404.

Geissler, L. R. (1917). The affective tone of color-combinations. *Studies in Psychology, Titchener Commemorative Volume*, 150–174.

Gordon, K. (1903). *The psychology of meaning*. Chicago: University of Chicago.

Gordon, K. (1912). Esthetics of simple color arrangements. *Psychological Review*, *19*, 352–363.

Gordon, K. (1923). A Study of esthetic judgments. *Journal of Experimental Psychology*, *6*, 36–43.

Gordon, K. (1925). The recollection of pleasant and of unpleasant odors. *Journal of Experimental Psychology*, *8*, 225–239.

Götz, K. O., Borisy, A. R., Lynn, R., & Eysenck, H. J. (1979). A new visual aesthetic sensitivity test: I Construction and psychometric properties. *Perceptual and Motor Skills, 49*, 795–802.

Graves, M. (1948). *Design judgement test*. San Antonio, TX: Psychological Corporation.

Greb, F., Elvers, P., & Fischinger, T. (2017). Trends in empirical aesthetics: A review of the journal *Empirical Studies of the Arts* from 1983 to 2014. *Empirical Studies of the Arts, 35*, 3–26. https://doi.org/10.1177/0276237415625258

Green, C. D. (1995). All that glitters: A review of psychological research on the aesthetics of the golden section. *Perception, 24*, 937–968.

Grove, M. S., & Eisenman, R. (1970). Complexity-simplicity, symmetry-asymmetry, and sociometric choice. *Perception & Psychophysics, 8*, 427–429.

Guernsey, M. (1928). The rôle of consonance and dissonance in music. *The American Journal of Psychology, 40*, 173–204.

Guilford, J. P., & Guilford, R. B. (1931). A prognostic test for students in design. *Journal of Applied Psychology, 15*, 335–345. https://doi.org/10.1037/h0069952

Gulliksen, H. (1968). Louis Leon Thurstone, experimental and mathematical psychologist. *The American Psychologist, 23*, 786–802. https://doi.org/10.1037/h0026696

Hall, G. S. (1912). *Founders of modern psychology*. New York, NY: D. Appleton and Company.

Handler, L. (2001). Assessment of men: Personality assessment goes to war by the Office of Strategic Services Assessment staff. *Journal of Personality Assessment, 76*, 558–578.

Haritos-Fatouros, M., & Child, I. (1977). Transcultural similarity in personal significance of esthetic interests. *Journal of Cross-Cultural Psychology, 8*, 285–298.

Hebb, D. E. (1949). *The organization of behavior. A neuropsychological theory*. New York. NY: John Wiley & Sons.

Heidelberger, M. (2004). *Nature from within. Gustav Theodor Fechner and his psychophysical worldview*. Pittsburgh, PA: University of Pittsburgh Press.

Heinlein, C. P. (1925). An experimental study of the Seashore Consonance Test. *Journal of Experimental Psychology, 8*, 408–433.

Heinlein, C. P. (1928). The affective characters of the major and minor modes in music. *Journal of Comparative Psychology, 8*, 101–142.

Hevner, K. (1930a). An empirical study of three psychophysical methods. *The Journal of General Psychology, 4*(1–4), 191–212. https://doi.org/10.1080/00221309.1930.9918310

Hevner, K. (1930b). Tests for aesthetic appreciation in the field of music. *Journal of Applied Psychology*, (14), 470–477.

Hevner, K. (1931). A study of tests for appreciation of music. *Journal of Applied Psychology, 15*, 575–583.

Hevner, K. (1935a). Experimental studies of the affective value of colors and lines. *Journal of Applied Psychology, 19*, 385–398.

Hevner, K. (1935b). Expression in music: A discussion of experimental studies and theories. *Psychological Review, 42*, 186–204.

Hevner, K. (1935c). The affective character of the major and minor modes in music. *The American Journal of Psychology, 47*, 103–118.

Hevner, K. (1936). Experimental studies of the elements of expression in music. *The American Journal of Psychology, 48*, 246–268.

Hevner, K. (1937a). An experimental study of the affective value of sounds in poetry. *The American Journal of Psychology, 49*, 419–434.

Hevner, K. (1937b). The aesthetic experience: A psychological description. *Psychological Review, 44*, 245–263.

Hevner, K., & Mueller, J. H. (1939). The effectiveness of various types of art appreciation aids. *Journal of Abnormal and Social Psychology*, *34*, 63–72. https://doi.org/10.1037/h0059214

Horst, P. (1955). L.L. Thurstone and the science of human behavior. *Science*, *122*, 1259–1260. https://doi.org/10.1126/science.122.3183.1259

Israeli, N. (1928). Affective reactions to painting reproductions. A study in the psychology of aesthetics. *Journal of Applied Psychology*, *12*, 125–139.

Iwao, S., & Child, I. L. (1966). Comparison of esthetic judgments by American experts and by Japanese potters. *The Journal of Social Psychology*, *68*, 27–33.

Iwao, S., Child, I. L., & García, M. (1969). Further evidence of agreement between Japanese and American esthetic evaluations. *The Journal of Social Psychology*, *78*, 11–15.

Iwawaki, S., Eysenck, H. J., & Götz, K. O. (1979). A new visual aesthetic sensitivity test (VAST): II. Cross-cultural comparison between England and Japan. *Perceptual and Motor Skills*, *49*, 859–862.

Jacobsen, T. (2006). Bridging the arts and sciences: A framework for the psychology of aesthetics. *Leonardo*, *39*, 155–162.

Katz, S. E., & Breed, F. S. (1922). Color preferences of children. *Journal of Applied Psychology*, *6*, 255–266.

Koffka, K. (1940). Problems in the psychology of art. In *Art: A Bryn Mawr Symposium* (pp. 179–273). Bryn Mawr, PA: Bryn Mawr College.

Külpe, O. (1895). *Outlines of psychology based upon the results of experimental investigation*. London: George Allen & Unwin.

Külpe, O. (1907). Der gegenwärtige Stand der experimentellen Ästhetik. In F. Schumann (Ed.), *Bericht über den II. Kongreß für experimentelle Psychologie in Würzburg vom 18. bis 21. April 1906* (pp. 1–57). Leipzig: Barth.

Külpe, O. (1921). *Grundlagen der Ästhetik*. Leipzig: S. Hirzel.

Lehman, P. R. (1969). A selected bibliography of works on music testing. *Journal of Research in Music Education*, *17*, 427–442. https://doi.org/10.2307/3344172

Logasa, H. A., & Wright, M. M. (1930). *Tests for the appreciation of literature*. Bloomington, IN: Public School Publishing Co.

Lundholm, H. (1921). The affective tone of lines: Experimental researches. *Psychological Review*, *28*, 43–60.

MacDougall, R. (1903). The structure of simple rhythm forms. In H. Münsterberg (Ed.), *Harvard psychological studies* (Vol. 1, pp. 309–412). Boston, MA: Houghton, Mifflin and Company.

Machotka, P. (2002). Irvin Long Child (1915–2000). *American Psychologist*, *57*, 794.

MacKenzie, D. (1976). Eugenics in Britain. *Social Studies of Science*, *6*, 499–532.

Madison, T. H. (1942). Interval discrimination as a measure of musical aptitude. *Archives of Psychology*, *268*, 5–99.

Martin, L. J. (1905). Psychology of æsthetics. I. experimental prospecting in the field of the comic. *The American Journal of Psychology*, *16*, 35–118.

Martin, L. J. (1906). An experimental study of Fechner's principles of aesthetics. *Psychological Review*, *13*, 142–219.

Martin, L. J., & Müller, G. E. (1899). *Zur Analyse der Unterschiedsempfindlichkeit. Experimentelle Beiträge*. Leipzig: Johann Ambrosius Barth.

Martindale, C. (2007a). Recent trends in the psychological study of aesthetics, creativity, and the arts. *Empirical Studies of the Arts*, *25*, 121–141.

Martindale, C. (2007b). The foundation and future of the Society for the Psychology of Aesthetics, Creativity, and the Arts. *Psychology of Aesthetics, Creativity, and the Arts, 1*, 121–132. https://doi.org/10.1037/1931-3896.1.3.121

McAdory, M. (1933). *The construction and validation of an art test.* New York, NY: Columbia University Press.

McCarthy, D. (1930). A study of the Seashore measures of musical talent. *Journal of Applied Psychology, 14*, 437–455. https://doi.org/10.1037/h0073360

McReynolds, P. (1987). Lightner Witmer. Little-known founder of clinical psychology. *American Psychologist, 42*, 849–858.

Meier, N. C. (1926). Aesthetic judgment as a measure of art talent. In *University of Iowa Studies. Series on Aims and Progress of Research* (Vol. 1). Iowa City, IA: University of Iowa.

Meier, N. C. (1927). Can art talent be discovered by test devices? *Western Arts Association Bulletin, 11*, 74–79.

Meier, N. C. (1928). A measure of art talent. *Psychological Monographs, 39*, 184–199.

Meier, N. C. (1939). Factors in artistic aptitude: Final summary of a ten-year study of a special ability. *Psychological Monographs, 51*, 140–158. https://doi.org/10.1037/h0093484

Meier, N. C. (1940). *Meier art tests. I. Art judgment.* Iowa City, IA: State University of Iowa, Bureau of Educational Research and Service.

Meier, N. C. (1942). *The Meier Art Judgment Test.* Iowa City, IA: Bureau of Educational Research and Service, University of Iowa.

Meier, N. C. (1963). *Meier art tests. II. Aesthetic perception.* Iowa City, IA: Bureau of Educational Research and Service, University of Iowa.

Meier, N. C., & Seashore, C. E. (1929). *The Meier-Seashore Art Judgment Test.* Iowa City, IA: Bureau of Educational Research, University of Iowa.

Meischner-Metge, A. (2010). Gustav Theodor Fechner: Life and work in the mirror of his diary. *History of Psychology, 13*, 411–423.

Metfessel, M. (1950). Carl Emil Seashore, 1866–1949. *Science, 111*, 713–717.

Meumann, E. (1908). *Einführung in die Ästhetik der Gegenwart.* Leipzig: Quelle & Meyer.

Meumann, E. (1919). *System der Aesthetik.* Leipzig: Quelle & Meyer.

Meyer, M. (1900). Elements of psychological theory of melody. *Psychological Review, 7*, 241–273. https://doi.org/10.1037/h0067387

Meyer, M. (1901). Contributions to a psychological theory of music. *University of Missouri Studies, 1*, 1–80. https://doi.org/10.2307/2177044

Meyer, M. (1903). Experimental studies in the psychology of music. *The American Journal of Psychology, 14*, 456–478. https://doi.org/10.2307/1412315

Meyer, M. (1911). *The fundamental laws of human behavior: Lectures on the foundations of any mental or social science.* Boston, MA: Richard G. Badger.

Michaels, G. M. (1924). Color preferences according to age. *The American Journal of Psychology, 35*, 79–87.

Montuori, A. (2003). Frank Xavier Barron (1922–2002). *American Psychologist, 58*, 492. https://doi.org/10.1037/0003-066x.58.6-7.492

Morgan, C. D., & Murray, H. A. (1935). A method for investigating fantasies: The thematic apperception test. *Archives of Neurology and Psychiatry, 34*, 289–306. https://doi.org/10.1001/archneurpsyc.1935.02250200049005

Murray, H. A., & Mackinnon, D. W. (1946). Assessment of OSS personnel. *Journal of Consulting Psychology, 10*, 76–80. https://doi.org/10.1037/h0057480

Myers, C. S., & Valentine, C. W. (1914). A study of the individual differences in attitude towards tones. *British Journal of Psychology, 1904–1920, 7*(1), 68–111. https://doi.org/10.1111/j.2044-8295.1914.tb00245.x

Myers, R. (1973). *Interview with Daniel Berlyne. Oral history of psychology in Canada.* Unpublished manuscript. Retrieved from http://www.utsc.utoronto.ca/publications/aestheticsofemotion/wp-content/uploads/sites/2/2016/07/DanBerlyneInterview_Oct14-1973.pdf

Norris, E. L., Twiss, A. G., & Washburn, M. F. (1911). An effect of fatigue on judgments of the affective value of colors. *The American Journal of Psychology, 22*, 112–114.

Norton, B. (1981). Psychologists and class. In C. Webster (Ed.), *Biology, medicine and society 1840–1940* (pp. 289–314). Cambridge: Cambridge University Press.

Ogden, R. M. (1938). *The psychology of art.* New York, NY: Charles Scribner's Sons.

Ortlieb, S. A., Kügel, W. A., & Carbon, C. C. (2020). Fechner (1866): The aesthetic association principle—A commented translation. *I-Perception, 1*, 1–20. https://doi.org/10.1177/2041669520920309

Ortmann, O. (1926). On the melodic relativity of tones. *Psychological Monographs, 35*, i–47.

Ortmann, O. (1928). Tonal intensity as an aesthetic determinant. *The Musical Quarterly, 14*, 178–191.

Peters, H. N. (1935). The judgmental theory of pleasantness and unpleasantness. *Psychological Review, 42*, 354–386.

Peters, H. N. (1938a). Experimental studies of the judgmental theory of feeling. I. Learning of positive and negative reactions as a determinant of affective judgments. *Journal of Experimental Psychology, 23*, 1–25. https://doi.org/10.1037/h0060310

Peters, H. N. (1938b). Experimental studies of the judgmental theory of feeling. II. Application of scaling to the measurement of relatively indifferent affective values. *Journal of Experimental Psychology, 23*, 258–269. https://doi.org/10.1037/h0056719

Peters, H. N. (1939a). Experimental studies of the judgmental theory of feeling: III. The absolute shift in affective value conditioned by learned reactions. *Journal of Experimental Psychology, 24*, 73–85. https://doi.org/10.1037/h0057546

Peters, H. N. (1939b). Experimental studies of the judgmental theory of feeling: IV. Retention of the effects of learned reactions on affective judgments. *Journal of Experimental Psychology, 24*, 111–134. https://doi.org/10.1037/h0053975

Peters, H. N. (1942). The experimental study of aesthetic judgments. *Psychological Bulletin, 39*, 273–305.

Peters, H. N. (1943a). Experimental studies of the judgmental theory of feeling: V. The influence of set upon the affective values of colors. *Journal of Experimental Psychology, 33*, 285–298. https://doi.org/10.1037/h0057467

Peters, H. N. (1943b). Experimental studies of the judgmental theory of feeling. VI. Concrete versus abstract sets in the preference judgments of pictures. *Journal of Experimental Psychology, 33*, 487–499. https://doi.org/10.1037/h0058653

Peters, H. N. (1955). Toward a behavioral theory of value. *ETC: A Review of General Semantics, 12*, 172–177.

Peters, H. N., & Rodgers, F. T. (1947). Experimental studies of the judgmental theory of feeling. VII. The influence of nonmanipulative responses. *Journal of Experimental Psychology, 37*, 59–68. https://doi.org/10.1037/h0055888

Pfuffer, E. D. (1903). Studies in Symmetry. In H. Münsterberg (Ed.), *Harvard psychological studies* (Vol. 1, pp. 467–539). Boston, MA: Houghton, Mifflin and Company.

Pierce, E. (1894). Aesthetics of simple forms. (I) Symmetry. *Psychological Review, 1*, 483–495.

Pillsbury, W. B. (1929). *The history of psychology*. London: George Allen & Unwin.

Pillsbury, W. B. (1940). Margaret Floy Washburn (1871–1939). *The Psychological Review, 47*, 99–109.

Poffenberger, A. T., & Barrows, B. E. (1924). The feeling value of lines. *Journal of Applied Psychology, 8*, 187–205.

Powelson, I., & Washburn, M. F. (1913). The effect of verbal suggestion on judgments of the affective value of colors. *The American Journal of Psychology, 24*, 267–269.

Reber, R., Schwarz, N., & Winkielman, P. (2004). Processing fluency and aesthetic pleasure: Is beauty in the perceiver's processing experience? *Personality and Social Psychology Review, 8*, 364–382.

Rieser, M. (1962). Contemporary aesthetics in Poland. *The Journal of Aesthetics and Art Criticism, 20*, 421–428. https://doi.org/10.2307/427904

Robbins, H., Smith, D., & Washburn, M. F. (1915). The influence of fatigue on affective sensitiveness to colors. *The American Journal of Psychology, 26*, 291–292.

Scheerer, E. (1987). The unknown Fechner. *Psychological Research, 49*, 197–202.

Seashore, C. E. (1930). Carl Emil Seashore. In C. Murchison (Ed.), *A history of psychology in autobiography Vol. 1* (pp. 225–297). Worcester, MA: Clark University Press.

Segal, J. (1905). Die bewußte Selbsttäuschung als Kern des ästhetischen Genießen. *Archiv Für Die Gesamte Psychologie, 6*, 254–270.

Segal, J. (1906). Über die Wohlgefälligkeit einfacher räumlicher Formen: Eine psychologische-ästhetische Untersuchung. *Archiv Für Die Gesamte Psychologie, 7*, 55–124.

Segal, J. (1907). Psychologische und normative Ästhetik. *Zeitschrift Für Ästhetik Und Allgemeine Kunstwissenschaft, 2*, 1–24.

Silvia, P. J. (2005). Cognitive appraisals and interest in visual art: Exploring an appraisal theory of aesthetic emotions. *Empirical Studies of the Arts, 23*, 119–133.

Smith, M. B., & Anderson, J. W. (1989). Henry A. Murray (1893–1988). *American Psychologist, 8*, 1153–1154. https://doi.org/10.1037/h0091919

Stanton, H. M. (1928). Seashore measures of musical talent. *Psychological Monographs, 2*, 135–144. https://doi.org/10.1037/h0093342

Staples, R. (1931). Color vision and color preference in infancy and childhood. *Psychological Bulletin, 28*, 297–308.

Stetson, R. H. (1903). Rhythm and rhyme. In H. Münsterberg (Ed.), *Harvard psychological studies* (Vol. 1, pp. 413–466). Boston, MA: Houghton, Mifflin and Company.

Stevens, G., & Gardner, S. (1982). Contributions to the History of Psychology: XXXI. Life as an Experiment—The Long Career of Lillien Jane Martin (1851–1942). *Psychological Reports, 51*(2), 579–590. https://doi.org/10.2466/pro.1982.51.2.579

Stoerring, G. (1923). Ernst Meumann 1862–1915. *The American Journal of Psychology, 34*, 271–274.

Stratton, G. M. (1897a). Vision without inversion of the retinal image. *Psychological Review, 4*, 341–360.

Stratton, G. M. (1897b). Vision without inversion of the retinal image (continued). *Psychological Review, 4*, 463–481.

Stratton, G. M. (1902). Eye-movements and the aesthetics of visual form. *Philosophische Studien, 20*, 336–359.

Stratton, G. M. (1906). Symmetry, linear illusions, and the movements of the eye. *Psychological Review, 13*, 82–96.

Stratton, G. M. (1923). The color red, and the anger of cattle. *Psychological Review, 30*, 321–325.

Tatarkiewicz, W. (1946). Jakub Segal. *Przegląd Filozoficzny, 42*, 327–328.

Taylor, R. E., & Eisenman, R. (1964). Perception and production of complexity by creative art students. *The Journal of Psychology, 57*, 239–242.

Taylor, Robert E., & Eisenman, R. (1968). Birth order and sex differences in complexity-simplicity, color-form preference and personality. *Journal of Projective Techniques & Personality Assessment, 32*, 383–387. https://doi.org/10.1080/0091651X.1968.10120501

Thorndike, E. L. (1913). The measurement of achievement in drawing. *Teachers College Record, 14*, 345–382.

Thorndike, E. L. (1916). Tests of esthetic appreciation. *The Journal of Educational Psychology, 7*, 509–522.

Thorndike, E. L. (1917). Individual differences in judgments of the beauty of simple forms. *Psychological Review, 24*, 147–153.

Thorndike, E. L. (1924). *A scale for general merit of children's drawings*. New York, NY: Teachers College, Columbia University.

Titchener, E. B. (1910). The past decade in experimental psychology. *The American Journal of Psychology, 21*, 404–421.

Triplet, R. G. (1992). Henry A. Murray: The making of a psychologist? *American Psychologist, 47*, 299–307. https://doi.org/10.1037/0003-066X.47.2.299

Valentine, C. W. (1913a). The aesthetic appreciation of musical intervals among school children and adults. *British Journal of Psychology, 1904–1920, 6*(2), 190–216. https://doi.org/10.1111/j.2044-8295.1913.tb00090.x

Valentine, C. W. (1913b). *An introduction to the experimental psychology of beauty*. London: T.C. & E.C. Jack.

Valentine, C. W. (1914). The method of comparison in experiments with musical intervals and the effect of practice on the appreciation of discords. *British Journal of Psychology, 1904–1920, 7*(1), 118–135. https://doi.org/10.1111/j.2044-8295.1914.tb00247.x

Valentine, C. W. (1919). *An introduction to the experimental psychology of beauty* (revised). London: T.C. & E.C. Jack.

Valentine, C. W. (1962). *The experimental psychology of beauty*. London: Methuen & Co.

Vartanian, O. (2014). Empirical aesthetics: hindsight and foresight. In P. P. L. Tinio & J. K. Smith (Eds.), *The Cambridge handbook of the psychology of aesthetics and the arts* (pp. 6–34). Cambridge: Cambridge University Press.

Verstegen, I. (1996). The thought, life, and influence of Rudolf Arnheim. *Genetic, Social, and General Psychology Monographs, 122*, 199–213.

Voss, M. D. (1939). A study of conditions affecting the functioning of the art appreciation process at the child-level. *Psychological Monographs, 48*, 1–39.

Washburn, M. F. (1911). A note on the affective values of colors. *The American Journal of Psychology, 22*, 114–115.

Washburn, M. F. (1932). Some recollections. In C. Murchison (Ed.), *History of psychology in autobiography* (pp. 333–358). Worcester, MA: Clark University Press.

Washburn, M. F., Haight, D., & Regensburg, J. (1921). The relation of the pleasantness of color combinations to that of the colors seen singly. *The American Journal of Psychology, 32*, 145–146.

Washburn, M. F., Hatt, E., & Holt, E. B. (1923). Affective sensitiveness in poets and in scientific students. *The American Journal of Psychology, 34*, 105–106.

Watson, J. B. (1913). Psychology as the behaviorist views it. *Psychological Review, 20*, 158–177.

Weber, C. O. (1931). The aesthetics of rectangles and theories of affection. *Journal of Applied Psychology*, *31*, 310–318.

Welsh, G. S. (1949). *A projective figure-preference test for diagnosis of psychopathology: i. A preliminary investigation*. Unpublished Doctor's Thesis. University of Minnesota.

Welsh, G. S., & Barron, F. X. (1949). *Barron-Welsh Art Scale*. Palo Alto, CA: Consulting Psychology Press.

White, R. W. (1992). Who was Morton Prince? *Journal of Abnormal Psychology*, *101*, 604–606.

Whiting, J. W. M., & Child, I. L. (1953). *Child training and personality: A cross-cultural study*. Yale, CT: Yale University Press.

Williams, E. D., Winter, L., & Woods, J. M. (1938). Tests of literary appreciation. *British Journal of Educational Psychology*, *8*, 265–284.

Wing, H. D. (1941). A factorial study of musical tests. *British Journal of Psychology*, *31*, 341–355.

Witmer, L. (1892). Some experiments upon the aesthetics of simple visual forms. *First Annual Meeting of the American Psychological Association*. Philadelphia, PA.

Witmer, L. (1894a). Zur experimentellen Aesthetik einfacher räumlicher Formverhältnisse, Schluss. *Philosophische Studien*, *9*, 209–263.

Witmer, L. (1894b). Zur experimentellen Aesthetik einfacher räumlicher Formverhältnisse. *Philosophische Studien*, *9*, 96–144.

Woleński, J. (2011). Jews in Polish Philosophy. *Shofar*, *29*, 68–82.

Woodward, W. R. (2015). *Hermann Lotze: An intellectual biography*. Cambridge, MA: Cambridge University Press.

Wooldrige, A. (1994). *Measuring the mind. Education and psychology in England, c.1860–c.1990*. Cambridge: Cambridge University Press.

Yokoyama, M. (1921). Affective tendency as conditioned by color and form. *The American Journal of Psychology*, *32*, 81–107.

CHAPTER 3

REVISITING FECHNER'S METHODS

GESCHE WESTPHAL-FITCH

INTRODUCTION

GUSTAV Theodor Fechner (see Figure 3.1) is widely regarded to be the founding father of empirical aesthetics (Green, 1995; Höge, 1995). Although this field has flourished in the last decades (Berlyne, 1971; Chaterjee, 2010; Eibl-Eibesfeldt, 1988; Leder, 2013; Leder and Nadal, 2014; Leder, Belke, Oeberst, & Augustin, 2004; Nadal, Munar, Capó, Rossello, & Cela-Conde, 2008; Ramachandran, 2004; Zaidel, Nadal, Flexas, & Munar, 2013; Zeki, 1998), my conviction in this chapter is that certain of Fechner's founding principles and guidelines have been more influential than others, and the goal of this chapter is to call attention to some of his less appreciated insights.

In this chapter my aim will be to encapsulate the key points of Fechner's approach to empirical aesthetics as laid out in Fechner (1871, 1876, 1865) in a manner that I hope will be useful for the reader who is unable to peruse the original German texts. Because Fechner's use of terms is both idiosyncratic and somewhat old-fashioned, I will make liberal use of quotations with direct translations into English. My goal here is to give the gist of Fechner's meanings without any claim to providing the definitive translation of his many difficult terms and turns of phrase. My main focus will be on Fechner's admonition about the need for a diversity of methodologies, so I will structure this chapter around his framework of three key methodologies in empirical aesthetics and his concept of aesthetics from below.

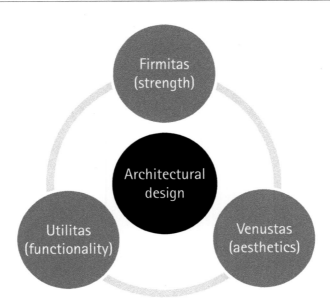

FIGURE 3.1. Gustav Theodor Fechner, 1801–1887.

AESTHETICS FROM ABOVE AND BELOW

Fechner was the first scientist to put empiricism at the heart of aesthetic research. Prior to his works, aesthetics was a purely philosophical (and thus theoretical) undertaking, going back to Alexander Baumgarten, who coined the term "aesthetics" in the eighteenth century (Baumgarten, 1986; Gregor, 1983). Not only did Fechner propose an empirical approach, he conducted empirical research himself, notably on the aesthetic aspects of the golden ratio.

Fechner differentiates between aesthetics from above and below. With this differentiation Fechner made a key contribution to empirical aesthetics, which has subsequently been fundamentally shaped by it. Aesthetics from above as he describes it is a philosophical endeavor, which entails starting with most general principles and proceeding from there to specifics without any empirical elements. It is important to realize that this is what the enquiry into aesthetics had traditionally been about before Fechner. In contrast, aesthetics from below is inherently empirical and deals with the simplest and most specific phenomena that eventually feed into broader and more general insights. If applied correctly, the two approaches do not necessarily contradict each other; instead, aesthetics from above can use and integrate insights generated by aesthetics from below, ultimately guiding "big picture" questions. Crucially, in Fechner's mind, aesthetics from below counts as one of the most central prerequisites ("zu den wesentlichsten Vorbedingungen") for aesthetics from above (Fechner, 1876, p. 4). This implies a sequence in which research into aesthetics should unfold, with empirical research preceding theoretical work.

In this vein, Fechner points out that when applying practical and specific empirical methods for aesthetics from below, researchers should take care not to be influenced by generalized, theoretical preconceptions:

> Wer Licht erst sucht, und der Weg von Unten ist ein Weg solchen Suchens, kann diesen Weg nicht mit schon fertigem Lichte beleuchten wollen.

> (Fechner, 1876, p. 5)

> Those who seek light, and the path from below constitutes a path of such a search, cannot want to illuminate this path with already prepared light.

Thus, the path of aesthetics from below should be guided by the facts it discovers, not by preconceived expectations or aesthetics from above.

Aesthetics from below in its pure form is not prescriptive; instead, it is a wholly descriptive approach, which entails breaking a phenomenon down into its component parts in order to understand it. It is important to realize that Fechner conceptualized aesthetics as a common thing and not a rare, elitist trait. Importantly, he put humans, not theories or norms, at its center, turning it into an undertaking that strives to understand the aesthetic proclivities of all humans, rather than a select few, studying common objects rather than rare artworks. Thus, Fechner's vision of an egalitarian, inclusive approach such as aesthetics from below is was surprisingly modern and relevant to current empirical research.

WHAT IS BEING MEASURED?

Intuitively, aesthetics is the study of beauty and its appreciation. Studying aesthetics from below with potentially quite simple stimuli, however, Fechner proposes *Wohlgefälligkeit* (pleasingness) as the dependent variable instead. Fechner suggests that there are two ways the pleasingness of an object may come about: by associative factors and by direct factors (physical properties of an object or artwork), which in turn can be intertwined:

> Nach Massgabe nun, als uns das gefällt oder missfällt, woran wir uns bei einer Sache erinnern, trägt auch die Erinnerung ein Moment des Gefallens oder Mißfallens zum ästhetischen Eindrucke der Sache bei, was mit anderen Momenten der Erinnerung und dem directen Eindrucke der Sache in Einstimmung oder Konflikt treten kann, woraus die mannigfachsten ästhetischen Verhältnisse fließen (...).

> (Fechner, 1876, p. 94)

Based on the stipulation that we like or dislike whatever a matter reminds us of, such a memory also contributes a moment of like or dislike to the aesthetic impression of the matter, which can be in harmony or conflict with other moments of memory and the direct impressions of the matter, which leads to the most diverse aesthetic relationships.

Here Fechner is emphasizing that an aesthetic impression is not only complex, consisting of multiple associative and direct elements, but can also be markedly different for each individual, depending on which associative memories are triggered by an object. It follows therefore that the pleasingness of an aesthetic object cannot be derived merely from its physical properties, but also arises from an interplay between object properties and the viewer's current internal mental state. Furthermore, the relation between associative and direct factors is also variable, as the following excerpt describes:

Kann man (...) dem Factor directer Wohlgefälligkeit selbst in den höhern Künsten der Sichtbarkeit seine wichtige Bedeutung nicht absprechen, so wächst doch dieselbe, wenn wir von Plastik und Malerei zur Architektur und von dieser zur Kunstindustrie oder den sog. technischen Künsten und der Ornamentik herabgehen; indem nach Maßgabe dieses Herabgehens einerseits der assoziative Factor selbst an Bedeutung in Verhältniss zum directen verliert, anderseits Conflicte des directen mit dem assoziativen minder leicht eintreten.

(Fechner, 1876, p. 183)

While one cannot dispute the important meaning of the factor of direct pleasingness for even the higher visual arts, it grows further when we descend from sculpture and painting to architecture and from there on to industrial art or the so called technical arts and ornament. As the associative factor loses meaning in relation to the direct factor proportionally to this descent, conflicts, on the other hand, occur less easily between the direct and associative factors.

The relationship between direct and associative factors therefore is quite fluid, and each may make varying contributions to the pleasingness of an object. It is important to note that Fechner does not value one over the other: both exist on an equal footing in his framework. Because the contributions of direct and associative factors can vary so much in various types of artwork, it follows that all types of artwork should be studied equally in order to gain a full picture of these factors.

USING MULTIPLE METHODS

Fechner was the first to suggest that not only would aesthetics benefit from an empirical approach, but that multiple approaches should be used in aesthetic research. He outlined three methods: the method of choice ("*Methode der Wahl*"), the method of production ("*Methode der Herstellung*"), and the method of use ("*Methode der Verwendung*"). Fechner introduced them extensively in Fechner (1871), which will be the basis of the following description of the methods.

Method of choice

The method of choice is the Fechnerian method most commonly used today. Fechner describes the method in some detail, including practicalities of data organization, which will not be reproduced here. The basic principles that Fechner describes, however, still hold true today:

> Man legt die, hinsichtlich ihrer relativen Wohlgefälligkeit zu vergleichenden, Verhältnisse in möglichst einfachen Schematen vielen Personen vor, lässt sie, wenn es sich um directe Wohlgefälligkeit handelt, mit ausdrücklicher Erinnerung an keine bestimmte Verwendung zu denken, das Verhältniss, was ihnen nach seiner eigenen Beschaffenheit am wohlfälligsten und was am missfälligsten erscheint, bezeichnen (...).
>
> (Fechner, 1871, p. 48)

> One shows the relations that are to be compared with regard to their relative pleasingness to many people in schemas that are as simple as possible. One lets them, if direct pleasingness is being examined, name that relation that seems most pleasing based on its properties and that which is least pleasing, while they [the participants] are explicitly reminded to not think of any particular use.

In his work on the golden ratio, Fechner himself employed the method of choice by showing multiple variants of rectangles simultaneously and asking participants to choose not only their favorite, but also their least favorite. Today, this design would be somewhat unorthodox. Nowadays participants in choice experiments are usually asked to make a positive choice of preference rather than indicating nonpreferred variants (although this is merely a matter of convention; of course these two approaches are merely two sides of the same coin). Furthermore, choices are typically made with only one or two images. Two images are usually presented in a two-alternative forced choice paradigm or in paired comparisons. Alternatively, individual images are often rated using (typically 5- or 7-point) Likert scales, which allow a degree of preference to be captured. Care is usually taken to randomize the order of images in order to minimize the effect of carryover from one image to the next. In its many variants, the method of choice is a pillar of empirical aesthetics today. However, as I hope to show in the next sections, much could be gained by extending the toolkit of empirical aesthetics as originally envisioned by Fechner.

Method of production

Studying creativity and artistic production in a laboratory setting might strike some as an inherent contradiction. While experiments by their very nature rely on predictable, broadly reproducible outcomes, the artistic process is often thought to be erratic and to rely on divine inspiration to a select few. However, as I have already laid out, Fechner was promoting an aesthetics from below when describing his vision of empirical aesthetics. This entails the reduction of aesthetic phenomena to their simplest possible form. Due to this reduction to simple shapes and figures, the method of production can be used with wide groups of people rather than a select few that are exceptionally artistically talented. Fechner describes his idea of production as follows:

> Man veranlasst viele Personen, statt unter mehreren vorgegebenen Verhältnissen das wohlgefälligste zu wählen, vielmehr dasselbe in einfachst möglichen Schematen selbst herzustellen, wonach man untersucht, bei welchem Verhältnisse die meisten Versuchssubjecte zusammentreffen oder um welches sich die einzelnen am dichtesten schaaren; die geringeren Grade der Wohlgefälligkeit aber nach der geringeren Zahl derer, die bei einem gegebenen Verhältnisse stehen bleiben, misst.
>
> (Fechner, 1871, pp. 48–49)

> Instead of asking many people to choose the most pleasing relation from multiple presented relations, one asks them to produce it in schemas that are as simple as possible. One analyzes which relation the most subjects converge on, or around which one the individuals cluster most closely. The low degrees of pleasingness are measured by the smaller number [of participants] that stop at a given relation.

The method of production is certainly in use, albeit rarely, see, for example, McManus, Zhou, L'Anson, Waterfield, Stöver, and Cook (2011). It should be noted that the advent of modern computer technology has broadened the horizon of possible aesthetic phenomena that might be investigated. While many participants might feel inhibited when asked to draw shapes and figures by hand, a software interface that participants can control with a mouse is often less of a barrier for those individuals who are well acquainted with the use of computers. An added advantage would be that digital output can be quantified more readily and reliably than drawings in an analogue form.

Some might argue that simplifying shapes and forms comes at the cost of aesthetic impact and thus validity. However, remember that Fechner put pleasingness rather than beauty at the center of his aesthetic enterprise. While most would not find beauty in a square, many would probably agree that there is something quite pleasing about it. While beauty is typically found only in rarefied moments with special objects, finding something pleasing is a common occurrence that many, if not most people can relate to. According to Fechner, there is no reason not to take it seriously and acknowledge it as a major factor in what we find aesthetically pleasing.

In Westphal-Fitch, Huber, Gómez, and Fitch (2012) my colleagues and I set out to extend the types of stimuli that might be used with the method of production by developing a software interface ("Flextiles") that allows participants to generate visual geometric patterns on a computer. While the basic grid of the pattern and the shape of its component parts are predetermined, participants can freely change the orientation of the shapes, thereby creating a wide range of different patterns that are visually striking and have an aesthetic impact. We maintain that such patterns are a useful bridge between maximally simple shapes, as proposed by Fechner, and fully fledged art, and studying their production can lead to insights into the aesthetic production processes in normal adults with no particular artistic training.

Method of use

The method of Use ("*Verwendung*") aims to quantify the physical properties of simple objects that are commonly in use, thereby allowing conclusions to be drawn about what is generally considered to be pleasing:

> Man misst die Dimensionen oder Abtheilungen der einfachsten, im Gebrauche, Verkehr, Handel und Wandel, kurz will ich sagen, im Leben, vorkommenden Gegenstände, bei welchen die Form vielmehr direct durch Rücksichten der Wohlgefälligkeit (vorausgesetzt, dass es sich um reine direct Wohlgefälligkeit handelt) als des Zwecks, der Bedeutung oder des Anpassens an andere Formen bestimmt ist, und welche keine Willkühr in der Anlegungsweise des Masses zulassen, wonach man wieder das relative Mass der Wohlgefälligkeit durch die relative Häufigkeit des Vorkommens dieses oder jenes Formverhältnisses bestimmt hält.
>
> (Fechner, 1871, p. 49)

> One measures the dimensions or compartments of the simplest objects in use, in trade, commerce, I'll say briefly in life, whose form is determined rather by pleasingness (if it is purely direct pleasingness) than by their purpose, meaning or accommodation of other forms and which do not allow an arbitrariness of the application of the measure. One determines the relative measure of pleasingness by the relative frequency with which this or that form-relation occurs.

As Fechner points out, it is in principle important to examine objects whose shape is determined by pleasingness rather than utilitarian considerations. This is a theoretical distinction that in practice, however, is never fully distinct. Insisting on pure pleasingness would limit researchers to fully ornamental objects and jewelry and yet even these will have also been shaped by some practical considerations (being able to lift them would limit size and weight, for example). Thus I would argue that in real life objects are shaped by both aesthetic factors and practical considerations, to varying degrees and both should be taken into account by researchers.

When applying the method of use, researchers should ideally endeavor to identify classes of objects that are *primarily* shaped by aesthetic factors. One example of the method is described in Westphal-Fitch and Fitch (2013). Here, the spatial properties of patterns used in quilts (a traditional type of hand-sewn blanket typically with complex geometrical patterns on the exposed side) were analyzed. While the quilts of course were shaped by practical considerations to some degree (a certain minimum size is required for a blanket to cover the body), most time and effort went into the aesthetic properties of the patterns used to embellish the quilts and thus it seems appropriate to make these the focus of an empirical investigation.

One weakness of the method of use is selection bias. It is rarely possible to completely sample the class of objects in question, and researchers by necessity will have to limit their sample size. Here it is critical that researchers have clear, unbiased criteria for selecting their sample that are laid out prior to data collection, in order to avoid criticism that certain items were preferentially chosen.

Combining methods

Fechner recognized that each of the three methods would possibly lead to different results by shedding light on different partial aspects of the same aesthetic phenomenon that is under examination. Naturally, researchers would want to avoid reaching a conclusion based on one-sided or incomplete data, and therefore Fechner, when he proposed his methods, also suggested that they should be combined, wherever possible:

> Jede der zwei ersten Methoden [Wahl und Herstellung] kann mit der dritten [Verwendung] gewissermassen verbunden werden, insofern man, anstatt der Wahl oder Herstellung abstracter Formen ohne Rücksicht auf Anwendung ausdrücklich die Wahl oder Herstellung mit dem Gedanken concreter Anwendung vornehmen lässt. [...] So viel als möglich wird man diese verschiedenen Methoden sich durch einander ergänzen und wechselseitig controliren lassen.
>
> (Fechner, 1871, p. 49)

> Each of the two first methods [choice and production] can be combined, so to speak, with the third [use] if one lets [participants] choose or produce with concrete application in mind instead of choice or production without taking an application into account. [...] One will let these methods complement each other and control each other as much as possible.

In 1871, Fechner suggested that the methods of either choice or production be mainly combined with the method of use. However, in his 1876 work, he only states that the results of all three methods should control each other, without specifying which combinations of methods he recommends. For practical work in empirical aesthetics, it would seem that many useful insights may be gleaned by combining the methods of choice and production. These two methods can easily be applied in a laboratory setting. Furthermore, the same participant can be tested using the creatively active method of production as well as the method of choice that relies purely on processing and assessment. Since these are two very different aspects of the aesthetic process, a larger window may be opened onto the aesthetic proclivities of any individual. For example, in visual experiments using geometric patterns, it has been shown that there are key differences in the type of patterns that participants prefer and those that they themselves choose to produce (Westphal-Fitch, Oh, & Fitch, 2013). In the preference task, patterns were chosen that had a good global fit, while during production patterns were predominantly produced that had a strong local fit. It is argued that these differences arise because the production task, which relies on small, local steps, biases participants toward focusing on local features, while the preference task, which forces participants to make fast decisions about patterns, encourages them to take global views of the patterns. If only one of the two methods had been employed to study the patterns, this contrast between global and local properties in geometrical patterns would not have been detectable. As this example shows, Fechner is right in promoting the use of multiple methods. I would argue that particularly the combination of the methods of choice and production can make a valuable contribution to our understanding of both sides of the aesthetic process, covering both production and appreciation side of aesthetics.

Participants

Fechner very astutely recognized that the selection of participants in experiments on aesthetics can be difficult in that extraneous factors may influence preferences:

> Auch durch die Bemerkung, dass Bildungszustand, Alter, Geschlecht, Individualität einen Einfluß auf die ästhetische Bevorzugung dieses oder jenes Verhältnisses haben können, wird der Kreis der Untersuchung nur erweitert, indem es gilt, diese Einflüsse mit in Rücksicht zu ziehen, und theils das durch alles Durchgreifende, theils das sich danach Modifizierende festzustellen; insofern es aber kurzen Ausspruch gilt, das was durchschnittlich für Erwachsene von mittlerem und höherem Bildungsgrade gilt, vor dem, was für das Kind und den rohen Menschen gilt, zu bevorzugen.
>
> (Fechner, 1876, p. 189)

The observation that education, age, sex, individuality have an influence on the aesthetic preferences for this or that relationship causes the scope of the study only to be extended by taking these influences into account and to partly determine that which permeates all, and partly to determine later, modifying factors. If a short dictum is required, then that which holds true for average adults of medium or higher education is to be preferred over that which holds true for children or raw people.

In his earlier work, Fechner points out that analyzing differences in aesthetic preferences between various groups is a central question in experimental aesthetics:

> Aber es hindert nicht nur nichts, die Unterschiede, die in dieser Hinsicht zwischen verschiedenen Klassen von Menschen nach Alter, Geschlecht, Race, Stand, Bildungsstufe, Klima, Zeitalter bestehen, zu verfolgen, indem man die Versuchssubjecte danach sondert, sondern es muss diess selbst als eine wesentliche Aufgabe der experimentalen Aesthetik gelten.
>
> (Fechner, 1871, p. 52)

> Not only is there no hindrance to pursuing the differences that exist in this regard between different classes of people depending on age, sex, race, standing, level of education, climate, era by differentiating subjects on these grounds, instead this must itself count as an essential task of experimental aesthetics.

The fundamental problem of selecting a representative sample of participants still poses a challenge today, not only in empirical aesthetics, but in science more generally. While Fechner's choice of words ("raw people") is of course not politically correct and is to be shunned, it is nonetheless true that most empirical data in science and the broad claims based on it are gathered from "WEIRD" participants: Western, Educated, Industrialized, Rich, and Democratic (Henrich, Heine, & Norensayan, 2010a, 2010b). While a certain selectivity, say for male over female participants, was not regarded as a problem in the nineteenth century, it is fair to say that attitudes have changed and awareness of this problem is increasing. In order to fully understand a wide-reaching phenomenon such as aesthetics that is universally shared in humans, many researchers today would agree that it is necessary to study a wide range of participants, including children and individuals from non-Western cultures. While the theoretical necessity is widely recognized, the practical reality of tight funding and project deadlines means that most research in empirical aesthetics will continue to be "WEIRD" in the foreseeable future. One way to partially alleviate the homogeneity of participants in the lab would be to recruit a wider range of participants for online experiments. Access to and familiarity with computers is increasingly common, and it is relatively straightforward to recruit potentially large numbers of participants through social media, etc. Although researchers lack the complete control of participant's characteristics that they have in lab experiments, web experiments do offer access to wider and larger numbers of participants at little cost and thus can make valuable contributions in empirical aesthetics.

GOLDEN RATIO

When a line is divided so that the relationship between the longer and shorter piece is the same as that between the longer piece and the whole line, then this relationship is the so-called golden ratio, a source of mathematical fascination since the ancient Greeks.

The golden ratio is an example of an aesthetic phenomenon that has been examined with all three methods, and where there is still no clear consensus. In this section, I highlight some of the work done on the preferences for the golden ratio with regard to Fechner's methods.

Interest in the golden section in aesthetics goes all the way back to Adolf Zeising's 1855 work "Aesthetische Forschung" (Aesthetic Research) (Zeising, 1855). When relations obey the golden ratio, Zeising said, a feeling of great contentment inevitably arises, even if the underlying reason is unclear:

> (...) [U]nd hieraus muß dem Gefühle, auch ohne daß es sich des Grundes bewußt wird, nothwendig eine hohe Befriedigung erwachsen.
>
> (Zeising, 1855, p. 184)

> And of it must grow a feeling of great contentment, without being conscious of the reason for it.

It is striking that even at this early stage of aesthetic research the stark mathematical relation that constitutes the golden ratio is connected with subjective, irrational feelings, encapsulating the inherently dual nature of the aesthetic process: while some properties of an artwork can be objectively quantified (size, color, shapes), the actual sensation of processing an artwork cannot be fully captured in numbers or words.

Fechner took up Zeising's idea that the golden ratio is inherently pleasing and set out to test it. He initially attempted to determine whether golden ratio relations were present in several Madonna statues (Fechner, 1865), which could be classified as an application of the method of use. Fechner finds deviations from the golden section, thus contradicting Zeising's idea, but suggests that the figures he chose were simply too complex, with too many intervening factors, to allow the golden ratio to be studied meaningfully. Fechner explains why formal principles may be more apparent in decorative art forms than in figurative art:

> Namentlich gewinnt in diesen Kunstgebieten die anschaulich verknüpfte Mannichfaltigkeit eine erhöhte Wichtigkeit, wohin die Symmetrie, der golden Schnitt, das regelmäßige Muster, die Wellenlinie, die Volute, der Mäander u.s.w. gehören, was Alles in den höhern Künsten der Sichtbarkeit leichter fehlen kann, und

aus angegebenen Gründen meist fehlen muss, weil man darin für die anschauliche Verknüpfung die associative durch die Idee hat.

(Fechner, 1876, p. 183)

In particular the clear connection of diverse elements gains importance in these art forms, to which symmetry, the golden section, regular patterns, the sinuous line, the volute, the meander etc. belong, and which can be absent more easily in the higher visual arts, and for the aforementioned reasons often must be absent, because one has the [artistic] idea as the associative [factor] to establish clear connections.

He therefore devised an experiment to empirically test for preferences in the width/ height ratio of simple rectangles and found a strong preference for rectangles that had the golden ratio (Fechner, 1871, 1876). Many attempts have been made to replicate his findings with the method of choice, with conflicting results (Godkewitsch, 1974; Green, 1995; Höge, 1995, 1997; McManus, 1980). It seems clear that preferences are a delicate measure that, depending on context, may not always reveal rather subtle effects. Indeed, there may be *several* peaks in the preferences indicated by participants (including squares, for example), suggesting that varying width/height ratios may be preferred, depending for example on how the shape is framed, as explored in Westphal-Fitch, Oh, and Fitch (2013). Here participants were asked to produce rectangles to their liking in a space that had no frame, a square frame or a golden ratio rectangle, either horizontal or vertical. This study was the first to show that there is a strong effect of framing on the types of rectangles that are produced, suggesting that some of the previous conflicting results may be due to the fact that rectangles were typically presented on a rectangular surface (table, paper, screen, etc.) that would have unintentionally acted as a frame, which in turn might have influenced preferences.

PRACTICAL APPLICATIONS

An area where Fechner's methods might be practically applied is museums. Museums are ideal places not only for visitors to expose themselves to beauty and culture, but also for researchers to learn more about the internal aesthetic processes of the viewer. Examining the behavior of visitors in museums is an active field of research (Brieber, Nadal, Leder, & Rosenberg, 2014; Heidenreich & Turano, 2011; Smith, Smith, & Tinio, 2017) that aims to draw conclusions about the inner workings of the visitor's mind.

The method of production could be used by museums to gather large quantities of data from a diverse set of people. Letting visitors manipulate artworks (on computer screens) to their liking could add another dimension to the aesthetic experience for visitors while simultaneously allowing researchers to gather data on aesthetic preferences. This is a constellation that to date has been underutilized in exhibitions. While offering researchers data from the visitors, such a setting might at the same time enrich a visitor's experience by offering the chance to actively interact with the artworks.

CHALLENGES AND SUGGESTIONS

Turning to some challenges for Fechner's framework, the method of use has strong practical limitations for researchers, such as sampling bias and determining sample size meaningfully. However, there are tantalizing new possibilities in the age of digital image searches and machine learning where exhaustive searches of images containing an aesthetic phenomenon of interest are becoming more and more feasible. Fechner's method of use may thus soon experience a renaissance.

A challenge for the method of production is finding tasks that are simple enough for many participants to do that nonetheless have aesthetic importance. In the past, this has limited the types of questions that could be addressed using analogue tools. Again, digital technology is starting to broaden the scope of this method, which should lead to an increase in popularity of this method with researchers.

The overarching goal of aesthetics should, in accordance with Fechner's ideas, be to achieve a full description in aesthetics using multiple methods. Importantly, a holistic view of aesthetics including both preferences and production is necessary in order to fully understand the phenomenon of human aesthetics fully. The challenge for the method of choice thus lies in combining it meaningfully with the rest of the Fechnerian toolkit.

Finally, it is an unfortunate fact that English translations of *Vorschule der Ästhetik* and *Zur experimentalen Ästhetik* are still unavailable. They would be a useful addition for anyone working in empirical aesthetics and who is not fluent in the intricacies of nineteenth-century scientific German, and one hopes that this deficit will be rectified soon.

DISCUSSION

As I hope to have shown in this chapter, empirical aesthetics as Fechner envisioned it continues to be highly relevant. His is an inclusive approach because it opens research to include most (if not all) types of participants and applies it to everyday, common phenomena. This inclusivity is necessary if we are to completely understand aesthetics as the universally shared trait that it seems to be.

Aesthetics as it occurs in the real world in cultures around the world is of course vastly complex and can be intermingled with other social and culturally specific issues such as status, fashion, and money. The value of Fechner's approach of aesthetics from below is that individual phenomena are isolated and studied in their simplest possible form, avoiding other factors as much as possible. Basic principles, perhaps widely shared across different groups, may thus be uncovered, without being masked by features specific to certain cultures.

However, the ultimate challenge will be to unify findings from these many strands of research and derive a big picture overview of aesthetics from them. Here, Fechner may have underestimated the role that "aesthetics from above" can play in this context, by offering frameworks that guide the interpretation of results (see, for example, Leder, Belke, Oeberst, & Augustin, 2004; Leder & Nadal, 2014, for such a guiding framework). Given that Fechner was trying to establish empirical aesthetics and differentiate it from the overwhelmingly theoretical tradition of aesthetics that had dominated the field until then, it is easy to see why he emphasized aesthetics from below as strongly as he did. As usual the solution may lie somewhere in the middle, with theoretical contributions inspiring empirical work and vice versa.

Modern empirical aesthetics is of course developing in exciting new directions. Neurological and biological approaches to aesthetics will (1) help to understand how assessment of beauty and pleasingness is anchored in the brain, and (2) try to explain how such a trait evolved and whether it or parts of it may be shared with other species (Darwin, 1874; Menninghaus, 2011; Prum, 2017; Ryan, 2018; Westphal-Fitch & Fitch, 2015, 2018). The wisdom of Fechner's words should however not be forgotten when venturing into these new areas of research. Using multiple methods to verify and test hypotheses should remain a guiding principle in traditional research in empirical aesthetics and become one in the newly developing areas of empirical aesthetics.

ACKNOWLEDGMENTS

I would like to thank Tecumseh Fitch for fruitful discussions about Fechner, and Marcos Nadal and Oshin Vartanian for the invitation to write on the topic. I acknowledge the Austrian Science Fund Firnberg Grant No. T827-B27 for financial support.

REFERENCES

Baumgarten, A. G. (1986). *Aesthetica*. Hildesheim: Olms (originally published 1750).

Berlyne, D. E. (1971). *Aesthetics and psychobiology*. New York: Appleton-Century-Crofts.

Brieber, D., Nadal, M., Leder, H., & Rosenberg, R. (2014). Art in time and space: Context modulates the relation between art experience and viewing time. *PLoS One, 9*(6), e99019.

Chaterjee, A. (2010). Neuroaesthetics: A coming of age story. *Journal of Cognitive Neuroscience, 23*, 53–62.

Darwin, C. (1874). *The descent of man and selection in relation to sex*. London: William Clowes and Son.

Eibl-Eibesfeldt, I. (1988). The biological foundation of aesthetics. *Beauty and the brain. Biological aspects of aesthetics*. Basel, Germany: Birkhäuser.

Fechner, G. T. (1865). Über die Frage des goldenen Schnittes. *Archiv für die zeichnenden Künste mit besonderer Beziehung auf Kupferstecher- und Holzschneidekunst und ihre Geschichte, 11,* 100–112.

Fechner, G. T. (1871). *Zur Experimentalen Aesthetik.* Leipzig, Germany: Breitkopf & Härtel.

Fechner, G. T. (1876). *Vorschule der Ästhetik.* Leipzig, Germany: Von Breitkopf & Härtel.

Godkewitsch, M. (1974). The "golden section": An artifact of stimulus range and measure of preference. *The American Journal of Psychology, 87,* 269–277.

Green, C. (1995). All that glitters: A review of psychological research on the aesthetics of the golden section. *Perception, 24,* 937–968.

Gregor, M. J. (1983). Baumgarten's "Aesthetica." *The Review of Metaphysics, 37,* 357–385.

Heidenreich, S. M., & Turano, K. M. (2011). Where does one look when viewing artwork in a museum? *Empirical Studies of the Arts, 29,* 51–72.

Henrich, J., Heine, S. J., & Norensayan, A. (2010a). Most people are not WEIRD. *Nature, 466,* 29.

Henrich, J., Heine, S. J., & Norenzayan, A. (2010b). The weirdest people in the world? *Behavioral and Brain Sciences, 33,* 61–135.

Höge, H. (1995). Fechner's experimental aesthetics and the golden section hypothesis today. *Empirical Studies of the Arts, 13,* 131–148.

Höge, H. (1997). The golden section hypothesis—its last funeral. *Empirical Studies of the Arts, 15,* 233–255.

Leder, H. (2013). Next steps in neuroaesthetics: Which processes and processing stages to study? *Psychology of Aesthetics, Creativity and the Arts, 7,* 27–37.

Leder, H., Belke, B., Oeberst, A., & Augustin, D. (2004.) A model of aesthetic appreciation and aesthetic judgements. *British Journal of Psychology, 95,* 489–508.

Leder, H., & Nadal, M. (2014). Ten years of a model of aesthetic appreciation and aesthetic judgments: The aesthetic episode—developments and challenges in empirical aesthetics. *British Journal of Psychology, 105,* 443–464.

McManus, I. C. (1980). The aesthetics of simple figures. *British Journal of Psychology, 71,* 502–524.

McManus, I. C., Zhou, F. A., L'Anson, S., Waterfield, L., Stöver, K., & Cook, R. G. (2011). The psychometrics of photographic cropping: The influence of colour, meaning and expertise. *Perception, 40,* 332–357.

Menninghaus, W. (2011). *Wozu Kunst? Ästhetik nach Darwin.* Berlin: Suhrkamp.

Nadal, M., Munar, E., Capó, M. À., Rossello, J., & Cela-Conde, C. J. (2008). Towards a framework for the study of neural correlates of aesthetic preference. *Spatial Vision, 21,* 379–398.

Prum, R. O. (2017). *The evolution of beauty. How Darwin's forgotten theory of mate choice shapes the animal world—and us.* New York: Doubleday.

Ramachandran, V. S. (2004). *The Artful Brain.* London: Fourth Estate.

Ryan, M. D. (2018). *A taste for the beautiful.* Princeton, NJ: Princeton University Press.

Smith, L. F., Smith, J. K., & Tinio, P. P. L. (2017). Time spent viewing art and reading labels. *Psychology of Aesthetics, Creativity and the Arts, 11,* 77–85.

Westphal-Fitch, G., & Fitch, W. T. (2013). Spatial analysis of "crazy quilts," a class of potentially random aesthetic artefacts. *PLoS ONE, 8,* e74055.

Westphal-Fitch, G., & Fitch, W. T. (2015). Towards a comparative approach to empirical aesthetics. In J. P. Huston, M. Nadal, F. Mora, L. F. Agnati, & C. J. Cela-Conde (Eds.), *Art, aesthetics and the brain.* Oxford: Oxford University Press, 385–407.

Westphal-Fitch, G., & Fitch, W. T. (2018). Bioaesthetics: The evolution of aesthetic cognition in humans and other animals. *Progress in Brain Research*, 237, 3–24.

Westphal-Fitch, G., Huber, L., Gómez, J. C., & Fitch, W. T. (2012). Production and perception rules underlying visual patterns: Effects of symmetry and hierarchy. *Philosophical Transactions of the Royal Society B*, 367, 2007–2022.

Westphal-Fitch, G., Oh, J., & Fitch, W. T. (2013). Studying aesthetics with the method of production: Effects of context and local symmetry. *Psychology of Aesthetics, Creativity, and the Arts*, 7, 13–26.

Zaidel, D. W., Nadal, M., Flexas, A., & Munar, E. (2013). An evolutionary approach to art and aesthetic experience. *Psychology of Aesthetics, Creativity and the Arts*, 7, 100–109.

Zeising, A. (1855). *Ästhetische Forschung*. Frankfurt am Main, Germany: Verlag von Weidingger Sohn & Comp.

Zeki, S. (1998). Art and the brain. *Daedalus*, *127*, 71–103.

CHAPTER 4

THE LINK BETWEEN EMPIRICAL AESTHETICS AND PHILOSOPHY

WILLIAM P. SEELEY

INTRODUCTION

EMPIRICAL aesthetics and philosophy of art are disciplines bound at the hip by a common research target: art. They are at the same time often more akin to feuding cousins than close friends. The trouble is methodological. Philosophers and psychologists use different sets of tools to approach, engage, and understand art. The focus of their attention is often, as a result, directed at different aspects of artworks and artistic practice. The solution to this trouble would seem to be simple. Reorient the discussion. Gather up the usual suspects and engage a conversation about common research targets. Experimental research is born of an insatiable impulse for creative problem solving. Interdisciplinary research harnesses the methodological slip between theoretical perspectives to drive collaborative problem solving in the lab. Reorienting cross-disciplinary perspectives to bring them into register is a powerful means to bring elusive research targets into focus. Cognitive science is grounded in the hope that comradery, collaboration, and creative problem solving will win the day in these design thinking contexts.

Unfortunately, things are rarely so simple. Ontology is not entirely a matter of discovery. It is more accurately seen as a reflection of the theoretical commitments of our best beliefs and desires. What we think there is is what our best epistemic apparatus suggests there is. What this entails is that methodological differences among theories are often reified as robust differences in ontology. The great divide between empirical aesthetics and philosophy of art is a case in point. Methodological differences manifest themselves there in a difference of opinion about what art is. Researchers in the two fields have different objects in view. Reorienting the exchange between them can therefore be more complicated than one might expect it should be. Nonetheless, it is the solution. Reorienting attention to common ground should suffice to bring the artifacts we call artworks into a common register and yield a shared ontology of art.

A SHORT REVISIONIST HISTORY

The art world is a complicated place. The nature of the artifacts and practices that fall within the scope of its governance are belied by commonsense aesthetic intuitions about artworks. These intuitions reflect an old fashioned model of linear progress toward clarity of aesthetic expression in art. The idea is, loosely, that there is an elusive form of aesthetic pleasure that is the mark of epistemic success in our engagement with artworks. Art may be about mimesis (Plato, 1989; Walton, 1990), the representation of rational ideas (Kant, 1790), the expression of a historical *weltanschauung*, the exploration and evaluation of socio-political issues, e.g., Adrian Piper, *Catalysis IV* (1971), or a reflexive examination of the nature of art itself (Danto, 2000; Greenberg, 1960). But the language of art, at least in the fine arts, is aesthetic. Medium-specific artistic methods, stereotyped productive strategies for making art, are tools for rendering the subject of a work in a way that expresses its content, its point, purpose, or meaning. Progress in art is progress in the clarity of the aesthetic expression of that content.

Commonsense aesthetic intuitions about art are reflected in an academic folk history of realistic depiction in European oil painting (Danto, 2000; Gombrich 1960). The development of painterly methods for depiction, e.g., formal compositional strategies for rendering space, skin tone, and dynamic anatomical relationships that animate living bodies, are imagined to have been driven by a common goal of representational clarity. Artworks that were the product of unsuccessful productive strategies were thought to be perceived as muddled and confused. Artworks that succeeded were thought to be perceived with aesthetic clarity.

This folk intuition borrows some philosophical baggage from the eighteenth century. Philosophers like Leibniz (1684), Hutcheson (1725), Baumgarten (1735), Mendelssohn (1757), and Kant (1790) thought that the compositional structure of successful works exhibited a quality of *uniformity amidst variety*. The *overallness* of this holistic compositional quality was, in turn, thought to resemble the structure of a sensuous manifold, e.g., the sensory inputs that support the visual recognition of the subject of a work (see Guyer, 1993). Some contemporary theorists have analogously thought that the formal composition of the painted canvas, the pattern of marks and texture gradients produced by the painter's brush, reflect the structure of an optic array or Marr's 2 ½ dimensional sketch (Gibson, 1971; Marr, 1982). Clarity in aesthetic expression, on this view, is thought to be achieved by producing works whose formal structure resonates with the range of sensory processes that support perceptual recognition. The ultimate expressive goal of an artwork need not therefore necessarily be aesthetic, but to be an artwork is to be written in an aesthetic vernacular that is recognizable in the affective profile of artistic experience.

Philosophers call this view an aesthetic theory of art. Ordinary individuals perceptually recognize a broad range of objects, actions, and events in everyday experience. But they do not have explicit cognitive access to the logical grounds for these perceptual judgments. The same is true of the defining aesthetic qualities of artworks. The nature of art is, like the nature of sensuous cognition itself, ineffable (at least from within the perspective of subjective experience). Aesthetic theories therefore treat art as a cognitively inscrutable method of perceptual expression. A commonsense understanding of the category of artifacts, actions, and events that we call "art" is nonetheless, like any other ontological category, tacitly encoded in our everyday epistemic practices. We perceptually recognize art. We talk about what we perceptually recognize in art. When we talk about art we are quite often art critically successful. This is true whether or not we are art experts. The goal of the ontology of art is to articulate the tacit commonsense understanding of art that is encoded in everyday artistic behaviors and practices. Philosophers approach this task via a method of conceptual analysis designed to cull foundational beliefs and intuitions about the nature of things from the muddy structure of ordinary linguistic practices.

Aesthetic theories of art make for an easy rapprochement between psychologists and philosophers of art. Theories in the ontology of art reflect the folk psychology of everyday artistic judgments. These epistemic and evaluative practices are cognitive practices. Aesthetic theories of art are therefore tacit models for our psychological engagement with artworks. They reflect our best psychological understanding of the cognitive and affective processes that underwrite everyday folk psychological behaviors. Interdisciplinary collaboration has become quite fashionable. There is no need however for the rapprochement between philosophy and psychology of art to be explicit, or even cooperative. It is sufficient that outcomes in each of the two fields indirectly influence the practice of the other via more general, culturally embedded, interdisciplinary discussions of each discipline individually. Philosophy and psychology are therefore tacitly interwoven fields of research, two strands of a common thread working together indirectly to triangulate the location of art in theoretical space over time.

The aesthetic story of art is a neat and tidy tale of artistic practice. It is a parable that we can use to open a conversation about the link between philosophy and psychology of art. But it is a revisionist history. The commonsense aesthetic model of art has been turned on its head in recent years. Art has always been about the expression of ideas.[1] Linear, historical models of artistic progress grounded in a psychological understanding of perceptual representation fell by the wayside in the middle of the last century. There is, nonetheless, a thread that ties the aesthetic model to contemporary artistic practice. Artworks are communicative vehicles. They are tools for the expression of ideas. This is as true of eighteenth-century aesthetic artworks as it is of contemporary conceptual performances and installations.

Arthur Danto (2000) argued that what it is to be an artwork is to be an occasion for art criticism. When we engage with an artwork we ask ourselves, "How should we recognize this artifact as a communicative event fit to a familiar category of art?" This kind of position is a cognitivist theory of art. Contrary to common intuition, its scope encompasses aesthetic theories of art. The aesthetic is just one among many categories of art governed by its own set of productive and evaluative conventions. A cognitivist view suggests that the question that binds philosophy and psychology together in discussions of art is not, "What is the nature of the aesthetic and how can it be used to articulate a common understanding of art?" It is rather, "How do the practices of philosophers and psychologists complement one another in explanations of the communicative practices that define art?"

STARTING POINTS

Philosophy has traditionally played a normative role within cognitive science. Philosophers can be thought of as part of its custodial staff. Ontology is the study of the range of explicit and implicit commitments encoded in commonsense beliefs and scientific theories. Terms are often used differently and for different purposes among fields with overlapping research interests. If so, researchers may unwittingly talk past one another. This is a common difficulty in nascent interdisciplinary collaboration. There is a need to settle collectively on shared language that supports a common ontology that can lead to complementary experimental goals in these contexts. Philosophers are, in this sense, ontological janitors. They employ a method of conceptual analysis to sort and trim ontological commitments, weed out theoretical inconsistencies, and generally enhance the coherence of interdisciplinary research.

We can use the example of aesthetic theories of art from above to illustrate this approach. Aesthetic theories of art define artworks as artifacts designed to trigger aesthetic experiences. The difficulties with this view are philosophically familiar. Art and the aesthetic represent overlapping domains. But the two categories are not coextensive. There are many artworks that simply are not aesthetic objects. The list includes Dada artworks and performances, Absurdist drama, Surrealist paintings, Rauschenberg's *Combines*, Mario Merz's *Arte Povera* installations, Vito Acconci and Adrian Piper's performance art, Tracy Emin's bed, and Martina Abromovic's *Imponderabilia* (1977), a work in which she and Uwe Laysiepen stood facing each other naked in a doorway through which audiences had to pass. There are, likewise, many aesthetic artifacts that are not artworks. Art Deco architecture, modernist kitchen design, Jaguars, and a Maykke Naples freestanding bathtub fit the bill (just to name a few). Aesthetic theories of art are, strictly speaking, committed to the judgment that these nonart aesthetic artifacts are, and anti-aesthetic artworks are not, artworks! The ontological commitments of the theory are therefore incompatible with the ontology of everyday artistic practice.

Aesthetic theories of art need amending. The first step is to restrict their scope. Aesthetic artworks represent just one category of art among many. The second is to recall the communicative nature of artworks. Aesthetic artworks employ an aesthetic vocabulary to express some range of conventionally appropriate ideas in an artistically salient way. The identity of an aesthetic artifact as an artwork is not tied to its aesthetic qualities per se. Rather what matters is the way those aesthetic properties have been used to express its artistically salient content. We may, for instance, easily recognize the aesthetic qualities of the compositional elements that categorize a painting as a seventeenth-century Dutch landscape, or a Cuyp or Van Ruisdael. But this does not entail that we see the artistic significance of these features. There is a reason artists like Cuyp and Van Ruisdael painted just those objects and events in just those configurations. The artistic salience of the perceptible features of the work is tied to those reasons, to their semantic role in the more general expressive point, purpose, or meaning of the work.

Philosophers who take their ontological role as conceptual custodians seriously see themselves as directing traffic in cognitive science. There are familiar shortcomings to this normative view of the role played by philosophy in cognitive science. It is commonplace in philosophy of science to note that theories and methods cannot be easily disentangled. The conceptual lens that theorists use to frame their subject matter is shaped by their means of measurement. Philosophical theories of art are no different. The conceptual analyses of ordinary language are more often than not divorced from the nitty gritty details of experimental psychology. Where the two diverge, philosophers distinguish between personal- and subpersonal-level analyses, or between explanations couched in terms of the explicit beliefs, desires, needs, and interests of conscious human agents in social contexts and explanations couched in terms of causal-psychological mechanisms. Skeptics consequently bracket off the relevance of psychology to art. They argue it at best provides an understanding of subpersonal level mechanisms that are equally relevant to understanding our engagement with art and nonart stimuli. Art is, alternatively, located in and among the conscious, personal-level, social interactions that are the proper subject of philosophy. There is a lot to get a grip on here. It suffices for now to note that the trouble with this approach is that the conscious mental lives of human agents supervene on, and so are constrained by, facts about causal-psychological processes. The normative role played by philosophers in cognitive science should not float free of experimental models and results. The two are inextricably tied.

COGNITIVE SCIENCE AND ART

Cognitive science and art are natural partners in crime. Cognitive science, in the most general sense, is an interdisciplinary field dedicated to the study of the way organisms acquire, represent, manipulate, and use information in the production of behavior. Artworks are communicative devices. They are artifacts intentionally designed to express some point, purpose, or meaning. Questions about the nature of art are, as a result, at least in part, questions about the ways that artists use medium-specific productive strategies to express these ideas. Answers to these questions can be culled from an understanding of the range of ways that consumers acquire, represent, manipulate, and use information in the perceptible surface of an artwork to recover and recognize its artistically salient formal-compositional, aesthetic, expressive, depictive, or representational content. We might coin an awkward acronym for this model for understanding art: ARMUIAC or the study of the way artists and consumers *acquire, represent, manipulate, and use information in artistic communication* (Seeley, 2011).

The ARMUIAC model can be articulated relative to what we might call *the problem of selectivity* for perceptual systems. The environment is replete with information. Only a small fraction of this information is, however, salient to the needs and interests of an organism at any particular time. The well-being of an organism often depends upon a capacity for swift responses in these contexts. Perceptual systems, therefore, need strategies to focus attention on task-salient features of the environment in a timely fashion. This problem is exacerbated by the fact that perceptual systems are limited capacity cognitive systems. How does this problem get solved? One suggestion is that we develop perceptual routines to focus attention on minimal sets of features sufficient to categorize, and so perceptually recognize, objects, events, and their task salient features (Ballard, Hayhoe, Pook, & Rao, 1997; Land & Hayhoe, 2002; Schyns, 1998).

Artists likewise develop medium-specific productive strategies that enable them to cull sets of diagnostic features from the environment sufficient for their expressive purposes. The representational power of exaggerated forms in caricature is a hackneyed example, but it is not the only one. The expressive power of choreographed movements, the dynamics of futurist sculpture, and the sparse narrative efficiency of film editing techniques are but a few of a cornucopia of others. These productive artistic strategies work simply because they are directed at the operations of perceptual systems. The suggestion of the ARMUIAC model is therefore that that there is a tight coupling between the range of category-specific productive practices in an artist's toolkit and the operations of perceptual systems that can be used to help explain the nature of art.

There is nothing new in this view of art. Nor is it unique to the lens of cognitive science and aesthetics. It can be traced back to E. H. Gombrich's discussions of the history of landscape painting (Gombrich, 1960). Gombrich was a psychologically minded art historian. He noted that it was an odd fact that realism in painting should have a history. Realistic depiction feels like a perceptual genre, like an illusory window on the world. Why, then, has it produced such a wide array of different, formal-compositionally unique artistic styles? Why shouldn't an artist simply copy what we all collectively see? The answer is that there is neither a unique, ideal set of diagnostic features necessary to perceptually recognize an object scene or event, nor a unique, ideal system of marks for rendering those diagnostic features in paint in a realistic depiction. Any of a vast array of formal vocabularies and compositional strategies will do. This fact is easily demonstrated by looking at realistic depictions from within and across different eras, e.g., landscape by Aelbert Cuyp, Jacob Van Ruisdael, John Constable, Edouard Manet, Winslow Homer, Robert Bechtel, Richard Estes, and Rackstraw Downes. The variance we observe among realistic styles in landscape painting demonstrates that artists must choose how to render the subject of their painting. What are the constraints on this process? The communicative intent of the artist within the context of their artistic community. The communicative exchange between an artist and a consumer is shaped by the aesthetic properties, expressive content, and semantic associations that an artist intends a consumer to recognize in the work as well as the norms and conventions governing communicative practices within their community.

Categories of art are defined by the range of productive and appreciative practices associated with different media, genres, and artists at a time within a community. These normative conventions for the production of, and engagement with, artworks are by-products of a back-and-forth communicative exchange between artists, consumers, and their precursors in a reflectively acknowledged history of art. The artistic styles that define different categories of art are therefore shared attributes of artistic communities, communicative devices that are artifacts of a complex social negotiation among artists and consumers. This raises a set of questions that are central to understanding art: what category of art does a work belong to, what are the productive strategies constitutive of that category of art, and how are they used to carry and communicate information (Carroll & Seeley, 2013)? Of course this is not to say that artistic production and appreciation are constrained by rigidly structured categories of art. The story of twentieth-century art is interdisciplinary in its own right. Traditional disciplinary boundaries among artistic media and schools of art have been exploded. What was left behind in their wake was an open-ended toolkit of expressive strategies. Contemporary artworks straddle media and categories of art with reckless abandon. Some capacity to perceptually recognize the array of categories of art an artist has drawn on in their work, and focus attention appropriately, is therefore critical to an understanding or appreciation of contemporary art.

Where does the link between empirical aesthetics and philosophy of art fall within the ARMUIAC model? Questions about the ontology of art are, ultimately, questions about the way artworks are structured to function as communicative devices. A range of disciplines contribute to our understanding of how artworks work this way. Art criticism can be thought of as a branch of art theory dedicated to understanding the particular content of individual artworks. Art criticism is paired with art history. We ask how a particular work might have emerged in a particular contemporary context framed by a range of art historical institutions and art critical questions. Philosophers paint art with broader strokes. Their interest is in more general structural questions that inform an understanding of how artworks work as communicative devices and how answers to these questions frame an understanding of the ontology of art. The answers to these questions depend on an understanding of both the social practices associated with artistic appreciation and the psychological processes that support them.

Judy Pfaff's sculptures and installations from the 1980s can be used to illustrate these sorts of analyses. Pfaff's works interweave painterly and sculptural methods to generate a dynamic formal aesthetic vocabulary for site-specific installations (Sandler, 2003; Smith, 1984). Pfaff is drawing in space. Some elements of the installations were tied to the wall, cantilevered into space from an available mechanism of support. We might, therefore, categorize the works as sculptural paintings. They are, however, also concerned with the enervation of space through the dynamics of three-dimensional form. We might, therefore, also think of them as painterly sculptures. Finally, the works are site-specific. They were not repeatable. They are each an installation, conceptualized for a particular location, and constructed onsite as a dynamic exploration of a unique architectural space. There is therefore a critical performative aspect to the works. They are installations that can be categorized as gestural expressions of Pfaff's embodied understanding of the space (Friedman, 1994, p. 16).

It is hard to know how to sort these ontological issues out. Which categorization should we prefer? It helps to know that Pfaff entered the MFA program at Yale as painter, not a sculptor, that she felt deeply dissatisfied by the conservative constraints of unique artistic media as a graduate student at Yale, and that she followed the advice of her professor Al Held, abandoned painterly methods, and exploded her imagery into physical space. It also helps to know that when she speaks about her installations she talks about reinvigorating the static mass of traditional sculpture (Friedman, 1994; Sandler, 2003).

These data points do not resolve questions about the identity of Pfaff's works, but they do inform them. And more importantly, they inform how we should interact with them, how we should recognize their formal and compositional features. This is where philosophers focus their attention. How do the elements of an artwork carry the communicative intentions of the artist and how do answers to these questions shape our understanding of the ontology of art. The ARMUIAC model suggests that the answer to the first question is that the artist provides clues as to how to categorize a work. Categories of art provide recipes for how to attend to the work. Our understanding of the categorical intentions of the artist, therefore, shape how we recognize the content of an artwork and interpret its meaning. These processes, in turn, shape how we perceive it. Of course, this is only one model among the many that philosophers have proposed over the years. But it has two critical attributes that point toward its broad applicability and elucidate the tacit structural link between empirical aesthetics and philosophy of art. It is a psychological model for our engagement with art that reflects the broader social nature of artistic practice.

Philosophical Skepticism about Empirical Aesthetics

Empirical aesthetics and philosophy of art have traditionally been portrayed as disciplines at loggerheads in a heated debate about the nature of art. At issue are questions of value. Philosophers have argued that what matters in matters of art is the normative value, aesthetic or otherwise, of artworks and associated experiences. A range of arguments have been brought forth to show that experimental psychology is not the right place to look for answers to normative questions. The fact that a culture exhibits some set of moral values, for instance, is not evidence that those moral values are ethically sound. Likewise, the fact that some large sample of ordinary perceivers exhibits some set of aesthetic preferences in the lab or at the museum is not evidence that those preferences are artistically sound (even if they do genuinely reflect the aesthetic preferences of that community).

Empirical aesthetics is often distinguished from what Gustav Fechner (1876) and Daniel E. Berlyne (1971) called *speculative aesthetics*. Fechner and Berlyne argued that philosophical and other speculative theories of art were born from a flawed methodology. Theories in speculative aesthetics are built from a priori principles derived from the aesthetic intuitions and artistic judgments of individual art critics, historians, and other experts via deductive methods. Theories derived in this way reflect the consensus preferences and subjective judgments of small, insulated communities of dedicated art consumers. The worry is that the sample is biased and that the only real criteria governing the validity of results would be their internal coherence. These are valid worries. They do not guarantee that speculative aesthetics misses the mark, but they raise the possibility that philosophy of art is a discipline dedicated to the logical exploration of the internal structure of arcane conceptual frameworks that are divorced from broader facts about the social behaviors they describe.

Berlyne replaced the art critical methods of speculative aesthetics with objective measures of verbal and physiological responses of average viewers to large sets of artworks and other aesthetic stimuli, e.g., aesthetic preferences and psychophysical measures of arousal. Berlyne's goal was an objective science of art grounded in the assumption that pleasingness (measured by levels of arousal) and attention (as indicated by fixation patterns and looking time) could be used as objective measures of aesthetic appraisal, cognitive engagement, and the artistic value of the formal-compositional elements of a work.

David Davies has identified a strain of philosophical skepticism that he calls *extreme pessimism* (Davies, 2013). Ludwig Wittgenstein famously quipped, "People still have the idea that psychology is one day going to explain all of our aesthetic judgments, and they mean experimental psychology. This is very funny – very funny indeed. There doesn't seem to be any connection between what psychologists do and any judgment about a work of art ... " (Wittgenstein, 1967, p. 19). This kind of extreme pessimism about empirical aesthetics has had a broad following and is shared by many contemporary philosophers. George Dickie, for instance, argued that exploring questions about the nature of art by polling the preferences of average audiences was like determining judgments of grammaticality by polling the judgments of toddlers. In each case what matters is not average measures of the behavior of large groups of individuals per se, but rather the measured responses of sample populations of experts, folks familiar with the salient normative conventions, or conventions governing artistic and linguistic practice for a community at a time (Dickie, 1962; see also McFee, 2011; Noë, 2015).

There is something to this line of reasoning. A distinction should be drawn between preferences and artistic judgments. Verbal responses and physiological measures of arousal and interest can reveal an individual's preferences, but they cannot tell us whether those preferences are categorically appropriate or not. We spend a lot of time in philosophy of art talking about naïve consumers who express artistically irrelevant preferences for artworks, e.g., preferences for performances of Simone Forti's

Slant Board (1961) or Robert Morris' *Sea Saw* (1971) that reflect memories of the kinds of games they might have played at summer camp. This phenomenon is not limited to nonexperts. People express all sorts of categorically inconsistent preferences for artworks, e.g., aesthetic preferences for the elements of anti-aesthetic Minimalist installations. Categories of art are composed of normative conventions, productive and related evaluative conventions that govern artistic expression for a medium, genre, school of art, etc. Artistic appreciation is driven by judgments of fit between an artifact and the normative conventions that define these categories of art. What matters for matters of art is whether those preferences are fit to the appropriate category of art.

Vito Acconci's *Following Piece* (1969) is one of my favorite examples of this phenomenon. Acconci would pick out the first person he noticed when he walked out of his building in New York City and follow them until they entered a private space. This often took him on rambling adventures across different subway lines and into different boroughs. Commonsense suggests that the work is voyeuristic. It appears as if Acconci is spying on someone's life. But commonsense gets the story wrong. Acconci's work is an example of late-twentieth-century nihilism in New York performance art (see also works by Chris Burden). The work is about the loss of control of one's body in the public space of contemporary society. Recognizing this fact may not resurrect the work for a consumer if they already don't like it—it may have no effect on their verbally and physiologically expressed preferences. But it should have a profound effect on their ability to understand it as an artwork—to evaluate how it carries information about its content, and thereby to recognize and evaluate its artistically salient features.

Extreme pessimism rests upon an assumption that the only questions germane to philosophy of art are normative questions about artistic value and appreciation and a related claim that results in experimental psychology are, strictly speaking, irrelevant in these matters. The trouble is that neither this assumption nor this claim is valid. Philosophers have always been interested in the psychological underpinnings of our engagement with artworks. Plato worried that the affective influence of fictional narratives was so strong that they could be used to sway political opinion. He banished art from the ideal polis as a result (Plato, 1989). Aristotle was likewise interested in the emotional effects of fictional narratives. He believed, loosely, that audiences experienced a form of transference he called *catharsis* in responses to tragic dramas (Aristotle, 1984). He, therefore, assigned drama a socially productive role. More recently, philosophers like Alvin Goldman (2006) and Gregory Currie (1995) have explored the relative roles that theory of mind and simulation theory can play in explanations of narrative understanding and audience engagement with characters. These examples suffice to demonstrate a longstanding interest in psychology among philosophers of art.

Extreme pessimists have a reply to this argument. The simple version goes as follows. Facts about the psychological processes underwriting our engagement with artworks apply equally in explanations of our affective, perceptual, and cognitive engagement with nonart artifacts. They therefore provide no information about the unique, defining characteristics of art. We may appeal to results from experimental psychology in explanations of our engagement with artworks and other aspects of artistic practice.

These data may corroborate or disconfirm existing theories, but they do not contribute anything to our understanding of the nature of art (Davies, 2013).

LOCATING ART

Alva Noë frames philosophical skepticism about empirical aesthetics as a question about *how to bring art into focus* in the lab. The target of his argument is research on art in what he calls the key of neuroscience. But its spirit generalizes more broadly to cognitive science and aesthetics. Noë uses jokes to illustrate his position. He provides an example: *Two Irishmen walk out of a bar. Yes this can happen.* We might ask a linguist to help us parse the surface structure of these sentences and recover their literal meanings. We might also ask psychologists to help articulate the cognitive processes involved. But if that were where we stopped we would miss the joke. The joke is not located in the sentences themselves. It lies in the way they are embedded in a social context. A listener must know far more than English grammar and the meanings of the words to recover the joke from its utterance. They have to at least know something about the relevant social stereotypes and the timing of one liners. It might also help to know something about the teller and the intended audience. It would certainly help to have an understanding of the boundaries of inappropriateness in humor. Jokes like this one play off of social biases. There are some contexts in which they really are not funny.

Artworks are like jokes. They are acts of communication. Philosophers of art often appeal to Paul Grice's (1957) theory of interpretation to frame these kinds of social interactions (Carroll, 1992; Fodor, 2012; see also Davidson, 1973; Dennett, 1981). Loosely, what it is to interpret someone's behavior is to frame it in the context of the body of beliefs and desires one would expect to have produced that behavior. Interpretation is a matter of attributing unseen beliefs and desires to others under the assumption that they are rational agents. In the case of verbal communication, we attribute the beliefs and desires to a speaker that make the best sense of their utterances in the context of our conversation. In the case of art, we attribute meaning to a work relative to our best sense of what it would have meant to make an artifact with that appearance in a historically particular social context. We expect that an artist produced their work under an assumption that we should recognize that they intended us to categorize and interpret it in a particular way, e.g., as a work of political satire, an Impressionist painting, or a work of performance art. Categorizing the work in the right way reveals the appropriate set of normative conventions for evaluating its content, or what it means to have rendered its subject in that particular way, e.g., as a joke among friends as opposed to a barbed expression of deep-seated social bias.

Normative conventions do the heavy lifting in philosophical skepticism about empirical aesthetics. The central claim is, again, that cognitive science is not well suited to explain the role these conventions play in our interactions with artworks. This is an important issue. The puzzle of locating art has plagued interdisciplinary research in cognitive science and aesthetics (Seeley, 2018). Nonetheless, extreme pessimists have overplayed their hand. Normative conventions are not magic totems. They are shared cognitive criteria governing artistic practices. They include productive conventions for making artworks of certain types and evaluative conventions for determining if those works have been done well or poorly. They also include communicative conventions for understanding what it means to have rendered the subject of a work in a particular way. If an artist wants to make an Impressionist painting there is a particular way they should manipulate their brushstrokes in order to capture their subject. They should also choose a subject fit to the representational and art theoretical goals of Impressionism. They might for instance choose an image that represents the fleeting dynamics of everyday life, e.g., a snapshot of the light on a field of haystacks at dusk or steam in a railroad yard, e.g., Claude Monet, *Wheatstacks, End of Summer* (1890–91) or Édouard Manet, *The Railway* (1873). Consumers recognize these conventions in a work, understand what it means to have articulated them in one way or another, and appreciate whether they have been utilized well or poorly.

Communicative conventions are a little more complex. They emerge in the context of broader social negotiations about how to interpret the actions and iconography employed by artists. We can return to landscape painting to illustrate what this means. Nineteenth-century American landscape paintings are, at first blush, pictorial representations of the sheer magnitude of the natural environment. They represent the spirit of North American expansion and a putatively vast and untamed new world. And they were seen that way, or so the story goes. But, this isn't the only tale we can tell about them. They were not pleine-air paintings. They were studio paintings; they were constructed, idealized pictures schematically composed from reams of drawings and color studies. They are therefore not snapshots of a wild and untamed natural environment. They are rather more like the vaudeville sideshow of a zoo or circus. They represent the taming of the wild by an increasingly industrialized society. We can see this quality in the crisp orderliness of their compositions. We can also see it in the emptiness of the depicted landscapes. The economic and social activities of their inhabitants are missing. The occupants of the landscape are, if they are depicted at all, depicted as inconsequentially small relative to its vastness. These paintings therefore represent an expanding Western society that was reifying the natural landscape, re-envisioning and re-purposing it in their own image for their own use. Shifting attention between the skew magnitude and mass of the depicted mountainscapes and the empty orderliness of their compositions reveals the contrasting semantic qualities of these two interpretations of this category of paintings.

Noë argues that art is a social activity that organizes us. We learn how to look at art. When we learn how to look at art we learn to see what it shows us against the backdrop of a range of normative conventions. He offers the social practice of "keeping score" at a baseball game as an illustration of this point (Noe, 2015).[2] It is a nice example. Keeping score is a rigidly structured social practice that is culturally unique. Baseball is played on four bases organized into a diamond with a vast outfield stretching beyond it. The pitcher stands on a small hill in the center of the diamond. The batter is positioned facing the pitcher and the outfield. There are nine players on a side. Each player is assigned a unique number by their team and each defensive position is assigned a number between one and nine. Fans are provided with scorecards in their programs and (in the old days) pencils as they enter the park. The scorecard provides a grid of small diamonds, each of which represents the infield of the playing surface. These images are arranged in columns and rows. They are used to keep track of at bats per inning for each team. Fans use a rudimentary system of marks to record the salient actions and events constitutive of the game. Hits are recorded by underscoring the sides of the diamond in a counter-clockwise direction to record the distance the batter traveled around the bases. Outs are recorded by marking the position numbers of the players involved in the play, e.g., if the shortstop (6) throws the batter out at first base with the pitcher (1) covering for the second out of the inning the first base line is underscored on the diamond and the play is recorded as ② 6–1. Keeping score is therefore a practice governed by a set of shared conventions that focus joint attention on the details of the game, collectively organizing the behavior of the fans in attendance. Likewise for art. Categorizing a work relative to the critical communicative conventions of an artistic community at a time focuses attention on its artistically salient features, the elements of the work diagnostic for its point, purpose, or meaning.

It is exactly here that the extreme pessimist has overplayed their hand. There are a range of psychological questions that seem fairly critical to understanding how art organizes us in this way. First, foremost, front, and center are questions about the way consumers perceptually recognize categories of art in the diagnostic cues carried in a work. Falling in not far behind are questions about the way perceptual recognition subsequently directs attention to artistically salient features and shapes the perception of a work. These might include questions about the nature of the concepts that encode categories of art (Dean, 2003; Knobe, Prosada, & Newman, 2013; Meskin, Robson, Ichino, Goffin, & Monseré, 2018). They might also include questions about levels of artistic salience. Is there a basic level of recognition for categories of art (Rosch & Mervis, 1975)? If so, are there expertise effects on what counts as a basic or subordinate level for different categories of art? What are the cognitive processes that facilitate the transition from basic level recognition to the meaning of a work? How do more detailed explorations of the semantic qualities of a work influence attention and perceptual experience? What role, if any, does affective processing play in these cognitive interactions with artworks? Affective attention plays a critical role in our engagement with the environment. Affective responses encode information about the biological salience of a stimulus or its utility to less pressing intermediate needs, interests, and goals. Affective attention, therefore, drives perception toward task-salient aspects of the environment critical to approach and withdrawal behaviors. Presumably, by parity of reasoning, affective responses to art are cognitively inflected physiological responses that drive attention toward artistically salient features of artworks diagnostic for their identities and meanings.

The list of psychological questions germane to understanding our engagement with artworks is too long to summarize here.[3] I leave it to readers to fill it in relative to their own research interests and theoretical biases. Critically, however, engaging with art is like keeping score. Categories of art are social constructs that organize us. They encode a shared understanding of the productive, evaluative, and communicative normative conventions that define different artistic genres, schools, movements, etc. Categorizing a work one way or another directs attention, shapes perception, and thereby reveals the features of a work diagnostic for its point, purpose, or meaning.

What are we to make, then, of the extreme pessimist claim that cognitive science is strictly irrelevant to understanding art? Cognitive science does not explain art, at least not in the philosopher's sense. Empirical aesthetics is not in the business of constructing theories of art per se. Rather, cognitive science contributes information that helps explain target aspects of artistic practice. Sometimes this information has a bearing on broader theoretical questions about the nature of art. It is hard to see how it could not. Where there is some slip between our best philosophical theories of art and results in empirical aesthetics those theories should require adjustment to accommodate it. Cognitive science is in the business of constructing models to test theories. These models provide guidance to help make the requisite adjustments. My guess is that this happens all the time. This makes me a *moderate optimist* (Davies, 2013). Moderate optimists are confident that when we look under the hood to see how artworks work we will find information germane to our understanding of the nature of art. The generality of moderate optimism is of course an empirical matter. The extent of the explanatory link between philosophy and psychology of art cannot be decided a priori. More importantly, neither philosophy of art nor empirical aesthetics float free of the other. They are rather linked in a dynamic exchange that unfolds in multiple waves over time.

Conclusions

Psychology provides a natural lens through which to interpret the history of art. Artworks are communicative events. They are cognitive, perceptual, and affective stimuli intentionally designed to express a point a purpose, articulate an idea, or convey some socially embedded meaning. Methodological progress in art is progress in a collective capacity to shape psychological responses in consumers germane to recovering this content. Understanding art in all of its variance is simply the process of tracking how artworks have been used as communicative devices within different social contexts. Philosophers and psychologists study complementary aspects of these communicative exchanges. Despite entrenched philosophical skepticism, the rich, longstanding, albeit often tacit, rapprochement between these two fields should therefore come as no surprise.

Notes

1. This fact about art plays a central role in the writings of Baumgarten, Mendelssohn, and Kant that form the basis for aesthetic models of art.
2. See *How to—quick scorebook guide*. Retrieved June 17, 2018: https://www.youtube.com/watch?v=82WJsBG5O3s.
3. See Currie, Kieran, Meskin, and Moore (2014), Currie, Kieran, Meskin, and Robson (2014), Minnisale (2013), and Schellekens and Goldie (2001) for reviews of interdisciplinary research that articulates points of contact between philosophy and psychology of art.

References

Aristotle (1984). *Poetics*. In Jonathan Barnes (Ed.), *The complete works of Aristotle* (pp. 2316–2340). Princeton, NJ: Bollinger Press.

Ballard, D. H., Hayhoe, M. M., Pook, P. K., & Rao, R. P. N. (1997). Deictic codes for the embodiment of cognition. *Behavioral and Brain Sciences, 20*, 723–767.

Baumgarten, A. G. (1735/1954). *Reflections on poetry*. Berkeley, CA: University of California Press.

Berlyne, D. E. (1971). *Aesthetics and psychobiology*. New York: Appleton-Century-Croft.

Carroll, N. (1992). Art, intention, and conversation. In G. Iseminger (Ed.), *Intention and interpretation* (pp. 97–131). Philadelphia, PA: Temple University Press.

Carroll, N., & Seeley, W. P. (2013). Kinesthetic understanding and appreciation in dance. *Journal of Aesthetics and Art Criticism, 72*(3), 177–186.

Currie, G. (1995). *Image and mind: Film, philosophy, and cognitive science*. New York: Cambridge University Press.

Currie, G., Kieran, M., Meskin, A., & Moore, M. (2014). *Philosophical aesthetics and the sciences of art*. New York: Cambridge University Press.

Currie, G., Kieran, M., Meskin, A., & Robson, J. (2014). *Aesthetics and the sciences of mind*. New York: Oxford University Press.

Danto (2000). Art and meaning. In N. Carroll (Ed.), *Theories of art today* (pp. 130–140). Madison, WI: University of Wisconsin Press.

Davidson, D. (1973). Radical interpretation. *Dialectica, 27*(3), 313–328.

Davies, D. (2013). Dancing around the issues: Prospects for an empirically grounded philosophy of dance. *The Journal of Aesthetics and Art Criticism, 71*(2), 195–202.

Dean, J. T. (2003). The nature of concepts and the definition of art. *Journal of Aesthetics and Art Criticism, 61*, 29–35.

Dennett, D. C. (1981). True believers: The intentional strategy and why it works. Reprinted in J. Haugeland (Ed.), *Mind design II: Philosophy, psychology, and artificial intelligence* (pp. 57–79). Cambridge, MA: MIT Press, 1997.

Dickie, G. (1962). Is psychology relevant to aesthetics? *The Philosophical Review, 71*(3), 285–302.

Fechner, G. (1876/1978). *Vorschule der aesthetik*. Leipzig: Breitkopf and Hartel.

Fodor, J. A. (2012). Deja-vu all over again: How Danto's aesthetics recapitulates the philosophy of mind. In Mark Rollins (Ed.), *Danto and his critics* (pp. 41–54). Malden, MA: Blackwell Publishers.

Friedman, M. (1994). As far as the eye can see. *Visions of America: Landscape as metaphor in the late twentieth century* (pp. 11–34). New York: Harry N. Abrams Publishers.

Gibson, J. J. (1971). The information available in pictures. *Leonardo*, 4(1), 27–35.

Goldman, G. (2006). *Simulating minds*. New York: Oxford University Press.

Gombrich, E. H. (1960). *Art and illusion*. Princeton, NJ: Princeton University Press.

Greenberg, C. (1960). Modernist painting. In John O'Brien (Ed.), *Clement Greenberg, the collected essays and criticism, volume 4. Modernism with a vengeance, 1957–1969* (pp. 85–93). Chicago, IL: University of Chicago Press.

Grice, P. (1957). Meaning. Philosophical Review, 66(3), 377–388.

Guyer, P. (1993). *Kant and the experience of freedom*. New York: Cambridge University Press.

Hutcheson, F. (1725/1972). In Peter Kivy (Ed.), *Inquiry concerning beauty, order, harmony and design*. Amsterdam: Springer Netherlands.

Kant, I. (1790). *Critique of judgement*. New York: Oxford University Press.

Knobe, J., Prosada, S., & Newman, G. E. (2013). Dual character concepts and the normative dimension of conceptual representation. *Cognition*, *127*, 242–257.

Land, M. F., & Hayhoe, M. (2002). In what ways do eye movements contribute to everyday activities. *Vision Research*, *41*, 3559–3565.

Leibniz, G. W. (1684). Meditation on knowledge, truth, and ideas. In R. Ariew & D. Garber (Trans.), *Philosophical essays of G. W. Leibniz* (pp. 23–34). Indianapolis, IN: Hackett Publishing Company.

Meskin, A. (2018). Philosophical aesthetics and cognitive science. *WIREs Cognitive Science*, *9*, e1445. doi:10.1002/wcs.1445.

Marr, D. (1982). *Vision*. Cambridge, MA: MIT Press.

McFee, G. (2011). *The philosophical aesthetics of dance: Identity, performance, and understanding*. Southwold: Dance Books Ltd.

Mendelssohn, M. (1757/1997). On the main principles of the fine arts and the sciences. In Daniel O. Dahlstrom (Ed.), *Moses Mendelssohn: Philosophical writings* (pp. 169–191). New York: Cambridge University Press.

Meskin, A., Robson, J., Ichino, A., Goffin, K., & Monseré, A. (2018). Philosophical aesthetics and cognitive science. *WIREs Cognitive Science*, *9*, e1445. doi:10.1002/wcs.1445.

Minnisale, G. (2013). *The psychology of contemporary art*. New York: Cambridge University Press.

Noë, A. (2015). *Strange tools*. New York: Hill and Wang.

Plato (1989). *Republic*. In Edith Hamilton, & Huntington Cairns (Eds.), *Plato: The collected dialogs* (pp. 575–874). Princeton, NJ: Bollinger Press.

Rosch, E., & Mervis, C. B. (1975). Family resemblances: Studies in the internal structure of categories. *Cognitive Psychology*, *7*(4), 573–605.

Sandler, I. (2003). *Judy Pfaff*. New York: Hudson Hills Press.

Schellekens, E., & Goldie, P. (2001). *The aesthetic mind: Philosophy and psychology*. New York: Oxford University Press.

Schyns, P. G. (1998). Diagnostic recognition: Task constraints, object information, and their interactions. *Cognition*, *67*, 147–179.

Seeley, W. P. (2011). What is the cognitive neuroscience of art … and why should we care? *Newsletter of the American Society for Aesthetics*, *31*(2), 1–4.

Seeley, W. P. (2018). Seeking salience in engaging art: A short story about attention, artistic value, and neuroscience. *Progress in Brain Research, 237*, 437–453.

Smith, R. (1984). *Judy Pfaff: Autonomous objects*. Charlotte, NC: Knight Gallery.

Walton, K. L. (1990). *Mimesis as make-believe: On the foundations of the representational arts*. Cambridge, MA: Harvard University Press.

Wittgenstein, L. (1967). *Lectures and conversations on aesthetics, psychology, and religious belief*. Berkeley, CA: University of California Press.

CHAPTER 5

APPRECIATION MODES IN EMPIRICAL AESTHETICS

ROLF REBER

AESTHETIC APPRECIATION AND APPRECIATION OF ART

AESTHETICS is often confounded with art, even in empirical aesthetics (see Bullot & Reber, 2013b; Carroll, 1999; 2002; Gopnik, 2012). According to the aesthetic theory of art, aesthetic experiences are a defining feature of art, and scientists saw for a long time the aesthetic experience as the main problem of the science of art. Contrary to this tenet, recent theories of art make a sharp distinction between art and aesthetic, even though both have undergone multiple changes in their definition (see Tatarkiewicz, 1980/1976). However, this is not the place to analyze such conceptual issues. Essential for the treatment of appreciation modes in empirical aesthetics is the rough distinction between art as an activity of people—for example, painters, poets, and composers—who produce artifacts within an institutional framework and aesthetics as the study of subjective experiences related to sensory input that lead to automatic evaluation. The most prominent example of such an evaluation is in terms of beauty that derives from an affective response to the object (see Reber, Schwarz, & Winkielman, 2004). There is some overlap between art and aesthetics; the perception of the form of artifacts made by artists within an institutional framework produces an evaluative response ("How beautiful!"). However, aesthetics goes beyond art. Alexander Gottlieb Baumgarten— who coined the term aesthetics—distinguished between "*cognitio intellectiva*" and "*cognitio sensitiva*"—an intellectual and a sensory understanding of the world—and revolutionized philosophical aesthetics when he claimed that the latter is inherently aesthetic (see Tatarkiewicz, 1980/1976). If we follow Baumgarten's lead, every sensory object can yield aesthetic experiences, an idea Dewey (2005/1934) followed up when he noted that a mechanic may see beauty in the neat sound of a perfectly tuned engine. The most prominent object of aesthetic scholarship outside art has been the appreciation of nature. Aesthetic principles also play a role in design where form and function are aligned. As our environments are either natural or designed by humans, every object has the potential to elicit an aesthetic response. In fact, recent studies found that basic perception is inherently affective, suggesting that an aesthetic response is inherent to any perception (Erle, Reber, & Topolinski, 2017; Topolinski, Erle, & Reber, 2015).

Art, on the other hand, may have little to do with aesthetics. Theorists like Noël Carroll (1999; 2002) or Blake Gopnik (2012) argue that art may be appreciated cognitively, without aesthetic response; in other words, the aesthetic does not constitute art. Perhaps the easiest way to explain this tenet is to assume that art has certain functions, such as making a political point, enabling religious contemplation, creating identity, or making a conceptual point about art. Enabling an aesthetic response (which may be always present, as we have shown above) may be one among many functions; the aesthetic function may be sufficient for a work to be art but it is not a necessary one.

In sum, there are two domains to be appreciated, art and aesthetics. Both fall within the realm of empirical aesthetics. Although there is some connection between the two, it is important to distinguish them. We may appreciate art in a nonaesthetic way, as we shall discuss in the last part of this chapter. On the other hand, we may appreciate natural and man-made patterns—both visual and auditory—that were never made with the intention to please the eye or the ear. Indeed, much research in empirical aesthetics is done with materials (stimuli) that do not come from art.

Three Modes of Appreciation: Aesthetic Pleasure, Aesthetic Emotions, and Artistic Understanding

Exploration of aesthetic pleasure stood at the beginning of empirical aesthetics when Gustav Theodor Fechner (1876) asked his participants—people older than 16 years from educated classes—to judge which one is most pleasing among various forms of rectangles. Since Fechner, judgments of aesthetic pleasure and—relatedly—of liking or beauty have become the main measurement in empirical aesthetics. More recently, models of aesthetic pleasure have been extended to include interest, which could be seen as a positive emotion. Indeed, art always afforded other effects on the viewer than eliciting feelings of pleasure, and researchers began to measure emotions in response to art. A philosophical treatise of the scope of appreciation of art has been presented by Tatarkiewicz (1980/1976). A prime example of how the breadth of appreciation can be examined is Gabrielsson's work on strong experiences in music. We explore the range of emotions that play a role here and consider Silvia's (2005a) appraisal model of interest in art. Recent research examined mixed feelings, such as being moved (Kuehnast, Wagner, Wassiliwizky, Jacobsen, & Menninghaus, 2014) or the pleasure of watching sad movies or listening to sad music (Eerola, Vuoskoski, Peltola, Putkinen, & Schäfer, 2018). Some theorists claim that evaluating art without understanding it is as meaningless as claiming to like the elegance of a mathematical proof without understanding it (Gilmore, 2013; Reber & Bullot 2013). In one study that examined how art is appreciated, experts provided higher scores than nonexperts on liking, arousal and emotions, and comprehension (Leder, Gerger, Dressler, & Schabmann, 2012). The last section looks at understanding as a cognitive form of art appreciation.

Aesthetic Pleasure

Given that beauty was an important purpose of art until the 19th century, it is not surprising that empirical aesthetics began with studies on aesthetic pleasure. There are three main approaches to define beauty, one as an objective feature of the object, another as a subjective judgment of taste, and finally an interactionist approach (for a historical overview, see Tatarkiewicz, 1980/1976). Objectivist approaches explore features of the object that are judged beautiful, such as symmetry (e.g., Jacobsen, Schubotz, Höfel, & von Cramon, 2006) or the golden section, which was already the object of Fechner's (1876) investigations. The golden section denotes the proportions of a rectangle, where a + b is the length and a is the height (see Figure 5.1). The golden section means that (a + b)/a equals a/b. Although of classical origin, modern research could not yield conclusive results. Some claim that there is no preference for the golden section (Höge, 1997) whereas others provide the more careful answer that if there were such a preference, it would be very fragile and susceptible to miniscule methodological changes (Green, 1995).

In contrast to objectivists interested in the characteristics of artworks and other objects to be appreciated, subjectivists were interested in the characteristics of persons that appreciate the arts. When beauty is a matter of taste, what determines differences of tastes? Arguably the most prominent factor in empirical psychology is expertise. For example, novices without art training prefer simplicity and symmetry whereas experts prefer complexity and asymmetry in visual elements (McWhinney, 1968).

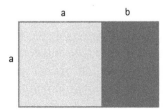

FIGURE 5.1. The golden section.

Brain researchers are interested in the biochemical and brain processes that lead to the subjective experience of beauty. One hypothesis is that beauty is related to the reward system and opioids contribute to its experience (for a theory, see Biederman & Vessel, 2006; for experiments, see Chelnokova et al., 2014; Goldstein, 1980). Theories in the field of neuroaesthetics hold that brain processes contribute to perceived beauty and other aesthetic responses (Cela-Conde, Agnati, Huston, Mora, & Nadal, 2011; Chatterjee, 2014; Ramachandran & Hirstein, 1999; Zeki, 1999).

The best solution seems to be an interactive approach that considers beauty as the function of both the features of the object and characteristics of the person. One such approach is the perceptual fluency theory of aesthetic pleasure (Reber et al., 2004). Perceptual fluency—the subjective ease with which an object can be perceived—depends on the one hand on features of the object, such as figure–ground contrast and symmetry, and on the other hand on the experience of the person with the object, such as familiarity or typicality. The perceptual fluency theory claims that ease of perception determines the perceived beauty of an aesthetic object. Indeed, a rich literature, reviewed in Reber et al. (2004), provided findings in line with the fluency theory. Many features that increase perceptual fluency also enhance aesthetic pleasure. The theory has various strengths. First, it combines research on individual features that were found to increase aesthetic pleasure into a unified theory. Thus, the fluency theory obviates the need for separate theories that explain the beauty of symmetry, familiarity, or typicality. Second, fluency theory can explain instances of preference for typical or average form (Halberstadt, 2006) and instances where individuals prefer extreme forms (see Ramachandran & Hirstein, 1999). Third, fluency theory explains the observation that newborns all seem to like consonant musical elements (Zentner & Kagan, 1996) whereas adults like different styles of music (e.g., Bourdieu, 1987/1979). As newborns can process consonant musical elements more easily (Trainor & Heinmiller, 1998), they prefer consonance. When growing up, children from different social classes and cultures are exposed to music of different styles. Familiarity with a style increases perceptual fluency, which, in turn, results in the preferences of adult life. Familiarization with different styles leads to different adult preferences. Finally, fluency theory can explain the long-standing anecdotes that mathematicians use beauty as a proxy for truth because research revealed that fluency underlies both beauty and truth. Such findings suggest that beauty might be a reliable cue to truth in mathematics (Reber, 2018).

Research published in the line of the fluency theory of aesthetic pleasure found that subjective fluency, not objective fluency, determines liking (Forster, Leder, & Ansorge, 2013). Recent research suggests that any successful perception results in positive affect, as already mentioned earlier. Together with results on perceptual fluency and affect (Reber, Winkielman, & Schwarz, 1998), this research shows that positive affect is inherent to the dynamics of perception (Erle et al., 2017; Topolinski, Erle, & Reber, 2015). Fluency theory has triggered much research in empirical aesthetics and design studies.

Despite the fact that the fluency theory of aesthetic pleasure can explain a broad range of observations with patterns, the theory has its critics. Silvia (2012) noted that most of the studies in support of fluency theory used visual patterns, not real artworks, to examine variables related to aesthetic pleasure, such as liking or beauty. Moreover, some authors questioned whether fluency influences real beauty or mere prettiness (Armstrong & Detweiler-Bedell, 2008; Silvia, 2012).

Although fluency theory helps explain some hitherto unexplained phenomena, such as the preference for prototypical stimuli (Martindale & Moore, 1988) and the mere-exposure effect (Zajonc, 1968), it cannot explain all results. Most prominently, it is difficult to explain nonlinear effects of complexity on aesthetic pleasure. Berlyne (1971) consistently found an inverted U-shaped function; with increasing complexity, pleasure increases from simple stimuli up to a point of medium complexity, and then decreases when the stimuli become more complex. A pure fluency theory cannot explain the observation that simple stimuli are liked less than stimuli of medium complexity. Additional theoretical assumptions are needed to be able to explain this inverted U-shaped function (e.g., Reber, 2012), but such additional assumptions render the theory less parsimonious and thus less elegant. One problem is that viewers do not like too complex artworks but neither too simple ones. This led to the notion that art or design has to be "Most Advanced Yet Acceptable," or the MAYA principle, which states that familiarity and novelty—two attributes that seem incompatible—increase liking together (Hekkert, Snelders, & Wieringen, 2003).

Beyond nonlinear relationships, there are empirical observations that are difficult if not impossible to reconcile with fluency theory. First, people like ambiguous stimuli, and ambiguity renders stimuli disfluent (Jakesch, Leder, & Forster, 2013). Second, fluency theory does not seem to apply to faces (Gerger, Forster, & Leder, 2017; Rhodes, 2006). Third, readers show interest in complicated poems when they have sufficient information to know what they are about (Silvia, 2005a). Such observations led to the conclusion that perceptual fluency has limited power to explain the experience of beauty. Fluency seems best suited to explain the pleasures of low-level bottom-up perceptual processes but does not cover more complex aesthetic responses to an aesthetic object (Armstrong & Detweiler-Bedell, 2008).

A COMPLEX MODEL OF
AESTHETIC PLEASURE

To address the criticism summarized above, Graf and Landwehr (2015) took a dual-process perspective to develop the Pleasure-Interest Model of Aesthetic Liking (PIA Model; see Figure 5.2). They assumed that processing is at first stimulus-driven. Low-level perceptual features like symmetry or fluency from familiarity determine whether the viewer likes the stimulus or not. If a stimulus is more fluent than expected, the resulting affect is positive; if a stimulus is less fluent than expected, the resulting affect is negative. This is an automatic evaluation of the stimulus that needs few cognitive resources. Stimulus-driven processing results in aesthetic pleasure that can be explained by the fluency theory discussed in the previous section. In contrast to the flu-ency theory, automatically elicited positive affect is not the end of the story. Graf and Landwehr assume that viewers of an artwork differ in their need for cognitive enrich-ment. If viewers are not motivated to process the stimulus further their feeling will be the same as the automatic response—positive for relatively fluent stimuli but negative for relatively disfluent stimuli. By contrast, if the viewer is highly motivated to process the stimulus more deeply, the resulting affect depends on the nature of disfluency reduc-tion. If disfluency is reduced (Yes DR in Figure 5.2) the viewer will feel interested, which is a positive emotion according to Silvia (2008). However, fluency reduction may lack in two ways. The first is that the viewer experiences disfluency at first but no reduction after further processing (No R in Figure 5.2). We could imagine that a museum visitor named Richard contemplates a complex abstract painting that he does not understand and therefore elicits disfluency. If he does not experience an increase in understanding and a concomitant reduction in disfluency after contemplating, he will be confused. The second way in which disfluency is not reduced occurs in a situation where there is no disfluency beforehand. When Richard's friend Sarah looks at a representational painting that reveals itself at once, she may not feel any disfluency (No D in Figure 5.2). Even if she contemplates the painting more deeply, no reduction in disfluency occurs because the painting is already fluent, and she feels bored.

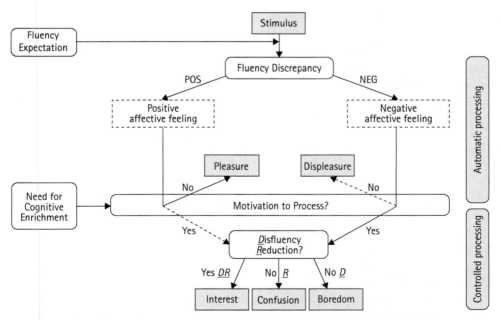

FIGURE 5.2. The Pleasure-Interest Model of Aesthetic Liking (PIA Model) by Graf & Landwehr (2015).

This dual-process model assumes a two-step process where the first step is automatic evaluation of the artwork based on stimulus-driven perceptual processes and the second a controlled evaluation based on perceiver-driven processes. This two-step model can also explain the inverted U-shaped function of complexity on pleasure. The automatic evaluation yields positive affect as a linear function of fluency, as indeed observed for simple stimuli across the whole spectrum of figure–ground contrast (Reber et al., 1998), but only when participants saw the stimuli for a short time (Reber & Schwarz, 2001). The second step yields boredom if people cannot reduce disfluency because a simple stimulus already is fluent, but it yields confusion when disfluency cannot be reduced because the stimulus is too complex.

Although we discussed the PIA Model under the heading of aesthetic pleasure, interest could be seen as an aesthetic emotion.

AESTHETIC EMOTIONS

Romantic artists like Caspar David Friedrich did not aim at conveying beauty but emotions. Indeed, emotions play a crucial role in art (Armstrong & Detweiler-Bedell, 2008), music (Eerola & Vuoskoski 2013; Gabrielsson, 2011; Zentner, Grandjean, & Scherer, 2008), and literature (Menninghaus, 2003).

Arguably, the most prominent theory of emotion is the appraisal theory, which states that people appraise a situation with regard to various factors, such as valence (positive versus negative), novelty, goal-conduciveness, and coping potential (e.g., Leventhal & Scherer, 1987; Scherer, 1984). Silvia (2005b) derived from this emotion theory an appraisal model of artistic interest. In one experiment, Silvia (2005a) presented a poem that was complex and obscure. However, when he explained to the participants that the poem is about sharks, readers had an easier time understanding the poem.

A COMPLEX MODEL OF
AESTHETIC EMOTIONS

It is uncontroversial that art, music, and literature elicit emotions. Yet how does this happen? It seems that art does not elicit the same emotions as in the real world. For example, a novel about the cruelties on the battlefields of World War I does not evoke the same panic and horror as the soldiers must have felt. Moreover, it is hard to conceive that a listener's romanticizing at hearing a love song has the same underlying processes as the thrill caused by a horror movie, which means that there probably cannot be one theory of emotion in art as there is one theory of aesthetic pleasure, such as the fluency theory or the PIA Model. A final question has been raised by Aristotle and is known as the paradox of fiction: Why do people enjoy sad music, frightening stories, or—nowadays—horror movies?

Recently, Menninghaus et al. (2017a) proposed a solution to this paradox, the distancing–embracing model of aesthetic emotions that is depicted in Figure 5.3. The first factor in the model is distancing. Imagine you walk in the inner city and see a murder live. You are shocked, frightened, maybe traumatized for life. These responses are unlikely to happen when the same murder is depicted in a story or shown in a movie. How hard it is to get real horror into the cinema is illustrated by a statement of movie director Samuel Fuller, who prior to his career in the movie industry experienced bloody fighting as a young soldier in World War II. "If you really want to make readers understand a battle, a few pages of your book would be booby-trapped. For moviegoers to get the idea of real combat, you'd have to shoot at them every so often from either side of the screen" (Fuller, Fuller and Rudes 2002, p.123).

Three features of an artwork allow distancing, the first step of Menninghaus et al.'s (2017a) two-step model: art schema, cognitive schema of representation, and the fiction schema. When we read a fictional murder story that happens in the inner city, we know that we are currently enjoying a novel in our garden and are therefore safe from danger (art schema). Relatedly, the action in the novel takes place in a different place—often in a different city—and at a different time (cognitive schema of representation). Finally, we know that in the realm of fiction, the event in the novel is not real (fiction schema). Together, the three schemata allow distancing because we feel safe, the event is remote in space and time, and we know that the event is not real despite our immersion in the story.

The second step in Menninghaus et al.'s (2017a) model is embracing. When the audience knows that it is safe and the event is remote and unreal, it is ready to cope with the negative emotions evoked by the artwork. Five mechanisms enable readers and viewers to turn negative emotion into pleasure and enjoyment of the artwork.

First, composition of the artwork may result in the interplay between negative and positive emotions. In his theory of dramatic plot, Zillmann (2006) proposed that negative emotions lead to physiological excitation that is transferred to the positive peak at the end. He derived this assumption from laboratory experiments that showed transfer of excitation from negative to positive emotions or vice versa. In one study, men were interviewed by a woman after they crossed a wobbly bridge. The results indicated that these men transferred arousal from anxiety of crossing the bridge to sexual attraction toward the female interviewer (Dutton & Aron, 1974). Zillmann, Katcher, and Milavsky (1972) showed that excitation caused by exercise may transfer to anger.

Second, mixed emotions may turn negative emotions into pleasure. For example, the mixed emotion that turns sadness into pleasure is being moved (Kuehnast et al., 2014; see also Vuoskoski & Eerola, 2017). The mixed emotion that turns horror into pleasure is suspense (see Hoffner & Levine, 2005).

Third, aesthetic virtues of the artistic representation result in positive emotions. Viewers of a painting or readers of a novel do not necessarily enjoy the contents but aesthetic properties, such as balance and other features of good form in the painting and

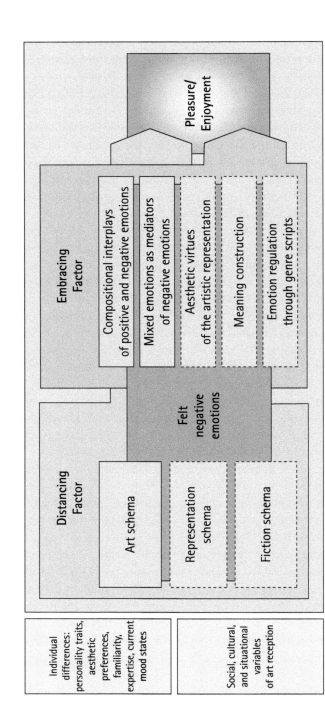

FIGURE 5.3. The distancing–embracing model of the enjoyment of negative emotions in art reception by Menninghaus et al. (2017a).

the beauty of the language in novels. Several studies cited in Menninghaus et al. (2017a) found positive correlations between aesthetic liking, the intensity of being affected, and felt negative emotions. One study on sadly moving poems observed that poetic diction—an aesthetic feature that enhances ease of processing—increased feelings of sadness, being moved, and positive affect (Menninghaus, Wagner, Wassiliwizky, Jacobsen, & Knoop, 2017b), pointing to the effect of aesthetic form on reappraisal of negative emotions in the artwork.

A fourth mechanism is meaning-making. The death of a soldier is sad. The death of a soldier that saved five other lives is heroic. When readers can make sense of a negative event, the situation is reappraised in a way that turns a negative emotion into a positive one.

Fifth, genre scripts might result in reappraisal of an artwork. For example, disgusting scenes within a horror movie or the uncanny within a fairytale may turn into positive emotions because viewers or readers anticipate and appreciate these negative emotions in horror movies and fairytales.

Taken together, these processes help explain how an audience feels complex emotions and at the same time can enjoy an artwork. As there are three distancing factors and five embracing factors, the theory does not claim that one process can explain all instances of emotional experience.

The distancing–embracing model is new and has to be tested more thoroughly but it is the most sophisticated model on aesthetic emotion to date. On the surface, the model is about complex emotions when appreciating works of art. However, beneath the surface, the model includes complex cognitive processes, as the last point in the distancing stage and the last two points of the embracing stage of the model testify. Retrieving a fiction schema that tells us that the event depicted in the artwork is not real; making meaning of negative events; retrieving genre scripts; all these processes involve cognitive processes that help the audience understand an artwork.

Understanding an Artwork

A final mode of appreciation consists of understanding an artwork. There is some terminological confusion about whether understanding is part of aesthetic appreciation or only a prerequisite. In empirical aesthetics, understanding did not play a role for a long time, and aesthetic pleasure and later aesthetic emotions were the most important research problems in the field.

The pinnacle of art expertise is the recognition of artists' style where characteristics of form are recognized across different content. Early studies explored understanding of style in children. Machotka (1966) found a developmental pattern that he aligned with Piaget's stages of development. Children aged 6–8 appreciated content and color. When they viewed the paintings, they simply identified the subject or activity being represented and sometimes identified with it (e.g., "Father has a hat like that"). At the second stage, children aged between 7 and 11 appreciated realistic representations, contrast, harmony, and clarity of expression. Children from 12 to 15 showed an interest in style, composition, and affective tone. In an elegant study, Gardner (1970) confirmed this development from content to style. In his study, ninth graders, compared with younger children, used more style-related characteristics to assign one of four test paintings (e.g., one Renoir and three other paintings) to two paintings by the same artist (here, Renoir). Whereas the oldest children were to a greater degree able to use style information, younger children used content and other salient features to solve this matching task. It seems that the older children become, the more they are able to abstract from content and recognize stylistic information in artworks.

Given the early interest in child development of understanding of artistic styles, it is not surprising that the arguably earliest psychological theory that included aesthetic understanding was Parsons' (1987) developmental model of art appreciation, based on theories of cognitive development. Parsons distinguished five stages of artistic understanding roughly related to five different phases of life (see also Reber, 2016). Preschool children see an artwork as an immediate source of delight. Subject matter enters the stage in elementary school children. A work of art is seen as beautiful if it is appealing and realistic. Adolescents begin to appreciate the expressive character of art. The more intense and the more interesting the experience a painting provides, the better it is. Beauty and subject matter, on the other hand, become secondary to expressiveness. Adult viewers consider a painting as a social rather than individual achievement. As artists and viewers share a tradition, objective norms of appreciation come to the fore. Paintings have public significance as they become carriers of thoughts and feelings in culture and history. Neither beauty nor meaningfulness nor mere expression by the artist, but style and form become relevant. The fifth and last stage is autonomy, where a viewer, listener, or reader has to weigh different aspects of a tradition and provide judgments that have to be based on reasons.

COMPLEX MODELS OF ARTISTIC APPRECIATION

A comprehensive model of aesthetic appreciation and aesthetic judgment was developed by Leder, Belke, Oeberst, & Augustin (2004). The model includes five stages of processes that finally affect aesthetic appreciation and aesthetic emotion (see Figure 5.4). An artwork, preclassified as such by being seen in a museum or gallery, first undergoes perceptual analysis. Variables such as complexity, symmetry, contrast, order, and grouping influence the affective state in response to the artwork. The second stage in this model is implicit memory integration. Here, familiarity or prototypicality of an artwork determines the affective response, as well as peak shifts that result in the preference of exaggerated forms (see Ramachandran & Hirstein, 1999). These processes depend on former experience. In line with the fluency theory reviewed earlier, having seen a painting makes it easier to process, which has effects on its evaluation even if the viewer no longer remembers having seen it. It follows the third stage, classification of the artwork along its style and content, which is a prerequisite for the fourth stage, which is cognitive mastery. This stage includes art-specific interpretation and self-related interpretation that depend on domain-specific expertise, knowledge, interest, and personal taste. The fifth stage includes evaluation, which has both a cognitive and an affective component. Cognitively, the viewer has to understand ambiguity. The affective state is a result of the previous stages, as the arrow under the five boxes that represent the five processing stages denotes (Figure 5.4). Aesthetic judgment results from the cognitive component and aesthetic emotion result from the affective state. Note that there are various feedback loops among the later stages in the model, and also from evaluation and social interaction to expertise, knowledge, interest, and taste.

The model by Leder et al. (2004) has been extended, first by Leder and Nadal (2014), who provided an update on the model, and later in the new Vienna Integrated Model of top-down and bottom-up processes in Art Perception (VIMAP; Pelowski, Markey, Forster, Gerger, & Leder, 2017). The latter model is highly ambitious in that it classifies bottom-up and top-down processes in art appreciation and aligns them to brain circuits.

Let us look at a problem—illustrated by an example—that has so far remained unsolved by psychological and neuroscientific models of art appreciation (Locher, 2012). After a failed career as a painter, the Dutch painter Han van Meegeren began in the 1930s to produce paintings that he later claimed to be unknown work of Vermeer's. After an authoritative Vermeer expert confirmed the authenticity of the paintings, van Meegeren could sell them to renowned museums and art collections (Coremans, 1949). After World War II, it became clear that all those newly discovered Vermeer paintings were forgeries produced by van Meegeren. From one day to another, the value of the paintings fell decreased to a

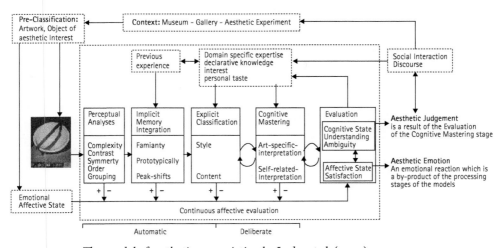

FIGURE 5.4. The model of aesthetic appreciation by Leder et al. (2004).

fraction of their former worth, and experts reassessed their artistic value as well. How could this sudden change in aesthetic appreciation and rapid devaluation happen, given that these were the same paintings, hung in the same museums and galleries?

A possible solution to this riddle and at the same time a criticism of psychological and neuroscientific models is the psycho-historical framework for the research on art appreciation by Bullot and Reber (2013a). All models before that time assumed that the artwork is a stimulus that viewers perceive and evaluate. This view neglects the fact that an artist, influenced by individual, historical, and cultural circumstances, plans and creates an artifact [but see Tinio's (2013) mirror model of art where art reception mirrors in art creation]. Exploring affective responses to artworks as stimuli is not enough because such responses are uninformed by understanding. However, an artwork cannot be understood just by perceiving it as a stimulus. The viewer, reader, or listener has to go beyond the information given and ask why the maker of the artwork designed it the way it is. Bullot and Reber used the term "designer stance" to denote this readiness to exploring the origin and art-historical background of an artwork "design stance." Such a stance is a necessary condition for understanding an artwork. Understanding is not limited to the meanings and patterns within the artwork as a stimulus but refers back to the art-historical context that includes the intentions and the personal history of the artist, the cultural and economic situation in which the artwork was created, and the technical possibilities to make the work (Figure 5.5).

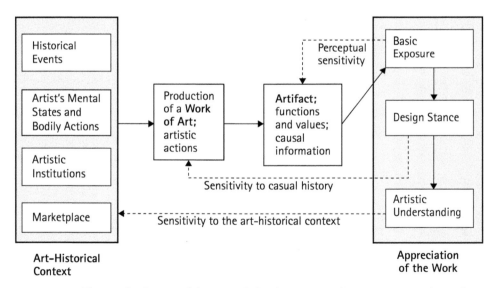

FIGURE 5.5. The psycho-historical framework for the science of art appreciation by Bullot & Reber (2013a).
Solid arrows indicate relations of causal and historical generation. Dashed arrows indicate information-processing and representational states in the appreciator's mind that refer back to earlier historical stages in the production and transmission of a work.

As Bullot and Reber (2013a) outline, van Meegeren's paintings lost their value because the history of the production of the works and their relations to their maker and the art-historical context matter to their artistic value. Van Meegeren's forgeries are misleading when they are taken to be material evidence of Vermeer's past artistic skill. The psycho-historical framework suggests that viewers of artworks dislike being misled by a forgery precisely because its lack of authenticity undermines their historical understanding of the artwork and their grasp of the correct intentional and causal history.

The most comprehensive and sophisticated traditional model, the one by Leder et al. (2004), discussed some variables included in the Bullot and Reber (2013a) model, such as cognitive mastery, which could be considered to be artistic understanding, and context. However, context in Leder et al.'s model is limited to the context of viewing the artwork, such as gallery or a psychological experiment. This is the context of the current viewing situation and does not need to refer to art-historical contexts; context that refers back in time has remained implicit in traditional models of empirical aesthetics. By contrast, context in Bullot and Reber's model spells out the role of the art-historical context in studying the appreciation of the artwork. Only when appreciators refer back to the history of the production of the artwork will they be able to fully appreciate the work.

The crucial difference between the two models—or of the psycho-historical approach to the psychological and neuroscientific models in empirical aesthetics—is that evaluation in the psychological models is based on perceived context; they are purely descriptive models. The psycho-historical approach by Bullot and Reber (2013a) adds a normative component by claiming that artistic understanding of the work has to be taken into account when assessing the subjective understanding of the work (see also Gilmore, 2013). Reber and Bullot (2013) used an analogy to illustrate the difference between understanding and evaluating an artwork. If a student claims that he likes to solve mathematical problems of a certain kind (let's say trigonometry) but the student is unable to solve simple trigonometric problems, we would be justified to argue that this is a shallow affective preference because the preference is not based on understanding. In a similar vein, the psycho-historical approach claims that art appreciation is shallow if not based on the understanding of the artwork. The task of the psychology of art is not just to inquire about liking and other indicators of aesthetic pleasure but to assess how much art evaluation is based on artistic understanding—for example, what were the intentions of the artist, or how did the artist use the techniques of her time to bring her intention into shape?

Note that this normative aspect is controversial and has not been accepted by most researchers in empirical aesthetics, who deny that a normative theory of aesthetic understanding is possible (e.g., Juslin, 2013). Other critics argue that the perceptual context is sufficient to appreciate a work as art and historical context is not necessary because the necessary information can be directly perceived within the artwork (Bundgaard, 2015)—a notion that may obviate the need for art-historical context and may render the perceptual context postulated in the Leder et al. (2004) model sufficiently. Finally, Kreuzbauer, King, & Basu (2015) presented evidence that people prefer handmade objects, such as watches, to functionally superior machine-made objects because people value unique personal expression in a particular object. This evidence points to the potential universality of appreciation and claims that hypotheses put forward by contextualist theories could be explained by observations that suggest universalist mechanisms.

In sum, there are two strategies to object to contextualist theories of appreciation. The first approach denies that such theories are necessary or even possible (Juslin, 2013); the other objects to traditional universalist views of art appreciation advocated in psychology and neuroscience, but claims that there are higher-order universals regarding the interaction of the artifact and the mind of its appreciators. The latter view, put forward by Kreuzbauer et al. (2015), has not yet attracted much attention but is perhaps the most promising approach to challenge contextualist theories.

Only a few studies have included historically relevant context information to study appreciation, some of them before the publication of Bullot and Reber's (2013a, b) psychohistorical framework (e.g., Jucker & Barrett, 2011; Newman & Bloom, 2012; Silvia, 2005a; Takahashi, 1995); and some of them thereafter (Jucker, Barrett, & Wlodarski, 2014; Locher, Krupinski, & Schaefer, 2015; Swami, 2013).

Conclusion

The variety of theories and empirical studies on aesthetic appreciation suggests that a unified theory of aesthetic experience and art appreciation has not yet been found. The question arises whether it will ever be possible to arrive at such a unified theory. It may well turn out that aesthetic appreciation is an ill-defined term that is based on family resemblance (Wittgenstein, 1953; see Tatarkiewicz, 1980/1976, for the notion that art is such a concept). Some aesthetic appreciation may reflect simple pleasure while other kinds of appreciation are more complex and lead to interest. Other forms of appreciation include aesthetic emotions, or understanding, or both. Pleasure, interest, emotions, and understanding may be interrelated or overlap but there are no clear definitional boundaries that distinguish aesthetic from nonaesthetic appreciation. The question becomes whether the ever more complex theories of art appreciation really capture the phenomenon well or whether researchers should aim to postulate and test simple laws of aesthetic appreciation that explain some instances of appreciation but not others.

When we look into the history of concepts of aesthetics, research on one notion of aesthetic appreciation is conspicuously lacking—the idea that aesthetic experience is a delirious state (see Tatarkiewicz, 1980/1976). Neither is it included in any of the theories of appreciation discussed above. There may be several reasons for the lack of research on delirium. First, such states are difficult to explore in experimental laboratory research. Second, delirious states may be rare in aesthetic appreciation in Western societies. Third, delirious states in the appreciation of music or dance may be connected to religion or to the intake of drugs. It might be difficult to separate delirious states owing to religious ecstasy or drugs from delirious states owing to aesthetic appreciation; the question arises what would be left for aesthetic appreciation after the contribution of nonaesthetic factors had been deducted.

Finally, there are various feelings related to beauty and aesthetic emotions that have not been explored in detail, such as the fascinating, moving, or surprising (Hosoya et al., 2017). The question arises whether various expressions to denote positive aesthetic qualities of an object are underpinned by corresponding psychological and physiological processes or—alternatively—could be defined in terms of a two- or more-dimensional semantic space similar to the one outlined for core affect (Russell, 2003).

To summarize, traditional models of aesthetic appreciation considered beauty and its correlates. Since the millennium, there has been a growing interest in (1) variables beyond beauty and liking, (2) more complex theoretical models, and (3) more variegated methods to explore aesthetic appreciation.

REFERENCES

Armstrong, T., & Detweiler-Bedell, B. (2008). Beauty as an emotion: The exhilarating prospect of mastering a challenging world. *Review of General Psychology*, *12*, 305–329.

Berlyne, D. E. (1971). *Aesthetics and psychobiology*. New York: Appleton-Century-Crofts.

Biederman, I., & Vessel, E. A. (2006). Perceptual pleasure and the brain: A novel theory explains why the brain craves information and seeks it through the senses. *American Scientist*, *94*(3), 247–253.

Bourdieu, P. (1987/1979). *Distinction: A social critique of the judgment of taste* (R. Nice, Trans.). Cambridge, MA: Harvard University Press.

Bullot, N. J., & Reber, R. (2013a). The artful mind meets art history: Toward a psycho-historical framework for the science of art appreciation. *Behavioral and Brain Sciences*, *36*, 123–137.

Bullot, N. J., & Reber, R. (2013b). A psycho-historical research program for the integrative science of art. *Behavioral and Brain Sciences*, *36*, 163–180.

Bundgaard, P. F. (2015). Feeling, meaning, and intentionality—A critique of the neuroaesthetics of beauty. *Phenomenology and the Cognitive Sciences*, *14*, 781–801.

Carroll, N. (1999). *Philosophy of art: A contemporary introduction*. London: Routledge.

Carroll, N. (2002). Aesthetic experience revisited. *British Journal of Aesthetics*, *42*(2), 145–168.

Cela-Conde, C. J., Agnati, L., Huston, J. P., Mora, F., & Nadal, M. (2011). The neural foundations of aesthetic appreciation. *Progress in Neurobiology*, *94*(1), 39–48.

Chatterjee, A. (2014). *The aesthetic brain. How we evolved to desire beauty and to enjoy art.* New York: Oxford University Press.

Chelnokova, O., Laeng, B., Eikemo, M., Riegels, J., Løseth, G., Maurud, H., ... Leknes, S. (2014). Rewards of beauty: The opioid system mediates social motivation in humans. *Molecular Psychiatry*, *19*(7), 746–747.

Coremans, P. B. (1949) *Van Meegeren's faked Vermeers and de Hooghs: A scientific examination*. Amsterdam: J. M. Meulenhoff.

Dewey, J. (2005/1934). *Art as experience*. London: Penguin.

Dutton, D. G., & Aron, A. P. (1974). Some evidence for heightened sexual attraction under conditions of high anxiety. *Journal of Personality and Social Psychology*, *30*(4), 510–517.

Eerola, T., & Vuoskoski, J. K. (2013). A review of music and emotion studies: Approaches, emotion models, and stimuli. *Music Perception*, *30*(3), 307–340.

Eerola, T., Vuoskoski, J. K., Peltola, H. R., Putkinen, V., & Schäfer, K. (2018). An integrative review of the enjoyment of sadness associated with music. *Physics of Life Reviews*, *25*, 100–121.

Erle, T. M., Reber, R., & Topolinski, S. (2017). Affect from mere perception. Illusory contour perception feels good. *Emotion*, *17*, 856–866.

Fechner, G. T. (1876). *Vorschule der Ästhetik*. Leipzig: Breitkopf & Härtel.

Forster, M., Leder, H., & Ansorge, U. (2013). It felt fluent, and I liked it: Subjective feeling of fluency rather than objective fluency determines liking. *Emotion*, *13*, 280–289.

Fuller, S., Fuller, C. L., & Rudes, J. (2002). *Third face: My tale of writing, fighting, and filmmaking*. New York: Alfred A. Knopf.

Gabrielsson, A. (2011). *Strong experiences with music: Music is much more than just music* (R. Bradbury, Trans.). Oxford: Oxford University Press.

Gardner, H. (1970). Children's sensitivity to painting styles. *Child Development*, *41*, 813–821.

Gerger, G., Forster, M., & Leder, H. (2017). It felt fluent but I did not like it: Fluency effects in faces versus patterns. *The Quarterly Journal of Experimental Psychology*, *70*(4), 637–648.

Gilmore, J. (2013). Normative and scientific approaches to the understanding and evaluation of art. *Behavioral and Brain Sciences*, *36*, 144–145.

Goldstein, A. (1980). Thrills in response to music and other stimuli. *Physiological Psychology*, *8*, 126–129.

Gopnik, B. (2012). Aesthetic science and artistic knowledge. In A. P. Shimamura & S. E. Palmer (Eds.), *Aesthetic science: Connecting minds, brains, and experience* (pp. 129–159). Oxford: Oxford University Press.

Graf, L. K., & Landwehr, J. R. (2015). A dual-process perspective on fluency-based aesthetics: The pleasure-interest model of aesthetic liking. *Personality and Social Psychology Review*, *19*, 395–410.

Green, C. D. (1995). All that glitters: A review of psychological research on the aesthetics of the golden section. *Perception*, *24*(8), 937–968.

Halberstadt, J. (2006). The generality and ultimate origins of the attractiveness of prototypes. *Personality and Social Psychology Review*, *10*(2), 166–183.

Hekkert, P., Snelders, D., & Wieringen, P. C. (2003). "Most advanced, yet acceptable": Typicality and novelty as joint predictors of aesthetic preference in industrial design. *British Journal of Psychology*, *94*(1), 111–124.

Hoffner, C. A., & Levine, K. J. (2005). Enjoyment of mediated fright and violence: A meta-analysis. *Media Psychology*, *7*(2), 207–237.

Höge, H. (1997). The golden section hypothesis—Its last funeral. *Empirical Studies of the Arts*, *15*(2), 233–255.

Hosoya, G., Schindler, I., Beermann, U., Wagner, V., Menninghaus, W., Eid, M., & Scherer, K. R. (2017). Mapping the conceptual domain of aesthetic emotion terms: A pile-sort study. *Psychology of Aesthetics, Creativity, and the Arts*, *11*(4), 457–473.

Jacobsen, T., Schubotz, R. I., Hofel, L., & von Cramon, D. Y. (2006). Brain correlates of aesthetic judgment of beauty. *Neuroimage*, *29*, 276–285.

Jakesch, M., Leder, H., & Forster, M. (2013). Image ambiguity and fluency. *PLoS ONE*, *8*(9), e74084.

Jucker, J. L., & Barrett, J. L. (2011). Cognitive constraints on the visual arts: An empirical study of the role of perceived intentions in appreciation judgements. *Journal of Cognition and Culture*, *11*(1), 115–136.

Jucker, J. L., Barrett, J. L., & Wlodarski, R. (2014). "I just don't get it": Perceived artists' intentions affect art evaluations. *Empirical Studies of the Arts*, 32(2), 149–182.

Juslin, P. N. (2013). The value of a uniquely psychological approach to musical aesthetics: Reply to the commentaries on "A unified theory of musical emotions". *Physics of Life Reviews*, 10, 281–286.

Kreuzbauer, R., King, D., & Basu, S. (2015). The mind in the object—Psychological valuation of materialized human expression. *Journal of Experimental Psychology: General*, 144(4), 764.

Kuehnast, M., Wagner, V., Wassiliwizky, E., Jacobsen, T., & Menninghaus, W. (2014). Being moved: Linguistic representation and conceptual structure. *Frontiers in Psychology: Emotion Science*, 5, 1242.

Leder, H., Belke, B., Oeberst, A., & Augustin, D. (2004). A model of aesthetic appreciation and aesthetic judgments. *British Journal of Psychology*, 95(4), 489–508.

Leder, H., Gerger, G., Dressler, S. G., & Schabmann, A. (2012). How art is appreciated. *Psychology of Aesthetics, Creativity, and the Arts*, 6(1), 2–10.

Leder, H., & Nadal, M. (2014). Ten years of a model of aesthetic appreciation and aesthetic judgments: The aesthetic episode—Developments and challenges in empirical aesthetics. *British Journal of Psychology*, 105(4), 443–464.

Leventhal, H., & Scherer, K. (1987). The relationship of emotion to cognition: A functional approach to a semantic controversy. *Cognition and Emotion*, 1, 3–28.

Locher, P. J. (2012). Factors contributing to a viewer's aesthetic experience with visual art. In A. P. Shimamura & S. E. Palmer (Eds.), *Aesthetic science: Connecting minds, brains, and experience* (pp. 163–188). Oxford: Oxford University Press.

Locher, P., Krupinski, E., & Schaefer, A. (2015). Art and authenticity: Behavioral and eye-movement analyses. *Psychology of Aesthetics, Creativity, and the Arts*, 9(4), 356–367.

Machotka, P. (1966). Aesthetic criteria in childhood: Justifications of preference. *Child Development*, 37, 877–885.

Martindale, C., & Moore, K. (1988). Priming, prototypicality, and preference. *Journal of Experimental Psychology: Human Perception and Performance*, 14, 661–670.

McWhinnie, H. J. (1968). A review of research on aesthetic measure. *Acta Psychologica*, 28, 363–375.

Menninghaus, W. (2003). *Disgust: The theory and history of a strong sensation*. Albany, NY: SUNY Press.

Menninghaus, W., Wagner, V., Hanich, J., Wassiliwizky, E., Jacobsen, T., & Koelsch, S. (2017a). The distancing-embracing model of the enjoyment of negative emotions in art reception. *Behavioral and Brain Sciences*, 40, e347, 1–63.

Menninghaus, W., Wagner, V., Wassiliwizky, E., Jacobsen, T., & Knoop, C. A. (2017b). The emotional and aesthetic powers of parallelistic diction. *Poetics*, 63, 47–59.

Newman, G. E., & Bloom, P. (2012). Art and authenticity: The importance of originals in judgments of value. *Journal of Experimental Psychology: General*, 141(3), 558–569.

Parsons, M. L. (1987). *How we understand art: A cognitive developmental account of aesthetic experience*. Cambridge: Cambridge University Press.

Pelowski, M., Markey, P. S., Forster, M., Gerger, G., & Leder, H. (2017). Move me, astonish me … delight my eyes and brain: The Vienna integrated model of top-down and bottom-up processes in art perception (VIMAP) and corresponding affective, evaluative, and neurophysiological correlates. *Physics of Life Reviews*, 21, 80–125.

Ramachandran, V. S., & Hirstein, W. (1999) The science of art: A neurological theory of aesthetic experience. *Journal of Consciousness Studies*, 6, 15–51.

Reber, R. (2012). Processing fluency, aesthetic pleasure, and culturally shared taste. In A. P. Shimamura, & Palmer S. E. (Eds.), *Aesthetic science: Connecting mind, brain, and experience* (pp. 223–249). New York: Oxford University Press.

Reber, R. (2016). *Critical feeling. How to use feelings strategically.* Cambridge: Cambridge University Press.

Reber, R. (2018). Beauty and truth in mathematics: Evidence from cognitive psychology. In S. Bangu (Ed.), *Naturalizing logico-mathematical knowledge: Perspectives from philosophy, psychology and cognitive science* (pp. 252–267). London: Routledge.

Reber, R., & Bullot, N. J. (2013). Artistic understanding matters to musical judgment. Comment on "From everyday emotions to aesthetic emotions: Towards a unified theory of musical emotions" by Patrik N. Juslin. *Physics of Life Reviews, 10,* 273–274.

Reber, R., & Schwarz, N. (2001). The hot fringes of consciousness: Perceptual fluency and affect. *Consciousness and Emotion, 2,* 223–231.

Reber, R., Winkielman, P., & Schwarz, N. (1998). Effects of perceptual fluency on affective judgments. *Psychological Science, 9,* 45–48.

Reber, R., Schwarz, N., & Winkielman, P. (2004). Processing fluency and aesthetic pleasure: Is beauty in the perceiver's processing experience? *Personality and Social Psychology Review, 8,* 364–382.

Rhodes, G. (2006). The evolutionary psychology of facial beauty. *Annual Review Psychology, 57,* 199–226.

Russell, J. A. (2003). Core affect and the psychological construction of emotion. *Psychological Review, 110,* 145–172.

Scherer, K. R. (1984). On the nature and function of emotion: A component process approach. In K. R. Scherer & P. Ekman (Eds.), *Approaches to emotion* (pp. 293–317). Hillsdale, NJ: Erlbaum.

Silvia, P. J. (2005a). Cognitive appraisals and interest in visual art: Exploring an appraisal theory of aesthetic emotions. *Empirical Studies of the Arts, 23*(2), 119–133.

Silvia, P. J. (2005b). What is interesting? Exploring the appraisal structure of interest. *Emotion, 5,* 89–102.

Silvia, P. J. (2008). Interest—The curious emotion. *Current Directions in Psychological Science, 17*(1), 57–60.

Silvia, P. J. (2012). Human emotions and aesthetic experience. In A. P. Shimamura & Palmer S. E. (Eds.), *Aesthetic science: Connecting mind, brain, and experience* (pp. 250–275). New York: Oxford University Press.

Swami, V. (2013). Context matters: Investigating the impact of contextual information on aesthetic appreciation of paintings by Max Ernst and Pablo Picasso. *Psychology of Aesthetics, Creativity, and the Arts, 7*(3), 285–295.

Takahashi, S. (1995). Aesthetic properties of pictorial perception. *Psychological Review, 102*(4), 671–683.

Tatarkiewicz, W. (1980/1976). *A History of Six Ideas. An Essay in Aesthetics* (C. Kasparek, Trans). Dordrecht: Kluwer.

Tinio, P. P. L. (2013). From artistic creation to aesthetic reception: The mirror model of art. *Psychology of Aesthetics, Creativity, and the Arts, 7*(3), 265–275.

Topolinski, S., Erle, T. M., & Reber, R. (2015). Necker's smile: Immediate affective consequences of early perceptual processes. *Cognition, 140,* 1–13.

Trainor, L. J., & Heinmiller, B. M. (1998). Infants prefer to listen to consonance over dissonance. *Infant Behavior and Development, 21,* 77–88.

Vuoskoski, J. K., & Eerola, T. (2017). The pleasure evoked by sad music is mediated by feelings of being moved. *Frontiers in Psychology, 8,* 439.

Wittgenstein, L. (1953). *Philosophical investigations.* Oxford: Blackwell.

Zajonc, R. B. (1968). Attitudinal effects of mere exposure. *Journal of Personality and Social Psychology, Monograph Supplement, 9,* 1–27.

Zeki, S. (1999). *Inner vision: An exploration of art and the brain.* Oxford: Oxford University Press.

Zentner, M., Grandjean, D., & Scherer, K. R. (2008). Emotions evoked by the sound of music: Characterization, classification, and measurement. *Emotion, 8*(4), 494–521.

Zentner, M. R., & Kagan, J. (1996). Perception of music by infants. *Nature, 383*(6595), 29.

Zillmann, D. (2006) Dramaturgy for emotions from fictional narration. In J. Bryant & P. Vorderer (Eds.), *Psychology of entertainment* (pp. 215–238). Mahwah, NJ: Erlbaum.

Zillmann, D., Katcher, A. H., & Milavsky, B. (1972). Excitation transfer from physical exercise to subsequent aggressive behavior. *Journal of Experimental Social Psychology, 8,* 247–259.

CHAPTER 6

....

EXPLORING THE LANDSCAPE OF EMOTION IN AESTHETIC EXPERIENCE

....

GERALD C. CUPCHIK

DEFINING THE PROBLEM: WHAT ARE "AESTHETIC EMOTIONS" AND DO THEY EXIST?

WHAT are "aesthetic emotions" and how do they differ from everyday emotions? There are at least three ways to think about the meaning of "aesthetic emotions." First, the word "aesthetic" can be used to modify "emotions" so that reference is being made to "aesthetic" rather than "everyday" emotions. The phrase implies that the emotional experience embodies a beautiful quality or takes place during an aesthetic episode. Second, one can imagine the reverse wherein the word "emotion" modifies "aesthetic" so that a person's relationship to art is expressive rather than logical or abstract. In this vein, Sparshott interpreted Langer's "aesthetic emotion" (Langer, 1942, p. 222) as the sense of elation or "the satisfaction of discovering truth" that might "be occasioned by works of art" (Sparshott, 1963, p. 265). He adds a cynical note, asking "Why should we invent spurious entities to support superfluous disciplines" (p. 265). The third variation is a hybrid concept such that "aesthetic emotions" are treated as a distinct class of emotions *sui generis*. This latter treatment of "aesthetic emotions," as a kind of hypothetical construct or entity, is a central concern in this chapter.

We would do well to recall William James's (1884) distinction between "subtler" and "coarse" emotions. He lamented that "the aesthetic sphere of the mind, its longings, its pleasures and pains, and its emotions, have been so ignored" (p. 188) and sought to redress the imbalance. Subtler emotions

... are the moral, intellectual, and aesthetic feelings. Concords of sounds, of colors, of lines, logical consistencies, teleological fitnesses, affect us with a pleasure that seems ingrained in the very form of the representation itself, and to borrow nothing from any reverberation surging up from the parts below the brain ... A mathematical demonstration may be as "pretty," and an act of justice as "neat," as a drawing or a tune, although the prettiness and neatness seem to have nothing to do with sensation. We have, then, or some of us seem to have, genuinely cerebral forms of pleasure and displeasure, apparently not agreeing in their mode of production with the "coarser" emotions... (James, 1890, p. 468)

One might argue that James resolved the problem right from the outset. "Aesthetic emotion" is just another way of talking about "subtler" emotions wherein form shapes the "the primary feeling of beauty, as a pure incoming sensible quality" (p. 470). However, "coarse emotions" of fear, anger, or disgust might also be elicited by the subject matter of a work of art, literature, or theater. Both "subtler" and "coarse" emotions, and the contexts within they are elicited, should be addressed in a unified aesthetic theory that examines their interactions with perception, cognition, and memory processes in episodes of creation and reception.

Some interesting issues arise when we apply an "ordinary language" approach to figuring out the meaning of the phrase "aesthetic emotions." Kurt Danziger (1997) warns against treating concepts such as emotion or memory as "natural kinds" that have an existence independent of how we think about them. It is important to realize that "the categories one meets in psychological texts are discursive categories, not the things themselves" (p. 186) and they are replete with "unexamined and unquestioned assumptions and preconceptions" (p. 8). Following Danziger's (2000) discussion of Lewin (1949/1999), if the term "aesthetic emotions" referred to a phenomenon in the world, an "ideal case" (Cassirer, 1910/1923) would have to be created (or re-created) in an empirical context to illustrate or represent it. The semiotician Paul Bouissac has similarly advised against falling into an ontological trap through the slippery slope of semantic categories. An "ontological trap" involves "confusing a hypothetical notion, a heuristic model, a semantic category (which depends on a particular language) with an actual observable object in the world endowed with its own ontological presence and opacity."[1] Accordingly, in what sense would "aesthetic emotions" be observable as a phenomenon in the world, distinct from everyday emotions and present only in aesthetic situations, and what kind of data would be needed to demonstrate their singular existence?

Aesthetic Emotions in the Late 19th and Early 20th Centuries

More than a century ago, in exploring "the nature of aesthetic emotion," Bosanquet (1894) described a process of communication whereby emotion is spontaneously embodied in a work by an artist/author and experienced by the viewer/audience; the experience of beauty yielding a state of pleasure. The power of aesthetic experience is to provide a sense for expressive utterances of the artist or poet. In short, the central quality of aesthetic emotion is that it involves "expression for expression's sake" and "the original feeling is prolonged and accentuated by help of positive symbols and presentations, so that the mind may dwell upon it ... " (p. 157). The central point is that the aesthetic work is intimately tied up with emotional expression and related experiences on the part of the artist *and* the beholder. Ultimately, we are dealing with "the relation of content, as expressed, to life."

Bosanquet turned to drama to illustrate how an everyday emotion, such as fear, can be *elevated* to an "aesthetic emotion." Following Aristotle's (1905) theory, tragedy produces "pleasure by means of two painful emotions, pity and fear" (p. 159). Artistic expression or representation makes this possible by offering an abstract treatment of emotion that is universally experienced in a particular situation (i.e., Cassirer's "ideal case"). The "fear, for art, is a fear idealised by expression or objective embodiment, while free utterance is not ... obstructed by any intrusion of the dumb shock of personal terror" (p. 159). In this way, fear becomes "an aesthetic emotion, a source of artistic enjoyment or the pleasure of tragedy" (p. 159). It is the author's aesthetic action that transforms everyday emotion to an idealized state separate from the pragmatics of everyday life. The point is well made that "Emotion brought up by mere associated content, irrelevant to a real or universal connexion with presented elements, is not aesthetic emotion" (p. 160). For Bosanquet, aesthetic works provide a context for elevating everyday emotions, such as fear and pity, to an abstract or universalized level. In contrast, 21st-century cognitive behaviorists such as Menninghaus and Scherer treat emotion words as concrete dependent measures that attain value through mere association in an empirical context.

In his ordinary language account of the "origins of the aesthetic emotion," Clay (1908) states simply that "The feeling for beauty plays an important part in life" and that "the basis of our pleasure in beautiful things is an emotional response to an appropriate combination of color, sounds, or rhythmical movement" (p. 282). As one might expect following the age of Darwin, Clay asks whether an aesthetic emotion has some kind of instinctual or survival value comparable with that of emotions such as love, hate, fear, curiosity, or acquisitiveness. Can it be that "some instinctive necessary function or activity, that subsequently, when refined and raised into the ideal regions by the intellect, becomes the artistic spirit"? (pp. 282–283). Clay plays a distinctly psychological card stating that "we must disabuse our minds of any transcendental beauty" (p. 288). Instead, he situates the basis for the experience of beauty and pleasure distinctly in the mind of the beholder. "Beauty is not a perfect thing, but as our senses and intellect become more developed, we shall, as we advance, be able to realize and to see and hear beauty" (p. 288) but "always guided and limited by the felt need for harmony" (p. 289).

Clay argues that, like other instincts, "emotions are raised either to serve the highest aspirations of man or to serve for simple sensual gratification" and this process will be driven by the "old very useful instinct of curiosity" (p. 289), much as Berlyne (1960) observed many years later. In essence, the locus of aesthetic experience lies within the individual and his or her past experiences. Thus, we find beauty within ourselves "under the stimulus of the emotional excitement" (p. 290). Accordingly, "the richer the mind, the wider the experience, the deeper the stored impressions of the memory, so the greater the response to beauty when once the emotion has been touched and the right store of associations tapped" (p. 290).

In his classic work on "psychical distance" (what we now call "aesthetic distance"), Bullough (see Cupchik, 2002) developed a metaphor for the space that "lies between our own self and such objects as are the sources or vehicles" (Bullough, 1912, p. 89) shaping our affections involving sensations, perceptions, emotional states, or ideas. Like Bosanquet, he was interested in a personal relation to the work that is "often highly emotionally colored, but of a peculiar character" (p. 91) because the practical side is filtered out. The central principle for both artists and beholders is maximal involvement without excessive self-absorption: "*utmost decrease of Distance without its disappearance*" (p. 94). In essence, the aesthetic state has a two-fold character "in which *we know* a thing *not* to exist, but *accept its existence*" (p. 113). This delicate balance between being overly engaged to the point of imagining the work to represent one's own life ("under-distancing") and overly detached while intellectualizing about the work ("over-distancing") represents the default conditions for a failed aesthetic experience. Bullough offers a process-oriented account of the optimal conditions underlying aesthetic experiences. Aesthetic experience removes the beholder or audience member from the judgmental criteria of everyday life; hence, aesthetic emotions.

Dewey (1934) emphasized active involvement during aesthetic episodes in a holistic relationship between artist and beholder. The artist must engage both in "artistic" (i.e., "doing") and "esthetic" (i.e., "undergoing") processes in the creation of a work. The beholder "must *create* his own experience" in a way that is "comparable to those which the original producer underwent" (p. 54). Thus, the beholder's "emotionalized imagination" (p. 73) produces representations rich in perceptual, meaningful, and affective qualities that are suffused with emotions nourished by past experiences. Arnheim (1954, 1971) continued this emphasis on the holistic and spontaneous experience of expression in the structure of an artwork. The metaphorical process is revealed by viewers who find "symbolic meanings expressed in concrete happening, the sensing of the universal in the particular" (1971, p. 436). The processes underlying emotion, perception, and cognition are intertwined in the organic unfolding of an aesthetic experience for both artist and beholder.

In summary, over a period of more than 50 years, scholars described a process of engagement between artist and beholder or playwright and audience. Bosanquet situated "aesthetic emotions" in a process of communication whereby emotions are spontaneously embodied in works and elevated to an idealized level by their aesthetic form that is experienced by an actively engaged beholder. His idea that aesthetic situations transform and elevate everyday emotions to a universal level can help illuminate today's controversy about "aesthetic emotions." Clay, too, emphasized the active role of the beholder who explored the aesthetic work in search of harmony and pleasure, given background knowledge and relevant life experiences. Bullough considered the beholder's optimal "aesthetic distance" from the work so as to be immersed without feeling overwhelmed or so detached as to lose interest. This optimal "psychical distance" contributes to the process of elevating emotions to an aesthetic "subtler" level filled with universal meaning.

Dewey and Arnheim treated emotion as part of a larger unfolding structure enriched by aesthetic knowledge and personal resonances. The sharing of meaningful experiences with viewers and readers is central to the creative process and mediated by relations between the subject matter and form of artifacts in culturally meaningful situations. Emotions do not exist in isolation from other noetic processes. Nor are expressive qualities detached from the subject matter and form of artworks (Cupchik, 2016). These scholars share an emphasis on elevating "coarse" emotions during aesthetic episodes of creation and reception to a more "subtle" and abstract level that universalizes their meaning for viewers, readers, and audience members.

Aesthetic Emotions in the 21st Century

The earlier holistic account of aesthetic communication, wherein the art or literary work unites creators and beholders, diminishes after the *cognitive turn* that marks the postinformation theory era of the 1960s. The role of creative processes on both sides of the communication paradigm disappears in behaviorist circles. Instead, an emphasis is placed on beholders who are motivated to experience beauty and pleasure in the form of a stimulus. This dualistic approach seeks to characterize the distinctive qualities of aesthetic experiences in response to particular kinds of stimuli. Scherer (2005), for example, offers an account of "aesthetic emotions" linked to appraisal theory that is consistent with Berlyne's (1971) focus on the importance of intrinsic motivation rather than extrinsically motivated problem solving. Rather than being adaptive, "aesthetic emotions are produced by the appreciation of the intrinsic qualities of the beauty of nature, or the qualities of a work of art or an artistic performance. Examples of such aesthetic emotions are being moved or awed, being full of wonder, admiration, bliss, ecstasy, fascination, harmony, rapture, solemnity" (Scherer, 2005, p. 706). These qualities are tied to intrinsically meaningful experiences in aesthetic situations rather than to ones requiring action. However, words like wonder, fascination, or admiration can relate to situations that have nothing to do with aesthetics as a cultural process. We can feel wonder watching a television program on outer space, admiration upon reflecting on the success enjoyed by a friend, bliss in the context of a loving relationship, and so forth. The creative artist, who embodied meanings and feelings in artwork, disappears into the behaviorist experimental paradigm. This also sets the stage for the experience of admiration or bliss being transformed into a concrete behavioral measure thereby losing reference to the underlying processes that shape them.

Marković (2012) adopts a similar cognitive approach but includes everyday emotions that might be stimulated by narrative situations (e.g., sentimental novels) and require empathic appraisals of internal emotional states of characters. Thus, "emotions can be used as constitutive parts of narratives which indirectly contribute to the generating of aesthetic emotions. In this case, the aesthetic emotion is an emotion which is emerging through the process of appraisal of more profound symbolic layers of a narrative" (p. 11). Accordingly, aesthetic emotion may reflect "the detection of deeper structural regularities is (collections of impressions) in both narrative (literature, film, theater, etc.) and non-narrative compositions (music, abstract art, architecture, etc.)" and involves "feelings of unity and exceptional relationship with the objects of aesthetic experience" (p. 12). Everyday and uniquely "aesthetic emotions" can live side-by-side in episodes involving real aesthetic materials.

The next stage of research on "aesthetic emotions" adopts a distinctly positivist turn with a focus on collecting well-attested facts about emotions that arise during aesthetic episodes. The notion of "aesthetic emotions" is operationally defined by word clusters using a bottom-up inductive method. Hosoya et al. (2017) used a technique in which participants sorted 75 relevant words into piles to explore the semantic structure of aesthetic terms. The authors found "well-interpretable and finely differentiated clusters" (p. 467) that related to established discourse in the discipline and could be used to develop a questionnaire. Working with the same research group, Schindler et al. (2017), in response to the question "How does beauty feel?", assumed that "aesthetic appeal is more felt than known" and that "Emotions accompany and inform our experiences of art … [and so on]" (p. 145). In other words, feelings and emotions necessarily accompany aesthetic experiences without a person's awareness. They asked roughly 500 people who attended 25 different events about the emotions they experienced, having collected 75 potentially relevant emotion words. The prototypical aesthetic emotions that arose in these diverse experiences included: the feeling of beauty/liking, fascination, being moved, and awe. Apart from beauty, the words listed here can be applied to all manner of experiences including being fascinated by a new idea, moved by someone's sad story or even a design object, or a feeling of awe in a religious setting. In this context, "aesthetic emotions" are methodological artifacts.

A distinctly top-down approach to the unpacking of fuzzy "aesthetic emotions" is demonstrated in the theory-building work of Menninghaus and his colleagues (Menninghaus et al., 2018). In their elaborate additive model, "aesthetic emotions" are defined as having four mandatory features: (1) full-blown discrete emotions involving relevant appraisals that relate to evaluation/appreciation, (2) association with specific attributes of aesthetic appeal assigned to the object or event (e.g., moving, surprising, fascinating, etc.), (3) reflecting subjectively felt pleasure (or displeasure), and (4) predicting resultant liking or disliking. This emphasis on appraisals producing feelings of pleasure that shape liking and lead to evaluations is consistent with a cognitive/behavioral approach in psychology in contrast to a phenomenological concern for finding emotional meaning in a work of art.

Aesthetic emotions are treated as a subgroup of emotions stimulated by particular features (termed "virtues") in an artwork and include feelings of being moved, fascinated, surprised, and the resulting liking. The causal role of the "virtues" is central to this linear and sequential model. Thus, "We enjoy and like a work of art *because* it moves, fascinates, elevates ... or dislike *because* it bores us ... " This model is reminiscent of processes associated with behavioral psychology in its early years (Danziger, 2000) where the effects of stimulus features are *local* (observed at a particular time and place), *proximal* (resulting from an immediately present effective agent or stimulus), *short-term* (generally lasting for the duration of the stimulus conditions), and *descomposable* (are analyzed into isolable components).

Working in the appraisal tradition of cognitive social psychology, this model focuses on aesthetic perception leading to the evaluation of objects. Emphasis is placed on a "special judgment focus on aspects of the objects under consideration that are *subjectively experienced as pleasing to our senses and/or our cognitive capacities.*" They propose a broad range of prototypical features that make it possible to determine "whether a given episode is an 'aesthetic emotion'" from a "multicomponent" perspective. Given that aesthetic features can appear in any stimulus, be it a beautiful face or building, the authors argue against the idea of an aesthetic "stance" or "attitude." This implies that the mere presence of a beautiful feature is sufficient to trigger an "aesthetic emotion." Aesthetic experiences and related judgments are fully decontextualized so that culturally meaningful events or episodes are not important. Nor is there any discussion of acts of creation or the relationship between creators of art (literature and so forth) and viewers or audiences. Aesthetic communication disappears and the potency of decontextualized features or (ironically) "virtues" is all that matters.

The approach of Menninghaus and his colleagues to "aesthetic emotions," both in theory and in practice, lies clearly in the behavioral/cognitive positivist tradition. The empirical account of "aesthetic emotions" instantiates a bottom-up approach that is part of the American regime initiated by Festinger (1953) and his students. As inferred hypothetical constructs, "aesthetic emotions" do not have an independent ontological status. Rather, they are operationally defined through associations with words such as "awe" and "fascination," which are measured in an empirical context. On the other hand, the top-down constraints of the model focus on pleasure and arousal as mediating variables that shape liking and, hence, evaluation. There are indeed many similarities to Berlyne's (1960, 1971, 1974) psychobiological and behavioral approach, which was itself influenced by information theoretic principles of the 1960s. His main theoretical concern was with modulations of ratings of interest, surprise, pleasure, and arousal by stimulus properties of aesthetic configurations both natural and contrived. For Berlyne, aesthetics had to do with evoking curiosity and related interest, while emotion was addressed in terms of pleasure or reward derived from engagement with art rather than "coarse" emotions.

Despite the great erudition behind this analysis of "aesthetic emotions," three things stand out. First, the approach to aesthetics adopted by the authors is atomistic, mechanistic, and objectivist. Focus is placed on feature-oriented analyses that occur at the front (i.e., perceptual) end of everyday and aesthetic encounters. There is an assumption that viewers "appraise" particular features or "virtues" of an aesthetic work impacting superficial aspects of reactions such as pleasure or arousal and consequent liking. This places Menninghaus and colleagues in a direct lineage with formalists of the earlier 19th century who believed that aesthetic pleasure was determined by the structural properties of artworks (Jahoda, 2005), along with motivational/cognitive theorists of the 20th century, such as Berlyne (1971) and Zillmann (1983), for whom arousal levels shape responses to evocative stimuli. Arnheim (1985) has referred to such a model as "hedonistic psychophysics." This exclusive focus on stimulus properties abandons a concern for *situations* within which aesthetic experiences take place and appropriate "aesthetic attitudes" that are adopted (Beardsley, 1958) through the mediation of neural processes (Cupchik, Vartanian, Crawley, & Mikulis, 2009).

The second thing is that they are allied with a tradition in emotion theory (see Cupchik, 2016) that includes appraisal theorists (Scherer, 2009) who focus on quantifiable "core affects" (Russell, 2003) that map onto dimensions of valence (pain–pleasure) and arousal and describe affective processes in a linear, sequential, and inferential manner (Russell & Barrett, 1999). This approach is "based on theories that treat emotion as the product of non-emotional processes, usually a synthesis of cognitive and autonomic motor reactions" rather than as "real" or "existent" (Leventhal, 1982, p. 126). As in the case of the cognitive/behavioral approach, everyday "coarse emotions" related to happiness, anger, or fear are marginalized. Aesthetic experience reflects the impact of stimulus "virtues" (i.e., properties) rather than an interaction between viewers (readers and so forth) with personally meaningful works.

Third, the established tradition in aesthetics that treats "aesthetics emotions" as part of a process linking artists/authors and beholders/readers has been lost in the swirl of the narrowly conceived empirical narratives. The larger process includes culturally grounded, long-term, and deeper efforts after meaning that encompass emotion, culture, and background knowledge as expressed in Dilthey (1976/1894), Wundt's (1896) *Völkerpsychologie*, Dewey (1934), and Arnheim's (1954, 1971) Gestalt approach. In conclusion, "aesthetic emotions" do not have independent ontological status but appear as an artifact of the behavioral method.

RETURNING TO A BALANCED AND CULTURALLY GROUNDED APPROACH TO AESTHETIC PROCESS

In 19th-century Germany, there was an ongoing controversy between aesthetic formalists and adherents to the Romantic Movement (Jahoda, 2005; see also Malgrave & Ikonomou, 1994). The formalists followed Kant and Herbart, "viewing art as the pleasurable interplay of our cognitive faculties with purposive form" (Malgrave & Ikonomou, 1994, p. 6). Zimmermann wanted to develop a "science of form" and Fechner sought empirical evidence (in an "aesthetics from below") to show how formal properties, such as the "golden section," shaped preferences, thereby quantifying relations between mind (i.e., perception) and body. In contrast, scholars adhering to ideas from the Romantic Movement emphasized the value of content and symbolism for evoking emotion. A leading figure was Robert Vischer, who first developed the concept of *Einfühlung* or empathy in 1873 (see Malgrave & Ikonomou, 1994). He proposed that the mind enhances sensations to create ideas or images and these produce emotions, when influenced by the self, which are then projected onto the work.

In comparing the two approaches, the contrast is between formal properties that shape feelings of pleasure and emotions that resonate to personally meaningful subject matter in the artwork. While Berlyne (1974) dismissed such ideas as "armchair speculation," these insights derived from skillful observations of aesthetic experiences. Their accounts of underlying bodily processes were limited by science in the later 19th century much like Berlyne's (1971) "psychobiology" reflected the boundaries of mid-20th-century knowledge of brain processes. The link with Scherer and Menninghaus's theoretical approaches is apparent.

Scholars in the late 19th and early 20th centuries balanced aesthetic creation and reception in relation to emotional experience. Perhaps the most important insight came from Bosanquet (1894), who described the transformation and "elevation" of everyday emotion to a universal status during aesthetic episodes. This fits nicely with Bullough's (1912) account of optimizing "psychical distance" so that everyday emotions do not overwhelm the audience member. Thus, emotional experiences occur during aesthetic episodes but have a more abstract purpose. While Aristotle's "fear" and "pity" responses to dramatic tragedy are based in everyday experiences, the purpose of catharsis is to release pent-up emotions while providing an opportunity for raising consciousness regarding the meaning of the play. A focus on universally meaningful situations was central to August Schlegel, who translated Shakespeare into German in the late 18th century (Burwick, 1991). Thus, emotional processes take place during aesthetic episodes but the question arises as to whether they are concrete and respond to *mimesis*, the successful simulation of everyday events, or more abstract and embody the higher meaning of a work.

Resolving the Conflict Between the Formalist and Romantic Approaches

The formalist and Romantic approaches to aesthetic engagement are in fact complementary and presume different kinds of cognitive and affective processes. The formalist model pairs the discerning of structural properties, such as complexity or symmetry with *feelings* of pleasure or arousal. There is a *match* between the formal properties of a work and the person's ability to discern them. Both Fechner (1876) and Berlyne (1971, 1974) maintained that people prefer (i.e., found pleasure in) moderate levels of complexity. This represents an instance of the principle *feelings are the shadow of cognition*, reflecting the affective resultant of cognitive operations (Cupchik, 2016).

The formalist model is highly objective and predicated on detached discerning of structural properties. This is a *self-terminating* process, to borrow a concept from cognitive psychology. In other words, if the focus is on particular features of the work, then one need not penetrate further once the property is discerned. This also has motivational and practical implications when it comes to making choices about media products. If a person's desire is to watch an exciting program or a more romantic one, then all they have to do is search for that particular quality and surf the resulting feelings of pleasure or arousal. This illustrates the principle of *affective covariation* whereby the desired property matches the motive and a deeper exploration of plot or character is unnecessary.

The Romantic model, on the other hand, pairs emotional experiences related to primary emotions (including happiness, sadness, fear, anger, interest, or disgust) with personally meaningful subject matter. The person perceives *coherent* meaning that resonates with personal experience. This is consistent with the definition of emotion as *feelings filled with meaning related to the self in situations* and the principle that *suggestion meets connection* (Cupchik, 2016). In other words, viewers, readers, or audience members experience blends of emotions in response to works that resonate with their lived experiences and episodic memories.

The Romantic model is highly subjective and based on an engaged exploration of subject matter and symbols in search of meaning. This is an *exhaustive* process because, as much as one explores, there is more left to be interpreted. The depth of aesthetic meaning is boundless, especially in relation to personal resonances. The *situation* or *context* of the work, both within and beyond the frame, is subject to the *emotional elaboration* principle such that the deeper the processing, the more memorable the work because the nuances cohere as if glued together (Cupchik, 2016).

A parallel interplay between objective and subjective processes applies to creative or artistic activity. The artist engages in a project and must balance the Thinking-eye and the Being-I. The Thinking-eye involves the action- or purpose-oriented part of the brain supported by aesthetic distance from the work. It is technically oriented and planning is central to action. The Being-I is engaged and shaped by the unfolding experience as deeper meanings are embodied in the work. While the Thinking-Eye corrals them together in accordance with principles of design that are appropriate to the artist and culture, the Being-I spontaneously expresses symbolic elements and images. Of course, the artist shows plasticity of attention, shifting between being absorbed in the unfolding work and standing back to critically analyze how the project is progressing. Creative inspiration must be complemented by careful elaboration so that "unity within diversity" is preserved.

The same reciprocal process applies to the viewer/reader. The Thinking-eye helps viewers find contours in the work, defining the elements, unpacking the iconography, and so forth. It gets to work right away, segmenting boundaries of objects, separating figure from ground (Cupchik & Berlyne, 1979; Mureika, Cupchik, & Dyer, 2004). With additional exploration of the work, the stylistic, thematic, and iconographic features become more clearly defined. This is the hallmark of expertise when it comes to aesthetic exploration (Reber, 2012). The role of the Being-I is more complex and, in a sense, more interesting. In accordance with the principle of *suggests meets* connection (Cupchik, 2016), one can form an attachment to an image or narrative that is deeply personal without even knowing that it is happening. At other times, a book may require several readings before gaps in the text are understood and "good continuation" is achieved in the act of reading (Iser, 1978); attachment is formed as closure is achieved. This suggests that one can become attached to books by coming to appreciate their intellectual subtlety. But a strong emotional attachment is predicated on a bridge between the book or play's themes and personal life experiences.

The Implications of a Process-Oriented Approach to Aesthetics

The main lesson from Bosanquet, Clay, and Bullough is that aesthetic episodes should be approached holistically. The creative product is a cultural artifact that brings together artist and viewer, author and reader, playwright and audience within the framework of aesthetic communication. The creative work embodies the principle of "unity within diversity" and has an intrinsic value to be appreciated outside the pragmatics of everyday life. Shklovsky (1988/1917) argued that the goal of art is to de-automatize perception through a process of "estrangement" by placing familiar objects in novel contexts. Thus, "The purpose of art is to impart the sensation of things as they are perceived and not as they are known" (Shklovsky, 1988, p. 20). The challenge for the viewer, reader, or audience member is to grasp the meaning of this "estrangement" so that aesthetic communication is successful.

In relation to "aesthetic emotions," the central point is that perception, cognition, imagination, emotion, memory, and so forth are integrated in a unified process. The goal is to search for principles to account for how these processes interact to shape experiences during episodes of creation and reception. The motivations behind these episodes can vary from person to person and situation to situation. A depth of aesthetic and affective processing is helpful here. Feelings of pleasure or excitement are sufficient to absorb someone interested in distracting entertainment. Deeper emotions are elicited when suggestions within the work resonate with emotional meanings in the person. Surface feelings of pleasure or excitement are less enduring than profound emotions that relate to personally meaningful situations. The experience of feelings related to pleasure or arousal and the experience of "coarse" emotions in the "effort after meaning" unfold in parallel.

Conclusion

What can we conclude about the nature of "aesthetic emotion" in relation to a process-oriented analysis? The problematic nature of "aesthetic emotions," as a hybrid and hypothetical construct, provided the occasion for this analysis of aesthetic process. Any empirical effort to find these "aesthetic emotions" is constrained by underlying assumptions of the method. The search for parsimony does not easily fit with a collection of emotion words that describe aesthetic experiences, if only because these words can be applied in everyday contexts.

Both the formalists and Romantics offered meaningful contributions to our understanding of "aesthetic" process. People do respond to formal properties of artworks that shape "unity within diversity." They also can respond to subject matter of the work that awakens or resonates with personal life experiences. In relation to "emotions," William James's (1890) distinction between "subtler" and "coarse" emotions is relevant. The "subtler" emotions are not just aesthetic but extend to elegant scientific solutions and ethical assertions as well. They apply to an appreciation of formalist properties in artworks that contribute to the experience of beauty. The "coarse" emotions are found in everyday life but are elevated to a level of universal meaning (and abstraction) in successful works of art and literature. A process-oriented approach describes how viewers, readers, or audience members respond to "subtle" and "coarse" aspects of aesthetic experience both in episodes of creation and reception. Emotion, perception, imagination, reason, and memory interact in the larger web of aesthetic processes linking mind and body. It is best not to isolate emotions in aesthetic contexts and treat them as entities or hypothetical constructs based on the co-presence of words in statistical analyses.

NOTE

1. Personal e-mail communications, May 1, 2014.

REFERENCES

Aristotle (1905). *Aristotle's poetics.* Oxford, UK: Clarendon Press. (Benajmin Jowett, trans.)

Arnheim, R. (1954). *Art and visual perception: A psychology of the creative eye.* Oakland, CA: University of California Press.

Arnheim, R. (1971). *Art and visual perception.* Berkeley, CA: University of California Press.

Arnheim, R. (1985). The other Gustav Theodor Fechner. In S. Koch & D. E. Leary (Eds.), *A century of psychology as science* (pp. 856–865). New York: McGraw-Hill.

Beardsley, M. C. (1958). *Aesthetics: problems in the philosophy of criticism.* New York: Harcourt Brace.

Berlyne, D. E. (1960). *Conflict, arousal and curiosity.* New York: McGraw-Hill.

Berlyne, D. E. (1971). *Aesthetics and psychobiology.* New York: Appleton-Century-Crofts.

Berlyne, D. E. (1974). *Studies in the new experimental aesthetics: Steps toward an objective psychology of aesthetic appreciation.* Washington, DC: Hemisphere.

Bosanquet, B. (1894). On the nature of aesthetic emotion. *Mind, 10,* 153–166.

Bullough, E. (1912). Psychical distance as a factor in art and an aesthetic principle. *British Journal of Psychology, 5*(2), 87–118.

Burwick, F. (1991). *Illusion and the drama: Critical theory of the enlightenment and romantic era.* University Park, PA: Pennsylvania State University.

Cassirer, E. (1923). *Substance and function*. Chicago, IL: Open Court (Reprinted Dover Publications, 1953. German original published 1910).

Clay, F. (1908). The origin of the aesthetic emotion. *Sammelbände der Internationalen Musikgesellschaft*, 9, 282–290.

Cupchik, G. C. (2002). The evolution of psychical distance as an aesthetic concept. *Culture and Psychology*, 8(2), 155–188.

Cupchik, G. C. (2016). *The aesthetics of emotion: up the down staircase of the mind-body*. Cambridge, UK: Cambridge University Press.

Cupchik, G. C., & Berlyne, D. E. (1979). The perception of collative properties in visual stimuli. *Scandinavian Journal of Psychology*, 20(1), 93–104.

Cupchik, G. C., Vartanian, O., Crawley, A., & Mikulis, D. J. (2009). Viewing artworks: Contributions of cognitive control and perceptual facilitation to aesthetic response. *Brain and Cognition*, 70, 84–91.

Danziger, K. (1997). *Naming the mind: How psychology found its language*. London: Sage.

Danziger, K. (2000). Making social psychology experimental: A conceptual history, 1920–1970. *Journal of the History of the Behavioral Sciences*, 36(4), 329–347.

Dewey, J. (1934). *Art as experience*. New York: Minton, Balch & Company.

Dilthey, W. (1976). Ideas about a descriptive and analytical psychology (H. P. Rickman, Trans.). In H. P. Rickman (Ed.), *W. Dilthey selected writings* (pp. 88–97). Cambridge, UK: Cambridge University Press (original work published 1894).

Fechner, G. T. (1876). *Vorschule der Ästhetik*. Leipzig: Breitkopf & Härtel.

Festinger, L. (1953). Laboratory experiments. In L. Festinger & D. Katz (Eds.), *Research methods in the behavioral sciences* (pp. 136–172). New York: Holt, Rinehart, & Winston.

Hosoya, G., Schindler, I., Beermann, U., Wagner, V., Menninghaus, W., Eid, M., & Scherer, K. R. (2017). Mapping the conceptual domain of aesthetic emotion terms: A pile-sort study. *Psychology of aesthetics, creativity, and the arts*, 11(4), 457–473.

Iser, W. (1978). *The act of reading: A theory of aesthetic response*. Baltimore, MD: The John Hopkins University Press.

Jahoda, G. (2005). Theodor Lipps and the shift from "sympathy" to "empathy." *Journal of the history of the behavioral sciences*, 41(2), 151–163.

James, W. (1884). That is an emotion? *Mind*, IX (34), 188–205.

James, W. (1890). *The principles of psychology, Vol. 2*. New York: Dover.

Langer, S. K. (1942). *Philosophy in a new key*. New York: Penguin Books.

Leventhal, H. (1982). The integration of emotion and cognition: A view from the perceptual-motor theory of emotion. In M. Clark & S. Fiske (Eds.), *Affect and cognition: The 17th Annual Carnegie Symposium on Cognition* (pp. 121–156). Hillsdale, NJ: Erlbaum.

Lewin, K. (1999). Cassirer's philosophy of science and the social sciences. In M. Gold (Ed.), *The complete scientist: A Kurt Lewin reader* (pp. 23–36). Washington, DC: American Psychological Association (original work published 1949).

Mallgrave, H. F., & Ikonomou, E. (Eds.). (1994). *Empathy, form, and space*. Santa Monica, CA: The Getty Center for the History of Art and the Humanities.

Marković, S. (2012). Components of aesthetic experience: aesthetic fascination, aesthetic appraisal, and aesthetic emotion. *i-Perception*, 3, 1–17.

Menninghaus, W., Wagner, V., Wassiliwizky, E., Schindler, I., Hanich, J., Jacobsen, T., and Koelsch, S. (2018). What are aesthetic emotions? *Psychological Review*, 126, 171–195.

Mureika, J. R., Cupchik, G. C., & Dyer, C. C. (2004). Multifractal fingerprints in the visual arts. *Leonardo*, 37(1), 53–56.

Reber, R. (2012). Processing fluency, aesthetic pleasure, and culturally shared taste. In Shimamura A. P., and Palmer, S. E. (Eds.), *Aesthetic science: Connecting minds, brains, and experience* (pp. 223–249). New York: Oxford University Press.

Russell, J. A. (2003). Core affect and the psychological construction of emotion. *Psychological Review, 110*(1), 145–172.

Russell, J. A., & Barrett, L. F. (1999). Core affect, prototypical emotional episodes, and other things called emotion: Dissecting the elephant. *Journal of Personality and Social Psychology, 76*(5), 805–819.

Scherer, K. R. (2005). What are emotions? And how can they be measured? *Social Science Information—Sur Les Sciences Sociales, 44*(4), 695–729.

Scherer, K. R. (2009). The dynamic architecture of emotion: Evidence for the component process model. *Cognition & Emotion, 23*(7), 1307–1351.

Schindler, I., Hosoya, G., Menninghaus, W., Beermann, U., Wagner, V., Eid, M., & Scherer, K. R. (2017). Measuring aesthetic emotions: A review of the literature and a new assessment tool. *PLoS ONE, 12*(6), e0178899.

Shklovsky, V. (1988). Art as technique. In D. Lodge (Ed.), *Modern criticism and theory* (pp. 16–30). New York: Longman (original work published in 1917).

Sparshott, F. E. (1963). *The structure of aesthetics*. Toronto: University of Toronto Press.

Wundt, W. (1896). *Grundriss der psychologie*. Stuttgart, Germany: Engelmann.

Zillmann, D. (1983). Transfer of excitation in emotional behavior. In J. T. Cacciopo, & R. E. Petty (Eds.), *Social psychophysiology: A sourcebook* (pp. 215–240). New York: Guilford Press.

CHAPTER 7

....

THE NEUROBIOLOGY OF SENSORY VALUATION

....

MARTIN SKOV

INTRODUCTION

....

WHEN I eat an ice cream or listen to David Bowie's song "Heroes" I feel, as part of both experiences, a pleasurable response. To express this feeling, I might say I *like* these two objects. In contrast, I *dislike* eating kale or listening to songs by Taylor Swift. Why is there this difference? Why do I experience some things as likable and others as dislikable?

Modern aesthetics was largely invented to address this question (Åhlberg, 2003; Dickie, 1996; Kivy, 2003). It was founded by philosophers in the eighteenth century, who wondered if there are specific psychological rules that dictate how liking responses form for particular sense impressions. These thinkers posed two cardinal questions that have continued to animate later scientific studies of sensory liking: (1) What are the mechanisms that compute and implement liking responses? (2) And what computational principles do these mechanisms employ in order to "calculate" how likable different objects are? This chapter reviews work from the neurosciences that has helped us address these two questions. Specifically, it provides a first introduction to research that illuminates the way the nervous system computes hedonic values for stimuli perceived by the five sensory systems. It outlines the neurobiological processes involved in computing such hedonic values, and discusses factors that influence the way these processes unfold.

While in my view understanding the neurobiology of hedonic valuation can be viewed as providing a biological foundation to the study of aesthetic appreciation, I am well aware that it represents a take on traditional concepts in empirical aesthetics that can seem alien, perhaps even orthogonal, to some members of the community (Skov, 2019; Skov & Nadal, 2021). I shall therefore begin the chapter by highlighting three issues where the neurobiological account of liking can be seen as diverging from traditional theories of aesthetic appreciation. First of all, in both philosophical aesthetics and empirical aesthetics aesthetic appreciation is often viewed as a distinct psychological mechanism attuned to a circumscribed set of object qualities. Thus, aesthetic appreciation is often assumed to produce a specific kind of psychological response (i.e., specialized emotions such as beauty, awe, rapture, etc.) to certain categories of objects—objects "containing" these qualities (especially art objects). The neurobiological account of liking disputes this hypothesis, finding, instead, that hedonic valuation is a *general* mechanism for assessing how pleasurable or unpleasurable any sense input is, irrespective of sense modality. Second, in most traditional models of aesthetic appreciation liking is conceived of as a response *to* specific object properties—an idea that essentially follows from the notion that aesthetic appreciation assesses specific object qualities. The neurobiological account of liking also disputes this idea. Instead, it finds that the same stimulus can give rise to different appreciation events, leading to different hedonic values. The biological reason for this is that aesthetic appreciation does not, in fact, "extract" aesthetic qualities from perceived objects, but calculates how beneficial an object is to survival concerns in the organism's current circumstances. This point ties in with the third issue where traditional aesthetics and neuroscience can be seen to part ways. While one of the core traits traditionally attributed to aesthetic appreciation is its "disinterestedness," a supposed confined focus on assessing an object's aesthetic quality for its own sake, the neuroscientific explanation of aesthetic appreciation roots hedonic liking in neurobiological processes whose purpose it is to regulate interactions between physiology and behavior. Far from being considered disinterested, a neurobiological account of liking suggests that aesthetic appreciation assesses sensory objects for their hedonic value in order to motivate behavior.

What, then, does neuroscience mean when it says that liking can be conceived of as a state of affective evaluation assigning a hedonic value to sensory stimuli? The key idea is that biological organisms have evolved a neurobiological system for tagging stimuli with an affective "gloss" that can aid the organism in deciding how to interact with the environment (Berridge, 2004; Berridge & Kringelbach, 2015; Cabanac, 1979; Ellingsen, Leknes, & Kringelbach, 2015; Panksepp, 1998). In neuroscientific parlance this affective gloss is referred to as a *hedonic* value. Hedonic values fluctuate between positive and negative, and can be felt as *pleasurable* on the positive end, and *unpleasurable* on the negative end (although in many circumstances hedonic values are not represented consciously). Critically, hedonic values are used to mediate between a sensory stimulus and the organism's behavioral interaction with it (Figure 7.1). Thus, sensory valuation can also be thought of as a regulatory interface between sensation and behavior (Dickinson & Balleine, 2010; Montague & King-Casas, 2007; Peters & Büchel, 2010; Symmonds & Dolan, 2012).

Hedonic values help regulate every important facet of animal and human behavior: whom we have sex with (Andersson & Simmons, 2006; Gangestad & Scheyd, 2005), what we eat and drink (Grabenhorst & Rolls, 2011; Rossi & Stuber, 2018; Zimmerman, Leib, & Knight, 2017), and why we interact socially with conspecifics the way we do (Forbes & Graffman, 2010; Loseth, Ellingsen, & Leknes, 2014; Ruff & Fehr, 2014). In humans, hedonic values also regulate consumer behavior (Hsu & Yoon, 2015; Knutson & Genevsky, 2018), economic decision making more generally (Krajbich &

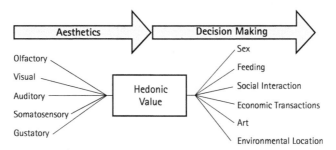

FIGURE 7.1. Hedonic valuation sits at the intersection between perception and behavior. It assigns an affective value to sensory stimuli, assessing what the object's impact will be on the biological state of the organism. In this way sensory valuation links aesthetic appreciation and decision making. Hedonic values have been found to influence behavioral decision making in a wide array of behavioral domains, including feeding and drinking, sex, economic transactions, and indeed art experience.

Dean, 2015; Pessiglione & Delgado, 2015), and art behavior: seeking out and enjoying music, paintings, or literature (Brattico & Pearce, 2013; Chatterjee & Vartanian, 2014). As a general rule, positive hedonic values facilitate *approach* behavior, for instance the seeking out and eating of an ice cream, or spending money on buying a CD by Bowie. Negative hedonic values, in contrast, promote *avoidance* behavior, such as shunning people, food, or artifacts that the hedonic valuation system suggests might be injurious or harmful to the organism (Lieberman, Billingsley, & Patrick, 2018; Tybur & Lieberman, 2016).

Because hedonic values underwrite all forms of motivated behavior, in reality the experimental study of "aesthetics"—i.e., establishing why a specific sensory stimulus elicits a specific hedonic value—is an important part of a wide range of scientific disciplines (Figure 7.2). For example, hedonic feeding studies try to understand why certain chemicals taste pleasant and others awful. Similarly, sexual selection research in animals and humans attempts to divine why certain body features are deemed attractive while others are not. Questions of aesthetic appreciation are found in consumer science, design studies, behavioral economics, etc. An important benefit of addressing the mystery of sensory valuation from the point of view of the brain is that this approach can help unify these diverse research disciplines—so rarely in contact with each other—into one explanatory framework.

Recognizing that hedonic values are computed with the purpose of motivating behavior also makes it clear that the way the brain valuates a sensory stimulus is intimately related to behavioral decision making (Figure 7.1). Indeed, for many disciplines in psychology and neuroscience the main reason for studying how liking works is that hedonic valuation is the principal gateway to understanding decision making. Thus, consumer psychology wants to understand how liking a product makes us buy it, sexual selection why attractiveness makes us seek out specific partners, and hedonic feeding why we choose to eat certain food items (and in some circumstances choose to overeat). This suggests that aesthetic appreciation and decision making are two sides of the same coin: We decide, in part, on the basis of the hedonic values our brain attributes to the sensory objects involved in a behavioral scenario. And, as I will show, how a stimulus is valuated is, in turn, partly informed by contextual decision making conditions.

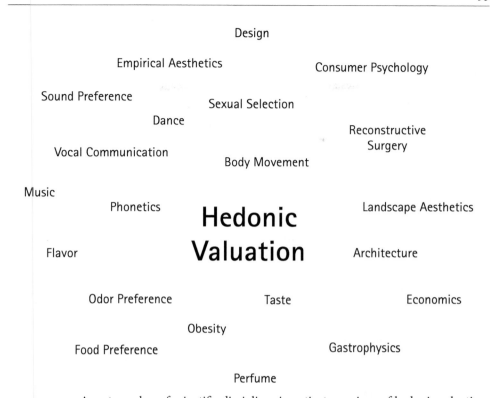

FIGURE 7.2. A vast number of scientific disciplines investigate versions of hedonic valuation. I suggest we bring these diverse disciplines, often ignorant about the accomplishments of other fields, together into a general framework.

In the following sections I explain which parts of the brain compute and implement hedonic valuation. I review what is known about this system in terms of anatomy, physiology and function. I also discuss experimental evidence that help us understand why hedonic values are modulated by regulatory and behavioral task demands, and why hedonic values vary as a function of both endogenous and external factors. At the end of the chapter I return to the question of how a general neurobiological account of hedonic valuation fits with traditional concerns in empirical aesthetics, especially the question of whether or not hedonic values for human cultural objects such as artworks in any way differ from hedonic values for more "basic," biological objects.

Hedonic Valuation: Regulating Behavior

All living organisms require maintenance of physiological systems in order to survive. The nervous system contains a number of regulatory systems that attempt to control behavior such that these physiological requirements are met. For instance, the cardiovascular system regulates blood flow, circulating nutrients, in part by modulating heart rate. Respiration controls breathing, allowing a steady supply of oxygen intake. Feeding and drinking regulate cell metabolism and fluid osmosis.

The brain controls these regulatory processes through a number of dedicated neural systems that project to the body's hollow organs, tissue, and viscera (Jänig, 2003). These regulatory systems are located in a so-called behavioral control column, comprising nuclei in the brainstem, hypothalamus, pituitary gland, and the mesocorticolimbic reward circuit (Swanson, 2000). These neural systems, in a sense, mediate between physiological needs and behavioral decision making. The brain's regulatory systems attempt to adapt behavior such that the organism's physiological states will not deviate from certain fixed optimal points that allow it to survive—a regulatory mechanism known as *homeostasis* (Berridge, 2004).

A short example can illustrate how metabolic regulation works. When fluid balance changes due to water deprivation—measured as an elevated ratio between solute and water—receptors in the blood detect this change and signal to neurons in the lamina terminalis (LT) in the hypothalamus (Zimmerman, Leib, & Knight, 2017). A network of neurons in the LT triggers a suite of responses the purpose of which is the restoration of fluid balance, increasing thirst and salt appetite. These processes initiate search for and procurement of a fluid in the environment that contains the physiological components needed to restore fluid balance (e.g., sodium). When such a fluid is found (or appears to be found), other neural processes stimulate its intake and ingestion. As the ingested molecules are absorbed and diffused out through the body, restoring homeostatic balance, updated changes to plasma osmolarity, volume, and pressure are signaled back to the regulatory system, inhibiting or decreasing neural activity there.

Together, metabolic regulation can be described as a behavioral cycle comprising three phases: an *appetitive phase*, a *consummatory phase*, and a *satiety phase* (Kringelbach & Berridge, 2017; see Figure 7.3). The appetitive phase registers a homeostatic imbalance and stimulates behavioral action to alleviate this inequity. The consummatory phase decides on which behavioral option will meet the regulatory goal, and implements it. The satiety phase registers what impact the behavioral decision has on the organism's physiological systems, calculating if the homeostatic goal is met.

In order to facilitate this mediation of behavior, regulatory systems intersect with a range of neural systems involved in the control of behavior. For instance, emotional systems signal homeostatic need and enact motivational drive (*hunger, thirst, urge*). Perceptional and cognitive systems become attuned to sensory information deemed relevant to solving the regulatory problem (e.g., recognizing if something in the vicinity of the organism is a suitable fluid object). Executive systems help decide whether or not to pursue an action, or choose between multiple options. Motor systems implement action choices. All of these processes are modulated by information generated in the regulatory systems.

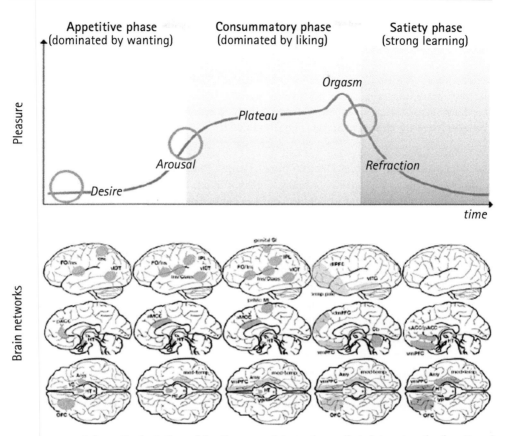

FIGURE 7.3. Schematic depiction of the three regulatory phases that determine the functional properties characterizing reward processing.

Reproduced with permission from Georgiadis and Kringelbach (2012).

Hedonic valuation

Hedonic values can be thought of as the central neural mechanism used by the brain's regulatory systems to motivate behavior in order to meet homeostatic goals. Hedonic values arise as states of positive or negative *emotional valence* at the intersection of sensory processing, interoceptive projections (signaling the body's homeostatic state), and executive mechanisms implementing unfolding behavior (Tye, 2018). The purpose of hedonic valuation is to evaluate sensory stimuli for their positive or negative impact on homeostatic regulation, with positive values promoting approach to, and interaction with, the stimulus at hand, and negative values discouraging contact (Figure 7.4). Thus, to *like* a sensory object is to deem it good for continued survival, whereas to *dislike* one is to find it threatening to survival—at least on an implicit, unconscious level. For example, hedonic values help categorize needed nutrients as desirable (Rolls, 2016), and

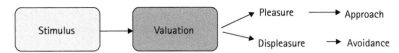

FIGURE 7.4. The key functional purpose of hedonic valuation is to promote adaptive behavior. In most cases, this means that positive (pleasurable) values will promote approach behavior (seeking out and eating an apple), while negative (unpleasurable) values will promote avoidance behavior (steering clear of pathogen-filled food stuff).

pathogens and other molecules that pose a danger to metabolic homeostasis as undesirable (Lieberman, Billingsley, & Patrick, 2018; Oaten, Stevsen, & Case, 2009; Tybur et al., 2018). Hedonic values also help select sexual partners deemed suitable—more attractive—for reproduction (Kuijper, Pen, & Weissing, 2012; Puts, 2015; Rhodes, 2006), and appear in general to control social interaction in populations (Ruff & Fehr, 2014), in humans playing a central role in modulating moral and economic decision making (Forbes & Graffman, 2010; Padoa-Schioppa, 2011).

The "valence" of a hedonic value is rooted in its activation of positive and negative affective states (Berridge & Kringelbach, 2015; Tye, 2018). Positive hedonic values are experienced as *pleasurable*, negative hedonic values as *unpleasurable* (Tybur & Lieberman, 2016). It is the affective impact of a hedonic value that makes it motivating. As first shown by Pavlov and Thorndike, experiencing a sensory object as pleasurable makes an animal crave it when encountered again at a later occasion (Berridge, 2004). Hence, positive hedonic values are said to *reward* or *reinforce* behavior. Similarly, negative hedonic values *punish* nonadaptive behavior. In short, hedonic values motivate behavior by "nudging" the organism to pursue actions that are accompanied by feelings of pleasure, and to avoid actions that give rise to displeasure (Rangel, Camerer, & Montague, 2008).

We can use the notion *aesthetic appreciation* to refer to the specific aspect of a sensory valuation event that concerns determining what value the brain will assign to a stimulus in a specific context. In this sense, the science of aesthetics is tasked with determining the computational principles and factors that influence how a specific stimulus is valuated. As should be clear from the discussion so far, these computational principles take into account not only the sensory information acquired via the perceptional representation of the stimulus at hand, but also other sources of information that reflect the ongoing regulatory concerns of the organism. Moreover, as we shall see, the brain does not in fact compute only a hedonic value signal for what we can call the *outcome* of the valuation process, but also a number of other value signals, including one that *predicts* how rewarding a stimulus will be, based on previously learned associations between sensory representations and liking outcomes.

Hedonic values promote action programs

Before I turn to a discussion of these computational principles, I will briefly mention the way hedonic valuation affects behavior by projecting its outputs to other neural systems

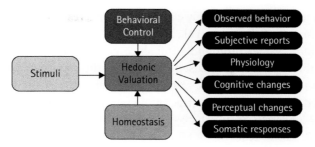

FIGURE 7.5. A key neural consequence of hedonic valuation is the occurrence of projections from value signals in the reward circuit to neural populations in other parts of the brain, eliciting various forms of action programs that are important to the implementation of value-based decisions. Action programs modulate activity in physiological, somatic, and cognitive systems.

involved in the implementation of action (Figure 7.5). These "consequences" of hedonic valuation can be characterized as what Damasio and Carvalho has called emotional *action programs* (Damasio & Carvalho, 2013).

Emotional action programs modulate a wide range of functions, including decision making, physiology, perception, and cognition, in order to facilitate motivated behavioral responses. I will mention three action programs important to sensory valuation events.

First, hedonic values bias decision making processes, affecting what we choose to eat (Hare, Camerer, & Rangel, 2009; Plassmann, O'Doherty, & Rangel, 2010), which partner people date (Cooper et al., 2012), the commercial success of songs (Berns & Moore, 2012; Salimpoor et al., 2013) and movies (Boksem & Smidts, 2015), and decisions with respect to a range of economic dilemmas (Calhoun & Hayden, 2015; Koechlin, 2016; O'Doherty, Cockburn, & Pauli, 2017). Experimental evidence suggests that such biases arise when unconscious hedonic values generated in striatum and amygdala (Bechara & Damasio, 2005; De Martino, Camerer & Adolphs, 2010; Knutson & Genevsky, 2018; Pessiglione et al., 2007) are integrated into executive processes in medial and lateral parts of the pre-frontal cortex, including orbitofrontal cortex (OFC), anterior cingulate cortex (ACC), and dorsolateral prefrontal cortex (dlPFC) (Rangel, Camerer, & Montague, 2008; Padoa-Schioppa, 2011; Wallis & Kennerley, 2007). Specifically, ventromedial structures appear important for integrating value signals with other sources of information (e.g., certainty or how available an object is; Clark et al., 2008; Knutson et al., 2007), and comparing and selecting between choice options (Blair et al., 2006; Grueschow et al., 2015; Padoa-Schioppa & Assad, 2008), while structures extending laterally from the ACC, via dlPFC, into premotor cortex implement and control decision processes (Hare, Camerer & Rangel, 2009; Wunderlich, Rangel, & O'Doherty, 2009).

Hedonic values also strongly modulate internal physiological systems such as heart rate, skin conductance, or respiration (Craig, 2005; Salimpoor et al., 2009). Arousal reliably fluctuates as a function of the hedonic value attributed to a stimulus (Bradley, 2000; Fuller, Sherman, Pedersen, Saper, & Lu, 2011), increasing both for positive and negative values (Ramsøy et al., 2012). Intense experiences of pleasure, such as those prompted by so-called musical "chills," strongly elevate heart rate, respiration, and arousal (Craig, 2005; Goldstein, 1980; Salimpoor et al., 2009).

Finally, hedonic values profoundly influence perception, biasing information processing such that attention is focused on parts of the sensory input that may be of relevance to the homeostatic task at hand. Experiments have revealed that sensory objects deemed more pleasurable attract rapid perceptual attention (e.g., di Pellegrino, Margarelli, & Mengarelli, 2011; Valuch et al., 2015), even when experienced subliminally (Hung, Nieh, & Hsieh, 2016; Sui & Liu, 2009). Similarly, hedonic valuation influences which parts of a crowded sensory environment perceptual systems expend computational resources on exploring (Chen, Liu, & Nakabayashi, 2012; Li, Oksama, & Hyönä, 2016; Liu & Chen, 2012). Being liked or disliked might even help a stimulus gain faster access to consciousness (Nakamura, Arai, & Kawabata, 2018; Ramsøy & Skov, 2014).

Value expectations, based on an object's reward history, also modulate neural activity throughout perceptual systems (e.g., Hikosaka, Nakamura, & Nakahara, 2006; Serences, 2008; Summerfield & de Lange, 2014). For example, electrophysiological studies of neural activity in V1 and V4 have found that, as a visual cue becomes associated with reward value, activity in a subset of neurons changes firing rates to reflect this value attribution (Baruni, Lau, & Salzman, 2015; Gavornik et al., 2009; Goltstein, Meijer, & Pennartz, 2018; Shuler & Bear, 2006; Zold & Shuler, 2015).

Together, action programs, prompted by sensory valuation, modulate perceptual, cognitive, and physiological activity in ways that help integrate a stimulus's perceived hedonic value into our behavioral responses to the surrounding world.

NEURAL SYSTEMS INVOLVED IN SENSORY VALUATION

We now turn to the question of where in the brain hedonic values are generated. As I have already noted, evidence suggests that hedonic valuation mechanisms are located in the brain's control column. In the following section I discuss evidence that links hedonic valuation specifically to nuclei located in the mesocorticolimbic reward circuit (Figure 7.6).

Experimental attempts to identify the precise location of sensory valuation mechanisms in humans have principally made use of noninvasive neuroimaging methods, especially functional magnetic resonance imaging (fMRI) and positron emission tomography (PET), that allow researchers to locate functional activity with a high degree of precision (Wang, Smith, & Delgado, 2016). In neuroimaging studies it is possible to monitor ongoing neural activity in human subjects as they engage in valuation assessments of a variety of stimulus categories. Different analysis techniques can dissociate neural correlates for positive or negative hedonic values by contrasting such states with control conditions, or identifying areas where neural activity scales with

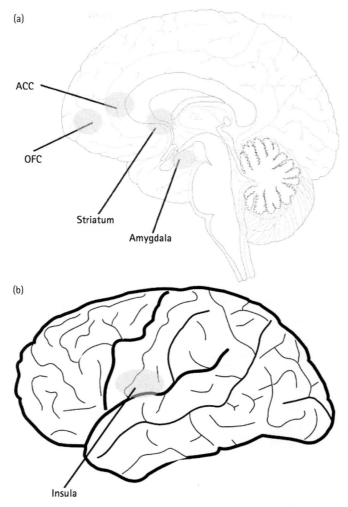

FIGURE 7.6. Core anatomical structures involved in the generation of hedonic values. (6A) Medial view of the brain depicting approximate locations of ACC, OFC, striatum (NAcc and pallidum), and amygdala. (6B) Lateral view of the brain depicting the approximate location of the insula.

variation in hedonic valuation. As a result, hedonic valuation for a wide range of sensory objects has been investigated, including *food* and *fluids* (Hinton et al., 2004; Kringelbach et al., 2003; Small et al., 1997; Small et al., 2003), *odors* (de Araujo et al., 2003; Gottfried, O'Doherty, & Dolan, 2003), human *faces* (Aharon et al., 2001; Nakamura et al., 1998; Winston et al., 2007), *bodies* (Martín-Loeches et al., 2014), *music* (Blood et al., 1999; Blood & Zatorre, 2001; Brattico et al., 2003; Menon & Levitin, 2005), *paintings* (Cela-Conde et al., 2004; Kawabata & Zeki, 2004; Vartanian & Goel, 2004), *sculpture* (Di Dio, Macaluso, & Rizzolatti, 2007), *architecture* (Kirk et al., 2009b; Vartanian et al., 2013), *dance* (Calvo-Merino et al., 2008, 2010), *consumer products* (Alba & Williams, 2013), or *monetary gains and losses* (O'Doherty et al., 2001; Thut et al., 1997).

Using statistical methods, it is possible to ask which parts of the brain are activated across a large number of such studies, using different objects categories and sensory modalities. The answer is that such meta-analyses repeatedly find hedonic valuation associated with elevated activity in key regions of the reward circuit: structures in the striatum (especially nucleus accumbens (NAcc) and pallidum), OFC, ACC, insula, and the amygdala (Table 7.1).

Thus, comparing neural activity across many hundreds of studies, involving the hedonic assessment of both primary reinforcers and cultural objects, suggests that the human brain employs a common system, located in the corticolimbic reward circuit, for computing hedonic values for all sensory stimuli. In other words, human neuroimaging suggests that assessing how much I like a song or a painting taps into the same

Table 7.1. Overview of statistical meta-analyses analyzing neural structures found commonly activated in imaging studies investigating sensory valuation in humans. Check mark indicates that one of the reward circuit's key structures was found to be involved in generating sensory valuation

Paper	Stimuli	OFC	ACC	Striatum	Insula	Amygdala
Bzdok et al., 2010	Faces	√				√
Brown et al., 2011	Visual	√	√	√	√	√
	Auditory	√	√	√	√	
	Olfactory	√	√		√	
	Gustatory				√	
Kühn & Gallinat, 2012	Faces/odor/drink/ food/International Affective Picture System (IAPS)/ paintings/music/ photos	√	√			
Sescousse et al., 2013	Taste		√	√	√	
	Money	√	√	√	√	√
	Erotic	√	√	√	√	√
Bartra et al., 2013	Monetary payoffs/ liquids/arousing pictures/social feedback	√	√	√	√	
Zou et al., 2016	Odors	√	√		√	√

neurobiological machinery as determining how tasty a steak is, relying on similar computational principles and molecular processes. Among neuroscientists, this hypothesis is known as the *common currency* hypothesis (Berridge & Kringelbach, 2015; Levy & Glimcher, 2012; Montague & King-Casas, 2007).

Intervention studies

While neuroimaging research is a powerful tool for probing the human brain, it comes with certain methodological limitations, especially the fact that imaging data are correlational in nature. This makes it difficult to ascertain exactly what causal role a given activation locus plays in generating hedonic values. Often neuroimaging experiments studying valuations events will yield widespread activity in many different neural structures, some of which will reflect core value computations—i.e., neural activity involved in increasing or decreasing liking—and other auxiliary processes associated with value computation (O'Doherty, 2014), including the action programs mentioned above. To determine which neural processes encode and amplify hedonic values we need various forms of intervention studies—paradigms where individual nuclei are systematically manipulated—to establish their impact on variation in hedonic valuation.

One powerful way liking can be changed is through the manipulation of the homeostatic state of the body. Recall that sensory valuation serves a regulatory purpose: assessing how rewarding or punishing a stimulus is in relation to a homeostatic problem. Therefore, appealing food items become more liked in depleted states than in sated states. Several studies have found that if subjects eat a food item to satiation, their hedonic response for it will change over time from liking to disliking as they become increasingly sated. In imaging studies this variation in liking can be modeled as a parametric regressor, identifying neural activity that reflects this change. Studies show that neural activity associated with a linear increase in liking is found in both striatum and the OFC (e.g., Kringelbach et al., 2003; Small et al., 2001). In animal studies firing in NAcc neurons is found to increase when salt-depleted rats are served even high concentrations of sodium, mirroring a change from dislike to like for salt intake (Tindell et al., 2006).

Another type of intervention study consists of stimulating cell activity in reward neurons, prompting a variation in liking even though the stimulus remains unchanged (e.g., Peciña, Smith, & Berridge, 2006; Peng et al., 2015). A similar effect can be achieved by manipulating neurochemicals involved in reward processing. For example, injecting a μ-opioid agonist in specific parts of NAcc or ventral pallidum selectively enhances liking responses in rats (Smith & Berridge, 2005, 2007). In humans, administration of a μ-opioid agonist enhances liking for faces and food (Chelnokova et al., 2014; Eikemo et al., 2016), while μ-opioid antagonists attenuate liking responses for music (Mallik, Chanda, & Levitin, 2017) and erotic images (Buchel, Miedl, & Sprenger, 2018); changes associated with modulation of neural activity in striatum, OFC, and amygdala (Buchel, Miedl, & Sprenger, 2018).

Together, intervention studies support a causal role in hedonic valuation for nuclei located in the mesocorticolimbic reward circuit, especially NAcc, ventral pallidum, OFC, and insula (Peciña, Smith, & Berridge, 2006). Neural activity in these nuclei appears to be under the control of specific neurochemicals such as opioids, orexin, and endocannabinoid neurotransmitters (Smith et al., 2010). This view is further supported by the recent finding that people suffering from a clinical condition called *specific musical anhedonia* (SMA) experience a markedly reduced liking for music, despite having an intact ability to represent music perceptually, and a preserved ability to feel pleasure for nonmusical stimuli such as visual art or monetary rewards (Mas-Herrero et al., 2014, 2018). A recent fMRI study by Martínez-Molina and colleagues found that this difference in liking responses can be explained by a difference in NAcc activity (Martínez-Molina et al., 2016)—intact for nonmusic stimuli; reduced for music—caused by diminished white matter connectivity between auditory areas and NAcc (Sachs et al., 2016). Lending further support to the idea that reward structures causally generate hedonic values, Loui and colleagues have shown that individual variability in connectivity between auditory cortex and the reward circuit also predicts individual differences in experience of musical pleasure in nonanhedonic subjects (Loui et al., 2017), suggesting that perceptual representations of stimuli must gain access to the reward circuit for the brain to be able to attach a hedonic value to it.

Hedonic hotspots

Does the reward circuit contain nuclei specialized for the generation of positive and negative hedonic values? Kent Berridge and his group have found that the mesocorticolimbic reward system in animals does indeed contain anatomically distinct regions that specifically generate pleasure—what he has dubbed hedonic *hotspots* (Berridge, 2018; Peciña, Smith, & Berridge, 2006; Smith et al., 2010). These neural populations can amplify liking reactions to sensory stimuli when they are selectively stimulated, for instance through microinjections of opioid agonists. Hedonic hotspots appears to be quite small—around 1 mm^3 in rats—and have been experimentally demonstrated to exist in structures such as NAcc, ventral pallidum, OFC, and the insula (Berridge, 2018; Smith et al., 2010). According to Berridge, hotspots in this distributed network act together so that stimulating one hotspot will recruit the others as well. He has suggested that "unanimous activation of multiple hotspots together appears required in order to amplify sensory pleasures" (Berridge, 2018, p. 10)—a hypothesis that conforms well to the observation that focal lesions to reward structures rarely extinguish the ability to generate hedonic values.

Work by Berridge and others also suggests that, in addition to hotspots for amplification of pleasure, the reward circuit also contains *coldspots* for generating displeasure or disgust (e.g., Berridge, 2018; Castro, Terry, & Berridge, 2016), as well as larger areas of tissue that enhance the motivational salience of a sensory object, leading to what Berridge calls increased *wanting* (Berridge, 2018; Berridge, Robinson, & Aldridge, 2009).

In humans, it is presently less clear which specific anatomical parts might subserve hotspots, coldspots, and wanting. As noted, neuroimaging studies indicate that a diffuse network of structures exhibits elevated activity for positive hedonic values (Table 7.1). They might all contain hotspots and coldspots akin to those found in animal models. In an early meta-analysis Morten Kringelbach observed that neural correlates for positive hedonic values coalesce around the medial parts of OFC, while neural correlates for negative hedonic values appear centered on lateral parts (Kringelbach, 2005; Kühn & Gallinat, 2012; Sescousse et al., 2013). Enhanced activity for positive hedonic values is also seen in striatum, especially its ventral parts (Kühn & Gallinat, 2012; Sescousse et al., 2013; Wang, Smith, & Delgado, 2016), and anteroventral parts of the insula (Brown et al., 2011; Sescousse et al., 2013). Meanwhile, apart from lateral OFC, negative hedonic values have been associated with activation of NAcc, amygdala, and the insula (Calder et al., 2007). Thus, as also suggested by animal research, sensory valuation in all likelihood recruits a complex network of nuclei in the reward circuit, with both positive and negative values—as hypothesized by Berridge—relying on the coordinated co-activation of multiple parts to be generated and implemented.

Reward prediction and outcome

A possible functional dissociation exists between value signals involved in *predicting* a future reward and value signals that integrate all available information to compute the subjective experience of reward—the reward *outcome*. Experimental evidence from human neuroimaging has specifically implicated ventral striatum in the computation of expected value signals (e.g., Knutson et al., 2001, 2005; Knutson & Greer, 2008; O'Doherty et al., 2002). This finding accords with the electrophysiological observation by Wolfram Schultz and others that a subset of neurons in central striatum fire when an animal is presented with a stimulus that predicts an upcoming reward, but not during the actual experience of the reward (Schultz 2016; Schultz et al., 1992). The functional purpose of these value signals is to trigger Berridge's "wanting," a state of *incentive salience* where stimuli assumed to be rewarding become more attention-grabbing and elicit approach behavior (Berridge, 2018; Berridge, Robinson, & Aldridge, 2009). As we have seen, value predictions not only motivate the organism to *want* a specific part of its surroundings (by predicting it will be rewarding), but also bias perception toward salient features, and modulate neural activity in perceptual and cognitive systems. Intriguingly, observed activity in ventral striatum better predicts the future *aggregate* behavior of a cohort than other value signals (Knutson & Genevsky, 2018).

In contrast, neural processes that integrate information from predictive value signals with other perceptual and cognitive sources of contextual information to form a subjective hedonic value appear to be associated with activity in ventromedial PFC, especially OFC. This makes some sense since, as we have seen, this part of the reward system seems important for integrating hedonic values with decision making (Padoa-Schioppa, 2011; Rushworth, Mars, & Summerfield, 2009), and also happens to receive projections from a wide range of neural structures (Haber & Knutson, 2010).

Factors Modulating Hedonic Valuation

The research reviewed so far makes clear that hedonic values are computed and generated by neural populations distributed across the mesocorticolimbic reward circuit. For a stimulus to be liked in a certain way, either acquiring a pleasurable or an unpleasurable gloss, it must reach and engage these nuclei. However, if we want to understand *why* this happens we also have to discuss the neurobiological factors that influence information transfer from perceptual-cognitive systems to the reward system, and the way processes here respond to this influx.

Factors modulating the representation of sensory objects

Since the purpose of sensory valuation is to imbue stimuli with affective import, motivating behavior, one might think that evolution would dictate iron-clad connections between specific perceptual states and reward structures, such that percepts important to survival would automatically trigger the required positive or hedonic responses. While we do find that certain stimuli have a propensity for activating either positive or negative hedonic values—sweet molecules or symmetrical faces positive values; bitter molecules or dissonant music negative values (e.g., Brattico & Pearce, 2013; Drewnowski, 1997; Peng et al., 2015; Schwartz, Howe, & Purves, 2003)—in reality no sensory stimulus produces uniform hedonic responses. Rather, empirical evidence finds that sensory valuation events are characterized by great *variance*, even for stimuli that are of great importance to homeostatic needs. Indeed, in humans it is very common for some people to like objects that should be distasteful or disgusting, by dint of their homeostatic qualities, such as fermented food items like cheese (Herz, 2018).

In aesthetics we use the notion *aesthetic sensitivity* to describe this variance in liking responses. People vary greatly in how sensitive they are to a given stimulus property when assessing its hedonic value (Corradi et al., 2020). For example, while some people enjoy cheese, others are disgusted by the mere smell or sight of it. This difference in liking is caused by a difference in reward activity as a response to the same stimulus (Royet et al., 2016). The question is why aesthetic sensitivity is the rule and not the anomaly.

One answer is found in individual differences in how brains represent stimuli and project information about them to the reward circuit. These differences likely occur at any functional node in the processing system. For instance, for genetic reasons people vary in how many bitter receptors their mouths contain, leading to a marked difference in how they respond to bitter fluids such as beer (Herz, 2018), with so-called super-tasters experiencing enhanced negative hedonic values for bitter molecules (Macht & Mueller, 2007). Similarly, Sherman, Grabowecky, and Suzuki (2015) found that a variance in working memory ability influences how images differing in complexity are appreciated, with subjects with high working memory capacity liking highly complex images more than subjects with low working memory capacity. But not only computational nodes are subject to individual variance. I have already mentioned how differences in white matter pathways between auditory cortex and ventral striatum explain variance in liking (Loui et al., 2017), suggesting the way the brain is able to transfer information also influences how hedonic valuation is modulated.

Aesthetic science is still far from being able to explain differences in aesthetic sensitivity as a function of individual structural and functional differences. It is well known that experience strongly changes both functional activity, and axonal connections between nuclei involved in the representation of sensory objects, and that these changes modulate liking responses (e.g., Calvo-Merino et al., 2008; Cross et al., 2011; Kirk et al., 2009b; Kirsch, Drommelschmidt, & Cross, 2013). While it can be surmised that experiental plasticity affects both the perceptual-cognitive system's ability to represent a stimulus and its expectations for it, as well as signaling pathways linking parts of the system, our understanding of what form these modifications take remains extremely superficial.

Factors modulating regulatory concerns

Apart from factors intrinsic to the representation of stimulus, and how it is relayed to the reward circuit, hedonic valuation is also influenced by what we can call *regulatory factors*. These are factors that reflect the regulatory context of an aesthetic appreciation event, that is to say circumstances that relate to the *use* of the hedonic value in guiding behavior. They are, as a rule, object-extrinsic, signaling information about the homeostatic state, knowledge about the object, its availability, and reward probability, which are important for assessing the object's precise impact on individual regulatory situations. Together, they modulate hedonic valuation to yield liking responses for stimuli that suit contextual demands.

We can distinguish between at least two categories of regulatory factors (Figure 7.7): (1) *Endogenous* factors that signal information about the body's physiological state to neurons in the brainstem, hypothalamus, and striatum. And (2) *executive* factors that project information related to decision making and control of behavior to parts of the reward circuitry, especially ventromedial prefrontal structures. These factors reflect behavioral goals and task demands inherent to the regulatory situation. Both types of factors modulate reward activity, amplifying how pleasant or unpleasant the stimulus is experienced to be.

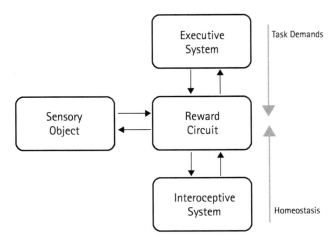

FIGURE 7.7. According to recent evidence, hedonic values for sensory inputs are computed by nuclei in the reward circuit. Value computations are, however, strongly modulated by inputs from interoceptive and executive systems, reflecting on-going contextual task demands and the homeostatic state of the organism.

I have already mentioned how imaging studies reveal that neurons associated with value assessment are strongly modulated by *satiation* (Kringelbach et al., 2003; Small et al., 2001). As noted, the reason for this is that the purpose of hedonic values is to motivate the organism to engage in optimal behavioral acts that help maintain homeostatic goal states. When hungry, an organism should put a premium on acquiring nutritious food stuff; when sated, it should value food stuff, no longer relevant, as less rewarding. To calibrate hedonic values in this way, the reward system integrates satiation level, as one parameter reflecting homeostatic state, into neural activity in structures such as nucleus accumbens, pallidum, or OFC (e.g., Führer, Zysset, & Stumvoll, 2008; Katsuura, Heckmann, & Taha, 2011; Siep et al., 2009; Thomas et al., 2015). Importantly, satiation has been demonstrated to not only modulate hedonic valuation for sensory objects with a direct impact on metabolism, but also for economic (de Ridder et al., 2014; Symmonds et al., 2010) and social (Damjanovic, Wilkinson, & Lloyd, 2018; Meier et al., 2012) objects, suggesting homeostatic state changes affect sensory valuation in a general manner.

Another example of an endogenous factor that influences reward activity, modulating hedonic valuation, is fluctuating hormone levels as a result of estrus. During the follicular phase, between the onset of menstruation and ovulation, estrogen rises while progesterone remains low. Then, after ovulation, progesterone levels sharply rise, until, at the end of the luteal phase, both estrogen and progesterone fall (Sakai & Mather, 2012; Roney, 2018). Studies in the female rat suggest that estrogen exhibits a dopamine-agonistic effect, increasing dopamine projections to the reward circuit during the follicular phase. As a consequence, reward sensitivity and motivation appear to increase (Diekhof, 2018; Yoest, Cummings, & Becker, 2014). In contrast, studies indicate that progesterone decreases reactions to rewards (Sakai & Mather, 2012).

Human research has found that changes in ovarian hormone levels also influence aspects of hedonic valuation in women, although it remains unclear what the effects of estrogen and progesterone on reward activity precisely are. Neuroimaging has shown activity in parts of the reward circuit to vary with women's menstrual cycle (Caldú & Dreher, 2009; Yoest, Quigley, & Becker, 2018), influencing hedonic valuation for various objects (Dreher et al., 2007; Frank et al., 2010; Ossewaarde et al., 2010; Rupp et al., 2009). An influential hypothesis has suggested that an increase in estrogen levels, signaling fertility, specifically promotes liking for masculinized male traits (Little, Jones, & DeBruine 2011). However, empirical evidence for this hypothesis has been inconclusive, and it is currently thought that estrus instead regulates women's general motivation for sexual rewards (Jones et al., 2018a, 2018b; Jones, Hahn, & DeBruine, 2019).

Turning to executive factors, the brain constructs cognitive models of reward contingencies that are used to guide behavior (O'Doherty, Cockburn, & Pauli, 2017; Padoa-Schioppa, 2011). These models influence how *risky* rewards and punishments are thought to be—i.e, how likely an object is to elicit a reward or a punishment (Rangel, Camerer, & Montague, 2008)—*when*, if at all, an object will yield a reward (Pessiglione & Delgado, 2015), or how pleasurable or unpleasant it will be. Such models affect the organism's expectations of how valuable a stimulus is going to be through top-down projections from anterior structures to nodes in the reward circuit. For example, what an organism thinks it knows about a sensory object influences its computational expectations for it. This can be demonstrated experimentally by presenting an experimental subject with information about a sensory object *before* it is perceived and valuated (Okamoto & Dan, 2013). In such framing studies semantic labels, names, titles, or other forms of information will exert a powerful influence on how the object is valuated (Fernqvist & Ekelund, 2014; Krishna, 2012; Okamoto & Dan, 2013; Piqueras-Fiszman & Spence, 2018), modulating activity in several parts of the reward circuit occurring during hedonic valuation (Kirk et al., 2009a; McClure et al., 2004; Plassmann, O'Doherty, Shiv, & Rangel, 2008). Intriguingly, people who are less susceptible to the framing effect have been shown to exhibit increased regulatory activity in the executive network, including dorsolateral prefrontal cortex (Aydogan et al., 2018; Schmidt et al., 2017).

Expectations set by cognitive models may play an especially important part in the assessment of temporally unfolding sensory objects. Musical objects, for instance, rely on the unfolding of temporal structures where the listener continuously predicts what must follow at a given time point (Koelsch, Vuust, & Friston, 2019). Such predictions take their departure from learned models about relations among tones, pitch, and other auditory elements, such as the probable progression of elements in a given harmonic system (Brattico & Pearce, 2013). Imaging research by Salimpoor and others has shown that confirmation of such expectations elicits activity in both striatum and OFC, prompting intense pleasurable responses (Salimpoor et al., 2011, 2013).

Cognitive models also influence processes involved in decision making, affecting hedonic valuation in the process. Evidence suggests that sensory objects are valuated differently when they are explicitly assessed as part of a behavioral choice, compared with when hedonic valuation unfolds implicitly (Chatterjee et al., 2009; Kim et al., 2007). For example, if people are asked to choose between two equally attractive objects, the mere act of choosing will often elevate liking for the chosen object (Ariely & Norton, 2008; Nakamura & Kawabata, 2013), a change in liking mirrored by changes to neural activity in the striatum and ACC (Izuma et al., 2010; Sharot, De Martino, & Dolan, 2009). Contrasting activation in reward structures during explicit and implicit valuation conditions—for instance reporting how likable an object is vs. reporting how round it is—reveals that activity unfolds differently, with more nodes in the ventromedial prefrontal cortex being recruited during explicit valuation events (Chatterjee et al., 2009; Jacobsen et al., 2006). A possible explanation for this difference could be the recruitment of integrative, executive processes when an object's hedonic value is being actively matched to cognitive models.

Hedonic Valuation and the "Aesthetic"

Understanding liking is an important problem in biology. All animals have to make decisions about which parts of the physical world to interact with, and which to avoid. They have to identify sources of energy and nourishment, whom to reproduce with, and which physical entities might be dangerous to come into contact with. One of the solutions to this problem devised by evolution is an affective system for assigning hedonic values to perceived stimuli, tagging sensory objects in the surrounding world with either a pleasurable or unpleasant emotional response that influences behavioral decision making.

Neuroscience has made great strides in charting the neurobiological mechanisms that constitute this system. Experiments in both animal models and humans convincingly show that a network of neural populations located in the mesocorticolimbic reward circuit compute and generate hedonic values for sensory input. What is less well known is under what conditions, and according to what rules, a specific stimulus becomes liked or disliked in varying circumstances. Evidence suggests that a number of factors modulate how a stimulus becomes represented and responded to by processes in the reward system, during hedonic valuation events. Crucially, a number of these factors reflect conditions that embed the unfolding hedonic valuation event within the organism's current homeostatic and behavioral context.

Liking paints the *Umwelt* an organism inhabits in a positive and negative glow. Importantly, because organisms differ in their adaptive needs, and occupy different ecological niches, hedonic valuation varies from species to species. Yet, comparative research suggests that valuation mechanisms are built on the same neurobiological principles, recycling a limited set of anatomical regions and neurochemical processes. The implication of this is that what we in humans call aesthetic appreciation must be yet another manifestation of this basic neurobiological system. The research I have reviewed in this chapter, including neuroimaging experiments demonstrating overlapping activity in the reward circuit for primary reinforcers and art, supports this conclusion.

Still, the notion of aesthetic appreciation is historically associated with a number of conceptual assumptions that cast "human" aesthetic appreciation as radically different from "animal" sensory valuation (Skov, 2019; Skov & Nadal, 2018, 2021). As C.W. Valentine famously quipped, "We should hardly call the pleasurable sensation due to a satisfying meal 'beautiful'" (Valentine, 1962, p. 9). It is worth examining the arguments for and against human hedonic valuation being distinct from animal hedonic valuation.

I should preface this discussion by making a point about the use of the word "aesthetic." While aesthetics was first used by Baumgarten and others to describe a general science of sensory evaluation (Åhlberg, 2003; Skov, 2019), it has never acquired a commonly accepted, precise meaning. In empirical aesthetics aesthetic appreciation in some circumstances refers broadly to the assessment of liking, in the vein also described here, but in others it is used to specifically signify the evaluation, by humans, of sensory qualities possessed by art objects. In the latter sense aesthetic appreciation evaluates not just liking, but also qualities as diverse as being moved, fascinated, awe-inspired, or shocked (Carbon, 2018; Menninghaus et al., 2019; Pelowski et al., 2017), psychological states that involve different neural mechanisms than the ones described in this chapter. I suppose it is a matter of semantic fiat if you prefer the former or the latter definition, but unfortunately they are often run together, conflating liking as a general phenomenon with ideas about art as a source of special experiental qualities that are unique to humans (Skov & Nadal, 2018, 2021). This conflation of liking and art appreciation has associated the concept of *aesthetic* appreciation with a number of tacit assumptions over the years: that artworks may elicit hedonic values that are different from "basic" pleasures, such as beauty, or that aesthetic appreciation in humans is "disinterested," an end to itself, whereas hedonic valuation in animals is always instrumental.

Here, I will focus on three questions that accept as fact that humans assess their liking for sensory objects using the same core neurobiological system as other animals, employing similar neurochemical processes located in the mesocorticolimbic reward circuit to generate pleasure and unpleasure/disgust for both primary reinforcers and complex cultural objects such as art. The three questions ask if human hedonic valuation, even if firmly rooted in homologous neural processes, may have acquired certain novel traits during hominin evolution that infuse human aesthetic appreciation with a set of exclusive functions. The first question is concerned with the degree to which animal and human sensory valuation overlap in terms of neurobiological processing. The second question asks if any evidence suggests that sensory pleasure is different in humans than in other animals. And the third asks if we have grounds to believe that the "disinterestedness" hypothesis is true, that aesthetic appreciation can occur for certain objects, without eliciting instrumental behavior.

The first question is really too extensive to do justice in a brief discussion, and deserves to be treated separately at some point. However, as the experimental evidence reviewed in this chapter makes clear there are ample reasons to think that sensory valuation in humans employs the same neural system as animal models when assessing how sensory objects are liked. Neuroimaging show activity in core corticolimbic structures during hedonic valuation, even for cultural objects. Manipulating elemental neurochemical processes in these structures, for instance by disrupting opioid signaling, changes liking responses, including for music and facial attractiveness. Moreover, human sensory valuation obeys similar computational principles as found in other animals, including a distinction between prediction and outcome signals, a neural dissociation between wanting and liking, and a fundamental intersection with behavioral decision making. On the other hand, some studies have found intriguing differences in how primary reinforcers and cultural objects are represented by the reward circuit. For instance, Morten Kringelbach, in a review of OFC activity associated with hedonic valuation, found "abstract" rewards—such as elicited by monetary gains and losses—to engage more anterior parts of the OFC than primary reinforcers such as food or fluids (Kringelbach, 2005). Similarly, Anjan Chatterjee and colleagues observed both overlapping and different activation patterns in OFC during hedonic valuation of face and places (Pegors et al., 2015). It remains unclear, though, what such regional differences in activity for different stimulus categories actually mean. It is possible that, as *Homo sapiens* expanded the domains of sensory objects it needed to be able to assess, parts of the reward circuit became specialized for these stimuli. It is also possible that neural processes associated with hedonic values—for instance, projections to perceptual, cognitive, or executive systems—activate different processes in the reward system. At the moment, we don't know what the correct explanation is.

While the reward circuit in humans may have evolved new sub-processes to deal with an expanding repertoire of sensory objects, such "human" objects do not appear to engage it in a novel functional way. Money, art, or artifacts all elicit reward predictions, motivating behavior. Hedonic valuation for such objects is susceptible to the same contextual factors that also drive valuation in animals, including risk assessment, temporal availability, and framing. Critically, hedonic values generated by primary reinforcers and cultural objects "interfere" with each other, suggesting a common base. For example, in a clever experiment by Chumbley, Tobler, and Fehr, male subjects learned to associate visual cues with sexual rewards (pictures of women in bikinis). Months later, they were asked to participate in an economic experiment, where the same cues were used to now signal upcoming monetary rewards. Astonishingly, the subjects exhibited a propensity to choose cues they had previously seen associated with high erotic rewards, even when in the new experiment these would lead to smaller economic gains (Chumbley, Tobler, & Fehr, 2014).

The ability of pleasure generated by hedonic valuation for art, design, music, money, or artifacts to affect pleasures generated by more "basic" biological objects implies that the human brain has coopted affective processes evolved to signal liking for the latter in order to compute liking for the former. Still, debate continues as to whether or not humans experience other, unique kinds of hedonic values, separating, say, beauty from pleasure (Brielmann & Pelli, 2018). In an fMRI study Ishizu and Zeki sought to identify the neural correlates of a possible beauty "faculty" by contrasting self-reported states of beauty for music and visual art with self-reported states of ugliness and indifference (Ishizu & Zeki, 2011). However, the region they found to correlate with beauty, located in the medial OFC, is routinely found to be activated by other pleasurable objects, casting into doubt whether their finding supports conceiving of beauty as a distinct affective state. Indeed, to the best of my knowledge no theory exists that has tried to describe, in terms of physiology, neural correlates, or neurobiological function, how beauty contrasts with pleasure. It may still turn out to have a distinct hedonic nature, but we need clear evidence in order to understand it as such.

The third question of relevance to our understanding of aesthetic appreciation as a possible idiosyncratic human version of sensory valuation is not related to putative distinct affective reactions to cultural objects, or special hedonic emotions, but to its role in regulating behavior. As I have described the neurobiological mechanism of sensory valuation in this chapter, its function can only be understood in light of the regulatory purpose it serves. The way hedonic values are computed and generated as a function of homeostatic needs and behavioral task demands only makes sense if we view hedonic values as affective tags that assign an instrumental relevance to perceived objects within a regulatory context. However, in the tradition of empirical aesthetics aesthetic appreciation is often seen as disinterested, no doubt fueled by the modern experience of art for "its own sake"—going to concerts, attending exhibitions, etc. What disinterestedness translates into with respect to a neurobiological theory of sensory valuation is more unclear, though. Julia Christensen has written a paper where she suggests that art pleasures are different from nonart pleasures by dint of being able to elicit more fulfilling hedonic values, without states of craving (Christensen, 2018). Anjan Chatterjee has floated the idea the arts might possibly engage the reward circuit's liking system without engaging its wanting system, thus eliminating impact on motivated behavior (Chatterjee, 2014; Chatterjee & Vartanian, 2016). Both of these hypotheses could find support in the future, but as of now no evidence exists that make them likely to be true (Nadal & Skov, 2018). Indeed, as I have shown, there is copious empirical evidence that suggests hedonic values for cultural objects—including art—do in fact engage processes associated with wanting and instrumental behavior: reward prediction, incentive salience, biasing of decision making, and reinforcement learning.

Characterizing sensory valuation in humans is an ongoing effort, and identifying unique facets to the neurobiological machinery that might have evolved in recent evolutionary history remains an important task. Yet, even though we are likely to find a number of distinctive traits, the general computational principles guiding hedonic valuation and liking responses appear not significantly different in humans. This suggests that important lessons about the mechanism of sensory valuation can be learned by pooling research in different disciplines, investigating different forms of aesthetic appreciation, and linking human research with studies conducted on animal models.

Conclusions

The body of work presented here hopefully will work as a first introduction to the neurobiology of sensory valuation. My aim has been to describe the neurobiological processes involved in hedonic valuation computations, and discuss some of the functional principles that influence the way individual stimuli acquire a specific hedonic value in particular contexts. I have put a special premium on emphasizing the regulatory role sensory valuation plays in biological organisms' quest for survival. We are endowed with a capacity for liking and disliking sensory objects because this ability helps us navigate the natural world, engaging with things that contribute to our homeostatic well-being, and avoiding things that imperil it. This neurobiological account of liking suggests that research into aesthetic appreciation should not study how pleasing objects with different features are in isolation, but how sensory objects acquire a hedonic value within the context of this regulatory framework.

References

Aharon, I., Etcoff, N., Ariely, D. Chabris, C. F., O'Connor, E., & Breiter, H. C. (2001). Beautiful faces have variable reward value. *Neuron, 32*, 537–551.

Åhlberg, L.-O. (2003). The invention of modern aesthetics: From Leibniz to Kant. *Historicni Seminar, 4*, 133–153.

Alba, J. W., & Williams, E. F. (2013). Pleasure principles: A review of research on hedonic consumption. *Journal of Consumer Psychology, 23*, 2–18.

Andersson, M., & Simmons, L. W. (2006). Sexual selection and mate choice. *Trends in Ecology and Evolution, 21*, 296–302.

Ariely, D., & Norton, M. I. (2008). How actions create—not just reveal—preferences. *Trends in Cognitive Sciences, 12*, 13–16.

Aydogan, G., Flaig, N., Ravi, S. N., Large, E. W., McClure, S. M., & Margulis, E. H. (2018). Overcoming bias: Cognitive control reduces susceptibility to framing effects in evaluating musical performance. *Scientific Report, 8*, 6229.

Bartra, O., McGuire, J. T., & Kable, J. W. (2013). The valuation system: A coordinate-based meta-analysis of BOLD fMRI experiments examining neural correlates of subjective value. *Neuroimage, 76*, 412–427.

Baruni, J. K., Lau, B., & Salzman, C. D. (2015). Reward expectation differentially modulates attentional behavior and activity in visual area V4. *Nature Neuroscience, 18*, 1656–1663.

Bechara, A., & Damasio, A. R. (2005). The somatic marker hypothesis: A neural theory of economic decision. *Games and Economic Behavior, 52*, 336–372.

Berns, G. S., & Moore, S. E. (2012). A neural predictor of cultural popularity. *Journal of Consumer Psychology, 22*, 154–160.

Berridge, K. C. (2004). Motivational concepts in behavioral neuroscience. *Physiology & Behavior, 81*, 179–209.

Berridge, K. C. (2018). Evolving concepts of emotion and motivation. *Frontiers in Psychology, 9*, 1647.

Berridge, K. C., & Kringelbach, M. L. (2015). Pleasure systems in the brain. *Neuron, 86*, 646–664.

Berridge, K. C., Robinson, T. E., & Aldridge, J. W. (2009). Dissecting components of reward: "Liking," "wanting," and learning. *Current Opinion in Pharmacology, 9*, 65–73.

Blair, K., Marsh, A. A., Morton, J., Vythilingam, M., Jones, M., Mondillo, K., ... Blair, J. R. (2006). Choosing the lesser of two evils, the better of two goods. *Journal of Neuroscience*, 26, 11379–11386.

Blood, A. J., & Zatorre, R. J. (2001). Intensely pleasurable responses to music correlate with activity in brain regions implicated in reward and emotion. *Proceedings of the National Academy of Sciences*, 98, 11818–11823.

Blood, A. J., Zatorre, R. J., Bermudez, P., & Evans, A. C. (1999). Emotional responses to pleasant and unpleasant music correlate with activity in paralimbic brain regions. *Nature Neuroscience*, 2, 382–387.

Boksem, M. A. S., & Smidts, A. (2015). Brain responses to movie trailer predict individual preferences for movies and their population-wide commercial success. *Journal of Marketing Research*, 52, 482–492.

Brattico, E, Jacobsen, T., De Baene, W., Nakai, N., & Tervaniemi, M. (2003). Electrical brain responses versus evaluative judgments of music. *Annals of the New York Academy of Sciences*, 999, 155–157.

Bradley, M. M. (2000). Emotion and motivation. In J. T. Caioppo, L. G. Tassinary, & G. G. Berntson (Eds.), *Handbook of psychophysiology* (pp. 581–607), 2nd ed. Cambridge, MA: Cambridge University Press.

Brattico, E., & Pearce, M. (2013). The neuroaesthetics of music. *Psychology of Aesthetics, Creativity, and the Arts*, 7, 48–61.

Brielmann, A. A., & Pelli, D. G. (2018). Aesthetics. *Current Biology*, R8, R859–R863.

Brown, S., Gao, X., Tisdelle, L., Eickhoff, S. B., & Liotti, M. (2011). Naturalizing aesthetics: Brain areas for aesthetic appraisal across sensory modalities. *Neuroimage*, 58, 250–258.

Buchel, C., Miedl, S., & Sprenger, C. (2018). Hedonic processing in humans is mediated by an opioidergic mechanism in a mesocorticolimbic system. *eLIFE*, 7, e39648.

Bzdok, D., Langner, R., Caspers, S., Kurth, F., Habel, U., Zilles, K., ... Eickhoff, S. B. (2010). ALE meta-analysis on facial judgments of trustworthiness and attractiveness. *Brain Structure and Function*, 215, 209–223.

Cabanac, M. (1979). Sensory pleasure. *The Quarterly Review of Biology*, 54, 1–28.

Calder, A. J., Beaver, J. D., Davis, M. H., van Ditzhuijzen, J., Keane, J., & Lawrence, A. D. (2007). Disgust sensitivity predicts the insula and pallidal response to pictures of disgusting food. *European Journal of Neuroscience*, 25, 3422–3428.

Caldú, X., & Dreher, J.-C. (2009). Gonadal steroid hormones' influence on decision making processes. In J.-C. Dreher, & L. Tremblay (Eds.), *Handbook of reward and decision making* (pp. 309–334). Amsterdam: Academic Press.

Calhoun, A. J., & Hayden, B. Y. (2015). The foraging brain. *Current Opinion in Behavioral Sciences*, 5, 24–31.

Calvo-Merino, B., Jola, C., Glaser, D. E., & Haggard, P. (2008). Towards a sensorimotor aesthetics of performing art. *Consciousness and Cognition*, 17, 911–922.

Calvo-Merino, B. Urgesi, C., Orgs, G., Aglioti, S. M., & Haggard, P. (2010). Extrastriate body area underlies aesthetic evaluation of body stimuli. *Experimental Brain Research*, 204, 447–456.

Carbon, C.-C. (2018). Empirical aesthetics: In quest of a clear terminology and valid methodology. In Z. Kaouta et al. (Eds.), *Exploring transdisciplinarity in art and sciences* (pp. 107–119). Berlin: Springer.

Castro, D. C., Terry, R. A., & Berridge, K. C. (2016). Orexin in rostral hotspots of nucleus accumbens enhances sucrose "liking" and intake, but scopolamine in caudal shell shifts "liking" toward "disgust" and "fear." *Neuropsychopharmacology, XX*, 1–11.

Cela-Conde, C. J., Marty, G., Maestú, F., Ortiz, T., Munar, E., Fernández, A., ... Quesney, F. (2004). Activation of the prefrontal cortex in the human visual aesthetic perception. *Proceedings of the National Academy of Sciences of the United States of America, 101*, 6321–6325.

Chatterjee, A. (2014). Scientific aesthetics: Three steps forward. *British Journal of Psychology, 105*, 465–467.

Chatterjee, A., Thomas, A., Smith, S. E., & Aguirre, G. K. (2009). The neural response to facial attractiveness. *Neuropsychology, 23*, 135–143.

Chatterjee, A., & Vartanian, O. (2014). Neuroaesthetics. *Trends in Cognitive Sciences, 18*, 370–375.

Chatterjee, A., & Vartanian, O. (2016). Neuroscience of aesthetics. *Annals of the New York Academy of Sciences, 1369*, 172–194.

Chelnokova, O., Laeng, B., Eikemo, M., Riegels, J., Løseth, G., Maurud, H., ... Leknes, S. (2014). Rewards of beauty: The opioid system mediates social motivation in humans. *Molecular Psychiatry, 19*, 746–747.

Chen, W., Liu, C. H., & Nakabayashi, K. (2012) Beauty hinders attention switch in change detection: the role of facial attractiveness and distinctiveness. *PLoS One, 7*(2), e32897.

Christensen, J. F. (2018). Pleasure junkies all around! Why it matters and why "the arts" might be the answer: A biopsychological perspective. *Proceedings of the Royal Society of London B, 284*, 20162837.

Chumbley, J. R., Tobler, P. N., & Fehr, E. (2014). Fatal attraction: Ventral striatum predicts costly choice errors in humans. *Neuroimage, 89*, 1–9.

Clark, L., Bechara, A., Damasio, H., Aitken, M. R., Sahakian, B. J., & Robbins, T. W. (2008). Differential effects of insular and ventromedial prefrontal cortex lesions on risky decision-making. *Brain, 131*, 1311–1322.

Cooper, J. C., Dunne, S., Furey, T., & O'Doherty, J. (2012). Dorsomedial prefrontal cortex mediates rapid evaluations predicting the outcome of romantic interactions. *Journal of Neuroscience, 32*, 15647–15656.

Corradi, G., Chuquichambi, E. G., Barrada, J. R., Clemente, A. S., & Nadal, M. (2020). A new conception of aesthetic sensitivity. *British Journal of Psychology, 111*(4), 630–658.

Craig, D. G. (2005). An exploratory study of physiological changes during "chills" induced by music. *Musicae Scientae, 9*, 273–282.

Cross, E. S., Kirsch, L., Ticini, L. F., & Schütz-Bosbach, S. (2011). The impact of aesthetic evaluation and physical ability on dance perception. *Frontiers in Human Neuroscience, 5*, 102.

Damasio, A., & Carvalho, G. B. (2013). The nature of feelings: Evolutionary and neurobiological origins. *Nature Reviews Neuroscience, 14*, 143–152.

Damjanovic, L., Wilkinson, H., & Lloyd, J. (2018). Sweet emotion: The role of odor-induced context in the search advantage for happy facial expressions. *Chemical Senses, 43*, 139–150.

De Araujo, I. E., Kringelbach, M. L., & Rolls E. T. (2003). Taste–olfactory convergence, and the representation of the pleasantness of flavour, in the human brain. *European Journal of Neuroscience, 18*, 2374–2390.

De Martino, B., Camerer, C. F., & Adolphs, R. (2010). Amygdala damage eliminates monetary loss aversion. *Proceedings of the National Academy of Sciences, 107*, 3788–3792.

De Ridder, D., Kroese, F., Adriaanse, M., & Evers, C. (2014). Always gamble on an empty stomach: Hunger is associated with advantageous decision making. *PLoS One, 9*, e111081.

di Pellegrino, G., Margarelli, S., & Mengarelli, T. (2011). Food pleasantness affects visual selective attention. *Quarterly Journal of Experimental Psychology, 64*, 560–571.

Di Dio, C., Macaluso, E., & Rizzolatti, G. (2007). The golden beauty: Brain responses to classical and renaissance sculptures. *PLoS ONE, 2*, e1201.

Dickie, G. (1996). *A century of taste*. Oxford: Oxford University Press.

Dickinson, A., & Balleine, B. W. (2010). Hedonics: The cognitive–motivational interface. In M. L. Kringelbach, & K. C. Berridge (Eds.), *Pleasures of the brain* (pp. 74–84). Oxford: Oxford University Press.

Diekhof, E. K. (2018). Estradiol and the reward system in humans. *Current Opinion in Behavioral Sciences, 23*, 58–64.

Dreher, J. C., Schmidt, P. J., Kohn, P., Furman, D., Rubinow, D., & Berman, K. F. (2007). Menstrual cycle phase modulates reward-related neural function in women. *Proceedings of the National Academy of Sciences, 104*, 2465–2470.

Drewnowski, A. (1997). Taste preferences and food intake. *Annual Review of Nutrition, 17*, 237–253.

Eikemo, M., Løseth, G. E., Johnstone, T., Gjerstad, J., Willoch, F., & Leknes, S. (2016). Sweet taste pleasantness is modulated by morphine and naltrexone. *Psychopharmacology, 233*, 3711–3723.

Ellingsen, D.-M., Leknes, S., & Kringelbach, M. L. (2015). Hedonic value. In T. Brosch, & D. Sanders (Eds.), *Handbook of value: Perspectives from neuroscience, philosophy, psychology and sociology* (pp. 265–286). Oxford: Oxford University Press.

Fernqvist, F., & Ekelund, L. (2014). Credence and the effect on consumer liking on food—A review. *Food Quality and Preference, 32*, 340–353.

Forbes, C. E., & Graffman, J. (2010). The role of the human prefrontal cortex in social cognition and moral judgment. *Annual Review of Neuroscience, 33*, 299–324.

Frank, T. C., Kim, G. L., Krzemien, A., & Van Vugt, D. A. (2010). Effect of menstrual cycle phase on corticolimbic brain activation by visual food cues. *Brain Research, 1363*, 81–92.

Führer, D., Zysset, S., & Stumvoll, M. (2008). Brain activity in hunger and satiety: An exploratory visually stimulated fMRI study. *Obesity, 16*, 945–950.

Fuller, P., Sherman, D., Pedersen, N. P., Saper, C. B., & Lu, J. (2011). Reassessment of the structural basis of the ascending arousal system. *Journal of Comparative Neurology, 519*, 933–956.

Gangestad, S. W., & Scheyd, G. J. (2005). The evolution of human physical attractiveness. *Annual Review of Anthropology, 34*, 523–548.

Gavornik, J. P., Shuler, M. G., Loewenstein, K., Bear, M. F., & Shuval, H. Z. (2009). Learning reward timing in cortex through reward dependent expression of syntactic plasticity. *PNAS, 106*, 6826–6831.

Georgiadis, J. R., & Kringelbach, M. L. (2012). The human sexual response cycle: Brain imaging evidence linking sex to other pleasures. *Progress in Neurobiology, 98*, 49–81.

Goldstein, A. (1980). Thrills in response to music and other stimuli. *Physiological Psychology, 8*, 126–129.

Goltstein, P. M., Meijer, G. T., & Pennartz, C. M. (2018). Conditioning sharpens the spatial representation of rewarded stimuli in the mouse primary visual cortex. *eLife, 7*, e37683.

Gottfried, J. A., O'Doherty, J., & Dolan, R. J. (2003). Encoding predictive reward value in human amygdala and orbitofrontal cortex. *Science, 301*, 1104–1107.

Grabenhorst, F., & Rolls, E. T. (2011). Value, pleasure and choice in ventral prefrontal cortex. *Trends in Cognitive Sciences, 15*, 56–67.

Grueschow, M., Polania, R., Hare, T. A., & Ruff, C. C. (2015). Automatic versus choice-dependent value-representations in the human brain. *Neuron, 85*, 875–885.

Haber, S. N., & Knutson, B. (2010). The reward circuit: Linking primate anatomy and human imaging. *Neuropsychopharmacology, 35*, 4–26.

Hare, T. A., Camerer, C. F., & Rangel, A. (2009). Self-control in decision-making involved modulation of the vmPFC valuation system. *Science, 324*, 646–648.

Herz, R. (2018). *Why you eat what you eat.* New York & London: W.W. Norton.

Hikosaka, O., Nakamura, K., & Nakahara, H. (2006). Basal ganglia orient eyes to reward. *Journal of Neurophysiology, 95*, 567–584.

Hinton, E., Parkinson, J. A., Holland, A. J., Arana, F. S., Robert, A. C., & Owen, A. M. (2004). Neural contributions to the motivational control of appetite in humans. *European Journal of Neuroscience, 20*, 1411–1418.

Hsu, M., & Yoon, C. (2015). The neuroscience of consumer choice. *Current Opinion in Behavioral Sciences, 5*, 116–121.

Hung, S. M., Nieh, C. H., & Hsieh, P. J (2016). Unconscious processing of facial attractiveness: Invisible attractive faces orient visual attention. *Scientific Reports, 6*, 37117.

Ishizu, T., & Zeki, S. (2011). Toward a brain-based theory of beauty. *PLoS ONE, 6*, e21852.

Izuma, K., Matsumoto, M., Murayamab, K., Samejimaa, K., Sadatoc, N., & Matsumotoa, K. (2010). Neural correlates of cognitive dissonance and choice-induced preference change. *Proceedings of the National Academy of Sciences, 107*, 22014–22019.

Jacobsen, T., Schubotz, R. I., Höfel, L., & von Cramon, D. Y. (2006). Brain correlates of aesthetic judgment of beauty. *NeuroImage, 29*, 276–285.

Jänig, W. (2003). The autonomic nervous system and its coordination by the brain. In R. J. Davidson, K. R. Scherer, & H. H. Goldsmith (Eds.), *Handbook of affective sciences* (pp. 135–186). Oxford: Oxford University Press.

Jones, B. C., Hahn, A. C., & DeBruine, L. M. (2019). Ovulation, sex hormones, and women's mating psychology. *Trends in Cognitive Sciences, 23*, 51–62.

Jones, B. C., Hahn, A. C., Fisher, C. I., Wang, H., Kandrik, M., & DeBruine, L. M. (2018b). General sexual desire, but not desire for uncommitted sexual relationships, tracks changes in women's hormonal status. *Psychoendocrinology, 88*, 153–157.

Jones, B. C., Hahn, A. C., Fisher, C. I., Wang, H., Kandrik, M., Han, C.-Y., … DeBruine, L. M. (2018a). No compelling evidence that preferences for facial masculinity track changes in women's hormonal status. *Psychological Science, 29*, 996–1005.

Katsuura, Y., Heckmann, J. A., & Taha, S. A. (2011) μ-Opioid receptor stimulation in nucleus accumbens elevates fatty tastant intake by increasing palatability and suppressing satiety signals. *American Journal of Physiology, 301*, R244–R254.

Kawabata, H., & Zeki, S. (2004). Neural correlates of beauty. *Journal of Neurophysiology, 91*, 1699–1705.

Kim, H., Adolphs, R., O'Doherty, J. P., & Shimojo, S. (2007). Temporal isolation of neural processes underlying face preference decisions. *Proceedings of the National Academy of Sciences, 104*, 18253–18258.

Kirk, U., Skov, M., Christensen, M. S., & Nygaard, M. S. (2009b). Brain correlates of aesthetic experience: A parametric fMRI study. *Brain & Cognition, 69*, 306–315.

Kirk, U., Skov, M., Hulme, O., Christensen, M. S., & Zeki, S. (2009a). Modulation of aesthetic value by semantic context: An fMRI study. *Neuroimage, 44*, 1125–1132.

Kirsch, L. P., Drommelschmidt, C., & Cross, E. S. (2013). Shaping and reshaping the aesthetic brain: Emerging perspectives on the neurobiology of embodies aesthetics. *Neuroscience and Biobehavioral Reviews, 62,* 56–68.

Kivy, P. (2003): *The seventh sense,* 2nd ed. Oxford: Clarendon Press.

Knutson, B., Adams, C. M., Fong, G. W., & Hommer, D. (2001). Anticipation of increasing monetary reward selectivity recruits nucleus accumbens. *Journal of Neuroscience, 21,* RC159.

Knutson, B., & Genevsky, A. (2018). Neuroforecasting aggregate choice. *Current Directions in Psychological Science, 27,* 110–115.

Knutson, B., & Greer, S. M. (2008). Anticipatory affect: Neural correlates and consequences for choice. *Philosophical Transactions of the Royal Society B, 363,* 3771–3786.

Knutson, B., Rick, S., Wimmer, G. E., Prelec, D., & Loewenstein, G. (2007). Neural predictors of purchases. *Neuron, 53,* 147–156.

Knutson, B., Taylor, J, Kaufman, M., Peterson, R., & Glover, G. (2005). Distributed neural representation of expected value. *Journal of Neuroscience, 25,* 4806–4812.

Koechlin, E. (2016). Prefrontal executive function and adaptive behavior in complex environments. *Current Opinion in Neurobiology, 37,* 1–6.

Koelsch, S., Vuust, P., & Friston, K. (2019). Predictive processes and the peculiar case of music. *Trends in Cognitive Sciences, 23,* P63–P77.

Krajbich, I., & Dean, M. (2015). How can neuroscience inform economics? *Current Opinion in Behavioral Sciences, 5,* 51–57.

Kringelbach, M. L. (2005). The human orbitofrontal cortex: Linking reward to the hedonic experience. *Nature Reviews Neuroscience, 6,* 691–702.

Kringelbach, M. L., & Berridge, K. C. (2017). The affective core of emotion: Linking pleasure, subjective well-being, and optimal metastability in the brain. *Emotion Review, 9,* 191–199.

Kringelbach, M. L., O'Doherty, J., Rolls, E. T., & Andrews, C. (2003). Activation of the human orbitofrontal cortex to a liquid food stimulus is correlated with subjective pleasantness. *Cerebral Cortex, 13,* 1064–1071.

Krishna, A. (2012). An integrative review of sensory marketing: Engaging the senses to affect perception, judgment, and behavior. *Journal of Consumer Psychology, 22,* 332–351.

Kühn, S., & Gallinat, J. (2012). The neural correlates of subjective pleasantness. *Neuroimage, 61,* 289–294.

Kuijper, B., Pen, I., & Weissing, F. J. (2012). A guide to sexual selection theory. *Annual Review of Ecology, Evolution, and Systematics, 41,* 287–311.

Levy, D. J., & Glimcher, P. W. (2012). The root of all value: A neural common currency for choice. *Current Opinion in Neurobiology, 22,* 1027–1038.

Li, J., Oksama, L., & Hyönä, J. (2016). How facial attractiveness affects sustained attention. *Scandinavian Journal of Psychology, 57,* 383–392.

Lieberman, D., Billingsley, K., & Patrick, C. (2018). Consumption, contact and copulation: How pathogens have shaped human psychological adaptations. *Philosophical Transactions of the Royal Society of London B, 373,* 20170203.

Little, A. C., Jones, B. C., & DeBruine, L. M. (2011). Facial attractiveness: Evolutionary based research. *Philosophical Transactions of the Royal Society of London B, 366,* 1638–1659.

Liu, C. H., & Chen, W. (2012). Beauty is better pursued: Effects of attractiveness in multiple-face tracking. *The Quarterly Journal of Experimental Psychology, 65,* 553–564.

Loseth, G. E., Ellingsen, D. M., & Leknes, S. (2014). State-dependent μ-opioid modulation of social motivation. *Frontiers in Behavioral Neuroscience, 8,* 430.

Loui, P., Patterson, S., Sachs, M. E., Leung, Y., Zeng, T., & Przysinda, E. (2017). White matter correlates of musical anhedonia: Implications for evolution of music. *Frontiers in Psychology*, 8, 1–10.

Macht, M., & Mueller, J. (2007). Increased negative emotional responses in PROP supertasters. *Physiology and Behavior*, 90, 466–472.

Mallik, A., Chanda, M. L., & Levitin, D. J. (2017). Anhedonia to music and mu-opioids: Evidence from the administration of naltrexone. *Scientific Reports*, 7, 41952.

Martín-Loeches, M, Hernández-Tamames, J. A., Martín, A., & Urrutia, M. (2014). Beauty and ugliness in the bodies and faces of others: An fMRI study of person esthetic judgement. *Neuroscience*, 277, 486–497.

Martínez-Molina, N., Mas-Herrero, E., Rodríguez-Fornells, A., Zatorre, R. J., & Marco-Pallares, J. (2016). Neural correlates of specific musical anhedonia. *Proceedings of the National Academy of Science*, 113, E7337–E7345.

Mas-Herrero, E., Karhulati, Marcos-Pallares, J., Zatorre, R. J., & Rodriguez-Fornells, A. (2018). The impact of visual art and emotional sounds in specific musical anhedonia. *Progress in Brain Research*, 237, 399–413.

Mas-Herrero, E., Zatorre, R. J., Rodriguez-Fornells, A., & Marco-Pallaes, J. (2014). Dissociation between musical and monetary reward responses in specific musical anhedonia. *Current Biology*, 24, 699–704.

McClure, S. M., Li, J., Tomlin, D., Cypert, K. S., Montague, L. M., & Montague, P. R. (2004). Neural correlates of behavioral preference for culturally familiar drinks. *Neuron*, 44, 379–387.

Meier, B. P., Moeller, S. K., Riemer-Pelz, M., & Robinson, M. D. (2012). Sweet taste preferences and experiences predict prosocial inferences, personalities and behaviors. *Journal of Personality and Social Psychology*, 102, 163–174.

Menninghaus, M., Wagner, V., Wassiliwizky, Schindler, I., Hanich, J., Jacobsen, T., & Koelsch, S. (2019). What are aesthetics emotions? *Psychological Review*, 126, 171–195.

Menon, V., & Levitin, D. J. (2005). The rewards of music listening: response and physiological connectivity of the mesolimbic system. *Neuroimage*, 28, 175–184.

Montague, P. R., & King-Casas, B. (2007). Efficient statistics, common currencies and the problem of reward-harvesting. *Trends in Cognitive Sciences*, 11, 514–519.

Nadal, M., & Skov, M. (2018). The pleasure of art as a matter of fact. *Proceedings of the Royal Society B: Biological Sciences*, 285, 20172252.

Nakamura, K., Arai, S., & Kawabata, H. (2018). Prioritized identification of attractive and romantic partner faces in rapid serial visual presentation. *Archives of Sexual Behavior*, 46, 2327–2338.

Nakamura, K., & Kawabata, H. (2013). I choose, therefore I like: Preference for faces induced by arbitrary choice. *PLoS ONE*, 8, e72071.

Nakamura, K., Kawashima, R., Nagumo, S., Ito, K., Sugiura, M., Kato, T., … Kojima, S. (1998). Neuroanatomical correlates of the assessment of facial attractiveness. *NeuroReport*, 9, 753–757.

Oaten, M., Stevsen, R. J., & Case, I. (2009). Disgust as disease-avoidance mechanism. *Psychological Bulletin*, 135, 303–321.

O'Doherty, J. P. (2014). The problem with value. *Neuroscience and Biobehavioral Reviews*, 43, 259–268.

O'Doherty, J. P., Cockburn, J., & Pauli, W. M. (2017). Learning, reward, and decision making. *Annual Review in Psychology*, 68, 73–100.

O'Doherty, J. P., Deichmann, R., Critchley, H. D., & Dolan, R. J. (2002). Neural responses during anticipation of a primary taste reward. *Neuron, 33*, 815–826.

O'Doherty, J. P., Kringelbach, M. L., Rolls, E. T., Hornak, J., & Andrews, C. (2001). Abstract reward and punishment representations in the human orbitofrontal cortex. *Nature Neuroscience, 4*, 95–102.

Okamoto, M., & Dan, I. (2013). Extrinsic information influence taste and flavor perception: A review from psychological and neuroimaging perspectives. *Seminars in Cell & Developmental Biology, 24*, 247–255.

Ossewaarde, L., van Wingen, G. A., Kooijman, S. C., Bäckström, T., Fernández, G., & Hermans, E. J. (2010). Changes in functioning of mesolimbic incentive processing circuits during the premenstrual phase. *Social Cognitive and Affective Neuroscience, 6*, 612–620.

Padoa-Schioppa, C. (2011). Neurobiology of economic choice: A good-based model. *Annual Review in Neuroscience, 34*, 333–359.

Padoa-Schioppa, C., & Assad, J. A. (2008). The representation of economic value in the orbitofrontal cortex is invariant for changes of menu. *Nature Neuroscience, 11*, 95–102.

Panksepp, J. (1998). *Affective neuroscience.* Oxford: Oxford University Press.

Peciña, S., Smith, K. S., & Berridge, K. C. (2006). Hedonic hot spots in the brain. *The Neuroscientist, 12*, 500–511.

Pegors, T. K., Kable, J. W., Chatterjee, A., & Epstein, R. A. (2015). Common and unique representations in pFC for face and place attractiveness. *Journal of Cognitive Neuroscience, 27*, 959–973.

Pelowski, M., Markey, P. S., Forster, M., Gerger, G., & Leder, H. (2017). Move me, astonish me ... delight my eyes and brain: The Vienna Integrated Model of top-down and bottom-up processes in Art Perception (VIMAP). *Physics of Life Reviews, 21*, 80–125.

Peng, Y., Gillis-Smith, S., Jin, H., Tränkner, D., Ryba, N. J., & Zuker, C. S. (2015). Sweet and bitter taste in the brain of awake behaving animals. *Nature, 527*, 512–515.

Pessiglione, M., & Delgado, M. R. (2015). The good, the bad and the brain: Neural correlates of appetitive and aversive values underlying decision making. *Current Opinion in Behavioral Sciences, 5*, 78–84.

Pessiglione, M., Schmidt, L., Draganski, B., Kalisch, R., Lau, H., Dolan, R., & Frith, C. (2007). How the brain translates money into force: A neuroimaging study of subliminal motivation. *Science, 316*, 904–906.

Peters, J., & Büchel, C. (2010). Neural representations of subjective reward value. *Behavioral and Brain Research, 213*, 135–141.

Piqueras-Fiszman, B., & Spence, C. (2018). Sensory expectations based on product-extrinsic food cues: An interdisciplinary review of the empirical evidence and theoretical accounts. *Food Quality and Preference, 40*, 165–179.

Plassmann, H., O'Doherty, J. P., & Rangel, A. (2010). Appetitive and aversive goal values are encoded in the medial orbitofrontal cortex at the time of decision making. *Journal of Neuroscience, 30*, 10799–10808.

Plassmann, H., O'Doherty, J., Shiv, B., & Rangel, A. (2008). Marketing actions can modulate neural representations of experienced pleasantness, *PNAS, 105*, 1050–1054.

Puts, D. (2015). Human sexual selection. *Current Opinion in Psychology, 7*, 28–32.

Ramsøy, T. Z., Friis-Olivarius, M., Jacobsen, C., Jensen, S. B., & Skov, M. (2012). Effects of perceptual uncertainty on arousal and preference across different visual domains. *Journal of Neuroscience, Psychology, and Economics, 5*, 212–226.

Ramsøy, T. Z., & Skov, M. (2014). Brand preference affects the threshold for perceptual awareness. *Journal of Consumer Behavior, 13*, 1–8.

Rangel, A., Camerer, C., & Montague, P. R. (2008). A framework for studying the neurobiology of value-based decision making. *Nature Reviews Neuroscience, 9*, 545–556.

Rhodes, G. (2006). The evolutionary psychology of facial beauty. *Annual Review of Psychology, 57*, 199–226.

Rolls, E. T. (2016). Reward systems in the brain and nutrition. *Annual Review of Nutrition, 36*, 435–470.

Roney, J. R. (2018). Functional roles of gonadal hormones in human pair bonding and secuality. In O. C. Schultheiss, & P. H. Metha (Eds.), *Routledge international handbook of social neuro-endocrinology* (pp. 239–255). Abingdon: Routledge.

Rossi, M. A., & Stuber, G. D. (2018). Overlapping brain circuits for homestatic and hedonic feeding. *Cell Metabolism, 27*, 42–56.

Royet, J.-P., Meunier, D., Torquet, N., Mouly, A.-M., & Jiang, T. (2016). The neural bases of disgust for cheese: An fMRI study. *Frontiers in Human Neuroscience, 10*, 511.

Ruff, C. C., & Fehr, E. (2014). The neurobiology of rewards and values in social decision making. *Nature Reviews Neuroscience, 15*, 549–562.

Rupp, H. A., James, T. W., Ketterson, E. D., Sengelaub, D. R., Janssen, E., & Heiman, J. R. (2009). Neural activation in the orbitofrontal cortex in response to male faces increases during the follicular phase. *Hormones and Behavior, 56*, 66–72.

Rushworth, F. S., Mars, R. B., & Summerfield, C. (2009). General mechanisms for decision making? *Current Opinion in Neurobiology, 19*, 1–9.

Sachs, M. E., Ellis, R. J., Schlaug, G., & Loui, P. (2016). Brain connectivity reflects human aesthetic responses to music. *Social Cognitive and Affective Neuroscience, 6*, 884–891.

Sakai, M., & Mather, M. (2012). How reward and emotional stimuli induce different reactions across the menstrual cycle. *Social and Personality Psychology Compass, 6*, 1–17.

Salimpoor, V. N., Benovoy, M., Larcher, K., Dagher, A., & Zatorre, R. J. (2011). Anatomically distinct dopamine release during anticipation and experience of peak emotion to music. *Nature Neuroscience, 14*, 257–262.

Salimpoor, V. N., Benovoy, M., Longo, G., Cooperstock, J. R., & Zatorre, R. J. (2009). The rewarding aspects of music listening are related to degree of emotional arousal. *PLoS One, 4*, e7487.

Salimpoor, V. N., van den Bosch, I., Kovacevic, N., McIntosh, A. R., Dagher, A., & Zatorre, R. J. (2013). Interactions between the nucleus accumbens and auditory cortices predicts music reward value. *Science, 340*, 216–219.

Schmidt, L., Skvortsova, Kullen, C., Weber, B., & Plassmann, H. (2017). How context alters value: The brain's valuation and affective regulation system link price cues to experienced taste pleasantness. *Scientific Reports, 7*, 8098.

Schultz, W. (2016). Dopamine reward prediction-error signaling: A two-component response. *Nature Reviews Neuroscience, 17*, 183–195.

Schultz, W., Apicella, P., Scarnati, E., & Ljungberg, T. (1992). Neuronal activity in monkey ventral striatum related to the expectation of reward. *Journal of Neuroscience, 12*, 4595–4610.

Schwartz, D. A., Howe, C. Q., & Purves, D. (2003). The statistical structure of human speech sounds predicts musical universals. *Journal of Neuroscience, 23*, 7160–7168.

Serences, J. T. (2008). Value-based modulations in human visual cortex. *Neuron, 60*, 1169–1181.

Sescousse, G., Caldú, X., Segura, B., & Dreher, J.-C. (2013). Processing of primary and secondary rewards: A quantitative meta-analysis and review of human functional neuroimaging studies. *Neuroscience and Biobehavioral Reviews*, *37*, 681–696.

Sharot, T., de Martino, B., & Dolan, R. J. (2009). How choice reveals and shapes expected hedonic outcome. *Journal of Neuroscience*, *29*, 3760–3765.

Sherman, A., Grabowecky, M., & Suzuki, S. (2015). In the working memory of the beholder: Art appreciation is enhanced when visual complexity is compatible with working memory. *Journal of Experimental Psychology: Human Perception and Performance*, *41*, 898–903.

Shuler, M. G., & Bear, M. F. (2006). Reward timing in the primary visual cortex. *Science*, *311*, 1606–1609.

Siep, N., Roefs, A., Roebroeck, A., Havermans, R., Bonte, M. L., & Jansen, A. (2009). Hunger is best spice: An fMRI study of the effects of attention, hunger and calorie content on food reward processing in the amygdala and the orbitofrontal cortex. *Behavioural Brain Research*, *198*, 149–158.

Skov, M. (2019). Aesthetic appreciation: The view from neuroimaging. *Empirical Studies of the Arts*, *37*, 220–248.

Skov, M., & Nadal, M. (2018). Art is not special: An assault on the last lines of defense against the naturalization of the human mind. *Reviews in the Neurosciences*, *29*, 699–702.

Skov, M., & Nadal, M. (2021). The nature of perception and emotion in aesthetic appreciation: A response to Makin's challenge to empirical aesthetics. *Psychology of Aesthetics, Creativity and the Arts*, *15*, 470–483.

Small, D. M., Gregory, M. D., Mak, Y. E., Gitelman, D., Mesulam, M. M., & Parrish, T. (2003). Dissociation of neural representation of intensity and affective valuation in human gustation. *Neuron*, *39*, 701–711.

Small, D. M., Jones-Gotman, M., Zatorre, R. J., Petrides, M., & Evans, A. C. (1997). Flavor processing: More than the sum of its parts. *Neuroreport*, *8*, 3913–3917.

Small, D. M., Zatorre, R. J., Dagher, A., Evans, A. C., & Jones-Gotman, M. (2001). Changes in brain activity related to eating chocolate. From pleasure to aversion. *Brain*, *124*, 1720–1733.

Smith, K. S., & Berridge, K. C. (2005). The ventral pallidum and hedonic reward: Neurochemical maps of sucrose "liking" and food intake. *Journal of Neuroscience*, *25*, 8637–8649.

Smith, K. S., & Berridge, K. C. (2007). Opioid limbic circuit for reward: Interaction between hedonic hotspots of nucleus accumbens and ventral pallidum. *Journal of Neuroscience*, *27*, 1594–1605.

Smith, K. S., Mahler, S., Peciña, S., & Berridge, K. C. (2010). Hedonic hotspots: Generating sensory pleasure in the brain. In M. L. Kringelbach, & K. C. Berridge (Eds.), *Pleasures of the brain* (pp. 27–49). Oxford: Oxford University Press.

Sui, J., & Liu, C. H. (2009). Can beauty be ignored? Effects of facial attractiveness on covert attention, *Psychonomic Bulletin and Review*, *16*, 276–281.

Summerfield, C., & de Lange, F. P. (2014). Expectation in perceptual decision making: Neural and computational mechanisms. *Nature Reviews Neuroscience*, *15*, 745–756.

Swanson, L. W. (2000). Cerebral hemisphere regulation of motivated behavior. *Brain Research*, *886*, 113–164.

Symmonds, M., & Dolan, R. J. (2012). The neurobiology of preferences. In R. J. Dolan, & T. Sharot (Eds.), *Neuroscience of preference and choice* (pp. 3–30). London: Academic Press.

Symmonds, M., Emmanuel, J. J., Drew, M. E., Batterham, R. L., & Dolan, D. J. (2010). Metabolic state alters economic decision making under risk in humans. *PLoS One*, *5*, e11090.

Thomas, J. M., Higgs, S., Dourish, C. T., Hansen, P. C., Harmer, C. J., & McCabe, C. (2015). Satiation attenuates BOLD activity in brain regions involved in reward and increases activity in dorsolateral prefrontal cortex: An fMRI study in healthy volunteers. *American Journal of Clinical Nutrition, 101,* 697–704.

Thut, G., Schultz, W., Roelcke, U., Nienhusmeier, M., Missimer, J., Maguire, R. P., & Leenders, K. L. (1997). Activation of the human brain by monetary reward. *Neuroreport, 8,* 1225–1228.

Tindell, A. J., Smith, K. S., Peciña, S., Berridge, K. C., & Aldridge, J. W. (2006). Ventral pallidum firing codes hedonic reward when a bad taste turns good. *Journal of Neurophysiology, 96,* 2399–2409.

Tybur, J. M., Çinar, C., Karinen, A. K., & Perone, P. (2018). Why do people vary in disgust? *Philosophical Transactions of the Royal Society B, 373,* 20170204.

Tybur, J. M., & Lieberman, D. (2016). Human pathogen avoidance adaptations. *Current Opinion in Psychology, 7,* 6–11.

Tye, K. M. (2018). Neural circuit motifs in valence processing. *Neuron, 100,* 436–452.

Valentine, C. W. (1962). *Experimental psychology of beauty.* London: Methuen.

Valuch, C., Pflüger, L. S., Wallner, B., Laeng, B., & Ansorge, U. (2015). Using eye tracking to test for individual differences in attention to attractive faces. *Frontiers in Psychology, 6,* 42.

Vartanian, O., & Goel, V. (2004). Neuroanatomical correlates of aesthetic preference for paintings. *NeuroReport, 15,* 893–897.

Vartanian, O., Navarrete, G., Chatterjee, A., Fich, L. B., Leder, H., Modroño, C., Nadal, M., Rostrup, N., & Skov, M. (2013). Impact of contour on aesthetic judgments and approach-avoidance decisions in architecture. *Proceedings of the National Academy of Sciences, 110,* 10446–10453.

Wallis, J. D., & Kennerley, S. W. (2007). Heterogeneous reward signals in prefrontal cortex. *Current Opinion in Neurobiology, 20,* 191–198.

Wang, K. S., Smith, D. V., & Delgado, M. R. (2016). Using fMRI to study reward processing in humans: Past, present, and future. *Journal of Neurophysiology, 115,* 1664–1678.

Winston, J. S., O'Doherty, J., Kilner, J. M., Perrett, D. I., & Dolan, R. J. (2007). Brain systems for assessing facial attractiveness. *Neuropsychologia, 45,* 195–206.

Wunderlich, K., Rangel, A., & O'Doherty, J. D. (2009). Economic choices can be made using only stimulus values. *Proceedings of the National Academy of Sciences, 107,* 15005–15010.

Yoest, K. E., Cummings, J. A., & Becker, J. B. (2014). Estradiol, dopamine and motivation. *Central Nervous System Agents in Medicinal Chemistry, 14,* 83–89.

Yoest, K. E., Quigley, J. A., & Becker, J. B. (2018). Rapid effects of ovarian hormones in dorsal striatum and nucleus accumbens. *Hormones and Behavior, 98,* 210–218.

Zimmerman, C. A., Leib, D. E., & Knight, Z. A. (2017). Neural circuits underlying thirst and fluid homeostasis. *Nature Reviews Neuroscience, 18,* 459–469.

Zold, C. L., & Shuler, M. G. (2015). Theta oscillations in visual cortex emerge with experience to convey expected reward time and experienced reward rate. *Journal of Neuroscience, 35,* 9603–9614.

Zou, L. Q., van Hartvelt, T. J., Kringelbach, M. L., Cheung, E. F., & Chan, R. C. (2016). The neural mechanism of hedonic processing and judgment of pleasant odors: An activation likelihood estimation meta-analysis. *Neuropsychology, 30,* 970–979.

CHAPTER 8

THE EVOLUTION OF AESTHETICS AND BEAUTY

DAHLIA W. ZAIDEL

INTRODUCTION

AESTHETICS and beauty-related issues were guided mainly by philosophical debates in the past several millennia (Goldblatt, Brown, & Patridge, 2017), and although the discussions were intellectually useful, the essence of aesthetics remained an enigma until relatively recently. Those debates tied the notion of aesthetics mainly to art, but current scientific explorations have profitably blurred the distinctions between art beauty, face beauty, and other sources of beauty, seeking insights, instead, through aesthetic/beauty reactions in the brain (reviewed in Nadal, 2013; Vartanian & Skov, 2014) as well as through biological explanations. The link to biology was introduced by Charles Darwin in the 1800s, and 100 years later elaborated upon substantially by other scientists (described below). In the 1970s, Amotz Zahavi, an evolutionary biologist, significantly advanced the biological link notion by explaining the intersection of mate selection strategies, art, and aesthetics (Zahavi, 1978). His ideas were subsequently richly developed by Geoffrey Miller, who shone additional well-thought-out light on the biological links (Miller, 2000, 2001).

Unlike Darwin, Alfred Wallace, an evolutionary biologist also working in the 1800s, steered away from the aesthetic issue, emphasizing instead that the basis of females' choice in procreation is an assessment of the qualities of health and strength in the male animal. Such factors underlie the choice since they lead to survival of the offspring (Cronin, 1992; Prum, 2012; Wallace, 1870). The logic behind species survival through selection based on high genetic qualities explains the evolutionary development of elaborate mate-attracting strategies upon which females can base their choice for mating, as in overly large physical characteristics (phenotypes). This exaggerated growth in size and color variations has come to be known as the Fisherian runaway principle (Fisher, 1915). In evolutionary perspectives, the advantage of exaggerated phenotypes is that they reveal multiple important health-related details that are predictive of fitness, and thus have a long-term adaptive value for the species, an advantage that outweighs the risks of exaggeration (susceptibility to predators, increased requirement for maintenance energy). The significance of such notions to the present discussion is that they have helped pave the intellectual road toward explaining aesthetics/beauty reactions in biological terms.

BIOLOGICAL FOUNDATION OF AESTHETICS/ BEAUTY AND ART

Zahavi (1978) proposed that the exaggerated phenotypes, although forming a platform for showcasing and assessing genetic qualities, carry a cost, a handicap. Maintaining the appearance of health requires much effort and only the strongest and fittest can sustain it. The two are intertwined—males' phenotypes allow inspection by the females of minute health-revealing fine details and at the same time the healthiest males, who have high-quality genes, possess the exaggerated physical characteristics. He considers them "decorative patterns" and likens them to the efforts humans put into art-making.

Against this pivoting theoretical backdrop, the artistic genetic qualities can be inferred: they are revealed in the artist's artwork. The more effort artists invest in their artwork, the more they exhibit their artistic genes, which encompass artistic cognition, talent, skill, and intellectual energy. The viewer of the artwork is basically assessing the artist's genes as they pertain to art. The aesthetic reactions in the viewer are positive when the artistic gene quality is high but low or neutral when quality is low. Aesthetics in art, then, using biological terms, are viewers' reactions to those artistic genetic qualities.

RELATIONSHIP OF MATE SELECTION STRATEGIES TO AESTHETICS/BEAUTY

In biological terms, the aim of breeding strategies is, ultimately, propagation of the species. The specifics of the displays are unique to each animal, and nature is replete with examples of the cleverness and variability that have evolved to attract a mate (Gould & Gould, 1989). Regardless of the animal and the details revealed in its unique physical exhibit, (1) the intensity and effort invested in advertising the signals form a fundamental aspect of signal generation, and (2) attention-getting is the overarching goal. Both of these aspects orchestrate the biological logic of the display. To be able to interpret the signals (3) multi-modal brain regions are required in the recipient and, by inference, (4) a co-evolution of the brain of the signaler and of attentional mechanisms of the recipient. These notions are developed further below.

The classic example is the courtship display of the peacock, *Pavo cristatus*, for the benefit of attracting a peahen (Cronin, 1992). The long-feathered peacock tail is lifted into a fan that the animal vibrates to display the "eyes" on the feathers as well as the physical strength required to maintain the vibration. Strutting back and forth in front of her allows the peahen to assess details that would otherwise be hidden when the tail (also known as train) is down and dragged behind. The vibration in the air caused by "rattling" of the raised fan-like tail is achieved not only through the biomechanics of feather structure but also by sheer motoric strength (Dakin, McCrossan, Hare, Montgomerie, & Amador Kane, 2016). The display requires the functionality of several modalities in the peahen's brain. She has to be capable of analyzing feather asymmetries, discoloration, and aberrant iridescence; all could be symptoms of parasite hosting (Balenger & Zuk, 2014; Hamilton & Zuk, 1982), disease manifestations, or outcomes of unsuccessful fights. These would indicate poor fitness qualities and not an inheritance the peahen wants to pass on to her offspring, since she alone carries the burden of hatching and caring for them.

Perceptually and cognitively, the brain of the peahen is suited to discern fitness and genetic qualities in the peacock. To the peahen, the purpose of the display is anchored in biologically practical, species-survival issues for that particular biological pheasant family, not at all what the peacock's physical features signify to human viewers. It is thus reasonable to assume that co-evolutionary processes were underway to match the courtship display needs with the brain and age of the animal observer (a topic elaborated upon subsequently). The animal observer possesses the neuroanatomical underpinning for perceptual and cognitive assessment of genetic qualities in her conspecific. Humans have no way of determining whether or not animals have aesthetic reactions.

To humans, on the other hand, the peacock's feathers are aesthetically pleasing—they provide material and ideas for home decoration, body ornaments, artistic design themes, and inspiration for color fads. None of the fitness signals emanating from the peacock is meaningful procreation-wise to the human observer, indeed they largely go unnoticed.

The feathers are elaborate physical "engineering feats" (Dakin et al., 2016; Yoshioka & Kinoshita, 2001; Zi et al., 2003), so much so as to suggest nothing but evolutionary progress in a trajectory that has been underway for hundreds of millions of years, its purpose being to maximize high genetic inheritance of future offspring. There is fossil evidence of colors and iridescence of feathers going back to the days of the dinosaurs (Hu et al., 2018; Zhou, 2014), long before the peacock and the peahen evolved. The patterns are designed for multi-modal perception, not just for visual assessment. Sounds, air vibrations, and biomechanical effects all require multiple processing of physical entities by the peahen. Indeed, peacocks are not alone among avians in producing multiple effects: several birds such as the hummingbird (Clark, Elias, & Prum, 2013), sage-grouse (Koch, Krakauer, & Patricelli, 2015), the manakin (Bostwick & Prum, 2005), among others (Bostwick, Elias, Mason, & Montealegre et al., 2010) have been found to use biomechanical features to attract a mate. These features send nonvocal signals not readily perceived by human sensory organs.

Additional physical phenotypes advertise fitness in male animals (Gould & Gould, 1989). Antlers are signals of maleness in sexual mate selection. They can be elaborate as in the red deer, elk, or in the caribou. Large bony structures protruding from males' heads, such as horns in cattle or in mountain sheep, are similarly used to advertise strength, dominance, and to win the right to procreate with females. Antlers and horns are cumbersome and pose obstacles in escaping predators. However, they, too, have been evolving in structural composition and function for hundreds of millions of years, and as fossil records indicate, were already present at the time of the dinosaurs (Farlow & Dodson, 1975; Hone, Wood, & Knell, 2016).

The time frame in the foregoing suggests that the basis for aesthetic sensibility in female animals, if it exists, has not changed much in millions of years, unlike aesthetic responses in humans where cultural habits and conventions have an impact, and many beauty-related habits have short duration times. The interaction of the biological roots with human fashion fads and ever-changing values enter into humans' aesthetic reactions. Thus, although Darwin was the first to think of biological reasons, significant insights, relevant ideas, and inferences regarding the relationship to art were discussed and gained much later (as reviewed above; and see Jones & Ratterman, 2009).

Darwin, when he suggested that the whole appearance of the peacock (and other male animals) was influenced by female aesthetic sensibility (the peahen's), could not have known that future scientific investigations would reveal, more than 150 years later, minute physical and chemical arrangements in the peacock's feathers, namely that bio-mechanical aspects of the feathers enter into the courtship display strategy, and any aesthetic "taste" in female animals could not have led to such a complex arrangement in the male. The most parsimonious explanation for so-called female choice strategies is to assume that natural selection "selected" those features that reveal genetic qualities the most even if that means extravagant appendages. In other words, the more is revealed, the more informed the choice. The biological evolution of the male's feathers could have evolved independently of the observer's "taste." It has been argued that male competition alone plays a major role in this process (see Moore & Martin, 2016). Whatever the form the physical appearance of the peacock has taken, intra-sexual factors (between the males) had an influence. In any case, the end result is that a match between the signaler and the recipient, between the courtship display and the brain of the animal observer, is crucial for successful mating and procreation.

HONEST SIGNALS OF HEALTH IN NATURE: HANDICAP PRINCIPLE IN BIOLOGY AND ART

Physical and mental effort, metabolic energy, muscle strength, immunocompetence, and high maintenance costs are required to display a perfectly healthy body to attract a mate for procreation. Having the elaborate appendages, which need to be displayed, takes a toll on the male animals and for that reason Zahavi suggested that honest signals carry a handicap (Zahavi, 1975, 1997). Only the strongest males can maintain a front that lures females. His theory has been debated and discussed by others and is now widely supported (Grafen, 1990). The costs of maintaining physical attributes that showcase fitness qualities are of and of themselves signals of genetic quality, the kind that maximize survival.

In essence, not only do the elaborate appendages hinder survival of the individual male, possessing them carries costs that are detrimental to health in the long run. Thus, male animals generally have lower life expectancy than females. Male big horn sheep butt heads with such force that the resounding head collisions are heard for long distances. But such battles cannot be maintained by the same ram year in and year out. The thick skull can absorb the impact for a long while until one ram collapses. The surviving ram wins the right to procreate with the females of the herd and thereby increase his progeny. Winning is physically costly.

Generalizing to art aesthetics/beauty, the greater the investment in the skillful execution of an artwork, the more it reflects favorable artistic genetic qualities, and the more likely it is to trigger aesthetic reactions in the viewer. The aesthetic response and the genetic qualities assessment pathways are assumed to share the same neural circuitry. Obviously, the artist is not promoting personal interest in procreation and attraction of a mate through the work. In producing the artwork, the artist is not "putting" the aesthetics into it; rather the work triggers the aesthetic reaction in the brain of the viewer.

The overall physical health of the artist is independent of the artistic cognitive abilities, although under some conditions it could shape the artwork (e.g., eye health conditions in some artists in the school of Impressionism). Countless renowned artists with serious health issues produced universally regarded, time-transcended valued artworks, among whom are Goya, Monet, Van Gogh, Mozart, Beethoven, and Schubert, to mention but a miniscule few (Zaidel, 2015b). It is the artistic cognition that is put on display and, ultimately, what is assessed by the viewer is the artistic genetic quality.

Considered within a biological and evolutionary framework, humans would not experience aesthetic reactions in the first place if there were no adaptive value to them. To wit, early on, both newborns and young children demonstrate selective response to beautiful faces (Bascandziev & Harris, 2014; Dion, 1973; Langlois, Ritter, Roggman, & Vaughn, 1991) attesting to the biological underpinning of the response.

HUMAN AESTHETIC/BEAUTY RESPONSE: BIOLOGICAL ROOTS AND EVOLUTIONARY CO-OPTION

Humans see beauty in the peacock's raised tail, its colors, iridescences, shades, and elegant crown, while peahens see an opportunity to inspect the peacock's health status. The brain of the observer limits what is sensed, perceived, and contemplated. Elliot Gould and Elisabeth Vreba developed the idea of co-option and labeled it exaptation: a structure or function originally arising to serve one biological purpose evolves further through environmental, physiological, and neural constraints to serve another function (Gould & Vrba, 1982). Here, it is argued that neural pathways that originally evolved to assess genetic qualities for mating and procreating have co-opted in the human brain to support nonbiological entities such as art and the aesthetic/beauty reactions to it. In human cultural existence, art has become a critical mode of social communication, symbolic expression of group unity, and display of genetic talent (Zaidel, 2017, 2018).

By inference, humans judge what they consciously think is artistic virtuosity but what enters the judgment formula without awareness is assessment of the artistic genetic quality. The assessment of health is a conserved trait inherited from animal ancestors, meant to serve a particular function for animals, but in humans it metamorphosed into an aesthetic/beauty response; that is, the response has co-opted to serve something immensely useful to humans, specifically the attentional honing to the message emanating from the source.

ATTENTION-ATTRACTION AND THE AESTHETIC/BEAUTY RESPONSE

An important aspect of the genetic fitness display is that it is strategically organized to attract attention. This aspect is factored into the logic of the display as a whole and it, too, has been biologically preserved in humans (minus procreation needs). Universal principles of attention are so basic and advantageous to survival that it is reasonable to assume that they would be incorporated into behaviors targeting species procreation.

Neural systems supporting attention have formed early on in biological organisms. Attentional channeling of resources optimizes successful perceptual and cognitive assessment of the source's signals (Mangun, 2012). Detecting objects, sounds, vibrations, touch, smells, taste, and minute changes in the environment is crucial. Slight alteration in the surroundings could determine life or death, eating or being eaten, being unmasked or hidden, and so on. Similarly, species survival depends heavily on attention-attraction to animals' mate selection displays, an extension of basic alertness since it is critical for successfully choosing the best mate.

Humans no longer need dedicated neural resources for prey detection given their capacity to control and modify their habitat for protection; unlike animals, humans are famously highly adapted to new terrain, weather, and food sources through their mechanical and technological skills. Moreover, most humans no longer share the same environmental niche with animals. The attentional system was modified through evolutionary pressures to serve human-unique survival needs, and the human aesthetic response could be viewed as an extension, a co-option, of the strong biological need to draw notice to mating displays.

Indeed, myriad sources unrelated to obvious genetic showcasing trigger aesthetic responses. What triggers our heightened aesthetic response to the rising full moon, sunsets over the Pacific Ocean, shades of red in autumn tree foliage, drops of rain on waterlily-filled ponds, fire sparks in shooting volcanoes, flights of hummingbirds, or the iridescent colors in a peacock's tail? And conversely, what lessens our aesthetic response when the same full moon is viewed at zenith, when torrential rains hit the ground, or when freshly fallen snow on city streets is trampled upon by cars and pedestrians? Such considerations are contemplated by the Japanese school of aesthetics, Wabi-Sabi, which considers aesthetic response to imperfect, so-called ugly things (Koren, 2008). In all of these conditions, attention-attraction to the signals emanating from the source is the critical element: the signals attract attention, much as when the peacock's display draws the peahen's attention (Zaidel, 2015a).

BIOLOGICAL AESTHETICS: PLEASURE VERSUS ATTENTION-ATTRACTION

In evolutionary terms, choosing and displaying for the purpose of procreation requires attention, concentration, energy, and efficiency. With animals, the role of pleasure in this whole endeavor is unknown. Some published studies of visual art evaluation (paintings) have reported increased activation in the "reward pathway," which encompasses a so-called "pleasure center" (Aharon et al., 2001; Ishizu & Zeki, 2011). The pathway was originally uncovered in rats, in whom pleasure was inferred but not objectively verified (Berridge & Kringelbach, 2013, 2015). The occasional finding of increased brain activation in these areas in humans has suggested that pleasure is involved in the aesthetic evaluation of art but this inference has been challenged (e.g., Ticini, 2017), and even on the face of it, does not hold much weight.

Thus, the subjective feeling humans become aware of sometimes upon experiencing aesthetic reactions may not have emerged from inherited neural pathways controlling mate selection. Indeed, one would have to wonder, why pleasure? Arguing that the biologically conserved system from whence aesthetic reactions emanate has been preserved for the sole purpose of generating pleasure is highly tenuous. Rather, it is more reasonable to suppose that the occasional and transient nature of pleasure associated with some aesthetic reactions is a secondary event controlled by separate neural pathways. The human-specific aesthetic response itself likely rests on evolutionary modification of the biologically tuned attentional system.

BIOLOGICAL AESTHETICS OF MUSIC

Music is an art form that is ubiquitously present in human cultures and this suggests a basis of inherited biological foundation for composing and performing it. Indeed, the human ear structure and the neural auditory system have origins in distant phylogenetic species, possibly emerging with fish (Manley, Popper, & Fay, 2004). With most animals, deciphering sounds is constrained by the environment and the functions subserved by those sounds, even while there is conservation of brain areas responding to music across widely divergent species such as crocodiles, birds, and humans (Behroozi et al., 2018). Similarly, human neural brain organization and functionality are likely to have shaped the upper limits of hearing the sounds of language and music (Ayala, Lehmann, & Merchant, 2017; Baumann, Petkov, & Griffiths, 2013).

Given conservation of sensory auditory neural systems, we need to explore the biological ancestry to gain an understanding of the human response to music. The principal reasons why animals produce sounds include declarations of territorial boundaries, predatory warning calls, physical strength displays, information sharing, and mate selection displays. Bird songs have been studied by far the most and provide a model for insights into human and animal communication (Knight & Lewis, 2017; Rothenberg, Roeske, Voss, Naguib, & Tchernichovski, 2014). Birds sing to signal their territory, bond with mates, declare affiliation, and display fitness strength; additional reasons remain to be uncovered. A clear sex difference in song production has been observed: males sing to attract mates while females rarely sing, and this male dominance suggests an early (evolutionary) sexual role of sound formation skills. Songs are learned through mimicking after birth. Learning from their conspecifics is achieved during a period of growth when brain plasticity mechanisms are functional; early isolation from conspecifics produces distorted songs (Nottebohm, 2005).

However, a driving evolutionary force in shaping the human brain is language communication, the antecedents of which have a long evolutionary history traced to nonhuman primates (Aboitiz, 2018), and to the adaptive strategy of social bonding and group belongingness (Zaidel, 2018). At the same time, our reactions to music are biologically linked to other animals' intra-species communication and mating fitness signals (Zatorre & Peretz, 2001). Indeed, human musical compositions share elements produced by birds, whales, frogs, and numerous other animals, despite evolutionary paths that diverged from our ancestors millions of years ago (Fitch, 2015; Honing et al., 2015). The fact that young babies and children react to music early on without any instruction, and the ubiquitous presence of music throughout human societies both attest to its strong biologically based social, emotional, and aesthetic appeal (Mithen, 2009).

Human brain neuroanatomy supporting the sounds of language specialization, asymmetrically emphasizing the left hemisphere, has been evolving in nonhuman primates (Aboitiz, 2018; Cantalupo & Hopkins, 2001; Hopkins et al., 2017), whereas musical processing, an art expression, involves activation of neural systems in both hemispheres, and musical compositions, too, lack robust asymmetrical hemispheric control (Zaidel, 2015b). The two human abilities, language and music, share neuroanatomical structures but are not organized similarly in the brain, although both have social and participatory communicative functions.

Music's Emotional Pleasure and Communication

In addition to the aesthetic/beauty issue, humans experience a variety of emotions evoked by music, including sadness, relaxation, melancholy, elation, excitement, arousal, and more. Pleasure is the most discussed in this context (Zatorre & Salimpoor, 2013). We verify the emotions explicitly ("I enjoy this music," "I love this music," "this music is beautiful," etc.) (Schaefer, 2017). Subjectively, peak emotions and pleasure with music are experienced as physical bodily chills, thrills, shivers, goosebumps, known scientifically as piloerections (Goldstein, 1980; Panksepp, 1995). How and why piloerections are triggered is not currently understood. Moreover, there is great variability in the response itself; some report not experiencing them at all while still reporting subjective pleasure.

The sympathetic branch of the autonomic nervous system controls the contraction of the skin muscles involved in piloerections (Benedek & Kaernbach, 2011). Anatomically, smooth muscles underlying skin hair follicles are stimulated by the sympathetic branch. In the brain, the autonomic system is controlled by the hypothalamus, which also controls heart rate, respiration, digestion, body temperature, and other functions normally not under voluntary control. The response of piloerections is involuntary in both humans and animals, whether it is caused by fear, flight, coldness, or stress. The relationship between the hypothalamus and music is not clear cut. However, this brain structure is part of the limbic system, which is known to be involved in emotional reactions, and receives input from widely distributed neuroanatomical structures in the cerebral cortex and brain stem.

Exploiting the deeply rooted biological, anatomical, and neural circuits to create and enjoy music is a natural step in the evolution of human social culture. Initially, early humans emerging in Africa, *Homo sapiens*, could easily have discovered that animal mimicry through modulation of guttural throat sounds, tongue clicks, and whistling provided the right kind of camouflage for successful hunting or scavenging (Zaidel, 2017, 2018). The same could be assumed for symbolic sound-making, through throat or instrumental production, by *Homo neanderthalensis* in Europe (d'Errico et al., 2017; Hoffmann, Angelucci, Villaverde, Zapata, & Zilhão, 2018), and, by extension, possibly even by *Homo erectus*, who dispersed away from Africa well over a million years earlier than *Homo sapiens*. Responding to these sounds meaningfully in musical rhythms, beats, and harmony with percussion on stones, wood, leather, bones, or through whistling with plant material (leaves, reeds) would have been a natural endeavor in the distant past (Zaidel, 2015b).

Although physical material artifacts of music-making are missing from the archeology of the very early hominin epochs in Africa, emerging only ~40,000–30,000 years ago in Europe, vocally produced nonlanguage, purposeful rhythmical human sound-making could nevertheless have been practiced for symbolic purposes denoting

social unity and cohesion (Zaidel, 2017). The archeological record shows consistent socially based group living dating all the way back to ~300,000 years ago (Brooks et al.,
2018; Potts et al., 2018; Tooby & Cosmides, 2016). A human musical chorus of voices
could easily have included all group members regardless of social hierarchy, age, or
sex. Aesthetic/beauty issues would have been secondary because they would have
emphasized individual displays of talent, potentially triggering competition among
individuals (jealousy and conflict?), instead of whole group displays (Zaidel, 2018). It
is parsimonious to assume that the primary reasons were the group's survival as a cooperative socially oriented unit. The fact that this strategy was successful can be seen in
the eventual spread of *Homo sapiens* to the rest of the world. Currently, we do witness
individual musical composers, single instrument players, and a range of vocal singers
displaying their virtuosity because the dynamics of flourishing societies have cultural
norms that allow such exhibits. Humans have become resourceful with regard to survival and can afford to practice expanded cultural repertoires.

Conclusion

The human aesthetics/beauty response has been linked to conserved biological
pathways inherited from the animal ancestry, particularly to mate selection strategies.
It plays a role in the arts, commercial advertisement, decision making, career paths, jury
selection, and mate attraction, and is also triggered by scenery, food, and parenthood.
The broad range of beauty triggers in human existence suggests the response has been
co-opted and modified to blend into the cultural reality of human survival practices. It
has an evolutionary adaptive purpose.

References

Aboitiz, F. (2018). A brain for speech: Evolutionary continuity in primate and human auditory-
vocal processing. *Frontiers in Neuroscience, 12,* 174.

Aharon, I., Etcoff, N., Ariely, D., Chabris, C. F., O'Connor, E., & Breiter, H. C. (2001). Beautiful
faces have variable reward value. *Neuron, 32,* 537–551.

Ayala, Y. A., Lehmann, A., & Merchant, H. (2017). Monkeys share the neurophysiological
basis for encoding sound periodicities captured by the frequency-following response with
humans. *Scientific Reports, 7,* 16687.

Balenger, S. L., & Zuk, M. (2014). Testing the Hamilton-Zuk hypothesis: Past, present, and future. *Integrative and Comparative Biology, 54,* 601–613.

Bascandziev, I., & Harris, P. L. (2014). In beauty we trust: Children prefer information from
more attractive informants. *British Journal of Developmental Psychology, 32,* 94–99.

Baumann, S., Petkov, C., & Griffiths, T. (2013). A unified framework for the organization of the
primate auditory cortex. *Frontiers in Systems Neuroscience, 7,* 11.

Behroozi, M., Billings, B. K., Helluy, X., Manger, P. R., Güntürkün, O., & Ströckens, F. (2018). Functional MRI in the Nile crocodile: A new avenue for evolutionary neurobiology. *Proceedings of the Royal Society B: Biological Sciences*, 285, 20180178.

Benedek, M., & Kaernbach, C. (2011). Physiological correlates and emotional specificity of human piloerection. *Biological Psychology*, 86, 320–329.

Berridge, K. C., & Kringelbach, M. L. (2013). Neuroscience of affect: Brain mechanisms of pleasure and displeasure. *Current Opinion in Neurobiology*, 23, 294–303.

Berridge, K. C., & Kringelbach, M. L. (2015). Pleasure systems in the brain. *Neuron*, 86, 646–664.

Bostwick, K. S., Elias, D. O., Mason, A., & Montealegre Z. F. (2010). Resonating feathers produce courtship song. *Proceedings of the Royal Society B: Biological Sciences*, 277, 835–841.

Bostwick, K. S., & Prum, R. O. (2005). Courting bird sings with stridulating wing feathers. *Science*, 309, 736.

Brooks, A. S., Yellen, J. E., Potts, R., Behrensmeyer, A. K., Deino, A. L., Leslie, D. E., … Clark, J. B. (2018). Long-distance stone transport and pigment use in the earliest Middle Stone Age. *Science*, 360, 90–94.

Cantalupo, C., & Hopkins, W. D. (2001). Asymmetric Broca's area in great apes: A region of the ape brain is uncannily similar to one linked with speech in humans. *Nature* 414, 505.

Clark, C. J., Elias, D. O., & Prum, R. O. (2013). Hummingbird feather sounds are produced by aeroelastic flutter, not vortex-induced vibration. *The Journal of Experimental Biology* 216, 3395–3403.

Cronin, H. (1992). *The ant and the peacock*. Cambridge: Cambridge University Press.

d'Errico, F., Banks, W. E., Warren, D. L., Sgubin, G., van Niekerk, K. L., Henshilwood, C., … Sánchez Goñi, M. F. (2017). Identifying early modern human ecological niche expansions and associated cultural dynamics in the South African Middle Stone Age. *Proceedings of the National Academy of Sciences USA*, 114, 7869–7876.

Dakin, R., McCrossan, O., Hare, J. F., Montgomerie, R., & Amador Kane, S. (2016). Biomechanics of the peacock's display: How feather structure and resonance influence multimodal signaling. *PLoS ONE*, 11, e0152759.

Dion, K. K. (1973). Young children's stereotyping of facial attractiveness. *Developmental Psychology*, 9, 183–188.

Farlow, J. O., & Dodson, P. (1975). The behavioral significance of frill and horn morphology in ceratopsian dinosaurs. *Evolution*, 29, 53–361.

Fisher, R. A. (1915). The evolution of sexual preference. *Eugenics Review*, 7, 184–192.

Fitch, W. T. (2015). Four principles of bio-musicology. *Philosophical Transactions of the Royal Society B: Biological Sciences*, 370, 20140091.

Goldblatt, D., Brown, L. B., & Patridge, S. (Eds.) (2017). *Aesthetics: A reader in philosophy of the arts*. New York: Routledge.

Goldstein, A. (1980). Thrills in response to music and other stimuli. *Physiological Psychology*, 8, 126–129.

Gould, J. L., & Gould, C. G. (1989). *Sexual selection*. New York: Scientific American Library.

Gould, S. J., & Vrba, E. S. (1982). Exaptation: A missing term in the science of form. *Paleobiology*, 8, 4–15.

Grafen, A. (1990). Biological signals as handicaps. *Journal of Theoretical Biology*, 144, 517–546.

Hamilton, W. D., & Zuk, M. (1982). Heritable true fitness and bright birds: A role for parasites? *Science*, 218, 384–387.

Hoffmann, D. L., Angelucci, D. E., Villaverde, V., Zapata, J., & Zilhão, J. (2018). Symbolic use of marine shells and mineral pigments by Iberian Neanderthals 115,000 years ago. *Science Advances, 4*, eaar5255.

Hone, D. W. E., Wood, D., & Knell, R. J. (2016). Positive allometry for exaggerated structures in the ceratopsian dinosaur *Protoceratops andrewsi* supports socio-sexual signaling. *Palaeontologia Electronica, 19.1.5A*, 1–13.

Honing, H., ten Cate, C., Peretz, I., & Trehub, S. E. (2015). Without it no music: Cognition, biology and evolution of musicality. *Philosophical Transactions of the Royal Society B: Biological Sciences, 370*, 20140088.

Hopkins, W. D., Meguerditchian, A., Coulon, O., Misiura, M., Pope, S., Mareno, M. C., & Schapiro, S. J. (2017). Motor skill for tool-use is associated with asymmetries in Broca's area and the motor hand area of the precentral gyrus in chimpanzees (*Pan troglodytes*). *Behavioural Brain Research, 318*, 71–81.

Hu, D., Clarke, J. A., Eliason, C. M., Qiu, R., Li, Q., Shawkey, M. D., ... Xu, X. (2018). A bony-crested Jurassic dinosaur with evidence of iridescent plumage highlights complexity in early paravian evolution. *Nature Communications, 9*, 217.

Ishizu, T., & Zeki, S. (2011). Toward a brain-based theory of beauty. *PLoS One, 6*, e21852.

Jones, A. G., & Ratterman, N. L. (2009). Mate choice and sexual selection: What have we learned since Darwin? *Proceedings of the National Academy of Sciences, 106*, 10001–10008.

Knight, C., & Lewis, J. (2017). Wild voices: Mimicry, reversal, metaphor, and the emergence of language. *Current Anthropology, 58*, 435–453.

Koch, R. E., Krakauer, A. H., & Patricelli, G. L. (2015). Investigating female mate choice for mechanical sounds in the male Greater Sage-Grouse. *The Auk, 132*, 349–358.

Koren, L. (2008). *Wabi-sabi for artists, designers, poets, and philosophers*. Point Reyes, CA: Imperfect Publishing.

Langlois, J. H., Ritter, J. M., Roggman, L. A., & Vaughn, L. S. (1991). Facial diversity and infant preferences for attractive faces. *Developmental Psychology, 27*, 79–84.

Mangun, G. R. (Ed.) (2012). *Neuroscience of attention: Attentional control and selection*. New York: Oxford University Press.

Manley, G. A., Popper, A. N., & Fay, R. R. (Eds.) (2004). *Evolution of the vertebrate auditory system*. Basel: Springer.

Miller, G. F. (2000). *The mating mind: How sexual choice shaped the evolution of human nature*. New York: Doubleday.

Miller, G. F. (2001). Aesthetic fitness: How sexual selection shaped artistic virtuosity as a fitness indicator and aesthetic preferences as mate choice criteria. *Bulletin of Psychology and the Arts, 2*, 20–25.

Mithen, S. (2009). The music instinct: The evolutionary basis of musicality. *Annals of the New York Academy of Sciences, 1169*, 3–12.

Moore, M. P., & Martin, R. A. (2016). Intrasexual selection favours an immune correlated colour ornament in a dragonfly. *Journal of Evolutionary Biology, 29*, 2256–2265.

Nadal, M. (2013). The experience of art: Insights from neuroimaging. *Progress in Brain Research, 204*, 135–158.

Nottebohm, F. (2005). The neural basis of birdsong. *PLOS Biology, 3*, e164.

Panksepp, J. (1995). The emotional sources of "chills" induced by music. *Music Perception, 13*, 171–207.

Potts, R., Behrensmeyer, A. K., Faith, J. T., Tryon, C. A., Brooks, A. S., Yellen, J. E., … Renaut, R. W. (2018). Environmental dynamics during the onset of the Middle Stone Age in eastern Africa. *Science, 360*, 86–90.

Prum, R. O. (2012). Aesthetic evolution by mate choice: Darwin's *really* dangerous idea. *Philosophical Transactions of the Royal Society B, 367*, 2253–2265.

Rothenberg, D., Roeske, T. C., Voss, H. U., Naguib, M., & Tchernichovski, O. (2014). Investigation of musicality in birdsong. *Hearing Research, 308*, 71–83.

Schaefer, H. E. (2017). Music-evoked emotions: Current studies. *Frontiers in Neuroscience, 11*, 600.

Ticini, L. (2017). The role of the orbitofrontal and dorsolateral prefrontal cortices in aesthetic preference for art. *Behavioral Science, 7*, 31.

Tooby, J., & Cosmides, L. (2016). Human cooperation shows the distinctive signatures of adaptations to small-scale social life. *Behavioral Brain Science, 39*, e54.

Vartanian, O., & Skov, M. (2014). Neural correlates of viewing paintings: Evidence from a quantitative meta-analysis of functional magnetic resonance imaging data. *Brain and Cognition, 87*, 52–56.

Wallace, A. R. (1870). *Contributions to the theory of natural selection*. London: Macmillan.

Yoshioka, S., & Kinoshita, S. (2001). Effect of macroscopic structure in iridescent color of the peacock feathers. *Forma, 17*, 169–181.

Zahavi, A. (1975). Mate selection—a selection for a handicap. *Journal of Theoretical Biology, 53*, 205–214.

Zahavi, A. (1978). Decorative patterns and the evolution of art. *New Scientist, 19*, 182–184.

Zahavi, A. (1997). *The handicap principle: a missing piece of Darwin's puzzle*. Oxford: Oxford University Press.

Zaidel, D. W. (2015a). Neuroesthetics is not just about art. *Frontiers of Human Neuroscience, 9*, 80.

Zaidel, D. W. (2015b). *Neuropsychology of art: Neurological, biological and evolutionary perspectives*, 2nd edition. Hove: Psychology Press.

Zaidel, D. W. (2017). Art in early human evolution: Socially driven art forms versus material art. *Evolutionary Studies in Imaginative Culture, 1*, 149–157.

Zaidel, D. W. (2018). Culture and art: Importance of art practice, not aesthetics, to early human culture. *Progress in Brain Research, 237*, 25–40.

Zatorre, R. J., & Peretz, I. (Eds.) (2001). *The biological foundations of music*. New York: New York Academy of Sciences.

Zatorre, R. J., & Salimpoor, V. N. (2013). From perception to pleasure: Music and its neural substrates. *Proceedings of the National Academy of Sciences of the United States of America, 110*, 10430–10437.

Zhou, Z. (2014). Dinosaur evolution: Feathers up for selection. *Current Biology, 24*, R751–R753.

Zi, J., Yu, X., Li, Y., Hu, X., Xu, C., Wang, X., … Fu, R. (2003). Coloration strategies in peacock feathers. *Proceedings of the National Academy of Sciences of the United States of America, 100*, 12576–12578.

SECTION 2

METHODS

CHAPTER 9

HISTORIOMETRIC METHODS

DEAN KEITH SIMONTON

AESTHETIC products, such as poems and paintings, are produced by creative artists, like poets and painters, who work within a given sociocultural milieu, such as the baroque, neoclassical, or romantic periods (Hasenfus, Martindale, & Birnbaum, 1983). Hence, one might think that researchers engaged in empirical aesthetics would devote considerable effort to studying artistic masterpieces, creative geniuses, and the golden ages of a given art form or style. After all, these research targets would represent the epitome of the phenomenon, much like targeting Olympic athletes to comprehend the basis for exceptional talent in sports. Yet many methods favored in empirical aesthetics are not well designed to focus on such entities. For example, experimental aesthetics is conducted in a laboratory setting most often using college undergraduates as participants. Furthermore, the products may actually entail specially devised "art-like" stimuli to permit direct experimental manipulation of the various components that contribute to aesthetic impact. To be sure, humanistic scholars have been studying real-world aesthetics for a considerable time, but their efforts do not usually contribute to an *empirical* aesthetics. Instead, their methods tend toward qualitative and speculative single-case studies that do not permit scientific inferences.

Happily for the field of empirical aesthetics, techniques do exist to permit scientific inquiries into products, artists, and contexts. These techniques are collectively referred to as historiometrics or historiometry, a term that was introduced more than a century ago (Woods, 1909, 1911). In brief, historiometric methods involve the application of quantitative measurement and analysis to multiple cases of historic individuals, products, or events in order to test nomothetic hypotheses about genius, creativity, leadership, talent, or aesthetics (cf. Simonton, 1990b). By "historic" we mean that the cases have in one way or another "made history" by entering into the archives of world civilization—such as masterworks, eminent architects, and major artistic trends or movements.

The adjective "nomothetic" in the definition just means a statement regarding some law or statistical regularity that is hypothesized to apply broadly across a large number of individuals, products, or events. An example would be a general claim about how artistic masterpieces are distinguished from works in the same genre that do not attain the same level of historical acclaim (e.g., Derks, 1989; Kozbelt & Burger-Pianko, 2007; Simonton, 2000c). For example, why do some symphonies become mainstays of the classical repertoire while other compositions, even those by the same composers, fall by the wayside, seldom to be performed or recorded? To offer a more specific illustration, historiometric research has managed to establish why the odd-numbered symphonies of Ludwig van Beethoven exhibit appreciably more aesthetic impact than his even-numbered symphonies (Simonton, 2015). The favoritism of audiences and connoisseurs is not arbitrary but rather reflects verifiable aesthetic differences.

Of course, the key to these empirical successes is the "metric" part of historiometric. Somehow, historic products, artists, and contexts are subjected to direct quantitative measurements. Only after these measurements are obtained can they then be subjected to the most appropriate statistical analyses, such as factor analysis, multiple regression, and structural equation modeling. Fortunately, historiometric researchers have a great many measurement techniques at their disposal (Simonton, 1990b). Of these various techniques, perhaps the most critical is content analysis, particularly when content analysis is carried out by computer programs that remove subjectivity from the quantifications. A well-known example in empirical aesthetics is the Regressive Imagery Dictionary that Martindale (1975, 1990) introduced to allow computerized content analysis of poetry and other literary texts (see also Derks, 1994; Simonton, 1989a). More accurately speaking, the term "content analysis" is misleading because the method can be used to assess style, not just content. This breadth applies to both manual and computerized content analysis. For instance, content analysis has assessed incongruous juxtapositions in plays (Derks, 1994; Simonton, 1997; cf. Martindale, 1990), the linguistic complexity of poetry (Simonton, 1989a, 1990a), the integrative complexity of screenplays (McCullough & Conway, 2018), and the melodic predictability of musical themes (Cerulo, 1988, 1989; Simonton, 1984b, 1994). Hence, this historiometric method might be better called "content and/or style analysis."

Although historiometrics inevitably incorporates a specific type of archival data analysis (Simonton, 2000a), not all historiometric measurements need be confined to archival sources. For example, Martindale (1975, 1984) exclusively used archival methods (e.g., his Regressive Imagery Dictionary) to test and develop his evolutionary theory of stylistic change in literature. Yet when he wanted to extend that theory to nonverbal forms of artistic expression, that approach would no longer work. To get around this impasse, he opted to use multiple and independent human raters to provide subjective but still reliable ratings of music recordings and art reproductions (Martindale, 1986b; Martindale & Uemura, 1983). In both cases the stimuli rated were representative products by the most eminent composers and artists of their generation, with the explicit goal of assessing stylistic fluctuations across the history of a given art form (see also Hasenfus, Martindale, & Birnbaum, 1983; Lindauer, 1993a; Simonton, 2007e; Sorokin, 1937–1941). So the empirical inquiries remain historiometric at their core.

In any case, we now turn to an overview of the application of historiometric methods to the three core phenomena in empirical aesthetics.

Aesthetic Products

....

The basics of conducting historiometric research do not differ all that much from other techniques in empirical aesthetics. Once the nomothetic research hypotheses or questions are given, the investigator must identify the samples, engage in the required measurements, and then conduct the necessary statistical analyses.

Product samples

The aesthetic products under investigation could represent any domain that is widely recognized as a bona fide form of artistic expression. Of course, what this precisely includes can change over time as civilization adds new genres. For example, film music can be said to have become a legitimate form of aesthetic creativity in 1935 when the Academy of Motion Picture Arts and Sciences instituted the first Award for Best Original Music Score. Only after sufficient awardees and nominees could such products become subject to historiometric analyses (e.g., Simonton, 2007a, c). As of today, graffiti art seems on the cusp of attaining such status, with Banksy as perhaps the first acclaimed creative genius. In contrast, other vehicles of aesthetic communication go way back to the Muses of ancient Greece, such as poetry, music, and dance.

Often it is possible to sample the entire population of products representing a well-defined domain, such as all poems reprinted in a specified set of prestigious literary anthologies, all musical compositions in the standard classical repertoire (as precisely defined by performance and recording frequencies), all films nominated for an Academy Award ("Oscar") in the principal categories of cinematic achievement (best picture, director, male and female leads and supporting actor, and screenplay), and so forth. If an utterly inclusive sample is prohibitively large, then the researcher may introduce some additional restrictions, like all aesthetic products by a particular artistic genius (Kozbelt, 2007; Simonton, 1987) or a small number of such geniuses (Hass & Weisberg, 2009; Jackson & Padgett, 1982). However, two sampling strategies are sometimes used despite having some conspicuous disadvantages.

First, a researcher might just take a random sample from a larger, well-defined population (e.g., Bazzini, McIntosh, Smith, Cook, & Harris, 1997). This is, quite frankly, an absolutely terrible strategy. Its use immediately destroys one big asset of historiometric research: replicability. Not relying on college undergraduates who happen to sign up for experimental participation, nor on those web surfers who chance upon an online survey, historiometric samples can be exactly defined so that subsequent research can potentially replicate any results exactly (Simonton, 2014b). Any replication failure *must* be ascribed to measurement differences (assuming that the statistical analyses are exactly duplicated). If that represents a unique asset of historiometric research, then why not exploit it rather than reduce the study to the same level of other methods that too often yield nonreplicable results? Another drawback is more subtle: a random procedure cannot guarantee that the most distinguished masterpieces end up in the sample. Yet what can it mean when a particular study inadvertently omits Beethoven's Fifth Symphony, Dante's *Divine Comedy*, Shakespeare's *Hamlet*, Tolstoy's *War and Peace*, Michelangelo's Sistine Chapel Ceiling, Rodin's *The Thinker*, or Welles's *Citizen Kane*? Shouldn't identifiable masterpieces be guaranteed inclusion into any "sample" dealing with a given artistic domain?

Second, researchers are often tempted to confine the sample to the most exemplary cases of a particular art form, that is, the unquestionable masterpieces. For instance, a sample of films might be confined to only those that won best picture awards or emerged as a blockbuster in the box office, and thereby ignore the vast majority of films released each year (cf. Beckwith, 2009). While this strategy avoids the problem introduced by random sampling, it introduces another issue altogether: it instantaneously reduces the variance on the dependent variable that often has the greatest interest, namely, the actual aesthetic impact of the cinematic products! Any predictors out there that distinguish the best pictures from mediocre pictures cannot be identified by any statistical method whatsoever. Even worse, the researcher often ends up identifying features of great films that are actually features of all films, great, mediocre, or terrible. For example, almost all films contain protagonists, but great films may have different kinds of protagonists than run-of-the-mill films.

Obviously, if the goal is to discern the predictors of aesthetic success, the cases must be heterogeneous on the chosen measure of aesthetic impact. The most common way to procure this heterogeneity is to simply make sure that the variance on the criterion is not truncated. Nonetheless, other strategies are possible, depending on the aim of the particular historiometric study. For instance, bestselling novels can be contrasted with a set of poorly selling novels that are otherwise matched on such variables as publicity and author prestige (Harvey, 1953). Most strikingly, the study might compare masterpieces with products that lie at the absolute opposite end of the evaluative continuum, such as notably "bad" or "kitsch" art (Simonton, 2007d; cf. Lindauer, 1990, 1991).

Lastly, on occasion the historiometric researcher decides on breaking an aesthetic product into smaller parts, a fragmentation that can lead to more fine-grained analysis of both aesthetics and creativity. For example, to discern why some of Shakespeare's sonnets are much more effective than others, each poem can be broken down into the three component quatrains and concluding couplet (Simonton, 1990a). In the case of music, an investigator might concentrate on the individual themes that make up a given a composition rather than the composition as a whole (Simonton, 1980a; cf. Simonton, 1986a). Even more remarkably, researchers can focus on the individual sketches that lead up to a given masterwork. The best illustrations are studies of the sketches that Pablo Picasso produced on route to his masterpiece *Guernica*, studies that shed considerable light on the creative process in a bona fide artistic genius (Damian & Simonton, 2011; Simonton, 2007e; Weisberg, 2004; cf. Arnheim, 1962).

Product measures

As suggested in the previous section, the products making up a given sample will very often get measured on one or more indicators of aesthetic impact. Depending on the particular domain of artistic creativity, these measures may include: number of citations in standard histories, performance, recording, or reproduction frequencies, reprinting in anthologies or other select collections, quotation or citation frequencies, ratings by experts, critical reviews, sales figures, download counts, box office, prestigious awards, and probability of representation in "greatest … " lists. For the most part, these alternative indicators will correlate very highly, sufficiently so that they can be taken as indicators of the same underlying construct or latent variable. To illustrate, an inquiry into the differential aesthetic impact of 496 operas constructed a global assessment using nine recording catalogues, three video guides, 11 performance tabulations, three dictionaries, five histories, and five rankings in reference works, obtaining a co-efficient alpha (internal consistency) reliability of 0.95 (Simonton, 1998). Besides the conspicuous consensus, it's also worth pointing out that the consensus on a product's aesthetic merit tends to be stable across considerable periods of time (Simonton, 1989a, 1998; see also Kozbelt, 2007). For example, the success of an opera in its first run predicts its later success decades, even centuries later (Simonton, 1998). So-called "sleepers" or "neglected masterpieces" are so rare as to constitute the exceptions rather than the rule (see also Simonton, 2009c). It is somewhat more common for once popular works to slowly vanish from the art scene, an event almost guaranteed by the constant addition of new artistic products into the competition. In the case of opera, for instance, Giovanni Paisiello's 1782 *The Barber of Seville* was his most successful work, and held its own for well over two decades, until Gioachino Rossini came out with his 1816 version of a very similar libretto, and Paisiello's masterpiece was gradually replaced by the upstart. Sometimes remakes surpass the original.

That all said, aesthetic evaluations can also split into separate, nearly orthogonal assessments because distinct audiences, consumers, or connoisseurs are involved. In such instances we must really recognize more than one consensus. The most obvious example is cinema, which can be considered as both an art form and a commercial product. Hence, not only will film critics often disagree with box office performance, but the industry professionals who bestow the major awards, such as the Oscars, may not completely concur with either of the previous two judgments (Simonton, 2009b). Likewise, how often do bestselling books win elite book awards?

Content analysis was already mentioned as a key measurement strategy for the study of artistic products, an approach that can assess both content and style. Yet depending on the specific art form under investigation, a host of more straightforward variables are easily coded directly from the archival sources. An example is the specific genre of a given work. Thus, dramas have long been classified as either tragedies or comedies (e.g., Derks, 1989; Simonton, 1983, 1986b), a genre distinction that still carries over to modern cinema (e.g., Simonton, 2002, 2009a). These various attributes often have demonstrable consequences for the aesthetic impact of a given creative product. For instance, when Kozbelt and Burger-Pianko (2007) attempted to predict the differential recording counts of Franz Schubert's 597 songs (Lieder), they assessed not only content analytical attributes, such as the melodic originality of the first six notes and the primordial and conceptual imagery of the text, but also such objective attributes as structural complexity, performance duration, major versus minor key, and the identity of the poet (see also Simonton, 1980b, 2000c).

In addition to various substantive variables, researchers are often compelled to define crucial control variables to avoid the statistical artifacts that can easily plague inferences in correlational research (Simonton, 1990b). Although these variables can be quite diverse, it is particularly common to introduce a control for the date when an artistic product was actually created.

Product analyses

Because historiometric research is necessarily correlational rather than experimental, researchers using this technique rely heavily on the full panoply of correlational statistics. These include factor analysis, multiple regression, path analysis, and structural equation modeling (e.g., Simonton, 2004a, 2004b, 2004c). The factor analysis may be used to consolidate a large number of variables into a more manageable set of meaningful dimensions, while the other methods are most often exploited to identify the primary predictors of some aesthetic impact criterion of interest. However, sometimes the investigator is interested in the predictors of content and style characteristics of each work. For example, historiometric research has shown that both content and style are influenced by contextual factors taking place at the time that the work was created (e.g., Cerulo, 1984; Simonton, 1980a, 1986a). Apparently, even the lone artistic genius cannot be completely isolated from his or her surroundings!

These statistical applications most often do not differ in any substantial way from the application of the same statistics to other correlational data, such as those gathered from psychometric and survey research. Even so, the analysis of artistic products features two distinctive characteristics that deserve special attention.

First, although standard inferential statistics assume that the cases are randomly sampled from a larger population, historiometric samples are most often defined by the *entire population* of interest (Simonton, 1990b). Sometimes the population is strictly defined by a specific art form and a particular composer who produced exemplary works in that art form. Besides the study of Schubert's songs mentioned earlier (Kozbelt & Burger-Pianko, 2007), other examples include inquiries into *all* compositions by Mozart (Kozbelt, 2005), *all* symphonies of Beethoven (Simonton, 2015; cf. Simonton, 1987), and *all* of the plays of Shakespeare (Brainerd, 1980; Derks, 1989, 1994; Simonton, 2004d). Moreover, even when the sample is more broadly defined, it still can encompass all artistic products of any genuine interest, such as *all* works that are regularly performed in the top opera houses of the world (Simonton, 2000b), *all* symphonies in the standard repertoire that were created by symphonists who contributed four or more works to that repertoire (Simonton, 1995), or *all* films nominated for the major cinema awards (Pardoe & Simonton, 2008; Simonton, 2005). Whatever the sampling specifics, it is manifest that effect sizes are far more meaningful than levels of statistical significance (Simonton, 2014b). After all, the effect sizes are not at all estimates but rather directly assess population characteristics (cf. Cohen, 1994). Confidence intervals have no real meaning whatsoever when the point estimate is not an estimate but a parameter.

Second, very often historiometric data have an implicit or explicit multilevel structure (cf. Silvia, 2007). At the very minimum, the aesthetic products are nested within artistic geniuses so that variables may be defined at both product and creator levels. This data structure then mandates that the investigator introduce hierarchical linear models (e.g., Kozbelt, 2011; Zickar & Slaughter, 1999). Overlooking this structure can lead to faulty inferences at the descriptive level, so it is not just a matter of inferential statistics. To illustrate, Simonton (1989b) claimed to have demonstrated a "swan-song phenomenon" in which classical works showed dramatic changes when created at the end of the composer's life. Yet Meredith and Kozbelt (2014) used multilevel modeling to show that these effects were not sufficiently robust to count as an empirically reliable phenomenon. Although such models could include more than two levels—such as musical themes nested within movements nested within compositions nested within composers—researchers have tended to confine themselves to just two levels.

Naturally, often the unit of analysis is not the single aesthetic product but rather the artistic creator who contributes those products, which brings us to the next phenomenon.

CREATIVE ARTISTS

Art is created by artists, not scientists, and great art is created by great artists, so what are the characteristics of historic artists that enable them to contribute to the canon of aesthetic masterworks in a given domain? That is the fundamental question addressed by historiometric studies that concentrate on the creative artist as the unit of analysis. Not surprisingly, then, historiometric research at this level closely parallels what was earlier described for artistic products. More specifically, we need to look at samples, measures, and analyses.

Artist samples

As noted with respect to products, it is rare that random sampling of artistic creators has any scientific justification. Instead, it makes more sense to define a "sample" that includes the entire population of undeniable exemplars, or what has been called a "significant sample" (Simonton, 1999). To provide some numbers to indicate what is meant, Murray (2003) used nearly a dozen standard histories of Western art to identify the "significant figures" who appear most often in every source. Confining the count to artists active after 1200, fully 455 were so identified, of whom 154 could be considered major figures. By comparison, when Simonton (1984a) collected a sample of post-medieval Western artists for a historiometric inquiry, he used a standard biographical dictionary to obtain a "sample" of 772 cases. In other words, this investigation not only encompassed universally recognized artistic geniuses like Michelangelo and Picasso, as well as very numerous also-rans, like the 18th-century Scottish painter William Dyce, but dipped down to include such obscure stragglers as the 17th-century Dutch painter Hendrick Bloemaert. Hence, the collective creative activity of these 772 figures pretty much defines the history of Western art after the end of the European Middle Ages.

To be sure, for various reasons the sample may be restricted to fewer than several hundred notables. For example, the significant sample might be defined by those who have received special awards or honors. Thus the number of creative writers who have won the Nobel Prize for Literature is only a little over 100. Other times the sample might be confined to those creators for whom the biographical data are most adequate to address the given nomothetic hypothesis. For instance, even though nearly 700 composers have contributed at least one enduring work to the classical repertoire (Simonton, 1977b), the sample might be cut to far less, such as 120, 57, or even just 10 (Meredith & Kozbelt, 2014; Simonton, 1977a, 1991a). More accurately, when the sample is reduced to a very small number, the investigator will often obtain a larger N by using a different unit of analysis. For example, the inquiry into 10 classical composers (viz. Bach, Handel, Mozart, Haydn, Beethoven, Schubert, Chopin, Brahms, Wagner, and Debussy) actually divided their productive careers into consecutive 5-year periods, thus generating 100 cases in a cross-sectional time-series analysis (Simonton, 1977a; see also Hass & Weisberg, 2015).

For reasons given earlier for artistic products, it seldom if ever makes sense to use random sampling in historiometric research. Why literally take the chance that the sample might inadvertently omit Beethoven, Dante, Shakespeare, Tolstoy, Michelangelo, Rodin, or Welles? Besides, significant samples do not have to be all that large. In Murray's (2003) comprehensive determination for creators in various world civilizations, the count of significant figures never exceeds a thousand, and more often numbers a few hundred or less. In fact, it is not impossible for historiometric publications to include a complete list of all subjects studied (e.g., Galton, 1869; Kozbelt, 2008a; Murray, 2003; Simonton, 2014a). Hence, if the sample sizes are not likely prohibitive, why not make sure that the study definitely includes the "best and the brightest"?

Artist measures

In a manner analogous to assessing products on aesthetic impact, a significant sample of artistic creators can be assessed on achieved eminence or posthumous reputation (e.g., Cox, 1926; Raskin, 1936). These measures most often entail composites of indicators drawing from histories, encyclopedias, biographical dictionaries, and other reference works. Sometimes these archival assessments will be supplemented or replaced by surveys of experts. For example, Farnsworth (1969) gauged the differential eminence of classical composers using both standard reference works (histories and encyclopedias) and a survey of musicologists. The exact choice of indicators does not really matter that much because alternative eminence indicators all reflect a single latent variable styled "Galton's *G*" after the first researcher to suggest that genius be measured by posthumous reputation (Simonton, 1991b). Any secondary factors merely represent shared method artifacts, such as scaling and distribution characteristics. As a result, composites consisting of linear sums of multiple indicators exhibit impressive internal consistency reliability coefficients (Simonton, 1990b). For instance, Murray (2003) reported the following reliabilities (Cronbach alphas) for creators who attained eminence in various aesthetic traditions (significant figures in parentheses): Chinese art .91 (111), Japanese art .93 (81), Western art .95 (479), Arabic literature .88 (82), Chinese literature .89 (83), Indian literature .91 (43), Japanese literature .86 (85), Western literature .95 (835), and Western music .97 (522). Even though Murray relied heavily on Western scholarship for his assessments, the reliabilities remain high for the non-Western artists and writers, who form a more selective group (Simonton & Ting, 2010).

In addition, the conspicuous consensus on eminence exhibits substantial temporal stability across decades, even centuries (Farnsworth, 1969; Ginsburgh & Weyers, 2014; Rosengren, 1985; Simonton, 1991b; Vermeylen, van Dijck, & de Laet, 2013). Just as significant is the fact that this enduring "test–retest" reliability cannot be attributed to one generation's evaluations borrowing from the evaluations of the preceding generation; more formally, consecutive assessments are not autoregressive (Simonton, 1991b). Apparently, each generation of historians, critics, and other scholars is making its own independent assessments based on each creator's lifetime contributions to an aesthetic domain. If those works stand the test of time, then so will the artists who produced those works. Hence, the contemporary judgments of the relative merits of Renaissance artists are in substantial agreement with those held today (Ginsburgh & Weyers, 2006a, b). To be sure, the transhistorical stability is not perfect (Runco, Acar, Kaufman, & Halliday, 2016; Weisberg, 2015). Just as was seen for artistic products, assessments will change with the addition of new creators to the pool. For instance, for centuries the top-rated Italian painters were Michelangelo, Raphael, and Leonardo da Vinci, with Michelangelo almost always placed first (cf. Ginsburgh & Weyers, 2006a, b). Yet once Picasso entered the competition, the last two Italian artists got bumped down to third and fourth place (Murray, 2003). In sum, assessment of achieved eminence is by means arbitrary or capricious.

Indeed, the last conclusion is reinforced when significant samples of artistic creators are assessed on a host of other variables that root eminence in concrete behavioral, developmental, and personality antecedents (Simonton, 2013). The most obvious of these concern various measures of creative productivity across the life span (e.g., Hass & Weisberg, 2009, 2015; Lindauer, 1993b). These include total lifetime output, maximum output rate, and the ages at which the creators make their first major contribution, their best single contribution, and their last major contribution (e.g., Kaufman & Gentile, 2002; Kaufman & Kaufman, 2007; Simonton, 1977a, 1977b). These straightforward behavioral assessments can be supplemented by historiometric "at-a-distance" measures of both development and personality (e.g., Cox, 1926; Raskin, 1936; Simonton, 1991a).

The developmental variables can include family background, such as birth order and socioeconomic status, education and special training, role models and mentors, and domain-specific social networks, such as artistic friends, colleagues, and rivals (e.g., Simonton, 1984a). Some recent work has also examined the developmental impact of diversifying experiences, such as parental loss, physical or cognitive disabilities, and minority status (e.g., Damian & Simonton, 2015). The personality variables can be equally diverse, but many historiometricians have taken an interest in symptoms of mental illness, both clinical and subclinical (e.g., Kaufman, 2001, 2005; Ludwig, 1998; Martindale, 1972; Ramey & Weisberg, 2004; Simonton, 2014a; Weisberg, 1994).

Needless to say, control variables also must be defined, the specific controls depending on the particular needs of the historiometric investigation (Simonton, 1990b). Yet it almost always makes sense to control for the artistic creator's date of birth to adjust for any gross secular trends.

Artist analyses

If the actual unit of analysis is the creative artist, then statistical analysis of the data resulting from the foregoing measurements involves nothing more than what is normally done with cross-sectional data. It is only when the cases are split into smaller units, such as the 5-year age periods mentioned earlier, that more sophisticated analytical methods come into play (cf. Meredith & Kozbelt, 2014; Zickar & Slaughter, 1999). Nevertheless, it must be repeated that inferential statistics have rather less relevance when dealing with significant samples that essentially incorporate the entire population of interest (Simonton, 2014b). The descriptive statistics are not estimates but rather actual parameter values—the actual correlations or mean differences sans confidence intervals or significance tests. Any artistic creators omitted from the sample are either (a) far less interesting than those in the sample or (b) do not represent a comparable population to which the researcher can generalize anyway. For instance, a given study might only include Western creators, such as the 772 artists study cited earlier (Simonton, 1984a), but those cases were not randomly sampled from the larger population that includes artists from other civilizations in East Asia, South Asia, or elsewhere. Cross-cultural contrasts can easily undermine the generalizability of any findings even if the results are statistically significant at the $p < .001$ level (Simonton & Ting, 2010).

Now that cross-cultural comparisons have been introduced, it becomes time to turn to the last major phenomenon in empirical aesthetics.

SOCIOCULTURAL MILIEU

All aesthetic products are produced by creators embedded within a larger social, cultural, political, and economic milieu—or what I will just call the "sociocultural context."

Moreover, the "cultural" environment can be taken to encompass specific artistic traditions, norms, or styles. Historiometric research operating at this level has three parts that closely parallel what was observed for persons and products, but with some quite distinctive methodological features.

Defining the units

A key component of studying sociocultural context is the need to aggregate either creators or creations into larger units. Hence, the sampling strategies discussed earlier automatically apply here: get a sample of aesthetic products or artistic creators. Once these have been determined, they can then be assigned to the appropriate sociocultural unit. These units may be either spatial, such as nations or civilizations, or temporal, such as years, decades, or generations. Of course, some historiometric inquiries may involve both types of units. In addition, the choice of units will often determine the sampling procedures, such as limiting the spatial units or determining the onset and termination of the temporal units. To illustrate, when Martindale and Uemura (1983) investigated stylistic change in Western music, they limited the spatial units to just four nations (France, Germany, the United Kingdom, and Italy) and the temporal units to the interval 1490 to 1909 CE (i.e., from the Renaissance to modern times). They then divided the latter interval into 21 consecutive 20-year periods. Next, they identified the three most eminent composers for each period within each nation, thus yielding a significant sample of 252 composers (= 21 × 4 × 3). Finally, they picked the single most famous work by each composer to obtain a representative theme for the subsequent content analysis.

In the above illustration, the investigators deliberately sought equal representation across nations and within periods, but frequently researchers want the samples to represent the actual differences in the representation of artistic products or creators across units (e.g., Borowiecki, 2014; Murray, 2003; Simonton, 1975, 1992). The resulting tabulations will then describe the fluctuations in aesthetic activity across and within the spatial units. In such instances the researcher will collect a significant sample of products or persons according to procedures already described and then aggregate them into the units. For instance, Murray (2003) used this method to scrutinize the generational rise and fall of creative activity in Western, Islamic, Indian, Chinese, and Japanese civilizations, where the sociocultural activity included art, literature, and music.

Measuring the milieu

Speaking more precisely, the tabulations mentioned in the previous paragraph will usually incorporate a methodological refinement: Rather than just count the number of artistic geniuses active in a given period (most often taken as a 20-year generation), the investigator will weight those counts according to differential achieved eminence, as assessed by the methods mentioned earlier (Murray, 2003; Simonton, 1975, 2017; Sorokin, 1937–1941). Hence, a tabulation of artists would have Michelangelo count much more than Hendrick Bloemaert. Fortunately, because the greatest creative artists tend to appear in the same eras when the most also-rans also appear, the details of the weighting scheme are less important than the assurance that the greatest figures fall during the peak periods (Simonton, 1988).

A wide range of other contextual variables can be assessed, such as the frequency and intensity of war (including both international and civil), political fragmentation, governmental stability, economic prosperity, population growth, cultural diversity, religious or philosophical ideology, etc. (e.g., Murray, 2003; Simonton, 1975, 1992, 2017; Sorokin, 1937–1941). In addition, content analysis can be directly applied to artistic products to assess various stylistic attributes that define a particular era (e.g., Kozbelt & Meredith, 2010). Indeed, Martindale (1990) devoted an entire career to studying aesthetic evolution based on the content analysis of literary, artistic, and musical products (see also Martindale, 1986a). Naturally, historiometric researchers will define pertinent control variables as well, such as controls for any linear or nonlinear historical trends.

Analyzing the data

Often data analyses at this level use the same techniques seen at the lower levels, whether product or person. Examples include factor analysis, multiple regression, and structural equation models. Yet frequently the statistical treatment can take advantage of the unique properties of many studies conducted at this level. This is especially true when the data consist of generational time series, that is, consecutive observations on 20-year units that span centuries if not millennia (e.g., Murray, 2003; Simonton, 1975, 1992, 2017; Sorokin, 1937–1941). The investigator can then employ the kinds of dynamic models so often seen in econometric analyses of macroeconomic data. Sociocultural creativity just replaces economic prosperity or other such measure of material conditions. These models can include various hypothesized external influences, such as political, social, or economic conditions (see also Borowiecki, 2014).

Yet these same models also incorporate an "autoregressive" factor representing internal influences (Murray, 2003; Simonton, 1975, 1988). In particular, aesthetic creativity at one generation is very often a positive function of aesthetic creativity at the previous generation. This cross-generational influence has been called "role-model availability," and its critical effect has been replicated across several world civilizations (Murray, 2003; Simonton & Ting, 2010; cf. Simonton, 2018). In formal terms, the representation of artistic geniuses in generation g is positively associated with the representation of artistic geniuses in generation $g - 1$. Moreover, this influence holds for both weighted and unweighted tabulations. Lastly, these internal effects function independently of the external effects.

CONCLUSION

Experimental aesthetics is often said to have begun with Gustav Fechner's (1876) pioneering efforts (Martindale, 2007). Yet surprisingly, the historiometric approach to empirical aesthetics is more than four decades older. The first such inquiry was a quantitative analysis of the relation between an eminent playwright's age and the production of dramatic masterworks in both English and French theater. This was published by Adolphe Quételet in 1835, albeit as just part of a much larger treatise devoted to applying statistics to the social sciences (Quételet, 1835/1968). Quételet helps illustrate another point: historiometric studies of the arts have always been a multidisciplinary effort. He himself was trained in mathematics and became a prominent statistician (see also Brainerd, 1980; Pardoe & Simonton, 2008), but other contributions have come from researchers in psychology (e.g., Kaufman, 2000–2001; Kozbelt, 2008b; Lindauer, 1993b; Martindale, 1995; Simonton, 2007b), psychiatry (e.g., Ludwig, 1998; Post, 1996), communication studies (e.g., Paisley, 1964; Rosengren, 1985), sociology (e.g., Accominotti, 2009; Borowiecki, 2014; Cerulo, 1984; Lincoln & Allen, 2004), anthropology (e.g., Dressler & Robbins, 1975; Richardson & Kroeber, 1940), marketing (e.g., Collins & Hand, 2006; Eliashberg & Shugan, 1997), and economics (e.g., Galenson, 2005; Ginsburgh, 2003; Hellmanzik, 2010). In the latter case, in fact, we can speak of the emergence of "cultural economics" as a frequent example of the practice (e.g., Ginsburgh & Weyers, 1999; Hellmanzik, 2009; Holbrook & Addis, 2008). *The Journal of Cultural Economics* (begun in 1977) can be considered a counterpart to *Empirical Studies of the Arts* (begun in 1983), but with an even higher percentage of historiometric articles. Some historiometricians will even publish in both journals (e.g., Ginsburgh & Weyers, 2005, 2006a, b, 2010). The only contrast is that economists are more likely to refer to their version of quantitative history as cliometrics rather than historiometrics (Simonton, 2008). But what's in a name? Both terms come from Greek, and with equivalent meanings, for Clio was the Muse of history.

Moreover, with the advent of internet databases, the ability to collect historiometric data for measurement and analysis has substantially improved. Now information can be downloaded regarding hundreds, even thousands of aesthetic products and creative artists. This opportunity is perhaps best illustrated by recent work on cinematic aesthetics and creativity, which often takes full advantage of such online sources as the Internet Movie Database, Metacritic, and Rotten Tomatoes (e.g., Plucker, Holden, & Neustadter, 2008; Simonton, Graham, & Kaufman, 2012). These sources have enabled investigators to tackle such questions as the actual impact of "sex and violence" on a film's financial performance, movie awards, and critical acclaim (Cerridwen & Simonton, 2009; Simonton, Skidmore, & Kaufman, 2012). Who would ever guess that sex *doesn't* sell, whether in the box office, critical reviews, or award ceremonies?

The emphasis of this chapter is on the method itself rather than the empirical results produced by that method. Fortunately, extensive reviews of key findings have already been published, and the contributions to empirical aesthetics are immense (e.g., Kozbelt, 2014; Simonton, 2013). Furthermore, these empirical results just cannot be attained by any other methodology, experimental or otherwise. For that reason, it is safe to predict that historiometric research will continue well into the future.

References

Accominotti, F. (2009). Creativity from interaction: artistic movements and the creativity careers of modern painters. *Poetics, 37*, 267–294.

Arnheim, R. (1962). *Picasso's Guernica: The genesis of a painting*. Berkeley, CA: University of California Press.

Bazzini, D. G., McIntosh, W. D., Smith, S. M., Cook, S., & Harris, C. (1997). The aging women in popular film: Underrepresented, unattractive, unfriendly, and unintelligent. *Sex Roles, 36*, 531–543.

Beckwith, D. C. (2009). Values of protagonists in best pictures and blockbusters: Implications for marketing. *Psychology and Marketing, 26*, 445–469.

Borowiecki, K. J. (2014). Artistic creativity and extreme events: The heterogeneous impact of war on composers' production. *Poetics, 47*, 83–105.

Brainerd, B. (1980). The chronology of Shakespeare's plays: A statistical study. *Computers and the Humanities, 14*, 221–230.

Cerridwen, A., & Simonton, D. K. (2009). Sex doesn't sell—nor impress: Content, box office, critics, and awards in mainstream cinema. *Psychology of Aesthetics, Creativity, and the Arts, 3*, 200–210.

Cerulo, K. A. (1984). Social disruption and its effects on music: An empirical analysis. *Social Forces, 62*, 885–904.

Cerulo, K. A. (1988). Analyzing cultural products: A new method of measurement. *Social Science Research, 17*, 317–352.

Cerulo, K. A. (1989). Variations in musical syntax: Patterns of measurement. *Communication Research, 16*, 204–235.

Cohen, J. (1994). The earth is round (p < 0.05). *American Psychologist, 49*, 997–1003.

Collins, A., & Hand, C. (2006). Vote clustering in tournaments: What can Oscar tell us? *Creativity Research Journal, 18*, 427–434.

Cox, C. (1926). *The early mental traits of three hundred geniuses*. Stanford, CA: Stanford University Press.

Damian, R. I., & Simonton, D. K. (2011). From past to future art: The creative impact of Picasso's 1935 *Minotauromachy* on his 1937 *Guernica*. *Psychology of Aesthetics, Creativity, and the Arts, 5*, 360–369.

Damian, R. I., & Simonton, D. K. (2015). Psychopathology, adversity, and creativity: Diversifying experiences in the development of eminent African Americans. *Journal of Personality and Social Psychology, 108*, 623–636.

Derks, P. L. (1989). Pun frequency and popularity of Shakespeare's plays. *Empirical Studies of the Arts, 7*, 23–31.

Derks, P. L. (1994). Clockwork Shakespeare: The Bard meets the Regressive Imagery Dictionary. *Empirical Studies of the Arts, 12*, 131–139.

Dressler, W. W., & Robbins, M. C. (1975). Art styles, social stratification, and cognition: An analysis of Greek vase painting. *American Ethnologist, 2*, 427–434.

Eliashberg, J., & Shugan, S. M. (1997). Film critics: Influencers or predictors? *Journal of Marketing, 61*, 68–78.

Farnsworth, P. R. (1969). *The social psychology of music*, 2nd edition. Ames, IA: Iowa State University Press.

Fechner, G. T. (1876). *Vorschule der Aesthetik* (2 vols.). Leipzig, Germany: Breitkopf & Härtel.

Galenson, D. W. (2005). *Old masters and young geniuses: The two life cycles of artistic creativity.* Princeton, NJ: Princeton University Press.

Galton, F. (1869). *Hereditary genius. An inquiry into its laws and consequences.* London, UK: Macmillan & Co.

Ginsburgh, V. (2003). Awards, success and aesthetic quality in the arts. *Journal of Economic Perspectives, 17*, 99–111.

Ginsburgh, V., & Weyers, S. (1999). On the perceived quality of movies. *Journal of Cultural Economics, 23*, 269–283.

Ginsburgh, V., & Weyers, S. (2005). Creativity and life cycles of artists. *Journal of Cultural Economics, 30*, 91–107.

Ginsburgh, V., & Weyers, S. (2006a). Comparing artistic values: The example of movies. *Empirical Studies of the Arts, 24*, 163–175.

Ginsburgh, V., & Weyers, S. (2006b). Persistence and fashion in art: Italian Renaissance from Vasari to Berenson and beyond. *Poetics, 34*, 24–44.

Ginsburgh, V., & Weyers, S. (2010). On the formation of canons: The dynamics of narratives in art history. *Empirical Studies of the Arts, 26*, 37–72.

Ginsburgh, V., & Weyers, S. (2014). Evaluating excellence in the arts. In D. K. Simonton (Ed.), *The Wiley handbook of genius* (pp. 511–532). Oxford, England: Wiley.

Harvey, J. (1953). The content characteristics of best-selling novels. *Public Opinion Quarterly, 17*, 91–114.

Hasenfus, N., Martindale, C., & Birnbaum, D. (1983). Psychological reality of cross-media artistic styles. *Journal of Experimental Psychology: Human Perception and Performance, 9*, 841–863.

Hass, R. W., & Weisberg, R. W. (2009). Career development in two seminal American songwriters: A test of the equal odds rule. *Creativity Research Journal, 21*, 183–190.

Hass, R. W., & Weisberg, R. W. (2015). Revisiting the 10-year rule for composers from the *Great American Songbook*: On the validity of two measures of creative production. *Psychology of Aesthetics, Creativity, and the Arts, 9*, 471–479.

Hellmanzik, C. (2009). Artistic styles: Revisiting the analysis of modern artists' careers. *Journal of Cultural Economics, 33*, 201–232.

Hellmanzik, C. (2010). Location matters: Estimating cluster premiums for prominent modern artists. *European Economic Review, 54*, 199–218.

Holbrook, M. B., & Addis, M. (2008). Art versus commerce in the movie industry: A two-path model of motion-picture success. *Journal of Cultural Economics, 32*, 87–107.

Jackson, J. M., & Padgett, V. R. (1982). With a little help from my friend: Social loafing and the Lennon-McCartney songs. *Personality and Social Psychology Bulletin, 8*, 672–677.

Kaufman, J. C. (2000–2001). Genius, lunatics and poets: Mental illness in prize-winning authors. *Imagination, Cognition & Personality, 20*, 305–314.

Kaufman, J. C. (2001). The Sylvia Plath effect: Mental illness in eminent creative writers. *Journal of Creative Behavior, 35*, 37–50.

Kaufman, J. C. (2005). The door that leads into madness: Eastern European poets and mental illness. *Creativity Research Journal, 17*, 99–103.

Kaufman, J. C., & Gentile, C. A. (2002). The will, the wit, the judgement: The importance of an early start in productive and successful creative writing. *High Ability Studies, 13*, 115–123.

Kaufman, S. B., & Kaufman, J. C. (2007). Ten years to expertise, many more to greatness: An investigation of modern writers. *Journal of Creative Behavior, 41*, 114–124.

Kozbelt, A. (2005). Factors affecting aesthetic success and improvement in creativity: A case study of musical genres in Mozart. *Psychology of Music, 33*, 235–255.

Kozbelt, A. (2007). A quantitative analysis of Beethoven as self-critic: Implications for psychological theories of musical creativity. *Psychology of Music, 35*, 144–168. doi:10.1177/0305735607068892

Kozbelt, A. (2008a). Longitudinal hit ratios of classical composers: Reconciling "Darwinian" and expertise acquisition perspectives on lifespan creativity. *Psychology of Aesthetics, Creativity, and the Arts, 2*, 221–235.

Kozbelt, A. (2008b). One-hit wonders in classical music: Evidence and (partial) explanations for an early career peak. *Creativity Research Journal, 20*, 179–195.

Kozbelt, A. (2011). Age and aesthetic significance in classical music: A multi-level reanalysis of Halsey's (1976) ratings. *Empirical Studies of the Arts, 29*, 129–148.

Kozbelt, A. (2014). Musical creativity over the lifespan. In D. K. Simonton (Ed.), *The Wiley handbook of genius* (pp. 451–472). Oxford, England: Wiley.

Kozbelt, A., & Burger-Pianko, Z. (2007).Words, music, and other measures: Predicting the repertoire popularity of 597 Schubert lieder. *Psychology of Aesthetics, Creativity, and the Arts, 1*, 191–203.

Kozbelt, A., & Meredith, D. (2010). A note on trans-historical melodic originality trends in classical music. *International Journal of Creativity and Problem Solving, 20*, 109–125.

Lincoln, A. E., & Allen, M. P. (2004). Double jeopardy in Hollywood: age and gender in the careers of film actors, 1926–1999. *Sociological Forum, 19*, 611–631.

Lindauer, M. S. (1990). Reactions to cheap art. *Empirical Studies of the Arts, 8*, 95–110.

Lindauer, M. S. (1991). Comparisons between museum and mass-produced art. *Empirical Studies of the Arts, 9*, 11–22.

Lindauer, M. S. (1993a). The old-age style and its artists. *Empirical Studies and the Arts, 11*, 135–146.

Lindauer, M. S. (1993b). The span of creativity among long-lived historical artists. *Creativity Research Journal, 6*, 231–239.

Ludwig, A. M. (1998). Method and madness in the arts and sciences. *Creativity Research Journal, 11*, 93–101.

Martindale, C. (1972). Father absence, psychopathology, and poetic eminence. *Psychological Reports, 31*, 843–847.

Martindale, C. (1975). *Romantic progression: The psychology of literary history*. Washington, DC: Hemisphere.

Martindale, C. (1984). Evolutionary trends in poetic style: The case of English metaphysical poetry. *Computers and the Humanities, 18*, 3–21.

Martindale, C. (1986a). Aesthetic evolution. *Poetics, 15*, 439–473.

Martindale, C. (1986b). The evolution of Italian painting: A quantitative investigation of trends in style and content from late Gothic to the Rococo period. *Leonardo, 19*, 217–222.

Martindale, C. (1990). *The clockwork muse: The predictability of artistic styles*. New York: Basic Books.

Martindale, C. (1995). Fame more fickle than fortune: On the distribution of literary eminence. *Poetics, 23*, 219–234.

Martindale, C. (2007). Recent trends in the psychological study of aesthetics, creativity, and the arts. *Empirical Studies of the Arts, 25*, 121–141.

Martindale, C., & Uemura, A. (1983). Stylistic evolution in European music. *Leonardo, 16*, 225–228.

McCullough, H., & Conway, L. G. III. (2018). "And the Oscar goes to … ": Integrative complexity's predictive power in the film industry. *Psychology of Aesthetics, Creativity, and the Arts, 12*, 392–398.

Meredith, D, & Kozbelt, A. (2014). A swan song for the swan-song phenomenon: Multi-level evidence against robust end-of-life effects for classical composers. *Empirical Studies of the Arts, 32*, 5–25.

Murray, C. (2003). *Human accomplishment: The pursuit of excellence in the arts and sciences, 800 B.C. to 1950.* New York: HarperCollins.

Paisley, W. J. (1964). Identifying the unknown communicator in painting, literature and music: The significance of minor encoding habits. *Journal of Communication, 14*, 219–237.

Pardoe, I., & Simonton, D. K. (2008). Applying discrete choice models to predict Academy Award winners. *Journal of the Royal Statistical Society: Series A (Statistics in Society), 171*, 375–394.

Plucker, J. A., Holden, J., & Neustadter, D. (2008). The criterion problem and creativity in film: Psychometric characteristics of various measures. *Psychology of Aesthetics, Creativity, and the Arts, 2*, 190–196.

Post, F. (1996). Verbal creativity, depression and alcoholism: An investigation of one hundred American and British writers. *British Journal of Psychiatry, 168*, 545–555.

Quételet, A. (1968). *A treatise on man and the development of his faculties.* New York: Franklin. (Reprint of 1842 Edinburgh translation of 1835 French original.)

Ramey, C. H., & Weisberg, R. W. (2004). The "poetical activity" of Emily Dickinson: A further test of the hypothesis that affective disorders foster creativity. *Creativity Research Journal, 16*, 173–185.

Raskin, E. A. (1936). Comparison of scientific and literary ability: A biographical study of eminent scientists and men of letters of the nineteenth century. *Journal of Abnormal and Social Psychology, 31*, 20–35.

Richardson, J., & Kroeber, A. L. (1940). Three centuries of women's dress fashions: A quantitative analysis. *Anthropological Records, 5*, 111–150.

Rosengren, K. E. (1985). Time and literary fame. *Poetics, 14*, 157–172.

Runco, M. A., Acar, S., Kaufman, J. C., & Halliday, L. R. (2016). Changes in reputation and associations with fame and biographical data. *Journal of Genius and Eminence, 1*(1), 50–58.

Silvia, P. J. (2007). An introduction to multilevel modeling for research on the psychology of art and creativity. *Empirical Studies of the Arts, 25*, 1–20.

Simonton, D. K. (1975). Sociocultural context of individual creativity: A transhistorical time-series analysis. *Journal of Personality and Social Psychology, 32*, 1119–1133.

Simonton, D. K. (1977a). Creative productivity, age, and stress: A biographical time-series analysis of 10 classical composers. *Journal of Personality and Social Psychology, 35*, 791–804.

Simonton, D. K. (1977b). Eminence, creativity, and geographic marginality: A recursive structural equation model. *Journal of Personality and Social Psychology, 35*, 805–816.

Simonton, D. K. (1980a). Thematic fame and melodic originality in classical music: A multivariate computer-content analysis. *Journal of Personality, 48*, 206–219.

Simonton, D. K. (1980b). Thematic fame, melodic originality, and musical zeitgeist: A biographical and transhistorical content analysis. *Journal of Personality and Social Psychology, 38,* 972–983.

Simonton, D. K. (1983). Dramatic greatness and content: A quantitative study of eighty-one Athenian and Shakespearean plays. *Empirical Studies of the Arts, 1,* 109–123.

Simonton, D. K. (1984a). Artistic creativity and interpersonal relationships across and within generations. *Journal of Personality and Social Psychology, 46,* 1273–1286.

Simonton, D. K. (1984b). Melodic structure and note transition probabilities: A content analysis of 15,618 classical themes. *Psychology of Music, 12,* 3–16.

Simonton, D. K. (1986a). Aesthetic success in classical music: A computer analysis of 1935 compositions. *Empirical Studies of the Arts, 4,* 1–17.

Simonton, D. K. (1986b). Popularity, content, and context in 37 Shakespeare plays. *Poetics, 15,* 493–510.

Simonton, D. K. (1987). Musical aesthetics and creativity in Beethoven: A computer analysis of 105 compositions. *Empirical Studies of the Arts, 5,* 87–104.

Simonton, D. K. (1988). Galtonian genius, Kroeberian configurations, and emulation: A generational time-series analysis of Chinese civilization. *Journal of Personality and Social Psychology, 55,* 230–238.

Simonton, D. K. (1989a). Shakespeare's sonnets: A case of and for single-case historiometry. *Journal of Personality, 57,* 695–721.

Simonton, D. K. (1989b). The swan-song phenomenon: Last-works effects for 172 classical composers. *Psychology and Aging, 4,* 42–47.

Simonton, D. K. (1990a). Lexical choices and aesthetic success: A computer content analysis of 154 Shakespeare sonnets. *Computers and the Humanities, 24,* 251–264.

Simonton, D. K. (1990b). *Psychology, science, and history: An introduction to historiometry.* New Haven, CT: Yale University Press.

Simonton, D. K. (1991a). Emergence and realization of genius: The lives and works of 120 classical composers. *Journal of Personality and Social Psychology, 61,* 829–840.

Simonton, D. K. (1991b). Latent-variable models of posthumous reputation: A quest for Galton's G. *Journal of Personality and Social Psychology, 60,* 607–619.

Simonton, D. K. (1992). Gender and genius in Japan: Feminine eminence in masculine culture. *Sex Roles, 27,* 101–119.

Simonton, D. K. (1994). Computer content analysis of melodic structure: Classical composers and their compositions. *Psychology of Music, 22,* 31–43.

Simonton, D. K. (1995). Drawing inferences from symphonic programs: Musical attributes versus listener attributions. *Music Perception, 12,* 307–322.

Simonton, D. K. (1997). Imagery, style, and content in 37 Shakespeare plays. *Empirical Studies of the Arts, 15,* 15–20.

Simonton, D. K. (1998). Fickle fashion versus immortal fame: Transhistorical assessments of creative products in the opera house. *Journal of Personality and Social Psychology, 75,* 198–210.

Simonton, D. K. (1999). Significant samples: The psychological study of eminent individuals. *Psychological Methods, 4,* 425–451.

Simonton, D. K. (2000a). Archival research. In A. E. Kazdin (Ed.), *Encyclopedia of psychology* (Vol. 1, pp. 234–235). Washington, DC: American Psychological Association; New York: Oxford University Press.

Simonton, D. K. (2000b). Creative development as acquired expertise: Theoretical issues and an empirical test. *Developmental Review, 20,* 283–318.

Simonton, D. K. (2000c). The music or the words? Or, how important is the libretto for an opera's aesthetic success? *Empirical Studies of the Arts, 18,* 105–118.

Simonton, D. K. (2002). Collaborative aesthetics in the feature film: Cinematic components predicting the differential impact of 2,323 Oscar-nominated movies. *Empirical Studies of the Arts, 20,* 115–125.

Simonton, D. K. (2004a). The "Best Actress" paradox: Outstanding feature films versus exceptional performances by women. *Sex Roles, 50,* 781–794.

Simonton, D. K. (2004b). Film awards as indicators of cinematic creativity and achievement: A quantitative comparison of the Oscars and six alternatives. *Creativity Research Journal, 16,* 163–172.

Simonton, D. K. (2004c). Group artistic creativity: Creative clusters and cinematic success in 1,327 feature films. *Journal of Applied Social Psychology, 34,* 1494–1520.

Simonton, D. K. (2004d). Thematic content and political context in Shakespeare's dramatic output, with implications for authorship and chronology controversies. *Empirical Studies of the Arts, 22,* 201–213.

Simonton, D. K. (2005). Film as art versus film as business: Differential correlates of screenplay characteristics. *Empirical Studies of the Arts, 23,* 93–117.

Simonton, D. K. (2007a). Cinema composers: Career trajectories for creative productivity in film music. *Psychology of Aesthetics, Creativity, and the Arts, 1,* 160–169.

Simonton, D. K. (2007b). Creative life cycles in literature: Poets versus novelists or conceptualists versus experimentalists? *Psychology of Aesthetics, Creativity, and the Arts, 1,* 133–139.

Simonton, D. K. (2007c). Film music: Are award-winning scores and songs heard in successful motion pictures? *Psychology of Aesthetics, Creativity, and the Arts, 1,* 53–60.

Simonton, D. K. (2007d). Is bad art the opposite of good art? Positive versus negative cinematic assessments of 877 feature films. *Empirical Studies of the Arts, 25,* 121–143.

Simonton, D. K. (2007e). The creative process in Picasso's *Guernica* sketches: Monotonic improvements or nonmonotonic variants? *Creativity Research Journal, 19,* 329–344.

Simonton, D. K. (2008). Cliometrics. In W. A. Darity, Jr. (Ed.), *International encyclopedia of the social sciences,* 2nd edition (Vol. 1, pp. 581–583). Detroit, MI: Macmillan Reference USA.

Simonton, D. K. (2009a). Cinematic success, aesthetics, and economics: An exploratory recursive model. *Psychology of Creativity, Aesthetics, and the Arts, 3,* 128–138.

Simonton, D. K. (2009b). Cinematic success criteria and their predictors: The art and business of the film industry. *Psychology and Marketing, 26,* 400–420.

Simonton, D. K. (2009c). Controversial and volatile flicks: Contemporary consensus and temporal stability in film critic assessments. *Creativity Research Journal, 21,* 311–318.

Simonton, D. K. (2013). Creative genius in literature, music, and the visual arts. In V. Ginsburgh, & D. Throsby (Eds.), *Handbook of the economics of art and culture* (Vol. 2, pp. 15–48). Amsterdam: Elsevier/North Holland.

Simonton, D. K. (2014a). More method in the mad-genius controversy: A historiometric study of 204 historic creators. *Psychology of Aesthetics, Creativity, and the Arts, 8,* 53–61.

Simonton, D. K. (2014b). Significant samples—not significance tests! The often overlooked solution to the replication problem. *Psychology of Aesthetics, Creativity, and the Arts, 8,* 11–12.

Simonton, D. K. (2015). Numerical odds and evens in Beethoven's nine symphonies: Can a computer really tell the difference? *Empirical Studies of the Arts, 33,* 18–35.

Simonton, D. K. (2018). Intellectual genius in the Islamic Golden Age: Cross-civilization replications, extensions, and modifications. *Psychology of Aesthetics, Creativity, and the Arts, 12*, 125–135.

Simonton, D. K., Graham, J., & Kaufman, J. C. (2012). Consensus and contrasts in consumers' cinematic assessments: Gender, age, and nationality in rating the top-250 films. *Psychology of Popular Media Culture, 1*, 87–96.

Simonton, D. K., Skidmore, L. E. & Kaufman, J. C. (2012). Mature cinematic content for immature minds: "Pushing the envelope" versus "toning it down" in family films. *Empirical Studies of the Arts, 30*, 143–166.

Simonton, D. K., & Ting, S.-S. (2010). Creativity in Eastern and Western civilizations: The lessons of historiometry. *Management and Organization Review, 6*, 329–350.

Sorokin, P. A. (1937–1941). *Social and cultural dynamics* (Vols. 1–4). New York: American Book.

Vermeylen, F., van Dijck, M., & de Laet, V. (2013). The test of time: Art encyclopedias and the formation of the canon of the 17th-century painters in the Low Countries. *Empirical Studies of the Arts, 31*, 81–105.

Weisberg, R. W. (1994). Genius and madness? A quasi-experimental test of the hypothesis that manic-depression increases creativity. *Psychological Science, 5*, 361–367.

Weisberg, R. W. (2004). On structure in the creative process: A quantitative case-study of the creation of Picasso's *Guernica*. *Empirical Studies of the Arts, 22*, 23–54.

Weisberg, R. W. (2015). On the usefulness of "value" in the definition of creativity. *Creativity Research Journal, 27*, 111–124.

Woods, F. A. (1909, November 19). A new name for a new science. *Science, 30*, 703–704.

Woods, F. A. (1911, April 14). Historiometry as an exact science. *Science, 33*, 568–574.

Zickar, M. J, & Slaughter, J. E. (1999). Examining creative performance over time using hierarchical linear modeling: An illustration using film directors. *Human Performance, 12*, 211–230.

CHAPTER 10

OBSERVATION METHOD IN EMPIRICAL AESTHETICS

PABLO P. L. TINIO AND EVA SPECKER

A museum visitor strolls into a museum gallery wearing audio tour headphones and holding a brochure with information about the exhibition. He walks up to the wall text and reads about the exhibition on display and makes mental notes of the details surrounding the works including the artists who made them, when they were made, and the art style to which they belong. The visitor proceeds to browse the individual pieces, briefly glancing at some and slowing down to look closely at others. He might stop by a specific work, read the label that accompanies it, and use the audio guide device to listen to information about the piece.

Across the gallery, a museum researcher observes this visitor. She watches his every move, making notes of which artworks he looks at and for how long he looks at them as well as whether or not he reads the labels accompanying the works. She might note details about the artworks that the visitor spent most time on and those that seemed to engage the visitor the most. The researcher might come up with questions about the visitor's aesthetic experience of the artworks, questions such as how the information from the audio guide, brochure, and wall texts influence the visitor's perception of, and engagement with, the artworks. Which work did the visitor look at the longest and what is it about that particular work that might have garnered so much attention? What motivated the visitor to go to the museum that day and what were his goals for his visit?

In the vignette above, both the visitor and researcher are using the most fundamental method for experiencing our world and for gathering information: observation. In empirical aesthetics research, as in the above example, observation occupies a dual role. On the one hand, an aesthetic experience is fundamentally a type of observation—looking at artworks in a museum (e.g., Smith & Smith, 2001), interacting with design objects at home (e.g., Hekkert & Leder, 2008), or perhaps appreciating modern architecture (e.g., Vartanian et al., 2013). On the other hand, the study of such experiences—the focus of this chapter and volume—involves some form of observation by a researcher, whether through direct observation of people's behaviors during aesthetic encounters, recording what people say in such situations, and noting features of the environments in which the aesthetic encounters take place; or through indirect observation, such as using advanced technologies to record what people look at when interacting with aesthetic objects and how museum visitors move around and physically interact with artworks in a gallery. All of these approaches—direct or indirect—fall under the purview of the observation method. It is important to note that empiricism itself, as a grand theory, is defined by the very act of making observations, and as Adler and Adler (1994) have stated, observation is "the fundamental base of all research methods" (p. 389).

In this chapter, we describe the observation method of research and its features and uses. We also provide examples of empirical aesthetics research that have used observation as the primary method for data collection. We subsequently use these examples as a foundation for providing guidelines on how to conduct observations while simultaneously considering issues related to reliability and validity as well as the challenges and limitations associated with the method. The chapter will focus on the method of observation employed for the purpose of gathering information about people's aesthetic experiences of stimuli such as artworks. In addition, although observation could be conducted both in the highly controlled context of the laboratory and in more natural contexts such as a museum, emphasis is placed on the use of observation in the latter context. Much of the discussion below is applicable to areas beyond aesthetics. However, the discussion and examples provided will focus on empirical aesthetics.

Uses of Observations

Observation, as the most basic method for conducting empirical research, is used for several specific purposes. First, observation could be used simply to describe an aesthetics phenomenon or set of phenomena. This mode of observation bears some resemblance to classic fieldwork methods in the social sciences, such as case studies and ethnographic research, both of which are used to provide rich and thick descriptions of a phenomenon, subject, or event (Creswell, 2014; Geertz, 1973; Holloway, 1997; Lincoln & Guba, 1985). An example of this type of observation is research on people's behaviors in museums, as illustrated in the opening vignette. The researcher stands at a distance and makes notes of art perceivers' behaviors, while being careful not to be obtrusive so as to preserve, as much as possible, people's natural behaviors. Another example is research on the creative art-making process in which the researcher directly observes an artist at work, typically in the artist's studio. The researcher is immersed in the artist's creative process, witnessing the different stages involved in the creation of an artwork from the initial conceptualization of an idea to its eventual realization in a tangible object (Locher, 2010). Because the focus of these observations is to obtain a near-exhaustive account of a phenomenon, subject, or event, and because the process is typically open-ended and emergent (i.e., divergent and deductive), the process requires a significant amount of time and resources. However, the amount and the quality of data gathered could be substantial and the insights gained could enhance not only the understanding of the creative art-making process, but also the art-viewing experience (Tinio, 2013).

Another important use of observation is to characterize or refine a research question and to identify key phenomena related to the question. For example, a researcher who is seeking to understand what types of artworks people are most likely to engage with might observe people at an art exhibition and then record which artworks in the exhibition are being looked at the most. The researcher could also speak with some of these visitors as they exit the gallery, asking them which artworks they looked at, how long and why they looked at them, and what they thought about their experience looking at the works. The information collected could then help to determine the features that are common to the artworks that were viewed the most. Perhaps it is the style of the works, their size, the subject that they depict (or do not depict in case of abstract works), and their placements within the physical space of the gallery. An account of the relationships among these factors could then be produced, and additional research questions and corresponding hypotheses could be developed for future study.

Researchers also rely on observations to test specific hypotheses, a process related to yet another purpose of observations in research, which is to confirm, refute, or revise theory. Theories are often inspired by informal observations from everyday life (e.g., seeing visitors' reactions to an installation artwork) or by data collected in a formal study (e.g., a novel finding that existing theories are unable to explain). Through these observations, patterns of behaviors or occurrences could be found, which in turn could lead to the development of a formal theory that could be tested, revised, and then perhaps tested again, and so on. The iterative process involved in the development of theory is one of the hallmarks of science. For example, a classic theory in empirical aesthetics, one that might explain why observers find some artworks more engaging than others, is Berlyne's (1971) *psychobiological theory*. A significant aspect of the theory suggests that the things that people find most interesting and pleasant are those that have moderate levels of complexity. According to the theory, the reason is that such stimuli elicit the optimal amount of arousal in viewers—neither too simple, nor too complex, but just the right amount of complexity to be interesting and pleasant. Berlyne and other researchers (e.g., Nadal, Munar, Marty, & Cela-Conde, 2010; Silvia, 2005) have further developed, refined, and adapted the psychobiological theory in light of new findings about the art experience as well as the development of new research technologies, such as those that allow direct measurements of physical arousal.

In addition to using observation as a primary method for data collection, it could also be used to augment other research methods (Adler & Adler, 1994), which typically occurs naturally in most studies: a researcher conducting experimental aesthetics research in the laboratory might observe participants' unusual or extreme overt emotional reactions to the presented stimuli; when conducting interviews, the interviewer could note the interviewee's nonverbal reactions and facial expressions when answering questions; when implementing a novel research procedure, the researcher might closely look for unforeseen reactions of participants or unintended consequences of the new procedure. Observation, therefore, has a multitude of uses, both as a primary and a secondary method for data collection as well as for the development of theory.

Empirical Aesthetics Research and the Observation Method

There are myriad examples in the history of empirical aesthetics of the use of observations—whether to test a hypothesis or theory, refine a research question, or characterize an aesthetics phenomenon. The field has its roots in philosophical aesthetics, which is associated with introspective and observational methods for studying phenomena (e.g., Baumgarten, 1735/1954). Toward the end of the 19th century, these methods gave way to more experimental approaches to research (Fechner, 1876), although observation remained an important empirical method. In the past 20 years, the method has had a resurgence after decades of emphasis on laboratory studies. In fact, Martindale (2007) describes psychologists as having "fled" into their laboratories in which the modus operandi has involved the following elements: recruit participants (typically college undergraduates who agree to participate in research for course credit or monetary compensation); present (in random order) to the participants a set of images of artworks on a computer screen; have participants use rating scales to evaluate each artwork for how much they like or prefer it, find it beautiful or interesting, or the extent to which they perceive it as pleasant, complex, symmetrical, novel, surprising, or dynamic; and compile and statistically analyze data across all participants. Laboratory studies that have employed these procedures for the purpose of increasing experimental control have reached important findings and have arguably advanced empirical aesthetics more than any other methodological approach. However, there are certain aspects of the aesthetic experience that are best examined when art is presented in more natural contexts. These are the circumstances in which observations conducted in galleries, museums, and other natural settings are useful (McKechnie, 2008).

Below, we describe empirical aesthetics research in which the observation method was used. Although observations could also be used in different research contexts, such as in the laboratory, we focus on observations that involve researchers watching people engage in the viewing of art in a natural setting such as a gallery or museum. It is in these settings where the observation method is typically used as the primary method for collecting data instead of being used to merely augment another method. Using the observation method, the researcher collects first-hand recordings of the key aspects of the aesthetic experience of art, such as the characteristics and behaviors of the perceivers and the attributes of the physical context of the aesthetic encounter, including information about the artwork (through wall text, brochures, or art labels) that is provided to the perceivers. It is important to note that this chapter is not meant to be an exhaustive review of all studies that have used observations; it is instead meant to describe a few key studies that illustrate what is possible with observations, in what contexts they could be optimally used, how observations may be used alongside other research methods, and how the type of observation used could be tailored to address specific research questions.

DIRECT OBSERVATION

The first set of studies involves researchers directly observing people experiencing art and recording their behaviors, which could include the amount of time that they spend looking at art, what types of art they look at, how they move through spaces such as galleries and museums, and other behavior tendencies during aesthetic experiences.

Time spent on art

In a now classic study that has used observation in its simplest form, Smith and Smith (2001) examined how much time people spend looking at art in a museum. Museum professionals had a notion that museum visitors do not spend a lot of time looking at each artwork, even those that are considered to be masterpieces. To test this notion empirically, Smith and Smith selected six artworks from the Metropolitan Museum of Art in New York. The artworks were known masterpieces by Rembrandt, Cezanne, Raphael, Bierstadt, Leutze, and Heade. A total of 150 museum visitors were observed. For each visitor, the researchers tracked the total time that he or she spent looking at the artwork and reading the accompanying label. They also recorded the visitor's gender, estimated age, and if the visitor was viewing art alone or with other people. Results showed that people, on average, spent 27.2 s looking at an artwork (including time spent reading the label) with the median time spent being 17 s. Some paintings received longer viewing times than others, with a range of 13.2–44.6s. Smith and Smith also found an effect of group size, noting that people who visited with others spent more time looking at individual artworks than people visiting alone. No effects of gender or age were observed.

This study was replicated by Smith, Smith, and Tinio (2017), who observed visitors to the Art Institute of Chicago. They found an average viewing time of 28.63 s with a median viewing time of 21 s. As with Smith and Smith (2001), Smith et al. (2017) found no effects of gender and age and a small effect of group size, with people visiting with others spending more time looking at artworks. Importantly, this study separated out the time that viewers spent looking at the artwork itself and the time viewers spent looking at the accompanying label. In the original study by Smith and Smith, both of these behaviors were included in the time spent with the artworks. Smith et al. found that 246 out of a total sample of 456 museum visitors read the accompanying labels. The visitors who read the labels spent, on average, about as much time reading the label (15.79 s) as they did viewing the artworks (17.26 s). Finally, during the observations, the researchers were struck by museum visitors taking *selfie* pictures with the artworks, which the authors then appropriately named *arties*. Noting this as a particularly frequent behavior after the first day of observation the authors decided to track this behavior for the remaining observation period. They found that 35% of museum visitors snapped arties with the artworks on display.

The two studies above (Smith & Smith, 2001; Smith et al., 2017) demonstrate the potential of observations for uncovering behaviors fundamental to the aesthetic experience. These researchers used a very direct and straightforward technique: stand beside an artwork, wait for a visitor to engage with the work, and measure the duration of the engagement while recording perceiver characteristics as well as other notable behaviors such as reading labels and taking photographs.

Recently, Carbon (2017) used a similar approach to Smith and Smith (2001) to study the behaviors of museum visitors to a Gerhard Richter exhibition at the Neues Museum in Nürnberg. In Smith and Smith as well as in Smith et al. (2017), only the viewing times of the first initial viewings of artworks were recorded. Carbon expanded on this method by examining repeated viewings of the same artworks by the same person during one visit. He found that people on average spent 32.9 s (median = 25.1 s) looking at individual artworks, a result that is relatively similar to those found by Smith and Smith. Furthermore, Carbon found that some paintings received longer viewing times than others, with a range of 25.7–41.0 s. Interestingly, more than half of the visitors (55.3%) returned to look at an artwork more than once, resulting in an average total viewing time of 50.5 s. It is worth noting that the initial viewing times of artworks that were later viewed again were shorter (mean = 25.8 s) than for artworks that were viewed only once (mean = 37.9 s). Carbon suggested that visitors may have realized during their visit that they looked at some artworks too briefly and therefore returned to look at them again. Another explanation may be that people initially wanted to spend more time looking at an artwork, but that their viewing may have been constrained by a number of factors. For example, people who are with others in a museum might feel pressured to stay with the group and forgo a closer, slower look at an artwork in order to move with the group to another artwork. Another possible explanation is that other visitors may block the path leading to, or line of sight toward, a particular work. In each of these situations, the amount of time that a visitor spends looking at an artwork would decrease and the motivation to want to return to a particular work later in the visit would increase. A carefully conducted observation, as Carbon had done, allows such interpretations to be made.

Physical movement and locomotion

The observation method also allows the measurement of people's location and movements in natural settings. Determining people's physical behaviors in a particular space is difficult, if not impossible, with other common methods of research such as surveys, questionnaires, and interviews because such methods depend heavily on memory of where one has been, of the exact path that one took to get to a location, of how long one spent at particular locations, and of how one has physically interacted with aesthetic objects. Observations allow minute-to-minute, if not second-to-second recording of such behaviors. For example, in addition to measuring the amount of time people spent looking at artworks, Carbon (2017) also observed museum visitors' viewing distances from the artworks. Inspired by Locher, Smith, and Smith (2001), who report that viewers in a museum had viewing distances from artworks ranging from 60–120 cm with the lower limit being the distance viewers had to the smallest artwork, Carbon's observations of viewing distances showed a range of 149–212 cm with a mean of 175 cm. His observation data also showed a direct relationship between viewing distance and the size of an artwork: the bigger the artwork, the farther the distance. For tackling such a research question regarding viewing distance, observation is the optimal method.

Similarly, regarding physical location and movement in museums, Pelowski, Liu, Palacios, and Akiba (2014) used observation as a method to better understand previous findings (Pelowski, 2012) which found that people in the Rothko room in the Kawamura Memorial DIC Museum of Art in Japan had less engaged aesthetic experiences as compared with visitors to the Rothko Chapel in Houston, United States, and to a room of Rothko artworks at the Tate Modern in London, United Kingdom. The researchers postulated that aesthetic experience may have been inhibited by the architectural features of the Kawamura room in which the space made it more difficult to avoid standing in another visitor's line of sight. Pelowski et al. observed 65 visitors to the Rothko Room in Kawamura and found that people indeed explicitly tried to avoid being in another person's field of vision, a finding that suggests the impact of social aspects of art viewing on the aesthetic experience of art. Following their initial observations, the Kawamura room was remodeled in order to eliminate the cramped viewing conditions and to create a space where physical movement and viewing were less restricted. Pelowski et al. returned to the Rothko room after it was remodeled and found evidence that art viewers had more profound aesthetic experiences than in the pre-remodeled room.

The art-making process

Another use of direct observation worth mentioning is the study of the creative art-making process, an area that aesthetics scholars have also delved into as a means of gaining additional insight into the aesthetic experience (e.g., Arnheim, 1954/1974, 1962, 1969; Gombrich, 1960). Recently, the field of empirical aesthetics has witnessed a push toward characterizing the relationship between art-making and aesthetic experiences (Specker, Tinio, & van Elk, 2017; Tinio, 2013), for example, by determining whether the emotional characteristics of artworks (i.e., their emotional affordance) can be experienced by the perceiver of the work. In other words, is there a correspondence between the emotional characteristics of a work that have resulted from specific steps that the artist took during the art-making process and art perceivers' aesthetic experiences of the artwork (Tinio & Gartus, 2018)? Observation is one method for gaining insight into the art-making process. An important characteristic of this type of observation is direct observation of an artist at work in the natural context of a studio for the purpose of obtaining a detailed description of the art-making process, which includes the materials and methods used by the artist as well as the making of photographic records of the artwork during different stages of its creation (Locher, 2010).

INDIRECT OBSERVATION USING ADVANCED TECHNOLOGIES

Various technologies could be used to conduct indirect observations. One of the strengths of this approach is that it allows for a more objective (i.e., a way of circumventing human bias and observation error) and unobtrusive measure of behaviors during aesthetic encounters. This could be accomplished through the use of technologies that, for example, record where people look and where they move within a given space as well as physiological measures that could be used to further shed light on aesthetic experiences. The following section describes research that has used such technologies to good effect.

An example of indirect observation research was conducted by Tschacher et al. (2012), who observed 517 visitors to the Kunstmuseum St. Gallen, Switzerland, during a period of several months. The visitors wore electronic gloves that contained a transponder that enabled precise recordings of visitors' movement patterns within the museum. The gloves also measured skin conductance level, skin conductance variability, heart rate, and heart rate variability. This technology allowed for indirect observations of visitors' behaviors in an unobtrusive and natural manner, with visitors able to determine how they spent their time at the museum and to choose freely what artworks they looked at and how long they looked at them. The research participants were visitors of the "11:1 (+3) = Eleven Collections for a Museum" exhibition that was curated specifically for the study. A total of 76 contemporary and modern paintings and sculptures comprised the exhibition. In addition to the objective measures, visitors also completed an aesthetics questionnaire that assessed the emotions conveyed by the artworks (e.g., joy, anger, sadness, and surprise) and the artworks' aesthetic qualities (e.g., beauty, artistic merit) as well as visitors' general aesthetic evaluations of the works (e.g., whether the works belonged in the gallery, how famous was the artist?). Tschacher et al. found that skin conductance variability, heart rate, and heart rate variability correlated highly with participants' responses regarding the artworks' aesthetic quality, surprise/humor, dominance, and curatorial quality.

The same glove technology used by Tschacher et al. (2012) was used by Trondle (2014) to further observe people's movements within a museum space. Detailed recordings were made of the physical movements of 50 visitors to the Kunstmuseum St. Gallen. Trondle found that specific features of the museum space influenced visitors' movements within the museum galleries as well as which artworks they looked at and for how long they looked at them. Through the use of the transponder technology to unobtrusively observe art perceivers' movements, Trondle was able to discover what he termed *space-cells*, or particular areas within the museum that encouraged very specific responses, such as slowing down and stopping to look at an artwork and corresponding label. Furthermore, an *orientation point* marks the beginning of a space-cell by orienting visitors' attention to a salient feature, such as a wall text introducing the artworks within a particular gallery. The totality of space-cells in a museum represents the general pattern of behavior exhibited by the visitors. Indirect observation, such as that used by Trondle, allowed for a characterization of art perceivers' behaviors that would have been extremely difficult using other methods.

Another technology, the Bluetooth proximity sensor, was used by Yoshimura et al. (2014) to indirectly observe visitor movements at the Louvre Museum. The researchers examined the flow of visitors from the entrance of the museum through the gallery spaces with specific attention to the volume of visitors within areas of the galleries and their sequence of movements as well as the length of time that they spent at the museum. Unlike the studies described above, such as those by Trondle (2014) and Tschacher et al. (2012), Yoshimura et al. focused entirely on visitor movements and did not gather other, more cognitive data, an approach that truly characterizes indirect observation. The Bluetooth technology also did not require visitors to carry or wear a tracking device, but instead, their movements were recorded by sensors placed in key locations around the museum. This method was highly unobtrusive, with visitors not being aware that their physical behaviors were being recorded. In total, data from over 20,000 visitors during a period of 1 month were analyzed.

Yoshimura et al. (2014) were able to determine, with extreme detail, the amount of time that each visitor spent at the museum, which ranged from less than 1 hr to 15 hr, with the majority of visitors staying between 4 and 6 hr. Regarding visitors' movements in the museum, the researchers found something surprising: the amount of time that visitors spent at the museum did not make a significant difference to how much of the museum these visitors explored. Both short-stay and long-stay visitors tended to visit the same areas of the museum that are typically popular to visitors. This is a notable finding given the vastness of the Louvre Museum as well as the size of its collection of art. Yoshimura et al.'s use of Bluetooth technology was an optimal method for indirectly observing the physical behaviors of museum visitors. The Bluetooth method is objective, precise, and unobtrusive as well as efficient in the sense that it enabled data gathering on a large scale for an extended period of time.

Another method for conducting indirect observations makes use of technology that records where people look (e.g., Brieber, Nadal, Leder, & Rosenberg, 2014). This allows the measurement of what objects people look at, how and how long they look at them, and, with the use of video recording of their visual attention, their movements, and other physical behaviors within a given space. An example of research that used this technology was conducted by Pelowski et al. (2018), who explored art perceivers' experience of installation art. The study was the first to systematically and empirically examine the aesthetic experience of this type of art. The two works under examination were part of the exhibition, "Baroque Baroque!" by artist Olafur Eliasson and were installed at the Belvedere Museum, Austria. By their very nature, installation artworks involve an interplay between the installed features and the environment in which they are installed. Pelowski et al. examined the interplay between elements of Eliasson's works and the Baroque interior of the museum's galleries: whether visitors engaged with the installed elements independent of their surroundings or whether they engaged with both aspects. The researchers found evidence for the latter, with people visually attending to both artworks and the gallery space in which they were installed. Interestingly, for both artworks, people looked more at (i.e., more and longer eye fixations) aspects of the rooms than elements of the artworks. One of the artworks, *Wishes versus Wonders*, consisted of a tall mirror that subdivided a room that had landscape and battlefield scenes painted on its walls. Pelowski et al. found evidence that people were highly engaged with the paintings and that visitors might have integrated the painted scenes into their experience of the art. Indirect observation using eye tracking and video recording technologies, as carried out by Pelowski et al., allows for rigorous and detailed accounts of people's behavior during aesthetic encounters with art.

AUGMENTED OBSERVATION

The observation method could be augmented with other methods in order to address one of its limitations, namely, its inability to tap into people's thoughts, emotions, and other internal processes. An example of a study that made use of augmented observations is that conducted by Specker et al. (2017). They observed people interact with artworks in a museum and in a lab. In both contexts, they used a think-aloud procedure where research participants verbalized their thoughts aloud while viewing William Gropper's *The Senate* (c. 1950), a painting on exhibit at the Queens Museum in New York. Participants used an audio recording device to record their verbalized thoughts. The researchers also took notes of other relevant behaviors such as how visitors physically looked at the painting as well as if they read the museum label or spoke to other visitors while looking at the artwork. The use of the think-aloud procedure allowed the researchers to gain knowledge about what the visitors were thinking about the painting. Observations, combined with the think-aloud procedure, allowed access to visitors' thoughts about the artwork while being less obtrusive to visitors' aesthetic experience of the artwork. Specker et al. performed a similar study in the lab by presenting a reproduction of the same Gropper painting.

Specker et al.'s (2017) use of augmented observation led to important findings, such as evidence that art perceivers' aesthetic engagement with the Gropper painting largely followed the information-processing stages described in models of the aesthetic experience (Chatterjee, 2003; Leder, Belke, Oeberst, & Augustin, 2004; Leder & Nadal, 2014; Pelowski, Markey, Forster, Gerger, & Leder, 2017; Tinio, 2013). The study also found that art perceivers generally had a strong motivation to derive meaning from the work, and they often described very specific emotional reactions to the piece, stating that the painting made them feel depressed or that it had a sense of eeriness. Augmented observation, in this sense, was used to empirically test various theories of the aesthetic experience of art as well as to characterize the nuances associated with this experience.

CONDUCTING OBSERVATIONS

The studies described in the previous sections illustrate the strengths of the observation method for empirically examining aesthetic experiences. As with all empirical methods, observation has practical, logistical, and psychometric properties—such as validity and reliability—that must be considered for the method to be effective (for a comprehensive overview of these properties, see Fendler, 2016). The following issues must be taken into account when using the observation method: *Appropriateness*—is the method appropriate for the research question being asked and is the research designed in a way that allows the benefits of the method to come through? *Comprehensiveness* and *reliability*— are the observations, whether performed solely by a researcher and/or augmented by advanced technology, performed in a comprehensive, objective, systematic, rigorous, detailed, and accurate manner? *Validity*—is the interpretation (and where appropriate, the *application*) of the results consistent with the data that are collected (Creswell, 2014)? The next section provides guidelines for the use of the observation method, and the studies above will be used to illustrate important concepts.

Appropriateness

As fundamental and powerful as the observation method is, care must be taken to ensure that it can effectively capture the data needed to answer the research question or to test a specific hypothesis (Silverman, 1993). Observation is optimal for measuring overt behaviors to answer research questions, such as which artworks within an exhibition appear to engage people the most as indicated by the number of people who approach the works and look at them as well as whether they read labels accompanying the works and discuss the works with others. Observation would also be appropriate for determining which of a number of design objects—smartphones, for instance—would people interact with the most when given the simple task of using the objects. It is important to note that these observations involve overt behaviors and directly address the research question of aesthetic engagement with visual stimuli of art or design objects.

If used beyond measuring overt behaviors, the appropriateness of the observation method becomes questionable. Observation is less effective at determining people's cognitions (how much they find a painting interesting, beautiful, or intellectually challenging), emotional reactions (if an installation artwork made them feel anxious, uncomfortable, or nostalgic), and knowledge and experiences (how much formal art education people have received and to what extent this influences their aesthetic experiences). Although observations could be augmented with other methods to gain insight into internal processes, such as Specker et al.'s (2017) use of the think-aloud procedure, the ultimate strength of observations involves what can be directly seen.

Comprehensiveness and reliability

The primary purpose of the observation method is to describe, and according to Patton (2002), it must have the following:

> Observational data must have depth and detail. The data must be descriptive—
> sufficiently descriptive that the reader can understand what occurred and how
> it occurred. The observer's notes become the eyes, ears, and perceptual senses for
> the reader. The descriptions must be factual, accurate, and thorough without being
> cluttered by irrelevant minutiae and trivia.
>
> (Patton, 2002, p. 23)

Observations are conducted through the lens of the observer. This may sound like a truism, but if steps are not taken to ensure that the process of observing is rigorous, systematic, detailed, and accurate, the quality and validity of the data will be compromised (Cotton, Stokes, & Cotton, 2010). The observer's own lens may lead to bias in what he or she actually observes, which would limit a study's comprehensiveness—the thorough sampling of the range of behaviors of interest including the minutiae of what people do and say. It could also include observing, in detail, the context in which the behaviors occur. Comprehensiveness also entails including the appropriate range of time during which the sampling of behavior occurs. It could involve seconds and minutes as in Smith and Smith's (2001) study of the amount of time people spend looking at paintings, or weeks and months as in Yoshimura et al.'s (2014) study of people's movements in a museum.

In addition to the need for observations to be comprehensive, they must also be reliable. There must be little variability in how observations are made and recorded. Accuracy is key. The exact behaviors of participants, their expression, and other features that are associated with them must be described in accurate detail (e.g., Creswell, 1998; Geertz, 1973; Holloway, 1997; Tjora, 2006), and such accuracy should apply to each and every research participant. Observations must also be consistent across different observers who are tasked with observing the same aesthetic phenomena; in other words, inter-rater reliability must be high (Creswell, 2014).

Reliability and objectivity are critical to ensuring the validity of observations, yet they are two of the most challenging issues to address. Observers are fallible. They are prone to mistakes and observer bias—seeing things in a manner that is consistent with their perspectives and beliefs and that may confirm their expectations, or hypotheses, for the study (e.g., Connor-Greene, 2007). Observations are typically recorded using checklists, rubrics, observational protocols, and often, rough field notes and short narratives that are quickly written as the events and behaviors are taking place. None of these recording methods is immune to inaccuracies. A rigorous approach to recording observations is therefore needed to minimize errors and ensure the quality of data (Creswell, 1998). Because of the complexities associated with observations, it is important for observers to be trained in the following skills (adapted from Patton, 2002):

- Noticing what there is to see and hear.
- Knowing what to pay attention to and what to ignore.
- Recording observations systematically, accurately, and descriptively.
- Recognizing and acknowledging the limitations of one's observations and potential biases.
- Minimizing any influence that one might have on the research context and participants' behaviors.

One way to address issues of reliability is through the use of technology. Observations made by a person could be augmented with technology, or as in studies such as that conducted by Yoshimura et al. (2014), observations could be solely technology-based. Whether it is video recording people engaging in a certain behavior or performing a task or using wearable devices that track locations and movements within a space, appropriate technology use could significantly increase the objectivity and reliability of observation data, which in turn would help increase the validity of the data.

Validity

Validity, within the context of observations, refers to the extent to which the observations made are appropriately interpreted and applied. Therefore, valid interpretations of observations are only possible when the observations themselves are highly objective and reliable. Once the conditions of objectivity and reliability are established at a sufficient level (which together signify the quality of the data and the strength of evidence to support predictions or to address the research questions), the next step would be to ensure that the interpretation of the results is consistent with the observation data and that any generalizations drawn from the study are appropriate, which requires careful determination of the representativeness of the data (Booth, Colomb, & Williams, 2008).

One important point to consider when interpreting and generalizing the results is the possibility that the observer's mere presence in the research context has influenced the events and behaviors of the participants under investigation (Silverman, 1985). Although the negative impact resulting from the presence of the observer could be mitigated by taking the necessary steps to be as inconspicuous as possible (e.g., blending in), such impact can never be fully ruled out. In presenting the results of an observation study, at the minimum, one must acknowledge the potential impact of the observer and to consider such impact when generalizing the results.

Conclusion

The observation method is arguably the most fundamental of all research methods (Adler & Adler, 1994). It could be used as a sole approach for data collection or to augment other methods (e.g., interviews and laboratory experiments) as well as to develop and refine theory. With these uses come some costs, such as the challenges associated with designing observation research. For the observation method to be effective, it must be appropriate for the research question being addressed. The observations themselves must be rigorously and systematically performed as well as comprehensive and reliable. The interpretation of the data must also be valid. Empirical aesthetics has depended on observations since its inception as a field of study (Fechner, 1876). Even with the continuous development and use of advanced technologies for conducting aesthetics research, researchers will always depend on the observation method as the most basic, yet one of the most powerful, methods for empirically examining aesthetics phenomena.

References

Adler, P. A., & Adler, P. (1994). Observational techniques. In N. K. Denzin & Y. S. Lincoln (Eds.), *Handbook of qualitative research* (pp. 377–392). London: Sage.

Arnheim, R. (1954/1974). *Art and visual perception*. Berkeley, CA: University of California Press.

Arnheim, R. (1962). *The genesis of a painting. Picasso's Guernica*. Berkeley, CA: University of California Press.

Arnheim, R. (1969). Visual thinking. Berkeley, CA: University of California Press.

Baumgarten, A. G. (1735/1954). Reflections on poetry. Berkeley, CA: University of California Press.

Berlyne, D. E. (1971). *Aesthetics and psychobiology*. New York: Appleton-Century-Crofts.

Booth, W. C., Colomb, G. G., Williams, J. M. (2008). *The craft of research*. Chicago, IL: University of Chicago Press.

Brieber, D., Nadal, M., Leder, H., & Rosenberg, R. (2014). Art in time and space: Context modulates the relation between art experience and viewing time. *PLoS ONE, 9*, e99019.

Carbon, C.-C. (2017). Art perception in the museum: How we spend time and space in art exhibitions. *I-Perception, 8*, 204166951769418.

Chatterjee, A. (2003). Prospects for a cognitive neuroscience of visual aesthetics. *Bulletin of Psychology and the Arts, 4*, 55–60.

Connor-Greene, P. A. (2007). Observation or interpretation? Demonstrating unintentional subjectivity and interpretive variance. *Teaching of Psychology, 34*, 167–171.

Cotton, D. R. E., Stokes, A., & Cotton, P. A. (2010). Using observational methods to research the student experience. *Journal of Geography in Higher Education, 34*, 463–473.

Creswell, J. W. (1998). *Qualitative inquiry and research design: Choosing among five traditions.* London: Sage.

Creswell, J. W. (2014). *Research design: Qualitative, quantitative, and mixed Methods approaches.* London: Sage.

Fechner, G. T. (1876). *Vorschule der Ästhetik* [Primary school of aesthetics]. Leipzig, Germany: Breitkopf & Härtel.

Fendler, L. (2016). Ethical implications of validity-vs.-reliability trade-offs in educational research. *Ethics and Education, 11*, 214–229.

Geertz, C. (1973). *The interpretation of cultures.* New York: Basic Books.

Gombrich, E. H. (1960). *Art and illusion: A study in the psychology of pictorial representation.* Princeton, NJ: Princeton University Press.

Hekkert, P., & Leder, H. (2008). Product aesthetics. In R. Schifferstein, & P. Hekkert (Eds.), *Product experience* (pp. 259–286). Abingdon, England: Elsevier.

Holloway, I. (1997). *Basic concepts for qualitative research.* London: Blackwell Science.

Leder, H., Belke, B., Oeberst, A., & Augustin, D. (2004). A model of aesthetic appreciation and aesthetic judgments. *British Journal of Psychology, 95*, 489–508.

Leder, H., & Nadal, M. (2014). Ten years of a model of aesthetic appreciation and aesthetic judgments: The aesthetic episode—Developments and challenges in empirical aesthetics. *British Journal of Psychology, 105*, 443–464.

Lincoln, Y. S., & Guba, E. G. (1985). *Naturalistic inquiry.* Beverly Hills, CA: Sage.

Locher, P., Smith, J. K., & Smith, L. F. (2001). The influence of presentation format and viewer training in the visual arts on the perception of pictorial and aesthetic qualities of paintings. *Perception, 30*, 449–465.

Locher, P. J. (2010). How does a visual artist create an artwork? In J. Kaufman & R. Sternberg (Eds.), *Cambridge handbook of creativity* (pp. 131–144). Cambridge, England: Cambridge University Press.

Martindale, C. (2007). Recent trends in the psychological study of aesthetics, creativity, and the arts. *Empirical Studies of the Arts, 25*, 121–141.

McKechnie, L. E. F. (2008). Observational research. In L. M. Given (Ed.), *The SAGE encyclopedia of qualitative research methods* (pp. 574–577). London: Sage.

Nadal, M., Munar, E., Marty, G., & Cela-Conde, C. J. (2010). Visual complexity and beauty appreciation: Explaining the divergence of results. *Empirical Studies of the Arts, 28*, 173–191.

Patton, M. Q. (2002). *Qualitative research and evaluation methods.* London: Sage.

Pelowski, M. (2012). (Not) myspace: Social interaction as detriment to cognitive processing and aesthetic experience in the museum of art. In Damiani, E., Howlett, R. J., Jain, L. C., Gallo, L., De Pietro, G. (Eds.): *Intelligent interactive multimedia: Systems and Services* (pp. 399–410). Berlin: Springer.

Pelowski, M., Leder, H., Mitschke, V., Specker, E., Tinio, P. P. L., Gerger, G., … Husslein-Arco, A. (2018). Capturing aesthetic experiences with Installation Art: An empirical assessment of emotion, valuations, and mobile eye tracking in Olafur Eliasson's "Baroque, Baroque!" *Frontiers in Psychology, 9*, 1255. doi: 10.3389/fpsyg.2018.01255.

Pelowski, M., Liu, T., Palacios, V., & Akiba, F. (2014). When a body meets a body: An exploration of the negative impact of social interactions on museum experiences of art. *International Journal of Education & the Arts, 15*, 1–47.

Pelowski, M., Markey, P. S., Forster, M., Gerger, G., & Leder, H. (2017). Move me, astonish me … delight my eyes and brain: The Vienna integrated model of top-down and bottom-up processes in art perception (VIMAP) and corresponding affective, evaluative, and neuro-physiological correlates. *Physics of Life Reviews, 21,* 80–125.

Silverman, D. (1985) *Qualitative methodology and sociology: Describing the social world.* Farnham, England: Gower Publishing Co.

Silverman, D. (1993) Interpreting qualitative data: Methods for analysing talk, text and interaction. London: Sage.

Silvia, P. J. (2005). Emotional responses to art: From collation and arousal to cognition and emotion. *Review of General Psychology, 9,* 342–357.

Smith, J. K., & Smith, L. F. (2001). Spending time on art. *Empirical Studies of the Arts, 19,* 229–236.

Smith, L. F., Smith, J. K., & Tinio, P. P. L. (2017). Time spent viewing art and reading labels. *Psychology of Aesthetics, Creativity, and the Arts, 11,* 77–85.

Specker, E., Tinio, P. P. L., & van Elk, M. (2017). Do you see what I see? An investigation of the aesthetic experience in the laboratory and museum. *Psychology of Aesthetics, Creativity, and the Arts, 11,* 265–275.

Tinio, P. P. L. (2013). From artistic creation to aesthetic reception: The mirror model of art. *Psychology of Aesthetics, Creativity, and the Arts, 7,* 265–275.

Tinio, P. P. L., & Gartus, A. (2018). Characterizing the emotional response to art beyond pleasure: Correspondence between the emotional characteristics of artworks and viewers' emotional responses. *Progress in Brain Research, 237,* 319–342.

Tjora, A. H. (2006). Writing small discoveries: an exploration of fresh observers' observations. *Qualitative Research, 6,* 429–451.

Trondle, M. (2014). Space, movement and attention: Affordances of the museum environment. *International Journal of Arts Management, 17,* 4–17.

Tschacher, W., Greenwood, S., Kirchberg, V., Wintzerith, S., van den Berg, K., & Trondle, M. (2012). Physiological correlates of aesthetic perception of artworks in a museum. *Psychology of Aesthetics, Creativity, and the Arts, 6,* 96–103.

Vartanian, O., Navarrete, G., Chatterjee, A., Fich, L. B., Leder, H., Modroño, C., … Skov, M. (2013). Impact of contour on aesthetic judgments and approach-avoidance decisions in architecture. *PNAS, 110,* 1–8.

Yoshimura, Y., Sobolevsky, S., Ratti, C., Girardin, F., Carrascal, J. P., Blat, J., & Sinatra, R. (2014). An analysis of visitors' behavior in the Louvre Museum: A study using Bluetooth data. *Environment and Planning B: Planning and Design, 41,* 1113–1131.

CHAPTER 11

....

OBSERVATIONAL DRAWING RESEARCH METHODS

....

JUSTIN OSTROFSKY

INTRODUCTION

....

THE production of drawings is a behavior that has been performed for most of human history, as evident by the discovery of the paintings found in the Chauvet Cave in France and the El Castillo Cave in Spain, respectively dated to be approximately 32,000 and 40,000 years old (Clottes, 2003). Additionally, drawing is a behavior people perform throughout most of their lifespan, as most children as early as 2 years old (and in many cases even younger) draw (Kellogg, 1970), and many motivated adults continue to create drawings into old age. Furthermore, the behavior of drawing is a culturally valued behavior for both aesthetic and communicative purposes, as evident, for example, by the fact that many paintings have been sold for millions of dollars, by the existence of many kinds of draftsman professions, and by the strong presence of required drawing/painting instruction in the United States' elementary and high school education systems. Thus, drawing is a universal and important human behavior.

Although there are many different types of drawings that each have their own depictive and creative goals (e.g., schematic drawings, expressive drawings, memory- or imagination-based drawings, abstract drawings), this chapter exclusively focuses on the activity of *observational* drawing. Observational drawing is the behavior of creating a recognizable depiction of a specific model object or scene that is directly perceived by the individual while they create the drawing (unless otherwise stated, all future mentions of "drawing" in this chapter will specifically refer to observational drawing). There is a high degree of variability in the quality of drawings individuals are capable of producing, with most adults finding it difficult to produce high-quality drawings. Indeed, extensive training in drawing is often required before individuals are capable of producing high-quality drawings. Why is this the case? What prevents most adults without formal training from producing high-quality drawings? What is acquired during formal training and practice that leads to the development of strong drawing skill? What differences exist between skilled and unskilled individuals that contribute to this individual variability in drawing performance?

This behavior and set of questions have attracted scientific interest from cognitive and developmental psychologists alike. Cognitive psychologists have pursued this line of questioning from an information-processing perspective, as the activity of drawing is supported by multiple cognitive processes. Individuals utilize perceptual, attentional, decision-making, and memory processes to guide the production of such drawings. Many cognitive psychologists have attempted to understand how individual variability in such cognitive processes contributes to variability in the quality of drawings (Chamberlain & Wagemans, 2016). Developmental psychologists have addressed this set of questions by studying how the quality of and production strategies used to create drawings vary over the lifespan. Some have studied the stereotypical changes in drawing production that occur from early childhood into late childhood and adulthood (e.g., Freeman & Janikoun, 1972). Others have adopted an expertise approach by studying how deliberate training and practice affects, or is associated with, drawing performance and performance in nondrawing tasks that assess various types of cognitive processing ability (Kozbelt & Ostrofsky, 2018; Kozbelt & Seeley, 2007).

Studies of drawing adopt one of two general focuses: a process-oriented approach or a product-oriented approach. Research adopting the process-oriented approach mainly studies the sequence of actions one engages in when producing a drawing. Some process-oriented studies have investigated how variability in the sequence of mark-making affects or is related to the quality of the final drawing (e.g., Cohen, 2005; Tchalenko, 2009). Other studies adopting this approach have investigated how the experimental manipulation of cognitive processing affects the sequence of marks made when producing a drawing (e.g., Sommers, 1984; Vinter, 1999). However, since this approach represents a small minority of drawing research that has been recently conducted, it will not be the focus of this chapter.

Rather, this chapter mainly focuses on research that has adopted the product-oriented approach, which represents the majority of the research that has been conducted on this topic over the past 20 years and is largely concerned with assessing the quality and content of the final drawing. A major focus is assessing the visual accuracy of the final drawing, which is commonly measured in such studies. Cohen and Bennett (1997) defined a visually accurate drawing as "one that can be recognized as a particular object at a particular time and in a particular space, rendered with little addition of visual detail that cannot be seen in the object represented or with little deletion of visual detail [seen in the object represented]" (p. 609). Studies that have adopted this approach have aimed to understand how drawing accuracy/skill is (a) affected by manipulating various cognitive and perceptual factors (e.g., Cohen & Earls, 2010; Ostrofsky, Kozbelt, Tumminia & Cipriano, 2016), and/or (b) associated with performance in nondrawing tasks that measure some aspect of cognitive ability (e.g., Ostrofsky, Kozbelt & Seidel, 2012).

In this chapter, I will provide an overview of the various methods used in laboratory-based observational drawing research that adopts a product-oriented approach. First,

I will describe the general questions and methodological designs used in such research. Next, I will summarize the various types of drawing tasks administered in studies focusing on this topic. Afterwards, I will summarize the various methods used to measure drawing skill/accuracy. Finally, I will end the chapter with a discussion of the challenges research in this area currently faces and suggestions as to the future directions research on this topic would benefit from by adopting.

General Questions and Methodological Strategies in Drawing Research

Multiple lines of general questions have been addressed in drawing research over the past 20 years. Below, I will identify each type of general question that has been studied and describe the methodological strategies that have been adopted to address them.

Relationship between drawing skill and performance in nondrawing tasks: Correlational studies

Since drawing is a complex behavior that is supported by perceptual and cognitive processing, researchers have been interested in determining which particular stages and components of perceptual/cognitive processing support skilled drawing. One way researchers have addressed this is by identifying a perceptual or cognitive process that is hypothesized to support drawing skill, and determining if individual variability in the ability to engage those processes is associated with variability in drawing performance. Examples of cognitive and perceptual processes that have been studied along these lines include:

- perceptual constancies pertaining to shape and size (Cohen & Jones, 2008; McManus, Loo, Chamberlain, Riley, & Brunswick, 2011; Ostrofsky et al., 2012; Ostrofsky, Cohen, & Kozbelt, 2014),
- various visual illusions (Chamberlain & Wagemans, 2015; Mitchell, Ropar, Ackroyd, & Rajendran, 2005; Ostrofsky, Kozbelt, & Cohen, 2015),
- local (in contrast to global) perceptual processing biases (Chamberlain, McManus, Riley, Rankin, & Brunswick, 2013; Drake, 2013; Drake & Winner, 2011),
- flexibility of visual attention (Chamberlain & Wagemans, 2015),
- efficiency of perceptually encoding the shape of an object (Perdreau & Cavanagh, 2014),
- integration of object-based visual information across eye movements (Perdreau & Cavanagh, 2013), and
- absolute and relative spatial positioning ability (Huang & Chen, 2017).

Correlational studies have been used to investigate such associations. In these studies, participants are required to create a drawing and complete at least one nondrawing task that has been designed to assess the perceptual or cognitive processing ability of interest. Statistically significant correlations between performance in the drawing and nondrawing tasks are the primary evidence used to support claims that drawing skill is associated with a particular perceptual or cognitive process.

Although much has been learned from such studies, this methodological strategy has important limitations one should be sensitive to when interpreting the correlational evidence. First, the observation of such statistically significant correlations is not solid evidence that drawing skill is directly related, in a causal manner, to the perceptual or cognitive process of interest. There is always the possibility that some unaccounted for variable exists that directly affects ability in drawing and perceptual/cognitive processing in parallel without drawing skill and perceptual/cognitive ability themselves being directly related. Second, even if ability in drawing and perceptual/cognitive processing were directly related, it is impossible to determine the direction of causality. Correlational evidence alone cannot be used to determine whether variability in perceptual/cognitive processing directly affects drawing performance, or vice versa. Thus, the safest conclusion one can draw from such studies is simply that a predictive association between drawing skill and perceptual/cognitive processing ability exists.

Differences in perceptual/cognitive processing ability between artists and nonartists: expertise studies

Expert-versus-novice differences in perception, cognition, and neural structure/function is a topic that has received a lot of attention from psychological researchers. For example, experts and novices in the domains of chess (Chase & Simon, 1973), action videogame playing (Green & Bavelier, 2003), musical notation reading (Wong & Gauthier, 2012), and navigation (Maguire et al., 2000) have been observed to differ with respect to a variety of perceptual, cognitive, and neural processes. Such studies are conducted for one of two general purposes. Some studies make such comparisons to provide clues pertaining to the perceptual, cognitive, or neural processes that support skilled performance. Other expert-versus-novice studies are performed to probe the plasticity of perceptual, cognitive, and neural systems that are associated with extensive experience in a specific domain.

Similar research has been conducted for the domain of drawing by comparing expert artists and novice nonartists (Kozbelt & Ostrofsky, 2018; Kozbelt & Seeley, 2007). Examples of processing abilities that have been compared between artists and nonartists include:

- the experience of perceptual constancies (Cohen & Jones, 2008; Ostrofsky et al., 2012; Perdreau & Cavanagh, 2011; McManus et al., 2011),
- susceptibility to various visual illusions (Chamberlain et al., 2019),

- perceptual grouping (Ostrofsky, Kozbelt, & Kurylo, 2013),
- perception of the size of angles (Carson & Allard, 2013),
- the flexibility of visual attention (Chamberlain & Wagemans, 2015),
- the ability to recognize objects found in degraded images (e.g., out-of-focus images, images of objects with segments deleted from the images) (Chamberlain et al., 2019; Kozbelt, 2001),
- visual memory ability (Perdreau & Cavanagh, 2014),
- the volume and activity of various brain regions (Chamberlain, McManus, Brunswicket al., 2014; Schlegel et al., 2015), and
- face recognition (Devue & Barsics, 2016; Tree, Horry, Riley, & Wilmer, 2017; Zhou, Cheng, Zhang, & Wong, 2012).

Such studies adopt a quasi-experimental approach where expertise (artist versus nonartist) is the independent variable and performance on a nondrawing task assessing perceptual, cognitive, or neural processing is the dependent variable. Although many interesting expertise-based differences (and nondifferences) have been observed in such studies, this type of research is generally similar to the correlational studies described above with respect to its limitations in supporting causal claims. First, perceptual, cognitive, and neural differences between artists and nonartists do not necessarily indicate that such differences are directly related to differences in drawing ability between the groups. Second, even if such perceptual, cognitive, and neural differences were directly related in a causal manner to expertise-based differences in drawing skill, it is unclear whether the differences in perceptual, cognitive, and neural processes preceded, were followed by or were developed in parallel with drawing expertise.

Another limitation of this line of research concerns the nonstandardized approach pertaining to how participants are classified as an expert (or artist). Different studies and/or different research groups vary with respect to the criteria used to classify a participant as an expert artist. The following groups have been recruited to serve expert participants: (a) undergraduate art students (sometimes just majors and other times both majors and minors), (b) graduate art students, (c) community members recruited via fliers and online advertisements, and (d) professional artists (most of the time, the criteria used to classify someone as a professional artist are not provided). Some studies use only one of these four groups to serve as expert participants, and other studies have mixed individuals from two or more of these groups. Sometimes, the qualification of an individual would lead them to be categorized as an expert via one study's criteria and a novice via another study's criteria. For instance, Tchlalenko (2009) assigned professional artists to an expert group and assigned both undergraduate art students and nonartists to a novice group. In contrast, many other studies have assigned undergraduate art students to an expert group. Finally, at least one study assigned participants to expert and novice groups based on their performance on a drawing task administered during the course of the study, where a median split was used to categorize the half who drew better as experts and the half who drew more poorly as novices (Perdreau & Cavanagh, 2014).

The nonstandardized approach in categorizing participants as experts and novices creates potential problems when attempting to assess cross-study reliability of specific expertise-based differences. For instance, if there are discrepancies between multiple studies concerning an expertise-based difference on a specific cognitive/perceptual/neural variable, it would be difficult to conclude that the effect is unreliable if the two studies adopted different criteria to categorize participants as experts and novices. Two studies provided discrepant findings concerning expertise-based differences concerning face recognition abilities, as assessed by performance on the Cambridge Face Memory Test. Here, Devue and Barsics (2016) observed artists performing significantly better than nonartists in this task, whereas Tree and colleagues (2017) found no expertise-based difference. The criteria used to categorize participants as expert artists varied between the two studies. The expert group in the Devue and Barsics (2016) study were recruited from internet advertisements, had an average age of 26 years, and varied according to whether they were professionally trained or self-taught. In contrast, the members of the artist group in the Tree et al. (2017) study were professional portrait artists (teachers or those who work for commission) who had a mean age of 42 years. Such differences in the characteristics of the expert samples make it difficult to determine the source of the discrepancy in findings between these two studies. It could be that the expertise-related effect on face recognition abilities is unreliable, or it could be that these two artist groups are not homogeneous, and thus, not comparable for the purposes of assessing cross-study reliability.

Extending on this point, even when it appears that two studies adopted the same criteria to define expert participants, the characteristics of the experts may still vary between the two studies. For example, imagine two studies that define artists as undergraduate and/or graduate art students. If the students are recruited from different institutions, the level of expertise and skill in drawing may vary if one institution's admissions process involves different standards than the other. In such a case, the level of expertise between the two samples of artists may substantially vary. In light of these considerations, future expertise-based research in this area may benefit from developing a standardized method of categorizing individuals as experts. This would facilitate researchers' ability to compare the results of different studies with each other. However, even if such standardization is too challenging to develop, one should always be cautious in evaluating such expertise-based differences and pay close attention to the precise criteria used to define expertise.

Factors that influence drawing performance: experimental studies

Understanding methods that can lead to direct changes in drawing ability is of interest to both psychologists evaluating theories of drawing performance and art instructors who wish to identify and/or validate instructional methods used for improving students' drawing ability. In the correlational and expertise-based studies described above, researchers were primarily interested in how participants' current drawing ability is associated with performance in nondrawing tasks. In contrast, other studies have been concerned with investigating methods that could be used to directly improve and/or impair drawing performance. Examples of factors that have been assessed to determine if they affect drawing performance include:

- level of familiarity with the object category of which the model (or, the physical object being drawn) is a member (Glazek, 2012; Sheppard, Ropar, & Mitchell, 2005),
- the orientation of the model (e.g., upright versus upside-down) (Cohen & Earls, 2010; Day & Davidenko, 2018; Kozbelt, Seidel, ElBassiouny, Mark, & Owen, 2010; Ostrofsky, Kozbelt, Cohen, Conklin, & Thomson, 2016),
- the presence versus absence of three-dimensional depth cues in the model (Mitchell et al., 2005; Ostrofsky et al., 2015; Sheppard et al., 2005),
- the presence or absence of declarative knowledge pertaining to the canonical structure of an object (Ostrofsky, Kozbelt, Tumminia et al., 2016),
- the isolation of high vs. medium vs. low spatial frequencies in the model image (Freeman & Loschky, 2011),
- the manipulation of the frequency in which individuals shift their gaze between the model and drawing during production (Cohen, 2005), and
- how individuals interpret the identity of the model object being drawn (Ostrofsky, Nehl, & Mannion, 2017; Vinter, 1999).

Experiments have been conducted to investigate these effects. In such experiments, a measure of drawing performance is used as the dependent variable and the independent variable is the researchers' manipulation of the factor that is hypothesized to have an effect on drawing performance. Significant differences in the mean values of the drawing performance measure between the different levels of the independent variable are the evidence used to claim that the independent variable has an effect on drawing performance.

One major limitation of such studies pertains to the generalizability of the effects observed in the experiments. In most cases, the model being drawn in a given experiment represents just one object category. For instance, in the experiments referenced above that investigated the effects of model orientation on drawing performance, the model being drawn was a face, and the researchers manipulated whether the model-face was displayed upright or upside-down (Cohen & Earls, 2010; Day & Davidenko, 2018; Ostrofsky, Kozbelt, Cohen et al., 2016). Across these studies, the results indicated that drawing performance was either impaired or not affected when drawing upside-down faces (relative to upright faces) depending on the particular measure of drawing performance analyzed. In no case was it observed that drawing performance was improved via face inversion. However, this is not strong evidence to conclude that inverting a model has no benefits to drawing performance in general, as these experiments only looked at performance in drawing faces. Further experimentation is required to assess whether inverting models of other object categories has similar or dissimilar effects as those observed in face drawings. More generally, the larger set of studies referenced above have the same limitation, in that drawing performance is typically measured with respect to drawing models that represent only one or just a few object categories. Furthermore, it is rare that researchers attempt to replicate such experimental effects using models of different object categories beyond those used in the experiments that originally demonstrated the effect. Thus, until such replication studies are conducted, one must avoid overgeneralizing experimental effects as existing for drawing perform-ance in general as opposed to drawing performance for a particular type of model object.

Types of Drawing Tasks Administered in Laboratory Research

For most drawing studies, drawing skill is based on an assessment of observational drawings produced by participants in the laboratory. This section focuses on describing the drawing tasks that have been administered and will highlight some of the common methodological features researchers have adopted.

Free-hand drawing tasks

Free-hand drawing tasks refer to participants being exposed to a model and being asked to draw a reproduction of it as it appears. In studies of observational drawing, such tasks often instruct participants to strive for accuracy above all else when reproducing a model via drawing. Commonly, instructions set the participants' goal to producing as accurate a copy of the model as the participant is capable of producing without neces-sarily striving for producing a highly creative or even aesthetically pleasing drawing.

Different types of models have been used in such drawing tasks. For instance, photographs are often used, especially those that depict a single object such as an octopus (Ostrofsky et al., 2014), a hand holding a pencil, a Lego-block configuration (Chamberlain et al., 2013), faces (Ostrofsky et al., 2014), and a generator (Cohen & Bennett, 1997). Physically present three-dimensional objects are also used at times, most often in the form of a "still-life" collection of objects. In some studies, the researchers standardize the distance and angle from the objects the participants are seated at (Chamberlain et al., 2013) and other studies allow participants to freely inspect the collection of objects by moving their head and sitting at different positions (Carson, Millard, Quehl, & Danckert, 2014).

Studies employing photographs and physically present objects as models represent the most complex free-hand drawing tasks. In order to skillfully draw such models, participants must accurately depict a wide variety of visual information that includes shading, angles, relative line length, detailed appearance of local features, linear per-spective, relative and absolute spatial positioning of different features, relative size of different features, etc. Thus, in order to create a high-quality drawing of such models, participants must exhibit skill in many aspects of drawing. In other studies, researchers have used simpler models that most commonly come in the form of simple line drawings. Examples of such simple models have included faces (Day & Davidenko, 2018; Tchalenko, 2009), full human bodies (Tchalenko, 2009), an eye, a wine glass, Chinese ideograms (Glazek, 2012), parallelograms (Mitchell et al., 2005), cylinders (Matthews & Adams, 2008), and abstract shapes not representing meaningful objects (Sheppard et al., 2005). One reason such simple models are used is to assess a very spe-cific aspect of drawing skill. For instance, Chamberlain, McManus, Riley et al. (2014) asked participants to draw multiple irregular hexagon models (the "Cain's House Task") in order to narrowly assess skill in drawing angles and relative line lengths. Another reason such simple models are used is to eliminate some aspects of drawing that are needed to be utilized in order to produce a high-quality drawing. For instance, copying line drawings of faces, wine glasses, eyes, and tables eliminates the need for participants to accurately shade in order to draw a high-quality reproduction of the model.

In most cases, the use of a free-hand drawing task is intended to allow researchers to have an ecologically valid assessment of general drawing skill where drawings are produced under natural conditions. Participants typically produce drawings on paper using pencil, are allowed to erase and modify their drawing during the course of its pro-duction, are free to utilize whatever drawing techniques they know/desire to use (with the exception of tracing), and are not constrained with respect to the sequential produc-tion of the drawing. However, one constraint most free-hand drawing tasks impose on participants that might reduce the ecological validity of the drawing assessment involves the time limits participants are often given to complete their drawings. Depending on the complexity of the model being drawn, this time limit can range from seconds (e.g., 30-s time limit used in Schlegel et al., 2015) to minutes (e.g., 15-min time limit used by Ostrofsky et al., 2012) to an hour (e.g., Huang & Chen, 2017). Such time limits are typ-ically used to standardize the drawing tasks across participants and, for convenience, to ensure that participants complete all of the study's required tasks within the allotted time for the data collection session. However, it is open to question as to how well timed tasks result in drawings that reflect a participant's maximum level of drawing skill. It is always possible that a participant would be able to produce a higher quality drawing if they were allotted more time to produce it or did not know from the outset that they had to complete the drawing within a specific time frame.

Tracing tasks

It is widely accepted that observational drawing is a complex behavior that is guided by multiple perceptual and cognitive processes. Cohen and Bennett (1997) identified four main processes that guide the production of a drawing: (a) perceptual encoding of the model; (b) representational decision-making as to what features from the model to emphasize, de-emphasize, or neglect in the drawing; (c) eye–hand motor coordination; and (d) evaluation of the quality of the emerging drawing and making necessary corrections when deviations between the model and drawing are perceived. Tracing tasks have generally been used by researchers in order to study, in an isolated fashion, the decision-making, and/or eye–hand motor coordination processes involved in drawing. Cohen and Bennett (1997, Experiment 1) asked participants to trace photographs. This task eliminated the need for participants to perceptually encode many aspects of the photograph that would have needed to be accurately encoded in a free-hand drawing task (e.g., one does not need to accurately encode size-proportions, relative spatial positioning of different features, angles, etc.). This task also substantially reduced the difficulty of the evaluation process, as the only evaluation participants needed to make was whether they missed any lines or if their drawn line deviated from the path of the printed line found in the photograph. Thus, the researchers isolated decision-making (i.e., deciding which lines to emphasize/de-emphasize and how thick to draw a specific line) and eye–hand coordination as the pertinent skills needed to produce a high-quality depiction. In their second experiment, the researchers asked participants to trace a tracing produced by another individual, which further isolated eye–hand motor coordination as the only pertinent skill needed to produce a high-quality tracing. Here, decision-making processes are eliminated, or at least are substantially reduced.

A variant tracing task that has been argued to more sensitively assess representational decision-making processes is the "limited-line tracing task" (Chamberlain et al., 2019; Kozbelt et al., 2010; Ostrofsky et al., 2012). A potential limitation of the traditional tracing method is that individuals are free to use an unlimited number of lines to trace the model. For studies that aim to compare representational decision-making differences between groups (e.g., artists versus nonartists), this freedom may mask any differences between individuals who make stronger versus weaker depictive decisions. The limited line tracing task controls the lines participants are allowed to use to trace the model, so that the number, thickness, and length of lines used for the tracing are standardized and equated across participants. Critically, the number of lines participants are allowed to use is fewer than what is required to trace the entire the image. This method forces participants to be more economical in their decision-making, forcing them to prioritize and decide which segments of the model are more or less important to depict. This method has been useful in establishing differences in decision-making quality between those who are more versus less skilled in drawing, as the quality of such limited line tracings have been found to be (a) rated significantly higher for those produced by expert artists than those produced by novices, and (b) positively correlated with the quality of free-hand drawings.

MEASURES OF DRAWING PERFORMANCE

Once drawings or tracings are produced, performance is measured using a variety of quantitative assessment methods. There are two general categories of quantitative measures of drawing performance that have been used in such research: (a) subjective rating methods that aim to assess perceived quality, and (b) objective measurement methods that aim to measure specific deviations in appearance between the drawing and the model. In most cases, the subjective and objective measurement methods aim to quantify how accurately the drawings reproduce the visual appearance of the model. Each will be described in detail below.

Subjective rating methods

Subjective accuracy ratings are used in cases where researchers are interested in understanding "perceived accuracy," or how accurate a drawing reproduces the model as visually perceived by independent observers. Studies that measure drawing performance via subjective accuracy ratings typically recruit a sample of independent judges who are instructed to view the drawings and the model side-by-side and provide judgments (most often in the form of Likert-type ratings) pertaining to how accurate the drawing reproduced the visual appearance of the model. Often, judges are instructed to base their ratings specifically on how well the drawing reproduced the visual appearance of the model without considering how creative or aesthetically pleasing the drawings are. Despite the subjective nature of this type of assessment, most studies employing this method find high levels of inter-rater reliability, as evident by observed Cronbach alpha levels of .70 or above, often exceeding levels of .90 (e.g., Chamberlain McManus, Riley et al., 2014; Cohen & Earls, 2010; Cohen & Jones, 2008; Ostrofsky et al., 2012). High reliability levels have been found in studies that employed expert judges, novice judges and both, and within studies that have sampled a relatively small (e.g., $N = 3$, Ostrofsky et al., 2012) and large (e.g., $N = 51$, Cohen & Jones, 2008) number of judges. This suggests that subjective accuracy ratings are a reliable method for assessing perceived accuracy, especially for the purposes of comparing the perceived accuracy between different drawings.

In many studies, each judge provides a single rating per drawing that represents overall perceived accuracy (e.g., Chamberlain et al., 2019; Cohen, 2005; Freeman & Loschky, 2011; Glazek, 2012; Ostrofsky et al., 2012). In some of these studies, judges are given little criteria to base their judgments on other than being asked to rate how accurately the drawing reproduced the appearance of the model (e.g., Ostrofsky et al., 2012). In other studies, researchers provide judges with a detailed rubric to review that specifies some aspects of the drawing they should attend to when determining what rating value to assign to a drawing (e.g., Chamberlain et al., 2019; Huang & Chen, 2017). For example, Huang and Chen (2017) provided a rubric that included the accuracy in reproducing: (a) the relative spatial positioning of multiple objects, (b) form and shape, (c) shadows, and (d) overall realism. Presumably, one goal of providing such rubrics is to increase inter-rater reliability, as one may expect higher reliability if all of the judges are basing their ratings on the same criteria as opposed to each judge utilizing their own idiosyncratic criteria of drawing accuracy in the absence of such a rubric. However, the effect of providing a rubric on such reliability has not been explored, as no study has compared rubric- vs. non-rubric-based ratings for a single set of drawings.

Furthermore, high reliability levels observed in studies employing non-rubric-based rating methods suggest that rubrics are not necessary to establish strong inter-rater reliability.

One criticism of measuring drawing performance using single ratings to represent overall perceived accuracy is that this type of measure does not capture the complex, multifaceted nature of drawing accuracy. A single drawing can be relatively accurate with respect to reproducing some aspects of a model but relatively inaccurate with respect to reproducing others. For instance, a drawing may be highly accurate with respect to reproducing the relative spatial positioning of features, but may be highly inaccurate with respect to reproducing shading gradients that are needed to convey depth or in drawing the detailed appearance of individual features. This complexity of drawing accuracy is masked when drawing performance is reduced to a single-value accuracy rating. This potentially creates problems of interpretation for the types of correlational and experimental studies described earlier. When significant correlations or experimental effects are observed, it is unclear which aspects of drawing accuracy are related to nondrawing task performance or which are affected by experimental manipulations when drawing accuracy is assessed via single-value accuracy ratings. The correlations or experimental effects could pertain to all or only some aspects of perceived drawing accuracy, and the use of single-value accuracy ratings makes it impossible to determine which is the case.

In order to assess perceived drawing accuracy in a more specific way, some studies have instructed judges to provide multiple ratings that each focus on a different aspect of drawing accuracy. For instance, two face-drawing studies reported by Cohen and colleagues asked judges to provide three ratings per drawing: (a) overall accuracy, (b) accuracy in drawing individual facial features, and (c) accuracy in drawing the relative spatial positioning of the features (Cohen & Earls, 2010; Cohen & Jones, 2008). As another example, Hayes and Milne (2011) instructed judges to rate the accuracy of face drawings according to 10 aspects, including face shape, eye spacing, eye size, nose length, nose width, distance between the nose and mouth, mouth width, lip fullness, distance between the mouth and chin, and chin size. However, even though such ratings can provide us with a more nuanced understanding of how accurate a drawing is perceived to be, the use of such ratings may still mask some of the complexities of drawing accuracy. For instance, although the studies by Cohen and colleagues cited above instructed judges to provide specific ratings concerning the accuracy of drawing the relative spatial positioning of features, there are many spatial relationships within a model that could be drawn with different levels of accuracy. Cohen and Earls (2010) found that drawings of upside-down faces are rated as less spatially accurate compared with upright face drawings, suggesting that face inversion impairs the ability to draw spatial relationships between features. But, when assessing specific spatial relationships in a later study, Ostrofsky, Kozbelt, Cohen et al. (2016) found that not all spatial relationships within a face are impaired by face inversion; inversion impaired drawing accuracy for one spatial relationship (the vertical distance between the eyes and mouth), but not others (e.g., the horizontal distance between the two eyes; the vertical distance between the nose and mouth). Thus, although subjective accuracy ratings are useful for broad-level assessments of perceived drawing accuracy (i.e., allowing one to empirically establish whether one drawing is, overall, more or less accurate than another), they may mask some nuanced, and potentially important, aspects of how well a drawing reproduced specific aspects of the visual appearance of a model.

Objective measurement methods

Although subjective accuracy ratings are useful for assessing how accurate a drawing is perceived to be by observers, they do not allow one to specifically assess how a drawing deviated in appearance from the model. Subjective accuracy ratings often fall short in specifying the aspects of a drawing that are more or less accurate, and they do not allow one to precisely quantify the magnitude of drawing error. Thus, some studies have assessed drawing performance using objective measurements of drawing error that precisely quantify specific deviations between a drawing and the model. Generally speaking, there are three categories of objective measurement methods that have been used in drawing research: (a) anthropometric measures, (b) landmark-based morpho-metric measures, and (c) feature counting measures.

Anthropometric measures refer to those that quantify spatial aspects of a drawing (e.g., size of a feature, distance between multiple features) using proportional variables. Although anthropometry was developed specifically for measures of the human body in nondrawing contexts, the basic method has been used to measure the accuracy of drawings based on a variety of model object categories, including faces (Costa & Corazza, 2006; Harrison, Jones, & Davies, 2017; Hayes & Milne, 2011; Ostrofsky et al., 2014), the human body (Tchalenko, 2009), cylinders (Matthews & Adams, 2008), parallelograms (Mitchell et al., 2005), and houses (Harrison et al., 2017). As one simple example, the width of an eye has been quantified as the eye width divided by the face width (Ostrofsky et al., 2014). As another example, the height of a house's second story window has been quantified as the height of the window divided by the overall height of the house (Harrison et al., 2017). Such proportioned measures control for differences in the absolute size between a model and drawing (and between different drawings) in order to facilitate comparisons, which is useful as it is generally accepted that the quality in drawing spatial aspects of an image is normally assessed based on accuracy in reproducing relative proportions rather than absolute sizes. Once the drawings and the model have been measured using this method, drawing errors can be computed using a variety of quantitative variables (e.g., computing the difference between the drawing and model measures, computing ratios of the drawing and model measures, computing the difference between the drawing and model measures and dividing this difference by the model measure to express error as a proportion or percentage of deviation from the model measure).

Anthropometric methods are useful in that they allow researchers to define specific spatial aspects of a drawing that are being assessed for accuracy, and provide precise measures of error in terms of direction and magnitude (e.g., by how much an eye was drawn too wide or narrow). However, they are not suited to assessing a drawing's overall accuracy for two major reasons. First, they are not capable of assessing important nonspatial aspects of a drawing, such as the accurate depiction of shadows and the detailed visual appearance of local features. Second, assessments of drawing accuracy are restricted to the specific spatial relationships selected by the researcher. In consideration of statistical power, researchers should be mindful of the number of spatial relationships assessed, as increases in the number of spatial relationships measured decreases statistical power if researchers appropriately control for inflated Type I error rates due to multiple comparisons. In cases where the model being drawn is visually complex and contains a large number of spatial relationships, this restriction may lead to researchers narrowly focusing on only some aspects of spatial drawing accuracy, leading them to potentially neglect assessing accuracy of important spatial aspects of the drawing that impact perceived accuracy or that are of potential theoretical interest. Thus, this method is generally best used in cases where a researcher wants to analyze the accuracy of a very specific subset of spatial relationships found in the depicted object rather than analyzing how accurately the drawing reproduced all possible spatial relationships (e.g., Mitchell et al., 2005; Ostrofsky, Kozbelt, Tumminia et al., 2016).

If a researcher is more interested in objectively measuring overall spatial accuracy rather than measuring drawing error for specifically defined spatial relationships, landmark-based morphometric measures are a useful alternative that have been used in multiple drawing studies (Chamberlain McManus, Riley et al., 2014; Day & Davidenko, 2018; Hayes & Milne, 2011; Perdreau & Cavanagh, 2014; for a general, nondrawing specific review of this method, see Webster & Sheets, 2010). Assessing drawing accuracy using this method entails first defining a number of landmarks in the model image, where the number and location of landmarks used are determined by the researcher. These landmarks are set to be positioned at easily identifiable locations in the image that can later be located in the drawings of that model. For instance, Chamberlain McManus, Riley et al. (2014) used photographic models of a Lego-block configuration and a hand holding a pencil. For the Lego-block model, the landmarks were set at most of the corners visible in the configuration of blocks. For the model depicting a hand holding a pencil, landmarks were placed at every knuckle on the hand and the two endpoints of the pencil. Once drawings of the model are produced, they are digitized and researchers place points at all of the predefined landmarks. The goal of the analysis is to determine the degree to which the drawings deviated from the model with respect to the relative positioning of the landmarks. This is often accomplished via Procrustes analysis. Here, the model and drawing landmarks are mapped in two-dimensional space and Euclidean transformations of position (translation), size (scaling), orientation (rotation), and reflection are applied to the drawings in order to minimize, as much as possible, the deviation in the relative spatial positioning (or coordinates) of all the landmarks between the drawing and model. After these transformations are applied, the deviation in the position of each landmark between the drawing and the model is computed as the Euclidean distance between them. Once the Euclidean distance has been computed for all of the landmarks, the Procrustes Distance statistic is calculated as (stated in an oversimplified manner) the sum of the Euclidean distances for all the landmarks. Thus, the greater the value of the Procrustes Distance statistic, the greater the drawing deviated from the model with respect to the relative spatial positioning of all the landmarks (or, in other words, the greater the degree of spatial drawing error).

As alluded to above, this method is only useful for assessing overall accuracy in drawing the relative spatial positioning of features. Unlike anthropometric measures, landmark-based morphometric statistics are not capable of determining the ways that a drawing erred with respect to reproducing specific spatial relationships between features found in a model. Further, like anthropometric measures, this method is only useful for assessing spatial drawing accuracy and cannot be used to assess other important aspects of drawing accuracy, like shading and the detailed appearance of local features.

At this point, we have discussed two major methods that are useful for objectively assessing spatial drawing accuracy. Moving beyond this, feature counting measures are another objective method for assessing drawing performance. Here, the researcher identifies a number of important visual features found in the model, and counts how many of them were included versus excluded from the drawing. For example, line junctions, or vertices, are an important visual feature that support object recognition in general (Biederman, 1987) and are useful in drawing in order to convey depth. Drawing and tracing performance has been partially assessed in some studies by counting the number of line junctions found in a model that were included in a drawing/tracing (Biederman & Kim, 2008; Ostrofsky et al., 2012). As another example, Drake (2013) assessed drawing performance in children by counting the presence versus absence of a number of important drawing features, such as the use of occlusion, foreshadowing, and the presence of single lines to represent the edges of objects as opposed to representing the entire object itself.

Such methods are useful in studying attentional and representational decision-making processes in drawing, as feature counting methods provide insights about what features individuals attend to versus neglect and/or what features individuals decide to include versus exclude from a drawing. For instance, in the two studies cited above that assessed drawings/tracings for the presence versus absence of line junctions, it was found that expert artists are more likely to depict line junctions than novice nonartists. This highlights that experts and novices differ in what visual features of the model they attend to and decide to include in their drawings, and thus, may be part of the reason why they differ in their ability to produce high-quality drawings. Skill in drawing may be associated with a greater sensitivity pertaining to the visual cues, like line junctions, that support strong object recognition (which is the essential goal of creating an observational drawing).

DIRECTIONS FOR FUTURE RESEARCH

In concluding this chapter, this section will highlight some suggested directions for future research, focusing on issues pertaining to the measurement of drawing performance and methodological approaches useful in assessing the causal relationships between drawing skill and perceptual/cognitive processing ability.

Measures of drawing performance

As explained in the prior section, subjective and objective measures of drawing accuracy differ in that subjective measures assess perceived accuracy whereas objective measures assess how drawings actually deviated in appearance from the model. Usually, studies utilize either subjective or objective measures. This results in a study either assessing how accurate a drawing is perceived to be by others without understanding how a drawing actually deviated in appearance from the model, or the study assessing how a drawing deviated in appearance from a model without understanding whether such deviations impacted perceived accuracy. Future drawing research would benefit by using subjective and objective measures in conjunction, as doing so would provide a more complete understanding of drawing performance within a study and may provide clues as to what types of objective drawing errors are more or less associated with how accurate a drawing is perceived to be by others. Just because a drawing objectively deviated from a model in some aspect does not necessarily mean that the specific drawing error is related to how accurate the drawing was perceived to be by others. For instance, the few studies that have assessed the relationship between subjective and objective accuracy measures for a single set of drawings have demonstrated that not all types of objective drawing errors are predictive of perceived accuracy. For example, face-drawing studies have demonstrated that subjective accuracy ratings are predicted by objectively measured errors in depicting some, but not all, spatial relationships between features (Hayes & Milne, 2011; Ostrofsky et al., 2014). Further, Chamberlain McManus, Riley et al. (2014) found that subjective accuracy ratings were predicted by objective, morphometric measures of error for drawings of some types of models (e.g., abstract hexagons, photographs of Lego blocks and hands) but not for others (e.g., the painting titled *Suprematism with Eight Red Rectangles* created by Malevich).

Despite the common use of subjective accuracy ratings to measure drawing performance, the factors that influence perceived drawing accuracy are currently not well understood. However, the common observation of high levels of inter-rater reliability of subjective accuracy ratings suggests that there are predictable properties of drawings that individuals attend to and evaluate in a consistent fashion when judging how accurate they perceive the drawing to be. Further, there have been observations of differences in the average subjective accuracy ratings provided by expert artists and nonartists (e.g., Kozbelt et al., 2010), suggesting that different populations vary in the criteria used when judging how accurate a depiction appears to be. Future research can be aimed at systematically analyzing how different aspects of drawing are weighted during the evaluation of perceived accuracy. What general properties of a drawing are more or less attended to when perceived accuracy judgments are being formed? What aspects of a drawing are weighted heavily versus moderately versus weakly in the judgment of perceived accuracy? How does the weighting of different aspects of drawing in this evaluation process vary across different populations? Such questions can be addressed via two approaches. One approach that has been used involves assessing correlations between subjective accuracy ratings and objective error measurements (Hayes & Milne, 2011; Ostrofsky et al., 2014). However, an observed correlation between subjective accuracy ratings and a particular objective error measure does not guarantee that the objective error directly influenced subjective accuracy ratings (due to the general limitations of correlational evidence). Alternatively, experimental methods could serve as another approach, where researchers systematically manipulate the appearance of drawings and determine how they affect individuals' perceptions of drawing accuracy. Here, participants can judge the accuracy of well-controlled stimuli that systematically vary the appearance of one aspect of drawing while holding all other aspects constant. In this way, researchers can determine the isolated contribution that the manipulated aspect has on perceived accuracy. In one of the only, if not the only, studies adopting this approach, Biederman and Kim (2008) presented participants with two drawings of a horse that were identical in every regard except the presence or absence of a particular line junction. They found that participants judged that the drawing with the line junction was a better depiction than the drawing without it, indicating that the presence versus absence of line junctions is an aspect of drawing that influences perceived drawing accuracy. This approach can conceivably be adapted to study how perceived accuracy is influenced by many different aspects of drawing accuracy.

Methods for understanding causal relationships between drawing skill and cognition/perception

As mentioned in an earlier section, correlational and expertise-based drawing studies generally aim to determine the differences in nondrawing-related cognitive/perceptual processes between skilled and unskilled drawers. Although the overarching aim of such studies is often to understand how cognitive/perceptual processing differences either support skilled drawing or are developed as a consequence of skill acquisition, the limitations of correlational and quasi-experimental evidence prevent one from understanding the specific causal relationships that produced the observed correlations between drawing and perceptual/cognitive processing ability or expertise-based differences in perceptual/cognitive processing ability. In order to advance our understanding of the cognitive/perceptual processes that directly impact drawing performance or to understand the cognitive/perceptual changes that occur as a result of the acquisition of drawing expertise, researchers can adopt an experimental, longitudinal methodological approach. If researchers are interested in understanding how a particular cognitive/perceptual process impacts drawing performance, researchers can conduct experiments where participants are trained over a long period of time in order to develop stronger ability for a particular cognitive/perceptual process, and then determine if that training results in improvements (or impairments) in drawing performance (relative to a baseline measure). Currently, I am unaware of any study that has adopted this approach, and thus, this void presents a great opportunity for novel and theoretically significant research on this topic. Alternatively, if researchers are interested in understanding how cognitive/perceptual processing ability changes as a result of the acquisition of drawing skill, researchers can conduct an experiment where participants are trained over a long period of time to improve their drawing skill, and then determine how cognitive/perceptual ability changes as a consequence of drawing training (relative to a baseline measure). There have only been a few studies that have adopted this approach (Kozbelt et al., 2016; Schlegel et al., 2015; Tree et al., 2017), and thus, there is a clear need for more research along these lines as changes in only a small number of cognitive/perceptual abilities have been assessed.

CONCLUSION

Observational drawing is a topic of scientific interest to psychologists. As reviewed in the chapter, there are various methods that have been used to understand individual variability in drawing ability and in order to measure drawing performance in laboratory-based studies. Although much can be learned from each method, this chapter highlighted significant limitations each method has pertaining to interpretations one can validly draw from the results of a study or pertaining to the aspects of drawing performance a particular measurement method is capable of assessing. However, such limitations do not indicate that drawing is a topic that cannot be subjected to scientific inquiry. Rather, such limitations simply highlight the need of researchers to critically evaluate the methods used by a particular study in order to draw valid scientific conclusions and to avoid overgeneralizing results in such a way that they are not supported by the methodological features used by a particular study. This is by no means unique to the study of observational drawing, as the study of all topics in scientific research is based on methods that have their own unique limitations. Since the scientific study of adult observational drawing performance is a relatively young field, one can expect refinements in the methods used to study this topic to be developed in the future. The preceding section of this chapter provided suggestions on how some of these limitations can be improved upon in future research, and thus, one can be optimistic that research on observational drawing will continue to develop and to provide more insights that can explain the tremendous range of individual variability in drawing performance that is found in the population.

REFERENCES

Biederman, I. (1987). Recognition-by-Components: A theory of human image understanding. *Psychological Review, 94,* 115–147.

Biederman, I., & Kim, J. G. (2008). 17,000 years of depicting the junction of two smooth shapes. *Perception, 37*, 161–164.

Carson, L. C., & Allard, A. (2013). Angle-drawing accuracy as an objective performance-based measure of drawing expertise. *Psychology of Aesthetics, Creativity, and the Arts, 7*, 119–129.

Carson, L. C., Millard, M., Quehl, N., & Danckert, J. (2014). Polygon-based drawing accuracy analysis and positive/negative space. *Art & Perception, 2*, 213–236.

Chamberlain, R., Drake, J. E., Kozbelt, A., Hickman, R., Siev, J., & Wagemans, J. (2019). Artists as experts in visual cognition: An update. *Psychology of Aesthetics, Creativity, and the Arts, 13*, 58–73

Chamberlain, R., McManus, I. C., Brunswick, N., Rankin, Q., Riley, H., & Kanai, R. (2014). Drawing on the right side of the brain: A voxel-based morphometry analysis of observational drawing. *NeuroImage, 96*, 167–173.

Chamberlain, R., McManus, I. C., Riley, H., Rankin, Q., & Brunswick, N. (2013). Local processing enhancements associated with superior observational drawing are due to enhanced perceptual functioning, not weak central coherence. *Quarterly Journal of Experimental Psychology, 66*, 1448–1466.

Chamberlain, R., McManus, I. C., Riley, H., Rankin, Q., & Brunswick, N. (2014). Cain's House Task revisited and revived: extending theory and methodology for quantifying drawing accuracy. *Psychology of Aesthetics, Creativity, and the Arts, 8*, 152–167.

Chamberlain, R., & Wagemans, J. (2015). Visual arts training is linked to flexible attention to local and global levels of visual stimuli. *Acta Psychologica, 161*, 185–197.

Chamberlain, R., & Wagemans, J. (2016). The genesis of errors in drawing. *Neuroscience & Biobehavioral Reviews, 65*, 195–207.

Chase, W. G., & Simon, H. A. (1973). Perception in chess. *Cognitive Psychology, 4*, 55–81.

Clottes, J. (2003). *Chauvet cave: The art of earliest times*. Salt Lake City, UT: University of Utah Press.

Cohen, D. J. (2005). Look little, look often: the influence of gaze frequency on drawing accuracy. *Perception and Psychophysics, 67*, 997–1009.

Cohen, D. J., & Bennett, S. (1997). Why can't most people draw what they see? *Journal of Experimental Psychology: Human Perception and Performance, 23*, 609–621.

Cohen, D. J., & Earls, H. (2010). Inverting an image does not improve drawing accuracy. *Psychology of Aesthetics, Creativity, and the Arts, 4*, 168–172.

Cohen, D. J., & Jones, H. E. (2008). How shape constancy relates to drawing accuracy. *Psychology of Aesthetics, Creativity, and the Arts, 2*, 8–19.

Costa, M., & Corazza, L. (2006). Aesthetic phenomena as supernormal stimuli: The case of eye, lip, and lower-face size and roundness in artistic portraits. *Perception, 35*, 229–246.

Day, J. A., & Davidenko, N. (2018). Physical and perceptual accuracy of upright and inverted face drawings. *Visual Cognition, 26*, 89–99.

Devue, C., & Barsics, C. (2016). Outlining face processing skills of portrait artists: Perceptual experience with faces predicts performance. *Vision Research, 127*, 92–103.

Drake, J. E. (2013). Is superior local processing in the visuospatial domain a function of drawing talent rather than ASD? *Psychology of Aesthetics, Creativity, and the Arts, 7*, 203–209.

Drake, J. E., & Winner, E. (2011). Realistic drawing talent in typical adults is associated with the same kind of local processing bias found in individuals with ASD. *Journal of Autism and Developmental Disorders, 41*, 1192–1201.

Freeman, N. H., & Janikoun, R. (1972). Intellectual realism in children's drawings of a familiar object with distinctive features. *Child Development, 43*, 1116–1121.

Freeman, T. L., & Loschky, L.C. (2011). Low and high spatial frequencies are most useful for drawing. *Psychology of Aesthetics, Creativity, and the Arts, 5*, 269–278.

Glazek, K. (2012). Visual and motor processing in visual artists: Implications for cognitive and neural mechanisms. *Psychology of Aesthetics, Creativity and the Arts, 6*, 155–167.

Green, C. S., & Bavelier, D. (2003). Action video game modifies visual selective attention. *Nature, 423*, 534–537.

Harrison, N. R., Jones, J., & Davies, S. J. (2017). Systematic distortions in vertical placement of features in drawings of faces and houses. *i-Perception, 8*, 204166951769105.

Hayes, S., & Milne, N. (2011). What's wrong with this picture? An experiment in quantifying accuracy in 2D portrait drawing. *Visual Communication, 10*, 149–174.

Huang, S. T., & Chen, I. P. (2017). The relationship between 2D positioning ability and realistic drawing skill. *Art and Design Review, 5*, 1–12.

Kellogg, R. (1970). *Analyzing children's art.* Mountain, CA: Mayfield Publishing Company.

Kozbelt, A. (2001). Artists as experts in visual cognition. *Visual Cognition, 8*, 705–723.

Kozbelt, A., Chamberlain, R., & Drake, J. E. (2016). Learning to see by learning to draw: a longitudinal study of perceptual changes among artists-in-training. Presented at the Congress of the International Association of Empirical Aesthetics, Vienna, Austria.

Kozbelt, A., & Ostrofsky, J. (2018). Expertise in drawing. In K. A. Ericsson, R. R. Hoffman, A. Kozbelt, & A. M. Williams (Eds.), *The Cambridge handbook of expertise and expert performance*, 2nd edition (pp. 576–596). Cambridge, England: Cambridge University Press.

Kozbelt, A., & Seeley, W. (2007). Integrating art historical, psychological, and neuroscientific explanations of artists' advantages in drawing and perception. *Psychology of Aesthetics, Creativity and the Arts, 1*, 80–90.

Kozbelt, A., Seidel, A., ElBassiouny, A., Mark, Y., & Owen, D. R. (2010). Visual selection contributes to artists' advantages in realistic drawing. *Psychology of Aesthetics, Creativity, and the Arts, 4*, 93–102.

Maguire, E. A., Gadian, D. G., Johnsrude, I. S., Good, C. D., Ashburner, J., Frackowiak, R. S. J., & Frith, C. D. (2000). Navigation-related structural change in hippocampi of taxi drivers. *Proceedings of the National Academy of Sciences of the United States of America, 97*, 4398–4403.

Matthews, W. J., & Adams, A. (2008). Another reason why adults find it hard to draw accurately. *Perception, 37*, 628–630.

McManus, I. C., Loo, P., Chamberlain, R., Riley, H., & Brunswick, N. (2011). Does shape constancy relate to drawing ability? Two failures to replicate. *Empirical Studies of the Arts, 29*, 191–208.

Mitchell, P., Ropar, D., Ackroyd, K., & Rajendran, G. (2005). How perception impacts on drawings. *Journal of Experimental Psychology: Human Perception and Performance, 31*, 996–1003.

Ostrofsky, J., Cohen, D. J., & Kozbelt, A. (2014). Objective versus subjective measures of face-drawing accuracy and their relations with perceptual constancies. *Psychology of Aesthetics, Creativity, and the Arts, 8*, 486–497.

Ostrofsky, J., Kozbelt, A., & Cohen, D. J. (2015). Observational drawing biases are predicted by biases in perception: Empirical support of the misperception hypothesis of drawing accuracy with respect to two angle illusions. *The Quarterly Journal of Experimental Psychology, 68*, 1007–1025.

Ostrofsky, J., Kozbelt, A., Cohen, D. J., Conklin, L., & Thomson, K. (2016). Face inversion impairs the ability to draw long-range, but not short-range, spatial relationships between features. *Empirical Studies of the Arts, 34*, 221–233.

Ostrofsky, J., Kozbelt, A., & Kurylo, D. (2013). Perceptual grouping in artists and non-artists: A psychophysical comparison. *Empirical Studies of the Arts, 31*, 131–143.

Ostrofsky, J., Kozbelt, A., & Seidel, A. (2012). Perceptual constancies and visual selection as predictors of realistic drawing skill. *Psychology of Aesthetics, Creativity, and the Arts, 6*, 124–136.

Ostrofsky, J., Kozbelt, A., Tumminia, M., & Cipriano, M. (2016). Why do non-artists draw the eyes too far up the head? How vertical eye-drawing errors relate to schematic knowledge, pseudoneglect and context-based perceptual biases. *Psychology of Aesthetics, Creativity and the Arts, 10*, 332–343.

Ostrofsky, J., Nehl, H., & Mannion, K. (2017). The effect of object interpretation on the appearance of drawings of ambiguous figures. *Psychology of Aesthetics, Creativity and the Arts, 11*, 99–108.

Perdreau, F., & Cavanagh, P. (2011). Do artists see their retinas? *Frontiers in Human Neuroscience, 5*, 1–10.

Perdreau, F., & Cavanagh, P. (2013). The artist's advantage: Better integration of object information across eye movements. *i-Perception, 4*, 380–395.

Perdreau, F., & Cavanagh, P. (2014). Drawing skill is related to the efficiency of encoding object structure. *i-Perception, 5*, 101–119.

Schlegel, A., Alexander, P., Foggelson, S. V., Li, X., Lu, Z., Kohler, P. J., Riley, E., Tse, P. U., & Meng, M. (2015). The artist emerges: Visual art learning alters neural structure and function. *NeuroImage, 105*, 440–451.

Sheppard, R., Ropar, D., & Mitchell, P. (2005). The impact of meaning and dimensionality on the accuracy of children's copying. *Journal of Autism and Developmental Disorders, 37*, 1913–1924.

Sommers, P. V. (1984). *Drawing and cognition: Descriptive and experimental studies of graphic production processes*. Cambridge, England: Cambridge University Press.

Tchalenko, J. (2009). Segmentation and accuracy in copying and drawing: Experts and beginners. *Vision Research, 49*, 791–800.

Tree, J. J., Horry, R., Riley, H., & Wilmer, J. B. (2017). Are portrait artists superior face recognizers? Limited impact of adult experience on face recognition ability. *Journal of Experimental Psychology: Human Perception and Performance, 43*, 667–676.

Vinter, A. (1999). How meaning modifies drawing behavior in children. *Child Development, 70*, 33–49.

Webster, M., & Sheets, H. D. (2010). A practical introduction to landmark-based geometric morphometrics. *Quantitative Methods in Paleobiology, 16*, 163–188.

Wong, Y. K., & Gauthier, I. (2012). Music-reading expertise alters visual spatial resolution for musical notation. *Psychonomic Bulletin & Review, 19*, 594–600.

Zhou, G., Cheng, Z., Zhang, X., & Wong, A. C.-N. (2012). Smaller holistic processing of faces associated with face drawing experience. *Psychonomic Bulletin & Review, 19*, 157–162.

CHAPTER 12

IMPLICIT MEASURES IN THE AESTHETIC DOMAIN

LETIZIA PALUMBO

AESTHETIC EXPERIENCE: AN OVERVIEW

SINCE the advent of experimental psychology in the nineteenth century the field of empirical aesthetics has offered a wide range of theoretical and functional models (Berlyne, 1960; 1971; Chatterjee, 2003; Cupchik, 1994; Fechner, 1871; Leder et al., 2004; Nadal, Munar, Capo, Rossello, & Cela-Conde, 2008; Marković, 2012; Silvia, 2005; Starr, 2013). Each with its focus on different components has enriched the debate on the nature of aesthetic experience and its function in everyday life. The complexity of the phenomenon has challenged the formulation of a unified framework and a variety of features have emerged across time. From a modern psychological perspective, aesthetic experience has been examined in terms of subjective variations along several continua: pleasure–unpleasure, like–dislike, positive–negative etc. (Silvia, 2009), hence shifting the attention away from the philosophical debate on the objective ideal of beauty. Here I will try to summarize those aspects of aesthetic experience that I believe are central for the analysis proposed in this chapter.

Aesthetic appreciation is an overarching term used by scholars in the field to include pleasure, interest, curiosity, fascination, wonder, and so on. It can be generally defined as an evaluative hedonic response to a given object, reflecting inner mental operations and underlying brain processes. The complexity of these mental operations is due to interconnections between different dimensions (perception, emotion, and cognition), which entail multilevel processes (implicit and explicit) and feedback loops (bottom-up and top-down). In synthesis, aesthetic experience reflects the intricate relationships among these mental processes and personal predispositions (knowledge, expertise, personality, attitudes, mood, taste, and motivations) (Leder et al., 2004; Silvia, 2009), cultural factors (canons, traditions, innovations, fashion, and trends) (Carbon, 2010; Ritterfeld, 2002), and art and historical context (Bullot & Reber, 2013; Jacobsen, 2010).

The role that each of those elements plays in the formation of aesthetic experience is subject to individual differences, or personal relevance (Vessel et al., 2012), and might depend on the type of object we are presented with (e.g., art vs. no art). In this respect, there is still some disagreement among scholars. Leder et al. (2004) proposed that for aesthetic experience to occur the observer needs to engage with a work of art, taken in its context. Marković (2012) re-valued the ideal of the "sublime," remarking that aesthetic experience reflects an exceptional state of mind. This does not belong to the ordinary experience (preference, liking, judgments of beauty) with everyday objects and does not have a pragmatic function. Although we cannot deny that everyday objects have also aesthetic qualia (Hekkert et al., 2003; Leder & Carbon, 2005), Marković (2012) pointed out that there is a difference between a beautiful object and an object of beauty. On the other hand, Starr (2013) affirms that "not only art can drive powerful aesthetic experience" (p. 25). The dispute on whether the affective events (i.e., reward) occurring during aesthetic experience belong to a special class of "aesthetic emotions" or to our ordinary experience is still ongoing. I will return to this debate at the end of the chapter.

What Are Implicit Processes and How Can We Measure Them?

Based on the principle of cognitive economy, we can differentiate between mental processes that are effortless and fast, such as perception and emotion, and more demanding mental operations involved in deliberate decision making, evaluations, or problem-solving strategies. Implicit processes have been defined as automatic and uncontrolled mental activities executed in absence of volition (Nosek & Hansen, 2008) and beyond conscious control (Bargh, 1989). As such, implicit processes are mental activities that the individual cannot recall or report in propositional terms (Bornstein & Pittman, 1992). The architecture of the mind comprises bottom-up (stimulus driven) and top-down (conceptually driven) processes, which entail different stages. For example, our senses encode low-level information (e.g., light, sound, odor etc.) received from the environment. This information proceeds from subcortical to cortical areas of the brain where isolated elements are finally combined into a mental representation. The single features of an object, for example in a visual stimulus: edges, size, orientation, motion, color etc. are organized, identified, and interpreted into a percept. The two processing stages, sensation and perception, advance in a bottom-up fashion, from particular to general, and do not necessitate conscious control. An observer cannot report how all the single elements have been bound together to form a particular configuration nor when the process occurred. Therefore, we can refer to bottom-up stimulus driven analysis as an implicit process. Automatic feedback loops can also link different cognitive domains. For example, a perceived feature in a target object might lead to implicit associations with semantics stored in memory. These automatic associations can, in turn, modulate the evaluation of the stimulus in question. In addition, our perceptual interpretations can also be influenced by other factors, such as expectations, existing beliefs, knowledge etc. In many cases we are not aware of these top-down (conceptually driven) influences, although they are effective.

De Houwer et al. (2009) defined implicit measures as outcomes of measurement procedures that are caused through automatic processes by psychological attributes. In their normative analysis, the authors stipulated the properties that an ideal implicit measure should have. These refer to (1) whether the outcome is causally produced by the psychological attribute it was meant to measure; (2) the nature of the processes involved in this cause–effect relation; and (3) whether these processes operate automatically.

In the area of social cognition and in social psychology the most common implicit measures are affective priming paradigms (Bargh et al., 1996; Fazio & Olson, 2003), the Implicit Association Test (IAT) (Greenwald et al., 1998; Nosek et al., 2005), as well as implicit measures of approach–avoidance (De Houwer et al., 2001). Other subdisciplines of psychology, such as clinical psychology and consumer psychology (see Gattol et al., 2011) have implemented these procedures to study affective dispositions, implicit attitudes, and preference.

In empirical aesthetics most research has implemented rating scales (i.e., Likert scales) or forced-choice responses that reflect explicit evaluations. These measures are not always appropriate to study the rich interconnections that characterize the formation of hedonic responses. Recently, the use of affective priming, the IAT, and approach–avoidance tasks have become more popular. The use of these measures has revealed associations between perceptual features and semantics or affective representations and how these might give rise to phenomena of appreciation for a variety of visual stimuli, from abstract patterns or shapes, paintings, to architecture and design (Bertamini et al., 2013; Flexas et al., 2013; Makin et al., 2012; Mastandrea et al., 2011; Mastandrea & Maricchiolo, 2014; Palumbo et al., 2015; Pavlović & Marković, 2012). In the text that follows, I will first introduce these implicit measures. In the next section, with reference to existing models in empirical aesthetics, we will see how the use of these implicit measures contributed to verify early processing stages of the aesthetic experience.

Affective priming

Priming effects reflect the strength of the association between a preceding prime and a target stimulus. The speed of a categorization response for a target stimulus is influenced by the congruency with an immediate preceding prime (Klauer & Musch, 2003). We can distinguish between semantic and affective priming (Fazio et al., 1986), depending on whether the congruency between the two stimuli is based on object category or valence, respectively. If the prime and target belong to the same object category (e.g., tiger and elephant) or have the same valence (both positive or both negative), namely congruent condition, the reaction times (RTs) for the target will be faster as compared with when the two stimuli differ (incongruent condition). A short interval between the two stimuli as well as short stimulus onset asynchrony (SOA) maximize the effect (Hermans et al., 2001). Another distinction is between subliminal and supraliminal priming (Murphy & Zajonc, 1993). In the first case the prime stimulus is presented below conscious detection thresholds. In the second case, participants can recall having seen the prime, although ignoring its potential influence. De Houwer et al. (2002) explained priming in terms of a conflict at the stage of response selection. In the incongruent condition the prime would prepare participants to press the wrong key and this would slow down RTs in this condition as compared with the congruent condition. Therefore, the outcome might be a consequence of a response conflict, which reflects the strength of the association between the two stimuli. The possibility of using pictures or sounds instead of words in affective priming paradigms makes it particularly suitable to examine the relation between affect and hedonic evaluations for a wider range of aesthetic stimuli. However, studies using affective priming paradigms in empirical aesthetics are still limited.

The Implicit Association Test (IAT)

The IAT (Greenwald et al., 1998) is another implicit measure that has been mainly adopted in social psychology to study implicit attitudes toward different social dimensions such as race or sex (Mitchell et al., 2003). Lately, its use has also been extended to empirical aesthetics to verify whether there is an association between some specific object features and semantics, including valence. The IAT allows determining the degree of implicit association between two categories (De Houwer et al., 2009). The underlying principle is similar to priming: if two elements have a strong association this is going to improve performance. However, the IAT procedure is substantially different. In the original task by Greenwald et al. (1998), participants used two buttons to classify four stimulus categories. On some trials they were presented with pictures of two different categories, for example flowers or insects. The instructions prompted participants to press one button for flower and the other button for insect. On interleaved trials, participants received either positive words (e.g., "love") or negative words (e.g., "hate"). The task was to press one button for positive, and the other for negative. In compatible blocks, the same button was used for "flower" or "love," and the other was used for "insect" or "hate." In incompatible blocks, the response mapping was reversed (one button was used for "flower" and "hate," the other was used for "insect" and "love"). Participants took longer to respond and made more errors in the incompatible trials because they were less likely to associate flowers with negative words and insects with positive words. Therefore, the implicit association between stimulus pairs is reflected in the difference on the RTs between compatible and incompatible blocks. The IAT, given its experimental structure, has been preferentially applied within the visual domain.

Approach–avoidance

The Manikin task (De Houwer et al., 2001) has been developed to examine implicit approach–avoidance responses. Assuming that the stimuli that are approached are implicitly evaluated as positive and those that are avoided as negative (Chen & Bargh, 1999), this procedure can be used as an indirect measure of preference. Similar to the other implicit measures, the design of this task also involves compatible and incompatible blocks of trials. The original version of this task consists of pressing one key as soon as possible to move a figure toward a stimulus and to press another key to move it away. Subsequently, Krieglmeyer et al. (2010) applied a modification using three key presses to give the impression to the observer that the manikin was walking, hence increasing ecological validity. In both cases "approach" or "avoidance" is recorded as RT needed to decide and react (RTs on first key press). In terms of data analysis, it is possible to take into account the first key press (how fast the participant decides to approach or avoid) as in De Houwer et al. (2001) and in Krieglmeyer et al. (2010) or to consider the time elapsed between the first key press (precisely when the manikin started to move) and the third key press (when the manikin stopped closed or away from the target stimulus). In the latter case, we obtain two measures: (1) how fast the participants decide the direction of the movement (response selection: approach or avoidance); and (2) how fast they keep the manikin going in that direction (Palumbo et al., 2015). As we will see in the next section, the Manikin task can be used in combination with the IAT to verify if associations with positive or negative attributes are also confirmed in terms of congruent approach and avoidance responses.

In addition to the Manikin task there are also other approach–avoidance procedures, such as, for example, the joystick task where participants pull and push a joystick, or the variant with the feedback (also called feedback joystick task) in which the actions of pulling or pushing a joystick cause the visual impression that the stimuli come closer or disappear. However, a comparative study (Krieglmeyer et al., 2010) showed that the Manikin task was more sensitive to stimulus valence and provided a better assessment of approach–avoidance than the other two tasks. Furthermore, with joystick procedures participants are more likely to experience self–other conflictual embodied responses (i.e., moving the joystick away from the object presented on screen would activate an embodied approach toward the self).

THE ROLE OF IMPLICIT PROCESSES IN AESTHETIC EVALUATION

Despite some key differences across models in empirical aesthetics (see Marković, 2012), a common feature is the distinction between implicit and explicit mental processes in the experience of an aesthetic object (Chatterjee et al., 2003; Chatterjee & Vartanian, 2016; Cupchik, 1994; Höfel & Jacobsen, 2007; Leder, 2013; Leder et al., 2004).

Leder et al. (2004) proposed an information-processing model to explain the formation of aesthetic experience mainly for visual art. A revised version was released a decade later (Leder & Nadal, 2014). This model presents early processing stages, which first involve a perceptual analysis and an implicit memory integration, followed by an explicit classification and cognitive mastering. These stages lead to two main outcomes: aesthetic judgment and aesthetic emotion. The focus of the next sections will be on the intersection between the first two processing stages.

Perceptual qualia, rewarding processes, or all at once?

The role of automaticity leading to aesthetic judgments has been central in some models (Cupchik, 1994). Ramachandran and Hirstein (1999) have identified some aesthetic principles, for example order and symmetry, as determinants of hedonic appreciation. One influential theory to explain visual preferences is that the visual system is tuned to specific object properties (Zeki, 1999); therefore, those features that optimally stimulate the visual system tend to assume an aesthetic connotation.

The study of visual perception has examined a wide range of parameters, features, and configurations in relation to positive and aesthetic responses. Symmetry, for example, is notoriously linked with beauty (Höfel & Jacobsen, 2007; Perrett et al., 1999) (for detailed information about symmetry, see Bertamini et al., 2016 and Bertamini and Rampone, Section 3, Chapter 22).

Winkielman et al. (2003) formulated the fluency hypothesis, which predicts a cause–effect relation between hedonic evaluations and ease of information processing (see also Reber et al., 2004). According to this theory, we tend to appreciate perceptual features that are easy, fast, and effortless to process. In this category, we can find perceptual qualia that meet Gestalt laws or that produce an optimal stimulation of the visual system. The ease of processing is not a necessary determinant of aesthetic value (i.e., beauty), but it is intended to operate as a mental lever for pleasure.

Recent research made use of implicit measures to establish a link between symmetry and positive valence. For example, Makin et al. (2012) tested whether the positive response to symmetry is elicited automatically. The authors used the IAT in a series of four experiments in absence of an explicit evaluation, to measure valence of different visual regularities (reflection, translation, rotation, and random). The strong association between reflection symmetry and positive words was interpreted as an implicit preference for this type of configuration. The authors also found that reflection symmetry was preferred to both rotation and translation and that rotation was preferred to random. Interestingly, in some cases there was no agreement between implicit responses and preference reported verbally, but the implicit preferences predicted detection speed. The authors confirmed an automatic affective response for symmetry, which was explained in terms of perceptual fluency.

Subsequently, Bertamini et al. (2013) found that symmetrical patterns were implicitly associated with positive and more arousing words, whereas random patterns were associated with lower arousal. Furthermore, symmetrical patterns were associated with mathematic expressions. In contrast, random patterns were associated with complex expressions. The authors concluded that aesthetic liking of symmetry involves emotional reactions that arise from perceptual simplicity of symmetry, hence supporting the fluency hypothesis in the formation of hedonic responses.

Another perceptual feature that has been the focus of research is curvature. Here I refer to smooth curvature as a single line parameter (Bertamini et al., 2016), as a contour line of a closed shape (Bar & Neta, 2006, 2007; Bertamini et al., 2016), or as a basic component embedded in more complex object designs (Leder & Carbon, 2005; Vartanian et al., 2013). In these studies, observers consistently expressed their preference for curvature (as opposed to angularity) directly, with stimuli selection procedures, or indirectly, rating one stimulus at a time. As for symmetry, the curvature effect is consistent, strong, and cuts across cultures (Munar et al., 2015). Unlike symmetry, the nature of the preference for curvature has not yet been properly assessed, although some hypotheses have been put forward (Bar & Neta, 2007; Bertamini et al., 2016; Bertamini et al., 2019). The studies conducted so far seem to suggest that visual preference for curvature is the result of a multifactorial interaction between low-level visual parameters, affect, personality traits, expertise, and context (Cotter et al., 2017; Palumbo et al., 2015; Vartanian et al., 2013). The use of implicit measures clarified the role of affect and the link with semantics.

Palumbo et al. (2015) implemented a multidimensional IAT (Gattol et al., 2011) to test implicit associations between curvature and three semantic dimensions (valence, danger, and gender). As in all our experiments we used unfamiliar abstract shapes (i.e., irregular polygons) to avoid familiarity effects. Based on consistent liking ratings for curvature, valence was the most obvious attribute. Therefore, we predicted implicit associations between curved shapes with positive words and between angular shapes with negative words. Danger was tested because preference for curvature was previously explained as a by-product of the dislike for angularity, which contains visual features, sharp angles, that signal a threat (Bar & Neta, 2007). The gender dimension was an interesting one because of the possible link between abstract curves and the female body, although here for consistency we used female and male names instead of body images. The results confirmed a strong association of curved shapes with positive and safety words, and with female names. In contrast, angular shapes were associated with negative and danger words and male names. The strength of the association was similar across dimensions. The IAT confirmed that we do implicitly associate abstract meaningless objects with semantics in the expected direction. However, it did not reveal which of the two associations (curved shapes with positive words or angular shapes with negative words) is stronger. Therefore, we employed the Manikin task in a subsequent experiment. Interestingly, this measure revealed a congruent approach response for curved shapes (RTs were faster for approach to curved shapes as compared with avoidance), whereas for angular shapes there was no significant difference between approach and avoidance.

The Manikin task clarified the nature of the associations that were previously found using the IAT procedure. From these two studies we concluded that hedonic responses for curvature might depend on an aesthetic quality contained in the curved contour itself, although it is also influenced by what curves can recall in terms of affective representations. This is in line with past research by Lundholm (1921) and Poffenberger and Barrows (1924), who found explicit associations between angular and curved stimuli with a variety of adjectives, although in these studies the congruency with valence did not always occur.

Implicit mental processes involve automatic processes executed in absence of volition. Perceptual features can automatically recall mental representations, symbolic (linguistic) or figurative (images) from our memory. Extensive research has been conducted to explain how our representations or schemas are automatically activated and which are the factors that might facilitate the accessibility of these schemas (see Fiske & Taylor, 2013). First impression formation, for example, is greatly influenced by familiarity, which is the amount of exposure to a given object, and prototypicality, which is the degree to which an object is representative of a general class of object. For example, the effect of familiarity on affective preference for a stimulus was first reported using the "mere exposure" paradigm (Zajonc, 1968). In Leder et al.'s (2004) model, familiarity, prototypicality, and peak-shift (exaggeration of features) have been located within the stage of "implicit memory integration." Based on cognitive fluency (Winkielman et al., 2003), the facilitation of the access to stored mental representations would ultimately lead to a positive response.

Mastandrea et al. (2011) used the IAT for the first time in the field of empirical aesthetics to test whether hedonic responses for visual arts and architecture might reflect implicit association with positive and negative attributes. The authors used two art styles (figurative vs. abstract) and two architectural styles (classic vs. contemporary), which, depending on the condition (compatible or incompatible), were paired with positive or negative words. The authors reported faster RTs when figurative art and classic architectural style were paired with positive words (compatible task) as compared with when these were paired with negative words (incompatible task). They concluded that an implicit aesthetic preference for figurative and classical architecture was driven by familiarity and prototypicality, hence suggesting that cognitive fluency might account for these results.

However, the implicit role played by fluency might be by other factors, such as expertise. In a subsequent study, Mastandrea and Maricchiolo (2014) extended the use of the IAT with classical and modern design objects (i.e., chairs) to compare implicit evaluation depending on participants' expertise. They found that in a group of laypeople there was not a significant difference in latency between compatible trials (classic design with positive words and modern design with negative words) and incompatible trials (classic design with negative words and modern design with positive words). In contrast, with design expert participants they found faster responses in the incompatible task as compared with the compatible task. This suggests that implicit preference for classic and modern design objects was modulated by expertise, as the aesthetic preference at an implicit level was only found for modern design objects and with experts. This confirms the thesis that novices tend to prefer figurative art because the meaning is more accessible, whereas experts find abstract art more rewarding (Leder et al., 2004).

On the other hand, Pavlović and Marković (2012) also used the IAT in two experiments to examine whether hedonic tone would influence automatic aesthetic evaluation for figural and abstract art. Participants' performance was faster in the compatible task (where hedonically "positive" paintings were paired with positive attributes and hedonically "negative" ones were paired with negative attributes) as compared with the incompatible task. Interestingly, the authors reported that explicit judgments of the hedonic tone were related to the individual IAT effects but only in the case of abstract art. Pavlović and Marković (2012) excluded the idea that their set of results could be explained in terms of higher processing of meaning, given that the effect was found only for abstract art.

Some recent research showed that at the neural level novices can process certain complex structural aspects of stimuli, such as harmonies in music or syntactic rules in poetry. One of the advantages of using neuroscience tools in the field of empirical aesthetics is that these can disclose pre-attentive processes underlying hedonic evaluations, which might not be explicated. For example, Vaughan-Evans et al. (2016) conducted an interesting study using electroencephalogram (EEG) to assess whether readers with no specific knowledge of Cynghanedd, a traditional form of Welsh poetry, could distinguish phrases conforming to its complex poetic construction rules from those that violate them. Importantly, the ability to distinguish between these conditions affects appreciation of poetry (Aryani et al., 2013). The participants' task was to explicitly distinguish between meaningful sentences with an ending word that either met the strict poetic construction rules, violated rules of consonantal repetition violated, stress pattern, or violated both. The results on the behavioral task showed that naive participants did not explicitly distinguish between conditions. However, in the case of violations, the critical word elicited a distinctive brain response for target detection, namely the P3b, as compared with the other conditions. This pattern of results showed that speakers of Welsh with no expertise in this particular form of poetry can detect its musical properties without conscious awareness. In other words, novices can implicitly detect complex structures of poetry harmonies that typically influence hedonic evaluations.

This is interesting also in relation to studies on music where the role of expertise examined with different harmonic variations has showed some discrepancies (Müller et al., 2010; Smith & Melara, 1990).

This study opens up a new territory of investigations on the role of implicit processing in the formation of aesthetic experience that can be extended to other forms of art. At present, current models seem to underestimate the role that implicit processing can have in directing our hedonic evaluations. One obvious reason why it is important to implement implicit measures is that a large amount of mental activity escapes awareness. Understanding what we can or cannot process and the effects that this might have on hedonic evaluations is fundamental to fully comprehending what aesthetic experience is.

THE INTERRELATION BETWEEN SENSATION AND EMOTION

There is substantial agreement that emotion is involved in aesthetic appraisal (Silvia, 2005, 2009) and for many scholars it is the core component of aesthetic experience (Starr, 2013). Phenomena of appreciation, pleasure, interest, attraction all denote a variation in the arousal levels and valence. Therefore, emotions not only constitute a response, but they actively contribute to the formation of aesthetic experience. In fact, emotions can direct or modulate aesthetic appreciation for artworks as shown by Flexas et al. (2013). The authors used facial expressions (happiness, disgust, or no emotion) as primes varying SOA (20 ms vs. 300 ms). The effect of priming was measured in terms of differences in aesthetic evaluations (i.e., liking) for abstract paintings depending on the emotion depicted in the preceding primes. The results in the longer SOA condition showed that artworks were liked more when preceded by happiness primes and they were liked less when preceded by disgust primes. In the subliminal condition, only happiness primes, not disgust, showed an effect. These results, therefore, established a link between the implicit influence of affect and aesthetic appreciation.

Leder et al. (2004) and Leder and Nadal (2014) acknowledged the role of the emotional component in aesthetic experience. From the moment that the attendee classifies the perceived object as a work of art, the emotional affective state informs all the other stages involved (continuous affective evaluation) until an emotional response is finally reached. However, it remains unclear how the emotional component operates in relation to the other processing stages, especially in consideration of the fact that affect is subject to changes.

The interconnection between implicit and explicit components of aesthetic experience was already theorized by Cupchik (1994), who proposed reflexive and reflective models of emotion in aesthetics. More recently, Chatterjee and Vartanian (2016) captured these two different levels (implicit and explicit) in their "aesthetic triad" model, which comprises sensorimotor, emotion-valuation, and knowledge-meaning. For the purposes of the current chapter, I will focus on the interconnection between the first two components. According to the authors, the sensorimotor component involves sensation, perception, and the activation of the motor system. In contrast, the emotional-valuation is characterized by the interaction between reward and emotion, as supported by numerous neuroscience studies (see Chatterjee & Vartanian, 2016; Nadal et al., 2008 for a review).

It is possible to investigate motor reactions in terms of a spontaneous response to he-donic stimuli. Spontaneous responses from facial muscles are reported during passive observation of facial expressions using facial electromyographical (EMG) responses (Dimberg et al., 2000). Gerger et al. (2011) used EMG to examine reactions to the attract-iveness of faces and abstract patterns varying presentation durations. The authors found a stronger activation of the zygomaticus major (ZM), the facial muscle responsible for smiling, for attractive stimuli and a stronger activation of the corrugator supercilii (CS), the facial muscle responsible for frowning, for unattractive stimuli. These results mirror several neuroimaging studies which showed that the perception of artworks elicits motor activity in the observer's brain (Cela-Conde et al., 2009; Cross & Ticini, 2012).

The role of the sensorimotor components in relation to emotional events involved during aesthetic experience was previously proposed by Freedberg & Gallese (2007). Their account emphasizes that the creation of artworks, such as paintings, involves an activation of the motor system and that what we process during passive observation of paintings also includes features that reflect the artists' actions. To test this hypothesis, Ticini et al. (2014) examined the link between art appreciation and automatic motor activity in the observer using an action priming paradigm. They presented participants with pointillist-style paintings where brushstrokes were crucially evident and asked them to rate how much they liked each canvas. An image priming the motor act con-gruent or incongruent with the simulation of the artists' movements preceded each target painting. The authors found higher liking ratings in the congruent as compared with the incongruent condition. In line with the account of Freedberg and Gallese (2007), this study provides evidence that automatic embodied simulation mechanisms might be involved in the formation of aesthetic experience.

THE SOCIAL FUNCTION OF AESTHETICS

At the end of my overview, I left the reader with some unresolved questions about the nature (exceptional or ordinary) of aesthetic experience and its objects (art vs. no art). The attempt to reconcile different positions leads to a final question: Does art have a pragmatic function? In Ancient Greece, tragedy had a cathartic function (Berczeller, 1967). Nowadays we can acknowledge that art has a powerful communicative, evoca-tive, and imaginative function. Whether this function can be considered pragmatic would depend on the effects that it produces. Assuming that art has a pragmatic function, we might need to reconsider the type of satisfaction aesthetic experience would generate.

At an individual level, art can potentially break intellectual routines, or promote a change in our internal homeostasis, thus bringing the mind to a different dimension. In this respect we can agree with Marković (2012) that aesthetic experience reflects an ex-ceptional state of mind. However, the lack of pragmatic function of aesthetic experience might be questionable. Aesthetic experience can contribute to our well-being, and as such art might be seen as a need, involving the same reward circuits as for food or sex. In this view we must accept that the reward system and emotions involved in ordinary life are the same as those involved during aesthetic experience. However, the way reward is experienced and the relevance that it assumes for the individual might differ from person to person.

On one hand, aesthetic experience reflects individual differences (expertise, attitudes etc.), but on the other it can turn into a collective response when shared with others. Therefore, aesthetic experience can have a social value. There are paintings or photographs, songs or performances that aesthetically move most people in a similar fashion and that we love to share with the belief that these pieces would be relevant to all. In some ways this "collective fascination" might also contribute to generate trends or styles, which feed back into hedonic evaluations, often implicitly. As such we can also ascribe a social function to aesthetic experience, which can, in turn, modulate aesthetic evaluations at an individual level.

The social function of art has been extensively discussed (Gombrich & Gombrich, 1999). Again, this function can have an implicit influence on aesthetic evaluations, which could be modulated by other factors. Experts would probably be more conscious of the effects that cultural norms, canons, art context etc. have on their own aesthetic judgment. In contrast, laypeople would probably engage more with the implicit, automatic components (sensorial, emotional, and associative) of the aesthetic experience. Hence, this would make aesthetic experiences different between experts and novices, although both would share the same ability to be aesthetically moved. Future research might direct efforts to reveal how implicit and explicit components of the models presented in this chapter would integrate with each other, under which circumstances in consideration of personal and cultural factors.

Conclusions and Final Remarks

This chapter offered a review of empirical works on implicit processes in relation to existing models in aesthetics. I showed how the adoption of implicit measures enriched our understanding of the reciprocal interactions between perceptual and emotional components and other factors such as art expertise. In conclusion, hedonic evaluations might be generated by: (1) perceptual qualia of the stimulus; (2) reward or satisfaction given by the facility with which the perceptual system can interpret the sensorial information (or perceptual fluency); (3) valence transferred to the stimulus via associative processes with semantics; and (4) reward or satisfaction given by the facility with which we form these associations (or cognitive fluency). The use of implicit measures helped establish the existence of automatic links among liking, semantics, and affective components for a variety of stimuli, from works of art or design, to abstract meaningless shapes or patterns. This confirms that the emotional component already plays a sub-stantial role in the early stages of information processing (Leder & Nadal, 2014; Leder et al., 2004). The link between the perceptual analysis of an artwork and the emotional reaction that it provokes might be reflected in sensory motor processes, as predicted by embodied cognition accounts.

The studies presented here confirmed some aspects of the existing models but also opened up new questions. For some scholars the contribution of automatic components (sensorial-motor-affective experience) is partial. There are other personal (i.e., expertise, personality) and contextual factors that can (top-down) influence, and in some cases overcome, first impression, thus fulfilling aesthetic experience (Leder & Nadal, 2014; Leder et al., 2004; Marković, 2012). However, it remains unclear whether these top-down influences operate at an explicit, controlled level of information pro-cessing or whether at least part of their role is played tacitly. Future studies in empirical aesthetics should extend the research enquiry and design their own paradigms to test specific hypotheses. For example, the use of different methods, such as implicit and ex-plicit procedures, would need to be combined with technological innovations (Mansilla et al., 2011), so as to include digital art, and with ecological settings (Brieber et al., 2015; Carbon, 2017).

Many scholars have addressed questions from different disciplines, from phil-osophy and history of art to psychology and neuroscience, marketing and design, using different levels of analysis. This has challenged the debate, although themes have been often approached in an isolated fashion, leading to resolutions that are still dependent on the theoretical and methodological specificity of each discipline. The translation of theoretical questions into operational paradigms has often imposed a reductionist approach. As we know, an empirical investigation that studies aesthetic experience taking its multifaceted components in isolation, although necessary, is not sufficient to provide a comprehensive understanding of its complexity.

The empirical investigation has started pushing the boundaries of each discipline as the demand to integrate the diversity of perspectives is rapidly increasing. I believe that the next challenge for this discipline is to embrace a multiperspective approach and val-idate new methods that could extend to other contexts. This would overcome current limitations and create a unified multidisciplinary ground for the future.

References

Aryani, A., Jacobs, A. M., & Conrad, M. (2013). Extracting salient sublexical units from written texts: "Emophon," a corpus-based approach to phonological iconicity. *Frontiers in Psychology, 4.* doi:10.3389/fpsyg.2013.00654.

Bar, M., & Neta, M. (2006). Humans prefer curved visual objects. *Psychological Science, 17*(8), 645–648. doi:10.1111/j.1467-9280.2006.01759.x.

Bar, M., & Neta, M. (2007). Visual elements of subjective preference modulate amygdala ac-tivation. *Neuropsychologia, 45*(10), 2191–2200. doi:10.1016/j.neuropsychologia.2007.03.008.

Bargh, J. A. (1989). Conditional automaticity: Varieties of automatic influence in social perception and cognition. In J. S. Uleman & J. A. Bargh (Eds.), *Unintended thought* (pp. 3–51). New York: Guilford Press.

Bargh, J. A., Chaiken, S., Raymond, P., & Hymes, C., (1996). The automatic evaluation effect: Unconditional automatic attitude activation with a pronunciation task. *Journal of Experimental Social Psychology, 32*(1), 104–128.

Berczeller, E. (1967). The "aesthetic feeling" and Aristotle's *Catharsis* theory. *The Journal of Psychology, 65*(2), 261–271, doi:10.1080/00223980.1967.10544870.

Berlyne, D. E. (1960). *McGraw-Hill series in psychology. Conflict, arousal, and curiosity.* New York: McGraw-Hill Book Company. doi:10.1037/11164-000.

Berlyne, D. E. (1971). *Aesthetics and psychobiology.* New York: Appleton-Century-Crofts.

Bertamini, M., Makin, A., & Rampone, G. (2013). Implicit association of symmetry with positive valence, high arousal and simplicity. *i-Perception, 4*(5), 317–327. doi:10.1068/i0601jw.

Bertamini, M., Palumbo, L., Gheorghes, T. N., & Galatsidas, M. (2016). Do observers like curvature or do they dislike angularity? *British Journal of Psychology, 107*(1), 154–178.

Bertamini, M., Palumbo, L., & Redies, C. (in press). An advantage for smooth compared to angular contours in the speed of processing shape. *Journal of Experimental Psychology: Human Perception and Performance.*

Bornstein, R., & Pittman, T. (1992). *Perception without awareness: Cognitive, clinical, and social perspectives.* New York: Guilford Press.

Brieber, D., Nadal, M., & Leder, H. (2015). In the white cube: Museum context enhances the valuation and memory of art. *Acta Psychologica, 154*, 36–42. doi:10.1016/j.actpsy.2014.11.004.

Bullot, N. J., & Reber, R. (2013). The artful mind meets art history: Toward a psycho-historical framework for the science of art appreciation. *Behavioral and Brain Sciences, 36*(2), 123–137. doi:10.1017/S0140525X12000489.

Carbon, C. C. (2010). The cycle of preference: Long-term dynamics of aesthetic appreciation, *Acta Psychologica, 134*(2), 233–244. doi:10.1016/j.actpsy.2010.02.004.

Carbon, C. C. (2017). Art perception in the museum: How we spend time and space in art exhibitions. *i-Perception, 8*(1). doi:10.1177/2041669517694184.

Cela-Conde, C. J., Ayala, F. J., Munar, E., Maestú, F., Nadal, M., Capó, M. A., … Marty, G. (2009). Sex-related similarities and differences in the neural correlates of beauty. *Proceedings of the National Academy of Sciences, 106*(10), 3847–3852. doi:10.1073/pnas.0900304106.

Chatterjee, A. (2003). Prospects for a cognitive neuroscience of visual aesthetics. *Bulletin of Psychology and the Arts, 4*, 55–60. doi:10.1037/e514602010-003.

Chatterjee, A., & Vartanian, O. (2016). Neuroscience of aesthetics. *Annals of the New York Academy of Sciences, 1369*(1), 172–194. doi:10.1111/nyas.13035.

Chen, M., & Bargh, J. A. (1999). Consequences of automatic evaluation: Immediate behavioral predispositions to approach or avoid the stimulus. *Personality and Social Psychology Bulletin, 25*(2), 215–224. doi:10.1177/0146167299025002007.

Cotter, K. N., Silvia, P. J., Bertamini, M., Palumbo, L., & Vartanian, O. (2017). Curve appeal: Exploring individual differences in preference for curved versus angular objects. *i-Perception, 8*(2). doi:10.1177/2041669517693023.

Cross, E. S., & Ticini, L. F. (2012). Neuroaesthetics and beyond: New horizons in applying the science of the brain to the art of dance. *Phenomenology and the Cognitive Sciences, 11*(1), 5–16. doi:10.1007/s11097-010-9190-y.

Cupchik, G. C. (1994). Emotion in aesthetics: Reactive and reflective models. *Poetics, 23*(1–2), 177–188. doi:10.1016/0304-422X(94)00014-W.

De Houwer, J., Crombez, G., Baeyens, F., & Hermans, D. (2001). On the generality of the affective Simon effect. *Cognition & Emotion, 15*(2), 189–206. doi:10.1080/0269993004200051

De Houwer, J. D., Hermans, D., Rothermund, K., & Wentura, D. (2002). Affective priming of semantic categorisation responses. *Cognition & Emotion, 16*(5), 643–666.

De Houwer, J., Teige-Mocigemba, S., Spruyt, A., & Moors, A. (2009). Implicit measures: A normative analysis and review. *Psychological Bulletin, 135*(3), 347–368. doi:10.1037/a0014211

Dimberg, U., Thunberg, M., & Elmehed, K. (2000). Unconscious facial reactions to emotional facial expressions. *Psychological Science, 11*(1), 86–89. doi:10.1111/1467-9280.00221

Fazio, R. H., & Olson, M. A. (2003). Implicit measures in social cognition research: Their meaning and use. *Annual Review of Psychology, 54*(1), 297–327. doi:10.1146/annurev.psych.54.101601.145225

Fazio, R. H., Sanbonmatsu, D. M., Powell, M. C., & Kardes, F. R. (1986). On the automatic activation of attitudes. *Journal of Personality and Social Psychology, 50*(2), 229–238. doi:10.1037/0022-3514.50.2.229

Fechner, G. T. (1871). *Zur experimentalen aesthetik [electronic resource]/* Leipzig: S. Hirzel, 1871. Electronic reproduction. New York: Columbia University Libraries, 2009.

Fiske, S. T., & Taylor, S. E. (2013). *Social cognition: From brains to culture.* London: Sage.

Flexas, A., Rosselló, J., Christensen, J. F., Nadal, M., La Rosa, A. O., & Munar, E. (2013). Affective priming using facial expressions modulates liking for abstract art. *PLoS ONE, 8*(11), e80154.

Freedberg, D., & Gallese, V. (2007). Motion, emotion and empathy in esthetic experience. *Trends in Cognitive Sciences, 11*(5), 197–203. doi:10.1016/j.tics.2007.02.003

Gattol, V., Sääksjärvi, M., & Carbon, C. C. (2011). Extending the Implicit Association Test (IAT): Assessing consumer attitudes based on multi-dimensional implicit associations. *PLoS ONE, 6*(1), e15849. doi:10.1371/journal.pone.0015849

Gerger, G., Leder, H., Tinio, P. P., & Schacht, A. (2011). Faces versus patterns: Exploring aesthetic reactions using facial EMG. *Psychology of Aesthetics, Creativity, and the Arts, 5*(3), 241–250. doi:10.1037/a0024154

Gombrich, E. H., & Gombrich, E. H. (1999). *The uses of images: Studies in the social function of art and visual communication* (p. 199). London: Phaidon.

Greenwald, A. G., McGhee, D. E., & Schwartz, J. L. (1998). Measuring individual differences in implicit cognition: The Implicit Association Test. *Journal of Personality and Social Psychology, 74*(6), 1464–1480. doi:10.1037/0022-3514.74.6.1464

Hekkert, P., Snelders, D., & Van Wieringen, P. C. W. (2003). Most advanced, yet acceptable: Typicality and novelty as joint predictors of aesthetic preference in industrial design. *British Journal of Psychology, 94*(1), 111–124. doi:10.1348/000712603762842147

Hermans, D., De Houwer, J., & Eelen, P. (2001). A time course analysis of the affective priming effect. *Cognition & Emotion, 15*(2), 143–165. doi:10.1080/02699930125768

Höfel, L., & Jacobsen, T. (2007). Electrophysiological indices of processing aesthetics: Spontaneous or intentional processes? *International Journal of Psychophysiology, 65*(1), 20–31. doi:10.1016/j.ijpsycho.2007.02.007

Jacobsen, T. (2010). Beauty and the brain: Culture, history and individual differences in aesthetic appreciation. *Journal of Anatomy, 216*(2), 184–191. doi:10.1111/j.1469-7580.2009.01164.x

Klauer, K. C., & Musch, J. (2003). Affective priming: Findings and theories. In J. Musch & K. C. Klauer (Eds.), *The psychology of evaluation: Affective processes in cognition and emotion* (pp. 7–49). Mahwah, NJ: Lawrence Erlbaum Associates Publishers.

Krieglmeyer, R., Deutsch, R., De Houwer, J., & De Raedt, R. (2010). Being moved: Valence activates approach-avoidance behavior independently of evaluation and approach-avoidance intentions. *Psychological Science, 21*(4), 607–613.

Leder, H., Belke, B., Oeberst, A., & Augustin, D. (2004). A model of aesthetic appreciation and aesthetic judgments. *British Journal of Psychology, 95*(4), 489–508. doi:10.1348/0007126042369811

Leder, H. (2013). Next steps in neuroaesthetics: Which processes and processing stages to study?. *Psychology of Aesthetics, Creativity, and the Arts, 7*(1), 27–37. doi:10.1037/a0031585

Leder, H., & Carbon, C. C. (2005). Dimensions in appreciation of car interior design. *Applied Cognitive Psychology, 19*(5), 603–618. doi:10.1002/acp.1088

Leder, H., & Nadal, M. (2014). Ten years of a model of aesthetic appreciation and aesthetic judgments: The aesthetic episode—developments and challenges in empirical aesthetics. *British Journal of Psychology, 105*(4), 443–464. doi:10.1111/bjop.12084

Lundholm, H. (1921). The affective tone of lines: Experimental researches. *Psychological Review, 28*(1), 43–60. doi:10.1037/h0072647

Makin, A. D. J., Pecchinenda, A., & Bertamini, M. (2012). Implicit affective evaluation of visual symmetry. *Emotion, 12*(5), 1021–1030. doi:10.1037/a0026924

Mansilla, W. A., Perkis, A., & Ebrahimi, T. (2011, November). Implicit experiences as a determinant of perceptual quality and aesthetic appreciation. In *Proceedings of the 19th ACM international conference on Multimedia* (pp. 153–162). ACM.

Marković, S. (2012). Components of aesthetic experience: Aesthetic fascination, aesthetic appraisal, and aesthetic emotion. *i-Perception, 3*(1), 1–17. doi:10.1068/i0450aap

Mastandrea, S., Bartoli, G., & Carrus, G. (2011). The automatic aesthetic evaluation of different art and architectural styles. *Psychology of Aesthetics, Creativity, and the Arts, 5*(2), 126–134. doi:10.1037/a0021126

Mastandrea, S., & Maricchiolo, F. (2014). Implicit and explicit aesthetic evaluation of design objects. *Art & Perception, 2*(1–2), 141–162. DOI:10.1163/22134913-00002015

Mitchell, J. P., Nosek, B. A., & Banaji, M. R. (2003). Contextual variations in implicit evaluation. *Journal of Experimental Psychology: General, 132*(3), 455–469. doi:10.1037/0096-3445.132.3.455

Müller, M., Höfel, L., Brattico, E., & Jacobsen, T. (2010). Aesthetic judgments of music in experts and laypersons—An ERP study. *International Journal of Psychophysiology, 76*(1), 40–51. doi:10.1016/j.ijpsycho.2010.02.002

Munar, E., Gómez-Puerto, G., Call, J., & Nadal, M. (2015). Common visual preference for curved contours in humans and great apes. *PloS ONE, 10*(11), e0141106. doi:10.1371/journal.pone.0141106

Murphy, S. T., & Zajonc, R. B. (1993). Affect, cognition, and awareness: Affective priming with optimal and suboptimal stimulus exposures. *Journal of Personality and Social Psychology, 64*(5), 723–739.

Nadal, M., Munar, E., Capo, M. A., Rossello, J., & Cela-Conde, C. J. (2008). Towards a framework for the study of the neural correlates of aesthetic preference. *Spatial Vision, 21*(3), 379–396. doi:10.1163/156856808784532653

Nosek, B., & Hansen, J. (2008). The associations in our heads belong to us: Searching for attitudes and knowledge in implicit evaluation. *Cognition and Emotion, 22*(4), 553–594. doi:10.1080/02699930701438186

Nosek, B. A., Greenwald, A. G., & Banaji, M. R. (2005). Understanding and using the Implicit Association Test: II. Method variables and construct validity. *Personality and Social Psychology Bulletin, 31*(2), 166–180. doi:10.1177/0146167204271418

Palumbo, L., Ruta, N., & Bertamini, M. (2015). Comparing angular and curved shapes in terms of implicit associations and approach/avoidance responses. *PloS ONE, 10*(10), e0140043.

Pavlović, M., & Marković, S. (2012). Automatic processes in aesthetic judgment: Insights from the implicit association test. *Psihologija, 45*(4), 377–393. doi:10.2298/PSI1204377P

Perrett, D. I., Burt, D. M., Penton-Voak, I. S., Lee, K. J., Rowland, D. A., & Edwards, R. (1999). Symmetry and human facial attractiveness. *Evolution and Human Behavior, 20*(5), 295–307. doi:10.1016/S1090-5138(99)00014-8

Poffenberger, A. T., & Barrows, B. E. (1924). The feeling value of lines. *Journal of Applied Psychology, 8*(2), 187–205. doi:10.1037/h0073513

Ramachandran, V. S., & Hirstein, W. (1999). The science of art: A neurological theory of aesthetic experience. *Journal of Consciousness Studies, 6*(6–7), 15–51.

Reber, R., Schwarz, N., & Winkielman, P. (2004). Processing fluency and aesthetic pleasure: Is beauty in the perceiver's processing experience? *Personality and Social Psychology Review, 8*(4), 364–382.

Ritterfeld, U. (2002). Social heuristics in interior design preferences. *Journal of Environmental Psychology, 22*(4), 369–386. doi:10.1006/JEVP.2002.0276

Silvia, P. J. (2005). Cognitive appraisals and interest in visual art: Exploring an appraisal theory of aesthetic emotions. *Empirical Studies of the Arts, 23*(2), 119–133. doi:10.2190/12AV-AH2P-MCEH-289E

Silvia, P. J. (2009). Looking past pleasure: Anger, confusion, disgust, pride, surprise, and other unusual aesthetic emotions. *Psychology of Aesthetics, Creativity, and the Arts, 3*(1), 48–51. doi:10.1037/a0014632

Smith, J. D., & Melara, R. J. (1990). Aesthetic preference and syntactic prototypicality in music: 'Tis the gift to be simple. *Cognition, 34*(3), 279–298. doi:10.1016/0010-0277(90)90007-7

Starr, G. G. (2013). *Feeling beauty: The neuroscience of aesthetic experience.* Cambridge, MA: The MIT Press.

Ticini, L. F., Rachman, L., Pelletier, J., & Dubal, S. (2014). Enhancing aesthetic appreciation by priming canvases with actions that match the artist's painting style. *Frontiers in Human Neuroscience, 8*, 391. doi:10.3389/fnhum.2014.00391

Vartanian, O., Navarrete, G., Chatterjee, A., Fich, L. B., Leder, H., Modroño, C., … Skov, M. (2013). Impact of contour on aesthetic judgments and approach-avoidance decisions in architecture. *Proceedings of the National Academy of Sciences, 110*(Supplement 2), 10446–10453. doi:10.1073/pnas.1301227110

Vaughan-Evans, A., Trefor, R., Jones, L., Lynch, P., Jones, M. W., & Thierry, G. (2016). Implicit detection of poetic harmony by the naïve brain. *Frontiers in Psychology, 7*, 1859. doi:10.3389/fpsyg.2016.01859

Vessel, E. A., Starr, G. G., & Rubin, N. (2012). The brain on art: Intense aesthetic experience activates the default mode network. *Frontiers in Human Neuroscience, 6*, Article ID 66. doi:10.3389/fnhum.2012.00066.

Winkielman, P., Schwarz, N., Fazendeiro, T., & Reber, R. (2003). The hedonic marking of processing fluency: Implications for evaluative judgment. In Musch, J. & Klauer, K. C. *The Psychology of Evaluation: Affective Processes in Cognition and Emotion,* (pp. 189–217). Mahwah, NJ: Lawrence Erlbaum Associates.

Zajonc, R. B. (1968). Attitudinal effects of mere exposure. *Journal of Personality and Social Psychology, 9*, 1–27. doi:10.1037/h0025848

Zeki, A. D. (1999). *Inner Vision: An Exploration of Art and the Brain.* Oxford: Oxford University Press. doi:10.1016/S1364-6613(00)01518-7

THE STUDY OF EYE MOVEMENTS IN EMPIRICAL AESTHETICS

PAUL LOCHER

THE STUDY OF EYE MOVEMENTS IN EMPIRICAL AESTHETICS

THE study of eye movements has for many decades been a very useful and popular technology in the field of experimental aesthetics. In fact, knowledge obtained using eye-tracking techniques has contributed in a major way to the development of contemporary cognitive and information processing-based models that detail the mechanisms and processes underlying the viewing of art (for detailed descriptions of these theoretical frameworks, see Pelowski, Markey, Lauring, & Leder, 2016). The models typically comprised three multilayered overarching components; namely, (1) the artwork as stimulus (e.g., its pictorial features, artistic style, thematic content, etc.), (2) the viewer's contribution (e.g., his or her personal history, personality, knowledge about art, etc.), and (3) the physical (e.g., the museum) and social (e.g., the human figure in art) contexts in which an artwork is perceived. In addition it is generally agreed that these components are subject to a continuous dynamic interplay between bottom-up (stimulus-driven) and top-down (perceiver-driven) influences across the time course of an aesthetic experience with art. Huge leaps in our knowledge of the interaction of these components have occurred in recent years as a consequence of the development of new methods for the visualization and analysis of eye movement data and the use of mobile eye-tracking techniques.

The purpose of this chapter is to present an overview of the findings of recent eye movement studies designed to expand the body of knowledge concerning the complex dynamic interactions among factors that underlie an aesthetic experience with visual art. Some of the factors included in the studies reviewed, such as observers' art expertise, have a long history of inclusion in eye movement research because of their demonstrated strong interactive impact on all aspects of the perception and evaluation of art. Other topics are new to the field (e.g., a painter's eye movements during the creation of art; the interplay between eye and body movements during the perception of art). The thematic development of this chapter and its organizational structure reflect the interactive nature of factors that underlie art perception. In almost all cases at least one factor in a labeled content area has been the focus of investigation (either as a manipulated or controlled variable) in studies described in other content areas. As mentioned, viewer sophistication in the arts is a factor that "runs throughout" the experimental aesthetics literature and has done so since the early eye movement research conducted by Yarbus (1967).

METHODS FOR VISUALIZATION AND ANALYZING EYE-TRACKING DATA

Two standard techniques used to visualize eye-tracking data collected during the viewing of artworks are scanpath representations and fixation heatmaps. A scanpath is the path taken by a viewer's eye during exploration of a visual display. It is an ordered pattern of fixations connected by saccades, depicted by circles and lines, respectively. Heatmap analysis is a procedure that graphically depicts in different colors the parts of a painting receiving the highest intensities of fixations or fixation durations by an individual observer or group of observers. Additional frequently used techniques to analyze eye movement data are fixation map analysis, fixation clustering, and fixation dwell map analysis (for descriptions of standard methods for analysis and visualization of eye-tracking data, see Kübler, Fuhl, Rosenberg, Rosenstiel, & Kasneci, 2016). The interested reader can find many state-of-the-art visualization and analysis techniques described in detail in almost every recent issue of the *Journal of Eye Movement Research*. These approaches are employed to identify the principal *regions of interest* (ROIs or *areas of interest*, AOIs) of observers viewing an artwork. They are all designed to answer the question, where in the pictorial field of an image did viewers tend to look?

MOBILE EYE-TRACKING INVESTIGATIONS OF ART—ADVANTAGES AND LIMITATIONS OF THIS ECOLOGICAL APPROACH

Commercial versions of mobile eye-trackers are now widely available and have been used in many recent investigations of the role of eye movements in real-world activities including perception of the visual arts. They enable a researcher to conduct investigations of factors underlying an aesthetic experience with art in a natural ecologically valid setting (e.g., a museum or gallery) while retaining some of the careful procedures and precise measurement of behaviors observed in a laboratory study. Lappi (2015) provides a very comprehensive discussion of the advantages and potential limitations of using a mobile eye-tracking approach compared with a laboratory design implemented in different real-world research environments. According to Lappi, a major limitation of naturalistic field studies using mobile eye-tracking is that the stimulus situation is typically complex, dynamic, and constantly evolving across the time course of the study. Stimuli are not presented on a fixed basis but change dynamically resulting from field factors interacting with a subject's body and head motion and eye movements. This may make it difficult to identify precisely the stimulus information used by a viewer, and correspondingly, to compare results of investigations of related patterns of behavior. This limitation is diminished somewhat when one conducts a mobile eye-tracking study in a museum setting because the artworks chosen as stimuli remain stationary in the field (the gallery) with the exception of the various forms of Kinetic Art. These art stimulus conditions constitute different levels of ecological naturalness discussed in Lappi's paper.

The possible advantages and limitations of using mobile eye-tracking techniques outlined by Lappi (2015) are elaborated upon in detail by Mitschke, Goller, and Leder (2017), who conducted a mobile eye-tracking study of how people respond to graffiti and sculptures in a complex real-world setting. The natural environment was a promenade section of the Danube Canal in Vienna along which are displayed graffiti and sculptures as well as other object categories such as natural sights, advertisements, and the walkway. Art-naïve adults equipped with a mobile eye-tracker engaged in a free exploration walk that lasted approximately 4 min. The researchers explained, as did Lappi, that because of the unpredictable events that occur in naturalistic field studies using mobile eye-tracking, the stimulus situation is typically complex, dynamic, and constantly evolving, and so they carefully monitored participants' behavior and environmental changes. Participants returned to a follow-up laboratory setting 1 week after the eye-tracking session at which time they viewed their personal eye-tracking video and commented on what they saw and what they liked and disliked. They then provided liking and interest ratings of screenshots from the eye-tracking camera.

Mitschke et al. (2017) present their findings in a figure showing total fixation duration for each of the nine participants for each of the six object categories. The pattern of results was very varied. For example, one participant spent only 13% of his overall fixation time looking at the graffiti and sculptures, whereas another participant spent more than 50% of his time looking at these objects. For the most part, the findings are presented in a descriptive fashion because, as the researchers point out, they faced many methodological issues, which they describe in much detail. This study expands the field of ecologically valid approaches into the realm of aesthetic experience with everyday street art and provides valuable insights into how this can be accomplished methodologically.

Most of the mobile eye-tracking studies in the field of experimental aesthetics to date have been conducted in museum settings and their findings are described in a later section of this chapter.

Art, Expertise in the Visual Arts, and Eye Movements

Observers' knowledge base about art (i.e., their "aesthetic fluency," Smith & Smith, 2006) acquired by formal training and/or through direct experience with art has consistently been shown to influence the visual scanning of art and related aesthetic tasks. In general, exploration of paintings by experts in the field of visual arts, compared with nonexperts, is characterized by longer saccades, less frequent and shorter fixations on narrative elements, and greater visual coverage of paintings, especially with respect to the relationship among pictorial elements and their structural organization (e.g., Nodine, Locher, & Krupinski, 1993; Vogt & Magnussen, 2007).

An eye movement investigation of the influence of expertise on the processes underlying an aesthetic episode with art was recently reported by Bauer and Schwan (2018). Participants were art history students and a group majoring in non-art-related fields. The Renaissance art stimuli consisted of full-length portraits with one central human figure and several objects that can be perceived either according to their literal meaning (e.g., keys) or with symbolic connotations (e.g., paleness of skin, holding hands) located at the pictorial field margins, and double portraits consisting of two peripheral human figures with symbolic details between them. Participants' eye movements were recorded in an initial session during which they examined each portrait for 10 s and in a second self-timed session their eye movements were recorded simultaneously with a think-aloud task. They then summarized their thoughts about a painting while viewing a blank screen.

For the purposes of the gaze-data analyses, Bauer and Schwan (2018) identified AOIs that could be taken in their literal or symbolic meaning in each portrait as well as AOIs for each part of the human figure (head, hands, torso). The principal finding was that in both sessions dwell time (the sum of all fixations and saccade times within an AOI) was higher for the art history students on symbols compared with human features than was the case for naïve participants. Additionally, participants in both groups looked more at symbolic AOIs in the self-timed session than during the initial session. Analyses of the think-aloud data revealed that the sophisticated participants interpreted the meaning of symbols more often than naïve individuals, especially for double rather than single portraits. Furthermore, compared with the art-naïve participants, the content of the art majors' thinking-aloud contained more interpretations and was more structured for double than for single portraits. According to Bauer and Schwan, their findings suggest that the trained participants' deeper engagement with higher levels of meaning than laypersons for the kind of art studied lead them to make more attempts to interpret a portrait's content.

Another recent eye movement study conducted by Francuz, Zaniewski, Augustynowicz, Kopiś, and Jankowski (2018) sheds light on the nature of the relationship between a painting's compositional balance, art sophistication of a beholder, and his or her familiarity with a work of art. Their stimuli consisted of reproductions of figurative paintings by famous artists likely known to all participants and an equal number of works by a relatively unknown painter. The original paintings were almost all perfectly balanced structurally. Three less balanced experimentally altered versions of each original were created for the study: slightly, moderately, or significantly imbalanced. Art-trained and art-naïve participants saw all altered versions of each picture paired with the original and selected the version they judged more pleasant. They had unlimited viewing time to examine each pair and their eye movements were recorded throughout the experimental session.

The principal finding of the study relevant to this topic area is that only for the art-sophisticated group was the number of fixations on unknown paintings significantly higher than the known ones. Furthermore, in the trained group the larger number of fixations predicted less accurately their choice of the original painting than its paired altered version. The researchers speculate that their findings reflect a greater need to explore unknown paintings by experts for whom composition is an important criterion for assessing an artwork's aesthetic value.

USING EYE-TRACKING TO ASSESS EFFECTIVENESS OF EDUCATIONAL INTERVENTION IN AESTHETIC FLUENCY

As previously mentioned, eye-tracking studies have shown that, when experiencing an artwork, unsophisticated viewers focus their attention on individual pictorial elements suggesting that they consider representational accuracy to be more important than design in judging the aesthetics of a visual composition. Art-trained viewers on the other hand spend more time discovering patterns and relationships among compositional elements located throughout the pictorial field. Thus, it appears that art training results in a shift of purpose of perceptual scanning away from local feature analysis and information gathering to global recognition of pictorial structures and their relationship to compositional design.

Ishiguro, Yokosawa, and Okada (2016) point out that there are many formal and informal institutions that provide educational programs designed to help art-naïve students gain knowledge about the creation and appreciation of artworks. However, the effectiveness of these interventions has typically been evaluated qualitatively by educators and researchers with measures of subjective interpretative change in various aspects of viewers' art sophistication. Ishiguro et al. addressed this limitation with an eye-tracking study designed to objectively assess the effectiveness of an artistic photo creation course to help students acquire procedural knowledge and techniques of photo creation that would result in changes in their viewing strategies in art appreciation. The course, attended by university students who had no previous professional education in artistic creation, consisted of 14 classes that covered sessions for acquiring fundamental techniques and procedural knowledge about photo creation as well as aesthetic appreciation instruction for works of art.

A pre- and post-test design was employed, with the same photographs shown randomly for 50 s during both testing sessions. Ishiguro et al.'s (2016) principal findings demonstrate that students' viewing strategies changed following completion of the course. For example, students' perceptual exploration became more global and active with photographs containing recognizable subjects (i.e., humans and objects) and their global scanning increased when they viewed examples of classic photography covered in the course. Interview data at the end of the course revealed that participants became aware of how technical effects were created in photographs, and important to the purpose of the study. Accordingly, their eye-tracking strategies reflected the desired shift from local feature analysis and information gathering to global recognition of pictorial structures and their relationship to compositional design. Ishiguro et al.'s findings demonstrate the importance to the field of art education of the untapped potential of eye-tracking techniques to objectively assess the effectiveness of different types of educational interventions designed to enhance students' aesthetic fluency.

MUSEUM VERSUS LABORATORY EYE MOVEMENT STUDIES

As stated earlier, the physical context in which an artwork is perceived is one of the key factors contributing to an aesthetic experience with art. Two research approaches employed to examine the influence of context on art viewing are laboratory-based and in-museum investigations. There are advantages and limitations to each approach. Simply put, experiments performed in a laboratory can be highly controlled and therefore lack ecological validity, whereas museum studies have some degree of ecological validity but lack control of the many variables included in models of the aesthetic experience with art (as previously discussed, use of mobile eye-tracking equipment in museum settings does not fully resolve the validity issue). Pelowski, Forster, Tinio, Scholl, and Leder (2017) present a very comprehensive literature review and theoretical discussion of the factors that underlie the experience of actual art in a museum setting that may differ when studied in a laboratory setting (see also Smith, 2014).

In the past decade there have been several eye-tracking studies conducted in a strictly controlled laboratory setting using static photographic or electronic images as stimuli contrasted with behavioral research conducted in a museum setting using mobile tracking. One such eye-tracking study was conducted by Quiroga, Dudley, and Binnie (2011). Participants in the gallery condition looked at the painting by Millais titled *Ophelia* hanging in the Tate Britain museum for a few minutes while wearing a mobile eye-tracker. Participants in the laboratory condition viewed a digital image of the same painting on the monitor of a stationary eye-tracker system for 1 min without being given any particular task.

The painting depicts Ophelia singing while floating in a river just before she drowns, and is known for its depiction of the detailed flora of the river and the riverbank, stressing the patterns of growth and decay in a natural ecosystem. Distinctly different fixation patterns were recorded for the two presentation formats in the study by Quirigo et al. (2011). The majority of fixations for the laboratory group clustered over the small pictorial areas of Ophelia's face and hands. In contrast, viewers wearing the mobile tracker explored the actual artwork more thoroughly by altering their stance to examine the painting from different angles and also moving closer to the painting to examine surface conditions; they distributed their gaze mostly over the vegetative undergrowth that served as the background surrounding Ophelia. The researchers suggest that it might be expected that both groups would focus their attention on Ophelia's face as the most salient feature, as has typically been reported in the face perception literature (e.g., Little, Jones, & DeBruine, 2011). This indeed was the finding for the laboratory group. The museum group on the other hand tended to explore the much larger background area of the pictorial field, which creates the context in which Ophelia lies. They had the obvious advantage of being able to adjust their physical behavior (i.e., eye, head, and body movements) to enhance their perception of global and local pictorial features of the artwork. Based on their findings, Quirigo et al. suggest that museum goers are likely to visually explore artworks more fully when they are seen in a museum than in a controlled laboratory environment.

Brieber, Nadal, Leder, and Rosenberg (2014) conducted an eye-tracking investigation to examine the influence of context (museum or laboratory) on the relationship between viewing time and viewing behaviors. The stimulus set consisted of art photographs depicting humans and objects embedded in several types of staged or composed urban and natural environments. Each image was accompanied by a label providing information about the artwork, its artist, and his oeuvre in general. Half of the student participants, who had little or no art expertise, saw the original photographs in a museum of contemporary art; the other half saw the same photographs on a screen in a laboratory setting. In both cases viewing times were recorded with a mobile eye-tracking system. Participants completed three tasks during the experimental session: an initial free-viewing task, a rating task, and a questionnaire task. In the rating task participants rated each artwork for liking, interest, understanding, and ambiguity, followed by two questionnaires measuring participants' general interest in and specific knowledge about art and photography. It is noteworthy that several technical procedures were employed during the free-viewing task in the laboratory that made it more comparable in stimulus presentation to viewing conditions in the museum. These included use of software that allowed participants to zoom in and out on the screen image and to go forward and backward through the order of photographs imitating exploration of the actual artworks in the museum.

Each artwork and its label were designated an ROI and the sum of all fixations and saccade durations for each ROI for each participant was employed as the viewing time measure. Some of the main findings are the following. Participants in the museum setting viewed the photographs longer than did people in the laboratory, demonstrating that the museum context fostered greater prolonged and focused attention to art. Participants in the museum condition found the photographs more interesting and liked them more than did laboratory participants. Viewing time decreased from the first to the last artwork for participants in both contexts. Findings for the artwork labels revealed that viewing time for labels was predicted by the number of words on labels, their presentation order, and participants' appreciation (a compounding of the liking and interest ratings). The findings of Brieber et al. (2014) demonstrate the need for more comparative studies between museum and laboratory contexts to ascertain which factors, processes, behaviors, and experiences incorporated in Pelowski et al.'s (2017) model are transferable between contexts.

Finally, a recent study conducted by Walker, Bucker, Anderson, Schreij, and Theeuwes (2017) examined the influence of bottom-up and top-down attentional processes on gaze behavior during the earliest stage of an aesthetic experience with visual art in a museum setting. They compared the eye movement patterns of children and adults (ages 11–12 years and 20–29 years, respectively) as they viewed five lesser-known Van Gogh paintings hanging in one gallery of the Van Gogh Museum in Amsterdam. The experiment was conducted in two phases during which participants looked at each painting for 30 s. In Phase 1 participants observed each painting freely (i.e., no top-down task was required) and bottom-up processes were quantified by comparing the locations in the pictorial field that participants fixated to a salience map for each painting showing pictorial elements and regions that stand out from their surroundings. Top-down processing was manipulated in Phase 2 by giving participants the background information available to museum visitors of the Van Gogh Museum about each painting prior to the second viewing. They did not see the paintings while being given their descriptions. Analyses of the eye movement data collected in Phase 2 utilized ROIs for each painting, based on the painting descriptions given to participants.

As one would expect, differences were observed between the children and adults with respect to their use of bottom-up- and top-down-driven gaze processes as they observed the paintings. Children initially focused their first five fixations on high-level salient elements of the paintings reflecting use of a bottom-up strategy during free viewing. After they received background information about the paintings during Phase 2 the children fixated on less salient regions first, indicating that their scanpaths were now driven much more by top-down knowledge about the works provided. The eye movement behaviors of adults on the other hand were very similar during both phases. They consistently fixated on areas with low salience value from the time of stimulus onset demonstrating that their eye movements in Phase 1 were already influenced by top-down factors such as the *painting gist*—one's first impression of an artwork (a term introduced by Locher, 2015). In sum, top-down factors played a relatively greater role throughout the time course of the aesthetic experience with paintings for adults compared with children.

TITLES AND WALL TEXTS OF PAINTINGS IN A MUSEUM INFLUENCE THEIR PERCEPTION

The use of labels (a painting's artist and title) and wall texts in museum galleries has been and continues to be a widely debated topic in museology, and there are numerous articles and websites that propose and discuss the best methods to use when writing wall labels and text. A number of eye-tracking studies have sought evidence of the ways in which the title and description of an artwork, typically in combination with other factors, affect how it is subsequently viewed. Kapoula, Daunys, Herbez, and Yang (2009) investigated the nature of the interaction between stimulus-driven (the degree of abstractness of a painting) and cognitively driven influences (manipulation of the information concerning a painting's title) on an aesthetic experience with art. The stimuli employed were three Cubist paintings by Fernand Léger: *The Wedding* (composed of fragments of human faces, limbs, and arbitrary pictorial fragments), *The Alarm Clock* (composed of pictorial fragments creating the perception of a person), and *Contrast of Forms* (consisting of forms and cylinders). Art-naïve adults explored each artwork either without knowing its title, with the instruction to invent a title for each work, or being told the actual title before viewing it. Participants' eye movements were recorded as they examined for an unlimited time each of the three paintings presented on a computer screen, after which they were interviewed about their perception and comprehension of each artwork.

Differences in exploratory behavior were observed as a function of title condition and artwork using a visual grid analysis procedure. Fixation durations were significantly different across all paintings, and among the three title conditions. Durations were longest when participants knew the actual title of a work before viewing it, shorter when asked to generate a title, and shortest when they were not given the title. Kapoula and her associates suggest that this is due to the different levels of cognitive activity required by the three tasks. For example, they speculate that being given the actual title of a painting caused viewers to implement a search strategy to fit the contents of the painting to its title, which engaged a deeper level of semantic analysis and correspondingly a greater number of long-dwell fixations than the strategies used in the other two task conditions.

The specific pictorial content of the paintings also contributed in a differential fashion to the participants' visual exploration. For example, *The Wedding* produced smaller saccade sizes (i.e., the distances between fixation locations) when participants were instructed to invent a title for the painting or when they knew the actual title before viewing it in the active and driven conditions than was the case for the other two paintings, presumably due to visual aspects of the composition, i.e., the higher density of small pictorial fragments and to the detailed semantic analysis required by the many real human faces and limbs contained in the composition. Finally, Kapoula et al. (2009) compared the distribution of fixation time during the first and last 5 s of exploration for each condition and found that in most cases fixation time was initially more concentrated on a few select areas than during the last 5 s. They conclude that their findings are due collectively to the interplay among a painting, title condition, and visual processing thereby providing additional support for the complex interaction of bottom-up and top-down influences on visual exploration during an aesthetic experience with art.

A more recent eye-tracking study to investigate the influence of descriptive text on viewers' exploration of artworks was conducted by Davies et al. (2017). One group of participants saw eight paintings without any prior description and a second group saw the same artworks each of which was preceded by a descriptive narrative. The paintings consisted of landscapes, portraits, and abstract works each seen for 10 s. Results showed that for seven of the eight paintings description texts did not affect the way participants viewed the paintings. The one exception was an abstract painting that did not have distinctive features differentiating one area from any other. The researchers suggest several limitations of their study that may account for their failure to demonstrate a descriptive text effect typically reported in the literature. First, paintings were viewed for only 10 s. It may be that the eyes would be drawn automatically to salient components regardless of the description utilized. And, it is always possible that another curatorial narrative would provide the type of information that would lead to a descriptive text effect.

Time Course of an Aesthetic Experience with Art

Eye-tracking investigations that examine fixation patterns across the time course of an aesthetic experience with an artwork are essential to identify the underlying dynamics of the perceptual/cognitive processes involved. Several studies that addressed the temporal aspects of scanning have been described throughout this chapter (and see Hristova & Grinberg, 2011). In one such study, Locher, Krupinski, and Schaefer (2015) sought evidence that knowledge of a painting's alleged authenticity status would serve as a context cue that influences in a top-down fashion the way a painting is visually scanned and aesthetically evaluated over time. Art-sophisticated and naïve adults were shown lesser-known paintings by major artists under each of three alleged authorship conditions (as originals, copies, or fakes). Participants were given unlimited viewing time to provide their self-perceived scanning strategies, verbal reactions to the paintings, and evaluations of the monetary value, pleasantness, and artistic merit of each painting. Following completion of the task, participants were asked if they saw differences of any kind between the paintings in each category and if they used a particular scanning approach or viewing strategy for looking at the three categories of paintings.

Statistical analyses of the eye movement data using a matrix cell procedure included the variable "scanpath segment" with three levels—first, second, third segments— to determine if participants changed their scanning strategies across the time course of observation of the paintings. Total cumulative coverage across the three segments was also subjected to separate analyses. Both naïve and sophisticated participants maintained approximately the same average percent of spatial coverage (52.9%) across the three scanpath segments and, for the most part, directed their gaze to the same pictorial elements in each artwork regardless of its label in the counterbalanced design employed. Spatial coverage was, however, significantly influenced by the interaction of participants' art sophistication and their perception of differences among works in the three alleged authenticity conditions. Specifically, no significant difference in cumulative coverage was reported between naïve participants who said they did and those who said they did not perceive differences in cumulative coverage as a function of authenticity. On the other hand, coverage by sophisticated participants who said they saw differences among works in the three authenticity conditions directed their gaze to a significantly smaller area of the pictorial fields than did sophisticated participants who saw no differences. According to Locher et al. (2015), this finding demonstrates that the often-reported finding that sophisticated individuals examine more of an artwork than naïve viewers must be modified to take into account the specific attention demands of a viewing task that drive the scanning strategies used by sophisticated viewers of art.

Another important finding of this study was that average coverage of the pictorial fields for the full set of data was 59.2%, with attention focused in the center areas of the image, leaving 40.8% of the artworks not directly fixated during completion of the task. This "central bias" is a common observation reported in the literature and is said to reflect the fact that areas in the outer regions of a painting serve as the peripheral backdrop for the pictorial features of central interest, and therefore receive little direct attention. The bias is readily apparent in the raw fixation scatter grams for five different artwork classes (abstract and depictive paintings, works by Cézanne, and two sets of photographs) presented for the eye-tracker study of salience effects reported by Fuchs, Ansorge, Redies, and Leder, 2011).

SOCIAL CONTEXT CREATED BY THE HUMAN FIGURE IN ART

Artists and scientists interested in aesthetics have long recognized that the human figure is a critical pictorial element that attracts a viewer's gaze during the exploration of art. Additionally it is recognized that the salience of the human figure, especially the face, is frequently subject to the simultaneous interaction with other major compositional components included in the theoretical frameworks of art perception described earlier. Research by Villani, Morganti, Cipresso, and Gilli (2015) used eye-tracking methodology to add to the existing body of knowledge concerning the influence of social context scenes on exploration of different parts of human figure elements in paintings. Their stimuli consisted of figurative-style classical paintings that included at least two but not more than four human figures. In some scenes several individuals were present but not interacting in any way and only one person was performing a bodily action (e.g., a peasant woman carrying brushwood). Other artworks depicted several persons in a scene either not interacting among themselves or they were interacting by performing complementary actions (e.g., two individuals touching each other). Analyses focused on two body parts in each artwork, the face and arms depicted in action.

The nonexpert student participants were first asked to fill out the *Interpersonal Reactivity Index*, an instrument used in this study to assess participants' empathic responsiveness to others, and to search for socially relevant information in artworks. They then were instructed to look at the human figures (i.e., the agents) in each artwork shown for 10 s. Results revealed that participants spent more time in terms of number and duration of fixations observing the face in social interaction conditions than in individual action scenes, while the agents' body parts significantly attracted eye movements only when the agents were involved in individual actions. Additionally, when social actions were depicted in scenes, participants scanned the scene with a greater number of fixations before examining the ROIs of arms and a smaller number of fixations before examining the face ROIs. A related key finding was that participants who showed high empathetic abilities as measured with the *Interpersonal Reactivity Index* became immediately fixated on faces with the onset of a painting. This behavior provides additional support for the notion of painting gist.

Another eye-tracking study that incorporates the human figure in its design as a social factor was conducted by Massaro et al. (2012). They also sought to demonstrate the complex interaction of bottom-up and top-down processes that contribute to a viewer's aesthetic experience with representational paintings. Their stimuli consisted of paintings that varied in color (color or experimentally modified black-and-white versions of the originals); dynamism (depicted dynamic movement or static); content (natural environments or human full-figure representations); and task (art displayed under aesthetic or movement rating conditions). The first two factors were included as bottom-up influences on art perception and the third and fourth factors as top-down influences. Exploration patterns of art-naïve participants were recorded in a laboratory setting as they viewed each art stimulus for 3 s in both rating tasks.

The principal results for the ROI analyses performed on gaze behavior showed that content-related top-down processes exerted a greater influence on low-level visually driven bottom-up processes when a human agent is depicted in a painting whereas bottom-up processes influenced scanning to a greater extent when participants were viewing nature-content paintings. With respect to the salience of the human figure in art, cluster analyses performed by Massaro et al. (2012) indicated that a smaller cluster

ROI size was observed for human than nature paintings. According to the researchers, this indicates that attractors (i.e., pictorial elements) in human images captured viewers' attention on specific narrower expected ROIs than nature images, which include a wider range of potential pre-defined attractors. Additionally, the first three clusters produced by the analyses revealed more and longer fixations, as well as greater returns to these areas in human paintings than to the initial clusters in nature paintings. These findings, coupled with the behavioral analyses results not reported here, add to a more comprehensive understanding of the saliency of the human image in art paintings.

The Potential Use of Eye-Tracking Methodology to Study Cultural Differences in Art Portraits

According to Schulz and Hayn-Leichsenring (2017) an observer of a portrait is directed toward at least two different aesthetic aspects, namely, the attractiveness of the depicted person and the artistic beauty of the portrait that refers to the way in which the face is presented in the portrait. Their research supports the conclusion that attractiveness is predominantly driven by perceptual processes, a finding consistent with most previous research that shows high agreement in the key features (e.g., averageness, symmetry, and certain facial properties) that contribute to facial attractiveness preferences within and across cultures. Zhang, Wang, Wang, Zhang, and Xiang (2017) point out, however, that very few of these studies used eye-tracking methodology to determine the ways specific facial features impact the evaluation of facial attractiveness. The goal of their study was to add to the dearth of eye-tracking investigations of female facial features that contribute to attractiveness in Chinese culture. Male and female Chinese university students rated the attractiveness of images of Chinese female faces displaying neutral emotional expressions. Participants' scanpaths for each stimulus were recorded for 20 s as they completed the task.

Zhang et al. (2017) analyzed their data using three facial ROIs (nose, mouth, and eyes) and participant gender (female and male) as factors. They found that with the onset of a stimulus participants fixated on the eyes and mouth first and then concentrated their gaze on the nose for the remaining allotted 20 s of viewing time. Males fixated on the nose area to a significantly greater extent than did females. Based on these findings, it appears that the nose is of greater importance in Chinese culture than the eyes or mouth in the judgment of facial attractiveness. Zhang et al. suggest that this fixation bias likely reflects the fact that direct or excessive eye contact in East Asian cultures is considered rude and is therefore to be avoided. They assert that their results warrant future cross-cultural eye movement investigations of facial attractiveness to expand and clarify knowledge of the factors that contribute to facial attractiveness, factors that may contribute to the composition, perception interpretation, and appreciation of portrait art.

INTERPLAY BETWEEN EYE MOVEMENTS AND BODY MOVEMENTS

In addition to eye movement investigations of the many factors that contribute to an aesthetic experience with art that have appeared in the recent literature, researchers have begun to investigate the functional relationship between eye movements and other sensory and perceptual processes. For example, Kapoula, Lang, Vernet, and Locher (2015) studied the impact of eye movement effects on postural adjustment of the body (posturography) of viewers of Op Art. Op Art (short for Optical Art) is a distinct style of art that creates the illusion of three-dimensional movement by the use of precision and mathematics, stark contrast, and abstract shapes that gives them a three-dimensional quality not seen in other styles of art. Kapoula et al. sought evidence that eye movements participate in this illusion. Their art stimuli consisted of two well-known Op Art paintings projected in their actual size: Bridget Riley's *Movement in Squares* and Akiyoshi Kitaoka's *Rollers*. Adults who had no formal training in the visual arts were instructed to either maintain fixation at the center of the pictorial field or to explore the artwork freely. Posture was measured for 30 s per condition using a body-fixed sensor (accelerometer) placed on a participant's lower back. After viewing each artwork participants rated their sensation of movement within the image.

The principal finding of this study was that the two Op Art paintings induced higher antero-posterior than medio-lateral body sway by participants both in terms of speed and body displacement and an increase in motion illusion in the free viewing compared with the fixation conditions. Antero-posterior movement is indicative of the illusion of movement in depth, and many participants agreed during debriefing that the images, especially the work by Kitaoka, produced a sense of motion in depth. Kapoula et al. (2015) provide a detailed explanation of the mediating processes among the visual properties of the two paintings, vergence and saccadic eye movements, and aspects of body sway that generate the illusory visual motion seen in Op Art.

A PAINTER'S EYE MOVEMENTS

Previous eye-tracking studies in the field of experimental aesthetics have focused almost exclusively on the processes that lead to viewers' perceptions and appreciation of completed artworks and very rarely on the actual working processes engaged in by artists as they create art. Most of what little is known about the picture-production process comes from two types of case study research; namely, archival case studies and real-life case studies (see Locher, 2010). Archival case studies analyze chronological versions of a single completed painting. One such study was conducted by Weisberg (2004), who investigated the development of Picasso's painting *Guernica*. Viewers described the central elements and overall structural arrangement of the composition of the 45 preliminary sketches for the work and the eight photographs of the developing artwork taken throughout the build-up of the completed work. An obvious limitation of this and other archival case studies is that they do not capture directly the actual art-making processes. Real-life eye-tracking studies, on the other hand, capture every pictorial detail of the actual on-going working processes used by an artist as he or she creates an artwork. Surprisingly, given the tremendous potential contribution of real-life eye-tracking studies of the art-making process, almost no such studies have been reported to date in the recent literature. For this reason the two studies described below are somewhat dated for this review, but are included to demonstrate the potential of eye-tracking studies to examine factors that contribute to the ways artists create paintings.

Miall and Tchalenko (2001) conducted a real-life eye movement study of the picture-production processes employed by the British portrait artist Humphrey Ocean, who was known for his skill in creating realistic portraits of models from life. During the first phase of the study the artist looked at four prospective males to select a model for the drawing. Ocean then drew each candidate in a small sketchpad to help him make a selection of the model. The actual picture-production phases followed after which the artist made a series of 1-min sketches from a black-and-white photograph of a face. To capture the nature of the perceptual/cognitive and drawing processes employed by the artist, the researchers utilized an eye-tracker to record his visual exploration strategies, a close-up video filming of the emerging portrait, and a hand-movement sensor recording the movements of the artist's pencil. The very large sets of data generated by these experimental systems provide very detailed descriptions of the interactive components of the artist's "online" picture-production processes provided by Miall and Tchalenko in their paper.

In a more recent real-life study, Cohen (2005) investigated the relationship between drawing accuracy and a visual analysis component of the drawing process; namely, the rate at which an artist glances between his/her drawing and the stimulus (termed gaze frequency by Cohen). Such shifts are made hundreds of times by an artist during picture production and are believed to be a direct reflection of the picture creation process. In each of the four experiments conducted by Cohen, university art majors and nonmajors were asked to render realistic drawings of the images in two photographs of the heads of males. Their eye movements were recorded as they looked back-and-forth between the photograph and their drawing. The location of the gaze (photograph, drawing, neither) and the time spent fixating on each view were the variables of interest. In Experiment 1, participants were given 10 min to draw each stimulus using whatever strategy they desired to complete their drawings. The speed of alternation between the two views was experimentally manipulated at intervals of 1, 3, 5, 8, or 15 s across the reaming three experiments to vary gaze frequency.

The principal findings of the study were that the art-trained students made more alternations between the stimulus and drawing than did untrained students, and that gaze frequency for both groups directly influenced drawing accuracy. Cohen (2005) suggests that the observed higher gaze frequencies (i.e., relatively fast alternations) for artists provide the perceptual system with only a small amount of pictorial information in working memory to be transferred to the drawing, thereby reducing memory distortion of perceptual information contained in the working memory, which in turn facilitates the reduction of stimulus and context effects through focused attention.

As mentioned, given the obvious contribution of the real-life case study approach to the observation of online creative processes used by artists at work, it is not clear to this author why so few eye-tracking studies like that reported by Miall and Tchalenko (2001) have been conducted to date. Clearly this is an area of eye movement research that deserves much additional attention.

Conclusion and Future Research

Knowledge obtained using eye-tracking techniques has historically contributed in a major way to the development of models that detail the mechanisms and processes underlying the experience of visual art. As emphasized throughout the review presented in this chapter, the experience of art viewing is the result of the complex dynamic interaction among factors incorporated in contemporary person–artifact–context relational models. Recent technical developments in eye-tracking apparatus and methods for visualization and analyzing eye-tracking data have played important roles in recent advances in understanding the nature of these complex interactions. However, given the complexity of the issues included in the various contemporary frameworks, and given the dynamic and interactive nature of the components, it would appear that there remain an almost infinite number of studies to be performed before anything approaching a truly comprehensive understanding of an aesthetic experience with art will be achieved. Yet, there are signs that progress is already being made toward this goal. For example, Rigas, Friedman, and Komogortsev (2018) report results of their study "of an extensive set of 101 categories of eye movement features from three types of eye movement events: fixations, saccades, and post-saccadic oscillations." They "present a unified framework of methods for the extraction of features that describe the temporal, positional and dynamic characteristics of eye movements" (p. 1). Although Rigas et al. collected data from subjects during a text reading task, they assert that their methods and analyses can provide a valuable tool for researchers in many fields to which I would add the study of eye movements in empirical aesthetics.

REFERENCES

Bauer, D., & Schwan, S. (2018). Expertise influences meaning-making with Renaissance portraits: Evidence from gaze and thinking-aloud. *Psychology of Aesthetics, Creativity, and the Arts, 12*, 193–204. doi:10.1037/aca0000264

Brieber, D., Nadal, M., Leder, H., & Rosenberg, R. (2014). Art in time and space: Context modulates the relation between art experience and viewing time. *PLoS ONE, 96*, e99019. doi:10.1371/journal.pone.0099019

Cohen, D. (2005). Look little, look often: The influence of gaze frequency on drawing accuracy. *Perception & Psychophysics, 67*, 997–1009.

Davies, A., Reani, M., Vigo, M., Harper, S., Grimes, M., Gannaway, C., & Jay, C. (2017). Does descriptive text change how people look at art? A novel analysis of eye-movements using data-driven Units of Interest. *Journal of Eye Movement Research, 10*, 1–13. doi:10.16910/jemr.10.4.4

Francuz, P., Zaniewski, I., Augustynowicz, P., Kopiś, N., & Jankowski, T. (2018). Eye movement correlates of expertise in visual arts. *Frontiers in Human Neuroscience, 12*, 87. doi:10.3389/fnhum.00087

Fuchs, I., Ansorge, U., Redies, C., & Leder, H. (2011). Salience in paintings: Bottom-up influences on eye fixation. *Cognitive Communication, 3*, 25–36. doi:10.1007/s12559-010-9062-3

Hristova, E., & Grinberg, M. (2011). Time course of eye movements during painting perception. In B. Kokinov, B. Karmiloff-Smith, & N. Nersessian (Eds.), *European Perspectives on Cognitive Science* (pp. 477–487). Sofia: New Bulgarian University Press.

Ishiguro, C., Yokosawa, K., & Okada, T. (2016). Eye movements during art appreciation by students taking a photo creation course. *Frontiers in Psychology, 7*, 1074. doi:10.3389/fpsyg.2016.01074

Kapoula, Z., Daunys, G., Herbez, O., & Yang, Q. (2009). Effect of title on eye movement exploration of cubist paintings by Fernand Léger. *Perception, 38*, 479–491. doi:10.1068/p6080

Kapoula, Z., Lang, A., Vernet, M., & Locher, P. (2015). Eye movement instructions modulate motion illusion and body sway with Op Art. *Frontier in Human Neuroscience, 9*, 121. doi:10.3389/fnhum.2015.00121

Kübler, T., Fuhl, W., Rosenberg, R., Rosenstiel, W., & Kasneci, E. (2016). Novel methods for analysis and visualization of saccade trajectories. ECCV Workshop—VISART. Retrieved from http://www.researchgate.net/publication/305787528

Lappi, O. (2015). Eye tracking in the wild: The good, the bad, and the ugly. *Journal of Eye Movement Research, 8*, 1–21. doi:10.16190/jemr.8.5.1

Little, A., Jones, B., & DeBruine, L. (2011). The many faces of research on face perception. *Philosophical Transactions of the Royal Society B, 366*, 1634–1637. doi:10.1098/rstb.2010.0386

Locher, P. (2010). How does a visual artist create an artwork? In J. Kaufman, & R. Sternberg (Eds.), *The Cambridge handbook of creativity* (pp. 131–144). Cambridge, England: Cambridge University Press.

Locher, P. (2015). The aesthetic experience with visual art "At first glance." In P. F. Bundgaard, & F. Stjernfelt (Eds.), *Investigations into the phenomenology and the ontology of the work of art* (pp. 75–88). New York: Springer Open. doi:10.1007/978-3-319-14090-2

Locher, P., Krupinski, E., & Schaefer, A., (2015). Art and authenticity: Behavioral and eye movement analyses. *Psychology of Aesthetics, Creativity, and the Arts, 9*, 356–367. doi:10.1037/aca0000026

Massaro, D., Savazzi, F., Di Dio, C., Freedberg, D., Gallese, V., Gilli, G., & Marchetti, A. (2012). When art moves the eyes: A behavioral and eye-tracking study. *PLoS ONE*, *7*(5), e37285. doi:10.1371/journal.pone.0037285

Miall, R., & Tchalenko, J. (2001). A painter's eye movements: A study of eye and hand movement during portrait drawing. *Leonardo*, *34*, 35–40. http://muse.jhu.edu/demo/leonardo/v034/34.1miall.html

Mitschke, V., Goller, J., & Leder, H. (2017). Exploring everyday encounters with street art using a multimethod design, *Psychology of Aesthetics, Creativity, and the Arts*, *11*, 276–283. doi:10.1037/aca0000131

Nodine, C., Locher, P., & Krupinski, E. (1993). The role of formal art training on the perception and aesthetic evaluation of art compositions. *Leonardo*, *26*, 219–227. doi:10.2307/1575815

Pelowski, M., Forster, M., Tinio, P., Scholl, M., & Leder, H. (2017). Beyond the lab: An examination of key factors influencing interaction with "real" museum-based art. *Psychology of Aesthetics, Creativity, and the Arts*, *11*, 245–264. doi:10.1037/aca0000141.supp

Pelowski, M., Markey, P., Lauring, J., & Leder, H. (2016). Visualizing the impact of art: An update and comparison of current psychological models of art experience. *Frontiers in Human Neuroscience*, *10*, 160. doi:10.3389/fnhum.2016.00160

Quiroga, R. Q., Dudley, S., & Binnie, J. (2011). Looking at Ophelia: A comparison of viewing art in the gallery and in the lab. *Advances in Clinical Neuroscience and Rehabilitation*, *11*, 15–18.

Rigas, I., Friedman, L., & Komogortsev, O. (2018). Study of an extensive set of eye movement features: Extraction methods and statistical analysis. *Journal of Eye Movement Research*, *11*(1), 3. doi:10.16910/jemr.11.13

Schultz, K., & Hayn-Leichsenring, G. (2017). Face attractiveness versus artistic beauty in art portraits: A behavioral study. *Frontiers in Psychology*, *8*, 2254. doi:10.3389/fpsyg.2017.02254

Smith, J. (2014). *The museum effect: How museums, libraries, and cultural institutions educate and civilize society*. Lanham, MD: Rowman & Littlefield.

Smith, L. F., & Smith, J. K., (2006). The nature and growth of aesthetic fluency. In P. Locher, C. Martindale, & L. Dorfman (Eds.), *New directions in aesthetic creativity and the arts* (pp. 47–58). Amityville, NY: Baywood.

Villani, D., Morganti, F., Cipresso, P., & Gilli, G. (2015). Visual exploration patterns of human figures in action: An eye tracker study with art paintings. *Frontiers in Psychology*, *6*, 1636. doi:10.3389/psyg.2915.01636

Vogt, S., & Magnussen, A. (2007). Expertise in pictorial perception: Eye movement patterns and visual memory in artists and laymen. *Perception*, *36*, 91–100. doi:10.1068/p5262

Walker, F., Bucker, B., Anderson, N., Schreij, D., & Theeuwes, J. (2017). Looking at paintings in the Vincent Van Gogh Museum: Eye movement patterns of children and adults. *PLoS ONE*, *12*(6), e0178912. doi:10.1371/journal.pone.0178912

Weisberg, R. (2004). On structure in the creative process: A quantitative case study of the creation of Picasso's *Guernica*. *Empirical Studies of the Arts*, *22*, 23–54.

Yarbus, A. L. (1967). *Eye movements and vision*. New York: Plenum Press. doi:10.1007/978-1-4899-5379-7

Zhang, Y., Wang, X., Wang, J., Zhang, L., & Xiang, Y. (2017). Patterns of eye movements when observers judge female facial attractiveness. *Frontiers in Psychology*, *8*, 1909. doi:10.3389/fpsyg.2017.01909

CHAPTER 14

ELECTROPHYSIOLOGY

THOMAS JACOBSEN AND STINA KLEIN

Introduction

RECENT bio-psychological accounts of aesthetic processing profess that aesthetic appreciation comprises both cognitive and affective components. According to these accounts, upon viewing an object of beauty, sensorial and perceptual processes construct mental representations of the object that form the basis of the aesthetically evaluative process. Then, activated mental scripts and schemata modulate the perceptual processes and form perceptual sets in the mind of the observer. These processes are followed by, or may interact with, genuinely affective processes of aesthetic appreciation.

Cognitive psychology, and, later on, cognitive neuroscience, have provided us with a good account of the mental processing architecture in perception, judgment and decision making, language, and other higher-order cognitive processes. In a multi-method approach, self-reports, response times, error data, physiological, and anatomical data are used. The employed methods differ with respect to their temporal and spatial resolutions. Some methods are very well versed for a precise localization of neural structures; for instance, functional magnetic resonance imaging (fMRI). Other methods are particularly suitable for the investigation of mental chronometry and its processing stages, because of their high temporal resolution. This holds, in particular, for electrophysiological methods as well as magnetoencephalography. One advantage of these methods pertains to the fact that they allow for the identification of several processing stages within a single experimental trial. This, of course, can be obtained with other methods as well, but often not as practically. The neurocognitive psychology of aesthetics, or neuroaesthetics, builds on these methodological advances. The present chapter reviews findings in the psychology of aesthetics that have been obtained using electrophysiological methods.

Background: Cognitive Electrophysiology

The synchronized electrical activity of large-scale and open field neural populations can be noninvasively recorded from the scalp. This electroencephalogram (EEG), first described by Hans Berger (1929), has become a standard method in research on human information processing. While its temporal resolution solely depends on the accuracy of the measurement equipment, its spatial resolution is limited, because multiple brain generators contribute to any scalp-recorded EEG signal. Localization of these electrical sources requires sophisticated algorithms with many degrees of freedom. The many sources of an EEG signal can be divided into those that contribute to the event-related activity of the brain and those that reflect spontaneous activity. Electrical brain activity can be related to external sensorial or response-related processes, or to internal events of mental processing.

In order to distinguish between event-related and spontaneous brain activity, the method of deriving event-related brain potentials (ERPs) from the spontaneous EEG signal is often used. ERPs are computed by averaging experimentally equivalent EEG-epochs. By discarding spontaneous EEG activity, this procedure results in voltage changes, which are characterized by peaks and troughs of positive and negative polarity over time and with a certain topography over the scalp. When a voltage change of a given polarity and latency—with a characterized amplitude maximum at a given scalp side—can be functionally specified, it is labeled a component (see e.g., Luck, 2005). Over the past few decades, cognitive electrophysiology has identified multiple ERP components reflecting mental processes ranging from early sensorial processes in the order of only a few milliseconds to higher-order cognitive processes lasting several hundreds of milliseconds (see e.g., Luck, 2005, for a review).

In ERP studies, usually group-averaged data are shown. This is required, if one wants to make inferences based on the investigated sample with respect to the underlying population. In addition, multiple epochs of EEG are required for an averaging method that extracts the event-related activity from any other ongoing electrical brain activity. This leads to certain requirements for the experimental design. In particular, interindividual variation has to be taken into account. This, again, poses a particular challenge, obviously, for processes that are often subject to individual differences, like aesthetic appreciation.

Psychology of Aesthetics

Aesthetic processing, as a multifaceted endeavor, is determined by a host of factors. Our aesthetics are governed by biological and human brain evolution, as well as by fashions, culture, subcultures, socially constituted conventions, and many other factors. Our individual dispositions interact with domain specificities and situational characteristics in any given episode of aesthetic appreciation (Jacobsen, 2006, 2010).

A FRAMEWORK FOR THE NEUROCOGNITIVE PSYCHOLOGY OF AESTHETICS

Empirical aesthetics can be pursued in multiple ways. It is deeply rooted in experimental psychology, as the founder of psychophysics, Gustav Theodor Fechner, had a profound interest in empirical aesthetics. He provided an inductive scientific approach to aesthetics via collecting data, in the form of "aesthetics from below," as contrasted with a theoretical deductive approach (i.e., "from above"). Since Fechner's seminal work (1876, *Vorschule der Aesthetik*), many scholars have contributed to the psychology of aesthetics. Jacobsen (2006; see Figure 14.1) has suggested a framework that comprises seven perspectives. In the so-called diachronic perspective one can account for changes in aesthetics over time. Such changes can be biological in nature, or of cultural origin. Therefore, the diachronic perspective helps to account for changes in, for instance, fashion, or, on the other hand, for phenomena of temporal stability. In a complementary way, the ipsichronic perspective can investigate and account for effects of culture or subculture. This perspective also accounts for social processes within a given time frame. Taken together, these two perspectives allow analyses of the phenomena on an individual or a group-level basis. According to the third perspective, aesthetic processing can be conceived as being governed by situational and person determinates, which, in turn, will also depend or be modulated by content domains (Jacobsen & Beudt, 2017). Taken together, then, these three perspectives (content, person, and situation) create a matrix, allowing for detailed investigations.

Empirical data suggest that the content domains of visual art and music differ in their underlying conceptual structure of aesthetic experiences (e.g., Augustin, Wagemans, & Carbon, 2012; see also Istók et al., 2009; Jacobsen, Buchta, Köhler, & Schröger, 2004; Knoop, Wagner, Jacobsen, & Menninghaus, 2016). This is reflected in the content perspective. In the domain of music, melody and harmony play important roles. These conceptual facets, of course, do not play roles in the aesthetic of visual objects (Jacobsen et al., 2004).

The framework proposed by Jacobsen contains two more perspectives: body and mind. These can be conceived of as the classical psychophysical dimensions. The mind perspective covers psychological theorizing from the first-person perspective, whereas the body perspective entails scientific concepts from biology in general and the neurosciences in particular. Here, we find the scientific paradigm currently adopted by cognitive neuroscience or, more generally, biological psychology. Research from functional neuroanatomy is combined with mental chronometry from cognitive science.

The remainder of this chapter will be devoted mainly to studies focusing on the mental chronometry of aesthetic processing. As discussed above, EEG, and derived

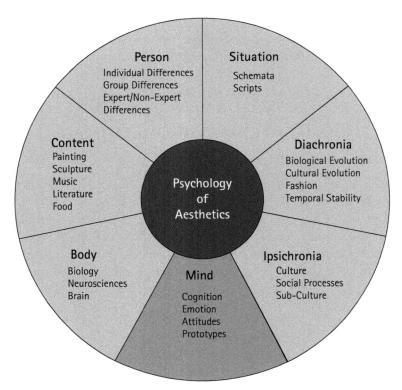

FIGURE 14.1. An illustration of a framework for the psychology of aesthetics. The topic is viewed from seven different vantage points that are not mutually exclusive. These are called: Diachronia, Ipsichronia, Mind, Body, Content, Person, and Situation. Eventually, this work can converge on a unified theory of processing aesthetics. Diachronia is the perspective that takes change over time into account. Ipsichronia is the vantage point focusing on comparisons within a given time slice, i.e., comparisons between cultures, subcultures, or social systems.

Source: Thomas Jacobsen, "Bridging the Arts and Sciences: A Framework for the Psychology of Aesthetics," *Leonardo*, 39:2 (April, 2006), pp. 155–162. © 2006 by the International Society for the Arts, Sciences and Technology (ISAST).

measures such as ERPs, allow for a good temporal resolution while showing limited spatial resolution of the processes under investigation (see also Jacobsen, 2010, 2013; cf. also de Tommaso et al., 2008; Lengger, Fischmeister, Leder, & Bauer, 2007).

COGNITIVE ELECTROPHYSIOLOGY OF AESTHETIC APPRECIATION

Using the ERP technique, Jacobsen and Höfel (2001, 2003) investigated the mental chronometry of aesthetic judgment by comparing data from an evaluative aesthetic judgment task with those from a nonaesthetic descriptive judgment task using the same stimulus material. Aesthetic judgments of beauty were contrasted with descriptive judgments of symmetry. To this end, 252 black-and-white graphic patterns were newly designed in the laboratory (see Figure 14.2). On each trial, participants were asked to perform each of the two tasks depending on a cue. Both judgment tasks appeared in a pseudorandom fashion. Participants could view any given stimulus for 3 s. Forming a judgment took, on average 1,300 ms.

Although presentation of the stimuli was counterbalanced across participants, there was a double dissociation in the EEG signatures of the two judgment processes: For the aesthetic judgment task, there was a negative-going fronto-central deflection between 300 and 400 ms after stimulus onset. This effect was taken to reflect impression formation in the brain of the subjects. This first effect was followed by a second deflection that was taken to be a late positive potential (LPP). The LPP had been reported in the earlier literature as reflecting evaluative categorization (Cacioppo, Crites, Berntson, & Coles, 1993). Judgments of symmetry, in contrast, resulted in a longer-lasting, late-onset, ERP deflection with a posterior distribution. This effect was interpreted to reflect a sustained analysis of symmetry in the presented stimulus.

This double dissociation in space and time suggested not only a difference in the quality of the judgment itself, evaluative versus descriptive, but also in the modes of processing underlying these two judgments tasks. The ERP technique provided time marks reflecting separate processing stages within the mental chronometry of aesthetic judgment. Importantly, aesthetic judgment of beauty of the novel graphic patterns seems to have been determined independently from symmetry and complexity, which were features built into the process of construction of these stimuli. Judgment analysis (e.g., Cooksey, 1996) was used for parametric modeling of individual aesthetic judgment strategies (Jacobsen, 2004; Jacobsen & Höfel, 2002; Höfel & Jacobsen, 2003).

First presented at the Annual Meeting of the Cognitive Neuroscience Society in 2000, Jacobsen and Höfel (2000) refrained from labeling the newly found ERP effects prematurely as components. Rather, they conducted a series of further ERP studies using derivates of the tasks employed in the 2003 study. In one follow-up study, they investigated whether the ERP deflections seemingly representing aesthetic judgments of beauty were due to judgment categorization or, rather, judgment report (Höfel & Jacobsen, 2007b). To this end, participants were asked to misreport their true judgments, e.g. to answer "no" when they meant "yes." While under the false judgment report condition, there was a superposition on the LPP. The earlier fronto-central effect between 300 and 400 ms after stimulus onset, however, remained unaffected in quality. It appeared about 100 ms later than in the earlier 2003 study. Under true judgment conditions the LPP occurred as in the 2003 study. These findings suggested that the fronto-central effect and the LPP indeed do reflect two separate processing stages of the aesthetic judgment of beauty of graphic stimuli. If both ERP deflections reflected one and the same process, then both deflections should have been affected by the false judgment report condition. The results also suggested that the LPP ERP effect predominantly reflects evaluative judgment categorization, rather than judgment report.

FIGURE 14.2. Stimulus examples.
The graphic patterns in rows 1 and 2 are not symmetric, ranging from not beautiful to beautiful (line by line). Patterns in row 3 and 4 are symmetric, also ranging from not beautiful to beautiful.

Source: Thomas Jacobsen, "Bridging the Arts and Sciences: A Framework for the Psychology of Aesthetics," *Leonardo*, 39:2 (April, 2006), pp. 155–162.
© 2006 by the International Society for the Arts, Sciences and Technology (ISAST).

In a further study, Höfel and Jacobsen (2007a) investigated whether or not the ERP deflections observed in earlier studies were contingent on the active judgment task, or whether they would occur spontaneously in a derived aesthetic contemplation task that did not require an overt judgment. To this end, the authors contrasted an aesthetic contemplation condition with a mere viewing condition. A probe detection task was interspersed to control for intentional effects. The results showed that the earlier fronto-central effect taken to reflect impression formation did not occur under conditions of mere aesthetic contemplation. Rather, the longer-lasting ERP effect showing a posterior distribution reflecting prolonged analysis of symmetry of the presented stimuli did occur spontaneously. The LPP reflecting evaluative categorization did not occur under either aesthetic contemplation or mere viewing.

Taken together, these results suggest that the fronto-central ERP deflection between 300 and 400 ms detected in the study of Jacobsen and Höfel (2003) was contingent on the intention to perform an aesthetic judgment. In contrast, aesthetic contemplation that does not imply the intention to produce a judgment did not result in this fronto-central ERP deflection. In sum, these three studies using identical stimulus material and parametric variations of the task allowed for a cognitive specification of the observed ERP effects.

Aesthetic Appreciation of Visual Art

De Tommaso et al. (2008) also investigated neural correlates of the aesthetic processing using geometric images, albeit their materials differed from the patterns of Jacobsen and colleagues greatly. Additional to the geometric images, artistic paintings were used as stimuli. Thus, by comparing the two types of stimuli, geometric and artistic, and simultaneously considering the aesthetic preference shed light on the processing of artworks. Participants were asked to rate the presented stimuli during EEG recording. Afterwards, the most beautiful and ugly stimuli as well as neutral stimuli were selected for geometric shapes and for the paintings. The chosen stimuli acted as targets in a subsequent second session. In the second session, participants were instructed to detect the targets as quickly as possible and to distinguish them from a green panel. The results showed that the amplitude of the P3 component was greater for beautiful shapes, independent of the type of stimuli, compared with neutral and ugly shapes. The P3 component is associated with a wide range of memory processes (e.g., Polich, 2007) and also emotional arousal (e.g., Johnston, Miller, & Burleson, 1986), thus, the authors suggest an attraction effect concerning beautiful stimuli, independent of the type of beauty.

Alongside the characteristics of the content of the stimulus, the characteristics of the evaluating person also have a significant influence on the aesthetic perception, which is also observable in the electrophysiological chronometry. For instance, the extent of art expertise influences the electrophysiological activation; a negative relationship between art expertise and amplitudes at parieto-occipital regions has been found (Pang,

Nadal, Müller-Paul, Rosenberg, & Klein, 2013). A study from Beudt and Jacobsen (2015) furthermore indicates that the mental perspective influences aesthetic judgments. Participants were asked to review paintings either from their own viewpoint or from the viewpoint of a fictitious artist. In the cue–target interval participants already showed a greater negativity in the condition of the artistic judgment compared with the condition of the personal judgment. After the target was presented, amplitudes in centro-parietal regions were also greater, albeit more positive, for judgments made from an external mental perspective than from the internal perspective. The authors suggested that more effort in general is needed when appreciating aesthetic work from a different mental perspective.

Even early components such as the P2 amplitude differentiate depending on the aesthetic appreciation. Wang, Huang, Ma, and Li (2012) proposed that negative emotions are evoked when being faced with aesthetically nonbeautiful stimuli. The amplitude of the P2 component was greater for less beautiful stimuli; accordingly, the amplitude for beautiful paintings was less pronounced. The P2 is a positivity-evoked component by visual stimuli and is associated with the affective content, especially for negative emotions. This result could not be expanded to another kind of artistic work; Noguchi and Murota (2013) also investigated the P2 component associated with aesthetic ratings. For that reason, participants were asked to explicitly review varying images of sculptures. In contrast to the findings of Wang et al. (2012), the relationship between the P2 amplitude and the rating was positive. Even though the two studies are reversed in their findings, there seems to be a modulation in this early component, however this is actually evoked.

Aside from the electroencephalography there are further electrophysiological techniques that allow insights into the operation of aesthetic appreciation. Such methods include electrodermal skin conductance, heart rate, and electromyography (EMG). For instance, EMG measures changes in facial muscles. In particular, the zygomaticus major (a.k.a., the smiling muscle) and the corrugator supercilii (a.k.a., the frowning muscle) show reversed activation according to the valence of the emotion.

Gerger, Leder, and Kremer (2014) explored the effect of the contextual setting on the ratings of aesthetical liking and on positive and negative emotion on artworks using the EMG technique. In addition to artworks as stimuli, pictures from the International Affective Picture System (IAPS) were used. However, IAPS stimuli depict explicit emotional situations and are not to be classified as works of art. The context was either of an artistic or realistic manner. The results showed that being in an art context influenced the liking as well as the affective sensation. Negative artworks can be associated with an increase in the rating of liking and an increase in positive emotion in the artistic context compared with the realistic context. No difference was found for negative emotions. There was no difference in liking ratings, in positive or in negative emotional reactions, when positive artworks were presented. The EMG data confirmed the results. The activation of the zygomaticus major was increased for negative artworks in the art context. It is concluded that the context of art influences the intensity of affective reaction.

Up to this point the experimental setting of the studies was predominantly in laboratories. The next one, however, is a field study and was conducted in a museum during an exhibition (Tschacher et al., 2012). Visitors to the exhibition could take part voluntarily. Each participant was equipped with a purpose-built glove. The glove recorded skin conductance and its variability, heart rate and its variability, and the position of the wearer in the exhibition at all times. After the visit, participants were asked to state their opinion of certain artworks regarding their aesthetic value and emotional appraisal. The authors aimed to investigate a possible connection between electrophysiological measures and aesthetic appreciation in an authentic environment. The examined variables explained between ~1 and 25% of the variance in the outcome measures of interest. It is concluded that physiological properties and aesthetic appreciation are linked. However, there are "no empirical grounds to claim that aesthetic experiencing could or should be reduced to its physiological embodiment" (Tschacher et al., 2012, p. 102).

Aesthetic Appreciation of Music and Poetry

With regard to the aesthetic appreciation in the content domain of music, Brattico, Jacobsen, De Baene, Glerean, and Tervaniemi (2010) used cadences of five chords in order to investigate aesthetic judgments of the beauty of music in contrast to descriptive judgments of the correctness of music. The newly composed cadences could either be correct, ambiguous, or incorrect, with reference to Western musical harmony. Participants were asked to perform either an aesthetic judgment task of beauty or a descriptive judgment task of correctness. In each of the cadences, the fifth and last chord would determine whether the entire cadence would be correct, ambiguous, or incorrect. ERPs time-locked to the last chord revealed that an LPP was elicited in the evaluative judgment condition, while a qualitatively different electrophysiological response was elicited in the descriptive correctness judgment condition. The earlier fronto-central deflection observed for the evaluative judgment of visual stimuli, however, was not observed in the domain of music. Several differences in the nature of the musical stimulation may account for these differences. In sum, the study demonstrated a clear-cut dissociation between affective and cognitive modes of listening to music and subsequent judgments. The finer structure of the mental architecture underlying these processes should be investigated in future studies.

As one of the possible follow-ups, Müller, Höfel, Brattico, and Jacobsen (2010) investigated the effect of musical expertise on the ERP effects introduced above using a similar experimental procedure with equal conditions. Auditory, cognitive, and affective aspects, and stages of processing could be differentiated between experts and laypersons. Experts showed differences in posterior regions after the initial presentation of the cue for the following task. When the cue for the correctness task was displayed, a more positive waveform could be distinguished from the waveform when experts prepared for the beauty task. Such differences in amplitudes could not be seen in laypersons. This indicates that experts prepare differently depending on task demands. Whereas experts differed in the early preparatory stage, laypersons' electrophysiological modulations differed in the late preparatory stages; during the presentation of the first four chords of the cadence, particularly 1,000 and 1,300 ms after the onset of the first chord, the amplitude was more negative for the correctness task compared with the beauty task in frontal regions. Possibly the layperson needs to invest more effort in order to answer correctly. As such, expertise leads to greater ease and higher precision during the construction of the mental representation of the stimulus, forming the cognitive basis for subsequent evaluative aesthetic processing. Furthermore, the previous findings for the LPP were replicated to some extent. In laypersons the beauty task elicited a greater positivity. On the contrary, for experts, such differences regarding the LPP could not be found. The authors suggested that laypersons rely more heavily on their internal affective state when evaluating the beauty of the cadences. Because of the knowledge of their role as musical connoisseurs, experts neglect their affective state and rely more on their professional view independently of the task.

Jaśkiewicz, Francuz, Zabielska-Mendyk, Zapała, and Augustynowicz (2016) also examined the influence of musical expertise on the shaping of the temporal course of the neural activity. The participants were also asked to indicate the beauty or correctness. They listened to excerpts of Johann Sebastian Bach's compositions, so-called chorales, lasting between 13 and 21 s. In the middle of the chorale one chord was manipulated and could therefore be either expected, unexpected, or very unexpected. Although the electrophysiological modulations of the LPP showed differences, these were reversed compared with Müller et al. (2010) in two ways. First, the waveform for the correction task did not differ between the beauty and correctness judgment when the participants did not possess any musical expertise. Second, when experts conducted the correctness task a greater positivity was observable compared with the beauty task between 500 and 650 ms. The authors attributed these results to a greater complexity of the stimuli.

Istók and colleagues (2013) have demonstrated that ERPs are sensitive to longer-term genre preferences. Latin American and heavy metal music enthusiasts performed liking judgments and a genre classification task on excerpts of both music genres. While the evaluative judgment task was reflected by an LPP between 600 and 900 ms after stimulus onset, ERP reflections of evaluation were also observed in the descriptive task. This finding clearly indicates that these music excerpts were evaluated spontaneously, even in the absence of a task demand.

Turning now toward the written arts, there is one study, at least known to us, that intentionally investigated the aesthetics of poetry using the EEG technique. Obermeier et al. (2016) chose 60 German stanzas as stimuli that were furthermore varied with regard to the rhyming and the meter and ended up with 240 stanzas (60 × rhyming/metered, 60 × rhyming/nonmetered, 60 × nonrhyming/metered, and 60 × nonrhyming/nonmetered). During EEG recording participants either judged the rhythmicity or the

linking of the stanzas. Unsurprisingly, rhymed and/or metered stanzas correlated positively with the rhythmicity ratings, but positive relationships between rhyme and liking
ratings as well as meter and liking ratings were also found. The interaction of rhymed
and metered variations of the short poems led to a reduction in the N400 component.
The N400 component is known to be sensitive to rhyme manipulation (e.g., Coch, Hart,
& Mitra, 2008; Khateb et al., 2007). The same effect, albeit weaker, was found in the
P600 component. The P600 component is affected by the metrical structure of written
and spoken words (e.g., Schmidt-Kassow & Kotz, 2009). The authors concluded that
rhyme and meter indicate a processing ease, which in turn correlates with the liking of
poetic work.

Aesthetic Appreciation of Faces

Concerning the aesthetics of the human face, several studies have revealed that the facial
stimuli itself, the task demands, and characteristics of the person influence the chronometry when perceiving faces. Early and late components are discussed in the available
research (e.g., Werheid, Schacht, & Sommer, 2007; van Hooff, Crawford, & van Vugt,
2010; Zhang et al., 2011); however, the following section focuses on the LPP because the
effects of facial attractiveness are recurring.

In two studies from Johnston and colleagues (Johnston & Oliver-Rodríguez, 1997;
Oliver-Rodríguez, Guan, & Johnston, 1999), participants viewed schematic portraits of
male and female faces that varied with respect to attractiveness. Amplitudes were larger
in posterior regions between 400 and 600 ms for attractive faces than for unattractive
ones. These findings are supported by a further study, in which participants actively
classified faces as attractive or unattractive during EEG recording. Attractive faces
elicited more positive amplitudes (Werheid, Schacht, & Sommer, 2007). This difference
was interpreted as a reflection of sensitivity to attractive faces. In the analysis of a
follow-up study Schacht, Werheid, and Sommer (2008) divided the facial stimuli into
five sections ranging from "most attractive" to "most unattractive." In contrast to the
three mid-sections, the two outer sections elicited larger amplitudes concluding in a U-
shaped association between attractiveness and the amplitude in the LPP. In contrast to
earlier studies, Schacht et al. (2008) argued that their stimuli showed greater deviation
with regard to facial aesthetics. Therefore, it was concluded that attractive as well as unattractive faces compared with average attractive faces have a higher valence and/or are
more salient. These modulations mentioned by Schacht et al. (2008) were only observable when participants rated the attractiveness explicitly. While doing an implicit descriptive task, more precisely identifying the gender of the presented face, there were no
significant differences between attractive and unattractive faces. Such task-dependent
modulations were also found by Roye, Höfel, and Jacobsen (2008). Interestingly, in this
study nonbeautiful faces elicited more positive waveforms than beautiful faces. These
results are contradictory to the remaining research. Additionally, the differences were

only observed in female faces and not in male facial stimuli. Gender differences were also found by van Hooff et al. (2010); however here, in accordance with the aforementioned research, attractive female faces elicited more positive amplitudes than unattractive female faces. Regardless of the direction, this implies different valences of male and female faces.

The attractiveness of faces also influenced the LPP when retrieving previously encoded stimuli (Marzi & Viggiano, 2010). In contrast, such differences could not be replicated in another study, also examining the influence of attractiveness on retrieval (Zhang, Wei, Zhao, Zheng, & Zhang, 2016). Also, modulations of the LPP are sensitive to one's own perception of the attractiveness of the participants (Morgan & Kinsley, 2014). The so-called market value of the male perceivers was experimentally influenced intraindividually. Each participant rated a set of images of female faces twice. Before each rating the participants themselves were informed about their attractiveness based on a fictitious rating. Either the rating was fairly high, ending in a high market value, or the rating was fairly low and accordingly the induced market value was also low. Interestingly, the LPP did not differ for attractive faces when comparing the high market value and the low market value conditions. However, the amplitude was higher for unattractive faces when participants had a low market value compared with having a high market value. The authors concluded that the resources used for the processing of attractiveness are influenced by the characteristics of the perceiver.

Aesthetic Appreciation of Everyday Objects

Though not content-related, a team of researchers investigated a possible association between aesthetics and Chinese typefaces. For that reason, Mandarin-speaking students served as participants and were asked to detect one single typeface as a target, while 175 other characters acted as nontarget stimuli. The subsequent analysis compared liked, disliked, and all other, nonselected characters. It was ascertained that disliked characters elicited a more pronounced negativity than liked or nonselected characters for the P2 and the LPP. Li, Qin, Zhang, Wu, and Zhou (2015) concluded that electrophysiological modulations of everyday encountered stimuli, in this case, typefaces, for Mandarin-speaking individuals, show a negativity bias.

Everyday objects of different quality are used repeatedly; for instance, a pen, a cup, or a paperclip. Compared with artistic works, such as paintings or musical compositions, the aesthetic or beauty of everyday objects is often not considered. However, Righi, Orlando, and Marzi (2014) addressed this research gap and investigated the connection between aesthetics and affordance of everyday tools. From the beginning of the ERP-induced waveform till late modulations positive interactions between affordance and attractiveness were repeatedly shown. Righi et al. (2014) concluded that the synergy of high affordance and high attractiveness facilitates the processing of everyday tools. A follow-up study focused on a possible influence of the aesthetics of everyday objects on different stages of cognitive processing (Righi, Gronchi, Pierguidi, Messina, & Viggiano, 2017). Therefore, Righi et al. (2017) compared highly aesthetic and less aesthetic everyday objects and their elicited patterns when presenting them in an oddball task. From early modulations to late components the patterns were distinguishable. It was concluded that aesthetics do influence cognitive processing: from perception up to the process of making a decision.

One device that is used daily by a growing percentage of the population is the smartphone. Ding, Guo, Hu, and Cao (2017) investigated whether the aesthetics of smartphones can be associated with early components of the mental chronometry. In an oddball task, images of landscapes acted as targets and images of smartphones as nontargets. The color, edges, and corners, as well as the size of the display varied over the pictured phones. Before the oddball task participants were presented with the smartphones and had to indicate the aesthetically preferred devices. The results showed that the latencies and the amplitudes of P200 were similar for high attractive and low attractive smartphones. However, for the N100 and the N200 in the frontal scalp regions the amplitude was greater for low attractive devices compared with high attractive smartphones. The first impression, as the authors concluded, is affected by the aesthetics of smartphones.

Conclusion

The cognitive electrophysiology of aesthetic appreciation forms a part of neuroaesthetics. In its correlational approach, it constructs "transformational relations between irreducibly and individually subjective mental processes and states, on the one hand, and their objectively, externally observed neural underpinnings on the other" (Jacobsen, 2010, p. 189). In so doing, it follows Fechner's tradition, even more in being an instantiation of inner psychophysics than merely providing "aesthetics from below" (Fechner, 1876, p. 1). The electrophysiological measures described here are used to inform us about the mental architecture of aesthetics.

Challenges, Goals, and Suggestions

With electrophysiological techniques, researchers have the possibilities to gain insight into the biological correlates of aesthetic processing and the corresponding temporal courses. EEG (including its derivates) is a very well established method in psychology and cognitive neuroscience. However, in the field of aesthetics, researchers still have many opportunities to discover new phenomena using these techniques. The first steps into the understanding of aesthetic processing have been made. Future research could, and maybe should, broaden the findings with the aim to have an elaborative understanding of aesthetics. As it stands, a systematic import of electrophysiology into empirical aesthetics has yet to be made.

References

Augustin, M. D., Wagemans, J., & Carbon, C. -C. (2012). All is beautiful? Generality vs. Specificity of word usage in visual aesthetics. *Acta Psychologica, 139*(1), 187–201. doi:10.1016/j.actpsy.2011.10.004

Berger, H. (1929). Über das Elektrenkephalogramm des Menschen. *Archiv für Psychiatrie und Nervenkrankheiten, 87*(1), 527–570. doi:10.1007/bf01797193

Beudt, S., & Jacobsen, T. (2015). On the role of mentalizing processes in aesthetic appreciation: An ERP study. *Frontiers in Human Neuroscience, 9*, 600. doi: 10.3389/fnhum.2015.00600

Brattico, E., Jacobsen, T., De Baene, W., Glerean, E., & Tervaniemi, M. (2010). Cognitive vs. affective listening modes and judgments of music—An ERP study. *Biological Psychology, 85*(3), 393–409. doi:10.1016/j.biopsycho.2010.08.014

Cacioppo, J. T., Crites, S. L., Berntson, G. G., & Coles, M. G. H. (1993). If attitudes affect how stimuli are processed, should they not affect the event-related brain potential? *Psychological Science, 4*(2), 108–112. doi:10.1111/j.1467-9280.1993.tb00470.x

Coch, D., Hart, T., & Mitra, P. (2008). Three kinds of rhymes: An ERP study. *Brain and Language, 104*(3), 230–243. doi:10.1016/j.bandl.2007.06.003

Cooksey, R. W. (1996). *Judgment analysis: Theory, methods, and applications.* San Diego, CA: Academic Press.

de Tommaso, M., Pecoraro, C., Sardaro, M., Serpino, C., Lancioni, G., & Livrea, P. (2008). Influence of aesthetic perception on visual event-related potentials. *Consciousness and Cognition: An International Journal, 17*(3), 933–945. doi:10.1016/j.concog.2007.09.003

Ding, Y., Guo, F., Hu, M., & Cao, Y. (2017). Using event related potentials to investigate visual aesthetic perception of product appearance. *Human Factors and Ergonomics in Manufacturing & Service Industries, 27*(5), 223–232. doi:10.1002/hfm.20704

Fechner, G. T. (1876). *Vorschule der Aesthetik [Experimental Aesthetics; "Pre-School" of Aesthetics].* Leipzig, Germany: Breitkopf & Härtel.

Gerger, G., Leder, H., & Kremer, A. (2014). Context effects on emotional and aesthetic evaluations of artworks and IAPS pictures. *Acta Psychologica, 151*, 174–183. doi:10.1016/j.actpsy.2014.06.008

Höfel, L., & Jacobsen, T. (2003). Temporal stability and consistency of aesthetic judgments of beauty of formal graphic patterns. *Perceptual and Motor Skills, 96*(1), 30–32. doi:10.2466/PMS.96.1.30-32

Höfel, L., & Jacobsen, T. (2007a). Electrophysiological indices of processing aesthetics: Spontaneous or intentional processes? *International Journal of Psychophysiology, 65*(1), 20–31. doi:10.1016/j.ijpsycho.2007.02.007

Höfel, L., & Jacobsen, T. (2007b). Electrophysiological indices of processing symmetry and aesthetics: A result of judgment categorization or judgment report? *Journal of Psychophysiology, 21*(1), 9–21. doi:10.1027/0269-8803.21.1.9

Istók, E., Brattico, E., Jacobsen, T., Krohn, K., Müller, M., & Tervaniemi, M. (2009). Aesthetic responses to music: A questionnaire study. *Musicae Scientiae, 13*(2), 183–206. doi:10.1177/1029864909013002O1

Istók, E., Brattico, E., Jacobsen, T., Ritter, A., & Tervaniemi, M. (2013). "I love rock 'n' roll"—music genre preference modulates brain responses to music. *Biological Psychology, 92*(2), 142–151. doi:10.1016/j.biopsycho.2012.11.005

Jacobsen, T. (2004). Individual and group modelling of aesthetic judgment strategies. *British Journal of Psychology, 95*(1), 41–56. doi:10.1348/000712604322779451

Jacobsen, T. (2006). Bridging the arts and sciences: A framework for the psychology of aesthetics. *Leonardo, 39*(2), 155–162. doi:10.1162/leon.2006.39.2.155

Jacobsen, T. (2010). Beauty and the brain: culture, history and individual differences in aesthetic appreciation. *Journal of Anatomy, 216*(2), 184–191. doi:10.1111/j.1469-7580.2009.01164.x

Jacobsen, T. (2013). On the electrophysiology of aesthetic processing. In S. Finger, D. W. Zaidel, F. Boller, & J. Bogousslavsky (Eds.), *Progress in Brain Research* (Vol. 204, pp. 159–168). Amsterdam: Elsevier.

Jacobsen, T., & Beudt, S. (2017). Stability and variability in aesthetic experience: A review. *Frontiers in Psychology, 8*, 143. doi:10.3389/fpsyg.2017.00143

Jacobsen, T., Buchta, K., Köhler, M., & Schröger, E. (2004). The primacy of beauty in judging the aesthetics of objects. *Psychological Reports, 94*(3, Pt. 2), 1253–1260. doi:10.2466/PR0.94.3.1253-1260

Jacobsen, T., & Höfel, L. (2000). Descriptive and evaluative judgment processes: an event-related potential analysis of processing symmetry and aesthetics. *Journal of Cognitive Neuroscience, 12*(Suppl.), 110.

Jacobsen, T., & Höfel, L. (2001). Aesthetics electrified: An analysis of descriptive symmetry and evaluative aesthetic judgment processes using event-related brain potentials. *Empirical Studies of the Arts, 19*(2), 177–190. doi:10.2190/P7W1-5F1F-NJK9-X05B

Jacobsen, T., & Höfel, L. (2002). Aesthetic judgments of novel graphic patterns: Analyses of individual judgments. *Perceptual and Motor Skills, 95*(3, Pt. 1), 755–766. doi:10.2466/PMS.95.7.755-766

Jacobsen, T., & Höfel, L. (2003). Descriptive and evaluative judgment processes: Behavioral and electrophysiological indices of processing symmetry and aesthetics. *Cognitive, Affective & Behavioral Neuroscience, 3*(4), 289–299. doi:10.3758/CABN.3.4.289

Jaśkiewicz, M., Francuz, P., Zabielska-Mendyk, E., Zapała, D., & Augustynowicz, P. (2016). Effects of harmonics on aesthetic judgments of music: An ERP study involving laypersons and experts. *Acta Neurobiologiae Experimentalis, 76*(2), 142–151.

Johnston, V. S., Miller, D. R., & Burleson, M. H. (1986). Multiple P3s to emotional stimuli and their theoretical significance. *Psychophysiology, 23*(6), 684–694.

Johnston, V. S., & Oliver-Rodriguez, J. C. (1997). Facial beauty and the late positive component of event-related potentials. *Journal of Sex Research, 34*(2), 188–198. doi:10.1080/00224499709551884

Khateb, A., Pegna, A. J., Landis, T., Michel, C. M., Brunet, D., Seghier, M. L., & Annoni, J.-M. (2007). Rhyme processing in the brain: An ERP mapping study. *International Journal of Psychophysiology, 63*(3), 240–250. doi:10.1016/j.ijpsycho.2006.11.001

Knoop, C. A., Wagner, V., Jacobsen, T., & Menninghaus, W. (2016). Mapping the aesthetic space of literature "from below." *Poetics, 56*, 35–49. doi:doi.org/10.1016/j.poetic.2016.02.001

Lengger, P. G., Fischmeister, F. P. S., Leder, H., & Bauer, H. (2007). Functional neuroanatomy of the perception of modern art: A DC-EEG study on the influence of stylistic information on aesthetic experience. *Brain Research, 1158*, 93–102. doi:10.1016/j.brainres.2007.05.001

Li, R., Qin, R., Zhang, J., Wu, J., & Zhou, C. (2015). The esthetic preference of Chinese typefaces—An event-related potential study. *Brain Research, 1598*, 57–65. doi:10.1016/j.brainres.2014.11.055

Luck, S. J. (2005). *An Introduction to the event-related potential technique.* Cambridge, MA: MIT Press.

Marzi, T., & Viggiano, M. P. (2010). When memory meets beauty: Insights from event-related potentials. *Biological Psychology, 84*(2), 192–205. doi:10.1016/j.biopsycho.2010.01.013

Morgan, L. K., & Kisley, M. A. (2014). The effects of facial attractiveness and perceiver's mate value on adaptive allocation of central processing resources. *Evolution and Human Behavior, 35*(2), 96–102. doi:10.1016/j.evolhumbehav.2013.11.002

Müller, M., Höfel, L., Brattico, E., & Jacobsen, T. (2010). Aesthetic judgments of music in experts and laypersons—An ERP study. *International Journal of Psychophysiology, 76*(1), 40–51. doi:10.1016/j.ijpsycho.2010.02.002

Noguchi, Y., & Murota, M. (2013). Temporal dynamics of neural activity in an integration of visual and contextual information in an esthetic preference task. *Neuropsychologia, 51*(6), 1077–1084. doi:10.1016/j.neuropsychologia.2013.03.003

Obermeier, C., Kotz, S. A., Jessen, S., Raettig, T., Koppenfels, M., & Menninghaus, W. (2016). Aesthetic appreciation of poetry correlates with ease of processing in event-related potentials. *Cognitive, Affective & Behavioral Neuroscience, 16*(2), 362–373. doi:10.3758/s13415-015-0396-x

Oliver-Rodríguez, J. C., Guan, Z., & Johnston, V. S. (1999). Gender differences in late positive components evoked by human faces. *Psychophysiology, 36*(2), 176–185. doi:10.1017/S0048577299971354

Pang, C. Y., Nadal, M., Müller-Paul, J. S., Rosenberg, R., & Klein, C. (2013). Electrophysiological correlates of looking at paintings and its association with art expertise. *Biological Psychology, 93*(1), 246–254. doi:10.1016/j.biopsycho.2012.10.013

Polich, J. (2007). Updating P300: An integrative theory of P3a and P3b. *Clinical Neurophysiology, 118*(10), 2128–2148. doi:10.1016/j.clinph.2007.04.019

Righi, S., Gronchi, G., Pierguidi, G., Messina, S., & Viggiano, M. P. (2017). Aesthetic shapes our perception of every-day objects: An ERP study. *New Ideas in Psychology, 47*, 103–112. doi:10.1016/j.newideapsych.2017.03.007

Righi, S., Orlando, V., & Marzi, T. (2014). Attractiveness and affordance shape tools neural coding: Insight from ERPs. *International Journal of Psychophysiology, 91*(3), 240–253. doi:10.1016/j.ijpsycho.2014.01.003

Roye, A., Höfel, L., & Jacobsen, T. (2008). Aesthetics of faces: Behavioral and electrophysiological indices of evaluative and descriptive judgment processes. *Journal of Psychophysiology, 22*(1), 41–57. doi:10.1027/0269-8803.22.1.41

Schacht, A., Werheid, K., & Sommer, W. (2008). The appraisal of facial beauty is rapid but not mandatory. *Cognitive, Affective & Behavioral Neuroscience, 8*(2), 132–142. doi:10.3758/CABN.8.2.132

Schmidt-Kassow, M., & Kotz, S. A. (2009). Event-related brain potentials suggest a late interaction of meter and syntax in the P600. *Journal of Cognitive Neuroscience, 21*(9), 1693–1708. doi:10.1162/jocn.2008.21153

Tschacher, W., Greenwood, S., Kirchberg, V., Wintzerith, S., van den Berg, K., & Tröndle, M. (2012). Physiological correlates of aesthetic perception of artworks in a museum. *Psychology of Aesthetics, Creativity, and the Arts, 6*(1), 96–103. doi:10.1037/a0023845

van Hooff, J. C., Crawford, H., & van Vugt, M. (2010). The wandering mind of men: ERP evidence for gender differences in attention bias towards attractive opposite sex faces. *Social Cognitive and Affective Neuroscience, 6*(4), 477–485. doi:10.1093/scan/nsq066

Wang, X., Huang, Y., Ma, Q., & Li, N. (2012). Event-related potential P2 correlates of implicit aesthetic experience. *NeuroReport: For Rapid Communication of Neuroscience Research, 23*(14), 862–866. doi:10.1097/WNR.0b013e3283587161

Werheid, K., Schacht, A., & Sommer, W. (2007). Facial attractiveness modulates early and late event-related brain potentials. *Biological Psychology, 76*(1–2), 100–108. doi:10.1016/j.biopsycho.2007.06.008

Zhang, Y., Kong, F., Chen, H., Jackson, T., Han, L., Meng, J., ... ul Hasan, A. N. (2011). Identifying cognitive preferences for attractive female faces: An event-related potential experiment using a study-test paradigm. *Journal of Neuroscience Research, 89*(11), 1887–1893. doi:10.1002/jnr.22724

Zhang, Y., Wei, B., Zhao, P., Zheng, M., & Zhang, L. (2016). Gender differences in memory processing of female facial attractiveness: Evidence from event-related potentials. *Neurocase, 22*(3), 317–323. doi:10.1080/13554794.2016.1151532

CHAPTER 15

FUNCTIONAL NEUROIMAGING IN EMPIRICAL AESTHETICS AND NEUROAESTHETICS

TOMOHIRO ISHIZU

INTRODUCTION

It has only been 15 years since neuroimaging techniques were first empirically used in the cognitive neuroscience of arts and aesthetics to study the relationships between the workings of the brain and our aesthetic experiences and artistic activities. The first of these functional neuroimaging studies were published in 2004 by three research groups (Cela-Conde et al., 2004; Kawabata & Zeki, 2004; Vartanian & Goel, 2004). In these studies, changes in the blood oxygenation level-dependent (BOLD) signals, or in the magnetic fields, were measured using functional magnetic resonance imaging (fMRI), or magnetoencephalography (MEG), while participants viewed visual artworks, including portraits, landscapes, still lifes, and abstract paintings, and rated them according to how much they experienced beauty (or aesthetic preferences). The results showed that declared intensity of the experience of beauty correlated with the strength of activity within the regions of the brain thought to be involved in the processing of reward and the experience of pleasure. These include the medial orbitofrontal cortex (mOFC), the ventromedial prefrontal cortex (vmPFC), the ventral anterior cingulate cortex (vACC), the anterior insula cortex, and the caudate nucleus.

Since then, several research papers have reported other brain regions generally related to perceiving, rating, or otherwise responding to art/nonart stimuli. Although perceiving art, much as any activity, involves almost all regions of the brain to some extent, a few recently published studies, mainly brain imaging studies (e.g., positron emission tomography (PET), functional/structural MRI, electro/magnetoencephalography (E/

MEG), near-infrared spectroscopy (NIRS)), theoretical reviews (e.g., Brattico & Pearce, 2013; Chatterjee, 2011; Chatterjee & Vartanian, 2014; Conway & Rehding, 2013; Cross & Ticini, 2012; Cinzia & Vittorio, 2009; Leder, 2013; Nadal & Pearce, 2011; Pearce et al., 2016; Pelowski, Markey, Forster, Gerger, & Leder, 2017; Zaidel, 2013), and meta-analysis studies of art viewing or aesthetic/beauty appraisals (e.g., Brown, Gao, Tisdelle, Eickhoff, & Liotti, 2011; Kuhn & Gallinat, 2012; Vartanian & Skov, 2014) have identified a handful of crucial regional activities and inter-regional connectivity (see subsequent sections).

Aesthetic experiences can be defined as psychological processes that occur during interactions between stimuli, such as visual artworks or musical pieces, and observers. These processes involve many aspects, such as perception and cognition, emotion, evaluation and judgment, and even social interactions (Chatterjee & Vartanian, 2014; Jacobsen, 2013; Pelowski et al., 2017). Aesthetic experiences are not limited to beauty. Therefore, this chapter includes brain responses engaged in other aesthetic experiences, such as those in which ugliness, sublimity, and negatively valenced aesthetic emotions. It should also be noted that these aesthetic experiences could be derived not only from the visual arts or music, but also from any other forms of stimuli including nature, landscapes, architectures, human figures, foods, or daily mundane activities. Some studies, nonetheless, have examined differences between artworks and their resemblances (nonart), and matched them for contents, to delineate the brain responses attributable to artistic status (see Lacey et al., 2011; Mizokami et al., 2014, for instance).

Neuroaesthetics

When it comes to art, some people may not be interested at all. Beauty, however, is different. While often discussed in the same context as art, beauty can be perceived anywhere and everywhere—in an ocean sunset, in a favorite painting, or in a loved one's face. The concept is not limited to appearance. One can speak of a person's "beautiful personality," or a "beautiful friendship" as well. Benevolence and justice may be two concepts treated as beautiful moral virtues, perhaps universally, across all cultures in the world. It is clear though, that our aesthetic sense is an undercurrent that runs through a diverse array of perceptions that are both concrete and figurative or abstract.

Neuroaesthetics is the scientific discipline for empirical and theoretical studies on the workings of the brain and our cognition in relation to aesthetic experiences and art (Zeki & Lamb, 1994). Researchers explore the brain's capacity to experience beauty and the neural mechanisms related to aesthetic appreciation, primarily through neuroimaging techniques. This subdomain of cognitive neuroscience is relatively new, but research institutions in several countries have already begun to emphasize cognitive neuroscience and psychological approaches to the study of aesthetic experience and art. Dedicated research chairs have been established at several major universities and research institutions in Europe and North America, including the University of London (University College London, City University, Goldsmiths University), the University of Vienna, University of the Balearic Islands, the Max Planck Institute for Empirical Aesthetics, the University of Pennsylvania, New York University, the University of California, Berkeley, and Massachusetts Institute of Technology to name a few. Additionally, the Psychology Department of Goldsmiths now offers a Master's program where students can officially study the field, which is anticipated to expand in the coming years.

The first attempt to study the relationship between perception, cognition, and the aesthetic experience can be traced back to the *experimental aesthetics* of Gustav Fechner in the late nineteenth century. Fechner sought to formally explain a diverse array of complex sensory experiences in terms of a single variable and uncover the elements that were common to all. For Fechner, however, the more important goal was to explain the association between the perception of beauty and *neural activity* that was presumed to govern one's responses to stimuli. In fact, this is a common goal for psychophysics and experimental aesthetics alike. Modern improvements and developments in non-invasive functional brain imaging and advances in cognitive neuroscience have strengthened neuroaesthetics' scientific rigor today, thereby allowing scientists to test and prove hypotheses on an empirical basis.

Before we delve into the literature, I would like for readers to take note of how aesthetic experience does and does not relate to the arts. Aesthetic experiences of the beautiful, ugly, or sublime can be triggered by a wide variety of subjects, not only by works of art. Nonetheless, the cognitive and perceptual processes that are involved in artistic appreciation and creation are not limited to aesthetic considerations. Despite the close association and multiple overlapping elements, we must be careful to distinguish these two concepts. We can broadly describe the scope and topics handled by neuroaesthetics according to the following categories: studies in cognitive neuroscience and evolutionary biology aiming to explain aesthetic experience and those exploring artistic cognition and creation (see more details in Pearce et al., 2016). The cognitive neuroscience research on beauty that is reviewed below falls primarily into the former category.

In the sections below, I will review neuroimaging studies on aesthetic experiences and evaluations in terms of the core brain regions (see also Figure 15.1).

Beauty in Sensory Perception

If someone asked you to give a few examples of things you find "beautiful," what would you respond? The adjective connotes different things for different people. You might regard a painting I find beautiful to be ugly, and vice versa. Beauty is a concept difficult to define, yet exceedingly familiar, and one that we all know well. If asked people to describe it, they might say it is something "pleasant," "good," or "of value," or perhaps "the opposite of ugliness." We all intuitively know and understand the sentiment and value of the judgments that beauty evokes. In essence, although you and I might perceive beauty in different things, our "inner psychological states" as we perceive it should

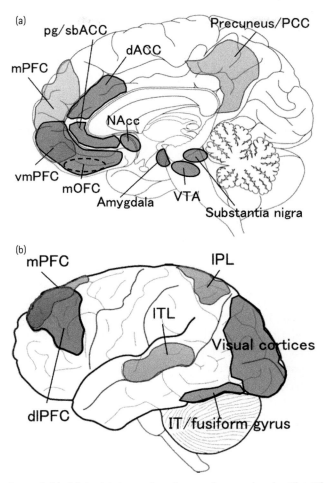

FIGURES 15.1. (a and b) Main brain regions/networks previously identified in aesthetic experiences and art appreciation researches; (upper) medial, (lower) lateral surface of the brain (abbreviations; dACC, dorsal anterior cingulate cortex; dlPFC, dorsolateral prefrontal cortex; IT, inferior temporal cortex; lPL, lateral parietal lobe; lTL, lateral temporal lobe; mOFC, medial orbitofrontal cortex; mPFC, medial prefrontal cortex; NAcc, nucleus accumbens; PCC, posterior cingulate cortex; pg/sbACC, pregenual/subgenual anterior cingulate cortex; vmPFC, ventro-medial prefrontal cortex;, VTA, ventral tegmental area). The mPFC, precuneus/PCC, lTL, and lPL form the DMN.

be somewhat similar. One of the first topics tackled by neuroaesthetics research was the question of which specific patterns of brain activity are associated with the common psychological state corresponding to an aesthetic experience, namely beauty, that can be elicited by different experiences for different people. This was the same question that motivated Fechner and his colleagues in empirical aesthetics to try to delineate the rules governing a wide variety of apparently loosely related aesthetic judgments.

Orbitofrontal Cortex (OFC)

How should we go about investigating how brain activity relates with aesthetic experience? Experiments using fMRI, which has been dominantly used in this field, generally use a method called *functional brain mapping* to identify brain regions that are intensely activated in response to specific sensory stimuli or during different mental states. In neuroaesthetics, the "state" of interest is the subjective experience of beauty (or ugliness). A typical research design would present subjects with an array of similar stimuli. If paintings are used, for example, they should be as uniform as possible in terms of their theme, brightness, composition, and other visual properties. Subjects are then asked to rate the subjective strength of the experience of beauty or ugliness for each painting, e.g., by Likert scale, while their neural activity is recorded. One way to detect correlations between brain responses and experimental variables/parameters is to statistically assess the difference between the averaged patterns of the BOLD signal of two experimental conditions (i.e., to "contrast" the two conditions against each other). A reliably detected difference is then assumed to relate to differential brain processing under the two conditions. Therefore, in theory, contrasting the activation patterns that characterize "beautiful" and "ugly" ratings on fMRI data should yield the so-called *neural correlate* of aesthetic experience. Studies employing figurative artworks, such as portraits and landscape paintings, have begun to shed light on the specific brain regions activated during the subjective experience of beauty. One of the core regions is the *medial orbitofrontal cortex* (mOFC), located in the base of frontal lobes just above the brow. Over a decade of research and repeated experiments and replications have confirmed the close relationship between the experience of beauty and the activity within the mOFC using a wide range of visual stimuli, including not only figurative paintings, but also abstract paintings, photos, statues, natural scenes, buildings, and faces, as well as more abstract stimuli such as the movement of dots and color combinations, morality, and even mathematics (Di Dio, Macaluso, & Rizzolatti, 2007; Ikeda, Matsuyoshi, Sawamoto, Fukuyama, & Osaka, 2015; Ishizu & Zeki, 2017; Kawabata & Zeki, 2004; Tsukiura & Cabeza, 2011; Vartanian et al., 2013; Zeki, Romaya, Benincasa, & Atiyah, 2014; Zeki & Stutters, 2012). The activity correlates parametrically with the strength of the declared experience of beauty given by a participant. Moreover, a recent study has reported an increase in aesthetic ratings of visual stimuli (Nakamura & Kawabata, 2015) following the application of anodal transcranial direct current stimulation (tDCS) to the cortical area including medial orbital cortex, presumably because of enhanced neural activity within it. Exploring the workings of the brain has linked diverse experiences of the beautiful—an ineffable, subjective, and extremely personal judgment—to the specific, objective commonality of enhanced activity in the mOFC.

At this point, one might argue that beauty as experienced in visual arts such as that evoked by a painting *feels* completely different from the "auditory beauty" perceived from musical pieces. However, research has shown that the brain responds similarly to both musical and visual beauty (Brown et al., 2011 for meta-analysis; Ishizu & Zeki, 2011). The revelation that these two forms of beauty activate the same area of the brain, despite music and the visual arts involving different sensory modalities, is a finding of great interest. Activity in the mOFC seems to function as a "common currency" in psychological appraisals of beauty, independent of the source (Pegors, Kable, Chatterjee, & Epstein, 2015). This common neurological basis for aesthetic judgments may allow us to compare or equate all manner of aesthetic experiences derived from different sources.

Such experiments cannot, of course, answer the question of what kinds of stimulus properties evoke beauty. Nevertheless, it seems undeniable that a specific, localized brain region(s) is involved in the experience of beauty, independent not only of stimulus features, but also of the type of media (visual, auditory, etc.) conveying the information.

Ventromedial Prefrontal Cortex (vmPFC)

Like the mOFC, the *ventromedial prefrontal cortex (vmPFC)* also plays a role in aesthetic experience and evaluation. This region is known as a part of brain's reward system engaged in reward seeking or response. The junction between the vmPFC and mOFC is especially argued to be a supramodal center for ongoing self-relevance detection, acting independently of stimulus type or valence (Northoff et al., 2006; Pelowski et al., 2017 for review; Schmitz & Johnson, 2007). These ventral regions are then further connected to the subcortical amygdala and insula, which may be activated in anticipation of further processing important stimuli or in identifying affective aspects (i.e., threat or relevance). The vmPFC, as well as the medial temporal lobe (MTL) and posterior cingulate cortex (PCC), also makes use of stored representations of former experiences in order to attribute meaning to affective input, which guides emotion categorization (Lindquist, Wager, Kober, Bliss-Moreau, & Barrett, 2012). Note that in practice, the specific distinction between the mOFC and the vmPFC is not always clear. While researchers may interpret their findings to be tied more to one area or the other, due to the spatial resolution of fMRI as well as the actual coordinates reported in several studies, it might be best to have unified and systematic labeling criteria for anatomical locations in the research community.

Inconsistent use of Anatomical Labels

The mOFC is a large expanse of cortex that has several architectonic areas (including Brodmann areas 10, 11, 12, 32, and 25). There seems to be inconsistent use of anatomical labels for the structures in the ventral frontal area, including the mOFC, the vmPFC, as well as the subgenual anterior cingulate cortex (ACC) (although this inconsistent use of the anatomical labels can be seen not only in neuroaesthetics studies but also in cognitive neuroscience in general, for example, in decision making and pleasure research). For example, Vartanian and Goel (2004) refer to their site of activation as being in the subgenual ACC although their locus of activation, at −10 42 −6 in the Montreal Neurological Institute (MNI) coordinates, is close to the locus of the mOFC in the study of Kawabata and Zeki (2004), that of Kirk, Skov, Hulme, Christensen, and Zeki (2009) and Ishizu and Zeki (2011, 2013, 2017). Similarly, Tsukiura and Cabeza (2011) attribute their locus of activation in response to facial attractiveness and moral goodness to the ACC but the site of activation, at −4 44 1, is again close to the one reported in the above studies labeling the region as the mOFC. On the other hand, Kawabata and Zeki (2004) and Ishizu and Zeki (2011) refer to their activation site as the mOFC at −3 41 −8; however, the activation expands to the more dorsal portion, which includes the vmPFC. The site reported by Kranz and Ishai (2006), Cloutier, Heatherton, Whalen, and Kelley (2008) and O'Doherty et al. (2003) for facial attractiveness is labeled as the OFC, but again, their activation also appears to expand to the vmPFC or subgenual ACC. This may cause confusion in interpretation of fMRI data. This could be solved by using a unified and systematic anatomical labeling system or by clearly reporting MNI coordinates of peak voxels, cluster sizes, and smoothing levels in spatial pre-processing, in addition to statistical methods.

Ventral Striatum and Nucleus Accumbens (NAcc)

Another key brain structure for aesthetic experience/judgment is the ventral striatum of the basal ganglia. The ventral striatum, notably the nucleus accumbens (NAcc), shows specific activation when rating something particularly beautiful, attractive, or pleasing (especially with music and poetry, e.g., Bohrn, Altmann, Lubrich, Menninghaus, & Jacobs, 2013; Salimpoor et al., 2013; Wassiliwizky, Koelsch, Wagner, Jacobsen, & Menninghaus, 2017). This region is again related to reward processing, together with the mOFC/vmPFC, and is considered a key node of the reward circuit (Heekeren et al., 2007; O'Doherty, 2004; Yacubian et al., 2007), along with the interconnected medial prefrontal and orbitofrontal areas, the amygdala, and dopaminergic midbrain nuclei (O'Doherty, 2004). However, the strongest activation in this area is found during reward anticipation rather than attainment (e.g., Knutson & Greer, 2008; O'Doherty, Deichmann, Critchley, & Dolan, 2002; Zatorre & Salimpoor, 2013), and thus may play an important role when individuals are interacting with a temporal medium—e.g., with a forthcoming rewarding element, a crescendo in music (Brown, Martinez, & Parsons, 2004; Koelsch, Fritz, v. Cramon, Müller, & Friederici, 2006), or poetry (Wassiliwizky et al., 2017), and is also connected to experiencing musical chills.

Both the NAcc and the OFC comprise the brain's reward circuitry, however, they may have different functions. A study by Kirk et al. (2009) used architecture pictures with expert architects and non-experts aesthetically evaluating them while being scanned with fMRI. They found that both the NAcc and the OFC were activated. They also found that only some regions associated with the processing of reward are modulated by expertise, namely, the OFC and ventral ACC, whereas, activity in the NAcc was observed in both expert and non-expert subject groups, suggesting that these regions play different roles in reward processing of aesthetic value (Kirk et al., 2009).

Similarly, a more recent fMRI study by Wang et al. (2015) also found differential profiles in the ventral basal ganglia and the OFC. They compared qualitatively different types of beauty judgments—facial beauty (physical attractiveness) and moral beauty (abstract and higher-order beauty)—to learn what brain mechanisms are activated during the evaluation of each type. The result showed that both types of beauty judgments commonly engaged the mOFC, which is consistent with the previous neuroaesthetics research; however, relative to moral beauty, only facial beauty judgment engaged the ventral striatum in addition to the mOFC (Wang et al., 2015). Brown et al. proposed in their meta-analysis that the OFC processes exteroceptive information through the ventral sensory pathways and computes a stimulus's valence working together with the anterior insula, which is another emotional portion of the brain, whereas, the ventral basal ganglia including ventral striatum works as a "hedonic hotspot" responding to rewarding stimuli (Brown et al., 2011).

Although a considerable number of papers have reported the engagement of the mOFC/vmPFC in aesthetic experiences, specifically the experience of beauty, functional neuroimaging studies using visual stimuli (both artworks or nonart objects) to investigate beauty have not yet yielded a consistent picture in terms of core brain regions across studies. Problems in comparing these studies include different stimuli (e.g., real artworks vs no-nart stimuli, facial vs other objects, etc.), participant populations, and different tasks (e.g., participants were asked about "attractiveness" in some studies but asked about "beauty" in other studies, etc.). Thus, future studies need more systematic approaches using standardized stimuli, tasks, instructions, and anatomical labeling to allow researchers a means to reliably compare results across studies.

AESTHETIC EXPERIENCES IN MUSIC AND BRAIN RESPONSES

Emotions induced from listening to music are thought to be multi-dimensional. For example, "beautiful" musical pieces can range from bright and cheerful orchestral pieces, to sorrowful but beautiful violin concerts, and to chill-inducing jazz performances, etc. Musical beauty engages not only the mOFC/vmPFC but other reward-related regions, such as the NAcc and insula cortex. Trost, Ethofer, Zentner, and Vuilleumier

(2012) mapped brain activities that correlated with each of the emotional dimensions measured by the Geneva Musical Emotion Scale with nine emotion scales. The results showed that activities within the mOFC and right NAcc correlated to the dimensions of "melancholy" and "tenderness," whereas the right ventral striatum and right insula activities correlated more to "joy" and "wonder" (Trost, Ethofer, Zentner, & Vuilleumier, 2012). These correlations between musical emotions and brain activities within various regions may reflect the variety and richness of emotions we derive from music.

Although there have been several neuroimaging reports of the mOFC's involvement in the perception of musical beauty (e.g., Brown et al., 2011; Ishizu & Zeki, 2011), it should be noted that this result is not as consistent as the results from the visual aesthetic studies. Activity within the NAcc, especially, has been more routinely reported in music studies (e.g., Zatorre & Salimpoor, 2013 for a review). For example, since the late 1990s, before visual neuroaesthetics studies became popular, a research group of Zatorre conducted a series of studies using PET and fMRI and found a correlation between preference rating in music and activation in the ventral striatum, including the NAcc (e.g., Blood & Zatorre, 2001). So far, there is no convincing explanation of the dissociation between the NAcc and the mOFC/vmPFC region. However, one can speculate that this might be due to (1) the differences in neurotransmitter profiles, e.g., the mOFC is a dopaminergic-dominant system, whereas the ventral striatum works with GABA, glutamate, in addition to dopamine, and the cortico-striatal-thalamic-cortical (CSTC) loop also plays an important role in its activity (Stahl, 2008); or (2) the difference in information processing in the two modalities, e.g., the evolving and therefore dynamic and transient nature of the musical stimuli as opposed to the set and static nature of the visual stimuli. This difference is interesting and worth pursuing in future studies in order to better understand the differences between the nature of musical and visual aesthetics. Cognitive neuroscience and empirical aesthetics studies on music and audition can be found in detail in Chapter 27.

NEGATIVELY VALENCED AESTHETIC EXPERIENCES

It is interesting to briefly discuss the brain responses to pleasure evoked by listening to sad music, which is regarded as being a positive aesthetic experience with a negatively charged emotional valence (Schubert, 1996). Such a contradictory experience can be seen in many forms of art, including painting and film (e.g., Hanich, Wagner, Shah, Jacobsen, & Menninghaus, 2014; Leder, Gerger, Brieber, & Schwarz, 2014), but is most notable and relatively well studied in the music domain. Among previous behavioral and neuroimaging studies on sad music (e.g., Kawakami, Furukawa, Katahira, & Okanoya, 2013; Suzuki et al., 2008; Taruffi and Koelsch, 2014), a recent one (Sachs, Damasio, & Habibi, 2015) has argued that sad music is found pleasurable when (1) it is perceived as non-life-threatening (not a "real" threat) and with no immediate real-life implication; (2) it is aesthetically pleasing; and (3) it has certain psychological benefits, such as mood regulation caused by recollection of personal past events.

It is also interesting in the study by Trost, Ethofer, Zentner, and Vuilleumier (2012) that the brain's reward system, namely, the mOFC and the NAcc, were stimulated with the perception of melancholy, which involves delicate sadness (negatively valenced emotion). The activity within the reward regions might have something to do with our enjoyment while listening to "heart-wrenching" sad music. Why we enjoy sad music or tragedies invoking negative emotions has been an age-old question in the humanities.

Recently in neuroaesthetics, there has been intense theoretical and empirical interest in understanding the nature of the aesthetic experiences derived from negatively charged emotions (Ishizu & Zeki, 2014; Pelowski et al., 2018). For example, a recent fMRI study, researching brain networks during enjoyment of emotionally negatively and positively valenced artistic photographs, found that the positive and negative photographic stimuli that were experienced as aesthetically preferable *both* coincided with higher activation in brain reward areas. More importantly, with the negatively valenced but aesthetically pleasing photographs alone, this higher activity in the reward areas was modulated by areas dedicated to empathy such as the supplementary motor area/mid cingulate cortex (Ishizu & Zeki, 2017). In another study, Menninghaus et al. (2017) provided a conceptual framework for considering the paradox of enjoying negative emotions with music and arts by proposing two interrelated processes, "distancing" and "embracing" (Menninghaus et al., 2017). The model suggests that an individual can undergo an engagement with a certain pre-state actualizing activation of a schema. It sets the stage for two sequential and intertwined processes consisting of the "distancing factor," which invokes existential safety and "control" over the situation, and "any involved (negative) emotion." This can then be followed by the process of "embracing," which presumably is the main component of interest, pleasure, and intellectually or hedonically enjoying art—and would presumably coincide with the main aspects of "mastery" or "savoring" in most discussions of art experience (e.g., Gerger, Ishizu, & Pelowski, 2017; Pelowski et al., 2017). Especially negative emotions are argued to be enjoyed if and only if at least one component of distancing in concert with one component of embracing are activated. This points to possible interesting future studies of how the brain reacts to the experience of sadness evoked by different sources.

Beauty and Pleasure

There is apparently a strong relationship between beauty and pleasure/reward. Since we have a pleasurable experience while we experience something as beautiful in most case, it seems that beauty and pleasure/reward are almost inseparable. As I summarized above regarding the brain responses to the experience of beauty, the experience of it generally engages brain sites that are also engaged in pleasure and reward including the mOFC, the vmPFC, and the ventral striatum, namely NAcc. That experiencing beauty activates the brain's reward system means that beauty itself includes reward values. This raises questions as to whether or not beauty itself is actually a reward. For example, let us say that there is a brain state "A" in which a person experiences beauty derived from looking at a masterpiece of art or listening to a piece of music. If the brain state "A" is the same as a brain state "B" in which the person experiences pleasure derived from something other than beauty, e.g., eating a delicious hamburger when hungry or getting high when taking a drug, then the finding of the association between the experience of beauty and the accompanied brain state "A" would not have any importance. This is because, if beauty is a reward, one cannot tell whether the brain state "A" is due to the experience of beauty or simply due to that of pleasure. Although it is difficult to distinguish beauty from pleasure, we must further discuss the relationship between the two. First of all, a question such as "Can beauty be equated with pleasure?" may not be a good place to start, because pleasure is apparently not necessarily beautiful. For example, food, sex, and drugs, which all provide a pleasurable experience, are not necessarily experienced as beautiful. In this sense, what should be asked first is whether there are any differences between "pleasure without the experience of beauty" and "pleasure derived from beauty," and whether or not the two can be distinguished in neural terms. There have been few empirical approaches to this question so far in neuroaesthetics.

One research group led by Sescousse, Redouté, and Dreher reported that the mOFC has functional subdivisions (Sescousse, Redouté, & Dreher, 2010). They examined activation patterns in the mOFC by contrasting when participants got monetary rewards and when they got sexually arousal rewards. They found that the medial and posterior portion of the OFC responded more to the sexual arousal reward and the lateral and anterior portion responded more to monetary reward. This means that the OFC may have functional subdivisions that possibly process different kinds of rewards.

It is also worth noting the functional differences among the reward centers, especially, between the mOFC and the ventral striatum, which has been found to be active in many examples of neuroaesthetics research. Both regions have been known to commonly respond to the primary and secondary reward, e.g., food and money (e.g., Sescousse, Caldú, Segura, & Dreher, 2013). However, past neuroimaging studies have suggested that some types of intrinsic reward may stimulate the two regions differently. Unlike the primary and secondary rewards, the intrinsic reward is not necessarily tied to physiological pleasure. For example, Moll and colleagues reported that altruistic behaviors such as charitable donation, which fall into the intrinsic reward category, activated the mOFC stronger than the ventral striatum (Moll et al., 2006). Another study on the experience of mathematical beauty, which is also an intellectual and intrinsic pleasure for mathematicians, found activation within the mOFC but not the ventral striatum (Zeki et al., 2014). On the contrary, "pure hedonic" experiences derived from physiological pleasure, such as food, water, mating, etc., is thought to stimulate the structures of the ventral striatum, in addition to the mOFC. Collectively, it might be hypothesized that the intrinsic rewards are probably processed predominantly in the mOFC rather than the ventral striatum, whereas pure hedonic pleasure can similarly activate both regions.

This framework may be applicable to the categorization of the experience of beauty and the question of beauty and pleasure. The experience of beauty could be categorized into two different types: one is to be derived from stimuli that can provide pure hedonic, physiological pleasure ("hedonic-based beauty"), and another is derived from stimuli that can lead to intrinsic, non-physiological pleasure ("high-order beauty"). For example, the former could be facial beauty or physical/bodily attractiveness that could be tied/lead to mating and romantic relationships, and the latter could be found in altruistic acts, such as moral beauty and self-sacrificing behaviors. The hedonic-based beauty may mobilize both the ventral striatum and the mOFC, whereas the high-order beauty may stimulate the mOFC more dominantly. A recent study has shown that evaluating physical attractiveness (facial beauty) activates both the mOFC and the basal ganglia including ventral striatum, but evaluating moral goodness (moral beauty) activates the mOFC alone (Wang et al., 2015). The discussion of separating beauty into two different kinds according to two different reward circuitries is hypothetical and currently not empirically tested; however, it is useful when we revisit and study the age-old question of the relationship between beauty and pleasure.

Although there have been no empirical neuroimaging studies, recently this topic has been gaining lots of scientific attention (e.g., Christensen, 2017; Nadal & Skov, 2018). Future studies, including neuroimaging, psychopharmacology, and comparative psychology approaches, may reveal whether or not beauty and pleasure engage different neural systems or if they engage a single common one.

DORSOLATERAL PREFRONTAL CORTEX (DLPFC)

Another key area is the dorsolateral prefrontal cortex (dlPFC). Recent neuroimaging studies, including brain stimulation experiments on beauty and aesthetic pleasantness have emphasized dlPFC involvement (Ticini, 2017). This cortical area, especially in the left hemisphere, has been found to be active while making aesthetic judgments (Cela-Conde et al., 2004; Nadal, Munar, Capo, Rossello, & Cela-Conde, 2008). Activity has also been found in both the reward and aversive conditions (Plassmann, O'Doherty, & Rangel, 2010). Studies with the use of brain stimulation, such as tDCS and transcranial magnetic stimulation (TMS), have also shown a possible causal relationship between the activity or disruption within the cortical zone and positive assessments (Cattaneo et al., 2014a, 2014b). A recent review by Ticini argues that "activity in the left DLPFC is triggered when participants are asked to express their preference" such as by pressing a button during or after a stimulus presentation (Ticini, 2017). A primate study demonstrated that there is a difference in the time course of the activation of the OFC and the dlPFC (Wallis & Miller, 2003), reporting that a peak selectivity associated with reward information appeared earlier in the OFC than in the dlPFC. The finding indicates that there is a direction of the reward information processing, which would enter the prefrontal cortex via the OFC area to be subsequently forwarded to the dlPFC in order to guide the forthcoming behavioral response (inputs to OFC might be from sensory pathways and subcortical dopaminergic areas, e.g., the ventral tegmental area or the NAcc). Collectively, this may indicate that "the left dlPFC is engaged in a subset of delayed computations used to control behaviour" and "that its activity is influenced by reward and other affective information passed on by the OFC" (Ticini, 2017, p. 3).

Previous studies have also implicated dlPFC involvement in cognitive and aesthetic judgments, with even more pronounced activity during the latter (Ishizu & Zeki, 2013; Sanfey, Rilling, Aronson, Nystrom, & Cohen, 2003). This region may especially relate to analytical assessments, which in some cases may overlap with inhibition or self-censorship (Pelowski et al., 2017). For example, Ellamil, Dobson, Beeman, and Christoff (2012), who compared generative and evaluative modes in creative drawing, found that when designers were explicitly evaluating their produced designs for quality, rather than coming up with aesthetic ideas, they had higher activation in the dlPFC and dorsal ACC (Ellamil, Dobson, Beeman, & Christoff, 2012). Meta-analyses have also shown strong connectivity between the lateral OFC (Zald et al., 2014) and the dlPFC. The dlPFC has also been found to be a major source of regulation for the mesolimbic dopamine pathway involving reward-related regions (NAcc, mOFC) (Spee et al., 2018), with the former acting as an identifier of stimuli or tasks that might be potentially rewarding. Thus, it regulates reward-seeking activity (Ballard et al., 2011). However, the relation of these findings to the above is still in question—potentially involving a more analytic mindset that lowers focus on one's feelings.

ANTERIOR CINGULATE CORTEX (ACC)

Activation within the ACC, especially the pregenual subdivision (pgACC), including the adjacent subgenual part (sbACC), has been found during the experience of aesthetically pleasing stimuli (Kawabata & Zeki, 2004; Vartanian et al., 2013; Vartanian & Goel, 2004). The ACC's diverse cognitive and emotional functions make it difficult to define each subdivision's involvement in a precise function. However, previous studies have suggested that the ventral and sub/pregenual areas are involved in the processing of emotion, especially that pgACC activity may correlate with the experience of positive emotions (see Etkin, Egner, & Kalisch, 2011 for a review). The pgACC has also been connected to the above-discussed mOFC/vmPFC network tied to identification of self-relevance (Northoff et al., 2006; Schmitz & Johnson, 2007). Thus, this region may be more active when, for example, a stimulus does have a more important connection because of one's background or past (cultural) experience (see Pelowski et al., 2017). This region may also be involved in the general assessment of task difficulty, allocation of additional resources, and effortful regulation. It may also be involved in specifically identifying discrepancy or "cognitive dissonance" and thus a need for more involved processing or resolution exists (Izuma et al., 2010; Jarcho, Berkman, & Lieberman, 2011; Schmitz & Johnson, 2007).

The dorsal subdivision (dACC), by contrast, is strongly associated with negative emotional states as well as cognitive components, as evident in a recent fMRI study demonstrating the dACC's involvement in emotionally negatively valenced beauty (Ishizu & Zeki, 2017). This region is also active during the experience of physical pain as well as social pain and social anxiety, which may be a key target for cultural studies (Eisenberger & Lieberman, 2004; Lamm et al., 2011 for a review). The dorsorostral and supragenual ACC and the dorsal part of the MPFC (notably the dorsomedial PFC) may show connection to posterior areas—PCC, retrosplenial cortex (RSC), medial parietal cortex (MPC)—and may be a second top-down sub-system related to introspective processes (self-reflection, evaluation) (Northoff et al., 2006; see Pelowski et al., 2017 for review; Schmitz & Johnson, 2007).

Insula Cortex

The insula is a cerebral cortex folded within the lateral sulcus. It has two major subdivisions: the anterior and posterior insula. This cortex is thought to be involved in various functions, including multimodal sensory integration, interoceptive perception, motor control, and emotional processing. The anterior insula, particularly, is of interest in aesthetic experiences in sculpture and body. For example, previous fMRI studies have reported that the anterior insula, especially in the right hemisphere, is engaged when viewing and aesthetically rating sculptures (e.g., Di Dio et al., 2007). Using fMRI, Di Dio et al. (2007) investigated brain responses when viewing and rating sculptures that had been manipulated in their foot-to-navel/navel-to-head proportions. They found increased neural responses in the anterior insula with the original proportions compared with the manipulated ones. In another study, they examined brain responses when viewing and rating sculptures versus real body counterparts posing in the same way (photographs of humans) (Di Dio, Canessa, Cappa, & Rizzolatti, 2011). The results showed again that, although the two conditions produced a similar global activation pattern, the activation within the anterior insula was found during sculpture viewing alone.

Later, this region emerges as one of the candidates of the supramodal area, with positive aesthetic experience in a meta-analysis paper (Brown et al., 2011). Considering the notion that the insula is a "hub" for integrating sensory information, especially in affective stimuli, the result sounds plausible. However, it should be noted that in the meta-analysis by Brown et al., they collected data for the activation likelihood estimation (ALE) analysis from 93 previously published papers in total, but the data set, especially for gustatory and olfactory modalities, includes studies that did not investigate aesthetic experiences and evaluation at all, but rather, preferences for food (chocolate, wine, glucose, etc.), water, or sexually arousing pictures. For example, in the gustatory modality, they used data from 16 papers but 8 of them were about preference for food or water (see their supplementary materials). As the insula is engaged in emotional valence and arousal, it is not surprising then, that the area survives with the ALE analysis.

SENSORY AND MOTOR CORTICES

The visual cortex has also shown specific patterns of activation. Previous fMRI studies have showed that activity within the visual areas (specifically V5 and fusiform face area (FFA)), is parametrically related to the declared intensity of aesthetic liking for kinetic visual stimuli (Zeki & Stutters, 2012) and facial stimuli (Chatterjee, Thomas, Smith, & Aguirre, 2009), though apparently V4 activity does not have such a relationship with beautiful chromatic stimuli (Ikeda et al., 2015). When participants rate a stimulus as aesthetically pleasing, there is also evidence for greater functional connectivity between the mOFC and the visual areas (FFA for facial stimuli and parahippocampus (PPA) for scenery; Kawabata & Zeki, 2004). An application of TMS to disrupt activity within the extrastriate body area (EBA), a region in the occipito-temporal cortex engaged in the processing of body information, during aesthetic judgment on body images decreased beauty rating selectively on the body stimuli (Calvo-Merino, Urgesi, Orgs, Aglioti, & Haggard, 2010). Another study using TMS (Cattaneo et al., 2015) to interfere with activity in the lateral occipital region during the viewing of abstract and representational paintings selectively reduced evaluation of representational paintings, although this did not impact abstract artworks or overall assessments of clearness, suggesting its role in object recognition.

Regarding body or motor reactions, Umilta, Berchio, Sestito, Freedberg, and Gallese (2012) have also shown activation in premotor areas when viewing paintings with salient evidence of artist actions. When observing static images of abstract paintings by Lucio Fontana consisting of cuts in canvas, versus computer-generated line patterns reproducing the same basic visual patterns, *mu* rhythm suppression located over the bilateral motor regions was observed, indicating activation within the regions. They argue that this supports an argument for a mirror neuron system or automatic mirroring of human actions or human bodies, when individuals engage in interactions with what they perceive to be human-derived artifacts.

Collectively, these results thus indicate that activity that is parametrically modulated with subjective, affective experiences is not restricted to "higher" cortical areas, such as the dlPFC or the mOFC/vmPFC, but may also involve visual sensory areas, possibly by feedback from other centers. Since neuroaesthetics studies on performing arts, including motor execution, observation, and evaluation in dance and ballet, are discussed in chapters by Brattico (this volume), Cross and Orlandi (this volume), and Merino (this volume), I will not go into further details in this chapter.

Default Mode Network (DMN)

Recent studies have also suggested the role of the DMN—including the mPFC, the PCC/praecuneus, the lateral temporal cortex, the superior frontal gyrus, and the temporo-parietal junction—may play a role in aesthetic appreciation (e.g., Chatterjee & Vartanian, 2016; Vessel, Starr, & Rubin, 2012). The network is specially activated during conditions of low cognitive control, absence of external stimuli, or introspection, whereas its activity should be decreased during cognitive tasks demanding attention (e.g., Raichle et al., 2001). However, recent fMRI studies have revealed that it showed heightened activation only in response to paintings found to be particular moving (using the high end of a Likert-type scale) (Belfi et al., 2019; Vessel, Starr, & Rubin, 2012). Among these regions, in particular the mPFC (tied to focus on self-reference and self-importance) and the PCC (potentially tied to recalling or savoring affective experience) (e.g., see Pelowski et al., 2017) may show a particular tie to deep appreciation. The activity in the DMN has also been suggested to facilitate an associative mode of processing that supports the generation of novel ideas (e.g., Limb & Braun, 2008; Mayseless, Eran, & Shamay-Tsoory, 2015). The importance of the network in aesthetic judgment has also been proposed in a MEG study by Cela-Conde et al. (2013). They suggested that detailed cognitive processes could be performed in a late latency, within the 1000–1500 ms after stimulus onset, following an initial aesthetic perception being formed in an earlier stage (250–750 ms), and this delayed process may engage the DMN (Cela-Conde et al., 2013). It could be interesting to apply effective connectivity analyses, which enable us to investigate directional influences of one neuronal system on another, such as Dynamic Causal Modeling, Granger causality mapping, and structural equation modeling (e.g., Friston, Harrison, & Penny, 2003; Goebel, Roebroeck, Kim, & Formisano, 2003; McIntosh & Gonzalez-Lima, 1994).

Amygdala and Motor Cortex with Ugliness

It should be useful to mention ugliness, which is often paired and contrasted with beauty in the general as well as the artistic mind. It is known that specific brain regions, namely the amygdala and the motor cortex (e.g., Di Dio et al., 2007; Ishizu & Zeki, 2011), are engaged when one experiences ugliness. Specifically, the activation of the motor cortex is of particular interest and is not observed in other aesthetic experiences (except for studies using dance or stimuli implying movements; e.g., Calvo-Merino, Jola, Glaser, & Haggard, 2008). Past studies suggest that perception of negatively emotionally charged stimuli, such as fearful stimuli, may mobilize the motor system in preparation for taking an action to avoid the fearful or aversive stimulus in a kind of defensive system (e.g.,

Armony & Dolan, 2002). Such a defensive reaction may occur instantly and automatically (reflexively) in the early processing stage. Specifically, a MEG study has shown
that there are stronger responses to ugly stimuli than to beautiful stimuli in an early
MEG component (Munar et al., 2012). Behavioral studies also suggest that reactions
occur faster to unpleasant stimuli related to survival or health than to pleasant ones
(Boesveldt, Frasnelli, Gordon, & Lundström, 2010). The reflex reaction associated with
motor preparation implies that our body reacts to ugly objects as if they are (becoming)
real threats.

Like other aesthetic experiences valenced with negative emotions, such as sublimity
or grotesqueness (e.g., Ishizu & Zeki, 2014), it is apparent that artworks featuring ugliness can achieve aesthetic value (Kayser, 1957). However, to enjoy abjection as art, the
"psychological distance" becomes more important than the appreciation of positive
art, as it is necessary to secure the personal safety of the viewer, which would then indicate that the negative emotions are non-threatening in real life (Sachs, Damasio, &
Habibi, 2015). Therefore, to appreciate ugliness as an aesthetic value, it is necessary that
(1) one suppresses physiological reactions that are associated with the rejection of the
ugly stimulus, and (2) the evaluative recurrent process in the later stage (as described in
the Vienna Integrated Model of top-down and bottom-up processes in Art Perception
(VIMAP) model; Pelowski et al., 2017) becomes active to override the initial automatic physiological reaction to the object (Ishizu & Sakamoto, 2017). Actual cognitive
processes and workings of the brain in relation to aesthetic appreciation of ugliness are
yet to be studied. However, it must be one of the important research questions in future
studies.

Interestingly, a MEG study reported that activity in the right lateral orbitofrontal
cortex (lOFC) was greater while participants rated visual stimuli as not beautiful than
when they rated them as beautiful in a relatively early latency between 300 and 400
ms after stimulus onset (Munar et al., 2012). However, there is still an argument as to
whether "not beautiful" images can be regarded as the same as "ugly" images, the result
of which might suggest a functional dissociation between the medial and lateral portion
of the OFC according to the stimulus's aesthetic values.

Cross-Cultural Aspects in
Neuroaesthetics

The neuroimaging studies summarized above normally use artworks and music from
Western cultures as experimental stimuli. However, other studies have examined
brain responses evoked by non-Western artworks. For example, Osaka and colleagues
conducted a neuroimaging study on aesthetic appreciation by using traditional
Japanese paintings (Osaka, Ikeda, Rentschler, & Osaka, 2007). Using fMRI, they
investigated brain responses correlating to the aesthetic ratings of Japanese paintings
given by the participants. Stimuli varied by style of painting (landscapes, portraits, still

lifes), and the participants were all Japanese. The stimulus paintings were rated by many Japanese subjects in preliminary testing and were selected based on consistent scoring across participants. Therefore, the stimulus paintings selected for the fMRI study were considered beautiful based on the ratings of Japanese subjects. Thus, this procedure allowed the researchers to explore how beauty and ugliness in Japanese paintings influence the brain activities of Japanese people. The results showed significant activation within the ventral ACC/mOFC, the visual cortices, and the inferior frontal gyrus with paintings rated as beautiful, whereas ones rated as ugly showed activation within the amygdala and the right lateral OFC. The activity in the ventral ACC/mOFC and the visual cortex with the beauty condition and amygdala with the ugliness condition is consistent with the many previous fMRI studies with Western populations and Western artworks. This provides evidence that these brain areas may universally play a fundamental role in aesthetic judgments. However, the engagement of the right lateral OFC with the experience of ugliness is interesting because it is not usually observed in Western populations (except for the study by Munar et al., 2012). The same research group also examined neural substrates on facial expressions, specifically using Noh masks. In the traditional Japanese Noh theater plays, performers use masks (e.g., "Ko-omote") to indicate many of the mental states of the characters they portray. They found that while participants viewed the masks, which were rated as "delicately" sad prior to the study, there was significant activation within the right amygdala. They suggested that such delicate sad masks in traditional Noh could activate the amygdala possible because of an underlying similarity to emotions such as fear or disgust (Osaka, Minamoto, Yaoi, & Osaka, 2012).

In the context of culturally based perception, it is also noteworthy to mention a current trend of studies on aesthetic appreciation in calligraphy and pictograms, especially in Far East Asian countries. For example, Zhang et al. tested perception and aesthetic appreciation in Chinese pictograms, which are language symbols having a graphical structure based on its referential objects, by conducting behavioral and brain imaging experiments (Zhang, Lai, He, Zhao, & Lai, 2016). Behavioral results showed pictographs that referred to beautiful objects were rated significantly higher on aesthetic rating than those that referred to ugly objects. Brain imaging data revealed activations in several regions including the visual cortex, the frontal lobe, and the inferior OFC with the contrast that those rated as beautiful were greater than in the control. It would be expected that more studies of this kind would come from those cultures where pictograms and calligraphy are regarded as a form of art, such as China, Arabic countries, Korea, and Japan. So far, cultural influences on art perception and aesthetic appreciation have not been well investigated in empirical neuroaesthetics research. The exploration of cross-cultural properties would be an interdisciplinary field integrated with humanities and cognitive sciences, and an important direction of neuroaesthetics research with cultural and ethnic value (Yongming, 2014). Since human art and aesthetic activities are enormously varied and culturally diverse, and yet also universal to all humans (Nadal & Chatterjee, 2018), theoretical consideration and an empirical approach to cross-cultural researches must be one of the vital components in future neuroaesthetics to elucidate a universally valid theory on our aesthetic activities.

BEAUTY IN ABSTRACTION

One of the important achievements of cognitive neuroscience research into beauty and aesthetics is the discovery that the brain responds to the aesthetic qualities of moral virtues such as goodness and truth in a similar manner to sensory beauty like visual and auditory beauty. For example, describing the act of helping others as a beautiful deed is not controversial. Many people agree that morality and friendship are some of the concepts we perceive as inherently beautiful. Research to date has shown that the mOFC/vmPFC reacts similarly when appraising an action as morally good to when judging a face as attractive (Tsukiura & Cabeza, 2011). Since one cannot characterize a "beautiful personality" based on visual information, the quality cannot be physically represented by good appearances, harmonious colors, or a pleasant melody. Indeed, most concepts central to what it means to be human—ethical values and goodness among them—involve abstract beauty in some way. The idea that "beauty is good" dates back to the idea of *kalon* in ancient Greek philosophy. Today, the relatedness of the two concepts has been demonstrated empirically in psychology and cognitive science. The stereotypical bias "beauty is good, and ugliness is evil" may well be inherent to human cognition. These revelations suggest a similar connection between beauty and morals. Indeed, patients with injuries to the ventromedial prefrontal cortex, immediately adjacent to the mOFC/vmPFC, reportedly suffer impairments when making moral judgments (Young et al., 2010).

Interestingly, another fMRI study on moral beauty reported that, when comparing facial (i.e., physical) and moral beauty, the former engaged not only the mOFC/vmPFC but the ventral basal ganglia as well, whereas the latter found activity within the mOFC/vmPFC alone. The study also showed that moral beauty activated a large-scale cortical network that included the precuneus, the rectus gyrus, the middle cingulate, and the middle occipital lobe, which are thought to play a role in empathy and self-reference (e.g., Bai et al., 2012; Moll et al., 2002). This indicates that "more advanced and complex cerebral representations" characterize moral beauty (Wang et al., 2015, p. 822).

BEAUTY IN CONTEXTUAL MODULATION

From a foundation of over a decade of research, neuroaesthetics has begun to move beyond mere neural correlates and abstractions of beauty, treading new ground by exploring the social and interpersonal factors that influence its perception. Generally speaking, beauty is a highly subjective and highly personal experience. We often speak of the "value" of a work of art; however, can we really argue that this value is absolute and immutable? For example, would you have the same emotional response and aesthetic evaluation to Monet's *Water Lilies* displayed on an artist's stand in a dirty back alley as in a gorgeous art museum? Studies to date have shown that our value judgments are rather vulnerable and subject to be modified (Kirk et al., 2009). The value we perceive in a work of art can be modulated merely by environmental and contextual information unrelated to the work per se.

Imagine you are presented with two similar abstract paintings. The first comes from the collection of a famous art museum; the second is a computer-generated image (CGI) modeled on the original. The task is to compare the pair and select the aesthetically more pleasing image. In the experiment done by Kirk et al. (2009), both are actually CGI created automatically using the same algorithm and only the labels are different—nothing else. They found that most participants rated "museum collection" images as more aesthetically pleasurable than the same images labeled as of "computer" origin, implying that aesthetic judgments of the works were influenced by the contextual information provided by the labels. Moreover, they noted that mOFC activity of participants, a known neural correlate of aesthetic experience, was enhanced more strongly by the images labeled as a museum collection.

Other contextual factors known to affect value judgments in such a paradigm include the authenticity of a work and peer's reviews, but these effects vary from person to person. For example, the contextual effect becomes considerably smaller when art experts such as art historians or art students serve as experimental subjects. The dlPFC may be a brain area thought to play some role in this effect. This cortical area is especially well developed in the human brain and handles higher-order functions such as the integration of sensory information and impulse control. In another study, Kirk et al. showed that the dlPFC is strongly activated in participants with expert knowledge who maintain their spontaneous opinions even when provided contextual information (Kirk et al., 2011). This activity was not observed, in contrast, in the brains of participants who readily changed their minds when presented with the same information. Interestingly, the authors reported enhanced functional coupling between the dlPFC and the mOFC during these judgments, speculating that the former modulates the activity of the latter by controlling the influence of information not directly related to the artwork in question. Thus, it seems that the dlPFC may contribute to how people form opinions about aesthetic value and, by extension, explain the mechanism behind an art connoisseur's cognition for evaluating art and beauty. We often speak of an aesthetic value of artworks or things. Above, we have seen how this "value" is not inherent to the work per se, but rather is dynamically shaped by contextual information such as its presentation and origin.

OTHER TECHNIQUES

Voxel-based morphometry and multivariate approaches

Although brain mapping has been a dominant method in cognitive neuroscientific studies on art and aesthetics, in recent years there have been new and powerful techniques emerging in both structural and functional imaging. Among them is analysis of structural changes in the brain. Voxel-based morphometry (VBM) is a method that can examine the gray and white matter volume of the whole brain or its subdivisions. VBM has recently received increasing attention as it allows investigation of focal changes and differences in brain anatomy using the statistical approach of parametric mapping and is useful to study brain plasticity (Bal, Goyal, Smith, & Demchuk, 2014). For example, researchers used VBM to study brain structural differences by comparing experts (art students) and naïve participants (Chamberlain et al., 2014).

Another promising technique is the multivariate approach for brain imaging data, such as multi-voxel pattern analysis (MVPA) and representation similarity analysis (RSA). These analyses evaluate correlation or covariance of activation across brain regions (as well as within a region-of-interest), rather than proceeding on a voxel-by-voxel basis, which allows researchers to study an inter-regional network that otherwise conventional univariate approaches cannot easily address (Habeck, 2010). Multivariate approaches can also be applied for brain "decoding" studies. The basic idea behind conventional brain mapping experiments is that, for example, a stimulus image that a participant views or an inner state which is evoked by a task is "encoded" in brain data (i.e., as the BOLD signals). On the contrary, a "brain decoding" method has been used to decode the inner state or the stimulus a participant viewed by applying machine learning to collected brain data (e.g., Norman, Polyn, Detre, & Haxby, 2006). Pegors et al. applied this technique and found that a "classifier" for facial beauty, which they produced from the patterns of voxel activities within the vmPFC/OFC, successfully decoded beauty judgments of other stimulus category, i.e., places. This suggests overlapping signals for face and place aesthetic evaluation in the vmPFC/OFC, thereby indicating that this region codes a signal for value that applies across different aesthetic judgments (Pegors et al., 2015). These new methods are promising tools to better understand the brain's systems for aesthetic experiences and evaluations.

Magnetoencephalography (MEG)

To date, neuroimaging studies in neuroaesthetics have been largely dependent on functional and structural MRI and electroencephalography (EEG) data (which is argued in detail in Chapter 12). The studies have revealed that specific brain structures and networks, such as the mOFC/vmPFC, the ventral striatum, the dlPFC, and the DMN, among them, are engaged in aesthetic experience, judgment, and evaluation as reviewed above. The fMRI technique, however, has a relatively low temporal resolution. To learn about the chronological order of cortical activation requires a different set of experiments, with the same psychophysical approach, such as EEG/ERP. However, since source localization using EEG suffers from some limitations, a more accurate source localization approach is needed. MEG has the theoretical advantage of being capable of localizing cortical activities owing to the reduced influence of the cerebrospinal fluid, skull, and skin. Moreover, the excellent temporal resolution of the MEG is the same as that of the EEG. For these, researchers use a MEG with high temporal resolution to determine whether there is a temporal difference in latency and time course of activity in brain areas when participants have aesthetic experiences belonging to various stimulus categories. A research group led by Cela-Conde has been taking the active contributions to the field. For example, a result from his group showed that the activity within the left dlPFC (prefrontal dorsolateral cortex) was greater when stimuli were judged as beautiful than when judged as not beautiful with natural and artistic photography stimuli (Cela-Conde et al., 2004). The dlPFC is known as a multifunctional area in the prefrontal cortex that integrates sensory information and regulates emotions, and especially with the left dlPFC, is thought to play a role in "the conscious deliberation about different options, influenced by emotional information from OFC and certain limbic areas" (Nadal et al., 2008, p. 390). The same group also proposed a theoretical framework on aesthetic appreciation based on their MEG results. In the framework, they argued that aesthetic appreciation relies on the activation of two different networks—an initial aesthetic network and a delayed network—engaged within distinct time frames. They hypothesized that the activation of the DMN might correspond mainly to the delayed aesthetic network processing with more cognitive analysis of a stimulus in a comparatively late stage (1000–1500 ms). This can be compared with the OFC, which may have an important role in the initial aesthetic network occurring in the earlier stage where a fast aesthetic appreciative perception is formed (Cela-Conde et al., 2013).

These MEG data could provide important information on the temporal course of the dynamic neuronal processes that underlie aesthetic appreciation. By combining the results from fMRI studies providing the spatial and regional activity, the inter-regional connectivity data, and those from E/MEG studies characterizing the temporal and spectral aspects, we could achieve significant advancements in our knowledge and understanding of the neural foundations of aesthetic appreciations.

CONCLUSION

Artistic beauty may be what we usually have in mind when we discuss beauty. However, as we have seen from the research reviewed in this chapter, aesthetic considerations pervade our judgments in all dimensions of life, regarding nature, people, morality, and lifestyle alike. It follows that humans access some cognitive function that serves as a mental framework when making a wide variety of decisions and appraisals. These criteria may be related to the concepts of goodness or truth. Truth, goodness, and beauty are three values that humans view as ideal and strive to pursue. Humans are highly susceptible to the cognitive bias of conflating what is beautiful with what is good, as mentioned above. In this light, perhaps aesthetic experience functions to mediate certain kinds of emotional information when judging a subject's rightness or goodness. Perceptions of what is good can be drastically transformed depending on the situation and the social context. The processes involved in aesthetics are likewise flexible, augmented, and dynamically formed by context. This mutability might be a product of interactions between neural networks for making aesthetic judgments, localized in the reward system including the mOFC/vmPFC, the NAcc, or insula, and cognitive processes in higher-order brain regions such as the dlPFC.

This chapter focused on neuroaesthetics research on beauty, but as mentioned at the beginning, the scope of the discipline is much wider than this. Other active research areas include the studies on artistic activities other than beauty, such as on artistic perception, cognition, and creativity. However, it is also true that many have criticized neuroscientific research on art and aesthetics on philosophical grounds. One argument for this is that a comprehensive understanding of our aesthetic sense is outside the purview of one-dimensional accounts of brain function. Researchers both in science and the humanities seem to have implicitly understood the limitations inherent to the purely quantitative study of beauty and subjectivity.

However, aesthetic experience seems to have physiological–physical correlates in the form of neural activity, as is clear from the findings of research on brain functions. This capacity is highly malleable, changing in response to artificial interventions, such as brain stimulation, and damage to the brain alike. In this light, we should be able to deepen our understanding and enrich our discussions of aesthetic experience by recognizing the validity of treating some of its qualities as objective and quantitatively measurable. Experimental approaches rooted in empirical sciences could give new insights regarding what beauty really means to humanity.

The concept of *"transcendent beauty"* no longer holds in modern theories of aesthetics and philosophy of aesthetics. And yet, aesthetic appreciation, this intense yet ineffable feeling, was hard-wired into our cognition and the brains long before we ever called it by that name. Beauty is shrouded in mystery, as if hidden behind many veils. Neuroaesthetics may only be capable of capturing a mere glimpse of the entity on the other side. However, techniques to measure psychological states objectively and empirically through neuroimaging may be able to open one of the veils, showing us more than Fechner could ever have seen in the past.

RECOMMENDED FURTHER READINGS

Chatterjee, A. (2014). *The aesthetic brain: How we evolved to desire beauty and enjoy art.* Oxford: Oxford University Press.

Zeki, S. (1999). Splendours and miseries of the brain. *Philosophical Transactions of the Royal Society of London B: Biological Sciences, 354*(1392), 2053–2065.

Zeki, S., & Nash, J. (1999). *Inner vision: An exploration of art and the brain* (Vol. 415). Oxford: Oxford University Press.

REFERENCES

Armony, J. L., & Dolan, R. J. (2002). Modulation of spatial attention by fear-conditioned stimuli: An event-related fMRI study. *Neuropsychologia, 40*(7), 817–826. https://doi.org/10.1016/S0028-3932(01)00178-6

Bai, F., Shi, Y., Yuan, Y., Wang, Y., Yue, C., Teng, Y., … Zhang, Z. (2012). Altered self-referential network in resting-state amnestic type mild cognitive impairment. *Cortex, 48*(5), 604–613. https://doi.org/10.1016/J.CORTEX.2011.02.011

Bal, S., Goyal, M., Smith, E., & Demchuk, A. M. (2014). Central nervous system imaging in diabetic cerebrovascular diseases and white matter hyperintensities. *Handbook of Clinical Neurology, 126*, 291–315. https://doi.org/10.1016/B978-0-444-53480-4.00021-7

Ballard, I. C., Murty, V. P., Carter, R. M., MacInnes, J. J., Huettel, S. A., & Adcock, R. A. (2011). Dorsolateral prefrontal cortex drives mesolimbic dopaminergic regions to initiate motivated behavior. *The Journal of Neuroscience: The Official Journal of the Society for Neuroscience, 31*(28), 10340–10346. https://doi.org/10.1523/JNEUROSCI.0895-11.2011

Belfi, A. M., Vessel, E. A., Brielmann, A., Isik, A. I., Chatterjee, A., Leder, H., … Starr, G. G. (2019). Dynamics of aesthetic experience are reflected in the default-mode network. *NeuroImage, 188*, 584–597. https://doi.org/10.1016/J.NEUROIMAGE.2018.12.017

Blood, A. J., & Zatorre, R. J. (2001). Intensely pleasurable responses to music correlate with activity in brain regions implicated in reward and emotion. *Proceedings of the National Academy of Sciences of the United States of America, 98*(20), 11818–11823. https://doi.org/10.1073/pnas.191355898

Boesveldt, S., Frasnelli, J., Gordon, A. R., & Lundström, J. N. (2010). The fish is bad: Negative food odors elicit faster and more accurate reactions than other odors. *Biological Psychology, 84*(2), 313–317. https://doi.org/10.1016/J.BIOPSYCHO.2010.03.006

Bohrn, I. C., Altmann, U., Lubrich, O., Menninghaus, W., & Jacobs, A. M. (2013). When we like what we know—a parametric fMRI analysis of beauty and familiarity. *Brain and Language, 124*(1), 1–8. https://doi.org/10.1016/J.BANDL.2012.10.003

Brattico, E., & Pearce, M. (2013). The neuroaesthetics of music. *Psychology of Aesthetics, Creativity, and the Arts, 7*(1), 48–61. https://doi.org/10.1037/a0031624

Brown, S., Gao, X., Tisdelle, L., Eickhoff, S. B., & Liotti, M. (2011). Naturalizing aesthetics: Brain areas for aesthetic appraisal across sensory modalities. *NeuroImage, 58*(1), 250–258. https://doi.org/10.1016/J.NEUROIMAGE.2011.06.012

Brown, S., Martinez, M. J., & Parsons, L. M. (2004). Passive music listening spontaneously engages limbic and paralimbic systems. *Neuroreport, 15*(13), 2033–2037. Retrieved from www.ncbi.nlm.nih.gov/pubmed/15486477

Calvo-Merino, B., Jola, C., Glaser, D. E., & Haggard, P. (2008). Towards a sensorimotor aesthetics of performing art. *Consciousness and Cognition, 17*(3), 911–922. https://doi.org/10.1016/J.CONCOG.2007.11.003

Calvo-Merino, B., Urgesi, C., Orgs, G., Aglioti, S. M., & Haggard, P. (2010). Extrastriate body area underlies aesthetic evaluation of body stimuli. *Experimental Brain Research, 204*(3), 447–456. https://doi.org/10.1007/s00221-010-2283-6

Cattaneo, Z., Lega, C., Ferrari, C., Vecchi, T., Cela-Conde, C. J., Silvanto, J., & Nadal, M. (2015). The role of the lateral occipital cortex in aesthetic appreciation of representational and abstract paintings: A TMS study. *Brain and Cognition, 95*, 44–53. https://doi.org/10.1016/J.BANDC.2015.01.008

Cattaneo, Z., Lega, C., Flexas, A., Nadal, M., Munar, E., & Cela-Conde, C. J. (2014a). The world can look better: Enhancing beauty experience with brain stimulation. *Social Cognitive and Affective Neuroscience, 9*(11), 1713–1721. https://doi.org/10.1093/scan/nst165

Cattaneo, Z., Lega, C., Gardelli, C., Merabet, L. B., Cela-Conde, C. J., & Nadal, M. (2014b). The role of prefrontal and parietal cortices in esthetic appreciation of representational and abstract art: A TMS study. *NeuroImage*, *99*, 443–450. https://doi.org/10.1016/J.NEUROIMAGE.2014.05.037

Cela-Conde, C. J., Garcia-Prieto, J., Ramasco, J. J., Mirasso, C. R., Bajo, R., Munar, E., … Maestu, F. (2013). Dynamics of brain networks in the aesthetic appreciation. *Proceedings of the National Academy of Sciences*, *110*(Supplement_2), 10454–10461. https://doi.org/10.1073/pnas.1302855110

Cela-Conde, C. J., Marty, G., Maestú, F., Ortiz, T., Munar, E., Fernández, A., … Quesney, F. (2004). Differential activation of the human orbital, mid-ventrolateral, and mid-dorsolateral prefrontal cortex during the processing of visual stimuli. *PNAS*, *99*(8), 5649–5654. https://doi.org/10.1073/pnas.072092299

Chamberlain, R., McManus, I. C., Brunswick, N., Rankin, Q., Riley, H., & Kanai, R. (2014). Drawing on the right side of the brain: A voxel-based morphometry analysis of observational drawing. *NeuroImage*, *96*, 167–173. https://doi.org/10.1016/J.NEUROIMAGE.2014.03.062

Chatterjee, A. (2011). Neuroaesthetics: A coming of age story. *Journal of Cognitive Neuroscience*, *23*(1), 53–62. https://doi.org/10.1162/jocn.2010.21457

Chatterjee, A., Thomas, A., Smith, S. E., & Aguirre, G. K. (2009). The neural response to facial attractiveness. *Neuropsychology*, *23*(2), 135–143. https://doi.org/10.1037/a0014430

Chatterjee, A., & Vartanian, O. (2014). Neuroaesthetics. *Trends in Cognitive Sciences*, *18*(7), 370–375. https://doi.org/10.1016/J.TICS.2014.03.003

Chatterjee, A., & Vartanian, O. (2016). Neuroscience of aesthetics. *Annals of the New York Academy of Sciences*, *1369*(1), 172–194. https://doi.org/10.1111/nyas.13035

Christensen, J. F. (2017). Pleasure junkies all around! Why it matters and why "the arts" might be the answer: A biopsychological perspective. *Proceedings of the Royal Society B: Biological Sciences*, *284*(1854), 20162837. https://doi.org/10.1098/rspb.2016.2837

Cinzia, D. D., & Vittorio, G. (2009). Neuroaesthetics: A review. *Current Opinion in Neurobiology*, *19*(6), 682–687. https://doi.org/10.1016/j.conb.2009.09.001

Cloutier, J., Heatherton, T. F., Whalen, P. J., & Kelley, W. M. (2008). Are attractive people rewarding? Sex differences in the neural substrates of facial attractiveness. *Journal of Cognitive Neuroscience*, *20*(6), 941–951. https://doi.org/10.1162/jocn.2008.20062

Conway, B. R., & Rehding, A. (2013). Neuroaesthetics and the trouble with beauty. *PLoS Biology*, *11*(3), e1001504. https://doi.org/10.1371/journal.pbio.1001504

Cross, E. S., & Ticini, L. F. (2012). Neuroaesthetics and beyond: New horizons in applying the science of the brain to the art of dance. *Phenomenology and the Cognitive Sciences*, *11*(1), 5–16. https://doi.org/10.1007/s11097-010-9190-y

Di Dio, C., Canessa, N., Cappa, S. F., & Rizzolatti, G. (2011). Specificity of esthetic experience for artworks: An fMRI study. *Frontiers in Human Neuroscience*, *5*, 139. https://doi.org/10.3389/fnhum.2011.00139

Di Dio, C., Macaluso, E., & Rizzolatti, G. (2007). The golden beauty: Brain response to classical and renaissance sculptures. *PLoS ONE*, *2*(11), e1201. https://doi.org/10.1371/journal.pone.0001201

Eisenberger, N. I., & Lieberman, M. D. (2004). Why rejection hurts: A common neural alarm system for physical and social pain. *Trends in Cognitive Sciences*, *8*(7), 294–300. https://doi.org/10.1016/J.TICS.2004.05.010

Ellamil, M., Dobson, C., Beeman, M., & Christoff, K. (2012). Evaluative and generative modes of thought during the creative process. *NeuroImage*, *59*(2), 1783–1794. https://doi.org/10.1016/J.NEUROIMAGE.2011.08.008

Etkin, A., Egner, T., & Kalisch, R. (2011). Emotional processing in anterior cingulate and medial prefrontal cortex. *Trends in Cognitive Sciences, 15*(2), 85–93. https://doi.org/10.1016/J.TICS.2010.11.004

Friston, K. J., Harrison, L., & Penny, W. (2003). Dynamic causal modelling. *NeuroImage, 19*(4), 1273–1302. https://doi.org/10.1016/S1053-8119(03)00202-7

Gerger, G., Ishizu, T., & Pelowski, M. (2017). Empathy as a guide for understanding the balancing of Distancing-Embracing with negative art. *Behavioral and Brain Sciences, 40*, e361. https://doi.org/10.1017/S0140525X17001698

Goebel, R., Roebroeck, A., Kim, D.-S., & Formisano, E. (2003). Investigating directed cortical interactions in time-resolved fMRI data using vector autoregressive modeling and Granger causality mapping. *Magnetic Resonance Imaging, 21*(10), 1251–1261. https://doi.org/10.1016/J.MRI.2003.08.026

Habeck, C. G. (2010). Basics of multivariate analysis in neuroimaging data. *Journal of Visualized Experiments: JoVE, 41*, e1998. https://doi.org/10.3791/1988

Hanich, J., Wagner, V., Shah, M., Jacobsen, T., & Menninghaus, W. (2014). Why we like to watch sad films. The pleasure of being moved in aesthetic experiences. *Psychology of Aesthetics, Creativity, and the Arts, 8*(2), 130–143. https://doi.org/10.1037/a0035690

Heekeren, H. R., Wartenburger, I., Marschner, A., Mell, T., Villringer, A., & Reischies, F. M. (2007). Role of ventral striatum in reward-based decision making. *NeuroReport, 18*(10), 951–955. https://doi.org/10.1097/WNR.0b013e3281532bd7

Ikeda, T., Matsuyoshi, D., Sawamoto, N., Fukuyama, H., & Osaka, N. (2015). Color harmony represented by activity in the medial orbitofrontal cortex and amygdala. *Frontiers in Human Neuroscience, 9*, 382. https://doi.org/10.3389/fnhum.2015.00382

Ishizu, T., & Sakamoto, Y. (2017). Ugliness as the fourth wall-breaker: Comment on "Move me, astonish me … delight my eyes and brain: The Vienna Integrated Model of top-down and bottom-up processes in Art Perception (VIMAP) and corresponding affective, evaluative, and neurophysiological correlates" by Matthew Pelowski et al. *Physics of Life Reviews, 21*, 138–139. https://doi.org/10.1016/J.PLREV.2017.06.003

Ishizu, T., & Zeki, S. (2011). Toward a brain-based theory of beauty. *PLoS ONE, 6*(7), e21852. https://doi.org/10.1371/journal.pone.0021852

Ishizu, T., & Zeki, S. (2013). The brain's specialized systems for aesthetic and perceptual judgment. *European Journal of Neuroscience, 37*(9), 1413–1420. https://doi.org/10.1111/ejn.12135

Ishizu, T., & Zeki, S. (2014). A neurobiological enquiry into the origins of our experience of the sublime and beautiful. *Frontiers in Human Neuroscience, 8*, 891. https://doi.org/10.3389/fnhum.2014.00891

Ishizu, T., & Zeki, S. (2017). The experience of beauty derived from sorrow. *Human Brain Mapping, 38*(8), 4185–4200. https://doi.org/10.1002/hbm.23657

Izuma, K., Matsumoto, M., Murayama, K., Samejima, K., Sadato, N., & Matsumoto, K. (2010). Neural correlates of cognitive dissonance and choice-induced preference change. *Proceedings of the National Academy of Sciences of the United States of America, 107*(51), 22014–22019. https://doi.org/10.1073/pnas.1011879108

Jacobsen, T. (2013). On the electrophysiology of aesthetic processing. *Progress in Brain Research, 204*, 159–168. https://doi.org/10.1016/B978-0-444-63287-6.00008-7

Jarcho, J. M., Berkman, E. T., & Lieberman, M. D. (2011). The neural basis of rationalization: Cognitive dissonance reduction during decision-making. *Social Cognitive and Affective Neuroscience, 6*(4), 460–467. https://doi.org/10.1093/scan/nsq054

Kawabata, H., & Zeki, S. (2004). Neural correlates of beauty. *Journal of Neurophysiology, 91*(4), 1699–1705. https://doi.org/10.1152/jn.00696.2003

Kawakami, A., Furukawa, K., Katahira, K., & Okanoya, K. (2013). Sad music induces pleasant emotion. *Frontiers in Psychology, 4*, 311. https://doi.org/10.3389/fpsyg.2013.00311

Kayser, W. (1957). *Das Groteske: Seine Gestaltung in Malerei und Dichtung.* Oldenburg, Germany: Gerhard Stalling.

Kirk, U., Harvey, A., & Montague, P. R. (2011). Domain expertise insulates against judgment bias by monetary favors through a modulation of ventromedial prefrontal cortex. *Proceedings of the National Academy of Sciences, 108*(25), 10332–10336. https://doi.org/10.1073/pnas.1019332108

Kirk, U., Skov, M., Hulme, O., Christensen, M. S., & Zeki, S. (2009). Modulation of aesthetic value by semantic context: An fMRI study. *NeuroImage, 44*(3), 1125–1132. https://doi.org/10.1016/J.NEUROIMAGE.2008.10.009

Knutson, B., & Greer, S. M. (2008). Anticipatory affect: Neural correlates and consequences for choice. *Philosophical Transactions of the Royal Society B: Biological Sciences, 363*(1511), 3771–3786. https://doi.org/10.1098/rstb.2008.0155

Koelsch, S., Fritz, T., v. Cramon, D. Y., Müller, K., & Friederici, A. D. (2006). Investigating emotion with music: An fMRI study. *Human Brain Mapping, 27*(3), 239–250. https://doi.org/10.1002/hbm.20180

Kranz, F., & Ishai, A. (2006). Face perception is modulated by sexual preference. *Current Biology, 16*(1), 63–68. https://doi.org/10.1016/J.CUB.2005.10.070

Kühn, S., & Gallinat, J. (2012). The neural correlates of subjective pleasantness. *NeuroImage, 61*(1), 289–294. https://doi.org/10.1016/J.NEUROIMAGE.2012.02.065

Lacey, S., Hagtvedt, H., Patrick, V. M., Anderson, A., Stilla, R., Deshpande, G., … Sathian, K. (2011). Art for reward's sake: Visual art recruits the ventral striatum. *NeuroImage, 55*(1), 420–433. https://doi.org/10.1016/J.NEUROIMAGE.2010.11.027

Lamm, C., Decety, J., & Singer, T. (2011). Meta-analytic evidence for common and distinct neural networks associated with directly experienced pain and empathy for pain. *NeuroImage, 54*(3), 2492–2502. https://doi.org/10.1016/J.NEUROIMAGE.2010.10.014

Leder, H. (2013). Next steps in neuroaesthetics: Which processes and processing stages to study? *Psychology of Aesthetics, Creativity, and the Arts, 7*(1), 27–37. https://doi.org/10.1037/a0031585

Leder, H., Gerger, G., Brieber, D., & Schwarz, N. (2014). What makes an art expert? Emotion and evaluation in art appreciation. *Cognition and Emotion, 28*(6), 1137–1147. https://doi.org/10.1080/02699931.2013.870132

Limb, C. J., & Braun, A. R. (2008). Neural substrates of spontaneous musical performance: An fMRI Study of Jazz Improvisation. *PLoS ONE, 3*(2), e1679. https://doi.org/10.1371/journal.pone.0001679

Lindquist, K. A., Wager, T. D., Kober, H., Bliss-Moreau, E., & Barrett, L. F. (2012). The brain basis of emotion: A meta-analytic review. *Behavioral and Brain Sciences, 35*(03), 121–143. https://doi.org/10.1017/S0140525X11000446

Mayseless, N., Eran, A., & Shamay-Tsoory, S. G. (2015). Generating original ideas: The neural underpinning of originality. *NeuroImage, 116*, 232–239. https://doi.org/10.1016/J.NEUROIMAGE.2015.05.030

McIntosh, A. R., & Gonzalez-Lima, F. (1994). Structural equation modeling and its application to network analysis in functional brain imaging. *Human Brain Mapping, 2*(1–2), 2–22. https://doi.org/10.1002/hbm.460020104

Menninghaus, W., Wagner, V., Hanich, J., Wassiliwizky, E., Jacobsen, T., & Koelsch, S. (2017). The Distancing-Embracing model of the enjoyment of negative emotions in art reception. *Behavioral and Brain Sciences, 40*, e347. https://doi.org/10.1017/S0140525X17000309

Mizokami, Y., Terao, T., Hatano, K., Hoaki, N., Kohno, K., Araki, Y., ... Kochiyama, T. (2014). Difference in brain activations during appreciating paintings and photographic analogs. *Frontiers in Human Neuroscience, 8*, 478. https://doi.org/10.3389/fnhum.2014.00478

Moll, J., Krueger, F., Zahn, R., Pardini, M., de Oliveira-Souza, R., & Grafman, J. (2006). Human fronto–mesolimbic networks guide decisions about charitable donation. *Proceedings of the National Academy of Sciences, 103*(42), 15623–15628. https://doi.org/10.1073/pnas.0604475103

Moll, J., Oliveira-Souza, R. de, Eslinger, P. J., Bramati, I. E., Mourão-Miranda, J., Andreiuolo, P. A., & Pessoa, L. (2002). The neural correlates of moral sensitivity: A functional magnetic resonance imaging investigation of basic and moral emotions. *Journal of Neuroscience, 22*(7), 2730–2736. https://doi.org/10.1523/JNEUROSCI.22-07-02730.2002

Munar, E., Nadal, M., Rosselló, J., Flexas, A., Moratti, S., Maestú, F., ... Cela-Conde, C. J. (2012). Lateral orbitofrontal cortex involvement in initial negative aesthetic impression formation. *PLoS ONE, 7*(6), e38152. https://doi.org/10.1371/journal.pone.0038152

Nadal, M., & Chatterjee, A. (2018). Neuroaesthetics and art's diversity and universality. *Wiley Interdisciplinary Reviews: Cognitive Science*, e1487. https://doi.org/10.1002/wcs.1487

Nadal, M., Munar, E., Capo, M. A., Rossello, J., & Cela-Conde, C. J. (2008). Towards a framework for the study of the neural correlates of aesthetic preference. *Spatial Vision, 21*(3), 379. https://doi.org/10.1163/156856808784532653

Nadal, M., & Pearce, M. T. (2011). The Copenhagen Neuroaesthetics conference: Prospects and pitfalls for an emerging field. *Brain and Cognition, 76*(1), 172–183. https://doi.org/10.1016/J.BANDC.2011.01.009

Nadal, M., & Skov, M. (2018). The pleasure of art as a matter of fact. *Proceedings of the Royal Society B: Biological Sciences, 285*(1875), 20172252. https://doi.org/10.1098/rspb.2017.2252

Nakamura, K., & Kawabata, H. (2015). Transcranial direct current stimulation over the medial prefrontal cortex and left primary motor cortex (mPFC-lPMC) affects subjective beauty but not ugliness. *Frontiers in Human Neuroscience, 9*, 654. https://doi.org/10.3389/fnhum.2015.00654

Norman, K. A., Polyn, S. M., Detre, G. J., & Haxby, J. V. (2006). Beyond mind-reading: Multi-voxel pattern analysis of fMRI data. *Trends in Cognitive Sciences, 10*(9), 424–430. https://doi.org/10.1016/J.TICS.2006.07.005

Northoff, G., Heinzel, A., de Greck, M., Bermpohl, F., Dobrowolny, H., & Panksepp, J. (2006). Self-referential processing in our brain—a meta-analysis of imaging studies on the self. *NeuroImage, 31*(1), 440–457. https://doi.org/10.1016/J.NEUROIMAGE.2005.12.002

O'Doherty, J. P. (2004). Reward representations and reward-related learning in the human brain: Insights from neuroimaging. *Current Opinion in Neurobiology, 14*(6), 769–776. https://doi.org/10.1016/J.CONB.2004.10.016

O'Doherty, J. P., Deichmann, R., Critchley, H. D., & Dolan, R. J. (2002). Neural responses during anticipation of a primary taste reward. *Neuron, 33*(5), 815–826. https://doi.org/10.1016/S0896-6273(02)00603-7

O'Doherty, J., Winston, J., Critchley, H., Perrett, D., Burt, D., & Dolan, R. (2003). Beauty in a smile: The role of medial orbitofrontal cortex in facial attractiveness. *Neuropsychologia, 41*(2), 147–155. https://doi.org/10.1016/S0028-3932(02)00145-8

Osaka, N., Ikeda, T., Rentschler, I., & Osaka, M. (2007). PPA and OFC correlates of beauty and ugliness: An event-related fMRI study. *Perception ECVP Abstract, 36*, S174–175.

Osaka, N., Minamoto, T., Yaoi, K., & Osaka, M. (2012). Neural correlates of delicate sadness. *NeuroReport, 23*(1), 26–29. https://doi.org/10.1097/WNR.0b013e32834dccda

Pearce, M. T., Zaidel, D. W., Vartanian, O., Skov, M., Leder, H., Chatterjee, A., & Nadal, M. (2016). Neuroaesthetics. *Perspectives on Psychological Science, 11*(2), 265–279. https://doi.org/10.1177/1745691615621274

Pegors, T. K., Kable, J. W., Chatterjee, A., & Epstein, R. A. (2015). Common and unique representations in pFC for face and place attractiveness. *Journal of Cognitive Neuroscience, 27*(5), 959–973. https://doi.org/10.1162/jocn_a_00777

Pelowski, M., Ishizu, T., & Leder, H. (2018). Sadness and beauty in art—do they really coincide in the brain? *Physics of Life Reviews, 25*, 124–127. https://doi.org/10.1016/j.plrev.2018.03.013

Pelowski, M., Markey, P. S., Forster, M., Gerger, G., & Leder, H. (2017). Move me, astonish me ... delight my eyes and brain: The Vienna Integrated Model of top-down and bottom-up processes in Art Perception (VIMAP) and corresponding affective, evaluative, and neurophysiological correlates. *Physics of Life Reviews, 21*, 80–125. https://doi.org/10.1016/J.PLREV.2017.02.003

Plassmann, H., O'Doherty, J. P., & Rangel, A. (2010). Appetitive and aversive goal values are encoded in the medial orbitofrontal cortex at the time of decision making. *Journal of Neuroscience, 30*(32), 10799–10808. https://doi.org/10.1523/JNEUROSCI.0788-10.2010

Raichle, M. E., Macleod, A. M., Snyder, A. Z., Powers, W. J., Gusnard, D. A., & Shulman, G. L. (2001). A default mode of brain function. *Proceedings of the National Academy of Sciences of the United States of America, 98*(2), 676–682. https://doi.org/10.1073/pnas.98.2.676

Sachs, M. E., Damasio, A., & Habibi, A. (2015). The pleasures of sad music: A systematic review. *Frontiers in Human Neuroscience, 9*, 404. https://doi.org/10.3389/fnhum.2015.00404

Salimpoor, V. N., van den Bosch, I., Kovacevic, N., McIntosh, A. R., Dagher, A., & Zatorre, R. J. (2013). Interactions between the nucleus accumbens and auditory cortices predict music reward value. *Science, 340*(6129), 216–219. https://doi.org/10.1126/science.1231059

Sanfey, A. G., Rilling, J. K., Aronson, J. A., Nystrom, L. E., & Cohen, J. D. (2003). The neural basis of economic decision-making in the Ultimatum Game. *Science, 300*(5626), 1755–1758. https://doi.org/10.1126/science.1082976

Schmitz, T. W., & Johnson, S. C. (2007). Relevance to self: A brief review and framework of neural systems underlying appraisal. *Neuroscience and Biobehavioral Reviews, 31*(4), 585–596. https://doi.org/10.1016/J.NEUBIOREV.2006.12.003

Schubert, E. (1996). Enjoyment of negative emotions in music: An associative network explanation. *Psychology of Music, 24*(1), 18–28. https://doi.org/10.1177/0305735696241003

Sescousse, G., Caldú, X., Segura, B., & Dreher, J. C. (2013). Processing of primary and secondary rewards: A quantitative meta-analysis and review of human functional neuroimaging studies. *Neuroscience & Biobehavioral Reviews, 37*(4), 681–696. https://doi.org/10.1016/j.neubiorev.2013.02.002

Sescousse, G., Redouté, J., & Dreher, J.-C. (2010). The architecture of reward value coding in the human orbitofrontal cortex. *Journal of Neuroscience, 30*(39), 13095–13104. https://doi.org/10.1523/JNEUROSCI.3501-10.2010

Spee, B., Ishizu, T., Leder, H., Mikuni, J., Kawabata, H., & Pelowski, M. (2018). Neuropsychopharmacological aesthetics: A theoretical consideration of pharmacological approaches to causative brain study in aesthetics and art. *Progress in Brain Research, 237*, 343–372. https://doi.org/10.1016/BS.PBR.2018.03.021

Stahl, S. M. (2008). *Stahl's essential psychopharmacology: Neuroscientific basis and practical applications.* Cambridge: Cambridge University Press.

Suzuki, M., Okamura, N., Kawachi, Y., Tashiro, M., Arao, H., Hoshishiba, T., ... Yanai, K. (2008). Discrete cortical regions associated with the musical beauty of major and minor chords. *Cognitive, Affective, and Behavioral Neuroscience, 8*(2), 126–131. https://doi.org/10.3758/CABN.8.2.126

Taruffi, L., & Koelsch, S. (2014). The paradox of music-evoked sadness: An online survey. *PLoS ONE, 9*(10), e110490. https://doi.org/10.1371/journal.pone.0110490

Ticini, L. (2017). The role of the orbitofrontal and dorsolateral prefrontal cortices in aesthetic preference for art. *Behavioral Sciences, 7*(2), 31. https://doi.org/10.3390/bs7020031

Trost, W., Ethofer, T., Zentner, M., & Vuilleumier, P. (2012). Mapping aesthetic musical emotions in the brain. *Cerebral Cortex, 22*(12), 2769–2783. https://doi.org/10.1093/cercor/bhr353

Tsukiura, T., & Cabeza, R. (2011). Shared brain activity for aesthetic and moral judgments: Implications for the Beauty-is-Good stereotype. *Social Cognitive and Affective Neuroscience, 6*(1), 138–148. https://doi.org/10.1093/scan/nsq025

Umiltà, M. A., Berchio, C., Sestito, M., Freedberg, D., & Gallese, V. (2012). Abstract art and cortical motor activation: An EEG study. *Frontiers in Human Neuroscience, 6*, 311. https://doi.org/10.3389/fnhum.2012.00311

Vartanian, O., & Goel, V. (2004). Neuroanatomical correlates of aesthetic preference for paintings. *Neuroreport, 15*(5), 893–897. https://doi.org/10.1097/00001756-200404090-00032

Vartanian, O., Navarrete, G., Chatterjee, A., Fich, L. B., Leder, H., Modroño, C., ... Skov, M. (2013). Impact of contour on aesthetic judgments and approach-avoidance decisions in architecture. *Proceedings of the National Academy of Sciences of the United States of America, 110*(Supplement 2), 10446–10453. https://doi.org/10.1073/pnas.1301227110

Vartanian, O., & Skov, M. (2014). Neural correlates of viewing paintings: Evidence from a quantitative meta-analysis of functional magnetic resonance imaging data. *Brain and Cognition, 87*, 52–56. https://doi.org/10.1016/J.BANDC.2014.03.004

Vessel, E. A., Starr, G. G., & Rubin, N. (2012). The brain on art: Intense aesthetic experience activates the default mode network. *Frontiers in Human Neuroscience, 6*, 66. https://doi.org/10.3389/fnhum.2012.00066

Wallis, J. D., & Miller, E. K. (2003). Neuronal activity in primate dorsolateral and orbital prefrontal cortex during performance of a reward preference task. *European Journal of Neuroscience, 18*(7), 2069–2081. https://doi.org/10.1046/j.1460-9568.2003.02922.x

Wang, T., Mo, L., Mo, C., Tan, L. H., Cant, J. S., Zhong, L., & Cupchik, G. (2015). Is moral beauty different from facial beauty? Evidence from an fMRI study. *Social Cognitive and Affective Neuroscience, 10*(6), 814–823. https://doi.org/10.1093/scan/nsu123

Wassiliwizky, E., Koelsch, S., Wagner, V., Jacobsen, T., & Menninghaus, W. (2017). The emotional power of poetry: Neural circuitry, psychophysiology and compositional principles. *Social Cognitive and Affective Neuroscience, 12*(8), 1229–1240. https://doi.org/10.1093/scan/nsx069

Yacubian, J., Sommer, T., Schroeder, K., Gläscher, J., Braus, D. F., & Büchel, C. (2007). Subregions of the ventral striatum show preferential coding of reward magnitude and probability. *NeuroImage, 38*(3), 557–563. https://doi.org/10.1016/J.NEUROIMAGE.2007.08.007

Yongming, Z. (2014). Neuroaesthetics research in the construction of Chinese character art. *Leonardo, 47*(3), 294–296. https://doi.org/10.1162/LEON_a_00785

Young, L., Bechara, A., Tranel, D., Damasio, H., Hauser, M., & Damasio, A. (2010). Damage to ventromedial prefrontal cortex impairs judgment of harmful intent. *Neuron, 65*(6), 845–851. https://doi.org/10.1016/J.NEURON.2010.03.003

Zaidel, D. W.. (2013). Art and brain: The relationship of biology and evolution to art. *Progress in Brain Research, 204*, 217–233. https://doi.org/10.1016/B978-0-444-63287-6.00011-7

Zald, D. H., McHugo, M., Ray, K. L., Glahn, D. C., Eickhoff, S. B., & Laird, A. R. (2014). Meta-analytic connectivity modeling reveals differential functional connectivity of the medial and lateral orbitofrontal cortex. *Cerebral Cortex, 24*(1), 232–248. https://doi.org/10.1093/cercor/bhs308

Zatorre, R. J., & Salimpoor, V. N. (2013). From perception to pleasure: Music and its neural substrates. *Proceedings of the National Academy of Sciences, 110*(Supplement 2), 10430–10437. https://doi.org/10.1073/pnas.1301228110

Zeki, S., & Lamb, M. (1994). The neurology of kinetic art. *Brain, 117*(3), 607–636. https://doi.org/10.1093/brain/117.3.607

Zeki, S., Romaya, J. P., Benincasa, D. M. T., & Atiyah, M. F. (2014). The experience of mathematical beauty and its neural correlates. *Frontiers in Human Neuroscience, 8*, 68. https://doi.org/10.3389/fnhum.2014.00068

Zeki, S., & Stutters, J. (2012). A brain-derived metric for preferred kinetic stimuli. *Open Biology, 2*(2), 120001. https://doi.org/10.1098/rsob.120001

Zhang, W., Lai, S., He, X., Zhao, X., & Lai, S. (2016). Neural correlates for aesthetic appraisal of pictograph and its referent: An fMRI study. *Behavioural Brain Research, 305*, 229–238. https://doi.org/10.1016/J.BBR.2016.02.029

....

CHAPTER 16

NONINVASIVE BRAIN STIMULATION

Contribution to Research in Neuroaesthetics

....

ZAIRA CATTANEO

NONINVASIVE BRAIN STIMULATION: AN OVERVIEW OF AVAILABLE TECHNIQUES AND THEIR FUNCTIONING

TRANSCRANIAL magnetic stimulation (TMS) and transcranial electrical stimulation (tES) are largely used in cognitive neuroscience research to investigate *causal* structure–function relationships. The rationale is that if stimulating a specific region (or node of a network) induces a significant modulation of task performance, said region (and/or the network it is part of) can be considered as causally relevant for that specific process (for reviews, see Filmer, Dux, & Mattingley, 2014; Hallett et al., 2017; Parkin, Ekhtiari, & Walsh, 2015; Valero-Cabré, Amengual, Stengel, Pascual-Leone, & Coubard, 2017). This section offers an overview of the basic mechanisms of action of noninvasive brain stimulation (NIBS) and of the main paradigms used in cognitive neuroscience in general, and in research in neuroaesthetics in particular (see Figure 16.1). Although clinical applications of NIBS are beyond the scope of this chapter, it is important to note that TMS and tES are increasingly employed to act on brain plasticity in treating clinical symptoms in several neurological and psychiatric diseases (Boes et al., 2018). Moreover, NIBS nowadays can be combined with neuroimaging and electrophysiological techniques that provide readouts of neural activity, thus enabling us to assess the

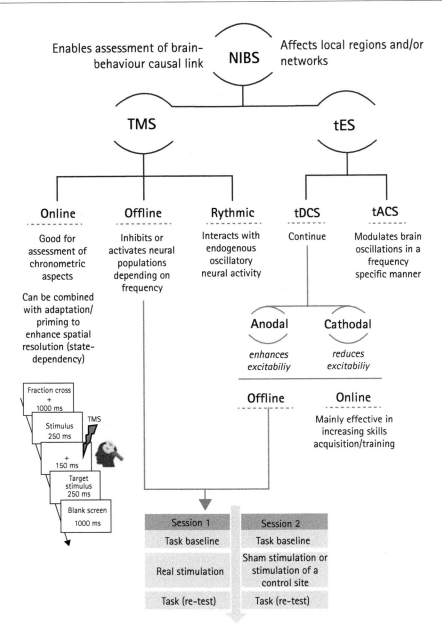

FIGURE 16.1. Overview of some of the main TMS and tES paradigms used in cognitive neuroscience that may be employed to gain insight into brain–behavior causal links in aesthetic evaluation of artworks. For online and offline protocols, a timeline of a typical experimental paradigm is shown. The figure also depicts the main mechanisms of action of the different techniques.

changes caused by stimulation but also to drive a more effective stimulation (Bergmann, Karabanov, Hartwigsen, Thielscher, & Siebner, 2016).

Transcranial magnetic stimulation

In TMS, a brief and high-amplitude current is delivered through a coil placed above the scalp, generating a perpendicular and rapidly changing magnetic field. Single-pulse TMS discharges a single magnetic pulse at a given time, whereas repetitive TMS (rTMS) delivers repeated single magnetic pulses of the same intensity to the targeted brain region. The magnetic pulses induce a transitory electric current in the cortical surface under the coil, which causes membrane depolarization in neuronal structures, initiation of action potential, and hence neuronal activation. By interfering with ongoing intrinsic neural activity, TMS affects functions that rely on the perturbated brain region. Although TMS effects on perceptual and cognitive abilities were initially described in terms of transient "virtual lesions" caused by noise induction (Pascual-Leone, Walsh, & Rothwell, 2000), TMS may also facilitate performance (Luber & Lisanby, 2014). Indeed, TMS may elicit enhancement or suppression of activity at the cortical level, depending on stimulation parameters—such as frequency, intensity, and duration of stimulation— but also on the ongoing state of the stimulated area (e.g., Romei, Thut, & Silvanto, 2016; Silvanto & Cattaneo, 2017).

The spatial resolution of TMS on cortical surfaces is moderately good (1–2 cm); subcortical regions cannot be directly stimulated, but their activity can be indirectly modulated via TMS by targeting cortical regions that are connected to them. For instance, by applying TMS to a region interconnected with the hippocampus, the posterior inferior parietal cortex, it is possible to affect hippocampal memory functions (Tambini, Nee, & D'Esposito, 2018). Similarly, TMS over the superior temporal sulcus affects activity in the amygdala during face processing, consistent with the existence of a cortico-amygdala pathway for processing face information (Pitcher, Japee, Rauth, & Ungerleider, 2017). Or again, stimulation of the (left) dorsolateral prefrontal cortex (DLPFC) affects not just the region beneath the coil but also the meso-cortico-limbic network (Tik et al., 2017). Also, specific coils are available that allow for deeper stimulation (Samoudi, Tanghe, Martens, & Joseph, 2018).

Many TMS paradigms have been used in cognitive neuroscience research (for a review, see Sandrini, Umiltà, & Rusconi, 2011). In *online* TMS paradigms, single-pulse or rTMS is given concurrently with the task. This enables us to investigate whether a region subserves a certain function but also to study *chronometric* aspects (Sliwinska, Vitello, & Devlin, 2014). TMS temporal resolution is indeed quite good, allowing the measurement of the contribution of an area to a specific process with a precision of tens of milliseconds. For instance, varying the asynchrony between visual stimulus onset and TMS pulse to the early visual cortex in studies of visual awareness has enabled the tracking of the time-course of the functional relevance of the early visual cortex for vision (de Graaf, Koivisto, Jacobs, & Sack, 2014). Typically, in online paradigms TMS is given over one or more regions that may be implicated in the process of interest; control conditions (like vertex or sham stimulation) are also included to control for unspecific effects of stimulation. In *offline* paradigms, stimulation and task execution occur separately; participants are typically required to first perform the task (with no stimulation) and subsequently receive repetitive TMS (generally 1-Hz TMS for 10–25 min to suppress neural activity). Repetitive TMS induces changes in brain activity that last beyond the stimulation period; hence, after stimulation, task performance is re-assessed to measure any stimulation-induced effect. The main advantage of offline protocols in cognitive neuroscience research is that they avoid unspecific effects of stimulation on performance (such as discomfort, muscle twitching, somatosensory sensation on the scalp, and auditory click evoked by the pulses). However, TMS-induced effects in offline paradigms tend to quickly decline with time (Thut & Pascual-Leone, 2010); more than one session of TMS (over different days) is needed to allow for proper control conditions (at least, in within-subjects designs), and the time-course of involvement of a specific region in a certain process cannot be assessed. In light of this, online TMS paradigms tend to be preferred by cognitive neuroscientists working in basic research (in turn, repeated sessions of rTMS are widely used in clinical settings to induce lasting changes in cortical excitability and guide plasticity with therapeutic intent).

Finally, recent paradigms have started employing repetitive "rhythmic" TMS to interact with endogenous oscillatory neural activity with the aim of driving network activity (and associated functions) through interaction with brain oscillations (Romei et al., 2016). For instance, theta-rhythmic TMS has been found to enhance auditory working memory (Albouy, Weiss, Baillet, & Zatorre, 2017); similar enhancing effects have also been obtained via rhythmic TMS for other functions, such as attention (Romei, Thut, Mok, Schyns, & Driver, 2012).

Transcranial electrical stimulation

tES is a noninvasive, neuro-modulation technique in which a small current (usually 1–2 mA) is delivered to the brain by means of electrodes applied over the scalp. The low-voltage current allows a reversible modulation of the excitability in a specific brain area by influencing the spontaneous neural activity (Bestmann & Walsh, 2017; Yavari, Jamil, Mosayebi Samani, Vidor, & Nitsche, 2018). tES is a generic term that refers to different techniques based on the modality of the applied electricity. The most widely used form of tES is transcranial direct current stimulation (tDCS).

In tDCS protocols, the current is most commonly delivered using a bipolar montage that consists of an "active" electrode (which could be the anode or the cathode, depending on the experimental design) located directly over the region of interest and a "reference" electrode located over either another cephalic site or over an extra-cephalic site such as the shoulder. Unlike TMS, the effects of tDCS are subthreshold; that is, the polarization induced is not sufficient to drive the generation of action potentials but it brings neurons closer or further from their threshold for firing an action potential (Stagg & Nitsche, 2011). Initial studies applied tDCS over the motor cortex and showed that anodal stimulation is effective in enhancing neural firing rates via up-regulation of the resting potential of the neurons' membrane voltage while cathodal stimulation reduces the firing rate via down-regulation of the membrane voltage (Nitsche & Paulus, 2000). Following the same rationale, tDCS has been applied to modulate excitability of other cortical regions, although mechanisms of anodal and cathodal stimulation may not be so straightforward outside the motor cortex (Bestmann & Walsh, 2017). Indeed, computational models and physiological measurements suggest that tDCS effects depend on multiple factors including properties of the current (duration, intensity, and frequency) and of the electrodes (shape, size, position) as well as individual differences in anatomy (e.g., skull thickness) and cortical excitability (Opitz et al., 2015; Woods et al., 2016). Critically, tDCS is able to induce prolonged shifts in cortical excitability, which can be desirable for treatment of many neurological and psychiatric disorders (Bikson et al., 2018).

Compared with TMS, spatial and temporal resolution of tDCS is poor. During stimulation, current flows between the electrodes; accordingly, tDCS effects are not very focal. Options to increase spatial resolution include the use of high-definition tDCS, in which a small central electrode positioned over the target region is surrounded by four return electrodes, or varying the size of the active and reference electrodes (Woods et al., 2016). Moreover, tDCS is not suited to assess the time-course of perceptual and cognitive functions, since current needs to be applied for several minutes to induce changes in cortical excitability. In a typical tDCS experiment in cognitive neuroscience, participants perform a task, 1–2-mA tDCS is then delivered for 10–20 min, after which the task is repeated a second time. Since the effects of tDCS tend to rapidly decline, the task performed after tDCS has to fall within a few minutes of the end of stimulation. A widely used control condition consists of a sham stimulation, in which the electrode montage is the same as for the real stimulation, but the current is ramped down after 30 s to 0 mA. Online tDCS protocols—in which participants perform the task while receiving stimulation—are also employed and seem to be particularly suited for enhancing skill acquisition (Martin, Liu, Alonzo, Green, & Loo, 2014).

A more recent tES approach to modulate neurophysiological activation patterns is transcranial alternating current stimulation (tACS), in which a current of a specific frequency is applied (Antal & Herrmann, 2016). In contrast to tDCS, there is no constant anode or cathode. The main potential of tACS relies on its capacity to modulate brain oscillations in a frequency-specific manner by entraining ongoing brain oscillations or synchronizing neuronal networks (the rationale is similar to rhythmic TMS described above). When using tACS, researchers have hence to refer to electrophysiological evidence about a specific brain oscillation or combination of oscillations characterizing the function they want to modulate. tACS has been successfully used to modulate perception (Cabral-Calderin & Wilke, 2020), attention (Hopfinger, Parsons, & Fröhlich, 2017), working memory, and fluid intelligence capacity (Albouy et al., 2018; Santarnecchi et al., 2016). Finally, protocols in which current intensity and frequency vary in a randomized manner (transcranial random noise stimulation, tRNS) are also employed. Studies using tRNS have found facilitatory effects of tRNS in several perceptual (e.g., Ghin, Pavan, Contillo, & Mather, 2018) and cognitive tasks (e.g., Popescu et al., 2016), but more research is needed to shed light on the underlying modulatory mechanisms.

NIBS Studies in Neuroaesthetics

Consistent neuroimaging evidence has shown that aesthetic appreciation relies on the activity of a broadly distributed neural network, involving both cortical and subcortical brain regions (for reviews, see Boccia et al., 2016; Chatterjee & Vartanian, 2016). Measurements of neural electrical and magnetic signals have greatly complemented localization information by offering insights into the chronometry of the aesthetic experience (e.g., Cela-Conde et al., 2004; Jacobsen, 2013; Pang, Nadal, Müller-Paul, Rosenberg, Klein, 2013). In this scenario, NIBS techniques have more recently entered the field enabling the investigation of the causal link between aesthetic preference decisions and underlying brain activity. The term "decision" is stressed here because NIBS techniques, when not combined with neuroimaging, electrophysiological, or electromyographic measurements, typically need a behavioral output in order to measure whether the targeted area is involved in a specific process. This section offers an overview of available TMS and tDCS studies investigating the possible causal role of different cortical regions in aesthetic evaluation of visual artworks. The final section will then touch on possible future scenarios (and current limits) of application of these techniques in the field of neuroaesthetics.

Aesthetic decisions and prefrontal cortex stimulation

Several studies have observed increased activity in the DLPFC, mainly in the left hemisphere, and in medial and orbital sectors of the prefrontal cortex while participants viewed aesthetically pleasing images (Cela-Conde et al., 2004; Cupchik et al., 2009; Ishizu & Zeki, 2011, 2017; Lengger et al., 2007; Vartanian and Goel, 2004; Vessel et al., 2012; Zhang, Lai, He, Zhao, & Lai, 2016). The increase in prefrontal activity observed during aesthetic appreciation is likely to be related to different processes, such as evaluation processes involved in aesthetic preference, orientation toward aesthetic qualities of the stimuli, salience/attention mechanisms, as well as emotional responses and reward computation.

tDCS and TMS have been recently employed to shed light on the possible causal role exerted by lateral and medial sectors of the prefrontal cortex in mediating aesthetic appreciation of visual artworks. In a first tDCS study (Cattaneo et al., 2014a), we employed anodal tDCS to enhance excitability of the left DLPFC and measured whether this would have an impact on liking of abstract and figurative artworks. We used both abstract and figurative artworks since prior evidence suggested that (left) DLPFC activation may be more relevant for liking of the figurative category: indeed, representational paintings elicit more semantic (memory) associations than abstract ones (at least in art-naïve observers) and are therefore more likely to activate prefrontal regions involved in high-level integrative processing (Lengger et al., 2007). Art-naïve participants were first presented with a subset of images and they were asked to indicate (moving the mouse cursor along an analogical bar) how much they liked them. This baseline assessment was followed by 20 min of 2-mA anodal tDCS over the left DLPFC, in order to increase excitability in this region. The reference electrode was placed over the contralateral supraorbital region, a standard montage when targeting the DLPFC (e.g., DaSilva, Volz, Bikson, & Fregni, 2011). Immediately following the end of the stimulation, participants had to evaluate a new subset of images. We found that enhancing excitability of the left DLPFC via anodal tDCS compared with sham stimulation (performed on a different day) resulted in a moderate (~3%) but statistically significant increase of aesthetic appreciation of figurative but not of abstract images. Critically, the effect of anodal tDCS over the left DLPFC was specific for aesthetic evaluation, as shown by a control experiment in which the same stimulation protocol did not affect evaluation of images' external features (color).

The findings by Cattaneo et al. (2014a) suggest that the left DLPFC plays a causal role in mediating aesthetic appreciation of visual artworks (at least of figurative ones, toward which art-naïve individuals may find it easier to orient aesthetically). However, the specific mechanisms by which left DLPFC-tDCS modulated aesthetic appreciation in this study remain to be clarified. tDCS may have affected emotional responses to artworks, with prior studies reporting consistent effects of DLPFC stimulation on affective processing (see Mondino, Thiffault, & Fecteau, 2015 for a review). Moreover, the observed effects on aesthetic decisions may have depended on tDCS affecting reward computations. Indeed, tDCS over the left DLPFC (Fonteneau et al., 2018) and repetitive (theta-burst) TMS over the left DLPFC (Ko et al., 2008) have been found to modulate striatal dopamine release, with the striatum being a key node of the rewarding system. Furthermore, tDCS may also have affected high-level processes mediated by the DLPFC and important in art appreciation, such as semantic processing, a function that has been found to be affected by DLPFC-tDCS (e.g., Mitchell, Vidaki, & Lavidor, 2016). Hence, if on the one hand Cattaneo and colleagues' (2014a) findings point to a role of the DLPFC in mediating aesthetic evaluation of visual artworks, on the other hand the specific mechanisms by which modulation of DLPFC activity leads to changes in aesthetic pleasure remain to be fully clarified.

To shed further light on the functional significance of DLPFC recruitment during aesthetic evaluation of paintings, we carried out a second study in which again we targeted the left DLPFC, this time with (online) TMS (Cattaneo et al., 2014b). The right parietal cortex was also stimulated in light of prior evidence reporting fronto-parietal activation during aesthetic experience (Cela-Conde et al., 2009, 2013); the vertex (top of the head; Cz in the EEG system) was used as a control site. Art-naïve participants were presented with a series of abstract and representational paintings, and had to indicate as fast as possible (note that decisions need to be fast for online TMS to affect responses) whether they liked them or not. Triple-pulse 10-Hz TMS was delivered over the target area immediately after the onset of each painting to interfere with underlying neural activity. Critically, when recruiting participants we also took into account individual preference for abstract and figurative art, as models of aesthetic appreciation point to individual stylistic preference as an important factor to be considered (Leder & Nadal, 2014; Pelowski, Markey, Forster, Gerger, & Leder, 2017). We found that interfering with DLPFC activity via online TMS decreased liking of artworks, but only of those belonging to the preferred category: in other words, following TMS to the DLPFC compared with the control site (vertex), participants preferring figurative art rated fewer figurative artworks as "liked," whereas their evaluation for abstract art was unaffected by TMS (and vice versa for participants preferring abstract art). The effects of TMS over the parietal cortex were less clear-cut, with parietal TMS only affecting liking of figurative paintings in participants preferring this kind of art (whereas decisions of participants preferring abstract artworks were not affected by stimulation). If the selective effects of TMS for the preferred art category are in line with models of aesthetic experience that emphasize the human contribution to the experience of art, at the physiological level they may reflect state-dependency mechanisms (Silvanto & Cattaneo, 2017; Silvanto et al., 2008), with preferred art probably eliciting different neural activation states compared with not-preferred art differently susceptible to TMS action.

Interestingly, stimulation of the DLPFC has been found to affect appreciation of other stimuli beyond visual artworks, such as music. In particular, Mas-Herrero and colleagues (Mas-Herrero, Dagher, & Zatorre, 2018) recently applied (theta-burst) ex-citatory and inhibitory TMS over the left DLPFC to directly modulate fronto-striatal function and then tested participants with measures of pleasure and motivation during music listening. They found that perceived pleasure, psychophysiological measures of emotional arousal, and the monetary value assigned to music were significantly increased by exciting fronto-striatal pathways, whereas inhibition of this system led to decreases in all of these variables compared with sham stimulation. Overall, the available findings (Cattaneo et al., 2014a, b; Mas-Herrero et al., 2018) suggest that (left) DLPFC stimulation is effective in modulating aesthetic decisions, possibly via modulation of meso-cortico-limbic dopamine transmission (Fonteneau et al., 2018; Ko et al., 2008).

Medial sectors of the PFC have also been stimulated to shed light on their possibly causal contribution to aesthetic appreciation of art. Nakamura and Kawabata (2015) used a bipolar tDCS montage to simultaneously modulate excitability of the medial prefrontal cortex (mPFC) and of the left primary motor cortex (lPMC), the latter responding during subjective experience of ugliness in art, as shown by prior neuroimaging evidence (Ishizu & Zeki, 2011; Kühn & Gallinat, 2012). Participants rated the subjective beauty and ugliness of abstract paintings before and after the application of ~15 min (the exact duration of stimulation was not provided) of 2-mA tDCS. Cathodal tDCS over the mPFC with anode electrode over the lPMC led to a decrease in beauty ratings but not in ugliness ratings. In turn, anodal or sham tDCS over the mPFC did not affect ratings of either beauty or ugliness. Results from this experiment suggest that the mPFC and the lPMC are causally involved in generating the subjective experience of beauty, with beauty and ugliness evaluations likely constituting two distinct dimensions.

Aesthetic evaluation along the dorsal and ventral streams

An interesting finding consistently emerging from neuroimaging studies is that regions along the dorsal and ventral streams, such as motion-sensitive area V5 and the lateral occipital complex, may not only mediate encoding of basic perceptual features of the stimulus but also respond to a different extent depending on individual preference for that particular stimulus. Although the functional significance of the observed enhanced activity in brain regions devoted to processing basic stimulus properties during aesthetic evaluation remains to be clarified, an interesting hypothesis is that it may reflect an increased orientation toward the perceptual features individuals find appealing (Cupchik et al., 2009).

It is well known—since seminal work by Semir Zeki—that area V5 in the occipito-temporal cortex encodes the direction and speed of moving objects (Zeki, 2015). Interestingly, in a fMRI study in which participants had to rate their preference for kinetic dot configurations, Zeki and Stutters (2012) found that preferred patterns produced stronger activity in V5 (as well in V3A/B and in the parietal cortex). Artists have largely exploited visual form resources to convey a sense of motion from static depictions in paintings, and it is known from fMRI evidence that V5 also responds to *implied* motion in static images (Kourtzi & Kanwisher, 2000). In line with the finding of Zeki and Stutters (2012), it may thus be expected that V5 also responds differently depending on level of preference for paintings implying motion (but see Thakral et al., 2012). Activity along the ventral stream has also been found to relate to aesthetic preference for visual art (Cupchik et al., 2009; Ishizu & Zeki, 2013; Lacey et al., 2011; Vartanian & Goel, 2004). For instance, Lacey et al. (2011) found that responses in the (right) lateral occipital area (LO)—a key node within the ventral object recognition pathway, involved in many aspects of objects processing (for a review, see Grill-Spector, 2003)—correlated positively with aesthetic preference for artistic images. As in the case of V5, neural responses along the ventral stream, in particular in LO, may not be confined to the extraction of low-level object information, but also reflect subjective preference for a certain image, at least when the image is artistic (Lacey et al., 2011). As mentioned in the previous section, TMS can be used to explore the causal role of specific cortical regions in mediating a certain function. With regard to increased activity in V5 and LO for preferred stimuli, TMS can shed light on whether such variations in activation are *causally* related to preference. Following this rationale, two TMS studies have investigated whether interfering with LO and V5's activity affects liking of paintings (Cattaneo et al., 2015; Cattaneo, Schiavi, Silvanto, & Nadal, 2017), as is detailed below.

In a first study (Cattaneo et al., 2015), we presented a group of art-naïve participants with a series of abstract and representational paintings, and we required them to indicate as fast as possible whether they liked them or not. Triple-pulse 10-Hz TMS was delivered over the target area LO and over the vertex as a control site at the onset of each painting. Our expectation was that if the contribution of LO to aesthetic processing is strictly related to object recognition mechanisms, then TMS over LO should have selectively interfered with liking of figurative paintings but not abstract artworks, since the latter (at least the ones we selected) lacked any discernible object content. Results confirmed our hypothesis. The effects of LO TMS on liking were not due to stimulation somehow affecting the overall sharpness/clarity of the images, as we assessed in a second control TMS experiment. In turn, TMS over LO likely interfered with processing of the individual objects depicted in figurative paintings, which indirectly impacted on their liking. Indeed, when viewing representational paintings, laypersons tend to fixate mostly on recognizable objects at the expense of background information, and their liking is linked to the identity and meaning attached to those objects (e.g., Vogt & Magnussen, 2007). This view accounts also for the lack of LO TMS effects on liking for abstract paintings that contained no meaningful objects (again, the main source of aesthetic appreciation in lay participants). Although LO TMS may have affected contour detection as well (Grill-Spector, 2003), with shapes being present also in abstract artworks, abstract art appreciation in art-naïve participants likely relies on evaluation of a number of visual characteristics other than shape, such as color, texture, or dynamism. Thus, even if stimulation of LO did interfere with shape processing, our data suggest that this was not sufficiently critical to affect liking of this class of artworks.

Following a similar rationale, in a second TMS study we focused on the role of V5 in mediating the liking of artworks implying motion (Cattaneo et al., 2017). The hypothesis was that if the strength with which motion is perceived in a painting affects its liking (as suggested by behavioral evidence for both figurative and abstract paintings; see Cattaneo et al., 2017; Massaro et al., 2012), then interfering with motion detection should have also resulted in a reduction in the liking for that specific artwork. The paradigm was very similar to that used for LO stimulation (Cattaneo et al., 2015; see Figure 16.2), with art-naïve participants being presented with a series of unfamiliar figurative and abstract paintings and required to express (as fast as possible) whether or not the paintings conveyed a sense of motion, and whether or not they liked them. Triple-pulse 10-Hz TMS was applied during presentation of each painting either over vertex (control condition) or over V5. We found that V5 TMS caused a significant reduction in the sense of motion participants perceived in both figurative and abstract paintings, but reduced liking for the latter category only. The interpretation is somehow symmetrical to that provided for LO effects. The abstract paintings we selected contained no meaningful objects and their processing was thus likely closely related to sensory processes (i.e., motion perception). In turn, when looking at representational paintings in which objects are clearly recognizable, preference may be tied to a relatively more conceptual as opposed to sensory process (see also Thakral et al., 2012). Content-related features,

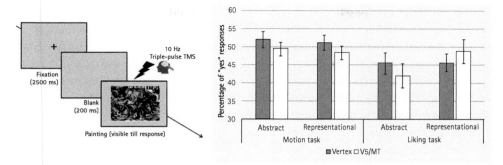

FIGURE 16.2. (Left) Example of an experimental trial in the study by Cattaneo et al. (2017). In each trial a painting was centrally presented on the screen and participants had to indicate as fast as possible whether they perceived the image as dynamic or not (sense of motion task) or whether they liked it or not (liking task). Triple-pulse TMS was given 100 ms from painting onset to interfere with the processing of implied motion conveyed by the images. The painting shown in this figure is *The Cyclist* by Natalia Goncharova (1913) (free from copyright at http://commons. wikimedia.org). (Right) Frequency histograms for "I find this dynamic" (Motion task) and "I like it" (Liking task) responses as a function of art style (figurative vs. abstract). V5-TMS reduced the number of paintings perceived as dynamic irrespective of art style. In turn, TMS over V5 selectively reduced appreciation for abstract artworks. Error bars depict ± 1 SEM.

such as familiarity or affective valence, may therefore matter more than the artwork's formal features in driving liking of figurative paintings (Nodine, Locher, & Krupinski, 1993; Winston & Cupchik, 1992). Abstract art, by definition, represents no recognizable objects, so liking can only be based on formal features, some of which constitute cues for motion.

Another region along the dorsal stream whose activity has been found to exhibit different activity for stimuli rated as beautiful compared with those rated as not beautiful is the parietal cortex (Cela-Conde et al., 2009). In the study by Cattaneo et al. (2014b) described above, interfering with parietal cortex activity with online TMS decreased liking for figurative paintings (but only in participants preferring figurative over abstract art), supporting prior neuroimaging evidence on the involvement of the parietal regions in aesthetic evaluation. The role of posterior parietal regions in directing spatial attention toward selective features salient for the ongoing task is well demonstrated (Gottlieb & Snyder, 2010), and recognizable objects is what laypersons primarily focus on when viewing artworks. Previous studies using paintings as stimuli reported that parietal activity is more closely tied to processing representational art (in which objects are visible) than abstract or indeterminate art (Fairhall & Ishai, 2008; Wiesmann and Ishai, 2010). The reduction in aesthetic appreciation induced by parietal TMS in our study may hence be linked to a disruption of Gestalt-like processing related to holistic spatial processing. Critically, parietal sectors are also involved in value-based decision making (Larsen & O'Doherty, 2014), with TMS also possibly interfering with initial stages of value computation in parietal regions.

It is worth mentioning here that effects of brain stimulation over the parietal cortex have also been studied in the context of aesthetic appreciation of dance, although with a different rationale compared with the study by Cattaneo et al. (2014b). Specifically, Grosbras and colleagues (2012) applied offline inhibitory TMS to a region of the right posterior parietal cortex that is part of the parieto-frontal executive system and is typically involved in cognitive control, whose activity (recorded with fMRI) was negatively correlated with the dynamic emotional reactions of participants while they watched a dance video. Grosbras et al. (2012) found that inhibition of this region led to an enhancement in the subjective emotion rating for specific moments in the dance, suggesting more sensitivity to emotional context. The authors interpreted these finding as suggesting that inhibiting the parieto-frontal executive control system could reduce the more cognitive processing of the dance watched (e.g., expectancies, judgment of the quality of movement, action observation mechanisms) and thereby "free" resources for emotional processing, resulting in higher appreciation. A similar approach has been adopted to study the contribution of two regions involved in body processing to appreciation of dance. In particular, Calvo-Merino et al. (2010) investigated whether and how the extrastriate body area (EBA, which houses a local representation of body parts; Urgesi et al., 2007) and the ventral premotor cortex (which houses a configural representation of complete body postures; Urgesi et al., 2007) are involved in aesthetic preference judgments for dance postures. Calvo-Merino et al. (2010) found that interfering with EBA reduced observers' aesthetic sensitivity by reducing the local processing of the stimuli. Conversely, disruption of the global route via TMS over the ventral premotor cortex increased aesthetic sensitivity by increasing the relative contribution of the local route via EBA. These findings suggest that regions specialized in global/local processing may be differently involved in aesthetic appreciation. Facilitation of a process (such as emotional engagement in the study by Grosbras et al., 2012 or local processing of the stimuli as in the case of Calvo-Merino et al., 2010) resulting from disinhibiting interactions between different processes through TMS has been observed in different contexts (for a review, see Luber & Lisanby, 2014) and may be another interesting approach to adopt when studying the neural underpinnings of aesthetic experiences.

Finally, TMS has also been used to investigate whether evaluation of emotional cues in portraits recruit the same neural mechanisms involved in processing emotional expressions in real faces (Ferrari, Schiavi, & Cattaneo, 2018). This study falls in a line of research that has compared neural responses to observation or evaluation of artworks (e.g., a painting, a sculpture) vs. photographs depicting a similar content (e.g., an everyday object, a face, a human body), finding indeed some relevant differences between artistic and nonartistic stimuli (e.g., Di Dio et al., 2011; Kesner & Horáček, 2017; Lutz et al., 2013). The superior temporal sulcus (STS), at the intersection of the ventral and dorsal stream, and the somatosensory cortex (SC), are critical regions for the processing and recognition of facial emotion expressions (Engell & Haxby, 2007; Winston, O'Doherty, & Dolan, 2003). In our study, we aimed to investigate whether interfering with STS and SC activity would have an impact on expressivity judgments about portrayed faces in paintings. Our results showed that TMS over the right STS significantly reduced the extent to which portraits (but not other paintings depicting human figures with faces only in the background) were perceived as expressive. However, TMS over the right STS did not affect the liking of portraits (again, since there are multiple factors feeding into aesthetic appreciation, selectively interfering with processing of one factor may not significantly affect the level of appreciation). These findings suggest that evaluation of emotional cues in artworks recruit (at least partially) the same neural mechanisms involved in processing genuine biological others.

Concluding Remarks: Limits and Potentials of NIBS in Neuroaesthetics

As described in this chapter, noninvasive brain stimulation may nicely complement neuroimaging and electrophysiological evidence on brain–behavioral causal links in aesthetic evaluation of artworks. However, some caveats in the use of NIBS deserve some consideration. Although NIBS techniques are safe when applied under strict guidelines (Antal et al., 2017; Rossi, Hallett, Rossini, Pascual-Leone, & Safety of TMS Consensus Group, 2009), there may be potential risks for participants that need to be carefully considered when designing experiments for basic research purposes. Moreover, there is a high interindividual variability in the effects of brain stimulation (e.g., Lee, Rastogi, Hadimani, Jiles, & Camprodon, 2018; Wiethoff, Hamada, & Rothwell, 2014) that needs to be taken into account when performing studies using TMS or tES. Also, stimulation may mainly reach cortical sites, whereas aesthetic experience heavily involves subcortical structures as well (Boccia et al., 2016), which can be only indirectly modulated by TMS or tDCS.

Notwithstanding the limitations in the use of NIBS mentioned above, there is a high potential for these techniques in developing research in neuroaesthetics. A future avenue for NIBS studies in neuroaesthetics is the use of online TMS to shed light on the time-course of the *causal* contribution of different cortical regions to aesthetic evaluation, in light of the different stages of the aesthetic process that have been identified in prior MEG and EEG research (Cela-Conde et al., 2009, 2013; Jacobsen, 2013). Furthermore, measurement of TMS-induced motor evoked potentials is another promising tool to gain insight into embodied mechanisms of aesthetic appreciation (Ardizzi et al., 2018). Another intriguing application would be the use of rhythmic TMS or tACS to interact with endogenous oscillatory neural activity during aesthetic engagement. Frequency-tuned NIBS is indeed a growing approach in cognitive neuroscience, and has already led to important developments in the understanding of the neural bases of cognitive functions, such as working memory (for a review, see Albouy et al., 2018). If, as animal and human studies consistently suggest, reward is associated with specific oscillatory neural activity (Levy, Zold, Namboodiri, & Hussain Shuler, 2017; Marco-Pallarés,

Münte, & Rodríguez-Fornells, 2015), NIBS may be used to boost oscillations related to art-related reward. State-dependency (Silvanto et al., 2008) is also an important manipulation that may benefit research in neuroaesthetics. Since ongoing brain activity critically interacts with the impact of brain stimulation (i.e., effects of stimulation are state-dependent), spatial resolution of TMS can be enhanced to target specific neuronal subpopulations/networks by changing the initial state activation of neurons with behavioral priming and adaptation protocols (Romei et al., 2016; Silvanto & Cattaneo, 2017). In the field of neuroaesthetics, combining TMS with adaptation to specific artistic styles or to a certain degree of "beauty" in art, would allow the teasing apart of the neural tuning properties of the cortical regions involved in aesthetic evaluation. The use of NIBS to modulate connectivity in the brain networks involved in aesthetic appreciation is another unexplored field of investigation. For instance, tDCS applied to nodes of the default mode network (DMN) has been found to effectively impact mind wandering (Kajimura, Kochiyama, Nakai, Abe, & Nomura, 2016), and may also affect aesthetic experiences that are known to recruit the DMN (Cela-Conde et al., 2013; Vessel, Starr, & Rubin, 2013). Research in neuroaesthetics may also benefit from the combination of NIBS with fMRI or EEG recording to better understand the interrelation between the physiological and behavioral impacts of brain stimulation on aesthetic evaluation; the combined use of these methods representing a growing approach in cognitive neuroscience (Farzan et al., 2016; Plow et al., 2014; Saiote, Turi, Paulus, & Antal, 2013).

References

Albouy, P., Baillet, S., & Zatorre, R. J. (2018). Driving working memory with frequency-tuned noninvasive brain stimulation. *Annals of the New York Academy of Sciences*.

Albouy, P., Weiss, A., Baillet, S., & Zatorre, R. J. (2017). Selective entrainment of theta oscillations in the dorsal stream causally enhances auditory working memory performance. *Neuron, 94*(1), 193–206.

Antal, A., Alekseichuk, I., Bikson, M., Brockmöller, J., Brunoni, A. R., Chen, R., ... Paulus W. (2017). Low intensity transcranial electric stimulation: Safety, ethical, legal regulatory and application guidelines. *Clinical Neurophysiology, 128*(9), 1774–1809.

Antal, A., & Herrmann, C. S. (2016). Transcranial alternating current and random noise stimulation: Possible mechanisms. *Neural Plasticity, 2016*, 3616807.

Ardizzi, M., Ferroni, F., Siri, F., Umiltà, M. A., Cotti, A., Calbi, M., Fadda, E., Freedberg, D., & Gallese, V. (2018). Beholders' sensorimotor engagement enhances aesthetic rating of pictorial facial expressions of pain. Psychology Research.

Bergmann, T. O., Karabanov, A., Hartwigsen, G., Thielscher, A., & Siebner, H. R. (2016). Combining non-invasive transcranial brain stimulation with neuroimaging and electrophysiology: Current approaches and future perspectives. *Neuroimage, 140*, 4–19.

Bestmann, S., & Walsh, V. (2017). Transcranial electrical stimulation. *Current Biology, 27*(23), 1258–1262.

Bikson, M., Brunoni, A. R., Charvet, L. E., Clark, V. P., Cohen, L. G., Deng, Z. D., ... Lisanby, S. H. (2018). Rigor and reproducibility in research with transcranial electrical stimulation: An NIMH-sponsored workshop. *Brain Stimulation, 11*(3), 465–480.

Boccia, M., Barbetti, S., Piccardi, L., Guariglia, C., Ferlazzo, F., Giannini, A. M., & Zaidel, D. W. (2016). Where does brain neural activation in aesthetic responses to visual art occur? Meta-analytic evidence from neuroimaging studies. *Neuroscience & Biobehavioral Reviews, 60*, 65–71.

Boes, A. D., Kelly, M. S., Trapp, N. T., Stern, A. P., Press, D. Z., & Pascual-Leone, A. (2018). Noninvasive brain stimulation: Challenges and opportunities for a new clinical specialty. *Journal of Neuropsychiatry and Clinical Neuroscience, 30*(3), 173–179.

Cabral-Calderin, Y., & Wilke, M. (2020). Probing the link between perception and oscillations: Lessons from transcranial alternating current stimulation. Neuroscientist, *26*(1), 57–73. doi:10.1177/1073858419828646

Calvo-Merino, B., Urgesi, C., Orgs, G., Aglioti, S. M., & Haggard, P. (2010). Extrastriate body area underlies aesthetic evaluation of body stimuli. *Experimental Brain Research, 204*(3), 447e56.

Cattaneo, Z., Lega, C., Ferrari, C., Vecchi, T., Cela-Conde, C. J., Silvanto, J., & Nadal, M. (2015). The role of the lateral occipital cortex in aesthetic appreciation of representational and abstract paintings: A TMS study. *Brain and Cognition, 95*, 44–53.

Cattaneo, Z., Lega, C., Flexas, A., Nadal, M., Munar, E., & Cela-Conde, C. J. (2014a). The world can look better: Enhancing beauty experience with brain stimulation. *Social Cognitive and Affective Neuroscience, 9*(11), 1713–1721.

Cattaneo, Z., Lega, C., Gardelli, C., Merabet, L. B., Cela-Conde, C., & Nadal, M. (2014b). The role of prefrontal and parietal cortices in aesthetic appreciation of representational and abstract art: A TMS study. *Neuroimage, 99*, 443–450.

Cattaneo, Z., Schiavi, S., Silvanto, J., & Nadal, M. (2017). A TMS study on the contribution of visual area V5 to the perception of implied motion in art and its appreciation. *Cognitive Neuroscience, 8*, 59–68.

Cela-Conde, C. J., Ayala, F. J., Munar, E., Maestú, F., Nadal, M., Capó, M. A., ... Marty, G. (2009). Sex-related similarities and differences in the neural correlates of beauty. *Proceedings of the National Academy of Sciences of the USA, 106*, 3847–3852.

Cela-Conde, C. J., García-Prieto, J., Ramasco, J. J., Mirasso, C. R., Bajo, R., Munar, E., ... Maestú, F. (2013). Dynamics of brain networks in the aesthetic appreciation. *Proceedings of the National Academy of Sciences of the USA, 110*(Suppl. 2), 10454–10461.

Cela-Conde, C. J., Marty, G., Maestú, F., Ortiz, T., Munar, E., Fernández, A., Roca, M., ... Quesney, F. (2004). Activation of the prefrontal cortex in the human visual aesthetic perception. *Proceedings of the National Academy of Sciences of the USA, 101*, 6321–6325.

Chatterjee, A., & Vartanian, O. (2016). Neuroscience of aesthetics. *Annals of the New York Academy of Sciences, 1369*(1), 172–194.

Cupchik, G. C., Vartanian, O., Crawley, A., & Mikulis, D. J. (2009). Viewing artworks: contributions of cognitive control and perceptual facilitation to aesthetic experience. *Brain Cognition, 70*, 84–91.

DaSilva, A. F., Volz, M. S., Bikson, M., & Fregni, F. (2011). Electrode positioning and montage in transcranial direct current stimulation. *Journal of Visualized Experiments*, (51), pii, 2744.

de Graaf, T. A., Koivisto, M., Jacobs, C., & Sack, A. T. (2014). The chronometry of visual perception: Review of occipital TMS masking studies. *Neuroscience and Biobehavioral Reviews, 45*, 295–304.

Di Dio, C., Canessa, N., Cappa, S. F., & Rizzolatti, G. (2011). Specificity of esthetic experience for artworks: An fMRI study. *Frontiers in Human Neuroscience, 5*, 139.

Engell, A. D., & Haxby, J. V. (2007). Facial expression and gaze-direction in human superior temporal sulcus. *Neuropsychologia, 45*(14), 3234–3241.

Fairhall, S. L., & Ishai, A. (2008). Neural correlates of object indeterminacy in art compositions. *Conscious Cognition, 17*, 923–932.

Farzan, F., Vernet, M., Shafi, M. M., Rotenberg, A., Daskalakis, Z. J., & Pascual-Leone, A. (2016). Characterizing and modulating brain circuitry through transcranial magnetic stimulation combined with electroencephalography. *Frontiers in Neural Circuits, 10*, 73. doi:10.3389/fncir.2016.00073

Ferrari, C., Schiavi, S., & Cattaneo Z. (2018). TMS over the superior temporal sulcus affects expressivity evaluation of portraits. Cognitive, Affective, and Behavioral Neuroscience.

Filmer, H. L., Dux, P. E., & Mattingley, J. B. (2014). Applications of transcranial direct current stimulation for understanding brain function. *Trends in Neuroscience, 37*(12), 742–753.

Fonteneau, C., Redoute, J., Haesebaert, F., Le Bars, D., Costes, N., Suaud-Chagny, M. F., & Brunelin, J. (2018). Frontal transcranial direct current stimulation induces dopamine release in the ventral striatum in human. *Cerebral Cortex, 28*(7), 2636–2646.

Ghin, F., Pavan, A., Contillo, A., & Mather, G. (2018). The effects of high-frequency transcranial random noise stimulation (hf-tRNS) on global motion processing: An equivalent noise approach. *Brain Stimulation, S1935-861X*(18), 30252–30253.

Gottlieb, J., & Snyder, L. H. (2010). Spatial and non-spatial functions of the parietal cortex. *Current Opinion in Neurobiology, 20*(6), 731–740.

Grill-Spector, K. (2003). The neural basis of object perception. *Current Opinion in Neurobiology, 13*(2), 159–166.

Grosbras, M. H., Tan, H., & Pollick, F. (2012). Dance and emotion in posterior parietal cortex: a low-frequency rTMS study. *Brain Stimulation, 5*(2), 130–136.

Hallett, M., Di Iorio, R., Rossini, P. M., Park, J. E., Chen, R., Celnik, P., … Ugawa, Y. (2017). Contribution of transcranial magnetic stimulation to assessment of brain connectivity and networks. *Clinical Neurophysiology, 128*(11), 2125–2139.

Hopfinger, J. B., Parsons, J., & Fröhlich, F. (2017). Differential effects of 10-Hz and 40-Hz transcranial alternating current stimulation (tACS) on endogenous versus exogenous attention. *Cognitive Neuroscience, 8*(2), 102–111.

Ishizu, T., & Zeki, S. (2011). Toward a brain-based theory of beauty. *PLoS ONE, 6*(7), e21852.

Ishizu, T., & Zeki, S. (2013). The brain's specialized systems for aesthetic and perceptual judgment. *European Journal of Neuroscience, 37*(9), 1413–1420.

Ishizu, T., & Zeki, S. (2017). The experience of beauty derived from sorrow. *Human Brain Mapping, 38*(8), 4185–4200.

Jacobsen, T. (2013). On the electrophysiology of aesthetic processing. *Progress in Brain Research, 204*, 159–168.

Kajimura, S., Kochiyama, T., Nakai, R., Abe, N., & Nomura, M. (2016). Causal relationship between effective connectivity within the default mode network and mind-wandering regulation and facilitation. *Neuroimage, 133*, 21–30.

Kesner, L., & Horáček, J. (2017). Empathy-related responses to depicted people in art works. *Frontiers in Psychology, 8*, 228. doi:10.3389/fpsyg.2017.00228

Ko, J. H., Monchi, O., Ptito, A., Bloomfield, P., Houle, S., & Strafella, A. P. (2008). Theta burst stimulation-induced inhibition of dorsolateral prefrontal cortex reveals hemispheric asymmetry in striatal dopamine release during a set-shifting task: A TMS-[(11)C]raclopride PET study. *European Journal of Neuroscience, 28*(10), 2147–2155.

Kourtzi, Z., & Kanwisher, N. (2000). Activation in human MT/MST by static images with implied motion. *Journal of Cognitive Neuroscience, 12*, 48–55.

Kühn, S., & Gallinat, J. (2012). The neural correlates of subjective pleasantness. *Neuroimage, 61*, 289–294.

Lacey, S., Hagtvedt, H., Patrick, V. M., Anderson, A., Silla, R., Deshpande, G., … Sathian, K., (2011). Art for reward's sake: visual art recruits the ventral striatum. *Neuroimage, 55*, 420–433.

Larsen, T., & O'Doherty, J. P. (2014). Uncovering the spatio-temporal dynamics of value-based decision-making in the human brain: A combined fMRI-EEG study. *Philosophical Transactions of the Royal Society London B: Biological Sciences, 369*(1655), pii, 20130473.

Leder, H., & Nadal, M. (2014). Ten years of a model of aesthetic appreciation and aesthetic judgments: The aesthetic episode—Developments and challenges in empirical aesthetics. *British Journal of Psychology, 105*(4), 443–464.

Lee, E. G., Rastogi, P., Hadimani, R. L., Jiles, D. C., & Camprodon, J. A. (2018). Impact of non-brain anatomy and coil orientation on inter- and intra-subject variability in TMS at midline. *Clinical Neurophysiology, 129*(9), 1873–1883.

Lengger, P. G., Fischmeister, F. P. S., Leder, H., & Bauer, H. (2007). Functional neuroanatomy of the perception of modern art: A DC-EEG study on the influence of stylistic information on aesthetic experience. *Brain Research, 1158*, 93–102.

Levy, J. M., Zold, C. L., Namboodiri, V. M. K., & Hussain Shuler, M. G. (2017). The timing of reward-seeking action tracks visually cued theta oscillations in primary visual cortex. *Journal of Neuroscience, 37*(43), 10408–10420.

Luber, B., & Lisanby, S. H. (2014). Enhancement of human cognitive performance using transcranial magnetic stimulation (TMS). *Neuroimage, 85*(3), 961–970.

Lutz, A., Nassehi, A., Bao, Y., Pöppel, E., Sztrókay, A., Reiser, M., Fehse, K., & Gutyrchik, E. (2013). Neurocognitive processing of body representations in artistic and photographic images. *Neuroimage, 66*, 288–292.

Marco-Pallarés, J., Münte, T. F., & Rodríguez-Fornells, A. (2015). The role of high-frequency oscillatory activity in reward processing and learning. *Neuroscience and Biobehavioral Reviews, 49*, 1–7.

Martin, D. M., Liu, R., Alonzo, A., Green, M., & Loo, C. K. (2014). Use of transcranial direct current stimulation (tDCS) to enhance cognitive training: Effect of timing of stimulation. *Experimental Brain Research, 232*(10), 3345–3351.

Mas-Herrero, E., Dagher, A., & Zatorre, R. J. (2018). Modulating musical reward sensitivity up and down with transcranial magnetic stimulation. *Nature Human Behavior 2*(1), 27–32.

Massaro, D., Savazzi, F., Di Dio, C., Freedberg, D., Gallese, V., Gilli, G., & Marchetti, A. (2012). When art moves the eyes: A behavioral and eye-tracking study. *PLoS ONE, 7*, e37285.

Mitchell, R. L. C., Vidaki, K., & Lavidor, M. (2016). The role of left and right dorsolateral prefrontal cortex in semantic processing: A transcranial direct current stimulation study. *Neuropsychologia, 91*, 480–489.

Mondino, M., Thiffault, F., & Fecteau, S. (2015). Does non-invasive brain stimulation applied over the dorsolateral prefrontal cortex non-specifically influence mood and emotional processing in healthy individuals? *Frontiers in Cellular Neuroscience, 9*, 399. doi:10.3389/fncel.2015.00399

Nakamura, K., & Kawabata, H. (2015). Transcranial direct current stimulation over the medial prefrontal cortex and left primary motor cortex (mPFC-lPMC) affects subjective beauty but not ugliness. *Frontiers in Human Neuroscience, 9*, 654.

Nitsche, M. A., & Paulus, W. (2000). Excitability changes induced in the human motor cortex by weak transcranial direct current stimulation. *Journal of Physiology, 527*(3), 633–639.

Nodine, C. F., Locher, P. J., & Krupinski, E. A. (1993). The role of formal art training on perception and aesthetic judgment of art compositions. *Leonardo, 26,* 219–227.

Opitz, A., Paulus, W., Will, S., Antunes, A., & Thielscher, A. (2015). Determinants of the electric field during transcranial direct current stimulation. *NeuroImage, 109,* 140–150.

Pang, C. Y., Nadal, M., Müller, J. S., Rosenberg, R., & Klein, C. (2013). Electrophysiological correlates of looking at paintings and its association with art expertise. *Biological Psychology, 93,* 246–254.

Parkin, B. L., Ekhtiari, H., & Walsh, V. F. (2015). non-invasive human brain stimulation in cognitive neuroscience: A primer. *Neuron, 87*(5), 932–945.

Pascual-Leone, A., Walsh, V., & Rothwell, J. C. (2000). Transcranial magnetic stimulation in cognitive neuroscience—Virtual lesion, chronometry and functional connectivity. *Current Opinion in Neurobiology, 10,* 232–237.

Pelowski, M., Markey, P. S., Forster, M., Gerger, G., & Leder, H. (2017). Move me, astonish me ... delight my eyes and brain: The Vienna integrated model of top-down and bottom-up processes in art perception (VIMAP) and corresponding affective, evaluative, and neurophysiological correlates. *Physics of Life Reviews, 21,* 80–125.

Pitcher, D., Japee, S., Rauth, L., & Ungerleider, L. G. (2017). The superior temporal sulcus is causally connected to the amygdala: A combined TBS-fMRI study. *Journal of Neuroscience, 37*(5), 1156–1161.

Plow, E. B., Cattaneo, Z., Carlson, T. A., Alvarez, G. A., Pascual-Leone, A., & Battelli, L. (2014). The compensatory dynamic of inter-hemispheric interactions in visuospatial attention revealed using rTMS and fMRI. *Frontiers in Human Neuroscience, 8,* 226.

Popescu, T., Krause, B., Terhune, D. B., Twose, O., Page, T., Humphreys, G., & Cohen Kadosh, R. (2016). Transcranial random noise stimulation mitigates increased difficulty in an arithmetic learning task. *Neuropsychologia, 81,* 255–264.

Romei, V., Thut, G., Mok, R. M., Schyns, P. G., & Driver, J. (2012). Causal implication by rhythmic transcranial magnetic stimulation of alpha frequency in feature-based local vs. global attention. *European Journal of Neuroscience, 35*(6), 968–974.

Romei, V., Thut, G., & Silvanto, J. (2016). Information-based approaches of noninvasive transcranial brain stimulation. *Trends in Neuroscience, 39*(11), 782–795.

Rossi, S., Hallett, M., Rossini, P. M., Pascual-Leone, A., & Safety of TMS Consensus Group (2009). Safety, ethical considerations, and application guidelines for the use of transcranial magnetic stimulation in clinical practice and research. *Clinical Neurophysiology, 120*(12), 2008–2039.

Saiote, C., Turi, Z., Paulus, W., & Antal, A. (2013). Combining functional magnetic resonance imaging with transcranial electrical stimulation. *Frontiers in Human Neuroscience, 7,* 435.

Samoudi, A. M., Tanghe, E., Martens, L., & Joseph, W. (2018). Deep transcranial magnetic stimulation: improved coil design and assessment of the induced fields using MIDA model. *BioMed Research International, 2018,* 7061420.

Sandrini, M., Umilta, C., & Rusconi, E. (2011). The use of transcranial magnetic stimulation in cognitive neuroscience: A new synthesis of methodological issues. *Neuroscience and Biobehavioral Reviews, 5*(3), 516–536.

Santarnecchi, E., Muller, T., Rossi, S., Sarkar, A., Polizzotto, N. R., Rossi, A., & Cohen Kadosh R. (2016). Individual differences and specificity of prefrontal gamma frequency-tACS on fluid intelligence capabilities. *Cortex, 75,* 33–43.

Silvanto, J., & Cattaneo, Z. (2017). Common framework for "virtual lesion" and state-dependent TMS: The facilitatory/suppressive range model of online TMS effects on behaviour. *Brain & Cognition, 119*, 32–38.

Silvanto, J., Muggleton, N., & Walsh, V. (2008). State-dependency in brain stimulation studies of perception and cognition. *Trends in Cognitive Science, 12*(12), 447–454.

Sliwinska, M. W., Vitello, S., & Devlin, J. T. (2014). Transcranial magnetic stimulation for investigating causal brain-behavioral relationships and their time course. *Journal of Visualizing Experiments, 89*, e51735. doi:10.3791/51735

Stagg, C. J., & Nitsche, M. A. (2011). Physiological basis of transcranial direct current stimulation. *Neuroscientist, 17*, 37–53.

Tambini, A., Nee, D. E., & D'Esposito, M. (2018). Hippocampal-targeted theta-burst stimulation enhances associative memory formation. *Journal of Cognitive Neuroscience, 30*(10), 1452–1472.

Thakral, P. P., Moo, L. R., & Slotnick, S. D. (2012). A neural mechanism for aesthetic experience. *NeuroReport, 23*, 310–313.

Thut, G., & Pascual-Leone, A. (2010). A review of combined TMS-EEG studies to characterize lasting effects of repetitive TMS and assess their usefulness in cognitive and clinical neuroscience. *Brain Topography, 22*(4), 219–232.

Tik, M., Hoffmann, A., Sladky, R., Tomova, L., Hummer, A., Navarro de Lara, L., ... Windischberger, C. (2017). Towards understanding rTMS mechanism of action: Stimulation of the DLPFC causes network-specific increase in functional connectivity. *Neuroimage, 162*, 289–296.

Urgesi, C., Calvo-Merino, B., Haggard, P., & Aglioti, S. M. (2007) Transcranial magnetic stimulation reveals two cortical pathways for visual body processing. *Journal of Neuroscience, 27*, 8023–8030.

Valero-Cabré, A., Amengual, J. L., Stengel, C., Pascual-Leone, A., & Coubard, O. A. (2017). Transcranial magnetic stimulation in basic and clinical neuroscience: A comprehensive review of fundamental principles and novel insights. *Neuroscience and Biobehavoural Reviews, 83*, 381–404.

Vartanian, O., & Goel, V. (2004). Neuroanatomical correlates of aesthetic preference for paintings. *Neuroreport, 15*, 893–897.

Vessel, E. A., Starr, G. G., & Rubin, N. (2012). The brain on art: Intense aesthetic experience activates the default mode network. *Frontiers in Human Neuroscience, 6*, 66.

Vessel, E. A., Starr, G. G., & Rubin, N. (2013). Art reaches within: Aesthetic experience, the self and the default mode network. *Frontiers Neuroscience, 7*, 258.

Vogt, S., & Magnussen, S. (2007). Expertise in pictorial perception: Eye-movement patterns and visual memory in artists and laymen. *Perception, 36*(1), 91–100.

Wiesmann, M., & Ishai, A. (2010). Training facilitates object recognition in cubist paintings. *Frontiers in Human Neuroscience, 4*, 11.

Wiethoff, S., Hamada, M., Rothwell, J. C. (2014). Variability in response to transcranial direct current stimulation of the motor cortex. *Brain Stimulation, 7*(3), 468–475.

Winston, A. S., & Cupchik, G. C. (1992). The evaluation of high art and popular art by naive and experienced viewers. *Visual Arts Research, 18*, 1–14.

Winston, J. S., O'Doherty, J., & Dolan, R. J. (2003). Common and distinct neural responses during direct and incidental processing of multiple facial emotions. *Neuroimage, 20*(1), 84–97.

Woods, A. J., Antal, A., Bikson, M., Boggio, P. S., Brunoni, A. R., Celnik, P., … Knotkova, H. (2016). A technical guide to tDCS, and related non-invasive brain stimulation tools. *Clinical Neurophysiology, 127*(2), 1031–1048.

Yavari, F., Jamil, A., Mosayebi Samani, M., Vidor, L. P., & Nitsche, M. A. (2018). Basic and functional effects of transcranial electrical stimulation (tES)—An introduction. *Neuroscience and Biobehavioral Reviews, 85,* 81–92.

Zeki, S. (2015). Area V5—A microcosm of the visual brain. *Frontiers in Integrative Neuroscience, 9,* 21.

Zeki, S., & Stutters, J. (2012). A brain-derived metric for preferred kinetic stimuli. *Open Biology, 2,* 120001.

Zhang, W., Lai, S., He, X., Zhao, X., & Lai, S. (2016). Neural correlates for aesthetic appraisal of pictograph and its referent: An fMRI study. *Behavioural Brain Research, 305,* 229–238.

CHAPTER 17

INTEGRATED METHODS

A Call for Integrative and Interdisciplinary Aesthetics Research

MARTIN TRÖNDLE, STEVEN GREENWOOD,
CHANDRASEKHAR RAMAKRISHNAN,
FOLKERT UHDE, HAUKE EGERMANN, AND
WOLFGANG TSCHACHER

INTRODUCTION

THE differences between qualitative and quantitative research have been discussed extensively, and a prominent example is C.P. Snow's speech in 1959 (Snow, 2001). Snow perceived a division of qualitative and quantitative disciplines as delineating two separate cultures, and this observation might be still relevant today (Tschacher et al., 2011). Before Snow, Wilhelm Dilthey, who significantly contributed to the academic humanities, made an effort in 1894 to differentiate in psychology the interpretative from the explanatory approach (Galliker, Klein, & Reikart, 2007).[1] A dichotomy between understanding and explaining is still found in the principles of qualitative-and/or phenomenological-orientated disciplines in the humanities versus those of quantitative-objectifying disciplines in the sciences.

Scientists are commonly committed to their home disciplines and their respective socializations. On the one side, proponents of the interpretative "soft sciences" of the humanities and cultural studies commonly adopt a constructivist philosophy of science, and thus are wary of statistical quantitative methodologies because they might lead to a misrepresentation of their fields. On the other side, researchers socialized with quantitative and statistical modeling often lack an understanding of qualitative research and its interpretative values. Some philosophers of science even argue that all sciences are interpretative: statistical significances without interpretation would make no sense, and all data have to be generated before they can be interpreted (Knorr-Cetina, 2002; Latour & Woolgar, 1979).

The division of interpretative versus statistical approaches is nourished by the self-preservation politics of university departments, as well as by funding agencies, which are commonly organized along disciplinary lines. Even interdisciplinary research often stays within the boundaries of either quantitative or qualitative research endeavors. Hammersley (2013) therefore interprets the competing paradigms as openly antagonistic: "one as the true way, the other as the way of error or even of sin" (p. 2). We do not support such polarity, and therefore wish to present an integrative methodology for the empirical study of aesthetics. A *Handbook of Empirical Aesthetics* clearly calls for the integration of the quantitative and qualitative traditions. In this chapter, we will present this integrated methodological approach in the form of seven theses for aesthetics research:

1. Aesthetics research must emphasize *ecological validity*.
2. Measurement shall be *unobtrusive*.
3. Measures must be *inclusive* and cover all aspects of art reception.
4. Cognition should be understood as *embodied*.
5. *Artistic research* can generate novel epistemologies.
6. Qualitative and quantitative data must be *integrated*.
7. Perspectives of *participating* disciplines must be considered.

We will present these theses against the background of two large-scale research projects that attempted to triangulate a common research object: the aesthetic experience. A brief description of the methodological designs of both projects is given in the following section.

DESCRIPTION OF THE TWO PROJECTS

eMotion: Mapping museum experience

The project *eMotion: mapping museum experience* investigated aesthetic experiences of artworks (painting, sculpture, installations) in the environment of a fine arts museum (www.mapping-museum-experience.com/en). The *eMotion* project was initiated in 2008 and terminated in 2016. All spontaneous adult visitors during a field research phase between June and August 2009 were invited to participate in the project. After informed consent, participants received a "data glove" and an identification number (ID). The glove contained three electronic components: a small sender that continually tracked the visitor's position in the museum space, electrodes that measured skin conductance between two fingers, and a photoplethysmographic sensor that determined

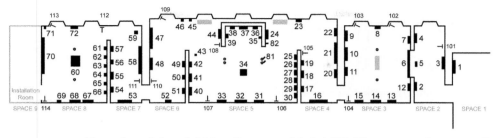

FIGURE 17.1. Floor plan of the exhibition. Spaces are labeled SPACE 1–9, artworks 1–81, wall texts 101–114. The three gray rectangles represent benches for sitting. Visitors started the tour in SPACE 1 and finished in SPACE 9.

blood pulse volume to infer heart rate. All information was transmitted and stored in a wireless network (WLAN) and labeled by the respective IDs anonymously. Before embarking on their tour (see Figure 17.1), participants completed an entry survey that collected sociodemographic characteristics, information on the frequency with which they visited museums, their expectations and motives for visiting the exhibition, their experiences and knowledge of modern fine art, and their momentary emotional state. The questionnaire contained short questions using 5-point Likert scales. The survey answers were entered directly into a computer and coded by the visitors' IDs. Following the entry survey, participants were able to move freely through the museum. At the end of the tour, the electronically enabled exit survey was conducted. Using similar quantitative scales, the particular focus was on experiences during the visit. Items on art experiences were formulated in analogy to the expectations items of the entry survey. Visitors evaluated the arrangement of the artworks and didactic panels of the exhibition. Further items concerned social interactions visitors may have had during their visit.

Of particular interest were responses to specific artworks to which the participant responded most ("peak artworks"). The criteria for selecting peak artworks were: time spent in front of the artwork, heart rate peaks, and skin conductance peaks. These criteria were assessed automatically by the system on the basis of the WLAN-collected tracking data (see Figure 17.2). For each of the three "peak" artworks, the participant was reshown the particular work on a computer screen and presented with items to assess it. Questions were given relating to theme and content, artistic technique, composition, beauty, the artwork's context (authorship, presentation of the artwork in the space, art historical significance, relation to other artworks in the exhibition), and its effect ("this artwork … surprised me; moved me; made me laugh, etc."). To provide comparison to these individually determined artworks, the same data were collected for three other artworks chosen by the investigators, which were identical for all participants. Four weeks after visitors toured the museum, they were invited by email to complete a follow-up survey (for detail, see Tröndle, Greenwood, Kirchberg, & Tschacher, 2014b).

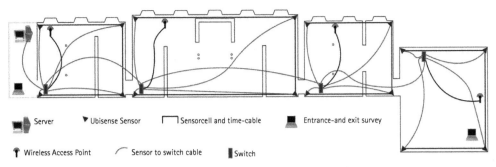

Server   ▼ Ubisense Sensor   ☐ Sensorcell and time-cable   ■ Entrance-and exit survey

⦗ Wireless Access Point   ⌒ Sensor to switch cable   ▮ Switch

FIGURE 17.2. *eMotion* network infrastructure.

ECR—Experimental Concert Research

The project *ECR—Experimental Concert Research*[2] was initiated in 2018 and is currently investigating aesthetic experiences in concerts of classical music (https://experimental-concert-research.org). The preconcert and postconcert surveys will be performed very similarly to the *eMotion* project, with items adapted to music listening in a concert (see Table 17.1).

Preconcert survey

A questionnaire will be designed on the basis of existing knowledge on concert attendance and concert experience. It will contain sociodemographic questions and questions on education level and vocational activities, together with a series of music-related questions expected to be covariates influencing the concert experience. We

Table 17.1. Overview of the stages of data acquisition.

Before the concert		During the concert	After the concert	
I. Approaching attendees: Informed consent of participants	II. Preconcert survey: Sociodemographics, assessment of knowledge, expectations, musical practice, etc.	III. Concert as experimental test series, collection of quantitative experimental data: Heart rate and skin conductance, motion tracking and facial expression, audience audio analysis	IV. Postconcert survey: Experience as regards expectations Inquiry into individual experiences of "peak passages" Additionally: Qualitative interviews	V. Delayed follow-up survey, 4 weeks after the concert: Asking for recall of the concert

Throughout the experimental phase: Taking ethnographic field notes during the experimental phase (I–IV)

will record the individual motivations for attending classical concerts, operationalized by items such as: "What was the main reason for your visit today?" "Why do you normally attend classical concerts?" We will assess musical taste ("How much do you like the following musical styles: … ?"), musical knowledge ("How well do you know the following composers, genres, pieces?" "How would you describe your musical knowledge?"), and personal musical practice (i.e., whether the participant plays an instrument or sings, for how long, and at what level). These items will be aggregated to a scaled measure of musical expertise, directly analogous to the psychometrically constructed Art Affinity Index (AAI) (Tschacher, Bergomi, & Tröndle, 2015). Further, we will assess the expectations concerning the upcoming concert by asking, "How important are the following aspects of a concert to you?" Participants will be asked to rate the following characteristics of a concert with a scale of 1 = unimportant, 2 = rather unimportant, 3 = neutral, 4 = important, to 5 = very important:

- the pieces that are played; the musicians;
- the interpretation of the pieces;
- the information about the pieces; to watch the musicians live;
- the opportunity to talk to others and get together before and after the concert;
- the concert venue; the choice of music pieces;
- the curation of the concert; the atmosphere of the concert; the intensity of the performance; etc.

All items will be formulated as closed questions to be ticked in a box (e.g., list of vocational activities) or rated on Likert scales. The questionnaire will be tested in pilot validation studies, and afterward used as the preconcert survey in the concert experiments (II. in Table 17.1). Parts of the preconcert survey will be applied in the postconcert survey (IV. in Table 17.1) in order to compare expectations with experiences and to evaluate the aesthetic responses to the particular experimental concert variation.

Physiological data

As in the *eMotion* project, in *ECR* heart rate, skin conductance, and additionally respiration of the participants will be monitored throughout the concert (concerning these measurements, see Thesis 3).

Body movement

ECR will use infrared-video recordings to measure body movement induced in the audience, as developed in projects based on motion energy analysis (MEA). MEA is a method of video analysis by which the amount of bodily movement in defined regions of a video can be objectively quantified by frame-to-frame pixel differencing (Ramseyer & Tschacher, 2010, 2011). We assume that listeners in concerts will tend to resonate to the music and thus possibly synchronize movement with each other. In a first study, the investigators found small to medium synchronization of the audience members, even within the behaviorally restrictive setting of a classical concert (Seibert, Greb, & Tschacher, 2019). This nonverbal synchrony might also be related to aspects of musical experience. In the mentioned pilot study, a complex interaction between the audience's focus on the music performance and the synchronization among co-listeners was found, which calls for further investigation. MEA is a novel and objective tool to study the embodied synchronization of a group to musical stimuli; in this way, it allows the evaluation of an aspect that is central for concert experience as a genuinely collective phenomenon. A similar methodological approach was used recently by Jakubowski et al. (2017).

Audience facial expression

The project is aiming for image-based detection, analysis, and interpretation of faces to analyze (aesthetic) emotion in the concert audience, using automated coding of facial expressions. Emotions can then be inferred based on these observations (e.g., positive and negative affect operationalized by activity of facial muscles involved in smiling and frowning, respectively). This approach will provide continuous measures of the audience's basic emotional states in response to different concert characteristics and enable them to be correlated with other collected data. Additionally, the musicians on the stage will be recorded by video.

As in *eMotion*, participants are given a unique ID. All data of the pre- and postconcert surveys can thus be linked and saved on a central server. No personal data will be collected that could lead to subsequent identification of the test person. As the audience is leaving the concert hall, project assistants will accompany their respective participants back to the questioning stations to conduct the postconcert survey, which will consist of items covering the general concert experience and appreciation and the experimental variation of the particular day or concert; for example, "Which of the following statements best fits your own experience during the concert tonight: the concert was thought-provoking; the concert's program composition was engaging; I enjoyed the atmosphere of the concert; I experienced a deep connection to the music, etc."

Subsequent to this standardized part of the postconcert survey, an automatically generated individualized part will relate to the specific "peak passages" identified for each individual based on the data. The participant will be confronted with moments of the concert when specific response patterns of skin conductance, heart rate, respiration, facial expression, and movement occurred. It is assumed that the selected musical passages (the participant will have to assess a video [items on Likert scale] of 10 s taken from when the peak was happening) may be linked to specific musical or performative attributes.

To enable this personalized postconcert survey and to match the quantitative and the qualitative data, a dedicated server-client architecture for time-indexed media streaming to multiple clients will be prototyped and implemented. The system will allow streaming audio-visual recordings of the concert to be included in the postconcert survey directly after they have been made. Additionally, the survey will be equipped with an ID-specific timeline indicating the general and individual peak passages as predefined, or else as identified by the automated peak moment analysis described above.

In analogy to the *eMotion* project (Tröndle, Greenwood, Bitterli, & van den Berg, 2014a; Tröndle & Tschacher, 2012), in *ECR* the aim is to test a series of situations or arrangements to investigate several hypotheses on the aesthetic experience. The

FIGURE 17.3. Radialsystem, Berlin, main hall. © Phil Dera, with permission.

underlying assumption is that the frame (the context and the way the concert is staged) in which the music is perceived heavily influences the aesthetic experience. To give an example: for testing the question "What is the difference between audience members' experience of a specific musical performance when the concert setting shifts from a contemporary location to a more traditional one?" the concert venues will thus serve as "laboratories" for the experiments. By staging the experimental concert similarly in two venues, Radialsystem in Berlin (see Figure 17.3) and the Pierre Boulez Saal Berlin (see Figure 17.4), with the same musicians and the same program, the effect of the spaces shall be investigated.

Several other hypotheses concerning the influence of the information given to the audience, moderation, and concert curation (*mise-en-scène*) on the framing will be tested incrementally, in eight different concerts with 100 participants each.

Additionally, to this quantitative survey we also aim to conduct qualitative, in-depth interviews with those concert attendees who did not participate in the experiment.

DISCUSSION OF THE SEVEN THESES

Thesis 1:   Research must emphasize ecological validity

In the *eMotion* project, the point of departure was to recruit participants who spontaneously visited a museum, and then to observe them in this very setting. In analogy, the

FIGURE 17.4. Pierre Boulez Saal, Berlin. Photo by Martin Tröndle.

ECR project addresses concertgoers and monitors their responses in the concert hall. The main motivation in both cases is ecological validity: research shall address the phenomenon of interest directly, not its laboratory derivative.

First, we believe that the motivation of participants might be essential for empirical aesthetics research—that is, we need to study people who become museumgoers or concert visitors of their own accord. Recruiting students who receive course credits for participation in a laboratory environment can be regarded only as an initial step of basic research, and one that severely lacks ecological validity.

Second, in the museum study, a visitor enters the exhibition, chooses freely which artworks to examine until he or she becomes captivated by a specific artwork, which may have a very specific and idiosyncratic attraction for this visitor. Gumbrecht (2004) suggests that the "presence" of art is perceived in such observations; this culture of presence is a novel aspect of art appreciation in contrast to the hermeneutical culture of meaning (the *Sinnkultur* prevalent in the humanistic sciences). Presence emphasizes the materiality and experiential nature of objects, highlighting the intensity of interaction between the observer and the object observed. Questionnaires can only be deployed at a temporal distance from these moments of presence (see Thesis 2), and they merely address the linguistically processed reports on previous "present" experiences. In *eMotion*, the focus therefore was on physiological responses to represent the present moment, analyzing physiological correlates by which the experience of beauty may be embodied (e.g., Jacobsen, Schubotz, Höfel, & Cramon, 2006; Kawabata

& Zeki, 2004; Nakahara, Furuya, Obata, Masuko, & Kinoshita, 2009). This physiological research tradition, however, is based almost exclusively on laboratory environments. The primary goal of the *eMotion* project in contrast was to develop a methodology that would allow for the mapping of aesthetic responses in the naturalistic environment of a fine arts museum. The original environment preserves the aura and affordances of the artworks in their context, allowing the observation of moments of presence (Tröndle et al., 2014b).

Given the goal of the *ECR* project—investigating the specificity and the constituents of the aesthetic experience of music in a concert in its totality, instead of focusing on the experience and appreciation of specific structural or expressive features of the music alone (e.g., Bharucha, Curtis, & Paroo, 2006; Dibben, 2001)—a naturalistic perspective is essential. Accordingly, the *ECR* project was based on theoretical considerations that conceptualize aesthetic experience as emerging from the interplay of an experiencing subject, the aesthetic object, and their situational, social, and institutional framing (Tröndle, 2018; Wald-Fuhrmann, Seibert, & Grüny, Forthcoming). Especially, *ECR* seeks to explore the extent to which a framing (the concert) co-creates and shapes the aesthetic object (the musical pieces to be played) and how the two interact and merge. The analysis of this interaction in its ecological setting is thus again mandatory to attain the goals of the *ECR* project.

Furthermore, concerts are generally characterized by a specific liveness and an interactive or participative potential (Auslander, 2008; Seibert, Toelle, & Wald-Fuhrmann, 2018). The liveness of a concert has several consequences: A concert hall provides a specific acoustic setting ideally optimized for musical performances, which affords unique musical experiences. Also, a concert provides a multimodal experience, with the visual component as an important influencing factor (e.g., Behne & Wöllner, 2011; Platz & Kopiez, 2012; Vuoskoski, Thompson, Clarke, & Spence, 2014). Finally, a concert performance is characterized by its specific presence and precariousness (e.g., Fischer-Lichte, 2004). The music is created in the moment and the performance is exposed to the possibility of failure and unexpectedness, which provides unique musical experiences.[3] As in the *eMotion* project, the focus in *ECR* stays on the presence of art reception. Ecological validity is key for measuring such effects.

An important concern and potential limitation of any integrated methodology is the reliability of in situ physiological measurements. Psychophysiological research has shown that heart activity and skin conductance, the two measures integrated into both projects, provide important cognitive and emotional information. But can these variables be assessed in a reliable way in a field setting? In the *eMotion* project, an encompassing analysis showed that the physiological data measured in specific locations of the exhibition halls were linked with self-report assessments obtained via questionnaire items in the exit survey (Tröndle & Tschacher, 2012; Tschacher et al., 2012). Physiological measures were significantly and meaningfully associated with aesthetic–emotional assessments in retrospect. Especially heart rate variability was a substantial marker: "beautiful" artworks and "surprising" or "humorous" artworks were significantly associated with increased heart rate variability. Heart rate level and skin conductance variability were also significant markers of the art-related experiences reported by the visitors. Skin conductance levels, however, were not significantly linked. This means that there is statistical evidence to demonstrate that three physiological parameters provided informative markers of aesthetic–emotional appraisal, supporting the validity and reliability of the measures obtained via physiological recordings in the field (Tröndle et al., 2014b).

Thesis 2: Measurement shall be unobtrusive

The very fact and awareness of measurement can distort the natural responses on the part of participants, and this confounding effect can be increased by the ethical necessity for investigators to obtain participants' informed consent, because information focuses participants' awareness on the topics under study. Confounding is a general problem of data acquisition in psychology and phenomenology, and thus not specific to integrative methodology or research in real-world settings (Thesis 1). Biases can lie in the reactivity of participants: technical measurement devices may have a considerable influence on what is observed, because they point the awareness of participants to the research questions (Cetina, 1999; Tröndle et al., 2011). Even the mere awareness of being observed, of being part of a research project, can change behavioral and cognitive responses. To minimize such biases—the "Hawthorne effect" (see Roethlisberger & Dickson, 2003) is a well-known example—measurement should be as noninvasive and nondistracting as possible. As much as possible, investigators must aim at a measurement design that allows participants to "forget" the fact that their data are being collected.

Some steps can be taken toward minimizing the obtrusiveness of data acquisition, and thus the possible bias. One step is that sensors must be lightweight and must allow free movement. Cables and plugs must be kept to a minimum, and fixing of electrodes and respiration belts must not entail uncomfortable sensations, or even pain, over the course of time—as in the 2 hr of a concert or during a prolonged museum visit. It is also important to design the informed consent adequately: the information has to be precise and objective, but it need not contain directed information on the investigators' hypotheses. It is important to address potential myths about physiological data (such as physiological measures having "lie detector" abilities), which may be more prevalent among museumgoers and concert audiences than among university students familiar with lab research.

In the *eMotion* project, the measurement bias exerted by physiological sensors on the "data glove" was consequently tested by a control group as well as by directly inquiring about the influence of measurements on the visitors' experiences. In sum, the influence of the glove and the survey resulted in small to minimal effects (for detail, see Tröndle et al., 2014b). There was no indication that the data collection itself had a directed influence on the participants' experiences of the artworks on display.

In the *ECR* project, the potential biases of the implementation of measurement (especially, again, the effect of wearing physiological sensors) will likewise be determined by collecting information on a control group. Therefore, during each concert, a randomized small control group will not be fitted with physiological sensors, but will still participate in all pre- and postconcert surveys. During the field phase, additional participant observations will be conducted for analyzing specificities of the single concert events that might influence the results on that specific day. The field notes will be analyzed and eventually transformed into a "thick" description of the experimental setting (Emerson, Fretz, & Shaw, 2007; Hitzler & Gothe, 2015). A specifically sensitive kind of data involves video recordings, a component of the *ECR* project, from which participants' body movement and facial expressions will be computed. The ethical implications (privacy, publication restrictions) are important, but are not the topic of this methodological chapter. The privacy invasion of video recordings may nevertheless influence behavior, even though ethical considerations are fully met. In the *ECR* project, participants will therefore be informed that infrared cameras and invisible infrared lighting are being used. Accordingly, the audience will remain in the traditional half-darkness of the music hall and video data can be obtained without interfering. Thus, the interference due to the lighting needs of the video is curbed.

Thesis 3: Measures must be inclusive and cover all aspects of art reception

In the *eMotion* methodology, three levels of data were integrated and merged into one dataset. The technological challenge was to join data with rather incongruent properties:

1. Sociological and psychological data: the electronically enabled entry and exit surveys for assessment of the visitors, as well as assessment of artworks by the visitors, were entered at two time points into two different computer stations. The senders of these data parcels were the two computer stations (see Figure 17.2).
2. Physiological data: heart rate and skin conductance were continuously measured throughout the exhibition visits, for up to eight simultaneous participants. Each participant wore a "data glove." This entailed two data streams for each participant being fed into the central server. The sender of this dataset was the moving participant.
3. Behavioral data: position tracking was performed to monitor the exact location and trajectory of each of up to eight participants.

The listed three sources of data are likewise recorded in the *ECR* concert project: sociological and psychological data will be collected by the electronically enabled entry and exit surveys; physiological data as heart rate and skin conductance, as well as respiration will be monitored by devices that are linked to a server; and behavioral data such as body movement will be tracked by video analyses, and facial expressions will also be collected by video analyses. All of these datasets will likewise be time stamped and integrated.

In *ECR*, multimodal data of each participant will be analyzed directly after the concert to identify individual peak passages; that is, moments where intense physiological, movement, and facial reactions were visible. It is expected that instances of special aesthetic experience will be reflected in these peak passages. For each individual, the analysis will isolate a number of the most prominent peak passages, which in turn will be used for presentation in a subsequent postconcert survey. Through this, the project hopes to gain physiological data that may be highly relevant to subjective aesthetic experience. To this end, efficient and robust analysis scripts must be newly developed or adapted from already existing ones. The identification of peak passages from multiple sources for use in the survey immediately after the concert is methodologically very challenging; however, the *eMotion* project has shown that the implementation in a naturalistic environment functioned robustly and reliably.

The multimethodological approach of *ECR* is designed to clarify how the various dimensions of aesthetic experience of music interact with the constitutive criteria and different manifestations of classical concerts. Furthermore, this approach will provide a large set of data for investigating subjective experiences.

More specifically, the project aims to address the interplay between the single components of a concert and the featured music with bodily and psychophysiological processes of attention, concentration, emotion, and evaluation. The premise is that attentiveness is a necessary condition for aesthetic experience. Therefore, directing audience attentiveness explicitly or implicitly toward the performance and the music played is the primary goal of the artistic setup of a concert with respect to its program, its interpretation, the dramaturgy, how it is staged, the acoustics, its rituals, and so on. Yet, this general attentiveness does not guarantee aesthetic experience; rather, it provides a fundamental precondition for conscious experience per se (Fazekas, 2016; Tröndle, 2018; Waldenfels, 2004). With regard to the allocation of attention, the project may ask whether the various aspects of a concert manipulated by the concert variations facilitate obtaining a general attentional focus on the music and its performance. If positive, a carefully arranged concert setting can support or even provoke a specific aesthetic attention.

We assume that emotional and intellectual experience cannot be completely reduced to cognitive processes (Clarke, 2005; Csikszentmihalyi & Robinson, 1990; Tröndle et al., 2014b). Embodied physiological and emotional states are insufficiently represented by the verbal reports of standardized surveys. We believe that only a combination of different data types, including peripheral physiological responses, audience motion, video recordings of the audience and the musicians, and facial expression measurement, will enable a holistic view of the experiential processes during the concert. To develop such a holistic, multifaceted understanding of the aesthetic experience, we also have to integrate manifold disciplinary understandings (e.g., musicological, sociological, psychological, artistic) of aesthetic experience.

Thesis 4:   Cognition should be understood as embodied

In recent years, researchers in psychology, cognitive science, and philosophy of mind have arrived at a novel understanding regarding the concept of cognition. Cognition is no longer understood as the mere processing and representation of abstract information—a "computer metaphor" of the mind that has long dominated the approach to cognition (Fodor, 1975). Even in computer science, the classical idea of artificial intelligence has given way to conceiving of cognition as always *embodied*: adaptive and intelligent cognition unfolds in immediate contact with the body, be it a robotic sensor–effector system or the perception–action loops of an animal or human. In living beings, the embodiment of mind in addition is "felt" qualitatively; for example, through the emotions that are associated with mental acts. Especially in the context of art reception, specific emotions such as "*kama muta*" and "being moved" (Menninghaus et al., 2015; Zickfeld et al., 2018) are of interest. The empirically backed theory of embodied cognition states that motor action and brain functioning rest on predictions of sensations, which are continuously compared to incoming, afferent real sensations. The neuronal structures involved is called the reafference system (von Holst & Mittelstaedt, 1950) and the mode of feedback is known as "active inference" (Friston et al., 2015), which together constitute the perspective of *enacted* cognition (Varela, Thompson, & Rosch, 1991). Furthermore, cognition always occurs in an environment, by which it becomes contextualized and "situated" (Greeno, 1994; Tschacher & Scheier, 1996). Thus, cognition is *embedded*. A fourth aspect of cognition related to this contextual embeddedness is sometimes labeled *extended* cognition (Clark & Chalmers, 1998), which becomes especially salient in the use of tools: when we drive a car, our sense of self can be extended to the very boundaries of the car. All these aspects are commonly summarized as "embodied cognition" or "embodiment" (Tschacher & Bergomi, 2011), or sometimes more explicitly as "4E cognition" (embodied, enacted, embedded, extended; Newen, De Bruin, & Gallagher, 2018).

The research methodology of both *eMotion* and *ECR* has attempted to accommodate the notion of 4E cognition in various ways. The focus on the aura and "presence" of the art, which is emphasized in both projects, points to the embeddedness of art reception; that is, art perception as being confronted with the affordance of an artwork and the exhibition hall or of a concert situation (Lewin, 1936; Tröndle, 2014, 2018). In the process of perception, there is a fleeting moment when an object is not yet thoroughly processed in the cognitive system: a stage of pure sensibility that may entail conscious representations and reflections. Following Immanuel Kant (section 1 of his *Critique of Pure Reason*, 1781) or Gumbrecht (2004), such moments of experienced presence are at the center of the perception of artworks. It is obvious that these aesthetic experiences are hard to monitor and assess; it is unlikely that they can be investigated in a reliable way via questionnaires or surveys alone, since those depict the conscious processing following the stages of experienced presence. The entirety of aesthetic experiences can be evoked most validly in the original setting, such as a fine art museum or a concert hall (Thesis 1). Thus, in the *eMotion* project, visitors were allowed to explore the gallery freely, without any restriction of movement, which is in obvious contrast to a standardized lab environment with a prescribed succession of stimuli. The preserved degrees of freedom of bodily movement allowed the capturing of the visitor's enactive dialog with an artwork, which may be expressed behaviorally by experimenting with different angles of viewing or trying different distances to the artwork. A further aspect of embodiment is the physiological–emotional response at the very moment of viewing the art. Online monitoring of physiological data of the participants is realized in the *eMotion* as well as the *ECR* project as a core property of data collection, with the goal of exploring the very moment of art appreciation, and of possibly being moved by the art. These moments are best detected when the participant is embedded in the context of art reception or music experience. Subsequently, the exit surveys elaborated the details in retrospect through stimulated recalls of the artworks (*eMotion*) or music passages (*ECR*), thus not influencing the original moments of experience (Thesis 2).

Experiencing art, including both fine art and music, can also be a social encounter with additional visitors or other members of a responsive audience, which adds to the embeddedness and situatedness of experiential processes. Thus, in *eMotion*, the sociality of art reception, that is, the effects of social exchanges while in the gallery, was one of the objects of museum research (Tröndle et al., 2012). In turn, the presence of others in art museums might be seen as a situational but nonetheless influential by-product, such that it must count as a defining factor in concerts that needs to be studied. In *ECR*, interaction within a concert may take place not only between the musicians but also between the musicians and audience and among the audience, even in the behaviorally restrictive setting of a classical concert. Therefore, it is important to consider phenomena of physiological or movement synchrony. In addition to applause, which plays an important role in the articulation of a concert ritual (Toelle, 2017, 2018), the fact that a certain number of people are jointly attending the concert bears a specific communicative and experiential potential (Burland & Pitts, 2014; Cochrane, 2009; Seibert, 2019).

Thesis 5: Artistic research can generate novel epistemologies

Only during the past decade has the discourse in philosophy of science become enriched by a third position: artistic research. Besides offering quantitative and qualitative research methods, artistic research is considered a third and enriching ontological methodology. As a starting point, we can see the overlapping of the fields of art and technology (see, e.g., Harris, 1999) and the steadily growing interest in the collaboration between artists and scientists from all kinds of disciplines since the 1970s (one of the pioneering journals encouraging a discourse between practitioners in art, science, and technology is *Leonardo* (MIT Press), and more recently the *Journal of Artistic Research*). Books that examine the relation between scientific research processes and creative artistic processes in diverse ways include *Laboratorium* (Obrist

& Vanderlinden, 2001), *Bridge the Gap?* (Obrist, Akiko, & Olson, 2002), *Art + Science Now* (Wilson, 2010), *Kunstforschung als ästhetische Wissenschaft* (Tröndle & Warmers, 2012), and *Subjectivity and Synchrony in Artistic Research* (Schindler, 2018), to name only a few. In the past few years, under the banner of artistic research, new modes of interaction and cooperation between art and science and the resulting epistemic potential have been tested (see e.g., Biggs & Karlsson, 2011; Bippus, 2009; Borgdorff, 2011; Caduff, 2007; Dertnig et al., 2014; Schwab, 2015). Key questions associated with all of the aforementioned publications are: How can artistic and scientific pursuits be combined successfully? What is the additional value of such a procedure (Tröndle et al., 2011)? The methodologies of artistic research are still evolving and there is by no means a "standard procedure." And herein lies the potential of this still-emerging field, which will remain at the crossroads of several disciplinary logics and methods. There are always spaces of possibilities to test novel procedures and to experiment off standardized methodological paths. Additionally, artistic research settings always require negotiating different theories and logics as well as formulating clear-cut theses to come up with scientifically valid claims (Schindler, 2018).

In both the *eMotion* and *ECR* projects, artists are involved. Steven Greenwood, Chandrasekhar Ramakrishnan, Folkert Uhde, and others have not just brought their own knowledge of information cartography and the sonification of data to the field, but have enlarged the projects by asking new questions, designing the research stimuli, and developing parts of the methodologies (e.g., physiological tracking in the field, experimental settings, audio analyses of body movement). It was via artistic representations that phenomena of the research subjects of *eMotion* and *ECR* became and continue to become visible, which would not have been possible using social science, statistical-mathematical, phenomenological, or critical research practices alone. The artistic displays became equivalent, valid instruments in the research process (for detail, see Tröndle et al., 2011). We therefore state that a holistic understanding of aesthetic experience can fruitfully be enhanced by novel research methods, and artistic representations (see the cartographies in *eMotion* such as in Figure 17.5) can enlarge and accomplish the insights gained by statistical analyses.

Thesis 6:   Qualitative and quantitative data must be integrated

The *eMotion* project integrated the multiple datasets (Thesis 3) originating from the entry and exit surveys, the locomotion data, and the physiological data, and inputted them into cartographic forms (e.g., Figure 17.5). The physiological markers were inserted in the cartographies as clouds of different colors, which depict points in a visitor's path where heart activity or skin conductance showed significant phasic shifts. These cartographies allow visual inspection and thus a qualitative understanding of what happened in the museum space.

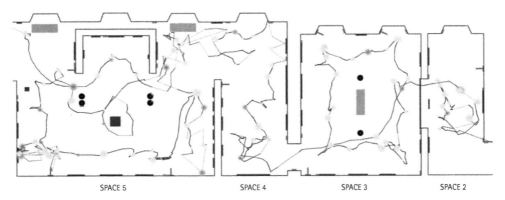

SPACE 5   SPACE 4   SPACE 3   SPACE 2

FIGURE 17.5. Path and physiological markers of Participant 802, Spaces 2–7. Changes in skin conductance level are depicted in yellow and light gray; changes in heart rate are depicted in orange and dark gray. With increasing magnitude, the physiological markers are rendered larger (in detail, see Tröndle et al., 2014a).

Using this methodology enabled the creation of mappings that compare various visitor qualities—for example, men/women, older/younger, novices/experts, being informed about the exhibition/not being informed—and the analysis of their behavior as well as their physiological responses. These cartographic mappings addressed and synthesized several questions: How do different artworks (small/large, famous/lesser known artists, various styles, etc.) affect the visitor (Tröndle & Tschacher, 2012)? Does the social situation affect the aesthetic experience (Tröndle et al., 2012)? Furthermore, the effects of curatorial arrangements and hangings on museum visitor behavior were investigated experimentally by arranging rehangings (Tröndle et al., 2014a; Tröndle & Tschacher, 2012). Several articles analyzed the effects of visitors' knowledge or priming on aesthetic experience (Tröndle, Kirchberg & Tschacher, 2014; Tröndle & Tschacher, 2016; Tschacher, Bergomi & Tröndle, 2015). The effect of the spatial layout and the visitors' locomotion on the visitors' attention was discussed in Tröndle (2014). Finally, analyzing visitors' self-reports as well as their spatial behavior and their physiological responses, three categories of museum visitors were identified (Kirchberg & Tröndle, 2015).[4]

Without these qualitative cartographic representations, many questions would not have been accessible and some questions would never have been asked. The explorative, interpretative analyses of the cartographies enabled the grasping of a novel understanding of what may constitute aesthetic experience. The current research project *ECR* is undertaking an exploration of analogous methods and data displays in order to allow a deeper insight into the aesthetic experience. Challenges will include integrating the manifold data sources in novel, artistically driven displays that allow a different reading of the data and therefore enable new epistemologies of aesthetic experiences.

Thesis 7: Perspectives of participating disciplines must be considered

Most real phenomena or "problems" are not restricted to or rooted exclusively in one discipline. This might be especially true if we are speaking about aesthetics, or the "aesthetic experience," which is discussed in psychology, sociology, philosophy, musicology, art history, neuroscience, and further disciplines, as well as in the artistic fields. Why, then, would one expect to find an answer or solution restricted to a single discipline or angle? A multi- or even transdisciplinary approach is needed: synergistically integrating the knowledge and competences from multiple and disparate disciplines, working with practitioners, bound around the phenomenon of aesthetic experience.

To engage scientists from different disciplines with various methodological competences, as well as artists, certainly widens the possibilities of observation and explanation. On the other hand, this engagement of arts, humanities, and sciences certainly also comes with manifold challenges: fruitfully integrating the different disciplines and habits of inquiry is an experiment in and of itself. It is important to note that not just the technical, methodological components have to be integrated, but also the individual, personal research approaches and the different academic and artistic habits, which all have to fit together. Frels, Newman, and Newman (2015) also speak of "synergistic mentoring and … conceptualizing skills, goals, and interactive dialogue specific to mixed and multiple research methodology" (p. 333). The research management is therefore crucial in such projects, to foster a mutual understanding and esteem for one another's perspectives (for detail, see Tröndle et al., 2011).

Also, the idea of authorship needs to be newly defined. Defining the research questions, the hypotheses, the experiments, the methodologies, and so on is a discursive–collaborative act, and responding to this, the concept of authorship likewise has to be collaborative. Thereby, articles about the projects *eMotion* and *ECR* must be multiauthored and written by researchers from various disciplines. Only via this procedure can a multifaceted perspective on the phenomenon of aesthetic experience be realized. We agree with Maxwell, Chmiel, and Rogers (2015), who point out: "The type of design, and the paradigm views of the researchers, are less important for integration than the ability to view the results using different mental models or 'lenses'" (p. 223). Expanding the study of aesthetics beyond a single method or disciplinary methodology also results in outcomes of greater validity than those that mirror only one discipline or methodology. Another benefit of such a collaborative research practice is that the results can echo in various disciplines: results of the *eMotion* project have been published in the fields of psychological empirical aesthetics, cultural sociology, arts management, museum studies, curatorial studies, behavioral studies, and many others.

Nonetheless, it is important to point out that writing in multidisciplinary teams brings forward a pluralistic perception, which comes along with a demand for high levels of communication and sometimes results in methodological tensions. We have found that journals were open for such multimethodological research, but we have also run into certain challenges regarding publication. Bazeley (2015) formulates: "Mixed methods research demands a level of integration of methods and/or analyses that is often difficult to achieve, especially within the writing phase .... Journal policies regarding word length or methodological focus often limit integration" (p. 296). Strategies of how to practically deal with this heterogeneity have to be agreed on, and sometimes even written consent within the research team has to be given to face possible tensions. Continuous research management, mentoring the different perspectives, is also needed. Nonetheless, taking the hurdles of this unconventional, off-the-beaten track research setting has thus paid out in terms of the levels of scientific and general media interest in the research projects.

Conclusions

We have summarized our approach to the study of aesthetics in the shape of seven theses. These theses may serve as a vantage point for studying aesthetic experiences by an integrated methodology. We have based this proposal on recent developments in cognitive science, using methods that are facilitated by technological advances of the recording and processing of large datasets. Projects of the size and approach of *eMotion* and *ECR* are embarking into new territory. Their ambition is to address aesthetic experience of art and music appreciation experimentally in real-world settings. The triangulation of qualitative self-report information; the collection of psychological, physiological, and behavioral data; and the experimental test series can foster a differentiated understanding of what constitutes the aesthetic experience conceptualized not only as a private but also as an embodied and social event. In other words, these different viewpoints must be integrated and such integration must be envisaged already in the design of a project.

Research findings on what influences aesthetic experience in the concert or in the museum space are of substantial interest to researchers in musicology and music psychology, curatorial studies, dramaturgy and performance studies, empirical aesthetics, cultural sociology, and not least to the artists themselves (see Scherer, Trznadel, Fantini, & Coutinho, 2019). Therefore, we have called for interdisciplinarity of research teams and the complementation of academic methods by artistic research. The choice of variables of interest and the generation of hypotheses will be more inclusive when interdisciplinarity is warranted.

We have emphasized the need for ecological validity and thus claimed that empirical aesthetics research should be conducted predominantly outside the laboratory. Recent developments in cognitive science have shown that cognition and experiencing must be viewed as embodied, extended, and enacted, meaning that the contextuality of experience is essential. This is especially true for aesthetic experience, which may strongly depend on the aura of an artwork or the atmosphere of a concert presentation. It is unlikely that this context can be provided in the lab. We are however also aware of the possible downsides of studies in the naturalistic setting—such research can turn out to be demanding and complex, and it is necessary to minimize the invasiveness of data acquisition.

High ecological validity of a research project carries the message of practical relevance, and is therefore noticed better by recipients from the classical music industry, including festivals, concert halls, orchestras, and ensembles, or in the case of the fine arts, by curators and managers of fine art museums, galleries, and biennales. Yet the significance of exploring aesthetic moments in the field setting goes well beyond fine art and music, as people experience "being moved" in many further contexts, such as in social and therapeutic interactions or in the reception of media messages. We therefore assume that an integrated methodology for studying aesthetic moments is of quite general concern.

NOTES

1. Wilhelm Dilthey, *Einleitung in die Geisteswissenschaften. Versuch einer Grundlegung für das Studium der Gesellschaft und der Geschichte*, vol. 1 (Leipzig, Duncker & Humblot, 1883).
2. This project is performed in a collaboration with the music department of the Max Planck Institute for Empirical Aesthetics.
3. The history of using the concert frame for research purposes is long: as early as 1892, Benjamin Ives Gilman organized a concert with a selection of pieces for violin and piano and subsequently asked the audience members a number of questions about the expressivity of the music (Gilman 1892). However, Gilman was not interested in the live setting per se, but rather had to rely on it because recorded music had only just started to become available and qualitatively acceptable.
4. For an overview of the various publications on *eMotion*, see www.mapping-museum-experience.com/en/publications.

REFERENCES

Auslander, P. (2008). *Liveness: Performance in a mediatized culture* (2nd ed.). London: Routledge.

Bazeley, P. (2015). Writing up multimethod and mixed methods research for diverse audiences. In S. Hesse-Biber & R. Johnson (Eds.), *The Oxford handbook of multimethod and mixed methods research inquiry* (1st ed.) (pp. 296–313). Oxford: Oxford University Press.

Behne, K.-E., & C. Wöllner, C. (2011). Seeing or hearing the pianists? A synopsis of an early audiovisual perception experiment and a replication. *Musicae Scientiae*, 15 (3), 324–342.

Bharucha, J., Curtis, M., & Paroo, K. (2006). Varieties of musical experience. *Cognition*, 100, 131–172.

Biggs, M., & Karlsson, H. (2011). *The Routledge companion to research in the arts*. London; New York, NY: Routledge.

Bippus, E. (2009). *Kunst des Forschens*. Zürich: Diaphanes.

Borgdorff, H. (2011). Künstlerische Forschung und akademische Forschung. In M. Tröndle & J. Wärmers (Eds.), *Kunstforschung als ästhetische Wissenschaft. Beiträge zur transdisziplinären Hybridisierung von Wissenschaft und Kunst* (pp. 69–90). Bielefeld: Transcript.

Burland, K., & Pitts, S. (Eds.) (2014). *Coughing and clapping: Investigating audience experience.* Farnham: Ashgate.

Caduff, C. (2007). *Autorschaft in den Künsten. Konzepte – Praktiken – Medien.* Zürich: Zürich University of the Arts.

Cetina, K. (1999). *Epistemic cultures: How the sciences make knowledge.* Cambridge, MA: Harvard University Press.

Clark, A., & Chalmers, D. (1998). The extended mind. *Analysis, 58,* 7–19.

Clarke, E. (2005). *Ways of listening: An ecological approach to the perception of musical meaning* (1st ed.). Oxford: Oxford University Press.

Cochrane, T. (2009). Joint attention to music. *British Journal of Aesthetics, 49,* 59–73.

Csikszentmihalyi, M., & Robinson, R. (1990). *The art of seeing: An interpretation of the aesthetic encounter.* Los Angeles, CA: J. P. Getty Museum.

Dibben, N. (2001). What do we hear, when we hear music?: Music perception and musical material. *Musicae Scientiae, 5*(2), 161–194.

Dertnig, C., Diederichsen, D., Holert, T., Porsch, J., Schaffer, J., Seibold, S., & Stockburger, A. (Eds.). (2014). *Troubling research. Performing knowledge in the arts.* Berlin: Sternberg Press.

Emerson, R., Fretz, R., & Shaw, L. (2007). *Writing ethnographic fieldnotes.* Chicago, IL: University of Chicago Press.

Fazekas, P. (2016). Attention and aesthetic experience. *Journal of Consciousness Studies, 23*(9–10), 66–87.

Fischer-Lichte, E. (2004). *Ästhetik des Performativeni.* Frankfurt: Suhrkamp.

Fodor, J. (1975). *The language of thought.* New York, NY: Crowell.

Frels, R., Newman, I., & Newman, C. (2015). Mentoring the next generation in mixed methods research. In S. Hesse-Biber & R. Johnson (Eds.), *The Oxford handbook of multimethod and mixed methods research inquiry* (pp. 333–355). Oxford: Oxford University Press.

Friston, K., Rigoli, F., Ognibene, D., Mathys, C., Fitzgerald, T., & Pezzulo, G. (2015). Active inference and epistemic value. *Cognitive Neuroscience, 6*(4), 187–214.

Galliker, M., Klein, M., & Reikart, S. (2007). *Meilensteine der Psychologie: Die Geschichte der Psychologie nach Personen, Werk und Wirkung.* Stuttgart: Kröner.

Gilman, I. B. (1892). Report on an experimental test of musical expressiveness. *American Journal of Psychology, 4*(4), 558.

Greeno, J. (1994). Gibson's affordances. *Psychological Review, 101,* 236–342.

Gumbrecht, H. (2004). *Diesseits der Hermeneutik: Die Produktion von Präsenz.* Frankfurt: Suhrkamp.

Hammersley, M. (2013). The relationship between qualitative and quantitative research: paradigm loyalty versus methodological eclecticism. In J. Richardson (Ed.), *Handbook of qualitative research methods for psychology and the social sciences* (pp. 1–27). Leicester: British Psychological Society Books, 1996. Retrieved from https://martynhammersley.files.wordpress.com/2013/03/relationship-between-qualitative-and-quantitative-research.pdf.

Harris, C. (1999). *Art and innovation. The Xerox PARC artist in residency program.* Cambridge, MA: MIT Press.

Hitzler, R., & Gothe, M. (Eds.). (2015). *Ethnographische Erkundungen, Erlebniswelten.* Wiesbaden: Springer.

Jacobsen, T., Schubotz, R., Höfel, L., & v. Cramon, D. (2006). Brain correlates of aesthetic judgment of beauty. *NeuroImage, 29,* 276–285.

Jakubowski, K., Eeruola, T., Alborno, P., Volpe, G., Camurri, A., & Clayton, M. (2017). Extracting coarse body movements from video in music performance: A comparison of automated computer vision techniques with motion capture data. *Frontiers in Digital Humanities, 4*, 9.

Kant, I. (1781). *Critique of pure reason.* Translated by N. Kemp Smith, 1929. Retrieved from www.hkbu.edu.hk/~ppp/cpr/aesth.html.

Kawabata, H., & Zeki, S. (2004). Neural correlates of beauty. *Journal of Neurophysiology, 91*, 1699–1705.

Kirchberg, V., & Tröndle, M. (2015). The museum experience: Mapping the experience of fine art. *Curator: The Museum Journal, 58*(2), 169–193.

Knorr-Cetina, K. (2002). *Die Fabrikation von Erkenntnis. Zur Anthropologie der Naturwissenschaft* (2nd ed.). Frankfurt: Suhrkamp.

Latour, B., & Woolgar, S. (1979). *Laboratory life: The social construction of scientific facts.* Los Angeles, CA: Sage.

Lewin, K. (1936). *Principles of topological psychology.* New York, NY: McGraw-Hill.

Maxwell, J., Chmiel, M., & Rogers, S. (2015). Designing integration in multimethod and mixed methods research. In S. Hesse-Biber & R. Johnson (Eds.), *The Oxford handbook of multimethod and mixed methods research inquiry* (pp. 223–239). Oxford: Oxford University Press.

Menninghaus, W., Wagner, V., Hanich, J., Wassiliwizky, E., Kuehnast, M., & Jacobsen, T. (2015). Towards a psychological construct of being moved. *PLoS ONE, 10*(6), e0128451.

Nakahara, H., Furuya, S., Obata, S., Masuko, T., & Kinoshita, H. (2009). Emotion-related changes in heart rate and its variability during performance and perception of music. *Annals of the New York Academy of Sciences, 1169*, 359–362.

Newen, A., De Bruin, L., & Gallagher, S. (Eds.). (2018). *The Oxford handbook of 4E cognition.* Oxford: Oxford University Press.

Obrist., H., Akiko, M., & Olson, S. (2002). *Bridge the gap?* Kitakyushu: Center for Contemporary Art Kitakyushu; Cologne: Walther König.

Obrist, H., & Vanderlinden, B. (2001). *Laboratorium.* Cologne: DuMont.

Platz, F., & Kopiez, R. (2012). When the eye listens: A meta-analysis of how audio-visual presentation enhances the appreciation of music performance. *Music Perception, 301*, 71–83.

Ramseyer, F., & Tschacher, W. (2010). Nonverbal synchrony or random coincidence? How to tell the difference. In A. Esposito, N. Campbell, C. Vogel, A. Hussain, & A. Nijholt (Eds.), *Development of multimodal interfaces: Active listening and synchrony* (pp. 182–196). Berlin: Springer.

Ramseyer, F., & Tschacher, W. (2011). Nonverbal synchrony in psychotherapy: coordinated body-movement reflects relationship quality and outcome. *Journal of Consulting and Clinical Psychology, 79*, 284–295.

Roethlisberger, F., & Dickson, W. (2003 [1939]). *An account of a research program conducted by the Western Electric Company, Hawthorne Works.* Cambridge, MA: Harvard University Press.

Scherer, K. R., Trznadel, S., Fantini, B., & Coutinho, E. (2019). Assessing emotional experiences of opera spectators in situ. *Psychology of Aesthetics, Creativity, and the Arts, 13*, 244–258. http://dx.doi.org/10.1037/aca0000163

Schindler, J. (2018). *Subjectivity and synchrony in artistic research: Ethnographic insights.* Bielefeld: Transcript.

Schwab, M. (2015). Experiment! Towards an artistic epistemology. *Journal of Visual Art Practice, 14*(2), 120–131.

Seibert, C. (2019). Situated approaches to musical experience. In R. Herbert, D. Clarke, & E. Clarke (Eds.), *Music and consciousness 2: Worlds, practices, modalities* (pp. 3–25). Oxford: Oxford University Press.

Seibert, C., Greb, F., & Tschacher, W. (2019). Nonverbale Synchronie und Musik-Erleben im klassischen Konzert. *Jahrbuch Musikpsychologie, 28*, 1–28. https://doi.org/10.5964/jbdgm.2018v28.18

Seibert, C., Toelle, J., & Wald-Fuhrmann, M. (2018). Live und interaktiv: ästhetisches Erleben im Konzert als Gegenstand empirischer Forschung. In M. Tröndle (Ed.), *Das Konzert II: Beiträge zum Forschungsfeld der Concert Studies* (pp. 425–447). Bielefeld: Transcript.

Snow, C. (2001). *The two cultures*. London: Cambridge University Press.

Toelle, J. (2017/18). Applaus. In D. Morat & H. Ziemer (Eds.), *Handbuch Sound. Geschichte—Begriffe—Ansätze* (pp. 178–182). Stuttgart: J. B. Metzler.

Tröndle, M. (2014). Space, movement and attention: Affordances of the museum environment. *International Journal of Arts Management, 17*(1), 4–17.

Tröndle, M. (2018). Eine Konzerttheorie. In M. Tröndle (Ed.), *Das Konzert II: Beiträge zum Forschungsfeld der Concert Studies* (pp. 25–51). Bielefeld: Transcript.

Tröndle, M., Kirchberg, V., & Tschacher, W. (2014). Subtle differences: Men, women and their art reception. *Journal of Aesthetic Education, 48*(4), 65–93.

Tröndle, M., & Tschacher, W. (2012). The physiology of phenomenology: The effects of artworks. *Journal of Empirical Studies of the Arts, 30*(1), 75–113.

Tröndle, M., & Tschacher, W. (2016). Art affinity influences art reception (in the eye of the beholder). *Journal of Empirical Studies of the Arts, 34*(1), 74–102.

Tröndle, M., Greenwood, S., Bitterli, K., & van den Berg, K. (2014a). The effects of curatorial arrangements. *Museum Management and Curatorship, 29*(2), 1–34.

Tröndle, M., Greenwood, S., Kirchberg, V., & Tschacher, W. (2014b). An integrative and comprehensive methodology for studying aesthetic experience in the field: merging movement tracking, physiology and psychological data. *Environment and Behavior, 46*(1), 102–135.

Tröndle, M., Greenwood, S., Ramakrishnan, C., Tschacher, W., Kirchberg, V., Wintzerith, S., . . . & Wäspe, R. (2011). The entanglement of arts and sciences: On the transaction costs of transdisciplinary research settings. *Journal for Artistic Research, 1*. Retrieved from www.researchcatalogue.net/view/12219/12220.

Tröndle, M., & Warmers, J. (2012). *Kunstforschung als ästhetische Wissenschaft. Zur transdiziplinären Hybridisierung von Wissenschaft und Kunst*. Bielefeld: Transcript.

Tröndle, M., Wintzerith, S., Wäspe, R., & Tschacher, W. (2012). A museum for the twenty-first century: The influence of 'sociality' on art reception in museum space. *Museum Management and Curatorship, 27*, 461–486.

Tschacher, W., & Bergomi, C. (Eds.). (2011). *The implications of embodiment: Cognition and communication*. Exeter: Imprint Academic.

Tschacher, W., Bergomi, C., & Tröndle, M. (2015). The Art Affinity Index (AAI): An instrument to assess art relation and art knowledge. *Empirical Studies of the Arts, 33*, 161–174.

Tschacher, W., Bischkopf, J. & Tröndle, M. (2011). Zwei Kulturen des Wissenschaftssystems? Betrachtungen aus dem Kunstprojekt eMotion. In E. Brunner, W. Tschacher, & K. Kenklies (Eds.), *Selbstorganisation von Wissenschaft* (pp. 57–75). Jena: IKS Garamond Verlag.

Tschacher W., Greenwood, S., Kirchberg, V., Wintzerith, S., van den Berg, K., & Tröndle, M. (2012). Physiological correlates of aesthetic perception of artworks in a museum. *Psychology of Aesthetics, Creativity and the Arts, 6*, 96–103.

Tschacher, W., & Scheier, C. (1996). The perspective of situated and self-organizing cognition in cognitive psychology. *Communication and Cognition—Artificial Intelligence (CCAI)*, 13, 161–188.

von Holst, E., & Mittelstaedt, H. (1950). Das Reafferenzprinzip. Wechselwirkung zwischen Zentralnervensystem und Peripherie. *Naturwissenschaften, 37*, 464–476.

Varela, F., Thompson, E., & Rosch, E. (1991). *The embodied mind*. Cambridge, MA: MIT Press.

Vuoskoski, J., Thompson, M., Clarke, E., & Spence, C. (2014). Crossmodal interactions in the perception of expressivity in musical performance. *Attention, Perception & Psychophysics*, 76, 591–604.

Wald-Fuhrmann, M., Seibert, C., & Grüny, C. (Forthcoming). *Aesthetic experiencing of music: A framework for empirical research*.

Waldenfels, B. (2004). *Phänomenologie der Aufmerksamkeit*. Frankfurt: Suhrkamp.

Wilson, S. (2010). *Art + science now: How scientific research and technological innovation are becoming key to 21st-century aesthetics*. London: Thames & Hudson.

Zickfeld, J., Schubert, T., Seibt, B., Blomster, J., Arriaga, P., Basabe, N., . . . & Fiske, A. (2018). Kama muta: Conceptualizing and measuring the experience often labelled being moved across 19 nations and 15 languages. *Emotion, 19*(3), 402–424.

SECTION 3

OBJECT FEATURES

THE ROLE OF COLLATIVE VARIABLES IN AESTHETIC EXPERIENCES

MANUELA M. MARIN

INTRODUCTION

THE systematic study of stimulus properties and their role in aesthetic responses can be traced back to the birth of empirical aesthetics, namely to Gustav Theodor Fechner's (1876) ground-breaking publication *Vorschule der Ästhetik*. Fechner describes a set of aesthetic principles of which some largely depend on object-related factors (e.g., the aesthetic threshold, which reflects his psychophysical approach), whereas other principles depend more on person-related factors (e.g., associations). It is not surprising that Fechner acknowledged the mutual role of stimulus properties and the perceiver in these early days of empirical aesthetics because they constitute essential pillars of aesthetic communication already known in antiquity: Greek architects were aware that corrections needed to be made to the canonical order of temples (taking into account visual perception) to obtain a regular, balanced, and pleasing result in the perceiver.

In the 20th century, psychological theories on aesthetic experiences and behavior ascribed a differential role to object- and person-related factors, generally depending on the psychological tradition in which they were developed. For example, stimulus properties were central to the work of Birkhoff (1932) and Eysenck (1941), who tried to predict an aesthetic response using mathematical formulae that were based on visual order and complexity. Stimulus properties were also at the core of subsequent theories that were influenced by information theory (Shannon, 1948). A case in point is Daniel Berlyne's (1924–1976) seminal arousal-based theory of aesthetic experience and behavior (Berlyne, 1960, 1971, 1974c). Berlyne, a motivational psychologist, greatly advanced the field of empirical aesthetics from around 1960 until his death in 1976 by introducing new approaches, methods, and aims, which led to a movement commonly referred to as the

New Experimental Aesthetics (Berlyne, 1971, 1974a). Berlyne and his numerous followers concentrated on (1) *collative* (structural, formal) stimulus properties, (2) motivational questions, (3) the measurement of nonverbal behavior and subjective judgments, and finally, (4) they tried to contribute to a better understanding of human psychology through the study of aesthetic phenomena (Berlyne, 1974a). Cupchik (1988) considered Berlyne as the "founder of modern experimental aesthetics" (p. 171), pointing toward Berlyne's reductionist and experimental approach, which gave a strong impetus to the research community in the 1970s and thereafter (Day, 1981). Consequently, Berlyne's *psychobiological model* (sometimes simply referred to as *arousal theory* or the *two-factor theory*) is widely known and frequently cited in reviews on the history and development of empirical aesthetics up to the 21st century (Palmer, Schloss, & Sammartino, 2013; Silvia, 2012; Vartanian, 2014).

Berlyne's research was largely guided by the question of why humans "display curiosity and explore their environment, why they seek knowledge and information, why they look at paintings and listen to music, [and] what directs their train of thought" (Konečni, 1978, p. 134). His answers to some of these fundamental questions were described in his book *Conflict, Arousal and Curiosity* (1960), which culminated in his general theory of *collative motivation*. This theory was later applied to the arts in his influential monograph *Aesthetics and Psychobiology* (1971). The intellectual achievement of Berlyne's work can be attributed to the introduction of an affective component (arousal) to the study of perceived stimulus features and their role in aesthetic responses. Specifically, he brought together aspects of Clark Hull's (1943) *drive reduction theory* (see also Bolles, 1975, for the history of its demise) with aspects of *information theory* by integrating them with the latest neurophysiological findings on reward processing of that time (Olds & Olds, 1965). Clearly, Berlyne's theoretical work was largely rooted outside aesthetics and Walker states that "it was Berlyne's ambition to achieve a truly general and universal theory, applicable to many, if not all, aspects of human activity" (1980, p. 110). Berlyne (1971) presented his theoretical arguments in a rigorous way and captured readers' attention by offering convincing examples stemming from music, poetry, and the visual arts alike. Berlyne was thus able to approach the study of empirical aesthetics from a broad perspective (Machotka, 1980)—a scientific approach that is nowadays not frequently followed (but see Brown, 2019; Marin, 2015; Tiihonen, Brattico, Maksimainen, Wikgren, & Saarikallio, 2017). It is worth noting that Berlyne's academic contributions and active scholarly involvement were already highly appreciated during his lifetime (Cupchik, 1988; Konečni, 1978; Machotka, 1980).

In brief and simplified terms, Berlyne (1960, 1971) argued that a stimulus possesses *arousal potential*, which he later described as the "overall power to excite the nervous system" (Berlyne & Madsen, 1973, p. 14), suggesting a very broad perspective on physiological arousal. Arousal potential is determined additively by three types of variables: *psychophysical* (e.g., intensity, brightness, and color), *ecological* (e.g., signal value, association with biologically significant events), and *collative* (e.g., novelty, complexity, and ambiguity). The term "collative variables" was coined by Berlyne because these variables "involve comparison, and thus response to degree and nature of similarity or difference, between stimulus elements that may be present together or at different times" (1971, p.

141). According to Berlyne (1960), collative variables are the primary drivers of arousal changes, which in turn are associated with changes in *hedonic value* (e.g., pleasure, preference, and beauty).

Berlyne's *arousal-boost* mechanism has been most frequently studied in the field and underlies the well-known inverted U-shaped curve, which is a function of a collative variable and a measure of hedonic value (Figure 18.1). It assumes that the perceiver is in a moderate arousal state *prior* to the perception of a stimulus; however, this person-related state is often ignored (but see, e.g., Konečni, 2011, for considering the immediate arousal context in relation to music choice). According to Berlyne (1971), activation of the primary reward system by a stimulus with moderate arousal potential may lead to maximum hedonic value. When the arousal potential of a stimulus is too large, hedonic value decreases and becomes negative due to activation of the aversion system, which has a higher activation threshold than the primary reward system. The *arousal-jag* mechanism, less known but still relevant, describes how positive hedonic value can be achieved in a case when arousal first increases markedly (high state of tension) but is then reduced, leading to relief from unpleasantness. In this case, the secondary reward system is active and there is an inhibition of the aversion system. This short description illustrates the core of Berlyne's theory by suggesting that the perception of object-related properties influences the arousal level of a person, which in turn motivates behavior (exploration, approach, and avoidance) and subjective affective experience (e.g., pleasure).

Berlyne (1965) argued that a work of art consists of a group of elements that can communicate four types of information, namely semantic, expressive, cultural, and syntactic, of which the latter three types can be grouped into *aesthetic information*. In abstract art forms, such as music and abstract paintings, syntactic information is the primary source of information (but see Koelsch, 2009; Koelsch et al., 2004, for

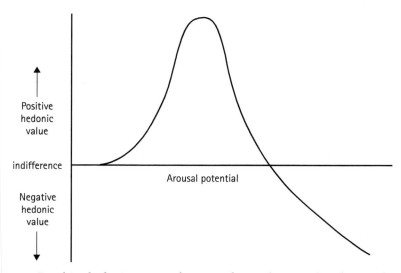

FIGURE 18.1. Resulting hedonic tone as a function of arousal potential, as discussed in Berlyne, 1971. (First developed by Wilhelm Wundt.)

neuroscientific evidence of how music can also convey semantic meaning). But even in works of art with semantic content, collative stimulus properties are crucial because artistic communication, within Berlyne's framework (1974), is largely determined by *how* something is communicated and not by *what* is communicated. In the *synthetic* research approach, Berlyne and collaborators constructed stimulus patterns that varied systematically along collative variables, whereas in the *analytic* approach, they studied actual artworks. These two empirical approaches, dating back to Fechner (Berlyne, 1971), are still pursued in parallel today.

Studying collative variables and their relation to aesthetic experience and behavior has received wide attention in the field since the 1970s—in and beyond the context of Berlyne's theory of collative motivation. Unsurprisingly, then, variables such as novelty, complexity, ambiguity, and so on also play a direct or indirect role in subsequent models of aesthetic experience (Carbon & Jakesch, 2013; Graf & Landwehr, 2015; Leder, Belke, Oeberst, & Augustin, 2004; Pelowski, Markey, Forster, Gerger, & Leder, 2017b; Van de Cruys & Wagemans, 2011). Arousal, regardless of its underlying (frequently vaguely defined) concept, is in most cases not regarded as an important factor in these models. Beyond the field of basic psychological research, collative variables have been of interest to those studying website aesthetics (Post, Nguyen, & Hekkert, 2017), online marketing (Sohn, Seegebarth, & Moritz, 2017; Wang & Li, 2017) brand logo design (Wang Duff, & Clayton, 2018), fashion (Tseng, 2018), and interior architectural design (Yeun, Eunsoo, & Jung, 2018), to name just a few examples from the visual domain. Collectively, this demonstrates the theoretical significance of collative variables and their practical relevance in aesthetic communication.

This chapter will critically review research on the role of collative variables in aesthetic experiences and behavior—within Berlyne's theoretical framework and beyond—as well as present challenges faced by the fields of psychology and cognitive neuroscience. Beginning with a more detailed presentation of Berlyne's theory from the perspective of current research in empirical aesthetics, insights gained from neuroaesthetics related to reward, motivational arousal, and pleasure will be presented. Next, findings and issues regarding individual collative variables (novelty, surprise, complexity, and ambiguity) will be discussed in more detail. Whenever appropriate, the examples will draw on various subfields of empirical aesthetics, mostly originating from the study of different types of visual stimuli, music, and poetry, which ultimately allows for a broad view on collative variables across the arts. Finally, this chapter concludes with a discussion of major challenges, goals, and suggestions for applications of current research findings regarding the role of collative variables in aesthetic experiences.

CURRENT PERSPECTIVES ON BERLYNE'S THEORY OF COLLATIVE MOTIVATION

Berlyne's psychobiological model (1971) is often reduced to his proposed inverted U-shaped curve, which does not do full justice to his contribution to the field. Berlyne not only tried to explain *how* stimulus properties are linked to hedonic responses, but he also provided an explanation for *why* humans engage with works of art although this behavior has no immediate survival value. Information-seeking, learning, and motivation are at the core of Berlyne's answers to this vital question when regarding animals and humans as curious beings that, depending on the context and their inner state, can show specific types of *curiosity*. Berlyne (1954) defined *perceptual curiosity* as being evoked by a complex or ambiguous sensory stimulus pattern that motivates exploration to gain information. *Epistemic curiosity* is evoked by complex ideas or conceptual ambiguities (e.g., scientific theories) that lead to further cognitive efforts to acquire knowledge, such as hypothesis testing. In this context, Berlyne further differentiates between *specific* and *diversive exploratory behaviors*. Specific exploration (e.g., due to uncertainty and conflict evoked by a stimulus and driven by both types of curiosity) may be rewarding through arousal reduction, whereas diversive exploration (due to boredom) may be rewarding through a moderate increase in arousal when searching for new information. Most current theoretical frameworks do not consider curiosity as a central concept driving aesthetic behavior (Pelowski, Markey, Lauring, & Leder, 2016); however, art museum visitors are clearly motivated by curiosity and learning among other things (for a review, see Pelowski, Forster, Tinio, Scholl, & Leder, 2017a; Slater, 2007). Thus, future theoretical work, based on the latest neuroscientific findings, may need to reconsider the role of motivation in aesthetic responses (see Silvia, 2005a).

The concept of *hedonic value*, as described and used by Berlyne with the background of learning, instrumental conditioning, and reward in mind, deserves some attention since it embraces a set of variables that can be measured either through verbal judgments or nonverbal behavior. *Positive hedonic value* refers to "pleasure, reward value, positive feedback, attractiveness (i.e., capacity to elicit approach), and positive incentive value," whereas *negative hedonic value* comprises "unpleasantness, punishment value, negative feedback, repulsiveness, and negative incentive value" (Berlyne, 1971, pp. 80–81). Berlyne (1974a) further introduced the term *hedonic tone* to refer to verbal judgments of pleasure, preference, beauty, and the like, and he was particularly interested in correlations between hedonic tone and nonverbal measures of hedonic value (e.g., Berlyne, 1972; Berlyne & Lawrence, 1964). Marin, Lampatz, Wandl, and Leder (2016) demonstrated that although measures of hedonic tone (beauty, pleasantness, and liking) are strongly correlated with each other when either viewing representational paintings or listening to music, their respective relationship with a collative variable, such as complexity, may differ. This suggests that the concept of hedonic tone may be less uniform than previously assumed, which should be taken into account in future experimental work (for a differentiation between concepts of hedonic value in current models of aesthetic experience, see, e.g., Brattico, Bogert, & Jacobsen, 2013; Pelowski et al., 2017b).

Berlyne's comprehensive research approach is nowadays not common, which is not only due to the emergence of neuroscientific methods. Researchers in Berlyne's tradition initially assessed a wide range of verbal ratings (descriptive, evaluative, internal-state, and stylistic scales) using the semantic differential, measured psychophysiological arousal, and employed behavioral measures of exploration time and exploratory choice (Berlyne, 1974c). They also measured interestingness (or interest, see also Silvia, 2008,

for defining *interest* as a knowledge emotion in the context of appraisal theory) besides pleasantness (or *pleasingness*, a term previously used) as an evaluative judgment.
Interest was understood as a measure of behavioral exploration, whereas pleasingness
was related to reward (Saklofske, 1975). Nowadays, researchers usually adhere to only
a few measures within the context of a study, such as one collative variable and one
measure of hedonic tone (e.g., Bohrn, Altmann, Lubrich, Menninghaus, & Jacobs,
2013; Cui, Collett, Troje, & Cuddy, 2015; Forsythe, Nadal, Sheehy, Cela-Conde, & Sawey,
2011). Studies considering two collative variables simultaneously are rare (Heyduk, 1975;
Jakesch & Leder, 2015; Madison & Schiolde, 2017; Seifert & Chattaraman, 2017; Tinio &
Leder, 2009), but interesting interaction effects on hedonic value may exist as already
reported by Berlyne (1970) regarding visual complexity and novelty. Moreover, partly
due to this reductionist approach when studying aesthetic responses, there is still an
ongoing discussion about the relative role of collative variables (in comparison with
other types of factors) in responses to music (North & Hargreaves, 2000; Schäfer &
Sedlmeier, 2010; Schubert, 2010), visual stimuli (Hekkert & Leder, 2008; Martindale,
Moore, & Anderson, 2005; Moshagen & Thielsch, 2010; Stich, Eisermann, Knäuper,
& Leder, 2007; Tuch, Presslaber, Stöcklin, Opwis, & Bargas-Avila, 2012), and literary
devices (Jacobs & Kinder, 2018). To clarify this debate will be a challenging endeavor
requiring rigorous experiments in the future, which will need to acknowledge the context in which aesthetic experiences happen to a much greater extent, as shown by recent
studies conducted in the museum (Brieber, Nadal, & Leder, 2015; Brieber, Nadal, Leder,
& Rosenberg, 2014).

There is a conceptual lack of clarity surrounding arousal, and its measurement has
been increasingly neglected in the field of empirical aesthetics. This may be either due
to the fact that Berlyne's original notion of arousal has considerably changed since his
theory was developed, or due to a general loss of interest in studying (motivational and
emotional) arousal. For instance, even within the framework of Berlyne's theory the
measurement of arousal changes is currently being ignored (e.g., Chmiel & Schubert,
2018; North & Hargreaves, 1995; Sun, Yamasaki, & Aizawa, 2018). In a similar fashion,
reviews on the inverted U-shaped relationship between collative variables and hedonic tone do not address empirical evidence for or against the mediation mechanism proposed by Berlyne in much depth (Chmiel & Schubert, 2017; Nadal, Munar,
Marty, & Cela-Conde, 2010; for recent studies assessing arousal within the context of
Berlyne's theory and beyond, see, e.g., Blijlevens, Carbon, Mugge, & Schoormans,
2012; Leder, Ring, & Dressler, 2013; Marin & Leder, 2013; Schäfer & Sedlmeier, 2011;
Steinbeis, Koelsch, & Sloboda, 2006; Tschacher et al., 2012; Tuch, Bargas-Avila, Opwis,
& Wilhelm, 2009). At the same time, arousal changes are still being studied when
exploring emotional peak experiences during aesthetic processing, such as the chill
response (Benedek & Kaernbach, 2011; Colver & El-Alayli, 2016), emotional lacrimation (Wassiliwizky, Jacobsen, Heinrich, Schneiderbauer, & Menninghaus, 2017a), or the
feeling of being moved (Menninghaus et al., 2015). Yet in these cases arousal is not necessarily considered within a motivational framework.

Emotions are central to our understanding of aesthetic responses, and there are several aspects of Berlyne's theory (1971) that are debated today with regard to emotion

processing. When discussing arousal dynamics and reward it is important to note that Berlyne regarded motivational arousal and pleasure (pleasantness) as dependent variables. Pleasure is also closely related to the affective concept of valence (pleasantness), and Berlyne was aware of emotion models that claimed the independence of arousal and pleasantness (Bradley & Lang, 1994; Osgood, Suci, & Tannenbaum, 1957; Wundt, 1896). Interestingly, the controversy surrounding the nature of the relationship between arousal and pleasantness/pleasure is still ongoing in emotion science (e.g., Bestelmeyer, Kotz, & Belin, 2017; Kragel & LaBar, 2016; Kuppens, Tuerlinckx, Russell, & Barrett, 2013) as well as among those studying aesthetic responses and reward (Blood & Zatorre, 2001; Marin & Leder, 2013; Salimpoor, Benovoy, Longo, Cooperstock, & Zatorre, 2009; Schäfer & Sedlmeier, 2010). Furthermore, Berlyne's focus on changes in hedonic value and pleasure has been criticized for ignoring the myriad of emotional responses an aesthetic experience may entail (Konečni, 1996; Silvia, 2005b). Another related issue already mentioned above concerns the relative contribution of psychophysical, ecological, and collative variables to the experience of pleasure. For instance, many types of visual artworks communicate (strong) emotions through semantic content and color, which alongside collative variables can generate pleasure, but still little is known about how aspects of emotional content interact with collative variables during visual aesthetic experiences (Marin & Leder, 2013). Indeed, the current neurocognitive literature on emotion–cognition interaction suggests that factors such as emotional content and complexity may interact at early stages of affective picture processing (e.g., Carretié, Hinojosa, López-Martín, & Tapia, 2007; Low, Bradley, & Lang, 2013; Schlochtermeier et al., 2013; but see also Bradley, Hamby, Löw, & Lang, 2007). Altogether, such findings may provide fruitful pathways for theoretical advances in the field.

Berlyne's arousal theory has been criticized despite its large influence (Konečni, 1996), and alternative theories have been proposed, such as Martindale's prototype theory of aesthetic preference (Martindale, 1984; Martindale & Moore, 1988), Silvia's appraisal account of aesthetic emotions and interest (Silvia, 2010, 2012), and the processing fluency theory of aesthetic pleasure (Reber, Schwarz, & Winkielman, 2004). Berlyne's theory has neither been further developed nor been integrated into other theoretical accounts, which is surprising because researchers are still frequently studying the inverted U-shaped curve using behavioral measures. In more recent times, the work on the role of neurotransmitters during aesthetic experiences has replaced work on arousal.

REWARD, MOTIVATIONAL AROUSAL, AND THE BRAIN

In his theoretical work, Berlyne (1971) focused much on arousal modulation in areas of the *ascending reticular activating system* (ARAS) in the brainstem (Moruzzi & Magoun, 1949). He assumed, mostly based on animal research, that the brain areas controlling fluctuations in arousal were the same as the ones processing reward and pleasure, or that these areas were at least close to each other. As discussed above, his theory on arousal fluctuation builds on the idea that there are three subcortical reward systems interacting with each other, two in the reticular activating system and one at the upper brainstem and in the limbic system. The notion of an involvement of several brain regions during aesthetic experiences is still valid today; however, Berlyne's conception of the reward and arousal systems is outdated.

Brain imaging has considerably changed our understanding of the human reward and arousal systems. Nowadays it is known that there is no uniform arousal system in humans and animals that can explain wake–sleep states, consciousness, as well as heightened attentional and general affective processing (Andretic, van Swinderen, & Greenspan, 2005; Lee & Dan, 2012; Picard, Fedor, & Ayzenberg, 2016; Robbins et al., 2006). The complexity of the neural underpinnings of general emotion processing in humans, for example, can be demonstrated by discussing the role of the brainstem (Venkatraman, Edlow, & Immordino-Yang, 2017), which is the oldest brain structure present in all vertebrates. The brainstem and its nuclei are particularly relevant in the discussion of appetitive motivation and motivational arousal associated with dopamine release (Wise, 2004).

The modulatory neurotransmitter network (another term for ARAS), projects to the hypothalamus, cortex, and forebrain and it controls arousal and consciousness by modulating interactions between the ascending and descending networks. This modulatory network comprises three major areas of dopaminergic neurons in the midbrain, with three different ascending pathways, that show both tonic and phasic firing patterns related to reward and motivational arousal. In addition, there are serotonergic neurons in the raphe nuclei that are functionally related to anxiety, stress, depression, and social behavior. Norepinephrine signaling in the locus coeruleus is relevant for the processing of emotionally salient information and alertness, and, together with dopaminergic pathways, it plays a role in learning and emotional memories. Moreover, cholinergic cell groups are part of the modulatory network and seem to play a role in emotion and reward processing by modulating dopaminergic signaling. It is generally agreed that the brainstem also receives input (top-down feedback) from rostral areas during bottom-up (sensory-based) emotion processing and concurrent fixed-pattern behavior (Venkatraman et al., 2017).

The above description of the brainstem circuits clearly suggests that any arousal-based theory of information processing in relation to art would need to consider the intricacy of the brainstem circuits in much more detail than Berlyne was able to do at his time. The involvement of the brainstem in a specific mechanism of emotion induction by music, the so-called *brainstem reflex*, has already been described by Juslin and Västfjäll (2008). Recent interdisciplinary models of emotion, such as the *Quartet Theory* (Koelsch et al., 2015), which is also applicable to music processing, also acknowledge the brainstem system as one of four core systems, alongside the diencephalon, hippocampal formation, and the orbitofrontal cortex. Another current model on visual art perception (VIMAP) also acknowledges the various brainstem functions at early processing stages (Pelowski et al., 2017b), but without considering the possibility of feedback loops from higher cortical areas. Modern brain-based models go beyond the idea that (de) activations of only a few brain regions can explain complex phenomena such as aesthetic experiences, decision making, and subsequent behaviors.

Berlyne developed his psychobiological model as a broad theory, and current neuroimaging results seem to support his idea that pleasure derived from art relies on similar brain networks as other fundamental pleasures. In fact, there is abundant evidence that light, food, sex, and social contact, as well as higher pleasures, such as money, music, and visual art, activate an overlapping and shared reward network (e.g., Blood & Zatorre, 2001; Brown, Gao, Tisdelle, Eickhoff, & Liotti, 2011; Koelsch, 2018; Lacey et al., 2011; Mallik, Chanda, & Levitin, 2017; Menon & Levitin, 2005; Montague & Berns, 2002; Sescousse, Caldu, Segura, & Dreher, 2013; Vartanian & Skov, 2014). This network comprises the prefrontal cortex (orbitofrontal, insula, and anterior cingulate cortices) and subcortical limbic structures (nucleus accumbens, ventral pallidum, and amygdala). A mid-anterior subregion of the orbitofrontal cortex has been associated with the subjective feeling of pleasure (Berridge & Kringelbach, 2015). These findings support the view that pleasure induced by artistic stimuli should be studied by comparing behavioral and neuroimaging results across stimulus categories to detect commonalities and differences (Jacobsen & Beudt, 2017; Johnson & Steinerberger, 2019; Marin, 2015; Mas-Herrero, Karhulahti, Marco-Pallarés, Zatorre, & Rodríguez-Fornells, 2018b; Tiihonen et al., 2017; Vessel, Maurer, Denker, & Starr, 2018).

Pleasure and reward are currently understood to involve three different psychological components, namely *liking* (hedonic impact), *wanting* (incentive salience), and *learning* (Pavlovian or instrumental associations and cognitive representations), each of them comprising specific neural networks that interact during a reward–behavior cycle. The neural networks underlying wanting are more largely distributed in the brain than the ones determining liking, which can be limited to several hot spots in the limbic system, but both networks seem generally to work in concert and overlap in the ventral striatum (Berridge & Kringelbach, 2015). All three components can be active at any time in the cycle, but wanting is dominant in the initial appetitive phase (approach behavior), liking in the consummatory phase, and finally, learning in the satiety phase. It is important to note that dopamine is generally not related to the experience of pleasure per se but to the appetitive phase of the reward cycle (Berridge & Kringelbach, 2008; Wise, 2004), regulating motivation and goal-directed behavior. The brainstem is particularly relevant in the discussion of appetitive motivation and motivational arousal associated with dopamine release. Subjective pleasure, in contrast, is primarily based on the release of opioid peptides in the nucleus accumbens (Wise, 2004).

Music, due to its temporal and dynamic nature, is an ideal stimulus to examine different phases of the reward cycle and its underlying neurochemical processes (Chanda & Levitin, 2013). Salimpoor, Benovoy, Larcher, Dagher, and Zatorre (2011) studied dopamine release and its dynamics by using the chill response as an index of pleasure. They found that dopamine release occurs during both the anticipatory and consummatory phases of the reward cycle in two anatomically different subcircuits of the striatum (for causal evidence for the role of dopamine in musical pleasure, see

Ferreri et al., 2019). Motivated by these findings, recent research on the aesthetics of poetry, involving neuroimaging, psychophysiological, and behavioral measures, has revealed that poetry can also induce strong emotions and chills (Wassiliwizky, Koelsch, Wagner, Jacobsen, & Menninghaus, 2017b). Interestingly, the authors only found some overlap between music and poetry regarding the reward-related brain regions, and their results showed in general more posterior activation in the cingulate, insula, and caudate, in comparison with previous reports for music. Differences in activation between music and poetry were also observed when comparing the temporal dynamics of the reward cycle, in which activation of the nucleus accumbens was reported prior, and not during, the emotional peak experience induced by poems.

Studying individual differences has revealed that people who are particularly sensitive to musical reward show an enhanced functional connectivity between the right auditory cortex and the ventral striatum/nucleus accumbens (Salimpoor et al., 2013). Interestingly, the reverse is observed in the case of *musical anhedonia* (Zatorre, 2015), a specific condition in which people do not experience pleasure when listening to music but show intact processing of fundamental pleasures (Martínez-Molina, Mas-Herrero, Rodríguez-Fornells, Zatorre, & Marco-Pallarés, 2016; Mas-Herrero, Zatorre, Rodríguez-Fornells, & Marco-Pallarés, 2014). Using transcranial magnetic stimulation, the same research group has recently provided causal evidence for a link between the activation of the fronto-striatal circuitry with the degree of music-induced pleasure, psychophysiological arousal, and motivational aspects of reward (Mas-Herrero, Dagher, & Zatorre, 2018a).

In the past 15 years, the emerging field of neuroaesthetics (Pearce et al., 2016) has largely advanced our knowledge about the underlying brain processes of aesthetic experiences. In a nutshell, the existing literature emphasizes that attentional, perceptual, affective, and cognitive processes closely interact with each other (Brown et al., 2011; Vartanian & Skov, 2014). For example, during the aesthetic experience of music, brain connectivity networks involving the auditory cortex, the reward system, and brain regions active during mind wandering come into play (Reybrouck, Vuust, & Brattico, 2018; Taruffi, Pehrs, Skouras, & Koelsch, 2017; Wilkins, Hodges, Laurienti, Steen, & Burdette, 2014). During visual aesthetic experiences, activation of the default mode network has also been reported (Belfi et al., 2018; Cela-Conde et al., 2013; Vartanian & Skov, 2014; Vessel, Starr, & Rubin, 2012), highlighting the role of introspective, self-referential thoughts and self-awareness. These findings suggest that there is much more to aesthetic experiences than emotion, pleasure, and reward, and that Berlyne's theory may be too simplistic (see also Pelowski et al., 2017b). Therefore, neuroaesthetics may clearly help determine the nature of aesthetic experiences in the future, for instance, by trying to elucidate whether aesthetic experiences can be characterized as *disinterested pleasure*, as famously proposed by Kant and the third Earl of Shaftesbury in the 18th century. The notion of disinterested pleasure implies that aesthetic experiences are mental states that do not involve the desire to acquire, control, or manipulate the object that induces the experience (we usually tend to want what we like) (Chatterjee & Vartanian, 2016). Chatterjee (2014) has proposed that during aesthetic experiences activation of the liking system can be observed without activation of the wanting system, but at the moment empirical evidence supporting this hypothesis is scarce (Leder, Gerger, Brieber, & Schwarz, 2014). In summary, the idea that motivational aspects are relevant for the discussion of the nature of aesthetic experiences has also found its place in neuroaesthetics, which in future will certainly employ neuropharmacological methods, enabling causative claims, to a greater extent (for a review, see Spee et al., 2018).

NOVELTY AND FAMILIARITY

Within Berlyne's framework, collative variables are means to either increase or decrease arousal in an individual, and they are tightly linked to information-theoretic concepts. *Novelty* is an arousal-increasing device related to high information content, whereas *familiarity* would be its counterpart; therefore, novelty/familiarity constitute anchors on a continuum. Novelty processing has been associated with the *orienting response* (or "What-is-it?" reflex), which signals changes in the sensory environment (Pavlov, 1927) and is thus essential for survival. At the behavioral level, orienting responses are associated with increased attention toward a stimulus. Repeated exposure to the same stimulus will lead to habituation. At the neural level, a hippocampal–neocortical network (Knight, 1996; Valenti, Mikus, & Klausberger, 2018) is involved in novelty processing and largely, but not only, driven by the dopaminergic system (Rangel-Gomez & Meeter, 2016). Early aestheticians such as Gerard (1764) and Home (1765) considered novelty as one of the main factors affecting aesthetic responses (see Berlyne, 1971), and empirical evidence has supported this view (Berlyne, 1970, 1974b; Leder, 2001; Park, Shimojo, & Shimojo, 2010; Seifert & Chattaraman, 2017; Tinio & Leder, 2009; and see Sluckin, Hargreaves, & Colman, 1983, for a review of older studies).

Berlyne differentiates between *absolute novelty* and *relative novelty*, with the former implying that a person has never interacted with a stimulus before, and the latter that perceived novelty depends on how, for instance, familiar elements appear in a new combination. Moreover, he differentiates between *short-term novelty* and *long-term novelty*, which refers to the time intervals between encountering stimuli or their elements. Examples of short-term novelty refer to the immediate context of elements experienced in aesthetic communication. In the case of music, Berlyne noted (1971) that "a music melody is not only a sequential pattern of pitches but also a sequential pattern of novelty values" (p. 145). In a similar vein, poetic devices such as different rhyme schemes and assonance also generate novelty, familiarity, and repetition through phonological structuring (Berlyne, 1971). Equally important, novelty/familiarity underlies the frequently applied principle of *variation* in music, in which, for example, a melody is repeated and altered by changing some musical features (Sluckin et al., 1983). In the visual domain, this artistic play with familiar and unfamiliar elements can be observed when painters create a series of paintings on one motif, such as Van Gogh's two series of *Sunflowers*, especially in cases where observers have the possibility to experience them together. The conceptual distinctions of novelty provided by Berlyne are still valid today and underlie current research strands, in which, for instance, memory processes (e.g., recognition) and repeated exposure as well as formed expectations during music and language processing are systematically studied (see also the following section).

Berlyne examined novelty by employing a familiarization paradigm, in which the same stimulus was repeatedly presented; that is, novelty was considered as an independent variable, whose impact on interestingness and hedonic value was measured. He also varied stimulus complexity alongside novelty, and in general, reported for both simple and complex visual stimuli a linear decrease in interestingness with repeated exposure, due to a reduction of uncertainty. For pleasantness ratings, an inverted U-shaped curve was reported only for complex stimuli, probably due to initial stimulus habituation and subsequent satiation (Berlyne, 1970, 1974b). Around the same time, Zajonc (1968) presented his affective model to explain the *mere-exposure effect*, predicting a positive linear relationship between repeated exposure and liking. Contrary to Berlyne, Zajonc argued that the increase in preference is due to the reduction of a negative affective state (i.e., a fear response) initially evoked by a novel stimulus. Since then many researchers have shown interest in the "what is familiar is preferred" phenomenon, which is not only germane to empirical aesthetics but also to fields such as social psychology (Soley & Spelke, 2016) and advertising psychology (Fang, Singh, & Ahluwalia, 2007).

In a very thorough meta-analysis, comparing three prominent theories that may underlie the mere-exposure effect (Berlyne's two-factor theory, fluency theory, and Zajonc's affective model), Montoya, Horton, Vevea, Citkowicz, and Lauber (2017) considered familiarity, recognition, and liking as dependent variables, and further, several moderators, such as age, presentation duration, and presentation type. Based on 268 curve estimates, they found support for an inverted U-shaped curve between exposure frequency and liking for visual, but not for auditory stimuli. In general, Berlyne's model seemed to account for this finding better than fluency theory. However, the authors developed a new theory—the *Representation Matching Model*—because older theories were not able to account for the specific results. This new model, congruent with established models of memory, explains the initial increase in liking with a matching mechanism that compares the incoming stimulus with a formed mental representation (cf. predictive coding in the following section). If the stimulus is perceived as "how it should be" and thus as "correct" and "good", the stimulus is liked. The negative quadratic effect is explained by a habituation via learning mechanism leading to a decrease in liking. In contrast to fluency theory (Reber et al., 2004), the increase in liking is not rooted in the ease of stimulus processing, and the decrease in liking is not explained by fatigue. The authors suggest studying the relationship between recognition, familiarity (as a dependent variable), and liking in greater depth in the future, including different types of stimuli.

Besides studying the mere-exposure effect, novelty/familiarity and its impact on aesthetic responses can be approached from diverse empirical perspectives. For example, researchers have investigated the effect of novelty on cognitive processing and experience (i.e., a stimulus is perceived as new vs. old; e.g., Bohrn et al., 2013; North & Hargreaves, 1995), and considered familiarity during stimulus selection procedures (Massaro et al., 2012; Nadal et al., 2010) or treated familiarity as a covariate while being primarily interested in other variables (e.g., Forsythe, Mulhern, & Sawey, 2008; Marin, Lampatz, Wandl, & Leder, 2016). This latter aspect is closely related to individual differences in art interest, training, and expertise (Kirk, Skov, Hulme, Christensen, & Zeki, 2009)—variables that are usually discussed in the context of person-related factors. Moreover, novelty/familiarity effects can be investigated at different hierarchical levels of stimulus features. Marin and Bhattacharya (2011) argued that, in the case of music processing, novelty/familiarity effects can be assessed regarding the culture-specific musical system, the musical style, the musical piece, the specific performance of a piece, parts of the musical structure (sections, themes, and motives), and their repetition within a piece, as well as note-by-note effects of musical structure (see the following section). It is a simple task to apply this differentiation to other temporal media, such as literature and dance, and in a slightly modified form, to the study of visual art, in which people may feel familiar or unfamiliar with art periods, styles, artists, as well as with specific artworks and their individual elements. Indeed, theoretical work on modeling aesthetic musical experiences also highlights the role of familiarity (in its different facets), formed mental representations, and spreading activation in associative networks, which may lead to pleasure by a very simple cognitive mechanism (Schubert, Hargreaves, & North, 2014). Hence, different types of novelty/familiarity effects may play a role during various cognitive processing stages of aesthetic stimuli, interacting with each other over time—a hypothesis that appears to be relatively empirically unexplored.

In the domain of music, novelty/familiarity effects are of particular interest, probably due to music's dynamic nature and its inherent repetition of musical elements, a key feature of musical communication (Margulis, 2014). The extant literature on repetition in music, for instance, has studied the detection of musical repetition by untrained listeners (Margulis, 2012), moderating effects of emotional content on psychophysiological (Iwanaga, Kobayashi, & Kawasaki, 2005; Witvliet & Vrana, 2007) and subjective responses (Ali & Peynircioğğlu, 2010), differences between focused and incidental listening (Schellenberg, Peretz, & Vieillard, 2008) as well as the role of the ecological validity of the stimuli (Szpunar, Schellenberg, & Pliner, 2004). Repetitiveness also seems to increase aesthetic responses to unfamiliar, contemporary art music (Margulis, 2013). It was even shown that repeated exposure to musical excerpts can lead to a transfer of preference to unfamiliar excerpts of the same stylistic genre (Johnston, 2016). Madison and Schiolde (2017) studied familiarity together with musical complexity and demonstrated for four levels of complexity a linear increase in liking ratings after repeated exposure. They also identified familiarity with musical style as a strong predictor of liking (see also Parncutt & Marin, 2006). Janata et al. (2018) manipulated novelty by several musical features and found that instrument entrances are a strong predictor of listening times. In short, this body of research illustrates a wide range of different aspects regarding musical repetition that are currently of interest to the community.

The effects of novelty/familiarity in response to sounds and music have also been investigated using neuroscientific methods. Using a mismatch-negativity (MMN) paradigm, Jacobsen, Schröger, Winkler, and Horváth (2005) showed in an electroencephalography (EEG) study that familiarity with the standard stimuli affected the processing of a deviant sound, as shown by a higher MMN response, in comparison with a condition with a sequence of unfamiliar standard stimuli (cf. predictive coding in the following section). Pereira et al. (2011), using functional magnetic resonance imaging (fMRI), studied "music lovers" with minimal musical training and found that familiar, in contrast to unfamiliar, musical pieces led to increased activation in limbic and paralimbic brain structures as well as in the reward circuit. Van Den Bosch, Salimpoor, and Zatorre (2013) demonstrated that repeated exposure to unfamiliar music increased electrodermal activity (physiological arousal) and felt pleasure. Novel music was able to induce pleasure, but there was no association between emotional arousal and pleasure in this case. Li, Chen, and Tsai (2015) studied repetition in music in relation to different stages of reward processing (reward-anticipation, -gain, and -loss) by focusing on popular songs and the verse–chorus form. Using fMRI they showed that activation of the bilateral temporo-parietal junctions and parts of the orbitofrontal cortex could be related to different stages of the reward cycle. Kumagai, Arvaneh, and Tanaka (2017) conducted an EEG study and were interested in how familiarity with piano music affects cortical entrainment to the musical signal. They found that the brain entrains more strongly to unfamiliar than to familiar music (see also Meltzer et al., 2015). In a thorough meta-analysis, Freitas et al. (2018) compared the neural correlates of familiar and unfamiliar music processing and reported for familiar music activation of the left superior frontal gyrus, the ventral lateral nucleus of the left thalamus, and the left medial surface of the superior frontal gyrus. Unfamiliar music activated the left insula and the right anterior cingulate cortex. Interestingly, limbic structures did not seem to play a role in familiarity processing. These intriguing examples demonstrate that subcortical and cortical brain regions are sensitive to novelty/familiarity during music processing, but at the moment it remains unclear how different facets of novelty/familiarity are represented in the brain and how they interact with each other, which leaves the doors wide open for future experiments.

SURPRISE AND EXPECTEDNESS

Berlyne (1971) argues that artists can induce arousal changes by playing with expectations, which are linked to the information-theoretic measure of uncertainty and probabilities of events. He states that artists can "violate an expectation by replacing the expected element with one that is distinct from it," they can "introduce a pattern that could be continued in any of several different ways, so that mutually contradictory hypotheses are entertained at once," or they can "introduce a pattern that induces no specifiable expectations at all, so that the appreciator is at complete loss to tell what might follow. All these possibilities are extensively utilized in all art forms" (1971, p. 145). Berlyne also differentiates between *surprise* and *incongruity*. Surprise can be evoked by elements that follow each other in time, with one element violating the expectations raised by the preceding elements, whereas incongruity may happen by unusual simultaneous combinations of elements. These concepts partly overlap, and during the perception of a painting, for example, there is a time-course of perceived events depending on eye movements, although the elements of a painting occur simultaneously (see Berlyne, 1971). Moreover, it is often the case that what is surprising is novel, and that what is expected is familiar, but as Berlyne pointed out (1971), novelty and surprise are distinct concepts and can occur independently of each other (see also Barto, Mirolli, & Baldassarre, 2013; Manahova, Mostert, Kok, Schoffelen, & de Lange, 2018; Miranda & Ullman, 2007, for some neuroscientific evidence).

Music offers the composer nearly unlimited possibilities to induce pleasure by using unexpected tones, rhythms, timbres, intensity levels, and formal structures—to name only a few options at the level of the musical piece. Haydn's second movement of his symphony No. 94 (popularly known as *Surprise Symphony*) is an example of how music can induce surprise in listeners by presenting a sudden fortissimo chord and then by continuing in a calm manner as if nothing has happened. Another example, at the music-syntactic level, is the *deceptive cadence*, a stylistic means in Western tonal music, in which a violation of the expected chord progression in a cadence (normally indicating the end of a theme or piece) occurs at the final chord, leaving the listener with the unexpected feeling of "oh, it's not over yet." These types of stylistic means are not only inherent to music, but unexpected violations of anticipated events play a role in most types of human works of art.

In literary works and the visual arts, surprise can be induced by violating expectations regarding form *and* semantic content. For instance, the underlying metrical structure of poems and the additional play with deviating stress patterns is a frequent mechanism of generating surprise (or novelty), thus affecting the interpretation of the poem and aesthetic appreciation. At the level of meaning, suspense and surprise-ending stories are commonly found in narrations. Even in static media elements of surprise are a frequent feature of art works, artistic styles, or artists. Some painters of the Renaissance (e.g., Hieronymus Bosch) painted fantastic creatures that were often based on reports of foreign animals, unknown to most people at that time, which probably led to surprise responses. Surprise is also a familiar reaction during the transition period of artistic styles, such as during Impressionism at the end of the 19th century, which violated not only the expected realistic depiction of scenes, but also confronted the audience with unexpected rough-and-ready brush strokes and an unusual use of color. Nowadays, surprise is an essential part of design (Ludden, Schifferstein, & Hekkert, 2008) as well as of performance art in which action artists often address political, social, or religious issues. The ubiquitous use of elements of surprise in various art forms over centuries and their theoretical relevance in philosophical aesthetics (Meyer, 1956b; Morreall, 2016; Skorin-Kapov, 2015, 2016) already hint at its deep root in human cognition (see Berlyne, 1971).

Based on prior experience and learning, expectancies play an essential role in biological functioning because they prepare an organism for reacting to future events and influence—or even determine—perception (de Lange, Heilbron, & Kok, 2018). The anticipation of future events is particularly necessary to avoid dangers, which is directly linked to survival. Due to the inherent uncertainty of future events, the correct prediction of an event is rewarded and induces a positive feeling state because the brain has found an adaptive response in a specific situation (Tooby & Cosmides, 1990). In contrast, surprising events are biologically "bad" and lead to heightened arousal and attention (*action-readiness*). In the context of art perception, however, surprises may initially lead to negative responses that are subsequently re-appraised as nonthreatening and positive (Huron, 2006).

Music is an ideal medium to generate surprise due to its temporal nature. The violation of expectations is one out of several mechanisms that may underlie emotion induction by music (Egermann, Pearce, Wiggins, & McAdams, 2013; Juslin & Västfjäll, 2008; Steinbeis et al., 2006), and strong reactions such as laughter, chills, and awe may be regarded as "flavors of surprise" (Huron, 2006, p. 25). For instance, chill responses, already discussed earlier regarding musical reward processing, are strong emotional responses that can be induced by unexpected changes in acoustic and musical features (Grewe, Nagel, Kopiez, Altenmüller, 2007; Sloboda, 1991). Sudden changes in loudness or harmony or entries of new voices are associated with specific psychophysiological processes including increased arousal (Laeng, Eidet, Sulutvedt, & Panksepp, 2016; Mori & Iwanaga, 2017; Sumpf, Jentschke, & Koelsch, 2015). Besides the possibility to generate surprise by playing with different musical features, surprises are most frequently evoked by violating mental representations of musical syntax (i.e., the structure of music). These cognitive representations are formed during musical enculturation through mechanisms of *implicit* and *statistical learning* (similar to the acquisition of language), which already take place early in life (Saffran, Aslin, & Newport, 1996). Since music is a rule-based system of communication, this enables the generation of schemas and concurrent probabilities of events during music processing (Rohrmeier & Rebuschat, 2012). The hierarchy of musical structures and violations of musical expectations have been intensively studied outside the context of aesthetics for a long time (Krumhansl & Kessler, 1982; Narmour, 1992; Schmuckler, 1989), generating a large body of psychological research on the expectation of melodic tones, chords, meter, and rhythm (Large & Kim, 2019; Rohrmeier & Koelsch, 2012). This research field is mostly characterized by using syntactic priming paradigms, determining the neural basis of expectancy violations, and developing computational models that can predict the probability of the next musical event (Pearce & Rohrmeier, 2018).

In the past two decades, computational models of perception such as *predictive coding* have tried to explain how the brain makes predictions about our environment (de Lange et al., 2018; Rao & Ballard, 1999). The idea that the brain matches sensory input with top-down expectations dates back to Helmholtz (1867), but only now it is possible to make use of computational models and neuroimaging data to test the theory that, for example, perception, decision making, and the processing of language largely depend on prior knowledge. This model assumes that the world surrounding us is normally stable and thus predictable, and that the brain has built-in internal models about the world (encoded in higher cortical regions) and is matching the incoming sensory input with these models. Prior knowledge not only refers to hierarchical syntactic structures, but also to knowledge about the environment that has been gained over a lifetime (e.g., sunlight comes from above) or to knowledge about the current context. Knowledge can also influence perception on short timescales (e.g., stimuli presented sequentially). If the expectation is fulfilled, this may lead to an increase in perceptual sensitivity for stimulus features and a reduced neural response (*expectation* or *repetition suppression*). On the other hand, an unexpected event may result in a *prediction error* leading to a neural signal. de Lange et al. (2018, p. 766) explain that "the relative impact of expectations versus sensory input on perception depends on their relative reliability (i.e., 'precision'). Observers rely most strongly on prior knowledge when expectations are reliable and stimuli are ambiguous, but rely most strongly on the input when expectations are weak and stimuli reliable." Bayesian probability theory is ideally suited to making such inferences and is used in this context. Importantly, predictive coding models of cortex make predictions about the current sensory input and not forecasts about the next incoming sensory input. This theory has been applied in the context of various types of sensory inputs, including static and dynamic (de Lange et al., 2018).

Predictive coding theory has been adopted to the perception of visual art (Consoli, 2016; Kesner, 2014; Van de Cruys & Wagemans, 2011); for example, suggesting that reward may be generated by an initial state of uncertainty, which turns into a state that is predictable. However, most of this work is of a theoretical nature and empirical evidence is still needed. In the domain of music, predictive coding has recently entered the field by modeling pitch (Chang, Bosnyak, & Trainor, 2018) and rhythm perception (Lumaca, Haumann, Brattico, Grube, & Vuust, 2019; Vuust, Dietz, Witek, & Kringelbach, 2018) as well as by discussing aspects of music-induced reward (Hansen, Dietz, & Vuust, 2017; Salimpoor, Zald, Zatorre, Dagher, & McIntosh, 2015). For instance, using three naturalistic pieces of Western art music with different elements of musical surprises, Shany et al. (2019) showed that surprising events led to an increase in subjective arousal and either an increase or decrease in pleasantness compared with unsurprising musical events. At the neuronal level, the authors observed a direct link between surprise-induced pleasantness and increased activation of the nucleus accumbens in a subgroup of participants who enjoyed listening to the music. Moreover, this subgroup also exhibited a stronger connectivity between the nucleus accumbens and auditory cortices related to musical surprises, which demonstrates an association between musical surprises and reward-related activation. In an fMRI study on suspense induced by literary texts, Lehne, Engel, Rohrmeier, Menninghaus, Jacobs, and Koelsch (2015) showed that the emotional experience of suspense was related to activation of regions known from studying social cognition as well as to those related to predictive inference (bilateral activations in inferior frontal regions extending into the lateral premotor cortex in the precentral gyrus). Activation of limbic brain structures was not modulated by suspense. In summary, a review of this current research has revealed that predictive coding has only recently gained attention in the field, and further, that in the context of dynamic stimuli the term *prediction* is frequently used to refer to anticipation and the prediction of upcoming events (Koelsch, Vuust, & Friston, 2019), which may be conceptually different from studying, for instance, the perception of static visual stimuli or individual musical sounds. In the future, predictive coding in relation to familiarity/novelty (e.g., Vladimirskiy, Urbanczik, & Senn, 2015) may also be studied in greater depth.

COMPLEXITY AND SIMPLICITY

Humans have to interact with a complex environment, and their sensory system has evolved to deal with this complexity (Godfrey-Smith, 2002). Unsurprisingly then, *complexity/simplicity* is a collative variable that has also gained much attention in the field of empirical aesthetics since the 1950s. The major intuitive determinant of perceived complexity is the number and variety of elements present in a stimulus. For example, a musical piece with several parts played by different instruments is considered as more complex than a piece played by one instrument (Marin & Leder, 2013). Berlyne (1971) argued that in narration, the addition of characters and incidents increases the degree of complexity in a similar way. However, the extensive literature on visual complexity has emphasized that subjective complexity is a multidimensional construct and determined by more than one objective stimulus feature (for a review, see Van Geert & Wagemans, 2020). In fact, the same notion of multidimensionality holds true for musical complexity (Streich, 2007) and literary complexity (Grishakova & Poulaki, 2019), indicating that research on complexity still leaves room for a great diversity of research programs within and across domains.

In the visual domain, complexity and its counterpart simplicity have been linked to concepts such as *goodness of configuration* (Koffka, 1935), information-theoretic concepts of *uncertainty, information content*, and *redundancy*, as well as to concepts of *order, diversity*, and *structure* (Berlyne, Ogilvie, & Parham, 1968). Berlyne (1960) argued that *subjective complexity* is positively correlated with the number of and dissimilarity between elements and negatively correlated with the perception of how these elements form a unit. Empirical evidence by Berlyne et al. (1968) supported this view by finding two dimensions of subjective complexity, one related to information content determined by "the number of independently selected component elements" (p. 383), and one related to "unitariness vs. articulation into recognizable parts" (p. 384). Whereas Chipman (1977) found that complexity is determined by an interplay between quantitative and structural variables (see also Gartus & Leder, 2017; Ichikawa, 1985; Marin & Leder, 2016), Nadal et al. (2010) suggested three underlying dimensions of subjective complexity, namely (1) the amount and variety of elements, (2) the disorganization of these elements, and (3) asymmetry. These dimensions may show different relationships with hedonic tone. Recent theoretical work by Van Geert and Wagemans (2020) argues that subjective visual complexity stems from *objective complexity* and *order* as two separate concepts. The authors define objective complexity as the "quantity and variety of information in a stimulus" (p. 4), similar to the first dimension of Berlyne et al. (1968) and Nadal et al. (2010). Objective order (e.g., symmetry, alignment, iteration) is related to the "structure and organization of the information in the stimulus" (p. 4), which reflects the second dimension of Berlyne et al. (1968) and the second and third dimensions of Nadal et al. (2010). In their framework, simplicity is defined as the opposite of complexity and disorder as the opposite of order. Both complexity and order are considered as multidimensional variables, and Van Geert and Wagemans (2020) suggest that a balance between these two variables may be a good predictor of aesthetic appreciation (see also Eysenck, 1942). Another line of research in the visual domain has focused on fractals, specifically the prevalence and complexity of fractal patterns in visual art (Taylor et al., 2005). Future research will also have to integrate aspects of conceptual and semantic dimensions of complexity (e.g., Commare, Rosenberg, & Leder, 2018; Madan, Bayer, Gamer, Lonsdorf, & Sommer, 2018; Nicki & Moss, 1975) into theories of structurally based complexity and order. Clearly, future studies will thus have to consider different definitions and operationalizations of visual complexity to be able to determine the relationship with aesthetic responses in greater detail.

The development of objective measures of visual complexity has had a long tradition in the field of empirical aesthetics and immensely contributed to our current understanding of subjective complexity. Here, *objective complexity* refers to the complexity that is physically present in a stimulus. Birkhoff (1932) conceived an aesthetic measure (i.e., an aesthetic response) as being determined by two factors, namely order and complexity: M (aesthetic measure) $= O$ (order)$/C$ (complexity). Order (unity or harmony) and complexity (multiplicity and diversity) have been thought to underlie beauty and related measures since the Greek antiquity (Boselie & Leeuwenberg, 1985). Birkhoff was the first to express this relation in a mathematical formula, arguing that order had a positive association with an aesthetic measure and complexity a negative one. However, empirical evidence for Birkhoff's formula, which was based on the perception of polygons, was scarce, which led Eysenck (1941) to develop a new empirical aesthetic formula, which he also based on studying polygons: $M = O \times C$. In his formula, both order and complexity had a positive contribution to an aesthetic measure, and Eysenck (1968) himself provided empirical evidence for this relationship.

After these initial efforts to formalize aesthetic responses, information-theoretic measures have entered the field, backed up by the growing use of automated algorithms to analyze (and create) artistic materials. Berlyne's *New Experimental Aesthetics* and his followers aimed at elucidating the relationship between objective measures of complexity (uncertainty) and subjective responses. It should be kept in mind that studies linking subjective responses to objective complexity measures have flourished in various fields over the past decades, ranging from basic research on visual aesthetics (for a review, see Van Geert & Wagemans, 2020) to more applied fields such as the aesthetics of food and beverages (Palczak, Blumenthal, Rogeaux, & Delarue, 2019) and the design of websites (Seckler, Opwis, & Tuch, 2015), to name only a few examples. In addition, a considerable amount of research has focused on *how* to measure complexity objectively in both the visual (Corchs, Ciocca, Bricolo, & Gasparini, 2016; Sun et al., 2018) and auditory domains (Mauch & Levy, 2011; Streich, 2007), proposing a wide range of computational measures detecting structural stimulus features. Needless to say, this endeavor has been largely dependent on computational advances in the field of image statistics and music information retrieval as well as on the development of algorithms and statistical models more generally.

In the field of visual aesthetics and digital image processing, the application of *compression algorithms* has become a widespread measure of complexity (Donderi, 2006; Forsythe et al., 2011; Marin & Leder, 2013). Authors usually report moderate to strong effect sizes regarding the relationship between subjective complexity ratings and image compression ratios, using formats such as *Joint Photographic Expert Group* (JPEG) or *Graphics Interchange Format* (GIF), whose performance depends on the types of images and employed statistical models (Fernandez-Lozano, Carballal, Machado, Santos, & Romero, 2019; Gartus & Leder, 2017; Machado et al., 2015; Marin & Leder, 2013). Compression ratios are an effective measure of visual complexity because, based on *Algorithmic Information Theory*, compression algorithms analyze an image's visual information and try to compress it to the degree that makes a valid reproduction of the input image possible (see also *Kolmogorov complexity*; Kolmogorov, 1968). The file size (in bits) then correlates positively with the complexity of the image. For instance, a simple figure-ground composition can be compressed more than a complex visual scene because simpler images are usually characterized by more redundant information that can be represented by a shorter string of bits (Donderi, 2006).

Other frequently applied measures of objective complexity are *edge detection algorithms*, such as *Perimeter edge detection* and *Canny edge detection* (Chikhman, Bondarko, Danilova, Goluzina, & Shelepin, 2012; Forsythe et al., 2008; Forsythe et al., 2011; Marin & Leder, 2013), and more complex measures such as *root-mean square* (RMS) *contrast* and *phase congruency* (Cavalcante et al., 2014; Gartus & Leder, 2017; Marin & Leder, 2013). These algorithms detect changes in intensity at an image's edges, revealing contours and a global measure of shape, and are sometimes employed in combination with compression rates (Gartus & Leder, 2017). The analysis of the degree of self-similarity constitutes another approach to measure image complexity. For instance, *PHOG self-similarity* is based on the *pyramid histogram of orientation gradients* and compares the similarity of these values for the entire image with the values for individual subparts (Lyssenko, Redies, & Hayn-Leichsenring, 2016; Redies, Amirshahi, Koch, & Denzler, 2012). This measure is closely related to the fractal geometrical properties of an image. Fractals show the same structure when zooming in and out of an image; in other words, there are similar structural patterns at different scales (Mandelbrot, 1967), and the measure of fractal dimension is an indicator of the self-similarity of an image (Theiler, 1990). The aesthetics of fractals has received some attention in the field (Forsythe et al., 2011; Spehar, Clifford, Newell, & Taylor, 2003; Spehar & Taylor, 2013; Taylor, Spehar, Clifford, & Newell, 2008; Viengkham & Spehar, 2018), but the relationship between fractal dimension and subjective aesthetic responses is still unclear. Furthermore, there is a growing body of research on intensity and color-based image statistics that have shown a relationship with perceived complexity, such as *PHOG anisotropy* (Lyssenko et al., 2016; Redies et al., 2012) and entropy (Marin & Leder, 2013), to name only a few (for a review, see also Van Geert & Wagemans, 2020). Marin & Leder (2016) studied affective environmental scenes and representational paintings, providing initial indications that objective measures may be sensitive to different sub-dimensions of visual complexity, that the subjective multidimensionality of visual complexity only emerges over time, and further, that the relationship between subjective and objective complexity may not depend significantly on the presentation duration of the stimuli. The application of *Convolutional Neural Networks* (CNNs), based on deep learning algorithms, to model visual complexity may also provide one avenue of future research (Krizhevsky, Sutskever, & Hinton, 2012; Simonyan & Zisserman, 2014). Altogether, using a wide range of visual stimuli, future studies will still have to shed more light on which factors determine the relationship between subjective and objective complexity.

Visual complexity has also been studied at the neurophysiological level and event-related potential (ERP) studies have associated visual complexity with early stages of stimulus processing (150 ms), showing effects of the affective image content (i.e., valence) on these early components (Bradley et al., 2007; for a review, see Olofsson, Nordin, Sequeira, & Polich, 2008). However, interaction effects between visual complexity and stimulus valence have also been reported, with complex, as well as more colorful, photographs of objects leading to stronger emotional responses at the neuronal level than simple pictograms (Schlochtermeier et al., 2013). Recently, an *arousal-complexity bias* for picture processing has been documented in a series of experiments, suggesting that arousal may affect the perception of visual complexity (Madan et al., 2018). There is some related neurophysiological evidence in support of this hypothesis (e.g., Schlochtermeier et al., 2013; Schupp, Junghofer, Weike, & Hamm, 2003), which also calls for a further discussion about the conceptual validity of a strict differentiation between emotion and cognition (Ochsner & Phelps, 2007; Okon-Singer, Hendler, Pessoa, & Shackman, 2015). In the field of neuroaesthetics, a recent study using EEG headsets during a museum visit of a large group of participants showed that visual complexity can be predicted above chance-level from EEG signals when viewing aesthetically pleasing art (Kontson et al., 2015). These are promising findings suggesting that combining technological advances with the endeavor to study aesthetic experiences in an ecologically valid setting may well be a fruitful path.

In the musical domain, subjective complexity has also been understood as a multidimensional concept (Conley, 1981; Pressing, 1999; Scheirer, Watson, & Vercoe, 2000; Streich, 2007), depending on a wide range of musical and acoustical features that can be measured objectively. Among the musical features determining general subjective complexity are those related to melody, harmony, rhythm, and meter (only melodic and rhythmic complexity are dealt here with greater detail). Relevant acoustic features of the auditory signal comprise changes in intensity and timbre (Streich, 2007). Numerous researchers have artificially varied one (or two) aspect(s) of musical complexity and investigated its link to hedonic tone, often by integrating objective measures of complexity into their research design, whereas other researchers have studied musical complexity more holistically with stimuli of higher ecological validity (e.g., Marin & Leder, 2013; North & Hargreaves, 1995). Studies also vary in how much they take into account the dynamic nature of music when modeling complexity by either considering the complexity of a musical excerpt as a whole, the complexity of different parts of an excerpt, or note-to-note relationships within an excerpt. This holds true for the development of cognitive models of musical complexity as well as for approaches aiming to objectively assess musical complexity. Furthermore, recent advances in the development of objective measures build on findings previously reported in the visual domain, such as the application of compression algorithms (e.g., MP3, FLAC, and Ogg Vorbis) to predict subjective musical complexity (de Fleurian, Blackwell, Ben-Tal, & Müllensiefen, 2017; Güçlütürk, Güçlü, van Gerven, & van Lier, 2018; Marin & Leder, 2013). Compression file sizes as measures of objective complexity have also proved to be good predictors when categorizing musical excerpts into musical styles (Cilibrasi, Vitányi, & Wolf, 2004), suggesting practical applications of fundamental research on musical complexity.

Melodic complexity has been widely studied in the field, especially regarding the predictability of note-to-note events (i.e., individual pitches within a sequence of pitches). Melodic complexity depends on music-theoretic factors such as pitch intervals, contours, and hierarchical pitch relationships. It is important to note that there is a conceptual overlap between expectancy violations (Meyer, 1956) and information-theoretic concepts of melodic complexity based on probabilities (Eerola, Himberg, Toiviainen, & Louhivuori, 2006). In simple terms, the less a melody is following our expectations, the more complex it will be perceived. Behind the background of information theory, one can argue that "the less probable a musical utterance is given some baseline probability—for example, the statistical regularities within a corpus—the higher the information entropy of that utterance and the more complex it is likely to be perceived" (Albrecht, 2016, p. 20). Indeed, models of melodic complexity based on either expectancy violations or redundancy appear to perform similarly (Eerola, 2016). Further evidence supporting this view stems from studying musical complexity within the framework of predictive coding: Delplanque, De Loof, Janssens, and Verguts (2019) showed that entropy measures of musical sound sequences (indicating the degree of disorder in a stimulus) may be a good predictor of preference. They authors reported an inverted U-shaped relationship between entropy and preference ratings, which is congruent with Berlyne's psychobiological model.

Drawing on the work of Berlyne and his approach to study both subjective and objective complexity, for example, Crozier (1974) calculated the uncertainty for specific sound sequences and asked how this measure is related to subjective responses to artificial sound-sequence structures in a series of experiments (for a similar approach, see also McMullen, 1974; Vitz, 1966). He reported a linear relationship between subjective complexity and uncertainty level, which was also observed for interestingness, and an inverted U-shaped function between pleasingness (beauty) and uncertainty level, which is in line with Berlyne's psychobiological model (1971). In more recent times, this approach has led to the development of computational models in music research that can not only analyze Shannon entropy as a measure of the uncertainty of the next note but also the information content of the note that follows as a measure of unexpectedness (Pearce, 2005). This suggests, as indicated above, that collative variables such as complexity and surprise are interwoven in dynamic musical stimuli when generating aesthetic responses (see also Eerola, 2016; Eerola & North, 2000). Melodic complexity has also been examined within the context of fractals (Beauvois, 2007), and an inverted U-shaped curve was also found between aesthetic preference (i.e., melodicity) and subjective and objective complexity measures, respectively. Martins, Gingras, Puig-Waldmueller, and Fitch (2017) also studied musical fractals and their results indicate that recursion and its cognitive presentation may be domain-general.

Recent neurophysiological studies have shown that, for example, event-related potential (ERP) markers, such as the N2, are sensitive to melodic complexity (Minati et al., 2010). In the context of predictive coding, several other studies have found correlates of the brain's precision of its predictive model regarding pitch sequences and their statistical properties (e.g., Garrido, Sahani, & Dolan, 2013; Heilbron & Chait, 2018; Hsu, Le Bars, Hämäläinen, & Waszak, 2015). Using more ecologically valid stimuli than previous studies, Quiroga-Martinez et al. (2019) employed magnetoencephalography to study expectancies within the context of low- and high-entropy melodies varying in their repetitiveness of pitches, which were assessed with a computational model of auditory expectation. Mismatch negativity (MMNm) amplitudes were used as a measure of prediction error, and pitch deviants in a high-entropy context yielded lower MMNm amplitudes than those in a low-entropy context. This finding is in line with theories suggesting that precision-weighted prediction error is a fundamental principle underlying brain function.

Rhythm is defined as a pattern of discrete durations of events that largely depend on perceptual grouping mechanisms (Fraisse, 1963), and that is usually studied by employing measures of human perception and performance (i.e., human reproduction ability, as measured in a tapping task, for instance). Cognitive models of *rhythmic complexity* (for a review, see Honing & Bouwer, 2019) have a long tradition in the field of music psychology (Povel & Essens, 1985; Shmulevich & Povel, 2000), and factors such as tempo and musical expertise have been found to play a role in rhythm perception and production. When we perceive a musical rhythm, we usually perceive a beat, because some musical events are more prominent than others due to accents. Rhythm (beat) perception was reported to activate motor regions of the brain (Grahn & Brett, 2007; Zatorre, Chen, & Penhune, 2007), and rhythmic complexity and musical expertise modulate the synchronization between auditory and motor areas in the brain (Chen, Penhune, & Zatorre, 2008). Musical rhythm has also been discussed within the framework of predictive coding (Vuust & Witek, 2014), and recent evidence suggests that rhythmic sequences of high entropy are more difficult to model for the brain (Lumaca et al., 2019; for a review on the neural underpinnings of rhythm processing, see Nguyen, Gibbings, & Grahn, 2018).

Several studies have also yielded important insights into how rhythmic complexity can be objectively measured, either from an abstract representation or directly from the audio signal. For instance, Alexander and Carey (1968) proposed that subjective complexity is negatively associated with the number of symmetric subsequences within a rhythmic pattern. This measure of *subsymmetry* was previously successfully applied to visual complexity by the same authors, and for musical rhythms, the measure of subsymmetry was also found to perform better than the *syncopation index* of Longuet-Higgins and Lee (1984) (see also Toussaint & Beltran, 2013, for more recent evidence). Another simple approach to model rhythmic complexity is to measure the rate of rhythmic activity and tempo of rhythms relative to other rhythms (Conley, 1981). de Fleurian et al. (2017) reported that information-theoretic measures based on Kolmogorov complexity and Shannon entropy were predictive of rhythmic complexity, and further, that musical expertise also affected rhythm perception. Other studies revealed that beat-based measures (Povel & Essens, 1985; Shmulevich & Povel, 2000) were good predictors of perceived rhythmic complexity, which also depended on tempo and musical training (Vinke, 2010). Rhythm has also been studied within the context of entrainment and groove (Levitin, Grahn, & London, 2018), and thus it is not surprising that an objective measure of *danceability* based on the audio signal has been proposed (Streich, 2007).

In both the visual and musical domains, individual differences regarding complexity perception have been observed. Berlyne (1971, 1974a) was already aware of individual differences regarding the relationship between complexity and preference (Lane, 1968; Vitz, 1966), and further, that these differences can also be due to how humans respond to ecological and semantic variables. With the advent of modern statistical modeling techniques, such as linear mixed models, which can account for individual differences and integrate them into statistical models, recent psychological research has shown an increased interest in participant-specific response patterns. For example, Güçlütürk, Jacobs, and Lier (2016) demonstrated that the inverted U-shaped function between complexity and liking for abstract computer-generated art can be explained by individual differences in preferences for complexity; namely, by two subgroups with one group preferring simple images and one complex ones. In a similar vein, Spehar, Walker, and Taylor (2016) reported four different subgroups of participants characterized by different preferences for fractal patterns. Street, Forsythe, Reilly, Taylor, and Helmy (2016) considered factors such as gender, age, and culture, and observed main effects of gender and culture as well as an interaction between gender and age on complexity responses to visual fractals. Personality traits can also explain why people respond differently to visual complexity. Marin and Leder (2018) showed that, among females, affect-related personality traits such as trait emotional intelligence, empathy, and stress reactivity modulate complexity and arousal responses to visual and musical stimuli. Güçlütürk and Lier (2019) reported that people can be separated into a subgroup preferring simple songs and one preferring complex songs, with age and gender as possible underlying factors explaining this group difference. Altogether, this current trend of studying individual differences is linked to the question of whether the field can make universal claims about the relationship of core variables such as complexity and liking, or whether a more nuanced way of looking at aesthetic responses is warranted in the future.

AMBIGUITY AND CLARITY

Ambiguities are common in everyday life, especially in verbal communication and humor (Martin & Ford, 2018; Rodd, Gaskell, & Marslen Wilson, 2002). According to Berlyne (1971), *ambiguity* and multiple meanings are also central concepts employed by artists and thus highly relevant in the perception of art (Zeki, 2002). The main difference between the perception of ambiguities in everyday life and their perception in relation to art may be that the former is based on prior knowledge and the latter mostly on conventions (Mamassian, 2008). The following examples demonstrate the widespread use of ambiguities in various art forms. In music, a chord can be ambiguous and give rise to different harmonic meanings, which can be resolved by the musical context that follows (Agawu, 1994). For instance, the familiar *Tristan chord* is highly ambiguous and has led to much theoretical speculation regarding its harmonic function in a tonal context. Another example is ambiguity in the analysis of musical form (de Clercq, 2017). In the realm of literature, ambiguity is a commonly found literary device, such as exemplified in *The Sick Rose* by William Blake, which leaves much room for interpretation because of several possible meanings of the words "Rose," "sick," and "worm." In visual arts, for instance, *Cubists* are known for applying ambiguities at several levels, such as depicting different profiles of faces at the same time (e.g., *Seated Woman* by Pablo Picasso) and overlapping shapes of objects with segments belonging to more than one object. Another example is *Op Art*, which is based on visual illusions based on Moiré patterns, figure-ground ambiguities, and three-dimensional appearances based on two-dimensional patterns (Berlyne, 1971, for other examples, see Mamassian, 2008).

Berlyne (1971) refers to Kaplan and Kris (1948), who differentiated between four types of ambiguity that can be discussed in relation to a pattern: (1) *disjunctive ambiguity* (i.e., several alternative and mutual exclusive meanings exist), (2) *additive ambiguity* (i.e., although meanings are mutually exclusive they overlap to a certain extent), (3) *conjunctive ambiguity* (i.e., the two meanings jointly affect the interpretation), and (4) *integrative ambiguity* (i.e., two meanings support each other and evoke one complex meaning). Although much theoretical work has been done on ambiguities (Berndt & Koepnick, 2018; Cross, 2005; Empson, 1930; Gamboni, 2002), empirical research on the role of ambiguity is rather limited in its scope and different conceptions of ambiguity are used, which makes it difficult to compare results across studies.

There is a growing body of research on visual ambiguity, in which, for instance, some researchers focus on *perceptual ambiguity* during early stimulus processing, which is sometimes discussed within the framework of processing fluency, and others on *cognitive ambiguity*, which refers to stable percepts (i.e., one visual experience) with more than one possible meaning or interpretation. Jakesch, Leder, and Forster (2013), for instance, investigated in six experiments how processing fluency (manipulated by presentation duration) and ambiguity interact during the perception of surrealist paintings by René Magritte. They reported that ambiguous paintings were preferred to nonambiguous paintings at presentation durations of 500 and 1,000 ms, and that ambiguous paintings were harder to process in general. In a follow-up study using the same type of stimuli and facial electromyography, Jakesch, Goller, and Leder (2017) demonstrated that ambiguous Magritte paintings elicited more positively valenced emotional responses than unambiguous paintings, although there was no difference in explicit liking ratings, which may have been due to individual differences. Another recent study by the same group (Markey, Jakesch, & Leder, 2019) explored ERP amplitudes in response to semantic and syntactic inconsistencies inherent to Magritte paintings and also to the photographic versions of these paintings. The data indicated that both types of stimuli were similarly processed and that the N400, a frequently reported ERP component regarding semantic violations, and the P600, an ERP component associated with syntactic violations, were not modulated by semantic and syntactic inconsistencies as expected. This may be due to a specific processing mode activated during the perception of these artworks.

Ambiguity in visual art can also be studied in relation to cognitive insight and the dynamics underlying this process. Muth and Carbon (2013) demonstrated that the level of insights into perceptual Gestalt affect liking and may enhance the appreciation of a stimulus after a perceptual insight (see also Muth, Ebert, Markovic, & Carbon, 2019). Muth, Hesslinger, and Carbon (2015) further reported that modern and contemporary ambiguous artworks that evoke cognitive challenges are appreciated and considered as interesting, and further, that the elaboration of an artwork may be an appealing process in itself. The same research group also developed a *Continuous Evaluation Procedure* (CEP) that allows for the dynamic assessment of subjective responses. This method was used to investigate changes in liking and interest while watching an artistic movie depicting the evolution and metamorphosis of an emerging Gestalt until moments of insights were reached. Their findings indicated that insights increase liking and that interest already increases 1,500 ms before the moments of insights. In a follow-up study using the same artistic video, Muth, Raab, and Carbon (2016) framed their research within the context of predictive coding and reward by having introduced the multidimensional concept of *semantic instability* (Muth & Carbon, 2016). Semantic instability comprises four clusters, namely integrative blend, multistability, indeterminacy, and contrast to perceptual habits (Muth, Hesslinger, & Carbon, 2018). Muth et al. (2016) specifically studied the role of the episodic context (increasing vs. decreasing visual determinacy) in the relationship between determinacy and liking, reporting that in the group that was exposed to an increase of visual determinacy of hidden Gestalts (i.e., the first episode was the least evocative of a clear Gestalt and had high semantic instability) determinacy was a good predictor of liking and that *Aesthetic Aha* effects (i.e., an increase in liking at moments of insight) were stronger in this condition than in the one of decreasing visual determinacy. In other words, the increase in certainty was probably more rewarding in the condition of increasing visual determinacy. The same research group also investigated whether experiencing the artistic video in a laboratory context vs. in an art gallery would affect determinacy and liking. Gallery visitors appreciated the video more and considered it as less semantically unstable than participants in the laboratory (Muth, Raab, & Carbon, 2017). In short, this research is a valuable contribution to our understanding of how aesthetic experiences may change over time, which also motivates a very naturalistic way of studying art perception by using advanced technological and statistical methods.

Empirical studies on ambiguities have also found its place outside the vision science community. A recent qualitative study by Maksimainen, Eerola, and Saarikallio (2019) examined *emotional ambiguities* present in the experience of either musical or visual objects. Participants were asked to think about an object that induced pleasure, and which was considered as meaningful in their daily lives. They freely reported on any emotions and emotional contradictions during such an experience, rated the strength of the felt pleasure and intensity of emotions as well as to what degree the experience could be regard as a bodily and aesthetic experience. The findings indicated that the majority of participants (~70%) experienced some degree of emotional ambivalence and that this was more frequently the case in response to musical than visual objects. Around half of the emotion terms (46%) used to describe ambivalence were positive, 36% negative, and around 14% both positive and negative. The findings also indicated that ambivalent emotions were associated with slightly higher emotional intensity and considered as aesthetic experiences. The authors also identified different categories of ambivalent attitude types inherent in their descriptions, demonstrating the need to integrate social, ideological, and contextual aspects in the discussion of ambivalent emotions.

One other line of research has tried to disambiguate the meaning and appreciation of paintings (or musical pieces) by offering various types of additional information at the cognitive level, such as the title of the paintings (musical pieces), the name of the painter (composer or performer), or statements about the paintings (music) (e.g., Anglada-Tort, Steffens, & Müllensiefen, 2019; Jakesch & Leder, 2009; Leder, Carbon, & Ripsas, 2006; Margulis, Levine, Simchy-Gross, & Kroger, 2017; Millis, 2001). Although these studies show interesting effects on aesthetic appreciation, they do not deal directly with the ambiguity of the actual stimulus characteristics and are thus not considered here in greater detail.

MAJOR CHALLENGES, GOALS, AND SUGGESTIONS

The current review of the literature on the role of collative variables in aesthetic experiences has shown that Berlyne's legacy is still strongly present among researchers in the field. Collative variables of different stimulus categories and sensory domains are widely studied, using behavioral, computational, and neuroscientific methods. However, Berlyne's theory of collative motivation has not been further developed and his conception of arousal systems is outdated. Notably, trying to replicate the inverted U-shaped curve between a collative variable and hedonic tone is a frequent endeavor, which has sometimes, but not always, failed. Thus, several major challenges and goals for researchers can be identified. First, if researchers in the field agree that collative variables play a role in aesthetic experiences and that Berlyne's theory is outdated, one challenge will be to integrate these variables into other, more recent and complex models of aesthetic experiences and to determine their relative role. Here I am not only referring to the relative role of collative variables among a set of a collative variables, but also to the relative role of collative variables with respect to other stimulus features (e.g., balance, color, and texture), person-related factors, and the (social) context of aesthetic experience. Second, current research has repeatedly demonstrated that individual differences in responses to collative variables do exist, as already indicated by Berlyne (1971). It will be a challenge to determine the factors underlying these individual differences, and more generally, to integrate individual differences to a larger extent into models of aesthetic experiences. Third, another recent trend is to compare aesthetic responses to collative variables across sensory or artistic domains. Future research will have to clarify whether specific or general models of aesthetic experiences are more appropriate, or in other words, whether we can identify an overlap in addition to domain/stimulus-specific facets at various levels of aesthetic processing and experience. It is also likely that a comparison will reveal differential results for individual collative variables. Fourth, Berlyne's idea to consider motivation in the study of aesthetic responses has recurred in the growing literature on pleasure, the brain, and the reward system. Here, the challenge will be to get a better understanding of the possible role of emotional and/or motivational arousal in relation to reward and pleasure. Fifth, the current review of previous research has revealed that there is much room for replication of reported effects and meta-analyses, considering more nuanced definitions underlying collative variables when generating stimuli for experiments, which may be achieved by acknowledging to a larger degree theoretical work rooted in the humanities. Finally, the field needs to tackle the challenge of studying conscious and nonconscious aspects of aesthetic responses to collative variables by embracing multiple empirical methods. This is especially true for the study of affective (arousal) responses during aesthetic experiences.

Collative variables have been widely studied outside the field of empirical aesthetics, as already mentioned. Examples range from website design to architecture and from music recommendation systems to music and consumer behavior, with frequent references to Berlyne's theory in these applied fields. This demonstrates that the study of collative variables has already found its place outside basic research, which indirectly highlights the relevance of collative variables for aesthetic responses. The literature stemming from more applied fields is growing in parallel to the one stemming from basic research in empirical aesthetics, which researchers working in the respective fields are often unaware of. This hinders fruitful communication across fields, which may be overcome in the future.

One practical suggestion for teaching theories of aesthetic responses at university level would be to avoid reducing Berlyne's theory to the well-known inverted U-shaped curve, as is often done, but to present it instead within the broader context of motivation, to teach its inherent complexity and roots in psychobiology, and finally, to relate it to the latest findings of neuroimaging research, which have recently put pleasure, re-ward, and predictive coding into the foreground. Such an approach would do justice to the theoretical contribution of Daniel Berlyne to the field of empirical aesthetics during the past decades, and also show how older theories may re-emerge, and, moreover, how they can be more easily empirically tested thanks to technological and methodological progress.

Acknowledgments

I would like to express my sincere appreciation to Bruno Gingras, Roberto Viviani, Helmut Leder, Martina Jakesch, and Andreas Gartus, whose comments have greatly improved this chapter.

References

Agawu, K. (1994). Ambiguity in tonal music: A preliminary study. In Pople, A. (Ed.), *Theory, analysis and meaning in music* (pp. 86–107). Cambridge, England: Cambridge University Press,

Albrecht, J. (2016). Modeling musical complexity: Commentary on Eerola (2016). *Empirical Musicology Review, 11*(1), 20–26.

Alexander, C., & Carey, S. (1968). Subsymmetries. *Perception and Psychophysics, 4,* 73–77.

Ali, S. O., & Peynircioğğlu, Z. F. (2010). Intensity of emotions conveyed and elicited by familiar and unfamiliar music. *Music Perception: An Interdisciplinary Journal, 27*(3), 177–182.

Andretic, R., van Swinderen, B., & Greenspan, R. J. (2005). Dopaminergic modulation of arousal in Drosophila. *Current Biology, 15*(13), 1165–1175.

Anglada-Tort, M., Steffens, J., & Müllensiefen, D. (2019). Names and titles matter: The impact of linguistic fluency and the affect heuristic on aesthetic and value judgements of music. *Psychology of Aesthetics Creativity and the Arts, 13*(3), 277–292.

Barto, A., Mirolli, M., & Baldassarre, G. (2013). Novelty or surprise? *Frontiers in Psychology, 4,* 907.

Beauvois, M. W. (2007). Quantifying aesthetic preference and perceived complexity for fractal melodies. *Music Perception, 24*(3), 247–264.

Belfi, A. M., Vessel, E. A., Brielmann, A., Isik, A. I., Chatterjee, A., Leder, H., ... Starr, G. G. (2018). Dynamics of aesthetic experience are reflected in the default-mode network. *NeuroImage, 188,* 584–597.

Benedek, M., & Kaernbach, C. (2011). Physiological correlates and emotional specificity of human piloerection. *Biological Psychology, 86*(3), 320–329.

Berlyne, D. E. (1954). A theory of human curiosity. *British Journal of Psychology, 45*(3), 180–191.

Berlyne, D. E. (1960). *Conflict, arousal, and curiosity.* New York, NY: McGraw-Hill.

Berlyne, D. E. (1965). *Structure and direction in thinking.* New York, NY: Wiley.

Berlyne, D. E. (1970). Novelty, complexity, and hedonic value. *Perception & Psychophysics, 8*(5), 279–286.

Berlyne, D. E. (1971). *Aesthetics and psychobiology.* New York, NY: Appleton-Century-Crofts.

Berlyne, D. E. (1972a). Ends and means of experimental aesthetics. *Canadian Journal of Psychology/Revue canadienne de psychologie, 26*(4), 303–325.

Berlyne, D. E. (1972b). Humor and its kin. In Goldstein, J. H., & McGhee, P. E. (Eds.), *The psychology of humor: Theoretical perspectives and empirical issues* (pp. 43–60), New York and London: Academic Press.

Berlyne, D. E. (1974a). The New Experimental Aesthetics. In D. E. Berlyne (Ed.), *Studies in the new experimental aesthetics: Steps towards an objective psychology of aesthetic appreciation* (pp. 1–26). Washington, DC: Hemisphere.

Berlyne, D. E. (1974b). Novelty, complexity, and interestingness. In D. E. Berlyne (Ed.), *Studies in the new experimental aesthetics: Steps toward an objective psychology of aesthetic appreciation* (pp. 175–180). Washington, DC: Hemisphere.

Berlyne, D. E. (1974c). *Studies in the New Experimental Aesthetics: Steps toward an objective psychology of aesthetic appreciation.* Washington, DC: Hemisphere.

Berlyne, D. E., & Lawrence, G. H. (1964). Effects of complexity and incongruity variables on GSR, investigatory behavior, and verbally expressed preference. *The Journal of General Psychology, 71*(1), 21–45.

Berlyne, D. E., & Madsen, K.B. (1973). *Pleasure, reward, preference: Their nature, determinants, and role in behavior.* Cambridge, England: Academic Press.

Berlyne, D. E., Ogilvie, J., & Parham, L. (1968). The dimensionality of visual complexity, interestingness, and pleasingness. *Canadian Journal of Psychology/Revue canadienne de psychologie, 22*(5), 376.

Berndt, F., & Koepnick, L. (Eds.). (2018). *Ambiguity in contemporary art and theory. Zeitschrift für Ästhetik und Allgemeine Kunstwissenschaft.* Hamburg: Felix Meiner Verlag.

Berridge, K. C., & Kringelbach, M. L. (2008). Affective neuroscience of pleasure: Reward in humans and animals. *Psychopharmacology, 199*(3), 457–480.

Berridge, K. C., & Kringelbach, M. L. (2015). Pleasure systems in the brain. *Neuron, 86*(3), 646–664.

Bestelmeyer, P. E. G., Kotz, S. A., & Belin, P. (2017). Effects of emotional valence and arousal on the voice perception network. *Social Cognitive and Affective Neuroscience, 12*(8), 1351–1358.

Birkhoff, G. D. (1932). *Aesthetic measure.* Cambridge, MA: Harvard University Press.

Blijlevens, J., Carbon, C. C., Mugge, R., & Schoormans, J. P. (2012). Aesthetic appraisal of product designs: Independent effects of typicality and arousal. *British Journal of Psychology, 103*(1), 44–57.

Blood, A. J., & Zatorre, R. J. (2001). Intensely pleasurable responses to music correlate with activity in brain regions implicated in reward and emotion. *Proceedings of the National Academy of Sciences, 98*(20), 11818–11823.

Bohrn, I. C., Altmann, U., Lubrich, O., Menninghaus, W., & Jacobs, A. M. (2013). When we like what we know—A parametric fMRI analysis of beauty and familiarity. *Brain and Language, 124*(1), 1–8.

Bolles, R. C. (1975). *Theory of motivation.* New York, NY: Harper & Row.

Boselie, F., & Leeuwenberg, E. (1985). Birkhoff revisited: Beauty as a function of effect and means. *The American Journal of Psychology, 98*(1), 1–39.

Bradley, M. M., Hamby, S., Löw, A., & Lang, P. J. (2007). Brain potentials in perception: Picture complexity and emotional arousal. *Psychophysiology, 44*(3), 364–373.

Bradley, M. M., & Lang, P. J. (1994). Measuring emotion: The Self-Assessment Manikin and the Semantic Differential. *Journal of Behavior Therapy and Experimental Psychiatry, 25*(1), 49–59.

Brattico, E., Bogert, B., & Jacobsen, T. (2013). Toward a neural chronometry for the aesthetic experience of music. *Frontiers in Psychology, 4*, 206.

Brieber, D., Nadal, M., & Leder, H. (2015). In the white cube: Museum context enhances the valuation and memory of art. *Acta Psychologica, 154,* 36–42.

Brieber, D., Nadal, M., Leder, H., & Rosenberg, R. (2014). Art in time and space: Context modulates the relation between art experience and viewing time. *PLoS ONE, 9*(6), e99019.

Brown, S. (2019). A unifying model of the arts: The Narration/Coordination Model. *Empirical Studies of the Arts, 37*(2), 172–196.

Brown, S., Gao, X., Tisdelle, L., Eickhoff, S. B., & Liotti, M. (2011). Naturalizing aesthetics: Brain areas for aesthetic appraisal across sensory modalities. *NeuroImage, 58*(1), 250–258.

Carbon, C. C., & Jakesch, M. (2013). A model for haptic aesthetic processing and its implications for design. *Proceedings of the IEEE, 101*(9), 2123–2133.

Carretié, L., Hinojosa, J. A., López-Martín, S., & Tapia, M. (2007). An electrophysiological study on the interaction between emotional content and spatial frequency of visual stimuli. *Neuropsychologia, 45*(6), 1187–1195.

Cavalcante, A., Mansouri, A., Kacha, L., Barros, A. K., Takeuchi, Y., Matsumoto, N., & Ohnishi, N. (2014). Measuring streetscape complexity based on the statistics of local contrast and spatial frequency. *PLoS ONE, 9*(2), e87097.

Cela-Conde, C. J., García-Prieto, J., Ramasco, J. J., Mirasso, C. R., Bajo, R., Munar, E., Flexas, A., … Maestú, F. (2013). Dynamics of brain networks in the aesthetic appreciation. *Proceedings of the National Academy of Sciences, 110*(Suppl. 2), 10454–10461.

Chanda, M. L., & Levitin, D. J. (2013). The neurochemistry of music. *Trends in Cognitive Sciences, 17*(4), 179–193.

Chang, A., Bosnyak, D. J., & Trainor, L. J. (2018). Beta oscillatory power modulation reflects the predictability of pitch change. *Cortex, 106,* 248–260.

Chatterjee, A. (2014). *The aesthetic brain: How we evolved to desire beauty and enjoy art.* Oxford, England: Oxford University Press.

Chatterjee, A., & Vartanian, O. (2016). Neuroscience of aesthetics. *Annals of the New York Academy of Sciences, 1369*(1), 172–194.

Chen, J. L., Penhune, V. B., & Zatorre, R. J. (2008). Moving on time: Brain network for auditory-motor synchronization is modulated by rhythm complexity and musical training. *Journal of Cognitive Neuroscience, 20*(2), 226–239.

Chikhman, V., Bondarko, V., Danilova, M., Goluzina, A., & Shelepin, Y. (2012). Complexity of images: Experimental and computational estimates compared. *Perception, 41*(6), 631–647.

Chipman, S. F. (1977). Complexity and structure in visual patterns. *Journal of Experimental Psychology: General, 106*(3), 269–301.

Chmiel, A., & Schubert, E. (2017). Back to the inverted-U for music preference: A review of the literature. *Psychology of Music, 45*(6), 886–909.

Chmiel, A. & Schubert, E. (2018). Emptying rooms: When the inverted-U model of preference fails—An investigation using music with collative extremes. *Empirical Studies of the Arts, 36*(2), 199–221.

Cilibrasi, R., Vitányi, P., & Wolf, R. D. (2004). Algorithmic clustering of music based on string compression. *Computer Music Journal, 28*(4), 49–67.

Colver, M. C., & El-Alayli, A. (2016). Getting aesthetic chills from music: The connection between openness to experience and frisson. *Psychology of Music, 44*(3), 413–427.

Commare, L., Rosenberg, R., & Leder, H. (2018). More than the sum of its parts: Perceiving complexity in painting. *Psychology of Aesthetics, Creativity, and the Arts, 12*(4), 380–391.

Conley, J. K. (1981). Physical correlates of the judged complexity of music by subjects differing in musical background. *British Journal of Psychology, 72*(4), 451–464.

Consoli, G. (2016). Predictive error reduction and the twofold nature of aesthetic pleasure. *Art & Perception*, *4*(4), 327–338.

Corchs, S. E., Ciocca, G., Bricolo, E., & Gasparini, F. (2016). Predicting complexity perception of real world images. *PLoS ONE*, *11*(6), e0157986.

Cross, I. (2005). Music and meaning, ambiguity and evolution. In D. Miell, R. MacDonald, & D. J. Hargreaves (Eds.), *Musical communication* (pp. 27–44). New York, NY: Oxford University Press.

Crozier, J. B. (1974). Verbal and exploratory responses to sound sequences varying in uncertainty level. In D. E. Berlyne (Ed.), *Studies in the new experimental aesthetics. Steps towards an objective psychology of aesthetic appreciation* (pp. 27–90). New York, NY: John Wiley & Sons.

Cui, A. X., Collett, M. J., Troje, N. F., & Cuddy, L. L. (2015). Familiarity and preference for pitch probability profiles. *Cognitive Processing*, *16*(2), 211–218.

Cupchik, G. C. (1988). The legacy of Daniel E. Berlyne. *Empirical Studies of the Arts*, *6*(2), 171–186.

Day, H. (Ed.). (1981). *Advances in intrinsic motivation and aesthetics*. New York, NY: Plenum Press.

de Clercq, T. (2017). Embracing ambiguity in the analysis of form in pop/rock music, 1982–1991. *Music Theory Online*, *23*(3), 1–20.

de Fleurian, R., Blackwell, T., Ben-Tal, O., & Müllensiefen, D. (2017). Information-theoretic measures predict the human judgment of rhythm complexity. *Cognitive Science*, *41*(3), 800–813.

de Lange, F. P., Heilbron, M., & Kok, P. (2018). How do expectations shape perception? *Trends in Cognitive Sciences*, *22*(9), 764–779.

Delplanque, J., De Loof, E., Janssens, C., & Verguts, T. (2019). The sound of beauty: How complexity determines aesthetic preference. *Acta Psychologica*, *192*, 146–152.

Donderi, D. C. (2006). Visual complexity: A review. *Psychological Bulletin*, *132*(1), 73–97.

Eerola, T. (2016). Expectancy-violation and information-theoretic models of melodic complexity. *Empirical Musicology Review*, *11*(1), 2–17.

Eerola, T., Himberg, T., Toiviainen, P., & Louhivuori, J. (2006). Perceived complexity of Western and African folk melodies by Western and African listeners. *Psychology of Music*, *34*(3), 337–371.

Eerola, T., & North, A. C. (2000). Expectancy-based model of melodic complexity. *Proceedings of the sixth international conference on music perception and cognition*. Keele, England: Department of Psychology. CD-ROM.

Egermann, H., Pearce, M. T., Wiggins, G. A., & McAdams, S. (2013). Probabilistic models of expectation violation predict psychophysiological emotional responses to live concert music. *Cognitive, Affective, & Behavioral Neuroscience*, *13*(3), 533–553.

Empson, W. (1930). *Seven types of ambiguity*. London: Random House.

Eysenck, H. J. (1941). The empirical determination of an aesthetic formula. *Psychological Review*, *48*(1), 83–92.

Eysenck, H. J. (1942). The experimental study of the "good Gestalt"—a new approach. *Psychological Review*, *49*(4), 344–364.

Eysenck, H. J. (1968). An experimental study of aesthetic preference for polygonal figures. *The Journal of General Psychology*, *79*(1), 3–17.

Fang, X., Singh, S., & Ahluwalia, R. (2007). An examination of different explanations for the mere exposure effect. *Journal of Consumer Research*, *34*(1), 97–103.

Fechner, G. T. (1876). *Vorschule der Ästhetik*. Leipzig, Germany: Breitkopf & Härtel.

Fernandez-Lozano, C., Carballal, A., Machado, P., Santos, A., & Romero, J. (2019). Visual complexity modelling based on image features fusion of multiple kernels. *PeerJ*, 7, 28.

Ferreri, L., Mas-Herrero, E., Zatorre, R. J., Ripollés, P., Gomez-Andres, A., Alicart, H., ... Rodriguez-Fornells, A. (2019). Dopamine modulates the reward experiences elicited by music. *Proceedings of the National Academy of Sciences*, 116(9), 3793–3798.

Forsythe, A., Mulhern, G., & Sawey, M. (2008). Confounds in pictorial sets: The role of complexity and familiarity in basic-level picture processing. *Behavior Research Methods*, 40(1), 116–129.

Forsythe, A., Nadal, M., Sheehy, N., Cela-Conde, C. J., & Sawey, M. (2011). Predicting beauty: Fractal dimension and visual complexity in art. *British Journal of Psychology*, 102, 49–70.

Fraisse, P. (1963). *The psychology of time*. New York, NY: Harper & Row.

Freitas, C., Manzato, E., Burini, A., Taylor, M. J., Lerch, J. P., & Anagnostou, E. (2018). Neural correlates of familiarity in music listening: A systematic review and a neuroimaging meta-analysis. *Frontiers in Neuroscience*, 12, 686.

Gamboni, D. (2002). *Potential images. Ambiguity and indeterminancy in modern art*. London: Reaction Books Ltd.

Garrido, M. I., Sahani, M., & Dolan, R. J. (2013). Outlier responses reflect sensitivity to statistical structure in the human brain. *PLoS Computational Biology*, 9(3), e1002999.

Gartus, A., & Leder, H. (2017). Predicting perceived visual complexity of abstract patterns using computational measures: The influence of mirror symmetry on complexity perception. *PLoS ONE*, 12(11), e0185276.

Gerard, A. (1764). *An essay on taste*. London: Millar.

Godfrey-Smith, P. (2002). Environmental complexity and the evolution of cognition. In R. J. Sternberg & J. C. Kaufman (Eds.): *The evolution of intelligence* (pp. 233–249). New Jersey: Lawrence Erlbaum Associates Publishers.

Graf, L. K. M., & Landwehr, J. R. (2015). A dual-process perspective on fluency-based aesthetics: The pleasure-interest model of aesthetic liking. *Personality and Social Psychology Review*, 19(4), 395–410.

Grahn, J. A., & Brett, M. (2007). Rhythm and beat perception in motor areas of the brain. *Journal of Cognitive Neuroscience*, 19(5), 893–906.

Grewe, O., Nagel, F., Kopiez, R., & Altenmüller, E. (2007). Listening to music as a re-creative process: Physiological, psychological, and psychoacoustical correlates of chills and strong emotions. *Music Perception: An Interdisciplinary Journal*, 24(3), 297–314.

Grishakova, M., & Poulaki, M. (2019). *Narrative complexity: Cognition, embodiment, evolution*. Lincoln, NB: University of Nebraska Press.

Güçlütürk, Y., Güçlü, U., van Gerven, M., & van Lier, R. (2018). Representations of naturalistic stimulus complexity in early and associative visual and auditory cortices. *Scientific Reports*, 8(1), 3439.

Güçlütürk, Y., Jacobs, R. H. A. H., & Lier, R. V. (2016). Liking versus complexity: Decomposing the inverted U-curve. *Frontiers in Human Neuroscience*, 10, 112.

Güçlütürk, Y., & Lier, R. V. (2019). Decomposing complexity preferences for music. *Frontiers in Psychology*, 10, 674.

Hansen, N. C., Dietz, M. J., & Vuust, P. (2017). Commentary: Predictions and the brain: How musical sounds become rewarding. *Frontiers in Human Neuroscience*, 11, 168.

Heilbron, M., & Chait, M. (2018). Great expectations: Is there evidence for predictive coding in auditory cortex? *Neuroscience*, 389, 54–73.

Hekkert, P., & Leder, H. (2008). Product aesthetics. In H. N. J. Schifferstein, & P. Hekkert (Eds.), *Product experience* (pp. 259–285). San Diego, CA: Elsevier.

Heyduk, R. G. (1975). Rated preference for musical compositions as it relates to complexity and exposure frequency. *Perception & Psychophysics, 17*(1), 84–90.

Home, H. (1765). *Elements of criticism*. London: Millar.

Honing, H., & Bouwer, F. L. (2019). Rhythm. In P. J. Rentfrow, & D. J. Levitin (Eds.), *Foundations in music psychology: Theory and research* (pp. 33–69). Cambridge, MA: MIT Press.

Hsu, Y.-F., Le Bars, S., Hämäläinen, J. A., & Waszak, F. (2015). Distinctive representation of mispredicted and unpredicted prediction errors in human electroencephalography. *Journal of Neuroscience, 35*(43), 14653–14660.

Hull, C. L. (1943). *Principles of behaviour*. New York, NY: Appleton-Century-Crofts.

Huron, D. B. (2006). *Sweet anticipation: Music and the psychology of expectation*. Cambridge, MA: MIT Press.

Ichikawa, S. (1985). Quantitative and structural factors in the judgment of pattern complexity. *Perception & Psychophysics, 38*(2), 101–109.

Iwanaga, M., Kobayashi, A., & Kawasaki, C. (2005). Heart rate variability with repetitive exposure to music. *Biological Psychology, 70*(1), 61–66.

Jacobs, A. M., & Kinder, A. (2018). What makes a metaphor literary? Answers from two computational studies. *Metaphor and Symbol, 33*(2), 85–100.

Jacobsen, T., & Beudt, S. (2017). Domain generality and domain specificity in aesthetic appreciation. *New Ideas in Psychology, 47*, 97–102.

Jacobsen, T., Schröger, E., Winkler, I., & Horváth, J. (2005). Familiarity affects the processing of task-irrelevant auditory deviance. *Journal of Cognitive Neuroscience, 17*(11), 1704–1713.

Jakesch, M., Goller, J., & Leder, H. (2017). Positive fEMG patterns with ambiguity in paintings. *Frontiers in Psychology, 8*, 785.

Jakesch, M., & Leder, H. (2009). Finding meaning in art: Preferred levels of ambiguity in art appreciation. *Quarterly Journal of Experimental Psychology, 62*(11), 2105–2112.

Jakesch, M., & Leder, H. (2015). The qualitative side of complexity: Testing effects of ambiguity on complexity judgments. *Psychology of Aesthetics, Creativity, and the Arts, 9*(3), 200–205.

Jakesch, M., Leder, H., & Forster, M. (2013). Image ambiguity and fluency. *PLoS ONE, 8*(9), e74084.

Janata, P., Peterson, J., Ngan, C., Keum, B., Whiteside, H., & Ran, S. (2018). Psychological and musical factors underlying engagement with unfamiliar music. *Music Perception, 36*(2), 175–200.

Johnson, S. G. B., & Steinerberger, S. (2019). Intuitions about mathematical beauty: A case study in the aesthetic experience of ideas. *Cognition, 189*, 242–259.

Johnston, R. R. (2016). The effect of repetition on preference ratings for select unfamiliar musical examples: Does preference transfer? *Psychology of Music, 44*(3), 514–526.

Juslin, P. N., & Västfjäll, D. (2008). Emotional responses to music: The need to consider underlying mechanisms. *Behavioral and Brain Sciences, 31*(5), 559–575; discussion 575–621.

Kaplan, A., & Kris, E. (1948). Esthetic ambiguity. *Philosophy and Phenomenological Research, 8*(3), 415–435.

Kesner, L. (2014). The predictive mind and the experience of visual art work. *Frontiers in Psychology, 5*, 1417.

Kirk, U., Skov, M., Hulme, O., Christensen, M. S., & Zeki, S. (2009). Modulation of aesthetic value by semantic context: An fMRI study. *NeuroImage, 44*(3), 1125–1132.

Knight, R. T. (1996). Contribution of human hippocampal region to novelty detection. *Nature*, *383*, 256–259.

Koelsch, S. (2009). Neural substrates of processing syntax and semantics in music. In R. Haas, & V. Brandes (Eds.), *Music that works: Contributions of biology, neurophysiology, psychology, sociology, medicine and musicology* (pp. 143–153). Vienna: Springer Vienna.

Koelsch, S. (2018). Investigating the neural encoding of emotion with music. *Neuron*, *98*(6), 1075–1079.

Koelsch, S., Jacobs, A. M., Menninghaus, W., Liebal, K., Klann-Delius, G., von Scheve, C., & Gebauer, G. (2015). The quartet theory of human emotions: An integrative and neurofunctional model. *Physics of Life Reviews*, *13*, 1–27.

Koelsch, S., Kasper, E., Sammler, D., Schulze, K., Gunter, T., & Friederici, A. D. (2004). Music, language and meaning: Brain signatures of semantic processing. *Nature Neuroscience*, *7*(3), 302–307.

Koelsch, S., Vuust, P., & Friston, K. (2019). Predictive processes and the peculiar case of music. *Trends in Cognitive Sciences*, *23*(1), 63–77.

Koffka, K. (1935). *Principles of Gestalt psychology*. New York: Harcourt, Brace.

Kolmogorov, A. N. (1968). Three approaches to the quantitative definition of information. *International Journal of Computer Mathematics*, *2*(1–4), 157–168.

Konecni, V. J. (2011). The influence of affect on music choice. In P. N. Juslin, & J. Sloboda (Eds.), *Handbook of music and emotion: Theory, research, applications* (pp. 697–723). Oxford, England: Oxford University Press.

Konecni, V. J. (1978). Daniel E. Berlyne: 1924–1976. *American Journal of Psychology*, *91*, 133–137.

Konecni, V. J. (1996). Daniel E. Berlyne (1924–1976): Two decades later. *Empirical Studies of the Arts*, *14*(2), 129–142.

Kontson, K., Megjhani, M., Brantley, J., Cruz-Garza, J., Nakagome, S., Robleto, D., ... Contreras-Vidal, J. (2015). "Your Brain on Art": Emergent cortical dynamics during aesthetic experiences. *Frontiers in Human Neuroscience*, *9*, 626.

Kragel, P. A. & LaBar, K. S. (2016). Decoding the nature of emotion in the Brain. *Trends in Cognitive Sciences*, *20*(6), 444–455.

Krizhevsky, A., Sutskever, I., & Hinton, G. E. (2012). Imagenet classification with deep convolutional neural networks. In P. Bartlett, F. C. N. Pereira, C. J. C. Burges, L. Bottou, & K. Q. Weinberger (Eds.), *Proceedings of the 25th international conference on neural information processing systems-volume 1 (NIPS'12)* (pp. 1097–1105). Red Hook, NY: Curran Associates Inc.

Krumhansl, C. L., & Kessler, E. J. (1982). Tracing the dynamic changes in perceived tonal organization in a spatial representation of musical keys. *Psychological Review*, *89*(4), 334–368.

Kumagai, Y., Arvaneh, M., & Tanaka, T. (2017). Familiarity affects entrainment of EEG in music listening. *Frontiers in Human Neuroscience*, *11*, 8.

Kuppens, P., Tuerlinckx, F., Russell, J. A., & Barrett, L. F. (2013). The relation between valence and arousal in subjective experience. *Psychological Bulletin*, *139*(4), 917–940.

Lacey, S., Hagtvedt, H., Patrick, V. M., Anderson, A., Stilla, R., Deshpande, G., ... Sathian, K. (2011). Art for reward's sake: Visual art recruits the ventral striatum. *Neuroimage*, *55*(1), 420–433.

Laeng, B., Eidet, L. M., Sulutvedt, U., & Panksepp, J. (2016). Music chills: The eye pupil as a mirror to music's soul. *Consciousness and Cognition*, *44*, 161–178.

Lane, S. H. (1968). Preference for complexity as a function of schematic orderliness and redundancy. *Psychonomic Science*, *13*(4), 209–210.

Large, E. W., & Kim, J. C. (2019). Musical expectancy. In P. J. Rentfrow, & D. J. Levitin (Eds.), *Foundations in music psychology: Theory and research* (pp. 221–263). Cambridge, MA: MIT Press.

Leder, H. (2001). Determinants of preference: When do we like what we know? *Empirical Studies of the Arts*, *19*(2), 201–211.

Leder, H., Belke, B., Oeberst, A., & Augustin, D. (2004). A model of aesthetic appreciation and aesthetic judgments. *British Journal of Psychology*, *95*(4), 489–508.

Leder, H., Carbon, C. C., & Ripsas, A. L. (2006). Entitling art: Influence of title information on understanding and appreciation of paintings. *Acta Psychologica*, *121*(2), 176–198.

Leder, H., Gerger, G., Brieber, D., & Schwarz, N. (2014). What makes an art expert? Emotion and evaluation in art appreciation. *Cognition and Emotion*, *28*(6), 1137–1147.

Leder, H., Ring, A., & Dressler, S. G. (2013). See me, feel me! Aesthetic evaluations of art portraits. *Psychology of Aesthetics Creativity and the Arts*, *7*(4), 358–369.

Lee, S.-H., & Dan, Y. (2012). Neuromodulation of brain states. *Neuron*, *76*(1), 209–222.

Lehne, M., Engel, P., Rohrmeier, M., Menninghaus, W., Jacobs, A. M., & Koelsch, S. (2015). Reading a suspenseful literary text activates brain areas related to social cognition and predictive inference. *PLoS ONE*, *10*(5), e0124550.

Levitin, D. J., Grahn, J. A., & London, J. (2018). The psychology of music: Rhythm and movement. *Annual Review of Psychology*, *69*(1), 51–75.

Li, C. W., Chen, J. H., & Tsai, C. G. (2015). Listening to music in a risk-reward context: The roles of the temporoparietal junction and the orbitofrontal/insular cortices in reward-anticipation, reward-gain, and reward-loss. *Brain Research*, *1629*, 160–170.

Longuet-Higgins, H. C., & Lee, C. S. (1984). The rhythmic interpretation of monophonic music. *Music Perception: An Interdisciplinary Journal*, *1*(4), 424–441.

Low, A., Bradley, M. M., & Lang, P. J. (2013). Perceptual processing of natural scenes at rapid rates: Effects of complexity, content, and emotional arousal. *Cognitive Affective & Behavioral Neuroscience*, *13*(4), 860–868.

Ludden, G. D., Schifferstein, H. N., & Hekkert, P. (2008). Surprise as a design strategy. *Design Issues*, *24*(2), 28–38.

Lumaca, M., Haumann, N. T., Brattico, E., Grube, M., & Vuust, P. (2019). Weighting of neural prediction error by rhythmic complexity: A predictive coding account using mismatch negativity. *European Journal of Neuroscience*, *49*(12), 1597–1609.

Lyssenko, N., Redies, C., & Hayn-Leichsenring, G. U. (2016). Evaluating abstract art: Relation between term usage, subjective ratings, image properties and personality traits. *Frontiers in Psychology*, *7*, 973.

Machado, P., Romero, J., Nadal, M., Santos, A., Correia, J., & Carballal, A. (2015). Computerized measures of visual complexity. *Acta Psychologica*, *160*, 43–57.

Machotka, P. (1980). Daniel Berlyne's contributions to empirical aesthetics. *Motivation and Emotion*, *4*(2), 113–121.

Madan, C. R., Bayer, J., Gamer, M., Lonsdorf, T. B., & Sommer, T. (2018). Visual complexity and affect: Ratings reflect more than meets the eye. *Frontiers in Psychology*, *8*, 2368.

Madison, G., & Schiolde, G. (2017). Repeated listening increases the liking for music regardless of its complexity: Implications for the appreciation and aesthetics of music. *Frontiers in Neuroscience*, *11*, 147.

Maksimainen, J. P., Eerola, T., & Saarikallio, S. H. (2019). Ambivalent emotional experiences of everyday visual and musical objects. *SAGE Open*, *9*(3).

Mallik, A., Chanda, M. L., & Levitin, D. J. (2017). Anhedonia to music and mu-opioids: Evidence from the administration of naltrexone. *Scientific Reports, 7*, 41952.

Mamassian, P. (2008). Ambiguities and conventions in the perception of visual art. *Vision Research, 48*(20), 2143–2153.

Manahova, M. E., Mostert, P., Kok, P., Schoffelen, J.-M., & de Lange, F. P. (2018). Stimulus familiarity and expectation jointly modulate neural activity in the visual ventral stream. *Journal of Cognitive Neuroscience, 30*(9), 1366–1377.

Mandelbrot, B. (1967). How long is the coast of Britain? Statistical self-similarity and fractional dimension. *Science, 156*(3775), 636–638.

Margulis, E. H. (2012). Musical repetition detection across multiple exposures. *Music Perception: An Interdisciplinary Journal, 29*(4), 377–385.

Margulis, E. H. (2013). Aesthetic responses to repetition in unfamiliar music. *Empirical Studies of the Arts, 31*(1), 45–57.

Margulis, E. H. (2014). *On repeat: How music plays the mind.* Oxford, England: Oxford University Press.

Margulis, E. H., Levine, W. H., Simchy-Gross, R., & Kroger, C. (2017). Expressive intent, ambiguity, and aesthetic experiences of music and poetry. *PLoS ONE, 12*(7), e0179145.

Marin, M. M. (2015). Crossing boundaries: Toward a general model of neuroaesthetics. *Frontiers in Human Neuroscience, 9*, 443.

Marin, M. M., & Bhattacharya, J. (2011). Music induced emotions: Some current issues and cross-modal comparisons. In J. Hermida, & M. Ferrero (Eds.), *Music education* (pp. 1–38). Hauppauge, NY: Nova Science Publishers.

Marin, M. M., Lampatz, A., Wandl, M., & Leder, H. (2016). Berlyne revisited: Evidence for the multifaceted nature of hedonic tone in the appreciation of paintings and music. *Frontiers in Human Neuroscience, 10*, 536.

Marin, M. M., & Leder, H. (2013). Examining complexity across domains: Relating subjective and objective measures of affective environmental scenes, paintings and music. *PLoS ONE, 8*(8), e72412.

Marin, M. M., & Leder, H. (2016). Effects of presentation duration on measures of complexity in affective environmental scenes and representational paintings. *Acta Psychologica, 163*, 38–58.

Marin, M. M., & Leder, H. (2018). Exploring aesthetic experiences of females: Affect-related traits predict complexity and arousal responses to music and affective pictures. *Personality and Individual Differences, 125*, 80–90.

Markey, P. S., Jakesch, M., & Leder, H. (2019). Art looks different—Semantic and syntactic processing of paintings and associated neurophysiological brain responses. *Brain and Cognition, 134*, 58–66.

Martin, R. A., & Ford, T. E. (2018). *The psychology of humor: An integrative approach.* London: Academic Press.

Martindale, C. (1984). The pleasures of thought: A theory of cognitive hedonics. *The Journal of Mind and Behavior, 5*(1), 49–80.

Martindale, C., & Moore, K. (1988). Priming, prototypicality, and preference. *Journal of Experimental Psychology: Human Perception and Performance, 14*(4), 661–670.

Martindale, C., Moore, K., & Anderson, K. (2005). The effect of extraneous stimulation on aesthetic preference. *Empirical Studies of the Arts, 23*(2), 83–91.

Martínez-Molina, N., Mas-Herrero, E., Rodríguez-Fornells, A., Zatorre, R. J., & Marco-Pallarés, J. (2016). Neural correlates of specific musical anhedonia. *Proceedings of the National Academy of Sciences, 113*(46), E7337–E7345.

Martins, M. D., Gingras, B., Puig-Waldmueller, E., & Fitch, W. T. (2017). Cognitive representation of "musical fractals": Processing hierarchy and recursion in the auditory domain. *Cognition, 161*, 31–45.

Mas-Herrero, E., Dagher, A., & Zatorre, R. J. (2018a). Modulating musical reward sensitivity up and down with transcranial magnetic stimulation. *Nature Human Behaviour, 2*(1), 27–32.

Mas-Herrero, E., Karhulahti, M., Marco-Pallares, J., Zatorre, R. J., & Rodriguez-Fornells, A. (2018b). The impact of visual art and emotional sounds in specific musical anhedonia. In J. F. Christensen, & A. Gomila (Eds.), *Arts and the brain: Psychology and physiology beyond pleasure* (pp. 399–413). Amsterdam: Elsevier Science.

Mas-Herrero, E., Zatorre, R. J., Rodriguez-Fornells, A., & Marco-Pallarés, J. (2014). Dissociation between musical and monetary reward responses in specific musical anhedonia. *Current Biology, 24*(6), 699–704.

Massaro, D., Savazzi, F., Di Dio, C., Freedberg, D., Gallese, V., Gilli, G., & Marchetti, A. (2012). When art moves the eyes: A behavioral and eye-tracking study. *PLoS ONE, 7*(5), e37285.

Mauch, M., & Levy, M. (2011). Structural change on multiple time scales as a correlate of musical complexity. In *Proceedings of the 12th international conference on music information retrieval (ISMIR 2011)*. http://matthiasmauch.net/_pdf/mauch_scm_2011.pdf

McMullen, P. T. (1974). Influence of number of different pitches and melodic redundancy on preference responses. *Journal of Research in Music Education, 22*(3), 198–204.

Meltzer, B., Reichenbach, C. S., Braiman, C., Schiff, N. D., Hudspeth, A. J., & Reichenbach, T. (2015). The steady-state response of the cerebral cortex to the beat of music reflects both the comprehension of music and attention. *Frontiers in Human Neuroscience, 9*, 436.

Menninghaus, W., Wagner, V., Hanich, J., Wassiliwizky, E., Kuehnast, M., & Jacobsen, T. (2015). Towards a psychological construct of being moved. *PLoS ONE, 10*(6), e0128451.

Menon, V., & Levitin, D. J. (2005). The rewards of music listening: Response and physiological connectivity of the mesolimbic system. *NeuroImage, 28*(1), 175–184.

Meyer, L. B. (1956). *Emotion and meaning in music*. Chicago, IL: University of Chicago Press.

Millis, K. (2001). Making meaning brings pleasure: The influence of titles on aesthetic experiences. *Emotion, 1*(3), 320–329.

Minati, L., Salvatoni, L., Rosazza, C., Pietrocini, E., Visani, E., Panzica, F., ... Franceschetti, S. (2010). Event-related potential (ERP) markers of melodic processing: The N2 component is modulated by structural complexity, not by melodic "meaningfulness." *Brain Research Bulletin, 83*(1–2), 23–28.

Miranda, R. A., & Ullman, M. T. (2007). Double dissociation between rules and memory in music: An event-related potential study. *NeuroImage, 38*(2), 331–345.

Montague, P. R., & Berns, G. S. (2002). Neural economics and the biological substrates of valuation. *Neuron, 36*(2), 265–284.

Montoya, R. M., Horton, R. S., Vevea, J. L., Citkowicz, M., & Lauber, E. A. (2017). A reexamination of the mere exposure effect: The influence of repeated exposure on recognition, familiarity, and liking. *Psychological Bulletin, 143*(5), 459–498.

Mori, K., & Iwanaga, M. (2017). Two types of peak emotional responses to music: The psychophysiology of chills and tears. *Scientific Reports, 7*, 46063.

Morreall, J. (2016). Philosophy of humor. In E. N. Zalta (ed.), *The Stanford encyclopedia of philosophy* (Winter 2016 edition). Stanford, CA: Stanford University. https://plato.stanford.edu/archives/win2016/entries/humor/.

Moruzzi, G., & Magoun, H. W. (1949). Brain stem reticular formation and activation of the EEG. *Electroencephalography and Clinical Neurophysiology, 1*(1–4), 455–473.

Moshagen, M., & Thielsch, M. T. (2010). Facets of visual aesthetics. *International Journal of Human-Computer Studies, 68*(10), 689–709.

Muth, C., & Carbon, C.-C. (2013). The Aesthetic Aha: On the pleasure of having insights into Gestalt. *Acta Psychologica, 144*(1), 25–30.

Muth, C., & Carbon, C.-C. (2016). SeIns: Semantic Instability in Art. *Art & Perception, 4*(1–2), 145–184.

Muth, C., Ebert, S., Markovic, S., & Carbon, C.-C. (2019). "Aha"ptics: Enjoying an Aesthetic Aha during haptic exploration. *Perception, 48*(1), 3–25.

Muth, C., Hesslinger, V. M., & Carbon, C.-C. (2015). The appeal of challenge in the perception of art: How ambiguity, solvability of ambiguity, and the opportunity for insight affect appreciation. *Psychology of Aesthetics, Creativity, and the Arts, 9*(3), 206–216.

Muth, C., Hesslinger, V. M., & Carbon, C.-C. (2018). Variants of semantic instability (SeIns) in the arts: A classification study based on experiential reports. *Psychology of Aesthetics, Creativity, and the Arts, 12*(1), 11–23.

Muth, C., Raab, M. H., & Carbon, C.-C. (2016). Semantic stability is more pleasurable in unstable episodic contexts. On the relevance of perceptual challenge in art appreciation. *Frontiers in Human Neuroscience, 10*, 43.

Muth, C., Raab, M. H., & Carbon, C.-C. (2017). Expecting the unexpected: How gallery visitors experience semantic instability in art. *Art & Perception, 5*(2), 121–142.

Nadal, M., Munar, E., Marty, G., & Cela-Conde, C. J. (2010). Visual complexity and beauty appreciation: Explaining the divergence of results. *Empirical Studies of the Arts, 28*(2), 173–191.

Narmour, E. (1992). *The analysis and cognition of melodic complexity: The implication-realization model.* Chicago, IL: University of Chicago Press.

Nguyen, T., Gibbings, A., & Grahn, J. (2018). Rhythm and beat perception. In R. Bader (Ed.), *Springer handbook of systematic musicology* (pp. 507–521). Berlin, Heidelberg, Germany: Springer.

Nicki, R., & Moss, V. (1975). Preference for non-representational art as a function of various measures of complexity. *Canadian Journal of Psychology/Revue canadienne de psychologie, 29*(3), 237–249.

North, A. C., & Hargreaves, D. J. (1995). Subjective complexity, familiarity, and liking for popular music. *Psychomusicology: A Journal of Research in Music Cognition, 14*(1–2), 77–93.

North, A. C., & Hargreaves, D. J. (2000). Collative variables versus prototypicality. *Empirical Studies of the Arts, 18*(1), 13–17.

Ochsner, K. N., & Phelps, E. (2007). Emerging perspectives on emotion-cognition interactions. *Trends in Cognitive Sciences, 11*(8), 317–318.

Okon-Singer, H., Hendler, T., Pessoa, L., & Shackman, A. J. (2015). The neurobiology of emotion–cognition interactions: Fundamental questions and strategies for future research. *Frontiers in Human Neuroscience, 9*(58).

Olds, J., & Olds, M. (1965). Drives, rewards, and the brain. *New Directions in Psychology, 2*, 327–410.

Olofsson, J. K., Nordin, S., Sequeira, H., & Polich, J. (2008). Affective picture processing: An integrative review of ERP findings. *Biological Psychology, 77*(3), 247–265.

Osgood, C. E., Suci, G. J., & Tannenbaum, P. H. (1957). *The measurement of meaning.* Chicago, IL: University of Illinois Press.

Palczak, J., Blumenthal, D., Rogeaux, M., & Delarue, J. (2019). Sensory complexity and its influence on hedonic responses: A systematic review of applications in food and beverages. *Food Quality and Preference, 71*, 66–75.

Palmer, S. E., Schloss, K. B., & Sammartino, J. (2013). Visual aesthetics and human preference. *Annual Review of Psychology, 64*, 77–107.

Park, J., Shimojo, E., & Shimojo, S. (2010). Roles of familiarity and novelty in visual preference judgments are segregated across object categories. *Proceedings of the National Academy of Sciences, 107*(33), 14552–14555.

Parncutt, R., & Marin, M. M. (2006). Emotions and associations evoked by unfamiliar music. In H. Gottesdiener, & J. C. Vilatte (Eds.), *Culture and communication: Proceedings of the XIXth conference of the international association of empirical aesthetics* (pp. 725–729). Avignon, France: IAEA.

Pavlov, I. P. (1927). *Conditional reflexes: An investigation of the physiological activity of the cerebral cortex.* Oxford, England: Oxford University Press.

Pearce, M. T. (2005). *The construction and evaluation of statistical models of melodic structure in music perception and composition.* Unpublished doctoral thesis, City University London.

Pearce, M. T., & Rohrmeier, M. A. (2018). Musical syntax II: Empirical perspectives. In R. Bader (Ed.), *Springer handbook of systematic musicology* (pp. 487–505). Berlin: Springer-Verlag.

Pearce, M. T., Zaidel, D. W., Vartanian, O., Skov, M., Leder, H., Chatterjee, A., & Nadal, M. (2016). Neuroaesthetics: The cognitive neuroscience of aesthetic experience. *Perspectives on Psychological Science, 11*(2), 265–279.

Pelowski, M., Forster, M., Tinio, P. P., Scholl, M., & Leder, H. (2017a). Beyond the lab: An examination of key factors influencing interaction with "real" and museum-based art. *Psychology of Aesthetics, Creativity, and the Arts, 11*(3), 245–264.

Pelowski, M., Markey, P. S., Forster, M., Gerger, G., & Leder, H. (2017b). Move me, astonish me … delight my eyes and brain: The Vienna Integrated Model of top-down and bottom-up processes in Art Perception (VIMAP) and corresponding affective, evaluative, and neurophysiological correlates. *Physics of Life Reviews, 21*, 80–125.

Pelowski, M., Markey, P. S., Lauring, J. O., & Leder, H. (2016). Visualizing the impact of art: An update and comparison of current psychological models of art experience. *Frontiers in Human Neuroscience, 10*, 160.

Pereira, C. S., Teixeira, J., Figueiredo, P., Xavier, J., Castro, S. L., & Brattico, E. (2011). Music and emotions in the brain: Familiarity matters. *PLoS ONE, 6*(11), 9.

Picard, R. W., Fedor, S., & Ayzenberg, Y. (2016). Multiple arousal theory and daily-life electrodermal activity asymmetry. *Emotion Review, 8*(1), 62–75.

Post, R., Nguyen, T., & Hekkert, P. (2017). Unity in variety in website aesthetics: A systematic inquiry. *International Journal of Human-Computer Studies, 103*, 48–62.

Povel, D.-J., & Essens, P. (1985). Perception of temporal patterns. *Music Perception: An Interdisciplinary Journal, 2*(4), 411–440.

Pressing, J. (1999). Complexity and the structure of musical patterns. *Noetica, 3*(8), 1–8.

Quiroga-Martinez, D. R., Hansen, N. C., Højlund, A., Pearce, M. T., Brattico, E., & Vuust, P. (2019). Reduced prediction error responses in high-as compared to low-uncertainty musical contexts. *Cortex, 120*, 181–200.

Rangel-Gomez, M., & Meeter, M. (2016). Neurotransmitters and novelty: A systematic review. *Journal of Psychopharmacology, 30*(1), 3–12.

Rao, R. P., & Ballard, D. H. (1999). Predictive coding in the visual cortex: A functional interpretation of some extra-classical receptive-field effects. *Nature Neuroscience, 2*(1), 79–87.

Reber, R., Schwarz, N., & Winkielman, P. (2004). Processing fluency and aesthetic pleasure: Is beauty in the perceiver's processing experience? *Personality and Social Psychology Review, 8*(4), 364–382.

Redies, C., Amirshahi, S. A., Koch, M., & Denzler, J. (2012). PHOG-derived aesthetic measures applied to color photographs of artworks, natural scenes and objects. In A. Fusiella, V. Murino, & R. Cucchiara (Eds.), *Lecture notes in computer science, Vol. 7583* (pp. 522–531), Berlin, Heidelberg, Germany: Springer.

Reybrouck, M., Vuust, P., & Brattico, E. (2018). Brain connectivity networks and the aesthetic experience of music. *Brain Sciences, 8*(6), E107.

Robbins, T. W., Granon, S., Muir J, L., Durantou, F., Harrison, A., & Everitt B, J. (2006). Neural systems underlying arousal and attention: Implications for drug abuse. *Annals of the New York Academy of Sciences, 846*(1), 222–237.

Rodd, J., Gaskell, G., & Marslen-Wilson, W. (2002). Making sense of semantic ambiguity: Semantic competition in lexical access. *Journal of Memory and Language, 46*(2), 245–266.

Rohrmeier, M. A., & Koelsch, S. (2012). Predictive information processing in music cognition. A critical review. *International Journal of Psychophysiology, 83*(2), 164–175.

Rohrmeier, M., & Rebuschat, P. (2012). Implicit learning and acquisition of music. *Topics in Cognitive Science, 4*(4), 525–553.

Saffran, J. R., Aslin, R. N., & Newport, E. L. (1996). Statistical learning by 8-month-old infants. *Science, 274*(5294), 1926–1928.

Saklofske, D. H. (1975). Visual aesthetic complexity, attractiveness and diversive exploration. *Perceptual and Motor Skills, 41*(3), 813–814.

Salimpoor, V. N., Benovoy, M., Larcher, K., Dagher, A., & Zatorre, R. J. (2011). Anatomically distinct dopamine release during anticipation and experience of peak emotion to music. *Nature Neuroscience, 14*, 257–262.

Salimpoor, V. N., Benovoy, M., Longo, G., Cooperstock, J. R., & Zatorre, R. J. (2009). The rewarding aspects of music listening are related to degree of emotional arousal. *PLoS ONE, 4*(10), e7487.

Salimpoor, V. N., van den Bosch, I., Kovacevic, N., McIntosh, A. R., Dagher, A., & Zatorre, R. J. (2013). Interactions between the nucleus accumbens and auditory cortices predict music reward value. *Science, 340*(6129), 216–219.

Salimpoor, V. N., Zald, D. H., Zatorre, R. J., Dagher, A., & McIntosh, A. R. (2015). Predictions and the brain: How musical sounds become rewarding. *Trends in Cognitive Sciences, 19*(2), 86–91.

Schäfer, T., & Sedlmeier, P. (2010). What makes us like music? Determinants of music preference. *Psychology of Aesthetics, Creativity, and the Arts, 4*(4), 223–234.

Schäfer, T., & Sedlmeier, P. (2011). Does the body move the soul? The impact of arousal on music preference. *Music Perception: An Interdisciplinary Journal, 29*(1), 37–50.

Scheirer, E. D., Watson, R. B., & Vercoe, B. L. (2000). On the perceived complexity of short musical segments. In C. Woods (Ed.), *Proceedings of the 2000 international conference on music perception and cognition.* Keele, England: University of Keele.

Schellenberg, E. G., Peretz, I., & Vieillard, S. (2008). Liking for happy- and sad-sounding music: Effects of exposure. *Cognition and Emotion, 22*(2), 218–237.

Schlochtermeier, L. H., Kuchinke, L., Pehrs, C., Urton, K., Kappelhoff, H., & Jacobs, A. M. (2013). Emotional picture and word processing: An fMRI study on effects of stimulus complexity. *PLoS ONE, 8*(2), e55619.

Schmuckler, M. A. (1989). Expectation in music: Investigation of melodic and harmonic processes. *Music Perception: An Interdisciplinary Journal, 7*(2), 109–149.

Schubert, E. (2010). Affective, evaluative, and collative responses to hated and loved music. *Psychology of Aesthetics, Creativity, and the Arts, 4*(1), 36–46.

Schubert, E., Hargreaves, D., & North, A. (2014). A dynamically minimalist cognitive explanation of musical preference: Is familiarity everything? *Frontiers in Psychology*, 5, 38.

Schupp, H. T., Junghofer, M., Weike, A. I., & Hamm, A. O. (2003). Emotional facilitation of sensory processing in the visual cortex. *Psychological Science*, 14(1), 7–13.

Seckler, M., Opwis, K., & Tuch, A. N. (2015). Linking objective design factors with subjective aesthetics: An experimental study on how structure and color of websites affect the facets of users' visual aesthetic perception. *Computers in Human Behavior*, 49, 375–389.

Seifert, C. & Chattaraman, V. (2017). Too new or too complex? Why consumers' aesthetic sensitivity matters in apparel design evaluation. *Journal of Fashion Marketing and Management*, 21(2), 262–276.

Sescousse, G., Caldu, X., Segura, B., & Dreher, J. C. (2013). Processing of primary and secondary rewards: a quantitative meta-analysis and review of human functional neuroimaging studies. *Neuroscience & Biobehavioral Reviews*, 37(4), 681–696.

Shannon, C. E. (1948). A mathematical theory of communication, *Bell System Technical Journal*, 27, 379–423, 623–656.

Shany, O., Hendler, T., Singer, N., Tarrasch, R., Gold, B. P., Jacoby, N., & Granot, R. (2019). Surprise-related activation in the nucleus accumbens interacts with music-induced pleasantness. *Social, Cognitive and Affective Neuroscience*, 14(4), 459–470.

Shmulevich, I., & Povel, D.-J. (2000). Measures of temporal pattern complexity. *Journal of New Music Research*, 29(1), 61–69.

Silvia, P. J. (2005a). Cognitive appraisals and interest in visual art: Exploring an appraisal theory of aesthetic emotions. *Empirical Studies of the Arts*, 23(2), 119–133.

Silvia, P. J. (2005b). Emotional responses to art: From collation and arousal to cognition and emotion. *Review of General Psychology*, 9(4), 342–357.

Silvia, P. J. (2008). Interest—The curious emotion. *Current Directions in Psychological Science*, 17(1), 57–60.

Silvia, P. J. (2010). Confusion and interest: The role of knowledge emotions in aesthetic experience. *Psychology of Aesthetics, Creativity, and the Arts*, 4(2), 75–80.

Silvia, P. J. (2012). Human emotions and aesthetic experience. In A. P. Shimamura, & S. E. Palmer (Eds.), *Aesthetic science: Connecting minds, brain and experience* (pp. 250–275). New York, NY: Oxford University Press.

Simonyan, K., & Zisserman, A. (2014). Very deep convolutional networks for large-scale image recognition. *arXiv preprint arXiv:1409.1556*.

Skorin-Kapov, J. (2015). *The aesthetics of desire and surprise: Phenomenology and speculation*. London: Lexington Books.

Skorin-Kapov, J. (2016). *The intertwining of aesthetics and ethics: Exceeding of expectations, ecstasy, sublimity*. London: Lexington Books.

Slater, A. (2007). "Escaping to the gallery": Understanding the motivations of visitors to galleries. *International Journal of Nonprofit and Voluntary Sector Marketing*, 12(2), 149–162.

Sloboda, J. A. (1991). Music structure and emotional response: Some empirical findings. *Psychology of Music*, 19(2), 110–120.

Sluckin, W., Hargreaves, D., & Colman, A. (1983). Novelty and human aesthetic preferences. In J. Archer, & L. I. A. Birke (Eds.), *Exploration in animals and humans* (pp. 245–269). Wokingham, England: Van Nostrand Reinhold.

Sohn, S., Seegebarth, B., & Moritz, M. (2017). The impact of perceived visual complexity of mobile online shops on user's satisfaction. *Psychology & Marketing*, 34(2), 195–214.

Soley, G., & Spelke, E. S. (2016). Shared cultural knowledge: Effects of music on young children's social preferences. *Cognition, 148*, 106–116.

Spee, B., Ishizu, T., Leder, H., Mikuni, J., Kawabata, H., & Pelowski, M. (2018). Neuropsychopharmacological aesthetics: A theoretical consideration of pharmacological approaches to causative brain study in aesthetics and art. In J. F. Christensen, & A. Gomila (Eds.), *Progress in brain research* (pp. 343–372). Amsterdam: Elsevier.

Spehar, B., Clifford, C. W., Newell, B. R., & Taylor, R. P. (2003). Universal aesthetic of fractals. *Computers & Graphics, 27*(5), 813–820.

Spehar, B., & Taylor, R. P. (2013). Fractals in art and nature: Why do we like them? In B. E, Rogowitz, T. N. Pappas, & H. DeRidder (Eds.), *Human vision and electronic imaging XVIII*. Proceedings of SPIE, Volume 8651. Burlingame, CA: SPIE.

Spehar, B., Walker, N., & Taylor, R. P. (2016). Taxonomy of individual variations in aesthetic responses to fractal patterns. *Frontiers in Human Neuroscience, 10*, 350.

Steinbeis, N., Koelsch, S., & Sloboda, J. A. (2006). The role of harmonic expectancy violations in musical emotions: Evidence from subjective, physiological, and neural responses. *Journal of Cognitive Neuroscience, 18*(8), 1380–1393.

Stich, C., Eisermann, J., Knäuper, B., & Leder, H. (2007). Aesthetic properties of everyday objects. *Perceptual and Motor Skills, 104*(3 suppl.), 1139–1168.

Street, N., Forsythe, A. M., Reilly, R., Taylor, R., & Helmy, M. S. (2016). A complex story: Universal preference vs. individual differences shaping aesthetic response to fractals patterns. *Frontiers in Human Neuroscience, 10*, 213.

Streich, S. (2007). *Music complexity: A multi-faceted description of audio content*. Unpublished doctoral dissertation, University of Pompeu Fabra.

Sumpf, M., Jentschke, S., & Koelsch, S. (2015). Effects of aesthetic chills on a cardiac signature of emotionality. *PLoS ONE, 10*(6), 16.

Sun, L., Yamasaki, T., & Aizawa, K. (2018). Photo aesthetic quality estimation using visual complexity features. *Multimedia Tools and Applications, 77*(5), 5189–5213.

Szpunar, K. K., Schellenberg, E. G., & Pliner, P. (2004). Liking and memory for musical stimuli as a function of exposure. *Journal of Experimental Psychology: Learning, Memory, and Cognition, 30*(2), 370–381.

Taruffi, L., Pehrs, C., Skouras, S., & Koelsch, S. (2017). Effects of sad and happy music on mind-wandering and the default mode network. *Scientific Reports, 7*(1), 14396.

Taylor, R. P., Spehar, B., Clifford, C. W. G., & Newell, B. R. (2008). The visual complexity of Pollock's dripped fractals. In A. A. Minai, & Y. Bar-Yam (Eds.), *Unifying themes in complex systems IV* (pp. 175–182). Berlin, Heidelberg, Germany: Springer.

Taylor, R. P., Spehar, B., Wise, J. A., Clifford, C., Newell, B. R., Hagerhall, C. M., ... Martin, T. P. (2005). Perceptual and physiological responses to the visual complexity of fractal patterns. *Nonlinear Dynamics,Psychology, and Life Sciences, 9*, 89–114.

Theiler, J. (1990). Estimating fractal dimension. *The Journal of the Optical Society of America A, 7*(6), 1055–1073.

Tiihonen, M., Brattico, E., Maksimainen, J., Wikgren, J., & Saarikallio, S. (2017). Constituents of music and visual-art related pleasure—A critical integrative literature review. *Frontiers in Psychology, 8*, 12.

Tinio, P. P. L., & Leder, H. (2009). Just how stable are stable aesthetic features? Symmetry, complexity, and the jaws of massive familiarization. *Acta Psychologica, 130*(3), 241–250.

Tooby, J., & Cosmides, L. (1990). The past explains the present: Emotional adaptations and the structure of ancestral environments. *Ethology and Sociobiology, 11*(4–5), 375–424.

Toussaint, G. T., & Beltran, J. F. (2013). Subsymmetries predict auditory and visual pattern complexity. *Perception, 42*(10), 1095–1100.

Tschacher, W., Greenwood, S., Kirchberg, V., Wintzerith, S., van den Berg, K., & Tröndle, M. (2012). Physiological correlates of aesthetic perception of artworks in a museum. *Psychology of Aesthetics, Creativity, and the Arts, 6*(1), 96–103.

Tseng, W. S.-W. (2018). Can visual ambiguity facilitate design ideation? *International Journal of Technology and Design Education, 28*(2), 523–551.

Tuch, A. N., Bargas-Avila, J. A., Opwis, K., & Wilhelm, F. H. (2009). Visual complexity of websites: Effects on users' experience, physiology, performance, and memory. *International Journal of Human-Computer Studies, 67*(9), 703–715.

Tuch, A. N., Presslaber, E. E., Stöcklin, M., Opwis, K., & Bargas-Avila, J. A. (2012). The role of visual complexity and prototypicality regarding first impression of websites: Working towards understanding aesthetic judgments. *International Journal of Human-Computer Studies, 70*(11), 794–811.

Valenti, O., Mikus, N., & Klausberger, T. (2018). The cognitive nuances of surprising events: Exposure to unexpected stimuli elicits firing variations in neurons of the dorsal CA1 hippocampus. *Brain Structure & Function, 223*(7), 3183–3211.

Van de Cruys, S., & Wagemans, J. (2011). Putting reward in art: A tentative prediction error account of visual art. *i-Perception, 2*(9), 1035–1062.

Van Den Bosch, I., Salimpoor, V., & Zatorre, R. J. (2013). Familiarity mediates the relationship between emotional arousal and pleasure during music listening. *Frontiers in Human Neuroscience, 7*, 534.

Van Geert, E., & Wagemans, J. (2020). Order, complexity, and aesthetic appreciation. *Psychology of Aesthetics, Creativity, and the Arts, 14*, 135–154.

Vartanian, O. (2014). Empirical aesthetics: Hindsight and foresight. In P. P. L. Tinio, & J. K. Smith (Eds.), *The Cambridge handbook of the psychology of aesthetics and the arts* (pp 6–34). Cambridge: Cambridge University Press.

Vartanian, O., & Skov, M. (2014). Neural correlates of viewing paintings: Evidence from a quantitative meta-analysis of functional magnetic resonance imaging data. *Brain and Cognition, 87*, 52–56.

Venkatraman, A., Edlow, B. L., & Immordino-Yang, M. H. (2017). The brainstem in emotion: A review. *Frontiers in Neuroanatomy, 11*, 12.

Vessel, E. A., Maurer, N., Denker, A. H., & Starr, G. G. (2018). Stronger shared taste for natural aesthetic domains than for artifacts of human culture. *Cognition, 179*, 121–131.

Vessel, E. A., Starr, G. G., & Rubin, N. (2012). The brain on art: Intense aesthetic experience activates the default mode network. *Frontiers in Human Neuroscience, 6*, 1–17.

Viengkham, C., & Spehar, B. (2018). Preference for fractal-scaling properties across synthetic noise images and artworks. *Frontiers in Psychology, 9*, 1439.

Vinke, L. N. (2010). *Factors affecting the perceived rhythmic complexity of auditory rhythms* Unpublished Master's thesis, Bowling Green State University.

Vitz, P. C. (1966). Affect as a function of stimulus variation. *Journal of Experimental Psychology, 71*(1), 74–79.

Vladimirskiy, B., Urbanczik, R., & Senn, W. (2015). Hierarchical novelty-familiarity representation in the visual system by modular predictive coding. *PLoS ONE, 10*(12), e0144636.

von Helmholtz, H. (1867). *Handbuch der physiologischen Optik.* Leipzig, Germany: Leopold Voss.

Vuust, P., Dietz, M. J., Witek, M., & Kringelbach, M. L. (2018). Now you hear it: A predictive coding model for understanding rhythmic incongruity. *Annals of the New York Academy of Sciences, 1423*(1), 19–29.

Vuust, P., & Witek, M. A. G. (2014). Rhythmic complexity and predictive coding: A novel approach to modeling rhythm and meter perception in music. *Frontiers in Psychology, 5*, 1111.

Walker, E. L. (1980). Berlyne's theoretical contributions to psychology. *Motivation and Emotion, 4*(2), 105–111.

Wang, M., & Li, X. (2017). Effects of the aesthetic design of icons on app downloads: Evidence from an android market. *Electronic Commerce Research, 17*(1), 83–102.

Wang, Z., Duff, B. R. L., & Clayton, R. B. (2018). Establishing a factor model for aesthetic preference for visual complexity of brand logo. *Journal of Current Issues & Research in Advertising, 39*(1), 83–100.

Wassiliwizky, E., Jacobsen, T., Heinrich, J., Schneiderbauer, M., & Menninghaus, W. (2017a). Tears falling on goosebumps: Co-occurrence of emotional lacrimation and emotional piloerection indicates a psychophysiological climax in emotional arousal. *Frontiers in Psychology, 8*, 41.

Wassiliwizky, E., Koelsch, S., Wagner, V., Jacobsen, T., & Menninghaus, W. (2017b). The emotional power of poetry: Neural circuitry, psychophysiology and compositional principles. *Social Cognitive and Affective Neuroscience, 12*(8), 1229–1240.

Wilkins, R. W., Hodges, D. A., Laurienti, P. J., Steen, M., & Burdette, J. H. (2014). Network science and the effects of music preference on functional brain connectivity: From Beethoven to Eminem. *Scientific Reports, 4*, 6130.

Wise, R. A. (2004). Dopamine, learning and motivation. *Nature Reviews Neuroscience, 5*, 483–494.

Witvliet, C. V. O., & Vrana, S. R. (2007). Play it again Sam: Repeated exposure to emotionally evocative music polarises liking and smiling responses, and influences other affective reports, facial EMG, and heart rate. *Cognition and Emotion, 21*(1), 3–25.

Wundt, W. (1896). *Grundriss der Psychologie*. Leipzig, Germany: Wilhelm Engelmann.

Yeun, J. J., Eunsoo, B., & Jung, C. H. (2018). Managing the visual environment of a fashion store: Effects of visual complexity and order on sensation-seeking consumers. *International Journal of Retail & Distribution Management, 46*(2), 210–226.

Zajonc, R. B. (1968). Attitudinal effects of mere exposure. *Journal of Personality and Social Psychology, 9*(2, Pt. 2), 1–27.

Zatorre, R. J. (2015). Musical pleasure and reward: Mechanisms and dysfunction. *Annals of the New Academy of Sciences, 1337*, 202–211.

Zatorre, R. J., Chen, J. L., & Penhune, V. B. (2007). When the brain plays music: Auditory-motor interactions in music perception and production. *Nature Reviews Neuroscience, 8*(7), 547–558.

Zeki, S. (2002). Neural concept formation & art. Dante, Michelangelo, Wagner something, and indeed the ultimate thing, must be left over for the mind to do. *Journal of Consciousness Studies, 9*(3), 53–76.

CHAPTER 19

PROCESSING FLUENCY

MICHAEL FORSTER

INTRODUCTION

IN empirical aesthetics, undoubtedly one of the major questions is which factors influence our aesthetic pleasure. Accordingly, in the present handbook entire chapters are devoted to single influencing factors such as symmetry, complexity, or balance. Striving for the most parsimonious explanation for why these factors might influence our aesthetic pleasure, Reber, Schwarz, and Winkielmann (2004) proposed the processing fluency account of aesthetic pleasure. In short, it is argued that "[t]he more fluently perceivers can process an object, the more positive their aesthetic response" (p. 364). Since 2004, the account has garnered widespread attention in the field of empirical aesthetics. Next to Berlyne's classical account of the relationship between arousal potential and hedonic response, processing fluency is often referred to as the main theory explaining aesthetic pleasure (for an overview, see Silvia, 2012). Since the first explicit attempt to explain aesthetic pleasure via processing fluency by Reber et al. (2004), multiple theoretical approaches have been proposed that incorporate the concept of processing fluency (Albrecht & Carbon, 2014; Forster, Fabi, & Leder, 2015; Graf & Landwehr, 2015). In this chapter, we will therefore take a closer look at the theory of processing fluency: where it comes from, how processing fluency works, and what the empirical evidence is. We will discuss in particular the evidence for processing fluency in empirical aesthetics. This should help to answer the main question of whether processing fluency lives up to the challenge of explaining aesthetic pleasure. Finally, we will relate the theory to other theoretical approaches explaining aesthetic pleasure and give an outlook on current challenges.

WHAT IS PROCESSING FLUENCY?

The concept of processing fluency as a distinct term originates from research on familiarity in memory (Jacoby, Kelley, & Dywan, 1989). Jacoby and colleagues argued that familiarity is a result of relative processing ease.[1] If a stimulus is easier to process than expected, a feeling of familiarity is experienced. This is because we infer from high processing fluency that the stimulus has been encountered before and is thus easy to process. Thus, the fluency of a stimulus is a metacognitive cue. Consecutive research has then shown that this metacognitive cue is not only attributed to familiarity, but can influence a variety of judgments (for an overview, see Alter & Oppenheimer, 2009).

Starting with the research on familiarity, we will see that throughout the chapter empirical findings on processing fluency are predominantly from the visual domain. Thus, processing fluency is mainly the ease of visual processing. Given that the visual sense is predominant in aesthetic processing, this focus on the visual domain should not limit the conclusions drawn from the empirical evidence. In other domains empirical evidence is rather sparse, but there are still some findings indicating that effects of processing fluency are also present in other domains, such as haptics (Hayes, Paul, Beuger, & Tipper, 2008; Jakesch & Carbon, 2012).

In the scope of this book, the most important finding is that processing fluency has been shown to influence judgments of liking (Reber, Winkielman, & Schwarz, 1998). This led Reber et al. (2004) to propose the processing fluency account of aesthetic pleasure. How does fluency now influence liking? Reber et al. (2004) argue as follows: (a) in general stimuli differ in their processing fluency; some things are easier and some harder to process (see Forster, Gerger, & Leder, 2015). (b) The fluency is per se hedonically marked (Topolinski, Likowski, Weyers, & Strack, 2009; Winkielman & Cacioppo, 2001) and is thus experienced as a positive feeling of fluency (see Forster, Leder, & Ansorge, 2013, 2016). In other words, one has an affectively positive reaction when processing something with ease. (c) When evaluating a stimulus, individuals draw on their subjective experiences with that stimulus (Schwarz, 2011), such as the experience of fluency. (d) The influence of fluency is moderated by expectations and attributions. Thus, fluency influences liking especially when something is unexpectedly fluent, i.e. when the relative fluency is high (see Wänke & Hansen, 2015), and when we are not aware that the fluency is the source of our positive feeling (Bornstein & D'Agostino, 1992, 1994).

After explaining how processing fluency influences liking, the question arises as to why it does so; especially, why fluency is experienced positively in the first place. Reber et al. (2004) explain this by arguing that high fluency indicates a positive state of affairs, availability of appropriate knowledge structures to interpret the stimulus, or progress toward successful recognition. Unfortunately, those explanations in the scope of processing fluency are only based on weak empirical grounds. Direct evidence for why fluency is positive is still lacking.

A potential candidate for why fluency is positive can be found in explanations of the so-called mere exposure effect (Zajonc, 1968, 2001). This effect describes the finding that liking of a stimulus increases with mere repetition (for an overview, see Bornstein, 1989). This effect can easily be explained by processing fluency. It is easy to show that mere repetition increases processing fluency: the more often something has been encountered, the easier it is to process. This experience of processing ease results in positive affect, which is then attributed to liking. Zajonc argued that repetition is positive, because it increases familiarity (Jacoby et al., 1989). Familiarity in turn indicates that past encounters with this stimulus were not harmful, thus resulting in positive affective reaction (Reber et al., 2004). This argument is however not backed by empirical findings.

Types of Fluency

Of course, stimuli, especially more complex ones such as artworks, can be easy or difficult to process on different levels. In processing fluency, this is accounted for by distinguishing between perceptual and conceptual fluency (for a more fine-grained differentiation of types of fluency, see Alter & Oppenheimer, 2009). That is, a stimulus can be on the one hand easy or difficult to perceive (perceptual fluency), and on the other hand easy or difficult to understand (conceptual fluency). Thus, processing fluency can operate on different levels of stimulus processing. Perceptual fluency is about early, rather low-level processes and is thus influenced by structural factors such as (visual) symmetry, contrast, perceptual congruence, or presentation duration. Conceptual fluency is about later, high-level processes of semantic relation, understanding, or meaning making. Thus, factors such as semantic congruence or expertise can influence conceptual fluency. There is ample evidence that different manipulations reliably influence either perceptual fluency (such as variation in presentation duration or contour priming (Forster et al., 2013; Reber et al., 1998)) or conceptual fluency (such as titles matching/ mismatching artwork content (Belke, Leder, Strobach, & Carbon, 2010), or sematic coherence of word triads (Topolinski et al., 2009)).

But how do these types of fluency relate to each other? Unfortunately, there is only very sparse evidence on this question. We can however draw on a study manipulating fluency in recognition memory. Lanska, Olds, & Westerman (2014) directly compared the effects of perceptual and conceptual fluency via priming and could show that both increased reports of recognition. In recognition memory, studies on processing fluency are based predominantly on the effect that higher fluency indicates familiarity (Jacoby et al., 1989). Thus, an effect of processing fluency on recognition means that participants incorrectly give more ratings of "yes, I have seen this stimulus before" in a recognition phase, when the stimuli were easy to process compared with when the stimuli were difficult to process. This is also termed false familiarity. Participants evaluate stimuli that have been made fluent in the recognition phase as having been presented before, because they attribute the fluency to previous exposure. It would thus be more appropriate to speak about subjective recognition instead of recognition to highlight that participants only believe that they have seen the stimulus before.

Malleability of Processing Ease

Another set of experiments by Lanska et al. (2014), however, showed another important factor in processing fluency, namely the malleability of processing fluency. They showed that, depending on the instructions either in the learning phase or the recognition phase, perceptual or conceptual fluency could be influenced to have a stronger influence on subjective recognition. If the instructions rendered the perceptual aspect of the stimuli more salient, perceptual fluency influenced subjective recognition more. If the instructions rendered the conceptual aspect of the stimuli more salient, conceptual fluency influenced subjective recognition more. Thus, the diagnosticity of different types of fluency depends on their relative salience. This is further in line with the theoretical assumption that processing fluency influences our judgments via naïve theories about what fluency indicates (Schwarz, 2011). This means our naïve theories tell us that higher processing fluency implies familiarity and consequently positivity via the above-mentioned connection between familiarity and positivity. Accordingly, experiments have shown that this naïve theory can be changed via learning phases that connect higher fluency with novelty, thus changing the naïve theory (Unkelbach, 2006, but see Olds & Westerman, 2012).

Thus, higher processing fluency might be positive, because our naïve theories tell us that higher fluency is good. In line with this, Song and Schwarz (2009) found that fictional food additives were judged more harmful when their names were harder to process. Furthermore, they could show that rollercoasters were judged as more exciting when their names were harder to process. These findings show the importance of the naïve theories when interpreting ease of processing. However, a recent failed replication casts doubt on the generality of this effect (Bahnik & Vranka, 2017).

Relative Fluency

Comparing the existing studies on processing fluency, it becomes apparent that studies have predominantly used within-participant manipulations of processing fluency. This means participants were presented with stimuli varying in how easily they could be processed. What on first glance looks like a methodological issue is however of paramount importance for the processing fluency theory. Obviously, the main difference between within- and between-participants manipulations of fluency is whether participants are able to experience (the experimentally manipulated) variations in fluency (within) or not (between). In a study Forster, Gerger, and Leder (2015) thus manipulated fluency either within or between participants and asked participants to evaluate liking and felt fluency, i.e., how easy it was to process the stimulus. It could be shown that reports of felt fluency were influenced regardless of the type of manipulation. However, liking evaluations were only influenced in a within-participants manipulation of fluency. This indicates that relative differences in experiences of fluency are necessary for the effect of fluency on liking (see also Wänke & Hansen, 2015).

Fluency and Aesthetic Responses

The main argument that processing fluency can straightforwardly explain aesthetic pleasure has been heavily criticized. In short, the main points of critique are: (a) relative rather than absolute fluency influences liking; (b) processing fluency can only explain shallow preferences, but not deep emotional reactions; (c) proponents of processing fluency extrapolate from experiments with simple stimuli to complex interactions with artworks without presenting empirical evidence; and (d) artworks are complex, rather disfluent stimuli, but perceivers still respond with pleasure. In turn, we will try to lay out each criticism and detail how it has been rebutted by proponents of the processing fluency account.

Considering aesthetic responses to, for example, art, critical readers might well argue that the statement "[t]he more fluently perceivers can process an object, the more positive their aesthetic response" (Reber et al., 2004, p. 364) cannot be that simple. A classical killer argument is that a drawing of a stick man is surely more fluent than the Mona Lisa, but hardly more aesthetically pleasing. This would be an apparent counterargument clearly falsifying the processing fluency account. However, the statement above is qualified by ancillary assumptions even in the original text, as laid out above. The counterargument comparing the Mona Lisa with the stick man furthermore reduces processing fluency to perceptual ease, which is only a part of the story. One could even argue that on a conceptual level the Mona Lisa might be more fluent. Most people have a richer knowledge about the background of the Mona Lisa than about the background of a random stick man drawing (for an elaborate discussion on conceptual fluency in the arts, see Bullot & Reber, 2012). Also in terms of relative fluency, the comparison between those two images is a bit of a stretch. When systematically studying effects of higher processing fluency on responses of aesthetic pleasure, one sensibly would rather compare the Mona Lisa with another critically acclaimed artwork. Taken together, the counterargument is more a criticism of the main statement for being too bold rather than a refutation of the whole theory of processing fluency.

The second main point of critique concerns the scope of the theory in explaining aesthetic responses. Those responses unarguably comprise a variety of reactions to aesthetic stimuli. This could range from complete indifference when encountering an artwork to instances of crying as a result of being overwhelmed by the beauty of the piece (Pelowski, 2015). A theory trying to explain both extremes at once thus has to live up to high expectations. Consequently, the processing fluency account has been criticized for not being able to explain especially intense emotions (Armstrong & Detweiler-Bedell, 2008). Thus, as Armstrong and Detweiler-Bedell argue in their article, it is necessary to distinguish between "mild pleasure associated with simple or familiar objects" and "more intense pleasure associated with complex or novel objects" (2008, p. 305). According to them, processing fluency is only able to explain mild pleasures, but not able to explain more intense reactions.

The distinction by Armstrong and Detweiler-Bedell (2008) between shallow and deep pleasure is well derived from philosophical aesthetics and definitely an interesting avenue for further research. It also touches on a larger issue in the whole field of empirical aesthetics. The terminology and definition of the main concepts are far from being clear. Although Reber et al. (2004) argue for why they equate beauty with aesthetic pleasure, there is little evidence that processing fluency alone leads to intense positive reactions in participants. Thus, processing fluency might indeed only influence shallow reactions of pleasure or displeasure. As we will see below, further developments of the processing fluency theory account for this.

A third and related criticism also concerns the scope of the theory, specifically regarding the typically used stimulus material in experiments on processing fluency. As Silvia (2012, p. 259) nicely put it: "[t]he scope of the research doesn't match on the scope of its claims. Essentially all of the studies use non-art or art-ish stimuli … " (p. 259). Indeed, most of the studies advancing the theory of processing fluency applied rather simple stimulus material, such as dot patterns (e.g., Reber et al., 1998) or simple line drawings (Forster et al., 2013). However, there are studies that tested effects of both perceptual and conceptual fluency on liking with artworks as stimuli. However, as we will see the results are less clear-cut.

Regarding conceptual fluency, in a study by Belke et al. (2010) artworks were presented with a matching title, a nonmatching title, or no title. Participants then evaluated liking of the artwork. Matching titles should make artworks conceptually more fluent than nonmatching titles or no titles. Thus, in this condition liking should be highest. The results showed that this was the case for representational and cubist, but not for abstract art (see also Russell & Milne, 1997). This pattern might be explained by the fact that there are discernable objects in representational and cubist art where titles clearly match or mismatch the depicted content. Abstract art, however, allows for multiple interpretations varying by participant. Thus, it seems plausible that in abstract art matching titles were not matching for all participants and thus did not lead to higher fluency.

Regarding perceptual fluency, in a study by Jakesch, Leder, & Forster (2013) ambiguous artworks by Rene Magritte were presented at different presentation durations. In this study, conceptual fluency was also varied by manipulating the ambiguous artworks to render them nonambiguous. Thus, higher liking for artworks presented at longer durations and/or for artworks with lower ambiguity would speak for effects of processing fluency. However, effects of presentation duration and ambiguity (high vs. low) on liking were not straightforward. In line with processing fluency, for ambiguous artworks liking increased with presentation duration. For their less ambiguous versions, this effect was only found for very short presentation durations. More importantly, at longer presentation durations (>500 ms) ambiguous, and thus harder to process, less fluent stimuli were liked more. This clearly goes against the theory of processing fluency.

This finding also brings us to the fourth and last criticism against the notion that in aesthetics fluency is liked. Given that artworks are both visually and semantically complex stimuli, they challenge our cognitive system to assess meaning. Thus, by definition, art should rather be disfluent than fluent. Take for example a visit to a museum of contemporary art. Most artworks there are made with the intention of challenging the visitors to understand them (for discussions, see Belke, Leder, & Carbon, 2015; Muth, Hesslinger, & Carbon, 2015). Even for works of classical art, such as for example *The Birth of Venus* by Sandro Botticelli, the amount of detail and the references to ancient

Greek mythology make the artwork far from easy to process. So why should we like what is fluent when we are looking at art?

Proponents of the processing fluency theory would argue that the theory already accounts for initial disfluency. According to the theory, effects of processing fluency are especially pronounced when something is unexpectedly, and thus relatively, easy to process. Thus, stimuli that get more fluent over time should be especially liked (Topolinski & Reber, 2010). Research on the effects of sudden insight, so-called "Aha" experiences, indeed has shown that insights, such as understanding or perceiving a Gestalt, lead to higher liking (Muth & Carbon, 2013). Thus, it is not only an absolute higher fluency that is positive, but also an increase in fluency over time.

This dynamic aspect of reduction in fluency is however only implicitly included in the processing fluency account as it is presented above. Without a clear theory of (a) when reduction of disfluency occurs, and (b) why a reduction in fluency is positive, it is hard to make clear predictions. It rather invites post hoc explanations that higher liking must be the result of a higher disfluency reduction.

The above-mentioned issues are however accounted for in another model, the Pleasure-Interest Model of Aesthetic Liking (PIA Model) by Graf and Landwehr (2015). Here, effects of disfluency reduction are explicitly accounted for and combined with the above-described theory of processing fluency.

THE PLEASURE-INTEREST MODEL OF AESTHETIC LIKING (PIA)

In the PIA Model (Graf & Landwehr, 2015) aesthetic evaluations can result from two distinct routes of processing a stimulus. Based on a dual-process account (Strack & Deutsch, 2004), there are two consecutive stages of processing (Graf & Landwehr, 2015): an initial automatic stage and a consecutive controlled stage. In the initial automatic stage, based on a fluency expectation, the relative fluency is automatically assessed. If fluency is higher than expected, a positive affective response occurs. If fluency is lower than expected, a negative affective response occurs. A crucial process in the model is that the next steps depend on the perceiver's motivation to further process the stimulus. This can now be initiated (a) by the stimulus, i.e., the stimulus affords deeper processing, or (b) by the perceiver, i.e., the person is both motivated and capable of further processing the stimulus. If there is no motivation to further process the stimulus, the resulting aesthetic response depends on the previous fluency experience. If fluency was high, pleasure occurs. If fluency was low, displeasure occurs. This is more or less the above-described account of processing fluency. However, if there is a motivation to further process the stimulus, a controlled processing stage is initiated. In this controlled stage, the need for disfluency reduction is assessed. Now the outcome of the aesthetic experience depends on the result of disfluency reduction.

There are three possible outcomes: If fluency was already high, no disfluency reduction is possible and needed. This, according to Graf & Landwehr (2015), leads
to boredom. This means a perceiver gets bored when she is motivated to further process the stimulus, but the stimulus was easy to process in the first place. Thus, there is
not much to further process and learn from the stimulus. If fluency was however low,
two outcomes are possible. If the perceiver is not able to reduce disfluency, confusion
results. This means, if a perceiver cannot make sense of the stimulus despite being
motivated to do so, he gets confused. If, however, the perceiver is able to reduce fluency, interest results. This means, if a perceiver can successfully reduce disfluency, she
gets interested in the stimulus. It is important to note that also here positive or negative
affect is postulated based on success or failure of disfluency reduction. However, unlike
in automatic processing this affect is not directly experienced as pleasure or displeasure.
In the controlled processing stage this affect is rather attributed to the interaction with
the stimulus (Graf & Landwehr, 2015), thus resulting in either interest (positive affect)
or confusion (negative affect). To sum it up, the outcome of the aesthetic evaluation
depends on two crucial things: (a) whether the perceiver is motivated to further process
the stimulus, and (b) whether then disfluency reduction is possible.

As an extension of the classical processing fluency account, the PIA Model allows for
richer and more diverse outcomes than just liking or disliking. Thus, it matches more
closely what perceivers actually experience when they are aesthetically processing
stimuli. It also introduces a more deliberate, controlled processing stage that accounts
for longer and deeper processing of stimuli. Thus, it accounts for the above-noted
criticism regarding the separation between shallow and deep pleasure (Armstrong &
Detweiler-Bedell, 2008). It also explicitly models that high processing fluency selectively influences shallow pleasure vs. displeasure. It finally also explicitly models dynamic changes in evaluations over time and accounts for reduction in disfluency.

These benefits of course come at a cost. The model is clearly less parsimonious. It
also postulates complex processing sequences, which remain to be tested. Initial evidence is generally in line with the main predictions (Graf & Landwehr, 2017). It however becomes apparent that given the complexity of the model simple relationships and
straightforward predictions are not to be expected.

Another potential criticism of the PIA Model is the conceptualization of interest as
the result of successful disfluency reduction (Consoli, 2017; but see Graf, 2018). Interest
has been rather conceptualized as the combination of an appraisal of something being
novel and an appraisal of coping potential (Consoli, 2017; Labroo & Pocheptsova, 2016;
Muth, Raab, & Carbon, 2015; Silvia, 2008). Thus, the crucial point is that interest typically is seen as the *expectation* of something being understandable or, in terms of processing fluency, the expectation of successful disfluency reduction. Graf and Landwehr,
however, conceive interest as the *result* of successful disfluency reduction. This is also
slightly at odds with findings on the positive affect of disfluency reduction and insight
(Muth, Raab, & Carbon, 2015). To be fair, this criticism can be easily accounted for by
slightly adapting the conceptualization of interest. The PIA Model remains an important
contribution in explaining aesthetic experience as a result of processing dynamics.

These dynamic changes of disfluency are also a crucial part of another theory, which has gained popularity and widespread interest as the potential grand theory explaining cognition: predictive coding (for a seminal introduction, see Clark, 2013). In short, predictive coding postulates that all cognition is an iterative process of the brain of drawing and testing hypotheses about the state of the environment. As we will see below, predictive coding can elegantly explain the pleasure derived from disfluency reduction.

PREDICTIVE CODING

The theory of predictive coding is tightly intertwined with the idea of bottom-up and top-down processing. Bottom-up processing is stimulus driven and based on sensory input; this means the processing in the brain is initiated by sensory perception of an external stimulus. Top-down processing is based on higher cognitive functions; this means the processing in the brain is initiated by internal goals and expectations. The classical view considers a sequence of initial bottom-up to subsequent top-down modulation of perception as the typical sequence of perception. This does not negate that top-down processing might take precedence in some cases, only that the route from bottom-up to top-down is the standard. Predictive coding now reverses this route. There is some discussion that predictive coding cannot easily be associated with top-down and bottom-up processing (Rauss & Pourtois, 2013). Nonetheless, given that most readers might be familiar with the concept of bottom-up and top-down, relating these to predictive coding should give an insight into the crucial differences.

In predictive coding all processing is purely top-down driven. As nicely put by Barrett (2017, p. 59): "And so, trapped within the skull, with only past experience as a guide, your brain makes predictions. [...] predictions at a microscopic scale as millions of neurons talk to one another. [...] These predictions are your brain's best guesses of what's going on in the world around you, and how to deal with it to keep you alive and well." Thus, the brain starting from the first firing of a neuron in the mother's womb constantly makes predictions about the state of the environment to reduce uncertainty. These predictions are then tested against sensory input from the senses and from interoception. When predictions and input perfectly align, the prediction is accepted as the state of the environment. This is however only a theoretical case. The typical view is that, given the complexity of the environment, predictions and input hardly ever align perfectly. The result is a certain amount of prediction error. The next step is now to reduce this prediction error by adapting the predictions based on the current information. This sequence of making predictions, testing them against input, and adapting them to minimize prediction error is constantly looping in our brain. Of course, prediction errors also lead to a tuning of future predictions. The next predictions are updated by the information gleaned from the current prediction (error). Thus, different from the classical bottom-up/top-down view, in predictive coding top-down takes clear precedence. Additionally, bottom-up processing is used to tune and adapt top-down predictions. In the classical view this was reversed; there top-down influence tuned and adapted bottom-up information.

If the basic human motivation is to reduce uncertainty via reduction of prediction error, the theory runs into a problem. This so-called "dark-room" problem states that given this motivation the optimal action would be to seek out a pitch-black room that gives no sensory stimulation. In this room prediction error would be minimal (see Clark, 2013). This problem is however circumvented by proposing that in our complex, sensory-rich, and challenging environment a dark room would be very unlikely and thus would actually lead to considerable prediction error. Humans have a prior expectation of a typical, complex external environment and make predictions based on this environment.

How does this theory now relate to processing fluency? One could easily conceptualize fluency as low prediction error and disfluency as high prediction error. In addition, disfluency reduction is conceptually very similar to prediction error reduction. Does that mean that predictive coding can now be explained in terms of processing fluency? Given that the theory of predictive coding is both more general and more elaborate on especially lower levels of perception, such as neuronal processing, it is rather that processing fluency can be explained in terms of predictive coding.

So far, we have presented predictive coding only as a theory of cognition. For the present chapter it is however much more interesting to ascertain whether and how affective processing can be explained in terms of predictive coding. In the end, aesthetics can be seen as the study of (disinterested) affective responses to sensory experiences (Shimamura, 2012). As we will see, the theory of predictive coding has an explanation for affective processing as well. It also should in turn become apparent that the classical distinction between cognition and emotion in predictive coding—and for that matter in aesthetics—is neither useful nor necessary, as both are two sides of the same coin of sensory experience.

To explain affective processing in terms of predictive coding the following basic assumption has to be made: the function of affect is to motivate humans to seek behavior that is beneficial for survival and to avoid behavior that is detrimental for survival (Van de Cruys & Wagemans, 2011). Thus, positive affect is a marker of something beneficial; negative affect a marker of something detrimental. Given this assumption, it is straightforward to postulate that low prediction error comes along with positive affect and high prediction error with negative affect (see Van de Cruys & Wagemans, 2011). This is because low prediction error indicates little uncertainty about the state of the environment. In other word, it indicates that the perceiver knows what the environment looks like. This information is helpful for survival. It allows the evaluation of whether there are threats that need appropriate actions to secure survival. Consequently, the reduction of prediction error is accompanied by positive affect, because uncertainty is reduced. Given the recency of the theory, empirical evidence for these assumptions is lacking as yet. In aesthetic processing, there is only indirect evidence from a meta-analysis on brain areas involved in processing stimuli aesthetically (Brown, Gao, Tisdelle, Eickhoff, & Liotti, 2011). Over all studies, an activation of the anterior insula was predominant, which is indicative of processing of negative emotions. However, a large-scale meta-analysis by Yarkoni, Poldrack, Nichols, Van Essen, and Wager (2011) could show that in most neuroimaging studies the anterior insula is active. On the one hand, this renders the area hardly specific for aesthetic processing. On the other hand, it still possible that the anterior insula is involved in affective reactions to prediction error, because, given the theory, prediction error is a crucial part of sensory processing in general.

Again, the explanation for why low prediction error is positive is very similar to the explanation for why processing fluency is positive. What however makes the theory of predictive coding more useful is the fact that it directly considers dynamic changes as the main source of affect. For example, the theory can easily explain why in the arts we can enjoy high uncertainty and thus, high prediction error, which by the definition of processing fluency should be negative. As Van de Cruys and Wagemans (2011, p. 1041) nicely put it:

> [I]n going into a museum, we expect the unexpected. [...] we can tolerate and even enjoy unpredictability because we expect to be surprised [...] This playful and safe as-if context of art, where our guards can be lowered and our actions suspended, allows for the usually negative prediction errors to be enjoyed. Hence, a positive reappraisal can immediately follow the negative gut reaction.

To expand on this with an example: consider trying to find your way with a map. If we made the map hard to read by distorting the lines and fiddling with the colors, readers would surely get frustrated and displeased. However, when the same person encounters the map as artwork in a museum, he might be interested and pleased. Predictive coding can easily explain both the perceptual process and, more importantly, the affective reaction of this interaction. When trying to find the way, one does not expect (i.e., predict) a map to be ambiguous and hard to decipher. The resulting prediction error is affectively negative. In the museum, however, one does expect the map, as an artwork, to contain some sort of ambiguity and thus one can indulge in the challenge posed by high prediction error. One might stay by the artwork to try to make sense of it; thus reduce prediction error, which is accompanied by positive affect.

The account of predictive coding does indicate that initial formulation of processing fluency—the higher the fluency the higher the liking—is too simplistic (see also, Consoli, 2016). Empirical evidence predominantly shows that it is rather the relative gain in fluency that is positive (see, for example, Muth, Hesslinger, & Carbon, 2015), rather than the absolute level of fluency. The predictive coding framework is able to explain this effect of disfluency reduction, as well as visual processing in general. Thus, it seems to be the more complete and more parsimonious account to explain why higher fluency is liked. The whole theory is however still in its infancy and needs to be experimentally tested on each level, from neuronal coding to behavioral outcomes. Furthermore, especially for aesthetics a crucial point is to solve the question of why prediction error reduction is intrinsically rewarding. Taken together predictive coding does have the potential to become one of the "grand theories" in science.

Major Challenges, Goals, and Suggestions

At this point, some readers might have the impression that the theory of processing fluency is dead, superseded by the PIA Model and ultimately predictive coding. In defense of the classical account of processing fluency, empirical evidence for the newer models is as yet rather sparse. Despite the criticism and limitations, the processing fluency account is currently much better tested empirically.

In our view, the main decision for researchers on processing fluency is whether to hold on to further specifying processing fluency or to jump on the train of reframing processing fluency in terms of predictive coding. The processing fluency account still offers many research questions to further specify the process. For example, proponents of processing fluency often fail to mention that fluency of course is only one factor influencing our aesthetic response. The relative weight of processing fluency in the aesthetic response in comparison with other factors, such as activation of memory, current mood, or social processes (see, for example, Lauring et al., 2016) has yet to be tested. Nonetheless, the processing fluency account still postulates that fluency can explain effects on aesthetic responses that previously have been ascribed to some other factors. These comprise more perceptual factors such as symmetry, balance, or contrast, but also more conceptual factors such as familiarity, meaning making, or understanding. One often has the impression that processing fluency can explain everything, but only in hindsight. This however renders the theory virtually worthless. It is thus necessary to specify concrete conditions when processing fluency is high (or increases) and when it influences our responses. This would allow clear predictions.

Additionally, it is as yet far from clear how processing fluency and especially the resulting positive affect is related to neuronal structures. Evidence for processing fluency effects can be found in a number of EEG studies (Li, Gao, Wang, & Guo, 2015; Paller, Voss, & Boehm, 2007; Vargas, Voss, & Paller, 2012; Voss, Lucas, & Paller, 2012; Voss & Paller, 2006, 2010; Voss, Reber, Mesulam, Parrish, & Paller, 2008; Wang, Li, Gao, Xiao, & Guo, 2015). Most of these studies try to dissociate brain structures active in explicit memory from those active in implicit memory. In a functional magnetic resonance imaging (fMRI) study (Dew & Cabeza, 2013) participants had to perform a word recognition task with masked priming. In the test phase, some words were preceded by conceptually related words, which were subliminally presented and masked. The results showed that "old" responses to new items led to reduced activity in the perirhinal cortex. This reduction has previously been mainly attributed to recovery of a long-term memory signal. However, as there is no long-term memory activation possible in new items, the activation in the perirhinal cortex indicates that this area might be involved in processing fluency. In a further study applying the same paradigm, Wang et al. (2015) we able to dissociate event-related potential (ERP) responses to perceptual fluency (ERPs at 150–250 ms) from ERP responses to conceptual fluency (FN400 effects). Taken together, processing fluency effects could be localized in brain structures. The relationship between processing fluency and positive affect has however yet to be established in neuroscientific studies. Despite ample evidence on neural correlates of pleasure responses (Kühn & Gallinat, 2012), it is as yet not clear how processing fluency activates responses of pleasure.

In terms of the predictive coding account these open questions apply, but can be embedded in a framework that allows clear inferences about possible effects. Regarding specific conditions when something is fluent, the predictive coding account would suggest the amount of prediction error should be considered. This is however not yet directly measurable. Furthermore, the relationship between processing fluency and pleasure is implicated in the amount of prediction error reduction, which should lead to pleasure. Again, empirical evidence is so far lacking.

Apart from lacking empirical evidence, another major upcoming challenge is to further specify these models allowing clear predictions of under which conditions aesthetic processing leads to which response. We are confident that further studies will advance the models step by step. A crucial point is here to combine evidence from processing on a neuronal level with evidence from behavior and subjective experiences to arrive at a unified theory of sensory processing.

Further specifying the models needs furthermore to go hand in hand with defining the crucial outcomes. This issue permeates the whole field of empirical aesthetics, not to mention the field of psychology. Contradictory conclusions among the models often stem from vague definitions of what these models actually intend to measure. As Armstrong and Detweiler-Bedell (2008) show, it is often not clear how beauty, aesthetic pleasure, liking, preference, positive affect, aesthetic emotions, or aesthetic experiences relate to each other. Of course, this is an ongoing challenge in all fields. It would still be worthwhile to invest some effort into a consensual definition of some of the concepts. This would allow us to clearly distinguish whether empirical results contradict each other or not. Taken together, the field of empirical aesthetics is thriving; it still offers many questions that await refinement.

Note

1. In the literature, processing fluency, processing ease, or ease of processing are often used interchangeably. To remain consistent throughout the chapter we will only use the term processing fluency or fluency, but where applicable also further explain that higher fluency means higher ease of processing.

References

Albrecht, S., & Carbon, C.-C. (2014). The Fluency Amplification Model: Fluent stimuli show more intense but not evidently more positive evaluations. *Acta Psychologica, 148*, 195–203.

Alter, A. L., & Oppenheimer, D. M. (2009). Uniting the tribes of fluency to form a metacognitive nation. *Personality and Social Psychology Review, 13*(3), 219–235.

Armstrong, T., & Detweiler-Bedell, B. (2008). Beauty as an emotion: The exhilarating prospect of mastering a challenging world. *Review of General Psychology, 12*(4), 305–329.

Bahnik, S., & Vranka, M. A. (2017). If it's difficult to pronounce, it might not be risky: The effect of fluency on judgment of risk does not generalize to new stimuli. *Psychological Science, 28*(4), 427–436.

Barrett, L. F. (2017). *How emotions are made: The secret life of the brain.* London: Pan Macmillan.

Belke, B., Leder, H., & Carbon, C.-C. (2015). When challenging art gets liked: Evidences for a dual preference formation process for fluent and non-fluent portraits. *PLoS ONE, 10*(8), e0131796.

Belke, B., Leder, H., Strobach, T., & Carbon, C. C. (2010). Cognitive fluency: High-level processing dynamics in art appreciation. *Psychology of Aesthetics, Creativity, and the Arts, 4*(4), 214–222.

Bornstein, R. F. (1989). Exposure and affect: Overview and meta-analysis of research, 1968–1987. *Psychological Bulletin, 106*(2), 265–289.

Bornstein, R. F., & D'Agostino, P. R. (1992). Stimulus-recognition and the mere exposure effect. *Journal of Personality and Social Psychology, 63*(4), 545–552.

Bornstein, R. F., & D'Agostino, P. R. (1994). The attribution and discounting of perceptual fluency: Preliminary tests of a perceptual fluency attributional model of the mere exposure effect. *Social Cognition, 12*(2), 103–128.

Brown, S., Gao, X., Tisdelle, L., Eickhoff, S. B., & Liotti, M. (2011). Naturalizing aesthetics: Brain areas for aesthetic appraisal across sensory modalities. *NeuroImage, 58*(1), 250–258.

Bullot, N. J., & Reber, R. (2012). The artful mind meets art history: Toward a psycho-historical framework for the science of art appreciation. *Behavioral and Brain Sciences, 36*(2), 123–137.

Clark, A. (2013). Whatever next? Predictive brains, situated agents, and the future of cognitive science. *Behavioral and Brain Sciences, 36*(3), 181–204.

Consoli, G. (2016). Predictive error reduction and the twofold nature of aesthetic pleasure. *Art & Perception, 4*(4), 327–338.

Consoli, G. (2017). Commentary: Aesthetic pleasure versus aesthetic interest: The two routes to aesthetic liking. *Frontiers in Psychology, 8*, 2.

Dew, I. T. Z., & Cabeza, R. (2013). A broader view of perirhinal function: From recognition memory to fluency-based decisions. *Journal of Neuroscience, 33*(36), 14466–14474.

Forster, M., Fabi, W., & Leder, H. (2015). Do I really feel it? The contributions of subjective fluency and compatibility in low-level effects on aesthetic appreciation. *Frontiers in Human Neuroscience, 9*, 373.

Forster, M., Gerger, G., & Leder, H. (2015). Everything's relative? Relative differences in processing fluency and the effects on liking. *PLoS ONE, 10*(8), e0135944.

Forster, M., Leder, H., & Ansorge, U. (2013). It felt fluent, and I liked it: Subjective feeling of fluency rather than objective fluency determines liking. *Emotion, 13*(2), 280–289.

Forster, M., Leder, H., & Ansorge, U. (2016). Exploring the subjective feeling of fluency. *Experimental Psychology, 63*, 45–58.

Graf, L. K. M. (2018). Response: Commentary: Aesthetic pleasure versus aesthetic interest: The two routes to aesthetic liking. *Frontiers in Psychology*, 9, 472.

Graf, L. K. M., & Landwehr, J. R. (2015). A dual-process perspective on fluency-based aesthetics: The Pleasure-Interest Model of Aesthetic Liking. *Personality and Social Psychology Review*, 19(4), 395–410.

Graf, L. K. M., & Landwehr, J. R. (2017). Aesthetic pleasure versus aesthetic interest: The two routes to aesthetic liking. *Frontiers in Psychology*, 8, 15.

Hayes, A. E., Paul, M. A., Beuger, B., & Tipper, S. P. (2008). Self produced and observed actions influence emotion: The roles of action fluency and eye gaze. *Psychological Research*, 72(4), 461–472.

Jacoby, L. L., Kelley, C. M., & Dywan, J. (1989). Memory attributions. In H. L. Roediger III, & F. I. M. Craik (Eds.), *Varieties of memory and consciousness: Essays in honour of Endel Tulving* (pp. 391–422). Hillsdale, NJ: Lawrence Erlbaum.

Jakesch, M., & Carbon, C.-C. (2012). The mere exposure effect in the domain of haptics. *PLoS ONE*, 7(2), e31215.

Jakesch, M., Leder, H., & Forster, M. (2013). Image ambiguity and fluency. *PLoS ONE*, 8(9), e74084.

Kühn, S., & Gallinat, J. (2012). The neural correlates of subjective pleasantness. *NeuroImage*, 61(1), 289–294.

Labroo, A. A., & Pocheptsova, A. (2016). Metacognition and consumer judgment: Fluency is pleasant but disfluency ignites interest. *Current Opinion in Psychology*, 10, 154–159.

Lanska, M., Olds, J. M., & Westerman, D. L. (2014). Fluency effects in recognition memory: Are perceptual fluency and conceptual fluency interchangeable? *Journal of Experimental Psychology: Learning, Memory, and Cognition*, 40(1), 1–11.

Lauring, J. O., Pelowski, M., Forster, M., Gondan, M., Ptito, M., & Kupers, R. (2016). Well, if they like it … Effects of social groups' ratings and price information on the appreciation of art. *Psychology of Aesthetics, Creativity, and the Arts*, 10(3), 344–359.

Li, B., Gao, C., Wang, W., & Guo, C. (2015). Processing fluency hinders subsequent recollection: An electrophysiological study. *Frontiers in Psychology*, 6, 863.

Muth, C., & Carbon, C.-C. (2013). The Aesthetic Aha: On the pleasure of having insights into Gestalt. *Acta Psychologica*, 144(1), 25–30.

Muth, C., Hesslinger, V. M., & Carbon, C. C. (2015). The appeal of challenge in the perception of art: How ambiguity, solvability of ambiguity, and the opportunity for insight affect appreciation. *Psychology of Aesthetics, Creativity, and the Arts*, 9(3), 206–216.

Muth, C., Raab, M. H., & Carbon, C.-C. (2015). The stream of experience when watching artistic movies. Dynamic aesthetic effects revealed by the continuous evaluation procedure (CEP). *Frontiers in Psychology*, 6, 365.

Olds, J. M., & Westerman, D. L. (2012). Can fluency be interpreted as novelty? Retraining the interpretation of fluency in recognition memory. *Journal of Experimental Psychology: Learning, Memory, and Cognition*, 38(3), 653–664.

Paller, K. A., Voss, J. L., & Boehm, S. G. (2007). Validating neural correlates of familiarity. *Trends in Cognitive Sciences*, 11(6), 243–250.

Pelowski, M. (2015). Tears and transformation: Feeling like crying as an indicator of insight or "aesthetic" experience with art. *Frontiers in Psychology*, 6, 1006.

Rauss, K., & Pourtois, G. (2013). What is bottom-up and what is top-down in predictive coding? *Frontiers in Psychology*, 4, 276.

Reber, R., Schwarz, N., & Winkielman, P. (2004) Processing fluency and aesthetic pleasure: Is beauty in the perceiver's processing experience? *Personality and Social Psychology Review*, 8(4), 364–382.

Reber, R., Winkielman, P., & Schwarz, N. (1998). Effects of perceptual fluency on affective judgments. *Psychological Science*, 9(1), 45–48.

Russell, P. A., & Milne, S. (1997). Meaningfulness and hedonic value of paintings: Effects of titles. *Empirical Studies of the Arts*, 15(1), 61–73.

Schwarz, N. (2011). Feelings-as-information theory. In P. Van Lange, A. Kruglanski, & E. T. Higgins (Eds.), *Handbook of theories of social psychology* (pp. 289–308). Thousand Oaks, CA: Sage.

Shimamura, A. P. (2012). Toward a science of aesthetics: Issues and ideas. In A. Shimamura, & S. E. Palmer (Eds.), *Aesthetic science: Connecting minds, brains, and experience* (pp. 3–30). New York: Oxford University Press.

Silvia, P. J. (2008). Interest—The curious emotion. *Current Directions in Psychological Science*, 17(1), 57–60.

Silvia, P. J. (2012). Human emotions and aesthetic experience: An overview of empirical aesthetics. In A. Shimamura, & S. E. Palmer (Eds.), *Aesthetic science: Connecting minds, brains, and experience* (pp. 250–275). New York: Oxford University Press.

Song, H., & Schwarz, N. (2009). If it's difficult to pronounce, it must be risky: Fluency, familiarity, and risk perception. *Psychological Science*, 20(2), 135–138.

Strack, F., & Deutsch, R. (2004). Reflective and impulsive determinants of social behavior. *Personality and Social Psychology Review*, 8(3), 220–247.

Topolinski, S., Likowski, K., Weyers, P., & Strack, F. (2009). The face of fluency: Semantic coherence automatically elicits a specific pattern of facial muscle reactions. *Cognition & Emotion*, 23(2), 260–271.

Topolinski, S., & Reber, R. (2010). Gaining insight into the "Aha" experience. *Current Directions in Psychological Science*, 19(6), 402–405.

Unkelbach, C. (2006). The learned interpretation of cognitive fluency. *Psychological Science*, 17(4), 339–345.

Van de Cruys, S., & Wagemans, J. (2011). Putting reward in art: A tentative prediction error account of visual art. *i-Perception*, 2(9), 1035–1062.

Vargas, I. M., Voss, J. L., & Paller, K. A. (2012). Implicit recognition based on lateralized perceptual fluency. *Brain Sciences*, 2(1), 22–32.

Voss, J. L., Lucas, H. D., & Paller, K. A. (2012). More than a feeling: Pervasive influences of memory without awareness of retrieval. *Cognitive Neuroscience*, 3(3–4), 193–207.

Voss, J. L., & Paller, K. A. (2006). Fluent conceptual processing and explicit memory for faces are electrophysiologically distinct. *Journal of Neuroscience*, 26(3), 926–933.

Voss, J. L., & Paller, K. A. (2010). Real-time neural signals of perceptual priming with unfamiliar geometric shapes. *Journal of Neuroscience*, 30(27), 9181–9188.

Voss, J. L., Reber, P. J., Mesulam, M. M., Parrish, T. B., & Paller, K. A. (2008). Familiarity and conceptual priming engage distinct cortical networks. *Cerebral Cortex*, 18(7), 1712–1719.

Wang, W., Li, B., Gao, C., Xiao, X., & Guo, C. (2015). Electrophysiological correlates associated with contributions of perceptual and conceptual fluency to familiarity. *Frontiers in Human Neuroscience*, 9, 321.

Wänke, M., & Hansen, J. (2015). Relative processing fluency. *Current Directions in Psychological Science*, 24(3), 195–199.

Winkielman, P., & Cacioppo, J. T. (2001). Mind at ease puts a smile on the face: Psychophysiological evidence that processing facilitation elicits positive affect. *Journal of Personality and Social Psychology, 81*(6), 989–1000.

Yarkoni, T., Poldrack, R. A., Nichols, T. E., Van Essen, D. C., & Wager, T. D. (2011). Large-scale automated synthesis of human functional neuroimaging data. *Nature Methods, 8*(8), 665–670.

Zajonc, R. B. (1968). Attitudinal effects of mere exposure. *Journal of Personality and Social Psychology, 9*(2, Pt. 2), 1–27.

Zajonc, R. B. (2001). Mere exposure: A gateway to the subliminal. *Current Directions in Psychological Science, 10*(6), 224–228.

CHAPTER 20

THE USE OF VISUAL STATISTICAL FEATURES IN EMPIRICAL AESTHETICS

DANIEL GRAHAM

INTRODUCTION: STATISTICAL REGULARITIES IN IMAGES

NEUROSCIENTIFIC investigations of statistical features in images are now a well-established field of study. A "feature" in this case means a characteristic or regularity of an image that is reflected in measures of image structure, such as pixel values. Statistical features in natural images are relevant to visual neuroscience because of evolutionary constraints on visual systems, which demand that sensory systems operate parsimoniously in their ecology. Neuroscience has come to see the brain more generally as capable of adapting over evolution and development to take advantage of the likely physical structure of the external world, whether the structure is the visual environment, the auditory scene, spoken language, or other inputs. In other words, the brain has been shaped by the need to take advantage of statistical regularities in the environment.

REGULARITIES IN SPATIAL STATISTICS

Power Spectra

In terms of vision, this line of argument can help explain the evolved structure of the early visual system. Consider spatial statistics. A simple relationship exists between any two neighboring points in a visual scene: on average, they are likely to be similar in terms of light intensity, and this similarity falls off as the two points become more dis-tantly separated. This regularity holds for the most part regardless of how big your two "points" are, or what you are looking at. By pointing your finger in a pseudorandom dir-ection in your environment and assessing light intensity at the pointed-to location, as well as immediately to its right (or left, up, down, etc.), you can confirm this for yourself. This property does not always hold, but it is likely to hold over many samples. As a regu-larity, this feature—a correlation in pairwise intensity—is something the visual system can take advantage of to make its job of encoding and transmitting information more efficient.

In the case of pairwise correlations, one can explain basic neural encoding strategies in the retina as an evolved processing strategy that takes advantage of such correlations. In other words, retinal interneurons assume that visual input from the world will have pairwise correlations like those in nature. Consequently, these cells mostly respond in areas of the scene where pairs of neighboring points are *not* correlated, such as edges (Atick & Redlich, 1992; Graham et al., 2006). This makes sense because edge contours often define objects, and object detection, segmentation, and recognition are among the most critical functions of primate vision. Efficient retinal processing strategies of this kind are shared by all primates and indeed nearly all mammals and other vertebrates. For reviews of statistical regularities in natural scenes and their relevance to models of vision coding, see for example, Field, 1994; Geisler, 2008; Simoncelli & Olshausen, 2001.

In vision science, basic spatial regularities are generally measured using the power spectrum of spatial frequencies in an image. The power spectrum measures the relative contributions of sine-wave patterns of varying spatial frequency in the composition of an image. The sine waves in this case describe the intensity of basis functions, which look like stripes of differing size, number, and orientation (see Figure 20.1A). Mathematically, such two-dimensional sine-wave basis functions vary in terms of frequency, amplitude, orientation, and phase. Any image can be broken down into a collection of such basis functions using Fourier analysis; it can also be reassembled from the appropriate "re-cipe" of basis functions using the same mathematical machinery.

The lowest spatial frequencies correspond to basis functions that alternate only once between white and black (we are ignoring color for the moment), at any orientation. A strong contribution to low frequency content in images would be a horizon line separating bright sky from darker land. And indeed, such ecological structure—being so common—contributes most to the typical power spectrum of the natural visual world. High frequencies, on the other hand, correspond to fine detail in a scene. Although humans glean important information from high spatial frequencies, they constitute only a small fraction of the image's spatial variation. Overall, when spatial frequency is plotted against the contribution of that frequency to image structure on logarithmic axes, we see a straight line with a negative slope. The relationship between power S and spatial frequency f can be approximated mathematically as: $S = f^p$, where p is about equal to -2 for natural images. As mentioned earlier, it does not matter how large the "points" are that one considers in pairwise correlations: this is the "scale invariance" implied by

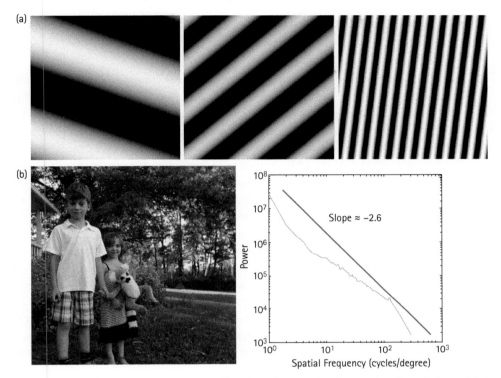

FIGURE 20.1. (A) Sine-wave gratings of various frequencies (increasing from left to right), amplitudes, and orientations. (B) Natural scene and its corresponding power spectrum. Any image can be decomposed into sine-wave components: the power spectrum (shown in blue) measures the contribution of each spatial frequency to the structure of the image, averaged over orientation. This function shows approximately linear fall off (shown in red) on logarithmic axes. Natural scenes typically have a slope of around –2 (this example has a slope of –2.6).

the relationship $S = f^{-2}$, which is equivalent to $S = 1/f^2$. That is, power spectra display "1/ f (one-over-f)" scaling (see e.g., Bak et al., 1987). Mathematically, p describes the fall off of the typical natural scene power spectrum with increasing spatial frequency. In particular, p describes the slope of the power spectrum when plotted on logarithmic axes. Note that some authors alternatively investigate the spatial frequency amplitude spectrum, which is the square root of the power spectrum; plotted on logarithmic axes, its typical slope for natural scenes is –1, or simply $p/2$. See Figure 20.1B.

The power spectrum description is equivalent to measuring pairwise similarities of each point (pixel) in an image with all of its neighbors; the power spectrum description is more flexible and formalized (and therefore in most common use in vision science), but thinking of the pairwise correlation structure can be more intuitive. This chapter will continue to refer to pairwise correlations where appropriate, though the following sections are primarily elaborated in terms of the power spectrum description.

Power Spectra and Aesthetics

Art Images

Given these relationships, one may suppose that what is "natural" in terms of statistical features has a special place in human visual aesthetics. To a first approximation, this is the case. Consider a class of images often created for aesthetic purposes: artwork. Diverse collections of art images are known to have similar regularities in terms of statistics relevant to vision coding. For example, large samples of art images have a similar pairwise correlation structure as natural scenes. In particular, Graham and Field (2007) and Redies et al. (2007a) separately found essentially the same spatial regularities in different samples of world artwork, with p having an average value of around -2 in both studies (see Graham & Redies, 2010, for a review).

To some extent this is unsurprising: although art styles vary widely within and across cultures, all art images are to a greater or lesser extent intended for the human eye and therefore must make use of visual patterns that our visual system is adapted to. Indeed, the variation in p for natural and artistic images of varying types is relatively small (see Table 20.1). This general consistency extends to abstract artwork including artwork produced with a degree of randomness, such as Jackson Pollock's drip paintings (Graham & Field, 2008a). Thus, even when artists are not depicting natural scenes, or when they employ randomness, they almost always follow the basic spatial regularities of natural scenes.

White Noise

However, it is not necessary to presume that artistic images have a special place in aesthetics (cf. Nadal & Skov, 2018) in order to find evidence in support of the idea that basic statistical regularities that are relevant to vision coding also shape our visual aesthetics. For example, one can see *prima facie* that very statistically unnatural images such as white noise (Figure 20.2A) are not attractive. White noise is created by randomly assigning the intensity at each pixel. This class of images has an average pairwise correlation of zero (since each pixel value is chosen independently of its neighbors), and, correspondingly, a power spectrum slope $p = 0$. The latter result indicates that the contribution to image structure across spatial frequency in white noise is uniform.[1]

Because white noise images are very unlike the natural visual world to which humans are evolutionarily adapted, there is a sense in which we can't even see them. For example, the white noise images shown in Figure 20.2A look indistinguishable, yet each one is utterly different from the others. Indeed, any pair of white noise images is likely to be far more different in terms of spatial structure than a given pair of natural images (see Chandler & Field, 2007). The visual system has adapted to a correlated world, and not to the uncorrelated world of white noise. In comparison, a random selection of images that has the pairwise regularities like those natural scenes but are otherwise completely random—$1/f$ noise—will appear rather pleasant, perhaps reminiscent of cloud-watching (Rogowitz & Voss, 1990); such images are also readily distinguishable (Figure 20.2B).

Table 20.1. Slope value (−p) for log–log plots of radially averaged Fourier power versus spatial frequency for different categories of natural and artistic images (from Graham & Redies, 2010)

	−p	SD[a]	n[b]
Natural scenes[c,d]	−2.0	0.3	208
Photographs of plants[c]	−2.9	0.4	206
Photographs of simple objects[c]	−2.8	0.3	179
Photographs of faces[e,f]	−3.5	0.2	3313
Graphic art of Western provenance[c]	−2.1	0.3	200
Artistic portraits (graphic art)[e]	−2.1	0.3	306
15th century	−2.0	0.2	20
16th century	−2.1	0.2	89
17th century	−2.1	0.4	34
18th century	−2.2	0.1	18
19th century	−2.2	0.4	50
20th century	−2.2	0.3	95
Etching	−2.0	0.3	50
Engraving	−2.1	0.2	17
Lithograph	−2.2	0.2	27
Woodcut	−2.4	0.4	13
Charcoal, chalk	−2.2	0.3	100
Pencil, silver point	−2.0	0.2	59
Pen drawing	−2.1	0.3	31
Scientific illustrations[c]	−1.6	0.3	209

[a] Standard deviation.

[b] Number of images in each category.

[c] Data from the study by Redies, Hasenstein et al. (2007).

[d] Images from the database of van Hateren and van der Schaaf (1998).

[e] Data from the study by Redies, Hänisch et al. (2007b).

[f] AR face database of Martinez and Benavente (1998).

In terms of production, white noise has probably been created only twice by hand: this feat of craft was first accomplished by Attneave (1954). In this seminal paper on efficient visual system encoding, two military enlistees darkened approximately 20,000 squares by hand according to randomly generated numerical values. This feat was also accomplished by the French artist François Morellet in his painting *Random Distribution of 40,000 Squares Using the Odd and Even Numbers of a Telephone Directory*, 1960 (Mather, 2013; see Figure 20.3A). Viewed from the perspective of art history, humans

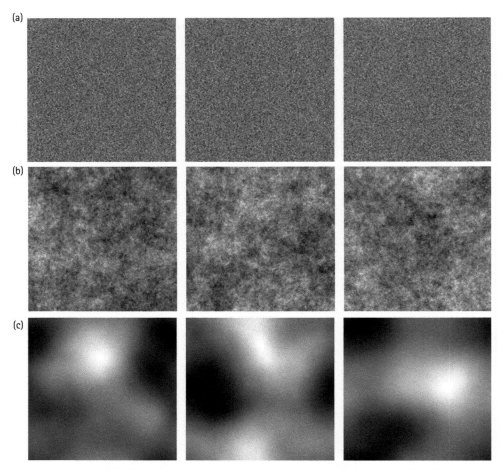

FIGURE 20.2. (A) White noise images, where each pixel value is chosen at random (in this case from a Gaussian distribution). In each image, a given pixel value is likely to be quite different from that of the corresponding pixel in the other images, and therefore these images are utterly different from one another. However, they are essentially indistinguishable. These images all have a flat power spectrum (slope = 0). (B) Noise images that possess $1/f$ scaling in their power spectra, i.e., $1/f$ noise. These images are also random, but have the same basic spatial statistical regularity as natural scenes, with a power spectrum slope of approximately −2.0. Such images are easily distinguished. (C) Blurry images that show power spectrum slope of around −6.0.

have produced copious numbers of monochrome paintings and other handmade images that are in a way imperceptible (in the sense of having no spatial variation), but only two that resemble white noise. Interestingly, however, the red and blue pigments Morrellet used are essentially equiluminant (Figure 20.3B), so the image may be processed more like a monochrome. Thus, in terms of empirical aesthetics, noise images hold a special place as an almost universally disliked stimulus. However, beyond dislike, it would be interesting to know how humans treat such images in an aesthetic context—do they

FIGURE 20.3. Luminance information present in the painting. François Morellet, *Random Distribution of 40,000 Squares Using the Odd and Even Numbers of a Telephone Directory, 1960.* Museum of Modern Art, New York. The painting was created with a random process that assigned red and blue pigments to a given location, making it something like white noise. However, if color information is removed, the image appears almost uniform.

feel disgust or other negative valence emotions, or no emotions at all? Do they prefer a disgusting image to white noise?

Blur

Images with power spectrum slope values of p much more negative than -2 are also difficult to perceive, and are also disliked. Such images appear very blurry. Randomly produced blurry images (e.g., generally those with $p > -3$, as in Figure 20.2C) are fairly easy to distinguish from one another due to differing location of the "blobs." However, they also seem to provoke frustration and aversion because of their indistinctness. When a natural scene is heavily blurred, the effect is the same. Conversely, anyone requiring strong optical correction can describe the pleasant sensation of seeing the world more clearly when they put on spectacles. That is, beyond the practical benefits of seeing the world without blur, there may be a related aesthetic dimension.

We can see this in artistic production as well: professional photographs are very rarely blurry. As Ke et al. (2006) showed, in a large and diverse set of viewer-rated photographs, the statistical presence of blur in an image is an excellent predictor of low image quality ratings. In fact, blur was a far better predictor of preference in this study than statistical models that considered contrast, color, edge structure, or brightness. Anecdotally, artwork that employs substantial blur exists (e.g., the work of South African painter Philip Barlow; see Figure 20.4), but is also very rare. However, even Barlow's work has a power spectrum that is well fit by a straight line on logarithmic axes. And though the image in Figure 20.4 has a slope p that is somewhat outside the normal range for natural scenes (around -3.5 by the author's calculation), it is not nearly as far as that of the very blurry images in Figure 20.2C.

FIGURE 20.4. Philip Barlow, Refuge II, n.d. http://www.philipbarlow.com. This image has a spatial frequency power spectrum slope of ~−3.5.

Barlow's work is of particular interest because he captures in paint something like the perceptual experience of humans with substantial optical errors. Since optical errors are highly prevalent in industrialized societies (e.g., 96% of 19-year-old males in Seoul were found to have myopia; Jung et al., 2012), perhaps researchers should consider how this myopia epidemic can affect aesthetics. If most adults see only a blur beyond a certain distance in depth (without optical correction), do they generally discount aesthetic considerations in this depth regime, for example in urban architecture? Such questions require research but it can be concluded that blur is rare and disliked aesthetically, though it is perhaps not as rare or as disliked as white noise.

There is also evidence that spatial statistics that differ in other ways from $1/f$ can be aversive. Fernandez and Wilkins (2008), for example, have shown that excess power in the mid-range of spatial frequency (especially high-contrast stripes at around 3 cycles/degree in spatial frequency)—relative to natural spectra—generates discomfort. They argue that this discomfort may be related to conditions of optically induced headache and seizure. Thus, images that deviate strongly from natural spatial statistics may be disliked not only because they are imperceptible, but perhaps also because they negatively interfere with other brain processes.

The Perceptibility Hypothesis

In terms of image statistics, then, we like what is typical. As it turns out, what is preferred is also what we see best, as has been shown by Spehar et al. (2015). These authors tested human viewers on preference and acuity—the latter measured as detection at increasing contrast and as discrimination in terms of just-noticeable differences—for random noise stimuli that varied in their power spectrum slope p from −0.2 to −5.0. They found that there was a strong relationship between images that were best perceived and those that were preferred, which in both cases corresponds to a value of p of roughly −2. In other words, there is a very similar inverted U-shaped distribution for both preference and visibility as a function of power spectrum slope p, which is centered around $p = -2$. At the extremes of the distribution of p values, blurry images were somewhat preferred to white noise-like images. The same relationship between acuity and preference held for sine-wave gratings of varying spatial frequency. Thus, humans cannot detect or discriminate images with statistical features characteristic of white noise and blur, and we dislike those images, too. Noise images with natural spatial statistics, on the other hand, can be readily detected and discriminated, and are therefore preferred (see Figure 20.2). The idea that we generally prefer what is typical because we see it best has been termed the *perceptibility hypothesis* (Graham & Field, 2008a).

Fractal Dimension Statistics

Before considering statistical features beyond power spectrum slope, it is worth a brief diversion to discuss the concept of "fractal dimension," since it is related to the power spectrum. Fractal dimension is defined as a measure of the degree to which a single line fills up a plane, or the degree to which a single plane fills up a volume, due to fractal structure (see e.g., Mandelbrot, 1982). Fractals in this case are mathematical objects that are both self-similar and scale invariant: they show the same patterns of structure at all spatial scales, and are generated according to deterministic recursive functions.

The idea of fractal dimension has been applied to real-world (nonmathematical) objects as well, but it is important to note that it can only be approximated. Often, fractal dimension is approximated by calculating *box dimension*, which works as follows: an object is defined in terms of a binary boundary. A grid of boxes is overlain on the boundary, and the fraction of filled boxes is tallied. This is repeated with larger and smaller grids over several orders of magnitude. The function relating box size to the fraction of boxes required to cover the boundary at that size determines the box dimension. This procedure can be used to understand the space-filling quality of real-world binary boundaries such as coastlines, where the boundary is meaningful. But its application to images is ambiguous. Typically, images are thresholded to produce such boundaries (e.g., Viengkham & Spehar, 2018). But thresholding produces quite unnatural silhouette-like images, whose power spectra (and other image statistics) are greatly altered relative to the original image. Indeed, few if any parts of the natural visual world consist solely of binary boundaries; most boundaries are in fact low contrast (Ruderman & Bialek, 1994), which is likely the case with artwork as well given the limitations in its dynamic range of luminances (see Graham, 2011).

Moreover, even if such boundaries were meaningful, Normant and Tricot (1991) have shown that the box dimension metric is only an accurate measure of fractal dimension for images that are both scale invariant and self-similar (see also Kube & Pentland, 1988). Since natural images and art images are not self-similar, box dimension measurement is an unreliable measure of their fractal dimension (see Soille & Rivest, 1996; Theiler, 1990). It should also be noted that the application of box dimension alone as a characteristic of authorship of abstract artwork (e.g., for stylometrics or attribution, e.g., Taylor et al., 1999) has been refuted (Jones-Smith & Mathur, 2006).

If a correspondence between visual perception and fractal dimension did exist, it would likely involve the "2D" box dimension (the degree to which a 2D plane fills 3D space), rather than the "1D" box dimension (the degree to which a 1D boundary fills a 2D plane). This could be done for example by considering an image as an intensity surface filling a 3D volume. In this case, fractal dimension D_f is linearly related to the slope p of the spatial frequency amplitude spectrum: $p = 8 - 2Df$ (Knill et al., 1990). This relation holds for all images whose spatial frequency power spectra are well-described by the function $1/f_p$. However, nearly all research concerning "fractal dimension" of images measures instead the "1D" box dimension. Ultimately, then, box dimension is a flawed statistical feature in natural and artistic images, whereas the spatial frequency power spectrum slope yields a principled measure of the same spatial regularities. Researchers are thus encouraged to work within spatial frequency statistics, a formalism particularly suited to patterns in the physical world, as opposed to fractal analysis, which is most germane to mathematical objects.

Higher-Order Spatial Statistics

Are Artistic Images Special?

So far we have only considered spatial regularities of the lowest statistical order, which concern relationships between pairs of points (pixels). In an image, there may exist relationships among more than two pixels, which are called higher-order spatial statistical regularities. Such regularities are generally difficult to measure in images because of the combinatoric explosion of possible triplets, quadruplets, and so on; the difficulty in measurement is further exacerbated by the difficulty of describing any such regularities graphically or numerically. However, higher-order structure that is relevant to vision coding can be explored using spatial filters that resemble those employed in early visual system spatial processing, such as the Gabor-like spatial filters of V1 simple cells. Because simple cell-like filters appear to efficiently encode "sparse" higher-order statistical structure in natural scenes (Bell & Sejnowski, 1997; Olshausen & Field, 1996), their responses give an indication of the higher-order spatial regularities most important to primate vision coding.

One line of argument holds that artistic images are a special class of images due to their higher-order statistical properties. Christoph Redies and colleagues have performed numerous experiments that provide evidence for this proposition.

First, consider faces: as a class, faces are processed in the visual system using specialized mechanisms. For example, face processing such as symmetry detection is most effective for upright faces (Rhodes et al., 2005). If artists aim to exploit these mechanisms, they should reproduce the typical statistics of real faces. However, artistic portraits deviate in their pairwise spatial statistics compared with photographs of human faces (Redies et al., 2007b). Similar findings have been found in terms of higher-order statistics, as described below. Graham and colleagues have found evidence for differences in basic structure between faces and handmade face representations, such as frontal portrait paintings (Graham et al., 2014), and masks from many world cultures (Prescott & Graham, 2020).

Special statistical features for artwork as an image class may not be limited to low-level structure. Redies and colleagues have also shown that, in artworks of different styles, local spatial structure is distinct from what is typical in other image classes, such as photographs of objects and facades. The higher-order structure they measured, termed edge orientation entropy, captures regularities in how edges continue in an image. In this analysis, edge elements are detected using a standard image-processing algorithm. Then each edge element's orientation is compared with that of its neighbors, or to all other edges in the image. One can then create a distribution of edge orientations as well as a distribution of edge relationships (as circular histograms). Uniformity in these distributions can be described in terms of their entropy. In the case of edge relationships, high entropy (i.e., uniformity) means that knowing a given edge's orientation tells one little about the orientation of other edges in the image, such as neighboring edges. Redies and colleagues found that artworks from numerous Western "high" art styles show quite similar distributions of edge orientation entropy, which are similar to those of certain natural scene categories such as large vistas. Similar results were found when the art was grouped by subject matter. Artworks are distinct in this sense from faces, as well as from several classes of human-created objects and architecture (Redies et al., 2017). Related results have been shown for artificial neural network systems that learn higher-order statistical regularities: diverse artwork from across Eurasia tends to group together in terms of its optimal neural network representation, in a way distinct from other human-created objects and buildings, as well as certain varieties of natural scenes (Brachmann et al., 2017; see also section Deep Learning, below). Also, when artists depict natural scenes, they tend to de-emphasize spatial frequency energy of horizontal and vertical orientations compared with natural scenes, which have disproportionate energy in cardinal orientations (Schweinhart & Essock, 2013).

However, it is not clear that all or even most artistic images occupy a special place in terms of human aesthetics because of their statistical properties (to say nothing of their purported specialness vis-à-vis cognitive appraisal or cultural context). To the extent that artwork is different from other image classes in terms of statistical features, this may be due to materials and compositional factors. For example, artists have freedom to create edges on a blank 2D canvas, typically using styli whose width falls in a small range. The 2D retinal image of the 3D physical world, on the other hand, can be modeled in a generative fashion from objects with power-law scaling in size, which can occlude each other, along with biases for cardinal orientations due to horizons, buildings, and trees (Ruderman, 1994, Switkes et al., 1978). In other words, the causes of statistical structure in natural images are distinct from those in art images because they are composed in fundamentally different ways. It is also possible that occlusions of objects in handmade art occur less or in different ways than in other classes of images. That is, humans may generally try to avoid depicting objects in handmade flat media using arrangements that produce a "bad" Gestalt due to occlusion. There is currently no evidence that "good" arrangements of objects are reflected in basic or higher-order spatial statistics. The distinctness of art from other artificial objects and buildings may also be explained by photographic biases in the former (McManus et al., 2011) and by rectilinearity in the latter. In any case, when considering the diversity of art styles beyond Western "high" art (Redies & Brachmann, 2017), as well as variations across time (Mather, 2018) and in art by neuroatypical individuals (Graham & Meng, 2011a), there is considerable variation in statistical regularities at low and high orders, which overlaps with what is typical in other image categories. However, to a first approximation, nearly all artwork shows the same $1/f$ power spectra as that typical of natural scenes. Moreover, despite differences in image statistics, artistic representations show similar basic perceptual responses: for example, portrait and landscape paintings can be discriminated by humans with similar accuracy compared with photographs of faces and landscapes when stimuli are presented rapidly (Graham & Meng, 2011b).

Bearing in mind these complexities, we may now ask whether variations in aesthetic response may be predicted by variations in higher-order statistical features. That is, given that low-level statistical regularities exist and are associated with preference, are variations in higher-order statistics correlated with or predictive of particular dimensions of aesthetic perception? Redies and colleagues have found that aesthetic ratings of images of several kinds of human-created objects and artificial patterns are correlated with higher entropy in edge orientations for those images, which is in turn partially predicted by the perceived curvilinearity of those images (Grebenkina et al., 2018). However, for the most nominally "artistic" of the image categories tested in this study—music album cover art—higher-order statistics (and post-hoc combinations thereof) explained only a quarter or less of data variance in aesthetic ratings. In this experiment, human-judged curvilinearity—a feature that to date has yet to be fully characterized in terms of low- or higher-order statistical regularities—explained much greater proportions of aesthetic rating data variance.

Though summarizing other research in this vein is beyond the scope of the present chapter (see Brachmann & Redies, 2017), we can summarize the affirmative statistical evidence related to the argument of Redies and colleagues as follows:

- Artwork of faces is different from real faces, and more like natural scenes.
- Artwork as a class is distinct from other human-created objects as well as faces and some natural scene categories.
- There is an association between aesthetic preference and a statistical feature that resembles curvilinearity for artificial objects and patterns.

Nevertheless, there is considerable ambiguity in the relationships between variations in higher-order statistics and aesthetics, and indeed in the statistical specialness of "artwork" (whether or not one believes artwork holds a special place in aesthetics).

On the other hand, it has been established that humans do have a preference for low-level spatial statistical regularities associated with natural and easily perceptible visual stimuli. One could speculate that, beyond general preference for pairwise spatial regularities due to efficient and widely shared coding strategies in the early visual system, visual aesthetics may not be an important enough neural function to warrant rigorous optimization for particular variations in low-order (or, for that matter, higher-order) spatial statistical features.

As we shall see once we look beyond spatial statistics, the visual system does not have a default aesthetic response to specific statistical properties in images, although general "rules" can be described for certain applied perceptual situations. Nor is what is most natural necessarily what is aesthetically preferred in these cases.

REGULARITIES IN LUMINANCE STATISTICS

One can appreciate the complexity of the situation by considering luminance distribution statistics, or the proportion of high-, middle-, and low-intensity light in an image. This area of research traces back to some of the first empirical work on efficient coding of natural scene regularities, which involved studies of natural luminances in insect vision (Laughlin, 1981). To a first approximation, scene luminances (light intensities) in natural daylight follow a lognormal distribution (Attewell & Baddeley, 2007; Brady & Field, 2000; Dror, Leung, Adelson, & Willsky, 2001). A lognormal distribution is a distribution whose logarithm is Gaussian. This means that most pixels in a natural scene send relatively low intensities of light to our eyes (the peak in the low intensities), but natural scenes also have intensities that extend far into the high intensities (the "heavy tail" of the distribution). In terms of descriptive statistics, symmetrical distributions like a Gaussian distribution have *skewness* (the third statistical moment) of 0, whereas natural scenes typically possess intensity distributions with skewness greater than 0, due to their approximately lognormal shape. See Figure 20.5.

Thus, we might expect to find that humans prefer this regularity. Indeed, this is what we would predict if we posit that low-level preferences follow from their statistical efficiency relative to sensory encoding. In particular, because cone photoreceptors respond in roughly logarithmic fashion at increasing light intensity, lognormally distributed scene intensities would be encoded as Gaussian responses, thereby making maximal information-theoretic use of the encoding mechanism of cone excitation.

In certain circumstances, there does appear to be a preference for high skew. For example, Yang et al. (2011) found that 7–8-month-old infants preferred to look at computer-simulated 3D objects that had high skewness in their intensity distributions

 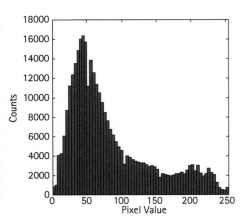

FIGURE 20.5. Natural scene and its intensity (pixel value) histogram. This histogram is roughly lognormal in shape and has a skewness of +1.1. Note that the scene image is not calibrated for luminance: because cameras compress high luminances in scenes more than low luminances, the true distribution of luminances in this scene extends much farther into the high luminances, and would likely have a correspondingly higher skewness.

(Figure 20.6). However, this was only the case when the high skewness corresponded with high glossiness (i.e., when bright highlights in the image accurately indicated glossy material reflectance). But there is also evidence that humans can accurately judge the freshness of photographs of real fruit and vegetables from small image patches, and that luminance distribution skewness by itself partly contributes to the accuracy of such judgments (Arce-Lopera et al., 2012; Wada et al., 2010). There is also evidence that higher values of luminance distribution kurtosis (the fourth statistical moment of the

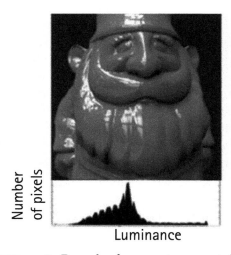 

FIGURE 20.6. Example of a computer generated object rendered with glossy (left) and non-glossy (right) materials, along with a historgram of the luminances in the corresponding image. Note that the glossy object has a much wider distribution of luminances that stretches to the high luminances, resulting in a highly skewed distribution (Yang et al., 2011).

distribution, which is generally higher for distributions with high skew) are associated with preference for abstract art, explaining 25% of data variance (Graham et al., 2010). Taken together, this line of work suggests that some image classes (including those depicting single glossy objects) that show high luminance distribution skewness may be generally preferred.

Conversely, however, Graham et al. (2016) have shown that versions of a natural image manipulated to have high skew are systematically disliked compared with those manipulated to have low skew. For outdoor scenes, Graham et al. (2016) found that humans generally prefer skew lower than what was present in the original scene. That is, we prefer natural scene images to be substantially altered in terms of their luminance distributions relative to what is natural. In a suite of studies, artistic photographs of Western U.S. landscapes as well as images from a standard natural scene database were manipulated to change their skew. This procedure leaves the mean and variance of the intensity distribution (and, of course, spatial relationships of pixels in the image) unchanged. Regardless of the inclusion of glossy objects in the scenes—and even when pixels were randomly scrambled—human viewers consistently preferred low-skew versions of the images. This finding may not be so surprising when we consider that human painters overwhelmingly produce low-skew images (Graham & Field, 2008a). In part, the low-skew bias in artwork is due to the limited dynamic range of luminances available for 2D reflective objects (see Graham et al., 2008b), but aesthetic demands may also bias human artists toward low-skew images. Indeed, it is possible to make high-skew images by hand, but because of the limited dynamic range, such images will necessarily be mostly quite dark, with a few highlights.

Otaka, Shimakura, and Motoyoshi (2019) have also investigated luminance regularities in images of skin patches. Since the material properties of skin are closely associated with biologically relevant aesthetic judgments such as attractiveness, this is a potentially useful arena for understanding statistical features related to aesthetics. Otaka and colleagues (2019) found that a range of perceptual judgments such as glossiness, smoothness, healthiness, and evenness can be summarized into two subjective factors: "goodness" and "glossiness." These factors in turn showed high correlations to simple luminance and color statistics, particularly the variance, skew, and kurtosis of the images' luminance and color distributions. Interestingly, both the glossiness attribute and the "goodness" factor were anticorrelated with luminance distribution skewness. In other words, low skew is preferred.

Thus, it appears that humans may have a general taste for low-skew scenes (at least for complex outdoor scenes, and to a lesser extent, skin), which artists have, on average, attempted to sate. Again, the artwork result (Graham & Field, 2008a) may be related to perceptibility: although one can make a high-skew image by hand, it will be mostly dark; lower-skew images may have more detail to explore, making them in a way more perceptible. However, in certain functional situations, on the other hand, such as judging fruit and vegetable ripeness we may be particularly attuned and attracted to high skewness associated with glossiness. But it should be said that researchers have criticized this approach on theoretical and empirical grounds (see e.g., Anderson & Kim; 2009;

Fleming, 2014). It is certainly not the case that a particular skew of the luminance distribution will guarantee preference (or, for that matter, glossiness). The possible neurobiological underpinnings of such a process also remain undefined.

REGULARITIES IN COLOR STATISTICS

Uniform Color Patches

Color is another realm where basic statistical features have been investigated in terms of empirical relationships with aesthetics.

Karen Schloss, Stephen Palmer, and colleagues have performed extensive research across diverse populations to determine mean preferences for small patches of color presented in isolation. In a series of experiments, Palmer and Schloss (2010) established a logical chain of evidence connecting numerical liking ratings for color patches and liking ratings of natural objects of the same color. In particular, color patches whose hue is commonly associated with objects whose average rated valence is positive are generally rated more highly than color patches whose hue is commonly associated with objects whose average rated valence is negative. For example, mean preference across individuals generally favors blue and disfavors brown: in turn, Palmer and Schloss (2010) show systematic evidence that humans judge canonically blue objects like clear sky and clean water as positive, while we judge canonically brown objects like feces and rotten food as negative.

What can these results tell us regarding color statistics? Generalizing from color patches to objects is difficult—we may make like a particular color only in a particular context, or in a particular functional situation (Schloss et al., 2013). Indeed, the spectral composition of the color could be the same in differing objects where a color is alternatively liked and disliked. We expect our food, for example, to have a predictable color appearance. Wheatley (1973), in a classic study, asked diners to enjoy a steak dinner in a room with dim lighting. When lighting was increased to a normal level partway through the meal, several diners reportedly became ill upon realizing that their otherwise delectable steak had been artificially colored blue (see Spence, 2015). So, whereas we may like a wavelength spectrum with increased energy in the short (blue) wavelengths when it is produced by, say, the sky, we will not necessarily like a similar collection of wavelengths when produced by something that does not normally appear blue. In any case, an understanding of the human species' most and least favorite colors is not necessarily a question that is usefully described using the language of statistics—this is in part because, even in a simple experiment, human responses can only be sampled for a limited number of the millions of discernible colors (Linhares et al., 2008); the combinatorics problem gets much worse when even simple color combinations are considered.

Artwork

Again bearing in mind the nonidentity of aesthetics and artwork, we can glean a meaningful understanding of relationships between color statistics and aesthetics by examining art. Empirical understanding of color statistics in art may be useful because Western artists in particular have historically paid close attention to natural color appearance and its vicissitudes, and they have invented diverse pigments for this purpose (though art traditions in the West and elsewhere have also greatly emphasized abstract color symbolism).

Montagner et al. (2016) used multispectral imaging to capture narrow-band measurements of wavelength content across the visible spectrum in Western painted artwork. They found that artists use more saturated red colors and fewer greens than are typical in natural scenes, but otherwise artists mostly matched natural colors. This result may be related to aesthetics, though other explanations are possible, such as the danger posed by standard green pigments, which were historically likely to contain arsenic (Zhao et al., 2008), leading to their disuse. There are also potential biases in natural scene image databases, which may include disproportionate amounts of greenery.

However, further experiments using multispectral images of paintings suggest additional links between preference and color statistics. In an innovative study, Nascimento et al. (2017) investigated preference for rotations of the color gamut in paintings. Such modifications have the effect of changing the color of each pixel according to its location in a perceptually uniform color space, but maintaining the geometric relationships among all pixel colors; light intensity (luminance) and spatial relationships of pixels remain constant as well. Thus, during gamut rotation, pixels with similar hues in the original painting will stay similar to one another as their hues change together, whereas pixels with very different original hues will maintain large differences as their hues change. Multispectral imaging—which captures fine-grained wavelength information invisible to the eye—is required in this case to accurately simulate images with rotated color gamuts. What is interesting with regard to empirical aesthetics is that when viewers are given a painting whose color gamut has been randomly rotated from its original state and are asked to rotate it according to their preference, they generally choose the original color axes. In particular, average viewer preference for the absolute colors in a given work of art is nearly indistinguishable perceptually from the preference for the original work created by the artist (Nascimento et al., 2017). This result holds for representational and highly abstract works, though, interestingly, preferred gamuts for naturalistic paintings were further away from the original colors compared with what was found for abstract works. This pattern holds for both art experts and laypersons. Thus, while artists do not necessarily all use the same approach to color harmony, each may find a maximally preferred color representation for her particular subject matter. However, preferred color gamuts do not fully align with what is typical in nature (nor, it was found, for represented materials of some aesthetic importance such as skin). Thus, from the point of view of color statistics, artists may in some respects prioritize aesthetic composition over natural rendering.

These results represent evidence both of the utility of empirical aesthetics investigations using digitized artwork, and the insights granted by statistical understanding of image features. As Nascimento et al. (2017) note, their conclusions are not predicted by the Palmer–Schloss model of preference for color patches in isolation.

In related experiments involving artworks and natural scenes, Nascimento and Masuda (2014) and Masuda and Nascimento (2012) used digital simulations of lighting changes as well as real-world lighting installations to investigate preferred illuminants. They found that humans preferred illumination to be rather different from what is typical in daylight: the preferred lighting spectra had more peaks and valleys across wavelength compared with natural daylight, which varies more smoothly. Also, humans preferred lighting that generated more saturated colors in the art and scenes compared with what is produced by daylight illumination.

Thus, while blue may be liked and brown disliked in general (due perhaps to these colors' associations with positive and negative valence natural substances, respectively), and while artists and viewers seem to agree on the most pleasing lighting and color relationships in artwork, there is variation in preference compared with what is natural—as with the preference for the distribution of luminances in scenes, described in the next section.

Regularities in Spatiotemporal Statistics

As we have seen, regularities of spatial, luminance, and color features can grant insight into empirical aesthetics, especially when considered in relation to natural regularities and the visual system mechanisms for encoding the retinal image. However, human vision is inherently dynamic: if one were to fully stabilize the retinal image, it would fade to nothingness (this so-called Troxler fading can be accomplished by physically affixing the image frame to the eyeball so that image and retina move together, or by mimicking the side-to-side jitter of the eyeball in a display; see, for example, Martinez-Conde et al., 2013).

Yet little research has been done to investigate spatiotemporal regularities from the point of view of empirical aesthetics. This may be because video stimuli take longer for viewers to evaluate compared with still images, and thus fewer can be shown during an experiment (though some researchers have developed novel methods for continuous evaluative responses, e.g., Muth et al., 2016). Many existing neuroscientific analyses of "natural" spatiotemporal patterns study instead Hollywood film (see Hasson et al., 2008) This is because it is very challenging to create natural movies that fully account for body, head, and eye movements, as well as accommodation and binocular disparity.

Summarizing how statistical regularities (especially higher-order spatial regularities) in static image statistics vary over time is also challenging.

As soon as humans developed the capability of manipulating images over time, they very quickly deviated from what is natural. In particular, they invented the cut, whereby two different scenes or two different views of the same scene (i.e., shots) are ordered in sequence. But while the approaches filmmakers employ within cuts—as well as the sequence of information displayed across cuts—differ from those we experience in daily life, their frequency appears to have grounding in natural vision. Cutting et al. (2010) have found that cut length in Hollywood film generally follows a $1/f$ temporal pattern. That is, the length of a given cut is well predicted by the length of cuts nearby in time, and the overall the distribution of cut lengths follows a $1/f$ distribution. Cutting et al. (2011) found that, over film history, absolute cut length has gone down, while camera and object motion within cuts has gone up. These results may be partly due to technological and cultural changes, but the $1/f$ nature of cuts may also reflect variations in human attentional capacity over time, which are also found to exhibit $1/f$ scaling in time (Gilden, 2001).

Of perhaps greater relevance to this chapter is the finding that mean intensity (pixel value) of frames in Hollywood film has gone down over time (Cutting et al., 2011). A further study by Cutting (2014) showed that pixel values show roughly lognormal (positively skewed) distributions throughout film history, though more recent films have a greater proportion of low- and high-intensity pixels compared with earlier film (suggesting higher skewness for recent films, though skewness was not reported). Thus, films considered as a whole share a basic regularity of natural luminance distributions. However, because of variability in luminance nonlinearities in film and projection, as well as considerable scattering of projected light in a large theater (which would make "black" pixels brighter), the luminances received by the retina may not be fully described by pixel value distributions.

Despite producing spatiotemporal sequences using cuts that would never be experienced in nature, filmmakers have produced temporal statistical regularities that may take advantage of statistical regularities in visual attention over time. This is perhaps not so surprising since human eye movements are so rapid and frequent that our instantaneous view of the world is itself fragmentary. The retinal image continually experiences large shifts, though not in the same way as film cuts, which are typically structured around story-related functions rather than egocentric exploration. In any case, given the dominance of film in the aesthetic marketplace, it is clear that capturing attention in this way is effective. It also appears that film generally reproduces the intensity distribution of natural scenes, which feature mostly low intensities.

THE RELIABILITY OF AESTHETIC RESPONSES

In this chapter, as in nearly all published research in empirical aesthetics, it has been assumed that human aesthetic responses can be accurately and consistently measured in humans using empirical methods. That is, when someone rates an image as a "5" in terms of liking on a 0–9 scale, we grant this measurement an implicit reliability. It is commonly acknowledged that individuals' aesthetics vary considerably, and for reasons that are poorly understood (but see recent work by Vessel et al., 2018 and Leder et al., 2016, addressing individual differences in aesthetics for certain image classes). And very few studies have investigated the ways our aesthetics vary at different stages of development. Nevertheless, we tend to assume that any individual's preferences are largely the same from one day or week to the next. Therefore, we assume that our measurements of their preferences are an accurate empirical gauge of an underlying psychological reality termed "aesthetics."

Yet humans at all stages of the lifespan have been found to be quite unreliable in their preferences for identical stimuli from week to week, with young children being most unstable. In the first study of its kind, Pugach et al. (2017) measured stability (i.e., test–retest reliability) in individuals age 3–99 using a suite of ranking tasks. Participants separately ranked images in four classes, containing face photographs, landscape photographs, and artistic paintings of the same faces and landscape features. They then repeated the same task 2 weeks later. In all age groups, participants made on average at least one rank change per image in each image class (young children made upwards of two rank changes per image).

Other studies, though not specifically concerned with stability/reliability, report correlations within observers of below .75 for aesthetic ratings of faces, natural images, and architecture over shorter intervals (Hönekopp, 2006). We can infer that, at most, around 50% of the variance of a given individual's preference for visual stimuli can be explained by their own previous ratings of the same stimuli. Indeed, even over very short (~15-min) intervals, individuals' aesthetic responses to the same stimuli can be rather different, with mean consistency measured at less than .9 for ratings of identical images (Vessel et al., 2018). This may in part be because of decreased liking with repeated exposures (Biederman & Vessel, 2006).

On the other hand, the same approach of studying stability/reliability has produced evidence that supports the notion of a "core" visual aesthetics, one that is surprisingly robust to brain damage. For example, in people with Alzheimer's related dementia and frontotemporal dementia, aesthetic stability for images is not significantly different from age-matched controls, though explicit memory is substantially worse in the diseased cohorts (Graham et al., 2013; Halpern et al. 2008; Halpern & O'Connor, 2013).

Thus, the study of aesthetic stability suggests that, on average, a hierarchy of basic preferences in the visual domain inheres in all individuals, even in the face of brain damage. However, the same research approach suggests that, outside of a fairly consistent aesthetic heuristic, there is considerable variability within all individuals in terms of their aesthetic responses to individual stimuli over the course of days or weeks. Fortuitously for researchers in empirical aesthetics, undergraduates are the most stable age cohort (Pugach et al., 2017). However, the variable nature of our aesthetic response for identical stimuli is a special concern when we try to discover empirical relationships between statistical features of images and measures of aesthetic response since statistical features in images are unchanging and devoid of context. Further, this problem is an impediment to a mechanistic neurobiological understanding of the relationships that may be observed between image statistics and aesthetics.

Summary

Given the evidence considered here, we can summarize how statistical features of images can illuminate the study of empirical aesthetics:

1) Humans prefer images with basic spatial statistics in a range around what is typical for natural scenes, and everybody dislikes images that have very different spatial statistics compared with what is typical in natural scenes, such as white noise and very blurry images. Irrespective of contextual factors, a $1/f$ power spectrum with slope around -2 is our default expectation for aesthetic images.

2) Smaller variation in slope around $p = -2$ is not known to be predictive of specific aesthetic responses. However, there is some evidence that artistic images from across cultures typically share distinctive higher-order statistical structure, though the influence of materials and composition cannot be ruled out.

3) Adults and children prefer high skew (i.e., less Gaussian) distributions of light intensity for isolated objects, fruits, and vegetables when there is associated glossiness. But more generally, we prefer lower-skew (i.e., more Gaussian) distributions of light intensity compared with what is natural. Handmade artwork is also low in skewness, though Hollywood films may have more highly skewed distributions of light intensity.

4) Observers prefer the way Western painters represent color compared with other color representations in a uniform space of color transformations. However, there are significant differences between natural color statistics and the preferred statistics of color use in artwork.

5) Temporal statistics of cuts in Hollywood films are also described by a $1/f$ distribution and therefore may fit human attentional capacity. However, cuts are themselves rather unnatural representations of spatiotemporal human vision.

Outlook: Where Do We Go From Here?

In conclusion, let us consider a variety of grand questions for future research.

Statistical Features: Comparative Approaches

Given the high similarity between human vision and other ape visual systems (as well as monkey visual systems, and indeed those of most other mammals), we can ask whether nonhuman animals experience the same generalized preferences for image statistical features such as natural scene-like power spectra. Our understanding of human visual aesthetics in the context of natural statistical regularities may tell us something about the "aesthetic primitives" that apply across many species. If other ape, primate, and mammal species show maximal preference and acuity for low-level natural scene-like regularities such as $1/f$ scaling, this would be strong evidence for the generality of the perceptibility hypothesis. As such, this finding would open new territory in the study of empirical aesthetics, since other species would be seen to operate on the same foundation of low-level visual biases or preferences. Studies of luminance statistics, color statistics, and other features in nonhuman animals may be profitable for similar reasons.

Spatiotemporal Features in Real Environments

Given the unnaturalness of film cuts, researchers have made efforts toward understanding more naturalistic aesthetic experiences that play out over time, such as museum visits (e.g., Pelowski et al., 2017). However, there is much yet to learn about how the statistics of spatiotemporal patterns of real-world visual stimulation relate to aesthetic experience. Indeed, as we go from considering single images to temporal sequences of images, the space of possible patterns of stimulation expands greatly. In relation to efficient coding of image statistical features, there is evidence that eye movements provide an important transformation of natural scenes (Kuang et al., 2012). However, accurately correlating eye movements in real environments to points of fixation in 3D space remains an unsolved problem.

Deep Learning

A new frontier in image statistics has opened in the recent acceleration in research on computer vision and machine learning systems that employ "deep" artificial neural networks. Such "deep learning" networks (e.g., convolutional neural networks) are powerful because they can learn higher-order spatial regularities of an input class of images. In particular, such systems find regularities by learning a set of basic representational units (i.e., spatial filters) that efficiently characterize commonalities of image structure within that image class. Basic spatial features are learned in lower levels of the network, while higher (deeper) levels use supervised learning to make more abstract associations between those features and semantic or conceptual categories. For example, such systems can learn to distinguish the stylistic category or authorship of patches extracted from artworks, and can match human performance on this task (see e.g., Gatys et al., 2016). It would not be inconceivable for such a system to learn to distinguish between aesthetic preferences of individual human observers, or to predict individual preference ratings in a given context.

However, the deep learning revolution has been countered by skeptics (e.g., Lake et al., 2017) who argue that a given deep learning network's performance is often poor when trained with a different set of images, applied to a different set of test images, or deployed to a related but distinct task. It is also impossible to interrogate a deep learning model to understand how it achieves a particular result since its "knowledge" consists entirely of thousands or millions of network weights, which together comprise a statistical model. That is, such models do not specify or describe mechanistic or functional relationships among real-world variables.

Thus, deep learning models that learn an individual's aesthetic taste might capture subtle higher-order idiosyncrasies in a particular set of images, and learn to associate these idiosyncrasies with what the subject reports to be their preference for a given tested image. Deep learning might then be able to accurately predict the individual's aesthetic judgments of previously untested images from the same set. However, even highly accurate models of this kind would likely fail in a different but related task or context. In addition, such models do not contribute to explaining human aesthetic preferences or their neural underpinnings.

In contrast, what is powerful about considering natural regularities in image statistical features is that we can generate explanatory models—at least about constraints on aggregate taste—which align with efficient neurobiological mechanisms in human vision.

ACKNOWLEDGMENTS

Thanks to Chris Redies, Andy Gartus, Patrick Markey, Helmut Leder, and Ed Vessel for helpful discussions.

NOTE

1. Curiously, we perceive white noise images as having only high frequency structure, despite having equivalent amounts of low, medium, and high frequency structure.

REFERENCES

Anderson, B. L., & Kim, J. (2009). Image statistics do not explain the perception of gloss and lightness. *Journal of Vision*, 9(11), 10.

Arce-Lopera, C., Masuda, T., Kimura, A., Wada, Y., & Okajima, K. (2012). Luminance distribution modifies the perceived freshness of strawberries. *i-Perception*, 3(5), 338.

Atick, J. J., & Redlich A. N. 1992. What does the retina know about natural scenes? *Neural Computing*, 4, 196–210.

Attewell, D., & Baddeley, R. J. (2007). The distribution of reflectances within the visual environment. *Vision Research*, 47(4), 548–554.

Attneave, F. (1954). Some informational aspects of visual perception. *Psychology Reviews, 61,* 183–193.

Bak, P., Tang, C., & Wiesenfeld, K. (1987). Self-organized criticality: An explanation of the 1/f noise. *Physical Review Letters, 59*(4), 381.

Bell, A. J., & Sejnowski, T. J. (1997). The "independent components" of natural scenes are edge filters. *Vision Research, 37,* 3327–3338.

Biederman, I., & Vessel, E. A. (2006). Perceptual pleasure and the brain: A novel theory explains why the brain craves information and seeks it through the senses. *American Scientist, 94*(3), 247–253.

Brachmann, A., Barth, E., & Redies, C. (2017). Using CNN features to better understand what makes visual artworks special. *Frontiers in Psychology, 8,* 830.

Brachmann, A., & Redies, C. (2017). Computational and experimental approaches to visual aesthetics. *Frontiers in Computational Neuroscience, 11,* 102.

Brady, N., & Field, D. J. (2000). Local contrast in natural images: Normalisation and coding efficiency. *Perception, 29,* 1–15.

Chandler, D. M., & Field, D. J. (2007). Estimates of the information content and dimensionality of natural scenes from proximity distributions. *The Journal of the Optical Society of America A, 24,* 922–941.

Cutting, J. E. (2014). How light and motion bathe the silver screen. *Psychology of Aesthetics, Creativity, and the Arts, 8*(3), 340.

Cutting, J. E., Brunick, K. L., DeLong, J. E., Iricinschi, C., & Candan, A. (2011). Quicker, faster, darker: Changes in Hollywood film over 75 years. *i-Perception, 2*(6), 569–576.

Cutting, J. E., DeLong, J. E., & Nothelfer, C. E. (2010). Attention and the evolution of Hollywood film. *Psychological Science, 21*(3), 432–439.

Dror, R. O., Leung, T. K., Adelson, E. H., & Willsky, A. S. (2001). Statistics of real-world illumination. Proceedings of the 2001 IEEE Computer Society Conference on Computer Vision and Pattern Recognition. CVPR 2001, Kauai, HI, USA, 2001, pp. II–II.

Fernandez, D., & Wilkins, A. J. (2008). Uncomfortable images in art and nature. *Perception, 37,* 1098–1113.

Field, D. J. (1994). What is the goal of sensory coding? *Neural Computation, 6*(4), 559–601.

Fleming, R. W. (2014). Visual perception of materials and their properties. *Vision Research, 94,* 62–75.

Gatys, L. A., Ecker, A. S., & Bethge, M. (2016). Image style transfer using convolutional neural networks. *2016 IEEE Conference on Computer Vision and Pattern Recognition (CVPR),* 2414–2423.

Geisler, W. S. (2008). Visual perception and the statistical properties of natural scenes. *Annual Review of Psychology, 59,* 167–192.

Gilden, D. L. (2001). Cognitive emissions of 1/f noise. *Psychological Review, 108*(1), 33.

Graham, D. J. (2011). Visual perception: Lightness in a high dynamic range world. *Current Biology, 21*(22), R914–R916.

Graham, D. J., Chandler, D. M., & Field, D. J. (2006). Can the theory of "whitening" explain the center-surround properties of retinal ganglion cell receptive fields? *Vision Research, 46,* 2901–2913.

Graham, D. J., & Field, D. J. (2007). Statistical regularities of art images and natural scenes: Spectra, sparseness and nonlinearities. *Spatial Vision, 21,* 149–164.

Graham, D. J., & Field, D. J. (2008a). Variations in intensity statistics for representational and abstract art, and for art from the eastern and western hemispheres. *Perception, 37,* 1341–1352.

Graham, D. J., & Field, D. J. (2008b). Global nonlinear compression of natural luminances in painted art. *Computer Image Analysis in the Study of Aart, 6810*, 68100K.

Graham, D. J., Friedenberg, J. D., McCandless, C. H., & Rockmore, D. N. (2010). Preference for artwork: Similarity, statistics, and selling price. *Proceedings of SPIE: Human Vision and Electronic Imaging, 7527*, 75271A.

Graham, D., & Meng, M. (2011a). Altered spatial frequency content in paintings by artists with schizophrenia. *i-Perception, 2*(1), 1–9.

Graham, D. J., & Meng, M. (2011b). Artistic representations: clues to efficient coding in human vision. *Visual Neuroscience, 28*(4), 371–379.

Graham, D.J., Pallett, P. M., Meng, M., & Leder, H. (2014). Representation and aesthetics of the human face in portraiture. *Art & Perception, 2*(1–2), 75–98.

Graham, D. J., & Redies, C. (2010). Statistical regularities in art: Relations with visual coding and perception. *Vision Research, 50*(16), 1503–1509.

Graham, D., Schwarz, B., Chatterjee, A., & Leder, H. (2016). Preference for luminance histogram regularities in natural scenes. *Vision Research, 120*, 11–21.

Graham, D., Stockinger, S., & Leder, H. (2013). An island of stability: art images and natural scenes–but not natural faces–show consistent esthetic response in Alzheimer's-related dementia. *Frontiers in Psychology, 4*, 107.

Grebenkina, M., Brachmann, A., Bertamini, M., Kaduhm, A., & Redies, C. (2018). Edge-orientation entropy predicts preference for diverse types of man-made images. *Frontiers in Neuroscience, 12*, 678.

Halpern, A. R., Ly, J., Elkin-Frankston, S., & O'Connor, M. G. (2008). "I know what I like": stability of aesthetic preference in Alzheimer's patients. *Brain and Cognition, 66*(1), 65–72.

Halpern, A. R., & O'Connor, M. G. (2013). Stability of art preference in frontotemporal dementia. *Psychology of Aesthetics, Creativity, and the Arts, 7*(1), 95.

Hasson, U., Landesman, O., Knappmeyer, B., Vallines, I., Rubin, N., & Heeger, D. J. (2008). Neurocinematics: The neuroscience of film. *Projections, 2*(1), 1–26.

Hönekopp, J. (2006). Once more: is beauty in the eye of the beholder? Relative contributions of private and shared taste to judgments of facial attractiveness. *Journal of Experimental Psychology: Human Perception and Performance, 32*, 199–209.

Jones-Smith, K., & Mathur, H. (2006). Fractal analysis: Revisiting Pollock's drip paintings. *Nature, 444*(7119), E9.

Jung, S. K., Lee, J. H., Kakizaki, H., & Jee, D. (2012). Prevalence of myopia and its association with body stature and educational level in 19-year-old male conscripts in Seoul, South Korea. *Investigative Ophthalmology & Visual Science, 53*(9), 5579–5583.

Ke, Y., Tang, X., & Jing, F. (2006). The design of high-level features for photo quality assessment. *2006 IEEE Computer Society Conference on Computer Vision and Pattern Recognition (CVPR'06), 1*, 419–426.

Knill, D. C., Field, D., & Kersten, D. (1990). Human discrimination of fractal images. *The Journal of the Optical Society of America A, 7*(6), 1113–1123.

Kuang, X., Poletti, M., Victor, J. D., & Rucci, M. (2012). Temporal encoding of spatial information during active visual fixation. *Current Biology, 22*(6), 510–514.

Kube, P., & Pentland, A. (1988). On the imaging of fractal surfaces. *IEEE Transactions on Pattern Analysis and Machine Intelligence, 10*(5), 704–707.

Lake, B. M., Ullman, T. D., Tenenbaum, J. B., & Gershman, S. J. (2017). Building machines that learn and think like people. *Behavioral and Brain Sciences, 40*, e253. doi:10.1017/S0140525X16001837

Laughlin, S. B. (1981) A simple coding procedure enhances a neuron's information capacity. *Z. Naturforsch*, 36c, 910–912.

Leder, H., Goller, J., Rigotti, T., & Forster, M. (2016). Private and shared taste in art and face appreciation. *Frontiers in Human Neuroscience, 10*, 155. doi:10.3389/fnhum.2016.00155

Linhares, J. M. M., Pinto, P. D., & Nascimento, S. M. C. (2008). The number of discernible colors in natural scenes. *The Journal of the Optical Society of America A, 25*(12), 2918–2924.

Mandelbrot, B. B. (1982). *The fractal geometry of nature* (Vol. 1). New York: WH Freeman.

Martinez, A. M., & Benavente, R. (1998). The AR face database. CVC Technical Report, 24.

Masuda, O., & Nascimento, S. M. (2012). Lighting spectrum to maximize colorfulness. *Optics Letters, 37*(3), 407–409.

Mather, G. (2013). *The psychology of visual art: Eye, brain and art.* Cambridge, England: Cambridge University Press.

Mather, G. (2018). Visual Image Statistics in the History of Western Art. *Art & Perception, 6*(2–3), 97–115.

Martinez-Conde, S., Otero-Millan, J., & Macknik, S. L. (2013). The impact of microsaccades on vision: Towards a unified theory of saccadic function. *Nature Reviews Neuroscience, 14*, 83–96.

McManus, I. C., Stöver, K., & Kim, D. (2011). Arnheim's Gestalt theory of visual balance: Examining the compositional structure of art photographs and abstract images. *i-Perception, 2*(6), 615–647.

Montagner, C., Linhares, J. M., Vilarigues, M., & Nascimento, S. M. (2016). Statistics of colors in paintings and natural scenes. *The Journal of the Optical Society of America A, 33*(3), A170–A177.

Muth, C., Raab, M. H., & Carbon, C. C. (2016). Semantic stability is more pleasurable in unstable episodic contexts. On the relevance of perceptual challenge in art appreciation. *Frontiers in Human Neuroscience, 10*, 43.

Nadal, M., & Skov, M. (2018). The pleasure of art as a matter of fact. *Proceedings of the Royal Society London B: Biological Sciences, 285*(1875), 20172252.

Nascimento, S. M., Linhares, J. M., Montagner, C., João, C. A., Amano, K., Alfaro, C., & Bailão, A. (2017). The colors of paintings and viewers' preferences. *Vision Research, 130*, 76–84.

Nascimento, S. M. C., & Masuda, O. (2014). Best lighting for visual appreciation of artistic paintings—experiments with real paintings and real illumination. *The Journal of the Optical Society of America A, 31*(4), A214–A219.

Normant, F., & Tricot, C. (1991). Method for evaluating the fractal dimension of curves using convex hulls. *Physical Review A, 43*(12), 6518.

Olshausen, B. A., & Field, D. J. (1996). Emergence of simple-cell receptive field properties by learning a sparse code for natural images. *Nature, 381*, 607–609.

Otaka, H., Shimakura, H., & Motoyoshi, I. (2019). Perception of human skin conditions and image statistics. *Journal of the Optical Society of America A, 36*, 1609–1616.

Palmer, S. E., & Schloss, K. B. (2010). An ecological valence theory of human color preference. *Proceedings of the National Academy of Sciences, 107*(19), 8877–8882.

Pelowski, M., Forster, M., Tinio, P. P., Scholl, M., & Leder, H. (2017). Beyond the lab: An examination of key factors influencing interaction with "real" and museum-based art. *Psychology of Aesthetics, Creativity, and the Arts, 11*(3), 245.

Prescott, N., & Graham, D. J. (2020). Face Representation and Perceptual Processing in Mask-making. PsyArXiv, doi:10.31234/osf.io/mdpaz<http://osf.io/mdpaz> Retrieved from psyarxiv.com/mdpaz<http://psyarxiv.com/mdpaz>

Pugach, C., Leder, H., & Graham, D. J. (2017). How stable are human aesthetic preferences across the lifespan? *Frontiers in Human Neuroscience*, *11*, 289.

Redies, C., & Brachmann, A. (2017). Statistical image properties in large subsets of traditional art, bad art, and abstract art. *Frontiers in Neuroscience*, *11*, 593.

Redies, C., Brachmann, A., & Wagemans, J. (2017). High entropy of edge orientations characterizes visual artworks from diverse cultural backgrounds. *Vision Research*, *133*, 130–144.

Redies, C., Hasenstein, J., & Denzler, J. (2007a). Fractal-like image statistics in visual art: Similarity to natural scenes. *Spatial Vision*, *21*(1), 137–148.

Redies, C., Hänisch, J., Blickhan, M., & Denzler, J. (2007b). Artists portray human faces with the Fourier statistics of complex natural scenes. *Network: Computation in Neural Systems*, *18*(3), 235–248.

Rhodes, G., Peters, M., Lee, K., Morrone, M. C., & Burr, D. (2005). Higher-level mechanisms detect facial symmetry. *Proceedings of the Royal Society of London B: Biological Sciences*, *272*(1570), 1379–1384.

Rogowitz, B. E., & Voss, R. F. (1990). Shape perception and low-dimensional fractal boundaries. *Proceedings of SPIE*, *1249*, 387–394.

Ruderman, D. L. (1994). The statistics of natural images. *Network: Computation in Neural Systems*, *5*(4), 517–548.

Ruderman, D. L., & Bialek, W. (1994). Statistics of natural images: Scaling in the woods. *Physical Review Letters*, *73*(6), 814–817.

Schloss, K. B., Strauss, E. D., & Palmer, S. E. (2013). Object color preferences. *Color Research & Application*, *38*(6), 393–411.

Schweinhart, A. M., & Essock, E. A. (2013). Structural content in paintings: Artists overregularize oriented content of paintings relative to the typical natural scene bias. *Perception*, *42*(12), 1311–1332.

Simoncelli, E. P., & Olshausen, B. A. (2001). Natural image statistics and neural representation. *Annual Review of Neuroscience*, *24*(1), 1193–1216.

Soille, P., & Rivest, J. F. (1996). On the validity of fractal dimension measurements in image analysis. *Journal of Visual Communication and Image Representation*, *7*(3), 217–229.

Spehar, B., Wong, S., van de Klundert, S., Lui, J., Clifford, C. W. G., & Taylor, R. (2015). Beauty and the beholder: The role of visual sensitivity in visual preference. *Frontiers in Human Neuroscience*, *9*, 514.

Spence, C. (2015). On the psychological impact of food colour. *Flavour*, *4*(1), 21.

Switkes, E., Mayer, M. J., & Sloan, J. A. (1978). Spatial frequency analysis of the visual environment: Anisotropy and the carpentered environment hypothesis. *Vision Research*, *18*, 1393–1399.

Taylor, R. P., Micolich, A. P., & Jonas, D. (1999). Fractal analysis of Pollock's drip paintings. *Nature*, *399*(6735), 422.

Theiler, J. (1990). Estimating fractal dimension. *The Journal of the Optical Society of America A*, *7*(6), 1055–1073.

Van Hateren, J. H., & van der Schaaf, A. (1998). Independent component filters of natural images compared with simple cells in primary visual cortex. *Proceedings of the Royal Society B: Biological Sciences*, *265*, 359–366.

Vessel, E. A., Maurer, N., Denker, A. H., & Starr, G. G. (2018). Stronger shared taste for natural aesthetic domains than for artifacts of human culture. *Cognition*, *179*, 121–131.

Viengkham, C., & Spehar, B. (2018). Preference for fractal-scaling properties across synthetic noise images and artworks. *Frontiers in Psychology, 9*, 1439. doi:10.3389/fpsyg.2018.01439

Wada, Y., Arce-Lopera, C., Masuda, T., Kimura, A., Dan, I., Goto, S. I., Tsuzuki, D. & Okajima, K. (2010). Influence of luminance distribution on the appetizingly fresh appearance of cabbage. *Appetite, 54*(2), 363–368.

Wheatley, J (1973) Putting colour into marketing. *Marketing, October*, 24–29, 67.

Yang, J., Otsuka, Y., Kanazawa, S., Yamaguchi, M. K., & Motoyoshi, I. (2011). Perception of surface glossiness by infants aged 5 to 8 months. *Perception, 40*(12), 1491–1502.

Zhao, Y., Berns, R. S., Taplin, L. A., & Coddington, J. (2008, February). An investigation of multispectral imaging for the mapping of pigments in paintings. *Computer Image Analysis in the Study of Art, 6810*, 681007).

CHAPTER 21

COLOR

OSHIN VARTANIAN

INTRODUCTION

OUR color preferences are an important aspect of our everyday lives, influencing our aesthetic choices in many domains, including consumer products and residential designs. Perhaps not surprisingly, scholars and thinkers have long been fascinated with the *psychological* effects of colors (see Elliot, 2019). For example, Johann Wolfgang von Goethe (1810/1967), Wilhelm Wundt (1897), and Grant Allen (1877) all pondered the impact of colors on feelings, emotions, and arousal (for a review, see Whitfield & Wiltshire, 1990). However, it was Charles Féré (1885, 1887) who appears to have conducted the first quantitative research that focused explicitly on the influence of color on downstream psychological functions (see Elliot, 2019). Specifically, he presented participants with a range of colors (e.g., red, blue, green, and violet) under various conditions—ranging from rooms illuminated with different colors, asking participants to look through colored glass or lenses, and presenting participants colored disks on a rotating presentation device—and was able to show that compared with other colors, red had a stimulating effect as measured by alterations in pulse rate, respiratory patterns, and physical strength.

Since those early years, several hundred studies have been published on color preference in adult humans (Elliot, 2019). However, careful analyses have revealed that many of the studies conducted in the 19th and first half of the 20th century on this topic suffered from a range of methodological shortcomings that rendered their results "generally worthless" (McManus, Jones, & Cottrell, 1981, p. 651). The methodological problems included reliance on nonrepresentative and small samples, insufficient color specification and standardization, lack of control over extraneous variables (e.g., background color and illumination), and atheoretical and underspecified means of measuring psychological responses to manipulations of color characteristics (Elliot, 2019; Gelineau, 1981; Valdez & Mehrabian, 1994; Whitfield & Wiltshire, 1990). However, since about the middle of the 20th century, color preference has been studied with substantial experimental rigor and sophistication, in the process yielding valid and reliable findings about this phenomenon. It is largely to this body of work that we turn to review our current understanding of color preference.

A System for Single Color Preference

We will discuss color preference in relation to the three properties based on which color stimuli are characterized: hue (i.e., wavelength or "basic color"), brightness (i.e., value or black-to-white quality), and saturation (i.e., chroma or purity/vividness). The well-known Munsell color system represents colors within this three-dimensional space. It is important to point out that unless otherwise stated, the literature discussed in this section concerns measurements based on single colors collected within context-free experimental designs.

Hue

Regarding hue, a number of early but well-conducted studies have already demonstrated that participants prefer the color blue the most, and yellow the least. For example, Granger (1955) instructed participants to rank order a set of Munsell colors based on preference. The results demonstrated that with remarkable similarity, participants preferred hues in the order blue, green, purple, red, and yellow. In turn, Guilford and Smith (1959) instructed their participants to rate Munsell color chips in terms of preference. Their results also demonstrated high consistency among the raters, and yielded a rank ordering of hues very similar to Granger (1955): blue, green, purple, violet, red, orange, yellow. Next, Helson and Lansford (1970) used a large set of Munsell color chips, and demonstrated that the participants preferred hues in the order blue, green, red, purple, yellow. These early studies using a standardized set of colors demonstrated consistently that people prefer blue the most, and yellow the least (see also Eysenck, 1941).

However, it is also important to note that despite group-level consistencies across studies, there are substantial individual differences in color preference. For example, despite showing a preference for blue and a dislike for yellow, McManus et al. (1981) noted that there were notable individual differences in taste: some participants preferred blue over yellow, whereas others preferred the opposite pattern, and yet others liked both hues. These observed differences in preference are reminiscent of early critics of this area of research such as Cohn (1894), von Allesch (1925), Dorcus (1926), and Chandler (1934), who felt that color preferences were too idiosyncratic to be amenable to systematic study. Such individual differences in the face of group-level regularities are also apparent in the results of more recent studies that draw on state-of-the-art methodologies for examining color preferences. For example, Palmer and Schloss (2010) administered 32 colors that were chosen systematically from the Munsell color system based on the perceptually salient dimensions of hue, brightness, and saturation to 48 participants, one at a time and in random order. In the color-preference condition they were instructed to rate how much they liked each color on a scale ranging from "not at all" to "very much" by sliding the cursor along the response scale and clicking to record their response. The expected hue preference profile was replicated, reflected in a clear preference maximum at blue, and a preference minimum at yellow to yellow-green. However, as illustrated in Schloss and Palmer (2017), the data were also marked by large individual differences in the shape of this profile among the 48 participants (Figure 21.1). To demonstrate this variation, the investigators calculated two sets of correlations. First, they computed the Pearson correlation coefficient between the mean preference z-scores for the eight hues in Figure 21.1 and the same participants' ratings of how blue vs. yellow the hues of these colors appeared to be. This correlation was strong and statistically significant, $r = .92$, $p < .01$. Next, they calculated the analogous correlation, but separately for each of the 48 participants whose data appear in Figure 21.1 (see thin gray lines). Those correlations exhibited a large spread, ranging from $r = .89$ ($p < .01$) to $r = .41$ ($p = .31$). This large spread demonstrates empirically that the grouped-average preference profile only reflects the pattern for some but not all participants in

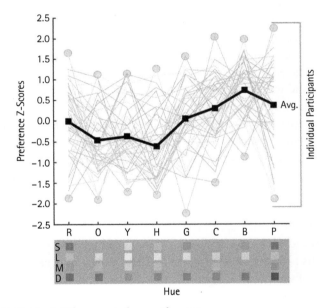

FIGURE 21.1. Individual differences in hue preference.
Z-scores of hue preference functions, after ratings were averaged over the saturated (S), light (L), muted (M), and dark (D) colors within each hue, for individual participants (thin gray curves) and averaged over participants (thick black curve). The x-axis represents hue (red, orange, yellow, chartreuse, green, cyan, blue, and purple). The colored squares below the x-axis approximate the Berkeley Color Project 32 (BCP-32) colors.

Source: Reprinted from *Vision Research*, 141, Karen B. Schloss and Stephen E. Palmer, 'An ecological framework for temporal and individual differences in color preferences', pp. 95–108, Figure 1, doi.org/10.1016/j.visres.2017.01.010

the sample, and that "for every individual who loves a given hue, there is another who hates it" (Schloss & Palmer, 2017, p. 96). Interest in uncovering the psychological and neurological bases for such important individual variation in color preference is reminiscent of similar approaches to understanding the common vs. shared aspects of aesthetic preference in various domains in empirical aesthetics, ranging from faces and scenes to visual art and architecture (Hönekopp, 2006; Vessel, Maurer, Denker, & Starr, 2018), and will likely be a fruitful area of inquiry in hue preference as well.

Furthermore, from an evolutionary perspective, McManus et al. (1981) pointed out that a preference for blue has also been shown to be the case in rhesus monkeys (Humphrey, 1972; Sahgal, Pratt, & Iversen, 1975) and pigeons (Sahgal and Iversen, 1975), although there, too, not all animals exhibited the same preference pattern (Karr & Carter, 1970). This suggests that when brightness and saturation are properly controlled for, then the animal and human data in the domain of hue preferences are largely similar. Such patterns of data suggest that there might be a common biological mechanism that underlies hue preference across species, similar to what has been proposed in other cases where humans and nonhuman animals exhibit similar aesthetic preference patterns in relation to other variables (see Munar, Gómez-Puerto, Call, & Nadal, 2015). Although there might be some ethological arguments in support of that view for color preference (Humphrey, 1976), clearly more empirical data are needed to substantiate it. Nevertheless, increasing our understanding of the evolutionary and biological underpinnings of hue preference is likely to lead to improved mechanistic explanations of this well-established effect.

Interestingly, and clearly relevant to considerations regarding the evolutionary and biological underpinnings of hue preference, there are lines of research that have focused on hue preference in infants, as well as cross-cultural differences in this effect. Regarding the former, there are a number of serious methodological issues that need to be overcome to enable the collection of valid and reliable data. First, and because of difficulties due to lack of verbalization ability in infants, viewing patterns in terms of duration and/ or precedence are used as implicit measures of preference (Teller, 1979). Second, as noted by Palmer and Schloss (2016), great care has to be taken to control for other variables to enable inferences about hue specifically, including luminance, brightness, discriminability, colorimetric purity, and saturation. Furthermore, it is necessary to wait at least until 3–4 months before studying infants to allow sufficient time for the development and maturation of short-wavelength sensitive cones, in the absence of which the infant will be functionally color deficient relative to adults (Palmer & Schloss, 2016). Elliot's (2019) review of this body of work demonstrated that although sample sizes for such infant studies have varied greatly—from one (Marsden, 1903; Myers, 1908; Valentine, 1914; Woolley, 1909) to 235 (Zemach, Chang, & Teller, 2007)—there is substantial evidence to suggest that red might be the most preferred color in infants (Adams, 1987; Franklin, Bevis, Ling, & Hurlbert, 2010; Franklin, Gibbons, Chittenden, Alvarez, & Taylor, 2012; Holden & Bosse, 1900; Jadva, Hines, & Golombok, 2010; Maier, Barchfeld, Elliot, & Pekrun, 2009; McDougall, 1908; Staples, 1932; Woolley, 1909). Of particular importance to the discussion at hand, Palmer and Schloss (2016) have pointed out that in relation to less saturated but better matched colors, not only is there a preference for red, but the preferences vary primarily on the red-to-green dimension rather than the blue-to-yellow dimension (Franklin et al., 2010). This suggests that experience and/or maturation likely play important roles in the development of hue preferences in adults. Despite such findings, it is also important to point out that preference for red hue in infants is far from universal. For example, when preference is measured for highly saturated colors, then the hue preference function appears to be quite similar to what is observed in adults—with a maximum around blue and a minimum around yellow to yellow-green (Teller et al., 2004). In other words, as is the case in adults, individual differences also exist among infants.

As noted by Elliot (2019), a largely similar conclusion can be drawn from the cross-cultural data, where different hue preference patterns have been observed in non-Western cultures and nonindustrialized societies (e.g., Al-Rasheed, 2015; Choungourian, 1968; D'Hondt & Vandewiele, 1983; Madden, Hewett, & Roth, 2000; Saito, 1996, 2016; Sorokowski, Sorokowska, & Witzel, 2014; Taylor, Clifford, & Franklin, 2013). On balance, it seems that despite well-established regularities among adults in Western cultures, hue preference is at least in part shaped by experience, as well as possibly developmental maturation.

Saturation

Although the literature involving the effect of saturation on preference is not nearly as large as the literature on hue preference, a number of fairly stable regularities have nevertheless emerged from the available data. Specifically, it has been shown that adults generally prefer colors of higher than lower saturation (McManus et al., 1981; Ou, Luo, Woodcock, & Wright, 2004; Palmer & Schloss, 2010), although colors of extremely high levels of saturation are not liked because of appearing "too vivid" (Granger, 1955). In addition, preference in relation to highly saturated colors has also been shown to vary by culture (see Palmer, Schloss, & Sammartino, 2013).

Brightness

The brightness of color has been shown to impact psychological states. For example, Valdez and Mehrabian (1994) demonstrated that the pleasure derived from a color patch was positively and most strongly influenced by its brightness. Brightness has also been associated with positivity (Specker et al., 2018), although the effect is stronger when measured implicitly than when measured explicitly (Specker & Leder, 2018). However, preference for brightness is not nearly as unequivocal as it is for hue, or even saturation. For example, in their review of this literature, Palmer et al. (2013) noted that although Western adults tend to prefer brighter colors, at least up to a point (Guilford & Smith, 1959; McManus et al., 1981), this is not always the case (Palmer & Schloss, 2010). The cause of this divergent pattern of results is not entirely clear. In their review of this literature, Palmer et al. (2013) do point out that brightness is confounded with saturation across hues, and because people generally prefer highly saturated colors, what this means is that different hues will have their peak preference at different brightness levels (Guilford & Smith 1959). As such, it is difficult to consider the effect of brightness on color preference without taking saturation into account as well.

Context Effects for Single Colors

The clear advantage of studying preference levels for context-free color patches is that this method provides the highest degree of experimental control over extraneous variables, in particular semantic influences. However, it is also a fact of life that we do not typically observe colors in context-free patches. Rather, we view and experience them as part of our environment, typically embedded within objects. As such, it is fair to ask whether the preference patterns that have been observed above for hue, saturation, and brightness also hold for actual or imagined objects that embody those colors. Interestingly, there has been much less research on color preferences situated in context, compared with studying the impact of context-free colors. Holmes and Buchanan (1984) instructed their participants to report verbally their favorite colors for a number of items (e.g., automobile), and then compared those context-dependent reports with their reports of context-free favorite colors. They found clear divergences between favorite colors under the two conditions. For example, certain colors that were never reported as a favorite in the context-free condition were nevertheless reported as a favorite in the context-dependent condition (e.g., the color brown for carpets and sofas). The authors concluded that "color preference cannot be asked independently of an object if that color preference is to have interpretive significance" (Holmes & Buchanan, 1984, p. 423). In turn, Saito (1983) presented participants with chips of 50 colors as well as the shape of an automobile with the identical colors, and instructed them to make preference judgments of the color chips with and without the shape in the experiment. The results demonstrated that there were some similarities in hue preference between the context-free and context-dependent conditions, but also marked differences in relation to saturation and brightness. Specifically, saturated and lighter colors were liked more in the context-free condition, whereas darker colors were liked more in the context-dependent condition.

Schloss, Strauss, and Palmer (2013) have conducted perhaps the most systematic study to date for examining the effect of context on color preference. Here I will focus on only a subset of their findings. In Experiment 1, in the context-free condition participants were presented with patches of 37 colored squares, and asked to rate how much they liked each color on a scale ranging from "not at all" to "very much." In turn, in the context-dependent condition, they were asked to imagine how much they liked various objects (i.e., walls, trim, couches, throw pillows, T-shirts, dress-shirts/blouses, and neckties/scarves) in those same 37 colors. Their results demonstrated that hue preferences for contextless squares generalize relatively well to hue preferences for imagined objects. However, there were a few exceptions. For example, participants liked purple objects relatively less than they liked purple contextless squares. In contrast to hue preference, major differences were observed in relation to saturation and brightness between the context-free and context-dependent conditions. For example, although previous research had shown that in general people tend to like more saturated over less saturated color patches, the results of Experiment 1 demonstrated that participants expressed lower preference for saturated colors for every object context tested. In addition, whereas preference for context-free color patches was relatively unaffected by variation in brightness, the experimenters observed greater preferences for most objects as they became darker, although wall and trim color preferences increased as the colors became lighter. As noted by the authors, preference for lighter wall and trim colors might be related to the notion of culturally conditioned appropriateness for different object types (see Sivik, 1974). Specifically, given that in naturalistic settings wall and trim colors tend to be light rather than dark, it is possible that the participants reported higher judgments of aesthetic preference for those color–object matches due to the higher degree of color–object appropriateness. In turn, in Experiment 2, they compared preference levels for imagined versus depicted object colors for a subset of their stimuli used in Experiment 1 (i.e., T-shirts, couches, walls, and two types of cars (VW Bugs and luxury sedans)). They opted to focus on a subset of objects from Experiment 1 so that they could compare the results of the two experiments with a manageable number of trials for a single experimental session, and included two cars to conduct within-category comparisons. The results demonstrated that despite some minor differences, preference profiles for imagined object colors were largely similar to the preference profiles when participants viewed pictures of the same objects—as exhibited by the high correlations observed between average color preferences for the imagined and depicted objects. In general, this overall pattern of results suggests that context—whether imagined or depicted—impacts color preference in relation to saturation and brightness more so than it does in relation to hue. As noted by Palmer and Schloss (2016), an additional factor to take into consideration in relation to context consists of our emotional reactions to various colors in different contexts. For example, people tend to prefer room colors that correspond to and reflect their desired feelings when inhabiting the room (Manav, 2007). Such findings suggest that the colors we prefer in specific contexts are also modulated by our feelings associated with those contexts.

WHY DO WE LIKE THE COLORS THAT WE DO?

Perhaps even more interesting than figuring out which colors we like is understanding the roots of our color preferences. In their review of this literature, Palmer et al. (2013) discussed four theories that have been proposed to explain our preferences for single colors (see also Palmer & Schloss, 2016). The first is a physiologically based theory proposed by Hurlbert and Ling (2007), according to which people's color preferences depend on a weighted average of cone contrasts relative to the background color, likely computed very early in visual processing based on the following fundamental neuronal mechanisms that encode colors: L-M ("red–green") and S-(L+M) ("blue–yellow"), where S, M, and L represent the outputs of cones maximally sensitive to short, medium, and long wavelengths of light.

The second theory is similar but purely psychophysical, according to which color preferences depend on the conscious appearance of colors (see Palmer & Schloss, 2010). This theory can be tested by using a weighted average of *observer-rated* redness-greenness, blueness-yellowness, saturation, and lightness of each color to predict preference levels. The third theory is based on emotion associations. Specifically, it has been proposed that people like colors to the extent that they like the emotions that are evoked by or associated with those colors (Ou et al., 2004).

Finally, according to the ecological valence theory (EVR), Palmer and Schloss (2010) have proposed that people's preferences for a color might be determined by the extent to which they like or dislike all of the environmental objects that are associated with that color. For example, our preference for blue might be based on our positive associations with clear skies and clean water, whereas our dislike for brown might be based on our negative associations with feces and rotting food. In a head-to-head comparison of the explanatory power of these four theories, Palmer and Schloss (2010) computed their respective model fits with an identical dataset, and found that they accounted for 37% (cone-opponent contrast model), 60% (color-appearance theory), 55% (color-emotion theory), and 80% (EVR) of the variance in observed preference ratings. Further experimental support for EVR was provided by Strauss, Schloss, and Palmer (2013), who demonstrated that color preferences could be changed by exposure to affectively biased samples of colored objects, offering confirmation for the idea that preferences for colored objects can causally influence preferences for their corresponding colors.

FROM SINGLE COLORS TO COLOR COMBINATIONS

The overwhelming majority of research on color preference has involved the study of specific colors in isolation. However, there is good reason to study preferences for color *combinations* because in our daily lives, colors are seldom viewed in isolation. Schloss and Palmer's (2011) review of art theoretical and empirical work on this phenomenon suggested that the literature was "riddled with confusions and contradictions," as a function of both methodological as well as conceptual shortcomings (p. 552; see also Elliot, 2019). To address the inconsistencies, they conducted four experiments. Critically, they argued that there are in fact three distinct ways of evaluating perceptual responses to color combinations, and that these distinctions are necessary for clarifying previous problems in the literature: (1) aesthetic preference for a given combination of colors, (2) perception of harmony for a given combination of colors, and (3) preference for a given figural color when it is viewed against a colored background. Building on those conceptual distinctions, they defined *pair preference* as how much an observer likes a given pair of colors as a whole, *pair harmony* as how strongly an observer experiences the combined colors as going or belonging together, and *figural preference* as how much the observer likes the figural color when viewed against a background color (Schloss & Palmer, 2011). The researchers found that pair preference and pair harmony both increase as hue similarity increases. In addition, figural preference increases as hue contrast with the background increases. As noted by Palmer and Schloss (2016), this latter effect is not surprising "because these would produce the strongest simultaneous color contrast effects, thus increasing the perceived saturation of the figural region" (p. 359).

Here, too, it is important to ask why we prefer certain color combinations over others. One reason could be that people have emotional associations with specific color combinations. For example, Schloss, Poggesi, and Palmer (2011) investigated preferences for color combination among students at Berkeley and Stanford, and found that Berkeley students preferred blue and gold whereas Stanford students preferred red and white (i.e., their own school color combinations). It may also be the case that colors that seem to go together are also those that are most likely to co-occur within the same object in natural images (see Palmer & Schloss, 2016). It is clear that more research is needed to explain our preferences for color combinations, including the holistic properties of color compositions in various contexts (see Altmann, Brachmann, & Redies, 2021).

Summary

A substantial body of research exists on human color preference, dating back to the very early days of the discipline of psychology. For single colors viewed out of context, there is a robust preference maximum for blue, and a minimum for yellow. Because infants prefer the color red the most, we can infer that experience and/or maturation play a role in shaping our adult color preferences. People also tend to prefer more saturated to less saturated colors. Theories that draw on physiology, psychophysics, emotion, and ecology have been proposed to explain why we like the colors that we do, with the latter fitting the data best. In addition, we now also know that our color preferences are affected by individual differences, context, and the presence of other colors. It can be concluded that important advances have been made to date to explain the aesthetics of color, although important challenges remain; in particular improved explanations of preference for color combinations. Importantly, this line of research has the potential to expand the scope of aesthetic research further to many applied settings ranging from consumer products to architecture.

REFERENCES

Adams, R. J. (1987). An evaluation of color preference in early infancy. *Infant Behavior & Development, 10,* 143–150. http://dx.doi.org/10.1016/0163-6383(87)90029-4

Al-Rasheed, A. S. (2015). An experimental study of gender and cultural differences in hue preference. *Frontiers in Psychology, 6,* Article 30. http://dx.doi.org/10.3389/fpsyg.2015.00030

Allen, G. (1877). *Physiological aesthetics.* London: Henry S. King & Company.

Altmann, C. S., Brachmann, A., & Redies, C. (2021). Liking of art and the perception of color. *Journal of Experimental Psychology: Human Perception and Performance.* https://doi.org/10.1037/xhp0000771

Chandler, A. R. (1934). *Beauty and human nature: Elements of psychological aesthetics.* New York: D. Appleton-Century Company.

Choungourian, A. (1968). Color preferences and cultural variation. *Perceptual and Motor Skills, 26,* 1203–1206. http://dx.doi.org/10.2466/pms.1968.26.3c.1203

Cohn, J. (1894). Experimentelle Untersuchungen über die Gefuehlsbeto- nung der Farben, Helligkeiten, und ihrer Kombinationen [Experimental investigations on the emotional emphasis of colors]. *Philosophische Studien, 10,* 562–603.

D'Hondt, W., & Vandewiele, M. (1983). Colors and figures in Senegal. *Perceptual and Motor Skills, 56,* 971–978. http://dx.doi.org/10.2466/pms.1983.56.3.971

Dorcus, R. M. (1926). Color preferences and color associations. *The Pedagogical Seminary and Journal of Genetic Psychology, 33,* 399–434. http://dx.doi.org/10.1080/08856559.1926.10532367

Elliot, A. J. (2019). A historically based review of empirical work on color and psychological functioning: Content, methods, and recommendations for future research. *Review of General Psychology, 23,* 177–200.

Eysenck, H. J. (1941). A critical and experimental study of colour preferences. *The American Journal of Psychology, 54,* 385–394. http://dx.doi.org/10.2307/1417683

Féré, C. (1885). Sensation et movement [Sensation and movement]. *Revue Philosophique de la France et de l'Etranger, 20,* 337–368.

Féré, C. (1887). Note sur les conditions physiologiques des émotions [Note on the physiological conditions of emotions]. *Revue Philosophique de la France et de l'Etranger, 24,* 561–581.

Franklin, A., Bevis, L., Ling, Y., & Hurlbert, A. (2010). Biological components of colour preference in infancy. *Developmental Science, 13,* 346–354. http://dx.doi.org/10.1111/j.1467-7687.2009.00884.x

Franklin, A., Gibbons, E., Chittenden, K., Alvarez, J., & Taylor, C. (2012). Infant color preference for red is not selectively context specific. *Emotion, 12,* 1155–1160. http://dx.doi.org/10.1037/a0025333

Gelineau, E. P. (1981). A psychometric approach to the measurement of color preference. *Perceptual and Motor Skills, 53,* 163–174. http://dx.doi.org/10.2466/pms.1981.53.1.163

Granger, G. W. (1955). An experimental study of colour harmony. *Journal of General Psychology, 52,* 21–35. http://dx.doi.org/10.1080/00221309.1955.9918341

Guilford, J. P., & Smith, P. C. (1959). A system of color-preferences. *The American Journal of Psychology, 72,* 487–502. http://dx.doi.org/10.2307/1419491

Helson, H., & Lansford, T. (1970). The role of spectral energy of source and background color in the pleasantness of object colors. *Applied Optics, 9,* 1513–1562. http://dx.doi.org/10.1364/AO.9.001513

Holden, W. A., & Bosse, K. K. (1900). The order of development of color perception and of color preference in the child. *Archives of Ophthalmology, 29,* 261–278.

Holmes, C. B., & Buchanan, J. A. (1984). Color preference as a function of the object described. *Bulletin of the Psychonomic Society, 22*, 423–425.

Hönekopp J. (2006). Once more: is beauty in the eye of the beholder? Relative contributions of private and shared taste to judgments of facial attractiveness. *Journal of Experimental Psychology: Human Perception and Performance, 32*, 199–209. https://doi.org/10.1037/0096-1523.32.2.199

Humphrey, N. K. (1972). Interest and pleasure: Two determinants of a monkey's visual preferences. *Perception, 1*, 395–416.

Humphrey, N. K. (1976). The colour currency of nature. In T. Porter & B. Mikellides (Eds.), *Colour in architecture* (pp. 95–98). London: Studio Vista.

Hurlbert, A., & Ling, Y. (2007). Biological components of sex differences in color preference. *Current Biology, 17*, 623–625.

Jadva, V., Hines, M., & Golombok, S. (2010). Infants' preferences for toys, colors, and shapes: Sex differences and similarities. *Archives of Sexual Behavior, 39*, 1261–1273. http://dx.doi.org/10.1007/s10508-010-9618-z

Karr, A. E., & Carter, D. E. (1970). Colour preferences in the pigeon: Measurement during extinction and during variable-interval reinforcement. *Proceedings of the 78th Annual Convention of the American Psychological Association*. Washington, DC: American Psychological Association.

Madden, T. J., Hewett, K., & Roth, M. S. (2000). Managing images in different cultures: A cross-national study of color meanings and preferences. *Journal of International Marketing, 8*, 90–107. http://dx.doi.org/10.1509/jimk.8.4.90.19795

Maier, M. A., Barchfeld, P., Elliot, A. J., & Pekrun, R. (2009). Context specificity of implicit preferences: The case of human preference for red. *Emotion, 9*, 734–738. http://dx.doi.org/10.1037/a0016818

Manav, B. (2007). Color-emotion associations and color preferences: A case study for residences. *Color Research & Application, 32*, 144–151.

Marsden, R. (1903). Discussion and apparatus: A study of the early color sense. *Psychological Review, 10*, 37–47. http://dx.doi.org/10.1037/h0071933

McDougall, W. (1908). An investigation of the colour sense of two infants. *British Journal of Psychology, 2*, 338–352. http://dx.doi.org/10.1111/j.2044-8295.1908.tb00185.x

McManus, I. C., Jones, A. L., & Cottrell, J. (1981). The aesthetics of colour. *Perception, 10*, 651–666. http://dx.doi.org/10.1068/p100651

Munar, E., Gómez-Puerto, G., Call, J., & Nadal, M. (2015). Common visual preference for curved contours in humans and great apes. *PLoS ONE, 10*, e0141106. https://doi.org/10.1371/journal.pone.0141106

Myers, C. S. (1908). Some observations on the development of the colour sense. *British Journal of Psychology, 2*, 353–362. http://dx.doi.org/10.1111/j.2044-8295.1908.tb00186.x

Ou, L., Luo., M. R., Woodcock, A., & Wright, A. (2004). A study of colour emotion and colour preference. Part III: Colour preference modeling. *Color Research & Application, 29*, 381–389.

Palmer, S. E., & Schloss, K. B. (2010). An ecological valence theory of human color preference. *PNAS Proceedings of the National Academy of Sciences of the United States of America, 107*, 8877–8882. doi: 10.1073/pnas.0906172107

Palmer, S. E., & Schloss, K. B. (2016). Human color preference. In N. Moroney (Ed.), *Encyclopedia of color science and technology* (pp. 354–360). New York: Springer.

Palmer, S. E., Schloss, K. B., & Sammartino, J. (2013). Visual aesthetics and human preference. *Annual Review of Psychology, 64,* 77–107. http://dx.doi.org/10.1146/annurev-psych-120710-100504

Sahgal, A., & Iversen, S. D. (1975). Colour preferences in the pigeon: A behavioural and psycho-pharmacological study. *Psychopharmacologia (Berlin), 43,* 175–179.

Sahgal, A., Pratt, S. R., & Iversen, S. D. (1975). The responsiveness of rhesus monkeys to visual stimuli differing in wavelength and angular orientation. *Journal of the Experimental Analysis of Behaviour, 24,* 377–381.

Saito, M. (1996). A comparative study of color preferences in Japan, China and Indonesia, with emphasis on the preference for white. *Perceptual and Motor Skills, 83,* 115–128. http://dx.doi.org/10.2466/pms.1996.83.1.115

Saito, M. (2016). A comparative study of color preferences in Japan, China and Indonesia, with emphasis on the preference for white. In M. Luo (Ed.), *Encyclopedia of color science and technology* (pp. 514–520). New York: Springer.

Saito, T. (1983). Latent spaces of color preference with and without a context: Using the shape of an automobile as the context. *Color Research & Application, 8,* 101–113.

Schloss, K. B., & Palmer, S. E. (2011). Aesthetic response to color combinations: Preference, harmony, and similarity. *Attention, Perception, & Psychophysics, 73,* 551–571.

Schloss, K. B., & Palmer, S. E. (2017). An ecological framework for temporal and individual differences in color preferences. *Vision Research, 141,* 95–108.

Schloss, K. B., Poggesi, R. M., & Palmer, S. E. (2011). Effects of university affiliation and "school spirit" on color preferences: Berkeley vs. Stanford. *Psychonomic Bulletin & Review, 18,* 498–504.

Schloss, K. B., Strauss, E. D., & Palmer, S. E. (2013). Object color preferences. *Color Research & Application, 38,* 393–411.

Sivik, L. (1974). Colour meaning and perceptual colour dimensions: A study of exterior colours. *Göteborg Psychological Reports, 4,* 1–24.

Sorokowski, P., Sorokowska, A., & Witzel, C. (2014). Sex differences in color preferences transcend extreme differences in culture and ecology. *Psychonomic Bulletin & Review, 21,* 1195–1201. http://dx.doi.org/10.3758/s13423-014-0591-8

Specker, E., & Leder, H. (2018). Looking on the bright side: Replicating the association between brightness and positivity. *Collabra: Psychology, 4, Article 34.* doi: https://doi.org/10.1525/collabra.168

Specker, E., Leder, H., Rosenberg, R., Hegelmaier, L. M., Brinkmann, H., Mikuni, J., & Kawabata, H. (2018). The universal and automatic association between brightness and positivity. *Acta psychologica, 186,* 47–53. https://doi.org/10.1016/j.actpsy.2018.04.007

Staples, R. (1932). The responses of infants to color. *Journal of Experimental Psychology, 15,* 119–141. http://dx.doi.org/10.1037/h0071205

Strauss, E. D., Schloss, K. B., & Palmer, S. E. (2013). Color preferences change after experience with liked/disliked color objects. *Psychonomic Bulletin & Review, 20,* 935–943.

Taylor, C., Clifford, A., & Franklin, A. (2013). Color preferences are not universal. *Journal of Experimental Psychology: General, 142,* 1015–1027. http://dx.doi.org/10.1037/a0030273

Teller, D. Y. (1979). The forced-choice preferential looking procedure: A psychophysical technique for use with human infants. *Infant Behavior and Development, 2,* 135–153.

Teller, D. Y., Civan, A., & Bronson-Castain, K. (2004). Infants' spontaneous color preferences are not due to adult-like brightness variations. *Visual Neuroscience, 21,* 397–401.

Valdez, P., & Mehrabian, A. (1994). Effects of color on emotions. *Journal of Experimental Psychology: General, 123*, 394–409. http://dx.doi.org/10.1037/0096-3445.123.4.394

Valentine, C. W. (1914). The colour perception and colour preferences of an infant during its fourth and eighth months. *British Journal of Psychology, 6*, 363–386. http://dx.doi.org/10.1111/j.2044-8295.1914.tb00099.x

Vessel, E. A., Maurer, N., Denker, A. H., & Starr, G. G. (2018). Stronger shared taste for natural aesthetic domains than for artifacts of human culture. *Cognition, 179*, 121–131. https://doi.org/10.1016/j.cognition.2018.06.009

von Allesch, G. J. (1925). Di ästhetische Erscheinungsweise der farben. *Psychologische Forschung, 6*, 1–91.

von Goethe, J. W. (1810/1967). *Theory of colors* (C. Eastlake, Trans.). London: Frank Cass & Company, LTD.

Whitfield, T. W. A., & Wiltshire, T. J. (1990). Color psychology: A critical review. *Genetic, Social, and General Psychology Monographs, 116*, 385–411.

Woolley, H. T. (1909). Some experiments on the color perceptions of an infant and their interpretation. *Psychological Review, 16*, 363–376. http://dx.doi.org/10.1037/h0074310

Wundt, W. M. (1897). *Outlines of psychology* (C. Judd, Trans.). London: Williams & Norgate. http://dx.doi.org/10.1037/12908-000

Zemach, I., Chang, S., & Teller, D. Y. (2007). Infant color vision: Prediction of infants' spontaneous color preferences. *Vision Research, 47*, 1368–1381. http://dx.doi.org/10.1016/j.visres.2006.09.024

CHAPTER 22

....

THE STUDY OF SYMMETRY IN EMPIRICAL AESTHETICS

....

MARCO BERTAMINI AND GIULIA RAMPONE

Symmetry has a central role in many fields. It has been studied formally in mathematics, but we can see its application also in art, religion, and ornamentation. Early thinkers, like Plato, were fascinated by symmetry. Although he did not discover what we now know as Platonic solids, he based a whole philosophy on them in the treatise *Timaeus*. There are five Platonic solids, which are polyhedra constructed by a set of identical polygonal faces: tetrahedron, cube, octahedron, dodecahedron, and icosahedron. Alternatively, using more than one type of face one can generate the 13 Archimedean solids (like the truncated icosahedron of a typical football with white hexagons and black pentagons). Aristotle also mentions symmetry as a form of beauty in his *Metaphisica*. The fascination continued through the centuries. Since the 19th century the treatment of symmetry has been based on *group theory* in physics and mathematics, and the underlying symmetry transformations can be thought of as operations. Based on this analysis we can then find, for example, that the icosahedron has 120 symmetries.

Our discussion will focus on patterns in two dimensions. Within the Euclidean plane there are four types of rigid transformations that preserve metric properties: translations, rotations, reflections, and glide reflections. These transformations form a symmetry group. For example, the human face is an example of reflection, and the pattern of footprints in the sand is a glide reflection, a combination of a reflection and a translation (Figure 22.1). For patterns that repeat along one dimension there are seven types (known as frieze patterns) and for patterns extending over two dimensions there are 17 types (known as wallpaper patterns) (Grünbaum & Shephard, 1987).

Why is symmetry so interesting to so many people? Mathematicians, such as Hermann Weyl, have noted the close link between symmetry and beauty ("Beauty is bound up with symmetry," Weyl, 1952, p. 1), and more recently Ian Stewart has titled a book *Why Beauty Is Truth: The History of Symmetry* (Stewart, 2007) (words taken from

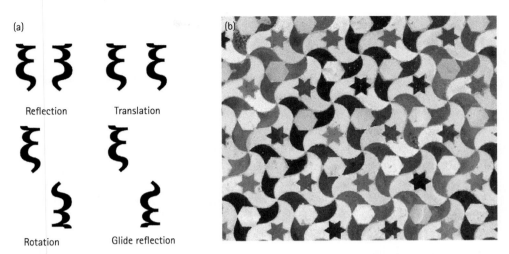

FIGURE 22.1. (A) The four rigid transformations in the Euclidian plane. (B) A digitally enhanced pattern from Alhambra. This is one type of wallpaper pattern, and its formal code is p3 because it has three different rotations of order three (120°), but no reflections or glide reflections.

a poem by Keats). Symmetry can be seen as a form of research strategy used by modern physicists (Zee, 2007). Biologists have also expressed great interest in symmetry. For instance, Darwin mentions symmetry specifically as a type of ornament in sexual selection (Darwin, 1882). In terms of artists, we could mention the fascination of M. C. Escher with the Moorish architecture of the Alhambra in Granada, and in particular with its mosaic patterns (Figure 22.1). In 1936 Escher traveled to Spain and he spent days making detailed drawings of the patterns and tessellations, which then figured in his own work.

Studies of symmetry perception have confirmed that symmetry can be detected quickly and efficiently (Barlow & Reeves, 1979; Julesz, 1971), and influences the salience of a pattern (Mach, 1886; Wenderoth, 1994), speed of responses (Bertamini, Friedenberg, & Kubovy, 1997; Royer, 1981), eye movement exploratory behavior (Locher & Nodine, 1987), and arousal as measured by skin conductance changes (Krupinski & Locher, 1988). For reviews, see Wagemans (1995), Treder (2010), or Bertamini and Makin (2014). In the case of Locher and Nodine (1987) and Krupinski and Locher (1988), the stimuli used were abstract paintings manipulated to add symmetry. With respect to memory, people tend to reproduce symmetric shapes more accurately and to make shapes more symmetrical than the original (Attneave, 1955; Perkins, 1932). Symmetric shapes appear also as more familiar (Brodeur, Chauret, Dion-Lessard, & Lepage, 2011). In summary, it is well established that symmetry is salient and can be detected efficiently by humans and other animals. Neurophysiological studies have also found strong and widespread activation in visual regions in response to presentation of symmetric patterns (for a review, see Bertamini, Silvanto, Norcia, Makin, & Wagemans, 2018).

Symmetry in Visual Arts

Scruton (2009) distinguished four types of beauty: human beauty (attractiveness), natural beauty, everyday beauty, and artistic beauty. We can find examples of symmetry for each of these categories, in the human body, in flowers, in architecture and design, and in recognized traditional and modern artworks. In the case of visual art, the role of symmetry is widespread, and we can find examples across the centuries and in all cultures (Arnheim, 1974; Deregowski, 1972; Washburn & Crowe, 1988).

A famous example of an explicit attempt to incorporate balance and symmetry is Leonardo da Vinci's *Vitruvian Man* (c.1490). It illustrates how human proportions are captured by simple geometrical forms, in particular a circle and a square. Da Vinci is elaborating the ideas of Marcus Vitruvius Pollio, a Roman author and architect from the 1st century BCE. In his book *De architectura* he discusses how important proportions that must guide architecture (in the broad sense) come from the human body. For example, with arms and legs outstretched the body can be placed inside a square and a circle and the navel is the center. Because da Vinci had familiarity with anatomy, in his drawing the arms are raised just as high as the top of the head and the navel is at the center of the circle, but not the square. He also deliberately chose a posture that was not perfectly symmetric, with the feet for example pointing in different directions. This shows that although symmetry can be found in the human body, one can overstate the regularity of the human proportions. It also shows that often artists contrast an overall symmetry with local deviations from regularity. The key proposal in *De architectura*, however, is that what we find pleasing derives from aspects of our physical body (Figure 22.2).

In addition to da Vinci, other Renaissance artists were fascinated by and wrote about symmetry. Albrecht Dürer included an acute rhombohedron (truncated on its axis of

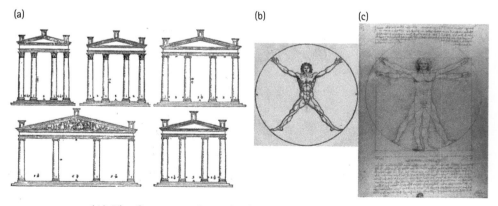

(a) (b) (c)

FIGURE 22.2. (A) The five types of temples listed by Vitruvius, in which spacing between columns is given as multiples of column width. (B) The body of a man inside a circle. These illustrations come from a translation of *De architectura* published in Venice in 1590. (B) Leonardo's *Vitruvian Man* (circa 1490), which is anatomically more accurate.

symmetry) in *Melancolia I* (1514) (Ritterbush, 1983), but also wrote a book on *Symmetry of the Human Body* (published posthumously in 1532).

Many authors have pointed out that we should not confine the study of preference for symmetry to established art forms. As noted by Gombrich (1979) humans like to surround themselves with symmetric objects and patterns. It is interesting that the two major figures in psychology of art of the 20th century, Gombrich and Arnheim, published books that, for all their differences, refer indirectly to symmetry in the title: *The Sense of Order* (Gombrich, 1979) and *The Power of the Centre* (Arnheim, 1982).

Symmetry and Complexity

It is necessary to consider symmetry together with complexity. This issue is central to work of early theoretical discussions in Birkhoff (1884–1944) and in the writing of Berlyne (1960). Birkhoff (1884–1944) was an American mathematician who developed a keen interest in aesthetics. He discussed the role of order, unity, or harmony and suggested that beauty is a direct function of order but decreases with complexity. Symmetry was part of what he referred to as order. He created a set of abstract stimuli and we show two examples in Figure 22.3. These are #1 and #90 in the series (Birkhoff, 1933). These stimuli were later employed in many studies by other researchers with mixed results. For example, Eysenck (1941) noted that some observers preferred simpler shapes and others preferred the more complex shapes.

Berlyne (1960) defined visual complexity in terms of three dimensions: the number of elements, their dissimilarity, and the regularity or irregularity of their arrangement. The presence of symmetry affects the level of objective as well as perceived complexity, something notoriously hard to quantify (Donderi, 2006). One can say that the number of nonredundant elements is reduced. For example, for bilateral symmetry one half of the configuration and a coding of symmetry are sufficient to describe the whole pattern. Various studies have noted how symmetry plays a role in perceived complexity of patterns (e.g., Berlyne, Ogilvie, & Parham, 1968; Chipman, 1977). In perception, the role of the number of transformations that generate a pattern of dots has been shown to predict the subjective "goodness" of that pattern (Garner, 1970). A different approach not based on transformations comes from structural information theory of perception (Leeuwenberg & van der Helm, 2013). Other authors, like Schmidhuber (1997), have claimed that art is based on minimal algorithmic complexity (Kolmogorov complexity).

The concept of symmetry is also closely linked to that of balance. This terminology has a long tradition, and a theoretical discussion can be found in Arnheim's book *The Power of the Centre* (Arnheim, 1982). Arnheim focuses on composition, and the fact that there is always a balance between centric and eccentric forces. This allows Arnheim to break away from a rigid interpretation of order, although it does not provide formal measures that can be used empirically.

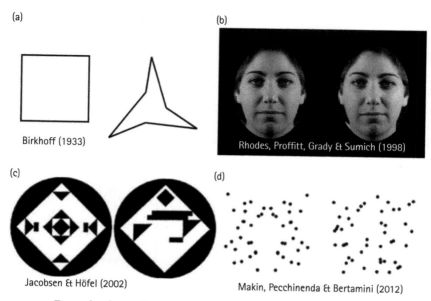

FIGURE 22.3. Example of stimuli used in studies of preference for symmetry. (A) These are two examples from a set of 90 created by Birkhoff (1933). They vary in order and complexity (as defined by Birkhoff). The one on the left has high order and low complexity, and the opposite for the example on the right (they are the first and the last in the original set of 90). (B) Faces manipulated so that the one on the left has perfect symmetry (courtesy of Gillan Rhodes; see Rhodes et al., 1998). The focus of this work was on perceived beauty and attractiveness. (C) Abstract patterns used by Jacobsen and Höfel (2002), symmetry and asymmetry. (D) Abstract patterns used by Makin, Wilton, Pecchinenda, and Bertamini (2012), bilateral symmetry and asymmetry.

EARLY EXPERIMENTAL WORK

Fechner cites symmetry ("symmetrie") approximately 50 times in his book (Fechner, 1876). He uses it as a clear example of visual preference, mentioning the kaleidoscope and the human body as examples. He also lists symmetry together with the golden section as examples of forms that we find pleasant independently from any learned association.

Eisenman (1967) and Eisenman and Rappaport (1967) used abstract shapes and asked participants to select the preferred ones. The stimuli in both studies were the same and included nine asymmetric and three symmetric polygons. The symmetric stimuli were taken from the set introduced by Birkhoff (1933). Eisenman concluded that there was a clear tendency to select symmetric shapes as preferred. Combined with the finding that complex shapes were never selected, this was seen as evidence against a preference for complexity, although only the preference for symmetry was replicated by Eisenman and Gillens (1968). In addition, the paper also suggests that there are individual differences and more creative people may prefer asymmetry to symmetry (see also Eysenck & Castle, 1970).

Eysenck developed a model that differed from Birkhoff's, and tried to support this empirically. He concluded that although order (including symmetry) was a key factor for visual preference, complexity was likely to contribute, and the two factors would interact in a multiplicative way (Eysenck, 1968). Eysenck was also a pioneer of cross-cultural studies of aesthetics. Two studies compared British and Egyptian samples using some Birkhoff stimuli. Symmetry had a similar influence in both cultures. This comparison has recently been replicated by Bode, Helmy, and Bertamini (2017) using abstract stimuli made with black-and-white matrices (see also Makin, Helmy, & Bertamini, 2017).

Preference for symmetry using abstract shapes (polygons) was confirmed by the experiments carried out by Munsinger and Kessen (1964). They concluded that symmetry contributed to preference because it reduced complexity and increased meaningfulness (something observers also rated).

We have already mentioned that Locher and Nodine (1987) and Krupinski and Locher (1988) used paintings manipulated to be more or less symmetric and measured eye movements and skin conductance. It is interesting that hedonic value was in their case reduced by symmetry. This is likely to be a result specific to these stimuli, and the fact that the symmetry was artificial and a deviation from what the artists had created. With respect to type of stimuli, in addition to abstract patterns and artworks, one study tested dynamic configurations (Wright & Bertamini, 2015). These dynamic stimuli were created as symmetric or random configurations of lines. Each line had a local rotation, and the configuration underwent a global transformation: translation, rotation, expansion, horizontal shear. Results confirmed a preference for dynamic symmetric patterns. Expansion was the preferred global dynamic transformation, and shear was the most disliked.

Finally, it is interesting to note that infants as young as 4 months old can discriminate symmetry (Humphrey and Humphrey, 1989), but there is no clear evidence of actual preference for the more symmetric patterns (Bornstein, Ferdinandsen, & Gross, 1981) or faces (Rhodes, Geddes, Jeffery, Dziurawiec, & Clark, 2002) at this age. Recently, Huang, Xue, Spelke, Huang, Zheng, and Peng (2018) have drawn explicit attention to this dissociation between perception and preference for symmetry in infants. Preschool children, when they start to draw, often use symmetry in their drawings, especially rotational symmetry for flowers (Villarroel, Merino, & Antón, 2019).

More Recent Studies and Models

Fechner (1876) had introduced three methods: choice, use, and production. Although production has not been employed as much as the others it can be very informative.

Westphal-Fitch, Oh, and Fitch (2013) gave participants an open-ended production task and a computer interface that constrained the generation of rectangles or complex patterns. They concluded that framing and local symmetries affected what people produce.

New techniques to study preference have also been developed. For example, Makin, Bertamini, Jones, Holmes, & Zanker (2016) used a gaze-driven evolutionary algorithm technique. An eye-tracker identified patterns (phenotypes) that were good at attracting and retaining the gaze of the observer. Resulting fitness scores determined the parameters (genotypes) used to create the next generation of patterns. This procedure tests whether people automatically evaluate symmetry without explicit instruction. When participants looked for symmetry, there was an increase in genes coding for symmetry. When participants looked for the patterns they preferred, there was a smaller increase in symmetry, indicating that people tolerated some imperfection. There was no increase in symmetry during free viewing.

In Leder et al.'s model of visual aesthetic judgment, symmetry is placed among other factors within the early perception analysis stage (Leder, Belke, Oeberst, & Augustin, 2004; see also Leder & Nadal, 2014). In this sense this formal aspect of the stimulus comes before later processing of factors like familiarity, prototypicality, and semantics. A large body of work has focused on symmetry and attractiveness, including the relationship between symmetry and prototypicality. This will be discussed in the following section.

If we look at ornamentation in different cultures, it is easy to find many examples of the use of symmetry (Brain, 1979; Gröning, 2002). This could be a strategy to signal biological fitness. Cárdenas and Harris (2006) tested the rating of attractiveness of human faces and added decorations that varied in symmetry. The addition of symmetric designs to asymmetric faces increased their attractiveness, and conversely the addition of asymmetric designs to symmetric faces decreased attractiveness.

Tinio and Leder (2009) studied the influence of familiarization on preference for symmetry and complexity. They found that massive familiarization generated contrast effects for complexity: participants familiarized with simple stimuli judged complex stimuli more beautiful and vice versa. This contrast effect was not present for symmetry, which appears to be more stable.

In an influential paper, Ramachandran and Hirstein (1999) claimed that artists deploy certain rules or principles to titillate the visual areas of the brain. One of these principles is symmetry. The argument relies on the evolutionary logic mentioned later, but they expand the idea. Symmetry, as a property of living organisms, is an early-warning system and grabs attention to facilitate further processing. It is therefore useful because it is geared toward discovering interesting object-like entities in the environment. Given these premises they say that "it is hardly surprising that we have a built-in aesthetic preference for symmetry" (p. 27).

Of the eight laws of aesthetic experience listed by Ramachandran and Hirstein (1999), in addition to symmetry there is a phenomenon known as "peak shift." This is relevant as one can argue that it applies to symmetry preference. In animal learning, after training with a stimulus, an animal may respond more strongly to the exaggerated version of the training stimulus. For example, if an animal is trained to choose a rectangle over a square the response may be stronger for rectangles that are more elongated than the stimulus used at training. In a study by Jansson, Forkman, and Enquist (2002) chickens were rewarded with two slightly asymmetric crosses that were mirror images of each other. After training, the animals preferred a novel symmetric cross to the asymmetric training stimuli. That is, the preferred stimulus was not the one that they had been rewarded with, but one that was novel but symmetric. The authors conclude that preference for symmetry arises as a consequence of generalization and without any link to quality of the signal.

Hypothesis About Why Symmetry is Linked to Beauty

One popular theory about symmetry and preference is based on an evolutionary hypothesis. During development organisms will deviate from symmetry when they are affected by genetic and environmental stresses. This process produces fluctuating asymmetry, and the degree of asymmetry is a proxy for quality of an individual and, in particular, quality of a mate (Watson & Thornhill, 1994). This role of symmetry in perceived attractiveness is supported by evidence that symmetry in faces and bodies affects preference (Bertamini, Byrne, & Bennett, 2013; Little & Jones, 2003; Little, Jones, & DeBruine, 2011; Perrett, Burt, Penton-Voak, Lee, Rowland, & Edwards, 1999; Rhodes, Proffitt, Grady, & Sumich, 1998), and symmetry as a factor in mating has been documented in many species. Møller and Thornhill (1998) conducted a meta-analysis on data from 42 species and concluded that there is a moderate significant negative relationship between fluctuation asymmetry and mating success.

Although testing symmetry separated from averageness is difficult, Rhodes, Sumich, and Byat (1999) confirmed that symmetric faces are attractive by statistically controlling for averageness. Jones et al. (2001) report evidence in support of the hypothesis that symmetry is a signal of genetic fitness. They found that attractiveness is mediated by a link between judgments of facial symmetry and of apparent health. The literature on attractiveness is vast and we cannot provide an exhaustive review here. We will just mention one last recent paper (Lewis, 2017) because it has demonstrated preference for symmetry in faces under naturalistic conditions (three-dimensional faces presented under rotation and with asymmetric lighting).

However, there is evidence that symmetry is preferred even when it does not serve any biologically relevant function, and as we have seen many studies have used abstract patterns (Eisenman, 1967; Humphrey, 1997). Even in animal work, mating is not the only factor. For example, bees are attracted to flower-like symmetric patterns (Lehrer, Horridge, Zhang, & Gadagkar, 1995; Rodríguez, Gumbert, Hempel de

Ibarra, Kunze, & Giurfa, 2004) and chicks prefer symmetric seeds (Clara, Regolin, & Vallortigara, 2007).

As an alternative view, preference for symmetry may be a byproduct of general properties of the sensory networks (Enquist & Johnstone, 1997; Jansson, Forkman, & Enquist, 2002), and the process of object recognition that needs to be robust to position and orientation changes (Enquist & Arak, 1994). It has been shown that trained networks prefer symmetric patterns because these patterns are close to the average of the training patterns, whether symmetry was present or not in the training set (Johnstone, 1994). This can explain the tuning of the visual system to symmetry but in itself it does not explain preference. To explain preference, one needs to assume that what is processed efficiently is also liked. This link has been made explicitly by various authors (Cavanagh, 2005; Latto, 1995; Zeki, 1999). In Latto's definition an aesthetic primitive is "intrinsically interesting, even in the absence of narrative meaning, because it resonates with the mechanisms of the visual system processing it" (Latto, 1995, p. 68). In this respect, symmetry lends itself as the ideal example of an aesthetic primitive. Other authors have developed the idea of a link between aesthetics and efficient coding by the brain (Redies, 2008).

Another hypothesis, also related to the existence of a tuning of the visual system to symmetry but more indirectly, is known as the fluency hypothesis. Fluency is the subjective ease with which a stimulus is processed. It has been proposed that fluent processing has a positive hedonic value, and that the fluent processing of symmetry directly produces a positive response (Reber, Schwartz, & Winkielman, 2004; Winkielman & Cacioppo, 2001). One possibility is that preference for symmetry is a form of affective misattribution due to the ease of processing symmetric objects (Pecchinenda, Bertamini, Makin, & Ruta, 2014).

It should be stressed that these hypotheses are not exclusive, and that they all capture some aspect of the phenomenon.

Evidence That Symmetry is Not Always Preferred to Asymmetry

Some authors have criticized the simplistic assumption that symmetry is always linked to beauty. For example, McManus (2005) has argued that there is always a tension between symmetry and asymmetry.

Although the examples of symmetry in art are widespread, it has been pointed out that symmetry is more important in Western culture than for instance in Japanese culture, which values asymmetry and irregularity (*fukinsei*) (Zeki, 2013).

Despite the many claims about the fundamental role of symmetry in aesthetics, the evidence provides some important qualifications. As a category, there is evidence that symmetry is linked with positive valence, as evidenced for instance by the implicit association test (IAT) (Bertamini, Makin, & Rampone, 2013; Makin, Pecchinenda, & Bertamini, 2012; Mastandrea, Bartoli, & Carrus, 2011). The IAT measures the strength of association between the category symmetry (represented by abstract patterns) and the category positive valence (represented by words). The strength of this association can be taken as an indirect, and implicit, measure of preference. However, preference measured by IAT does not always match the preference expressed explicitly, in particular in the case of rotational symmetry (Makin, Pecchinenda, & Bertamini, 2012). Bertamini, Makin, and Rampone (2013) confirmed an implicit association between symmetry and positive valence; in addition symmetry was associated with arousal, and with simplicity.

Although these implicit measures are interesting and confirm that people tend to think of symmetry in positive terms, they do not test the idea of a direct positive experience as a result of processing of symmetry. A more direct test of fast affective responses is provided by affective priming. Bertamini, Makin, and Pecchinenda (2013) report a series of experiments in which abstract symmetry was used as a prime, following by words that could have positive or negative valence. Here the evidence is that there is no automatic priming by symmetry of positive words. However, priming can take place under some conditions, in particular when the symmetry category is processed (Bertamini, Makin, & Pecchinenda, 2013).

Pecchinenda et al. (2014) used a priming task that involved reading the target words aloud, and they measured voice onset latency. When the word is read, this response is unique to each target. This has the advantage of avoiding Stroop-like mechanism interference at the response stage. There were faster vocal responses to positive target words preceded by symmetric patterns. In their final experiment, they used the affect misattribution procedure (AMP). The AMP is a variant of the affective priming paradigm in which symmetric and random patterns are presented incidentally, and the targets are unfamiliar and neutral. Results showed that the positive affect elicited by the brief presentation of symmetry (75 ms) was (mis)attributed to the targets (Chinese pictograms).

In the context of the link between symmetry and attractiveness, the evidence is not entirely univocal (see Rhodes, 2006, for discussion and evaluation). For humans and other animals, attractiveness is not always associated with symmetry. In particular there is mixed evidence for a role of symmetry in animal mating strategies (e.g., Dufour & Weatherhead, 1998; Palmer, 1996). With respect to facial attractiveness, some studies found evidence of reduced attractiveness for perfect symmetry, for example using computer generated faces (Zaidel & Deblieck, 2007). Scheib, Gangestad, and Thornhill (1999) and also Zaidel and Hessamian (2010) tested attractiveness of faces when only half of the face was visible. They found that images of half faces were rated as beautiful as the full faces.

Because symmetry is a nonaccidental property, it is associated with the presence of an object (Bertamini, 2010; Tyler, 1995). As we have seen symmetry is preferred across a range of different objects, familiar and abstract. In a recent study, Bertamini, Rampone, Makin, and Jessop (2019) interleaved male faces, female faces, polygons, smoothed versions of the polygons, flowers, and landscapes. For each category there were symmetric and asymmetric stimuli. Participants expressed a rating of beauty and also rated the salience of symmetry (in a separate block of trials). Landscapes that were artificially made to appear symmetric were liked less than the original landscapes, suggesting that symmetry is expected to belong to individual objects and not to scenes.

A recent study (Leder et al., 2019) investigated another factor: the role of art expertise on evaluations of beauty of patterns with different degrees of symmetry and complexity. Unlike the nonart experts, art experts (artists and art-historians) preferred simple and asymmetric shapes. This preliminary evidence suggests that we should update the view of a universal preference for symmetry by recognizing some mitigating factors (e.g. context, culture, personality traits, expertise). We should, however, make a distinction between explicit rating of preference and more indirect measures. Weichselbaum, Leder, & Ansorge (2018) found that art expertise did not alter the preference for symmetric over asymmetric patterns when measured with the IAT.

Moreover, in the study by Bertamini et al. (2019), within the category where symmetry was liked less than asymmetry (landscapes), the analysis of the modified stimuli (half of the total stimuli) showed that salience of symmetry was nevertheless correlated positively with preference.

In summary, in this section we have listed some examples of the literature that provide important counterexamples to a simple equation between symmetry and aesthetic beauty; for example, in different cultures, between symmetry and positive affect, depending on the measure of positive affect used, and between symmetry and attractiveness.

Neurophysiological Evidence

As we have seen a fundamental aspect of symmetry is its role in vision. There is agreement that a brain network in ventral extrastriate visual regions of the occipital cortex (but not of the primary visual areas) is tuned to symmetry (for a review, see Bertamini et al., 2018). Functional magnetic resonance imaging (fMRI) work has identified enhanced activation in these areas (Sasaki, Vanduffel, Knutsen, Tyler, & Tootell, 2005; Tyler et al., 2005), and electroencephalogram (EEG) work has showed negative deflection (e.g., Makin, Wilton, Pecchinenda & Bertamini, 2012) for symmetric configurations, compared with random. One question is whether this symmetry-related activation plays any role in determining the affective status of symmetry, and whether this role can be identified at the neural level.

Neural correlates of the link between symmetry and beauty were first explored by Jacobsen and Höfel (2001, 2002, 2003; see also Höfel & Jacobsen, 2003). The authors measured event-related potentials (ERPs) and aimed to identify indexes of judgments of beauty using abstract patterns that contained either symmetry (*beautiful* judgment-driving factor) or random configuration (*not beautiful* judgment-driving factor). They measured ERPs to the stimuli in descriptive (i.e., report whether the stimulus is symmetric or not) versus aesthetic evaluative judgments (i.e., rate how much you like the stimulus) in a trial-by-trial cueing task design, using binary responses (beautiful, not beautiful; symmetric, not symmetric). While early perceptual components (P1, N1) were present in all conditions, indicating visual processing of the stimulus, the two judgment types gave different later ERP responses. Evaluative judgments tasks led to early frontal negative deflection (Fz, 300–400 ms) for stimuli judged as *not beautiful*, and right lateralized late positivity (C4, 440–880 ms) in the evaluative task compared with the symmetry judgment task. Importantly, a response to symmetry vs. random was only evident in the symmetry categorization task, as a sustained negative deflection over parieto-occipital areas. This sustained visual analysis did not occur under the aesthetic judgment task. However, Jacobsen, Klein, and Löw, (2018) re-analyzed these data using different analysis parameters and showed an enhanced negativity to the symmetric stimuli also during evaluative aesthetic judgments. An fMRI study (Jacobsen, Schubotz, Höfel, & Cramon, 2006) provided similar results. Symmetry judgments triggered activation of regions related to visuospatial analysis, while aesthetic judgments elicited activation within fronto-temporal regions (although *beautiful*-judged stimuli elicited higher activation in both areas involved in aesthetic judgments (fronto-median) and areas involved in symmetry judgment (left intraparietal sulcus).

The dissociation, both in time (different response latency) and space (different neural generators), between the two types of tasks suggests aesthetic judgment of beauty may not originate from the mere processing of symmetry, despite the fact that both symmetry discrimination and aesthetic evaluation relied on the same stimulus feature. The same stimulus can be processed differently depending on the type of task.

In an original design, Höfel and Jacobsen (2007a) looked at the effect of misreporting a judgment (i.e., saying "no" to respond "yes"). Both true and false judgments triggered the earlier fronto-central negativity for *actual* not-beautiful patterns, while the right lateralization of the late positivity amplitude was cancelled when false judgments were made. The posterior sustained negativity for symmetry was not affected by the validity of the responses. The same authors (Höfel & Jacobsen, 2007b) then explored the role of performing an active judgment, as opposed to engaging in mere contemplation, on these ERP responses. Participants performed either an *aesthetic contemplation* or a *mere viewing* task. In both cases they did not make any explicit judgment. In both tasks there was no fronto-central ERP deflection, and the late positive potential was only present during the contemplation task. The sustained posterior negative ERP (index of symmetry processing) was always present.

Together these findings show that the recruitment of fronto-central networks underpins processes of self-reflection and subjective evaluation and is contingent on the *intention* to perform a judgment about the aesthetic quality of the pattern. A visual analysis of the stimulus characteristics is necessary (i.e., parieto-occipital deflection) but it is not sufficient to elicit aesthetic processing.

It is possible that abstract configurations contain information to make a *cold* judgment of symmetry, but this is not sufficient to elicit a spontaneous aesthetic experience (Makin, 2017). By contrast, faces are biologically and socially relevant stimuli. Neural correlates of face attractiveness have been recorded, although they are mainly associated with reward (e.g., Winston, O'Doherty, Kilner, Perrett, & Dolan, 2007). Other studies showed that attractive faces did not elicit any spontaneous response unless beauty was intentionally assessed (Roye, Höfel, & Jacobsen, 2008; Schacht, Werheid, & Sommer, 2008).

A strategy to identify an ERP index of the automatic association between symmetry and beauty/positive valence is the use of implicit measures. Rampone, Makin, and Bertamini (2014) used an affective picture–word interference task, with a word (positive or negative) superimposed on a pattern (symmetry or random). They investigated whether and how visual processing of symmetry is influenced when processing valence. When participants classified the valence of the word (and ignored the pattern underneath), the symmetry-related parieto-occipital negativity was recorded only for *positive words–symmetry* pairs but not for *negative words–symmetry* pairs. The authors proposed that preattentive tuning of the visual system to symmetry was enhanced when processing positive-valenced words, a similar conclusion to that drawn by Jacobsen et al. (2006).

Other electrophysiological measures have been used to index neural correlates of aesthetic experience. For example, electromyography (EMG) detects spontaneous affective responses. The activation of zygomaticus mayor (ZM—or smiling muscle) signals a positive emotional response (Achaibou, Pourtois, Schwartz, & Vuilleumier, 2008) and fluently processed stimuli (Cannon, Hayes, & Tipper, 2010; Winkielman & Cacioppo, 2001; Winkielman, Halberstadt, Fazendeiro, & Catty, 2006). Stimuli with negative valence, on the other hand, activate the corrugator supercilii (CS or frowning muscle) (Lishner, Cooter, & Zald, 2008). Gerger, Leder, Tinio, and Schacht (2011) used abstract patterns (asymmetric/symmetric) and faces (attractive/unattractive). They found that symmetric patterns and faces elicited higher ZM activations whereas unattractive patterns and faces elicited higher CS activations. Moreover, abstract patterns elicited fluency-related effects (greater ZM activation for longer stimulus presentations). In a 2AFC discrimination task (symmetry vs. random) Makin, Wilton, Pecchinenda, & Bertamini (2012) observed greater ZM activation for symmetry. However, in a second experiment, participants categorized the target with a dichotomous response (yes to symmetry, no to asymmetry for one group, the opposite for another group). Interestingly, ZM activation was stronger for trials that required a yes response, irrespective of target identity. In line with the aforementioned studies (Jacobsen & Höfel, 2007b; Jacobsen et al., 2006) this study showed that processing symmetry per se does not produce a positive response as measured by (neuro)physiological measures. What is true is that symmetry is spontaneously categorized as target (or *figure of interest*), unless other task requirements are present, and this categorization has positive effects, measured for example by the ZM response.

CLINICAL EVIDENCE

Preference for symmetry, order, and balance may be an adaptive natural behavior, but in some cases it can be manifested in extremes forms, becoming a marker of maladaptive compulsive behaviors.

Preoccupation with symmetry and ordering/arranging is one of the symptoms of obsessive compulsive disorder (OCD) (Lochner et al., 2016; Radomsky & Rachman, 2004). Symptoms include an obsession with symmetry and regularity in the physical environment, and a need for arranging elements in balanced and orderly structures. OCD individuals can experience a tormenting sense of dissatisfaction and *incompleteness* when things in the physical world are perceived as *not just right* (NJR-Experiences) (Coles, Frost, Heimberg, & Rhéaume, 2003). Incompleteness is a discomforting sense that involves all sensory modalities and is caused by a deficit in the ability to integrate emotional experience and sensory feedback in guiding behavior (Summerfeldt, 2004).

The need for symmetry and order lies on a continuum from healthy behavior to a clinically impairing behavior and can be measured in the nonclinical population. There are scales to measure OCD symptoms in the general population, in particular the *Symmetry, Ordering, and Arranging Questionnaire* (SOAQ, Radomsky & Rachman, 2004) assesses beliefs and behaviors associated with ordering and arranging, while the *NJRE Questionnaire (Revised*; Coles, Frost, Heimberg, & Rhéaume, 2003) assesses the intensity of subjective not-just-right experiences. High scores on these scales are related to high levels of discomfort when in disorderly environments (Coles, Heimberg, Frost, & Steketee, 2005), which can impact completion of ordinary tasks (Radomsky & Rachman, 2004).

A recent study investigated aesthetic preference for symmetry in individuals with OCD-like *incompleteness* traits (Summerfeldt, Gilbert, & Reynolds, 2015). Participants performed two aesthetic tasks on novel abstract stimuli, in which symmetry was either the primary (Assessment of Preference for Balance task, BT; Wilson & Chatterjee, 2005), or the secondary (Maitland Graves Design Judgment Test, DJT) dimension. Participants were asked to make objective estimates of the aesthetic value of an object (i.e., judge the degree of harmony and balance of the image) or to report their aesthetic preference (i.e., judge liking for the image). High scores on *incompleteness* traits and self-perceived symmetry-related concerns and behaviors (SOAQ scores) were associated with greater preference for symmetry (although there were no differences in the ability to estimate objectively the aesthetic value of the stimulus).

It is possible that strong preference for symmetry may result from a need to correct for sensory-emotional dysregulations. Summerfeldt et al. (2015) proposed there may be a link between the *perceptual fluency* account of preference for symmetry and the nature of this behavior. OCD individuals may show accentuated need for easily processed visual cues that can facilitate the achievement of a satisfactory sensory-emotional state.

Other studies have looked at EEG/ERP markers for preference for symmetry in OCD symmetry-related traits (Evans et al., 2012; Evans & Maliken, 2011). *Oddball tasks* have been shown to elicit atypical cortical activity in patients with OCD. Typically, processing a rare (oddball) stimulus elicits a positive component over centro-parietal areas (electrode Pz) that peaks around 300 ms from stimulus onset (P300). In OCD patients, P300 has a more pronounced amplitude and earlier onset. In one study (Evans et al., 2012) participants performed an oddball task with two sets of stimuli. One set consisted of alternating images of symmetric (parallel) and asymmetric (displaced) lines. A control set consisted of alternating blue and red colored spheres. Results showed stronger sensory conflict (i.e., more positive peak and faster latency of the P300) for oddball asymmetric stimuli in participants showing greater preference for symmetry and order. Similar results were observed in children with typical arranging compulsions (Evans & Maliken, 2011). These results suggest that greater sensitivity for oddball asymmetry may reflect a reaction to the occurrence of not-just-right experiences. A preference for organization is associated with several disorders, but is present in the general population as well. Langeslag (2018) measured ERP responses to objects arranged with various degrees of organization (sorted by shape and color from totally organized to totally disorganized). Participants rated the displays in terms of valence (i.e., pleasant/unpleasant feeling) and arousal (i.e., calming/arousing feeling); their *desire for order* and *organization behaviors* were also measured. There was a linear inverse relationship between level of disorganization and pleasantness (totally disorganized were least pleasant); no differences were observed with arousal. ERP measures showed a frontal negativity (at electrodes Fz, Cz) at 200–400 ms for the totally disorganized displays compared with organized, slightly disorganized, and control images. It is interesting that this negativity resembles the early frontal negative deflection (Fz, 300–400 ms) for stimuli judged as *not beautiful* observed with symmetric patterns (Höfel & Jacobsen, 2003; Jacobsen & Höfel, 2002, 2003). However, ERP amplitude did not correlate with valence ratings in this study.

Other clinical evidences of a bias toward symmetry have been found in patients with body dysmorphic disorder (BDD) (Lambrou, Veale, & Wilson, 2011) and autism spectrum disorder (Perreault, Gurnsey, Dawson, Mottron, & Bertone, 2011). Potentially, some of these common symptoms can be reunited under a similar endophenotype that involves an augmented perceptual sensitivity to symmetry and regularity.

Conclusion

Interest in symmetry is widespread and symmetry has been studied in many fields, from empirical aesthetics, evolutionary psychology, and psychology of art to neuroscience. Many thinkers, including early Greek philosophers, have linked symmetry with beauty. Empirical work has also produced a large literature. In general observers do like symmetry in novel and abstract configurations, in objects, and in the human body.

One issue that is central to this literature is how symmetry relates to complexity. Symmetry can be understood as regularity and redundancy, and this redundancy can be used for encoding of shape information. However, there is no clear and strong link between beauty and simplicity. For example, what makes bilateral symmetry more salient than rotational symmetry may have to do with visual perception, but not with the properties of the two transformations (both rigid transformations in the plane).

Although symmetry drives aesthetic judgments, it is difficult to isolate a neural correlate of this link. It seems that a spontaneous aesthetic response to symmetry (in abstract and unfamiliar stimuli) is not elicited in the brain unless people are explicitly processing symmetry aesthetically.

Finally, preference for symmetry, order, and balance lies on a continuum ranging from a universal tendency to prefer symmetry to pathological obsessive compulsion. It seems that dysfunctional perceptual mechanisms may play a role in excessive preferences for symmetry in disorders such as OCD, BDD, and autism. This area of research, however, is still in its infancy.

Symmetry will continue to be a central topic in empirical aesthetics as it is a paradigmatic tool to study order and complexity, and to test hypotheses about the potential adaptive function of certain patterns of preference.

References

Achaibou, A., Pourtois, G., Schwartz, S., & Vuilleumier, P. (2008). Simultaneous recording of EEG and facial muscle reactions during spontaneous emotional mimicry. *Neuropsychologia, 46*, 1104–1113.

Arnheim, R. (1974). *Art and visual perception: A psychology of the creative eye.* Berkeley, CA: University of California Press.

Arnheim, R. (1982). *The power of the centre. A study of composition in the visual arts.* Berkeley, CA: University of California Press.

Attneave, F. (1955). Symmetry, information, and memory for patterns. *The American Journal of Psychology, 68*, 209–222.

Barlow, H. B., & Reeves, B. C. (1979). The versatility and absolute efficiency of detecting mirror symmetry in random dot displays. *Vision Research, 19*, 783–793.

Berlyne, D. E. (1960). *Conflict, arousal and curiosity.* New York: McGraw-Hill.

Berlyne, D. E., Ogilvie, J. C., & Parham, L. C. C. (1968). The dimensionality of visual complexity, interestingness, and pleasingness. *Canadian Journal of Psychology, 22*, 376–387.

Bertamini, M. (2010). Sensitivity to reflection and translation is modulated by objectness. *Perception, 39*(1), 27–40.

Bertamini, M., Byrne, C., & Bennett, K. M. (2013). Attractiveness is influenced by the relationship between postures of the viewer and the viewed person. *i-Perception, 4*(3), 170–179.

Bertamini, M., Friedenberg J., & Kubovy M. (1997). Detection of symmetry and perceptual organization: How a lock-and-key process works. *Acta Psychologica, 95*, 119–140.

Bertamini, M., & Makin, A. D. J. (2014). Brain activity in response to visual symmetry. *Symmetry, 6*(4), 975–996.

Bertamini, M., Makin, A. D. J., & Rampone, G. (2013). Implicit association of symmetry with positive valence, high arousal and simplicity. *I-Perception, 4*(5), 317–327.

Bertamini, M., Makin, A. D. J., & Pecchinenda, A. (2013). Testing whether and when abstract symmetric patterns produce affective responses. *PLoS ONE, 8*(7), e68403.

Bertamini, M., Rampone, G., Makin, A. D. J., & Jessop, A. (2019). Symmetry preference in shapes, faces, flowers and landscapes. *PeerJ, 7*, e7078.

Bertamini, M., Silvanto, J., Norcia, A. M., Makin, A. D. J., & Wagemans, J. (2018). The neural basis of visual symmetry and its role in mid- and high-level visual processing. *Annals of the New York Academy of Sciences, 1426*(1), 111–126.

Birkhoff, G. D. (1933). *Aesthetic measure.* Cambridge, MA: Harvard University Press.

Bode, C., Helmy, M., & Bertamini, M. (2017). A cross-cultural comparison for preference for symmetry: comparing British and Egyptians non-experts. *Psihologija, 50, 3*, 383–402.

Bornstein, M. H., Ferdinandsen, K., & Gross, C. G. (1981). Perception of symmetry in infancy. *Developmental Psychology*, *17*(1), 82–86.

Brain, R. (1979). *The decorated body*. New York: Harper & Row.

Brodeur, M. B., Chauret, M., Dion-Lessard, G., & Lepage, M. (2011). Symmetry brings an impression of familiarity but does not improve recognition memory. *Acta Psychologica*, *137*(3), 359–370.

Cannon, P. R., Hayes, A. E., & Tipper, S. P. (2010). Sensorimotor fluency influences affect: Evidence from electromyography. *Cognition & Emotion*, *24*(4), 681–691.

Cardenas, R. A., & Harris, L. J. (2006). Symmetrical decorations enhance the attractiveness of faces and abstract designs. *Evolution and Human Behavior*, *27*, 1–18.

Cavanagh, P. (2005) The artist as neuroscientist. *Nature*, *434*(7031), 301–307.

Chipman, S. F. (1977). Complexity and structure in visual patterns. *Journal of Experimental Psychology: General*, *106*(3), 269–301.

Clara, E., Regolin, L., & Vallortigara, G. (2007). Preference for symmetry is experience dependent in newborn chicks (*Gallus gallus*). *Journal of Experimental Psychology: Animal Behavior Processes*, *33*(1), 12–20.

Coles, M. E., Frost, R. O., Heimberg, R. G., & Rhéaume, J. (2003). "Not just right experiences": perfectionism, obsessive–compulsive features and general psychopathology. *Behaviour Research and Therapy*, *41*(6), 681–700.

Coles, M. E., Heimberg, R. G., Frost, R. O., & Steketee, G. (2005). Not just right experiences and obsessive-compulsive features: Experimental and self-monitoring perspectives. *Behaviour Research and Therapy*, *43*(2), 153–167.

Darwin, C. (1882). *The descent of man and selection in relation to sex*. London: John Murray.

Deregowski, J. (1972). The role of symmetry in pattern reproduction by Zambian children. *Journal of Cross-Cultural Psychology*, *3*, 303–307.

Donderi, D. C. (2006). Visual complexity: a review. *Psychological Bulletin*, *132*(1), 73.

Dufour, K. W., & Weatherhead, P. J. (1998). Reproductive consequences of bilateral asymmetry for individual male red-winged blackbirds. *Behavioral Ecology*, *9*, 232–242.

Eisenman, R. (1967). Complexity-simplicity: I. Preference for symmetry and rejection of complexity. *Psychonomic Science*, *8*(4), 169–170.

Eisenman, R., & Gillens, H. (1968). Preferences for complexity-simplicity and symmetry-asymmetry. *Perceptual and Motor Skills*, *26*, 888–890.

Eisenman, R., & Rappaport, J. (1967). Complexity preference and semantic differential ratings of complexity-simplicity and symmetry-asymmetry. *Psychonomic Science*, *7*(4), 147–148.

Enquist, M., & Arak, A. (1994). Symmetry beauty and evolution. *Nature*, *372*, 169–170.

Enquist, M., & Johnstone, R. A. (1997). Generalization and the evolution of symmetry preferences. *Proceedings of the Royal Society of London. Series B: Biological Sciences*, *264*(1386), 1345–1348.

Evans, D. W., & Maliken, A. (2011). Cortical activity and children's rituals, habits and other repetitive behavior: A visual P300 study. *Behavioural Brain Research*, *224*(1), 174–179.

Evans, D. W., Orr, P. T., Lazar, S. M., Breton, D., Gerard, J., Ledbetter, D. H., ... Batchelder, H. (2012). Human preferences for symmetry: subjective experience, cognitive conflict and cortical brain activity. *PLoS ONE*, *7*(6), e38966.

Eysenck, H. J. (1941). The empirical determination of an aesthetic formula. *Psychological Review*, *48*(1), 83–92.

Eysenck, H. J. (1968). An experimental study of aesthetic preference for polygonal figures. *The Journal of General Psychology*, *79*(1), 3–17.

Eysenck, J., & Castle, M, (1970). Training in art as a factor in the determination of preference judgments for polygons. *British Journal of Psychology, 61*, 65–81.

Fechner, G. T. (1876). *Vorschule der Ästhetik.* Leipzig, Germany: Breitkopf und Härtel.

Garner, W. R. (1970). Good patterns have few alternatives. *American Scientist, 58*, 34–42.

Gerger, G., Leder, H., Tinio, P. P. L., & Schacht, A. (2011). Faces versus patterns: Exploring aesthetic reactions using facial EMG. *Psychology of Aesthetics, Creativity, and the Arts, 5*(3), 241–250.

Gombrich, E. H. (1979). *The Sense of order: A study of the psychology of decorative art.* Ithaca, NY: Cornell University Press.

Gröning, K. (2002). *Decorated skin: A world survey of body art.* London: Thames & Hudson.

Grünbaum, B., & Shephard, G. C. (1987). *Tilings and patterns.* New York: Freeman.

Höfel, L., & Jacobsen, T. (2003). Temporal stability and consistency of aesthetic judgments of beauty of formal graphic patterns. *Perceptual and Motor Skills, 96*(1), 30–32.

Höfel, L., & Jacobsen, T. (2007a). Electrophysiological indices of processing symmetry and aesthetics: A result of judgment categorization or judgment report? *Journal of Psychophysiology, 21*(1), 9–21.

Höfel, L., & Jacobsen, T. (2007b). Electrophysiological indices of processing aesthetics: Spontaneous or intentional processes? *International Journal of Psychophysiology, 65*(1), 20–31. doi:10.1016/j.ijpsycho.2007.02.007

Huang, Y., Xue, X., Spelke, E., Huang, L., Zheng, W., & Peng, K. (2018). The aesthetic preference for symmetry dissociates from early-emerging attention to symmetry. *Scientific reports, 8*(1), 6263.

Humphrey, D. (1997). Preferences in symmetries and symmetries in drawings: Asymmetries between ages and sexes. *Empirical Studies of the Arts, 15*, 41–60.

Humphrey, G. K., & Humphrey, D. E. (1989). The role of structure in infant visual pattern perception, *Canadian Journal of Psychology, 43*, 165–182.

Jacobsen, T., & Höfel, L. (2001). Aesthetics electrified: An analysis of descriptive symmetry and evaluative aesthetic judgment processes using event-related brain potentials. *Empirical Studies of the Arts, 19*(2), 177–190.

Jacobsen, T., & Höfel, L. E. A. (2002). Aesthetic judgments of novel graphic patterns: Analyses of individual judgments. *Perceptual and Motor Skills, 95*(3), 755–766.

Jacobsen, T., & Höfel, L. (2003). Descriptive and evaluative judgment processes: Behavioral and electrophysiological indices of processing symmetry and aesthetics. *Cognitive, Affective, & Behavioral Neuroscience, 3*(4), 289–299.

Jacobsen, T., Klein, S., & Löw, A. (2018). The posterior sustained negativity revisited—An SPN reanalysis of Jacobsen and Höfel (2003). *Symmetry, 10*(1), 27.

Jacobsen, T., Schubotz, R. I., Höfel, L., & Cramon, D. Y. V. (2006). Brain correlates of aesthetic judgment of beauty. *Neuroimage, 29*(1), 276–285.

Jansson L., Forkman B, & Enquist M. (2002). Experimental evidence of receiver bias for symmetry. *Animal Behavior, 63*, 617–621.

Johnstone, R. A. (1994). Female preference for symmetrical males as a by-product of selection for mate recognition. *Nature, 372*, 172–175.

Jones, B. C., Little, A. C., Penton-Voak, I. S., Tiddeman, B. P., Burt, D. M., & Perrett, D. I. (2001). Facial symmetry and judgments of apparent health: support for a good genes explanation of the attractiveness-symmetry relationship. *Evolution and Human Behavior, 22*, 417–429.

Julesz, B. (1971). *Foundations of cyclopean perception.* Chicago, IL: University of Chicago Press.

Krupinski, E., & Locher, P. (1988). Skin conductance and aesthetic evaluative responses to nonrepresentational works of art varying in symmetry. *Bulletin of the Psychonomic Society*, *26*, 355–358.

Lambrou, C., Veale, D., & Wilson, G. (2011). The role of aesthetic sensitivity in body dysmorphic disorder. *Journal of Abnormal Psychology*, *120*, 443e453.

Langeslag, S. J. E. (2018). Effects of organization and disorganization on pleasantness, calmness, and the frontal negativity in the event-related potential. *PLoS ONE*, *13*(8), 1–13.

Latto, R. (1995). The brain of the beholder. In R. L. Gregory, J. Harris, P. Heard, & D. Rose (Eds.), *The artful eye* (pp. 66–94). Oxford, UK: Oxford University Press.

Leder, H., & Nadal, M. (2014). Ten years of a model of aesthetic appreciation and aesthetic judgments. *British Journal of Psychology*, *105*(4), 443–464.

Leder, H., Belke, B., Oeberst, A., & Augustin, D. (2004). A model of aesthetic appreciation and aesthetic judgments. *British Journal of Psychology*, *95*(4), 489–508.

Leder, H., Tinio, P. P. L., Brieber, D., Kröner, T., Jacobsen, T., & Rosenberg, R. (2019). Symmetry is not a universal law of beauty. *Empirical Studies of the Arts*, *37*(1), 104–114.

Leeuwenberg, E. L. J., & van der Helm, P. A. (2013). *Structural information theory: The simplicity of visual form*. Cambridge, UK: Cambridge University Press.

Lehrer, M., Horridge, G. A., Zhang, S. W., & Gadagkar, R. (1995). Shape vision in bees: Innate preference for flower-like patterns. *Philosophical Transactions of the Royal Society London B*, *347*, 123–137.

Lewis, M. B. (2017). Fertility affects asymmetry detection not symmetry preference in assessments of 3D facial attractiveness. *Cognition*, *166*, 130–138.

Lishner, D. A., Cooter, A. B., & Zald, D. H. (2008). Rapid emotional contagion and expressive congruence under strong test conditions. *Journal of Nonverbal Behavior*, *32*, 225–239.

Little, A. C., & Jones, B. C. (2003). Evidence against perceptual bias views for symmetry preferences in human faces. *Proceedings of the Royal Society: Biological Sciences*, *270*, 1759–1763.

Little, A. C., Jones, B. C., & DeBruine, L. M. (2011). Facial attractiveness: Evolutionary based research. *Philosophical Transactions of the Royal Society B: Biological Sciences*, *366*(1571), 1638–1659.

Locher, P., & Nodine, C. (1987). Symmetry catches the eye. In J. K. Q'Reagan, & A. Levy-Schoen (Eds.), *Eye movements: From physiology to cognition* (pp. 353–361). Amsterdam: Elsevier.

Lochner, C., McGregor, N., Hemmings, S., Harvey, B. H., Breet, E., Swanevelder, S., & Stein, D. J. (2016). Symmetry symptoms in obsessive-compulsive disorder: Clinical and genetic correlates. *Revista Brasileira de Psiquiatria*, *38*(1), 17–23.

Mach, E. (1886). *Beiträge zur Analyse der Empfindungen* (Contributions to the Analysis of Sensations). Jena, Germany: Gustav Fisher.

Makin, A. D. J. (2017). The gap between aesthetic science and aesthetic experience. *Journal of Consciousness Studies*, *24*(1–2), 184–213.

Makin, A. D. J., Bertamini, M., Jones, A., Holmes, T., & Zanker, J. M. (2016). A gaze-driven evolutionary algorithm to study aesthetic evaluation of visual symmetry. *I-Perception*, *7*(2): 2041669516637432. doi:10.1177/2041669516637432

Makin, A. D. J., Helmy, M., & Bertamini, M. (2017). Visual cortex activation predicts visual preference: Evidence from Britain and Egypt. *Quarterly Journal of Experimental Psychology*, *71*(8), 1771–1780.

Makin, A.D.J., Pecchinenda, A., & Bertamini, M. (2012). Implicit affective evaluation of visual symmetry. *Emotion*, *12*(5), 1021–1030.

Makin, A. D. J., Wilton, M., Pecchinenda, A., & Bertamini, M. (2012). Symmetry perception and affective responses: A combined EEG/EMG study. *Neuropsychologia, 50*(14), 3250–3261.

Mastandrea, S., Bartoli, G., & Carrus, G. (2011). The automatic aesthetic evaluation of different art and architectural styles. *Psychology of Aesthetics, Creativity, and the Arts, 5*(2), 126.

McManus, I. C. (2005). Symmetry and asymmetry in aesthetics and the arts. *European Review, 13*, 157–180.

Møller, A. P., & Thornhill, R. (1998). Bilateral symmetry and sexual selection: A meta-analysis. The *American Naturalist, 151*(2), 174–192.

Munsinger, H., & Kessen, W. (1964). Uncertainty, structure, and preference. *Psychological Monographs: General and Applied, 78*, 1–24.

Palmer, A. R. (1996). Waltzing with asymmetry. *Bio Science, 46*(7), 518–532.

Pecchinenda, A., Bertamini, M., Makin, A. D. J., & Ruta, N. (2014). The pleasantness of visual symmetry: Always, never or sometimes. *PLoS ONE, 9*(3), e92685.

Perkins, T. (1932). Symmetry in visual recall. *The American Journal of Psychology, 44*, 473–490.

Perreault, A., Gurnsey, R., Dawson, M., Mottron, L., & Bertone, A. (2011). Increased sensitivity to mirror symmetry in autism. *PLoS ONE, 6*(4), e19519.

Perrett, D. I., Burt, D. M., Penton-Voak, I. S., Lee, K. J., Rowland, D. A., & Edwards, R. (1999). Symmetry and human facial attractiveness. *Evolution and Human Behavior, 20*, 295–307.

Radomsky, A. S., & Rachman, S. (2004). Symmetry, ordering and arranging compulsive behaviour. *Behaviour Research and Therapy, 42*(8), 893–913.

Ramachandran, V. S., & Hirstein, W. (1999). The science of art: A neurological theory of aesthetic experience. *Journal of Consciousness Studies, 6–7*, 15–51.

Rampone, G., Makin, A. A. D. J., & Bertamini, M. (2014). Electrophysiological analysis of the affective congruence between pattern regularity and word valence. *Neuropsychologia, 58*(1), 107–117. doi:10.1016/j.neuropsychologia.2014.04.005

Reber, R., Schwartz, N., & Winkielman, P. (2004). Processing fluency and aesthetic pleasure: Is beauty in the perceiver's processing experience? *Personality and Social Psychology Review, 8*, 364–382.

Redies, C. (2008). A universal model of esthetic perception based on the sensory coding of natural stimuli. *Spatial Vision, 21*(1), 97–117.

Rhodes, G. (2006). The evolutionary psychology of facial beauty. *Annual Review Psychology, 57*, 199–226.

Rhodes, G., Geddes, K., Jeffery, L., Dziurawiec, S., & Clark, A. (2002). Are average and symmetric faces attractive to infants? Discrimination and looking preferences. *Perception, 31*(3), 315–321.

Rhodes, G., Proffitt, F., Grady, J. M., & Sumich, A. (1998). Facial symmetry and the perception of beauty. *Psychonomic Bulletin & Review, 5*(4), 659–669.

Rhodes, G., Sumich, A., & Byatt, G. (1999). Are average facial configurations attractive only because of their symmetry? *Psychological Science, 10*, 52–58.

Ritterbush, P. C. (1983). Dürer and geometry: Symmetry in an enigma. *Nature, 301*(5897), 197–198.

Rodríguez, I., Gumbert, A., Hempel de Ibarra, N., Kunze, J., & Giurfa, M. (2004). Symmetry is in the eye of the beeholder: Innate preference for bilateral symmetry in flower-naïve bumblebees. *Naturwissenschaften, 91*(8), 374–377.

Roye, A., Höfel, L., & Jacobsen, T. (2008). Aesthetics of faces: Behavioral and electrophysiological indices of evaluative and descriptive judgment processes. *Journal of Psychophysiology, 22*(1), 41–57. doi:10.1027/0269-8803.22.1.41

Royer, F. L. (1981). Detection of symmetry. *Journal of Experimental Psychology: Human Perception & Performance, 7*, 1186–1210.

Sasaki, Y., Vanduffel, W., Knutsen, T., Tyler, C., & Tootell, R. (2005). Symmetry activates extrastriate visual cortex in human and nonhuman primates. *Proceedings of the National Academy of Sciences of the United States of America, 102*(8), 3159.

Schacht, A., Werheid, K., & Sommer, W. (2008). The appraisal of facial beauty is rapid but not mandatory. *Cognitive, Affective and Behavioral Neuroscience, 8*(2), 132–142. doi:10.3758/CABN.8.2.132

Scheib, J. E., Gangestad, S. W., & Thornhill, R. (1999). Facial attractiveness, symmetry and cues of good genes. *Proceedings of the Royal Society of London. Series B: Biological* Sciences, *266*, 1913–17.

Schmidhuber. (1997). Low-complexity art. *Leonardo, 30*(2), 97–103.

Scruton, R. (2009). *Beauty.* Oxford, UK: Oxford University Press.

Stewart, I. (2007). *Why beauty is truth: A history of symmetry.* New York: Basic Books.

Summerfeldt, L. J. (2004). Understanding and treating incompleteness in obsessive-compulsive disorder. *Journal of Clinical Psychology, 60*(11), 1155–1168.

Summerfeldt, L. J., Gilbert, S. J., & Reynolds, M. (2015). Incompleteness, aesthetic sensitivity, and the obsessive-compulsive need for symmetry. *Journal of Behavior Therapy and Experimental Psychiatry, 49*, 141–149.

Tinio, P. P. L., & Leder, H. (2009). Just how stable are stable aesthetic features? Symmetry, complexity, and the jaws of massive familiarization. *Acta Psychologica, 130*(3), 241–250.

Treder, M. S. (2010). Behind the looking-glass: A review on human symmetry perception. *Symmetry, 2*(3), 1510–1543.

Tyler, C. W. (1995). Empirical aspects of symmetry perception. *Spatial Vision, 9*, 1–7.

Tyler, C. W., Baseler, H. A., Kontsevich, L. L., Likova, L. T., Wade, A. R., & Wandell, B. A. (2005). Predominantly extra-retinotopic cortical response to pattern symmetry. *Neuroimage, 24*(2), 306–314.

Villarroel, J. D., Merino, M., & Antón, Á. (2019). Symmetrical motifs in young children's drawings: A study on their representations of plant life. *Symmetry, 11*(1), 26.

Wagemans, J. (1995). Detection of visual symmetries. *Spatial Vision, 9*, 9–32.

Washburn, D. K., & Crowe D. S. (1988). *Symmetries of culture.* Washington, DC: University of Washington Press.

Watson, P. J., & Thornhill, R. (1994). Fluctuating asymmetry and sexual selection. *Trends in Ecology & Evolution, 9*(1), 21–25.

Weichselbaum, H., Leder, H., & Ansorge, U. (2018). Implicit and explicit evaluation of visual symmetry as a function of art expertise. *I-Perception, 9*(2). doi:10.1177/2041669518761464

Wenderoth, P. (1994). The salience of vertical symmetry. *Perception, 23*(2), 221–236.

Westphal-Fitch, G., Oh, J., & Fitch, W. (2013). Studying aesthetics with the method of production: Effects of context and local symmetry. *Psychology of Aesthetics, Creativity, and the Arts, 7*(1), 13–36.

Weyl, H. (1952). *Symmetry.* Princeton, NJ: Princeton University Press.

Wilson, A., & Chatterjee, A. (2005). The assessment of preference for balance: Introducing a new test. *Empirical Studies of the Arts, 23*(2), 165–180.

Winkielman, P., & Cacioppo, J. T. (2001). Mind at ease puts a smile on the face: Psychophysiological evidence that processing facilitation leads to positive affect. *Journal of Personality and Social Psychology, 81*, 989–1000.

Winkielman, P., Halberstadt, J., Fazendeiro, T., & Catty, S. (2006). Prototypes are attractive because they are easy on the mind. *Psychological Science, 17*(9), 799–806.

Winston, J., O'Doherty, J., Kilner, J., Perrett, D., & Dolan, R. (2007). Brain systems for assessing facial attractiveness. *Neuropsychologia, 45*, 195–206.

Wright, D., & Bertamini, M. (2015). Aesthetic judgements of abstract dynamic configurations. *Art and Perception, 3*(3), 283–301.

Zaidel, D. W., & Deblieck, C. (2007) Attractiveness of natural faces compared to computer constructed perfectly symmetrical faces. *International Journal of Neuroscience, 117*, 423–431.

Zaidel, D. W., & Hessamian, M. (2010). Asymmetry and symmetry in the beauty of human faces. *Symmetry, 2*(1), 136–149.

Zee, A. (2007). *Fearful symmetry: The search for beauty in modern physics.* Princeton, NJ: Princeton University Press.

Zeki, S. (1999). Art and the brain. *Journal of Consciousness Studies, 6*(6–7), 76–96.

Zeki, S. (2013). Clive Bell's "Significant Form" and the neurobiology of aesthetics. *Frontiers in Human Neuroscience, 7*: 730. doi:10.3389/fnhum.2013.00730

CHAPTER 23

THE CURVATURE EFFECT

GUIDO CORRADI AND ENRIC MUNAR

Contour is a fundamental basic visual attribute to properly shape an object's form. As Marr (1982) indicated, contour in a single two-dimensional image conveys unambiguous and often quite detailed information about the three-dimensional form. Shaping the object's form is a crucial visual process in order to recognize and appraise it. Thus, it is reasonable to think that different contours and lines—which make up contours—give rise to different feelings.

Even before the foundations of empirical aesthetics as an academic discipline were laid, Hogarth (1753), an English painter and writer, argued that curved lines are ornamental because they can vary in length and also in degrees of curvature, whereas straight lines vary only in length, and therefore are less ornamental. He added that the wavy line—which he called "the line of beauty"—is "more productive of beauty," because it is composed of two contrasted curves and varies more insomuch as the hand makes a lively movement when drawing it with a pencil. It is probably the earliest study in which we can find a theoretical account of why curvature is a key factor in visual aesthetics (Bertamini & Palumbo, 2015; Bertamini, Palumbo, Gheorghes, & Galatsidas, 2016).

Quite a few studies have since shown that curved contours are preferred or involve more positive feelings than sharp-angled ones (Bar & Neta, 2006; Gerardo Gómez-Puerto, Munar, & Nadal, 2016; Leder & Carbon, 2005). Preference for curvature has been shown with different kinds of stimuli: lines (Bertamini et al., 2016; Hevner, 1935; Lundholm, 1920; Poffenberger & Barrows, 1924; Uher, 1991), typefaces (Kastl & Child, 1968; Velasco, Woods, Hyndman, & Spence, 2015), car interior designs (Leder & Carbon, 2005), familiar objects (Bar & Neta, 2006, 2007; Gómez-Puerto et al., 2017; Leder, Tinio, & Bar, 2011; Munar, Gómez-Puerto, Call, & Nadal, 2015), meaningless patterns (Bertamini et al., 2016; Cotter, Silvia, Bertamini, Palumbo, & Vartanian, 2017; Palumbo & Bertamini, 2016; Palumbo, Ruta, & Bertamini, 2015; Quinn, Brown, & Streppa, 1997; Silvia & Barona, 2009; Velasco, Salgado-Montejo et al., 2016), wrapped candies (Munroe, Munroe, & Lansky, 1976), toys (Jadva, Hines, & Golombok, 2010), furniture (Dazkir & Read, 2012), interior design (Banaei, Hatami, Yazdanfar, & Gramann, 2017; Van Oel & Van den Berkhof, 2013; Vartanian et al., 2013, 2017), product design (Westerman et al., 2012), dancers (Aronoff, 2006; Aronoff, Woike, & Hyman, 1992; Christensen, Pollick,

Lambrechts, & Gomila, 2016), interactive objects (Soranzo, Petrelli, Ciolfi, & Reidy, 2018), and even haptic forms (Jakesch & Carbon, 2011). Moreover, the effect has been shown in adults—most of the aforementioned studies, newborns (Amir, Biederman, & Hayworth, 2011; Fantz, 1961; Fantz & Miranda, 1975; Quinn et al., 1997; Ruff & Birch, 1974), infants (Hopkins, Kagan, Brachfeld, Hans, & Linn, 1976; Jadva et al., 2010; Munroe et al., 1976), Western and non-Western participants (Gómez-Puerto et al., 2017), and even in great apes (Munar et al., 2015) and chicks (Fantz, 1961; Schneirla, 1965). Nowadays, we can state that the "preference for curvature" or the "smooth curvature effect" or simply the "curvature effect" is a well-established phenomenon.

SPORADIC STUDIES OVER THE 20TH CENTURY

The earliest experimental research about preference for curvature that we found was described in Stratton (1902, 1906). He related the pleasure derived from the observation of curved lines to the concurrent movements of the extra-ocular muscles. He hypothesized that eye movements required to follow sharp lines must be more abrupt and, consequently, less pleasant than those required to follow curved lines. Stratton recorded gaze patterns while participants viewed different kinds of curved and sharp-angled stimuli using a rudimentary eye-tracking device. He noted that participants' eyes moved jerkily and similarly in relation to both curved and sharp-angled stimuli. However, despite the fact that his proposal was unsupported based on his own observations, his seminal work included interesting reflections on the two issues that have become central in the current research (Gómez-Puerto et al., 2016). The first one was about the mechanism underlying preference for curvature. He believed that curves provide observers with a continuous flow of information that is easy to process. However, he noticed that experience, environment, and cultural cues might influence the appraisal of lines. The second issue was about the functional significance of this preference. Most movements in nature are curvilinear, which makes us perceive the curved lines as an indication of a functional, normal behavior. On the other hand, angled lines convey a stronger sense of power.

Despite Stratton's inspiring experimental beginning to study the curvature effect, there were very few empirical attempts to delve into this issue during the 20th century. In the first half of the century, some studies related specific lines to specific feelings (Hevner, 1935; Lundholm, 1920; Poffenberger & Barrows, 1924). Participants received either (1) a series of words or (2) a series of lines, and they had either (1) to draw lines matching the words, or (2) to match some feelings to the lines. Some of the results related curved lines to *sad, quiet, lazy, merry, dead, playful, weak, gentle, serious, graceful,* and *serene*; and in turn sharp lines to *agitating, furious, robust, vigorous,* and *hard*. The patterns of response were quite consistent and uniform for most participants.

In an applied approach, Kastl and Child (1968) supported the notion that distinct feelings conveyed by isolated lines remain relevant when the stimuli are more complex. Using typefaces, they found that, in general, moods such as sprightly, sparkling, dreamy, calm, and soaring tend to be matched to the curved type, whereas moods such as dignified are matched to the angular type. Nevertheless, it should be noted that their findings indicated that angular types appeared to be sadder, contravening those of Lundholm (1920).

Valentine (1950) suggested that the curvature effect might be connected with the appeal of curves in the human form. McElroy (1954) indicated that the form most strongly appreciated as beautiful is the opposite sex, and much of the pleasure in works of art may be due to their appeal to sex-related emotions. He considered the role played by symbolism in mental life and alleged that sex differences must also exist regarding symbolic representations of male and female forms. Male perception of any suitable symbolic representation of the female form might be accompanied by a surplus of pleasurable affect, with a converse process applying to female perception of any suitable representation of the male form. As simple curved figures may represent female forms and pointed forms are typical male symbols (Franck & Rosen, 1949; Krout, 1950), McElroy constructed a 12-item aesthetics test to measure sex differences in aesthetic perception. Each item consisted of a pair of line drawings, one selected on account of its curved features (feminine) and the other selected because of its pointed properties (masculine). From a psychoanalytic hypothesis, he predicted that "surplus of affect" would exist and would be distributed in opposite directions for male and female groups. The results partially supported his prediction and showed that this sex difference increased with age. In this sense, McElroy interpreted this as implying that the difference was culturally delimited.

In the same line, Jahoda (1956) used McElroy's test with 858 boys and girls from Ghana. The results showed reduced but significant sex differences. He argued that the psychoanalytic hypothesis was supported and that the smaller differences in Ghana's group were due to a different cultural situation where there was less sexual repression. In contrast, Munroe et al. (1976) asked 175 children to select between two pieces of wrapped candies, one spherical and the other cube-shaped. Participants from both sexes chose the spherical candy more frequently. However, girls chose it (83%) significantly more than boys (57%). Since then, current studies have not found any sex differences in the curvature effect (Bar & Neta, 2007; Jadva et al., 2010; Palumbo et al., 2015).

In a subliminal perception study, Guthrie and Wiener (1966) presented drawings to participants who had to make judgments about a man in the drawing, using a list of several trait-dimensions (pleasant–unpleasant, helpful–harmful, etc.). They created two different versions of each image with sharp and smooth contours. The results showed that it was the overall sharpness, and not the presence of a gun, that determined whether the image was perceived as threatening and negative.

In the seventies, it was shown that 13-week-old infants (Ruff & Birch, 1974) and even 1-week-old neonates (Fantz & Miranda, 1975) fixated longer on curved contour forms than on straight or sharp-angled contours, respectively. The view of the infants was limited to two stimulus patterns. Hopkins and colleagues' (1976) results also implied that curvature appeared to have a special attention-recruiting quality for 10-month-old infants. Once infants were habituated, pressing a lever, to a straight or curved line, the experimenter changed the type of line that appeared when the infant pressed the lever and the dishabituation process was measured by means of several variables. Results showed that sustained reinforced responding and visual fixation were greater when dishabituation involved a change from straight to curved, rather than a change from curved to straight form. This greater responsivity, when the change is from a straight to a curved segment than the opposite direction, seems due to a greater interest and excitement for curved lines for the infant.

Uher (1991) presented stimuli with zigzags and wavy lines to 1,100 participants of various ages, genders, and occupations from Central Europe. They rated the emotional qualities on 24 semantic differential scales. Her results showed significant associations with antagonistic characteristics for the zigzag and with affiliative ones for the wavy lines. Interestingly, the author, from an ethological perspective, concluded that the zigzag motifs were likely to represent entoptic phenomena; that is, visual effects whose source is within the eye itself.

Aronoff et al. (1992) hypothesized that geometric patterns permit observers to recognize the meaning of threat or warmth. They used videotapes of classical ballet performances in Study 1, and lines and elliptical forms in Study 2. In Study 1, they analyzed three main visual configurations in human movement in a ballet performance: body display, arm display, and movement path. The *body display* was categorized in diagonal and round movements. The *arm display* and the *movement path* were categorized in angled, straight, and round movements. Roundness in the visual displays was strongly associated with warm characters, whereas the reverse visual display was strongly associated with threatening characters. They concluded that it was the abstract geometric form made in the body's presentation that provided the meaning. Christensen et al. (2016) replicated these results. In Study 2, Aronoff et al. (1992) carried out three experiments with diagonal lines and elliptical forms that were rated on a semantic differential scale with 12 adjective pairs. Again, roundedness produced a very large effect on the evaluation dimension, with a more rounded form seen as being better. A V-shaped figure—with a downward vertex—was perceived to be significantly worse than all the other diagonally shaped forms. The authors concluded that there is some neural mechanism that may respond to rounded visual forms with the meaning of warmth and may respond to diagonal, linear, and angular visual forms with the meaning of threat, whether the actual physical object that manifests the shape is a face, a line, a schematic drawing, or a body movement (Aronoff, 2006).

Quinn et al. (1997) showed that Gestalt organizational effects and preference for curvature are both involved in the initial parsing and subsequent organization of complex visual patterns. Using a familiarization-novelty preference procedure, the authors found that 3- and 4-month-old infants segregated the contours of two intersecting visual forms, and that they did so relying on the Gestalt principle of good continuation. Moreover, they argued that spontaneous preference for curvature facilitated the Gestalt organization of complex configurations into coherent forms.

THE 21ST CENTURY

Most of the 20th-century contributions to the study of the curvature effect were incidental and sporadic. They did not construct a body of knowledge about the psychological and biological functions of the phenomenon. In the 21st century, something in this regard has changed. In the first decade of the current century, several systematic studies focused on this effect (Bar & Neta, 2006, 2007; Leder & Carbon, 2005; Silvia & Barona, 2009; Zhang, Feick, & Price, 2006) and helped to increase interest about preference for curvature. Currently, we can find quite a few studies that have brought into focus the effect and have contributed to a better understanding of the phenomenon. However, these studies do not comprise a unified set that shares a common viewpoint. Actually, they make use of different frameworks. For example, some of them come from the applied perspective (Carbon, 2010; Dazkir & Read, 2012; Leder, Carbon, & Ripsas, 2006; Zhang et al., 2006), whereas others come from a more basic, experimental standpoint (Bar & Neta, 2006, 2007; Leder et al., 2011; Silvia & Barona, 2009; Vartanian et al., 2013). Some of the contributions are unconnected, and we cannot yet offer a cohesive account that encapsulates the available evidence. Nonetheless, we are going to present the salient issues of the current studies in order to provide a constructive development.

An Evolved or a Learnt Preference?

According to Carbon (2010), it is questionable whether the curvature effect can be demonstrated in all domains and for all times, especially when we take artificial, human-made objects into account. Leder and Carbon (2005) and Carbon (2010) relied on familiarity, mere exposure, and innovativeness to explain results from their studies on car design. When curved interiors were preferred to straight ones, the authors argued that straight lines were innovative and, therefore, the mere exposure effect could be held accountable for effects of preference for straightness, angularity, or curvature in different cases. To further explore this possibility, Carbon (2010) showed participants images of cars representing different epochs and styles. He indicated that curved car exteriors were only preferred when the design itself belonged to an epoch in which the trend was to build a more curved chassis. He claimed that preference for curvature was not static and uniform, but instead was under the influence of the aesthetic *Zeitgeist* of a given time. This reasoning supports a learned curvature effect as well as Zhang and colleagues' (2006) findings could do. According to them, countries high on individualism tend to use more angular brand logos than countries high on collectivism.

On another hand, before any experimental study about preference for curvature had been performed, Allen (1877) claimed a biological origin of some aesthetic features, including the curvature effect. According to this line of reasoning, Uher (1991) linked the use of zigzag motifs among different cultures to ancient environmental pressures.

Her evidence supported the influence of our biological heritage in the use of zigzag motifs, an influence that, nonetheless, was susceptible to cultural modulation. There are some other results that support the idea of an evolutionary origin of the curvature effect. Fantz and Miranda (1975) showed that 1-week-old infants tended to look longer at curved stimuli than at sharp ones. Moreover, findings from our group revealed that preference for curvature is also present in non-Western cultures (Gómez-Puerto et al., 2017; Munar, Gómez-Puerto, & Gomila, 2014) and even among nonhuman primates (Munar et al., 2015), using in both cases a particular approach–avoidance paradigm.

The approach–avoidance paradigm, due to its relationship with the evolutionary perspective and the embodied mind framework, deserves a separate mention in this section. It brings experimental aesthetics closer to the most basic and primary behaviors, while avoiding, as much as possible, complicated cognitive interpretations both by participants and researchers (Elliot & Covington, 2001; Munar et al., 2014). Some studies using approach–avoidance tasks found the curvature effect (Bertamini et al., 2016; Cotter et al., 2017; Gómez-Puerto et al., 2017; Munar et al., 2015; Palumbo et al., 2015), whereas others have not (Vartanian et al., 2013; Velasco, Salgado-Montejo, et al., 2016). However, they used different tasks: Bertamini et al. (2016) and Palumbo et al. (2015) used the manikin task; Munar et al. (2015) and Gómez-Puerto et al. (2017) used a pair-comparison task with an approach simulation after response; and Velasco et al. (2016) asked participants to categorize shapes in terms of approach/avoidance words. Conversely, Vartanian et al. (2013, 2017) used the same task in both studies in which participants rated interior design images on a dichotomous willingness-to-enter scale (enter versus exit), obtaining opposing results. They did not find a curvature effect in the former but they did in the latter. The authors indicated methodological considerations to account for the difference in results. The response window in the former study was limited to 3 seconds, whereas there was no time limit in the latter study. It is possible that longer viewing time triggers top-down processes that might alter the initial, rapid response to contour. The direction of this alteration would vary as a function of the task under consideration (i.e., beauty judgment vs. approach–avoidance decisions). In addition, the two studies differed in the number of stimuli, as well as the settings in which the data were collected. Perhaps most importantly, whereas one study involved naïve subjects, the other involved experts in the form of architects and designers. It is possible that expertise alters one's response to curvature in the context of approach–avoidance decisions. Further research is needed to clear up these aspects.

Overall, there is a certain amount of evidence supporting a possible evolutionary origin for the curvature effect, and several hypotheses that could explain it. One of them has been the *threat hypothesis* (Bar & Neta, 2006, 2007), which we will expound later. Another one is based on the neotenic features that tend to result in salient curved configurations, such as a rounded face or large rounded eyes, and seem to have been favored by sexual selection (Bertamini et al., 2016).

A Sensorimotor or an Appraisal Mechanism?

Some explanations of the curvature effect are based on specific sensorimotor systems, and others on appraisal processes (Gómez-Puerto et al., 2016). The sensorimotor explanation comes from the way in which curved stimuli directly interact with specific activation of the sensorimotor mechanisms (Amir et al., 2011; Fantz & Miranda, 1975; Ruff & Birch, 1974; Stratton, 1902, 1906). This research line is partly related to the processing fluency theory of aesthetic pleasure (Reber, Wurtz, & Zimmermann, 2004). Accordingly, fluent processing of an object leads to positive aesthetic responses. From this perspective, preference for curvature is greater than preference for angularity because curvature facilitates processing fluency. Some studies have reported that participants carry out different tasks faster using stimuli with curvilinear features than rectilinear ones (Álvarez, Blanco, & Leirós, 2002; LoBue, 2014; Quinn et al., 1997; Ruta, Palumbo, & Bertamini, 2014; Treisman & Gelade, 1980; Wolfe, Yee, & Friedman-Hill, 1992). However, Bar and Neta (2006, 2007) found no difference in the time it took participants to rate curved and sharp stimuli, even when curved ones were preferred. So far, only one preference-for-curvature study has reported significant differences between curved and sharp stimuli in response time. Experiment 1 in Palumbo and Bertamini (2016) showed that responses for the curved shapes were faster compared with responses for the sharp-angled shapes. This led to thinking that people perform general tasks faster with curvilinear than sharp-angled stimuli but this is not usually the case in tasks related to preference.

Amir et al. (2011) found that adults and infants looked first, and adults looked longer, at curved and nonparallel geons than at straight and parallel ones. According to them, human saccades tend to maximize the rate of information acquisition. First fixations tend to go to salient locations (Itti & Koch, 2001) and to locations that present greater uncertainty or a maximum amount of local information (Renninger, Verghese, & Coughlan, 2007). Amir et al. (2011) also found that curved geons produced great blood oxygen level dependence (BOLD) activity in human shape-selective cortex; that is, lateral occipital cortex and posterior fusiform gyrus. The importance of curvature in the occipito-temporal cortex is emphasized by the existence of a distributed network of cortical patches that respond maximally to curved stimuli (Yue, Pourladian, Tootell, & Ungerleider, 2014). Curved stimuli activate most V4 sites, and concave curvature—relative to fixation point—activates many posterior infero-temporal cortex sites (Ponce, Hartmann, & Livingstone, 2017).

Other explanations for the curvature effect have focused on appraisal mechanisms (Bar & Neta, 2006, 2007; Leder et al., 2011; Vartanian et al., 2013). These appraisal approaches are motivated by early findings about the emotional evaluation of straight, sharp, and curved lines (Lundholm, 1920; Poffenberger & Barrows, 1924), and abstract shapes (Hevner, 1935). Guthrie and Wiener's (1966) findings, which showed that the overall sharpness of a drawing determined that the image was perceived as threatening and negative, and Kastl and Child's (1968) findings about the emotional meaning of different typographies lent additional support to this approach. This research line is based on implicit and explicit appraisal processes and the way in which they impact aesthetic experience. These authors tend to agree that curvature is imbued with nonrepresentational semantic meaning and relate it to emotional processes. According to Vartanian et al. (2013), the effect is probably driven by pleasantness. Their results showed that judging the beauty of curvilinear spaces was associated with an increase in anterior cingulate cortex (ACC) activity. They indicated the contribution of ACC to reward and emotional and affective processing. Using mobile electroencephalography (EEG) and head-mounted virtual reality, Banaei et al. (2017) also found stronger theta synchronization in the ACC with curved forms.

Implicit measures might reveal more information about the semantic/affective processes underlying preference as compared with explicit evaluations. Palumbo et al. (2015) tested implicit associations between shapes' contour line (curved vs. sharp-angled) and attributes: valence, danger, and gender. They used an Implicit Association Test (IAT) with irregular polygons that allowed the control of familiarity and semantic processes, which typically influence liking evaluations. Curved shapes were implicitly associated with safe and positive words and with female names. In contrast, angular shapes were associated with danger and negative words and with male names. The test revealed affective processes underlying the curvature effect, which might not be accessible with explicit evaluations. The authors suggested that preference for curved contours might be triggered by an aesthetic quality contained in the curved contour itself, but it is also mediated by what curves can evoke in terms of affective representations. They indicated that preference for curves might be boosted by positive feedback from second-order associative processes.

The Threat Hypothesis

Aiken (1998) argued that preference for curvature is actually motivated by fear induced by sharp lines. Such fear had served an adaptive function in our past to help us rapidly detect and avoid possible threats. The author stated that primitive emotions, which originated initially as a response to environmental pressures, have been repurposed, giving rise to the aesthetic experience.

Bar and Neta (2006, 2007) tested the hypothesis that curved stimuli are preferred because sharp contours evoke a sense of threat. They confirmed the curvature effect with images of familiar objects and meaningless patterns. Participants were asked to make a like/dislike choice about stimuli varying in their contour: curved, sharp, or mixed. Curved stimuli were liked more than mixed and sharp ones (Bar & Neta, 2006). In another experiment, participants had to respond "threatening" or "nonthreatening" to each stimulus. Sharp-angled objects and patterns were rated as significantly more threatening

than curved ones. The authors interpreted their findings as being consistent with the proposal that objects may be perceived as threatening based on the nature of their contour.

Moreover, in a functional magnetic resonance imaging (fMRI) study, Bar and Neta
(2007) observed a bilateral increase in amygdala activity when participants were
presented with sharp stimuli. The authors expected this result, as amygdala activity is
related to threat perception. Grassini and colleagues' (2019) results supported this line
of argument, but with other stimuli: the curved ones. In Experiment 1, they compared
snakes, ropes, and other items, and the results showed that both snake and rope images
elicited enhanced P1 and N1 event-related potential components as well as early posterior negativity (EPN). In Experiment 2, they studied whether nonthreatening curvilinear images (i.e., ropes) still elicited the enhanced electrophysiological responses when
snake images were not presented as stimuli, and therefore, the context did not provoke
top-down attention to curvilinear shapes. Rope images still evoked an enhanced EPN—
but not P1 and N1. However, this effect was smaller than in Experiment 1, in which
snake images were present. According to the authors, a stronger EPN response can be
considered an index of reflexive attention and increased activity at the level of visual
cortex, and might be the result of the influence of the amygdala activation on the visual
areas. The authors suggested that the results might be due to a high-level, top-down attentional effect, such that the participants voluntarily directed attention toward curvilinear shapes when snakes were present as stimuli. Bottom-up attentional processes
might also be involved, because the participants may have been automatically more
aroused when snake images were present in the experiment.

As Bar and Neta (2006, 2007) used objects whose semantic meaning was emotionally
neutral, Leder et al. (2011) further explored the contour effect with objects of negative
valence. They hypothesized that if the perception of threat produced by an object was
related to preference, then the negative valence could override other positive cues such
as the curvature of its contour. Thus, they presented new stimuli depicting images of real
objects that had been manipulated to create a curved and a sharp contoured version of
each object. These objects were selected according to their emotional valence: positive
or negative. They digitally manipulated one version of the object—curved or sharp—
to create the other new version—sharp or curved. As predicted, curved stimuli were
preferred to sharp ones, but only when the objects had a positive or neutral valence.
They argued that this showed how threat and preference are interconnected, and that
semantic evaluation takes precedence over the evaluation of contour, overriding the
effects that curvature might have in preference.

However, some findings have questioned the *threat hypothesis*. In an fMRI study
with images of interior architectural spaces, Vartanian et al. (2013) found no increase
in amygdala activity when viewing rooms with sharp-angled contours compared with
rooms with curved contours, which were preferred to the former. The authors suggested
that sharp cues in buildings could have lost their threatening nature through learning
and exposure.

Bertamini et al. (2016) and Palumbo et al. (2015) showed that angles are not necessary to generate preference for curvature. Bertamini et al. (2016) (Experiment 2) tested

whether the effect was modulated by distance. If angular shapes were associated with threat, then the effect might be stronger when they were presented within peripersonal space. In the experiment, the shapes appeared at different perceived distances. The task was to rate preference for each shape after judging whether the object was within reach. According to the threat hypothesis, the effect should be stronger when shapes were presented near the observer, because any threat in near space is more noticeable than a threat farther away. However, the results showed that the curvature effect was not modulated by perceived distance. In Experiment 3, they used lines seen through an aperture so that there was no closed shape to form an object. There were straight lines with no angles, lines with an angle, and parabolas. If curvature was pleasant in itself, it should be preferred to straight lines, even in the absence of angles. The results revealed that curvature was preferred over angularity even for simple lines. Moreover, there was no difference in preference for angular and straight lines. In Experiment 4, they used a manikin task in which participants had to move a stick figure closer or farther, as instructed, from a series of curved or sharp polygons. Participants moved the manikin faster when presented with sharp polygons, independently of whether they brought it closer or moved it farther away. But when presented with curved polygons, they reacted faster only when they brought it closer to the stimuli. This is not the behavior that would be expected if sharp angles were perceived as threatening. Using the same task, Palumbo et al. (2015) found the same tendency with polygons with more and less pronounced vertices. The authors concluded that, in these cases, preference is due to the intrinsic characteristics of curvature and not to a rejection of sharp contours. However, they also indicated that the two proposals are not necessarily contradictory but instead, in some cases, might be complementary.

Soranzo et al. (2018) showed that sharp-angled objects displaying behaviors were preferred over quiescent objects and that the difference between preference for curved contours against sharp contours actually decreased when the object displayed behaviors. It is reasonable to believe that a potentially threatening motionless object would be more threatening if it were to display a behavior. Particularly, if an angularly shaped object exhibits behavior, this should be considered more threatening than a similar object that is quiescent. This finding also supports the hypothesis that the curvature effect is a genuine preference for curvature, rather than an avoidance of sharp-angled objects.

Beyond Visual Contour

Related to an evolutionary perspective, the idea that the curvature effect could be present in other sensory modalities has been widely expressed but little empirical evidence has demonstrated it. Jakesch and Carbon (2011) argued that the haptic sense should be less affected by cultural and *Zeitgeist* aspects and thus, should be more directly affected by evolutionary-based influences. Consequently, they used 3D plotted artificial stimuli with two types of contours (curved and sharp-angled) and two complexity levels (low and high). They used two types of responses: a like/dislike response and a 7-point scale. Curved stimuli were significantly rated as preferable in both types of responses.

Soranzo et al. (2018) reported the curvature effect with 3D objects that were both looked at—sight—and manipulated—touch. It seems therefore that the effect is not limited to pictorial representations and to visual processing, but it might be a general feature that extends to 3D objects and influences experience in more perceptual domains, such as touch.

Besides visual and tactile contour, preference for curvature has also been revealed in another perceptual attribute; that is, body movement. As mentioned previously, warmth has been related to curved body movements, curved arm movements, and curved movement paths in ballet performances (Aronoff, 2006; Aronoff et al., 1992; Christensen et al., 2016).

On another hand, there are several findings that showed a significant relation between sweet taste and curved shapes (Blazhenkova & Kumar, 2018; Salgado-Montejo et al., 2015; Velasco, Woods, Petit, Cheok, & Spence, 2016). If sweet tastes are considered to be preferred to other tastes, an indirect relationship between curved shapes and preferred taste can be established. However, empirical support for this association is required.

More studies are needed to confirm or reject the curvature effect in nonvisual modalities, especially in audition. In any case, the previous findings are indicating a possible similar effect in other modalities. If the effect were confirmed in other sensory modalities, then we should wonder about a possible common origin among modalities or specific sources for each modality. These visual and haptic preferences might have a common origin, with one perhaps being a consequence of the other, a matter that should be solved empirically. Following Dewey's (1922) principle of continuity, it would also be interesting to study whether these preferences could be recruited for higher cognitive consequences, as some instances in language could show: "well rounded," "sharp practice," "come round," "a short, sharp shock," "the sharp end," and "sharp" as "not quite honest" (Munar et al., 2014).

Individual and Contextual Differences

As the curvature effect has been firmly demonstrated across age groups, cultures, and species, a logical step is to explore different moderators such as personal and contextual features to shed light on its nature and mark the boundaries of the effect. In this line, several studies have focused on individual differences regarding the curvature effect (Cotter et al., 2017; Silvia & Barona, 2009; Vartanian et al., 2017; Zhang et al., 2006).

Using brand logos as stimuli, Zhang et al. (2006) found that people with an activated inter-independent self-construal (i.e., emphasizing compromise and collectivism) perceived curved shapes as more attractive than people with an activated independent self-construal (i.e., emphasizing confrontation and individualism). Moreover, they showed that countries high on collectivism (Hong Kong, Korea, and Japan) tended to use less angular logos than countries high on individualism (United States, Canada,

United Kingdom, and Germany). Tzeng et al. (1990) also found intercultural differences in the perception of what they called the "rounded factor" despite some similarities between cultures. They used 21 semantic differential scales, 10 graphic stimuli, and three groups of participants from Japan, Mexico, and Columbia. The "rounded factor" was the factor that accounted for more variance in a principal component analysis based on the data from the semantic differential scale. The Japanese sample liked roundness more than Mexican and Columbian samples.

However, Gómez-Puerto et al. (2017) investigated whether preference for curved contours was common across different cultures. They tested preference for curvature in two small-scale societies relatively uninfluenced by Western culture (Oaxaca, Mexico, and Bawku, Ghana) and a university sample from a Western country (Majorca, Spain). Participants performed a two-alternative, forced-choice task, in which they had to choose between curved and sharp-angled versions of the same real objects. The results showed that participants in all of the three countries chose the curved-contour version significantly more often than the sharp-angled one. Moreover, preference did not differ significantly among the three samples. The authors concluded that the curvature effect seems to be common across cultures and the conjecture that it is a constituent of a natural propensity for aesthetics.

On another hand, some findings indicate that artistic expertise interacts with the curvature effect (Cotter et al., 2017; Silvia & Barona, 2009; Vartanian et al., 2017). This interaction seems to depend on the type of stimuli. With asymmetrical complex patterns (Silvia & Barona, 2009) or irregular polygons (Cotter et al., 2017), participants higher in artistic expertise showed a greater curvature effect. Conversely, with arrays of simple objects—circles and hexagons—either there was no difference between experts and novices (Cotter et al., 2017) or the novices presented the effect and the experts did not (Silvia & Barona, 2009). Circles and hexagons are familiar objects, but the irregular stimuli used by Silvia and Barona (2009) and Cotter et al. (2017) were novel. As a possible explanation of the results, the authors indicated that people possess linguistic labels for circles and hexagons with a set of established semantic associations. It is likely that these stimuli already possess valence, which can take precedence over curvature (Leder et al., 2011).

Vartanian et al. (2017) studied the effect of interior space contour—curvilinear versus rectilinear—with architects, designers, and nonexperts. Participants rated photographs of architectural spaces—half on a dichotomous beauty scale and half on a dichotomous willingness-to-enter/exit scale—to indicate whether it was a space they would like to enter or leave. With the beauty scale, experts showed preference for curvature but nonexperts did not. With the enter–exit scale, nonexperts presented the curvature effect but experts did not. The nonexperts' results were the opposite of those of Vartanian et al. (2013). They showed the curvature effect with the beauty scale and not with the enter–exit scale. Aside from the fact that some of the photographs were the same in the two studies, there were some differences between the two procedures. The authors focused on the deduction that contour might be a more salient variable to architects and designers when assessing beauty. Another possibility is that contour could be a function of negative associations toward rectilinear contours, honed through professional practice and training. In relation to the enter–exit results, they suggested that experts might be trained to view images of architectural spaces dispassionately and be less subject to implicit behavioral biases rendered by their visual features. On another hand, the functionality or usability of a space becomes the relevant frame for choice for nonexperts.

Another trait that seems to moderate the curvature effect is openness to experience. Cotter et al. (2017) measured this trait with the HEXACO Inventory, the Neo-Five-Factor Inventory, and the Big Five Aspects Scale. Participants scoring higher on these scales showed greater curvature effect in irregular polygons, but not in arrays of circles and hexagons.

Type of Stimuli and Presentation Time

Besides personal and situational features, there are some other moderators of the effect that come from the stimuli. As Cotter et al. (2017) found, irregular polygons and arrays of circles and hexagons interact differentially with expertise. Regarding the familiarity of the stimuli, Bar and Neta (2006) reported a slightly larger effect size using meaningful images than meaningless patterns. However, Leder et al. (2011) reported a slightly larger effect size with abstract patterns than with real object images. Both studies used the same presentation time (84 ms), the same like–dislike task, and the same stimuli. Westerman et al. (2012) found similar effect sizes in meaningless patterns and real objects, using designs of packaging and until-response conditions.

In Corradi et al. (2018) we found similar effect sizes with real objects and meaningless patterns presented for short–medium times (84, 150, 300 ms), but different effect sizes for long times. The effect faded in the presentation time until-response with images of real objects as in Munar et al. (2015), whereas it increased with meaningless patterns. We interpreted this as implying that the processing of the two types of stimuli must be different. We hypothesized that long presentations give rise to an increasing contribution of semantic content that leads to preference based on such content instead of on curvature. When shapes have no meaning, the curvature effect is preserved or even heightened in long presentations. According to our results, this might come from the intensified weight of the curvature in the discrimination and decision processes.

Palumbo and Bertamini (2016) also varied the presentation time using the same meaningless patterns as we did: 120 ms in Experiment 1 and until-response in Experiments 2 and 3. The effect size was slightly higher in Experiment 1 than in Experiments 2 and 3. However, the difference between their results and ours could come from several sources: instructions, type of presentation, and kind of response. Palumbo and Bertamini's instructions were about liking in Experiments 1 and 2, and about attractiveness in Experiment 3. Our instructions were about selecting one of the two stimuli presented at once. On another hand, they used a like/dislike response in Experiment 1 and a rating scale in Experiments 2 and 3. They also manipulated the number of vertices and concavities. In this line, they concluded that parametric manipulations of complexity produce small but significant effects on preference. In particular, more concavities within curved shapes introduce more changes in curvature—and higher curvature magnitude—in turn, decreasing liking.

Applied Science

In the past decade, quite a few research lines have focused on understanding how object contours influence people to design more adaptive interactions between objects, or arrangements, and individuals. Some of them have tried to link basic scientific findings with applied aims, and others have had more direct business purposes. Because of the applied orientation, some of the tasks in these studies have not been about direct preference but about feelings that curvature can convey. Research from domains such as advertising, marketing, packaging, interior design, and planning of urban and recreational environments has taken interest in the curvature effect. We distinguish three types of applied studies according to their focus: (1) item forms (Ghoshal, Boarwright, & Malika, 2016; Hareli, David, Lev-Yadun, & Katzir, 2016; Hůla & Flegr, 2016; Soranzo et al., 2018); (2) product packaging, logos or shape of graphics on the package (Fang & Mowen, 2005; Westerman et al., 2012; Zhang et al., 2006); and (3) general settings (Banaei et al., 2017; Dazkir & Read, 2012; Hess, Gryc, & Hareli, 2013; Leder & Carbon, 2005; Van Oel & Van den Berkhof, 2013; Vartanian et al., 2013, 2017).

Items

Regarding the first group of studies, Ghoshal et al. (2016) asked participants to rate the hedonic value and functionality of a selection of 30 common products. They rated higher hedonic perceptions for curved products and higher functional perceptions for angular products. The impact of curvature or angularity was moderated by individual differences such as need for cognition and involvement with the category.

Soranzo et al. (2018) created 3D physical artifacts that combined four characteristics: contour (curved vs. sharp), size (small vs. large), surface texture (rough vs. smooth), and behavior of the objects (lighting, sounding, vibrating, and quiescent). Participants had to interact with the object and rate it on each of seven dimensions: interesting, comfortable, playful, surprising, pleasant, special, and relaxing. For all dimensions except surprising, the curvature effect was significant. That is, curved objects were more interesting, more comfortable, more playful, more special, and more relaxing.

Another two studies focused on specific organic items: flowers (Hůla & Flegr, 2016) and leaves (Hareli et al., 2016). Hůla and Flegr (2016) determined which, if any, flower colors and shapes were more preferred than others. The set of flower stimuli consisted of 52 photographs, which varied in different features: symmetry, form contour, color, complexity, and prototypicality. Twenty-one of them were classified as round, 15 as sharp, and 16 as mixed. According to their analyses, sharp contours positively affected the flower beauty scores, whereas mixed contours had no effect.

However, we have to consider that the different features were not combined system-atically. On another hand, the authors indicated the possibility that the curvature effect could be context-specific and, for some unspecified reason, does not apply to flowers. Despite its relative robustness, the curvature effect remains sensitive to methodological variations.

Hareli et al. (2016) asked participants to evaluate leaves—sharp-angled or curved—on a set of semantic differential scales. Curved shaped leaves were rated as more beau-tiful, friendlier, more comforting, and warmer than the sharp-angled ones. However, they also found a consistent pattern in which houses surrounded by sharp-leafed vegetation were evaluated as more expensive, compared with houses surrounded by round-leafed vegetation. In another experiment, they found that sharp leaf vegetation houses were evaluated as safer. They inferred that the characteristics associated with sharp shapes confer protection to the house. This way, we have to bear in mind that aesthetic preference is not the only way people choose between objects with different shapes.

Product Packaging and Brand Logos

Fang and Mowen (2005) showed that product category moderated the effects of curva-ture on evaluations of brand logos. Specifically, participants preferred a round logo for vases but an angular logo for buildings. They proposed a match-up explanation to account for this finding. That is, when a logo matches the typical form of an object that is stored in consumers' mind, their evaluation tends to be more positive. However, Westerman et al. (2012) found no beneficial effect of semantic congruence associated with using angular and round shapes, demonstrating preference for curved designs for different types of products (chocolate, water, and bleach) and different packaging designs (box vs. bottle). They manipulated images of product packaging regarding the shape of both contour and graphics. There was a preference for curved designs that extended to self-report purchase likelihood. They also showed additive effects of con-tour and graphic shape that could not be accounted for by design typicality or perceived ease of use.

Also, Jiang et al. (2016) showed that the curved shape of a logo influenced consumers' inferences about products and their attitudes toward them. They showed that a curved brand logo activated mental associations related to "softness" and a sharp-angled brand logo activated mental associations related to "hardness," and these activated associations subsequently influenced product and company attribute judgments. The authors proposed mental imagery as the underlying mechanism driving the effect of logo shape on consumer judgments. Support was obtained from two experiments: One showing that the logo shape effects were eliminated under conditions of visual load but not cog-nitive load, because only the former type of load constrained the available resources in visuospatial working memory necessary for imagery generation; a second experiment showed that the shape effect was reduced when people had a lower predisposition to generate mental images.

General Settings

Several studies examined how variation in the contour of interior spaces impacts explicit responses such as pleasure, aesthetics judgments, choices, and approach decisions (Banaei et al., 2017; Hess et al., 2013; Liu, Bogicevic, & Mattila, 2018; Van Oel & Van den Berkhof, 2013; Vartanian et al., 2013, 2017; Zhu & Argo, 2013). In this line, Dazkir and Read (2012) tested pleasure and approach reactions toward curvilinear and rectilinear simulated interior settings. They focused specifically on furniture forms. The curvilinear forms elicited higher amounts of pleasant emotions (feeling relaxed, peaceful, calm) than the rectilinear forms. Also, the participants desired to approach curvilinear settings more compared with the rectilinear ones.

Van Oel and Van den Berkhof (2013) investigated the way passengers value architectural airport design characteristics, using visualizations of hypothetical areas. They used eight design characteristics with two levels each. The "form" characteristic was elaborated in the roof construction, as either a curvilinear or an orthogonal roof. The results showed that form was the most influential characteristic in choosing the most preferred passenger area. The curvilinear form was more preferred than the orthogonal form. The "layout" characteristic was the third most influential characteristic. The layout was elaborated as a straight area layout or a curved area layout. In general, passengers had a clear preference for an area with curved hallways.

In Vartanian et al. (2013), naïve participants were more likely to judge spaces as beautiful if they had curvilinear rather than rectilinear contours. In contrast, contour had no effect on approach–avoidance decisions. In a second article, Vartanian et al. (2017) found that experts assessed curvilinear spaces as more beautiful than rectilinear spaces, whereas contour had no effect on beauty judgments among nonexperts. Interestingly, when making approach–avoidance decisions, nonexperts were more likely to choose to enter curvilinear rather than rectilinear spaces, whereas contour had no effect on approach–avoidance decisions among experts. Possible explanations of these results have been presented in the previous section about individual differences.

When contemplating architectural interiors as beautiful, Vartanian et al. (2013) found that curvilinear contour activated the anterior cingulate cortex (ACC) exclusively, a region strongly responsive to the reward properties and emotional salience of objects. The ACC also showed pronounced activity when participants in Banaei et al. (2017) presented higher responses in terms of pleasure and arousal related to rooms with more curved geometries. These authors investigated human brain dynamics connected to the affective impact of interior forms when the perceiver actively explored an architectural space. They used a mobile EEG set-up synchronized to head-mounted virtual reality. Rooms associated with lower pleasure and arousal ratings contained more linear geometries, whereas rooms with higher pleasure and arousal ratings contained more curved geometries.

Other studies investigated the indirect influence of shapes on social attitudes and decisions (Hess et al., 2013; Liu et al., 2018; Zhu & Argo, 2013). Hess et al. (2013) indicated that participants who were exposed to sharp shapes perceived other participants as more aggressive and were more likely to make an aggressive decision. In Experiment 1, participants assembled a puzzle. It was a face photo cut into round or sharp-edged puzzle pieces. After completion of the puzzle, they rated the person whose photo they had assembled. When the photo was assembled from round shapes, participants rated the individual on the photo as significantly less aggressive than when the photo was assembled from sharp shapes. In Experiment 2, participants played a game and were told that their decisions would be paired with the decisions made by another unknown participant at a later time. The room was decorated with round or sharp objects of different materials. When the room was decorated with sharp objects, participants chose the aggressive option relatively more often than when the room was decorated with round shapes.

Zhu and Argo (2013) found that when seating arrangements were circular, consumers evaluated persuasive material more favorably when it was consistent with a belongingness need (i.e., it included family-oriented information or a majority endorsement). In contrast, when a seating arrangement contained angles, consumers preferred a persuasive message when it related to a uniqueness need (i.e., it included self-oriented information or a minority endorsement).

Liu et al. (2018) examined the impact of shape cues—curved versus sharp-angled—on customer satisfaction. The findings suggested that in nonbusy settings, curved shape cue enhanced customer satisfaction. In contrast, sharp-angled shape cues increased customer satisfaction in busy settings. Customer satisfaction enhancement in nonbusy settings was via warmth perceptions, and satisfaction enhancement in busy settings was through competence perceptions. The authors suggested that a service incorporating curved cues will activate customers' warmth associations, and one with sharp-angled cues will activate competence associations.

Major Challenges, Goals, and Suggestions

In the last section, we have seen that some studies about the curvature effect have been related to applied research in the past decade. It has been related to innovative sensory marketing strategies (Fang & Mowen, 2005; Ghoshal et al., 2016; Liu et al., 2018; Schweinsberg et al., 2016; Zhang et al., 2006), social cognition (Hess et al., 2013; Zhu & Argo, 2013), architecture (Banaei et al., 2017; Van Oel & Van den Berkhof, 2013; Vartanian et al., 2013), security perception (Hareli et al., 2016), interior design (Dazkir & Read, 2012), and car design (Carbon, 2010; Leder & Carbon, 2005). We think this trend will continue in quite a few applied disciplines and is a great opportunity for researchers from empirical aesthetics. Interestingly, the effect has not yet been studied in the fields of painting, sculpture, and music, although some studies have shown its influence in dance and ballet (Aronoff, 2006; Aronoff et al., 1992; Christensen et al., 2016).

From another perspective, a comprehensive understanding of preference for curvature must go beyond the mere accumulation of data. According to Gómez-Puerto et al. (2016), research about the curvature effect needs to form some foundations of a unified framework to advance its understanding. For this purpose, we consider that there are some points that require research and refinement. Some of them are:

1. *A conceptual approach.* The concepts of *curvature* and *curved* are widely used throughout most published research. However, *roundness* and *round* are also used in some of the articles. It seems appropriate to clarify whether they refer to the same feature or whether there is some specific difference between the concepts. If there is consensus that they are referring to the same meaning, it may be preferable to use only one pair of concepts to strengthen the field and avoid misunderstanding. Something similar is observed with *sharpness* and *angularity*. Gómez-Puerto et al. (2016) proposed the use of the dichotomy *curvature/sharpness* to describe the object of study, and *curved/sharp-angled* to characterize the stimuli causing the effect. Defining central concepts clearly and univocally should be the first step to build compelling and testable explanations of preference for curvature.

2. *A psychophysical project.* A disentanglement of the psychophysical nature of this feature is needed. We should know more about what is deemed to be curved, and what physical factors (number of vertices, concavity, size, complexity, and others) affect perceived curvature. Perhaps there are other nonphysical factors that can also affect it. For instance, Carbon (2010) mentioned the images of shark teeth, the outline of a shark, and a rose thorn as paradigmatical examples of sharp transitions in nature, but it could be argued that these stimuli are actually curved in contour, not sharp-angled. The psychophysical nature of the feature needs to be explored in order to determine which contours and lines people consider curved and which sharp-angled.

3. *Preference for curvature, avoidance of sharpness, or both?* Evidence for a genuine preference for curvature has been increasing in the past few years, but there is also some evidence supporting the threat hypothesis. There is also a possibility that we are dealing with two cognitive phenomena or maybe only with one. When proposing an evolutionary origin, it is not enough to suggest a plausible explanation. A detailed scenario with testable predictions is required for both hypotheses to be useful.

4. *Contextual and individual differences.* Situations and personal characteristics can affect perceived curvature and preference of the contour. Previously, we have seen some of these characteristics that influence the curvature effect: self-construal, country, expertise, and openness to experience. However, we need some systematic studies that also help us to know more about the processes that moderate and mediate the curvature effect.

5. *One or several preference mechanisms?* We need to clarify whether we are dealing with a general preference for curvature or with specific dissociable preferences for curvatures. Is the mechanism that gives rise to preference for curved lines the same that gives rise to preference for curved contours? We can extend this question to 3D objects and also to different sensorial attributes and modalities. It is unclear whether this is a unimodal or a multimodal phenomenon.

Finally, we would like to include a suggestion for researchers, especially for beginners in research. Most of the studies used experimental designs to determine whether the effect is present in a particular situation, but it is appropriate to introduce manipulations of the participants' state and situations in order to reveal when the effect is present or when it increases or decreases in magnitude. This can be done using different experimental paradigms—implicit measures, eye movements, neuroimaging, among others—and would inform us more about the underlying cognitive processes that give rise to the preference for curvature.

References

Aiken, N. E. (1998). *The biological origins of art*. Westport, CT: Praeger Publishers/Greenwood.

Allen, G. (1877). *Physiological aesthetics*. New York, NY: D. Appleton & Company.

Álvarez, A., Blanco, M., & Leirós, L. (2002). Influencia de la simetría y la curvilinealidad en el procesamiento de estímulos cerrados. *Psicothema, 14*(3), 597–604.

Amir, O., Biederman, I., & Hayworth, K. J. (2011). The neural basis for shape preferences. *Vision Research, 51*(20), 2198–2206. doi:10.1016/j.visres.2011.08.015

Aronoff, J. (2006). How we recognize angry and happy emotion in people, places, and things. *Cross-Cultural Research, 40*(1), 83–105. doi:10.1177/1069397105282597

Aronoff, J., Woike, B. A., & Hyman, L. M. (1992). Which are the stimuli in facial displays of anger and happiness: Configurational bases of emotion recognition. *Journal of Personality and Social Psychology, 62*(6), 1050. doi:10.1037/0022-3514.62.6.1050

Banaei, M., Hatami, J., Yazdanfar, A., & Gramann, K. (2017). Walking through architectural spaces: The impact of interior forms on human brain dynamics. *Frontiers in Human Neuroscience, 11*(September), 477. doi:10.3389/FNHUM.2017.00477

Bar, M., & Neta, M. (2006). Humans prefer curved visual objects. *Psychological Science, 17*(8), 645–648. doi:10.1111/j.1467-9280.2006.01759.x

Bar, M., & Neta, M. (2007). Visual elements of subjective preference modulate amygdala activation. *Neuropsychologia, 45*(10), 2191–2200. doi:10.1016/j.neuropsychologia.2007.03.008

Bertamini, M., & Palumbo, L. (2015). The aesthetics of smooth contour curvature in historical contest. In *Art and its role in the history of the Balkans*. Kosovska, Mitrovica: Faculty of Philosophy, University of Pristina. Retrieved from https://www.bertamini.org/lab/Publications/BertaminiPalumbo2015.pdf.

Bertamini, M., Palumbo, L., Gheorghes, T. N., & Galatsidas, M. (2016). Do observers like curvature or do they dislike angularity? *British Journal of Psychology, 107*(1), 154–178. doi:10.1111/bjop.12132

Blazhenkova, O., & Kumar, M. M. (2018). Angular versus curved shapes: Correspondences and emotional processing. *Perception, 47*(1), 67–89. doi:10.1177/0301006617731048

Carbon, C. C. (2010). The cycle of preference: Long-term dynamics of aesthetic appreciation. *Acta Psychologica, 134*(2), 233–244. doi:10.1016/j.actpsy.2010.02.004

Christensen, J. F., Pollick, F. E., Lambrechts, A., & Gomila, A. (2016). Affective responses to dance. *Acta Psychologica, 168*, 91–105. doi:10.1016/j.actpsy.2016.03.008

Corradi, G. B., Rosselló, J., Vañó, J., Chuquichambi, E., Bertamini, M., & Munar, E. (2018). The effects of presentation time on preference for curvature of real objects and meaningless novel patterns. *British Journal of Psychology, 110*(4), 670–685. doi:10.1111/bjop.12367

Cotter, K. N., Silvia, P. J., Bertamini, M., Palumbo, L., & Vartanian, O. (2017). Curve appeal: Exploring individual differences in preference for curved versus angular objects. *I-Perception, 8*(2), 1–17. doi:10.1177/2041669517693023

Dazkir, S. S., & Read, M. A. (2012). Furniture form and their influence on our emotional responses toward interior environments. *Environment and Behavior, 44*(5), 722–732. doi:10.1177/0013916511402063

Dewey, J. (1922). *Human nature and conduct.* Carbondale, IL: Southern Illinois University Press.

Elliot, A. J., & Covington, M. V. (2001). Approach and avoidance motivation. *Educational Psychology Review, 13*(2), 73–92. doi:10.1023/A:1009009018235

Fang, X., & Mowen, J. C. (2005). Exploring factors influencing logo effectiveness. An experimental inquiry. *Advances in Consumer Research, 32,* 161.

Fantz, R. L. (1961). The origin of form perception. *Scientific American, 204*(5), 66–72. doi:10.1038/scientificamerican0561-66

Fantz, R. L., & Miranda, S. B. (1975). Newborn-infant attention to form of contour. *Child Development, 46*(1), 224–228. doi:10.2307/1128853

Franck, K., & Rosen, E. (1949). A projective test of masculinity-femininity. *Journal of Consulting Psychology, 13*(4), 247–256.

Ghoshal, T., Boarwright, P., & Malika, M. (2016). Curvature for all angles. In R. Batra, C. Seifert, & D. Brei (Eds.), *The Psychology of Design* (pp. 91–106). New York, NY: Routledge.

Gómez-Puerto, G., Munar, E., & Nadal, M. (2016). Preference for curvature: A historical and conceptual framework. *Frontiers in Human Neuroscience, 9*(January), 1–8. doi:10.3389/fnhum.2015.00712

Gómez-Puerto, G., Rosselló, J., Corradi, G., Acedo-Carmona, C., Munar, E., & Nadal, M. (2017). Preference for curved contours across cultures. *Psychology of Aesthetics, Creativity, and the Arts, 12*(4), 432–439. doi:10.1037/aca0000135

Grassini, S., Railo, H., Valli, K., Revonsuo, A., & Koivisto, M. (2019). Visual features and perceptual context modulate attention towards evolutionarily relevant threatening stimuli: Electrophysiological evidence. *Emotion, 19*(2), 348–364. doi:10.1037/emo0000434

Guthrie, G., & Wiener, M. (1966). Subliminal perception or perception of partial cue with pictorial stimuli. *Journal of Personality and Social Psychology, 3*(6), 619–628. doi:10.1037/h0023197

Hareli, S., David, S., Lev-Yadun, S., & Katzir, G. (2016). Money in your palm: Sharp shaped vegetation in the surroundings increase the subjective value of houses. *Journal of Environmental Psychology, 46,* 176–187. doi:10.1016/j.jenvp.2016.04.014

Hess, U., Gryc, O., & Hareli, S. (2013). How shapes influence social judgments. *Social Cognition, 31*(1), 72–80. doi:10.1521/soco.2013.31.1.72

Hevner, K. (1935). Experimental studies of the affective value of colors and lines. *Journal of Applied Psychology, 19*(4), 385–398.

Hogarth, W. (1753). *The analysis of beauty: Written with a view of fixing the fluctuating ideas of taste.* Ann Arbor, MI: University of Michigan Library.

Hopkins, J. R., Kagan, J., Brachfeld, S., Hans, S., & Linn, S. (1976). Infant responsivity to curvature. *Child Development, 47*(4), 1166–1171.

Hůla, M., & Flegr, J. (2016). What flowers do we like? The influence of shape and color on the rating of flower beauty. *PeerJ, 4,* e2106. doi:10.7717/peerj.2106

Itti, L., & Koch, C. (2001). Computational modeling of visual attention. *Nature Reviews Neuroscience, 2*(3), 194–203.

Jadva, V., Hines, M., & Golombok, S. (2010). Infants' preferences for toys, colors, and shapes: Sex differences and similarities. *Archives of Sexual Behavior, 39*(6), 1261–1273. doi:10.1007/s10508-010-9618-z

Jahoda, G. (1956). Sex differences in preferences for shapes: A cross-cultural replication. *British Journal of Psychology, 47*(2), 126–132.

Jakesch, M., & Carbon, C.-C. (2011). Humans prefer curved objects on basis of haptic evaluation. *Perception, 40*(Supplement), 219. doi:10.1068/v110148

Jiang, Y., Gorn, G. J., Galli, M., & Chattopadhyay, A. (2016). Does your company have the right logo? How and why circular- and angular-logo shapes influence brand attribute judgments. *Journal of Consumer Research, 42*(5), 709–726. doi:10.1093/jcr/ucv049

Kastl, A. J., & Child, I. L. (1968). Emotional meaning of four typographical variables. *Journal of Applied Psychology, 52*(6, Pt.1), 440–446. doi:10.1037/h0026506

Krout, J. (1950). Symbol elaboration test (S.E.T.): The reliability and validity of a new projective technique. *Psychological Monographs: General and Applied, 64*(4), 1–67.

Leder, H., & Carbon, C.-C. (2005). Dimensions in appreciation of car interior design. *Applied Cognitive Psychology, 19*(5), 603–618. doi:10.1002/acp.1088

Leder, H., Carbon, C.-C., & Ripsas, A.-L. (2006). Entitling art: Influence of title information on understanding and appreciation of paintings. *Acta Psychologica, 121*(2), 176–198. doi:10.1016/j.actpsy.2005.08.005

Leder, H., Tinio, P. P. L., & Bar, M. (2011). Emotional valence modulates the preference for curved objects. *Perception, 40*(6), 649–655. doi:10.1068/p6845

Liu, S. Q., Bogicevic, V., & Mattila, A. S. (2018). Circular vs. angular servicescape: "Shaping" customer response to a fast service encounter pace. *Journal of Business Research, 89*(April), 47–56. doi:10.1016/j.jbusres.2018.04.007

LoBue, V. (2014). Deconstructing the snake: The relative roles of perception, cognition, and emotion on threat detection. *Emotion, 14*(4), 701–711. doi:10.1037/a0035898

Lundholm, H. (1920). The affective tone of lines: Experimental researches. *Psychological Review, 28*(1), 43–60.

Marr, D. (1982). *Vision. A computational investigation into the human representation and processing of visual information.* Cambridge, MA: MIT Press. doi:10.7551/mitpress/9780262514620.001.0001

McElroy, W. A. (1954). A sex difference in preferences for shapes. *British Journal of Psychology, 64*(4), 209–216.

Munar, E., Gómez-Puerto, G., Call, J., & Nadal, M. (2015). Common visual preference for curved contours in humans and great apes. *PLoS ONE, 10*(11), e0141106. doi:10.1371/journal.pone.0141106

Munar, E., Gómez-Puerto, G., & Gomila, A. (2014). The evolutionary roots of aesthetics: An approach-avoidance look at curvature preference. In A. Scarinzi (Ed.), *Embodied Aesthetics* (pp. 3–17). Leiden, the Netherlands: Brill.

Munroe, R. H., Munroe, R. L., & Lansky, L. M. (1976). A sex difference in shape preference. *The Journal of Social Psychology, 98*, 139–140.

Palumbo, L., & Bertamini, M. (2016). The curvature effect: A comparison between preference tasks. *Empirical Studies of the Arts, 34*(1), 35–53. doi:10.1177/0276237415621185

Palumbo, L., Ruta, N., & Bertamini, M. (2015). Comparing angular and curved shapes in terms of implicit associations and approach/avoidance responses. *PLoS ONE, 10*(10), e0140043. doi:10.1371/journal.pone.0140043

Poffenberger, A. T., & Barrows, B. E. (1924). The feeling value of lines. *Journal of Applied Psychology*, 8(2), 187–205.

Ponce, C. R., Hartmann, T. S., & Livingstone, M. S. (2017). End-stopping predicts curvature tuning along the ventral stream. *The Journal of Neuroscience*, 37(3), 648–659. doi:10.1523/JNEUROSCI.2507-16.2017

Quinn, P. C., Brown, C. R., & Streppa, M. L. (1997). Perceptual organization of complex visual configurations by young infants. *Infant Behavior and Development*, 20(1), 35–46. doi:10.1016/S0163-6383(97)90059-X

Reber, R., Wurtz, P., & Zimmermann, T. D. (2004). Exploring "fringe" consciousness: The subjective experience of perceptual fluency and its objective bases. *Consciousness and Cognition*, 13(1), 47–60. doi:10.1016/S1053-8100(03)00049-7

Renninger, L. W., Verghese, P., & Coughlan, J. (2007). Where to look next? Eye movements reduce local uncertainty. *Journal of Vision*, 7(3), 6. doi:10.1167/7.3.6.

Ruff, H. A., & Birch, H. G. (1974). Infant visual fixation: The effect of concentricity, curvilinearity and number of directions. *Journal of Experimental Child Psychology*, 17, 460–473.

Ruta, N., Palumbo, L., & Bertamini, M. (2014). Comparing angular and smooth polygons. Exploring the link between preference, response time and contour integration. *Proceedings of the 23rd IAEA Conference*, pp. 571–575.

Salgado-Montejo, A., Alvarado, J. A., Velasco, C., Salgado, C. J., Hasse, K., & Spence, C. (2015). The sweetest thing: The influence of angularity, symmetry, and the number of elements on shape-valence and shape-taste matches. *Frontiers in Psychology*, 6(April), 1–17. doi:10.3389/fpsyg.2015.01382

Schneirla, T. C. (1965). Aspects of stimulation and organization in approach/withdrawal processes underlying vertebrate behavioral development. *Advances in the Study of Behavior*, 1(C), 1–74. doi:10.1016/S0065-3454(08)60055-8

Schweinsberg, M., Madan, N., Vianello, M., Sommer, S. A., Jordan, J., Tierney, W., . . . Uhlmann, E. L. (2016). The pipeline project: Pre-publication independent replications of a single laboratory's research pipeline. *Journal of Experimental Social Psychology*, 66, 55–67. doi:10.1016/j.jesp.2015.10.001

Silvia, P. J., & Barona, C. M. (2009). Do people prefer curved objects? Angularity, expertise, and aesthetic preference. *Empirical Studies of the Arts*, 27(1), 25–42. doi:10.2190/EM.27.1.b

Soranzo, A., Petrelli, D., Ciolfi, L., & Reidy, J. (2018). On the perceptual aesthetics of interactive objects. *Quarterly Journal of Experimental Psychology*, 71(12), 2586–2602. doi:10.1177/1747021817749228

Stratton, G. (1902). Eye-movements and the aesthetics of visual form. *Philosophische Studien*, 20, 336–359.

Stratton, G. (1906). Symmetry, linear Illusions, and the movements of the eye. *Psychological Review*, 13(2), 82–96. doi:10.1037/h0072441

Treisman, A. M., & Gelade, G. (1980). A feature-integration theory of attention. *Cognitive Psychology*, 12(1), 97–136.

Tzeng, O. C., Trung, N. T., & Rieber, R. W. (1990). Cross-cultural comparisons of psychosemantics of icons and graphics. *Internationa Journal of Psychology*, 25(1), 77–97.

Uher, J. (1991). On zigzag designs: Three levels of meaning. *Current Anthropology*, 32(4), 437–439.

Valentine, C. (1950). *Psychology and its bearing on education*. Hove, England: Routledge.

Van Oel, C. J., & Van den Berkhof, F. W. D. (2013). Consumer preferences in the design of airport passenger areas. *Journal of Environmental Psychology, 36,* 280–290. doi:10.1016/j.jenvp.2013.08.005

Vartanian, O., Navarrete, G., Chatterjee, A., Fich, L. B., Leder, H., Modrono, C., . . . Skov, M. (2013). Impact of contour on aesthetic judgments and approach-avoidance decisions in architecture. *Proceedings of the National Academy of Sciences of the United States of America, 110,* 10446–10453. doi:10.1073/pnas.1301227110

Vartanian, O., Navarrete, G., Chatterjee, A., Fich, L. B., Leder, H., Rostrup, N., . . . Skov, M. (2017). Preference for curvilinear contour in interior architectural spaces: Evidence from experts and nonexperts preference. *Psychology of Aesthetics, Creativity, and the Arts, 13*(1), 110–116. doi:10.1037/aca0000150

Velasco, C., Salgado-Montejo, A., Elliot, A. J., Woods, A. T., Alvarado, J., & Spence, C. (2016). The shapes associated with approach/avoidance words. *Motivation and Emotion, 40*(5), 689–702. doi:10.1007/s11031-016-9559-5

Velasco, C., Woods, A. T., Hyndman, S., & Spence, C. (2015). The taste of typeface. *I-Perception, 6*(4), 1–10.

Velasco, C., Woods, A. T., Petit, O., Cheok, A. D., & Spence, C. (2016). Crossmodal correspondences between taste and shape, and their implications for product packaging: A review. *Food Quality and Preference, 52*(4), 17–26. doi:10.1016/j.foodqual.2016.03.005

Westerman, S., Gardner, P. H., Sutherland, E. J., White, T., Jordan, K., Watts, D., & Wells, S. (2012). Product design: Preference for rounded versus angular design elements. *Psychology & Marketing, 29*(August), 595–605. doi:10.1002/mar

Wolfe, J. M., Yee, A., & Friedman-Hill, S. R. (1992). Curvature is a basic feature for visual search tasks. *Perception, 21,* 465–480.

Yue, X., Pourladian, I. S., Tootell, R. B. H., & Ungerleider, L. G. (2014). Curvature-processing network in macaque visual cortex. *Proceedings of the National Academy of Sciences, 111*(33), E3467–E3475. doi:10.1073/pnas.1412616111

Zhang, Y., Feick, L., & Price, L. J. (2006). The impact of self-construal on aesthetic preference for angular versus rounded shapes. *Personality and Social Psychology Bulletin, 32*(August), 794–805. doi:10.1177/0146167206286626

Zhu, R., & Argo, J. J. (2013). Exploring the impact of various shaped seating arrangements on persuasion. *Journal of Consumer Research, 40*(2), 336–349. doi:10.1086/670392

CHAPTER 24

FACIAL ATTRACTIVENESS

ALEKSANDRA MITROVIC AND JÜRGEN GOLLER

FACIAL ATTRACTIVENESS IN
EMPIRICAL AESTHETICS

There are few more pleasurable sights than a beautiful face. (Rhodes, 2006, p. 200)

ALTHOUGH probably more examples of pleasurable sights can be found throughout this book, it indeed seems to be the case that facial attractiveness is one of the commonest, strongest, and most consequential forms of beauty (Little, 2014; Thornhill & Gangestad, 1999). Faces are so outstanding and essential for human vision that humans have developed brain networks specifically dedicated to face processing (Liu, Harris, & Kanwisher, 2010). Without much effort, in the blink of an eye, we can readily assess a face's attractiveness (Olson & Marshuetz, 2005; Sui & Liu, 2009; Willis & Todorov, 2006). Facial attractiveness is also a pervasive factor in everyday life. Even though people are often not aware of its impact, attractiveness affects our social perception and interactions in various ways (Brand, Bonatsos, D'Orazio, & DeShong, 2012; Dion, Berscheid, & Walster, 1972; Langlois et al., 2000; Tsukiura & Cabeza, 2011). Thus, it is not surprising that facial attractiveness is important for a positive self-concept, becoming more and more important with the revolution in modern social media (e.g., selfies). Consequently, to improve their looks, people spend more and more money on cosmetics and plastic surgery, with about 4 million facial surgical procedures and over 8 million nonsurgical facial procedures (e.g., Botox injections) occurring worldwide per year (International Society of Aesthetic Plastic Surgery, 2016). The basic principles of facial appearance in the alignment of eyes, nose, and mouth even generalize to other forms of beauty, as for example in design elements, cars, or architecture. To structure this multi-faceted phenomenon, we have divided this chapter into four main sections, each taking a different perspective on facial attractiveness: (a) the face, (b) the face bearer, (c) the observer, and (d) the research.

THE FACE

The most obvious and mandatory question in a chapter about facial attractiveness is: what makes a face attractive? There are many interesting answers to this question that refer to different facial characteristics found at different levels of facial appearance. We cover basic local features, like the eyes, nose, mouth, and their spatial configuration, and describe the differences between feminine and masculine faces. We also include more global features, like skin complexion, facial hair, and head hair. The most extensively studied characteristics however are symmetry and averageness, which are powerful shortcuts to describe the combination of any characteristics.

Facial features

A face is an anatomical farrago of skull bones, fat layers, blood vessels, blemishes, hair, skin, and other organic elements. However, in everyday language, faces are usually understood in terms of how they appear on the surface. For example, eyes are associated with oval-shaped objects, surrounded by lids, lashes, and eyebrows, rather than a sensory bulb rolling around in a skull. At this surface level, local features and their spatial configuration come in very handy to describe facial appearance. The eyes, nose, mouth, and ears are not only essential sensory organs in perception, but their distinguished appearance also makes them the most salient local features in faces. Consequently, the appearance of these local features and their spatial configuration are essential to the evaluation of facial attractiveness (Shen et al., 2016). However, less frequently mentioned features like the forehead, cheekbones, or chin, and more distinctive features, like chin dimples, earlobes, freckles, and moles, among others, can also be important factors (Bovet, Barthes, Durand, Raymond, & Alvergne, 2012). Whatever local feature or characteristic is considered, it is necessary to first distinguish between female and male faces, which show systematic differences in their appearance.

In female faces, many aspects of attractiveness are related to youthfulness and the presence of neotenic features (cf. babyface(d)ness). Lifetime changes in facial appearance affect the relative size of local features and their configuration in a systematic way. A young or youthful female face is characterized by a high forehead and high eyebrows (Berry & McArthur, 1985; Cunningham, 1986; Geldart, 2010; Grammer, Fink, Moeller, & Thornhill, 2003; Jones, 1996; Perrett, May, & Yoshikawa, 1994; Valenzano, Mennucci, Tartarelli, & Cellerino, 2006), larger eyes and pupils (Cunningham, Barbee, & Pike, 1990), a small nose (Jones et al., 1995; Thornhill & Gangestad, 1999), a small chin and a smaller lower half of the face (Grammer & Thornhill, 1994; Johnston & Franklin,

1993), and finally, a small mouth but full lips (Bovet et al., 2012; Jones, 1995; Schaefer et al., 2006; Thornhill & Gangestad, 1993). Such neotenic features are more prominent in female faces, but the same general concept can also be applied to male faces (Cunningham et al., 1990; McArthur & Apatow, 1984), although slightly different characteristics are decisive (e.g., forehead and nose size are less important; Berry & McArthur, 1985). In general, neotenic features have been found to increase facial attractiveness in female faces (Baudouin & Tiberghien, 2004; Grammer & Thornhill, 1994), although, there seem to be exceptions to this general rule. Neotenic features influence facial attractiveness more when located in the center of the face and sexual maturity features at the periphery of the face (Cunningham, Roberts, Barbee, Druen, & Wu, 1995).

Besides neotenic features and youthfulness, additional features that are typically feminine further increase attractiveness in female faces (Komori, Kawamura, & Ishihara, 2009; Little, Burt, Penton-Voak, & Perrett, 2001; Penton-Voak et al., 1999; Perrett et al., 1998; Rhodes, 2006). These feminine features are high and prominent cheekbones, thinner eyebrows (Baudouin & Tiberghien, 2004; Bovet et al., 2012), and the absence of facial hair, as a strong natural indicator of high estrogen and low androgen levels (Fink, Grammar, & Thornhill, 2001; Symons, 1995). For male faces, on the other hand, facial hair is a strong secondary sex characteristic and a clear indicator of masculinity (Cunningham et al., 1990; Neave & Shields, 2008; Terry, 1994). However, the appearance of facial hair is very diverse, and it is not easy to find systematic patterns in preferences. Whether a male beard is preferred or not seems to be more a question of individual taste than a general rule (for exceptions, see Feinman & Gill, 1977; Pancer & Meindl, 1978). Besides facial hair, typical masculine—and therefore attractive—faces are often associated with higher muscularity (Dixson, Dixson, Bishop, & Parish, 2009), more prominent cheekbones, a large chin, wide jaw, and a generally bigger lower half of the face (Cunningham et al., 1990; Grammer & Thornhill, 1994; Thornhill & Gangestad, 1999).

The eyes

When people are asked what they consider important in facial attractiveness, it is most likely that the eyes will be mentioned (Cross & Cross, 1971). The eyes are probably the most idiosyncratic visual feature of a person, shrouded in many myths, often considered a window to the soul. Visually, the appearance of human eyes can vary along many different dimensions, such as color, shape, size, eyelashes, eyebrows, eyelids, and so forth. Also important is the spatial configuration of the eye in that the vertical eye placement and the horizontal eye separation is attractive within a middle range (Cunningham et al., 1990; Faure, Rieffe, & Maltha, 2002). Probably the most salient feature in eyes is the color of the iris, which can range from light green to dark brown with all variations and indistinct gradients in between. Although this diversity is prominent in Caucasians, it has little significance on a global scale, where most people have brown eyes (Frost, 2006). Blue eyes for example, only evolved about 7,000 years ago (Olalde et al., 2014), making it unlikely that eye color preferences are the product of any evolutionary adaptation. Previous research has limited itself to simple differentiations, as for example that lighter eyes are statistically preferred in female faces and darker eyes in male faces (Feinman & Gill, 1977). This general preference seems to interact with the eye color of the observer, in that similar coloring and brightness are statistically preferred (Bovet et al., 2012; Laeng, Mathisen, & Johnsen, 2007; also see assortative mating later in this chapter).

The skin

The color of human skin varies greatly across the globe, cultures, ethnicities, and people (Jablonski & Chaplin, 2000). The widely used Fitzpatrick scale (Fitzpatrick, 1988) differentiates between six types of skin colors, ranging from pale white (Type I) to black (Type VI). Within a given color type, female skin coloration is statistically lighter than male skin coloration (Jablonski & Chaplin, 2000). However, whether lighter skin is perceived as more attractive than darker skin remains inconclusive (Fink et al., 2001; Frost, 1988; Van den Berghe & Frost, 1986). Besides the lightness of the skin, a reddish taint was repeatedly found to make faces more attractive (Elliot, Tracy, Pazda, & Beall, 2013). Especially the cheeks are sensitive to changes in blood circulation, which might make reddish cheeks more attractive because they indicate a healthy state (Fink et al., 2001; Symons, 1995; Zahavi & Zahavi, 1997). Far more important than reddish cheeks however, is that the skin is free from blemishes and flaws and that its color is homogeneously distributed across the face (Barber, 1995; Etcoff, 1999; Morris, 1967; Symons, 1995). Flawless, smooth skin is assessed as younger, healthier, and consequently more attractive, for female and male faces alike (Fink, Butovskaya, Sorokowski, Sorokowska, & Matts, 2017; Fink et al., 2001; Matts, Fink, Grammer, & Burquest, 2007). This empirical finding seems to be intuitive and widely accepted, since efforts in enhancing these characteristics by applying color to the face date back at least 50,000 years (Zilhão, 2012). Especially women (but increasingly also men) frequently use make-up and facial cosmetics to mask certain flaws and produce a smooth color distribution to enhance their own attractiveness (Graham & Jouhar, 1980; Smith et al., 2006). The usage of cosmetics—in earlier times almost exclusively used by people of higher social status— has become accessible and they are mass produced by a constantly growing mega industry, reaching a market of US$390 billion in 2020 (Allied Analytics LLP, 2016), with skincare and make-up comprising more than 50% of that market.

Head hair

A seldom-considered aspect of facial attractiveness is the head hair, which strongly influences facial perception and facial attractiveness assessments (Fink et al., 2016; Mesko & Bereczkei, 2004; Saegusa, Intoy, & Shimojo, 2015). Head hair is a source of nearly unlimited within-person variation: hairstyles are probably the most efficient and easiest way to increase facial attractiveness (Fink et al., 2016). As they are different and difficult to classify, systematic research on hairstyle is rare. Previous studies have focused on single features, like hair texture (Bovet et al., 2012), hair length (Cunningham et al., 1990; Mesko & Bereczkei, 2004; Swami, Furnham, & Joshi, 2008), and hair color (Bovet et al., 2012; Clayson & Klassen, 1989; Cunningham et al., 1990; Feinman & Gill, 1977; Swami & Barrett, 2011). A well-controlled study used a combination of several factors in presenting computer-generated, rendered human head hair, systematically manipulating the diameter, hair density, and hairstyle of women (Fink et al., 2016). Overall, this study showed that long, thin, and straight hair was judged to be more attractive than short, thick, and wavy hair. It has also been shown that darker hair (medium copper and brown) is judged as more attractive than blonde hair, whereas earlier findings had shown the opposite effect (Sorokowski, 2008).

Global characteristics

On the level of local features like the eyes, nose, and mouth, facial appearance can be easily described. However, on a more detailed level, it becomes very complicated to describe facial appearance based on its actual visual characteristics (Gill, 2017). For example, it is more feasible to simply say that intermediate fat levels are more attractive than high or low fat levels (Clayson & Klassen, 1989; Coetzee, Perrett, & Stephen, 2009; Coetzee, Re, Perrett, Tiddeman, & Xiao, 2011; Little, 2014), rather than describing the actual differences on a visual level. Consequently, in research on facial attractiveness it is feasible to use global factors to describe facial appearance. Some of these global factors have already been mentioned above, such as the age of the face. Systematic changes in facial appearance over a lifetime, like changes in the soft tissue (Borelli & Berneburg, 2010), clearly affect facial attractiveness in that young faces are perceived as more attractive (Ebner, 2008; Foos & Clark, 2011; Henns, 1991; Kiiski, Cullen, Clavin, & Newell, 2016; Korthase & Trenholme, 1982; Kwart & Foulsham, 2012; Little, 2014; McKelvie, 1993; McLellan & McKelvie, 1993; Teuscher & Teuscher, 2007; Zebrowitz, Montepare, & Lee, 1993). This correlation between attractiveness and youthfulness seems to be especially important for female faces (Maestripieri, Klimczuk, Traficonte, & Wilson, 2014; Palumbo, Adams, Hess, Kleck, & Zebrowitz, 2017). However, relative to one's own age group, facial attractiveness seems to be somewhat stable throughout the lifespan (Alley, 1993; Pittenger, Mark, & Johnson, 1989; Sussman, Mueser, Grau, & Yarnold, 1983; Tatarunaite, Playle, Hood, Shaw, & Richmond, 2005; Yerkes & Pettijohn II, 2008; Zebrowitz et al., 1993). Thus, a child who, compared with their own age group, is attractive will still be attractive when growing up, compared with other peers. Another example is sexual dimorphism, in which specific features systematically differ between the sexes. Such features, be they more typically feminine or more masculine, are generally considered attractive (Perrett et al., 1998).

The two most extensively studied global factors in describing facial appearance regarding facial (and bodily) attractiveness are symmetry and averageness. Symmetry in faces refers to mirror symmetry, in which a vertical line across the middle of the face mirrors the left and the right half of the face. Mirror symmetry is the most salient form of symmetry, generally preferred in visual perception (Julesz, 1971; Treder, 2010). It is therefore not surprising that symmetry in faces is associated with higher attractiveness (Grammer & Thornhill, 1994; Little & Jones, 2006; Perrett et al., 1998; Rhodes, Proffitt, Grady, & Sumich, 1998). The simplest method to produce a perfectly symmetric face is to vertically cut an image of a face in two halves, and simply mirror one half to the other side. However, such a face also looks unnatural and lacks the beauty of naturally symmetric faces (Grammer & Thornhill, 1994; Rhodes et al., 1998), in which small deviations from perfect symmetry make a face even more attractive (Mentus & Marković, 2016; Swaddle & Cuthill, 1995; Zaidel & Hessamian, 2010).

Averageness is a concept that cannot only be applied to any individual characteristic of faces but also to other global concepts. In theory, this makes averageness a simple and powerful concept: whatever individual characteristic is used to describe a face, an average face is simply the face that reflects the population's average magnitude of this characteristic. In computer-generated faces, averageness can easily be produced by shifting all sliders of all characteristics to the middle position. For real faces however, such an approach is inapplicable, because the population parameters are unknown. However, average faces can be produced (and studied) by morphing. Morphing takes two or more images of faces, makes them partially transparent and overlays the single faces to produce one (average) face—put simply. This technique was already used by Francis Galton (1878), who created such composite portraits to study beauty in faces. Digital morphing has become much more sophisticated, resulting in amazingly realistic faces (a quick Internet search gives some impressive examples). Morphing was extensively used in facial attractiveness research revealing a clear effect: a morphed face is more attractive than single faces, and the more faces are morphed together, the more attractive the composite face (Grammer & Thornhill, 1994; Halberstadt & Rhodes, 2003; Komori et al., 2009; Langlois & Roggman, 1990; Rhodes, 2006; Rhodes & Tremewan, 1996). Consequently, it was stated that attractive faces are average (Baudouin & Tiberghien, 2004; Langlois & Roggman, 1990). In everyday language, this notion sounds counterintuitive, because an average-looking face could easily be interpreted as a not-so-good-looking face (Rhodes et al., 2005). Therefore, instead of using the term averageness, distinctiveness is often used as an opposing concept (Wickham & Morris, 2003), showing a negative correlation with facial attractiveness (Deffenbacher, Johanson, & O'Toole, 1998; Rhodes & Tremewan, 1996; Wickham & Morris, 2003). To that end, the perfect or Golden Ratio of facial attractiveness probably simply resembles an average face (Pallett, Link, & Lee, 2010). However, research has shown that there is not necessarily a linear relation between averageness and attractiveness, but rather that very attractive faces show deviations from averageness in the form of distinct features (Alley & Cunningham, 1991; Baudouin & Tiberghien, 2004; Little & Hancock, 2002; Wickham & Morris, 2003).

Within-person variation

Within-person variation in facial appearance has a long research tradition in face recognition, but was highly neglected in facial attractiveness research until recently (Jenkins, White, Van Montfort, & Burton, 2011). Given that facial appearance influences the valuation of facial attractiveness, it is quite common to observe within-person variation in facial attractiveness. It has even been shown that within-face variation of facial appearance and, in turn, facial attractiveness, can be even larger than between-face variation (Jenkins et al., 2011). The sources for within-person variation in facial appearance and consequently facial attractiveness can be manifold, comprising changes in blood flow and hence skin coloration, hairstyle, make-up, and accessory usage like glasses (Forster, Gerger, & Leder, 2013). Most importantly, our facial muscles are constantly in motion for various unintentional and intentional reasons. Highly relevant for facial attractiveness are facial muscle activations and movements reflecting emotional expressions and states. The quickest way to exploit within-person variation and (slightly) improve facial attractiveness judgments might therefore be simply by smiling (Cunningham et al., 1990; Mehu, Little, & Dunbar, 2008; Morrison, Morris, & Bard, 2013; Mueser, Grau, Sussan, & Rosen, 1984; Tatarunaite et al., 2005).

THE FACE BEARER

Evolution

One of the most frequently asked questions about facial attractiveness is why this phenomenon exists, and why it exists the way it does. The valuation of facial attractiveness is an innate and hard-wired process, shared across the world, that evolved over millions of years (Buss, 1995; Penton-Voak et al., 2003; Rhodes, 2006; Thornhill & Gangestad, 1999). It is therefore highly likely that facial attractiveness is the product of evolutionary adaptations, and not simply a by-product of other evolutionary processes. Whatever function facial attractiveness plays in evolution, it must have been beneficial for natural and/or for sexual selection. Although being attractive is advantageous in social perception and interactions (see next section), hence potentially being beneficial for natural selection, most of the evidence points toward sexual selection. One factor could be that facial attractiveness is part of a person's general attractiveness, which helps to motivate sexual behavior. However, pure sexual motivation cannot explain why we find a relatively high amount of shared taste in facial attractiveness assessments (Leder, Goller, Rigotti, & Forster, 2016). This finding requires that there is a positive correlation between perceived facial attractiveness and certain personal characteristics as indicators of mate quality. Mate quality is not easy to define but relates to genetic fitness and reproductive potential (Bovet et al., 2012;

Little, 2014). The list of facial characteristics at the beginning of this chapter is full of promising examples of such associations. For example, symmetry indicates a low level of fluctuating asymmetry (Gangestad, Thornhill, & Yeo, 1994; Schaefer et al., 2006; see Moller & Thornhill, 1998 for a review) and therefore indicates successful gene expression and consistent development of both body (and consequently also face) halves (e.g., Jones et al., 2001; Mealey, Bridgstock, & Townsend, 1999; Penton-Voak et al., 2001; Perrett, May, & Yoshikawa, 1994; Rhodes et al., 1998, 2001; Scheib, Gangestad, & Thornhill, 1999; Thornhill & Gangestad, 1999; Van Dongen & Gangestad, 2011). In turn, averageness is an indicator of high protein heterozygosity, enhancing the body's defenses against parasites (Langlois & Roggman, 1990; Rhodes, Sumich, & Byatt, 1999; Rhodes & Tremewan, 1996; Valentine, Darling, & Donnelly, 2004). Smooth skin was shown to correlate with high parasitic resistance (Barber, 1995; Symons, 1995). Rosy cheeks indicate a healthy level of blood pressure (Fink, Grammer, & Thornhill, 2001). Neotenic features and youthfulness signal higher fertility and the absence of senescence (Jones, 1995; Kenrick & Keefe, 1992; Thornhill & Gangestad, 1999), and sexual dimorphism—feminine or masculine traits—reflects hormonal health (Thornhill & Gangestad, 1999). However, the ultimate connection between facial attractiveness and mate quality as pinned down by specific genes is still lacking (Senior, 2003; Thornhill & Gangestad, 1993, 1999; Thornhill & Grammer, 1999).

Halo effects and consequences of facial attractiveness

Being attractive has mostly positive social consequences for a person. The so-called "what is beautiful is good" stereotype (Dion et al., 1972) is based on the perception that attractive people possess more favorable traits than less attractive people. To put it in another way, the perceiver is carried away by beauty. Moreover, attractive people are treated preferentially, a phenomenon that is often referred to as the halo effect of beauty. For example, attractive people are perceived to be more intelligent and healthier, although the correlation between measured intelligence (Fink et al., 2014; Kanazawa, 2011; Mitchem et al., 2015) and actual health (see Weeden & Sabini, 2005 for a review) with attractiveness ranges from small to nonexistent. Instances in which attractive people are treated differently than their less attractive counterparts are widespread: attractive infants receive more attention from their mothers and mothers of attractive infants are more affectionate (Langlois, Ritter, Casey, & Sawin, 1995), attractive criminals receive milder sentences (Sigall & Ostrove, 1975; see Mazzella & Feingold, 1994 for a review), attractive women are imitated more by people high in empathy (Mueller, Van Leeuwen, Van Baaren, Bekkering, & Dijksterhuis, 2013), attractive students get better grades in school (Dunkake, Kiechle, Klein, & Rosar, 2012), facial attractiveness influences hiring decisions (Chiu & Babcock, 2002), and even political election results (Budesheim & DePaola, 1994; Praino et al., 2014; for a review, see Little & Roberts, 2012). It could be assumed that only younger people with less life experience are carried away by beauty; however, this halo effect of attractiveness occurs also in older adults (Zebrowitz

& Franklin Jr., 2014; see also Adams, 1977; Burns & Farina, 1992; Eagly, Ashmore, Makhijani, & Longo, 1991; Feingold, 1992; Frevert & Walker, 2014; and Langlois et al., 2000 for reviews on attractiveness stereotypes, on how attractive people are viewed and responded to, how these different responses lead to differences in treatment, and how this different treatment leads to differences in adjustment between attractive and less attractive people). However, being attractive it is not always positive. For example, for female job applicants it can be disadvantageous to be attractive when applying for a typically masculine job, which is called the "beauty is beastly" effect (Heilman & Saruwatari, 1979; Paustian-Underdahl & Walker, 2015).

Familiarity

As discussed above, facial attractiveness influences the perception of the person, but, in turn, personal characteristics also influence perceived facial attractiveness. The most basic and best-studied variable is the familiarity of a person, which is a measure of how well observers know someone. Whether familiarity breeds attraction or contempt is a long-discussed question in psychology. Whereas early deliberations (Fechner, 1876) and empirical studies (Maslow, 1937) predicted both directions, depending on various contextual factors, it was the seminal work on the mere exposure effect that was most influential for our understanding of familiarity in face perception. The mere exposure effect states that sheer repetition—the mere exposure to a stimulus—increases its attraction (Zajonc, 1968). This basic finding has been repeatedly replicated for all kinds of visual object categories, including faces and facial attractiveness (for a review, see Bornstein, 1989). In one study, original and mirrored versions of photos of a face were presented to the face bearer and to some of their friends (Mita, Dermer, & Knight, 1977). Both groups preferred the version they had seen most often in their life: the face bearers preferred the mirrored version of their own faces and friends preferred the original version—a finding that is perfectly in line with the mere exposure effect in faces. However, as convincing as this study and others might be, familiarity effects with faces are more complicated, especially when social categories become more apparent. For example, in a heterosexual, opposite-sexed mating situation, familiarity breeds attraction in women but contempt in men (Little, DeBruine, & Jones, 2013; also compare the Coolidge effect, Fisher, 1962). Although these interactions are not large, they question the generality of the mere exposure effect and ask for a more differentiated account. A promising approach comes from social psychology, where the direction of familiarity effects depends on the stage of the relationship between the observer and the face bearer (Finkel et al., 2015). In most studies in perceptual psychology the faces are unfamiliar prior to the study. In that case, a mere exposure effect is likely because no further information about the person is available and the suffusion of familiarity enhances perceptual fluency (Reber, Schwarz, & Winkielman, 2004; Rhodes, Halberstadt, & Brajkovich, 2001; for the opposite effect see the "warm glow heuristic," Monin, 2003). The Coolidge effect on the other hand occurs at the surface contact stage, when people and faces are already familiar to some extent.

At this stage, social variables such as likeability might override the basic effect of mere exposure (Finkel et al., 2015).

THE OBSERVER

From a psychological perspective, facial attractiveness is neither in the face itself nor a personal characteristic but accrues in the mind and the brain of the observer. In this section, we will examine the extent to which facial attractiveness is in the eye of the beholder, and how much is shared across people and different cultures. We will seek out commonalities between observers and find variables that explain systematic differences in evaluating facial attractiveness. We will also discuss some cognitive and neuronal mechanisms in perceiving facial attractiveness.

Agreement

How much do people agree on attractiveness assessments and what does it mean to say that beauty is in the eye of the beholder? Two studies used variance components analyses in random effects models to estimate the ratio between shared and individual taste (Hoenekopp, 2006; Leder, Goller, Rigotti, & Forster, 2016). Both studies found that shared taste accounted for about 60% of the variance, whereas individual taste accounted for the remaining 40%. Based on these findings, the answer to the above question falls somewhere in between. Although facial attractiveness assessments are somewhat in the eye of the beholder, agreement across observers is stronger (see also research on inter-rater reliability conducted by Downs & Wright, 1982; Harrison, Shortall, Dispenza, & Gallup, 2011; Vessel, Maurer, Denker, & Starr, 2018; Zebrowitz et al., 1993). The agreement is especially high when there are clear-cut differences in the attractiveness of the assessed faces (e.g., Bernstein, Lin, & McCellan, 1982; Coetzee, Greeff, Stephen, & Perrett, 2014; Cunningham et al., 1995; Langlois et al., 2000; Rhodes, 2006). An extreme comparison illustrates this effect: giving raters the choice to decide which of two faces is more attractive between a highly attractive face and a highly unattractive face would probably result in perfect shared taste. Furthermore, people from different cultures, both industrialized and socially isolated, agree on the attractiveness of certain facial features (e.g., Apicella, Little, & Marlowe, 2007; Fink et al., 2017; Rhodes, Yoshikawa et al., 2001), and cross-cultural agreement is generally large (Cunningham et al., 1995). Together, it seems that facial attractiveness assessments are remarkably consistent (Perrett et al., 1994). However, there are also geographical, cultural, historical, and individual differences (Gao, Niddam, Noel, Hersant, & Meningaud, 2018; Thayer & Dobson, 2013). Ideals of beauty not only differ across the globe but also over time. A good example is the fall and rise of freckles as a marker of (un)attractiveness. Freckles result from sunlight exposure, which in certain European historic periods was a sign of (hard) outdoor labor. The absence of freckles was therefore associated with a higher social status and therefore considered attractive. Consequently, the cosmetic industry of the late 19th century aggressively advertised mercury-based remedies to get rid of freckles. This view completely changed over the decades, making freckles these days even an ideal of beauty, demonstrating the powerful effect of fashion on facial attractiveness assessments.

In contrast to inter-rater agreement, less research has been conducted on intra-rater reliability or stability over time. A problem in assessing intra-rater reliability is that raters must judge the same faces (at least) twice. This makes it difficult to disentangle the stability in the judgment from memory effects and the measurement error (cf. Leder, Goller, Forster, Schlageter, & Paul, 2017). This, together with different operationalizations, leads to inconclusive inferences regarding intra-rater reliability, with results ranging between low and high stability (Bronstad & Russell, 2007; Hoenekopp, 2006; Howells & Shaw, 1985; Kiekens, Maltha, Hof, & Kuijpers-Jagtman, 2006; Knight & Keith, 2005; Peerlings, Kuijpers-Jagtman, & Hoeksma, 1995; Phillips, Tulloch, & Dann, 1992; Pugach, Leder, & Graham, 2017). Another approach in assessing stability in ratings involves research on patients with Alzheimer's disease. Although memory is severely impaired in Alzheimer's patients, judgments of facial attractiveness seem to be remarkably consistent over time (Graham, Stockinger, & Leder, 2013).

Sexual factors

Across all research on facial attractiveness, we expect an interaction between the sex of the faces and the sex of the observers. Female faces are often perceived as more attractive than male faces, by both men and women (Harrison et al., 2011; Leder, Mitrovic, & Goller, 2016; Palumbo et al., 2017). Additionally, for men and women, attractiveness in a partner has different significance. Usually, men put more emphasis on (facial) attractiveness in a partner than women (Berscheid, Dion, Walster, & Walster, 1971; Bleske-Rechek & Ryan, 2015; Buss, 1989; Buss & Barnes, 1986; Feingold, 1990; Li, Bailey, Kenrick, & Linsenmeier, 2002; Lippa, 2007; Waynforth & Dunbar, 1995). From an evolutionary point of view, it was important for women to mate with a man who is interested in providing for offspring. The good genes advertised by facial attractiveness could also be obtained via extra-pair mating. Men were looking for women to sire and rear their offspring—therefore women had to be young, fertile, and attractive. This differential emphasis between men and women still applies to contemporary mating, especially for long-term relationship contexts. In short-term relationships, both men and women consider attractiveness equally important (Buunk, Dijkstra, Fetchenhauer, & Kenrick, 2002; Regan, Levin, Sprecher, Christopher, & Gate, 2000; Regan, Medina, & Joshi, 2001). A study on the continuity and changes in mate preferences over time found that the emphasis appears somewhat stable (Bleske-Rechek & Ryan, 2015).

Observer variables

Various observer variables influence the perception of facial attractiveness. A lot of research targeting women's hormonal changes has been conducted. The menstrual cycle of women changes their preferences in male faces, and consequently whom they find attractive, especially in the context of partner choice for a short-term relationship (Johnston, Hagel, Franklin, Fink, & Grammer, 2001; Jones et al., 2005; Penton-Voak et al., 1999; Penton-Voak & Perrett, 2000; Roney & Simmons, 2008; but see DeBruine et al., 2010, and Harris, 2010; for a review, see Jones et al., 2008). Naturally cycling women and pregnant women do not differ significantly regarding their preference for masculinity, yet they differ from postmenopausal women (Marcinkowska, Jasienska, & Prokop, 2017). However, differences between pregnant and nonpregnant women were found, specifically a clear preference for feminine male faces by women in the third trimester of pregnancy (Limoncin et al., 2015). The usage of hormonal contraceptives influences female preferences, for example for masculinity in male faces and voices (Feinberg, DeBruine, Jones, & Little, 2008; Vukovic et al., 2008). The menstrual cycle not only influences the preferences of women, but also changes women's appearance and consequently how attractive women are judged to be (Bobst & Lobmaier, 2012; Oberzaucher et al., 2012). Photos taken in the fertile phase are judged to be more attractive, tested between subjects (Smith et al., 2006) but also within subjects (Puts et al., 2013; Roberts et al., 2004; Samson, Fink, & Matts, 2011). The perceivers' personality also seems to influence attractiveness perception, at least in high-macho and low-macho men when judging female attractiveness (Keisling & Gynther, 1993).

Important variables related to motives and goals that change the perception of facial attractiveness are relationship status, sexual orientation, socio-sexual orientation, and motivational states, among others. It is likely that perceivers who are in a relationship, perceive and rate attractiveness differently than perceivers who are single (Maner et al., 2003). Cognitive processes might change when entering a relationship, so that indeed perception is altered. However, we know of no study that has compared the same people when in a relationship and single to test this directly. Another possible explanation is more motivational in nature. It could be that in a relationship, psychological mechanisms are activated to maintain the relationship (satisfaction) and (highly) attractive faces of potential mates are devaluated (Karremans, Dotsch, & Corneille, 2011; Karremans & Verwijmeren, 2008; Koranyi & Rothermund, 2012; Maner, Gailliot, & Miller, 2009; Maner, Gailliot, Rouby, & Miller, 2007; Maner, Rouby, & Gonzager, 2008; Miller, 1997; Miller & Maner, 2010; Plant, Kunstman, & Maner, 2010; Simpson, Gangestad, & Lerma, 1990). Sexual orientation influences attention to faces (Mitrovic, Tinio, & Leder, 2016; Vasquez-Amezquita et al., 2017), and heterosexual and homosexual perceivers differ in the importance they ascribe to facial attractiveness. While attractiveness is similarly important for both hetero- and homosexual men, it is less important for homosexual women compared with heterosexual women, for whom attractiveness is already not very important to begin with (Bailey, Gaulin, Agyei, & Gladue, 1994; Ha, van den Berg, Engels, & Lichtwarck-Aschoff, 2012; Russock, 2011). Another influencing variable is a person's socio-sexual orientation. Socio-sexual orientation indicates how much emotional commitment people need before they would engage in sexual behavior (Penke & Asendorpf, 2008). More socio-sexually unrestricted people need less emotional commitment, are more likely male than female, and engage in more short-term relationships (Oliver & Hyde, 1993; Rammsayer & Troche, 2013; Schmitt, 2005; Schwarz & Hassebrauck, 2007). As noted above, for short-term relationships, attractiveness is more important than for long-term relationships. Consequently, attractiveness is more important for more socio-sexually unrestricted people (Simpson & Gangestad, 1992).

There are even drug-induced influences on facial attractiveness assessments. It seems that even nicotine consumption (of the observer) makes faces more attractive (Attwood, Penton-Voak, Goodwin, & Munafò, 2012). In addition, the so-called "beer goggles" effect states that alcohol consumption (slightly) increases perceived attractiveness (Attwood et al., 2012; Jones, Thomas, & Piper, 2003; Mitchell et al., 2015; Parker, Penton-Voak, Attwood, & Munafò, 2008; but see Neave, Tsang, & Heather, 2009 for a null result). Interestingly, this effect of increased attractiveness also applies to the person who consumed the alcohol. In other words, not only are other people perceived to be more attractive when the observer has drunk alcohol, but the drinker themselves is perceived to look more attractive by others, as long as only small amounts of alcohol are consumed (Van Den Abbeele, Penton-Voak, Attwood, Stephen, & Munafò, 2015). The beer goggles effect seems to persist for up to a day, although the effect lasts longer for men assessing female faces (Parker et al., 2008). In general, this effect seems to be stronger for other-sex faces compared with same-sex faces. It also seems to depend on the attractiveness of the perceived face: the increase in attractiveness was higher for low and average attractive faces, but for highly attractive faces, consuming alcohol hardly made any difference at all (Chen, Wang, Yang, & Chen, 2014).

Mating

Our skill in judging facial attractiveness so easily and quickly is often argued to be related to mate selection. From an evolutionary point of view, it would be optimal to reproduce with highly attractive other-sex individuals, as these provide good genes that are passed on to offspring. Therefore, the chances to be chosen as a mate should be higher for attractive people. Further, following evolutionary ideas, it could be expected that only highly attractive people would reproduce as they are the most desirable mating partners owing to their good genes expressed in their attractive faces. However, daily life shows us that this is not the case. Not every person, one might say even very few of us, have highly attractive partners. If that were the case, then only highly attractive people would populate the world as they are the only ones who would reproduce—less attractive people on the other hand would never reproduce. A process called assortative mating (homogamy) appears on the scene to prevent mankind from extinction

(Burley, 1983; Vandenberg, 1972). Assortative mating states that a person will look for partners who are somewhat similar to them, for example in age, intelligence, personality, ethnical background, religious views, but also facial appearance and, relatedly, attractiveness (Berscheid et al., 1971; Burriss, Roberts, Welling, Puts, & Little, 2011; Buston & Emlen, 2003; Feingold, 1988; Gyuris, Járai, & Bereczkei, 2010; Laeng, Vermeer, & Sulutvedt, 2013; Price & Vandenberg, 1980; Rammstedt & Schupp, 2008; Spuhler, 1968; Vandenberg, 1972; Zietsch, Verweij, Heath, & Martin, 2011). Another mechanism that is suggested as an explanation of how people choose their mates is "sexual imprinting." On the one hand, proximity and resemblance—in the sense of incest prevention—should be aversive. However, on the other hand, a certain amount of resemblance is positive, as otherwise there would be no positive assortative mating. People find (other-sex) faces that resemble themselves (Sulutvedt & Laeng, 2014; Watkins et al., 2011; but see Nojo, Ihara, Furusawa, Akamatsu, & Ishida, 2011) and faces that are presented after pictures of their parents more attractive. However, when told that faces resemble themselves and having been told the study is about incest, then faces in general were rated to be less sexually attractive (Fraley & Marks, 2010). This is in line with the above-mentioned assortative mating principle, in which a certain amount of resemblance is positive. There is evidence that suggests that people mainly "imprint" on other-sex parents in comparison with same-sex parents and with other- and same-sex siblings (Griffee et al., 2017) and that partners resemble (other-sex) parents phenotypically and with regard to personality (Gyuris et al., 2010; Little, Penton-Voak, Burt, & Perrett, 2003; Marcinkowska & Rantala, 2012; Saxton, 2016; but see Nojo et al., 2011; Nojo, Tamura, & Ihara, 2012; Zietsch et al., 2011). This is influenced by the relationship context (short-term vs. long-term) (Nojo et al., 2011; for a review on sexual imprinting in mate choice, see Rantala & Marcinkowska, 2011).

Age and developmental aspects

Earlier in this chapter, we discussed changes in facial attractiveness within faces over the lifespan. The age of the face also interacts with the age of the observer. Young raters judge young faces to be more attractive compared with middle-aged and old faces; middle-aged raters judge young and middle-aged faces to be more attractive compared with old faces; and for old raters there are no differences (Foos & Clark, 2011; but see Kiiski et al., 2016). In general, it seems that older people judge the same faces to be of higher attractiveness compared with younger people (Palumbo et al., 2017). However, attractiveness is often evaluated in a similar way by children and adults (Cavior & Lombardi, 1973; Cross & Cross, 1971; Dion, 1973; Kościński, 2010), although this also depends on the age of the face to be rated. For example, no differences were found between mothers and daughters when looking at adult female faces (Kissler & Baeuml, 2000). However, for girls' faces there were differences. Additionally, the age of the perceiver is important. The older the children are, the higher is their agreement with peers and adults (Saxton, Caryl, & Craig Roberts, 2006). Children's preferences for characteristics that are deemed attractive according to adults' standards change from 4 years to 17 years of age (Boothroyd, Meins, Vukovic, & Burt, 2014). However, such studies, in which children rated attractiveness or ranked faces according to their attractiveness, have been conducted less often compared to research with adults. Additionally, little research has been conducted with children younger than 11 years of age (e.g., Boothroyd et al., 2014; Cavior & Lombardi, 1973; Cross & Cross, 1971; Dion, 1973; Kissler & Baeuml, 2000). Moreover, the younger the children are, the more the paradigms must be adapted. As ratings or rankings are not possible when children are younger than a certain age, attractiveness preferences in infants are usually researched via analyzing looking duration. Such studies found that infants who are only a few days old prefer to look at more attractive faces compared with less attractive faces (Langlois, Ritter, Roggman, & Vaughn, 1991; for a review, see Damon, Mottier, Méary, & Pascalis, 2017). Possibly owing to the biological relevance, more studies addressed women's than men's age. When boys reach sexual maturity, they stay fertile up until old age whereas women are not fertile anymore after menopause. Consequently, questions arise if and how age influences women's preferences for faces, like for example whether there are similarities between younger infertile girls and older infertile women, or differences between young fertile women and older infertile women. There is inconclusive evidence regarding the preference for facial features in male faces of women within and outside of the reproductive age range. Some research suggests that pubescent girls, postmenopausal women, and women within the reproductive age range differ with regard to their preferences for facial features, such as youthfulness (Kościński, 2011; Little et al., 2010). However, it was shown that girls react similarly to adult women especially when evaluating facial attractiveness in general (Kościński, 2011, 2013). Often, the similar preferences between children and adults and the increase in similarity with an increase in age of the children—especially in the case of female observers—are ascribed to hormonal changes throughout life (Kościński, 2011). For example, facial averageness, male facial symmetry, and male facial femininity (only when judged by girls) were perceived as more attractive by 13-year-old children compared with 11-year old children (Saxton, DeBruine, Jones, Little, & Roberts, 2009).

Own attractiveness

There is evidence that one's own attractiveness, possibly as an indicator of social or sexual market value, influences the perception and preferences for facial attractiveness. Studies have shown that self-assessed facial attractiveness and facial attractiveness assessed by others only show small correlations and are not highly aligned (Downs, 1990; Downs & Wright, 1982; Feingold, 1992; Penton-Voak et al., 2003), possibly because own attractiveness is often overestimated (Brewer, Archer, & Manning, 2007; Donaghue & Smith, 2008). Especially men overestimate their attractiveness whereas women are more accurate and thus seem to be more modest (Gabriel, Critelli, & Ee, 1994; Rand & Hall, 1983). This overestimation by men seems to depend also on the context—in an ultimatum game, men's overestimation was stronger when their competitor was a man compared with when the competitor was a woman (Saad & Gill, 2009). However, how does own attractiveness influence preferences? For men, own attractiveness affects selection of romantic partners to a lesser extent than for women (Lee, Loewenstein, Ariely, Hong, & Young, 2008). Following this, less research has been conducted concerning male attractiveness. However, it has been found that (self-reported and other-rated) attractive men prefer feminine female faces (Burriss, Welling, & Puts, 2011), and that men with serious health conditions seem to lower their attractiveness criteria (Danel et al., 2017).

On the other hand, women who perceive themselves to be more attractive prefer more attractive men, but not necessarily masculine male faces (Cornwell et al., 2006). However, the results regarding masculinity are mixed, since there is research that found that the higher self-rated attractiveness, the stronger the increase in the preference for masculinity (Little et al., 2001). Married women who are rated to be attractive expressed higher standards concerning good genes, including physical attractiveness, investment abilities, parenting indicators, and partner traits (Buss & Shackelford, 2008). Women who perceive themselves to be attractive make higher demands in lonely hearts advertisements than men. However, wealthier men name attractiveness as a criterion in a partner more frequently (Waynforth & Dunbar, 1995). Women's attractiveness, as an indicator of market value, also influences the relation between preferences for healthy partners and health in their actual partners in that the relation is stronger for women who are rated to be attractive by others (Wincenciak et al., 2015). Women who perceive themselves to be attractive prefer masculinized men's voices (Feinberg et al., 2012; Vukovic et al., 2008) and an increase in other-rated facial attractiveness leads to higher preferences for masculinity in male faces (Penton-Voak et al., 2003).

Reward and physiology

Facial attractiveness has numerous effects on cognitive, emotional, behavioral, and physiological levels. Event-related potentials have been used to identify systematic patterns in the brain response to facial attractiveness. Systematic differences between more and less attractive faces have been found in the sensitivity of an early negative component (N200, N300; Jin, Fan, Dai, & Ma, 2017; Werheid, Schacht, & Sommer, 2007; Zhang et al., 2011) and an enhanced late positive potential (Johnston & Oliver-Rodriguez, 1997; Ma, Hu, Jiang, & Meng, 2015; Oliver-Rodriguez, Guan, & Johnston, 1999). These components further show that brain responses to attractiveness occur fast and fairly automatically (Schacht, Werheid, & Sommer, 2008).

Facial attractiveness is generally pleasurable and rewarding. Facial attractiveness is associated with positive facial expressions as measured by facial electromyogram (fEMG; Gerger, Leder, Tinio, & Schacht, 2011). People are willing to exert additional effort (in the form of key presses) to make it possible to look longer at attractive faces (Hayden, Parikh, Deaner, & Platt, 2007; Wang, Hahn, DeBruine, & Jones, 2016). Brain imaging studies using functional magnetic resonance imaging (fMRI) have shown that besides face-specific areas, the putatively rewarding circuits are involved in processing attractive faces, which is similar to when other rewarding stimuli are processed (Aharon et al., 2001; Cloutier, Heatherton, Whalen, & Kelley, 2008; Hahn & Perrett, 2014; Vartanian, Goel, Lam, Fisher, & Granic, 2013; Winston, O'Doherty, Kilner, Perrett, & Dolan, 2007). As attractiveness can be rewarding, unattractiveness or ugliness can be something aversive (Cloutier et al., 2008; Kampe, Frith, Dolan, & Frith, 2001). Moreover, different brain regions are involved in the processing of attractive and unattractive faces (Aharon et al., 2001).

Visual attention

Facial attractiveness has an influence on overt and covert visual attention (Koranyi & Rothermund, 2012; Maner et al., 2003). The relation between facial attractiveness and overt visual attention was measured by analyzing gaze movements and gaze durations spent on faces. The earliest studies analyzed gaze duration by coding the gaze behavior in a face-to-face interaction. They found a positive relation between facial attractiveness and gaze (Fugita, Agle, Newman, & Walfish, 1977; Kleck & Rubenstein, 1975; for a more recent study, see van Straaten, Holland, Finkenauer, Hollenstein, & Engels, 2010). Subsequent studies used eye trackers to replicate this basic finding, but at the same time also drew a more comprehensive and differentiated picture (Aharon et al., 2001; Leder, Tinio, Fuchs, & Bohrn, 2010; Maner et al., 2003; Mitrovic et al., 2016; Shimojo, Simion, Shimojo, & Scheier, 2003). The effect is not limited to highly attractive faces or pronounced contrasts in attractiveness but also works within a small range of differences in a linear manner (Leder, Mitrovic, & Goller, 2016). As already mentioned above, the effect even applies to newborns and infants, a particularly strong case that facial attractiveness is an innate ability (Langlois et al., 1987; Langlois et al., 1991; Slater et al., 1998). Moreover, not only other-sexed beauty captures attention ("opposite-sexed beauty captures the mind" hypothesis; Maner et al., 2003), but the effect also applies to same-sexed faces in heterosexual observers (Leder, Mitrovic, & Goller, 2016).

Facial attractiveness not only influences overt visual attention, but also the increased exposure to faces can enhance facial attractiveness in return (Little, DeBruine, & Jones, 2013; Zajonc, 1968). This loop of a circular enhancement leads to the gaze-cascade effect, in which attractiveness captures attention, enhancing attractiveness in turn, enhancing visual attention, and so on and so forth (Shimojo et al., 2003). The relation between facial attractiveness and visual attention has also been studied in covert attention, where facial attractiveness seems to temporarily bind attention using cognitive resources (for a review, see Lindell & Lindell, 2014). This attention capture by attractive faces is thought to be an automatic effect that is hard to evade (Chen, Liu, & Nakabayashi, 2012; DeWall & Maner, 2008; Liu & Chen, 2012; Ogden, 2013). For example, it is harder to shift attention away from an attractive face (Valuch, Pflueger, Wallner, Laeng, & Ansorge, 2015), and attractive faces capture attention even when presented peripherally (Sui & Liu, 2009).

This attention capture seems to also temporarily bind our attention—when two attractive faces are presented shortly after each other, the identification of the second face is impaired (Nakamura & Kawabata, 2014).

Face inversion

Humans have such an expertise in processing the subtle nuances of faces because of millions of years of evolutionary adaptation. Face processing is therefore hard-wired to the perception of faces in upright orientation. Turning faces upside-down disrupts the ability to read emotions and intentions, make social inferences, and identify people (Bartlett & Searcy, 1993; Civile, McLaren, & McLaren, 2014; Farah, Tanaka, & Drain, 1995; Rhodes, Brake, & Atkinson, 1993; Rossion & Gauthier, 2002; Schwaninger & Mast, 2005; Taubert, van Golde, & Verstraten, 2016; for reviews, see Burke & Sulikowski, 2013; McKone & Yovel, 2009; Valentine, 1988). Since faces are more affected by inversion than other object categories, face processing has been claimed to be somehow special (Yin, 1969). This impairment of face processing by inversion has also been exploited in facial attractiveness research. For example, it has been shown that the discrimination between more and less attractive faces is more reliable for upright faces than for inverted faces (Baeuml, 1994) and that observers show less consistency in assessing inverted faces (Santos & Young, 2008). The attention-binding effect of attractive faces in infants also disappears when faces are presented inverted (Slater et al., 2000). Another study showed that facial attractiveness systematically increases in inverted faces. This effect interacts with the general attractiveness of a face: the less attractive the face, the more it gains by inversion. This interaction was interpreted as an unattractiveness counter in facial attractiveness assessments. Observers use inner templates of attractive faces to assess actual faces—each deviation from these templates reduces the resulting perceived attractiveness. By face inversion, detecting such (unattractive) deviations is impaired, and perceived facial attractiveness increases in turn (Leder et al., 2017).

Research Limitations

Research on facial attractiveness is subject to all the challenges and problems that affect empirical and psychological science in general. The various problems of the replication crisis in psychological research therefore limit the generalizability, reliability, and trustworthiness of the results and theories on facial attractiveness. In this chapter, we have tried to give an extensive overview of topics in facial attractiveness research that are often studied. However, as the field is very broad, it is impossible to cover everything within the scope of a book chapter. We note that there is much literature regarding facial attractiveness from a medical perspective, covering dentofacial and maxillodental topics, guidelines for surgeons, and much more (see e.g., *American Journal of Orthodontics, Journal of Dentistry, Journal of Dental Research, The Journal of the American Dental Association, British Dental Journal, Journal of Public Health Dentistry,* etc.). In the following paragraphs, we will address some issues that are specifically relevant for studying facial attractiveness.

Serial dependency

One factor that influences our judgments of faces is which faces were seen beforehand or are simultaneously seen with the face that is to be judged. Serial dependency, sequential effects, contrast and assimilation effects are well studied in other domains (Herr, 1986; Herr, Sherman, & Fazio, 1983; Parducci & Marshall, 1962; Schwarz, Strack, & Mai, 1991; Sherif, Taub, & Hovland, 1958). Recently, interest in these effects has also increased in research on faces and facial attractiveness (Cogan, Parker, & Zellner, 2013; Forsythe, Zellner, Cogan, & Parker, 2014; Furl, 2016; Kok, Taubert, Van der Burg, Rhodes, & Alais, 2017; MacDonald, Baratta, & Tzalazidis, 2015; Pegors, Mattar, Bryan, & Epstein, 2015; Taubert & Alais, 2016; Taubert, Van der Burg, & Alais, 2016; Xia, Leib, & Whitney, 2016). The findings of these studies are inconclusive: some find assimilation effects and others contrast effects. In assimilation effects, the differences get smaller between the previous face and the face to be rated. The reason is either a decrease in perceived attractiveness of the rated face when the previous face is less attractive, or an increase, when the previous face is more attractive. Contrast effects are found when the difference between the previous and the face to be rated becomes more pronounced. Such contrast effects occur for example in ratings of one's own attractiveness, in which looking at attractive same-sex faces lowers self-ratings of attractiveness for women and their preference for masculine male faces, whereas looking at less attractive faces increases self-ratings and masculinity preferences (Little & Mannion, 2006).

Related to research on assimilation and contrast effects is research on aftereffects. Results when observers are exposed to one specific kind of a face (e.g., attractive, or with specific features or distortions) show that recent experiences influence whom we find attractive (Little, DeBruine, & Jones, 2005; Rhodes, Jeffery, Watson, Clifford, & Nakayama, 2003). Moreover, it is not only the attractiveness of the previous face that is influential. For example, if a face is paired with a same-sex and sex-typical (feminine or masculine) face, it will be rated to be less attractive, whereas pairing with a sex-untypical and therefore less attractive face leads to an increase in attractiveness (Little, Caldwell, Jones, & DeBruine, 2011). Serial dependency in facial attractiveness assessments may be less relevant for everyday perception but all the more important for face research. If the attractiveness of a previously seen and rated face influences the attractiveness of a following face, then facial attractiveness is no absolute measure but only relative to previously seen faces. For example, if a highly attractive face precedes an average face, the average face will—owing to sequential effects—be rated as more attractive (assimilation) or less attractive (contrast).

Operationalization and stimuli

In general, there is a lot of variation in how facial attractiveness is measured, including Likert scales, visual analogue scales, ranking faces, key-press tasks, eye movements, and physiological measures. In addition, many different terms have been used to assess attractiveness, including attractiveness, beauty, sexual attractiveness, attraction, handsomeness, liking, wanting, and many more. Although most of the terms used to assess attractiveness are highly correlated (see Augustin, Wagemans, & Carbon, 2012 for a general discussion on the topic), it is often unclear how these concepts are defined by the authors and conceived by the participants. Participants certainly have somehow individual definitions of terms like attractiveness or liking, and even a given definition might not change those internal representations.

Another factor is the inconsistent labeling of rating scales. In particular, the seemingly arbitrary switch between one-dimensional (e.g., less to more attractive) and two-dimensional (e.g., unattractive versus attractive) operationalizations of attractiveness is problematic. The question remains unclear whether a less attractive face is conceived to be the same as an unattractive face. Another factor is that facial attractiveness is measured inconsistently across studies, ranging from n-point Likert-type scales to visual analogue scales. Although that makes comparison between studies difficult, a high positive correlation between the measures is likely (Rosas, Paço, Lemos, & Pinho, 2017).

Most previous research has used two-dimensional images of faces. In some more recent studies, these images were photographs of real (ambient) faces. More often, however, isolated, bodiless faces, even without hair and ears, or even computer-generated faces have been used to assess facial attractiveness. Such stimuli are highly controlled and very important for experimental research, but at the same time, they are artificial and hardly reflect everyday perception. This raises questions about the generalizability of research on facial attractiveness. For example, is attractiveness deduced from a photo the same as attractiveness from a video or even from face-to-face interactions? Moreover, often highly attractive faces are compared with nonattractive faces, hardly reflecting usual everyday encounters. Finally, instead of individual ratings, most studies use mean ratings of faces across many subjects. Such mean ratings ignore private taste, resulting in an information loss for statistical analyses. These methodological issues must be considered when interpreting findings from this vast and diverse literature.

References

Adams, G. R. (1977). Physical attractiveness research: Toward a developmental social psychology of beauty. *Human Development*, 20(4), 217–239.

Aharon, I., Etcoff, N., Ariely, D., Chabris, C. F., O'Connor, E., & Breiter, H. C. (2001). Beautiful faces have variable reward value: fMRI and behavioral evidence. *Neuron*, 32, 537–551.

Alley, T. (1993). The developmental stability of facial attractiveness: New longitudinal data and a review. *Merrill-Palmer Quarterly, 39*, 265–278.

Alley, T. R., & Cunningham, M. R. (1991). Averaged faces are attractive, but very attractive faces are not average. *Psychological Science, 2*, 123–125.

Allied Analytics LLP (2016). World cosmetics market—opportunities and forecasts, 2014–2022). Retrieved from https://www.researchandmarkets.com/reports/3275915/world-cosmetics-market-opportunities-and

Apicella, C. L., Little, A. C., & Marlowe, F. W. (2007). Facial averageness and attractiveness in an isolated population of hunter-gatherers. *Perception, 36*, 1813–1820.

Attwood, A. S., Penton-Voak, I. S., Goodwin, C., & Munafò, M. R. (2012). Effects of acute nicotine and alcohol on the rating of attractiveness in social smokers and alcohol drinkers. *Drug and Alcohol Dependence, 125*(1–2), 43–48.

Augustin, M. D., Wagemans, J., & Carbon, C. C. (2012). All is beautiful? Generality vs. specificity of word usage in visual aesthetics. *Acta Psychologica, 139*, 187–201.

Bailey, J. M., Gaulin, S., Agyei, Y., & Gladue, B. A. (1994). Effects of gender and sexual orientation on evolutionarily relevant aspects of human mating psychology. *Journal of Personality and Social Psychology, 66*(6), 1081–1093.

Bartlett, J. C., & Searcy, J. (1993). Inversion and configuration of faces. *Cognitive Psychology, 25*, 281–316.

Baudouin, J. Y., & Tiberghien, G. (2004). Symmetry, averageness, and feature size in the facial attractiveness of women. *Acta Psychologica, 117*, 313–332.

Baeuml, K. H. (1994). Upright versus upside-down faces: How interface attractiveness varies with orientation. *Perception & Psychophysics, 56*, 163–172.

Barber, N. (1995). The evolutionary psychology of physical attractiveness: Sexual selection and human morphology. *Ethology and Sociobiology, 16*, 395–424.

Bernstein, I. H., Lin, T.-D., & McClellan, P. (1982). Cross- vs. within-racial judgments of attractiveness. *Perception & Psychophysics, 32*, 495–503.

Berry, D. S., & McArthur, L. Z. (1985). Some components and consequences of a babyface. *Journal of Personality and Social Psychology, 48*(2), 312–323.

Berscheid, E., Dion, K., Walster, E., & Walster, G. W. (1971). Physical attractiveness and dating choice: A test of the matching hypothesis. *Journal of Experimental Social Psychology, 7*(2), 173–189.

Bleske-Rechek, A., & Ryan, D. E. (2015). Continuity and change in emerging adults' mate preferences and mating orientations. *Personality and Individual Differences, 72*, 90–95.

Bobst, C., & Lobmaier, J. S. (2012). Men's preference for the ovulating female is triggered by subtle face shape differences. *Hormones and Behavior, 62*(4), 413–417.

Boothroyd, L. G., Meins, E., Vukovic, J., & Burt, D. M. (2014). Developmental changes in children's facial preferences. *Evolution and Human Behavior, 35*(5), 376–383.

Borelli, C., & Berneburg, M. (2010). "Beauty lies in the eye of the beholder"? Aspects of beauty and attractiveness. *Journal of the German Society of Dermatology, 8*, 326–330.

Bornstein, R. F. (1989). Exposure and affect: Overview and meta-analysis of research, 1968–1987. *Psychological Bulletin, 106*, 265–289.

Bovet, J., Barthes, J., Durand, V., Raymond, M., & Alvergne, A. (2012). Men's preference for women's facial features: Testing homogamy and the paternity uncertainty hypothesis. *PLoS ONE, 7*(11), e49791.

Brand, R. J., Bonatsos, A., D'Orazio, R., & DeShong, H. (2012). What is beautiful is good, even online: Correlations between photo attractiveness and text attractiveness in men's online dating profiles. *Computers in Human Behavior, 28*(1), 166–170.

Brewer, G., Archer, J., & Manning, J. (2007). Physical attractiveness: The objective ornament and subjective self-ratings. *Journal of Evolutionary Psychology*, 5(1), 29–38.

Bronstad, P. M., & Russell, R. (2007). Beauty is in the "we" of the beholder: Greater agreement on facial attractiveness among close relations. *Perception*, 36, 1674–1681.

Budesheim, T. L., & DePaola, S. J. (1994). Beauty or the beast? The effects of appearance, personality, and issue information on evaluations of political candidates. *Personality and Social Psychology Bulletin*, 20(4), 339–348.

Burke, D., & Sulikowski, D. (2013). The evolution of holistic processing of faces. *Frontiers in Psychology*, 4, Article 11. doi:10.3389/fpsyg.2013.00011

Burley, N. (1983). The meaning of assortative mating. *Ethology and Sociobiology*, 4(4), 191–203.

Burns, G. L., & Farina, A. (1992). The role of physical attractiveness in adjustment. *Genetic, Social, and General Psychology Monographs*, 118(2), 157–194.

Burriss, R. P., Roberts, S. C., Welling, L. L. M., Puts, D. A., & Little, A. C. (2011). Heterosexual romantic couples mate assortatively for facial symmetry, but not masculinity. *Personality and Social Psychology Bulletin*, 37(5), 601–613.

Burriss, R. P., Welling, L. L. M., & Puts, D. A. (2011). Men's attractiveness predicts their preference for female facial femininity when judging for short-term, but not long-term, partners. *Personality and Individual Differences*, 50(5), 542–546.

Buss, D. M. (1989). Sex differences in human mate preferences: Evolutionary hypotheses tested in 37 cultures. *Behavioral and Brain Sciences*, 12(1), 1–14.

Buss, D. M. (1995). Psychological sex-differences—Origins through sexual selection. *American Psychologist*, 50, 164–168.

Buss, D. M., & Barnes, M. (1986). Preferences in human mate selection. *Journal of Personality and Social Psychology*, 50(3), 559–570.

Buss, D. M., & Shackelford, T. K. (2008). Attractive women want it all: Good genes, economic investment, parenting proclivities, and emotional commitment. *Evolutionary Psychology*, 6(1), 134–146.

Buston, P. M., & Emlen, S. T. (2003). Cognitive processes underlying human mate choice: The relationship between self-perception and mate preference in Western society. *Proceedings of the National Academy of Sciences*, 100(15), 8805–8810.

Buunk, B. P., Dijkstra, P., Fetchenhauer, D., & Kenrick, D. T. (2002). Age and gender differences in mate selection criteria for various involvement levels. *Personal Relationships*, 9(3), 271–278.

Cavior, N., & Lombardi, D. A. (1973). Developmental aspects of judgment of physical attractiveness in children. *Developmental Psychology*, 8(1), 67–71.

Chen, W., Liu, C. H., & Nakabayashi, K. (2012). Beauty hinders attention switch in change detection: The role of facial attractiveness and distinctiveness. *PLoS ONE*, 7, e32897.

Chen, X., Wang, X., Yang, D., & Chen, Y. (2014). The moderating effect of stimulus attractiveness on the effect of alcohol consumption on attractiveness ratings. *Alcohol and Alcoholism*, 49(5), 515–519.

Chiu, R. K., & Babcock, R. D. (2002). The relative importance of facial attractiveness and gender in Hong Kong selection decisions. *The International Journal of Human Resource Management*, 13(1), 141–155.

Civile, C., McLaren, R. P., & McLaren, I. P. L. (2014). The face inversion effect—Parts and wholes: Individual features and their configuration. *Quarterly Journal of Experimental Psychology*, 67, 728–746.

Clayson, D. E., & Klassen, M. L. (1989). Perception of attractiveness by obesity and hair color. *Perceptual and Motor Skills, 68,* 199–202.

Cloutier, J., Heatherton, T. F., Whalen, P. J., & Kelley, W. M. (2008). Are attractive people rewarding? Sex differences in the neural substrates of facial attractiveness. *Journal of Cognitive Neuroscience, 20,* 941–951.

Coetzee, V., Greeff, J. M., Stephen, I. D., & Perrett, D. I. (2014). Cross-cultural agreement in facial attractiveness preferences: The role of ethnicity and gender. *PLoS ONE, 9,* e99629.

Coetzee, V., Perrett, D. I., & Stephen, I, D. (2009). Facial adiposity: A cue to health? *Perception, 38,* 1700–1711.

Coetzee, V., Re, D., Perrett, D. I., Tiddeman, B. P., & Xiao, D. (2011). Judging the health and attractiveness of female faces: Is the most attractive level of facial adiposity also considered the healthiest? *Body Image, 8,* 190–193.

Cogan, E., Parker, S., & Zellner, D. A. (2013). Beauty beyond compare: Effects of context extremity and categorization on hedonic contrast. *Journal of Experimental Psychology: Human Perception and Performance, 39*(1), 16–22.

Cornwell, R. E., Law Smith, M. J., Boothroyd, L. G., Moore, F. R., Davis, H. P., Stirrat, M., Tiddeman, B., & Perrett, D. I. (2006). Reproductive strategy, sexual development and attraction to facial characteristics. *Philosophical Transactions of the Royal Society B: Biological Sciences, 361*(1476), 2143–2154.

Cross, J. F., & Cross, J. (1971). Age, sex, race, and the perception of facial beauty. *Developmental Psychology, 5*(3), 433–439.

Cunningham, M. R. (1986). Measuring the physical in physical attractiveness: Quasi-experiments on the sociobiology of female facial beauty. *Journal of Personality and Social Psychology, 50*(5), 925–935.

Cunningham, M. R., Barbee, A. P., & Pike, C. L. (1990). What do women want? Facial metric assessment of multiple motives in the perception of male facial physical attractiveness. *Journal of Personality and Social Psychology, 59,* 61–72.

Cunningham, M. R., Roberts, A. R., Barbee, A. P., Druen, P. B., & Wu, C.-H. (1995). "Their ideas of beauty are, on the whole, the same as ours": Consistency and variability in the crosscultural perception of female physical attractiveness. *Journal of Personality and Social Psychology, 68,* 261–279.

Damon, F., Mottier, H., Méary, D., & Pascalis, O. (2017). A review of attractiveness preferences in infancy: From faces to objects. *Adaptive Human Behavior and Physiology, 3*(4), 321–336.

Danel, D. P., Siennicka, A. E., Fedurek, P., Frackowiak, T., Sorokowski, P., Jankowska, E. A., & Pawlowski, B. (2017). Men with a terminal illness relax their criteria for facial attractiveness. *American Journal of Men's Health, 11*(4), 1247–1254.

DeBruine, L., Jones, B. C., Frederick, D. A., Haselton, M. G., Penton-Voak, I. S., & Perrett, D. I. (2010). Evidence for menstrual cycle shifts in women's preferences for masculinity: A response to Marris (in press). "Menstrual cycle and facial preferences reconsidered." *Evolutionary Psychology, 8*(4), 768–775.

Deffenbacher, K. A., Johanson, J., & O'Toole, A. J. (1998). Facial aging, attractiveness, and distinctiveness. *Perception, 27,* 1233–1243.

DeWall, C. N., & Maner, J. K. (2008). High status men (but not women) capture the eye of the beholder. *Evolutionary Psychology, 6,* 328–341.

Dion, K. K. (1973). Young children's stereotyping of facial attractiveness. *Developmental Psychology, 9*(2), 183–188.

Dion, K. K., Berscheid, E., & Walster, E. (1972). What is beautiful is good. *Journal of Personality and Social Psychology, 24*(3), 285–290.

Dixson, B., Dixson, A., Bishop, P., & Parish, A. (2009). Human physique and sexual attractiveness in men and women: A New Zealand-US comparative study. *Archives of Sexual Behavior, 39*, 798–806.

Donaghue, N., & Smith, N. (2008). Not half bad: Self and others' judgements of body size and attractiveness across the life span. *Sex Roles, 58*(11–12), 875–882.

Downs, A. C. (1990). Objective and subjective physical attractiveness judgments among young adults. *Perceptual and Motor Skills, 70*(2), 458.

Downs, A. C., & Wright, A. D. (1982). Differential conceptions of attractiveness: Subjective and objective ratings. *Psychological Reports, 50*(1), 282.

Dunkake, I., Kiechle, T., Klein, M., & Rosar, U. (2012). Schöne Schüler, schöne Noten? Eine empirische Untersuchung zum Einfluss der physischen Attraktivität von Schülern auf die Notenvergabe durch das Lehrpersonal. *Zeitschrift für Soziologie, 41*, 142–161.

Eagly, A. H., Ashmore, R. D., Makhijani, M. G., & Longo, L. C. (1991). What is beautiful is good, but … : A meta-analytic review of research on the physical attractiveness stereotype. *Psychological Bulletin, 110*(1), 109–128.

Ebner, N. C. (2008). Age of face matters: Age-group differences in ratings of young and old faces. *Behavior Research Methods, 40*, 130–136.

Elliot, A., Tracy, J., Pazda, A., & Beall, A. (2013). Red enhances women's attractiveness to men: First evidence suggesting universality. *Journal of Experimental Social Psychology, 49*, 165–168.

Etcoff, N. (1999). *Survival of the prettiest: The science of beauty.* New York: Anchor Books/Doubleday.

Farah, M. J., Tanaka, J. W., & Drain, H. M. (1995). What causes the face inversion effect? *Journal of Experimental Psychology: Human Perception and Performance, 21*, 628–634.

Faure, J. C., Rieffe, C., & Maltha, J. C. (2002). The influence of different facial components on facial aesthetics. *European Journal of Orthodontics, 24*(1), 1–7.

Fechner, G. T. (1876). *Vorschule der Aesthetik.* Leipzig, Germany: Breitkopf & Haertel.

Feinberg, D. R., DeBruine, L. M., Jones, B. C., & Little, A. C. (2008). Correlated preferences for men's facial and vocal masculinity. *Evolution and Human Behavior, 29*(4), 233–241.

Feinberg, D. R., DeBruine, L. M., Jones, B. C., Little, A. C., O'Connor, J. J. M., & Tigue, C. C. (2012). Women's self-perceived health and attractiveness predict their male vocal masculinity preferences in different directions across short- and long-term relationship contexts. *Behavioral Ecology and Sociobiology, 66*(3), 413–418.

Feingold, A. (1988). Matching for attractiveness in romantic partners and same-sex friends: A meta-analysis and theoretical critique. *Psychological Bulletin, 104*(2), 226–235.

Feingold, A. (1990). Gender differences in effects of physical attractiveness on romantic attraction: A comparison across five research paradigms. *Journal of Personality and Social Psychology, 59*(5), 981–993.

Feingold, A. (1992). Good-looking people are not what we think. *Psychological Bulletin, 111*(2), 304–341.

Feinman, S., & Gill, G. W. (1977). Females' response to males' beardedness. *Perceptual and Motor Skills, 44*, 2.

Fink, B., Butovskaya, M. Sorokowski, P., Sorokowska, A., & Matts, P. (2017). Visual perception of British women's skin color distribution in two nonindustrialized societies, the Maasai and the Tsimane. *Evolutionary Psychology, 15*, 147470491771895.

Fink, B., Grammer, K., & Thornhill, R. (2001). Human (*Homo sapiens*) facial attractiveness in relation to skin texture and color. *Journal of Comparative Psychology, 115*(1), 92–99.

Fink, B., Hufschmidt, C., Hirn, T., Will, S., McKelvey, G., & Lankhof, J. (2016). Age, health and attractiveness perception of virtual (rendered). human hair. *Frontiers in Psychology, 22*(7), 1893.

Fink, B., Kleisner, K., Chvátalová, V., & Flegr, J. (2014). Perceived intelligence is associated with measured intelligence in men but not women. *PLoS ONE, 9*(3), e81237.

Finkel, E. J., Norton, M. I., Reis, H. T., Ariely, D., Caprariello, P. A., Eastwick, P. W., Frost, J. H., & Maniaci, M. R. (2015). When does familiarity promote versus undermine interpersonal attraction? A proposed integrative model from erstwhile adversaries. *Perspectives on Psychological Science, 10*(1), 3–19.

Fisher, A. E. (1962). Effects of stimulus variation on sexual satiation in male rat. *Journal of Comparative and Physiological Psychology, 55*, 614–620.

Fitzpatrick, T. B. (1988). The validity and practicality of sun-reactive skin types i through vi. *Archives of Dermatology, 124*, 869–871.

Foos, P. W., & Clark, M. C. (2011). Adult age and gender differences in perceptions of facial attractiveness: Beauty is in the eye of the older beholder. *The Journal of Genetic Psychology, 172*, 162–175.

Forster, M., Gerger, G., & Leder, H. (2013). The glasses stereotype, revisited. *The Jury Expert, 25*, 1–9.

Forsythe, M., Zellner, D., Cogan, E., & Parker, S. (2014). Attractiveness difference magnitude affected by context, range, and categorization. *Perception, 43*(1), 59–69.

Fraley, R. C., & Marks, M. J. (2010). Westermarck, Freud, and the incest taboo: Does familial resemblance activate sexual attraction? *Personality and Social Psychology Bulletin, 36*(9), 1202–1212.

Frevert, T. K., & Walker, L. S. (2014). Physical attractiveness and social status. *Sociology Compass, 8*(3), 313–323.

Frost, P. (1988). Human skin color: A possible relationship between its sexual dimorphism and its social perception. *Perspectives in Biology and Medicine, 32*, 38–58.

Frost, P. (2006). European hair and eye color: A case of frequency-dependent sexual selection? *Evolution and Human Behavior, 27*, 85–103.

Fugita, S. S., Agle, T. A., Newman, I., & Walfish, N. (1977). Attractiveness, self-concept, and a methodological note about gaze behavior. *Personality and Social Psychology Bulletin, 3*, 240–243.

Furl, N. (2016). Facial-attractiveness choices are predicted by divisive normalization. *Psychological Science, 27*(10), 1379–1387.

Gabriel, M. T., Critelli, J. W., & Ee, J. S. (1994). Narcissistic illusions in self-evaluations of intelligence and attractiveness. *Journal of Personality, 62*(1), 143–155.

Galton, F. (1878). Composite portraits. *Journal of the Anthropological Institute of Great Britain and Ireland, 8*, 132–142.

Gangestad, S. W., Thornhill, R., & Yeo, R. A. (1994). Facial attractiveness, developmental stability, and fluctuating asymmetry. *Ethology and Sociobiology, 15*, 73–85.

Gao, Y., J. Niddam, J., Noel, W., Hersant, B., & Meningaud, J. P. (2018). Comparison of aesthetic facial criteria between Caucasian and East Asian female populations: An esthetic surgeon's perspective. *Asian Journal of Surgery, 41*, 4–11.

Geldart, S. (2010). That woman looks pretty, but is she attractive? Female perceptions of facial beauty and the impact of cultural labels. *European Review of Applied Psychology, 60*, 79–87.

Gerger, G., Leder, H., Tinio, P. P. L., & Schacht, A. (2011). Faces versus patterns: Exploring aesthetic reactions using facial EMG. *Psychology of Aesthetics, Creativity, and the Arts, 5,* 241–250.

Gill, D. (2017). Women and men integrate facial information differently in appraising the beauty of a face. *Evolution and Human Behavior, 38,* 756–760.

Graham, J. A., & Jouhar, A. J. (1980). Cosmetics considered in the context of physical attractiveness—A review. *International Journal of Cosmetic Science, 2,* 77–101.

Graham, D. J., Stockinger, S., & Leder, H. (2013). An island of stability: Art images and natural scenes—but not natural faces—show consistent esthetic response in Alzheimer's-related dementia. *Frontiers in Psychology, 4,* 8.

Grammer, K., Fink, B., Moeller, A. P., & Thornhill. R. (2003). Darwinian aesthetics: Sexual selection and the biology of beauty. *Biological Reviews of the Cambridge Philosophical Society, 78*(3), 385–407.

Grammer, K., & Thornhill, R. (1994). Human (*Homo sapiens*), facial attractiveness and sexual selection: The role of symmetry and averageness. *Journal of Comparative Psychology, 108*(3), 233–242.

Griffee, K., Stroebel, S. S., O'Keefe, S. L., Harper-Dorton, K. V., Beard, K. W., Young, D. H., … Elmer, S. (2017). Sexual imprinting of offspring on their parents and siblings. *Cogent Psychology, 4,* 1307632.

Gyuris, P., Járai, R., & Bereczkei, T. (2010). The effect of childhood experiences on mate choice in personality traits: Homogamy and sexual imprinting. *Personality and Individual Differences, 49*(5), 467–472.

Ha, T., van den Berg, J. E., Engels, R. C., & Lichtwarck-Aschoff, A. (2012). Effects of attractiveness and status in dating desire in homosexual and heterosexual men and women. *Archives of Sexual Behavior, 41*(3), 673–682.

Hahn, A. C., & Perrett, D. I. (2014). Neural and behavioral responses to attractiveness in adult and infant faces. *Neuroscience & Biobehavioral Reviews, 46,* 591–603.

Halberstadt, J., & Rhodes, G. (2003). It's not just average faces that are attractive: Computer-manipulated averageness makes birds, fish, and automobiles attractive. *Psychonomic Bulletin & Review, 10,* 149–156.

Harris, C. R. (2010). Menstrual cycle and facial preferences reconsidered. *Sex Roles, 64*(9–10), 669–681.

Harrison, M. A., Shortall, J. C., Dispenza, F., & Gallup, G. G. (2011). You must have been a beautiful baby: Ratings of infant facial attractiveness fail to predict ratings of adult attractiveness. *Infant Behavior and Development, 34*(4), 610–616.

Hayden, B. Y., Parikh, P. C., Deaner, R. O., & Platt, M. L. (2007). Economic principles motivating social attention in humans. *Proceedings of the Royal Society B: Biological Sciences, 274,* 1751–1756.

Heilman, M. E., & Saruwatari, L. R. (1979). When beauty is beastly: The effects of appearance and sex on evaluations of job applicants for managerial and nonmanagerial jobs. *Organizational Behavior & Human Performance, 23*(3), 360–372.

Henss, R. (1991). Perceiving age and attractiveness in facial photographs. *Journal of Applied Social Psychology, 21,* 933–946.

Herr, P. M. (1986). Consequences of priming: Judgment and behavior. *Journal of Personality and Social Psychology, 51*(6), 1106–1115.

Herr, P. M., Sherman, S. J., & Fazio, R. H. (1983). On the consequences of priming: Assimilation and contrast effects. *Journal of Experimental Social Psychology, 19*(4), 323–340.

Hoenekopp, J. (2006). Once more: Is beauty in the eye of the beholder? Relative contributions of private and shared taste to judgments of facial attractiveness. *Journal of Experimental Psychology: Human Perception and Performance, 32,* 199–209.

Howells, D. J., & Shaw, W. C. (1985). The validity and reliability of ratings of dental and facial attractiveness for epidemiologic use. *American Journal of Orthodontics, 88,* 402–408.

International Society of Aesthetic Plastic Surgery (2016). The international study on aesthetic/cosmetic procedures performed in 2016. Retrieved from https://www.isaps.org/wp-content/uploads/2017/10/GlobalStatistics2016-1.pdf.

Jablonski, N. G., & Chaplin, G. (2000). The evolution of human skin coloration. *Journal of Human Evolution, 39*(1), 57–106.

Jenkins, R., White, D., Van Montfort, X., & Burton, M. (2011). Variability in photos of the same face. *Cognition, 121,* 313–323.

Jin, J., Fan, B., Dai, S., & Ma, Q. (2017). Beauty premium: Event-related potentials evidence of how physical attractiveness matters in online peer-to-peer lending. *Neuroscience Letters,* 640, 130–135.

Johnston, V. S., & Franklin, M. (1993). Is beauty in the eye of the beholder? *Ethology and Sociobiology, 14,* 183–199.

Johnston, V. S., Hagel, R., Franklin, M., Fink, B., & Grammer, K. (2001). Male facial attractiveness: Evidence for hormone-mediated adaptive design. *Evolution and Human Behavior,* 22(4), 251–267.

Johnston. V. S., & Oliver-Rodriguez, J. C. (1997). Facial beauty and the late positive component of event-related potentials. *The Journal of Sex Research, 34,* 188–198.

Jones, D. (1995). Sexual selection, physical attractiveness, and facial neoteny. *Current Anthropology, 36,* 723–748.

Jones, D. (1996). An evolutionary perspective on physical attractiveness. *Evolutionary Anthropology, 5*(3), 97–109.

Jones, D., Brace, C. L., Jankowiak, W., Laland, K. N., Musselman, L. E., & Langlois, J. H. (1995). Sexual selection, physical attractiveness, and facial neoteny: Cross-cultural evidence and implications. *Current Anthropology, 36*(5), 723–748.

Jones, B. C., DeBruine, L. M., Perrett, D. I., Little, A. C., Feinberg, D. R., & Law Smith, M. J. (2008). Effects of menstrual cycle phase on face preferences. *Archives of Sexual Behavior,* 37(1), 78–84.

Jones, B. C., Little, A. C., Penton-Voak, I. S., Tiddeman, B. P., Burt, D. M., & Perrett, D. I. (2001). Facial symmetry and judgements of apparent health: Support for a "good genes" explanation of the attractiveness-symmetry relationship. *Evolution and Human Behavior,* 22, 417–429.

Jones, B. C., Perrett, D. I., Little, A. C., Boothroyd, L., Cornwell, R. E., Feinberg, D. R., Tiddeman, B. P., ... Moore, F. R. (2005). Menstrual cycle, pregnancy and oral contraceptive use alter attraction to apparent health in faces. *Proceedings of the Royal Society B: Biological Sciences, 272*(1561), 347–354.

Jones, B. T., Jones, B. C., Thomas, A. P., & Piper, J. (2003). Alcohol consumption increases attractiveness ratings of opposite-sex faces: A possible third route to risky sex. *Addiction,* 98(8), 1069–1075.

Julesz, B. (1971). *Foundations of cyclopean perception.* Chicago, IL: University of Chicago Press.

Kampe, K. K., Frith, C. D., Dolan, R. J., & Frith, U. (2001). Reward value of attractiveness and gaze. *Nature, 413*(6856), 589.

Kanazawa, S. (2011). Intelligence and physical attractiveness. *Intelligence, 39*(1), 7–14.

Karremans, J. C., Dotsch, R., & Corneille, O. (2011). Romantic relationship status biases memory of faces of attractive opposite-sex others: Evidence from a reverse-correlation paradigm. *Cognition, 121*(3), 422–426.

Karremans, J. C., & Verwijmeren, T. (2008). Mimicking attractive opposite-sex others: The role of romantic relationship status. *Personality and Social Psychology Bulletin, 34*(7), 939–950.

Keisling, B. L., & Gynther, M. D. (1993). Male perceptions of female attractiveness: The effects of targets' personal attributes and subjects' degree of masculinity. *Journal of Clinical Psychology, 49*(2), 190–195.

Kenrick, D., & Keefe, R. (1992). Age preferences in mates reflect sex differences in human reproductive strategies. *Behavioral and Brain Sciences, 15*(1), 75–91. doi:10.1017/S0140525X00067595

Kiekens, R., Maltha, J., Hof, M., & Kuijpers-Jagtman, A. (2006). Objective measures as indicators for facial esthetics in white adolescents. *The Angle Orthodontist, 76*, 551–556.

Kiiski, H., Cullen, B., Clavin, S. L., & Newell, F. N. (2016). Perceptual and social attributes underlining age-related preferences for faces. *Frontiers in Human Neuroscience, 10*, 1497.

Kissler, J., & Baeuml, K.-H. (2000). Effects of the beholder's age on the perception of facial attractiveness. *Acta Psychologica, 104*(2), 145–166.

Kleck, R. E., & Rubenstein, C. (1975). Physical attractiveness, perceived attitude similarity, and interpersonal attraction in an opposite-sex encounter. *Journal of Personality and Social Psychology, 31*, 107–114.

Knight, H., & Keith, O. (2005). Ranking facial attractiveness. *European Journal of Orthodontics, 27*, 340–348.

Kok, R., Taubert, J., Van der Burg, E., Rhodes, G., & Alais, D. (2017). Face familiarity promotes stable identity recognition: Exploring face perception using serial dependence. *Royal Society Open Science, 4*(3), 160685.

Komori, M., Kawamura, S., & Ishihara, S. (2009). Averageness or symmetry: Which is more important for facial attractiveness? *Acta Psychologica, 131*(2), 136–142.

Koranyi, N., & Rothermund, K. (2012). When the grass on the other side of the fence doesn't matter: Reciprocal romantic interest neutralizes attentional bias towards attractive alternatives. *Journal of Experimental Social Psychology, 48*(1), 186–191.

Korthase, K. M., & Trenholme, I. (1982). Perceived age and perceived physical attractiveness. *Perceptual and Motor Skills, 54*, 1251–1258.

Kościński, K. (2010). The pattern of facial preferences in boys at early adolescence. *Anthropological Review, 73*(1), 3–20.

Kościński, K. (2011). Life history of female preferences for male faces. *Human Nature, 22*(4), 416–438.

Kościński, K. (2013). Facial preferences in early adolescent girls: Pubertal maturity predicts preferences maturity. *Collegium Antropologicum, 37*(3), 735–743.

Kwart, D., & Foulsham, T. (2012). Age and beauty are in the eye of the beholder. *Perception, 41*, 925–938.

Laeng, B., Mathisen, R., & Johnsen, J.-A. (2007). Why do blue-eyed men prefer women with the same eye color? *Behavioral Ecology and Sociobiology, 61*, 371–384.

Laeng, B., Vermeer, O., & Sulutvedt, U. (2013). Is beauty in the face of the beholder? *PLoS ONE, 8*(7), e68395.

Langlois, J. H., Kalakanis, L., Rubenstein, A. J., Larson, A., Hallam, M., & Smoot, M. (2000). Maxims or myths of beauty? A meta-analytic and theoretical review. *Psychological Bulletin, 126*(3), 390–423.

Langlois, J. H., Ritter, J. M., Casey, R. J., & Sawin, D. B. (1995). Infant attractiveness predicts maternal behaviors and attitudes. *Developmental Psychology*, *31*(3), 464–472.

Langlois, J. H., Ritter, J. M., Roggman, L. A., & Vaughn, L. S. (1991). Facial diversity and infant preferences for attractive faces. *Developmental Psychology*, *27*(1), 79–84.

Langlois, J. H., & Roggman, L. A. (1990). Attractive faces are only average. *Psychological Science*, *1*, 115–121.

Langlois, J. H., Roggman, L. A., Casey, R. J., Ritter, J. M., Rieser-Danner, L. A., & Jenkins, V. Y. (1987). Infant preferences for attractive faces: Rudiments of a stereotype? *Developmental Psychology*, *23*, 363–369.

Leder, H., Goller, J., Rigotti, T., & Forster, M. (2016). Private and shared taste in art and face appreciation. *Frontiers in Human Neuroscience*, *10*, 155.

Leder, H., Mitrovic, A., & Goller, J. (2016). How beauty determines gaze! Facial attractiveness and gaze duration in images of real world scenes. *I-Perception*, *7*(4), 1–12.

Leder, H., Goller, J., Forster, M., Schlageter, L., & Paul, M. A. (2017). Face inversion increases attractiveness. *Acta Psychologica*, *178*, 25–31.

Leder, H., Tinio, P. P. L., Fuchs, I. M., & Bohrn, I. (2010). When attractiveness demands longer looks: The effects of situation and gender. *The Quarterly Journal of Experimental Psychology*, *63*(9), 1858–1871.

Lee, L., Loewenstein, G., Ariely, D., Hong, J., & Young, J. (2008). If I'm not hot, are you hot or not? Physical attractiveness evaluations and dating preferences as a function of one's own attractiveness. *Psychological Science*, *19*(7), 669–677.

Li, N. P., Bailey, J. M., Kenrick, D. T., & Linsenmeier, J. A. W. (2002). The necessities and luxuries of mate preferences: Testing the tradeoffs. *Journal of Personality and Social Psychology*, *82*(6), 947–955.

Limoncin, E., Ciocca, G., Gravina, G. L., Carosa, E., Mollaioli, D., Cellerino, A., … Jannini, E. A. (2015). Pregnant women's preferences for men's faces differ significantly from nonpregnant women. *The Journal of Sexual Medicine*, *12*(5), 1142–1151.

Lindell, A. K., & Lindell, K. L. (2014). Beauty captures the attention of the beholder. *Journal of Cognitive Psychology*, *26*, 768–780.

Lippa, R. A. (2007). The preferred traits of mates in a cross-national study of heterosexual and homosexual men and women: An examination of biological and cultural influences. *Archives of Sexual Behavior*, *36*(2), 193–208.

Little, A. C. (2014). Facial attractiveness. *Wiley Interdisciplinary Reviews—Cognitive Science*, *5*(6), 621–634.

Little, A. C., Burt, D. M., Penton-Voak, I. S., & Perrett, D. I. (2001). Self-perceived attractiveness influences human female preferences for sexual dimorphism and symmetry in male faces. *Proceedings of the Royal Society B: Biological Sciences*, *268*(1462), 39–44.

Little, A. C., Caldwell, C. A., Jones, B. C., & DeBruine, L. M. (2011). Effects of partner beauty on opposite-sex attractiveness judgments. *Archives of Sexual Behavior*, *40*(6), 1119–1127.

Little, A. C., DeBruine, L. M., & Jones, B. C. (2005). Sex-contingent face after-effects suggest distinct neural populations code male and female faces. *Proceedings of the Royal Society B: Biological Sciences*, *272*(1578), 2283–2287.

Little, A. C., DeBruine, L. M., & Jones, B. C. (2013). Sex differences in attraction to familiar and unfamiliar opposite-sex faces: Men prefer novelty and women prefer familiarity. *Archives of Sexual Behavior*, *43*, 973–981.

Little, A. C., & Hancock, P. J. (2002). The role of masculinity and distinctiveness in judgments of human male facial attractiveness. *British Journal of Psychology*, *93*, 451–464.

Little, A. C., & Jones, B. C. (2006). Attraction independent of detection suggests special mechanisms for symmetry preferences in human face perception. *Proceedings of the Royal Society B: Biological Sciences*, 22, 3093–3099.

Little, A. C., & Mannion, H. (2006). Viewing attractive or unattractive same-sex individuals changes self-rated attractiveness and face preferences in women. *Animal Behaviour*, 72(5), 981–987.

Little, A. C., Penton-Voak, I. S., Burt, D. M., & Perrett, D. (2003). Investigating an imprinting-like phenomenon in humans. Partners and opposite-sex parents have similar hair and eye colour. *Evolution and Human Behavior*, 24(1), 43–51.

Little, A. C., & Roberts, S. C. (2012). Evolution, appearance, and occupational success. *Evolutionary Psychology*, 10(5), 782–801.

Little, A. C., Saxton, T. K., Roberts, S. C., Jones, B. C., Debruine, L. M., Vukovic, J., ... Chenore, T. (2010). Women's preferences for masculinity in male faces are highest during reproductive age range and lower around puberty and post-menopause. *Psychoneuroendocrinology*, 35(6), 912–920.

Liu, C. H., & Chen, W. F. (2012). Beauty is better pursued: Effects of attractiveness in multiple-face tracking. *Quarterly Journal of Experimental Psychology*, 65, 553–564.

Liu, J., Harris, A., & Kanwisher, N. (2010). Perception of face parts and face configurations: An FMRI study. *Journal of Cognitive Neuroscience*, 22(1), 203–211.

Ma, Q., Hu, Y., Jiang, S., & Meng, L. (2015). The undermining effect of facial attractiveness on brain responses to fairness in the Ultimatum Game: An ERP study. *Frontiers in Neuroscience*, 9, 77.

MacDonald, G., Baratta, P. L., & Tzalazidis, R. (2015). Resisting connection following social exclusion: Rejection by an attractive suitor provokes derogation of an unattractive suitor. *Social Psychological and Personality Science*, 6(7), 766–772.

Maestripieri, D., Klimczuk, A. C. E., Traficonte, D. M., & Wilson, M. (2014). A greater decline in female facial attractiveness during middle age reflects women's loss of reproductive value. *Frontiers in Psychology*, 5, 179.

Maner, J. K., Gailliot, M. T., & Miller, S. L. (2009). The implicit cognition of relationship maintenance: Inattention to attractive alternatives. *Journal of Experimental Social Psychology*, 45(1), 174–179.

Maner, J. K., Gailliot, M. T., Rouby, D. A., & Miller, S. L. (2007). Can't take my eyes off you: Attentional adhesion to mates and rivals. *Journal of Personality and Social Psychology*, 93(3), 389–401.

Maner, J. K., Kenrick, D. T., Becker, D. V., Delton, A. W., Hofer, B., Wilbur, C. J., & Neuberg, S. L. (2003). Sexually selective cognition: Beauty captures the mind of the beholder. *Journal of Personality and Social Psychology*, 85(6), 1107–1120.

Maner, J. K., Rouby, D. A., & Gonzaga, G. C. (2008). Automatic inattention to attractive alternatives: The evolved psychology of relationship maintenance. *Evolution and Human Behavior*, 29(5), 343–349.

Marcinkowska, U. M., Jasienska, G., & Prokop, P. (2017). A comparison of masculinity facial preference among naturally cycling, pregnant, lactating, and post-menopausal women. *Archives of Sexual Behavior*, 47(5), 1367–1374.

Marcinkowska, U. M., & Rantala, M. J. (2012). Sexual imprinting on facial traits of opposite-sex parents in humans. *Evolutionary Psychology*, 10(3), 621–630.

Maslow, A. H. (1937). The influence of familiarization on preference. *Journal of Experimental Psychology*, 21, 162–180.

Matts P. J., Fink, B., Grammer, K., & Burquest, M. J. (2007). Color homogeneity and visual perception of age, health, and attractiveness of female facial skin. *Journal of the American Academy of Dermatology, 57,* 977–984.

Mazzella, R., & Feingold, A. (1994). The effects of physical attractiveness, race, socioeconomic status, and gender of defendants and victims on judgments of mock jurors: A meta-analysis. *Journal of Applied Social Psychology, 24*(15), 1315–1338.

McArthur, L. Z., & Apatow, K. (1984). Impressions of baby-faced adults. *Social Cognition, 2*(4), 315–342.

McKelvie, S. (1993). Stereotyping in perception of attractiveness, age, and gender in schematic faces. *Social Behavior and Personality, 21,* 121–128.

McKone, E., & Yovel, G. (2009). Why does picture-plane inversion sometimes dissociate perception of features and spacing in faces, and sometimes not? Toward a new theory of holistic processing. *Psychonomic Bulletin & Review, 16,* 778–797.

McLellan, B., & McKelvie, S. J. (1993). Effects of age and gender on perceived facial attractiveness. *Canadian Journal of Behavioural Science, 25,* 135–142.

Mealey, L., Bridgstock, R., & Townsend, G.C. (1999). Symmetry and perceived facial attractiveness: A monozygotic co-twin comparison. *Journal of Personality and Social Psychology, 76,* 151–158.

Mehu, M., Little, A. C., & Dunbar, R. I. M. (2008). Sex differences in the effect of smiling on social judgments: An evolutionary approach. *Journal of Social, Evolutionary, and Cultural Psychology, 2*(3), 103–121.

Mentus, T., & Marković, S. (2016). Effects of symmetry and familiarity on the attractiveness of human faces. *Psihologija, 49,* 301–311.

Meskó, N., & Bereczkei, T. (2004). Hairstyle as an adaptive means of displaying phenotypic quality. *Human Nature, 15,* 251–270.

Miller, R. S. (1997). Inattentive and contented: Relationship commitment and attention to alternatives. *Journal of Personality and Social Psychology, 73*(4), 758–766.

Miller, S. L., & Maner, J. K. (2010). Evolution and relationship maintenance: Fertility cues lead committed men to devalue relationship alternatives. *Journal of Experimental Social Psychology, 46*(6), 1081–1084.

Mita, T. H., Dermer, M., & Knight, J. (1977). Reversed facial images and the mere-exposure hypothesis. *Journal of Personality and Social Psychology, 35*(8), 597–601.

Mitchell, I. J., Gillespie, S. M., Leverton, M., Llewellyn, V., Neale, E., & Stevenson, I. (2015). Acute alcohol consumption and secondary psychopathic traits increase ratings of the attractiveness and health of ethnic ingroup faces but not outgroup faces. *Frontiers in Psychiatry, 6,* 25.

Mitchem, D. G., Zietsch, B. P., Wright, M. J., Martin, N. G., Hewitt, J. K., & Keller, M. C. (2015). No relationship between intelligence and facial attractiveness in a large, genetically informative sample. *Evolution and Human Behavior, 36*(3), 240–247.

Mitrovic, A., Tinio, P. P. L., & Leder, H. (2016). Consequences of beauty: Effects of rater sex and sexual orientation on the visual exploration and evaluation of attractiveness in real world scenes. *Frontiers in Human Neuroscience, 10,* 122.

Moller A. P., & Thornhill R. (1998). Bilateral symmetry and sexual selection: A meta-analysis. *The American Naturalist, 151,* 174–192.

Monin, B. (2003). The warm glow heuristic: When liking leads to familiarity. *Journal of Personality and Social Psychology, 85,* 1035–1048.

Morris, D. (1967). *The naked ape: A zoologist's study of the human animal.* London: Jonathan Cape Publishing.

Morrison, E. R., Morris, P. H., & Bard, K. A. (2013). The stability of facial attractiveness: Is it what you've got or what you do with it? *Journal of Nonverbal Behavior, 37,* 59–67.

Mueser, K. T., Grau, B. W., Sussman, S., & Rosen, A. J. (1984). You're only as pretty as you feel: Facial expression as a determinant of physical attractiveness. *Journal of Personality and Social Psychology, 46*(2), 469–478.

Mueller, B. C., Van Leeuwen, M. L., Van Baaren, R. B., Bekkering, H., & Dijksterhuis, A. (2013). Empathy is a beautiful thing: Empathy predicts imitation only for attractive others. *Scandinavian Journal of Psychology, 54*(5), 401–406.

Nakamura, K., & Kawabata, H. (2014). Attractive faces temporally modulate visual attention. *Frontiers in Psychology, 5,* 7.

Neave, N., & Shields, K. (2008). The effects of facial hair manipulation on female perceptions of attractiveness, masculinity, and dominance in male faces. *Personality and Individual Differences, 45*(5), 373–377.

Neave, N., Tsang, C., & Heather, N. (2009). Effects of alcohol and alcohol expectancy on perceptions of opposite-sex facial attractiveness in university students. *Addiction Research and Theory, 16*(4), 359–368.

Nojo, S., Ihara, Y., Furusawa, H., Akamatsu, S., & Ishida, T. (2011). Facial resemblance and attractiveness: An experimental study in rural Indonesia. *Letters on Evolutionary Behavioral Science, 2*(1), 9–12.

Nojo, S., Tamura, S., & Ihara, Y. (2012). Human homogamy in facial characteristics. *Human Nature, 23*(3), 323–340.

Oberzaucher, E., Katina, S., Schmehl, S. F., Holzleitner, I. J., Mehu-Blantar, I., & Grammer, K. (2012). The myth of hidden ovulation: Shape and texture changes in the face during the menstrual cycle. *Journal of Evolutionary Psychology, 10*(4), 163–175.

Ogden, R. S. (2013). The effect of facial attractiveness on temporal perception. *Cognition & Emotion, 27,* 1292–1304.

Olalde, I., Allentoft, M. E., Sánchez-Quinto, F., Santpere, G., Chiang, C. W. K., DeGiorgio, M., … Lalueza-Fox, C. (2014). Derived immune and ancestral pigmentation alleles in a 7,000-year-old Mesolithic European. *Nature, 507,* 225–228.

Oliver, M. B., & Hyde, J. S. (1993). Gender differences in sexuality: A meta-analysis. *Psychological Bulletin, 114*(1), 29–51.

Oliver-Rodriguez, J. C., Guan, Z., & Johnston, V. S. (1999). Gender differences in late positive components evoked by human faces. *Psychophysiology, 36*(2), 176–185.

Olson, I. R., & Marshuetz, C. (2005). Facial attractiveness is appraised in a glance. *Emotion, 5*(4), 498–502.

Pallett, P. M., Link, S., & Lee, K. (2010). New "golden" ratios for facial beauty. *Vision Research, 50,* 149–154.

Palumbo, R., Adams Jr., R. B., Hess, U., Kleck, R. E., & Zebrowitz, L. (2017). Age and gender differences in facial attractiveness, but not emotion resemblance, contribute to age and gender stereotypes. *Frontiers in Psychology, 8,* 1704.

Pancer, S. M., & Meindl, J. R. (1978). Length of hair and beardedness as determinants of personality impressions. *Perceptual and Motor Skills, 46*(3), 1328–1330.

Parducci, A., & Marshall, L. M. (1962). Assimilation vs. contrast in the anchoring of perceptual judgments of weight. *Journal of Experimental Psychology, 63*(5), 426–437.

Parker, L. L. C., Penton-Voak, I. S., Attwood, A. S., & Munafò, M. R. (2008). Effects of acute alcohol consumption on ratings of attractiveness of facial stimuli: Evidence of long-term encoding. *Alcohol and Alcoholism, 43*(6), 636–640.

Paustian-Underdahl, S. C., & Walker, L. S. (2015). Revisiting the beauty is beastly effect: Examining when and why sex and attractiveness impact hiring judgments. *The International Journal of Human Resource Management, 27*(10), 1034–1058.

Peerlings, R. H., Kuijpers-Jagtman, A. M., & Hoeksma, J. B. (1995). A photographic scale to measure facial aesthetics. *The European Journal of Orthodontics, 17*, 101–109.

Pegors, T. K., Mattar, M. G., Bryan, P. B., & Epstein, R. A. (2015). Simultaneous perceptual and response biases on sequential face attractiveness judgments. *Journal of Experimental Psychology: General, 144*(3), 664–673.

Penke, L., & Asendorpf, J. B. (2008). Beyond global sociosexual orientations: A more differentiated look at sociosexuality and its effects on courtship and romantic relationships. *Journal of Personality and Social Psychology, 95*(5), 1113–1135.

Penton-Voak, I. S., Jones, B. C., Little, A. C., Baker, S., Tiddeman, B., Burt, D. M., & Perrett, D. I. (2001). Symmetry, sexual dimorphism in facial proportions and male facial attractiveness. *Proceedings of the Royal Society of London. Series B: Biological Sciences, 268*, 1617–1623.

Penton-Voak, I. S., Little, A. C., Jones, B. C., Burt, D. M., Tiddeman, B. P., & Perrett, D. I. (2003). Female condition influences preferences for sexual dimorphism in faces of male humans (*Homo sapiens*). *Journal of Comparative Psychology, 117*(3), 264–271.

Penton-Voak, I. S., & Perrett, D. I. (2000). Female preference for male faces changes cyclically: Further evidence. *Evolution and Human Behavior, 21*(1), 39–48.

Penton-Voak, I. S., Perrett, D. I., Castles, D. L., Kobayashi, T., Burt, D. M., Murray, L. K., & Minamisawa, R. (1999). Menstrual cycle alters face preference. *Nature, 399*, 741–742.

Perrett, D. I., Lee, K. J., Penton-Voak, I., Rowland, D., Yoshikawa, S., Burt, D. M., Henzi, S. P. … Akamatsu, S. (1998). Effects of sexual dimorphism on facial attractiveness. *Nature, 394*, 884–887.

Perrett, D. I., May, K. A., & Yoshikawa, S. (1994). Facial shape and judgements of female attractiveness. *Nature, 17*, 368(6468), 239–242.

Phillips, C., Tulloch, C., & Dann, C. (1992). Rating of facial attractiveness. *Community Dentistry and Oral Epidemiology, 20*, 214–220.

Pittenger, J. B., Mark, L. S., & Johnson, D. F. (1989). Longitudinal stability of facial attractiveness. *Bulletin of the Psychonomic Society, 27*, 171–174.

Plant, E. A., Kunstman, J. W., & Maner, J. K. (2010). You do not only hurt the one you love: Self-protective responses to attractive relationship alternatives. *Journal of Experimental Social Psychology, 46*(2), 474–477.

Praino, R., Stockemer, D., & Ratis, J. (2014). Looking good or looking competent? Physical appearance and electoral success in the 2008 congressional elections. *American Politics Research, 42*(6), 1096–1117.

Price, R. A., & Vandenberg, S. G. (1980). Spouse similarity in American and Swedish couples. *Behavior Genetics, 10*(1), 59–71.

Pugach, C., Leder, H., & Graham, D. J. (2017). How stable are human aesthetic preferences across the lifespan? *Frontiers in Human Neuroscience, 11*, 289.

Puts, D. A., Bailey, D. H., Cardenas, R. A., Burriss, R. P., Welling, L. L., Wheatley, J. R., & Dawood, K. (2013). Women's attractiveness changes with estradiol and progesterone across the ovulatory cycle. *Hormones and Behavior, 63*(1), 13–19.

Rammsayer, T. H., & Troche, S. J. (2013). The relationship between sociosexuality and aspects of body image in men and women: A structural equation modeling approach. *Archives of Sexual Behavior, 42*(7), 1173–1179.

Rammstedt, B., & Schupp, J. (2008). Only the congruent survive—Personality similarities in couples. *Personality and Individual Differences, 45*(6), 533–535.

Rand, C. S., & Hall, J. A. (1983). Sex differences in the accuracy of self-perceived attractiveness. *Social Psychology Quarterly, 46*(4), 359–363.

Rantala, M. J., & Marcinkowska, U. M. (2011). The role of sexual imprinting and the Westermarck effect in mate choice in humans. *Behavioral Ecology and Sociobiology, 65*(5), 859–873.

Reber, R., Schwarz, N., & Winkielman, P. (2004). Processing fluency and aesthetic pleasure: Is beauty in the perceiver's processing experience? *Personality and Social Psychology Review, 8*, 364–382.

Regan, P. C., Levin, L., Sprecher, S., Christopher, F. S., & Gate, R. (2000). Partner preferences: What characteristics do men and women desire in their short-term sexual and long-term romantic partners? *Journal of Psychology & Human Sexuality, 12*(3), 1–21.

Regan, P. C., Medina, R., & Joshi, A. (2001). Partner preferences among homosexual men and women: What is desirable in a sex partner is not necessarily desirable in a romantic partner. *Social Behavior and Personality, 29*(7), 625–633.

Rhodes, G. (2006). The evolutionary psychology of facial beauty. *Annual Review of Psychology, 57*, 199–226.

Rhodes, G., Brake, S., & Atkinson, A. P. (1993). What's lost in inverted faces? *Cognition, 47*, 25–57.

Rhodes, G., Halberstadt, J., & Brajkovich, G. (2001). Generalization of mere exposure effects to averaged composite faces. *Social Cognition, 19*(1), 57–70.

Rhodes, G., Jeffery, L., Watson, T. L., Clifford, C. W., & Nakayama, K. (2003). Fitting the mind to the world: Face adaptation and attractiveness aftereffects. *Psychological Science, 14*(6), 558–566.

Rhodes, G., Proffitt, F., Grady, J. M., & Sumich, A. (1998). Facial symmetry and the perception of beauty. *Psychonomic Bulletin & Review, 5*, 659–669.

Rhodes, G., Robbins, R., Jaquet, E., McKone, E., Jeffery, L., & Clifford, C. W. (2005). Adaptation and face perception: How aftereffects implicate norm-based coding of faces. In C. W. G. Clifford & G. Rhodes (Eds.) *Fitting the mind to the world: Adaptation and after-effects in high-level vision* (pp. 213–240). Oxford: Oxford University Press.

Rhodes, G., Sumich, A., & Byatt, G. (1999). Are average facial configurations attractive only because of their symmetry? *Psychological Science, 10*, 52–58.

Rhodes, G., & Tremewan, T. (1996). Averageness, exaggeration, and facial attractiveness. *Psychological Science, 7*, 105–110.

Rhodes, G., Yoshikawa, S., Clark, A., Lee, K., McKay, R., & Akamatsu, S. (2001). Attractiveness of facial averageness and symmetry in non-western cultures: In search of biologically based standards of beauty. *Perception, 30*, 611–625.

Roberts, S. C., Havlicek, J., Flegr, J., Hruskova, M., Little, A. C., Jones, B. C., … & Petrie, M. (2004). Female facial attractiveness increases during the fertile phase of the menstrual cycle. *Proceedings of the Royal Society B: Biological Sciences, 271*, 270–272.

Roney, J. R., & Simmons, Z. L. (2008). Women's estradiol predicts preference for facial cues of men's testosterone. *Hormones and Behavior, 53*(1), 14–19.

Rosas, S., Paço, M., Lemos, C., & Pinho, T. (2017). Comparison between the visual analog scale and the numerical rating scale in the perception of esthetics and pain. *International Orthodontics, 15*(4), 543–560.

Rossion, B., & Gauthier, I. (2002). How does the brain process upright and inverted faces? *Behavioral and Cognitive Neuroscience Reviews, 1*, 63–75.

Russock, H. (2011). An evolutionary interpretation of the effect of gender and sexual orientation on human mate selection preferences, as indicated by an analysis of personal advertisements. *Behaviour, 148*(3), 307–323.

Saad, G., & Gill, T. (2009). Self-ratings of physical attractiveness in a competitive context: When males are more sensitive to self-perceptions than females. *The Journal of Social Psychology, 149*(5), 585–599.

Saegusa, C., Intoy, J., & Shimojo, S. (2015). Visual attractiveness is leaky: The asymmetrical relationship between face and hair. *Frontiers in Psychology, 6*, 377.

Samson, N., Fink, B., & Matts, P. (2011). Does a woman's skin color indicate her fertility level? *Swiss Journal of Psychology, 70*(4), 199–202.

Santos, I. M., & Young, A. W. (2008). Effects of inversion and negation on social inferences from faces. *Perception, 37*, 1061.

Saxton, T. K. (2016). Experiences during specific developmental stages influence face preferences. *Evolution and Human Behavior, 37*(1), 21–28.

Saxton, T. K., Caryl, P. G., & Craig Roberts, S. (2006). Vocal and facial attractiveness judgments of children, adolescents and adults: The ontogeny of mate choice. *Ethology, 112*(12), 1179–1185.

Saxton, T. K., Debruine, L. M., Jones, B. C., Little, A. C., & Roberts, S. C. (2009). Face and voice attractiveness judgments change during adolescence. *Evolution and Human Behavior, 30*(6), 398–408.

Schacht, A., Werheid, K., & Sommer, W. (2008). The appraisal of facial beauty is rapid but not mandatory. *Cognitive, Affective & Behavioral Neuroscience, 8*(2), 132–142.

Schaefer, K., Fink, B., Grammer, K., Mitteroecker, P., Gunz, P., & Bookstein, F. L. (2006). Female appearance: Facial and bodily attractiveness as shape. *Psychology Science, 48*(2), 187–204.

Scheib, J. E., Gangestad, S. W., & Thornhill, R. (1999). Facial attractiveness, symmetry and cues of good genes. *Proceedings of the Royal Society B: Biological Sciences, 266*, 1913–1917.

Schmitt, D. P. (2005). Sociosexuality from Argentina to Zimbabwe: A 48-nation study of sex, culture, and strategies of human mating. *Behavioral and Brain Sciences, 28*(2), 247–311.

Schwaninger, A., & Mast, F. W. (2005). The face-inversion effect can be explained by the capacity limitations of an orientation normalization mechanism. *Japanese Psychological Research, 47*, 216–222.

Schwarz, N., Strack, F., & Mai, H.-P. (1991). Assimilation and contrast effects in part-whole question sequences: A conversational logic analysis. *Public Opinion Quarterly, 55*(1), 3–23.

Schwarz, S., & Hassebrauck, M. (2007). Interindividuelle Unterschiede in Beziehungspräferenzen. *Zeitschrift für Sozialpsychologie, 38*(3), 179–193.

Senior, C. (2003). Beauty in the brain of the beholder. *Neuron, 38*, 525–528.

Shen, H., Chau, D. K., Su, J., Zeng, L. L., Jiang, W., He, J., ... Hu, D. (2016). Brain responses to facial attractiveness induced by facial proportions: Evidence from an fMRI study. *Scientific Reports, 25*(6), 35905.

Sherif, M., Taub, D., & Hovland, C. I. (1958). Assimilation and contrast effects of anchoring stimuli on judgments. *Journal of Experimental Psychology, 55*(2), 150–155.

Shimojo, S., Simion, C., Shimojo, E., & Scheier, C. (2003). Gaze bias both reflects and influences preference. *Nature Neuroscience, 6*, 1317–1322.

Sigall, H., & Ostrove, N. (1975). Beautiful but dangerous: Effects of offender attractiveness and nature of the crime on juridic judgment. *Journal of Personality and Social Psychology, 31*(3), 410–414.

Simpson, J. A., & Gangestad, S. W. (1992). Sociosexuality and romantic partner choice. *Journal of Personality, 60*(1), 31–51.

Simpson, J. A., Gangestad, S. W., & Lerma, M. (1990). Perception of physical attractiveness: Mechanisms involved in the maintenance of romantic relationships. *Journal of Personality and Social Psychology, 59*(6), 1192–1201.

Slater, A., Quinn, P. C., Hayes, R., & Brown, E. (2000). The role of facial orientation in newborn infants' preference for attractive faces. *Developmental Science, 3,* 181–185.

Slater, A., Von der Schulenburg, C., Brown, E., Badenoch, M., Butterworth, G., Parsons, S., & Samuels, C. (1998). Newborn infants prefer attractive faces. *Infant Behavior & Development, 21,* 345–354.

Smith, M. J., Perrett, D. I., Jones, B. C., Cornwell, R. E., Moore, F. R., Feinberg, D. R., ... Hillier, S. G. (2006). Facial appearance is a cue to oestrogen levels in women. *Proceedings of the Royal Society B: Biological Sciences, 273*(1583), 135–140.

Sorokowski, P. (2008). Attractiveness of blonde women in evolutionary perspective: Studies with two polish samples. *Perceptual and Motor Skills, 106,* 737–744.

Spuhler, J. N. (1968). Assortative mating with respect to physical characteristics. *Eugenics Quarterly, 15*(2), 128–140.

Sui, J., & Liu, C. H. (2009). Can beauty be ignored? Effects of facial attractiveness on covert attention. *Psychonomic Bulletin & Review, 16*(2), 276–281.

Sulutvedt, U., & Laeng, B. (2014). The self prefers itself? Self-referential versus parental standards in face attractiveness. *PeerJ, 2,* e595.

Sussman, S., Mueser, K., Grau, B., & Yarnold, P. (1983). Stability of facial attractiveness during childhood. *Journal of Personality and Social Psychology, 44,* 1231–1233.

Swaddle, J. P., & Cuthill, J. C. (1995). Asymmetry and human facial attractiveness: Symmetry may not always be beautiful. *Proceedings of the Royal Society, London, B, 261,* 111–116.

Swami, V., & Barrett, S. (2011). British men's hair color preferences: An assessment of courtship solicitation and stimulus ratings. *Scandinavian Journal of Psychology, 52,* 595–600.

Swami, V., Furnham, A., & Joshi, K. (2008). The influence of skin tone, hair length, and hair colour on ratings of women's physical attractiveness, health and fertility. *Scandinavian Journal of Psychology, 49,* 429–437.

Symons, D. (1995). Beauty is in the adaptations of the beholder: The evolutionary psychology of human female sexual attractiveness. In P. R. Abramson & S. D. Pinkerton (Eds.), *Sexual nature, sexual culture* (pp. 80–119). Chicago, IL: University of Chicago Press.

Tatarunaite, E., Playle, R., Hood, K., Shaw, W., & Richmond, S. (2005). Facial attractiveness: A longitudinal study. *American Journal of Orthodontics and Dentofacial Orthopedics, 127,* 676–682.

Taubert, J., & Alais, D. (2016). Serial dependence in face attractiveness judgements tolerates rotations around the yaw axis but not the roll axis. *Visual Cognition, 24*(2), 103–114.

Taubert, J., Van der Burg, E., & Alais, D. (2016). Love at second sight: Sequential dependence of facial attractiveness in an on-line dating paradigm. *Scientific Reports, 6,* 22740.

Taubert, J., van Golde, C., & Verstraten, F. A. J. (2016). Faces in context: Does face perception depend on the orientation of the visual scene? *Perception, 45,* 1184–1192.

Terry, R. L. (1994). Effects of facial transformations on accuracy of recognition. *Journal of Social Psychology, 134*(4), 483–492.

Teuscher, U., & Teuscher, C. (2007). Reconsidering the double standard of aging: Effects of gender and sexual orientation on facial attractiveness ratings. *Personality and Individual Differences, 42*, 631–639.

Thayer, Z. M., & Dobson, S. D. (2013). Geographic variation in chin shape challenges the universal facial attractiveness hypothesis. *PLoS ONE, 8*, e60681.

Thornhill, R., & Gangestad, S. W. (1993). Human facial beauty: Averageness, symmetry, and parasite resistance. *Human Nature, 4*(3), 237–269.

Thornhill, R., & Gangestad, S. W. (1999). Facial attractiveness. *Trends in Cognitive Sciences, 3*(12), 452–460.

Thornhill, R., & Grammer, K. (1999). The body and face of woman: One ornament that signals quality? *Evolution and Human Behavior, 20*(2), 105–120.

Treder, M. S. (2010). Behind the looking-glass: A review on human symmetry perception. *Symmetry, 2*, 1510–1543.

Tsukiura, T., & Cabeza, R. (2011). Shared brain activity for aesthetic and moral judgments: Implications for the beauty-is-good stereotype. *Social Cognitive and Affective Neuroscience, 6*(1), 138–148.

Valentine, T. (1988). Upside-down faces: A review of the effect of inversion upon face recognition. *British Journal of Psychology, 79*, 471–491.

Valentine, T., Darling, S., & Donnelly, M. (2004). Why are average faces attractive? The effect of view and averageness on the attractiveness of female faces. *Psychonomic Bulletin & Review, 11*, 482–487.

Van Den Abbeele, J., Penton-Voak, I. S., Attwood, A. S., Stephen, I. D., & Munafò, M. R. (2015). Increased facial attractiveness following moderate, but not high, alcohol consumption. *Alcohol and Alcoholism, 50*(3), 296–301.

Vandenberg, S. G. (1972). Assortative mating, or who marries whom? *Behavior Genetics, 2*(2/3), 127–157.

Van den Berghe, P. L., & Frost, P. (1986). Skin color preference, sexual dimorphism and sexual selection: A case of gene-culture co-evolution? *Ethnic and Racial Studies, 9*, 87–113.

Van Dongen, S., & Gangestad, S. W. (2011). Human fluctuating asymmetry in relation to health and quality: A meta-analysis. *Evolution and Human Behavior, 32*, 380–398.

Van Straaten, I., Holland, R. W., Finkenauer, C., Hollenstein, T., & Engels, R. C. (2010). Gazing behavior during mixed-sex interactions: Sex and attractiveness effects. *Archives of Sexual Behavior, 39*, 1055–1062.

Valenzano, D. R., Mennucci, A., Tartarelli, G., & Cellerino, A. (2006). Shape analysis of female facial attractiveness. *Vision Research, 46*(8–9), 1282–1291.

Valuch, C., Pflueger, L. S., Wallner, B., Laeng, B., & Ansorge, U. (2015). Using eye tracking to test for individual differences in attention to attractive faces. *Frontiers in Psychology, 6*, Article 42.

Vartanian, O., Goel, V., Lam, E., Fisher, M., & Granic, J. (2013). Middle temporal gyrus encodes individual differences in perceived facial attractiveness. *Psychology of Aesthetics, Creativity, and the Arts, 7*, 38–47.

Vasquez-Amezquita, M., Leongomez, J. D., Seto, M. C., Bonilla, M., Rodriguez-Padilla, A., & Salvador, A. (2017). Visual attention patterns differ in gynephilic and androphilic men and women depending on age and gender of targets. *The Journal of Sex Research, 56*, 1–17.

Vessel, E. A., Maurer, N., Denker, A. H., & Starr, G. G. (2018). Stronger shared taste for natural aesthetic domains than for artifacts of human culture. *Cognition, 179*, 121–131.

Vukovic, J., Feinberg, D. R., Jones, B. C., DeBruine, L. M., Welling, L. L. M., Little, A. C., & Smith, F. G. (2008). Self-rated attractiveness predicts individual differences in women's preferences for masculine men's voices. *Personality and Individual Differences, 45*(6), 451–456.

Wang, H., Hahn, A. C., DeBruine, L. M., & Jones, B. C. (2016). The motivational salience of faces is related to both their valence and dominance. *PLoS ONE, 11*(8), e0161114.

Watkins, C. D., DeBruine, L. M., Smith, F. G., Jones, B. C., Vukovic, J., & Fraccaro, P. (2011). Like father, like self: Emotional closeness to father predicts women's preferences for self-resemblance in opposite-sex faces. *Evolution and Human Behavior, 32*(1), 70–75.

Waynforth, D., & Dunbar, R. I. M. (1995). Conditional mate choice strategies in humans: Evidence from "Lonely Hearts" advertisements. *Behaviour, 132*(9/10), 755–779.

Weeden, J. & Sabini, J. (2005). Physical attractiveness and health in western societies: A review. *Psychological Bulletin, 131*(5), 635–653.

Werheid, K., Schacht, A., & Sommer, W. (2007). Facial attractiveness modulates early and late event-related brain potentials. *Biological Psychology, 76*, 100–108.

Wickham, L. H. V., & Morris, P. E. (2003). Attractiveness, distinctiveness, and recognition of faces: Attractive faces can be typical or distinctive but are not better recognized. *American Journal of Psychology, 116*, 455–468.

Willis, J., & Todorov, A. (2006). First impressions: Making up your mind after a 100-ms exposure to a face. *Psychological Science, 17*(7), 592–598.

Wincenciak, J., Fincher, C. L., Fisher, C. I., Hahn, A. C., Jones, B. C., & DeBruine, L. M. (2015). Mate choice, mate preference, and biological markets: The relationship between partner choice and health preference is modulated by women's own attractiveness. *Evolution and Human Behavior, 36*(4), 274–278.

Winston, J. S., O'Doherty, J., Kilner, J. M., Perrett, D. I., & Dolan, R. J. (2007). Brain systems for assessing facial attractiveness. *Neuropsychologia, 45*, 195–206.

Xia, Y., Leib, A. Y., & Whitney, D. (2016). Serial dependence in the perception of attractiveness. *Journal of Vision, 16*(15), 28.

Yerkes, M. J., & Pettijohn II, T. F. (2008). Developmental stability of perceived physical attractiveness from infancy to young adulthood. *Social Behavior and Personality, 36*, 691–692.

Yin, R. K. (1969). Looking at upside-down faces. *Journal of Experimental Psychology, 81*, 141–145.

Zahavi A., & Zahavi A. (1997). *The handicap principle: a missing piece of Darwin's puzzle.* New York: Oxford University Press.

Zaidel, D. W., & Hessamian, M. (2010). Asymmetry and symmetry in the beauty of human faces. *Symmetry, 2*, 136–149.

Zajonc, R. B. (1968). Attitudinal effects of mere exposure. *Journal of Personality and Social Psychology, 9*(2), 1–27.

Zebrowitz, L. A., & Franklin Jr., R. G. (2014). The attractiveness halo effect and the babyface stereotype in older and younger adults: Similarities, own-age accentuation, and older adult positivity effects. *Experimental Aging Research, 40*(3), 375–393.

Zebrowitz, L. A., Montepare, J. M., & Lee, H. K. (1993). They don't all look alike: Individuated impressions of other racial groups. *Journal of Personality and Social Psychology, 65*, 85–101.

Zhang, Y., Kong, F., Chen, H., Jackson, T., Han, L., Meng, J., … Najam ul Hasan, A. (2011). Identifying cognitive preferences for attractive female faces: An event-related potential experiment using a study-test paradigm. *Journal of Neuroscience Research, 89*, 1887–1893.

Zietsch, B. P., Verweij, K. J. H., Heath, A. C., & Martin, N. G. (2011). Variation in human mate choice: Simultaneously investigating heritability, parental influence, sexual imprinting, and assortative mating. *The American Naturalist, 177*(5), 605–616.

Zilhão, J. (2012). Personal ornaments and symbolism among the Neanderthals. *Developments in Quaternary Science, 16*, 35–49.

SECTION 4

ARTFORMS

CHAPTER 25

THE EMPIRICAL AESTHETICS OF MUSIC

ELVIRA BRATTICO

INTRODUCTION

IN the 1960s, the American psychologist A. H. Maslow found music to be one of the most common ways people create intense, transcendent experiences that are critical for self-actualization (Maslow, 1961). He called them peak experiences. Indeed, later in the 1990s, more than 1,300 people were surveyed about the strongest, most intense experience with music they had had in their life, with responses spanning from weeping or hair standing up on the back of the neck to the elicitation of personally important and emotional memories. To mention a recent real-life example, the benefit concert *One Love Manchester*, organized by American pop singer Ariana Grande two weeks after a tragic bomb attack, was attended by 55,000 people, broadcast in over 38 countries around the world, raised more than £10 million, and was the most watched television event in the United Kingdom in 2017.

Along with peak experiences, music also provides a soundtrack for our everyday life. In about 40% of thousands of randomly sampled episodes, people were listening to music (Juslin et al., 2008; North, 2004; Sloboda, O'Neill, & Ivaldi, 2001). In around 60% of these music episodes, music was influencing the listeners' emotions (Juslin & Laukka, 2004; Juslin et al., 2008). Going back in time, music appeared with *Homo sapiens* in parallel with figurative art (cave paintings), or perhaps even earlier (Brattico, Brattico, & Jacobsen, 2009). Flutes as old as 40,000 years were discovered in caves used by Neanderthals, perhaps suggesting that artistic activities had existed even in human ancestors who were previously considered as devoid of symbolic thinking (Fink, 1997; Wong, 1997). Some scholars have proposed that humans possess an innate, evolutionarily old craving for beauty, especially in terms of harmony and symmetry (Chatterjee,

2013; Conway & Rehding, 2013; Pearce et al., 2016; Smith, 2011). This behavior already exists from the first days of life: newborns already possess the neural circuitry to process musical sounds (Perani et al., 2010) and are calmed down by music (Cirelli, Trehub, & Trainor, 2018; Trehub et al., 2013).

Aesthetic appreciation of music and indeed other arts is therefore universal and as such can be the target of systematic investigation. This realization has led to the development of the *empirical aesthetics of music*, which uses multidisciplinary methodologies of both experimentation and naturalistic observations borrowed from experimental psychology, musicology, social psychology, cognitive neuroscience, and cognitive science in the common pursuit of understanding our universal drive for musical aesthetic activities. In empirical aesthetics, there is a consensus in defining an *artwork* (whether consisting of sounds or images) as characterized by a set of qualities or features that are favored or unfavored according to stable or changing conditions. The experience of being exposing to the artwork, namely the *aesthetic experience*, instead depends on the subject who decides to invest attentional, emotional, and cognitive resources toward the artwork. In Dewey's words: "By common consent, the Parthenon is a great work of art." Yet it has esthetic standing only as the work becomes an experience for the human being (Dewey, 2005, p. 2).

In spite of an abundance of findings, these have only rarely been organized in a systematic overview and when that has happened (e.g., Hargreaves & North, 1993; Tervaniemi, 2018) more emphasis has been given to perception, pleasure, and liking at the expense of other aesthetically tinged dimensions, beauty being the central one (Tiihonen, Brattico, Maksimainen, Wikgren, & Suvi Saarikallio, 2017). In this sense, Helmholtz was ahead of his time when he observed that music has a more immediate connection with pure sensation than any other of the fine arts, and, consequently … the theory of the sensations of hearing is destined to play a much more important part in musical esthetics, than, for example, the theory of chiaroscuro or of perspective in painting (von Helmholtz & Ellis, 1875, p. 3). This reductionist stance can nevertheless be contrasted with the common conception of musical aesthetics in the general population (Istók et al., 2009). Art first of all puts something beautiful before us, as (Hanslick & Cohen, 1892, p. 4) stated. Likewise, in their review on empirical aesthetics of music, Hargreaves and North (1993) admitted that our own principal interest has been in trying to account for everyday likes and dislikes in music rather than covering also other kinds of musical aesthetic responses such as aesthetic emotions, value attribution, or judgment and attitudes. Other authors have instead been limited to neuroimaging findings, only marginally touching on the broader empirical music–aesthetic field (Brattico, 2015, 2019; Brattico, Bogert, & Jacobsen, 2013; Brattico, Brattico, & Vuust, 2017; Hodges, 2016; Nieminen, Istók, Brattico, Tervaniemi, & Huotilainen, 2011; Reybrouck & Brattico, 2015; Reybrouck, Vuust, & Brattico, 2018). The present review, therefore, aims to provide a bird's eye view snapshot of the empirical aesthetics of music without neglecting core aesthetic properties, such as beauty judgments and preference.

Major Theories in the Empirical Aesthetics of Music

Today, aesthetic responses are seen as an outcome of several factors, and the various theories and research programs can be classified on the basis of the factors they focus on. In this section I will first discuss the historical beginnings of empirical aesthetics of music that emphasized the low-level sensory properties of the aesthetic object, that is, the stimulus itself. Next, I discuss models according to which pleasure originates from the learned, statistical properties of the object. These models thus add the aesthetic subject (listener/perceiver) to the model who learns and familiarizes with the stimulus features. They can be labeled as cognitivist theories, because, according to them, aesthetic responses constitute something akin to a cognitive puzzle. The group of models I discuss emphasize features of the art and music appreciation that rely on their context and other nonappearance properties, such as the historical context of the work, the intentions of the artist and the listener, and so on. A fourth set of emotivist models emphasize the psychological mechanisms that generate emotions from music. Finally, the neuroscientific theories identify the secret codes in neural mechanisms predicting positive aesthetic responses to music.

Historical beginnings

Perhaps the first to relate properties of sounds to aesthetic responses was Pythagoras (circa 570–500 BCE), who associated vibrating strings with lengths forming simple numerical ratios with pleasant, harmonious sensations (Crocker, 1963; Krumhansl, 2000). Above all, however, it was Hermann von Helmholtz who in his treatise *On the Sensations of Tone as a Physiological Basis for the Theory of Music* (von Helmholtz & Ellis, 1875) gave the first physiological explanation for the phenomenon. He was inspired by German post-Kantian philosophy and physiology as well as by Hanslick's view of musical aesthetics, which departed from exaggerated sentimentalism toward the search for elementary, natural forces determining the psychological responses to sounds. Helmholtz was aware that he was initiating a new interdisciplinary discipline bridging art and science. In the present work, he wrote, an attempt will be made to connect the boundaries of two sciences, which, although drawn toward each other by many natural affinities, have hitherto remained practically distinct—I mean the boundaries of physical and physiological acoustics on the one side, and of musical science and esthetics on the other (von Helmholtz & Ellis, 1875, p. 1). To achieve such synthesis, Helmholtz linked, for example, simple integer ratios with the amplitude modulations (i.e., beats) that occur when neighboring sounds with complex ratios to each other are played simultaneously, thus activating adjacent hair cells of the organ of Corti, in the inner ear. This produces a processing peculiarity that is translated into the unpleasant sensation of sensory dissonance. Much later, Reber (Reber, Schwarz, & Winkielman, 2004; Ashley & Timmers, 2017) used the term cognitive fluency to explain aesthetic pleasure of stimuli that are easily decoded as compared with the negative attribution of value to stimuli that are hard to decipher. In this formulation, perceptual fluency, namely the ease of identifying the features of the stimulus, works in concert with conceptual fluency, related to the stimulus interpretation and semantics to explain pleasure responses. Both processes are mediated by the subjective experience and familiarity with the object of the recipient (e.g., Obermeier et al., 2016).

Another major German exponent of empirical aesthetics was Carl Stumpf, who in a two-volume treatise *Tonpsykologien* (1883–1890, not yet translated into English although the first volume will soon appear for Ashgate and the second in 2019) proposed an alternative theory of musical consonance based on a psychological property of tones simultaneously perceived, that is, tonal fusion, in which consonant tones blend to form a unique percept. His students, the three influential founders of Gestalt psychology, Max Wertheimer (1880–1943), Wolfgang Köhler (1887–1967), and Kurt Koffka (1886–1941), then went on to contribute to the understanding of musical melody as an outcome of perceptual Gestalt laws. Gestalt laws are organizing principles of perception and later inspired, among others, the first theory of melodic *expectations* by Meyer (1973) and, more recently, the implication–realization model of melodic expectation by Eugene Narmour (1992).

Another work of historical importance and influence was the theory proposed by Daniel Berlyne in the 1960s and later reformulated as optimum stimulation by Zuckerman (1979). According to Berlyne, the listener collates the different properties of a given musical piece (e.g., complexity, familiarity, surprisingness) and these collative variables, alongside with the psychophysical properties of the stimulus and their ecological properties (their signal value or meaningfulness) converge to predict the level of arousal of the listeners' autonomic nervous system, specifically the ascending reticular activating system (ARAS). This level of physiological arousal induced by a stimulus determines the aesthetic preference along an inverted-U-shaped curve. This function was inspired by the curve relation between appreciation and stimulus intensity proposed by Wilhelm Wundt, a one-time assistant of Helmholtz (Ziche, 1999). According to Berlyne's formulation, medium amounts of arousal potential in the stimulus lead to the highest levels of preference. However, this medium optimal level varies across individuals and across time, as it depends on both the biological and cultural repertoire of each individual. This theory, receiving support from three decades of empirical research, dominated empirical aesthetics for over three decades and some variations of it are still present in modern cognitive theories of musical pleasure. For instance, several behavioral studies, reviewed by Hargreaves and North (1993), confirmed the inverted-U-relationship between ratings of pleasantness and the information content of the melodic or rhythmic complexity. Many of these studies referred to the notion of complexity as defined by Berlyne, namely in relation to the number of distinguishable elements. Other studies instead defined complexity by using the information theory concept of redundancy as conceptualized by Shannon and Weaver (1949), namely the extent to which a stimulus reduces uncertainty. By experimentally manipulating the melodic complexity it was found that even school-age children prefer melodies of medium complexity (McMullen, 1974).

Zajonc suggested that even the simplest objects might have certain features (preferenda) that are more susceptible to affective processing than others, and which allow the emergence of affective reaction early after the stimulus onset (Zajonc, 1980). Typically, these features are local and specific to the sensory modality of the aesthetic experience. On top of these, Zajonc (1968) put forward the listening experience of the individual by emphasizing the importance of repetition to boost a positive aesthetic response. The listener might reach enjoyment thanks to the mere exposure effect, namely the positive effect of prior listening on liking (Montoya, Horton, Vevea, Citkowicz, & Lauber, 2017). This kind of strategy is well known by music companies and radios, which broadcast the same song repetitively in order to allow the listeners time to learn and appreciate it. However, exposure and familiarity also have an inverted-U relationship with preference (Hargreaves & North, 1993). In support of this, Finnish musicologist Tuomas Eerola computationally calculated a score of complexity for the 12 UK albums by The Beatles and compared that figure with the number of weeks for which that album stayed in the chart after its release (Eerola, 1998). The results supported an inverted-U relationship between liking, complexity, and familiarity. In terms of the inverted-U curve, the less complex albums peaked early and then tailed off in popularity, and the more complex ones peaked later but then tailed off slowly.

In direct opposition to Berlyne's theory, Colin Martindale (Martindale & Moore, 1988) argued that the leading factor for determining aesthetic preference was prototypicality: more prototypical exemplars of a category, such as themes of classical music, are preferred to nonprototypical ones. Object representations are supposed to be kept in interconnected units of the mind that become activated more frequently by prototypical stimuli. The higher activations are related to preference. Marin, Lampatz, Wandl, and Leder (2016) hinted that the basis of both the mere exposure effect and the prototype-preference theory might be the cognitive fluency theory (Reber, Schwarz, & Winkielman, 2004), which states that the ease of processing determines preference.

Cognitivist theories

So far, two major lines of thought have been proposed to account for how music is perceived and appreciated. Some researchers, who can be called probabilists, use information theory to analyze music perception. They describe pitch and meter schemata in music as fundamentally probabilistic in nature and hence learned by exposure. This is opposed by the cognitivists, who describe musical phenomena as emerging from fixed cognitive templates or schemata that are activated (rather than learned) after acculturation and that are used, implicitly, by the human brain to discern musical structures (Cheung, Meyer, Friederici, & Koelsch, 2018; Jackendoff & Lerdahl, 2006; Koelsch, 2012;

Peretz & Coltheart, 2003). Tonality, for instance, can be viewed by the cognitivists as a cognitive bias for organizing sounds according to universal and innate preferences (Krumhansl, 2000). For the probabilists, in contrast, tonality is seen as a property emerging from the repetition of certain pitches over others, which in turn results in statistical learning (Loui, 2012a, 2012b; Pearce, 2018). A third, mediating viewpoint that can be referred to as evolutionist, proposes that universals for music, defined as the statistically recurrent features appearing in the different cultures around the world (Savage, Brown, Sakai, & Currie, 2015), emerge in the course of human evolution via intergenerational transmission as a result of the constraints imposed by the central nervous system (Lumaca, Ravignani, & Baggio, 2018; Lumaca, Trusbak Haumann, Vuust, Brattico, & Baggio, 2018; Ravignani, Delgado, & Kirby, 2016; Trainor, 2015).

Huron (2006) proposed a probabilistic framework called ITPRA (imagination, tension, prediction, reaction, and appraisal) dealing primarily with musical predictability and surprise. The assumptions of this model stem from the evolutionary theory: human and nonhuman animal brains evolved originally to make probabilistic estimates regarding their environment by using prior experiences (statistical learning) to achieve fast responses to danger (e.g., Bar, 2007; Friston, Kilner, & Harrison, 2006). Anticipation of musical stimuli facilitates the processing of upcoming data (how we become attentive toward a stimulus with potential survival value), and expectations serve to access memory and to project that information on the upcoming stimuli. Musical expectations become cues for pleasure and reward, being adaptive mechanisms in the service of driving the body toward a prepared state with feelings of anticipation (Huron, 2006; Salimpoor & Zatorre, 2013b). In other words, reminiscent of Husserl's (1991) considerations on internal time, Huron states that during music listening we are continuously anticipating (whether consciously or unconsciously) the outcomes of the temporally unfolding musical paths and wondering where they might lead us.

Contextual theories

LeBlanc (1982) proposed a variation of cognitive models that included three variable groups: the music, the listener, and the environment. Music preference decisions are based upon the action of input information and the characteristics of the listener, with input information consisting of the musical stimulus and the listener's cultural environment (LeBlanc, 1982, p. 4). This three-component model was developed further in their reciprocal feedback model (Hargreaves, Hargreaves, & North, 2011; Hargreaves & North, 1993), which was termed like that because any one of these three main components can exert an influence on each of the other two, and because these influences are bidirectional.

In the 1980s Vladimir Konečni conducted a massive amount of research to account for the social context. In his view (Konečni, 1982), the individual is in constant interaction with the social and nonsocial environment. Different aesthetic choices are made depending on the situation in which the individual finds themselves and in turn these choices affect the listener's emotional state and behavior toward others in the situation in a constant feedback loop. An ethically controversial study, Konečni et al. (1976) tested the model comparing listeners in an angry or relaxed mood and computer-generated melodies of high or low complexity. The participants in the annoy–wait group were repeatedly insulted by an accomplice of the experimenter, posing as another participant, then waited alone in a room, as opposed to the participants in the annoy–shock group, who were given the chance to retaliate by delivering fake electric shocks. The participants who were not insulted at all (no annoy–wait) or who were given the chance to retaliate did not show any preference for low- versus high-complexity melodies. In contrast, the stressed participants of the annoy–wait group listened more often to the simple melodies than the complex ones. Scholars (Hargreaves & North, 1993; Konečni, 1982) have suggested that these and similar findings have to do with arousal moderation or arousal-state goals, in that people select music that reduces high levels of arousal or increases low levels.

Emotivist theories

In the psychological literature, the most influential models focus on the psychological mechanisms that predict emotional reactions to music. Most models use the framework of everyday emotions, in which arousal constitutes one dimension and accounts for the activating or relaxing effects of music, together with valence or pleasantness as the second dimension accounting for the positive or negative value attribution accompanying an appraisal of an emotion-inducing event (Eerola & Vuoskoski, 2013). Other models have attempted to identify feelings and emotions that are specific to aesthetic contemplation of music such as in concerts, and that are not (easily) induced by other stimuli, such as sublime and awe (Zentner, Grandjean, & Scherer, 2008).

Some of these models, furthermore, aim to isolate a set of psychological mechanisms that explains the induction of emotions by music. One such model, termed BRECVEM (Juslin & Västfjäll, 2008), lists six mechanisms for music–emotion induction: (a) brain-stem reflexes (the immediate reactions to salient features of sounds), (b) evaluative conditioning (deriving from repeated association of music to positive or negative stimuli), (c) emotional contagion (when music mimics a vocal or bodily emotional expression), (d) visual imagery (association with visual images during listening), (e) episodic memory (elicitation of a memory for a particular event), and (f) rhythmic entrainment (an external rhythm influences some internal bodily rhythm in the listener—such as heart rate—such that the latter one locks in). On top of these six mechanisms, musical expectancy is also listed as an intra-musical mechanism, also encompassing then in this model the cognitive theories listed in the previous section. A similar view is taken by Vuust and Kringelbach (2010). In the slightly revised version of the BRECVEM model, aesthetic judgment is added as the final outcome of the summation of different emotion-inductive mechanisms (Juslin, 2013). This accounts for the aesthetic attitude adopted before listening and the individual criteria determining preferences associated with particular musical pieces or genres. In this sense (similarly to what was proposed in Brattico et al., 2013), aesthetic judgment can explain why music emotions are different from mundane emotions, and how it is possible to enjoy listening to a sad song.

In most of the cognitive psychological models, positive responses to music are often identified with pleasure, which is itself often measured by using the chill response. This refers to the physiological reaction involving goose bumps or shivers down the spine at peak moments of intense pleasure (Grewe, Nagel, Kopiez, & Altenmüller, 2005, 2007; Panksepp & Bernatzky, 2002; Salimpoor, Benovoy, Longo, Cooperstock, & Zatorre, 2009; Sumpf, Jentschke, & Koelsch, 2015). Chills have also been described as a subtle nervous tremor caused by intense emotion (Grewe et al., 2007, p. 297) or skin orgasms (Harrison & Loui, 2014). Although not every person experiences them (Goldstein, 1980; Grewe et al., 2007; Sloboda, 1991), the chill responses have inspired scientists owing to their reliability, and because they make it possible to translate the subjective emotional experiences of pleasure into objective physiological measures of autonomic nervous system changes. Chills are related to the experience of increased subjective emotion and pleasure and are associated with enhanced physiological arousal (Grewe et al., 2005; Mori & Iwanaga, 2017; Rickard, 2004; Salimpoor et al., 2009).

While most studies in music psychology and neuroscience have used pleasure as a stereotypical positive aesthetic outcome, some scholars have promoted other types of aesthetic responses to music (Chatterjee, 2013; Pelowski, Markey, Forster, & Gerger, 2017; Pelowski, Markey, Lauring, & Leder, 2016; Schindler et al., 2017). Among them, Konečni (2005) has posited an aesthetic trinity of three aesthetic responses: awe, being moved, and thrills. Nostalgia is featured by some scholars as an important kind of aesthetic emotional response, tinged with a predominant positive valence but also including a negative emotional dimension (Lahdelma & Eerola, 2015).

Neuroscientific models

In addition to the psychological models discussed above, the field has recently witnessed the emergence of several frameworks accounting for neural substrates, and the succession of information-processing stages in the brain. Several of these models can be termed multicomponent since they describe aesthetic experiences by modeling the relationship between bottom-up and top-down processes as well as their neural determinants (Brattico et al., 2013; Pelowski et al., 2017). These models are motivated by findings from neuroimaging, which makes it possible to study the human brain in real action. The neuroaesthetics of music (Brattico & Pearce, 2013) uses brain research techniques to study the neural principles underlying the human aesthetic experience of music. Initial attempts in this direction emerged more than five years ago, and the field is growing (Brattico, 2019).

A leading neuroscientific proposal on the aesthetic responses to music concentrates on the neural activity and neuronal connectivity between brain regions during music-induced pleasure, often marked by chills (Salimpoor et al., 2015). These studies have found that music enjoyment is associated with neuronal activity in the brain's reward circuit, a set of regions that include the nucleus accumbens, the ventral tegmental area, the amygdala, the insula, the orbitofrontal cortex, and the ventromedial prefrontal cortex. All these regions rely on the neurotransmitter dopamine for transmission (Chanda & Levitin, 2013; Salimpoor et al., 2015). Based on recent findings (Salimpoor, Benovoy, Larcher, Dagher, & Zatorre, 2011; Salimpoor et al., 2013), it has also been proposed that the neural mechanism predicting musical pleasure is the increased functional connectivity between the superior temporal gyrus where the auditory cortex is located and sounds are processed, the inferofrontal cortex where hierarchical predictions for sounds are computed, and reward regions where the bodily changes and the conscious awareness of pleasurable sensations are produced (Salimpoor & Zatorre, 2013a, 2013b; Zatorre & Salimpoor, 2013). When the anatomical connections between these brain regions perform poorly, musical anhedonia (absence of pleasure specific to music) results (Martínez-Molina, Mas-Herrero, Rodríguez-Fornells, Zatorre, & Marco-Pallarés, 2016).

Based on the suggestions of Salimpoor and Zatorre (2013a, 2013b; Zatorre & Salimpoor, 2013), and in line with the Kantian notion of aesthetic pleasure that distinguishes contemplation of beauty from mere sensory gratification, such as in eating or drinking (Brattico, 2015; Brattico & Pearce, 2013; Bundgaard, 2014; Kant, 2007; Zangwill, 1995), Brattico et al. (2013) proposed a chronometric model of the musical aesthetic experience, discerning between an immediate bottom-up pleasurable reaction to the object's features, and a reflective, top-down conscious pleasure involving a conscious decision concerning the music heard. Evidence from affective neuroscience suggests that sensory pleasure is immediately and involuntarily activated by the sensory properties of the stimulus and associated with the fast firing of dopaminergic neurons of the mesolimbic and nigrostriatal pathways, which, in turn, modulate the neuroendocrine, visceral, and muscle responses of the autonomic nervous system, altering the bodily state (Kringelbach & Berridge, 2009). A slower, voluntary pathway, recruiting frontal lobe structures, mediates instead conscious pleasure or enjoyment. This view agrees with a mainstream visual–neuroaesthetic view, according to which art emerges from the interaction between three main neural systems, a sensory–motor one (sensation, perception, motor system), a knowledge–meaning one (expertise, context, culture), and an emotion–evaluation one (reward, emotion, wanting/liking) (Chatterjee & Vartanian, 2016).

Other existing overviews of neuroscientific studies on music perception that also touch upon aesthetics tend to rely on the neural processing of individual musical sounds. Far fewer in number are those that refer explicitly to aesthetic responses, including not only pleasure but also preference, beauty, and other judgments related to value attribution. Hodges (2016) called the former accounts broad and the latter narrow, although when considering the efforts at covering the variety of human functions that are used in an aesthetic experience, the terminology could be reversed as well. Future research should perhaps take new steps toward studying the neural correlates of value attribution to sounds and the formation of musical taste, thus finally tackling the neural code underlying decisions of beauty.

The Aesthetic Object: Stimulus Features Driving Aesthetic Outcomes

In this section I will review the main findings on the stimulus features that most consistently predict aesthetic responses to musical sounds. These findings are transversal to theories in the sense that they have a factual value irrespectively of how researchers fit them into their models (Table 25.1).

Table 25.1. Stimulus–specific variables determinant for the aesthetic experience of music.

Variable	Abbreviation	Explanation and feature manipulation
Complexity	com	Complexity can be defined as the amount of information contained in the signal
Musical mode	mod	Musical mode is a series of pitches organized into a distinct order (scale), and characterized by certain relationships between each pitch. In Western music, the most used modes are the major and minor, differing mainly in the third pitch
Timbral features	tim	Timbral features, including fullness, brightness, spectral complexity, refer to a set of variables related to the sound wave and depending on the source that has generated the sound as well as the medium in which the sound is transduced. Overall, timbre describes the perceived quality or color of a sound
Tonal features	ton	Tonal features include pitch, melody, and harmony. They refer to the spectral aspects of auditory sequences that in Western tonal music are organized according to a discrete set of accepted units, the musical scale
Tempo and rhythm	tem	Tempo refers to the pace in which the music proceeds. Faster music, when other factors such as pitch are controlled, tends to evoke higher arousal while slower music lower level of arousal. Rhythm refers to the perceived temporal patterns in auditory sequences
Dissonance	dis	The unpleasant aversive sensation of two neighboring sounds, especially when played simultaneously, related to the physical phenomenon of beats, namely slow amplitude fluctuations
Musical texture	tex	A summary of local auditory features such as pitch, timbre, tempo, loudness, etc.

Tonal features: dissonance, pitch, melody, and harmony

In the music domain, one of the most studied features eliciting fast affective reactions is sensory dissonance, which is defined as the unpleasant and rough sensation of two neighboring sounds played simultaneously. Its music theory counterpart of musical dissonance consists of the incongruity of a chord to the dominant key and has been used by composers since the beginning of Western tonal music to create emotional dynamism by building up tension with incongruous, dissonant chords, followed by a resolution by consonant chords that clearly state the main tonality (Meyer, 2008). The unpleasant, aversive sensation of listening to a dissonant and rough sound is almost immediate, occurring less than 100 ms after sound onset (Schön, Regnault, Ystad, & Mireille Besson, 2005). This response appears very early on in development: even newborns turn their head away from dissonant chords whereas they keep watching the source producing consonant chords (Zentner & Kagan, 1996). A *Nature* paper showed dichotomous ratings in listeners exposed to Western music but not in non-Western tribal listeners (McDermott, Schultz, Undurraga, & Godoy, 2016). In a comprehensive empirical investigation of the aesthetic (preference) and emotional connotations of chords, namely simultaneously played pitches (Lahdelma & Eerola, 2015, 2016), it was found that mild dissonance of single chords (minor ninth, major minth, and minor seventh) were more preferred than consonances, showing also for chords an inverted-U relationship with preference. This was, however, not found using sine wave tones (Martindale & Moore, 1990). Neuroimaging and brain lesion studies have provided evidence for the role of the parahippocampal gyrus and the amygdala for the processing of dissonant chords both when presented in isolation (Pallesen, Brattico, & Bailey, 2005) and when inserted in a musical sequence (Blood, Zatorre, Bermudez, & Evans 1999; Gosselin et al., 2006).

The most pleasant pitch frequencies for humans range from 400–750 Hz in an inverted-U-shaped function over tones from 60–5,000 Hz, as measured with sinusoidal tones (Vitz, 1972). The preference for different tuning of musical scales has also been studied, with varying results depending on the instrument played: violinists seem to prefer Pythagorean intonation whereas pianists prefer well-tempered tuning (Loosen, 1994). As reviewed above, melodies of medium complexity and familiarity and complying with Gestalt laws are the most favored. However, a recent detailed listening experiment with melodies supported Berlyne's inverted-U relationship for complexity and beauty ratings when controlling for familiarity, but not for complexity and pleasantness nor complexity and liking (which were linear) (Marin et al., 2016). This suggests that people indeed differentiate between pleasure, liking, and beauty responses, as supposed by several scholars (e.g., Brattico et al., 2013).

Musical mode

Another important dichotomy of Western tonal music is the major/minor mode, which consists of a single pitch variation of the third note of the scales. The musical mode has been associated with replicable and robust affective responses in adults and school-age children: without changes in other sensory features (e.g., intensity, tempo, rhythm, and timbre), music using the intervals of the major scale is perceived as more happy and bright, whereas music using the minor scale tends to be perceived as more sad, subdued, dark, and wistful (Brattico et al., 2011; Bowling, Gill, Choi, Prinz, & Purves, 2010; Crowder, 1985; Dalla Bella, Peretz, Rousseau, & Gosselin, 2001; Hevner, 1935; Lahdelma & Eerola, 2016; Nieminen, Istók, Brattico, & Tervaniemi, 2012; Parncutt, 2014). In some studies, even isolated chords (played with different timbres) were perceived as happier when containing major intervals and sadder when containing minor intervals (Brattico et al., 2009), and were associated with brain activity in the amygdala, retrosplenial cortex, brainstem, and cerebellum (Pallesen, Brattico, & Bailey, 2005). The relation between modality and emotions exists from a young age although it seems that children associate major music with happiness at a younger age than they associate minor music with sadness (Cunningham & Sterling, 1988; Dolgin & Adelson, 1990; Gerardi & Gerken, 1995).

Tempo and rhythm

Along with musical mode, tempo has a major influence over emotional and aesthetic responses to music that are perceived and even felt in the listener. The recurrent finding indicates that fast tempos are related with physiological arousal and more positive emotions than slow tempo, which is in turn perceived as soothing and relaxing. Moreover, tempo seems to be the first feature driving sad/happy ratings of music in children of pre-school age (Dalla Bella et al., 2001). The relation between tempo and emotions, though, is not strictly linear when subjects are asked to classify their own (highly familiar) musical playlists as happy or sad (Brattico et al., 2015). In addition to studying the isolated or combined contribution of mode and tempo to the emotional connotations of music, Webster and Weir (2005) looked at the interaction between those musical features with each other and with harmonization. Results showed that major keys, nonharmonized simple melodies, and faster tempos are related to happier ratings and their opposites to sadder ratings, when considered separately. However, when considering major music only, happiness increased at a decreasing rate as tempo increased, whereas the opposite was observed with minor music. When including harmonization, they reported a decrease in happiness with increasing tempo for nonharmonized minor music, in contrast to all major and harmonized minor music, which showed a positive relation between tempo and happiness. These effects were further modulated by gender and musical experience since women rated minor music and slow music as sadder than men, and nonmusicians rated minor harmonized music as sadder than musicians.

Rhythm, and particularly its complexity or predictability, has also been associated with aesthetic responses since the early times of empirical–aesthetic research (e.g., McMullen & Arnold, 1976). Recent behavioral findings have combined information theory calculations of rhythmic complexity with self-ratings of pleasure and drive to move. Results showed that simple rhythmic patterns or too-complex variations from the rhythmic beat, namely syncopations, are less preferred and less associated with the drive to move (less groovy) than medium levels of syncopation (Witek, Clarke, Wallentin, Kringelbach, & Vuust, 2014, 2017). This inverted-U-shaped function of syncopation with aesthetic preference and drive to move has been related to theories on the role of musical anticipation and expectancy (Gebauer, Kringelbach, & Vuust, 2012; Juslin & Västfjäll, 2008; Vuust & Kringelbach, 2010).

Other local and global sensory features

In addition to the noted features, which are directly linked with notions from Western tonal music theory, there are other aesthetically relevant features of responses to sounds that can be local or even global in nature (Brattico et al., 2017). Local features are best illustrated by the musical score or by separate tracks in a digital audio workstation, where each sound appears in isolation and carries information about timbre, dynamics, pitch, or rhythm. In turn, global musical features are related to the summation of all features from a musical piece, which form a Gestalt unit that can be identified as separate from the sum of its components. One can refer to this global summation of all local features in a piece as the musical texture. Currently, the search for these local or global features can profit from the advancements in the audio engineering field of music information retrieval (MIR) and from its combination with psychology and neuroscience methods (Aucouturier & Bigand, 2013). Thanks to such approaches, the field is expanding away from music theory-based constructs toward identification of stimulus features relevant for a realistic aesthetic experience of music. For instance, Coutinho and Cangelosi (2011) combined computational analysis for acoustic feature retrieval with empirical measures (self-report and physiological data) in order to test whether a set of six local features, namely loudness, pitch level, pitch contour, tempo, multiplicity, and sharpness, could predict induced emotions in listeners. This study established positive linear correlations among felt arousal and loudness, tempo, pitch level, and sharpness. Furthermore, felt valence was positively correlated with tempo and pitch level.

Using neuroimaging methods in combination with MIR, a first study by Alluri et al. (2012) and the replication study by Burunat et al. (2016) showed that the timbral and global features of the acoustic stream, such as fullness, brightness, spectral complexity, and activity, were associated with neural activity in the auditory cortex, cerebellar cognitive areas, somatomotor cortex, and midline structures of the default-mode system. Higher-order structural features of key clarity and pulse clarity showed neural activity also in motor and emotion-related (limbic) areas. The computational feature extraction for controlling the effects of acoustic features on the phenomena of interest has become a standard in music psychology and neuroscience (e.g., Bogert et al., 2016; Brattico et al., 2011, 2015; Gosselin, Paquette, & Peretz, 2015; Siedenburg, Jones-Mollerup, & McAdams, 2015; Sturm, Dähne, Blankertz, & Curio, 2015), although its combination with functional magnetic resonance imaging (fMRI), apart from our efforts, is still rare (Trost, Frühholz, Cochrane, Cojan, & Vuilleumier, 2015; Vuilleumier & Trost, 2015).

A variety of other local features have also been associated with physiological changes related to emotional induction by music in the seminal experiment by Sloboda (1991). For instance, tears were most reliably provoked by musical passages featuring melodic appoggiaturas, or melodic/harmonic sequences, or descending harmonic movements through the cycle of fifths to the tonic. In turn, shivers down the spine were most reliably induced by surprising harmonies. However, the study also evidenced that only around a third of the responses were explained by a specific feature in the music, suggesting that overall emotions occur as a response to other more global aspects (Sloboda, 1991).

Most studies investigating the physiological changes in the autonomic nervous system during affective listening to music focused on basic emotions of sadness and happiness. Results converge in indicating changes in zygomatic facial muscle activity, skin conductance, and finger temperature according to the emotional feelings induced by the music (Lundqvist, Carlsson, Hilmersson, & Juslin, 2008). Fewer studies have explored the physiological responses to aesthetic pleasure and most of them have focused on the chill response, indicating peaks in muscle activity, depth of breathing, and heart pulse coinciding with the chill moment.

THE AESTHETIC SUBJECT: TOP-DOWN FACTORS DETERMINING THE AESTHETIC EXPERIENCE AND ITS OUTCOMES

In several music–aesthetic accounts, the external and/or internal state of the subject and her external context are supposed to play a role in the listening experience. These subject-related top-down factors are *domain-general* and not restricted to any modality and/or stimulus features (Table 25.2).

Age and gender

The two simplest subject-related variables to investigate are age and gender. Simple preferences for certain sound combinations and particularly for consonance, as well as spontaneous movements to rhythmic music appear already in infancy (reviewed in Nieminen et al., 2011). Contrarily, other musical abilities appear later: the representations of tonality and modality appear between five and six years of age, and this possibly explains why prettiness or beauty judgments for tonal music (especially when familiar) over atonal music increase with age (Nieminen et al., 2012), along with

Table 25.2. Domain–general variables determinant for the aesthetic experience of music.

Variable	Abbreviation	Explanation and feature manipulation
Gender	gen	Being male or female seems to affect the emotional and aesthetic responses to music
Age	age	An effect of age has been observed in several studies investigating musical aesthetic experience
Attitude	att	An attitude relates to a long-term memory association with an object that includes an evaluation and an action tendency. ATT can be, for example, manipulated by mimicking in the laboratory scanner a situation prompting for an aesthetic listening mode or for incidental listening
Culture	cul	Culture here refers to background information constructs that are acquired after learning. The role of music- and context-related CUL is typically studied by contrasting groups of music experts with laypersons
Motivation	mot	Motivation is intended as the drive to seek a stimulus or an experience. The baseline MOT state of an individual toward music is determined by questionnaires and can also be manipulated experimentally
Traits	tra	Individual traits such as personality and sensitivity to musical rewards are important to determine the baseline reactions to music. They are typically assessed by questionnaires

the recognition of happy and sad emotions from major and minor melodies (Dalla Bella et al., 2001). The sensitivity to musical style depends on age, with preference for more styles in childhood according to the open-earedness hypothesis and a strong preference for rock in adolescence (LeBlanc et al., 1996). Even some instrumental timbres seem to be preferred depending on age, as well as culture. For instance, in a survey study of fourth graders in the United States, they preferred the timbres of band instruments, while fourth graders in Greece liked the timbres of nonband instruments more (Cutietta & Foutalieraki, 1990). The age of the listener is also consistently related to the quality of the emotional experience of music, with older participants reporting more positive emotions from music and less negative emotions as compared with younger participants. However, according to Parsons (1976), it is only in preadolescence that listeners start to adopt the artist's intentions for judging the music heard. Furthermore, a systematic survey study of factors influencing preferences for pop music showed that teenagers rated melody, instruments, and especially peer influence (the influence that is exerted by members of one's own peer group and is brought to bear on the decision process) as the most important determinants of preference (Boyle, Hosterman, & Ramsey, 1981). From third grade through college, people seemed to prefer faster tempos to slower ones, especially with jazz music (LeBlanc, Colman, McCrary, Sherrill, & Malin,

1988; LeBlanc & McCrary, 1983). Moreover, the complexity of musical features affects listeners differently, depending on their age, as revealed in the early music empirical–aesthetic studies reviewed above. The frequency of using music for mood regulation also changes with age and peaks in adolescence (Robazza, Macaluso, & D'Urso, 1994; Saarikallio, 2007).

Gender can influence the emotional reactions to music as well: women report feeling emotions more frequently than men (Juslin et al., 2011). Moreover, females tend to use music in everyday life for regulating mood by distracting from negative thoughts with the outcome of forgetting the current mood (Carlson et al., 2015). To my knowledge, gender differences in other aesthetic responses, such as preference or beauty judgments, remain to be explored.

Aesthetic attitude and intentionality

Among the factors that might bypass the early sensory responses to sounds is what Hodges (2016) has termed focus, namely the act of paying attention to the music. This concept can be expanded to include the aesthetic attitude as an internal state motivating to attentive watching/listening in the case of performance arts or contemplation in the case of static arts. Although this factor is amenable to study, very little research has been dedicated to determining its role in the aesthetics of music.

The composition by John Cage entitled 4'33" is an extreme case where the stimulus features and structure are only minimally present: the piece is divided into three parts of silence during which instrumentalists are present but do not play. What makes this a musical piece are its many nonappearance, nonperceptual properties, including its title, history, creator, background, and context, which allow the audience to identify the intentional message by the artist (Brattico et al., 2017; Quinn & Danto, 1983). Among these sparse studies one cannot neglect the work done by Brattico et al. (2017) and Steinbeis and Koelsch (2008), who manipulated not the object, but the attitude of the subject toward it, and specifically the attribution of intentions (mental state) to the music. In one condition subjects believed they were listening to a piece of music written by a composer, and in another condition they believed the piece was generated by a computer. The subjects were deceived since they were not told that all music excerpts were MIDI (Musical Instrument Digital Interface) reproductions of pieces by either Schönberg or Webern and were asked to rate the pleasantness of the music. The attribution of mental intention to the composed pieces recruited the anterior medial frontal cortex and other areas belonging to the theory of mind network.

Some scholars consider art as one instance of a theory of theory of mind, where individuals are imaging what others are thinking when relating to each other, involving a continuous dialogue or interplay between one's own self and others, and with the self that evaluates one's own interaction with others. In the context of an aesthetic experience, for instance, attending a concert by a pianist, this intentional process can be fractionated into three components, extending an initial suggestion by Acquadro,

Congedo, and De Riddeer (2016): (a) the internal attitude and intention to approach an artwork, from which the attentional focus that is put into this act derives; (b) the efforts to capture the external intentions of the artist; and (c) the meta-dialogue with one's own self involved in the interactive experience, evaluating the success in understanding the other's intention. This intentional process needs further systematic investigation.

Culture: mere exposure effect and cognitive mastering

A related factor that has been put forward as an important predictor of individual aesthetic responses is culture, also termed cultural matrix (Hodges, 2016), which results in the neural/cultural adaptation from long-term exposure or cognitive mastering (Leder & Nadal, 2014; Reybrouck & Brattico, 2015). The effects of previous knowledge on emotional and evaluative responses during music listening are still underexplored compared with those effects on perceptual and cognitive processes and their neural mechanisms (Miendlarzewska & Trost, 2013; Reybrouck & Brattico, 2015). For instance, according to an investigation combining an information-theoretic model of melodic expectation with behavioral ratings (Hansen, Vuust, & Pearce, 2016), expertise with a specific musical style that is acquired after long-term musical education and performance modifies the ratings of explicit uncertainty, expectedness, and liking for different melody continuations. The 20 melodies used in the study were transcriptions of solo performances by the American jazz saxophonist Charlie Parker (in bebop style) that were classified based on the information-theoretic model as containing high or low uncertainty according to bebop style but the opposite according to tonal music. The results showed that "while classical musicians had internalized key aspects of the bebop style implicitly, only jazz musicians' explicit uncertainty ratings reflected the computational estimates, and jazz-specific expertise modulated the relationship between explicit and inferred uncertainty data" (Hansen, Vuust, & Pearce, 2016, p. 1).

Behavioral studies comparing emotional responses between music experts (professional musicians) and nonmusicians are rare, though. Indeed, musicians are trained to recognize and reproduce emotional expressions with sounds by means of acoustic features such as tempo, harmony, intensity, and timbral variations. Overall, the findings obtained in the scarce studies converge in indicating enhanced aesthetic and emotional responses to music in musicians as opposed to nonmusicians. For instance, in a behavioral and physiological study with sad, happy, and scary unfamiliar tunes played by a violinist in an expressive or mechanical way, musicians gave higher ratings of emotional intensity for the expressive excerpts as compared with nonmusicians (Vieillard, Roy, & Peretz, 2012). On the other hand, only the corrugator face muscle showed myographic activity in musicians and this was interpreted as a possibly conscious dislike reaction of musicians to the stimuli. In a neuroimaging study, higher arousal ratings and increased activity in the right frontoparietal brain areas were found in musicians vs nonmusicians in response to sad and fearful music (Park et al., 2014). Other cross-sectional studies contrasting musicians to nonmusicians demonstrate enhanced regional activity in subcortical emotion- and homeostasis-related regions (e.g., thalamus, caudate, nucleus accumbens, insula) in musically experienced individuals as compared with laypersons (Brattico et al., 2015; Chapin, Jantzen, Kelso, Steinberg, & Large, 2010) and a reliance on cognitive evaluation rather than self-emotional state for beauty judgments (Müller, Höfel, Brattico, & Jacobsen, 2009). Nevertheless, a pretest–posttest causal evidence of a relation between prior knowledge and aesthetic responses is still to come.

Individual traits

Inter-individual *variation* has often been considered as random noise, or else has substantiated relativistic views of emotional, and even more, aesthetic processing, reducing any subjective experience to an emergent state associated with dynamically varying (and hard to measure) processes and to a variety of cognitive functions. Lately, though, consistent sources of individual variation have been identified. One of them is personality, which is studied by relating music responses (whether self-reported, behavioral, or neural) to questionnaire scores of personality traits. For instance, the personality trait of agreeableness (characterized by cooperation, empathy, and altruism) has been correlated with more frequent occurrence of positive emotional states (such as happiness and relaxation) and less frequent occurrence of negative emotional states (such as boredom and disappointment) in response to music (Juslin et al., 2011; Liljeström, Juslin, & Västfjäll, 2012). In turn, individuals with high scores in the personality trait of extraversion, characterized by warmth, gregariousness, positive emotions, activity (Costa & McCrae, 1992), feel more positive emotional states (happiness, relaxation, tenderness) and more intense emotions from music as compared with those with low scores (Juslin et al., 2008; Vuoskoski & Eerola, 2011). Rentfrow and Gosling (2003) also associated extraversion with preference for musical genres that "emphasize positive emotions and are structurally simple" (Rentfrow & Gosling, p. 1241) with clear and fast rhythms. Based on an experience sampling study, extroverts had a higher frequency of musical episodes in their daily life as compared with introverts.

The personality trait openness to experience, characterized by imagination, aesthetic sensitivity, and attention to subjective feeling and values (Costa & McCrae, 1992), shows divergent relations with emotional responses to music. For instance, on one hand, it correlates positively with intensity of emotions (Juslin et al., 2011) and with experiencing awe (Silvia et al., 2015) and chills (Colver & El-Alayli, 2015; Silvia & Nusbaum, 2011) while listening to music, and it is also associated with a cognitive use of music (Chamorro-Premuzic & Furnham, 2007). On the other hand, in an experience sampling study, openness to experience correlated positively with anxiety/fear and negatively correlated with pleasure/enjoyment induced by music (Juslin et al., 2008). Related to this, Kreutz, Schubert, and Mitchell (2008) proposed that these music emotional responses interact with psychological traits to create a personal tendency toward experiencing music in either a cognitive or affective way. Unclear associations were also found for the personality trait of conscientiousness with low values being related to a stronger tendency of using music for mood regulation (Chamorro-Premuzic & Furnham, 2007). Unclear associations have been found also for neuroticism, characterized by anxiety, self-consciousness, hostility, vulnerability, rumination, state negative affect (Costa & McCrae, 1992), with musical responses, even if some weak positive correlations have been observed with liking for reflective and complex music (Rentfrow & Gosling, 2003) and with higher felt sadness from music (Ladinig & Glenn Schellenberg, 2012; Vuoskoski & Eerola, 2011). In turn, emotional stability has been associated with decreased negative affect and increased pleasure in laboratory experiments (Liljeström, Juslin, & Västfjäll, 2012; Vuoskoski & Eerola, 2011), although in an experience sampling study it was linked with decreased pleasure (Juslin et al., 2008, 2011; Liljeström, Juslin, & Västfjäll, 2012). In sum, although a meta-analysis of the results is still missing, some associations exist between personality traits and emotional and aesthetic responses to music, with certain traits being more reliable in predicting musical responses than others.

Another yet-little-exploited way to study the origin of individual differences in aesthetic musical responses is behavioral genetics, which involves examining heritability and genetic data in combination with behavioral data, or imaging genetics, which combines heritability and genetic data with neuroimaging data (Dixson, Tost, & Meyer-Lindenberg, 2018). Indeed, a large variation exists in proneness to experience musical reward (in the presence of normal discriminatory skills), ranging from musicophilia to music-specific anhedonia (Mas-Herrero, Zatorre, Rodríguez-Fornells, & Marco-Pallarés, 2014). While the heritability of reward sensitivity to music has not been established thus far, recent studies combining survey data, behavioral ratings, psychophysiological measures, and diffusion tensor imaging (DTI) revealed that individual variations in reward sensitivity to music can be traced back to the white matter connectivity between auditory processing areas in the superior temporal gyrus and emotion- and reward-related areas such as the insula and medial prefrontal cortex (Martínez-Molina et al., 2016; Sachs, Ellis, Schlaug, & Loui, 2016). The neural transmission between these brain areas is regulated by the monoamine neurotransmitter dopamine, which has been linked to incentive salience and motivation for acting, namely to the wanting phase of the pleasure cycle (Kringelbach & Berridge, 2017). A recent investigation has discovered a link between affective sensitivity to sounds and dopamine functionality (Quarto et al., 2017), specifically demonstrating that a functional variation in a dopamine receptor gene modulates the impact of music and noise on mood states and emotion-related prefrontal and striatal brain activity. Hence, it is plausible to assume that, along with the environmental factors listed above (culture, attitudes, internal state; see also Gebauer, Kringelbach, & Vuust, 2012) and with basic biological factors (gender and age), the genes regulating the efficacy of neurotransmission in mesolimbic dopaminergic circuits would partially account for intersubject variation in motivational drive toward music (Blum et al., 2010).

THE EXTERNAL CONTEXT: PHYSICAL AND SOCIAL ENVIRONMENT AFFECTING AESTHETIC RESPONSES

In empirical aesthetics of music, the external context is intended not just as the mere presence (or absence) of others during a musical activity, but the communicative interaction between a perceiver and a performer or between performers. Several accounts of the musical aesthetic experience (Brattico et al., 2013; Hargreaves, Hargreaves, & North, 2011; Konečni, 2008) cover the relevance of the environment and situation of the listener (whether music is consumed alone or with peers, in a concert hall, or at home). The experience sampling method (ESM) (Csikszentmihalyi & LeFevre, 1989) is the best suited for addressing questions related to the impact of the environment and situation on listening choices and responses. ESM findings (Krause & North, 2016) obtained from 177 UK participants confirmed previous studies on the prevalence of listening privately at home over public locations (Greasley & Lamont, 2011; North, 2004), although with some variation depending on the time of the day and day of the week as well as on the age of the listener. Indeed, it was noticed that younger individuals and those who spend more time listening to music on average experience more music in public than private settings. When in public settings, people more often use mobile technology for listening, precisely, 44.3% of all public music listening (Krause & North, 2016). When instead music is imposed in a public place such as in a restaurant, liking ratings are lower compared with the overall mean, whereas they are significantly higher when listening is done at home and via mobile devices within public transportation.

Some attempts have also been made to investigate whether a particular type of context, namely the social presence or absence of other listeners, would affect aesthetic responses to music. Social facilitation has been hypothesized and has received some empirical support. Anecdotally, even the famous tenor Caruso claimed he could only sing his top Cs if he was in front of an audience. Several listening tests (Finnas, 1989; Furman & Duke, 1988), Internet surveys (Salganik, Dodds, & Watts, 2006), and even a behavioral and neuroimaging study converge in demonstrating that emotion and liking ratings of music excerpts are affected by the behavior of others (social feedback). The general trend is that responses align with the majority peer group opinion, especially for unfamiliar music (Furman & Duke, 1988), and especially when listeners are adolescents (Finnas, 1989). Recently, Egermann and colleagues (2011) collected psychological and physiological data from 14 participants while listening to 10-minute-long music pieces alone or in a group. For the physiological data they used an interconnected innovative digital interface that could register when a chill was experienced even concurrently on all participants and similarly for the physiological measurements a custom-made device could simultaneously record skin conductance changes in all participants. While emotional reports did not differ between listening conditions (alone or in groups), significantly higher levels of physiological responses during chills were obtained in the listening alone condition. These findings contradict the social facilitation hypothesis and instead point toward higher arousal of the sympathetic nervous system when listening alone to music. However, here participants did not receive any social feedback from their peers. Moreover, the musical pieces were specifically chosen to elicit chills and were mostly from the classical style. More research should continue to examine the various factors that intersect with the influence of social context (e.g., stimulus, age, situation, feedback).

MAJOR CHALLENGES, GOALS, AND SUGGESTIONS

We live in an inherently musical society. As a comparison, in the nineteenth century there were over 1,000 active orchestras in Italy, and it was necessarily to go to concert halls to listen to them play. Nowadays there are not more than 50 orchestras in Italy, but music can be listened to through many channels and environments, and it is less elitist than before. Moreover, talent shows and videos with musical content dominate media channels, the entertainment industry scores profits that surpass those of pharmaceutical companies, and smartphones as well as dedicated mobile devices keep people constantly exposed to musical sounds. Hence, it is compelling to understand the secrets of the music aesthetic *object*, namely how a song can become a worldwide hit or a music video can be visualized billions of time on social media; and the aesthetic *subject*, namely why many individuals seek to be surrounded by musical sounds daily and for several hours as well as when and where (the *context*).

The empirical aesthetics of music addresses all these questions using a variety of approaches, measurement methods, and stimulation paradigms. Useful knowledge has accumulated but more work needs to be done to increase the external validity of the findings, often restricted to laboratory situations. Moreover, while most music aesthetics laboratory studies focus on the single sensory modality of audition, recent work shows cross-modality of aesthetic responses with amplification or inhibition of, for instance, emotional induction or pleasure when sounds are concurrently presented with visual images or when movement is allowed (Baumgartner, Lutz, Schmidt, & Jäncke, 2006; Eldar, Ganor, Admon, Bleich, & Hendler, 2007). Moreover, the behavioral naturalistic approach can account for both generalization of findings by sampling behavioral and physiological data from lifelike conditions and for studying multimodal aesthetic experiences. For instance, the ESM asks the study participant to answer a set of questions prompted by alarms in a mobile device. Similarly, wearable physiological devices allow sampling of data during daily activities. A late trend is concert research, possible only in few locations in the world (LiveLab at McMaster University with 106 seats, and ArtLab at Max Planck Institute for Empirical Aesthetics in Frankfurt with 36 seats but to be expanded next year), in which a concert hall has been transformed into a laboratory by incorporating devices for behavioral ratings, motion capture, and for collection of physiological and even electroencephalogram (EEG) signal in the seats. When it comes to sampling of brain signals to understand the brain determinants of aesthetic responses to music, the possibilities to recreate a real-life situation are more limited. Methodological advances though allow the synchronous EEG collection of musically interacting agents under the hyperscanning approach. Nothing similar has been tried yet with other neuroimaging modalities, although hyperscanning with dual MEG (Magnetoencephalography) and fMRI have been tried for other cognitive functions (Konvalinka & Roepstorff, 2012). A pseudo-hyperscanning situation has been created with data analysis, looking at the synchronous brain activity of individuals being subjected to the same music stimulation (for reviews, see Ashley & Timmers, 2017).

In neuroimaging, improvement of ecological validity has been reached by adopting the naturalistic stimulation paradigm, namely by presenting subjects with real music and allowing them to listen attentively to the music without being disturbed by interruptions or unnatural behavioral tasks (Alluri et al., 2012; Haumann, Kliuchko, Vuust, & Brattico, 2018; Poikonen et al., 2016). This approach has been made possible in fMRI, EEG, and MEG by combining the time series of the brain signal with the time series of the acoustic features of the music heard, extracted computationally. The correlational analysis of both time series permits the drawing of statistical inferences on how the stimulus features change the brain responses. When isolating the most consistent peaks in beauty ratings focal activity from the medial orbitofrontal cortex was obtained. Furthermore, the latest trends indicate the behavioral interactions between individuals as well as the brain activity patterns within individuals have interconnected dynamic networks affecting the behavior of each single network node. Network science is a mathematics branch that provides laws of explanation for and prediction of these complex behaviors, which are then also applicable to human aesthetics.

Future directions should not neglect the extension of investigation to the wide variety of musical styles and cultures existing in the world. For instance, modern music is exemplary of top-down subjective factors in aesthetic responses to music. Modern music, initiated by Arnold Schönberg along with the Second Viennese School (Webern and Berg), is a special case of musical genre since it is characterized by local sensory features that are sensorily unpleasant and dissonant, and it lacks a tonal structure. In spite of these aversive local features, it is enjoyed by a group of enthusiastic listeners, with a growing number of specialist ensembles (e.g., Ensemble Intercontemporain in France, London Sinfonietta in the United Kingdom), performances, and festivals around the world. A recent proposal puts forward some putative top-down mechanisms that might explain the conscious pleasure derived from atonal music (Mencke et al., 2019): (a) the presentation of the music in an artistic context (framing); (b) repeated exposure leading to higher predictability; (c) cognitive mastering, that is, the use of knowledge about the piece of art or the artist in the aesthetic evaluation process; and (d) appreciation derived from low predictability (or low uncertainty of predictions) in itself owing to personality traits of individuals (openness and novelty-seeking) driving them toward novel and arousing stimuli.

In sum, future studies should exploit the advancement of technology and mathematical science to explain in the most accurate and veridical way the complexity of aesthetic processes. These explanations should be informed by systematic frameworks that account also for the multimodality of musical aesthetics, which is not limited to audition but also exploits and affect other sensory channels (e.g., vision, proprioception). The cross-modal effects of affective states from auditory stimuli to visual stimuli and vice versa should become a central topic in empirical aesthetics of music. Related to this, the role of the motor system needs to be accounted for: music is strictly linked with drive for action, namely dance or music-induced spontaneous movements. Another topic that should become more central to empirical research in the future is the development of aesthetic responses from childhood to adulthood. Considering the beneficial effects of music training and education, in a society that is inherently musical, predicting the effects of music exposure on the formation of self-confident, civilized individuals is deemed pivotal.

Acknowledgments

I wish to thank Nicola Di Stefano and Massimo Lumaca for useful comments on a previous version of the manuscript, Pauli Brattico for help with language editing of the manuscript, and Hella Kastbjerg for proofreading it. The Center for Music in the Brain is funded by the Danish National Research Foundation (grant number DNRF 117).

References

Acquadro, M. A. S., Congedo, M., & De Riddeer, D. (2016). Music performance as an experimental approach to hyperscanning studies. *Frontiers in Human Neuroscience*, *10*(May), 242.

Alluri, V., Toiviainen, P., Jääskeläinen, I. P., Glerean, E., Sams, M., & Brattico, E. (2012). Large-scale brain networks emerge from dynamic processing of musical timbre, key and rhythm. *NeuroImage*, *59*(4), 3677–3689.

Ashley, R., & Timmers. R. (2017). *The Routledge companion to music cognition*. Abingdon: Routledge.

Aucouturier, J.-J., & Bigand, E. (2013). Seven problems that keep MIR from attracting the interest of cognition and neuroscience. *Journal of Intelligent Information Systems*, *41*(3), 483–497.

Bar, M. (2007). The proactive brain: Using analogies and associations to generate predictions. *Trends in Cognitive Sciences*, *11*(7), 280–289.

Baumgartner, T, Lutz, K., Schmidt, C. F., & Jäncke, L. (2006). The emotional power of music: How music enhances the feeling of affective pictures. *Brain Research*, *1075*(1), 151–164.

Blood, A. J., Zatorre, R. J., Bermudez, P., & Evans, A. C. (1999). Emotional responses to pleasant and unpleasant music correlate with activity in paralimbic brain regions. *Nature Neuroscience*, *2*(4), 382–387.

Blum, K., Chen, T. J. H., Chen, A. L. H., Madigan, M., Downs, B. W., Waite, R. L., . . . Gold, M. S. (2010). Do dopaminergic gene polymorphisms affect mesolimbic reward activation of music listening response? Therapeutic impact on reward deficiency syndrome (RDS). *Medical Hypotheses, 74*(3), 513–520.

Bogert, B., Numminen-Kontti, T., Gold, B., Sams, M., Numminen, J., Burunat, I., . . . Brattico, E. (2016). Hidden sources of joy, fear, and sadness: Explicit versus implicit neural processing of musical emotions. *Neuropsychologia, 89*(August), 393–402.

Bowling, D. L., Gill. K., Choi, J. D., Prinz, J., & Purves, D. (2010). Major and minor music compared to excited and subdued speech. *The Journal of the Acoustical Society of America, 127*(1), 491–503.

Boyle, J. D., Hosterman, G. L., & Ramsey, D. S. (1981). Factors influencing pop music preferences of young people. *Journal of Research in Music Education, 29*(1), 47–55.

Brattico, E., & Pearce, M. (2013). The neuroaesthetics of music. *Psychology of Aesthetics, Creativity, and the Arts, 7*(1), 48–61.

Brattico, E. (2015). From pleasure to liking and back: Bottom-up and top-down neural routes to the aesthetic enjoyment of music. In J. P. Huston, M. Nadal, F. Mora, L. F. Agnati, & C. J. Cela Conde (Eds.), *Art, aesthetics, and the brain* (pp. 303–318). Oxford: Oxford University Press.

Brattico, E. (2019). The neuroaesthetics of music: A research agenda coming of age. In M. Thaut & D. Hodges (Eds.), *The Oxford handbook of music and the brain*. Oxford: Oxford University Press.

Brattico, E., Alluri, V., Bogert, B., Jacobsen, T., Vartiainen, N., Nieminen, S., & Tervaniemi, M. (2011). A functional MRI study of happy and sad emotions in music with and without lyrics. *Frontiers in Psychology, 2*, 308.

Brattico, E., Bogert, B., Alluri, V., Tervaniemi, M., Eerola, T., & Jacobsen, T. (2015). It's sad but i like it: The neural dissociation between musical emotions and liking in experts and laypersons. *Frontiers in Human Neuroscience, 9*, 676.

Brattico, E., Bogert, B., & Jacobsen, T. (2013). Toward a neural chronometry for the aesthetic experience of music. *Frontiers in Psychology, 4*(May), 206.

Brattico, E., Brattico, P., & Jacobsen, T. (2009). The origins of the aesthetic enjoyment of music—A review of the literature. *Musicae Scientiae: The Journal of the European Society for the Cognitive Sciences of Music, 13*(2_suppl.), 15–39.

Brattico, E., Pallesen, K. J., Varyagina, O., Bailey, C., Anourova, I., Järvenpää, M., . . . Tervaniemi, M. (2009). Neural discrimination of nonprototypical chords in music experts and laymen: An MEG study. *Journal of Cognitive Neuroscience, 21*(11), 2230–2244.

Brattico, P., Brattico, E., & Vuust, P. (2017). Global sensory qualities and aesthetic experience in music. *Frontiers in Neuroscience, 11*(April), 159.

Bundgaard, P. F. (2014). Feeling, meaning, and intentionality—A critique of the neuroaesthetics of beauty. *Phenomenology and the Cognitive Sciences, 14*(4), 781–801.

Burunat, I., Toiviainen, P., Alluri, V., Bogert, B., Ristaniemi, T., Sams, M., & Brattico, E. (2016). The reliability of continuous brain responses during naturalistic listening to music. *NeuroImage, 124*(Pt A), 224–231.

Carlson, E., Saarikallio, S., Toiviainen, P., Bogert, B., Kliuchko, M., & Brattico, E. (2015). Maladaptive and adaptive emotion regulation through music: A behavioral and neuroimaging study of males and females. *Frontiers in Human Neuroscience, 9*, 466.

Chamorro-Premuzic, T., & Furnham, A. (2007). Personality and music: Can traits explain how people use music in everyday life? *British Journal of Psychology, 98*(Pt 2), 175–185.

Chanda, M. L., & Levitin, D. J. (2013). The neurochemistry of music. *Trends in Cognitive Sciences, 17*(4), 179–193.

Chapin, H., Jantzen, K., Kelso, J. A. S., Steinberg, F., & Large, E. (2010). Dynamic emotional and neural responses to music depend on performance expression and listener experience. *PLoS ONE, 5*(12), e13812.

Chatterjee, A. (2013). *The aesthetic brain: How we evolved to desire beauty and enjoy art*. Oxford: Oxford University Press.

Chatterjee, A., & Vartanian, O. (2016). Neuroscience of aesthetics. *Annals of the New York Academy of Sciences, 1369*(1), 172–194.

Cheung, V. K. M., Meyer, L., Friederici, A. D., & Koelsch, S. (2018). The right inferior frontal gyrus processes nested non-local dependencies in music. *Scientific Reports, 8*(1), 3822.

Cirelli, L. K., Trehub, S. E., & Trainor, L. J. (2018). Rhythm and melody as social signals for infants. *Annals of the New York Academy of Sciences, March*. doi:10.1111/nyas.13580

Colver, M. C., & El-Alayli, A. (2015). Getting aesthetic chills from music: The connection between openness to experience and frisson. *Psychology of Music, 44*(3), 413–427.

Conway, B. R., & Rehding, A. (2013). Neuroaesthetics and the trouble with beauty. *PLoS Biology, 11*(3), e1001504.

Costa, P. T., & McCrae, R. R. (1992). Normal personality assessment in clinical practice: The NEO personality inventory. *Psychological Assessment, 4*(1), 5–13.

Coutinho, E., & Cangelosi, A. (2011). Musical emotions: Predicting second-by-second subjective feelings of emotion from low-level psychoacoustic features and physiological measurements. *Emotion, 11*(4), 921–937.

Crocker, R. L. (1963). Pythagorean mathematics and music. *The Journal of Aesthetics and Art Criticism, 22*(2), 189.

Crowder, R. G. (1985). Perception of the major/minor distinction: III. Hedonic, musical, and affective discriminations. *Bulletin of the Psychonomic Society, 23*(4), 314–316.

Csikszentmihalyi, M., & LeFevre, J. (1989). Optimal experience in work and leisure. *Journal of Personality and Social Psychology, 56*(5), 815–822.

Cunningham, J. G., & Sterling, R. S. (1988). Developmental change in the understanding of affective meaning in music. *Motivation and Emotion, 12*(4), 399–413.

Cutietta, R. A., & Foutalieraki, M. (1990). Preference for selected band and non-band instrument timbres among students in the United States and Greece. *Bulletin of the Council for Research in Music Education, 105*, 72–80.

Dalla Bella, S., Peretz, I., Rousseau, L., & Gosselin, N. (2001). A developmental study of the affective value of tempo and mode in music. *Cognition, 80*(3), B1–B10.

Dewey, J. (2005). *Art as experience*. London: Penguin.

Dixson, L., Tost, H., & Meyer-Lindenberg, A. (2018). Imaging genetics. In T. Schulze & F. J. McMahon (Eds.), *Psychiatric genetics: A primer for clinical and basic scientists* (pp. 107–123). New York: Oxford University Press.

Dolgin, K. G., & Adelson, E. H. (1990). Age changes in the ability to interpret affect in sung and instrumentally-presented melodies. *Psychology of Music, 18*(1), 87–98.

Eerola, T. (1998). The rise and fall of the experimental style of the Beatles. *Beatlestudies, 1*, 33–60.

Eerola, T., & Vuoskoski, J. K. (2013). A review of music and emotion studies: Approaches, emotion models, and stimuli. *Music Perception, 30*, 307–340.

Egermann, H., Sutherland, M. E., Grewe, O., Nagel, F., Kopiez, R., & Altenmüller, E. (2011). Does music listening in a social context alter experience? A physiological and psychological perspective on emotion. *Musicae Scientiae: The Journal of the European Society for the Cognitive Sciences of Music, 15*(3), 307–323.

Eldar, E., Ganor, O., Admon, R., Bleich, A., & Hendler, T. (2007). Feeling the real world: limbic response to music depends on related content. *Cerebral Cortex, 17*(12), 2828–2840.

Fink, R. (1997). *Neanderthal flute: Oldest musical instrument: matches notes of do, re, mi scale: Musicological analysis.* Greenwich: Robert Martin Fink.

Finnas, L. (1989). A comparison between young people's privately and publicly expressed musical preferences. *Psychology of Music, 17*(2), 132–145.

Friston, K., Kilner, J., & Harrison, L. (2006). A free energy principle for the brain. *Journal of Physiology, Paris, 100*(1–3), 70–87.

Furman, C. E., & Duke, R. A. (1988). Effect of majority consensus on preferences for recorded orchestral and popular music. *Journal of Research in Music Education, 36*(4), 220.

Gebauer, L., Kringelbach, M. L., & Vuust, P. (2012). Ever-changing cycles of musical pleasure: The role of dopamine and anticipation. *Psychomusicology: Music, Mind, and Brain, 22*(2), 152–167.

Gerardi, G. M., & Gerken, L. (1995). The development of affective responses to modality and melodic contour. *Music Perception: An Interdisciplinary Journal, 12*(3), 279–290.

Goldstein, A. (1980). Thrills in response to music and other stimuli. *Physiological Psychology, 8*(1), 126–129.

Gosselin, N., Paquette, S., & Peretz, I. (2015). Sensitivity to musical emotions in congenital amusia. *Cortex; a Journal Devoted to the Study of the Nervous System and Behavior, 71*(October), 171–182.

Gosselin, N., Samson, S., Adolphs, R., Noulhiane, M., Roy, M., Hasboun, D., … Peretz, I. (2006). Emotional responses to unpleasant music correlates with damage to the parahippocampal cortex. *Brain: A Journal of Neurology, 129*(Pt 10), 2585–2592.

Greasley, A. E., & Lamont, A. (2011). Exploring engagement with music in everyday life using experience sampling methodology. *Musicae Scientiae: The Journal of the European Society for the Cognitive Sciences of Music, 15*(1), 45–71.

Grewe, O., Nagel, F., Kopiez, R., & Altenmüller, E. (2005). How does music arouse 'chills'? Investigating strong emotions, combining psychological, physiological, and psychoacoustical methods. *Annals of the New York Academy of Sciences, 1060*(December), 446–449.

Grewe, O., Nagel, F., Kopiez, R., & Altenmüller, E. (2007). Listening to music as a re-creative process: Physiological, psychological, and psychoacoustical correlates of chills and strong emotions. *Music Perception: An Interdisciplinary Journal, 24*(3), 297–314.

Hansen, N. C., Vuust, P., & Pearce, M. (2016). "If you have to ask, you'll never know": Effects of specialised stylistic expertise on predictive processing of music. *PLoS ONE, 11*(10), e0163584.

Hanslick, E., & Cohen, G. (1892). The beautiful in music. A contribution to the revisal of musical æsthetics. *The Musical Times and Singing Class Circular, 33*(587), 44.

Hargreaves, D. J., Hargreaves, J. J., & North, A. C. (2011). Imagination and creativity in music listening. In D. Hargreaves, D. Miell and R. MacDonald (Eds.), *Musical imaginations: Multidisciplinary perspectives on creativity, performance and perception.* Oxford: Oxford University Press (pp. 156–172).

Hargreaves, D. J., & North, A. C. (1993). Experimental Aesthetics and Liking for Music. In P. N. Juslin and J. A. Sloboda (Eds.), *Handbook of music and emotion: Theory, research, applications* (pp. 515–546). Oxford: Oxford University Press.

Harrison, L., & Loui, P. (2014). Thrills, chills, frissons, and skin orgasms: Toward an integrative model of transcendent psychophysiological experiences in music. *Frontiers in Psychology, 5*(July), 790.

Haumann, N., Kliuchko, M., Vuust, P., & Brattico, E. (2018). Applying acoustical and musicological analysis to detect brain responses to realistic music: A case study. *NATO Advanced Science Institutes Series E: Applied Sciences, 8*(5), 716.

Helmholtz, H. von, & Ellis, A. J. (1875). *On the sensations of tone as a physiological basis for the theory of music.* London: Longmans, Green and Company.

Hevner, K. (1935). The affective character of the major and minor modes in music. *The American Journal of Psychology, 47*(1), 103.

Hodges, D. A. (2016). The neuroaesthetics of music. In S. Hallam, I. Cross, & M. Thaut (Eds.), *The Oxford handbook of music psychology*. Oxford: Oxford University Press.

Huron, D. B. (2006). *Sweet anticipation: Music and the psychology of expectation*. Cambridge, MA: MIT Press.

Husserl, E. (1991). *On the phenomenology of the consciousness of internal time (1893–1917)*. Dordrecht, the Netherlands: Springer.

Istók, E., Brattico, E., Jacobsen, T., Krohn, K., Müller, M., & Tervaniemi, M. (2009). Aesthetic responses to music: A questionnaire study. *Musicae Scientiae: The Journal of the European Society for the Cognitive Sciences of Music, 13*(2), 183–206.

Jackendoff, R., & Lerdahl, F. (2006). The capacity for music: What is it, and what's special about it? *Cognition, 100*(1), 33–72.

Juslin, P. N. (2013). From everyday emotions to aesthetic emotions: Towards a unified theory of musical emotions. *Physics of Life Reviews, 10*(3), 235–266.

Juslin, P. N., & Laukka, P. (2004). Expression, perception, and induction of musical emotions: A review and a questionnaire study of everyday listening. *Journal of New Music Research, 33*(3), 217–238.

Juslin, P. N., Liljeström, S., Laukka, P., Västfjäll, D., & Lundqvist, L.-O. (2011). Emotional reactions to music in a nationally representative sample of Swedish adults: Prevalence and causal influences. *Musicae Scientiae: The Journal of the European Society for the Cognitive Sciences of Music, 15*(2), 174–207.

Juslin, P. N., Liljeström, S., Västfjäll, D., Barradas, G., & Silva, A. (2008). An experience sampling study of emotional reactions to music: Listener, music, and situation. *Emotion, 8*(5), 668–683.

Juslin, P. N., & Västfjäll, D. (2008a). Emotional responses to music: The need to consider underlying mechanisms. *The Behavioral and Brain Sciences, 31*(5), 559–575; discussion 575–621.

Kant, I. (2007). *Critique of judgement*. Oxford: Oxford University Press.

Koelsch, S. (2012). *Brain and music*. Hoboken, NJ: John Wiley & Sons.

Konečni, V. J. (1982). Social interaction and musical preference. In D. Deutsch (Ed.), *The psychology of music* (pp. 497–516). New York: Academic Press.

Konecni, V. J. (2005). The aesthetic trinity: Awe, being moved, thrills. *PsycEXTRA Dataset*. doi:10.1037/e674862010-005

Konečni, V. J. (2008). Does music induce emotion? A theoretical and methodological analysis. *Psychology of Aesthetics, Creativity, and the Arts, 2*(2), 115.

Konečni, V. J., Crozier, J. B., & Doob, A. N. (1976). Anger and expression of aggression: Effects on aesthetic preference. *Scientific Aesthetics, 1*, 47–55.

Konvalinka, I., & Roepstorff, A. (2012). The two-brain approach: How can mutually interacting brains teach us something about social interaction? *Frontiers in Human Neuroscience, 6*(July), 215.

Krause, A. E., & North, A. C. (2016). Pleasure, arousal, dominance, and judgments about music in everyday life. *Psychology of Music, 45*(3), 355–374.

Kreutz, G., Schubert, E., & Mitchell, L. A. (2008). Cognitive styles of music listening. *Music Perception, 26*(1), 57–73.

Kringelbach, M. L., & Berridge, K. C. (2009). Towards a functional neuroanatomy of pleasure and happiness. *Trends in Cognitive Sciences, 13*, 479–487.

Kringelbach, M. L., & Berridge, K. C. (2017). The affective core of emotion: Linking pleasure, subjective well-being, and optimal metastability in the brain. *Emotion Review: Journal of the International Society for Research on Emotion, 9*(3), 191–199.

Krumhansl, C. L. (2000). Rhythm and pitch in music cognition. *Psychological Bulletin, 126*(1), 159–179.

Ladinig, O., & Schellenberg, E. G. (2012). Liking unfamiliar music: Effects of felt emotion and individual differences. *Psychology of Aesthetics, Creativity, and the Arts, 6*(2), 146–154.

Lahdelma, I., & Eerola, T. (2015). Theoretical proposals on how vertical harmony may convey nostalgia and longing in music. *Empirical Musicology Review: EMR, 10*(3), 245.

Lahdelma, I., & Eerola, T. (2016). Mild dissonance preferred over consonance in single chord perception. *I-Perception, 7*(3), 2041669516655812.

LeBlanc, A. (1982). An interactive theory of music preference, *Journal of Music Therapy, 19*, 28–45.

LeBlanc, A., Colman, J., McCrary, J., Sherrill, C., & Malin, S. (1988). Tempo preferences of different age music listeners. *Journal of Research in Music Education, 36*(3), 156.

LeBlanc, A., & McCrary, J. (1983). Effect of tempo on children's music preference. *Journal of Research in Music Education, 31*(4), 283–294.

LeBlanc, A., Sims, W. L., Siivola, C., & Obert, M. (1996). Music style preferences of different age listeners. *Journal of Research in Music Education, 44*(1), 49–59.

Leder, H, & Nadal, M. (2014). Ten years of a model of aesthetic appreciation and aesthetic judgments: The aesthetic episode—Developments and challenges in empirical aesthetics. *British Journal of Psychology, 105*(4), 443–464.

Liljeström, S., Juslin, P. N, & Västfjäll, D. (2012). Experimental evidence of the roles of music choice, social context, and listener personality in emotional reactions to music. *Psychology of Music, 41*(5), 579–599.

Loosen, F. (1994). Tuning of diatonic scales by violinists, pianists, and nonmusicians. *Perception & Psychophysics, 56*(2), 221–226.

Loui, P. (2012a). Learning and liking of melody and harmony: Further studies in artificial grammar learning. *Topics in Cognitive Science, 4*(4), 554–567.

Loui, P. (2012b). Statistical learning: What can music tell us? In P. Rebuschat & J. Williams (Eds.). *Statistical learning and language acquisition.* Berlin: Mouton de Gruyter.

Lumaca, M., Haumann, N. T., Vuust, P., Brattico, E., & Baggio, G. (2018). From random to regular: Neural constraints on the emergence of isochronous rhythm during cultural transmission. *Social Cognitive and Affective Neuroscience, July.* doi:10.1093/scan/nsy054

Lumaca, M., Ravignani, A., & Baggio, G. (2018). Music evolution in the laboratory: cultural transmission meets neurophysiology. *Frontiers in Neuroscience, 12*(April), 246.

Lundqvist, L.-O., Carlsson, F., Hilmersson, P., & Juslin, P. N. (2008). Emotional responses to music: experience, expression, and physiology. *Psychology of Music, 37*(1), 61–90.

Marin, M. M., Lampatz, A., Wandl, M., & Leder, H. (2016). Berlyne revisited: Evidence for the multifaceted nature of hedonic tone in the appreciation of paintings and music. *Frontiers in Human Neuroscience, 10*(November), 536.

Martindale, C., & Moore, K. (1988). Priming, prototypicality, and preference. *Journal of Experimental Psychology. Human Perception and Performance, 14*(4), 661–670.

Martindale, C., & Moore, K. (1990). Intensity, dissonance, and preference for pure tones. *Empirical Studies of the Arts, 8*(2), 125–134.

Martínez-Molina, N., Mas-Herrero, E., Rodríguez-Fornells, A., Zatorre, R. J., & Marco-Pallarés, J. (2016). Neural correlates of specific musical anhedonia. *Proceedings of the National Academy of Sciences, 113*(46), E7337–E7345.

Mas-Herrero, E., Zatorre, R. J., Rodriguez-Fornells, A., & Marco-Pallarés, J. (2014). Dissociation between musical and monetary reward responses in specific musical anhedonia. *Current Biology, 24*(6), 699–704.

Maslow, A. H. (1961). Peak experiences as acute identity experiences. *American Journal of Psychoanalysis, 21*(2), 254–262.

McDermott, J. H., Schultz, A. F., Undurraga, E. A., & Godoy, R. A. (2016). Indifference to dissonance in native Amazonians reveals cultural variation in music perception. *Nature, 535* (7613), 547–550.

McMullen, P. T. (1974). Influence of number of different pitches and melodic redundancy on preference responses. *Journal of Research in Music Education, 22*(3), 198–204.

McMullen, P. T., & Arnold, M. J. (1976). Preference and interest as functions of distributional redundancy in rhythmic sequences. *Journal of Research in Music Education, 24*(1), 22–31.

Mencke, I., Omigie, D., Wald-Fuhrmann, M. & Brattico, E. (2019). Atonal music: Can uncertainty lead to pleasure? *Frontiers in Neuroscience 12* , 979. doi:10.3389/fnins.2018.00979

Meyer, L. B. (1973). *Explaining music: Essays and explorations*. Berkeley, CA: University of California Press.

Meyer, L. B. (2008). *Emotion and meaning in music*. Chicago, IL: University of Chicago Press.

Miendlarzewska, E. A., & Trost, W. J. (2013). How musical training affects cognitive development: Rhythm, reward and other modulating variables. *Frontiers in Neuroscience, 7*, 279.

Montoya, R. M., Horton, R. S., Vevea, J. L., Citkowicz, M., & Lauber, E. A. (2017). A reexamination of the mere exposure effect: The influence of repeated exposure on recognition, familiarity, and liking. *Psychological Bulletin, 143*(5), 459–498.

Mori, K., & Iwanaga, M. (2017). Two types of peak emotional responses to music: The psychophysiology of chills and tears. *Scientific Reports, 7*(April), 46063.

Müller, M., Höfel, L., Brattico, E., & Jacobsen, T. (2009). Electrophysiological correlates of aesthetic music processing. *Annals of the New York Academy of Sciences, 1169*(1), 355–358.

Narmour, E. (1992). *The analysis and cognition of melodic complexity: The implication-realization model*. Chicago, IL: University of Chicago Press.

Nieminen, S., Istók, E., Brattico, E., Tervaniemi, M., & Huotilainen, M. (2011). The development of aesthetic responses to music and their underlying neural and psychological mechanisms. *Cortex; a Journal Devoted to the Study of the Nervous System and Behavior, 47*(9), 1138–1146.

Nieminen, S., Istók, E., Brattico, E., & Tervaniemi, M. (2012). The development of the aesthetic experience of music: Preference, emotions, and beauty. *Musicae Scientiae: The Journal of the European Society for the Cognitive Sciences of Music, 16*(3), 372–391.

North, A. C. (2004). Uses of music in everyday life. *Music Perception: An Interdisciplinary Journal, 22*(1), 41–77.

Obermeier, C., Kotz, S. A., Jessen, S., Raettig, T., von Koppenfels, M., & Menninghaus, W. (2016). Aesthetic appreciation of poetry correlates with ease of processing in event-related potentials. *Cognitive, Affective & Behavioral Neuroscience, 16*(2), 362–373.

Pallesen, K. J., Brattico, E., & Bailey, C. (2005). Emotion processing of major, minor, and dissonant chords. *Annals of the New York Academy of Sciences, 1060*, 450–453.

Panksepp, J., & Bernatzky, G. (2002). Emotional sounds and the brain: The neuro-affective foundations of musical appreciation. *Behavioural Processes, 60*(2), 133–155.

Park, M., Gutyrchik, E., Bao, Y., Zaytseva, Y., Carl, P., Welker, L., … Meindl, T. (2014). Differences between musicians and non-musicians in neuro-affective processing of sadness and fear expressed in music. *Neuroscience Letters, 566*(April), 120–124.

Parncutt, R. (2014). The emotional connotations of major versus minor tonality: One or more origins? *Musicae Scientiae: The Journal of the European Society for the Cognitive Sciences of Music, 18*(3), 324–353.

Parsons, M. T. (1976). A suggestion concerning the development of aesthetic experience in children. *The Journal of Aesthetics and Art Criticism, 34*(3), 305–314.

Pearce, M. T. (2018). Statistical learning and probabilistic prediction in music cognition: Mechanisms of stylistic enculturation. *Annals of the New York Academy of Sciences, 1423,* 378–395. doi:10.1111/nyas.13654

Pearce, M. T., Zaidel, D. W., Vartanian, O., Skov, M., Leder, H., Chatterjee, A., & Nadal, M. (2016). Neuroaesthetics: The cognitive neuroscience of aesthetic experience. *Perspectives on Psychological Science: A Journal of the Association for Psychological Science, 11*(2), 265–279.

Pelowski, M., Markey P. S., Forster, M., & Gerger, G. (2017). Move me, astonish me … delight my eyes and brain: The Vienna integrated model of top-down and bottom-up processes in art perception (VIMAP) and corresponding affective, evaluative, and neurophysiological correlates. *Physics of Life Reviews, 21,* 80–125.

Pelowski, M., Markey, P. S., Lauring, J. O., & Leder, H. (2016). Visualizing the impact of art: An update and comparison of current psychological models of art experience. *Frontiers in Human Neuroscience, 10*(April), 160.

Perani, D., Saccuman, M. C., Scifo, P., Spada, D., Andreolli, G., Rovelli, R., … Koelsch, S. (2010). Functional specializations for music processing in the human newborn brain. *Proceedings of the National Academy of Sciences of the United States of America, 107*(10), 4758–4763.

Peretz, I., & Coltheart, M. (2003). Modularity of music processing. *Nature Neuroscience, 6*(7), 688–691.

Poikonen, H., Alluri, V., Brattico, E., Lartillot, O., Tervaniemi, M., & Huotilainen, M. (2016). Event-related brain responses while listening to entire pieces of music. *Neuroscience, 312*(January), 58–73.

Quarto, T., Fasano, M. C., Taurisano, P., Fazio, L., Antonucci, L. A., Gelao, B., … Brattico, E. (2017). Interaction between DRD2 variation and sound environment on mood and emotion-related brain activity. *Neuroscience, 341*(January), 9–17.

Quinn, W., & Danto, A. C. (1983). The transfiguration of the commonplace. *The Philosophical Review, 92*(3), 481.

Ravignani, A., Delgado, T., & Kirby, S. (2016). Musical evolution in the lab exhibits rhythmic universals. *Nature Human Behaviour, 1*(1), 0007.

Reber, R., Schwarz, N., & Winkielman, P. (2004). Processing fluency and aesthetic pleasure: Is beauty in the perceiver's processing experience? *Personality and Social Psychology Review, 8*(4), 364–382.

Rentfrow, P. J., & Gosling, S. D. (2003). The do re mi's of everyday life: The structure and personality correlates of music preferences. *Journal of Personality and Social Psychology, 84*(6), 1236–1256.

Reybrouck, M., & Brattico, E. (2015). Neuroplasticity beyond sounds: Neural adaptations following long-term musical aesthetic experiences. *Brain Sciences, 5*(1), 69–91.

Reybrouck, M., Vuust, P., & Brattico, E. (2018). Brain connectivity networks and the aesthetic experience of music. *Brain Sciences, 8*(6). doi:10.3390/brainsci8060107

Rickard, N. S. (2004). Intense emotional responses to music: A test of the physiological arousal hypothesis. *Psychology of Music, 32*(4), 371–388.

Robazza, C., Macaluso, C., & D'Urso, V. (1994). Emotional reactions to music by gender, age, and expertise. *Perceptual and Motor Skills, 79*(2), 939–944.

Saarikallio, S. (2007). *Music as mood regulation in adolescence.* Jyväskylä: University of Jyväskylä.

Sachs, M. E., Ellis, R. J., Schlaug, G., & Loui, P. (2016). Brain connectivity reflects human aesthetic responses to music. *Social Cognitive and Affective Neuroscience, 11*(6), 884–891.

Salganik, M. J., Sheridan Dodds, P., & Watts, D. (2006). Experimental study of inequality and unpredictability in an artificial cultural market. *Science, 311*(5762), 854–856.

Salimpoor, V. N., Benovoy, M., Larcher, K., Dagher, A., & Zatorre, R. J. (2011). Anatomically distinct dopamine release during anticipation and experience of peak emotion to music. *Nature Neuroscience, 14*(2), 257–262.

Salimpoor, V. N., Benovoy, M., Longo, G., Cooperstock, J. R., & Zatorre, R. J. (2009). The rewarding aspects of music listening are related to degree of emotional arousal. *PLoS ONE, 4*(10), e7487.

Salimpoor, V. N., van den Bosch, I., Kovacevic, N., Randal McIntosh, A., Dagher, A., & Zatorre, R. J. (2013). Interactions between the nucleus accumbens and auditory cortices predict music reward value. *Science, 340*(6129), 216–219.

Salimpoor, V. N., Zald, D. H., Zatorre, R. J., Dagher, A., & Randal McIntosh, A. (2015). Predictions and the brain: How musical sounds become rewarding. *Trends in Cognitive Sciences, 19*(2), 86–91.

Salimpoor, V. N., & Zatorre, R. J. (2013a). Complex cognitive functions underlie aesthetic emotions. *Physics of Life Reviews, 10*(3), 279–280.

Salimpoor, V. N., & Zatorre, R. J. (2013b). Neural interactions that give rise to musical pleasure. *Psychology of Aesthetics, Creativity, and the Arts, 7*(1), 62–75.

Savage, P. E., Brown, S., Sakai, E., & Currie, T. E. (2015). Statistical universals reveal the structures and functions of human music. *Proceedings of the National Academy of Sciences, 112*(29), 8987–8992.

Schindler, I., Hosoya, G., Menninghaus, W., Beermann, U., Wagner, V., Eid, M., & Scherer, K. R. (2017). Measuring aesthetic emotions: A review of the literature and a new assessment tool. *PLoS ONE, 12*(6), e0178899.

Schön, D., Regnault, P., Ystad, S., & Besson, M. (2005). Sensory consonance. *Music Perception, 23*(2), 105–118.

Shannon, C. E., & Weaver, W. (1949). *The mathematical theory of communication.* Champaign, IL: University of Illinois Press.

Siedenburg, K., Jones-Mollerup, K., & McAdams, S. (2015). Acoustic and categorical dissimilarity of musical timbre: Evidence from asymmetries between acoustic and chimeric sounds. *Frontiers in Psychology, 6,* 1977.

Silvia, P. J., Fayn, K., Nusbaum, E. C., & Beaty, R. E. (2015). Openness to experience and awe in response to nature and music: Personality and profound aesthetic experiences. *Psychology of Aesthetics, Creativity, and the Arts, 9*(4), 376–384.

Silvia, P. J., & Nusbaum, E. C. (2011). On personality and piloerection: Individual differences in aesthetic chills and other unusual aesthetic experiences. *Psychology of Aesthetics, Creativity, and the Arts, 5*(3), 208–214.

Sloboda, J. A. (1991). Music structure and emotional response: Some empirical findings. *Psychology of Music, 19*(2), 110–120.

Sloboda, J. A., O'Neill, S. A., & Ivaldi, A. (2001). Functions of music in everyday life: An exploratory study using the experience sampling method. *Musicae Scientiae: The Journal of the European Society for the Cognitive Sciences of Music, 5*(1), 9–32.

Smith, M. (2011). Triangulating aesthetic experience. In A. P. Shimamura & S. Palmer (Eds.). *Aesthetic science: Connecting minds, brains, and experience* (pp. 80–102). New York: Oxford University Press.

Steinbeis, N., & Koelsch, S. (2008). Shared neural resources between music and language indicate semantic processing of musical tension-resolution patterns. *Cerebral Cortex, 18*(5), 1169–1178.

Sturm, I., Dähne, S., Blankertz, B., & Curio, G. (2015). Multi-variate EEG analysis as a novel tool to examine brain responses to naturalistic music stimuli. *PLoS ONE, 10*(10), e0141281.

Sumpf, M., Jentschke, S., & Koelsch, S. (2015). Effects of aesthetic chills on a cardiac signature of emotionality. *PLoS ONE, 10*(6), e0130117.

Tervaniemi, M. (2018). Musical sounds in the human brain. In M. Skov & O. Vartanian (Eds.). *Neuroaesthetics* (pp. 221–231). Amityville, NY: Baywood Publishing Company Inc.

Tiihonen, M., Brattico, E., Maksimainen, J., Wikgren, J., & Saarikallio, S. (2017). Constituents of Music and visual-art related pleasure—A critical integrative literature review. *Frontiers in Psychology, 8*(July), 1218.

Trainor, L. J. (2015). The origins of music in auditory scene analysis and the roles of evolution and culture in musical creation. *Philosophical Transactions of the Royal Society of London. Series B, Biological Sciences, 370*(1664), 20140089.

Trehub, S. E., Plantinga, J., Brcic, J., & Nowicki, M. (2013). Cross-modal signatures in maternal speech and singing. *Frontiers in Psychology, 4*(November), 811.

Trost, W., Frühholz, S., Cochrane, T., Cojan, Y., & Vuilleumier, P. (2015). Temporal dynamics of musical emotions examined through intersubject synchrony of brain activity. *Social Cognitive and Affective Neuroscience, 10*(12), 1705–1721.

Vieillard, S., Roy, M., & Peretz, I. (2012). Expressiveness in musical emotions. *Psychological Research, 76*(5), 641–653.

Vitz, P. C. (1972). Preference for tones as a function of frequency (Hertz) and intensity (decibels). *Perception & Psychophysics, 11*(1), 84–88.

Vuilleumier, P., & Trost, W. (2015). Music and emotions: From enchantment to entrainment. *Annals of the New York Academy of Sciences, 1337*(March), 212–222.

Vuoskoski, J. K., & Eerola, T. (2011). The role of mood and personality in the perception of emotions represented by music. *Cortex, 47*(9), 1099–1106.

Vuust, P., & Kringelbach, M. L. (2010). The pleasure of making sense of music. *Interdisciplinary Science Reviews, 35*(2), 166–182.

Webster, G. D., & Weir, C. G. (2005). Emotional responses to music: Interactive effects of mode, texture, and tempo. *Motivation and Emotion, 29*(1), 19–39.

Witek, M. A. G., Clarke, E. F., Wallentin, M., Kringelbach, M. L., & Vuust, P. (2014). Syncopation, body-movement and pleasure in groove music. *PLoS ONE, 9*(4), e94446.

Witek, M. A. G., Popescu, T., Clarke, E. F., Hansen, M., Konvalinka, I., Kringelbach, M. L., & Vuust, P. (2017). Syncopation affects free body-movement in musical groove. *Experimental Brain Research. Experimentelle Hirnforschung. Experimentation Cerebrale, 235*(4), 995–1005.

Wong, K. (1997). Neanderthal notes. Did ancient humans play modern scales? *Scientific American, 277*(3), 28, 30.

Zajonc, R. B. (1980). Feeling and thinking: Preferences need no inferences. *The American Psychologist, 35*(2), 151–175.

Zajonc, R. B. (1968). Attitudinal effects of mere exposure. *Journal of Personality and Social Psychology, 9*(2, Pt. 2), 1–27.

Zangwill, N. (1995). Kant on pleasure in the agreeable. *The Journal of Aesthetics and Art Criticism, 53*(2), 167.

Zatorre, R. J., & Salimpoor, V. N. (2013). From perception to pleasure: music and its neural substrates. *Proceedings of the National Academy of Sciences of the United States of America, 110*(Suppl. 2, June), 10430–10437.

Zentner, M., Grandjean, D., & Scherer, K. R. (2008). Geneva emotional music scale. *PsycTESTS Dataset.* doi:10.1037/t27579-000

Zentner, M. R., & Kagan, J. (1996). Perception of music by infants. *Nature, 383*(6595), 29.

Ziche, P. (1999). Neuroscience in its context. Neuroscience and psychology in the work of Wilhelm Wundt. *Physis; Rivista Internazionale Di Storia Della Scienza, 36*(2), 407–429.

Zuckerman, M. (1979). *Sensation seeking: Beyond the optimal level of arousal.* Hillsdale, NJ: Erlbaum

CHAPTER 26

THE AESTHETICS OF ACTION AND MOVEMENT

EMILY S. CROSS AND ANDREA ORLANDI

INTRODUCTION

As many of the other chapters in this volume will attest, many, if not most, published studies within the domain of empirical aesthetics have focused on the aesthetic appraisal of physically tangible objects, such as paintings, sculpture, and architecture. However, a cursory skim through this entire volume will also highlight that many other kinds of stimuli are worthy of consideration and investigation by those interested in empirical aesthetics, including music, poetry, mathematics, the human face, and, the focus of the present chapter, movements made by the human body. The human body in motion forms a special class of aesthetic stimulus. Since antiquity, we know that the human body in motion has served as the object of aesthetic evaluation. As empirical aesthetics has developed as a discipline, so has our understanding of how we value movements made by the human body, whether as an actor or an observer. Over the past decade and a half or so, the burgeoning discipline of neuroaesthetics has accelerated our understanding of the relationship between the bidirectional relationship between action and perception, and how this relationship influences or informs our aesthetic preferences.

In the present chapter, we aim to provide a brief overview of several themes that relate to the aesthetics of action and movement. We begin with theoretical considerations of the role of the body and action in aesthetic appraisals, and follow this with two sections that highlight early experimental psychology work that informs our understanding of the relationship between how movements are performed and preferences, and then the relationship between embodied experience and aesthetic evaluations, per se. This is followed by two sections that delve more deeply into the cognitive neuroscience research that informs our understanding of how we perceive others in action and how our own prior (visuo)motor experience shapes this perception and aesthetic preferences. We conclude with considerations of experimental challenges for future studies in this domain to consider, both in terms of methodology and open questions. The overarching aim of this chapter is to highlight the rich insights that can be gained by examining the relationships among embodiment, aesthetics, and the performing arts (dance in particular) that enrich our understanding of aesthetics more broadly.

THEORETICAL CONSIDERATIONS

A seminal theoretical contribution to the understanding of mechanisms associated with the aesthetic experience of action comes from a paper by Freedberg and Gallese (2007). In this work, the authors propose an embodied simulation account of aesthetic perception of an artwork. Via this account, they sought to combine the introspective and metaphysical concept of a viewer's empathic response with hard evidence from the neuroscience of perception. At the same time, they highlighted the role of the body of an observer in the process of art evaluation. Specifically, they identified the importance of embodied empathetic feelings about two key elements of a piece of art: the representational content of what a piece depicts, and the visible traces of the author that characterize the artwork. The idea of an observer's *embodied* experience was boosted following the discovery of so-called mirror neurons in the macaque (monkey) brain (Di Pellegrino, Fadiga, Fogassi, Gallese, & Rizzolatti, 1992) and evidence for a homologues system in the human brain (Rizzolatti, Fadiga, Gallese, & Fogassi, 1996). What the early neurophysiology work on mirror neurons showed is that observing another individual perform a motor act engages cortical regions in the observer that are also active during actual execution of the same action, including the ventral premotor cortex and inferior parietal lobule. Some authors have suggested that this simulation system linking action with perception means that observing (or possibly even thinking about) any action automatically engages the neural representation of the specific motor program and body sensation associated with that action (Gallese & Goldman, 1998). Authors such as Gallese and Goldman (1998) go further to propose that this system supports our understanding of the intentions and goals of other individuals, as well as their relative physical sensations and emotions. Thus, the observer could feel as he/she is performing the actual action. These resonance mechanisms have provided a possible neural substrate underlying social capabilities, including intersubjectivity and empathy feelings (Iacoboni, 2009).

Returning to the framework proposed by Freedberg and Gallese (2007), similar simulation processes could also shape a perceiver's aesthetic experience in response to the cognitive, sensory, and emotional content of paintings or sculptures. For instance, the actions depicted in the artwork would lead to visuomotor resonance processes, allowing the understanding of the intentions and emotions of the characters. This would account for the physical sensations that have been reported by the observers located in the body parts involved in the observed action (Freedberg & Gallese, 2007). Furthermore, Di Dio, Canessa, Cappa, & Rizzolatti (2011) showed similarities and differences during the aesthetic perception of artwork and real-life stimuli. These authors presented participants with images depicting classical sculptures and young athletes and asked them to make aesthetic judgments of both kinds of images during functional magnetic resonance imaging (fMRI) scanning. The observation of both categories of stimuli engaged a similar brain network, which included the occipito-temporal visual cortex and fronto-parietal mirror regions (intraparietal sulcus, ventral premotor cortex, and inferior frontal gyrus), hippocampus, and amygdala. However, the direct comparison between sculptures and real bodies showed a specific engagement of the right anterior amygdala and the fusiform gyrus. The opposite contrast revealed increased activity in the superior temporal sulcus when viewing real bodies compared with sculptures. Similar resonance processes have also been shown to take place in response to the observation of familiar manipulable objects (such as tools; Proverbio, Adorni, & D'Aniello, 2011), and emotional body expressions (Heberlein et al., 2004; Proverbio, Gabaro, Orlandi, & Zani, 2015). In one electroencephalographic (EEG) study by Proverbio and colleagues (2011), the observation of manipulable objects (tools) compared with non-tool objects elicited larger negativity over frontal portions of participants' scalps. The source reconstruction of the signal in that time window suggested specific engagement of the left postcentral gyrus and premotor cortex bilaterally in response to tools (vs. equally familiar non-tool objects). The authors suggest that this pattern reflects the automatic recall of the motor proprieties of the tools. A second hypothesized key component of the aesthetic experience of the artwork is the relation between the embodied concept of empathy and the visible traces of the artistic creations. In this regard, being able to see the traces left by the brushes or hand movements that characterize the style and technique of the artist would lead to a simulation of the relative motor programs (Gallese, 2017). Thus, the viewer would have the sensation of experiencing the painting from a first-person perspective.

An example of this effect has been found in the famous cuts on canvas by Lucio Fontana (Umiltà, Berchio, Sestito, Freedberg, & Gallese, 2012), and the dynamic brushstrokes by Franz Kline (Sbriscia-Fioretti, Berchio, Freedberg, Gallese, & Umiltà, 2013). In the EEG study by Umiltà and colleagues, participants were presented with images of Lucio Fontana artworks (cuts on canvas) and modified versions of the same stimuli (graphically modified versions of the Fontana artworks, where the cuts were visualized as black lines on a white surface) during a secondary attentional task. The volunteers also rated all the stimuli along different factors, including familiarity, aesthetic appraisal, amount of movement, and perceived artistic nature (i.e., is this a real artwork or not?). Umiltà and colleagues reported increased bilateral Mu rhythm suppression (8–12 Hz) in response to the original artworks (vs. baseline) compared with the control stimuli (vs. baseline), over sensorimotor regions of the scalp. Moreover, participants' reported visual familiarity with the stimuli did not affect the desynchronization of the Mu rhythm. This result was seen as an index of the engagement of the cortical motor system during the observation of abstract visual art. Finally, the original artworks also received higher ratings of pleasantness and amount of movement perceived, compared with the graphically modified versions.

EXPERIMENTAL PSYCHOLOGICAL STUDIES OF
ACTION AND PREFERENCES

Additional evidence that sheds light on the relationship between aesthetic perception and visuomotor simulation can be found in studies that have examined the observation of non-artistic actions, including eye movements (Topolinski, 2010) and finger movements (Beilock & Holt, 2007). In a series of experiments, Topolinski presented participants with sequences of dots moving on the screen depicting an L shape, and asked these participants to rate the likability of these movements. Before each trial, volunteers were asked to move the head (staring at a fixation cross) along the vertical and horizontal axis tracing a similar L shape. Matching movements rather than non-matching movements of dots and head resulted in a more positive aesthetic appraisal. Moreover, a progressive decrease in likability was found as a function of a deviation (rotation angle) between the two trajectories (dots and head). This result seemed to suggest an additional influence of the motor system, or perhaps motor fluency, in modulating the aesthetic judgment of simple actions (cf. Hayes, Paul, Beuger, & Tipper, 2008).

Similar results were previously reported by Beilock and Holt during the observation of finger movements (Beilock & Holt, 2007). In this study, skilled and novice typists were trained to reproduce different finger movement sequences (using the left and right index and middle fingers) associated with specific cue symbols. Then, the volunteers were presented with two pairs of letters (requiring the same finger or different fingers to be typed with the two hands) and instructed to choose the preferred one. Under a specific condition (dual-task), each trial was preceded by the presentation one training-related symbol, so that volunteers had to recall the motor pattern and execute it after the preference (or aesthetic) judgment. Only the experts showed a preference for the dyads requiring different fingers to be typed. However, this preference was attenuated when they had to keep in mind a motor pattern compatible with the dyads. Overall, this evidence suggested an influence of covert visuomotor simulation in the aesthetic appraisal of action stimuli. The more familiar the movement, the more fluent is the processing of the stimulus.

One final study whose findings further reinforce the role of the motor system in aesthetic judgment was performed by Hayes and colleagues (2008). In this study, the authors were interested in how the fluency of physical interactions with objects influences people's preferences for those objects. In the first experiment, participants were asked to either physically perform a reaching action to grasp an object (and this reaching action could be smooth and fluent, with no obstacles in the way, or participants would have to perform a more awkward reach around an obstacle in order to grasp the object). Participants rated the objects that they were able to reach with a fluent grasp as more likable than objects they had to grasp awkwardly. In two subsequent experiments, the authors examined whether similar preferences for objects that were grasped in a fluent manner also exist in the perceptual domain (i.e., if participants make no reaching movements themselves, but simply observe someone else grasping objects in a fluent or awkward manner). Here again, the authors found that objects were preferred that an actor has been able to grasp smoothly, compared with those reached via an awkward grasp around an obstacle (but, interestingly, only when the actor's eye gaze was visible). The authors suggest these findings illustrate how non-emotive actions can lead to empathic states in observers (as well as actors). When these findings are considered in light of Freedberg and Gallese's embodied theory of aesthetics, it is perhaps unsurprising that the motor systems of actors, as well as observers, play such a pronounced role in shaping preferences.

Experimental Psychological Studies of Embodiment and Aesthetics

At this point, at least three questions arise. First, is it possible to find a similar link between enjoyment and motor practice for more complex actions involving the entire body? Second, what is the role of extended visuomotor practice or expertise with a specific motor repertoire in modulating this relationship? Finally, to what extent might studies in this domain inform our understanding of how audiences evaluate (and value) the performing arts? In an early study by Cross and colleagues (2011), the authors sought to examine the relationship between embodiment and aesthetics at the brain and behavioral levels. They did this by asking participants to watch over 80 different short video clips of professional dancers performing a range of movements, ranging from mundane (such as walking in a circle or stretching the arms above the head) to extremely technical (such as a triple pirouette or a split leap). After each video clip, participants were asked to rate either how much they liked each movement, or how well they could physically reproduce the movement if asked to do so at present. The behavioral data revealed, contrary to the long-held assumption that familiarity breeds liking (also known as the "mere exposure effect"; Zajonc, 1968), a strong negative relationship between participants' motor familiarity (or ability to perform an action), and how much they liked watching a particular action. In other words, participants assigned a much higher aesthetic value (in this case, measured by liking) to the most complex, unfamiliar movements, and the lowest aesthetic value to the most simple, mundane movements. The authors referred to this finding as a possible "Cirque du Soleil" effect, and suggest that it intuitively makes sense that people would value spectacular, unfamiliar motor acts being performed by others more than simple movements they could easily perform themselves (Cross, Kirsch, Ticini, & Schutz-Bosbach, 2011).

However, it is important to note that in this study, all participants were non-dancers who were explicitly chosen as individuals who had never taken any dance classes and did not regularly (or even occasionally) attend dance performances. An important follow-up question concerns how actual physical experience or expertise might shape aesthetic processing and preferences. Kirsch and colleagues ran a between-groups training study to begin to address this question, recruiting dance-naïve participants and inviting them to the lab for a week to learn several hip-hop dance sequences using the popular video game *Dance Central 2* with the Xbox Kinect system (Kirsch, Drommelschmidt, & Cross, 2013). One group of participants learned the movements by physically practicing them, a second group simply watched the movements and listened to the soundtracks, and a third group listened to the soundtracks only. Participants' aesthetic preferences for individual dance movements were surveyed before and after the training intervention (as was their perceived ability to perform each movement). In contrast to what was observed by Cross et al. (2011), Kirsch and colleagues found that with actual dance training, physical practice not only improved participants' ability to perform dance movements (as would naturally be expected), but also led to higher ratings of enjoyment when watching those movements (compared with individuals in the audiovisual training and auditory training only groups). Subsequent work by Kirsch and colleagues asked related questions about actual physical experience and aesthetic preferences, and improved upon the first study by devising within-subjects designs to test these questions, which enabled the researchers to examine the influence of motor experience per se, as separated from visual and auditory experience (Kirsch, Dawson, & Cross, 2015). Here again, the authors found that asking participants to learn, via physical practice, dance movements that they later would watch and rate on aesthetic value increased participants' enjoyment of these movements. Furthermore, a recent study with participants who ranged from early adolescence through to older adulthood (12–69 years of age) expanded these insights to show that individuals at earlier and later life stages also enjoy watching dance movements more after they have gained physical experience performing these movements (Kirsch & Cross, 2018).

One final study by Kirsch and colleagues worth considering further illuminates the relationship between physical abilities and aesthetic preferences (Kirsch, Snagg, Heerey, & Cross, 2016). In this study, the authors used electromyography (EMG) to study spectators' facial muscle activity while they observed a range of short dance video clips. EMG allows researchers to gain insights into subtle emotional reactions by observers when they observe stimuli they find pleasant or unpleasant (perhaps boring or ugly) by recording subthreshold (or unobservable to the naked eye) engagement of facial musculature that is involved in smiling (shown to be engaged when we view pleasant stimuli) or frowning (shown to be engaged when we view less or unpleasant stimuli). Using a between-subjects design, Kirsch and colleagues recorded facial EMG signals from a group of experienced dancers as well as a group of dance-naïve participants while they watched short video clips of professional dancers performing a range of different movements. Later, the participants were asked to rate how much they enjoyed watching each movement. The authors found that the dancers' faces were more reactive than the non-dancers when watching dance movements overall, and further that dancers showed more engagement of "smiling" muscles when watching movements they later rated as enjoyable to watch and more engagement of "frowning" muscles when watching movements they later rated as less enjoyable to watch. This same relationship did not exist among the novice dancers. Similar findings using a different electro-physiological technique (galvanic skin response) and professional ballet dancers and control participants reported data broadly consistent with the findings of Kirsch and colleagues (Christensen, Gomila, Gaigg, Sivarajah, & Calvo-Merino, 2016). Together, the findings from this study and the others covered in this section begin to illustrate how an observer's physical capabilities and prior experience shape their enjoyment of dance (though, for deeper exploration of this relationship, see Kirsch, Urgesi, & Cross, 2016). In the next section, we describe how brain-based methods further our understanding of this relationship, in both everyday perception as well as when viewing artworks.

Cognitive Neuroscience Insights into the Aesthetics of Action

The growing application of neuroimaging techniques to better understand the neurocognitive mechanisms that support perception led to the identification of a network within the human brain that is thought to help the observer bridge the gap between her own body and bodily experience and the body of an observed individual. Building off the mirror neuron neurophysiology work originally performed in non-human primates, a large number of neuroimaging studies performed with humans show that the observation of an action performed by another individual engages an extensive network of fronto-parieto-temporal brain regions collectively referred to as action observation network (AON; Cross, Kraemer, Hamilton, Kelley, & Grafton, 2009; Caspers, Zilles, Laird, & Eickhoff, 2010; Grafton, 2009; Molenberghs, Cunnington, & Mattingley, 2012). The brain regions that compose the AON include multisensory areas that are active during the execution and observation of action, including the ventral premotor cortex (PMv), inferior frontal gyrus (IFG), intraparietal (IPS), and superior temporal sulcus (STS). Given the similarities with the mirror neurons identified within the ventral premotor cortex of the monkey (Gallese, Fadiga, Fogassi, & Rizzolatti, 1996), these frontoparietal regions are also sometimes referred to as the human mirror neuron system (Rizzolatti & Sinigaglia, 2016). In addition, several visual association areas located within the occipito-temporal cortex are part of the AON, including brain regions that show a preferential response to the human body (extrastriate and fusiform body areas), face (occipital and fusiform face areas), and motion (MT/V5; Peelen & Downing, 2007). According to the direct matching hypothesis (Rizzolatti, Fogassi, & Gallese, 2001), when we watch another person in action, the neural representation of the corresponding motor program supporting their movements is recalled and simulated through the observer's motor system. Thus, some manner of direct experience with the observed action would be possible (what is often referred to as a resonance process). This resonance process has been credited with helping us comprehend, for example, the goals and intentions of other individuals (Grafton & Hamilton, 2007). In line with this view, prior work has shown that increasing engagement of the AON is related to increased familiarity with the observed motor act (e.g., Buccino et al., 2004; Calvo-Merino, Glaser, Grezes, Passingham, & Haggard, 2005). A related idea of embodied cognition (Wilson, 2002) has also paved the way for new theories and approaches in the study of cognitive processes and the role played by the body and lived experience of actors and perceivers. However, more recently, other authors have proposed an alternative theory about the role of the AON in action understanding. This theory aligns with a predictive coding framework, and is based on empirical Bayesian processing (Kilner, Friston, & Frith, 2007). According to this theory, when we observe another person in action, if that person is moving in a predictable and familiar way (such as making a cup of coffee), then we would rapidly be able to understand the meaning of their action as a result of a process of minimizing prediction error at all levels of the cortical hierarchy (intention, goal, motor, and kinematics). In other words, the brain (and the AON in particular) is constantly comparing predicted and observed kinematics of a movement, and deviations from what is expected results in greater prediction error, which is then used to update the representation of the motor command (cf. Gardner, Goulden, & Cross, 2015). These deviations could be substantial, both when an observer is highly skilled/familiar with an observed action, or when the observed action is entirely novel and unfamiliar. Such a characterization of the AON accounts for enhanced activity seen in response to well-known/predictable movements but also very unfamiliar/unpredictable movements. An example was given by imaging studies in which participants were presented with physically impossible (vs. possible) finger movements (Costantini et al., 2005) and rigid robot-like (vs. human-like) actions (Cross et al., 2012). However, more evidence needs to be provided to corroborate or refute both the direct matching and predictive coding hypotheses, which should also help to resolve outstanding issues concerning how our motor systems help us to make sense of others in action.

Speaking more to the role of an observer's lived sensorimotor experience, and how this shapes perception, over the past decade, several research teams have explored questions along these lines by recruiting participants who vary in the level of acquired physical experience and motor knowledge (expertise) with a selected action repertoire (Calvo-Merino et al., 2005; Cross, Hamilton, & Grafton, 2006). The comparison between experts and non-experts from dance (Orgs, Dombrowski, Heil, & Jansen-Osmann, 2008; Orlandi, Zani, & Proverbio, 2017), sport (Smith, 2016), and music (Pau, Jahn, Sakreida, Domin, & Lotze, 2013) has enabled researchers to investigate further how motor knowledge is coded and represented in the human brain. The intense and extended training required to perform physical tasks (such as dance, sport, or music) at a professional level not only results in the acquisition of new motor skills from a body perspective, but also leads to refined and enriched perceptual representations of those motor acts. This is likely the result of structural and functional changes that happen in experts' brains over many hundreds (or thousands) of hours of practice (Giacosa, Karpati, Foster, Penhune, & Hyde, 2016; Karpati, Giacosa, Foster, Penhune, & Hyde, 2017). A classic example regards the fMRI study by Calvo-Merino and colleagues (2005), in which the brain activity of professional ballet and capoeira dancers was compared with that of non-dancer control participants during the observation of repertoire-specific movements. Participants were presented with videos displaying an expert performing dance steps from ballet and capoeira techniques. The researchers found greater activity within the ventral premotor cortex (vPM), intraparietal sulcus (IPS), right superior parietal lobule (SPL), and left posterior superior temporal sulcus (pSTS) in the brains of experts compared with non-experts, and these regions were most engaged while expert dancers were observing steps from their own technique (i.e., capoeira dancers watching capoeira movements) rather than kinematically comparable movements from the other dance style (i.e., capoeira dancers watching classical ballet). No difference in response to both categories of stimuli was found within the brains of control participants.

From an electrophysiological perspective, the observation of familiar compared with unfamiliar actions has been shown to result in a modulation of brain rhythms within specific frequency bands. In this study, Orgs and colleagues (2008) presented contemporary dancers and non-dancers with videos showing a performer reproducing daily actions as well as movements from the dancers' training routine. Participants were instructed to categorize each movement (daily life vs. dance) after observing it, and EEG recordings were taken throughout these tasks. A reduction of power (event-related desynchronization) in alpha and beta frequency bands during the observation of dance steps was found only in the brains of dancers. As in the study by Calvo-Merino et al. (2005), the modulation elicited by the two categories of moves was not significant in controls, likely due to a lack of any specific motor knowledge with the observed movements. Furthermore, Cross and colleagues (2006) showed that an increased response of AON is even possible after intensive training for few weeks. A group of expert contemporary dancers were taught novel sequences of whole-body movements for 5 weeks. At the end of each week, they were presented with videos representing fragments of movement from learned sequences and novel (not learned) sequences during fMRI scanning. They were instructed to imagine performing each move and rate their ability to do so. These authors reported that watching trained compared with non-trained movements elicited enhanced responses within STS, PMv, IPS, and the rostral part of the supplementary motor area (SMA). Moreover, activity in left IPL and PMv was correlated with feasibility ratings, showing an increased response with increasing ratings of performance competence. The authors interpreted this as a possible neural signature of embodiment; in other words, the better you are at performing an observed action yourself, the more you simulate it within premotor and parietal nodes of the AON.

Similar results were reported by Kirsch and colleagues (2015), who trained non-dancer participants across 4 days on a series of hip-hop/street dance sequences, through several different sensory modalities: visuomotor + acoustic, visual + acoustic and acoustic only. Participants' brain activity before and after the training intervention was then compared during the observation of trained and novel sequences. The activity in left premotor, left STG, and right IPC showed modulation based on the type of training experience participants had, such that these regions were more strongly engaged the more sensory modalities through which participants had learned the movements. Moreover, the premotor cortical engagement was positively correlated with participants' individual dance performance scores recorded after training. Overall, this evidence seems to suggest that motor resonance processes are stronger in response to well-known rehearsed movements, which was likely the result of the acquisition of a more detailed neural representation of action after extended and intense practice.

The recall of sophisticated movement representations might also explain the reason why experts showed a refined ability to anticipate the outcome of an action (Aglioti, Cesari, Romani, & Urgesi, 2008) and perceive errors (Amoruso et al., 2014) and variations in action execution (Orlandi et al., 2017). In this regard, Orlandi and colleagues (2017) showed that only professional dancers were able to automatically recognize small changes between two almost identical novel complex moves. Contemporary dancers and non-dancers were presented with video pairs of whole-body movements depicting the same step or a slight variation of it (in time, space, or body parameters). Participants were instructed to press a button in response to rare target images during video observation, while EEG recordings were taken over the scalp. An increased fronto-central negative potential (N400 effect) at approximately 450 ms was found in response to varied (compared with identical) movements, as was a greater modulation of a late centro-parietal positive potential (late positivity, LP) among the group of expert dancers. Contrarily, the lack of modulation in controls suggested their inability to detect these variations. In a subsequent study, Orlandi, D'Incà, and Proverbio (2020) investigated further the degree of detail and refinement that action representation can reach (see also Orlandi & Proverbio, 2019), by focusing on how perceivers encode muscular effort. Expert ballet dancers and non-dancers were presented with videos of effortful and relatively effortless technical steps from a classical ballet repertoire. Volunteers were asked to observe each video and imagine reproducing it when presented with a visual cue. Watching effortful compared with effortless moves elicited a more positive frontal component (P300) at approximately 1,100 ms, which was concurrent with the maximum peak of displayed effort, but only within the brains of the expert ballet dancers. The authors interpreted this as an index of increased effort encoding due to motor expertise. Similarly, over parietal sites, an LP component (1,400–1,600 ms) was also larger in response to effortful movements among the expert dancer group. Contrarily, this LP component was only visible over occipital sites among the control participants, which the authors interpret as likely indexing an increase in the number or complexity of kinematic parameters to encode. A source reconstruction of the event-related potential (ERP) recorded over the scalp in the LP time windows (on the difference wave effortful minus effortless movement) seemed to confirm the hypothesis of engagement of prefrontal working memory and occipito-temporal regions in controls. At the same time, activity in visuomotor regions (i.e., IPL and PM) was shown in dancers. Furthermore, in the same study, the authors found evidence of a refined tuning of early responses of the occipito-temporal cortex to action kinematics as a result of intense and extensive whole-body training (Orlandi & Proverbio, 2019). Regardless of the motor content (effort), the observation of dance moves elicited an occipito-temporal N2 component (240–300 ms) that was larger over the left hemisphere of dancers compared with controls. The neural sources of the negativity were bilaterally distributed in expert dancers, including inferior and middle temporal regions (together with visuomotor cortices). This suggested increased functional symmetry during action observation. In contrast, the visual and prefrontal areas in the right hemisphere were more engaged in control participants. Furthermore, the expert dancers (relative to controls) showed an early P2 component followed by a larger P300 (360–560 ms), which suggested, respectively, faster movement processing and enhanced recognition. At the same time, the larger P2 over body-related regions in controls (compared with expert dancers) indicated greater stimulus encoding, but weaker recognition ability (smaller P300). Only the dancers exhibited more sophisticated and refined action processing within 300 ms after the occurrence of the movement. Together, these findings provide a rich array of evidence to show that the lived experience of action experts (at least in the realm of dance) leads to pronounced changes in how we perceive others moving around us. In the next section, we explore what the brain imaging tools featured above might contribute to our knowledge about how dance experience (or lack thereof) shapes our aesthetic evaluation of others' movements.

COGNITIVE NEUROSCIENCE INSIGHTS INTO EMBODIMENT AND AESTHETICS

The earliest study to use brain imaging techniques to examine the relationship between observers' motor skills and their preferences for others' actions in a performing arts domain was published by Calvo-Merino and colleagues in 2008. Using the same brain imaging data collected from their 2005 study (Calvo-Merino et al., 2005), the authors invited a subset of the control participants back to the laboratory to rate 24 different classical ballet and capoeira dance movements on several established aesthetic dimensions (as defined by Berlyne, 1974). The authors then averaged the ratings of these six participants and used these ratings to identify brain regions that received higher average ratings of liking compared with lower average ratings of liking. The authors found that not only were occipital cortical regions more robustly engaged when naïve participants viewed dance movements they later rated as more likable, but the premotor cortex also showed this relationship. This was the first evidence that brain regions involved in action also support the aesthetic processing of bodily movements.

The subsequent study performed by Cross and colleagues (2011), which was introduced in the previous section, found further support for this relationship between brain regions implicated in action perception and production links. In this study, however, a larger sample of dance-naïve participants watched a broad range of dance movements and rated the aesthetic value of each movement individually after watching it, and the authors used individual participant preference scores (rather than group averages) to interrogate brain regions that responded more robustly to movements participants rated as most enjoyable to watch. These authors report that when participants watched movements they rated as most enjoyable (and also as most diffi-cult to reproduce, as discussed above), strong bilateral engagement of occipito-temporal brain regions, as well as right supramarginal gyrus/intraparietal sulcus, emerged. The authors suggest that this finding corroborates what Calvo-Merino and colleagues reported in 2008, as well as suggests that it is not simply motor resonance or physical ability that leads to stronger engagement of core nodes of the AON when watching others in action, but aesthetic preferences also shape this relationship.

One final brain imaging study worth considering in this section examined the rela-tionship between observers' bodies and physical abilities and their aesthetic evaluation of observed dancers' movements, but this time used a dance training manipulation to determine how the acquisition of motor experience shaped preferences (Kirsch, Dawson, & Cross, 2015). This study used the same participants and data from the Kirsch & Cross (2015) study described two sections previously, and focused on different analyses. Specifically, as in the Cross et al. (2011) study, after watching each video in the scanner, participants rated either how much they liked watching the previous video or how well they could reproduce the movement displayed. Following the week-long dance training intervention (described above), participants completed an identical scanning session. At the brain level, the authors found that the brain regions mediating aesthetic preferences shifted from subcortical regions associated with dopaminergic reward processing before training to temporal multisensory integration regions after training. The authors interpret this shift as possibly suggestive of more emotion-based processing for aesthetics before action experience is gained, and then after physical ex-perience is acquired, the brain regions implicated in integrating across emotion, vision, and action play a more dominant role. Together, the studies reviewed in this section pro-vide a glimpse of the utility of using brain imaging tools to not only study the relation-ship between perception and action, but also among perception, action, an observer's embodied experience, and aesthetic preferences. This work is still in its infancy, but many exciting new avenues are open for future research, as we explore in the next section.

Major Challenges, Goals, and Future Directions

As in any research area, and particularly in research areas that draw upon multiple disciplines spanning the arts and sciences, the study of the aesthetics of action is not free from considerable challenges. One major one is the issue of replicability of experimental results, a challenge that impacts psychologists, cognitive neuroscientists, and indeed any researcher working with empirical data (Lakens et al., 2018; Munafo et al., 2017). Despite good convergence of evidence toward similar engagement of brain regions during action observation, several major questions remain unresolved. For instance, an agreement does not exist on the specific contribution of distinct areas or circuits within the AON in encoding different aspects of an action (i.e., intentions/goals, outcome, and kinematic features). In addition, our understanding of specific contributions by the left and right hemispheres to action resonance processes and aesthetic evaluations remains rudimentary. This is due, in part, to the variety of methodological approaches and foci used by different research groups. For instance, the use of multiple experimental tasks and designs (i.e., passive observation, n-back task, explicit judgment) ensures the investigation of a broad range of cognitive processes, but also makes it difficult to compare findings across studies. Moreover, volunteers are quite often presented with a small set of stimuli (images or videos). On the one hand, this ensures good control of the relevant parameters between stimulus categories, but on the other hand, it could lead to habituation and familiarity effects. This might be particularly problematic when studying aesthetic processes, as it is well known that novelty and familiarity impact such evaluations (e.g., Zajonc, 1968). In addition, each experiment differs in the manipulation of the considered features of the stimuli, such as motion kinematics (i.e., simple vs. complex actions, whole-body vs. body parts), background, staging context, the gender of the actor or dancer, body shape, and clothing.

Another critical point concerns the exploitation of similarity between groups of participants rather than an emphasis on their differences, regarding both behavioral and neural responses to perception and aesthetic judgment of action. A comparison between participants with acquired expertise and motor skills (i.e., musicians, athletes, and dancers) is certainly a good way to investigate action representation. However, it would be useful to further investigate the commonalities and differences in the neural substrate of experts from different fields (i.e., dancers vs. musicians; cf. Giacosa et al., 2016; Karpati et al., 2017). Also, we predict that the role of previously acquired motor skills in shaping aesthetic preferences will remain a topic of great interest as we better understand how early arts education might shape children's preferences for the arts for the duration of their lifetime. In addition, gender and sexuality differences, as well as the ethnic and cultural background of viewers, should be taken into account when studying aesthetic perception (c.f. Darda). As this field becomes ever more interdisciplinary, it will be valuable to consider how insights from the humanities, social sciences, and technology might enable us to further develop an understanding of preferences in the performing arts. Finally, a clearer understanding of the developmental trajectory of aesthetic judgments and preferences will require further research attention, to investigate, for instance, how preferences and the relationship between one's body and the body being observed on stage changes as we develop and age (cf. Kirsch & Cross, 2018).

Beyond empirical neuroaesthetics itself, work within this domain has the potential to inform and advance a range of other domains as well. One clearly relevant area concerns the contribution of aesthetic research on action perception on marketing and advertising (cf. Ariely & Berns, 2010; Krishna, 2012). For example, with the growth of digital advertising not just on our computer screens, but also in public places, those working in advertising might be interested in how to maximize interest and attention among a group of individuals walking on a crowded street with the type of movement presented on a screen (or, indeed, in real life, as flash mobs have proven to be extremely effective marketing tools as well; cf. Cross, 2015). Moreover, returning to the importance of understanding developmental differences in aesthetic preferences, a deeper understanding of how aging and social context influence preferences could make it possible for advertisers to reach their intended audience in a more targeted way (which, of course, has its pros and cons). The communicative aspects of body and movement, in both emotional and conceptual terms, also need to be emphasized. Greater focus should be given to the role of elements of one's personal history (i.e., expertise, emotions, skills, creativity) on interpretation and ascription of significance to others' actions. In this regard, it would be interesting to create a vocabulary of movement to be associated with a specific brand. This could lead to novel insights into the long-term effects of acquired visual familiarity with a specific motor repertoire on brand reputation and related variations on sales.

In light of this consideration, a more ambitious goal may be drawing up a set of golden rules or principles, based on evidence from aesthetics research, which could guide the creation of a performative artwork (i.e., choreography). In this regard, the contribution of movement timings, space parameters, and body shape to aesthetic perception should be investigated both individually and in combination with each other (cf. Vicary, Sperling, von Zimmermann, Richardson, & Orgs, 2017; von Zimmerman, Vicary, Sperling, Orgs, & Richardson, 2018; Orlandi, Cross, & Orgs, 2020; Smith & Cross, 2022). For instance, it would be interesting to study whether a range of preferred speed for human action exists (i.e., natural vs. unnatural movement; cf. Casile et al., 2009), and if this is the case, how modulation of this speed may evoke different emotional reactions in the observer. Moreover, which kinematic parameters or body postures lead to increased attention or arousal during action observation can also be explored, which should help to futher illuminate the relationships between action, perception, and aesthetics.

Finally, as immersive technologies become ever more ubiquitous in our working and social lives, important contributions may be further provided through the innovative application of virtual reality (VR) to neuroaesthetic research questions that involve the human body in motion (cf. Bohil, Alicea, & Biocca, 2011). Using VR in aesthetics research would make it possible to manipulate the point of view of the observer, enabling them to explore a moving body (such as that of a dancer) from different perspectives that might not be possible in traditional theater or screen viewing settings. The viewer could be included in a moving group, becoming part of a dance ensemble himself, facing the audience, or a member of a symphonic orchestra, following the conductor. Such approaches would provide the opportunity to study the reaction of people previously less interested in or drawn to the performing arts, before and after exposure to a simulated live exhibition. Moreover, VR might aid an observer to approximate the performance of a dancer while executing a duet with a partner, which could in turn enable closer investigation of the role of proximity between two people in modulating effort perception and aesthetic appreciation. Overall, VR could lead to a more ecological way to study movement and human interactions while remaining in a tightly controlled environment, and is one of just several exciting possible avenues to explore over the coming years on the topic of the aesthetics of action and movement.

REFERENCES

Aglioti, S. M., Cesari, P., Romani, M., Urgesi, C. (2008). Action anticipation and motor resonance in elite basketball players. *Nature Neuroscience, 11*(9), 1109–1116.

Amoruso, L., Sedeño, L., Huepe, D., Tomio, A., Kamienkowski, J., Hurtado, E., ... Ibáñez, A. (2014). Time to tango: Expertise and contextual anticipation during action observation. *NeuroImage, 98,* 366–385.

Ariely, D., & Berns, G. S. (2010). Neuromarketing: the hope and hype of neuroimaging in business. *Nature Reviews Neuroscience, 11*(4), 284.

Beilock, S. L., & Holt, L. E. (2007). Embodied preference judgments: Can likeability be driven by the motor system? *Psychological Science, 18*(1), 51–57.

Berlyne, D. E. (1974). *Studies in the new experimental aesthetics: Steps toward an objective psychology of aesthetic appreciation.* Washington, DC: Hemisphere Co.

Bohil, C. J., Alicea, B., & Biocca, F. A. (2011). Virtual reality in neuroscience research and therapy. *Nature Reviews Neuroscience, 12*(12), 752.

Buccino, G., Lui, F., Canessa, N., Patteri, I., Lagravinese, G., Benuzzi, F., Porro, C.A., & Rizzolatti, G. (2004). Neural circuits involved in the recognition of actions performed by nonconspecifics: An fMRI study. *Journal of Cognitive Neuroscience, 16*(1), 114–126.

Calvo-Merino, B., Glaser, D. E., Grezes, J., Passingham, R. E., & Haggard, P. (2005). Action observation and acquired motor skills: An FMRI study with expert dancers. *Cerebral Cortex, 15*(8), 1243–1249.

Calvo-Merino, B., Jola, C., Glaser, D. E., & Haggard, P. (2008). Towards a sensorimotor aesthetics of performing art. *Consciousness and Cognition, 17*(3), 911–922.

Casile, A., Dayan, E., Caggiano, V., Hendler, T., Flash, T., & Giese, M. A. (2009). Neuronal encoding of human kinematic invariants during action observation. *Cerebral Cortex, 20*(7), 1647–1655.

Caspers, S., Zilles, K., Laird, A. R., & Eickhoff, S. B. (2010). ALE meta-analysis of action observation and imitation in the human brain. *NeuroImage, 50*(3), 1148–1167.

Christensen, J. F., Gomila, A., Gaigg, S. B., Sivarajah, N., & Calvo-Merino, B. (2016). Dance expertise modulates behavioral and psychophysiological responses to affective body movement. *Journal of Experimental Psychology: Human Perception and Performance, 42*(8), 1139–1147.

Costantini, M., Galati, G., Ferretti, A., Caulo, M., Tartaro, A., Romani, G. L., & Aglioti, S. M. (2005). Neural systems underlying observation of humanly impossible movements: An fMRI study. *Cerebral Cortex, 15*(11), 1761–1767.

Cross, E. S. (2015). Beautiful embodiment: The shaping of aesthetic preferences by personal experience. In J. P. Huston, M. Nadal, F. Mora, L. F. Agnati, & C. J. Cela-Conde (Eds.), *Art, aesthetics, and the brain* (pp. 189–208). Oxford, England: Oxford University Press.

Cross, E. S., Hamilton, A. F., & Grafton, S. T. (2006). Building a motor simulation de novo: Observation of dance by dancers. *NeuroImage, 31,* 1257–1267.

Cross, E. S., Kirsch, L., Ticini, L. F., & Schutz-Bosbach, S. (2011). The impact of aesthetic evaluation and physical ability on dance perception. *Frontiers in Human Neuroscience, 5,* 102.

Cross, E. S., Kraemer, D. J., Hamilton, A. F., Kelley, W. M., & Grafton, S. T. (2009). Sensitivity of the action observation network to physical and observational learning. *Cerebral Cortex*, *19*(2), 315–326.

Cross, E. S., Liepelt, R., de C. Hamilton, A. F., Parkinson, J., Ramsey, R., Stadler, W., & Prinz, W. (2012). Robotic movement preferentially engages the action observation network. *Human Brain Mapping*, *33*(9), 2238–2254.

Darda, K. M. & Cross, E. S. (in press). A unifying model of visual art appreciation: The role of expertise and culture. Scientific Reports.

Di Dio, C., Canessa, N., Cappa, S. F., & Rizzolatti, G. (2011). Specificity of esthetic experience for artworks: An fMRI study. *Frontiers in Human Neuroscience*, *5*, 139.

Di Pellegrino, G., Fadiga, L., Fogassi, L., Gallese, V., & Rizzolatti, G. (1992). Understanding motor events: A neurophysiological study. *Experimental Brain Research*, *91*(1), 176–180.

Freedberg, D., & Gallese, V. (2007). Motion, emotion and empathy in esthetic experience. *Trends in Cognitive Sciences*, *11*(5), 197–203.

Gallese, V. (2017). Visions of the body. Embodied simulation and aesthetics experience. *Aisthesis*, *1*(1), 41–50.

Gallese, V., Fadiga, L., Fogassi, L., & Rizzolatti, G. (1996). Action recognition in the premotor cortex. *Brain*, *119*(2), 593–609.

Gallese, V., & Goldman, A. (1998). Mirror neurons and the simulation theory of mindreading. *Trends in Cognitive Sciences*, *2*, 493–501.

Gardner, T., Goulden, N., & Cross, E. S. (2015). Dynamic modulation of the action observation network by movement familiarity. *Journal of Neuroscience*, *35*(4), 1561–1572.

Giacosa, C., Karpati, F. J., Foster, N. E., Penhune, V. B., & Hyde, K. L. (2016). Dance and music training have different effects on white matter diffusivity in sensorimotor pathways. *NeuroImage*, *135*, 273–286.

Grafton, S. T. (2009). Embodied cognition and the simulation of action to understand others. *Annals of the New York Academy of Sciences*, *1156*, 97–117.

Grafton, S. T., & Hamilton, A. F. de C. (2007). Evidence for a distributed hierarchy of action representation in the brain. *Human Movement Science*, *26*(4), 590–616.

Hayes, A. E., Paul, M. A., Beuger, B., & Tipper, S. P. (2008). Self produced and observed actions influence emotion: The roles of action fluency and eye gaze. *Psychological Research*, *72*(4), 461–472.

Heberlein, A. S., Adolphs, R., Tranel, D., and Damasio, H. (2004). Cortical regions for judgments of emotions and personality traits from point-light walkers. *Journal of Cognitive Neuroscience*, *16*, 1143–1158.

Iacoboni, M. (2009). Imitation, empathy, and mirror neurons. *Annual Review of Psychology*, *60*, 653–670.

Karpati, F. J., Giacosa, C., Foster, N. E., Penhune, V. B., & Hyde, K. L. (2017). Dance and music share gray matter structural correlates. *Brain Research*, *1657*, 62–73.

Kilner, J. M., Friston, K. J., & Frith, C. D. (2007). Predictive coding: An account of the mirror neuron system. *Cognitive Processing*, *8*(3), 159–166.

Kirsch, L.P., & Cross, E.S. (2015). Additive routes to action learning: Layering experience shapes engagement of the action observation network. *Cerebral Cortex*, *25*(12), 4799–4811.

Kirsch, L. P., & Cross, E. S. (2018). The influence of sensorimotor experience on the aesthetic evaluation of dance across the life span. *Arts and the Brain: Psychology and Physiology beyond Pleasure*, *237*, 291–316.

Kirsch, L. P., Dawson, K., & Cross, E. S. (2015). Dance experience sculpts aesthetic perception and related brain circuits. *Annals of the New York Academy of Sciences*, *1337*, 130–139.

Kirsch, L. P., Drommelschmidt, K. A., & Cross, E. S. (2013). The impact of sensorimotor experience on affective evaluation of dance. *Frontiers in Human Neuroscience*, *7*(521).

Kirsch, L. P., Snagg, A., Heerey, E., & Cross, E. S. (2016). The impact of experience on affective responses during action observation. *PLoS ONE*, *11*(5), e0154681.

Kirsch, L. P., Urgesi, C., & Cross, E. S. (2016). Shaping and reshaping the aesthetic brain: Emerging perspectives on the neurobiology of embodied aesthetics. *Neuroscience and Biobehavioral Reviews*, *62*, 56–68.

Krishna, A. (2012). An integrative review of sensory marketing: Engaging the senses to affect perception, judgment and behavior. *Journal of Consumer Psychology*, *22*, 332–351.

Lakens, D., Adolfi, F. G., Albers, C. J., Anvari, F., Apps, M. A. J., Argamon, S. E., ... Zwaan, R. A. (2018). Justify your alpha. *Nature Human Behaviour*, *2*(3), 168–171.

Molenberghs, P., Cunnington, R., & Mattingley, J. B. (2012). Brain regions with mirror properties: A meta-analysis of 125 human fMRI studies. *Neuroscience & Biobehavioral Reviews*, *36*(1), 341–349.

Munafo, M. R., Nosek, B. A., Bishop, D. V. M., Button, K. S., Chambers, C. D., du Sert, N. P., ... Ioannidis, J. P. A. (2017). A manifesto for reproducible science. *Nature Human Behaviour*, *1*, 0021.

Orgs, G., Dombrowski, J.-H., Heil, M., & Jansen-Osmann, P. (2008). Expertise in dance modulates alpha/beta event-related desynchronization during action observation. *European Journal of Neuroscience*, *27*, 3380–3384.

Orlandi, A., Cross, E. S., & Orgs, G. (2020). Timing is everything: Dance aesthetics depend on the complexity of movement kinematics. *Cognition*, *205*, 104446. https://doi.org/10.1016/j.cognition.2020.104446

Orlandi, A., D'Incà, S., & Proverbio, A. M. (2020). Muscular effort coding in action representation in ballet dancers and controls: Electrophysiological evidence. *Brain Research*, *1733*, 146712.

Orlandi, A., & Proverbio, A. M. (2019). Bilateral engagement of the occipito-temporal cortex in response to dance kinematics in experts. *Scientific Reports*, *9*(1), 1000.

Orlandi, A., Zani, A., & Proverbio, A. M. (2017). Dance expertise modulates visual sensitivity to complex biological movements. *Neuropsychologia*, *104*, 168–181.

Pau, S., Jahn, G., Sakreida, K., Domin, M., & Lotze, M. (2013). Encoding and recall of finger sequences in experienced pianists compared with musically naive controls: A combined behavioral and functional imaging study. *NeuroImage*, *64*, 379–387.

Peelen, M.V., & Downing, P.E. (2007). The neural basis of visual body perception. *Nature Reviews Neuroscience*, *8*(8), 636–648.

Proverbio, A. M., Adorni, R., & D'Aniello, G. E. (2011). 250 ms to code for action affordance during observation of manipulable objects. *Neuropsychologia*, *49*(9), 2711–2717.

Proverbio, A. M., Gabaro, V., Orlandi, A., & Zani, A. (2015). Semantic brain areas are involved in gesture comprehension: An electrical neuroimaging study. *Brain and Language*, *147*, 30–40.

Rizzolatti, G., Fadiga, L., Gallese, V., & Fogassi, L. (1996). Premotor cortex and the recognition of motor actions. *Cognitive Brain Research*, *3*(2), 131–141.

Rizzolatti, G., Fogassi, L., & Gallese, V. (2001). Neurophysiological mechanisms underlying the understanding and imitation of action. *Nature Reviews Neuroscience*, *2*(9), 661.

Rizzolatti, G., & Sinigaglia, C. (2016). The mirror mechanism: A basic principle of brain function. *Nature Reviews Neuroscience*, *17*(12), 757–765.

Sbriscia-Fioretti, B., Berchio, C., Freedberg, D., Gallese, V., & Umiltà, M. A. (2013). ERP modulation during observation of abstract paintings by Franz Kline. *PLoS ONE, 8*(10), e75241.

Smith, D. M. (2016). Neurophysiology of action anticipation in athletes: A systematic review. *Neuroscience & Biobehavioral Reviews, 60*, 115–120.

Smith, R. A., & Cross, E. S. (2022). The McNorm library: creating and validating a new library of emotionally expressive whole body dance movements. *Psychological research*, 1–25. Advance online publication. https://doi.org/10.1007/s00426-022-01669-9

Topolinski, S. (2010). Moving the eye of the beholder: Motor components in vision determine aesthetic preference. *Psychological Science, 21*(9), 1220–1224.

Umiltà, M. A., Berchio, C., Sestito, M., Freedberg, D., & Gallese, V. (2012). Abstract art and cortical motor activation: An EEG study. *Frontiers in Human Neuroscience, 6*, 311.

Vicary, S., Sperling, M., von Zimmermann, J., Richardson, D. C., & Orgs, G. (2017). Joint action aesthetics. *PLoS ONE, 12*(7), e0180101. doi:10.1371/journal.pone.0180101

von Zimmermann, J., Vicary, S., Sperling, M., Orgs, G., & Richardson, D. C. (2018). The Choreography of Group Affiliation. *Topics in Cognitive Science, 10*(1), 80–94.

Wilson, M. (2002). Six views of embodied cognition. *Psychonomic Bulletin & Review, 9*(4), 625–636.

Zajonc, R. B. (1968). Attitudinal effects of mere exposure. *Journal of Personality and Social Psychology, 9*(2, pt. 2), 1–27.

CHAPTER 27

....

AESTHETICS OF DANCE

....

BEATRIZ CALVO-MERINO

INTRODUCTION

....

DANCE is one of the latest art forms that has captured the attention of empirical aesthetics. Since Fechner's (1876) work, research on empirical aesthetics has been concerned mainly with understanding the affective, perceptual, and cognitive mechanisms that participate in the appreciation of painting, music, and architecture. Interest in other art domains, such as dance, has developed more prominently at the beginning of the 21st century. The past two decades have witnessed a steady growth of publications focusing on the relationship between the dance and the observer, and on revealing the interplay among the subjective, the cognitive, and the neural mechanisms in aesthetic appreciation of this performing art.

The concept of aesthetics has been explained on several occasions in this volume. This chapter focuses initially on the concept of dance, and later, on the bond between dance and aesthetics. The answer to the question "what is dance?" may vary if explained from an artistic context or from a more scientific or experimental perspective. The general definition provided by *Encyclopedia Britannica* (www.britannica.com) explains dance as an art form that generally involves body movements, which are usually rhythmic and performed to music, used as a form of expression, social interaction, or presented in a spiritual or performance setting. From here, we can infer multiple elements that play a significant role in dance (for a detailed description of multiple dance components, see Christensen & Calvo-Merino, 2013). Most of us will agree that core elements of dance include the body (i.e., the performing dancer) and the movement (i.e., the dancer's movements). However, this alone cannot distinguish dance from everyday action. Music and rhythm often accompany the visual display, but they are not intrinsic or necessary features of dance. Music is another extraordinarily complex art form and has been discussed in this volume (see Brattico, this volume). A third essential component included in this definition helps bring dance to a dimension beyond mundane actions (Kreitler & Kreitler, 1972), and it refers to the idea of the use of body movement to enhance the limits of bodily expressions (Laban, 1950). Together, these three components form a fascinating type of art ready to evoke an aesthetic experience in the observer, and from which an experimental perspective can be measured at the subjective, cognitive, neural, and physiological levels.

Beyond this schematic and simple conceptualization of dance, there are complex dance universals that have been described in different cultures. These include similar dance movements and dance positions across dance styles with different geographical or cultural origins, comparable patterns in the dance structure and physical properties of the dance (i.e., symmetry, synchronization, lines, and solos), or the use of ornamentation (i.e., tutus, fans, ankle bells, specific types of shoes—tap shoes, point shoes, flamenco shoes, etc.) (Christensen & Calvo-Merino, 2013). This idea of dance universals may be related to its counterpart in visual perception. Specifically, research in visual perception has shown the existence of universal visual preferences; for example, general preference for curved vs. sharp objects (Bar & Neta, 2006), or preference for cardinal vs. oblique lines (Latto, Brain, & Kelly, 2000; Palumbo & Bertamini, 2016). These preferences are normally explained in terms of evolutionary advantages. In the dance domain, it is been shown that smooth and fluent dance movements are preferred over awkward ones (Miura et al., 2010). While the same level of visual research has not been done on dance aesthetics as compared with objects/space aesthetics, some authors suggest an underlying universal aesthetic preference for visual features also in dance (Hagendoorn, 2005).

These ideas have driven research on aesthetics of dance toward the understanding not only of dance as a whole, but also of the interplay of its different elements. Therefore, before understanding visual preference for dance, we need to revise how the individual features of dance are processed. The following section aims to provide a basic description of the universal processing underlying what we have called the *dance triad*: the body, the movement, and the expression (see Figure 27.1). It dissects how each of these dance components is perceived in the human brain and associated cognitive systems, in order to be able to tell the dancer from the dance and understand how each of those components contributes to the final aesthetic percept responsible for our aesthetic experience.

THE DANCE TRIAD: BODY, MOVEMENT AND EXPRESSION

The body

Dance emerges from the dynamics of the body. We can understand the dancer's body as a tool that expresses movement. Basic research in cognitive neuroscience has described the neural processes that occur in the brain when a body is perceived by an observer.

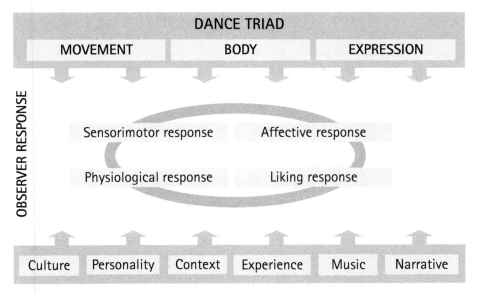

FIGURE 27.1. Schema of the dance triad.
Top: The three basic elements of dance influence how an observer responds. Middle: Types of an observer's response to the observation of dance. Bottom: Factors that may modulate the observer's response to the perception of dance.

Bodies are highly intertwined with movements, and several classical movement areas do engage in body perception, mostly if the bodies carry some movement information, as can be the case if a still image were taken from a movement sequence. Among these regions, we can find complex visual motion areas (Kourtzi & Kanwisher, 2000; Senior et al., 2000) and motor regions (Urgesi, Moro, Candidi, & Aglioti, 2006). Besides these movement-sensitive areas, there are at least two brain regions particularly tuned to the perception of bodies. These are the extrastriate body area (EBA) in the extrastriate cortex (Downing, Jiang, Shuman, & Kanwisher, 2001), and the fusiform body area (FBA), located in the fusiform gyrus (Peelen & Downing, 2005). The EBA responds to the observation of human bodies or body parts (e.g., arms, legs, etc.), as well as to the observation of bodies depicted in photographs, drawings, or movies (Peelen & Downing, 2005). The FBA is anatomically very close to the classical neural regions selective for faces, the face fusiform area (FFA) (Kanwisher, McDermott, & Chun, 1997), and responds to the observation of whole bodies and body parts. The type of processing carried out in each of these body areas is complementary, while the EBA is highly engaged with simple presentation of bodies and body parts, the FBA area seems to be driven by processing that requires the analysis of complex body representations (rather than just the perception of a body part) (Taylor et al., 2007). From a cognitive perspective, these two different processes fit well with an analytical and configural style of processing, respectively. Regions like the EBA may trigger an analytical perception, paying more attention to the morphology of the body rather than its configuration.

On the contrary, the region FBA will represent bodies in a more holistic or configural manner, in a similar way to that in which the FFA processes configural faces. Configural processing has been interpreted as a piece of efficient and fluent machinery for understanding external events developed through visual exposure over our evolutionary history. Other highly familiar stimuli, like faces, tend also to be processed in a configural manner (Reed et al., 2003; Valentine, 1988).

The movement

Movement is one of the very exclusive means that humans use to interact with the environment. While the importance of human movement for social interactions is indisputable, it has been only toward the end of the 20th century when cognitive neuroscience revealed parts of the fine machinery that the brain has developed to perceive, encode, understand, and evaluate observed movements. Very briefly, as this has been addressed elsewhere in this volume, each learned movement is internally represented in our own neural and cognitive systems in the form of a motor representation (Jeannerod, 1997). Motor representations (also known as action representations) are central in movement execution, but importantly to the purpose of this chapter, motor representations play a crucial role in action observation. In the early 1990s, the group led by Giacomo Rizzolatti in Parma University in Italy described a group of neurons in the ventral premotor cortex of the nonhuman primate that behaved in a similar fashion when the monkey was making a movement, and when the animal was only observing the experimenter performing the same movement (di Pellegrino, Fadiga, Fogassi, Gallese, & Rizzolatti, 1992; Rizzolatti et al., 1996). These results were followed up in additional experiments including the recording of cells in parietal cortex regions (Gallese et al., 1996). Overall the Parma group proposed the existence of neurons that reflect, like a mirror, the observed action to the one that the observer has in their motor repertoire (for a review, see Rizzolatti & Craighero, 2004). Neuroimaging studies using functional magnetic resonance imaging (fMRI) have reported a set of regions in the human brain that respond in a similar fashion when we perform or observe a movement. This mechanism has been coined the *mirror neuron system* (or action observation network—for a more extensive version), and fits with classical simulation theories when we reactivate internally the observed movement (Calvo-Merino et al., 2005, 2006). This network has been reported to participate in movement imitation, action understanding, and emotion recognition in movements, among other processes (Rizzolatti & Craighero, 2004). The main idea relevant for aesthetics of dance is that observing a movement elicits a type of brain activation that engages your own motor representations. This brings into aesthetics of dance an additional layer of brain regions and mental representations that participate when observing a dance movement, beyond the classical visual perception areas (Calvo-Merino et al., 2015).

The expression

The ability to express through movement is a key element in dance. When performed on the stage, movements often carry a communicative intention, which generally has a strong emotional component. Processing that additional emotional layer in the movement is an integral component of dance appreciation. A large number of studies have focused on how emotional information is extracted from faces (Adolphs, 2002; Bastiaansen, Thioux, & Keysers, 2009; Little, Jones, & Debruine, 2011; Sel, Forster, & Calvo-Merino, 2014), static bodies (de Gelder, 2009; Pichon, de Gelder, & Grèzes, 2008), and movement (Atkinson, Vuong, & Smithson, 2012; Pollick, Lestou, Ryuand, & Cho, 2002). The main message from these studies is that beyond classical visual perception areas related to face, body, or movement processing, understanding the emotions of others engages brain regions normally involved in experiencing the same emotion ourselves (Bastiaansen, Thioux, & Keysers, 2009; Keysers, Kaas, & Gazzola, 2010; Wicker et al., 2003). For example, the same area in the insula is activated when experiencing disgust and when seeing someone else being disgusted (Wicker et al., 2003). Another example, in the body perception domain, shows that the observation of whole-body gestures with emotional information elicits activity in classical body areas (EBA) and also emotion and reward-related regions such as the ventral striatum (Peelen & Downing, 2007). The accumulation of evidence for this idea suggests an emotion perception process that internally allows the observer to re-experience the observed emotion. These results fit nicely to a framework bridging sensorimotor simulation theories, like the ones proposed for movement perception in the previous section, and an embodied emotion framework (Niedenthal, 2007). Moreover, the embodied response is multisensory. For example, watching a musician interpreting a piece of music (in silence—without sounds) evokes activation in emotion regions such as the insula, similar to the ones that are found when listening to the music (Petrini, Crabbe, Sheridan, & Pollick, 2011).

While expressions of emotion in dance may be displayed in different forms, research has shown that observers are able to recognize the desired portrayed emotion in dance movements (Camurri, Lagerlof, & Volpe, 2003; Christensen et al., 2016; Hejmadi, Davidson, & Rozin, 2000; van Meel, Verburgh, & de Meijer, 1993). The levels of this emotional recognition seem to be enhanced when dance is accompanied by congruent music (Christensen et al., 2014).

At the neural level, Grosbras, Tan, and Pollick (2012) have shown that applying low-frequency repetitive magnetic stimulation to the posterior cortices prior to observing a dance performance enhances the emotional values observers give to the dance, as compared with those same ratings occurring in control conditions. In a similar fashion, recent work looking into classical signatures of motor resonance using electroencephalography (i.e., mu dyssynchronization during action observation) has shown a differential sensorimotor response when watching dance videos depicting movements with positive (happy) and negative (sad) valence (Corradi et al., 2020). Overall, these studies highlight the importance of an internal mechanism in the observer that resonates with the observed dance expressions, both at an emotional and a sensorimotor level.

Aesthetics of dance

The end of the 20th century witnessed pioneering work on neuroaesthetics, when cognitive scientists, neurobiologists, and curious minds from diverse disciplines including the arts, philosophy, and history started a search to understand how beauty is processed in the brain and to describe the neural and cognitive mechanisms responsible for aesthetic experiences. Most of the earlier work focused on visual aesthetics such as paintings (Zeki, 1999; Zeki & Lamb, 1994) or faces (Chatterjee et al., 2009). Around that time, since the discovery of a mirror neuron mechanism for observing others in nonhuman primates and humans, many studies in cognitive science focused on understanding how the human brain process others' actions, movements, bodies, and their intentions (such as communication, expression, and emotion). Among these earlier questions, one that was particularly important was to clarify the nature of the internal neural simulation during action observation. Calvo-Merino and colleagues (2005, 2006) designed a series of studies that provided evidence to support the claim (already proposed in research with primates) that when we observe an action we activate our neural representation of the motor action we are observing. The essence of these studies relies on the comparison of brain activity in observers with different types of acquired motor skills while observing different types of actions (that may be familiar or nonfamiliar to them). For this purpose, the authors recorded brain activity of ballet dancers while watching familiar ballet movements and unfamiliar movements (capoeira moves) inside the brain scanner. Capoeira dancers' brain activity was also recorded observing familiar capoeira moves and unfamiliar ballet movements. Brain responses in mirror neuron areas in premotor and parietal cortices responsible for representing actions were stronger during the observation of familiar movements, suggesting that knowing the observed movements evokes a stronger motor representation in the observer.

An interesting collateral effect of the series of studies performed by Calvo-Merino and her colleagues was starting a dialogue between neuroscience and dance. Calvo-Merino's study was the first on playing dance videos inside the scanner, and to scan the brain activity of professional dancers. Other studies followed, using a variety of paradigms such as training (e.g., Cross, Hamilton, & Grafton, 2006; Cross et al., 2011) and methodologies such as electroencephalography (e.g., Orgs, Dombrowski, Heil, & Jansen-Osmann, 2008). While the studies mentioned above did not directly aim to answer questions related to aesthetics, they highlighted the fascinating neural effects of being an expert dancer and opened a path for science and dance collaborations. These led to a series of studies that aimed to answer some of the following questions: How do we see movements we like? Do we perceive them differently than movements we like less? What do we like in a movement? Do I need to understand the content of the dance (e.g., its emotion, its narrative) to enjoy it? Is being an expert dancer changing the way

I feel dance? In the section below, I will aim to provide preliminary answers to some of these questions.

Implicit aesthetic appreciation of dance

"Towards a sensorimotor approach of performing arts" was the title of the first study published in 2008 that described the neural correlates of implicit aesthetic appreciation of dance (Calvo-Merino, Glaser, Jola, & Haggard, 2008). The experiment was divided into two sessions. In the first session, brain activity of observers without dance experience was recorded while they laid in the scanner and observed a variety of dance movements from different dance disciplines (ballet and capoeira), representing a variety of kinematic properties such as speed (fast or slow) or amount and direction of displacement (vertical or horizontal). During this first session, there was no reference to the quality or aesthetic properties of the dance movements. In a second session outside the scanner, observers watched the movements again, and rated them according to the five classical Berlyne (1974) dimensions: liking–disliking, simple–complex, interesting–dull, tense–relaxed, weak–powerful. Researchers looked at what brain areas were sensitive to any of these five dimensions. Only ratings in one of these dimensions (liking–disliking) showed differential patterns of brain activity. Specifically, the results showed stronger activation in the premotor cortex in the right hemisphere and visual cortices (in the medial region—precuneus) when observers watched dance movements that had higher liking ratings as compared with those with lower liking ratings. These findings suggest an automatic stronger sensorimotor response when we observe dance we like, and links for the first-time classical areas related to movement perception from the mirror neuron network to other levels of human cognition such as aesthetic appreciation (Calvo-Merino et al., 2008).

Explicit aesthetic appreciation of dance

How we make aesthetic judgments on dance movements is a question that has been asked (and partially answered) in cognitive neuroscience. Cross and her collaborators (2011) performed a study where participants watched dance videos inside the scanner while they rated how much they liked each dance movement. Results showed a set of brain areas that positively correlated with the intensity of the liking (brain areas in which responses increased when seeing movements that were liked more, and brain areas in which responses decreased when seeing movements that were liked less). Among these areas, Cross and her collaborators report those included in the body and movement perception (as described in the above section), namely the right parietal cortex (inferior parietal lobe, IPL) and occipitotemporal cortices (namely, motion area V5, MT, and body regions in the inferior temporal gyrus, ITG, and the middle temporal gyrus, MTG) (for a more detailed description, see the chapter by Cross and Orlandi in this volume; Calvo-Merino, 2015). In order to investigate if the role of sensorimotor regions is just a collateral effect of another type of processing, Calvo-Merino et al. (2010) performed a study employing transcranial magnetic stimulation (TMS). By applying TMS pulses over the scalp of a participant performing a task, we can enhance or disrupt the ongoing activity in that particular region, and modulate the performance on the ongoing task. During the aesthetic rating of a series of dance postures (depicted with a body), Calvo-Merino and colleagues applied repetitive TMS (rTMS) over two areas classically involved in sensorimotor processing of the body: the premotor cortex and EBA. The results showed that, in comparison with the pattern of aesthetic preference observed for each participant in a rating session without TMS stimulation, rTMS over the EBA blunted aesthetic judgments of body postures relative to the application of rTMS over the premotor cortex. These effects were found only when rating aesthetically body postures, but not when rating control stimuli like scrambled bodies. The main conclusions of these studies are in line with the proposed sensorimotor framework for dance aesthetics, as they provide classic visual perception and sensorimotor areas that normally were just known for participating in the observation of bodies and actions with a new cognitive role in higher human cognition, such as aesthetic appreciation (Calvo-Merino, 2015; Cross & Calvo-Merino, 2016).

Embodied aesthetics of dance

Theories of embodied cognition suggest that our perception is shaped by aspects of the entire body (Freedberg & Gallese, 2007). Within this framework, the term "embodied perception" has been used to highlight the internal re-enactment at the cognitive, emotional, and physiological levels of the observed action or emotion (Niedenthal, 2007). And in the aesthetic context, the term "embodied aesthetics" suggests that when observing an artwork (a painting, for example), we embody the motor acts that the artist has used to perform that painting (Freedberg & Gallese, 2007; Ticini, Urgesi, & Calvo-Merino, 2015; Umilta et al., 2012). The above-mentioned studies on implicit and explicit aesthetics of dance provide evidence to consider a very similar framework on aesthetic of dance. These studies show that perception of dance movements activates a set of regions that involve the premotor cortex and parietal cortex, and areas related to body processing (Calvo-Merino et al., 2008; Cross et al., 2011). These regions have two functions in common: they are activated during action observation and action execution. Therefore, the evidence supports the idea of an embodied aesthetic of dance (Ticini et al., 2015). A recent study provides direct evidence for the embodied aesthetic framework by measuring the activity in another brain area that holds a concrete representation of the human body, the primary somatosensory cortex (SCx). By using somatosensory evoked potentials (SEPs, by applying a small tap to the body), researchers measured direct activity over the SCx during the visual aesthetic judgment of dance body postures. The data showed that during aesthetic judgment there is a modulation of the activity over the SCx (interestingly, at the level of the somatosensory representation), but not during a control nonaesthetic visual task over the same dance body stimuli (Calvo-Merino, 2019).

Overall the above-mentioned studies and other work that provide data in the same direction (Fink, Graif, & Neubauer, 2009; Jang & Pollick, 2011; Orgs et al., 2008) suggest that when observing a dance movement, the internal motor simulation experienced by the observer (we could also call it internal embodiment) plays a crucial role in the process that leads to the final aesthetic judgment or aesthetic experience.

What Else Matters in Dance Aesthetics: The Observer

The long-term dance training that is necessary to become a professional dancer has been associated with changes in brain structure, especially in sensorimotor regions (Hänggi, Koeneke, Bezzola, & Jäncke, 2010). Dance expertise facilitates sensorimotor activations when watching familiar movements (Calvo-Merino et al., 2005, 2006; Cross et al., 2006). It has also been reported that dance expertise enhances visual sensitivity (Calvo-Merino, Ehrenberg, Leung, & Haggard, 2010). For example, the ability to discriminate between two very similar dance movements is higher if the observer knows the observed movements (an expert ballet dancer watching ballet movements), as opposed to a nondancer who is not familiar with the movements (see Bläsing et al., 2012 for a full review of how dance expertise influences other cognitive functions).

Art expertise also facilitates the processing of emotional information. Artists are experts in expressing or portraying different emotional expressions. It is being proposed that such individuals (i.e., artist, who in theory are experts in conveying emotions) have an enhanced affective response compared with controls. For example, musicians recognize better vocal expressions of emotions, as compared with nonmusicians (Lima & Castro, 2011). Actors show more empathy than nonactors (Goldstein, 2009; Goldstein & Winner, 2012). In the dance domain, Petrides and colleagues have shown that greater emotional intelligence is associated with the ballet dance ability (Petrides, Niven, & Mouskounti, 2006). Finally, in relation to aesthetics of dance, dance experience with the observed movements modulates the aesthetic neural response when observing these familiar movements (Kirsch, Drommelschmidt, & Cross, 2013; Kirsch, Dawson, & Cross, 2015).

Dance expertise goes beyond neural and behavioral modulations on perception. Christensen et al. (2016) have shown that dance expertise modulates the autonomic response related to recognizing dance expressions. Observers with experience in performing those dance movements had a differential physiological response while watching them (and rating them according to their emotion) than did observers without any experience in performing or watching dance. A second interesting bit of data from this study is that as a control stimuli, the experimenters presented the same sets of videos, only played backward. Both the controls and the expert group were able to categorize the videos according to their positive and negative valence (regarding the manner of the presentations). However, dance experts were also sensitive to this manipulation at the autonomic level (measured via galvanic skin response during observation). This suggests that affective expertise can influence internal physiological responses by a direct correspondence between the observer's motor expertise and its associated affective response and the kinematic properties of the observed movement (Christensen et al., 2016). These data fit well with classical theories of emotion proposing according to which autonomic expressions of emotion influence perceived emotions (James, 1894; Niedenthal, 2007). Observer experience is certainly an influential factor in the ongoing process associated with the aesthetic appreciation of dance. The interplay between the parallel modulations at the behavioral, neurological, and physiological levels is certainly at the core of the aesthetic experience in dance perception.

The above studies highlight the role of motor or affective experts in enhancing affective perfection. But performance theaters are packed with observers that have no motor or affective experience with dance in particular, or maybe not even with the arts in general. However, there are several other factors that influence our aesthetic preferences. For example, individual personality traits play an important role in how we experience the world and our preferences (Jola, Pollick, & Calvo-Merino, 2012). Another factor that can influence the aesthetic experience is the level of effort perceived by the observer in the dance. For example, nondancer participants rated the level of enjoyment of a series of dance videos, and they were also asked to rate their own ability to reproduce each of those dance moves. The authors found a negative correlation between the enjoyment and the ability levels, suggesting that aesthetic appeal in dance may be related to the capability to reproduce the observed dance actions (Kirsch et al., 2016). This has been framed as the classical "Cirque du Soleil" effect: artworks perceived as difficult to make are preferred to artworks that appear easy to make.

How to Study the Aesthetics of Dance Empirically? Challenges, Goals, and Suggestions

Investigating complex phenomena is a challenge for experimental science. It requires one to understand the individual pieces, and at the same time how they play at the system level. We have decomposed individual elements of dance, described how they are processed, and we have gained a little knowledge about a series of mechanisms that contribute to the final aesthetic percept. But this road has not arrived at an end yet. On the contrary, we are only starting the journey. Beyond earlier work on basic processing of individual components of dance (i.e., body, movement), recent studies have worked with more ecological types of stimuli. In the past five years, a series of dance libraries have been published that will allow a series of studies using normed stimuli (Christensen, Nadal, & Cela-Conde, 2014; Christensen, Lambrechts, & Tsakiris, 2018). Another aspect to consider is the temporal context. Daprati, Iosa, and Haggard (2009) provide a beautiful example of how dance preference changes, and how individual artists' creativity and their wider environmental context are in constant interaction with the audience preferences.

Finally, we would like to call for experimentation on dance aesthetics outside of the laboratory. Knowledge from ecological research in dance needs to be combined with existing knowledge from the laboratory, providing space for dialogue and flexibility in the interpretation of new venues for understanding the delightful world of the aesthetics of dance. Among these studies and toward this end, it is important to highlight those that aimed to measure brain activity in the dance theater (Jola & Grosbras, 2013; Jola et al., 2012), those combining more than one dance element, for example including dance and music (Christensen, Gaigg, Gomila, Oke, & Calvo-Merino, 2014), or those including multiple agents (i.e., more than one performer) (Vicary, Sperling, von Zimmermann, Richardson, & Orgs, 2017).

REFERENCES

Adolphs, R. (2002). Recognizing emotion from facial expressions: Psychological and neurological mechanisms. *Behavioral and Cognitive Neuroscience Reviews, 1*, 21–62.

Atkinson, A. P., Vuong, Q. C., & Smithson, H. E. (2012). Modulation of the face- and body-selective visual regions by the motion and emotion of point-light face and body stimuli. *NeuroImage, 59*, 1700–1712.

Bar, M., & Neta, M. (2006). Humans prefer curved visual objects. *Psychological Science, 17*, 645–648.

Bastiaansen, J. A., Thioux, M., & Keysers, C. (2009). Evidence for mirror systems in emotions. *Philosophical Transactions of the Royal Society of London, Series B: Biological Sciences, 364*, 2391–2404.

Berlyne, D. E. (1974). *Studies in the new experimental aesthetics: Steps toward an objective psychology of aesthetic appreciation.* Washington, DC: Hemisphere Publishing Corporation.

Bläsing, B., Calvo-Merino, B., Cross, E. S., Jola, C., Honisch, J., & Stevens, C. J. (2012). Neurocognitive control in dance perception and performance. *Acta Psychologica, 139*, 300–308.

Calvo-Merino, B. (2015). Sensorimotor aesthetics: Neural correlates of aesthetic perception of dance. In M. Nadal, J. P. Huston, L. Agnati, F. Mora, & C. José Cela-Conde (Eds.), *Art, aesthetics, and the brain* (pp. 209–222). New York: Oxford University Press.

Calvo-Merino, B. (2019). An embodied approach to understanding visual aesthetics. *Perception, 48*, 14.

Calvo-Merino, B., Glaser, D.E., Grèzes, J., Passingham, R. E., & Haggard, P. (2005). Action observation and acquired motor skills: An fMRI study with expert dancers. *Cerebral Cortex, 15*, 1243–1249.

Calvo-Merino, B., Grèzes, J., Glaser, D.E., Passingham, R. E., & Haggard, P. (2006). Seeing or doing? Influence of visual and motor familiarity in action observation. *Current Biology*, *16*, 2277.

Calvo-Merino, B., Jola, C., Glaser, & Haggard, P. (2008). Towards a sensorimotor aesthetics of performing art. *Consciousness and Cognition*, *17*, 911–922.

Calvo-Merino, B., Urgesi, C., Orgs, G., Aglioti, S. M., & Haggard, P. (2010). Extrastriate body area underlies aesthetic evaluation of body stimuli. *Experimental Brain Research*, *74*, 400–406.

Camurri, A., Lagerlof, I., & Volpe, G. (2003). Recognizing emotion from dance movement: Comparison of spectator recognition and automated techniques. *International Journal of Human–Computer Studies*, *59*, 213–225.

Chatterjee, A., Thomas, A., Smith, S. E., & Aguirre, G. K. (2009). The neural response to facial attractiveness. *Neuropsychology*, *23*, 135–143.

Christensen, J. F., & Calvo-Merino, B. (2013). Dance as a subject for empirical aesthetics. *Psychology of Aesthetics, Creativity, and the Arts*, *7*, 76–88.

Christensen, J. F., Gaigg, S. B., Gomila, A., Oke, P., & Calvo-Merino, B. (2014). Enhancing emotional experiences to dance through music: The role of valence and arousal in the cross-modal bias. *Frontiers in Human Neuroscience*, *8*, Article 757.

Christensen, J. F., Gomila, A, Gaigg, S, B., Sivarajah, N., & Calvo-Merino, B. (2016). Dance expertise modulates behavioral and psychophysiological responses to affective body movement. *Journal of Experimental Psychology: Human Perception and Performance*, *42*, 1139–1147.

Christensen, J. F., Lambrechts, A., & Tsakiris M., (2018). The Warburg dance movement library—The WADAMO Library: A validation study. *Perception*, *48*, 26–57.

Christensen, J. F., Nadal, M., & Cela-Conde, C. J. (2014). A norming study and library of 203 dance movements. *Perception*, *43*, 178–206.

Corradi, C., Almansa, J., Sabel, E., Silas, J., Jones, A., & Calvo-Merino, B. (2020). Perception of dance movements modulates sensorimotor activity: Mu suppression as an index for embodied emotions. *Cognitive Neuroscience Society Annual Meeting*. Virtually May 2–5, 2020.

Cross, E. S., & Calvo-Merino, B. (2016). The impact of action expertise on shared representations. In S. Sukhvinder, S. S. Obhi, & E. S. Cross (Eds.) *Shared Representations: Sensorimotor Foundations of Social Life* (pp. 541–564). Cambridge: Cambridge University Press.

Cross, E. S., Hamilton, A. F., & Grafton, S. T. (2006). Building a motor simulation de novo: Observation of dance by dancers. *NeuroImage*, *31*, 1257–1267.

Cross, E. S., Kirsch, L., Ticini, L. F., & Schütz-Bosbach, S. (2011). The impact of aesthetic evaluation and physical ability on dance perception. *Frontiers in Human Neuroscience*, *5*, 102.

Daprati, E., Iosa, M., & Haggard, P. (2009). A dance to the music of time: Aesthetically-relevant changes in body posture in performing art. *PLoS ONE*, *4*, e5023.

di Pellegrino, G., Fadiga, L., Fogassi, L., Gallese, V., & Rizzolatti, G. (1992). Understanding motor events: A neurophysiological study. *Experimental Brain Research*, *91*, 176–180.

de Gelder, B. (2009). Why bodies? Twelve reasons for including bodily expressions in affective neuroscience. *Philosophical Transactions of the Royal Society of London, Series B: Biological Sciences*, *12*, 3475–3484.

Downing, P. E., Jiang, Y., Shuman, M., & Kanwisher, N. (2001). A cortical area selective for visual processing of the human body. *Science*, *293*, 2470–2473.

Fechner, G. T. (1876). *Vorschule der Asthetik*. Leipzig, Germany: Breitkopf und Härtel.

Fink, A., Graif, B., & Neubauer, A. C. (2009). Brain correlates underlying creative thinking: EEG alpha activity in professional vs. novice dancers. *NeuroImage, 46*, 854–862.

Freedberg, D., & Gallese, V. (2007). Motion, emotion and empathy in esthetic experience. *Trends in Cognitive Sciences, 11*, 197–203

Gallese, V., Fadiga, L., Fogassi, L., & Rizzolatti, G. (1996). Action recognition in the premotor cortex. *Brain, 119*, 593–609.

Goldstein, T. R. (2009). Psychological perspectives on acting. *Psychology of Aesthetics, Creativity, and the Arts, 3*, 6–9.

Goldstein, T. R., & Winner, E. (2012). Enhancing empathy and theory of mind. *Journal of Cognition and Development, 13*, 19–37.

Grosbras, M. H., Tan, H., & Pollick, F. (2012). Dance and emotion in posterior parietal cortex: A low-frequency rTMS study. *Brain Stimulation, 5*, 130–136.

Hagendoorn, I. (2005). Dance perception and the brain. In R. Grove, C. Stevens, & S. McKechnie (Eds.) *Thinking in four dimensions: Creativity and cognition in contemporary dance* (pp. 137–148). Melbourne, Australia: Melbourne University Press.

Hänggi, J., Koeneke, S., Bezzola, L., & Jäncke, L. (2010). Structural neuroplasticity in the sensorimotor network of professional female ballet dancers. *Human Brain Mapping, 31*, 1196–1206.

Hejmadi, A., Davidson, R. J., & Rozin, P. (2000). Exploring Hindu Indian emotion expressions: Evidence for accurate recognition by Americans and Indians. *Psychological Science, 11*, 183–187.

James, W. (1894). Discussion: The physical basis of emotion. *Psychological Review, 1*, 516–529.

Jang, S. H., & Pollick, F. E. (2011). Experience influences brain mechanisms of watching dance. *Dance Research, 29*, 352–377.

Jeannerod, M. (1997). *The cognitive neuroscience of action*. Oxford: Wiley-Blackwell.

Jola, C., Abedian-Amiri, A., Kuppuswamy, A., Pollick, F. E., & Grosbras, M.-H. (2012). Motor simulation without motor expertise: Enhanced corticospinal excitability in visually experienced dance spectators. *PLoS ONE, 7*, e33343.

Jola, C., & Grosbras, M.-H., (2013). In the here and now: Enhanced motor corticospinal excitability in novices when watching live compared to video recorded dance. *Cognitive Neuroscience, 4*, 90–98.

Jola, C., Pollick, F. E., & Calvo-Merino, B. (2012). "Some like it hot": Spectators who score high on the personality trait openness enjoy the excitement of hearing dancers breathing without music. *Frontiers in Human Neuroscience, 11*, Article 718.

Kanwisher, N., McDermott, J., & Chun, M. M. (1997). The fusiform face area: A module in human extrastriate cortex specialized for face perception. *Journal of Neuroscience, 17*, 4302–4311.

Keysers, C., Kaas, J. H., & Gazzola, V. (2010). Somatosensation in social perception. *Nature Reviews Neuroscience, 11*, 417–428.

Kirsch, L. P., Dawson, K., & Cross, E. S. (2015). Dance experience sculpts aesthetic perception and related brain circuits. *Annals of the New York Academy of Sciences, 1337*, 130–139.

Kirsch, L. P., Drommelschmidt, K. A., & Cross, E. S. (2013). The impact of sensorimotor experience on affective evaluation of dance. *Frontiers in Human Neuroscience, 7*, Article 521.

Kirsch, L. P., Snagg, A., Heerey, E., & Cross, E. S. (2016). The impact of experience on affective responses during action observation. *PLoS ONE, 11*, e0154681.

Kreitler, H., & Kreitler, S. (1972). *Psychology of the arts*. Durham, NC: Duke University Press.

Kourtzi, Z., & Kanwisher, N. (2000). Activation in human MT/MST by static images with implied motion. *Journal of Cognitive Neuroscience, 12,* 48–55.

Laban, R. (1950). *The mastery of movement on the stage.* London: Macdonald & Evans.

Latto, R., Brain, D., & Kelly, B. (2000). An oblique effect in aesthetics: Homage to Mondrian (1872–1944). *Perception, 29,* 981–987.

Lima, C. F., & Castro, S. L. (2011). Speaking to the trained ear: Musical expertise enhances the recognition of emotions in speech prosody. *Emotion, 11,* 1021–1031.

Little, A. C., Jones, B. C., & Debruine, L. M. (2011). The many faces of research on face perception. *Philosophical Transactions of the Royal Society of London, Series B: Biological Sciences, 12,* 1634–1637.

Miura, N., Sugiura, M., Takahashi, M., Sassa, Y., Miyamoto, A., Sato, S., … Kawashima, R. (2010). Effect on motion smoothness on brain activity while observing a dance: An fMRI study using a humanoid robot. *Social Neuroscience, 5,* 40–58.

Niedenthal, P. M. (2007). Embodying emotion. *Science, 316,* 1002–1005.

Orgs, G., Dombrowski, J. H., Heil, M., & Jansen-Osmann, P. (2008). Expertise in dance modulates alpha/beta event-related desynchronization during action observation. *European Journal of Neuroscience, 27,* 3380–3384.

Palumbo, L., & Bertamini, M. (2016). The curvature effect: A comparison between preference tasks. *Empirical Studies of the Arts, 34,* 35–53

Peelen, M.V., & Downing, P. E. (2005). Selectivity for the human body in the fusiform gyrus. *Journal of Neurophysiology, 93,* 603–608.

Peelen, M. V., & Downing, P. E. (2007). The neural basis of visual body perception. *Nature Reviews Neuroscience, 8,* 636–648.

Petrini, K., Crabbe, F., Sheridan, C., & Pollick, F. E. (2011). The music of your emotions: Neural substrates involved in detection of emotional correspondence between auditory and visual music actions. *PLoS ONE, 6,* e19165.

Petrides, K. V., Niven, L., & Mouskounti, T. (2006). The trait emotional intelligence of ballet dancers and musicians. *Psicothema, 18,* 101–107.

Pichon, S., de Gelder, B., & Grèzes, J. (2008). Emotional modulation of visual and motor areas by dynamic body expressions of anger. *Social Neuroscience, 3,* 199–212.

Pollick, F. E., Lestou, V., Ryu, J., & Cho, S. B. (2002). Estimating the efficiency of recognizing gender and affect from biological motion. *Vision Research, 42,* 2345–2355.

Reed, C. L., Stone, V. E., Bozova, S., & Tanaka, J. (2003). The body inversion effect. *Psychological Science, 14,* 302–308.

Rizzolatti, G., & Craighero, L. (2004). The mirror-neuron system. *Annual Review of Neuroscience, 27,* 169–192.

Rizzolatti, G., Fadiga, L., Matelli, M., Bettinardi, V., Paulesu, E., Perani, D., & Fazio, F. (1996). Localization of grasp representations in humans by PET: 1. Observation versus execution. *Experimental Brain Research, 111,* 246–252.

Sel, A., Forster, B., & Calvo-Merino, B. (2014). The emotional homunculus: ERP evidence for independent somatosensory responses during facial emotional processing. *The Journal of Neuroscience, 34,* 3263–3267.

Senior, C., Barnes, J., Giampietro, V., Simmons, A., Bullmore, E. T., Brammer, M., & David, A. S. (2000). The functional neuroanatomy of implicit-motion perception or "representational momentum." *Current Biology, 10,* 16–22.

Taylor, J. C., Wiggett, A. J., & Downing, P. E. (2007). Functional MRI analysis of body and body part representations in the extrastriate and fusiform body areas. *Journal of Neurophysiology*, *98*, 1626–1633.

Ticini L. F., Urgesi C., & Calvo-Merino B. (2015). Embodied aesthetics: Insight from cognitive neuroscience of performing arts. In A. Scarinzi (Ed.), *Aesthetics and the embodied mind: Beyond art theory and the Cartesian mind–body dichotomy. Contributions To phenomenology (In Cooperation with The Center for Advanced Research in Phenomenology)*, Vol. 73 (pp. 103–115). Dordrecht, The Netherlands: Springer.

Umiltà, M. A., Berchio, C., Sestito M., Freedberg, D., & Gallese, V. (2012). Abstract art and cortical motor activation: An EEG study. *Frontiers in Human Neuroscience*, *6*, Article 311.

Urgesi, C., Moro, V., Candidi, M., & Aglioti, S. M. (2006). Mapping implied body actions in the human motor system. *The Journal of Neuroscience*, *26*, 7942–7949.

Valentine, T. (1988). Upside-down faces—a review of the effect of inversion upon face recognition. *British Journal of Psychology*, *79*, 471–491.

van Meel, J., Verburgh, H., & de Meijer, M. (1993). Children's interpretations of dance expressions. *Empirical Studies of the Arts*, *11*, 117–133.

Vicary, S., Sperling, M., von Zimmermann, J., Richardson, D. C., & Orgs, G. (2017). Joint action aesthetics. *PLoS ONE*, *12*, e0180101.

Wicker, B., Keysers, C., Plailly, Royet, J. P., Gallese, V., & Rizzolatti, G. (2003). Both of us disgusted in My insula: The common neural basis of seeing and feeling disgust. *Neuron*, *40*, 655–664.

Zeki, S. (1999). *Inner vision: An exploration of art and the brain*. Oxford: Oxford University Press.

Zeki, S., & Lamb, M. (1994). The neurology of kinetic art. *Brain*, *117*, 607–636.

CHAPTER 28

....

THE AUDIO-VISUAL AESTHETICS OF MUSIC AND DANCE

....

GUIDO ORGS AND CLAIRE HOWLIN

Dance and music are cultural practices with shared evolutionary origins. In fact, rhythmical structure and performing in groups are arguably the only two universally shared features of music performance across the globe (Savage, Brown, Sakai, & Currie, 2015). Evolutionary theory suggests that dance and music co-evolved across all known cultures (Brown, Merker, & Wallin, 2001; Laland, Wilkins, & Clayton, 2016; Ravignani & Cook, 2016). The origin of the word music itself from ancient Greek *mousiké* encompasses several rhythmical art forms including music and dance, but also poetry (Merker, 2001); separating dance and music into different art forms is a relatively recent cultural phenomenon. Evolutionary accounts indeed focus on two putatively adaptive functions common to both: mate selection and social bonding.

Mate selection

Good dancers are attractive. Female observers associate attractive male dancing with positive personality attributes (Weege, Barges, Pham, Shackelford, & Fink, 2015). Proficient male dancers are rated as more extroverted, conscientious, and less neurotic. The perceived quality of male dancing correlates with grip strength, suggesting that dancing may indeed serve as an honest signal to male fitness or at least competitiveness (Hugill, Fink, Neave, N., & Seydel, 2009). Similarly, males spend more time looking at attractive females dancing than looking at unattractive females dancing (Röder et al., 2016) and women appear to dance more attractively during high-fertility periods (Fink, Hugill, & Lange, 2012). These findings suggest a clear link between attractiveness and dancing skill. Though less frequently studied, making music can also boost attractiveness. Female listeners prefer composers of more complex music during high-fertility periods than during low-fertility periods (Charlton, 2014). Together, these findings illustrate that being a good dancer or making music are attractive attributes of a person, yet whether greater attraction to good dancers or musicians indeed predicts greater reproductive success is an open question.

Social bonding

People rarely dance and make music alone. Dance and music are inherently social art forms and the acquisition of both relies on social learning, for example imitation (Flinn, 1997; Laland et al., 2016). Dancing together promotes bonding in groups of people. In one of the first experiments to study social bonding in the context of dance, Tarr, Launay and Dunbar (2016) assigned four groups of 60 high school students to perform a sequence of dance moves either in synchrony or asynchronously. Some people performed movements that required substantial effort and involved the entire body; other people performed smaller movements that were less demanding and limited to a few body parts only. Groups that had exhausted themselves reported greater mutual liking than those groups that had exerted themselves less. Exertion also increased a person's pain threshold. Importantly, group bonding and pain threshold reductions were greatest if participants had performed the movements in synchrony. The study shows that dancing together can act as a "social glue" that binds people together. Such bonding is not simply the result of exercising together, but requires synchronizing movements in time, (Reddish, Fischer, & Bulbulia 2013). Singing in choirs can similarly bind people together and reduce people's sensitivity to pain (Weinstein, Launay, Pearce, Dunbar, & Stewart, 2016).

Moving in synchrony fosters social affiliation. But is it important that people perform the same movements in unison? To answer this question Zimmermann, Vicary, Sperling, Orgs, & Richardson (2018) tested people without any dance experience performing simple group dances, such as walking or running in circles. As in previous studies, these tasks were either performed in synchrony or out of synchrony. Wrist sensors recorded the movement of all participants to provide two objective indicators of behavioral coordination. *Unitary synchrony* implies performing the same movements at the same time. *Distributed coordination* on the other hand merely implies that movements of one person are coupled in time to the movements of another person, but does not require the same movements to be performed. In ballroom dancing for example, partners don't perform the same movements at the same time. Instead, movements complement each other, so that one person "answers" the movements of the other (Amoruso et al., 2014). Immediately after participating in the dance workshop, measures of group affiliation, bonding, and conformity were collected. Identification with the group, conformity, and mutual liking were correlated with distributed coordination, but not unitary synchrony. In other words, the prosocial effects of dancing together do not require for everyone to do the same thing; only that people tune into each other's actions and time their movements closely to the movements of the other.

The role of movement synchrony for social bonding among performers has been well documented, but does synchrony also carry aesthetic value? To explore the role of synchrony for dance aesthetics, Vicary, Sperling, von Zimmerman, Richardson, and Orgs (2017) measured synchrony among dancers during a 30-min live dance performance. During the show, groups of spectators provided continuous ratings of enjoyment and perceived "togetherness" of the group of performers on stage. Using Granger causality analyses, Vicary et al. (2017) showed that dynamic synchrony (distributed coordination, see above) predicted aesthetic ratings and spectators' heart rates. Importantly however, these predictive relationships were only apparent for those audience groups that formed a stable aesthetic evaluation of the entire choreography, suggesting that the aesthetic impact of synchrony strongly depends on the live performance context. Yet measures of performed synchrony contributed more to the aesthetic judgments than overall amount of movement or perceived togetherness. The importance of synchrony for aesthetics may well be rooted in an evolutionary function of social signaling: synchrony in dance and music performance not only promotes group cohesion among performers, but can signal the relative strength of social affiliation to groups of allies or opponents in line with coalition signaling (Hagen & Bryant, 2003).

In sum, these studies testify to the growing evidence in support of the "social bonding hypothesis." Dance and music share a social function that may provide an adaptive evolutionary advantage. They establish kinship and belonging between people and transmit social signals between groups.

RHYTHM IN DANCE AND MUSIC

Music making and dancing involve similar brain mechanisms. Often, dancing requires synchronizing movement to a musical rhythm or a beat (Su & Keller, 2020). Similarly, musicians produce sounds with their rhythmically and collectively timed movements (D'Ausilio et al., 2015). Sensorimotor integration and entrainment to a beat or rhythm are therefore essential to both art forms and mediated by the same brain areas and mechanisms (Brown, Martinez, Parsons, 2006; Iversen & Balasubramaniam, 2016; Karpati, Giacosa, Foster, Penhune, & Hyde, 2017; Penhune, Zatorre, & Evans, 1998). These brain areas include the cerebellum, the superior temporal gyrus (STG), the superior temporal sulcus (STS), the middle temporal gyrus (MTG), and the inferior frontal gyrus (Levitin, Grahn, & London, 2018; Penhune et al., 1998). The cerebellum mediates entrainment of movement to visual and auditory stimuli, while the basal ganglia have been shown to be sensitive to the metrical regularity of dance (Brown et al., 2006). Moreover, dancers and musicians exhibit increased cortical thickness in the STG, the STS, and the MTG. These brain areas have been reliably shown to mediate perception of the human body and human movement, but also respond to movement sounds (Keysers et al., 2003) and even movement execution (Orlov, Makin, & Zohar, 2010). Other brain mechanisms respond more selectively to dance or music only; for example, the right medial geniculate nucleus and the posterior cerebellar lobules are only activated in response to dance in the presence of music, and music alone, suggesting that these regions process visual stimuli and rhythms but are not involved in dancing without music (Brown et al., 2006). STG, STS, and MTG are all part of the human mirror neuron system (Kilner & Lemon, 2013; Rizzolatti & Sinigaglia, 2010), which plays a crucial role in dance aesthetics (see previous chapters on this topic in this handbook).

AUDIO-VISUAL AESTHETICS OF DANCE AND MUSIC

Music and dance interact in complex ways. Combining information from two or more senses leads to cross-modal biases whereby perceiving a stimulus in one domain is altered by simultaneous perception of a stimulus in a different modality. A classic example of audio-visual bias is the McGurk effect: people blend the sound of a person saying "Ga" with the sight of a person saying "Ba" and hear a person saying "Da" (McGurk & MacDonald, 1976). Similarly, affective perception of body movements is influenced by affective information transmitted via voice or music (Van den Stock, Grèzes, & de Gelder et al., 2008; Van den Stock, Grèzes, & de Gelder, 2009). Emotion recognition relies on a combination of visual cues of facial expression with auditory voice cues, i.e. Massaro & Egan (1996). Using abstract simple stimuli, it has been shown that the relative dominance of each modality on the cross-modal experience depends on a mixture of saliency, reliability temporal alignment of the unimodal information (Noppeney & Lee, 2018; Parise & Ernst, 2016). We will look at the interaction of sound and movement from two perspectives: Firstly, we will review studies that examine how sound and music influence the aesthetic experience of dance. Secondly, we will look at how the aesthetics of music depend on dance with a specific focus on the idea of "groove."

MUSIC INFLUENCES ON DANCE PERCEPTION

In one of the first experimental studies on how the experience of dance depends on music, Krumhansl and Schenk (1997) showed videos of George Balanchine's choreography to Mozart's Divertimento No. 15 to three groups of participants. The first group watched the video in silence (dance only), the second group listened to the music without seeing the video (music only), and a third group watched the video with sound (music and dance). All participants were asked to identify meaningful structural segments and to provide continuous ratings of tension and expressed emotion. Segmentation of the dance performance was similar across all three conditions, but the lowest amount of agreement was seen among participants in the dance-only condition. Continuous ratings of tension and emotional valence in the dance-only and music-only conditions correlated strongly with tension and emotional ratings for the combined dance and music condition. Interestingly, the music-only condition was a better predictor of the dance and music condition than the dance-only condition, suggesting that the aesthetic experience of the dance performance was primarily determined by the music, rather than the dancing.

Emotional responses

Different pieces of music can influence emotional responses to the same dance performance. In order to delve deeper into the audience experience, Christensen, Gaigg, Gomila, Oke, and Calvo-Merino (2014) decided to focus not only on how different interactions change how the audience see the dance, but also on how it makes the audience actually feel. To achieve this, they examined affective responses to "happy" and "sad" ballet video excerpts using the classic cross-modal paradigm, with congruent, incongruent, or no music (Christensen et al., 2014). Two pieces of music with matching emotional valence were chosen and combined with the dance videos either congruently or incongruently. Participants were asked to rate how the dance clip made them feel after each clip. Additionally, skin conductance was measured as an index of emotional arousal. A cross-modal bias between music and dance was identified. Participants rated the sad dance as significantly sadder in the presence of sad music, and significantly happier in the presence of happy music, compared with a third control condition where videos were viewed in silence. Interestingly, for the happy dance, a cross-modal bias was only observed in the context of sad music but not in the happy music condition. Moreover, low-arousal dance videos were rated as inducing more sadness and high-arousal videos induced more happiness regardless of the intended emotion being expressed. This underlines that the perceived emotional content of the dance performance is influenced by the perceived arousal of the performance. Dance and music combinations that were congruent in terms of arousal and valence led to the greatest physiological arousal responses. In contrast, stimuli that were incongruent in terms of valence and arousal reduced the saliency of the emotion felt, regardless of whether it was positive or negative. This demonstrates that congruence of arousal can be differentiated from congruence of valence. Overall this pattern of results show that there are particular dance and music dynamics that result in a stronger affective engagement than others, with the valence of the music capable of overriding the intended emotion expressed by the dance. This may be due to changes in eye movements in the presence of music, which encourage observers to search the visual display for movements that are in synchrony with the sounds being heard (Woolhouse & Lai, 2014). However, it is possible that such *aesthetic capture* of dance by music is related to the study design. Music was played continuously even after the dance clips had ended, and during the affective ratings, leading to a dominant influence of music on affective judgments. In line with existing theoretical models of aesthetic capture, the degree to which music or dance dominates is likely to depend on specific presentation contexts (Fogelsanger & Afanador, 2006; Mitchell & Gallaher, 2001). Additionally, while Christensen et al. (2014) made some attempt to account for individual differences by administering an art experience questionnaire (Chatterjee, Widick, Sternschein, Smith, & Bromberger, 2010), this questionnaire only examined experience with visual art, but did not assess musicality or musical experience of the participants.

Understanding and learning choreography

Combining dance with music can also reduce the perceived structural complexity of a choreography, and aid memory for the observed movements. Bläsing (2015) studied event segmentation for complex sequences of dance with and without music. Groups of professional dancers and athletes with no dance experience watched contemporary dance videos; the first 15 videos were played in silence; only the final five videos were played with music chosen by the choreographer. The soundtrack did not have any metric rhythm or pulse but consisted of slowly rising and falling chords. In order to examine the impact of music on dance aesthetics, dancers and athletes were asked to press a response button each time a part of the dance phrase ended and a new one began, based on their own subjective criteria. Expert dancers identified fewer segments than novice spectators, suggesting superior chunking strategies for watching and memorizing movement. Movement segmentation further depended on the presence of music. For dancers, music reduced the number of identified segments. In contrast, athletes identified *more* movement segments when watching the dance performance with music. When asked how the music affected their segmentation decisions, the dancers indicated that music had a binding effect, and gave the impression that the movement slowed. In contrast music was reported to confuse the nondancing group, leading to a greater number of segments as the music disrupted their ability to recognize previously clear segmentation cues. Therefore, combining dance with music can be both beneficial and detrimental to identifying and understanding choreographic or musical structure, depending on the spectator's prior experience with the art form. Bläsing (2015) argues that for novice spectators, music added a new layer of complexity that effectively interfered with understanding the structural properties of the choreography. For expert spectators, music had the opposite effect.

Bläsing (2015) reported a second experiment that indicated that the disruptive effect of the music disappeared after a small group of participants learned to perform the dance over a 6-week training period. This was accounted for by the fact that the nondancers practiced the dance routine alongside the music in training sessions. The authors suggest that the dance was not subsequently experienced in isolation from the music and was instead part of a combined integrated representation of the music and dance in their long-term memory (Land, Volchenkov, Bläsing, & Schack, 2013). The study demonstrates that dance expertise and competence with the task at hand directly modulate the way a person interprets, understands and subsequently appreciates interactions between dance and music. Moreover it suggests that abstract musical relationships with dance can lead to increased uncertainty at musical transition points that might otherwise be clearly discernible (Sridharan, Levitin, Chafe, Berger, & Menon, 2007). Perhaps with increased expertise the uncertainty caused by the abstract relationship is lessened and reduces the potential for confusion. As people become more familiar with the relationship, music provides additional cues to the structure of the choreography, and binds movement segments together that otherwise appear distinct. If music helps to structure choreography, it may also amplify aesthetic pleasure. Spectators who are sensitive to intentional matching of sound and movement recognize temporal structures between music and dance intended to go together, even when each form is presented independently, and can differentiate between dance choreography and music that are intended to match and those that are not (Mitchell & Gallaher, 2001).

A detrimental effect of music on memory for movement sequences was also observed by Betteridge, Stevens, & Bailes, (2014). Novice dancers remembered complex sequences better if they learned them with an underlying pulse provided by a metronome. If movements were learned while music was playing, recall deteriorated. A shared rhythmical structure therefore provides additional cues that help encoding and retrieval. In contrast, nonrhythmical features of music seemed to distract from learning the dance movements. Neither study collected aesthetic ratings, yet other studies with similar learning paradigms (Kirsch, Drommelschmidt, & Cross, 2013) clearly suggest that acquiring experience in performing and watching specific dance sequences increase the aesthetic appeal of both movements and music. Arguably, the effect of music on the aesthetic experience of dance may thus be related to improving memory and segmentation of dance movements.

Together these studies demonstrate that music can act as a scaffold to learning and segmenting dance, but sufficient expertise is required to cognitively benefit from structural interactions between music and dance. If the relationship between music and dance is too complex, the spectator-listener may become confused or overwhelmed by both inputs. At the same time sufficient complexity between the music and dance interaction needs to be present to provide ambiguity and surprise, and can enrich aesthetic experience by generating more opportunities for discovering structural relationships between the two modalities.

Visual attention

Music influences where spectators allocate their visual attention while watching dance. Woolhouse and Lai (2014) conducted an eye-tracking study to investigate the factors within dance and music that impact visual attention to dancers. This was a lab-based experiment in which participants were asked to tap along to a piece of music while simultaneously watching videos of two dancers; only one of the dancers was synchronized to the music. Woolhouse and Lai (2014) found that there was a greater proportion of dwell time for the synchronous dancer compared with the silent or asynchronous dancer, when two dancers were presented at the same time. This means that people prioritized looking at the dancer with movements matched to the music, compared with the dancer who did not move in time to the music. Moreover, this effect was present regardless of the musical tempo, but disappeared when the dancers moved in silence, with equal dwell time observed to the fast, medium, and slow moving dancers in the silent condition. An additional finding from this study was that participants exhibited exaggerated scan paths, with fixations at relatively distant locations on the dancer's body, when observing out-of-step dancers on their own. These exaggerated scan paths indicate that observers search more of the visual display when presented with incongruent presentations, which aligns with multi-modal models of neuroaesthetics that emphasize curiosity and exploration (Marin, 2015). Woolhouse and Lai (2014) conclude that observers search for time points when music and dance correspond, by integrating perceptually disparate sensory information. An important aspect of this study is that it demonstrates quite clearly that dwell time to dancers is influenced by the presence of music irrespective of whether it is synchronous or asynchronous with the dancing. However, previous studies without music reveal expertise effects, with dancers having shorter fixation times while watching dance movements compared with nondancers (Stevens et al., 2010). It is thus likely that dance expertise also modulates eye movements in the presence of music.

Aesthetic perception of dance

We have seen that combining dance and music can both enhance and diminish the aesthetic experience of each art form individually. Not surprisingly, Western artistic traditions in dance choreography and music composition have extensively explored this relationship (Jordan, 2011): Some 20th-century choreographers have eliminated music from their choreography altogether, often arguing that music "takes over" if combined with dance. Other choreographers and composers explicitly avoid choreomusical parallels: dance and music are created and presented alongside one another. In these cases any illustrative relationships should be accidental rather than intentional (Cunningham & Lesschaeve, 1985). In the next section we will discuss some of the psychological mechanisms that underlie the audio-visual aesthetics of movement, and in particular the idea that one modality might dominate over the other. Although not specifically focused on the aesthetics of dance and music, research on cross-modal biases will help us to understand some of the determinants of dance capturing music, or music capturing dance. Furthermore, Gestalt laws play a prominent role in aesthetic perception (Wagemans et al., 2012). Combining dance and music, perceptual grouping operates within modalities and across modalities (Sloboda, 1985). For example, perception of meter in dance choreography has been shown to be disrupted by a competing musical meter, and this effect is even stronger when well-known choreography is used, such as the popular dance to "Gangnam Style" (Lee, Barrett, Kim, Lim, & Lee, 2015).

So far, we have discussed laboratory experiments which typically use recordings of dance and music. This approach allows movements to be randomly paired with a sound-track. Unimodal control conditions can be created easily by muting the soundtrack to a dance, or playing music without showing the video. While this approach provides good experimental control, it lacks ecological validity. Dance performances in particular are typically experienced live. The live aesthetic experience can be substantially different from the experience of recorded dance. To address the need for enhanced eco-logical validity, several researchers have begun to examine aesthetic experience of live dance performances (Jola, Pollick, & Calvo-Merino, 2014; Reason et al., 2016; Vicary et al., 2017).

The first two studies to examine music and dance interactions in a theater setting used the same dance performance, "Double Points: 3X," in the presence of either classical music composed by Bach, electronic music, or a soundtrack of the dancers breathing (Jola et al., 2014; Reason et al., 2016). Jola et al. (2014) asked 52 participants to rate how much they liked each combination of dance and music at the end of each performance. Participants rated the nonmusic condition as being significantly different than either of the music conditions, but no difference was found between the two music conditions. The personality trait openness to experience predicted peoples' preference for dance with or without music: Spectators who scored highly on openness enjoyed dance without music – when only the dancers' breathing and footfalls could be heard – and responded less favorably to dance paired with classical music. The second study, by Reason et al. (2016) used a similar research paradigm in that they asked 15 participants to watch three live performances of "Double Points: 3X" in combination with the same three sound conditions mentioned above. Unlike the first study, Reason et al. (2016) used focus groups to gain a greater insight into the phenomenological experience of watching the dance, as well as a follow-up functional magnetic resonance imaging (fMRI) study using a recording of the same performance. Similar to Jola et al. (2014), there was a bigger difference in the aesthetic evaluation made between the music and no-music conditions compared with the two music conditions, and this finding was not related to the level of dance-*watching* experience. However, it was noted by participants that the different soundtracks produce different emotional characterizations of the dance performance, and led to the illusory impression that different dance moves were used in each condi-tion. Specifically participants characterized the performance alongside Bach as more "flowing," "elegant," and "relaxing," while the performance alongside the electronic music was characterized as "big," and "brighter" with "more competition between the dancers." Additionally, they found that audience members found the nonmusic condition more intense with a heightened sense of physical presence due to the sound of the dancers breathing. Interestingly, for many audience members this sense of bodily awareness was a negatively valenced experience, particularly for those who scored low on the openness personality trait. While this study maintained the ecological validity of a real dance performance, Reason et al. (2016) did not assess aesthetic preferences for each soundtrack, leaving open the possibility that preferences for certain combinations of dance and music reflected specific preferences for different musical compositions (Fogelsanger & Afanador, 2006; Howlin, Vicary, & Orgs, 2020). Nonetheless these two studies suggest important differences between sounds that are arbitrarily added to the dance, such as music and sounds that are produced by the performers themselves. Moreover, they show that the audio-visual aesthetics of dance and music depend on personality traits of the spectator.

Congruency and Aesthetic Capture

More recently, attempts have been made to control the congruency of the soundtrack more rigorously, while maintaining an ecologically valid atmosphere in which aesthetic evaluation could occur in response to the dance performance (Howlin et al., 2020). In this study 34 participants were randomly assigned to watch a 34-min video of a full-length contemporary dance performance, "Group Study," with a soundtrack that included the performer's steps, breathing sounds, and vocalizations, but no music. Dance and sound were paired congruently, i.e., as recorded, or incongruently with the same soundtrack played back in reverse so that the performers' sounds no longer aligned with their movement. In a third condition the dance video was shown in complete silence. This allowed the researchers to isolate the effect of congruency, since soundtrack and video were identical in congruent and incongruent conditions, only their temporal alignment was altered. Audience members were asked to continuously rate how much they enjoyed the performance on a tablet computer, and physiological responses were continuously collected using a wrist sensor throughout each performance. Some participants had completed some formal dance training, but both dance experience and musicality were comparable among the three groups. Surprisingly, the incongruent condition was rated as more enjoyable than the congruent and silent conditions. Furthermore, only the incongruent pairing of sound and movement elicited an electrodermal activity (EDA) response coupled to the synchrony of the group dancers. Conversely the silent and congruent conditions were rated as less enjoyable and the features in these videos were not related to spectator arousal. This corresponds with the finding of Reason et al. (2016) showing that audience members often dislike the sounds of dancers breathing. Importantly, Howlin et al. (2020) found that sound itself did not predict spectator arousal directly but that the performed synchrony predicted arousal in combination with the incongruent soundtrack. This suggests an indirect influence of the sound on the way the audience viewed the movements, because the sound was no longer coupled in time to the dance movements that produced the sounds. This corresponds to the concept of "capture," whereby the presence of one element affects how the other element is perceived (Mitchell & Gallagher, 2001). It also coincides with the previous finding that people use different strategies depending on whether the music is in time or out of time with the dancers (Woolhouse & Lai, 2014). It seems that by removing the direct link between the performers' actions and the corresponding sounds, an arbitrary relationship was created, similar to the arbitrary relationships observed when dance is presented with music. This lack of an explicit connection in turn invited spectators to actively search for structural correspondences between movement and sound, emphasizing the role of exploration and meaning making for the audiovisual aesthetics of combined dance and music (Marin, 2015; Woolhouse & Lai, 2014). Howlin et al. (2020) suggest that the incongruent condition created accidental audiovisual gestalts, paradoxically heightening the experience of congruency, with one participant explicitly reporting a sense of congruency in the incongruent condition. This sense of accidental or unintended congruency has been reported in previous studies (Bolivar, Cohen, & Fentress, 1994; Chion, 1994; Iwamiya, 1994; Lipscomb & Kendall, 1994). It seems the occurrence of accidental congruency may be what leads to aesthetically interesting correspondences and conflicts between music and dance stimuli.

Looking at these results together, it seems that congruency between music and dance is not strictly preferred by the audience. In a dance context, perfect congruency between movement and sound, such as the sounds of the moving and breathing dancers, does not seem to lead to superior aesthetic outcomes (Howlin et al., 2020). Instead, optimal combinations of sound and movement appear to be characterized by two features: structural and expressive scaffolding, and a certain level of ambiguity. Audiences use one stimulus to interpret features in the other stimulus (Bläsing, 2015). Arbitrary and somewhat ambiguous relationships between dance and music may increase enjoyment because they honor individual differences in what might constitute an optimal pairing between dance and music. Less obvious relationships between dance and music allow spectators to experience surprise and discover idiosyncratic patterns between the music and dance (Muth & Carbon, 2013).

These ideas align with Berlyne's (1971) optimal arousal hypothesis: an optimal amount of complexity is required to facilitate aesthetic pleasure. One way to achieve such optimal arousal, increasing arousal-based aesthetic responses, is to present two discriminately different qualities simultaneously. Therefore, the role of congruency in dance may depend on the perceived complexity between the performers' actions and their auditory consequences, with complexity providing an opportunity for perceptual and intellectual analysis. This would correspond to a changing role of congruency depending on the complexity of the movements involved. Future studies should seek to delineate the relative contributions of stimulus complexity and congruency to the audiovisual aesthetics of dance with music.

DANCE INFLUENCES ON MUSIC PERCEPTION

So far, this chapter has focused on the impact of music on our perception of dance, but dance also alters music perception. Much of classical Western music is designed for listening only, yet even passive listening often involves not just auditory but also motor processing in the brain. The experience of musical tempo is closely linked to body movement (Dahl & Huron, 2007; Fitch, 2016; MacDougall & Moore, 2005; Todd et al., 2007; Trainor, 2007) and activations in motor brain areas are most pronounced if people listen to musical tempos that they prefer (Kornysheva, von Cramon, Jacobsen, & Schubotz, 2009). The link between making and experiencing rhythm is most obvious in playing percussive instruments. Fitch (2016) argues that the origin of 4/4 meter lies in the natural rhythm of human walking. Downbeats signify making contact with the floor; quite literally upbeats are related to lifting the foot off the ground. More complex rhythmical patterns then result from placing notes in upbeat positions (Janata, Tomic, & Haberman, 2012; Madison, 2006).

Indeed, evidence suggests a close link between beat perception and walking (Dahl & Huron, 2007; MacDougall & Moore, 2005; Todd et al., 2007; Trainor, 2007). People's tendency to walk at a rate of 120 steps/min (MacDougall & Moore, 2005) is mirrored by the popularly preferred tempo of 120 beats/min, which pervades much of popular music (Fraisse, 1982; Moelants, 2002). Similarly, individual preference for musical tempo has been related to differences in body sizes (Trainor, 2007). Listening to a sequence of clicks resembling the rhythm of the Christmas carol "Jingle Bells," people with increased body size tended to prefer slower beat rates (Todd et al., 2007). A similar relationship between body size and preferred tempo emerges if listeners freely choose which songs they would like to dance to (Dahl, Huron, Brod, & Altenmüller, 2014). Leg length is the strongest predictor of preferred beat rate in music, followed by height (Dahl & Huron, 2007; Dahl et al., 2014), accounting for 16% of the variance. In order to understand how beat preferences emerge from rhythmical movement, Phillips-Silver and Trainor showed that bouncing impacts preferences for musical meter in both infants (Phillips-Silver & Trainor, 2005) and adults (Phillips-Silver & Trainor, 2007). In these experiments, infants were bounced, and adults were asked to bounce to every second or third beat to an ambiguous rhythm pattern, and then listened to music in either double or triple time. As predicted, both infants and adults tended to prefer the metrical structure that reflected their previous bouncing experience. This effect was not dependent on visual information, or transmitted when the participants stayed still, emphasizing the role of movement in mitigating this effect. Subsequently, Philips-Silver and Trainor (2008) demonstrated that even passive movements can impact preferences for musical meter, where the participant did not initiate any movements.

Groove and danceability

Music varies in how much it induces an urge to dance (Rose et al., 2020). Listeners prefer groovy music even if people don't actually dance to it (Fitch, 2016; Janata et al., 2012). Groove can be defined as the desire to move some part of the body in relation to some aspect of a musical pattern (Etani, Marui, Kawase, & Keller, 2018; Janata et al., 2012; Madison, 2006; Madison, Gouyon, Ullén, & Hörnström, 2011; Witek, Clarke, Wallentin, Kringlebach, & Vuust, 2014), such as repetitive rhythm at a comfortable tempo (Madison et al., 2011). High-groove music is associated with greater excitability of the motor cortex (Stupacher, Hove, Novembre, Schütz-Bosbach, & and Keller 2013), and is often linked to specific genres such as funk, soul, hip-hop, and electronic dance music (Witek et al., 2014), as well as jazz, salsa, and waltz (Fitch, 2016). Rhythmic movement is naturally a core factor in a wide variety of musical genres, despite the tendency of contemporary art forms to separate the two (Fitch, 2016). Additionally, groove has been linked to Japanese definitions of *nori*, which is related to sensations of vertical and horizontal movement, indicating that the appreciation of music through danceability may be shared across cultures (Etani et al., 2018). Both groove and nori highlight the sensation of wanting to move the body in different directions. Importantly, it has been shown that the more people desire to move to the music, the more they enjoy the music (Janata et al., 2012). Significant correlations are found between groove and enjoying music or pleasure responses to music (Labbé & Grandjean, 2014; Witek et al., 2014), with syncopations in the music seen as the common denominator (Witek et al., 2014).

In order to gain greater insight into how musical preferences are shaped by perceived danceability, several studies have examined the factors that create a sense of groove, namely tempo and syncopations. Initially it was thought that decreasing the tempo of the music would also decrease the potential for groove (Madison, 2003); however, more recent studies indicate that there is in fact an optimal tempo for groove. Etani et al. (2018) used a series of drum breaks to investigate how the sensation of wanting to move in particular patterns or directions is influenced by varying tempos. They found that the relationship between groove and tempo was an inverted U-shaped relationship, with very low and very high tempo music rated as having the least amount of groove. Groove ratings were higher at tempos between 100 and 120 beats/min, with tempos between 107 and 126 beats/min considered optimal. Interestingly, the optimal tempo for groove overlaps with the optimal tempo for enjoying listening to music (~108 beats/min; Holbrook & Anand, 1990), and the preferred tempo peak seen in dance music, 120–130 beats/min (Moelants, 2002). Along with optimal tempo the second prerequisite for a grooving rhythm is optimal syncopations. Syncopations involve introducing sounds that are asynchronous to the tempo of the music, and in theory should create a sense of cognitive dissonance since they violate the pattern. However, syncopations on the downbeat make perfect sense when seen in the context of dancing, since they energize the second half of the periodic movement, which allows people to finish or close the circular movements with a renewed energy (Fitch, 2016). The relative contribution of syncopations to groove was demonstrated in an online survey examining desire to move in response to listening to a series of drum breaks with varying degrees of syncopation (Witek et al., 2014). Sixty-six participants completed the survey, which included questions on musical training, groove familiarity, and dance experience. Witek et al. (2014) demonstrate that rhythms that elicit feelings of wanting to move elicit feelings of pleasure characterized by an inverted U-shaped relationship in line with Berlyne's (1971) inverted U-shaped hypothesis. Intermediate levels of syncopation elicited the greatest degree of desire to move and pleasure associated with groove. This means that people prefer some structural resistance against the regular meter in the music to make the music more interesting, but not so much that the secondary rhythm overrides or drowns out the primary meter. Additionally, Witek et al. (2014) also found that dance experience but not musical training or familiarity with groove affected subjects' aesthetic ratings of the music. This demonstrates that knowledge of dance movements affects how people interpret musical beats. It also lends support to the claim that knowing the dance movements to a particular style of music can enrich the musical experience leading to a greater appreciation of the music, even in the absence of dancing activity (Fitch, 2016; Kirsch Drommelschmidt, & Cross, 2013). This further emphasizes the importance of action for the aesthetic experience of music, as knowledge of body movements in dance influences the effect of syncopation on subjective experience of groove more robustly than musical training. This is mirrored by studies that demonstrate that dance performance can be improved by simply listening to the sound of the dance steps combined with accompanying music (Kirsch, Drommelschmidt, & Cross, 2013). This is an interesting finding and may be accounted for by audio-motor coupling, which outlines that sound–movement pairings can reinforce kinesthetic learning (Altenmüller, Marco-Pallares, Münte, & Schneider, 2009).

Taking these studies together it seems that physical size and simple movements can influence our preference for musical tempo, while experience of more complex movements through dance training helps us to appreciate more complex musical patterns such as syncopations, with people preferring music that combines tempo and syncopations in an optimal fashion so that the music induces a desire to move. This process facilitates the reciprocal transfer of musical metrical information and kinesthetic metrical information (Brown et al., 2006), which in turn results in dance as the embodiment of music. In this way it seems that the body plays an integral role in interpreting if not feeling the music. Future studies should examine whether groove happens as a matter of purely auditory pattern recognition, or whether muscle responses occur automatically as part of groove perception. This would help to determine whether physical responses to music moderate aesthetic responses in a bottom-up or top-down manner.

Methodological Challenges
to Studying Dance and
Music Interactions

Examining the interaction of music and dance in aesthetic judgments is challenging methodologically due to the presence of two dynamic stimuli and the importance of the live performance context for dance in particular (Howlin et al., 2020; Christensen & Jola, 2015; Stevens et al., 2009). Generally, it is important that full-length performances designed by dance professionals are used to investigate aesthetic interactions between music and dance (Christensen & Jola, 2015). Moreover, composers and choreographers should lead on the design of congruent and incongruent experimental conditions to guarantee ecological validity (Bläsing, 2015). This will help to ensure that there is an intended aesthetic quality within the stimulus presentation, while controlling for tempo relationships within the music (Woolhouse & Lai, 2014), to facilitate a measurable disruption of congruency.

Additionally, to account for the dynamic experience of the performing arts (Orgs, Caspersen, & Haggard, 2016; Vicary et al., 2017), it may be preferable to use continuous rather than discrete measures to capture audience enjoyment as performances unfold (Schubert, Vincs, & Stevens, 2013; Stevens et al., 2009; Isik & Vessel, 2019). This involves the introduction of continuous enjoyment response tools, which have benefits over a paper-based questionnaire in that they capture audience reaction as the performance unfolds and so give a more complete picture of audience enjoyment (Stevens et al., 2009; Millman et al., 2022). This method can also be used to evaluate audience agreement in response to disrupted audio-visual components of dance performance (Cohen, 2016), and has been introduced in the context of dance and sound interaction (Howlin et al., 2020). Measuring audience responses over time allows the interaction between music and dance to be examined at individual moments as well as across longer durations.

Finally, the role of individual differences should be explored in the audio-visual aesthetics of music and dance. It is well documented that personality traits such as openness to experience and extraversion modulate levels of appreciation of dance with and without sound (Jola et al., 2014). People scoring high on the personality trait openness to experience are more likely to appreciate dance without music, because dance without music violates the mainstream conceptualization of dance as movement to music. It would be interesting to see if openness could also account for more unusual combinations of music and dance depending on the complexity, congruency, or abstract nature of the combination. Similarly, since understanding and familiarity are well documented as modulating factors in music appreciation (Brattico, 2015; Brattico & Pearce, 2013) as well as dance appreciation (Calvo-Merino, Glaser, Grèzes, Passingham, & Haggard, 2005, 2006), studies on the aesthetics of both music and dance need to account for musical expertise and dance expertise (Rose et al., 2020; Müllensiefen et al., 2014. To date most studies only measure expertise in one domain (Bläsing, 2015; Jola et al., 2014; Reason et al., 2016), or examine art experience more generally (Christensen et al., 2014), with only a minority of studies accounting for music and dance experience (Howlin et al., 2020; Witek et al., 2014; Woolhouse & Lai, 2014). Future studies should evaluate the relative contributions between music and dance expertise in modulating the cross-modal bias and determine whether expertise in either domain predicts how people prioritize different aspects of music and dance combinations. Moreover, experience needs to be carefully delineated in terms of visual experience of dance, as opposed to professional dance experience, and musicality, as opposed to professional musicianship.

Summary

The relationship between music and dance is complex, and while participants tend to be good at identifying music and dance that are intended to match (Mitchell & Gallagher, 2001), it almost seems more challenging for people to dissociate the dance and music stimuli. This may be due to the shared evolutionary origins of music and dance (Hagen & Bryant, 2003). It may also be because the 20th century has seen an increasing aesthetic tendency towards dance compositions where sound and movement tend to be only loosely related. In this regard, arbitrary combinations of dance and music benefit from being relatively abstract, allowing people to project their own interpretation onto the performance. In contemporary dance, cross-modal incongruence can be perceived as aesthetically more pleasing. This is likely due to the fact that viewers actively look for cross-modal perceptual congruence formed by capture (Fogelsanger & Afanador, 2006; Mitchell & Gallaher, 2001), where each separate stimulus is perceived to complement the other rather than compete with it. This suggests that searching for a meaningful relationship between sound and movement is aesthetically pleasing, and more enjoyable than perfectly congruent relationships. Future studies should try to understand the different conditions in which the visual or auditory elements will dominate, assess which combinations are perceived as the most enjoyable, and integrate this information with current models of aesthetic experience, which tend to focus on single artforms and sensory modalities.

References

Altenmüller, E., Marco-Pallares, J., Münte, T. F., & Schneider, S. (2009). Neural reorganization underlies improvement in stroke-induced motor dysfunction by music-supported therapy. *Annals of the New York Academy of Sciences, 1169*(1), 395–405. doi:10.1111/j.1749-6632.2009.04580.x

Amoruso, L., Sedeño, L., Huepe, D., Tomio, A., Kamienkowski, J., Hurtado, E., ... & Ibáñez, A. (2014). Time to Tango: Expertise and contextual anticipation during action observation. *NeuroImage, 98*, 366–385. doi:10.1016/j.neuroimage.2014.05.005

Berlyne, D. E. (1971). *Aesthetics and psychobiology*. New York: Appleton-Century-Crofts.

Betteridge, G. L., Stevens, C. J., & Bailes, F. A. (2014). Beat it! Music overloads novice dancers. *Applied Cognitive Psychology*, 28(5), 765–771. doi:10.1002/acp.3044

Bläsing, B. E. (2015). Segmentation of dance movement: Effects of expertise, visual familiarity, motor experience and music. *Frontiers in Psychology*, 5, 1500. doi:10.3389/fpsyg.2014.01500

Bolivar, V. J., Cohen, A. J., & Fentress, J. C. (1994). Semantic and formal congruency in music and motion pictures: Effects on the interpretation of visual action. *Psychomusicology: A Journal of Research in Music Cognition*, 13(1–2), 28.

Brattico, E. (2015). From pleasure to liking and back: Bottom-up and top-down neural routes to the aesthetic enjoyment of music. In J. P. Huston, M. Nadal, F. Mora, L. F. Agnati, & C. J. Cela-Conde (Eds.), *Art, aesthetics, and the brain* (pp. 303–318). Oxford, England: Oxford University Press.

Brattico, E., & Pearce, M. (2013). The neuroaesthetics of music. *Psychology of Aesthetics, Creativity and the Arts*, 7(1), 48–61.

Brown, S., Martinez, M. J., & Parsons, L. M. (2006). The neural basis of human dance. *Cerebral Cortex*, 16(8), 1157–1167. doi:10.1093/cercor/bhj057

Brown, S., Merker, B., & Wallin, N. L. (2001). An introduction to evolutionary musicology. In N. L. Wallin, B. Merker, & S. Brown (Eds.), *The origins of music* (pp. 3–24). Cambridge, MA: MIT Press.

Calvo-Merino, B., Glaser, D. E., Grezes, J., Passingham, R. E., & Haggard, P. (2005). Action observation and acquired motor skills: An FMRI study with expert dancers. *Cerebral Cortex*, 15, 1243–1249.

Calvo-Merino, B., Grèzes, J., Glaser, D. E., Passingham, R. E., & Haggard, P. (2006). Seeing or doing? Influence of visual and motor familiarity in action observation. *Current Biology*, 16, 1905–1910.

Charlton, B. D. (2014). Menstrual cycle phase alters women's sexual preferences for composers of more complex music. *Proceedings of the Royal Society B: Biological Sciences*, 281, 1784. doi:10.1098/rspb.2014.0403

Chatterjee, A., Widick, P., Sternschein, R., Smith, W. B., & Bromberger, B. (2010). The assessment of art attributes. *Empirical Studies of the Arts*, 28, 207–222.

Chion, M. (1994). *Audio-vision: Sound on screen*, ed. and trans. C. Gorbman. New York: Columbia University Press.

Christensen, J. F., Gaigg, S. B., Gomila, A., Oke, P., & Calvo-Merino, B. (2014). Enhancing emotional experiences to dance through music: The role of valence and arousal in the cross-modal bias. *Frontiers in Human Neuroscience*, 8, 359. doi:10.3389/fnhum.2014.00757

Christensen, J. F., & Jola, C. (2015). Moving towards ecological validity in empirical aesthetics of dance. In Nadal, M., Huston, J. P., Agnati, L., Mora, F., & Cela-Conde, C. J. (Eds.), *Art, Aesthetics and the brain* (pp. 223–262). New York, NY: Oxford University Press.

Cohen, A. J. (2016). Music in performance arts: film, theatre, and dance. In S. Hallam, I. Cross, & M. Thaut (Eds.), *The Oxford handbook of music psychology*, 2nd edition (pp. 725–743). Oxford, England: Oxford University Press.

Cunningham, M., & Lesschaeve, J. (1985). *The dancer and the dance* (Vol. 1). London: Marion Boyars Publishers.

Dahl, S., & Huron, D. (2007). The influence of body morphology on preferred dance tempos. In K. K. Jensen (Ed.), *Proceedings of the 2007 International Computer Music Conference*, 2 (pp. 1–4). International Computer Music Association.

D'Ausilio, A., Novembre, G., Fadiga, L., & Keller, P. E. (2015). What can music tell us about social interaction?. *Trends in cognitive sciences, 19*(3), 111–114.

Dahl, S., Huron, D., Brod, G., & Altenmüller, E. (2014). Preferred dance tempo: Does sex or body morphology influence how we groove? *Journal of New Music Research, 43*(2), 214–223. doi:10.1080/09298215.2014.884144

Etani, T., Marui, A., Kawase, S., & Keller, P. E. (2018). Optimal tempo for groove: Its relation to directions of body movement and Japanese nori. *Frontiers in Psychology, 9*, 462. doi:10.3389/fpsyg.2018.00462

Fink, B., Hugill, N., & Lange, B. P. (2012). Women's body movements are a potential cue to ovulation. *Personality and Individual Differences, 53*(6), 759–763. doi:10.1016/j.paid.2012.06.005

Fitch, W. T. (2016). Dance, music, meter and groove: A forgotten partnership. *Frontiers in Human Neuroscience, 10*, 64. doi:10.3389/fnhum.2016.00064

Flinn, M. V. (1997). Culture and the evolution of social learning. *Evolution and Human Behavior, 18*(1), 23–67. doi:10.1016/S1090-5138(96)00046-3

Fogelsanger, A., & Afanador, K. (2006). Parameters of perception: Vision, audition, and twentieth-century music and dance. Paper presented at the 38th Congress on Research in Dance, Tempe, Arizona.

Fraisse, P. (1982). Rhythm and tempo. In D. Deutsch (Ed.), *The psychology of music* (pp. 149–180). Cambridge, MA: Academic Press.

Guéguen, N., Meineri, S., & Fischer-Lokou, J. (2013). Men's music ability and attractiveness to women in a real-life courtship context. *Psychology of Music, 42*(4), 545–549. doi:10.1177/0305735613482025

Hagen, E. H., & Bryant, G. A. (2003). Music and dance as a coalition signaling system. *Human Nature, 14*(1), 21–51.

Holbrook, M. B., & Anand, P. (1990). Effects of tempo and situational arousal on the listener's perceptual and affective responses to music. *Psychology of Music, 18*(2), 150–162. doi:10.1177/0305735690182004

Howlin, C., Vicary, S., & Orgs, G. (2020). Audiovisual aesthetics of sound and movement in contemporary dance. *Empirical Studies of the Arts, 38*(2), 191–211. doi:10.1177/0276237418818633

Hugill, N., Fink, B., Neave, N., & Seydel, H. (2009). Men's physical strength is associated with women's perceptions of their dancing ability. *Personality and Individual Differences, 47*(5), 527–530. doi:10.1016/j.paid.2009.04.009

Isik, A. I., & Vessel, E. A. (2019). Continuous ratings of movie watching reveal idiosyncratic dynamics of aesthetic enjoyment. *PLoS One, 14*(10), e0223896. doi:10.1371/journal.pone.0223896

Iversen, J. R., & Balasubramaniam, R. (2016). Synchronization and temporal processing. *Current Opinion in Behavioral Sciences, 8*, 175–180. doi:10.1016/j.cobeha.2016.02.027

Iwamiya, S. (1994). Interactions between auditory and visual processing when listening to music in an audio visual context: 1. matching, 2. audio quality. *Psychomusicology, 13*, 133–154.

Janata, P., Tomic, S. T., & Haberman, J. M. (2012) Sensorimotor coupling in music and the psychology of the groove. *Journal of Experimental Psychology: General, 141*, 54–75.

Jola, C., Pollick, F. E., & Calvo-Merino, B. (2014). "Some like it hot": Spectators who score high on the personality trait openness enjoy the excitement of hearing dancers breathing without music. *Frontiers in Human Neuroscience, 8*, 718. doi:10.3389/fnhum.2014.00718

Jordan, S. (2011). Choreomusical conversations: Facing a double challenge. *Source: Dance Research Journal, 43*(1), 43–64. doi:10.5406/danceresearchj.43.1.0043

Karpati, F. J., Giacosa, C., Foster, N. E. V., Penhune, V. B., & Hyde, K. L. (2017). Dance and music share gray matter structural correlates. *Brain Research*, *1657*, 62–73. doi:10.1016/j.brainres.2016.11.029

Keysers, C., Kohler, E., Umiltà, M. A., Nanetti, L., Fogassi, L., & Gallese, V. (2003). Audiovisual mirror neurons and action recognition. *Experimental Brain Research*, *153*(4), 628–636. doi:10.1007/s00221-003-1603-5

Kilner, J. M., & Lemon, R. N. (2013). What we know currently about mirror neurons. *Current Biology*, *23*(23), R1057–R1062. doi:10.1016/j.cub.2013.10.051

Kirsch, L., Drommelschmidt, K. A., & Cross, E. S. (2013). The impact of sensorimotor experience on affective evaluation of dance. *Frontiers in Human Neuroscience*, *7*, 521. doi:10.3389/fnhum.2013.00521

Kornysheva, K., von Cramon, D. Y., Jacobsen, T., & Schubotz, R. I. (2009). Tuning-in to the beat: Aesthetic appreciation of musical rhythms correlates with a premotor activity boost. *Human Brain Mapping*. doi:10.1002/hbm.20844

Krumhansl, C. L., & Schenck, D. L. (1997). Can dance reflect the structural and expressive qualities of music? A perceptual experiment on Balanchine's choreography of Mozart's Divertimento No. 15. *Musicae Scientiae*, *1*(1), 63–85. doi:10.1177/102986499700100105

Labbé, C., & Grandjean, D. (2014). Musical emotions predicted by feelings of entrainment. *Music Perception*, *32*, 170–185. doi:10.1525/mp.2014.32.2.170

Land, W. M., Volchenkov, D., Bläsing, B., & Schack, T. (2013). From action representation to action execution: exploring the links between cognitive and biomechanical levels of motor control. *Frontiers Computational Neuroscience*, *7*, 127, doi:10.3389/fncom.2013.00127

Laland, K., Wilkins, C., & Clayton, N. (2016). The evolution of dance. *Current Biology : CB*, *26*(1), R5–9. doi:10.1016/j.cub.2015.11.031

Lee, K. M., Barrett, K. C., Kim, Y., Lim, Y., & Lee, K. (2015). Dance and music in "Gangnam Style": How dance observation affects meter perception. *PLoS One*, *10*(8), e0134725.

Levitin, D. J., Grahn, J. A., & London, J. (2018). The psychology of music: Rhythm and movement. *Annual Review of Psychology*, *69*, 51–75.

Lipscomb, S. D., & Kendall, R. A. (1994). Perceptual judgement of the relationship between musical and visual components in film. *Psychomusicology*, *13*, 60–98.

MacDougall, H. G., & Moore, S. T. (2005). Marching to the beat of the same drummer: The spontaneous tempo of human locomotion. *Journal of Applied Physiology*, *99*, 1164–1173.

Madison, G. (2003). Perception of jazz and other groove- based music as a function of tempo. In R. Kopiez, A. C. Lehmann, I. Wolther, & C. Wolf (Eds.), *Proceedings of the 5th Triennial ESCOM Conference* (pp. 365–367). Hannover: School of Music and Drama.

Madison, G. (2006). Experiencing groove induced by music: consistency and phenomenology. *Music Perception*, *24*, 201–208. doi:10.1525/mp.2006.24.2.201

Madison, G., Gouyon, F., Ullén, F., & Hörnström, K. (2011). Modeling the tendency for music to induce movement in humans: First correlations with low-level audio descriptors across music genres. *Journal of Experimental Psychology: Human Perception and Performance*, *37*, 1578.

Marin, M. (2015). Crossing boundaries towards a general model of neuroaesthetics. *Frontiers in Human Neuroscience*, *9*, 443.

Massaro, D. W., & Egan, P. B. (1996). Perceiving affect from the voice and the face. *Psychonomic Bulletin & Review*, *3*(2), 215–221.

McGurk, H., & MacDonald, J. (1976). Hearing lips and seeing voices. *Nature*, *264*, 746–748.

Merker, B. (2001). Synchronous chorusing and human origins. In N. L. Wallin, B. Merker, & S. Brown (Eds.), *The origins of music* (pp. 315–328). Cambridge, MA: MIT Press.

Millman, L. M., Richardson, D. C., & Orgs, G. (2022). Continuous and collective measures of real-time audience engagement. *Routledge Companion to Audiences and the Performing Arts*, 293–307

Mitchell, R. W., & Gallagher, M. C. (2001). Embodying music: Matching music and dance in memory. *Music Perception*, *19*(1), 65–68.

Moelants, D. (2002). Preferred tempo reconsidered. In C. Stevens, D. Burnham, G. McPherson, E. Schubert, & J. Renwick (Eds.), *Seventh international conference on music perception and cognition*. Rundle Mall, Australia: Causal Productions.

Müllensiefen, D., Gingras, B., Musil, J., & Stewart, L. (2014). The musicality of non-musicians: an index for assessing musical sophistication in the general population. *PloS one, 9*(2), e89642.

Muth, C., & Carbon, C.-C. (2013). The aesthetic aha: On the pleasure of having insights into Gestalt. *Acta Psychologica, 144*, 25–30.

Noppeney, U., & Lee, H. L. (2018). Causal inference and temporal predictions in audiovisual perception of speech and music. *Annals of the New York Academy of Sciences*, 1423(1), 102–116. doi:10.1111/nyas.13615

Orgs, G., Caspersen, D., & Haggard, P. (2016). You move, I watch, it matters: Aesthetic communication in dance. In S. S. Obhi, & E. S. Cross, (Eds.), *Shared representations: Sensorimotor foundations of social life*. Cambridge, England: Cambridge University Press.

Orlov, T., Makin, T. R., & Zohary, E. (2010). Topographic representation of the human body in the occipitotemporal cortex. *Neuron, 68*(3), 586–600.

Parise, C. V., & Ernst, M. O. (2016). Correlation detection as a general mechanism for multisensory integration. *Nature Communications, 7*, 11543. doi:10.1038/ncomms11543

Penhune, V. B., Zatorre, R. J., & Evans, A. C. (1998). Cerebellar contributions to motor timing: A PET study of auditory and visual rhythm reproduction. *Journal of Cognitive Neuroscience, 10*, 752–765.

Phillips-Silver, J., & Trainor, L. J. (2005). Feeling the beat: Movement influences infants' rhythm perception. *Science, 308*, 1430.

Phillips-Silver, J., & Trainor, L. J. (2007). Hearing what the body feels: Auditory encoding of rhythmic movement. *Cognition, 105*, 533–546. doi:10.1016/j.cognition.2006.11.006.

Philips-Silver, J., & Trainor, L. J. (2008). Vestibular influence on auditory metrical interpretation. *Brain and Cognition, 67*, 94–102.

Ravignani, A., & Cook, P. F. (2016). The evolutionary biology of dance without frills. *Current Biology : CB, 26*(19), R878–R879. doi:10.1016/j.cub.2016.07.076

Reason, M., Jola, C., Kay, R., Reynolds, D., Kauppi, J. P., Grobras, M. H, … & Pollick, F. E. (2016). Spectators' aesthetic experience of sound and movement in dance performance: A transdisciplinary investigation. *Psychology of Aesthetics Creativity and the Arts, 10*(1), 42–55.

Reddish, P., Fischer, R., & Bulbulia, J. (2013). Let's dance together: Synchrony, shared intentionality and cooperation. *PLoS One, 8*(8), e71182. doi:10.1371/journal.pone.0071182

Rizzolatti, G., & Sinigaglia, C. (2010). The functional role of the parieto-frontal mirror circuit: Interpretations and misinterpretations. *Nature Reviews. Neuroscience, 11*(4), 264–274. doi:10.1038/nrn2805

Röder, S., Carbon, C.-C., Shackelford, T. K., Pisanski, K., Weege, B., & Fink, B. (2016). Men's visual attention to and perceptions of women's dance movements. *Personality and Individual Differences, 101*, 1–3. doi:10.1016/j.paid.2016.05.025

Rose, D., Müllensiefen, D., Lovatt, P., & Orgs, G. (2020). The Goldsmiths Dance Sophistication Index (Gold-DSI): A psychometric tool to assess individual differences in dance experience. *Psychology of Aesthetics, Creativity, and the Arts.*

Savage, P. E., Brown, S., Sakai, E., & Currie, T. E. (2015). Statistical universals reveal the structures and functions of human music. *Proceedings of the National Academy of Sciences of the United States of America, 112*(29), 8987–8992. doi:10.1073/pnas.1414495112

Schubert, E., Vincs, K., & Stevens, C. J. (2013). Identifying regions of good agreement among responders in engagement with a piece of live dance. *Empirical Studies of the Arts, 31*(1), 1–20.

Sloboda, J. A. (1985). *The musical mind: The cognitive psychology of music.* Oxford, England: Oxford University Press.

Sridharan, D., Levitin, D. J., Chafe, C. H., Berger, J., & Menon, V. (2007). Neural dynamics of event segmentation in music: converging evidence for dissociable ventral and dorsal networks. *Neuron, 55,* 521–532. doi:10.1016/j.neuron.2007.07.003

Stevens, C. J., Schubert, E., Morris, R. H., Frear, M., Chen, J., Healey, S., & Hansen, S. (2009). Cognition and the temporal arts: Investigating audience response to dance using PDAs that record continuous data during live performance. *International Journal of Human-Computer Studies, 67,* 800–813.

Stevens, C., Winskel, H., Howell, C., Vidal, L. M., Latimer, C., & Milne-Home, J. (2010). Perceiving dance schematic expectations guide experts' scanning of a contemporary dance film. *Journal of Dance Medicine & Science, 14*(1), 19–25.

Stupacher, J., Hove, M. J., Novembre, G., Schütz-Bosbach, S., & Keller, P. E. (2013). Musical groove modulates motor cortex excitability: A TMS investigation. *Brain Cognition, 82,* 127–136. doi:10.1016/j.bandc.2013.03.003

Su, Y. H., & Keller, P. E. (2020). Your move or mine? Music training and kinematic compatibility modulate synchronization with self-versus other-generated dance movement. *Psychological Research, 84*(1), 62–80.

Tarr, B., Launay, J., & Dunbar, R. I. M. (2016). Silent disco: Dancing in synchrony leads to elevated pain thresholds and social closeness. *Evolution and Human Behavior, 37*(5), 343–349. doi:10.1016/j.evolhumbehav.2016.02.004

Todd, N. P., Cousins, R., & Lee, C. S. (2007). The contribution of anthropometric factors to individual differences in the perception of rhythm. *Empirical Musicology Review, 2*(1), 1–13.

Trainor, L. J. (2007). Do preferred beat rate and entrainment to the beat have a common origin in movement? *Empirical Musicology Review, 2*(1), 17–20.

Van den Stock, J., Grèzes, J., & de Gelder, B. (2008). Human and animal sounds influence recognition of body language. *Brain Research, 1242,* 185–195. doi:10.1016/j.brainres.2008.05.040

Van den Stock, J. B., Peretz, I., Grèzes J., & de Gelder, B. (2009). Instrumental music influences recognition of emotional body language. *Brain Topography, 21,* 216–220. doi:10.1007/s10548-009-0099-0

Vicary, S., Sperling, M., von Zimmerman, J., Richardson, D. C., & Orgs, G. (2017). Joint action aesthetics. *PLoS One, 12*(7), e0180101. doi:10.1371/journal.pone.0180101

Wagemans, J., Elder, J. H., Kubovy, M., Palmer, S. E., Peterson, M. A., Singh, M., & von der Heydt, R. (2012). A century of Gestalt psychology in visual perception: I. Perceptual grouping and figure-ground organization. *Psychological Bulletin, 138*(6), 1172–1217. doi:10.1037/a0029333

Wallin, N. L., Merker, B., & Brown, S. (Eds.). (2001). *The origins of music.* Cambridge, MA: MIT press.

Weege, B., Barges, L., Pham, M. N., Shackelford, T. K., & Fink, B. (2015). Women's attractiveness perception of men's dance movements in relation to self-reported and perceived personality. Evolutionary Psychological Science, 1(1), 23–27. doi:10.1007/s40806-014-0004-2

Weinstein, D., Launay, J., Pearce, E., Dunbar, R. I. M., & Stewart, L. (2016). Group music performance causes elevated pain thresholds and social bonding in small and large groups of singers. *Evolution and Human Behavior: Official Journal of the Human Behavior and Evolution Society, 37*(2), 152. doi:10.1016/j.evolhumbehav.2015.10.002

Witek, M. A., Clarke, E. F., Wallentin, M., Kringelbach, M. L., & Vuust, P. (2014). Syncopation, body-movement and pleasure in groove music. *PLoS One, 9*, e94446. doi:10.1371/journal.pone.0094446

Woolhouse, M. H., & Lai, R. (2014). Traces across the body: Influence of music-dance synchrony on the observation of dance. *Frontiers in Human Neuroscience, 8*, 965. doi:10.3389/fnhum.2014.00965

Zimmermann, J. von, Vicary, S., Sperling, M., Orgs, G., & Richardson, D. C. (2018). The choreography of group affiliation. *Topics in Cognitive Science, 10*(1), 80–94. doi:10.1111/tops.12320

CHAPTER 29

AESTHETIC RESPONSES TO ARCHITECTURE

ALEXANDER COBURN AND ANJAN CHATTERJEE

HISTORICAL CONTEXT

IN cultures across the globe, *beauty* has long been considered an integral dimension of architectural design. The notion that architectural aesthetics can be critically examined dates back at least to the writing of Roman architect Vitruvius, who identified beauty as one of the three core dimensions of architectural design. His Vitruvian Triad (Figure 29.1) illustrated that a building must be structurally sound (*firmitas*), while accommodating the functional needs of its users (*utilitas*) and engaging their aesthetic sensibilities (*venustas*). For thousands of years, construction practices like the Chinese *feng shui* and the Indian *vaastu shastra* offered concrete guidelines for creating coherence and harmony in the built environment. In Europe, the study of architectural aesthetics generated interest from Goethe, Ruskin, and Kant, among others. The work of these philosophers suggests that aesthetic qualities of buildings can have a meaningful impact on everyday human experience.

The aesthetic dimension of architecture was deemphasized in the 20th century as the creed of "form follows function" began to dictate design practices. Architects of the past century often focused on advancing easily measurable dimensions of the built environment such as construction costs, fire safety, and energy efficiency (Vaughan, 2013). Structural engineers leveraged technological and material advances to construct taller and stronger buildings than was possible previously (Ali & Moon, 2007). The rise of utilitarianism in design aligned with a philosophical shift in architectural practice, whereby the notion of buildings as machines encouraged architects and planners to focus on improving mechanistic aspects of architecture while discarding aesthetic

FIGURE 29.1. The Vitruvian Triad.

Credit: Alex Coburn, Oshin Vartanian and Anjan Chatterjee, 'Buildings, beauty, and the brain: A neuroscience of architectural experience,' *Journal of Cognitive Neuroscience, 29*:9(September, 2017), pp. 1521–1531. © 2017 by the Massachusetts Institute of Technology, reprinted courtesy of the MIT Press.

considerations like human scaling and ornamentation. The reductive forms generated by this approach represented a new aesthetic ideal in which notions of architectural beauty were closely linked to functionalism (Venturi, Scott Brown, Rattenbury, & Hardingham, 2007). This philosophy pushed the investigation of aesthetic experience to the periphery of architectural research.

In the 21st century, however, a new line of research emerged exploring how aesthetic features of the built environment influence occupants' psychological experiences. People spend most of their lives in buildings (Evans & McCoy, 1998), and architecture can affect mood, cognition, and psychological wellbeing (Adams, 2014; Cooper, Burton, & Cooper, 2014; Hartig, 2008; Joye, 2007). While some studies have investigated the theoretical intersection of neuroscience *and* architecture (Dance, 2017; Eberhard, 2008; Mallgrave, 2010; Robinson & Pallasmaa, 2015), few experiments have been conducted on the neuroscience *of* architecture, wherein architectural experiences are the target of empirical investigation.

The field of neuroaesthetics offers important lessons for the emerging discipline of neuroarchitecture. Neuroaesthetics studies the neurophysiological underpinnings of aesthetic experiences in response to beauty and art (Chatterjee & Vartanian, 2016).

Many of the ideas and research methods of neuroaesthetics also apply to the study of psychological experiences in the built environment (Eberhard, 2009). Fifteen years ago, the field of neuroaesthetics reached an important point in its development. The first papers emerged using functional magnetic resonance imaging (fMRI) to investigate neural responses to art (Vartanian & Goel, 2004) and to review the neuropsychology of art (Chatterjee, 2004a, 2004b). Initial frameworks were also proposed outlining the key neural and cognitive systems that generate aesthetic experiences (Chatterjee & Vartanian, 2014; Leder, Oeberst, Augustin, & Belke, 2004). These frameworks motivated a wave of hypothesis-testing experiments and enabled neuroaesthetics to enter into the mainstream of scientific research (Chatterjee, 2011).

The neuroscience of architecture may be approaching a similar turning point in its development. Many studies to date have been *descriptive* in that they qualitatively relate neuroscientific insights to architectural experiences (Brown & Lee, 2016; Eberhard, 2008; Mallgrave, 2010). Some empirical research has also emerged linking architectural parameters to neurophysiological responses (Choo, Nasar, Nikrahei, & Walther, 2017; Marchette, Vass, Ryan, & Epstein, 2015; Shemesh et al., 2017; Vartanian et al., 2013, 2015). However, these studies are typically disconnected from any general neuroscientific framework. It is therefore difficult to place them within a cohesive research program. In the text that follows, we discuss how a general model of aesthetic experience can be applied to the neuroscience of architecture. This model is intended to help contextualize past research and to motivate future empirical studies.

THE AESTHETIC TRIAD

The *aesthetic triad* model (Chatterjee, 2013) outlines key neural systems that generate aesthetic experiences in response to visual art. This model can also be applied to frame empirical research on the neuroscience of architecture. This framework highlights three neural systems that are engaged when people experience the built environment: sensorimotor, emotion-valuation systems, and knowledge-meaning systems. Architecture interacts with sensory networks by engaging visual, auditory, olfactory, somatosensory, and vestibular systems, while also engaging approach-avoidance behavior and other motor responses. Buildings also trigger feelings and emotions, which are mediated by emotion-valuation networks. Finally, knowledge-meaning systems shaped by culture, education, and personal experiences influence how people engage with architectural spaces. Each of these systems is discussed in greater detail later in the chapter. These networks presumably do not act in isolation, but rather interact with each other to generate integrated aesthetic experiences in response to the built environment. Furthermore, these neural systems likely respond differently to architecture than to visual art. We discuss some important distinctions later in the chapter, including differences in dimensionality and the relatively longer time span of architectural encounters as compared with visual art. Finally, we consider how the effects of architecture on wellbeing might be mediated by acute aesthetic experiences in the built environment.

Sensory-motor systems

Sensory networks might be thought of as the gatekeepers of architectural experience because they mediate the influence of the built environment on downstream cognitive and affective experiences. Sensory features of architectural spaces engage visual, auditory, olfactory, somatosensory, and vestibular neural networks, while also modulating motor responses to buildings such as navigation and approach-avoidance decisions. Here, we focus primarily on *visual perception* of architecture, simply because vision dominates the existing literature related to perception of architectural spaces. However, nonvisual sensory networks undoubtedly play an important role in generating aesthetic responses to buildings.

Vision

Vision is the most widely studied sensory system in the existing literature on the neuroscience of architecture. Visual perception of architecture begins with the processing of low-level spatial and color features such as edges, brightness, and hue (Chatterjee, 2004a; Ibarra et al., 2017; Kotabe, Kardan, & Berman, 2016). These low-level visual features are then integrated into meaningful information by high-level neural systems such as the parahippocampal place area (PPA), the retrosplenial cortex (RSC), and the occipital place area (OPA) (Marchette et al., 2015). The PPA is specifically sensitive to environmental scenes such as buildings and landscapes. This area also plays an important role in spatial navigation (Epstein & Kanwisher, 1998; Mégevand et al., 2014) and in assessing the size of spaces (Kravitz, Peng, & Baker, 2011). The OPA may be responsible for processing mid-level visual features that help people recognize visual landmarks. The RSC, meanwhile, plays a role in retrieving conceptual information (e.g., memories) associated with these landmarks (Marchette et al., 2015). The hippocampus and entorhinal cortex also play important roles in processing architectural information during spatial navigation (Spiers & Barry, 2015).

The visual cortex may be particularly sensitive to a key aesthetic properties of architectural design, including contrast, order, complexity, and naturalness. The importance of visual contrast in the built environment has been widely discussed among architectural theorists (Alexander, 2002; Salingaros, 2007; Venturi, Scully, & Drexler, 1977). Neurons in the occipital cortex and cells in the retina are more sensitive to edges, or regions of high visual contrast, than to regions of homogenous brightness in a scene (Brady & Field, 2000; Geisler, 2007; Ramachandran & Hirstein, 1999). High-contrast regions are thought to capture interest because they contain a high density of visual information that is useful for identifying objects in scenes (Alexander, 2002; Hagerhall, Purcell, & Taylor, 2004; Leder et al., 2004; Ramachandran & Hirstein, 1999).

Order is also a key variable in architectural aesthetics. An important concept in empirical aesthetics is the notion of processing fluency, which states that people prefer visual patterns which can be processed more easily, or fluently, by the brain (Birkhoff, 1933; Eysenck, 1957; Oppenheimer & Frank, 2008; Palmer, Schloss, & Sammartino, 2013; Reber, Schwarz, & Winkielman, 2004). This phenomenon may extend to physical spaces. Evidence suggests that people tend to prefer more ordered environments, i.e., spaces that are processed more fluently (Kaplan & Kaplan, 1989; Kotabe, Kardan, & Berman, 2017). Environmental disorder, by contrast, has been linked to heightened anxiety (Tullett, Kay, & Inzlicht, 2015), increased rule-breaking behavior (Kotabe et al., 2016), reduced cognitive performance (Evans, Gonnella, Marcynyszyn, Gentile, & Salpekar, 2005), and a diminished sense of meaning in life (Heintzelman & King, 2014).

Environmental order implies both an absence of randomness (Tullett et al., 2015) and the presence of predictable patterns in scenes (Alexander, 2002; Reber et al., 2004; Salingaros, 2007). Two such patterns, grouping and symmetry, may be particularly relevant to visual perception of architectural scenes. Grouping, or visual redundancy, is a fundamental Gestalt principle that describes the process by which the visual system organizes repeated information in a scene. Examples of repeated patterns in architecture include alternating archways and columns in a colonnade, or repeated color patterns dispersed throughout a stained glass window (Alexander, 2002). Grouped spatial and structural features trigger synchronized action potential among the neurons that are responsible for processing those features (Ramachandran & Hirstein, 1999; Singer & Gray, 1995). These neural mechanisms may help generate the aesthetic pleasure response that people often experience when they encounter ordered patterns of color and form in the built environment (Alexander, 2002).

Balance and symmetry may also contribute to the perception of order and aesthetic preference in architectural scenes (Alexander, 2002; Wilson & Chatterjee, 2005). Experiments have shown that people often exhibit preferences for symmetrical geometric shapes and faces, compared with objects that are asymmetrical. Our species may have evolved these innate preferences through natural selection as a result of the evolutionary importance of symmetrical information for human survival (Frith & Nias, 1974; Jacobsen, Schubotz, Höfel, & Cramon, 2006; Ramachandran & Hirstein, 1999; Rhodes, Proffitt, Grady, & Sumich, 1998). Research also suggests that symmetry plays an important role in object identification and memory formation. One study, for instance, showed that the number of local symmetries present in a visual pattern strongly predicted the ease with which participants could find, remember, and describe that pattern (Alexander & Carey, 1968). The cognitive salience of symmetry may help explain why symmetrical patterns appear so often in human design at many scales.

Visual complexity may also influence the ease with which humans identify objects and extract information from the built environment. Complexity refers to "the volume of information present in a space" (Dosen & Ostwald, 2016, p. 3) and the informational "richness" of a scene (Kaplan & Kaplan, 1989, p. 53). Moderate correlations have been found between complexity and preference in various contexts, including the evaluation of artwork (Day, 1967; Leder et al., 2004; Taylor, Micolich, & Jonas, 1999), natural landscapes (Kaplan, 1987; Ulrich, 1977, 1983), and built environments (Imamoglu, 2000; Kaplan, Kaplan, & Wendt, 1972). Preferences often follow an inverted U-shaped curve in relation to complexity (Berlyne, 1970, 1971; Güçlütürk, Jacobs, & van Lier, 2016; Imamoglu, 2000), although the relationship between complexity and aesthetic preference generally varies as a function of how complexity is conceptualized (e.g., amount, variety or organization of elements within a scene) (Nadal, Munar, Marty, & Cela-Conde, 2010). Salingaros postulated that buildings stripped of visual complexity, like prisons and ultra-minimalist spaces, impoverish sensory experience by denying the visual system meaningful information (Salingaros, 2003). Excess architectural complexity can also overwhelm the visual system, particularly if the information is experienced as disorganized (Kotabe et al., 2016; Salingaros, 2003, 2007).

Fractal dimension, a popular measure of complexity in aesthetics research, may prove useful for evaluating the complexity of architectural spaces. Fractals are "fractured shapes [that] possess repeating patterns when viewed at increasingly fine magnifications" (Hagerhall et al., 2004, p. 247). Examples of objects with fractal properties include mountains, coastlines, and many other complex shapes in nature (Hagerhall et al., 2004). Whereas a smooth Euclidean curve has a fractal dimension close to 1, a densely convoluted line that approximates the appearance of a two-dimensional surface has a fractal dimension approaching 2. Higher fractal dimension therefore indicates greater visual complexity, as well as a higher degree of self-similarity, in an object or scene. Research suggests that people often exhibit strong preferences for natural scenes and visual art with fractal dimensions in the range of 1.3–1.5 (Spehar, Clifford, Newell, & Taylor, 2003; Taylor et al., 2005), although these claims remain controversial (Jones-Smith & Mathur, 2006). In principle, these findings suggest that the visual cortex may also be attuned to architectural spaces exhibiting moderate to high values of fractal dimension, such as Gothic cathedrals. In general, there are many quantifiable image statistics, in addition to fractal dimension, which are useful for predicting aesthetic responses to objects, art, and natural landscapes (Berman et al., 2014; Graham & Field, 2007; Graham & Redies, 2010; Graham, Schwarz, Chatterjee, & Leder, 2016; Kotabe et al., 2016; Redies, 2007). Many of these statistical measures could be used to investigate aesthetic responses to architecture (see, for instance, Coburn et al., 2019).

Naturalness is an important aesthetic dimension of the physical environment. Exposure to natural environments and natural features of the built environment has been shown to confer important psychological benefits such as improved mood (Barton & Pretty, 2010; Bowler, Buyung-Ali, Knight, & Pullin, 2010; Valtchanov, Barton, & Ellard, 2010), reduced stress (Valtchanov et al., 2010; Villani & Riva, 2011), and heightened cognitive performance on attention and working memory tasks (Berman et al., 2012; Berman, Jonides, & Kaplan, 2008; Berto, 2005; Bratman, Daily, Levy, & Gross, 2015; Kaplan, 1995). Two predominant psychological theories help frame these findings: Kaplan's *attention restoration theory* (ART) and E.O. Wilson's *biophilia hypothesis* (BH). ART addresses the cognitive benefits of exposure to nature. According to ART, the "softly fascinating" sensory stimuli of nature capture our attention in an automatic, bottom-up fashion, thereby restoring attentional resources and facilitating better performance on demanding cognitive tasks (Kaplan, 1995; Kaplan & Berman, 2010). The BH, which means "love of life," emphasizes the emotional benefits of interacting with the living and life-like forms often encountered in nature (Wilson, 1984; Wilson & Kellert, 1995). This theory postulates that people have an innate desire to seek contact with plants, animals, and natural habitats, which stems from our species' evolution in "biological – not artificial or manufactured – environment[s]" (Kellert, 2005, p. 123). Together, these two theories offer complementary perspectives on why interacting with nature may facilitate pleasurable and restorative psychological experiences.

Although natural and built environments are often classified as distinct spatial categories, many buildings exhibit nature-like visual characteristics. Indeed, builders throughout history have often endowed their structures with naturalistic visual qualities by drawing inspiration from the "monumental design model" of nature (Kellert, 2003, p. 36). Examples include architectural ornamentation depicting literal representation of plants and animals, engineering strategies that mimic the structural support mechanisms of trees, and biomimetic patterns of scaling and proportionality abstracted from biological systems (Alexander, 2002; Coburn et al., 2019; Kellert, 2005). Several scholars hypothesize that people may be innately attuned to naturalistic patterns in architecture, and that these patterns may confer similar psychological benefits as interacting with nature itself (Alexander, 2002; Joye, 2007; Salingaros, 2007). Supporting this view, evidence suggests that curvilinear spaces trigger distinct neural responses in visual and emotional brain regions from rectilinear spaces (Banaei, Hatami, Yazdanfar, & Gramann, 2017; Vartanian et al., 2013), and that naturalistic visual patterns are strongly predictive of aesthetic preferences for both interior and exterior architectural scenes (Coburn et al., 2019).

Appleton's *habitat theory* offers a complementary evolutionary framework of architectural aesthetics. This theory postulates that humans evolved to prefer physical environments containing features that were favorable to survival (Appleton, 1975). According to this view, people are often attracted to moderately complex, savannah-like landscapes (Balling & Falk, 1982; Joye, 2007), in part because they provide many areas of prospect and refuge. Clumps of trees and grass scattered throughout the savannahs offered early hominids places to hide from predators while simultaneously surveying the landscape for food and resources (Appleton, 1975). Points of prospect and refuge correlate with aesthetic preferences for both natural environments and architectural spaces (Dosen & Ostwald, 2016), suggesting that evolved landscape preferences may influence how modern humans experience the built environment. In one study, participants preferred architectural interiors that afforded more visual prospect (open rooms and rooms with high ceilings) over spaces that offered less visual prospect (enclosed rooms and rooms with low ceilings). Open interiors activated structures in the temporal lobes associated with perceived visual motion (left middle temporal gyrus and right superior temporal gyrus), and high ceilings activated structures in the dorsal stream associated with visuospatial attention and exploration (left precuneus and the left middle frontal gyrus) (Vartanian et al., 2015). These findings offer preliminary insight into how evolutionarily relevant features of the built environment are processed in the brain.

Audition, olfaction, and somatosensation

Sound, smell, and touch play an important role in shaping an occupant's aesthetic experiences in the built environment, but relatively little research has been conducted on nonvisual responses to architectural design. Multisensory inputs from the built environment are processed by the brain's auditory, olfactory, and somatosensory networks. Understanding how environmental features interact with these neural systems will be an important step for advancing the neuroscience of architecture. Odor may play an important role in shaping an occupant's affective response to an architectural space (Barbara & Perliss, 2006). The direct link between the olfactory bulb and the limbic system may contribute to the emotional salience of a building's smell (Ward, 2015). When a person visits their childhood home, for instance, the smell of the space can trigger vivid memories of their past experiences by engaging neural systems that govern memory and emotion (Lehrer, 2008). Sound also influences aesthetic experiences in the built environment. Acoustic information, such as reverberation time, can help generate useful information about a room's shape and size (Ward, 2015) and can influence whether a space is perceived as quiet and contemplative (as in a monastery) or loud and exciting (as in a stadium). Additionally, the temperature of a building and tactile quality of its materials feed into an occupant's overall architectural experience. These design factors are processed in the somatosensory cortex of the brain. Temperature has been shown to modulate occupants' perceptions of comfort and beauty in architectural environments (Fanger, 1973; Nicol & Humphreys, 2002; Thorsson, Honjo, Lindberg, Eliasson, & Lim, 2007), which speaks to the importance of multisensory interactions in environmental processing.

Movement and navigation

Unlike most forms of visual art, interacting with buildings involves planning and execution of movement. Design features of buildings may therefore interact with neural areas involved in navigation and coordination of motor activity. One study showed that beauty judgments of architectural interiors covaried with neural activity in the global pallidus (Vartanian et al., 2013), which may correspond to the anticipation of motion (Nambu, Tokuno, & Takada, 2002). Design variables may impact occupants' approach-avoidance decisions in the built environment. In one study, participants were more likely to enter rooms with high ceilings than those with low ceilings (Vartanian et al., 2015). Another group of researchers found that participants experienced greater immobility and responded more slowly on a manual clicking task when exposed to images of tall buildings, as compared with images of low buildings (Joye & Dewitte, 2016). Motor responses may be mediated by affective and reward processing areas in the brain, including the anterior insula, the nucleus accumbens, and the basolateral amygdala (Vartanian et al., 2013).

Knowledge-meaning systems

Neural responses to architecture relate to sensory features, which are processed in a bottom-up fashion. Top-down inputs such as expertise, personal experiences, memories, and context also interact with these bottom-up sensory inputs to influence a person's aesthetic responses to architectural spaces.

Expertise has a meaningful impact on aesthetic experiences in the built environment. Architecture students, for instance, recruit distinct neural regions from nonarchitecture students when viewing images of buildings (Wiesmann & Ishai, 2011). In another study, architects exhibited significantly greater neural activity in the reward areas of the brain, such as the bilateral medial orbitofrontal cortex and the subcallosal cingulate gyrus, than nonarchitects when evaluating architectural scenes on beauty (Kirk, Skov, Christensen, & Nygaard, 2009). Architects also had greater activation of the precuneus and hippocampus relative to nonarchitects when viewing buildings, but not when viewing faces. This finding suggests that domain-specific memories related to education and expertise may have enhanced the reward responses associated observed in the group of architects.

Memory and spatial learning can also influence how well people navigate urban and architectural environments. Repeated exposure to a given place generates a cognitive map of the physical environment in the grid cells of the hippocampus (McNaughton, Battaglia, Jensen, Moser, & Moser, 2006; O'Keefe & Nadel, 1978). These spatial maps then enable more efficient navigation in future visits to the same environment (Astur, Taylor, Mamelak, Philpott, & Sutherland, 2002; Maguire et al., 2000). The physical layout of architectural spaces also plays an important role in episodic memory, given that episodic events are encoded in grid cells along with their spatial context (Edelstein et al., 2008). Sensory features of architectural environments can influence spatial learning and navigation. For example, views to the exterior and clear visual reference points can improve navigation, whereas homogenous visual composition of interior spaces can hinder navigation for people with Alzheimer's disease (Passini, Pigot, Rainville, & Tétreault, 2000).

Architectural experience is influenced by top-down factors such as expectations, context, and inferred meaning. For instance, expectations about environmental control can affect perceptions of comfort. People are willing to tolerate a wider temperature range inside buildings when they have access to architectural features that allow them to control the indoor temperature, such as thermostats, fans, and operable windows (Nicol & Humphreys, 2002). In fact, the mere perception of control can increase occupants' tolerance for above-average and below-average indoor temperatures (Bauman et al., 1994; Brager, Paliaga, & De Dear, 2004). Furthermore, neuroaesthetics research has previously shown that cultural value and context can influence aesthetic responses to visual art. In one study, people were more likely to rate abstract visual artworks as beautiful if the images were labeled as gallery art pieces than if they were labeled as computer-generated graphics. Images assigned to the gallery condition also elicited heightened neural activity in reward centers of the brain, including the orbitofrontal cortex, suggesting that the cultural significance communicated by the label alone influenced participants' emotional responses (Kirk, Skov, Hulme, Christensen, & Zeki, 2009). Similar research could be undertaken in order to assess how context and cultural significance influence aesthetic responses to architecture. Culture-related factors that may influence aesthetic experiences include perceived cost, location, building function, and whether or not the building was designed by a well-known architect.

Emotion-valuation systems

The brain's reward circuitry plays a key role in modulating the emotions people feel when immersed in architectural spaces. Brown and colleagues proposed that aesthetic emotions are processed via a neural circuit that involves activation of the anterior insula, the orbitofrontal cortex (OFC), the anterior cingulate cortex (ACC), and the basal ganglia (Brown, Gao, Tisdelle, Eickhoff, & Liotti, 2011). They are likely involved in generating pleasurable experiences in the built environment.

In one study, images of curved buildings generated significantly greater activity in the ACC than images of rectilinear buildings when participants performed a beauty rating task (Vartanian et al., 2013). Curved interiors were also judged as significantly more beautiful and pleasing than rectilinear spaces in that experiment, suggesting that ACC activation was associated with a greater reward response generated by curvilinear architectural forms. In a follow-up study, participants showed a greater inclination to exit closed rooms compared with open rooms. These avoidance decisions in response to closed spaces were associated with significant activation of the anterior midcingulate cortex (aMCC) (Vartanian et al., 2015), which connects directly to the amygdala (Vogt & Pandya, 1987) and helps govern the emotion of fear (Whalen et al., 1998). Brain systems involved in processing negative emotions may therefore play an important role in how people experience the built environment. Supporting this possibility, another study found that subjects who took a stress test while immersed in a virtual simulation of a closed space experienced a greater stress response than subjects who took the test in a more open virtual room. The closed-room condition was associated with heightened and prolonged spikes in salivary cortisol compared with the open-room condition (Fich et al., 2014). It is not surprising that more closed spaces were associated with fear and elevated cortisol levels in these two studies, respectively, given that the limbic system influences the downstream release of stress hormones via the neuroendocrine and autonomic nervous systems (Ulrich-Lai & Herman, 2009). The close relationship between emotion-regulating neural networks, such as the limbic system, and stress response represents a possible mechanism by which maladaptive architectural spaces might damage a person's physical health over the long term (Joye, 2007).

An important question in environmental psychology is the extent to which emotional responses to environments are governed by bottom-up processing of low-level sensory information, or by top-down cognitive appraisals of high-level semantic content (Ibarra et al., 2017). Ulrich's psychoevolutionary framework proposes that affective experiences in the physical environment are heavily influenced by innate, unconscious responses to stimuli based on their relevance to human survival (Ulrich, 1983). Presumably, such responses would be adaptive, written into our biology over the course of evolutionary history. Supporting this view, some research suggests that affective responses to environmental scenes involve rapid, automatic response mechanisms (Hietanen & Korpela,

2004; Joye & Dewitte, 2016; Korpela, Klemettilä, & Hietanen, 2002; Valtchanov & Ellard, 2015). Adaptive mechanisms of aesthetic response could be viewed as advantageous to survival because they enable individuals to identify favorable environments based on ancestral experience (Joye, 2007; Kaplan, 1987; Ulrich, 1983).

If aesthetic emotions are partially rooted in human evolution, then could architects manipulate sensory features of the built environment to trigger favorable affective responses? Alexander and colleagues believe that builders, for millennia, have been doing just that. They identified a series of visual patterns that are commonly found in vernacular architecture across the globe. Patterns like incremental scaling and local symmetries, they contend, transcend cultural boundaries precisely because they generate positive human emotions (Alexander, 1977, 2002; Salingaros, 2007). Further research is needed to identify the neural circuitry involved in generating diverse emotions in response to the built environment, including liking, wanting, contemplation, and awe, all of which may be associated with distinct patterns of neural activation (Chatterjee & Vartanian, 2014).

Emotional responses to architectural spaces may also be somewhat distinct from cognitive evaluations of the built environment. In aesthetics research, participants are often asked to evaluate stimuli using metrics of beauty or attractiveness (Bermudez, 2016). These cognitive judgments of architecture tend to covary with neural activity in the prefrontal cortex, specifically the superior frontal gyrus and the frontopolar cortex, as well as with neural areas responsible for memory retrieval like the parahippocampus (Vartanian et al., 2013). These brain regions are somewhat different from the reward pathways associated with emotional responses to architecture. Neural activity in the prefrontal cortex indicates that high-level reasoning and intellectual analysis can play a meaningful role in aesthetic evaluation. Activation of the hippocampus during beauty judgments, furthermore, suggests that aesthetic evaluations may be influenced by memories, education, and expertise. In other words, it is possible that beauty judgments are more affected by top-down processing in knowledge-meaning systems than emotional responses to architecture, which may depend more directly on bottom-up sensory inputs from the environment itself.

If aesthetic judgments and emotions involve distinct types of neural processing, then it is possible that a person's conscious evaluations of an architectural space might be quite different from their unconscious affective responses to their surroundings. Architectural theorists have long debated this tension between "thinking" and "feeling" in the built environment,1 and neuroscientific research could meaningfully inform this debate. Similar work has already emerged in the neuroaesthetics literature. Di Dio and colleagues, for instance, found that aesthetic judgment tasks may interact or even interfere with emotional responses to visual art. In one of their fMRI studies, participants who made beauty ratings of Renaissance sculptures exhibited decreased neural activity in the right insula, which is part of the brain's reward system, compared with subjects who did not make beauty ratings but instead were instructed to observe the sculptures passively (Di Dio, Macaluso, & Rizzolatti, 2007). Similar studies could examine potential interactions between aesthetic emotions and evaluations in the built environment.

Major Challenges, Goals, and Suggestions

We outlined three large-scale neural systems that we believe to be most relevant to architectural experience. This neuroscientific model is intended to help neuroarchitecture transition from a descriptive to an experimental discipline. However, neuroscientific research on the built environment faces several practical challenges related to psychology, measurement, and application. Addressing these challenges will provide structure to the discipline as it develops.

Advancing the psychology of architecture

Psychology and neuroscience are closely linked disciplines, and behavioral research is an important tool for understanding and interpreting patterns of neural activity. As such, the maturation of neuroaesthetics as a scientific discipline has drawn on previous advances in empirical aesthetics, dating back to Fechner's work in the late 19th century relating inner and outer psychophysics (Fechner, 1876). These theoretical and empirical advances include Arnheim's perceptual psychology (Arnheim, 1954), Berlyne's work on complexity and arousal (Berlyne, 1971), and Martindale's historical-cultural analysis (Martindale, 1990). Although some architecturally relevant behavioral research has emerged from the disciplines of environmental psychology and sociology (Baum & Davis, 1980; Baum, Singer, & Baum, 1981; Baum, Valins, & others, 1977; Case, 1981; Case & Schlagel, 1980; Graham, Gosling, & Travis, 2015), there currently exists no academic tradition grounded specifically in the psychology of architecture. A robust literature on the psychology of architecture may be a necessary foundation for the development of an insightful neuroscience of architecture.

Measurement challenges

The neuroscience of architecture faces at least four measurement challenges: dimensionality, multi-modality, temporality, and depth of psychological processing. Dimensionality challenges include the difficulty of operationalizing three-dimensional environments, as well as the difficulty of quantifying nonvisual sensory dimensions of architectural experience. Neuroaesthetics research generally involves using two-dimensional images as experimental stimuli. Images can provide somewhat representative simulations of flat paintings. By contrast, much of the depth and immersive quality of architectural spaces is lost when buildings are represented in photographs. Virtual reality could become a useful tool for approximating architectural experience in future research. Another solution would be to use emerging technology like mobile electroencephalogram (EEG) (Kontson et al., 2015; Tröndle & Tschacher, 2012) to infer neural activity "in the field," while people are interacting with real buildings. However, technological issues with EEG remain. For instance, it is still difficult to infer mental states from EEG signals, and it is also difficult to separate signal from noise. Another challenge involves research on nonvisual experience in the built environment. Most neuroaesthetics research has focused on the perception of visual art, and neuroarchitecture research to date has been similarly biased toward visual experience in the built environment. However, researchers cannot hope to make comprehensive insights about architectural experience without including nonvisual sensory modalities, like audition and somatosensation, in their work.

Another measurement challenge for neuroarchitecture relates to the extended time course of aesthetic experiences in the built environment. Neuroaestheticians generally measure aesthetic responses to artwork that last no more than a few seconds (Cela-Conde et al., 2013). Although real-world interactions with art typically last longer than a few seconds (Chatterjee, 2014; Leder & Nadal, 2014), people generally spend less than 20 s looking at paintings (Smith & Smith, 2001). By contrast, encounters with buildings typically occur on the scale of minutes to hours. Furthermore, people are often exposed to the same buildings on a daily basis over the course of months or years, as in the case of homes and offices. Moving forward, it will be important to measure both psychological and neurophysiological data over the course of time in order to understand the chronic implications of long-term environmental exposure.

Moving beyond aesthetic preference, it will also be valuable to investigate the neural correlates of deeper and more complex mental states that can be induced by the built environment. Some architectural spaces (including places of worship) are specifically designed to foster deep psychological states like contemplation, whereas others (such as schools) are built to foster learning. Still other buildings (like artists' studios) are intended to inspire creative thought. It is therefore important for researchers to understand how design features of buildings might drive these nuanced mental states.

Applicability of research

One of the goals of neuroarchitectural research is to inform the design of more enriching buildings to promote flourishing in mental health and wellbeing (Eberhard, 2009). As such, studies in this discipline need to test hypotheses that can meaningfully inform architectural practice. Most studies to date have focused on measuring isolated variables in the built environment, including room color (Küller, Mikellides, & Janssens, 2009), lighting (Shin et al., 2015), ceiling height (Vartanian et al., 2015), and contour of architectural surfaces (Banaei et al., 2017; Shemesh et al., 2017; Vartanian et al., 2013). An advantage of using these straightforward variables is that they can easily be isolated and manipulated in an experimental framework. However, if the variables tested are simple, they might fail to adequately capture meaningful aesthetic qualities of the built environment (Cooper & Burton, 2014). Reductive environmental measures could also alienate practicing architects by promoting oversimplified dialogue about complex architectural and urban systems. As one pair of scholars asserted, "the currently dominating theoretical approaches … that focus on a limited number of individual measures should give way to ecological models; that is, the analysis of complex, situational processes at different scales of the environment" (Kyttä, Kahila, & Broberg, 2011, p. 633).

Some researchers have developed more dynamic and nuanced measures of the physical environment. In one study, researchers used a combination of low-level visual features (i.e., image statistics) and high-level visual features (e.g., lighting, windows, skyline geometry) to predict aesthetic responses to images of urban landscapes (Ibarra et al., 2017). Future studies could also focus on how architectural *processes*, e.g., how a building is constructed, influence psychological experiences in the built environment, as proposed by Alexander (2004). This proposed research would be analogous to empirical aesthetics studies exploring the psychological implications of different painting techniques (see, for instance, Taylor, Micolich, & Jonas, 2002).

CONCLUSION

Since ancient times, philosophers have acknowledged the experiential importance of architectural *beauty*. However, this topic has only received attention from the scientific community within the past decade. The goal of this chapter is to introduce a neuroscientific model, the *aesthetic triad*, which serves as a useful framework for investigating perceptions of beauty in the built environment. Within this framework, we discussed how sensory and emotional experiences in the built environment relate to biological response mechanisms shaped by human evolution. We also considered how these basic response patterns are influenced by a person's expertise, culture, and personal experiences. This model provides a theoretical context for researchers interested in exploring the sensory, emotional, and cognitive dimensions of architectural experience. Many challenges remain regarding experimental design, theoretical framing, and practical application. Despite these challenges, however, neuroarchitecture is at the brink of an important transition away from theoretical inquiry and toward empirical research in which architecture itself is the target of neuroscientific investigation. We hope that this emerging discipline will offer new insights into the human–environment connection and that these findings will inform that design of more beautiful and restorative architectural spaces in the years ahead.

ACKNOWLEDGMENTS

This chapter is adapted from a review previously published as Alex Coburn, Oshin Vartanian, and Anjan Chatterjee, "Buildings, beauty, and the brain: A neuroscience of architectural experience," *Journal of Cognitive Neuroscience*, 29:9 (September, 2017), pp. 1521–1531. © 2017 by the Massachusetts Institute of Technology. It is reprinted courtesy of the MIT Press.

NOTE

1. See, for instance, "Contrasting concepts of harmony in architecture," a publication of the 1982 debate between Peter Eisenmann and Christopher Alexander at Harvard (Steil, 2004).

REFERENCES

Adams, M. (2014). Quality of urban spaces and wellbeing. In R. Cooper, E. Burton, & C. L. Cooper (Eds.), *Wellbeing and the environment* (Vol. 2, pp. 249–270). Chichester, England: John Wiley & Sons Inc.

Alexander, C. (1977). *A pattern language: Towns, buildings, construction*. New York: Oxford University Press.

Alexander, C. (2002). *The phenomenon of life: An essay on the art of building and the nature of the universe* (Vol. 1). Berkeley, CA: Center for Environmental Structure.

Alexander, C., & Carey, S. (1968). Subsymmetries. *Perception & Psychophysics, 4*, 73–77.

Ali, M. M., & Moon, K. S. (2007). Structural developments in tall buildings: Current trends and future prospects. *Architectural Science Review, 50*, 205–223.

Appleton, J. (1975). *The experience of landscape*. London: John Wiley & Sons.

Arnheim, R. (1954). *Art and visual perception: A psychology of the creative eye*. Berkeley, CA: University of California Press.

Astur, R. S., Taylor, L. B., Mamelak, A. N., Philpott, L., & Sutherland, R. J. (2002). Humans with hippocampus damage display severe spatial memory impairments in a virtual Morris water task. *Behavioural Brain Research, 132*, 77–84.

Balling, J. D., & Falk, J. H. (1982). Development of visual preference for natural environments. *Environment and Behavior, 14*, 5–28.

Banaei, M., Hatami, J., Yazdanfar, A., & Gramann, K. (2017). Walking through architectural spaces: The impact of interior forms on human brain dynamics. *Frontiers in Human Neuroscience, 11*, 477.

Barbara, A., & Perliss, A. (2006). *Invisible architecture: Experiencing places through the sense of smell*. Milan: Skira.

Barton, J., & Pretty, J. (2010). What is the best dose of nature and green exercise for improving mental health? A multi-study analysis. *Environmental Science & Technology, 44*, 3947.

Baum, A., & Davis, G. E. (1980). Reducing the stress of high-density living: An architectural intervention. *Journal of Personality and Social Psychology, 38*, 471.

Baum, A., Singer, J. E., & Baum, C. S. (1981). Stress and the environment. *Journal of Social Issues, 37*, 4–35.

Baum, A., Valins, S., & others. (1977). *Architecture and social behavior: Psychological studies of social density*. Hillsdale, NJ: L. Erlbaum Associates.

Bauman, F., Arens, E. A., Fountain, M., Huizenga, C., Miura, K., Xu, T., … Borgers, T. (1994). *Localized thermal distribution for office buildings; final report—Phase III*. Berkeley, CA: Center for the Built Environment.

Berlyne, D. E. (1970). Novelty, complexity, and hedonic value. *Perception & Psychophysics, 8*, 279–286.

Berlyne, D. E. (1971). *Aesthetics and psychobiology*. New York: Appleton-Century-Crofts.

Berman, M. G., Hout, M. C., Kardan, O., Hunter, M. R., Yourganov, G., Henderson, J. M., … Jonides, J. (2014). The perception of naturalness correlates with low-level visual features of environmental scenes. *PLoS One, 9*, e114572.

Berman, M. G., Jonides, J., & Kaplan, S. (2008). The cognitive benefits of interacting with nature. *Psychological Science, 19*, 1207–1212.

Berman, M. G., Kross, E., Krpan, K. M., Askren, M. K., Burson, A., Deldin, P. J., … Jonides, J. (2012). Interacting with nature improves cognition and affect for individuals with depression. *Journal of Affective Disorders, 140*, 300–305.

Bermudez, J. (2016, September). *Contemplative neuroaesthetics*. Presented at the AFNA 2016: Connections—Bridgesynapses, La Jolla, California.

Berto, R. (2005). Exposure to restorative environments helps restore attentional capacity. *Journal of Environmental Psychology, 25*, 249–259.

Birkhoff, G. D. (1933). *Aesthetic measure*. Cambridge, MA: Harvard University Press.

Bowler, D. E., Buyung-Ali, L. M., Knight, T. M., & Pullin, A. S. (2010). A systematic review of evidence for the added benefits to health of exposure to natural environments. *BMC Public Health, 10*, 1–10.

Brady, N., & Field, D. J. (2000). Local contrast in natural images: Normalisation and coding efficiency. *Perception, 29*, 1041–1055.

Brager, G., Paliaga, G., & De Dear, R. (2004). Operable windows, personal control and occupant comfort. *ASHRAE Transactions, 110*, 17–35.

Bratman, G. N., Daily, G. C., Levy, B. J., & Gross, J. J. (2015). The benefits of nature experience: Improved affect and cognition. *Landscape and Urban Planning, 138*, 41–50.

Brown, M. G., & Lee, C. C. (2016). From savannas to settlements: Exploring cognitive foundations for the design of urban spaces. *Frontiers in Psychology, 7*, 1–8.

Brown, S., Gao, X., Tisdelle, L., Eickhoff, S. B., & Liotti, M. (2011). Naturalizing aesthetics: Brain areas for aesthetic appraisal across sensory modalities. *Neuroimage, 58*, 250–258.

Case, F. D. (1981). Dormitory architecture influences patterns of student social-relations over time. *Environment and Behavior, 13*, 23–41.

Case, F. D., & Schlagel, B. (1980). Designer intentions and user evaluations: Two college residence hall lounges. *Housing and Society, 7*, 35–53.

Cela-Conde, C. J., García-Prieto, J., Ramasco, J. J., Mirasso, C. R., Bajo, R., Munar, E., … Maestú, F. (2013). Dynamics of brain networks in the aesthetic appreciation. *Proceedings of the National Academy of Sciences, 110*, 10454–10461.

Chatterjee, A. (2004a). Prospects for a cognitive neuroscience of visual aesthetics. *Bulletin of Psychology and the Arts, 4*, 56–60.

Chatterjee, A. (2004b). The neuropsychology of visual artistic production. *Neuropsychologia, 42*, 1568–1583.

Chatterjee, A. (2011). Neuroaesthetics: A coming of age story. *Journal of Cognitive Neuroscience, 23*, 53–62.

Chatterjee, A. (2013). *The aesthetic brain: How we evolved to desire beauty and enjoy art*. Oxford, England: Oxford University Press.

Chatterjee, A. (2014). Scientific aesthetics: Three steps forward. *British Journal of Psychology, 105*, 465–467.

Chatterjee, A., & Vartanian, O. (2014). Neuroaesthetics. *Trends in Cognitive Sciences, 18,* 370–375.

Chatterjee, A., & Vartanian, O. (2016). Neuroscience of aesthetics. *Annals of the New York Academy of Sciences, 1369,* 172–194.

Choo, H., Nasar, J. L., Nikrahei, B., & Walther, D. B. (2017). Neural codes of seeing architectural styles. *Scientific Reports, 7,* 1–8.

Coburn, A., Kardan, O., Kotabe, H. P., Steinberg, J., Hout, M. C., Robbins, A., ... Berman, M. G. (2019). Psychological responses to natural patterns in architecture. *Journal of Environmental Psychology, 62,* 133–145.

Coburn, A., Vartanian, O., & Chatterjee, A. (2017). Buildings, beauty, and the brain: A neuro-science of architectural experience. *Journal of Cognitive Neuroscience, 29,* 1521–1531.

Cooper, R., & Burton, E. (2014). Wellbeing and the environmental implications for design. In R. Cooper, E. Burton, & C. L. Cooper (Eds.), *Wellbeing and the environment* (Vol. 2, pp. 653–668). Chichester, England: John Wiley & Sons Inc.

Cooper, R., Burton, E., & Cooper, C. L. (Eds.). (2014). *Wellbeing and the environment* (Vol. 2). Chichester, England: John Wiley & Sons Inc.

Dance, A. (2017). Science and culture: The brain within buildings. *Proceedings of the National Academy of Sciences, 114,* 785–787.

Day, H. (1967). Evaluations of subjective complexity, pleasingness and interestingness for a series of random polygons varying in complexity. *Perception & Psychophysics, 2,* 281–286.

Di Dio, C., Macaluso, E., & Rizzolatti, G. (2007). The golden beauty: Brain response to classical and renaissance sculptures. *PloS One, 2,* e1201.

Dosen, A. S., & Ostwald, M. J. (2016). Evidence for prospect-refuge theory: A meta-analysis of the findings of environmental preference research. *City, Territory and Architecture, 3,* 1–14.

Eberhard, J. P. (2008). *Brain landscape: The coexistence of neuroscience and architecture.* Oxford, England: Oxford University Press.

Eberhard, J. P. (2009). Applying neuroscience to architecture. *Neuron, 62,* 753–756.

Edelstein, E. A., Gramann, K., Schulze, J., Shamlo, N. B., van Erp, E., Vankov, A., ... Macagno, E. (2008). Neural responses during navigation in the virtual aided design laboratory: Brain dynamics of orientation in architecturally ambiguous space. In S. Haq, C. Hölscher, & S. Torgrude (Eds.), *Movement and Orientation in Built Environments: Evaluating Design Rationale and User Cognition* (pp. 35–41). Veracruz, Mexico: SFB/TR8 Spatial Cognition.

Epstein, R., & Kanwisher, N. (1998). A cortical representation of the local visual environment. *Nature, 392,* 598–601.

Evans, G. W., Gonnella, C., Marcynyszyn, L. A., Gentile, L., & Salpekar, N. (2005). The role of chaos in poverty and children's socioemotional adjustment. *Psychological Science, 16,* 560–565.

Evans, G. W., & McCoy, J. M. (1998). When buildings don't work: The role of architecture in human health. *Journal of Environmental Psychology, 18,* 85–94.

Eysenck, H. J. (1957). *The dynamics of anxiety and hysteria: An experimental application of modern learning theory to psychiatry.* London: Routledge & Kegan.

Fanger, P. O. (1973). Assessment of man's thermal comfort in practice. *British Journal of Industrial Medicine, 30,* 313–324.

Fechner, G. T. (1876). *Vorschule der Aesthetik.* Leipzig: Breitkopf & Hartel.

Fich, L. B., Jönsson, P., Kirkegaard, P. H., Wallergård, M., Garde, A. H., & Hansen, Å. (2014). Can architectural design alter the physiological reaction to psychosocial stress? A virtual TSST experiment. *Physiology & Behavior, 135,* 91–97.

Frith, C. D., & Nias, D. K. B. (1974). What determines aesthetic preferences? *Journal of General Psychology, 91*, 163–173.

Geisler, W. S. (2007). Visual perception and the statistical properties of natural scenes. *Annual Review of Psychology, 59*, 167–192.

Graham, D. J., & Field, D. J. (2007). Statistical regularities of art images and natural scenes: Spectra, sparseness and nonlinearities. *Spatial Vision, 21*, 149–164.

Graham, D. J., & Redies, C. (2010). Statistical regularities in art: Relations with visual coding and perception. *Vision Research, 50*, 1503–1509.

Graham, D., Schwarz, B., Chatterjee, A., & Leder, H. (2016). Preference for luminance histogram regularities in natural scenes. *Vision Research, 120*, 11–21.

Graham, L. T., Gosling, S. D., & Travis, C. K. (2015). The psychology of home environments: A call for research on residential space. *Perspectives on Psychological Science, 10*, 346–356.

Güçlütürk, Y., Jacobs, R. H. A. H., & van Lier, R. (2016). Liking versus complexity: Decomposing the inverted U-curve. *Frontiers in Human Neuroscience, 10*, 1–11.

Hagerhall, C. M., Purcell, T., & Taylor, R. (2004). Fractal dimension of landscape silhouette outlines as a predictor of landscape preference. *Journal of Environmental Psychology, 24*, 247–255.

Hartig, T. (2008). Green space, psychological restoration, and health inequality. *The Lancet, 372*, 1614–1615.

Heintzelman, S. J., & King, L. A. (2014). (The feeling of) meaning-as-information. *Personality and Social Psychology Review, 18*, 153–167.

Hietanen, J. K., & Korpela, K. M. (2004). Do both negative and positive environmental scenes elicit rapid affective processing? *Environment and Behavior, 36*, 558–577.

Ibarra, F. F., Kardan, O., Hunter, M. R., Kotabe, H. P., Meyer, F. A. C., & Berman, M. G. (2017). Image feature types and their predictions of aesthetic preference and naturalness. *Frontiers in Psychology, 8*, 632. doi:10.3389/fpsyg.2017.00632

Imamoglu, Ç. (2000). Complexity, liking and familiarity: Architecture and non-architecture Turkish students' assessments of traditional and modern house facades. *Journal of Environmental Psychology, 20*, 5–16.

Jacobsen, T., Schubotz, R. I., Höfel, L., & Cramon, D. Y. V. (2006). Brain correlates of aesthetic judgment of beauty. *Neuroimage, 29*, 276–285.

Jones-Smith, K., & Mathur, H. (2006). Fractal analysis: Revisiting Pollock's drip paintings. *Nature, 444*, E9–E10.

Joye, Y. (2007). Architectural lessons from environmental psychology: The case of biophilic architecture. *Review of General Psychology, 11*, 305–328.

Joye, Y., & Dewitte, S. (2016). Up speeds you down. Awe-evoking monumental buildings trigger behavioral and perceived freezing. *Journal of Environmental Psychology, 47*, 112–125.

Kaplan, R., & Kaplan, S. (1989). *The experience of nature—A psychological perspective.* Cambridge: Cambridge University Press.

Kaplan, S. (1987). Aesthetics, affect, and cognition: Environmental preference from an evolutionary perspective. *Environment and Behavior, 19*, 3–32.

Kaplan, S. (1995). The restorative benefits of nature: Toward an integrative framework. *Journal of Environmental Psychology, 15*, 169–182.

Kaplan, S., & Berman, M. G. (2010). Directed attention as a common resource for executive functioning and self-regulation. *Perspectives on Psychological Science, 5*, 43–57.

Kaplan, S., Kaplan, R., & Wendt, J. S. (1972). Rated preference and complexity for natural and urban visual material. *Perception & Psychophysics, 12*, 354–356.

Kellert, S. R. (2003). *Kinship to mastery: Biophilia in human evolution and development.* Washington, DC: Island Press.

Kellert, S. R. (2005). *Building for life: Designing and understanding the human-nature connection.* Washington, DC: Island Press.

Kirk, U., Skov, M., Christensen, M. S., & Nygaard, N. (2009). Brain correlates of aesthetic expertise: A parametric fMRI study. *Brain and Cognition, 69*, 306–315.

Kirk, U., Skov, M., Hulme, O., Christensen, M. S., & Zeki, S. (2009). Modulation of aesthetic value by semantic context: An fMRI study. *NeuroImage, 44*, 1125–1132.

Kontson, K. L., Megjhani, M., Brantley, J. A., Cruz-Garza, J. G., Nakagome, S., Robleto, D., … Contreras-Vidal, J. L. (2015). Your brain on art: Emergent cortical dynamics during aesthetic experiences. *Frontiers in Human Neuroscience, 9*, 1–17.

Korpela, K. M., Klemettilä, T., & Hietanen, J. K. (2002). Evidence for rapid affective evaluation of environmental scenes. *Environment and Behavior, 34*, 634–650.

Kotabe, H. P., Kardan, O., & Berman, M. G. (2016). The order of disorder: Deconstructing visual disorder and its effect on rule-breaking. *Journal of Experimental Psychology: General, 145*, 1713–1727.

Kotabe, H. P., Kardan, O., & Berman, M. G. (2017). The nature-disorder paradox: A perceptual study on how nature is disorderly yet aesthetically preferred. *Journal of Experimental Psychology: General, 146*, 1126–1142.

Kravitz, D. J., Peng, C. S., & Baker, C. I. (2011). Real-world scene representations in high-level visual cortex: It's the spaces more than the places. *Journal of Neuroscience, 31*, 7322–7333.

Küller, R., Mikellides, B., & Janssens, J. (2009). Color, arousal, and performance—A comparison of three experiments. *Color Research & Application, 34*, 141–152.

Kyttä, M., Kahila, M., & Broberg, A. (2011). Perceived environmental quality as an input to urban infill policy-making. *Urban Design International, 16*, 19–35.

Leder, H., & Nadal, M. (2014). Ten years of a model of aesthetic appreciation and aesthetic judgments : The aesthetic episode—Developments and challenges in empirical aesthetics. *British Journal of Psychology, 105*, 443–464.

Leder, H., Oeberst, A., Augustin, D., & Belke, B. (2004). A model of aesthetic appreciation and aesthetic judgments. *British Journal of Psychology, 95*, 489–508.

Lehrer, J. (2008). *Proust was a neuroscientist.* Boston, MA: Houghton Mifflin Harcourt.

Maguire, E. A., Gadian, D. G., Johnsrude, I. S., Good, C. D., Ashburner, J., Frackowiak, R. S. J., & Frith, C. D. (2000). Navigation-related structural change in the hippocampi of taxi drivers. *Proceedings of the National Academy of Sciences, 97*, 4398–4403.

Mallgrave, H. F. (2010). *The architect's brain: Neuroscience, creativity, and architecture.* Malden, MA: Wiley-Blackwell.

Marchette, S. A., Vass, L. K., Ryan, J., & Epstein, R. A. (2015). Outside looking in: Landmark generalization in the human navigational system. *Journal of Neuroscience, 35*, 14896–14908.

Martindale, C. (1990). The clockwork muse: The predictability of artistic change. *Journal of Aesthetics and Art Criticism, 50*(2), 171–173.

McNaughton, B. L., Battaglia, F. P., Jensen, O., Moser, E. I., & Moser, M.-B. (2006). Path integration and the neural basis of the "cognitive map." *Nature Reviews Neuroscience, 7*, 663–678.

Mégevand, P., Groppe, D. M., Goldfinger, M. S., Hwang, S. T., Kingsley, P. B., Davidesco, I., & Mehta, A. D. (2014). Seeing scenes: Topographic visual hallucinations evoked by direct electrical stimulation of the parahippocampal place area. *The Journal of Neuroscience, 34*, 5399–5405.

Nadal, M., Munar, E., Marty, G., & Cela-Conde, C. J. (2010). Visual complexity and beauty appreciation: Explaining the divergence of results. *Empirical Studies of the Arts, 28*, 173–191.

Nambu, A., Tokuno, H., & Takada, M. (2002). Functional significance of the cortico-subthalamo–pallidal "hyperdirect" pathway. *Neuroscience Research, 43*, 111–117.

Nicol, J. F., & Humphreys, M. A. (2002). Adaptive thermal comfort and sustainable thermal standards for buildings. *Energy & Buildings, 34*, 563–572.

O'Keefe, J., & Nadel, L. (1978). *The hippocampus as a cognitive map*. New York: Oxford University Press.

Oppenheimer, D. M., & Frank, M. C. (2008). A rose in any other font would not smell as sweet: Effects of perceptual fluency on categorization. *Cognition, 106*, 1178–1194.

Palmer, S. E., Schloss, K. B., & Sammartino, J. (2013). Visual aesthetics and human preference. *Annual Review of Psychology, 64*, 77–107.

Passini, R., Pigot, H., Rainville, C., & Tétreault, M.-H. (2000). Wayfinding in a nursing home for advanced dementia of the Alzheimer's type. *Environment and Behavior, 32*, 684–710.

Ramachandran, V. S., & Hirstein, W. (1999). The science of art: A neurological theory of aesthetic experience. *Journal of Consciousness Studies, 6*, 15–51.

Reber, R., Schwarz, N., & Winkielman, P. (2004). Processing fluency and aesthetic pleasure: Is beauty in the perceiver's processing experience? *Personality and Social Psychology Review, 8*, 364–382.

Redies, C. (2007). A universal model of esthetic perception based on the sensory coding of natural stimuli. *Spatial Vision, 21*, 97–117.

Rhodes, G., Proffitt, F., Grady, J. M., & Sumich, A. (1998). Facial symmetry and the perception of beauty. *Psychonomic Bulletin & Review, 5*, 659–669.

Robinson, S., & Pallasmaa, J. (Eds.). (2015). *Mind in architecture: Neuroscience, embodiment, and the future of design*. Cambridge, MA: The MIT Press.

Salingaros, N. A. (2003). The sensory value of ornament. *Communication and Cognition, 36*, 331–352.

Salingaros, N. A. (2007). *A theory of architecture*. Solingen, Germany: ISI Distributed Titles.

Shemesh, A., Talmon, R., Karp, O., Amir, I., Bar, M., & Grobman, Y. J. (2017). Affective response to architecture—Investigating human reaction to spaces with different geometry. *Architectural Science Review, 60*, 116–125.

Shin, Y.-B., Woo, S.-H., Kim, D.-H., Kim, J., Kim, J.-J., & Park, J. Y. (2015). The effect on emotions and brain activity by the direct/indirect lighting in the residential environment. *Neuroscience Letters, 584*, 28–32.

Singer, W., & Gray, C. M. (1995). Visual feature integration and the temporal correlation hypothesis. *Annual Review of Neuroscience, 18*, 555–586.

Smith, J. K., & Smith, L. F. (2001). Spending time on art. *Empirical Studies of the Arts, 19*, 229–236.

Spehar, B., Clifford, C. W., Newell, B. R., & Taylor, R. P. (2003). Universal aesthetic of fractals. *Computers & Graphics, 27*, 813–820.

Spiers, H. J., & Barry, C. (2015). Neural systems supporting navigation. *Current Opinion in Behavioral Sciences, 1*, 47–55.

Steil, L. (2004). Contrasting concepts of harmony in architecture. In B. Hanson, M. Mehaffy, & N. Salingaros (Eds.), *Contrasting concepts of harmony in architecture*. London: Katarxix Publications. Retrieved from http://www.katarxis3.com/Alexander_Eisenman_Debate.htm.

Taylor, R. P., Micolich, A., & Jonas, D. (2002). The construction of Jackson Pollock's fractal drip paintings. *Leonardo, 35,* 203–207.

Taylor, R. P., Micolich, A. P., & Jonas, D. (1999). Fractal analysis of Pollock's drip paintings. *Nature, 399,* 422.

Taylor, R. P., Spehar, B., Wise, J. A., Clifford, C. W., Newell, B. R., Hagerhall, C. M., … Martin, T. P. (2005). Perceptual and physiological responses to the visual complexity of fractal patterns. *Nonlinear Dynamics, Psychology, and Life Sciences, 9,* 89–114.

Thorsson, S., Honjo, T., Lindberg, F., Eliasson, I., & Lim, E.-M. (2007). Thermal comfort and outdoor activity in Japanese urban public places. *Environment and Behavior, 39*(5), 660–684.

Tröndle, M., & Tschacher, W. (2012). The physiology of phenomenology: The effects of artworks. *Empirical Studies of the Arts, 30,* 75–113.

Tullett, A. M., Kay, A. C., & Inzlicht, M. (2015). Randomness increases self-reported anxiety and neurophysiological correlates of performance monitoring. *Social Cognitive and Affective Neuroscience, 10,* 628–635.

Ulrich, R. S. (1977). Visual landscape preference: A model and application. *Man-Environment Systems, 7,* 279–293.

Ulrich, R. S. (1983). Aesthetic and affective response to natural environment. In I. Altman, & J. Wohlwill (Eds.). *Behavior and the natural environment* (pp. 85–125). Boston, MA: Springer.

Ulrich-Lai, Y. M., & Herman, J. P. (2009). Neural regulation of endocrine and autonomic stress responses. *Nature Reviews Neuroscience, 10,* 397–409.

Valtchanov, D., Barton, K. R., & Ellard, C. (2010). Restorative effects of virtual nature settings. *CyberPsychology, Behavior & Social Networking, 13,* 503–512.

Valtchanov, D., & Ellard, C. G. (2015). Cognitive and affective responses to natural scenes: Effects of low level visual properties on preference, cognitive load and eye-movements. *Journal of Environmental Psychology, 43,* 184–195.

Vartanian, O., & Goel, V. (2004). Neuroanatomical correlates of aesthetic preference for paintings. *Neuroreport, 15,* 893–897.

Vartanian, O., Navarrete, G., Chatterjee, A., Fich, L. B., Gonzalez-Mora, J. L., Leder, H., … Skov, M. (2015). Architectural design and the brain: Effects of ceiling height and perceived enclosure on beauty judgments and approach-avoidance decisions. *Journal of Environmental Psychology, 41,* 10–18.

Vartanian, O., Navarrete, G., Chatterjee, A., Fich, L. B., Leder, H., Modrono, C., … Skov, M. (2013). Impact of contour on aesthetic judgments and approach-avoidance decisions in architecture. *Proceedings of the National Academy of Sciences, 110,* 10446–10453.

Vaughan, E. (2013, September 30). The value and impact of building codes. Environmental and Energy Study Institute. Retrieved from http://www.eesi.org/papers/view/the-value-and-impact-of-building-codes.

Venturi, R., Scott Brown, D., Rattenbury, K., & Hardingham, S. (2007). *Learning from Las Vegas.* Abingdon, England: Routledge.

Venturi, R., Scully, V., & Drexler, A. (1977). *Complexity and contradiction in architecture* (2nd ed.). New York: The Museum of Modern Art, New York.

Villani, D., & Riva, G. (2011). Does interactive media enhance the management of stress? Suggestions from a controlled study. *Cyberpsychology, Behavior, and Social Networking, 15,* 24–30.

Vogt, B. A., & Pandya, D. N. (1987). Cingulate cortex of the rhesus monkey: II. Cortical afferents. *Journal of Comparative Neurology, 262,* 271–289.

Ward, J. (2015). *The student's guide to cognitive neuroscience.* New York: Psychology Press.

Whalen, P. J., Rauch, S. L., Etcoff, N. L., McInerney, S. C., Lee, M. B., & Jenike, M. A. (1998). Masked presentations of emotional facial expressions modulate amygdala activity without explicit knowledge. *The Journal of Neuroscience, 18,* 411–418.

Wiesmann, M., & Ishai, A. (2011). Expertise reduces neural cost but does not modulate repetition suppression. *Cognitive Neuroscience, 2,* 57–65.

Wilson, A., & Chatterjee, A. (2005). The assessment of preference for balance: Introducing a new test. *Empirical Studies of the Arts, 23,* 165–180.

Wilson, E. O. (1984). *Biophilia.* Harvard, CT: Harvard University Press.

Wilson, E. O., & Kellert, S. R. (1995). *The biophilia hypothesis.* Washington, DC: Island Press.

CHAPTER 30

AESTHETICS, TECHNOLOGY, AND POPULAR MOVIES

JAMES E. CUTTING

AESTHETICS is about sensory and emotional values, preferences, and tastes. It is also about recognizing style and virtuosity. It often reflects and creates nonutilitarian pleasure (or pain, or horror, or disgust) and it has a central but nonexclusive focus on the arts (Dutton, 2009). Technology is not far removed, being the science of craft. Indeed, much of making art is in the control and crafting of material, wherein style and virtuosity can reign. Thus, art and craft are inherently conjoined.

Moreover, across the centuries technology has driven our arts. Painting was changed by the technologies of dyes, binding oils, and then reproduction; dance of various kinds has been changed with the inventions of smooth floors, talcum, and even spandex; music wouldn't be as rich without strings, reeds, valves, pedals, synthesizers, and recording equipment; literature and poetry would not have taken their present form without movable type and now text editors and the newer technologies of printing. And the list goes on. More focally for this chapter, movies wouldn't exist without the earlier developments of cameras and photographic plates, the inventions by George Eastman and Thomas Edison of rolled film and sprocket holes, respectively, and many more.

Given such technological forces behind these and other arts, one can ask: What psychological needs are served by these technological changes? What aesthetics underlie the making and the made? In most artistic domains, precise answers are likely to be either overly general or extremely difficult to come by. However, film—and in particular popular film—is an artistic venue in which such questions can be posed and reasonably crisp answers offered.

The fact that movies are the youngest broad-reaching art form on Earth means that their history and technological progression are well described and perhaps most advanced, their psychological underpinnings can be readily inferred, and their effects on viewers reasonably discerned. Below, I offer eight questions and their psychological answers in a chronology of relevance to the technology and aesthetics of popular movies.

Circa 1895 and Beyond: Why Are Movies Projected in Theaters?

The answer to this question might appear to be completely obvious, but it is not. On the obvious side, there is contingent history. Theaters were used because popular entertainment in the late 19th century was already taking place there. That is, musical events and vaudeville were offered in large halls, typically with rows of seats. Moreover, movies were initially only several minutes long and could be slotted into a larger mixed-media show of slapstick, singing, and dancing.

However, in France the first movies, such as *The Arrival of a Train* (1895), were shown by the Lumière brothers to the public as single events in theaters for 1 Franc (roughly US$6 today). Per minute of viewing time and adjusting for inflation, this is a bit like paying US$650 to see a feature-length movie. Yet viewers flocked to see these films (Toulet, 1988), even endangering their lives due to the extremely flammable nitrate film base. Why were they so popular? Novelty, realism, and their nonevanescent nature (they could be seen many times) certainly played a role. However, other factors discussed below are pertinent.

The public display of movies in theaters is only the obvious half of the argument. The less obvious counterargument arises with the peep show (Belton, 1992). Thomas Edison, ever the inventor, was not satisfied with sprockets to advance roll film. He needed a projection system that suited his vision of movie-watching—the private viewing kiosk, called the kinetoscope (e.g., Rossell, 1988). The kinetoscope contained a loop of film rolling between pulleys (so that it could be repeated without rewinding), a small projector, a viewing lens, and an eye shield. It could be used only by one person at a time. Thus, Edison thought that the movie experience should be private and short. The 1-min film *Blacksmith Scene* (Dickson, 1893), showing three blacksmiths pounding on metal, was among the first kinetoscope movies publicly shown to viewers—but one at a time.

Early on Edison didn't imagine that people would want to view movies in public or that movies might actually tell complex stories. To be sure, there could be advantages in presenting potentially racy short movies to male viewers who didn't want to have it known to others what they were watching. But one can bend over and view such things only for so long. Later and fairly independently of Edison, his former cameraman Edwin Porter, directed the 10-min theater film *The Great Train Robbery* (1903), which spurred the genre of Westerns that flourished for 60 years.

The drive for personal over public viewing did not go away. Until the 1950s people could not watch a popular movie outside a movie theater. That changed, slowly at first, with television. Over the next decade, theater movie viewing declined from more than ten to about five films per year, where it has generally stayed ever since. Initially, television wasn't truly personal viewing; it would be better described as family viewing. But over the decades and with more televisions, the invention of videotape, then DVDs (digital versatile discs), and now streaming, movie viewing has become personal, and especially so with the capability of viewing them on laptops and handhelds. Currently, an estimated 90% of all movie viewing is done on TVs and personal devices. But surprisingly, movie theater attendance has not actually declined over the past 60 years. Instead, movie viewing itself has increased by roughly an order of magnitude. Whereas we might have watched eight movies a year in mid-20th century, we may have watched as many as 80 movies a year at the end of the first decade of the 21st century (British Film Institute, 2012).

So, what is the psychological difference between theater and personal viewing? Part of the answer stems from the distance to, and the relative size of, the viewed image. Two prominent sources of information for the layout of proximal objects are accommodation and convergence (see Cutting & Vishton, 1995). Accommodation is the thinning and thickening of the lens of the eye—thicker for things close and thinner for things farther away. Convergence is the canting inward of the eyes when looking at things close by (looking cross-eyed). Most peep-show devices were for one eye only, with the other eye closed to inhibit binocular interference. Nonetheless, accommodation and convergence are normally yoked reflexively, so using one eye will likely engage the ocular responses of the other.

What this means here is that these perceptual cues are telling the perceiver that the image is very close, that the characters are very small, and that this is not quite like real life. Yet cognitively, the people looked more or less normal and not small. Thus, a perceptual and cognitive conflict was present. One advantage of theater viewing is that the screen is much farther away, that no cues to closeness are present, and that watching the movie is much more like looking, unencumbered, through a window—often called the Albertian window after Leon Battista Alberti, who formalized the technology of perspective drawing in the 15th century—onto the diegetic (story) world. This information spatially separates the viewer from the object, allowing the viewer to diminish a sense of self.

But, of course, looking at the screen of a laptop, tablet, or smartphone is much the same as a peep show, except that the distance is increased a bit and it is binocular. Thus, there is ample information about closeness and smallness from eye convergence. Although such displays are relatively small, they can be quite convincing. Moreover, it is clear that people enjoy watching movies on them. But they are not quite like the full experience of theater viewing, as I will re-address in answering Question 5.

Another advantage of a theater is that it can be made darker than the typical living room or a normal environment when using a personal device. Darkness is important because it enhances viewing contrast in the image (the ratio in light units of the lightest to the darkest parts), and contrast contributes to vividness and image sharpness. White and black on a sheet of paper (or in a painting) will rarely have a luminance difference, or contrast ratio, of greater than about 90 (white) to 1 (black), or 90:1. The contrast in an image on a 20th-century cathode-ray tube TV set was about 300:1, and those on contemporary HDTVs can approach 2000:1 or more.[1] The problem with the latter is that such ratios can only be achieved in near-complete darkness, otherwise the reflected light in a room (called a veiling luminance) will lighten the blacks and considerably diminish the ratios.[2] Movie theaters take care of this by dimming the lights. Yet, partly because the movie image is so much larger (light diminishing by the square of the distance from its source), the contrast ratio in theaters is only about 500:1.

Finally, when a close-up is shown of a character (most often a protagonist), the size of her face is roughly the size of a person standing at arm's length from you, if not a bit closer. This size and its associated familiar distance signals intimacy or close friendship—why else would you have let this person appear so close to you?—and is likely to contribute to your identification with and empathy for that character (Balázs, 1952). To be sure, close-ups were not particularly common in popular film until about four or more decades after its beginning (Salt, 2009), but the effect is strong in the viewing of movies in theaters today.

On the other hand, one must schedule one's life around theater viewing times but the readily available personal device can be activated at any time. Thus, the aesthetic payoffs of theater versus personal viewing are presence and vividness versus convenience and privacy, respectively. All of these features seem sufficiently important that neither mode will likely go away any time soon.

Circa 1900 and Beyond: Why Are Movies Composed of Transitions and Shots?

The first movies consisted of single shots. There were no transitions—cuts, dissolves, or fades. These movies were *actualités*, or slices of life—dances, sneezes, kisses, trains, factory workers. They had little narrative content, and most of these films are only about a minute in length. But the advent of storytelling in this medium soon began. At the turn into the 20th century, filmmakers began to use multiple shots with transitions between them. The first may have been *Come Along, Do* (Paul, 1898), where an older couple sits outside a museum, the man drinks, and they then enter the museum. Across a cut they appear inside as he inspects a nude statue to his partner's dismay.

A larger issue in movie storytelling is that narrative time (the diegetic time in the story) and narrational time (the time presenting the film) must typically diverge (Genette, 1980). Stories often cover long periods, and they jump ahead or occasionally backward in time. Moreover, these time shifts are often accompanied by location shifts and, as filmed stories became more complex, time and location shifts were used to separate storylines with different characters. Parallel action was born, and narrative structure became more complex. Transitions were enlisted to present these narrative jumps quickly and convincingly. They are like "later," "meanwhile," and "then" in textual and oral storytelling.

Transitions are of three general kinds—*cuts*, or instantaneous changes, which were initially thought to be disorienting, brutal, and unstylish; *dissolves*, which showed the gradual, optical replacement of the first setting with that of the next; and *fades out and in*, which are like dissolves but longer and which go through black (see, Cutting, Brunick, & DeLong, 2011). Cultural familiarity is important, and dissolves were a natural extension from magic lantern shows, popular through the latter half of the 19th century (Rossell, 1988). These shows often were then-exotic travelogues with the adventurer giving a voice-over description and elaboration while showing glass slides of touristic highlights. Typically, two projectors were used (or one with dual lamps and slide holders) and, with slides in place, one lamp was dimmed and the other brightened. This procedure could also be used to simulate motion, and it was used by Muybridge in some presentations of his tachistoscopic images of race horses (Warner, 2015).

Early on cuts or fades were the only available transitions. Cuts were done in the editing room but fades could be done in the camera, gradually closing the aperture at the end of one shot, halting the camera during a change of location, and then restarting the camera and opening the lens for the next shot. But soon cameras, which were hand-cranked, could be run backward and a dissolve could be created in camera. The photographer could cup a hand over the lens, gradually occluding the aperture as with the fade, but then rewind the film, hold his hand over the lens, and gradually dis-occlude it.

From the 1930s through the 1940s the separate uses of these three transition types were roughly codified, sometimes with a fourth. The fade was typically used between major sections of the narrative, the dissolve was most often used to separate scenes implying the passage of time, a wipe (the change of image behind a line sweeping across the screen) denoted a change of place and characters but not time (later repopularized by Steven Spielberg), and the cut was initially only used to separate shots within a scene (Cutting et al., 2011). Thus, narrative structure (the hierarchical sectioning of the story) was indicated by a narrational use of transitions. This made storytelling clearer in the new medium. However, this system began to break down by the 1940s through the 1960s and today almost 99% of all transitions are cuts.

It would seem that, as viewers became more educated to filmic storytelling devices, wipes, dissolves, and fades were thought to draw too much attention to themselves. Moreover, as the pace of movies increased, filmmakers probably felt that dissolves and fades significantly slowed down narrative progression. But dissolves and fades haven't completely disappeared; they are still sometimes used to denote the passage of time, the change of state in a character (waking to dreaming), or precisely to slow the narrative pace of the movie.

The reciprocal of the transition is the shot—the length of the series successive static frames between transitions—and these have tended to get shorter over time. Over the past 60 years, the average shot durations of popular movies have gotten considerably shorter—ranging from as much as 12–15 s in the 1950s to about 3–5 s in the past decade. Why? One reason concerns rehearsals. Short shots can typically be done in few takes and thus are less costly. More importantly, however, short shots (with many cuts) allow the filmmaker better control over the viewers' gaze, and thus provide more control over the audience's attention. Viewers have a strong tendency to look at faces, and 90% of all movie shots have faces (Cutting, 2015). By quickly moving from face to face, filmmakers forcefully grab the attention of the viewer, making them move their eyes across the screen. And finally, shorter shot durations increase the pace of movies, a feature that contemporary audiences appear to appreciate (Bordwell, 2006).

But long duration shots—called *long* takes—also have an appeal. Throughout the analog film era (~1895 to ~1995) the longest shots in a movie were rarely greater than 1 min in duration, although almost every film had at least one long take. The reasons for this general limit are twofold. First, it became clear that longer duration shots required more rehearsal—more things could go wrong during any given take (the performance of action in front of the camera), and takes are expensive.[3] Second, there was an upper limit on the duration of a shot. Without gimmicks and in the pre-digital era, such as hiding a cut during a pan over the back of a man's dark coat, as in *Rope* (Hitchcock, 1948), the limit was about 10–12 min—the amount of film that could fit in a standard cartridge.

Indeed, this is also the duration of a reel, a segment of a movie shown before either rewinding or another reel could be shown. Standard feature-length films began to appear in the 1910s and they were typically four, five, and six reels. Later, the Academy of Motion Picture Arts and Sciences (AMPAS) would declare that to be a feature-length film and become eligible for standard Oscars a movie needed to be 40 min in length (at least a four-reeler). Because early theaters typically had only one projector and a limited number of blank reels, a reel had to be rewound before the next reel could be shown. This downtime—a very long and different type of transition—may have forced filmmakers to create stories with end-of-reel tension that would hold the interest of the audience during rewinding (Bordwell, 2008, p. 104). Larger scale story construction had begun.

In the digital era (after ~1995), there has emerged an increasing fascination with the long take—a shot of unusually long duration, as in the Dunkirk naval landing scene in *Atonement* (Wright, 2005; 5 min). Such shots are often placed at the beginning of a film—as in *Spectre* (Mendes, 2015; 4 min) and *Gravity* (Cuarón, 2013; 17 min)—and sometimes with the impression of enveloping the whole film, as in *Birdman* (Iñárritu, 2014). Most of these long takes consist of shorter (but still long) segments that are digitally knitted together. Such shots add a sense of virtuosity, even "showoffishness" to the movie (Bordwell, 2012), but they also can add a sense of involvement to the viewer, a breathlessness and intimacy, as if one really is a spectator present on scene. In an era when temporal and spatial jumps are extremely common, long takes can force a sense of immediacy by yoking narrative and narrational time.

Thus, the aesthetic impact of multiple shots and transitions is to allow for true storytelling, and to mark (when necessary) a hierarchy of narrative boundaries. Also, with shorter shots and more cuts filmmakers gain control viewers' gaze and increase the pace of the story; with longer shots and fewer cuts they can enhance the impression of virtuosity in filmmaking and intimacy with the characters.

CIRCA 1905 AND BEYOND: WHY WERE MOVIES CALLED FLICKS?

Edison's sprockets and sprocket holes allowed analog film to advance within a projector, frame by frame. By the early 1920s the mechanical sequence grew to be complicated, with the rapid and staccato advance of frames accompanied by an episcotister (or rotating blade shutter), cutting off the light two or three times before the advance of a frame.[4] At 24 frames/s the latter would create 72 flicks/s and the motion in an analog projected movie will typically appear quite smooth. The reason for this is that, at 72 light pulses/s, there is typically no perceived flicker—the rapid ons and offs of light. Indeed, alternating current in North America is 60 cycles/s (reversals of current direction, which create such ons and offs within an incandescent light bulb) precisely to avoid seeing flicker. The European standard of 50 Hz is almost as good.

But the flicker of movies didn't initially exceed the critical flicker fusion threshold— the rate beyond which continuous light is perceived. Frame rates were variable, cameras were hand-cranked, and not all early projectors (which were essentially cameras with open backs and an arc light source) had episcotisters.[5] Initial recording speeds with these cameras was at about 12 frames/s, which is close to the peak of our sensitivity—a 12 -Hz flicker rate is quite aversive (Zacks, 2015). Early projectionists knew this and typically projected (by hand cranking) early movies at about 16 frames/s, giving actors a jerky motion quality and increasing the risk of igniting the nitrate film. But even this increased rate was a bit troubling. Soon, filmmakers had cameras with motors that advanced the film and, with the invention of embedded sound, they switched to 24 frames/s and projectors followed—a compromise between the cost of film stock and the decrease in aversiveness.

The term "flick" came to be associated with movies themselves, but across generations the term seems to be dying out. Indeed, the usage of the English term "flicker" and the phrase "go to the flicks" seems to have peaked in the 1940s,[6] and one of the only other allusions reasonably current among students, having burgeoned in the 1990s, seems to be that of the "chick flick"—a movie made predominantly for a female audience. To be sure, the name Netflix may preserve the term for a while, but perhaps without signaling the original referent. The change to and the effects of digital cinema, where flicker is nonexistent, will be discussed in Question 8.

Thus, the aesthetic benefit of reducing flicker was to make the movie action appear smoother without light-pulsing distraction. Indeed, as many as 3% of people have symptoms of photosensitive epilepsy and would be distressed by film flicker.[7] With flicker eliminated viewers can more easily become engrossed in the narrative of the film.

CIRCA 1927 AND BEYOND: WHAT WERE THE EFFECTS OF ADDED SOUND?

A major event in the history of popular movies was the appearance of *The Jazz Singer* (Crosland, 1927), a mostly silent film with about one-third native sound, both music and voice. It was a sensation when it appeared. Hollywood rushed to make many more "talkies," and tried to convert silent films in the pipeline to sound as well. By 1929 nearly all Hollywood films were made with sound, although Charles Chaplin continued in the silent vein with *City Lights* (1931) and *Modern Times* (1936), although both had a track with sound effects.

The inclusion of sound tracks on film necessarily stabilized frame rates. Variations in soundtrack speed interfere with the pitch of music or of a speaker's voice more noticeably than do variations in visual frame rates. This fact forced an industry standard, and at the end of the 1920s Warner Brothers fixed the rate at a motor-controlled 24 frames/s. This complicated the structure of projectors even more—the sound track had to move smoothly through the device, but the frames had to move jerkily, frame by frame. This problem was solved by displacing the sound track along the length of film from its corresponding images, having the sound read at a different location in the projector than where the frames are shown. Interestingly, the tolerance for asynchrony of auditory and visual channels is reasonably large. In visible speech, for example, the auditory signal can lead the visual signal in time by as much as 45 ms and lag it by as much as 200 ms with no discrepancy detected (van Wassenhove, Grant, & Poeppel, 2007).

Live music almost always accompanied the public presentation of movies although it was seldom effectively synchronized to shots or frames. In the late 1910s, other sounds and voice also accompanied film but were played on separate devices—sound as a record on a turntable and visuals in a projector for the film. Projectionists had the duty to keep them in sync, and this wasn't easy. Once sound was bound into the film, and that became the norm, it completely changed the medium.

Three effects are prominent. First and most obviously, the actors' lips were synchronized with their voices and they were clearly perceived to speak. This enthralled audiences, who were quite used to music accompanying movies but had never heard and seen "talking pictures." It also gave an immediacy to the action. Viewers did not have to wait for dialog intertitles to know what was said, or wait through expositional intertitles to know if a location or time frame had changed.

Second, shot durations burgeoned. The average shot duration for silent films in the mid to late 1920s was about 5 s, a rate not attained again until the 1990s (see Cutting & Candan, 2015). By 1930 it quickly lengthened to an average of about 10 s and longer, and stayed there for two decades. In many ways, it was as if filmmakers had to relearn how to make movies and, in particular, how to film conversations. As a result, late silent films can appear surprisingly modern, and early sound films clunky and poorly timed.

A third effect was culturally more profound. Sound crashed the continuing emergence of a global cinema. For example, in the 1920s the UFA (Universum Film AG) Studio was the major German producer of movies, and it released about as many films as did Hollywood. It could hire, for example, Danish actresses, French actors, and through the use of intertitles in any language it could blanket the world with new movies every year. With "talkies" and with audiences' rapid endorsement of them, however, the global market gradually evaporated for many national cinemas (Thompson, 1985).

By the early 1930s movies were expected to be delivered in the spoken language of the audience. Moreover, those with dubbing or language-particular subtitles added in postproduction were more expensive. Lip motion generally mismatched sound, and reading subtitles while trying to discern facial expressions is visually cumbersome, essentially doubling the number of viewer saccades and halving fixation durations (Smith, 2015).

Soon, Hollywood and English-language film began to dominate worldwide, but sound film also allowed more diversification across national markets (O'Brien, 2005)— German expressionism burgeoned, Italian film flourished, the French New Wave emerged, and Japan and Sweden produced striking and strikingly different cinema before Hollywood, Bollywood, and Hong Film action films swallowed up most of the global market by the 1980s. Experimentation in different national cinemas fed new styles across them. Long takes and deep focus spread from Germany to Hollywood, and later the jump cuts (the deletion of a middle section from a longer shot) of French films eventually became relatively commonplace in Hollywood.

Thus, the aesthetics of synchronized sound naturalized film but, at least for a while, it also nationalized it. Cinema was initially global, then deglobalized, only to become more global again with the dominance of Hollywood, Bollywood, and Chinese film.[8] It also shifted storytelling to an emphasis on dialog. Today, almost 70% of all shots in Hollywood movies show one character talking to another (Cutting & Candan, 2015).

CIRCA 1939, BEFORE, AND BEYOND: WHAT ARE THE EFFECTS OF COLOR?

Most early films were in black and white because that is how photography began. Two-color photographic film stock became available in the early 20th century but it was not generally adapted to movies. The early color used in cinema was done in postproduction by painting each frame by hand. George Méliès used hand painters for many of his fantasies around 1900. An even more time-intensive technique was stenciling (Pathécolor) in which as many as six stencils were used on each frame to control the addition of color.[9]

Many silent films underwent toning or tinting (Yumibe, 2012). Toning changed the darks into a given color, leaving the lighter areas unchanged; tinting, on the other hand, changed the lighter areas, leaving the darks unchanged. One early purpose of these processes was to guard against bootleg copies, but the process was extended to most movies in part to set moods. In general, the use of certain colors was codified—daytime shots were tinted slightly amber and nighttime shots slightly blue, but other colors were used as well. As coloring improved the process also became expensive and began to die out in the 1920s, just as early color film processes matured. Early technicolor (a three-color process) shorts were produced by Walt Disney as early as 1932.

Commercially viable three-color film was produced by Eastman Kodak in 1935 and it was soon adopted for live action by the movie industry. The first large-scale color films in the USA were *The Wizard of Oz* (Fleming, 1939b) and *Gone with the Wind* (Fleming, 1939a). Color film was expensive, and the appearance of these films soon contributed to the production system of A (big budget) and B (low budget) movies, which were often paired and shown in double-feature format. Through the 1940s and into the 1950s the A movies were typically in color, and the B movies in black and white. The films noir of that era were typically in black and white and often survive with more critical acclaim than the A-listers they were paired with. Budget constraints foster creative solutions, which can make for fine art; as Orson Welles said "the enemy of art is the absence of limitations" (Jaglom, 1992, p. 78). Nonetheless, few popular films after 1960 were produced in black and white, and *Schindler's List* (Spielberg, 1993b) and *The Artist* (Hazanavicius, 2011) are the only such films to win Academy Awards for best picture after *The Apartment* (Wilder, 1960).[10]

But what does color offer the film viewer? Aside from contributing naturalism to the image, color can affect mood, although the exact effects may depend on context and individuality (Leibowitz, 1991). Color also improves recognition and enhances memory for scenes (Gegenfurtner & Rieger, 2000). Thus, it can be used by the filmmaker and the viewer to help segment scenes of movies, changing the visual tone when moving from one location to another. During its most furious changes among four levels of dream state, *Inception* (Nolan, 2010) helps guide the viewer by the predominant colors of a gray and rainy cityscape, a rich brown hotel interior, a white and mountainous snowscape, and relatively normal-colored limbo. Indeed, after longer shot durations and wider shot scale, color is the strongest indicant for the viewer that a scene change has occurred (Cutting, Brunick, & Candan, 2012).

Thus, the aesthetics of color are manifold. Color adds naturalness, it adds emotional tone, it increases discrimination of objects, and it can serve as a perceptual and memory aid about narrative structure. But there is no denying that black-and-white movies, like black-and-white photography, have a certain and admirable aesthetic. Wide-ranging attempts at digital colorization of old movies was begun in the 1980s to the horror of many film buffs, and the process largely ceased. As Roger Ebert (Ebert, 1986), an important film critic, asked in an episode of *At The Movies*: "What was so wrong about black and white movies in the first place? By filming in black and white, movies can sometimes be more dreamlike and elegant and stylized and mysterious. They can add a whole additional dimension to reality, while color sometimes just supplies additional unnecessary information."

CIRCA 1952 AND BEYOND: WHY DID MOVIE IMAGES GROW WIDER?

The image shape of movies was essentially unstandardized in the USA until the early 1930s when AMPAS set the aspect ratio to 1.33 (now called the Academy ratio). This numerical expression represents the width of the image divided by its height.[11] This ratio continued in almost all movies until 1952. To be sure, before that time it did not vary greatly. Many of the Kodak still cameras of the 1890s and 1900s had an aspect ratio of 1.33, but they also varied between about 1.2 and 1.5 (see Belton, 1992). Moreover, this general image shape was inherited from earlier photography and earlier still from art canvases. The view-camera images of the late 19th century were about 1.33, as were daguerreotypes. In turn, the ratios for landscape canvases in the 19th century are about 1.3 and those of portraits the inverse (Cutting, 2014).

In 1953, however, wider images erupted into and disrupted American movie venues. Why wider? If the goal is to project a large picture, image height has more architectural constraints than does image width—it is easier to make wider rooms within existing buildings than taller ones. Thus, aspect ratios generally grew bigger, and images wider. In some cases, as with Cinerama, they were curved, used multiple projectors, and had image ratios as great as 3.0. Wider film images became the rage, with many popular films made in a 2.55 ratio. Various formats were tried by different production companies over the next decades, 1.33 and 2.55 all but dropped out, and by the 1980s things basically settled to two formats: 1.85 (widescreen) and 2.35 (cinemascope). Initially most action and adventure films were 2.35 and animations, comedies, and dramas were 1.85. Most movies are now 2.35, with animations the last genre to generally achieve that width. The reason is that with animation one has to manually draw or compute the wings of the image; with live-action they come optically for free.

But what does a wider image offer? In general, for the purposes of film audience engagement, a bigger image is better. For optical reasons image size is measured in degrees—360° surrounds your head, 90° is a right angle, and 45° is the current standard for the width of a 2.35 movie image from a seat in the center of the theater.[12] If one balls up one's fist at arm's length and looks at the back of it, the width of your hand, from the fleshy bulge of your folded pinky to the thumb metacarpal, is about 10°. So, the theatrical movie image should be a bit more than four fist widths wide. Why?

Bigger images contribute strongly to the impression of "being there," looking through the Albertian window onto the diegetic world. In the domain of virtual reality this is often called *presence* (e.g., McMahan, 2003). The central cause of presence is a small visual subsystem called the accessory optic system (e.g., Giolli, Blanks, & Lui, 2006), in which large patches of slow motion in the visual field are registered and communicate with the brain stem and cerebellum to potentiate balance. With it, even when sitting safely in a cineplex rocking chair, one's visual system is sending messages about being ready to move and respond to the motion on the screen.

The accessory optic system is undemanding as to whether this slow movement is in the side wings of the image or above and below it. But again, architecturally it is easier to widen an image. Thus, movies in ratios of 2.35 do well in creating presence, a bit better than those of 1.85, which are much better than those of 1.33. Unsurprisingly, because the images are relatively small (about 20°in width or less), laptop and handheld movie viewing do not create this effect. And, of course, IMAX movie viewing is more physiologically stimulating than normal movie viewing because it both widens and heightens the image.

A small benefit to viewing certain movies on small screens is that queasicam (jerky, handheld camera) movies might be enjoyed more. *The Blair Witch Project* (Myrick, 1999), *Cloverfield* (Reeves, 2008), and even *The Bourne Ultimatum* (Greengrass, 2007) can be effectively seen on a small screen without making one sick. The accessory optic system is less stimulated.

Thus, the aesthetics of larger projection ratios (wider images) is that they enhance *presence* in the viewer, making her feel more like a direct observer of the diegetic world. The neural underpinnings of presence are that the periphery of the viewer's visual field engages her mechanisms of balance. Handhelds do none of this, and laptops only marginally.

CIRCA 1952 AND BEYOND: WHAT DOES 3D ADD TO MOVIES?

Perhaps no technological feature divides the opinions of cinemaphiles more than three-dimensional (3D) projection. At about the same time as widescreen movies were becoming popular, 3D was introduced to feature-length American movies. *Bwana Devil* (Oboler, 1952) was the first, an adventure film that often broke through the "fourth wall." This occurs when characters and objects reach out of the screen due to crossed stereoscopic disparities in the two eyes (see Manning, Finlay, Neill, & Frost, 1987).

This early 3D era saw a number of influential horror films, such as the *House of Wax* (de Toth, 1953), which was also the first feature with stereophonic sound. Even Alfred Hitchcock tried 3D in *Dial M for Murder* (1954), but he quickly withdrew most copies of that film. And 3D is expensive to execute—the filmmaker needs two cameras, rigidly mounted close to one another (Zone, 2012). In addition, until single-strip 3D films were produced (alternating frames for the left and right eyes), two projectionists might be needed and they would occasionally have to deal with twice the likelihood of deterioration—particularly, the resplicing of broken film.

Studios got rid of the necessity of theatrical two-projector systems as quickly as they could but there were other problems. One was that the highly reflective projection screens were necessary. 3D dimmed the movie image from seats even slightly to the side. Another was that viewers with a strongly dominant eye would see misaligned images and weak or no depth. As many as 30% of all people are stereoweak or stereoblind (Hess, To, Zhou, Wang, & Cooperstock, 2015). Yet another issue is eye strain. In normal vision convergence and accommodation are reflexively yoked, but these are necessarily dissociated in 3D movies. The 3D image is not nearby, requiring distance accommodation, but the image still requires convergence, implying near-distance convergence. As much as 50% of audiences felt negative aftereffects of watching feature-length 3D movies (Zone, 2012).

Most 3D films required polarized lenses mounted in frames. The two images were also polarized, projected on the screen, and reflected back to the eyes of the viewer. The lenses let in light that was polarized at 90° angles, either vertically and horizontally or on opposite diagonals. A cheaper method, less often used, employed glasses with two color filters—red and cyan—with the camera projection treated the same. In both cases the image brightness was less than a standard "flat" film, and contrast was similarly diminished. 3D movies were made throughout the period from the 1960s to 1990s but without much commercial success. Indeed, down-budget (soft and hard pornographic movies) and specialty films (Disney animation and live-action movies, and IMAX productions) dominated this market for decades.

Widely distributed digital 3D began again with the animated film *Chicken Little: 3D* (Dindal, 2005), which was very successful. Live-action 3D recaptured the public imagination with *Avatar* (Cameron, 2009), and other filmmakers followed with other movies to considerable box office success. Standard 2D movies were often rushed into postproduction to give them a 3D quality. This was done by digitally tracking object edges and rough distances from the camera to create the disparities in the two images, but the quality of postproduction 3D has never been perceptually successful. It yields what early 3D photographs often created, called the *coulisse* effect, from the French word for placard. That is, objects and people appear flat in front of their backgrounds.

Over the past decade the percentage theater gross captured by 3D in the USA has declined (Giardina & McClintock, 2017). Nonetheless, one cinematic distinction has become apparent: Live-action 3D is not nearly as good as computer-graphic imagery (CGI) in 3D. There are several reasons for this. First, camera pans with focal-depth changes are difficult to manage in live action. One image will likely be slightly out of focus compared with the other, and some viewers find this bothersome. This contrasts with CGI, where there are no real cameras, and the two images are computed, matched in sharpness, and rendered with the desired focal depth and depth of field.

Second, CGI movies have the advantage of being able to dynamically alter the inter-axial distance (the distance between the principal rays of the cameras) and convergence, and thus the apparent inter-ocular distance. Normally, a person's eyes are a bit more than 2 in. (about 6 cm) apart. Moreover, as stereoscopic photographers of the 19th century knew, when this distance is increased the objects in the world appear smaller. This was particularly salient in early 3D photographs of giant sequoia trees. The cameras were often as much as a foot or more apart and the impression was that the trees weren't giant at all. It was thought that a solution would be to place people beneath the trees, but this only made the people look extremely small (Scharf, 1974). Most 3D movies are made with an inter-axial distance of *less* than the mean inter-ocular distance to enhance depth, and few 3D movies now project crossed-disparities, which make people and objects loom out into the audience. This is regarded as too gimmicky.

Again, decreasing the inter-axial distance enhances size and depth, and early animated movies took advantage of this, as in *Antz* (Darnell & Johnson, 1998). Indeed, the inter-axial distance can be made to be zero, and a striking depth effect can be obtained (Koenderink, van Doorn, & Kappers, 1994). But the best use of inter-axial distance may occur when it can be dynamically changed. An effective use of this is in the Disney movie *Up* (Docter & Peterson, 2009). When the protagonist's house is carried aloft by balloons until it lands in the Amazon, the inter-axial distance is generally constant, but when they land atop a flat mountain and look into the distance at a waterfall the inter-axial distance is diminished, creating the sudden effect of immense distance. Moreover, it appears that this change can be obtained when the distance is gradually changed, either within a shot or from about 250 ms before a cut through about the same interval after the cut (Zone, 2012).

Thus, the aesthetics of 3D movies is that they enhance the depth contrast in the diegetic world. A drawback is that previous and current technology dims the image, reducing contrast. Other major issues are eye strain, and that 3D viewing through glasses can feel cumbersome and can detract from the movie experience. But perhaps more importantly, 3D viewing puts the viewer metrically "in" the movie. And the ultimate question is: Does the viewer really want to be physically "in" the movie? I think not. The movie viewer appreciates presence, which can be achieved by higher aspect ratios or larger screens (as with IMAX), but not necessarily immersion (McMahan, 2003).

Circa 1995 and After: What Has the Digital Era Brought Us?

After the increase in aspect ratios the development of technologies for movies themselves fell upon a quiescent period. To be sure, huge changes in our viewing habits arose with inexpensive VCRs (videocassette recorders) in the late 1970s, DVDs in the late 1990s, and now streaming. Our movie-watching increased by almost an order of magnitude. But moviemaking marched along quite incrementally—improving cameras, improving film stock, settling in on widescreen (1.85) and cinemascope (2.35), but not much else.

Then the digital era hit, and one of the first new changes was the Avid Technology video editor, which allowed *nonlinear editing* (which might be better described as nondestructive editing). That is, editors could rework their edits without destroying the original. This, and other digital technologies, changed cinema. I discuss aspects of these changes below, but the digital era brought other changes as well. It isn't possible to outline all these here (for a start, see Prince, 2011), but let me briefly consider three issues connected to previous questions—the cessation of flicker and the consequent increase in luminance, contrast, and resolution; the emergence of high dynamic range photography; and the flirtation with higher frame rates. Afterwards, I reconsider the idea of whether or not movies should be considered like photographs.

Flicker, Luminance, Contrast, and Resolution

In the analog film era, theater presentations were intermittent flashes, with up to 72 flicks/s. Once films began to appear on television the conversion of the 24 native frames to 60 cycles (30 interlaced pairs of frames) was necessary, typically by doubling every fourth frame but not altering the soundtrack. The contrast and resolution of analog televisions was poor, but they were bright. Logically, since there was no darkness half-cycle of flicker, they could be twice as bright. Flicker was eliminated since the screen was never dark—rasters (horizontal lines of phosphor elements) were written across the screen in alternating sequences of odd and even, each pixel replaced (extremely rapidly) one at the time. With the change to high-definition television (HDTV) at the turn into this century contrast ratios (~2,000:1) would seem to have been better than movie theaters (~500:1) but, with veiling luminances discussed above, they are probably about the same.

Resolution is a critical contributor to image quality. The resolution of an analog television image was roughly 760×575 pixels, whereas an equivalent resolution of a 35-mm film image is about 5600×3600, or about 45 times greater. High-definition televisions (HDTVs) and computers typically have a resolution of 1280×720, with analog theater projection about 22 times greater. Digital projection in theaters has a current standard of 4K (4048×2160), although 8K and 16K are being discussed for theaters and television as well. Increased resolution certainly improves the image but also increases the expense. That said, 8K resolution in a theater would reasonably approximate the resolution of the fovea in the human eye for viewing anywhere on the screen, and 16K would serve in IMAX.

High Dynamic Range (HDR)

Normal film and normal computer-graphic images do not reproduce nearly the dynamic range that viewers can see, which can be upwards of 10,000:1. This can be demonstrated by taking an analog photograph indoors with a large window behind or adjacent to the focal object, where you want the content indoors and outdoors beyond the window to be seen. With normal photography the indoor setting may appear fine but the outdoor setting would be bleached white, or the outdoor setting might be fine with the indoor setting dark and indistinct.

Two options are available to overcome this image deficit. The first is projective— "simply" to produce and project images with this much range. Unfortunately, although research continues in attempts to do this, it is very difficult and, so far, largely un-successful. The second method is receptive and more relevant to photography and movies—compress the dynamic range of the natural image. That is, rather than re-produce only the lower range (the visible indoor scene with bleached white outdoors) or the upper range (the dark interior and the visible outdoor scene), try to reproduce both. This is done by taking several simultaneous images of the same scene through a range of underexposed (and quite dark) to overexposed (and quite light) pictures. These images can then be merged (added together) in real time with a quite satisfactory result. Once one has a digital camera, the process is quite inexpensive. Indeed, contemporary smartphone photographs do exactly this and new movies and television shows are now providing HDR content. To many people, however, HDR images can appear garish, par-ticularly those with enhanced color, but they don't have to be (Lucas, 2015).

Flirtation with Higher Frame Rates (HFR)

The Hobbit: An Unexpected Journey (Jackson, 2012) and its sequels were released in both 3D and in an unusual projection speed—48 frames/s, double the norm. This high frame rate created great controversy, with viewers claiming that the resulting image had lost its cinematic quality, possibly because it was closer to television frame rates (Watson, 2013). The increased temporal resolution also added a clarity in movement that, at times, seemed unwanted. This less than enthusiastic reception, combined with the extra ex-pense of the appropriate theater projection system, likely means that HFR will be slow in coming, if at all, to be a new norm.

Should We Think of Movies as Moving Photographs?

There is no question that movies originated primarily in photography and live action. The rolled film of Eastman and the sprockets of Edison assured this. But at almost every moment in the history of movies and even before, there have been assaults on this notion. The phenakistoscope and zoetrope (Rossell, 1988), with their viewing slits and revolving disks and cylinders, are undeniable predecessors.[13] Moreover, special effects have always been part of cinema. At the turn into the 20th century Georges Méliès was famous for his fantasies and trick photography. Later, the various tricks of animation—the stop-action photography of Willis O'Brien (*The Lost World*, 1925; *King Kong*, 1933) and particularly the "dynamation" of Ray Harryhausen (*Mighty Joe Young*, 1949; *The Beast from 20,000 Fathoms*, 1953) that integrated live-action and animated models, brought fantastical worlds with fantastical beasts to the silver screen. The 21st-century eye would immediately see these effects as unconvincing, but the audiences at the time seemed to relish their naturalness. And throughout the same 60-year span, animations also captivated audiences, from *Pauvre Pierrot* (Reynaud, 1892) to *Gertie the Dinosaur* (McCay, 1914) to Disney's *Steamboat Willie* (Iwerks, 1928) and beyond.

But parlor tricks, fantasy, and animations seemed to have been regarded as quite specialized genres, not in the mainstream of film. Yet I would argue that they are central to what film tries to do. Moreover, they and their successors have become integrated into the visual stream of contemporary cinema. As the enhanced use of miniatures was gradually replaced by computer graphics imagery (CGI; *Star Trek II: The Wrath of Khan*, Meyer, 1982) for film segments and eventually mainstreamed by *Jurassic Park* (Spielberg, 1993a),[14] *Avatar* (2009) with its motion capture, and *Cinderella* (Branagh, 2015), we have truly entered a new era.

The aesthetics of digital imagery are that diegetic worlds and actions can be created that are vivid and realistic looking but that could not be created in live-action photography. Through fantasy, science fiction, and historical re-creation this greatly enlarges the storytelling venues that can be portrayed. And audiences appear to love this extension of reality. The reason would appear to be, as Zunshine (2006, 2012) has noted, that a major attraction of the narrative arts is that they can place us in a situation that is foreign, exotic, and even logically impossible, and have us work with the minds of the protagonists, as if to figure out what we would do in similar circumstances. This is called *theory of mind*, and the narrative arts exercise this skill in us. Indeed, we find it pleasurable.

Major Challenges, Goals, and Suggestions

The major challenges and opportunities confronting the study of the aesthetics of movies are several. One challenge, as Dargas (2014) noted, is that there are simply too many movies. The movie industry has thrived (despite occasional claims to the contrary) and the decreasing expense of digital cameras and the emergence of laptop editing and production have made small-budget "indie" films a realizable goal. Indeed, more than 4000 features were submitted to the Sundance Festival in 2019 alone. But one could equally say that today there are also too many books, too many plays, too much music, too much art, and so forth. Life is short, and tokens of every art form are many. Moreover, one doesn't need to see all movies to discuss movie aesthetics, only a reasonable sample.

Another challenge is to study those few people on the planet who have never seen a movie while they still remain naïve. The study of these individuals is extremely important for understanding the roles of learning in understanding the composition of film (Ildirar, Levin, Schwan, & Smith, 2017; Ildirar & Schwan, 2015). These studies provide an important parallel to the myriad studies of children and their acquisition of movie-watching skill (e.g., Rider, Coutrot, Pellicano, Dakin, & Mareschal, 2018; Wass & Smith, 2014).

And a significant opportunity is that we live at the beginning of an era of big data. A frame of digital imagery could have 10 million pixels and at 24 frames/s and a mean of about 165,000 frames per average feature-length movie, the result is close to 2 trillion pixels. If one is interested in the structure of the stimulus, there is a lot there to analyze (see Cutting, 2016a, b). In addition, increasing access to functional magnetic resonance imaging (Bezdek et al., 2015; Hasson, Malach, & Heeger, 2009; Magliano & Zacks, 2011) and to eye movement recording equipment (Smith, 2013; Smith & Henderson, 2008) makes movies a wonderful venue to study the human mind.

Finally, given the development of movies over the past 125 years it is important to try to capture the changing tastes and aesthetics of audiences over time. Baxandall (1972) wrote of the *period eye*, the modes of perception deeply embedded in time, culture, and in this case technology. In this sense, it important to try to understand the reactions of the contemporary audiences to Méliès, to Lubitsch, to Wilder, to Altman, and of every other major filmmaker in a more quantitative way, to determine how they differ from those of the early 21st century.

Notes

1. See, https://en.wikipedia.org/wiki/Contrast_ratio. Accessed January 26, 2018.
2. For example, if the luminance ratio of a screen is 1,000:1 but the ambient light in a room is 10 and is reflected off the screen, this makes the situation 1,000 + 10:1 + 10, or 1,010:11, or about 90:1.
3. https://www.quora.com/When-shooting-a-long-take-how-many-times-would-you-need-to-rehearse-for-one-long-take-to-go-perfectly-Do-actors-improvise-if-they-for get-their-lines-while-shooting-a-long-take. Accessed January 29, 2018.
4. The three-blade shutter, whose job it was to increase flicker rate, was invented by Theodor Pätzold of Berlin in 1902 (Fielding, 1967, p. 110), although it is not clear when they appeared on American projectors, like the Simplex, but certainly by the 1920s (Enticknap, 2005, p. 139).
5. Episcotister is a device for reducing the intensity of light in known ratio by means of rapidly rotating opaque and transparent sectors (https://www.merriam-webster.com).
6. These data were gathered through Google Ngram searches, January 25, 2018.
7. See https://www.epilepsy.com/learn/triggers-seizures/photosensitivity-and-seizures. Accessed January 29, 2018.
8. Although Hollywood, Bollywood, and Chinese film dominate the global audience, the country that produces the most movies is India, with the USA third. Nigeria has the second highest output of movies, and its multilingual industry is often called Nollywood. The largest numbers of tickets are sold in China, India, and the USA, respectively.
9. See Barbara Flueckiger's timeline of color and film: http://zauberklang.ch/filmcolors/
10. Of course, there is a small amount of color in *Schindler's List*: the little girl's red coat, as well as the scenes of the present at the beginning and end of the film.
11. There are myriad aspect ratios across films, many beyond the three discussed here. For a more detailed selection, see https://en.wikipedia.org/wiki/Aspect_ratio_(image). Accessed January 29, 2018.

12. For details for the certification of theatrical projection standards, see http://www.thx.com/certification/thx-cinema-certification-program/. Accessed January 29, 2018.

13. Zoetrope is an optical device in which figures on the inside of a revolving cylinder are viewed through slits in its circumference and appear like a single animated figure. A phenakistoscope is an optical toy resembling the zoetrope in principle and use and in one form consisting of a disk with the figures arranged about the center and having near the edge radial slits through which the figures are viewed by means of a mirror (https://www.merriam-webster.com).

14. To be sure *Jurassic Park* mixed animatronics (animated models), puppets, and CGI, but the CGI was the most impressive and would eventually become no more expensive (Prince, 2011).

REFERENCES

Balázs, B. (1952). *Theory of the film: Character and growth of a new art.* (E. Bone, Trans.) London: Dennis Dobson.

Baxandall, M. (1972). *Painting & experience in fifteenth-century Italy.* Oxford, England: Oxford University Press.

Belton, J. (1992). *Widescreen cinema.* Cambridge, MA: Harvard University Press.

Bezdek, M. A., Gerrig, R. J., Wenzel, W. G., Shin, J., Pirog Revill, K., & Schumacher, E. H. (2015). Neural evidence that suspense narrows attentional focus. *Neuroscience, 303,* 338–345. doi:10.1016/j.neuroscience.2015.06.066

Branagh, K., director. (2015). *Cinderella.* USA & UK: Walt Disney Home Entertainment. DVD.

British Film Institute (2012). *Statistical yearbook, 2012.* http://www.bfi.org.uk/sites/bfi.org.uk/files/downloads/bfi-statistical-yearbook-2012.pdf. Accessed 31 Jan. 2018.

Bordwell, D. (2006). *The way Hollywood tells it: Story and style in modern movies.* Berkeley, CA: University of California Press.

Bordwell, D. (2008). *The poetics of cinema.* New York: Routledge.

Bordwell, D. (October 7, 2012). Stretching the shot. *Observations on film art.* http://www.davidbordwell.net/blog/2012/10/07/stretching-the-shot/. Accessed 31 Jan. 2018.

Cameron, J., director (2009). *Avatar.* USA: Twentieth Century Fox Home Entertainment. DVD.

Chaplin, C., director (1931). *City Lights.* USA: Warner Home Video. DVD.

Chaplin, C., director (1936). *Modern Times.* USA: Warner Home Video. DVD.

Cooper, M. C., director (1933). *King Kong.* USA: Warner Home Video. DVD.

Crosland, A., director (1927). *The Jazz Singer.* USA: Warner Home Video. DVD.

Cuaròn, A., director (2013). *Gravity.* UK & USA: Warner Home Video. DVD.

Cutting, J. E. (2014). How light and motion bathe the silver screen. *Psychology of Aesthetics, Creativity, and the Arts, 8*(3), 340–353. doi:10.1037/a0036174

Cutting, J. E. (2015). The framing of characters in popular movies. *Art & Perception, 3*(2), 191–212. doi:10.1163/22134913-00002031

Cutting, J. E. (2016a). Narrative theory and the dynamics of popular movies. *Psychonomic Bulletin & Review, 23*(6), 1713–1743. doi:10.3758/s13423-1051-4

Cutting, J. E. (2016b). The evolution of pace in popular movies. *Cognitive Research: Principles and Implications, 1*(1), Article 30, 1–21. doi:10.1186/s41235-016-0019-0138

Cutting, J. E., Brunick, K. L., & Candan, A. (2012). Perceiving event dynamics and parsing Hollywood films. *Journal of Experimental Psychology: Human Perception and Performance, 38*(6), 1476–1490. doi:10.1017/a0027737

Cutting, J. E., Brunick, K. L., & DeLong, J. E. (2011). The changing poetics of the dissolve in Hollywood film. *Empirical Studies in the Arts*, 29(2), 149–169. doi:10.2190/EM.29.2.b

Cutting, J. E., & Candan, A. (2015). Shot durations, shot classes, and the increased pace of popular movies. *Projections: The Journal for Movies and Mind*, 9(2), 40–52. doi:10:3167/proj.2015.090204

Cutting, J. E., & Vishton, P. M. (1995). Perceiving layout and knowing distances: The interaction, relative potency, and contextual use of different information about depth. In W. Epstein, & S. Rogers (Eds.), *Perception of space and motion* (pp. 69–117). San Diego, CA: Academic Press.

Dargas, M. (January 9, 2014). As Indies explode, an appeal for sanity. *New York Times*. https://www.nytimes.com/2014/01/12/movies/flooding-theaters-isnt-good-for-filmmakers-or-filmgoers.html?_r=0. Accessed 30 Jan. 2018.

Darnell, E., & Johnson, T., directors (1998). *Antz*. USA: DreamWorks Home Entertainment.

de Toth, A., director (1953). *House of Wax*. USA: Warner Home Video. DVD.

Dickson, W. K. L., director (1893). *Blacksmith Scene*. USA: Edison Manufacturing Company. https://www.youtube.com/watch?v=cm5g7CfXYYE. Accessed 1 Feb. 2018.

Dindal, M., director (2005). *Chicken Little*. USA: Walt Disney Home Entertainment. DVD.

Docter, P., & Peterson, B., directors (2009). *Up*. USA: Walt Disney Studios Home Entertainment. DVD.

Dutton, D. (2009). *The art instinct*. New York: Bloomsbury Press.

Ebert, R. (1986). Colorizing—Hollywood's new vandalism. Siskel & Ebert (hosts) *Siskel & Ebert & the Movies*, Buena Vista Television, 1986; air date unknown. https://www.youtube.com/watch?v=6t91-JBI-Cw. Accessed 31 Jan. 2018.

Enticknap, L. (2005). *Moving image technology: From zoetrope to digital*. London: Wallflower Press.

Fielding, R. (Ed.) (1967). *A technological history of motion pictures and television*. Berkeley, CA: University of California Press.

Fleming, V., director (1939a). *Gone with the Wind*. USA: Warner Home Video. DVD.

Fleming, V., director (1939b). *The Wizard of Oz*. USA: Warner Home Video. DVD.

Gegenfurtner, K. R., & Rieger, J. (2000). Sensory and cognitive contributions of color to the recognition of natural scenes. *Current Biology*, 10(13), 805–808. doi:10.1016/S0960-9822(00)00563-7

Genette, G. (1980). *Narrative discourse: An essay on method*. (J. W. Lewin, Trans.) Ithaca, NY: Cornell University Press.

Giardina, C., & McClintock, P. (August 3, 2017). Is the golden age of 3D officially over? *Hollywood Reporter*. https://www.hollywoodreporter.com/behind-screen/is-golden-age-3d-officially-1025843. Accessed 30 Jan. 2018.

Giolli, R. A., Blanks, R. H., Lui, F. (2006). The accessory optic system: Basic organization with an update on connectivity, neurochemistry, and function. *Progress in Brain Research*, 151, 407–420. doi:10.1016/S0079-6123(05)51013-6

Greengrass, P., director (2007). *The Bourne Ultimatum*. USA: Universal Pictures Home Video. DVD.

Hasson, U., Malach, R., & Heeger, D. J. (2009). Reliability of cortical activity during natural stimulation. *Trends in Cognitive Sciences*, 14(1), 40–48. doi:10.1016/j.tics.2009.10.011

Hazanavicius, M., director (2011). *The Artist*. France: Sony Pictures Home Entertainment. DVD.

Hess, R. F., To, K., Zhou, J., Wang, G., & Cooperstock, J. R. (2015). Stereo vision: The haves and have-nots. *i-Perception*, 6(3), 1–5. doi:10.1177/2041669515593028

Hitchcock, A., director (1948). *Rope*. USA: Universal Pictures Home Entertainment. DVD.

Hitchcock, A., director (1953). *Dial M for Murder*. USA: Warner Home Video. DVD.

Hoyt, H. O., director (1925). *The Lost World*. USA: Ventura Distribution. DVD.

Ildirar, S., Levin, D. T., Schwan, S., & Smith, T. J. (2017). Audio facilitates the perception of cinematic continuity by first-time viewers. *Perception*, 47(3), 276–295. doi:10.1177/0301006617745782

Ildirar, S., & Schwan, S. (2015). First-time viewers' comprehension of films: Bridging shot transitions. *British Journal of Psychology*, 106(1), 133–151. doi:10.1111/bjop.12069

Iñárritu, A. G., director (2014). *Birdman (or the Unexpected Virtue of Ignorance)*. USA: Twentieth Century Fox Home Entertainment.

Iwerks, U. (1928). *Steamboat Willie*. USA: Walt Disney Productions. Film.

Jackson, P., director (2012). *The Hobbit: An Unexpected Journey*. USA and New Zealand: Warner Home Video. DVD.

Jaglom, J. (1992). The independent filmmaker. In J. E. Squire (Ed.), *The Movie Business Book*, 2nd edition (pp. 74–81). New York: Simon & Schuster.

Koenderink, J. J., van Doorn, A. J., & Kappers, A. M. (1994). On so-called paradoxical monocular stereoscopy. *Perception*, 23(5), 583–594. doi:10.1068/p230583

Leibowitz, F. (1991). Movie colorization and the expression of mood. *Journal of Aesthetics and Art Criticism*, 49(4), 363–365. http://www.jstor.org/stable/431036

Lourié, E., director (1953). *The Beast from 20,000 Fathoms*. USA: Warner Home Video. DVD.

Lucas, B. (March 29, 2015). Busted! 7 myths about high dynamic range photography. https://photography.tutsplus.com/articles/busted-7-myths-about-high-dynamic-range-photography--cms-23674. Accessed 29 Jan. 2018.

Lumière, A. & L. (1895). *L'Arrivé d'un train à La Ciotat (Arrival of a Train)*. France: Kino Video. https://www.youtube.com/watch?v=b9MoAQJFn_8. Accessed 1 Feb. 2018.

Magliano, J. P., & Zacks, J. M. (2011). The impact of continuity editing in narrative film on event segmentation. *Cognitive Science*, 35(6), 1489–1517. doi:10.1111/j.1551.-6709.2001.01202.x

Manning, M. L., Finlay, D. C., Neill, R. A., & Frost, B. G. (1987). Detection threshold differences to cross and uncrossed disparities. *Vision Research*, 27(9), 1683–1686. doi:10.1016/0042-6989(87)90173-8

McCay, W., director. (1914). *Gertie the Dinosaur*. USA: Milestone Film & Video. DVD.

McMahan, A. (2003). Immersion, engagement, and presence: A method for analyzing 3-D video games. In M. J. P. Wolf, & B. Perron (Eds.), *The video game, theory reader* (pp. 67–86. New York: Routledge, Taylor, & Francis.

Mendes, S., director (2015). *Spectre*. UK: Twentieth Century Fox Home Entertainment. DVD.

Meyer, N., director (1982). *Star Trek II: The Wrath of Khan*. Paramount Home Video. DVD.

Myrick, D., director (1999). *The Blair Witch Project*. USA: Artisan Entertainment. DVD.

Nolan, C., director (2010). *Inception*. USA & UK: Warner Home Video. DVD.

Oboler, A., director (1952). *Bwana Devil*. USA: United Artists. Film.

O'Brien, C. (2005). *Cinema's conversion to sound: Technology and film style in France and the U.S.* Bloomington, IN: Indiana University Press.

Paul, R., director (1898). *Come Along, Do*. UK: Kino Video. https://www.youtube.com/watch?v=ScD_yiykAro.

Porter, E., director (1903). *The great train robbery*. USA: The Edison Manufacturing Company. Film. https://www.youtube.com/watch?v=zuto7qWrplc. Accessed 31 Jan. 2018.

Prince, S. (2011). *Digital visual effects in cinema: The seduction of reality*. New Brunswick, NJ: Rutgers University Press.

Reeves, M., director (2008). *Cloverfield*. USA: Paramount Home Entertainment. DVD.

Reynaud, C.-E., director. (1892). *Pauvre Pierrot*. France: NickelOdeansChannel. Retrieved from https://www.youtube.com/watch?v=426mqlB-kAY

Rider, A. T., Coutrot, A., Pelicano, E., Dakin, S. C., & Mareschal, I. (2018). Semantic content outweighs low-level saliency in determining children's and adult's fixation of movies. *Journal of Experimental Child Psychology*, *166*, 293–309. doi:10.1016/jecp.2017.09.002

Rossell, D. (1988). *Living pictures: The origins of movies*. Albany, NY: The State University of New York Press.

Salt, B. (2009). *Film style and technology: History and analysis*. 3rd ed. London: Starword.

Scharf, A. (1974). *Art and photography*, 2nd edition. London: Penguin Books.

Schoedsack, E. B., director (1949). *Mighty Joe Young*. USA: Warner Home Video. DVD.

Smith, T. J. (2013). Watching you watch movies: Using eye tracking to inform cognitive film theory. In A. P. Shimamura (Ed.), *Psychoncinematics: Exploring cognition at the movies* (pp. 165–191). New York: Oxford University Press.

Smith, T. J. (2015). Read, watch, listen: A commentary on eye tracking and moving images. *Refractory: A Journal of Entertainment Media*, *25*(9). http://eprints.bbk.ac.uk/12583/. Accessed 29 Jan. 2018.

Smith, T. J., & Henderson, J. M. (2008). Edit blindness: The relationship between attention and global change blindness in dynamic scenes. *Journal of Eye Movement Research*, *2*(2), Article 6, 1–17. doi:10.16910/jemr.2.2.6

Spielberg, S., director (1993a). *Jurassic Park*. USA: Universal Studios Home Video. DVD.

Spielberg, S., director (1993b). *Schindler's List*. USA: Universal Studios Home Video. DVD.

Thompson, K. (1985) *Exporting entertainment: American in the world film market, 1907–1934*. UK: British Film Institute Publishing.

Toulet, E. (1988). *Cinématographie, invention du siècle*. Paris: Découvertes Gallimard.

van Wassenhove, V., Grant, K. W., & Poeppel D. (2007). Temporal window of integration in auditory-visual speech perception. *Neuropsychologia*, *45*(3), 598–607. doi:10.1016/j.neuropsychologia.2006.01.001

Warner, J. (2015). *Murder in motion: The strange life of photographer (and murderer) Eadweard Muybridge*. Hustonville, KY: Golgotha Press/Bookcaps.

Wass, S. V. & Smith, T. J. (2014). Individual differences in infant oculomotor behavior during the viewing of complex naturalistic scenes. *Infancy*, *19*(4), 352–384. doi:10.1111/infa.12049

Watson, A. B. (2013). High frame rates and human vision: A view through the window of visibility. *SMPTE Motion Imaging Journal*, *122*(2), 18–32. doi:10.5594/j18266

Wilder, B., director (1960). *The Apartment*. USA: MGM Home Entertainment. DVD.

Wright, J., director (2005). *Atonement*. UK: Universal Pictures Home Entertainment. DVD.

Yumibe, J. (2012). *Moving color: Early film, mass culture, modernism*. New Brunswick, NJ: Rutgers University Press.

Zacks, J. M. (2015). *Flicker: Your brain on movies*. New York: Oxford University Press.

Zone, R. (2012). *3-D revolution: The history of modern stereoscopic cinema*. Lexington, KY: University of Kentucky Press.

Zunshine, L. (2006). *Why we read fiction*. Columbus, OH: The Ohio State University Press.

Zunshine, L. (2012). *Getting inside your head: What cognitive science can tell us about popular culture*. Baltimore, MD: The Johns Hopkins University Press.

CHAPTER 31

......

EMPIRICAL AESTHETICS
OF POETRY

......

WINFRIED MENNINGHAUS AND STEFAN BLOHM

INTRODUCTION

THIS chapter presents a selective survey of *empirical* investigations into the *aesthetic perception and evaluation of poetry*. By implication, the rich humanist tradition of nonempirical poetics and literary studies is not in itself an object of this chapter. Still, this tradition provides crucial help in identifying both the (potentially) most relevant features of poetic texts and the most pertinent dimensions of recipients' responses to poetry. General and comparative studies in metrics, statistical analyses of the affective dictionaries and sounds of poems, and computational studies on corpora of poetry are only covered if and to the extent that they include empirical data on readers' actual aesthetic appreciation of the analyzed poems. Similarly, studies from cognitive psychology that pursue a more general interest in the cognitive processes involved in poetry comprehension are included only if they also help to elucidate genuine aesthetic appreciation.

Classical poetics distinguished three dimensions of text production and detailed how their execution affects text perception: the *selection/invention* (Lat. *inventio*) of a text's content (personae and their relations, situational setting, emotional content, mood, atmosphere), the *compositional arrangement* of this content (Lat. *dispositio*), and its linguistic realization (Lat. *elocutio*). Empirical research has predominantly focused on the third of these components, i.e., poetic diction.

AESTHETIC VIRTUES ASSOCIATED WITH POETRY

The aesthetic virtues of poetry differ strikingly from those of other literary genres. Whereas novels, short stories, and plays are primarily associated with *suspense*, poetry is primarily supposed to be *beautiful, romantic, poetic,* and *sad* (Knoop, Wagner, Jacobsen, & Menninghaus, 2016). Crucially, poetry's aesthetic virtues show more conceptual overlap with those of music than with those of other literary genres; specifically, poetry is unique among literary genres in its clear association with the music-related attributes *harmonious, melodious,* and *rhythmic.*

In studies that compare experimenter-selected dimensions of perceived aesthetic and emotional appeal (rather than free associations), *vivid* (Belfi, Vessel, & Starr, 2017) and (*emotionally*) *moving* (Menninghaus, Wagner, Wassiliwizky, Jacobsen, & Knoop, 2017) have been shown to be two additional preeminent virtues of poetry and good predictors of overall liking and/or beauty attributions.

The degree of literary expertise appears to modulate some of the dimensions of reading poetry. Thus, compared with nonexperts, expert readers are more likely to embrace semantic opacity as part of the subjective reading experience, and their judgments are altogether more complex and more stable (Nenadić, Vejnović, & Marković, 2019).

CORRECTNESS, CLARITY, AND THE SPECIAL "LICENSE" OF POETIC DICTION

The single most general virtue of diction is linguistic *correctness* (Kirchner, 2007; Quintilian, 1920), or skillful adherence to the rules of a given language. Poetic language, while also subject to these rules, takes greater liberties than any other genre of literature in departing from conversational language use (Aristotle, 1911; Mukařovský, 1964; Pathak, 1982; Quintilian, 1920; Sanni, 1993). The theory of "poetic license" is therefore a key element in theorizing poetic diction.

Ellipses and inversions of sentence constituents, word-form alterations, and morphophonological reductions and distortions (Quintilian, 1920) frequently appear in prototypical poems (and also in proverbs and dramatic verse) across many traditions and epochs. At the same time, the range of acceptable detours from ordinary language use depends on literary conventions and the grammatical properties of the language in question. For instance, Shakespeare's noun-to-verb conversions, such as in "Then I am *kinged* again," artfully exploit a word-formational potential of English that may not be equally available in other languages. For speakers of English, these formally striking expressions combine perceptual disfluency with conceptual fluency; that is, error detection and repair during early syntactic parsing with effortless semantic integration (Thierry et al., 2008).

Such poetic licenses may allow poets to adhere to the strict constraints of systematic rhyme and meter (Rice, 1997; Youmans, 1983), yet they also increase the cognitive complexity of grammatical processing during comprehension (Blohm, Wagner, Schlesewsky, & Menninghaus, 2018; Menninghaus et al., 2015). Thus, rhyme, meter, and the grammatical licenses that support them (e.g., ellipses) make German proverbs harder to read, less comprehensible, and—in line with Jakobson's (Jakobson, 1960, pp. 370–371) proposal that ambiguity is an "intrinsic feature" of poetic language use (Jakobson, 1960, pp. 370–371)—also more ambiguous (Wallot & Menninghaus, 2018).

However, despite such disfluency effects, detours from ordinary language use are widely accepted as inherent properties of poetic language and contribute to the categorization of texts as poetry (Hanauer, 1996). English word strings, for instance, sound more "poetic" if they deviate within limits from actual English text (Martindale, 1973). Similarly, in German, lines of traditional verse as well as regular sentences are perceived as more poetic if they feature noncanonical grammatical structures but not clear ungrammaticalities (Blohm et al., 2018). However, there is little research on modern poetry that goes far beyond these limitations and frequently subverts even the most basic linguistic standards (e.g., Cureton, 1979, 1980).

Poems depart not only from standards of formal linguistic correctness, but also often from standards of high (*conceptual*) *clarity*. Indeed, low conceptual clarity may render sentences and short texts, such as poems, richer in associative and affective meaning and thus engage readers in an active search for significance (Blohm, Menninghaus, & Schlesewsky, 2017; Gibbs, Kushner, & Mills, 1991; Peskin, 1998).

POETIC PHONOLOGY: THE VIRTUES OF PARALLELISTIC DICTION

Following the discussion of ongoing "parallelistic" structures in Lowth (1787), Hopkins (1865/1959), and Jakobson (1960), we use the term *parallelism* to denote not only the varied repetitions of the syntax and/or semantics of entire lines or sentences (the so-called "isokola" in classical rhetoric; Lausberg, 1998, §§ 719–754), but also recurrences at lower, sound-related levels of linguistic organization, such as meter, rhyme, alliteration, and assonance (see Fabb, 1997; Frog & Tarkka, 2017; Jakobson, 1960, 1966). Parallelistic patterns are revealed over time to the attentive recipient, shaping a poem's unfolding gestalt and contributing prediction- and surprise-based tension and release to the trajectory of reading. While parallelistic patterning per se appears to be a universal feature of poetry, poetic traditions and texts differ widely with regard to the special forms of parallelism they employ (e.g., Fabb, 2015; Küper, 1996).

The cognitive benefits of phonological parallelism for the processing of ordinary language are well attested: words, phrases, and sentences that feature ongoing prosodic alternation are segmented—and generally processed—more fluently than irregular alternatives (Bohn, Knaus, Wiese, & Domahs, 2013; Henrich, Alter, Wiese, & Domahs, 2014; Kelly, 1988). Like ritual language (Bauman & Briggs, 1990; Fox, 1988; Severi, 2002), poetry draws on this general preference and "artifies" it. Notably, both preverbal and the first verbal communication between parents and children similarly show pronounced rhythmical regularities beyond levels observed in ordinary language (Dissanayake, 2000; Falk, 2004).

Meter

Meter, which is arguably the most basic phonological parallelism, is found across virtually all poetic traditions in a multitude of language- and culture-specific variants (Fabb, 2015; Turner & Pöppel, 1988). Meter constrains and determines the number of phonological units (e.g., syllables) that can constitute a line of verse and/or the permissible distributions of rhythmic or melodic features across these units, such as syllable stress in English verse or tone in Chinese poetry. As in music, the continous repetition of complex prosodic patterns in poetry provides a sound-based grid for other systematic sound patterns like rhyme and alliteration (Žirmunskij, 1966).

Evidence from Dutch indicates that (stress-based) meter increases the perceived "smoothness" and comprehensibility of verse (Van Peer, 1990). A series of behavioral and electrophysiological experiments in German has provided further evidence that the continuous parallelism of meter makes verse more aesthetically appealing and more fluently readable (Menninghaus, Bohrn, Altmann, Lubrich, & Jacobs, 2014; Obermeier et al., 2016; Obermeier et al., 2013).

In traditional poetics, specific metrical patterns have often been assigned a special expressive character. For instance, both the dactylic hexameter of Greek and Latin antiquity and the iambic pentameter of English 17th- and 18th-century epic poetry have been dubbed *heroic verse*. (However, in both cases, the attribute *heroic* may simply be an associative transfer from the themes of the poems to the qualities of their rhythmic pattern.) Hevner (1937) constructed nonsense verse in both binary and ternary metrical feet to explore how different metrical patterns differ in their overall expressive character. Recipients perceived two-syllable feet as *solemn, earnest, dignified*, and *sad*, whereas three-syllable feet were instead perceived as *joyous, light, sparkling, spirited*, and *gay*. While this provides initial evidence that particular metrical patterns may support special expressive qualia and stylistic effects on their own, it remains an open question whether or not the same expressive characters of the two metrical forms are also found in meaningful verse.

Rhyme

Like sustained meter, systematic rhyme facilitates neural processing and increases liking (Obermeier et al., 2016), as it generates predictions whose fulfillment facilitates phonological and lexical processing. Frustration of these expectations, as reflected in electrophysiological responses, can be noticed as early as 150 ms after the onset of words during reading (Chen et al., 2016; Hoorn, 1996), and it is also reflected in pupillary responses (Scheepers, Mohr, Fischer, & Roberts, 2013). Based on the measure of reading times, different rhyme schemes do not differentially affect processing fluency (Carminati, Stabler, Roberts, & Fischer, 2006). However, other measures of cognitive (dis)fluency might well reveal differences that are dependent on rhyme schemes.

Many poetic traditions license imperfect rhymes/near rhymes in end rhyme position, i.e., word pairs in which the rhyming syllables are only partially rather than fully identical, e.g., English *was/pass* or *rock/stop*. The acceptability of such imperfect rhymes increases with the presence of a verse context (as compared with word pairs) and seems to benefit from the predictability of linguistic and parallelistic structures, e.g., meter (Knoop, Blohm, Kraxenberger, & Menninghaus, 2019). It remains unclear, though, how far imperfect rhyme shares the aesthetic and stylistic effects supported by perfect rhyme (see below).

Aesthetic and emotional effects of meter and rhyme

The effects of meter and rhyme are manifold. Rhyme tends to render aphorisms more convincing and accurate (McGlone & Tofighbakhsh, 2000), and proverbs more beautiful, succinct, and persuasive (Menninghaus et al., 2015). Unconventional and imperfect rhymes may have a comical effect and render humoristic verse funnier (Menninghaus et al., 2014). Multiple parallelistic patterns (meter, rhyme, and several local sound parallelisms) conjointly enhance impressions of *beauty, sadness, joy, being moved, melodiousness*, and *positive feelings* in response to poetry (Menninghaus et al., 2017). In all of these cases, the actual aesthetic effects of parallelistic features are strongly dependent on the context in which they are employed.

Concurrent phonological parallelisms also increase the aesthetic measure, that is, the order/complexity ratio, as formulated for relevant sound-related aspects of poetic composition (Birkhoff, 1933). This measure predicts liking for individual lines of pseudo-word verse that are devoid of semantic content; however, its predictive power is strongly reduced for meaningful verse (Beebe-Center & Pratt, 1937).

Poetic speech melody

Systematic *tonal parallelism* is a common feature of poetry in tone languages, for example, Chinese. But there is also evidence of a genuine *melodic parallelism* in the poetry of nontonal languages: recitations of traditional German poems feature text-specific pitch contours and rhythm patterns that recur over higher-order poetic structures, such as couplets or stanzas (Menninghaus, Wagner, Knoop, & Scharinger, 2018; for initial evidence from English, see Schramm, 1935), and that can be quantified by an autocorrelation measure developed for the analysis of music (Korotkov, Korotkova, Frenkel, & Kudryashov, 2003). Importantly, pitch-based autocorrelation coefficients not only correlate positively with subjective impressions of *melodiousness*, but also predict how likely it is that these poems have been set to music by professional composers (for the affinity between linguistic parallelism in poetry and musical form, see also Zeman, Milton, Smith, & Rylance, 2013). A particular affinity of poems to music has also been corroborated by a study that revealed the existence of naturally biased semantic associations in the general population (measured on a set of semantic differentials) between a series of musical selections and a series of quatrains (Albertazzi et al., 2017).

Sporadic parallelism

The recurrence of metrical patterns and of systematic parametrical parallelism in poetry (e.g., rhyme schemes) is regular and predictable. Additionally, there usually are local and sporadically recurring features that may or may not depend on the presence of a metrical grid: assonances (i.e., vowel repetitions in adjacent prominent syllables), consonances (i.e., consonant repetitions in adjacent prominent syllables), and alliterations (i.e., repetitions of word-initial speech sounds). These unsystematic parallelisms have been shown to attract attention to single words and phrases and to increase their emotional impact (Kraxenberger & Menninghaus, 2016a).

Expectancies and cadences

The compositional features of traditional poetry allow readers to build strong expectations regarding upcoming input and its unfolding gestalt. Thus, the reception of poetry may include tension-resolution trajectories similar to those found in the processing of music (Huron, 2006; Meyer, 1961). Across cultures, powerful cadences that bring these trajectories and the reader's constant updating of his/her anticipations (i.e., predictions) to a pleasurable conclusion are of preeminent importance in artful speech (Lausberg, 1998; Smith, 1968; Ye, 1996). This "sense of appropriate cessation" (Smith, 1968) is supported by an investigation of peak emotional experiences in response to (German) poetry, indicating that these episodes—as evidenced by both physiological measures (i.e., chills and goosebumps) and self-report—seem to be frequently elicited by the closures of verse lines, stanzas, and, most notably, entire poems (Wassiliwizky, Koelsch, Wagner, Jacobsen, & Menninghaus, 2017). Moreover, these peak emotional episodes are associated with neural activation of the primary reward circuitry: a largely (but not fully) convergent neural signature was previously reported for chills in response to music (Panksepp, 1995; Salimpoor, Benovoy, Larcher, Dagher, & Zatorre, 2011).

In sum, poetic parallelism and its implications for predictive coding of sensory information have a strong impact on the aesthetic and emotional perception of poetry along a great variety of dimensions far beyond mere euphony. Whereas readers are typically consciously aware of the regularly recurrent patterns of meter and rhyme, other dimensions of poetic phonology demonstrably affect readers while escaping their conscious awareness. For example, nonexpert readers of the Welsh poetic form Cynghanedd—which involves complex and sustained restrictions on the recurrence of consonants—cannot consciously tell apart lines that adhere to these restrictions from lines that violate them. At the same time, their neural responses indicate a clear difference in the processing of well- and ill-formed lines (Vaughan-Evans et al., 2016), suggesting that complex formal regularities of poems can be unconsciously perceived in low-level processing routines even by readers with no special poetic expertise (for evidence from tonal patterns in Chinese poetry, see Jiang et al., 2012).

Parallelistic phonology and poetic license in interaction

In their entirety, the parallelistic features of poetic language can be considered as linguistic analogues to multilayered patterns of recurrence and symmetry in visual (Berlyne, 1974; Palmer & Hemenway, 1978) and music (Lerdahl & Jackendoff, 1977; Margulis, 2014) aesthetics. They increase aesthetic liking and, depending on their context, affect a broad variety of specific aesthetic and emotional response dimensions. The mnemonic effects of phonological parallelism are also well established and have been reported for the form-based retrieval cues of meter (Van Peer, 1990), alliteration (Atchley & Hare, 2013; Lea, Rapp, Elfenbein, Mitchel, & Romine, 2008; Lindstromberg & Boers, 2008), and rhyme (Bower & Bolton, 1969; Rubin & Wallace, 1989) as well as for combinations of these patterns (deCastro-Arrazola & Kirby, 2019; Rubin, Ciobanu, & Langston, 1997; Tillmann & Dowling, 2007).

By enhancing ease of phonological processing and by yielding a variety of additional positive effects on aesthetic appreciation, the features of parallelistic phonology appear to more than compensate for the adverse effects of poetic diction on correctness, clarity, and overall ease of syntactic and semantic processing. At the same time, the frequent co-occurrence of parallelistic features with poetically licensed distortions of ordinary sentence structure and word forms support the general notion that the aesthetic appreciation of poems, like that of other artworks, is not just driven by increased fluency of processing, as proposed by standard variants of the cognitive fluency hypothesis (cf. Reber, Schwarz, & Winkielman, 2004). Rather, it involves dimensions of *both* enhanced and reduced ease of processing at different levels of stimulus processing (Alter, 2013; Graf & Landwehr, 2015). Specifically, poetic and rhetorical language frequently combine (low-level) *perceptual fluency* and (high-level) *conceptual disfluency* (Menninghaus et al., 2015; Song & Schwarz, 2009), resulting in ambiguities, lack of clarity, and other types of extra cognitive demands.

Other aspects of low-level (dis)fluency appear to modulate aesthetic liking of poetry as well: a hard-to-read font, which affects early stages of language comprehension (e.g., word recognition), decreases appreciation for poems that are formally and conceptually easier to read and understand, but appears to have no effect on the evaluation of more difficult poems (Gao, Dera, Nijhof, & Willems, 2019).

SEMANTIC FIGURES

Poetic language also makes frequent uses of semantic figures, including metaphors, similes, poetic imagery, paradoxical combinations, and other figures that prompt readers to construe coherent mental images by modifying and integrating the source and target concepts (Pagán Cánovas, Valenzuela, & Santiago, 2015). Apart from metaphor, few of these semantic figures in poetry have been systematically studied with regard to their aesthetic effects.

In both ordinary language use and literature, there seems to be a general preference for metaphors that combine a high level of concreteness/imageability and a rich interpretive potential with intermediate levels of cognitive challenge and surprise (Jacobs & Kinder, 2018; Littlemore, Sobrino, Houghton, Shi, & Winter, 2018; Utsumi, 2006). Moreover, metaphors that draw on infrequently used or negative-valence vehicle words are particularly likely to be considered high-quality metaphors (Littlemore et al., 2018).

The full appreciation of poetry seems to presuppose the reader's willingness to actively search for additional significance beyond the plain sense of the words. For instance, readers perceive poetic metaphors as more meaningful, emotional, and aesthetically enjoyable when they believe them to be intentionally composed (Gibbs et al., 1991; Peskin, 2007). A similar meaningfulness effect has been observed for sentences that contain apparent semantic incongruities; this effect is absent or greatly reduced in the case of literal and semantically congruent statements (Blohm et al., 2017). Moreover, metaphors are perceived as more likable and emotionally more moving when the reading stance promotes conscious metaphor identification (Gibbs, 2002). However, there is also evidence for an inverse mechanism: if the reading stance favors emotional engagement, then figurative language appears more salient to readers (Eva-Wood, 2004).

Sound-Iconic Expressions of Emotions

Against the background of the predominant assumption that the exact sound shape of linguistic signs is "arbitrary" (Saussure, 1916/1960), there has been speculation about an inherently motivated and in this sense "iconic" relation of sound and meaning in language and literature, particularly in poetry (Jakobson & Waugh, 1979/2002; Sapir, 1929; Schmidtke, Conrad, & Jacobs, 2014). Based on cross-linguistic data, Auracher, Albers, Zhai, Gareeva, and Stavniychuk (2010) argued that the dominant emotional content or tone of a poem is systematically reflected in the iconic use of certain classes of speech sounds and articulatory gestures. However, a replication of this study using a larger and more varied corpus of poetry could only confirm a link between the expressed emotion and some phenomenological sound dimensions (sounding bright vs. sounding dark), rather than a link between the dominant emotional tone and the occurrence of certain speech sounds (Kraxenberger & Menninghaus, 2016b).

Focusing on a collection of poems by the German author Enzensberger, two studies (Aryani, Kraxenberger, Ullrich, Jacobs, & Conrad, 2016; Ullrich, Aryani, Kraxenberger, Jacobs, & Conrad, 2017) have demonstrated that the affective states the author himself attributed to the poems (sad, friendly, spiteful) were correctly perceived by readers not only through the denotational or connotational meaning of the words, but also by reference to their phonological shape. Corroborating evidence stems from an experimental study that presented poem recitations with original or manipulated (sad vs. joyful) prosody; even nonnative listeners correctly used the cues of emotional prosody to identify the expressed emotion (Kraxenberger, Menninghaus, Roth, & Scharinger, 2018).

Mood Representation, Mood Empathy, and Poetic Diction

Most poems do not involve elaborate narratives, but instead represent momentary mood states or situational atmospheres that are particularly rich in memories, anticipations, and emotional meaning (Meyer-Sickendiek, 2011; Steiger, 1946; Ye, 1996). Not only do readers correctly decode these mood cues; they also experience mood-empathic affective responses (Lüdtke, Meyer-Sickendieck, & Jacobs, 2014). However, their aesthetic liking (as evidenced in ratings for *liking*, *beauty*, and *fascination*) does not depend on these mood-empathic responses (comprising measures for felt mood, atmosphere, and situation), but rather on the features of poetic form (summarized as *style*). Still, there seems to be an indirect relation between the two variables, as both mood empathy and aesthetic liking increase with imageability (Jacobs, Lüdtke, Aryani, Meyer-Sickendieck, & Conrad, 2016).

Digital Analyses of Poetry

Computational analyses of poetry are attracting increased interest, both in the digital humanities and among poetry scholars. As emphasized in the introduction, since this chapter is on the empirical aesthetics of poetry, it only covers studies that not only computationally identify and analyze various properties of poems, but also correlate these with measures of aesthetic perception and evaluation.

Kao and Jurafsky (2012) identified statistical features of hypothetically "good" poems by comparing poems written by professional poets that are included in well-acknowledged anthologies with poems written by amateur poets that are published only in internet fora. Professional poems show higher type–token ratios and contain fewer perfect end rhymes, fewer instances of alliteration, fewer positive outlook words, fewer negative emotion words, more references to concrete objects, fewer references to abstract concepts, and fewer generalizations. However, these findings are limited to a broad group effect, and we do not know of any studies to date in the digital humanities that provide evidence regarding how well distinct qualities of poetic diction predict relevant dimensions of the aesthetic appreciation of individual poems.

Using two sets of human- and machine-written poems, Lau et al. (2018) asked nonexperts for categorical attributions to human or machine authorship. The results for the two groups of poems did not differ significantly. However, beyond mere accept-ability ratings, the authors did not administer pertinent scales for genuine aesthetic evaluation. Moreover, an expert rated the computer-generated poems as lower in read-ability and emotional power compared with the human-composed poems. Other poetry generation studies (Colton, Goodwin, & Veale, 2012; McGregor, Purver, & Wiggins, 2016) have likewise administered rating scales that primarily capture the extent to which an artificially generated poem meets prototypical expectations of a particular poetic subgenre. Overall, the relevant dimensions of genuine aesthetic evaluation are to date clearly underrepresented in studies on poetry in the digital humanities.

A study that combined computational text analysis with eye-tracking revealed that reading behavior during poetry reading not only reflects the relevant text properties (e.g., word length) known from ordinary reading but also the sonority of speech sounds (Xue, Lüdtke, Sylvester, & Jacobs, 2019).

Who Likes Which Kind of Poetry?

It generally takes a certain affinity for poetry to fully enjoy it (Kraxenberger & Menninghaus, 2017). But which kinds of readers seek which kinds of poetry? Eysenck (1940) identified two factors that influence readers' preferences for poetry: formal com-positional principles and emotional expressiveness. The form- and cognition-related factor *simple–complex* correlates with readers' level of extra-/introversion, with extra-verted persons tending to prefer relatively simple poetic structures and introverted persons relatively complex ones. The emotion-related factor *sentimental–restrained* reflects readers' responses to the selection and treatment of themes. Susceptibility to the aesthetic effects of formal poetic composition has further been linked to readers' openness to absorbing experiences (Glicksohn, Tsur, & Goodblatt, 1991; Tsur, Glicksohn, & Goodblatt, 1991). More generally, and in line with findings for other art forms, readers prefer poems that match their linguistic, pragmatic, and literary knowledge and that offer an optimal balance between ease and difficulty of processing (Kammann, 1966).

Future Directions

The empirical research on poetry reviewed in this chapter is very strongly focused on the formal features of poetic diction. Most of the other distinctive features recently identified in a comprehensive theoretical account of the genre of poetry (Schlaffer, 2012) are barely covered, if at all. These include the content of poems (agents, situations, themes, and their respective unfolding), characteristic speech acts (such as addresses to absent or nonexistent persons, invocations, and analogues of magic spells), distinctive features of particular subgenres of poetry, and the functions of (reading) poems. Hence there is much room for broadening the scope of empirical research on poetry. Moreover, even though substantial work has already been devoted to the aesthetic effects of both parallelistic features and poetic license and on the psychological mechanisms explaining these effects (as discussed in the pertinent sections above), it remains largely unknown, beyond the overall correlations of these features with aesthetic and emotional ratings, how their concrete *temporal trajectory* interacts with unfolding themes and meanings to shape aesthetic experiences of poetry.

The most-cited models of aesthetic processing/evaluation in empirical aesthetics have been developed with a near-exclusive focus on the visual arts (Pelowski, Markey, Lauring, & Leder, 2016). At the same time, even the *Neurocognitive Poetics Model* (NCPM) of literary reading (Jacobs, 2015a, 2015b) does not entail any special provisions that account for the substantial differences between narratives, plays, and poems, which are clearly aesthetically relevant and reflected in readers' expectations (see the section "Aesthetic Virtues Associated with Poetry"). Still, the NCPM can guide future research on poetry if it is augmented with basic theoretical categories that allow accounting for systematic differences between the basic genres of literature. In any event, future work on the empirical aesthetics of poetry should have a stronger focus on theory formation.

As poetic traditions are inextricably tied to their respective languages, the understanding of the universal and language-specific aspects of the aesthetics of poetry could also be advanced by systematic cross-linguistic comparisons of poetic forms and their cognitive and aesthetic effects (deCastro-Arrazola, 2018). Finally, digital analyses of poetry's verbal material in general and of sentiment specifically may help to address the underrepresentation of thematic aspects in the empirical aesthetics of poetry (Barnes, Klinger, & Walde, 2017; Bostan & Klinger, 2018; Whissell, 2003). Combining the tools of digital text analysis with the methods of empirical aesthetics promises great potential for future advances in both fields.

References

Albertazzi, L., Canal, L., Micciolo, R., Ferrari, F., Sitta, S., & Hachen, I. (2017). Naturally biased associations between music and poetry. *Perception*, 46(2), 139–160.

Alter, A. L. (2013). The benefits of cognitive disfluency. *Current Directions in Psychological Science*, 22(6), 437–442.

Aristotle (1911). Poetics. In D. S. Margoliouth (Ed.), *The poetics of Aristotle*. London: Hodder and Stoughton.

Aryani, A., Kraxenberger, M., Ullrich, S., Jacobs, A. M., & Conrad, M. (2016). Measuring the basic affective tone of poems via phonological saliency and iconicity. *Psychology of Aesthetics, Creativity, and the Arts*, 10(2), 191–204.

Atchley, R. M., & Hare, M. L. (2013). Memory for poetry: More than meaning? *International Journal of Cognitive Linguistics*, 4(1), 35–50.

Auracher, J., Albers, S., Zhai, Y., Gareeva, G., & Stavniychuk, T. (2010). P is for happiness, N is for sadness: Universals in sound iconicity to detect emotions in poetry. *Discourse Processes*, 48(1), 1–25.

Barnes, J., Klinger, R., & Walde, S. S. I. (2017). Assessing state-of-the-art sentiment models on state-of-the-art sentiment datasets. In A. Balahur, S. M. Mohammad, & E. van der Goot (Eds.), *Proceedings of the 8th Workshop on Computational Approaches to Subjectivity, Sentiment and Social Media Analysis*, Copenhagen, Denmark (pp. 2–12). Retrieved from: https://www.aclweb.org/anthology/W17-52

Bauman, R., & Briggs, C. L. (1990). Poetics and performances as critical perspectives on language and social life. *Annual Review of Anthropology, 19*(1), 59–88.

Beebe-Center, J. G., & Pratt, C. C. (1937). A test of Birkhoff's aesthetic measure. *The Journal of General Psychology, 17*(2), 339–353.

Belfi, A. M., Vessel, E. A., & Starr, G. G. (2017). Individual ratings of vividness predict aesthetic appeal in poetry. *Psychology of Aesthetics, Creativity, and the Arts, 12*(3), 341–350.

Berlyne, D. E. (Ed.) (1974). *Studies in the new experimental aesthetics: Steps toward an objective psychology of aesthetic appreciation*. Oxford, England: Hemisphere.

Birkhoff, G. D. (1933). *Aesthetic measure*. Cambridge, MA: Harvard University Press.

Blohm, S., Menninghaus, W., & Schlesewsky, M. (2017). Sentence-level effects of literary genre: Behavioral and electrophysiological evidence. *Frontiers in Psychology, 8*, 1887. doi:10.3389/fpsyg.2017.01887

Blohm, S., Wagner, V., Schlesewsky, M., & Menninghaus, W. (2018). Sentence judgments and the grammar of poetry: Linking linguistic structure and poetic effect. *Poetics, 69*, 41–56.

Bohn, K., Knaus, J., Wiese, R., & Domahs, U. (2013). The influence of rhythmic (ir)regularities on speech processing: Evidence from an ERP study on German phrases. *Neuropsychologia, 51*(4), 760–771.

Bostan, L. A. M., & Klinger, R. (2018). An analysis of annotated corpora for emotion classification in text. In E. M., Bender, L. Derczynski, & P. Isabelle (Eds.), *Proceedings of the 27th International Conference on Computational Linguistics*, Santa Fe, NM (pp. 2104–2119). Retrieved from: https://www.aclweb.org/anthology/C18-1000

Bower, G. H., & Bolton, L. S. (1969). Why are rhymes easy to learn? *Journal of Experimental Psychology, 82*(3), 453–461.

Carminati, M. N., Stabler, J., Roberts, A. M., & Fischer, M. H. (2006). Readers' responses to sub-genre and rhyme scheme in poetry. *Poetics, 34*(3), 204–218.

Chen, Q., Zhang, J., Xu, X., Scheepers, C., Yang, Y., & Tanenhaus, M. K. (2016). Prosodic expectations in silent reading: ERP evidence from rhyme scheme and semantic congruence in classic Chinese poems. *Cognition, 154*, 11–21.

Colton, S., Goodwin, J., & Veale, T. (2012). Full-FACE Poetry Generation. In M. L. Maher, K. Hammond, A. Pease, R. Pérez y Pérez, D. Ventura & G. Wiggins (Eds.), *Proceedings of the International Conference on Computational Creativity* (ICCC 2012), Dublin, Ireland (pp. 95–102). Retrieved from: http://www.computationalcreativity.net/proceedings/ICCC-2012-Proceedings.pdf

Cureton, R. (1979). EE Cummings: a study of the poetic use of deviant morphology. *Poetics Today, 1*(1/2), 213–244.

Cureton, R. (1980). Poetic syntax and aesthetic form. *Style, 14*(4), 318–340.

deCastro-Arrazola, V. (2018). *Typological tendencies in verse and their cognitive grounding*. Doctoral thesis, Leiden University. Retrieved from http://hdl.handle.net/1887/61826

deCastro-Arrazola, V., & Kirby, S. (2019). The emergence of verse templates through iterated learning. *Journal of Language Evolution, 4*(1), 28–43.

Dissanayake, E. (2000). Antecedents of the temporal arts in early mother-infant interactions. In N. L. Wallin, B. Merker, & S. Brown (Eds.), *The origins of music* (pp. 389–410). Cambridge, MA: MIT Press.

Eva-Wood, A. L. (2004). How think-and-feel-aloud instruction influences poetry readers. *Discourse Processes*, *38*(2), 173–192.

Eysenck, H. J. (1940). Some factors in the appreciation of poetry, and their relation to temperamental qualities. *Journal of Personality*, *9*(2), 160–167.

Fabb, N. (1997). *Linguistics and literature: Language in the verbal arts of the world*. Oxford, England: Blackwell.

Fabb, N. (2015). *What is poetry? Language and memory in the poems of the world*. Cambridge, England: Cambridge University Press.

Falk, D. (2004). Prelinguistic evolution in early hominins: Whence motherese? *Behavioral and Brain Sciences*, *27*(4), 491–503.

Fox, J. J. (Ed.) (1988). *To speak in pairs: Essays on the ritual languages of eastern Indonesia*. Cambridge, England: Cambridge University Press.

Frog, M., & Tarkka, L. (Eds.). (2017). *Parallelism in verbal art and performance* (Vol. 31). Columbia, MO: Center for Studies in Oral Tradition.

Gao, X., Dera, J., Nijhof, A. D., & Willems, R. (2019). Is less readable liked better? The case of font readability in poetry appreciation. *PLoS ONE*, *14*, e0225757. doi:10.1371/journal.pone.0225757

Gibbs, R. W., Jr. (2002). Identifying and appreciating poetic metaphor. *Journal of Literary Semantics*, *31*(2), 101.

Gibbs, R. W., Jr., Kushner, J. M., & Mills, W. R., 3rd (1991). Authorial intentions and metaphor comprehension. *Journal of Psycholinguistic Research*, *20*(1), 11–30.

Glicksohn, J., Tsur, R., & Goodblatt, C. (1991). Absorption and trance-inductive poetry. *Empirical Studies of the Arts*, *9*(2), 115–122.

Graf, L. K. M., & Landwehr, J. R. (2015). A dual-process perspective on fluency-based aesthetics: The pleasure-interest model of aesthetic liking. *Personality and Social Psychology Review*, *19*(4), 395–410.

Hanauer, D. (1996). Integration of phonetic and graphic features in poetic text categorization judgements. *Poetics*, *23*(5), 363–380.

Henrich, K., Alter, K., Wiese, R., & Domahs, U. (2014). The relevance of rhythmical alternation in language processing: An ERP study on English compounds. *Brain and Language*, *136*, 19–30.

Hevner, K. (1937). An experimental study of the affective value of sounds in poetry. *The American Journal of Psychology*, *49*(3), 419–434.

Hoorn, J. F. (1996). Psychophysiology and literary processing: ERPs to semantic and phonological deviations in reading small verses. In R. J. Kreuz & M. S. MacNealy (Eds.), *Empirical approaches to literature and aesthetics* (pp. 339–358). Norwood, NJ: Ablex.

Hopkins, G. M. (1865/1959). Poetic diction. In H. House (Ed.), *The journals and papers of Gerard Manley Hopkins*. London: Oxford University Press.

Huron, D. (2006). *Sweet anticipation: Music and the psychology of expectation*. Cambridge, MA: MIT Press.

Jacobs, A. M. (2015a). Neurocognitive poetics: Methods and models for investigating the neuronal and cognitive-affective bases of literature reception. *Frontiers in Human Neuroscience*, *9*, 186. doi:10.3389/fnhum.2015.00186

Jacobs, A. M. (2015b). Towards a neurocognitive poetics model of literary reading. In R. M. Willems (Ed.), *Cognitive neuroscience of natural language use* (pp. 135–159). Cambridge, England: Cambridge University Press.

Jacobs, A. M., & Kinder, A. (2018). What makes a metaphor literary? Answers from two computational studies. *Metaphor and Symbol, 33*(2), 85–100.

Jacobs, A. M., Lüdtke, J., Aryani, A., Meyer-Sickendieck, B., & Conrad, M. (2016). Mood-empathic and aesthetic responses in poetry reception. *Scientific Study of Literature, 6*(1), 87–130.

Jakobson, R. (1960). Closing statement: Linguistics and poetics. In T. A. Sebeok (Ed.), *Style in language* (pp. 350–377). Cambridge, MA: MIT Press.

Jakobson, R. (1966). Grammatical parallelism and its Russian facet. *Language, 42*(2), 399–429.

Jakobson, R., & Waugh, L. R. (1979/2002). *The sound shape of language.* Berlin: de Gruyter.

Jiang, S., Zhu, L., Guo, X., Ma, W., Yang, Z., & Dienes, Z. (2012). Unconscious structural knowledge of tonal symmetry: Tang poetry redefines limits of implicit learning. *Consciousness and Cognition, 21*(1), 476–486.

Kammann, R. (1966). Verbal complexity and preferences in poetry. *Journal of Verbal Learning and Verbal Behavior, 5*(6), 536–540.

Kao, J., & Jurafsky, D. (2012). A computational analysis of style, affect, and imagery in contemporary poetry. In D. Elson, A. Kazantseva, R. Mihalcea, & S. Szpakowicz (Eds.), *Proceedings of the NAACL-HLT 2012 Workshop on Computational Linguistics for Literature*, Montréal, Canada (pp. 8–17). Retrieved from: https://www.aclweb.org/anthology/W12-25

Kelly, M. H. (1988). Rhythmic alternation and lexical stress differences in English. *Cognition, 30*(2), 107–137.

Kirchner, R. (2007). Elocutio: Latin prose style. In W. Dominik & J. Hall (Eds.), *A companion to Roman rhetoric.* (pp 181–194) Malden, MA: Blackwell.

Knoop, C. A., Blohm, S., Kraxenberger, M., & Menninghaus, W. (2019). How perfect are imperfect rhymes? Effects of phonological similarity and verse context on rhyme perception. *Psychology of Aesthetics, Creativity, and the Arts*, Advance Online Publication.

Knoop, C. A., Wagner, V., Jacobsen, T., & Menninghaus, W. (2016). Mapping the aesthetic space of literature "from below." *Poetics, 56*, 35–49.

Korotkov, E. V., Korotkova, M. A., Frenkel, F. E., & Kudryashov, N. A. (2003). The informational concept of searching for periodicity in symbol sequences. *Molecular Biology, 37*(3), 372–386.

Kraxenberger, M., & Menninghaus, W. (2016a). Emotional effects of poetic phonology, word positioning and dominant stress peaks in poetry reading. *Scientific Study of Literature, 6*(2), 298–313.

Kraxenberger, M., & Menninghaus, W. (2016b). Mimological reveries? Disconfirming the hypothesis of phono-emotional iconicity in poetry. *Frontiers in Psychology, 7*(1779).

Kraxenberger, M., & Menninghaus, W. (2017). Affinity for poetry and aesthetic appreciation of joyful and sad poems. *Frontiers in Psychology, 7,* 2051. doi:10.3389/fpsyg.2016.02051.

Kraxenberger, M., Menninghaus, W., Roth, A., & Scharinger, M. (2018). Prosody-based sound-emotion associations in poetry. *Frontiers in Psychology, 9,* 1284. doi:10.3389/fpsyg.2018.01284.

Küper, C. (1996). Linguistic givens and metrical codes: Five case studies of their linguistic and aesthetic relations. *Poetics Today, 17*(1), 89–126.

Lau, J. H., Cohn, T., Baldwin, T., Brooke, J., & Hammond, A. (2018). Deep-speare: A joint neural model of poetic language, meter and rhyme. In I. Gurevych & Y. Miyao (Eds.), *Proceedings of the 56th Annual Meeting of the Association for Computational Linguistics* (ACL), Melbourne, Australia (pp. 1948–1958). Retrieved from: https://www.aclweb.org/anthology/P18-1181

Lausberg, H. (1998). *Handbook of literary rhetoric: A foundation for literary study*. Leiden, Germany: Brill.

Lea, R. B., Rapp, D. N., Elfenbein, A., Mitchel, A. D., & Romine, R. S. (2008). Sweet silent thought—Alliteration and resonance in poetry comprehension. *Psychological Science, 19*(7), 709–716.

Lerdahl, F., & Jackendoff, R. (1977). Toward a formal theory of tonal music. *Journal of Music Theory, 21*(1), 111–171.

Lindstromberg, S., & Boers, F. (2008). The mnemonic effect of noticing alliteration in lexical chunks. *Applied Linguistics, 29*(2), 200–222.

Littlemore, J., Sobrino, P. P., Houghton, D., Shi, J., & Winter, B. (2018). What makes a good metaphor? A cross-cultural study of computer-generated metaphor appreciation. *Metaphor and Symbol, 33*(2), 101–122.

Lowth, R. (1787). *Lectures on the sacred poetry of the Hebrews*. London: J. Johnson.

Lüdtke, J., Meyer-Sickendieck, B., & Jacobs, A. M. (2014). Immersing in the stillness of an early morning: Testing the mood empathy hypothesis of poetry reception. *Psychology of Aesthetics, Creativity, and the Arts, 8*(3), 363–377.

Margulis, E. H. (2014). *On repeat: How music plays the mind*. Oxford, England: Oxford University Press.

Martindale, C. (1973). Approximation to natural language, grammaticalness, and poeticality. *Poetics, 3*(1), 21–25.

McGlone, M. S., & Tofighbakhsh, J. (2000). Birds of a feather flock conjointly (?): Rhyme as reason in aphorisms. *Psychological Science, 11*(5), 424–428.

McGregor, S., Purver, M., & Wiggins, G. (2016). Process based evaluation of computer generated poetry. In M. Purver, P. Gervás, & S. Griffiths (Eds.), *Proceedings of the INLG 2016 Workshop on Computational Creativity in Natural Language Generation*, Edinburgh, Scotland (pp. 51–60). Retrieved from: http://www.aclweb.org/anthology/W16-55

Menninghaus, W., Bohrn, I. C., Altmann, U., Lubrich, O., & Jacobs, A. M. (2014). Sounds funny? Humor effects of phonological and prosodic figures of speech. *Psychology of Aesthetics, Creativity, and the Arts, 8*(1), 71–76.

Menninghaus, W., Bohrn, I. C., Knoop, C. A., Kotz, S. A., Schlotz, W., & Jacobs, A. M. (2015). Rhetorical features facilitate prosodic processing while handicapping ease of semantic comprehension. *Cognition, 143*, 48–60.

Menninghaus, W., Wagner, V., Knoop, C. A., & Scharinger, M. (2018). Poetic speech melody: A crucial link between music and language. *PLoS ONE, 13*(11), e0205980.

Menninghaus, W., Wagner, V., Wassiliwizky, E., Jacobsen, T., & Knoop, C. A. (2017). The emotional and aesthetic powers of parallelistic diction. *Poetics, 63*, 47–59.

Meyer, L. B. (1961). *Emotion and meaning in music*. Chicago, IL: University of Chicago Press.

Meyer-Sickendiek, B. (2011). *Lyrisches Gespür: Vom geheimen Sensorium moderner Poesie*. Paderborn, Germany: Fink.

Mukařovský, J. (1964). Standard language and poetic language. In P. L. Garvin (Ed.), *A Prague School reader on esthetics, literary structure, and style* (pp. 17–30). Washington, DC: Georgetown University Press.

Nenadić, F., Vejnović, D., & Marković, S. (2019). Subjective experience of poetry: Latent structure and differences between experts and non-experts. *Poetics, 73*, 100–113.

Obermeier, C., Kotz, S. A., Jessen, S., Raettig, T., von Koppenfels, M., & Menninghaus, W. (2016). Aesthetic appreciation of poetry correlates with ease of processing in event-related potentials. *Cognitive Affective & Behavioral Neuroscience, 16*(2), 362–373.

Obermeier, C., Menninghaus, W., von Koppenfels, M., Raettig, T., Schmidt-Kassow, M., Otterbein, S., & Kotz, S. A. (2013). Aesthetic and emotional effects of meter and rhyme in poetry. *Frontiers in Psychology, 4,* 10. doi:10.3389/fpsyg.2013.00010

Pagán Cánovas, C., Valenzuela, J., & Santiago, J. (2015). Like the machete the snake: Integration of topic and vehicle in poetry comprehension reveals meaning construction processes. *Psychology of Aesthetics, Creativity, and the Arts, 9*(4), 385–393.

Palmer, S. E., & Hemenway, K. (1978). Orientation and symmetry: Effects of multiple, rotational, and near symmetries. *Journal of Experimental Psychology: Human Perception and Performance, 4*(4), 691–702.

Panksepp, J. (1995). The emotional sources of "chills" induced by music. *Music Perception: An Interdisciplinary Journal, 13*(2), 171.

Pathak, R. S. (1982). The Indian theory of Vakrokti in relation to the stylistic concept of deviance. *Annals of the Bhandarkar Oriental Research Institute, 63*(1/4), 195–211.

Pelowski, M., Markey, P. S., Lauring, J. O., & Leder, H. (2016). Visualizing the impact of art: An update and comparison of current psychological models of art experience. *Frontiers in Human Neuroscience, 10,* 160.

Peskin, J. (1998). Constructing meaning when reading poetry: An expert-novice study. *Cognition and Instruction, 16*(3), 235–263.

Peskin, J. (2007). The genre of poetry: High school students' expectations and interpretive operations. *English in Education, 41*(3), 20–36.

Quintilian, M. F. (1920). Institutio Oratoria, trans. H. E. Butler, *The Institutio Oratoria of Quintilian.* Cambridge, MA: Harvard University Press.

Reber, R., Schwarz, N., & Winkielman, P. (2004). Processing fluency and aesthetic pleasure: Is beauty in the perceiver's processing experience? *Personality and Social Psychology Review, 8*(4), 364–382.

Rice, C. (1997). Ranking components: The grammar of poetry. In G. Booij, & J. van de Weijer (Eds.), *Phonology in progress—Progress in phonology* (pp. 321–332). The Hague, the Netherlands: Holland Academic Graphics.

Rubin, D. C., Ciobanu, V., & Langston, W. (1997). Children's memory for counting-out rhymes: A cross-language comparison. *Psychonomic Bulletin & Review, 4*(3), 421–424.

Rubin, D. C., & Wallace, W. T. (1989). Rhyme and reason: Analyses of dual retrieval cues. *Journal of Experimental Psychology-Learning Memory and Cognition, 15*(4), 698–709.

Salimpoor, V. N., Benovoy, M., Larcher, K., Dagher, A., & Zatorre, R. J. (2011). Anatomically distinct dopamine release during anticipation and experience of peak emotion to music. *Nature Neuroscience, 14,* 257.

Sanni, A. (1993). A fourth century contribution to literary theory: Ibn Fāris's treatise on poetic licenses. *Journal of Arabic Literature, 24*(1), 11–20.

Sapir, E. (1929). A study in phonetic symbolism. *Journal of Experimental Psychology* (12), 225–239.

Saussure, F. d. (1916/1960). *Course in general linguistics.* London: Owen.

Scheepers, C., Mohr, S., Fischer, M. H., & Roberts, A. M. (2013). Listening to limericks: A pupillometry investigation of perceivers' expectancy. *PLoS ONE, 8*(9), e74986.

Schlaffer, H. (2012). *Geistersprache: Zweck und Mittel der Lyrik.* Stuttgart, Germany: Reclam.

Schmidtke, D., Conrad, M., & Jacobs, A. M. (2014). Phonological iconicity. *Frontiers in Psychology, 5,* 80. doi:10.3389/fpsyg.2014.00080.

Schramm, W. L. (1935). The melodies of verse. *Science, 82*(2116), 61–62.

Severi, C. (2002). Memory, reflexivity and belief. Reflections on the ritual use of language. *Social Anthropology*, 10(1), 23–40.

Smith, B. H. (1968). *Poetic closure: A study of how poems end*. Chicago, IL: University of Chicago Press.

Song, H., & Schwarz, N. (2009). If it's difficult to pronounce, it must be risky: Fluency, familiarity, and risk perception. *Psychological Science*, 20(2), 135–138.

Steiger, E. (1946). *Grundbegriffe der Poetik*. Zürich, Switzerland: Atlantis.

Thierry, G., Martin, C. D., Gonzalez-Diaz, V., Rezaie, R., Roberts, N., & Davis, P. M. (2008). Event-related potential characterisation of the Shakespearean functional shift in narrative sentence structure. *NeuroImage*, 40(2), 923–931.

Tillmann, B., & Dowling, W. J. (2007). Memory decreases for prose, but not for poetry. *Memory and Cognition*, 35(4), 628–639.

Tsur, R., Glicksohn, J., & Goodblatt, C. (1991). Gestalt qualities in poetry and the reader's absorption style. *Journal of Pragmatics*, 16(5), 487–500.

Turner, F., & Pöppel, E. (1988). Metered poetry, the brain, and time. In I. Rentschler, B. Herzberger, & D. Epstein (Eds.), *Beauty and the brain* (pp. 71–90). Basel, Switzerland: Birkhäuser Basel.

Ullrich, S., Aryani, A., Kraxenberger, M., Jacobs, A. M., & Conrad, M. (2017). On the relation between the general affective meaning and the basic sublexical, lexical, and inter-lexical features of poetic texts: A case study using 57 poems of H. M. Enzensberger. *Frontiers in Psychology*, 7: 2073. doi:10.3389/fpsyg.2016.02073

Utsumi, A. (2006). A cognitive approach to poetic effects of rhetorical figures: Toward a unified theory of cognitive rhetoric. Paper presented at the *19th Congress of the International Association of Empirical Aesthetics (IAEA2006)*, Avignon, France. Retrieved from: http://www.utm.se.uec.ac.jp/~utsumi/paper/iaea2006-utsumi.pdf

Van Peer, W. (1990). The measurement of metre: Its cognitive and affective functions. *Poetics*, 19(3), 259–275.

Vaughan-Evans, A., Trefor, R., Jones, L., Lynch, P., Jones, M. W., & Thierry, G. (2016). Implicit detection of poetic harmony by the naïve brain. *Frontiers in Psychology*, 7: 1859. doi:10.3389/fpsyg.2016.01859

Wallot, S., & Menninghaus, W. (2018). Ambiguity effects of rhyme and meter. *Journal of Experimental Psychology: Learning, Memory, and Cognition*, 44(12), 1947–1954.

Wassiliwizky, E., Koelsch, S., Wagner, V., Jacobsen, T., & Menninghaus, W. (2017). The emotional power of poetry: Neural circuitry, psychophysiology and compositional principles. *Social Cognitive and Affective Neuroscience*, 12(8), 1229–1240.

Whissell, C. (2003). Readers' opinions of romantic poetry are consistent with emotional measures based on the *Dictionary of Affect in Language*. *Perceptual and Motor Skills*, 96(3), 990–992.

Xue, S., Lüdtke, J., Sylvester, T., & Jacobs, A. M. (2019). Reading Shakespeare sonnets: Combining quantitative narrative analysis and predictive modeling—an eye tracking study. *Journal of Eye Movement Research*, 12, 5. doi:10.16910/jemr.12.5.2

Ye, Y. (1996). *Chinese poetic closure*. New York: Peter Lang.

Youmans, G. (1983). Generative tests for generative meter. *Language*, 59(1), 67–92.

Zeman, A., Milton, F., Smith, A., & Rylance, R. (2013). By heart: An fMRI study of brain activation by poetry and prose. *Journal of Consciousness Studies*, 20(9–10), 132–158.

Žirmunskij, V. M. (1966). *Introduction to metrics: The theory of verse*. Berlin, Boston, MA: De Gruyter Mouton.

....

CHAPTER 32

AESTHETIC RESPONSES TO THE CHARACTERS, PLOTS, WORLDS, AND STYLE OF STORIES

....

MARTA M. MASLEJ, JOSHUA A. QUINLAN, AND RAYMOND A. MAR

As humans, we spend an inordinate amount of time engaging with narratives. A large chunk of our leisure time is spent watching television, reading novels, going to movies, seeing plays, reading comic books or graphic novels, listening to podcasts, or playing videogames (Statistics Canada, 2011). What many of these activities tend to share is a narrative element: they are all different ways of telling stories. A story can be defined as the representation of causally and temporally organized events that take place within a context or world, centered around a relatable goal-based agent. These events typically begin with an inciting incident, which leads to rising action in terms of a succession of progress and setbacks, culminating in a resolution of the central conflict, followed by a brief denouement (Rumelhart, 1975; Stein & Glenn, 1975). Every human culture produces stories and their universal appeal would seem to reflect an intrinsic human interest in social relations: we are social animals and stories inevitably portray the complexities and difficulties of social interactions (Boyd, 2009; Hogan, 2003; Oatley, 1999a). In addition, stories are frequently objects of aesthetic appreciation. There is a beauty to be found in these varied representations of human psychology and human experiences. Moreover, because stories contain multiple facets, each aspect of a story can be an object that elicits an aesthetic response. Considering our definition of a story, it would seem that our appreciation of stories might well be organized around the various components of a story: its characters, the plot events portrayed, the world in which the story takes place, and finally the style in which all of these different aspects are represented. In this chapter, we provide a very brief introduction into the empirical investigation of our aesthetic responses to each of these facets of a narrative, before closing with a discussion of the challenges and goals for this field moving forward.

CHARACTER

Arguably, the most important feature of a fictional narrative is its characters (Hogan, 2003; Miall, 1988). Our interest in a story depends quite a lot on whether it depicts people we care about (Jose & Brewer, 1984), and this is perhaps why so much of a novel or film is dedicated to introducing and developing its protagonists. Through stories, we get to know fictional characters extremely well, with unheralded access to their experiences, relationships, goals, and dreams. In fact, we may well know familiar characters better than we know our close friends and relations. When we get to know characters in this way, we become more invested in what happens to them. For example, *Titanic* (1997) is one of the highest grossing films of all time, accumulating over 135 million views in North America alone. And this is despite the fact that the film takes 3 h to tell a story about a sinking ship, the outcome of which almost all viewers already know. So, the interest in this film does not derive from a curiosity regarding the outcome, or how the film ends. Of course, *Titanic* is not just a story about a ship. Half of the movie is spent acquainting viewers with its two protagonists, Jack and Rose, and revealing their forbidden love affair. Rather than watching what happens to the ship, viewers stay tuned to observe the development of Jack and Rose's relationship and its tragic end. It is the characters in narratives like *Titanic* that attract and maintain our attention, and our reactions are primarily in response to what these characters do and what happens to them (Hoffner & Cantor, 1991; Katz & Liebes, 1990).

We might care so much about characters in part because we tend to perceive and respond to them as if they were real people. For example, we might feel as though these fictional characters have an actual physical presence, and change our own behavior as we would in front of other people. In a set of clever experiments exploring this idea, Gardner and Knowles (2008) found that when participants were exposed to images of their favorite television characters, they exhibited a psychological phenomenon known as social facilitation. Social facilitation occurs when our performance improves on a well-learned task (and worsens on a novel task) in the presence of other people. And so, when their participants were in the presence of their favorite television character, they responded in the same way they would if they were among real people. Importantly, participants did not exhibit this effect when exposed to images of nonfavorite characters, which they reported as being less "real" than favorite characters (Gardner & Knowles, 2008). Since television characters are represented by actors, it is easy to see why we might think of them being real. However, it appears that we also attribute book characters with life-like physical characteristics. In one qualitative study, readers stated that they could easily imagine how characters sound, and most reported hearing characters' voices in their inner speech as they read (Alderson Day, Bernini, & Fernyhough, 2017).

Perceptions of characters' voices were rich and dynamic, varying in volume, pitch, and tone, and fluctuating in response to characters' emotional states. Some characters even spoke in accents the readers themselves could not speak, suggesting that our tendency to think of characters as real people with bodies and voices is not limited to characters we see on-screen. Writers have also described a similar sense of characters being "real" and independent, even when they have created that character. Marjorie Taylor, Hodges, and Kohanyi (2003) interviewed creative writers and found that many reported that the characters they created while writing at some point became very real to them, even independent of them and resistant to their wishes.

Wishful identification

If we tend to experience our favorite characters as being real, it is perhaps not surprising that we react to them as we would to people we meet in our day-to-day lives. We assess their personalities, evaluate our similarities to them, and can even find them attractive (Cohen, 2001; Hoffner & Buchanan, 2005). In other words, unsurprisingly, we can find beauty in the portrayal of characters, much like we can find beauty in our intimate partners and close relations. Sometimes, we might imitate or model them, which is referred to as wishful identification. Given the influence of role models in early development, the research on wishful identification has focused a fair bit on children and youth. Adolescents have been known to change their appearance, attitudes, and behaviors to become more like the celebrities they admire, such as dressing a certain way or dyeing their hair (Boone & Lomore, 2001; Murray, 1999). This drive to appear like a desired other, even one we do not know personally, strikes us as an aesthetic response. One topic of concern is how wishful identification might promote unhealthy habits or behaviors. For example, links have emerged between wishful identification with thin characters and disordered eating in college women (Harrison, 1997) as well as between wishful identification with aggressive characters and aggressive behavior in children (Huesmann, Lagerspetz, & Eron, 1984). However, characters can model positive behaviors as well. Dore and colleagues (2017) reported that children who listened to a script told from the perspective of a professor spent longer playing with an analytical toy (i.e., a Rubik's cube) than children who listened to the perspective of a cheerleader (Dore, Smith & Lillard, 2017).

To better understand the factors affecting wishful identification, researchers have conducted interviews and administered questionnaires asking both adults and children about their favorite television characters (Hoffner, 1996; Hoffner & Buchanan, 2005). Perhaps not surprisingly, similarities between characters and viewers emerge as important factors when it comes to wishful identification. Children tend to be influenced by demographic similarities (e.g., gender and race; Austin, Roberts & Nass, 1990; Greenberg, 1972; Hoffner, 1996; McDonald & Kim, 2001; Miller & Reeves, 1976), and participants of all ages tend to wishfully identify with characters that resemble them in personality and attitude. This effect appears across all kinds of different narratives, extending even to video games as well (Eyal & Rubin, 2003; Hoffner & Buchanan, 2005; McDonald & Kim, 2001). Wishful identification also occurs in response to characters that exhibit valued traits. Children tend to emulate male characters that are intelligent, powerful, and strong (Hoffner, 1996; Miller & Reeves, 1976; Reeves & Greenberg, 1977; cf. Reeves & Lometti, 1979), whereas attractiveness is the only predictor of wishful identification with female characters (Hoffner, 1996). In late adulthood however, both men and women are more likely to identify with characters that are intelligent, with women additionally identifying with characters that they find attractive (Hoffner & Buchanan, 2005). In sum, people appear drawn to characters who are already somewhat like them, but also characters that represent who they would like to be.

Parasocial interactions and relationships

Because story characters can feel so real to us, we not only want to be like them but we also feel as though we can interact with them. We might even talk to them, for example, cheering them on as they score a winning goal or urging them not to go to the basement to investigate a scary noise, if even only in our heads (Bezdek, Foy, & Gerrig, 2013). We might also feel betrayed or offended when we find out that they have done something distasteful, or chastise them when we disapprove of their actions. Our tendency to interact with characters as if they were real is known as parasocial interaction (Tian & Hoffner, 2010). Over time, we might begin to consider characters as friends or people we know, discussing them with others, seeking out information about them, and even missing them when they are not there (Dibble & Rosaen, 2011; Rubin, Perse, & Powell, 1985). This enduring bond with a character that continues after we watch a movie or read a book is called a parasocial relationship (Klimmt, Hartmann, & Schramm, 2006). Perhaps because parasocial interactions and relationships were first observed with media personalities, such as gameshow hosts and news broadcasters (Horton & Wohl, 1956), they have been primarily studied with on-screen characters, reality stars, and celebrities. Recently, however, parasocial relationships have been investigated with book characters as well (Liebers & Schramm, 2017).

Initially, researchers assumed that people formed parasocial relationships because they were lonely or had difficulties forming relationships in the real world (Rubin & McHugh, 1987), but this assumption has not been fully supported empirically. Although it is true that, on average, people who are shy and lonely are more likely to form parasocial relationships (Schiappa, Allen, & Gregg, 2007), watching a favorite television program is one of the most common things people do when feeling lonely (Gardner & Knowles, 2008; Rubin, Perse, & Powell, 1985). So people who are lonely might form parasocial relationships simply because they watch more television, and not because they lack closeness with others. Furthermore, there is also research that seems to directly contradict this idea that parasocial relationships emerge from loneliness. For example, parasocial relationships are linked with characteristics that predict sociability, such as empathy, extraversion, and positive self-esteem (Tsao, 1996; Turner, 1993).

Although loneliness or poor social skills are not prerequisites for parasocial relationships, these relationships can buffer against social rejection. In a set of studies, researchers manipulated opportunities for participants to write about their favorite television program after being reminded of a social rejection (i.e., a time when they fought with a close other) (Derrick, Gabriel, & Hugenberg, 2009). As compared with participants who wrote about their favorite program, participants who did not have this opportunity reported decreased self-esteem and increased feelings of rejection. These participants also filled out a word stem completion task with more words related to social exclusion, suggesting that, unlike those who wrote about their favorite television program, their thoughts were still occupied with the social rejection. Although these researchers did not ask participants to focus their writing on characters, they noted that many of the participants did so anyway, so it is possible that parasocial relationships are motivated by a need to feel included or to belong.

Rather than thinking of parasocial relationships as substitutes for those we might have in the real world, researchers consider them to be extensions of real-world relationships, perhaps because the two have many parallels (Cohen, 2004). As with real-world relationships, we are more likely to bond with characters we consider attractive or similar to us (for a meta-analysis, see Schiappa et al., 2007). Both real-world and parasocial relationships also seem to develop by way of uncertainty reduction. Berger and Calabrese (1975) argue that over the course of interacting with others, our ability to predict their behavior increases, which strengthens our relationships with them. Perse and Rubin (1989) proposed that the same process might occur when we watch or read about characters. In their study, the longer participants knew a person in their social group, the better able they were to predict his or her behavior, which was related to the strength of their relationship. Importantly, the same was true of the connection between participants and their favorite soap opera characters. Furthermore, parasocial relationships are affected by attachment styles. Attachment styles are stable tendencies in the way in which we respond to close others, which develop out of early experiences with our primary caregivers (Bowlby, 1969). These attachment styles can also predict the strength of parasocial relationships (Cole & Leets, 1999), as well as participants' reactions to the dissolution of these relationships (e.g., the death of a character or the cancellation of a television program) (Cohen, 2004). In general, these parasocial "break-ups" can have real-world negative outcomes, such as stress, depression, and loneliness (Cohen, 2004). Our relationships with fictional characters therefore seem to have a meaningful impact, and this suggests they are not just lesser versions of the relationships we have with other people in our lives. Much as we find deep appreciation in our close relationships with real-world peers, we find a similar sort of appreciation for the fictional characters we visit in narratives.

IDENTIFICATION

Another widely studied response to fictional characters is identification. Although identification is defined differently by literary critics or cultural theorists, researchers in psychology typically view it as a temporary process of imagining ourselves as being a character. During this time, we share this character's knowledge about the narrated events, adopt the character's goals, understand events according to these goals (i.e., cognitive empathy), and share the character's emotions (i.e., emotional empathy) (Altenbernd & Lewis, 1969; Cohen, 2001, 2004; Jose & Brewer, 1984; Oatley 1994; Tal-Or & Cohen, 2010). A distinguishing feature of identification is that we become so absorbed into the text that our own identity and self-awareness is diminished: we experience a temporary loss of ourselves (Cohen, 2001).

As with wishful identification and parasocial relationships, our tendency to identify with characters is influenced by different factors. We are more likely to identify with characters we perceive as being real, ones that we like or find physically attractive (Cohen, 1999; Hoffner, 1996; Hoffner & Cantor, 1991), and ones that carry out good deeds (Jose & Brewer, 1984; Tal-Or & Cohen, 2010). We might identify with characters that have these positive characteristics because we tend to think of ourselves as resembling good characters more than bad ones (Jose & Brewer, 1984), and similarity is a consistent predictor of identification (Maccoby & Wilson, 1957; Tian & Hoffner, 2010). This includes similarity in demographic characteristics like gender (Jose & Brewer, 1984), as well as in attitude and emotional reactions to events (Maccoby & Wilson, 1957; Turner, 1993).

In contrast to parasocial relationships, much of the work on identification has focused on characters from books (for a review, see Cohen, 2001), and some researchers argue that it is difficult to identify with on-screen characters. When watching television or a film, we sit opposite the screen and see the characters, which could make it difficult to imagine being them (Houston, 1984). Texts, on the other hand, can use first-person narratives to facilitate identification, giving readers complete access to the perceptions, feelings, and thoughts of a character (Oatley, 1999b; Sanders & Redeker, 1996). However, this claim regarding the benefits of first-person narration in writing has received mixed empirical support. Some researchers have successfully manipulated identification using first-person narration in stories (e.g., De Graaf, Hoeken, Sanders & Beentjes, 2012; Kerr, 2005), but other research suggests that the consequences of using first- or third-person narration are the same (Hartung, Hagoort, & Willems, 2017). In film and television, directors may be able to use camera angles to create perspective and foster identification (Cohen, 2001). An interesting direction for future research involves examining how manipulating camera angles affects identification. For instance, programs or films shot from the point of view of a protagonist in such a way that the audience sees what the character sees might be very successful at promoting identification. On the other hand, having a character address the viewer might elicit parasocial interaction, such as when a character "breaks the third wall" to confide in the audience.

Identification influences our appreciation or enjoyment of a story. Given that it requires us to adopt a character's goals, identification can make us more emotionally invested in how the narrative will be resolved. Since a story's success depends, in part, on the degree to which it rouses our emotions (Brewer & Lichtenstein, 1982), it is not surprising then that identification with a character can make the experience of reading or viewing more enjoyable. Many studies suggest that the more we identify with a film's characters, the more likely we are to enjoy the film (Busselle & Bilandzic, 2009; de Wied, Zillmann & Ordman, 1994; Igartua & Paez, 1997; cf. Tal-Or & Cohen, 2010) and this effect does not appear to depend on genre. Igartua (2010) interviewed participants leaving a movie theater after they watched different films and found that that this was true for comedies, thrillers, and dramas.

One important feature of identification is that it provides opportunities for vicarious experience. We enjoy identifying with different characters because it allows us to take on different and exciting identities, such as that of a millionaire, a high-powered attorney, or an international spy. In this way, identification can open us to new perspectives (Basil, 1996), and it can even lead to shifts in attitudes. In a set of experiments, participants who read stories from the perspective of one character (e.g., a disabled job applicant or a woman against euthanasia) identified more with that character, and they demonstrated opinions on relevant topics that were consistent with the experiences or opinions of those characters (De Graaf et al., 2012). Importantly, identification mediated the effects of the character's perspective on attitudes. In a different experiment, Igartua (2010) measured participants' beliefs about immigration either before or after watching a film about the lives of Mexican immigrants. Participants assessed after the film were more likely to express positive attitudes about immigration, agreeing that immigrants make valuable contributions to the economies of host countries, for example. Individuals that were more likely to identify with characters in the film also expressed more positive attitudes toward immigration (Igartua, 2010). These studies suggest that identification with book and on-screen characters may promote positive attitudes about people who often face discrimination or marginalization. Identifying with a character requires us to imagine what it would be like to have different feelings, thoughts, and goals, and in doing so we might engage in deeper reflection about the experiences of other people who are different from us (Igartua, 2010). Identifying with characters facing hardships that we would not otherwise experience (e.g., being disabled or immigrating to a new country) can help us form a richer representation of their experiences, which perhaps can lead to us being more positive, open, and sympathetic to others. In this way, identification might be useful for reducing prejudice and improving social relations (Paluck & Green, 2009).

PLOT

Another important aspect of a fictional narrative that can evoke an aesthetic response is the plot, or the way that story events are structured over narrative time. Aristotle posited that a successful story is composed of two parts: complication (i.e., the onset of conflict, an obstacle or problem) and unraveling (i.e., its eventual resolution) (Butcher, 1907). Another widely held conceptualization of plot is Freytag's pyramid, which divides Aristotle's story structure into five parts. First, the exposition introduces the elements of the plot, such as the setting and its characters. Next, a series of events (i.e., the rising action) leads to a climax, or the point of greatest interest in the story. At this point, the climax unravels and the protagonist's fate is revealed in the falling action, which concludes with a denouement (Freytag, 1863).

Plot structures

The theories of Aristotle and Freytag identify one type of plot structure, but theorists and researchers have since argued that there are a variety of plot structures and that these types can be revealed through empirical investigation. In a lecture entitled *The Shapes of Stories*, the writer Kurt Vonnegut (1995) describes several differentiable plot structures. Some resemble Aristotle's complication and unraveling, such as a plot he refers to as *Man in a Hole*. Other plots describe a nearly opposite unfolding of events. In *Boy Gets Girl* for example, the protagonist leads an average or dull existence, acquires something wonderful (e.g., falls in love), but loses it, and in some variations of this plot, he eventually gains it back. Other writers and researchers have also vouched for the existence of many plot structures, identifying from three to over 30 different types (Booker, 2004; Harris, 1959; Polti, 1916; Tobias, 1993).

Like many others, Vonnegut suggested that a story's ups and downs, or its positive and negative events, can be arranged in different ways, but he pioneered the notion that these arrangements can be "fed into computers," or graphed to reveal stories' shapes. Archer and Jockers (2016) implemented this suggestion to analyze the plots of over 40,000 English novels. Using a statistical program (Jockers, 2015), they graphed each novel's sentiment (the positive or negative tone of the content) over the course of the narrative, using a mathematical formula to account for different text lengths. Based on the graphed data, they created a matrix of the distance between every pair of novels, and from it, generated a tree diagram. The two primary branches of the diagram resembled Vonnegut's *Man in a Hole* and *Boy Gets Girl* plot structures, which further branched into what Archer and Jockers interpreted as six or seven fundamental plot shapes (Archer & Jockers, 2016). Although the computer-derived sentiment plots are rough proxies of plot development, they seem to closely resemble the shapes produced by human coders (Gao, Jockers, Laudun, & Tangherlini, 2016). Researchers are increasingly using computational methods to better understand plot and other literary topics (e.g., Mohammad, 2011). For instance, rather than categorizing novels into groups, Piper (2015) analyzed structural similarities within novels to identify the presence of a single plot type, and Schmidt (2015) showed that this method can be applied to the study of plots for different television genres.

Although the temporal arrangement of positive and negative events differs across stories, every story seems to involve a negative event, obstacle, or conflict. Conflict (either in love or political power) is a universal property of narratives found across different cultures and geographies (Hogan, 1997), and stories without some aspect of tension or complication are considered boring and unsuccessful (Fiedler, 1960). Our preference for conflict in fiction may be part of a well-evidenced negativity bias in our attentional and cognitive processes (Baumeister, Bratslavsky, Finkenauer, & Vohs, 2001), which is thought to have evolved so we can quickly react to aversive or threatening circumstances in the environment (Ohman, Flykt, & Esteves, 2001). We might learn from stories that depict difficult or challenging circumstances because they provide us with information on how best to cope with them (Nabi, Finnerty, Domschke, & Hull, 2006; Zillmann, 2000). This is perhaps why we consider stories that depict evolutionarily-relevant topics like social relationships to be of a higher quality than those that do not (e.g., espionage) (Carney, Wlodarski, & Dunbar, 2014). The degree to which negative events in fiction elicit our enjoyment or interest is a direction for future research. Incorporating computational methods, it may even be possible to empirically examine our preferences for certain plot structures, and how these preferences might interact with our personal histories and individual differences.

Emotional reactions to plot

Researchers have long argued that emotion is central to the experience of fiction (Frijda, 1989; Mar, Oatley, Djikic, & Mullin, 2011; Tan, 2000) and that good stories must succeed in both arousing and resolving our emotions (Brewer & Lichtenstein, 1982). However, these emotions may be subtler than the types of emotions we feel in our daily lives (Miall & Kuiken, 2002; Oliver, 1993). When consuming fiction, we can experience evaluative feelings (e.g., deriving enjoyment or satisfaction from reading or watching), or narrative feelings, which are evoked by aspects of the plot, such as feeling sad when reading about a funeral (Miall & Kuiken, 2002). Passages toward the beginning of a fictional work (i.e., in the exposition), or those that are descriptively dense, tend to evoke relived emotions, which are emotions that we feel when we remember a personal experience (Cupchik, Oatley, & Vorderer, 1998). Descriptive passages might prompt relived emotions because of their role in creating rich mental representations of situations or scenes (Mar et al., 2011). In contrast, fresh emotions, which occur when readers are surprised or taken aback by a new realization they have made about the story, tend to occur toward the end of a story (Cupchik et al., 1998; Miall & Kuiken, 2002).

Some research on evaluative and narrative feelings has been dedicated to understanding the appeal of negative content in stories. It seems intuitive that we might seek out stories to make us feel happy (Bryant & Zillmann, 1984; Zillmann & Cantor, 1977), yet the research suggests otherwise. For example, Igartua (2010) and Oliver (1993) found that when participants elected to view a dramatic or sad film (i.e., a "tearjerker"), the more negatively they felt while watching the film, the more they reported enjoying it (Oliver, 1993). Similarly, a video game that includes a dangerous or threatening backstory, as opposed to a pleasant one, induces feelings of suspense, and importantly, enjoyment (Klimmt, Rizzo, Vorderer, Koch, & Fischer, 2009). There are many reasons why we might enjoy stories that arouse negative emotions. When we feel unhappy, observing a protagonist who is in a bad situation may make us feel better about our own circumstances (Mares & Cantor, 1992). Experiencing negative emotions in response to plot events (i.e., negative narrative feelings) may also be cathartic, offering an opportunity to express negative feelings we have about our own lives in a safe way (Cornelius, 1997). These negative narrative feelings may therefore elicit positive evaluative feelings, such as enjoyment or gratification (Oliver, 1993), with our ability to control the narrative feelings possibly playing a role. By experiencing and resolving a manageable version of a negative emotion, readers might gain control over the emotion and feel a sense of mastery (Nell, 1988). For these reasons, we might seek out stories that make us feel sad or scared, especially if we know that we can put down a book or stop a movie, if necessary.

Part of the reason we enjoy negative narrative feelings might be due to our anticipation of a happy or uplifting ending and the positive feelings associated with it, like relief for a character we like. Indeed, in a story, resolving emotions may be as important to us as their arousal (Brewer & Lichtenstein, 1982). However, as Oliver (1993) points out, there are many popular stories that do not end happily. In fact, Archer and Jockers' (2016) analysis yields various plot structures that end on a negative note, suggesting that there is more to our enjoyment of these negative emotions than the promise of a positive outcome. This enjoyment might instead depend on how we feel about its characters. Specifically, we might enjoy stories in which characters we like succeed and ones we dislike fail (Chatman, 1978; Friedman, 1975). Jose and Brewer (1984) examined whether this principle holds among elementary school children in different grades. Children in the sixth grade enjoyed stories with happy endings but only when they featured characters they liked, but children in grade two enjoyed stories with happy endings, regardless of how they felt about the characters. Thus, we might develop a sophistication in our enjoyment of story outcomes over time, which eventually involves making moral judgments about what the characters deserve. Consistent with this finding, other research suggests that the ability to abstract morals or lessons from stories develops only in late childhood (Walker & Lombrozo, 2017).

Cognitive reactions to plot

Our reactions to narratives are not just based on our feelings. Stories can inspire us to think and reflect, changing our understanding of the story events and perhaps even of ourselves or human nature (Koopman & Hakemulder, 2015). These types of reactions are referred to as self-modifying feelings (Miall & Kuiken, 2002). Researchers usually study these reactions by asking participants to read stories and mark in the margins whenever they have an emotion, thought, or memory. After reading, participants return to each mark and report on what they experienced (Kuiken & Miall, 2001; Larsen & Seilman,

1988). This research suggests that although stories evoke different experiences across readers, the emotions, thoughts, and memories do tend to occur in similar places. That is, the sequences of plot events seem to guide readers' reactions (Miall & Kuiken, 2002).

Self-modifying feelings might contribute to the appeal of stories that make us feel sad or experience other negative emotions. Oliver and Raney (2011) argue that we have an intrinsic need to gain insight into human nature by deriving meaning, truth, or purpose from the world around us, which includes narratives. Gaining this insight can be unpleasant when exploring topics such as failure, frailty, or mortality. Since characters that grapple with these types of circumstances tend to pose questions about human nature and gain these insights, sad films may be more likely to fulfill our need for self-modifying feelings. In other words, we might seek out stories that make us feel sad because we wish to better understand ourselves and human nature, at the expense of our enjoyment.

Not all people achieve insights or self-modifying feelings when reading narratives however (Miall & Kuiken, 2002), which suggests that these reactions may depend on individual differences, such as in personal experience. By making connections between our experiences and the text, we can come to a deeper or renewed understanding of ourselves (Miall, 2004; Miall & Kuiken, 2002) but this understanding may require some personal experience with the story content. In two studies, readers who experienced a significant loss were more likely to report self-modifying feelings when they read a poem or story about loss than readers who had not experienced a loss (Kuiken, Miall & Sikora, 2004; Sikora, Kuiken & Miall, 2010). Interestingly, readers were less likely to report these feelings when the loss was recent, as compared with a loss that occurred over 2 years ago, suggesting that the recency of personal experience might also be important. When individuals are recently bereaved, they may react negatively to memories of the deceased, preventing self-modifying feelings during reading (Sikora et al., 2010). In another study, participants were randomly assigned to read a text about either depression or grief one week, then read the unread text the following week (Koopman, 2015a). These texts were literary narratives, life narratives, or expository texts. The literary narratives evoked more and longer-lasting thoughts and reflections compared with the other text types. Furthermore, people who experienced a past bout of depression reported more reflection when reading the texts about depression, and the same was true for texts about grief. Thus, it seems that insightful and reflective thoughts might be elicited by personally relevant stories. Perhaps stories about conflict and negative experiences resound with most of us because they document a universal feature of the human experience. We can probably easily think back to a negative situation or problem we once encountered, and stories might help us to work through or come to terms with past difficult experiences of our own.

Physiological responses to plot

Another empirical approach to studying our cognitive and emotional responses to stories involves looking at the underlying physiology behind these responses. One way that researchers have examined the ups and downs of a story's plot is by measuring peripheral physiology, such as heart rate and respiration, with physiological arousal tending to mirror the shape of a plot. The association between plot and arousal is not clear-cut, but there seems to be a correspondence between evaluative or narrative feelings and peripheral physiology. Nell (1988) found increases in heart rate, respiration, and facial muscle activity when participants read passages of stories they enjoyed, but this effect was rather weak. In a different study, the emotional intensity of a story influenced heart rate variability, an index of emotional arousal (Wallentin et al., 2011). In that study, the participants rated the emotional valence and arousal in a version of *The Ugly Duckling*. Based on these ratings, the researchers identified the most emotionally intense parts of the story (e.g., the duckling turning into a swan). Interestingly, these emotionally intense passages were associated with increased heart rate variability in a different group of participants who listened to the story.

Measures of peripheral physiology have also been useful in examining the effects of plot twists, or surprising events in stories. When we read a story or watch a television program, we create and update mental representations, also known as situation models, for the plot (Johnson-Laird, 1983). These situation models help us understand the text and infer what will happen next (Glenberg & Mathew, 1992). However, when new information does not match our situation models, in the form of a plot twist for example, we are forced to orient to this information and update our models. These types of narrative surprises are associated with slower reading times, perhaps allowing for deeper processing of the incompatible or surprising information (Rapp & Gerrig, 2006). Interestingly, plot twists are also associated with a specific pattern of autonomic activity called the orienting response. The orienting response comprises reactions we might have when we are startled or surprised, including an increase in heart rate and skin conductance (i.e., having sweatier palms) (Sukalla, Shoenberger, & Bolls, 2016). Thus, specific events in a story's plot (i.e., that are emotionally intense or surprising) can reliably elicit physiological responses. Future studies might examine whether other emotional reactions (such as fear or sadness) in response to reading a book or watching a film can be detected in our peripheral physiology, or perhaps if individual differences in our physiological reactions predict whether we will enjoy a certain genre, like horror or drama.

WORLD

A major aspect of any narrative is the world in which it takes place. Narrative worlds can be dark and gritty noir cityscapes, colorful and fantastic alien domains, or familiar and banal suburbs; the tone of these worlds will invariably color the audience's experiences and appreciation of character and plot. Visiting these narrative worlds can offer us new and exciting adventures (without the associated risks) or familiar and soothing experiences to escape the stressors of the real world. The role of the world in narrative also seems to be expanding; our media is increasingly built around extensive shared narrative worlds that invite us to revisit familiar realms but with novel characters and plots (e.g., the Marvel Cinematic Universe, which currently comprises more than 15 films and a dozen television series). When we engage with these narrative worlds, we are not just passively reading about (or watching or playing in) an alternative reality. Instead, we often feel absorbed into the world, focusing our attention on the narrative and losing awareness of the (nonnarrative) world around us. This feeling of absorption is likely to impact enjoyment, emotional responses, and any other aesthetic evaluation of a narrative, and is thought to be "the key determinant of narrative impact" (Green & Brock, 2000; p. 703). However, different narrative worlds are likely to elicit different responses from different people, and thus the role that the world plays in affecting aesthetic responses is subject to individual differences.

Transportation

To describe the experience of being strongly immersed in a narrative, Gerrig (1993) uses a metaphor of transportation: we travel some distance to a narrative world, are partially absent from the world of origin, and return from the journey changed (p. 10). In this way, Gerrig suggests that we actually feel present in the narrative world and can be meaningfully affected by what transpires therein. Green and Brock (2000) expanded on this work by describing transportation as a "distinct mental process, an integrative melding of attention, imagery, and feelings" (p. 701). That is, a transported individual's attention becomes focused on the narrative such that they lose some awareness of the world around them, becoming less likely to notice someone walking into the room or to recall a fact that contradicts the narrative. A transported individual also has vivid mental imagery of the narrative's world, characters, and plot. Lastly, transported individuals respond emotionally to narratives as if they were experiencing them directly, despite knowing it is not the case.

This theorizing has since received considerable empirical support. Green and Brock (2000) developed a scale to measure state transportation, which featured items such as "I could picture myself in the scene of the events described in the narrative" and "The narrative affected me emotionally." This measure was found to include three separate factors, which the authors labeled as cognitive, affective, and imagery. In support of Gerrig's (1993) suggestion that the traveler can be changed by the narrative world, Green and Brock (2000) also suggest that transportation is likely to facilitate persuasion, leading transported individuals to form and endorse beliefs that are consistent with the narrative. For example, in one study, Green and Brock (2000) had participants read a story about a psychiatric patient murdering a child in a mall. Participants who were more transported endorsed story-consistent beliefs, such as the need to restrict the freedoms of the mentally ill, more strongly than did participants who were less transported. This effect of transportation on narrative persuasion has since been frequently replicated (for a review, see Bilandzic & Busselle, 2013).

One of the ways that transportation promotes persuasion is by making the virtual seem real. Because a transported individual feels as if she is experiencing the plot and narrative world directly, the narrative feels like a personal experience and is thus influential in affecting beliefs and attitudes (Green & Brock, 2000). Transportation correlates positively with the perceived realism of a story, and experimentally encouraging transportation in the reading instructions increases this perceived realism (Green, 2004). Thus, in addition to describing a feeling of engagement with a narrative, transportation encourages us to process that narrative as if it represented real personal experiences. In this way, transportation is a major determinant of the impact of a narrative. For fantastical and banal worlds alike, if a narrative does not *feel* real, then we are unlikely to enjoy engaging with it or find much appreciation or beauty in it.

This relationship between enjoyment and transportation has also been a focus of research, with Green and colleagues (2004) identifying transportation and enjoyment as closely related concepts. They propose that transportation can be used to explain how and why we enjoy engaging with narratives: transportation allows us to become fully concentrated on visiting a new world, achieving a flow-like state while leaving behind our worries and self-consciousness. These researchers also observe that lack of enjoyment for media is often defined as an absence of transportation: "I just couldn't get into it" (p. 314). Transportation and enjoyment have also been found to be highly correlated, providing empirical support for this idea (Green, Brock, & Kaufman, 2004). This account also helps to explain the apparent paradox of enjoying negative affective responses to narratives, such as fear or sadness: transportation gives us an ultimately safe opportunity to vicariously experience thrilling, dangerous, or tragic events and the cathartic responses that they elicit. In this way, we can use narratives to explore nuanced emotional experiences and to contemplate grand questions about existence, mortality, and the meaning of life (Oliver & Raney, 2011).

Ultimately, transportation describes one of the dominant aspects of the experience of engaging with a narrative. Regardless of what type of narrative world we are encountering or the modality through which we are visiting it, we are unlikely to really enjoy a narrative if we do not feel "sucked into it." Transportation describes this feeling of escape, which is one of the most attractive features of narratives. It allows us to lose our awareness of ourselves and the nonnarrative world, explore new worlds as if they were real, and experience vivid emotions in a safe environment.

Revisiting narrative worlds

Although visiting narrative worlds can certainly offer us novel experiences and perspectives, we also interact with narrative worlds in other ways. Rather than constantly seeking out new worlds to visit, we often revisit the same worlds, either through other media set in the same universe (e.g., watching *Fantastic Beasts and Where to Find Them* because you enjoyed the *Harry Potter* films), through re-exposing oneself to the same media (e.g., rereading the *Harry Potter* books), or through engaging with the same narrative in a different format (e.g., watching the *Harry Potter* films because you enjoyed the *Harry Potter* books). Revisiting the same story has an apparent disadvantage of reducing suspense, since one already knows how the plot will develop. However, if novel experiences were the only draw of visiting narrative worlds, then we would seldom re-read books, rewatch movies or television shows, or ever engage with narratives whose endings we already know (e.g., *Titanic*).[1] Instead, there appear to be other things that are attractive about revisiting narrative worlds. One possibility is that revisiting a familiar narrative world helps us to feel less lonely and gives us a sense of belonging. Derrick and colleagues (2009) found that people report turning to their favorite television shows when they feel lonely, with these familiar and beloved shows helping to ease this loneliness. They also found that thinking about one's favorite show helped to protect oneself against the threats to self-esteem and feelings of rejection. This suggests that revisiting narrative worlds can be beneficial in a way that visiting new narrative worlds might not be.

That said, it is not completely accurate to claim that one does not have novel experiences when revisiting a narrative world. Although the content of the narrative has not changed, our perspective on that world may have. When revisiting a narrative world we typically have a richer holistic understanding of the world from the outset, allowing us to process information about it more fluently and thereby free up resources to detect information that might be more subtle (Dixon, Bortolussi, Twilley, & Leung, 1993). For example, we may better understand the quaint serenity of the Shire in *The Lord of the Rings* after seeing the turmoil that engulfs the rest of Middle-earth. This experience is commonly reported as "picking up on new things" on a second viewing or feeling like revisiting a world has helped one "better flesh it out." In this way, revisiting the same narrative may offer novel experiences in the form of a richer understanding of a narrative world. This phenomenon may also help to explain the surge in popularity in shared narrative universes (e.g., the Marvel Cinematic Universe). Revisiting familiar narrative worlds that have new plots may offer the best of both worlds, so to speak: we can further deepen our understanding of a narrative world in addition to experiencing new plots and character interactions.

Genres

One of the primary ways narrative worlds are defined is through genre. To say that a novel is a fantasy book, for example, tells us much about the content and tone that is likely to appear. Empirical work has shown that people are generally familiar with most common genres (e.g., sci-fi) and what type of content to expect from each (e.g., futuristic technologies in sci-fi) (Dixon & Bortolussi, 2009; Piters & Stokmans, 2000). Genre preference is likely to be the primary determinant of whether we enjoy visiting a given narrative world. However, regardless of preference, different genres are likely to elicit different aesthetic responses due to their differences in content and tone. For example, Gavaler and Johnson (2017) manipulated a short story to make it seem like a sci-fi narrative by changing its setting to a space station. Despite no major changes to the text's content, tone, or plot, participants randomly assigned to read the sci-fi version rated the story as lower in literary quality. Additionally, participants who thought they were reading a sci-fi short story expended more effort in making inferences about the world and less effort in making inferences about the characters' mental and emotional states. This was likely due to the readers' assumptions that a sci-fi story would focus more on a new and unfamiliar world compared with focusing on interpersonal relationships. This study illustrates that even small cues about the genre of a narrative can affect how we engage with that narrative. Assumptions about genre may determine which aspects of a narrative we attend to, how likely we are to identify with characters in the story, or what emotional responses we have to a narrative.

Genre is also an important determinant of other aesthetic responses to narrative. For example, although lifetime exposure to literary fiction is positively associated with interpersonal sensitivity (Mar, Oatley, Hirsh, dela Paz, & Peterson, 2006; Mar, Oatley, & Peterson, 2009), the strength of this relationship differs between genres (Fong, Mullin, & Mar, 2015). Specifically, exposure to romance or suspense/thriller narratives is more strongly associated with interpersonal sensitivity than exposure to domestic fiction and sci-fi/fantasy. Fong and colleagues (2015) suggest that the relationship between literary fiction and interpersonal sensitivity is stronger for genres that focus on portraying social experiences and interpersonal relationships. Building upon Gavaler and Johnson's (2017) finding that cues about genre may determine how we attend to different aspects of a narrative, it may be that these genres differ less in how much they portray interpersonal relationships and more in how they direct the attention of the audience to such aspects of the story. The audience of a fantasy narrative, for example, may focus more on developing an understanding of the narrative world than on the interpersonal relationships portrayed in the narrative, even if the relationship-related content in the narrative is plentiful. Genre may operate in a similar way with regard to affective responses. Different genres may be more or less likely to elicit certain emotions, regardless of content. For example, a stranger knocking at the door in the middle of the night may elicit fear in a horror or thriller narrative, but mere curiosity in a fantasy narrative. In this way, previous knowledge of a genre may affect how we engage with a given narrative and what aesthetic responses that narrative is likely to elicit.

Style

The appreciation of narrative extends beyond the characters, the events they experience, and the world they inhabit, to the formal characteristics of how all of these things are portrayed. We refer to the various ways in which narrative elements are portrayed as *style*, recognizing that the same event, involving the same characters in the same world, can be represented in a broad variety of ways. These choices on the part of a creator regarding how to tell a story, as opposed to what story to tell, are perhaps the most obvious target of aesthetic evaluation and most likely elicitor of aesthetic responses. Not surprisingly then, most of the empirical work to date on narrative has typically focused on style. This is no more pronounced than in the case of literary narratives, where the unique use of language in telling a story is known as foregrounding.

Foregrounding and literary narratives

Recognizing that the contents of a story can be communicated in unique ways, and that these unique stylistic choices can have various effects on a reader, has a long history in literary theory and elsewhere (Miall & Kuiken, 1994a). Employing language in novel ways has come to be known as foregrounding, with Koopman (2016) providing a concise review of its origins, identifying Mukařovský (1976) as the source of the term and Shklovsky (1965) as the progenitor of its most commonly associated outcome: defamiliarization. Defamiliarization refers to the sense that familiar concepts and experiences can become strange and unfamiliar once they are foregrounded by use of a unique portrayal. Essentially, something as banal as a conversation between two people can be highlighted and experienced as somewhat strange and new once it is described as a "meeting of the minds," for example. Creative language choices serve to draw a reader's attention (Sanford & Emmott, 2012), inviting pause and reflection on both the meaning being communicated and its relevance to the reader (Miall & Kuiken, 1994a). Moreover, content can be foregrounded by creating deviations from the norm along several dimensions, including phonetic, grammatical, and semantic conventions (Miall & Kuiken, 1994a; Mukařovský, 1976). Leech and Short (2007) provide an extensive discussion of the different stylistic choices available to writers, all of which may be employed to foreground story content.

Although it has long been recognized that literature embraces novel language use and that these unique constructions are salient or foregrounded, empirical research into foregrounding and its effects is comparatively nascent. Willie van Peer's (1986) book, *Stylistics and Psychology: Investigations of foregrounding*, was one of the first empirical investigations into literary style. The empirical studies by van Peer (1986) confirmed that foregrounded portions of a text do indeed succeed in drawing a reader's attention. This finding has proven to be robust, with other studies also reporting that readers take longer to read portions of a text that include more foregrounding (Miall & Kuiken, 1994b; Sopčák, 2007). Importantly, there may be some differences in how reading time relates to foregrounding depending on the type of foregrounding being employed (Sopčák, 2007). Deviations in writing with respect to grammar slow reading times as one might predict, but deviations along phonemic dimensions might actually result in faster reading times. This result that makes sense in hindsight when one considers the fluency afforded by techniques like alliteration (Sopčák, 2007).

Choosing a unique style to represent narrative content not only draws a reader's attention, it also serves to elicit aesthetic responses to the text (Miall & Kuiken, 1994a). In empirical studies of foregrounding, readers routinely identify passages that contain more novel uses of language as more striking or notable in nature (Miall & Kuiken, 1994b). Moreover, experimentally manipulating the level of foregrounding in a text appears to produce the same effect, with greater aesthetic responses observed in response to text that has been manipulated to include more foregrounding (Hakemulder, 2004; Van Peer, Hakemulder, & Zyngier, 2007). These aesthetic responses often emerge upon second encounter with a text, based on a rereading procedure in which texts or passages are presented more than once (Dixon et al., 1993). In light of the fact that foregrounding involves the introduction of novelty to a representation, it is intuitive that responses to this novelty might only emerge over time or after re-encountering the portrayal: our minds often need time or repeated exposure to adjust to novelty. Very much along these lines of thinking, Fialho (2007) has described a process of refamiliarization, in which content that has been defamiliarized through foregrounding is reintegrated into our schemas for familiar representations. One open area of inquiry is whether foregrounding might draw us out of a story, reducing our transportation and engagement, or whether foregrounding helps to facilitate our engagement and absorption with stories (Bálint, Hakemulder, Kuijpers, Doicaru, & Tan, 2017).

Not all of the research in foregrounding has revealed consistent findings. An interesting question regarding foregrounding is whether these effects are tied to expertise in any way: are individuals who read more often, or perhaps trained to read more critically, more or less susceptible to foregrounding effects? Would literary scholars be more likely to experience an aesthetic response to a passage rife with unique metaphors and alliteration? Empirical investigations of this possibility have produced rather mixed results. Some studies find that foregrounding effects emerge regardless of past training or experience (Miall & Kuiken, 1994b; van Peer, 1986), other studies have found that those with more experience or expertise are more sensitive to foregrounding (Andringa, 1996; Hakemulder, 2004), whereas still other studies find the exact opposite: that experienced readers are less sensitive to foregrounding (Koopman, 2015b). In order to reconcile these divergent findings, it will likely be necessary to more closely distinguish between the identification or perception of foregrounding and the various different kinds of responses to foregrounded texts that readers might have, in addition to the different dimensions along which foregrounding varies.

One of the most promising directions for work in this area is the incorporation of a wider variety of methodological approaches and tools. For example, neuroimaging research on foregrounding has begun to emerge, confirming past demonstrations that unique stylistic choices attract attention (Bohrn, Altmann, Lubrich, Menninghaus, & Jacobs, 2012). This work has also provided new insight into foregrounding, demonstrating that aesthetic responses to foregrounded text appear to occur spontaneously, even when readers are not explicitly asked about them (Bohrn, Altmann, Lubrich, Menninghaus, & Jacobs, 2013). Importantly, this sort of insight into the spontaneity or automatic nature of aesthetic responses can be derived from psychophysiological measures that do not rely on explicit report. In addition to neuroimaging, studies employing eye-tracking have shown similar promise, once again confirming past reports that foregrounding results in slower reading times, but also providing some unique insight tied to this methodology, for example informing us that readers are more likely to return their attention to foregrounded segments of a text (van den Hoven, Hartung, Burke, & Willems, 2017). Moreover, this same study has revealed that there are substantial differences between individuals in how they respond to foregrounded text, which highlights a very promising avenue for future investigation. Future investigations into how individual differences relate to foregrounding could perhaps build on past work showing that the moderating role of experience and expertise on foregrounding appears to be rather complex, as well as intriguing work on possible cultural differences when it comes to the influence of foregrounding (Zyngier, van Peer, & Hakemulder, 2007).

Foregrounding in other media

Although the bulk of empirical research on foregrounding has been devoted to understanding reader responses to literary texts, there is no a priori reason to believe that stylistic choices are not also important for other narrative media. That said, applying empirical approaches to the study of audio-visual or multimodal narratives brings additional challenges relative to studying text alone thanks to the additional dimensions that must be considered. Despite these challenges, a number of researchers are exploring the nature of film, including the role of stylistic choices in foregrounding narrative elements. Cutting (2016), for example, has analyzed large sets of films in order to determine the basic dimensions in which they differ and how these dimensions co-vary. This provides a promising launching point for studying deviations from various norms in film, which would constitute cinematic foregrounding. There are also direct investigations of foregrounding in film, such as the study by Hakemulder (2004). He found that foregrounded scenes from films are rated as more enjoyable by viewers, as well as more significant or noteworthy, based on a rewatching paradigm. These findings parallel the most robust results from foregrounding studies of literature, raising the intriguing possibility that foregrounding may produce similar effects across different narrative media. In all likelihood, however, there are likely to be foregrounding effects that are both universal across media and also some that are unique to specific narrative forms.

FUTURE GOALS AND CHALLENGES

In this chapter we have reviewed how people respond to various aspects of a story, and how empirical techniques have been employed to study these responses. Although brief, we have hopefully communicated the wide-ranging nature of these types of investigation. Despite the wealth of research in this area, there are many exciting directions for future work along with some puzzling aspects of our current understanding that require further investigation.

In taking a very broad perspective of aesthetic responses to stories, we have somewhat glossed over a major distinction that has been put forth in the literature between emotional responses tied to aspects of the story content (e.g., identification with characters, emotional responses to plot events, transportation into story worlds), known as narrative emotions, and the appreciation of beauty for the form or foregrounding in a story (e.g., responses to stylistic choices), known as aesthetic feelings (Miall & Kuiken, 2002; see also Tan, 2000). We chose to discuss all of these responses because not all aesthetic responses are affective in nature (they can also be cognitive; van Peer et al., 2007), because many of the responses to story content struck us as possible forms of positive evaluation or aesthetic appreciation, and because narrative and aesthetic emotions have been found to be rather closely related, empirically (Koopman, 2011; Koopman, Hilscher, & Cupchik, 2012). Whether and how these two types of responses to narrative diverge, as well as how they relate to similar outcomes, is a challenge for future research.

Despite the diverse set of empirical studies reviewed, there are some coherent themes that have emerged with respect to future directions. This field is blessed in its diversity of empirical approaches that have been adopted, with qualitative interview studies contributing just as much as neuroimaging investigations. It would be beneficial to see things continue in this direction, with more researchers adopting a wider variety of tools and perspectives to study this fascinating topic. Naturalistic observation in the field, for example, would likely provide some fascinating nuance to our understanding, as would more qualitative interview studies, case studies, and investigations using eye-tracking and psychophysiological measurement. Similarly, researchers have begun to branch out from literary texts to explore other narrative media, and we would love to see more investigations of aesthetic responses to video games, graphic novels, podcasts, film, and theater, among others. Although narrative has often been treated in a somewhat monolithic fashion in most studies to date, greater nuance with respect to types of stories (e.g., plots) and different genres of stories would certainly be welcome. Lastly, there is a growing acknowledgment that individual differences in aesthetic response, as well as cultural differences, are all going to be important when it comes to understanding when and how people appreciate stories. Overall, the future for empirical investigations of aesthetic responses to narrative appears very bright, and we remain excited and optimistic about what is to come.

Note

1. Although it is popularly-believed that the suspense created by an unknown ending is crucial to the enjoyment of a narrative, there is empirical evidence that suggests that this is not always the case. Leavitt and Christenfeld (2011) randomly assigned participants to read a story whose ending was either unspoiled or spoiled in the story's introduction. Across three different stories, participants enjoyed the spoiled version of the story significantly more. However, a later study showed that this effect is moderated by individual differences, such that those high in need for affect prefer unspoiled stories (Rosenbaum & Johnson, 2016).

References

Alderson-Day, B., Bernini, M., & Fernyhough, C. (2017). Uncharted features and dynamics of reading: Voices, characters, and crossing of experiences. *Consciousness and Cognition, 49*, 98–109.

Altenbernd, L., & Lewis, L. L. (1969). *Introduction to literature: Stories*. London: Macmillan.

Andringa, E. (1996). Effects of 'narrative distance' on readers' emotional involvement and response. *Poetics, 23*, 431–452.

Archer, J., & Jockers, M. L. (2016). *The bestseller code: Anatomy of the blockbuster novel*. New York: St. Martin's Press.

Austin, E. W., Roberts, D. F., & Nass, C. I. (1990). Influence of family communication on children's television-interpretation processes. *Communication Research, 17*, 545–564.

Bálint, K., Hakemulder, F., Kuijpers, M., Doicaru, M., & Tan, E. S. (2017). Reconceptualizing foregrounding. *Scientific Study of Literature, 6*(2), 176–207.

Basil, M. D. (1996). Identification as a mediator of celebrity effects. *Journal of Broadcasting & Electronic Media, 40*, 478–495.

Baumeister, R. F., Bratslavsky, E., Finkenauer, C., & Vohs, K. D. (2001). Bad is stronger than good. *Review of General Psychology, 5*(4), 323–370.

Berger, C. R., & Calabrese, R. J. (1975). Some explorations in initial interaction and beyond: Toward a developmental theory of interpersonal communication. *Human Communication Research, 1*(2), 99–112.

Bezdek, M. A., Foy, J. E., & Gerrig, R. J. (2013). Run for it!: Viewers' participatory responses to film narratives. *Psychology of Aesthetics, Creativity, and the Arts, 7*(4), 409–416.

Bilandzic, H., & Busselle, R. (2013). Narrative persuasion. In J. P. Dillard, & L. Shen (Eds.), *The SAGE handbook of persuasion: Developments in theory and* practice, 2nd edition (pp. 200–219). Thousand Oaks, Ca: Sage.

Bohrn, I. C., Altmann, U., Lubrich, O., Menninghaus, W., & Jacobs, A. M. (2012). Old proverbs in new skins—an fMRI study on defamiliarization. *Frontiers in Psychology, 3*, 204.

Bohrn, I. C., Altmann, U., Lubrich, O., Menninghaus, W., & Jacobs, A. M. (2013). When we like what we know—A parametric fMRI analysis of beauty and familiarity. *Brain and Language, 124*, 1–8.

Booker, C. (2004). *The seven basic plots: Why we tell stories*. New York: A&C Black.

Boon, S. D., & Lomore, C. D. (2001). Admirer-celebrity relationships among young adults: Explaining perceptions of celebrity influence on identity. *Human Communication Research, 27*(3), 432–465.

Bowlby, J. (1969). *Attachment and loss: Vol. 1. Attachment*. New York: Basic Books.

Boyd, B. (2009). *On the origin of stories: Evolution, cognition, and fiction*. Cambridge, MA: Harvard University Press.

Brewer, W. F., & Lichtenstein, E. H. (1982). Stories are to entertain: A structural-affect theory of stories. *Journal of Pragmatics, 6*(5–6), 473–486.

Bryant, J., & Zillmann, D. (1984). Using television to alleviate boredom and stress: Selective exposure as a function of induced excitational states. *Journal of Broadcasting & Electronic Media, 28*(1), 1–20.

Busselle, R., & Bilandzic, H. (2009). Measuring narrative engagement. *Media Psychology 12*(4), 321–347.

Butcher, S. H. (1907). *The Poetics of Aristotle*. New York: Macmillan.

Carney, J., Wlodarski, R., & Dunbar, R. (2014). Inference or enaction? The impact of genre on the narrative processing of other minds. *PLoS ONE, 9*(12), e114172.

Chatman, S. (1978). *Story and discourse narrative structure: Fiction and film.* New York: Cornell University Press.

Cohen, J. (1999). Favorite characters of teenage viewers of Israeli serials. *Journal of Broadcasting and Electronic Media, 43,* 327–345.

Cohen, J. (2001). Defining identification: A theoretical look at the identification of audiences with media characters. *Mass Communication & Society, 4*(3), 245–264.

Cohen, J. (2004). Parasocial break-up from favorite television characters: The role of attachment styles and relationship intensity. *Journal of Social and Personal Relationships, 21*(2), 187–202.

Cole, T., & Leets, L. (1999). Attachment styles and intimate television viewing: Insecurely forming relationships in a parasocial way. *Journal of Social and Personal Relationships, 16,* 495–511.

Cornelius, R. R. (1997). Toward a new understanding of weeping and catharsis? In A. J. J. M. Vingerhoets, F. J. Van Bussell, & A. J. W. Boelhouwer (eds.), *The (non) expression of emotions in health and disease* (pp. 303–321). Tilburg, the Netherlands: University Press.

Cupchik, G. C., Oatley, K., & Vorderer, P. (1998). Emotional effects of reading excerpts from short stories by James Joyce. *Poetics, 25,* 363–377.

Cutting, J. E. (2016). Narrative theory and the dynamics of popular movies. *Psychonomic Bulletin & Review, 23*(6), 1713–1743.

De Graaf, A., Hoeken, H., Sanders, J., & Beentjes, J. W. (2012). Identification as a mechanism of narrative persuasion. *Communication Research, 39*(6), 802–823.

de Wied, M., Zillmann, D., & Ordman, V. (1994). The role of empathic distress in the enjoyment of cinematic tragedy. *Poetics. Journal of Empirical Research on Literature, Media and the Arts, 23,* 91–106.

Derrick, J. L., Gabriel, S., & Hugenberg, K. (2009). Social surrogacy: How favored television programs provide the experience of belonging. *Journal of Experimental Social Psychology, 45*(2), 352–362.

Dibble, J. L., & Rosaen, S. F. (2011). Parasocial interaction as more than friendship: Evidence for parasocial interactions with disliked media figures. *Journal of Media Psychology: Theories, Methods, and Applications, 23*(3), 122–132.

Dixon, P., & Bortolussi, M. (2009). Readers' knowledge of popular genre. *Discourse Processes, 46*(6), 541–571.

Dixon, P., Bortolussi, M., Twilley, L. C., & Leung, A. (1993). Literary processing and interpretation: Toward empirical foundations. *Poetics, 22,* 5–33.

Dore, R. A., Smith, E. D., & Lillard, A. S. (2017). Children adopt the traits of characters in a narrative. *Child Development Research,* Article ID 6838079.

Eyal, K., & Rubin, A. M. (2003). Viewer aggression and homophily, identification, and parasocial relationships with television characters. *Journal of Broadcasting & Electronic Media, 47*(1), 77–98.

Fialho, O. (2007). Foregrounding and refamiliarization: Understanding readers' response to literary texts. *Language and Literature, 16*(2), 105–123.

Fiedler, L. A. (1960). *Love and death in the American novel.* Champaign, IL: Dalkey Archive Press.

Fong, K., Mullin, J. B., & Mar, R. A. (2015). How exposure to literary genres shapes attitudes toward gender roles and sexual behaviour. *Psychology of Aesthetics, Creativity, and the Arts, 9,* 274–285.

Freytag, G. (1863). *Freytag's technique of the drama*. New York: Benjamin Blom.

Friedman, N. (1975). *Form and meaning in fiction*. Athens, Georgia: University of Georgia Press.

Frijda, N. H. (1989). Aesthetic emotions and reality. *American Psychologist, 44*(12), 1546–1547.

Gao, J., Jockers, M. L., Laudun, J., & Tangherlini, T. (2016, November). A multiscale theory for the dynamical evolution of sentiment in novels. In *Behavioral, Economic and Socio-cultural Computing (BESC), 2016 International Conference* (pp. 1–4). Piscataway, NJ: IEEE.

Gardner, W. L., & Knowles, M. L. (2008). Love makes you real: Favorite television characters are perceived as "real" in a social facilitation paradigm. *Social Cognition, 26*(2), 156–168.

Gavaler, C., & Johnson, D. (2017). The genre effect: A science fiction (vs. realism) manipulation decreases inference effort, reading comprehension, and perceptions of literary merit. *Scientific Study of Literature, 7*(1), 79–108.

Gerrig, R. J. (1993). *Experiencing narrative worlds: On the psychological activities of reading*. New Haven, CT: Yale University Press.

Glenberg, A. M., & Mathew, S. (1992). When minimalism is not enough: Mental models in reading comprehension. *Psycoloquy, 92*, 3(64).

Green, M. C. (2004). Transportation into narrative worlds: The role of prior knowledge and perceived realism. *Discourse Processes, 38*(2), 247–266.

Green, M. C., & Brock, T. C. (2000). The role of transportation in the persuasiveness of public narratives. *Journal of Personality and Social Psychology, 79*(5), 701–721.

Green, M. C., Brock, T. C., & Kaufman, G. F. (2004). Understanding media enjoyment: The role of transportation into narrative worlds. *Communication Theory, 14*(4), 311–327.

Greenberg, B. S. (1972). Children's reaction to TV Blacks. *Journalism Quarterly, 49*, 5–14.

Hakemulder, J. (2004). Foregrounding and its effects on readers' perception. *Discourse Processes, 38*, 193–218.

Harris, W. F. (1959). *The basic patterns of plot*. Norman, OK: University of Oklahoma Press.

Harrison, K. (1997). Does interpersonal attraction to thin media personalities promote eating disorders? *Journal of Broadcasting & Electronic Media, 41*(4), 478–500.

Hartung, F., Hagoort, P., & Willems, R. M. (2017). Readers select a comprehension mode independent of pronoun: Evidence from fMRI during narrative comprehension. *Brain and Language, 170*, 29–38.

Hoffner, C. (1996). Children's wishful identification and parasocial interaction with favorite television characters. *Journal of Broadcasting & Electronic Media, 40*(3), 389–402.

Hoffner, C., & Buchanan, M. (2005). Young adults' wishful identification with television characters: The role of perceived similarity and character attributes. *Media Psychology, 7*(4), 325–351.

Hoffner, C., & Cantor, J. (1991). Perceiving and responding to mass media characters. In J. Bryant & D. Zillmann (Eds.), *Responding to the screen: Reception and reaction processes* (pp. 63–101). Mahwah, NJ: Lawrence Erlbaum Associates Publishers.

Hogan, P. C. (1997). Literary universals. *Poetics Today, 18*(2), 223–249.

Hogan, P. C. (2003). *The mind and its stories: Narrative universals and human emotion*. Cambridge, England: Cambridge University Press.

Horton, D., & Wohl, R. (1956). Mass communication and para-social interaction: Observations on intimacy at a distance. *Psychiatry, 19*(3), 215–229.

Houston, B. (1984). Viewing television: The metapsychology of endless consumption. *Quarterly Review of Film & Video, 9*(3), 183–195.

Huesmann, L. R., Lagerspetz, K., & Eron, L. D. (1984). Intervening variables in the TV violence–aggression relation: Evidence from two countries. *Developmental Psychology, 20*(5), 746–775.

Igartua, J. J. (2010). Identification with characters and narrative persuasion through fictional feature films. *Communications*, 35, 347–373.

Igartua, J., & Paez, D. (1997). Art and remembering traumatic collective events: The case of the Spanish Civil War. In W. Pennebaker, D. Paez, & B. Rimé (Eds.), *Collective memory of political events: Social psychological perspectives* (pp. 79–101). Mahwah, NJ: Lawrence Erlbaum Associates, Inc.

Jockers, M. (2015). *Syuzhet: Extract Sentiment and Plot Arcs from Text*. Retrieved from https://github.com/mjockers/syuzhet.

Johnson-Laird, P. N. (1983). *Mental models: Towards a cognitive science of language, inference, and consciousness*. Cambridge, MA: Harvard University Press.

Jose, P. E., & Brewer, W. F. (1984). Development of story liking: Character identification, suspense, and outcome resolution. *Developmental Psychology*, 20(5), 911–924.

Katz, E., & Liebes, T. (1990). Interacting with "Dallas": Cross cultural readings of American TV. *Canadian Journal of Communication*, 15(1), 45–66.

Kerr, A. (2005). *Towards a therapeutics of reading literature: The influence of aesthetic distance and Attachment*, Unpublished doctoral dissertation, University of Toronto.

Klimmt, C., Hartmann, T., & Schramm, H. (2006). Parasocial interactions and relationships. In J. Bryant & P. Vorderer (Eds.), *Psychology of entertainment* (pp. 291–313). Mahwah, NJ: Lawrence Erlbaum Associates Publishers.

Klimmt, C., Rizzo, A., Vorderer, P., Koch, J., & Fischer, T. (2009). Experimental evidence for suspense as determinant of video game enjoyment. *CyberPsychology & Behavior*, 12(1), 29–31.

Koopman, E. M. (2011). Predictors of insight and catharsis among readers who use literature as a coping strategy. *Scientific Study of Literature*, 1, 241–259.

Koopman, E. M. (2015a). How texts about suffering trigger reflection: Genre, personal factors, and affective responses. *Psychology of Aesthetics, Creativity, and the Arts*, 9(4), 430–441.

Koopman, E. M. (2015b). Empathic reactions after reading. The role of genre, personal factors and affective responses. *Poetics*, 50, 62–79.

Koopman, E. M. (2016). Effects of "literariness" on emotions and on empathy and reflection after reading. *Psychology of Aesthetics, Creativity, and the Arts*, 10(1), 82–98.

Koopman, E. M., Hilscher, M., & Cupchik, G. C. (2012). Reader responses to literary depictions of rape. *Psychology of Aesthetics, Creativity, and the Arts*, 6, 66–73.

Koopman, E. M. E., & Hakemulder, F. (2015). Effects of literature on empathy and self-reflection: A theoretical-empirical framework. *Journal of Literary Theory*, 9(1), 79–111.

Kuiken, D., & Miall, D. S. (2001). Numerically aided phenomenology: Procedures for investigating categories of experience. *Forum Qualitative SozialForschung*, 2, Article 15, http://nbn-resolving.de/urn:nbn:de:0114-fqs0101153.

Kuiken, D., Miall, D. S., & Sikora, S. (2004). Forms of self-implication in literary reading. *Poetics Today*, 25(2), 171–203.

Larsen, S. F., & Seilman, U. (1988). Personal remindings while reading literature. *Text*, 8, 411–429.

Leavitt, J. D., & Christenfeld, N. J. S. (2011). Story spoilers don't spoil stories. *Psychological Science*, 22(9), 1152–1154.

Leech, G. N., & Short, M. (2007). *Style in fiction: A linguistic introduction to English fictional prose*, 2nd edition. London: Pearson Education.

Liebers, N., & Schramm, H. (2017). Friends in books: The influence of character attributes and the reading experience on parasocial relationships and romances. *Poetics*, 65, 12–23.

Maccoby, E. E., & Wilson, W. C. (1957). Identification and observational learning from films. *The Journal of Abnormal and Social Psychology*, 55(1), 76–87.

Mar, R., Oatley, K. & Peterson, J. (2009). Exploring the link between reading fiction and empathy: Ruling out individual differences and examining outcomes. *Communications*, 34(4), 407–428.

Mar, R. A., Oatley, K., Djikic, M., & Mullin, J. (2011). Emotion and narrative fiction: Interactive influences before, during, and after reading. *Cognition & Emotion*, 25(5), 818–833.

Mar, R. A., Oatley, K., Hirsh, J., dela Paz, J., & Peterson, J. B. (2006). Bookworms versus nerds: Exposure to fiction versus non-fiction, divergent associations with social ability, and the simulation of fictional social worlds. *Journal of Research in Personality*, 40, 694–712.

Mares, M. L., & Cantor, J. (1992). Elderly viewers' responses to televised portrayals of old age: Empathy and mood management versus social comparison. *Communication Research*, 19(4), 459–478.

McDonald, D. G., & Kim, H. (2001). When I die, I feel small: Electronic game characters and the social self. *Journal of Broadcasting & Electronic Media*, 45(2), 241–258.

Miall, D. S. (1988). Affect and narrative: A model of response to stories. *Poetics*, 17(3), 259–272.

Miall, D. S. (2004). Episode structures in literary narratives. *Journal of Literary Semantics*, 33(2), 111–129.

Miall, D. S., & Kuiken, D. (1994a). Beyond text theory: Understanding literary response. *Discourse Processes*, 17, 337–352.

Miall, D. S., & Kuiken, D. (1994b). Foregrounding, defamiliarization, and affect. Response to literary stories. *Poetics*, 22, 389–407.

Miall, D. S., & Kuiken, D. (2002). A feeling for fiction: Becoming what we behold. *Poetics*, 30(4), 221–241.

Miller, M. M., & Reeves, B. (1976). Dramatic TV content and children's sex-role stereotypes. *Journal of Broadcasting & Electronic Media*, 20(1), 35–50.

Mohammad, S. (2011, June). From once upon a time to happily ever after: Tracking emotions in novels and fairy tales. In *Proceedings of the 5th ACL-HLT Workshop on Language Technology for Cultural Heritage, Social Sciences, and Humanities* (pp. 105–114). Stroudsburg, PA: Association for Computational Linguistics.

Mukařovský, J. (1976). *On poetic language*. Lisse, the Netherlands: De Ridder Press.

Murray, S. (1999). Saving our so-called lives: Girl fandom, adolescent subjectivity, and My So-Called Life. In M. Kinder (Ed.), *Kids' media culture* (pp. 221–235). Durham, NC: Duke University Press.

Nabi, R. L., Finnerty, K., Domschke, T., & Hull, S. (2006). Does misery love company? Exploring the therapeutic effects of TV viewing on regretted experiences. *Journal of Communication*, 56(4), 689–706.

Nell, V. (1988). The psychology of reading for pleasure: Needs and gratifications. *Reading Research Quarterly*, 23(1), 6–50.

Oatley, K. (1994). A taxonomy of the emotions of literary response and a theory of identification in fictional narrative. *Poetics*, 23, 53–74.

Oatley, K. (1999a). Why fiction may be twice as true as fact: Fiction as cognitive and emotional simulation. *Review of General Psychology*, 3(2), 101–117.

Oatley, K. (1999b). Meeting of minds: Dialogue, sympathy, and identification in reading fiction. *Poetics*, 26, 439–454.

Öhman, A., Flykt, A., & Esteves, F. (2001). Emotion drives attention: Detecting the snake in the grass. *Journal of Experimental Psychology: General*, 130(3), 466–478.

Oliver, M. B. (1993). Exploring the paradox of the enjoyment of sad films. *Human Communication Research, 19*(3), 315–342.

Oliver, M. B., & Raney, A. A. (2011). Entertainment as pleasurable and meaningful: Identifying hedonic and eudaimonic motivations for entertainment consumption. *Journal of Communication, 61*(5), 984–1004.

Paluck, E. L., & Green, D. P. (2009). Prejudice reduction: What works? A critical look at evidence from the field and the laboratory. *Annual Review of Psychology, 60,* 339–367.

Perse, E. M., & Rubin, R. B. (1989). Attribution in social and parasocial relationships. *Communication Research, 16*(1), 59–77.

Piper, A. (2015). Novel devotions: Conversional reading, computational modeling, and the modern novel. *New Literary History, 46*(1), 63–98.

Piters, R. A. M. P., & Stokmans, M. J. W. (2000). Genre categorization and its effect on preference for fiction books. *Empirical Studies of the Arts, 18*(2), 159–166.

Polti, G. (1916). *The thirty-six dramatic situations.* Boston, MA: The Writer.

Rapp, D. N., & Gerrig, R. J. (2006). Predilections for narrative outcomes: The impact of story contexts and reader preferences. *Journal of Memory and Language, 54*(1), 54–67.

Reeves, B., & Greenberg, B. S. (1977). Children's perceptions of television characters. *Human Communication Research, 3*(2), 113–127.

Reeves, B., & Lometti, G. E. (1979). The dimensional structure of children's perceptions of television characters: A replication. *Human Communication Research, 5*(3), 247–256.

Rosenbaum, J. E., & Johnson, B. K. (2016). Who's afraid of spoilers? Need for cognition, need for affect, and narrative selection and enjoyment. *Psychology of Popular Media Culture, 5*(3), 273–289.

Rubin, A. M., Perse, E. M., & Powell, R. A. (1985). Loneliness, parasocial interaction, and local television news viewing. *Human Communication Research, 12*(2), 155–180.

Rubin, R. B., & McHugh, M. P. (1987). Development of parasocial interaction relationships. *Journal of Broadcasting & Electronic Media, 31*(3), 279–292.

Rumelhart, D. E. (1975). Notes on a schema for stories. In D. G. Bobrow & A. Collins (Eds.), *Representation and understanding: Studies in cognitive science* (pp. 2–34). New York: Academic Press.

Sanders, J., & Redeker, G. (1996). Perspective and the representation of speech and thought in narrative discourse. In G. Fauconnier & E. Sweetser (Eds.), *Spaces, worlds and grammar* (pp. 290–317). Chicago, IL: University of Chicago Press.

Sanford, A. J., & Emmott, C. (2012). Attention in text: foregrounding and rhetorical focusing. In A. J. Sanford & C. Emmott (Eds.), *Mind, brain and narrative* (pp. 72–102). Cambridge, England: Cambridge University Press.

Schiappa, E., Allen, M., & Gregg, P. B. (2007). Parasocial relationships and television: A meta-analysis of the effects. In R. W. Preiss, B. M. Gayle, N. Gayle, M. Allen, & J. Bryant (Eds.), *Mass media effects research: Advances through meta-analysis* (pp. 301–314). Mahwah, NJ: Lawrence Erlbaum Associates Publishers.

Schmidt, B. M. (2015, October). Plot arceology: A vector-space model of narrative structure. In *Big Data (Big Data), 2015 IEEE International Conference* (pp. 1667–1672). Piscataway, NJ: IEEE.

Shklovsky, V. (1965). Art as technique. In L. T. Lemon & M. J. Reis (Eds.), *Russian formalist criticism: Four essays* (pp. 3–24). Lincoln, NE: University of Nebraska Press.

Sikora, S., Kuiken, D., & Miall, D. S. (2010). An uncommon resonance: The influence of loss on expressive reading. *Empirical Studies of the Arts, 28*(2), 135–153.

Sopčák, P. (2007). Creation from nothing—A foregrounding study of James Joyce's drafts for Ulysses. *Language and Literature, 16*(2), 183–196.

Statistics Canada. (2011). General Social Survey–2010: Overview of the time use of Canadians. 89-647-X.

Stein, N. L., & Glenn, C. G. (1975). An analysis of story comprehension in elementary school children: A test of a schema. *New Directions in Discourse Processing, 2*, 53–120.

Sukalla, F., Shoenberger, H., & Bolls, P. D. (2016). Surprise! An investigation of orienting responses to test assumptions of narrative processing. *Communication Research, 43*(6), 844–862.

Tal-Or, N., & Cohen, J. (2010). Understanding audience involvement: Conceptualizing and manipulating identification and transportation. *Poetics, 38*(4), 402–418.

Tan, E. (2000). Emotion, art, and the humanities. In M. Lewis, & J. M. Haviland-Jones (Eds.), *Handbook of emotions* (pp. 116–136). New York: Guilford Press.

Tan, E. S. H. (1995). Film-induced affect as a witness emotion. *Poetics, 23*(1–2), 7–32.

Taylor, M., Hodges, S. D., & Kohanyi, A. (2003). The illusion of independent agency: Do adult fiction writers experience their characters? *Imagination, Cognition and Personality, 22*(4), 361–380.

Tian, Q., & Hoffner, C. A. (2010). Parasocial interaction with liked, neutral, and disliked characters on a popular TV series. *Mass Communication and Society, 13*(3), 250–269.

Tobias, R. B. (1993). *20 master plots*. Cincinnati, OH: Writer's Digest.

Tsao, J. (1996). Compensatory media use: An exploration of two paradigms. *Communication Studies, 47*, 89–109.

Turner, J. (1993). Interpersonal and psychological predictors of parasocial interaction with different television performers. *Communication Quarterly, 41*, 443–453.

van den Hoven, E., Hartung, F., Burke, M., & Willems, R. M. (2017). *Effects of foregrounding on reading behavior: Evidence from eye-tracking study*. Unpublished Master's thesis, Tilburg University.

van Peer, W. (1986). *Stylistics and psychology: Investigations of foregrounding*. London: Croom Helm.

van Peer, W., Hakemulder, J., & Zyngier, S. (2007). Lines on feeling: Foregrounding, aesthetics and meaning. *Language and Literature, 16*, 197–213.

Vonnegut, K. (1995). Shapes of stories. Retrieved from https://www.youtube.com/watch?v=oP3c1h8v2ZQ 20

Walker, C. M., & Lombrozo, T. (2017). Explaining the moral of the story. *Cognition, 167*, 266–281.

Wallentin, M., Nielsen, A. H., Vuust, P., Dohn, A., Roepstorff, A., & Lund, T. E. (2011). Amygdala and heart rate variability responses from listening to emotionally intense parts of a story. *Neuroimage, 58*(3), 963–973.

Zillmann, D., & Cantor, J. R. (1977). Affective responses to the emotions of a protagonist. *Journal of Experimental Social Psychology, 13*(2), 155–165.

Zillmann, D. (2000). Mood management in the context of selective exposure theory. *Annals of the International Communication Association, 23*(1), 103–123.

Zyngier, S., Van Peer, W., & Hakemulder, J. (2007). Complexity and foregrounding: In the eye of the beholder? *Poetics Today, 28*(4), 653–682.

SECTION 5

THE PERSON

CHAPTER 33

THE ROLE OF ATTENTION, EXECUTIVE PROCESSES, AND MEMORY IN AESTHETIC EXPERIENCE

JOHN W. MULLENNIX

COGNITION AND AESTHETICS

IN recent years, a number of researchers have turned their attention toward investigating the cognitive processes involved in the appreciation of art. Researchers have brought an impressive array of behavioral and neuroscientific techniques to bear on this task, with converging results from behavioral experiments and brain imaging studies used to refine theoretical models proposed to explain how cognitive processes factor into the aesthetic experience. As discussed below, some of the basic structural components and mental processes that make up the human cognitive system, including perception, attention, memory, bottom-up processing, and top-down processing have been incorporated into these models. The goal of this research is to understand how cognitive structures and processes are employed during the appreciation of art. Although this work is scientific in nature, it's important to note that the findings from this research are of interest to others beside research scientists. Creative artists, advertisers, designers of consumer products, art gallery and museum personnel, and those who market art may find this theoretical and empirical work useful in terms of practical applications that would enhance appeal to consumers of art and art-related products.

One approach to examining cognitive processes and the appreciation of art is to formulate information-processing models where specific hypotheses emerging from the models can be produced and empirically tested. One such model was proposed by Leder, Belke, Oeberst, and Augustin (2004; see also Leder & Nadal, 2014). Leder et al. described an information-processing "box model" that laid out a specific temporal sequence of five perceptual/cognitive stages involved in processing modern visual art. These stages were (in sequence): perceptual analysis, memory integration, explicit classification, cognitive mastering, and evaluation. Their model also included a pathway for the simultaneous processing of affective information generated by the act of viewing art. Leder et al. suggested that cognitive and affective processes interact during the viewing of art and constrain each other. This follows from observations of viewers whose aesthetic experiences can arise from emotional (affective) reactions to art, cognitive judgments of art, or various combinations thereof. Certainly, we know that cognitive and affective systems are interconnected in various behavioral and neuroanatomical ways (Cabeza & Nyberg, 2000; Gray, 1990; Ledoux, 1989; Phan, Wager, Taylor, & Liberzon, 2002; Schwarz, 2000). In terms of affective information, it is important to note that "aesthetic emotions" are not the same as basic or "utilitarian" emotions (Scherer, 2004, 2005; Silvia, 2009). In Leder et al.'s model, the end result of the information-processing sequence is the experience of aesthetic emotion and/or the production of an aesthetic judgment by the viewer of the artwork, which together comprise a complete aesthetic experience.

A more recent information-processing model was proposed by Pelowski, Markey, Forster, Gerger, and Leder (2017). This model is called the Vienna Integrated Model of Top-Down and Bottom-Up Processes in Art Perception (VIMAP). The VIMAP model represents a substantial modification and expansion of the basic premises of the Leder et al. (2004) model. Pelowski et al. (2017) proposed a stage-processing sequence that added a pre-classification stage preceding Leder et al.'s perceptual analysis stage and replaced Leder et al.'s evaluation stage with two stages called secondary control and self-reflection/metacognitive assessment. Pelowski et al. also included three "processing check" mechanisms that are able to modify the results of these stages of processing and allow flexibility for producing different outcomes in the art viewer's experience.

The VIMAP framework specifies in detail the relative contributions of bottom-up (artwork-driven) processes and top-down (viewer-centered, knowledge-based, executive-related) processes to the aesthetic experience. Pelowski et al. (2017) attempted to match up research findings in neuroaesthetics (primarily neuroimaging studies) with their processing stages to delineate the brain areas related to each stage of processing. As they stated, "We identify regions that are posited to be main centers of the processes argued above, as well as those which correspond to main checks, and thus which might serve as a basis for future integrated art research" (p. 107). As they appropriately acknowledged, ultimately the behavioral and cognitive components of an information-processing model of art appreciation need to be linked up with the underlying biological basis for those components to properly evaluate and refine the model.

Other processing models of art appreciation are based on the concept of processing fluency dynamics (Albrecht & Carbon, 2014; Belke, Leder, Strobach, & Carbon, 2010; Forster, Leder, & Ansorge, 2013; Gerger, Forster, & Leder, 2017; Graf & Landwehr, 2015; Reber, 2012; Reber, Schwarz, & Winkielman, 2004). As defined by Reber et al., processing fluency is the "ease of processing" a stimulus. There are two types of fluency: perceptual fluency and conceptual fluency. Perceptual processing fluency is the ease with which the physical stimulus is identified, with the emphasis on how perceptual features are processed. Perceptual fluency depends on early automatic and implicit levels of processing in the cognitive system (Belke et al., 2010). Conceptual processing fluency (also known as higher-order fluency) is related to the ease of processing the stimulus meaning and its relationship to semantic knowledge structures. Conceptual fluency most likely involves later, higher-level processes requiring mental effort (Belke et al., 2010).

Graf and Landwehr (2015) outlined a fluency-based processing model called the Pleasure-Interest Model of Aesthetic Liking (PIA model). Their model incorporates two hierarchical fluency-based processes that produce pleasure and interest in the aesthetic object. When a viewer makes a quick, spontaneous judgment about an artwork, they rely on stimulus driven processes that produce pleasure or displeasure. When stimulus or motivational components become more pronounced, and the viewer processes the artwork more elaborately at a higher level, then aesthetic evaluations of interest, boredom, or confusion ensue. Their model suggests that the processing approach of the viewer determines the level of cognitive processing engaged and the resulting aesthetic experience produced.

When considering these recent cognitive information-processing models of aesthetics, one important theme that runs through them is a division of information processing into lower-level processes and higher-level processes. The language used to describe this varies. For example, Leder et al. (2004) divide their stages into lower-level "automatic" processes and higher-level "deliberate" processes. Pelowski et al. (2017) divide their stages into lower-level "bottom-up" processes and higher-level "top-down" processes. Graf and Landwehr (2015) discuss a distinction between lower-level "stimulus driven" processes and higher-level "perceiver driven" processes. Across these models of processing and others (Belke et al., 2010), there is an implicit assumption that some stages of processing proceed with little to no cognitive control and other stages require selective control of processing and effortful deliberation. In the following section, this distinction is examined in further detail.

DUAL-MODE PROCESSING FRAMEWORKS

Theoretical concepts emerging from research on human attention have had a major influence on cognitive models of art appreciation. In the early empirical work on attention in the 1950s and 1960s, researchers suggested that attention should be viewed as a filter or a bottleneck (Broadbent, 1958; Cherry, 1953; Treisman, 1964). Over the years, this view gave way to a more sophisticated perspective of attention that captured the flexibility of human information processing. This view, which became known as the dual-mode processing perspective, posited two types of processes, originally referred to as automatic and controlled processes (Hasher & Zacks, 1979; Schneider & Shiffrin, 1977; Shiffrin & Schneider, 1977). Other terms have been used to describe these processes, such as Type 1 and Type 2 processes (Evans & Stanovich, 2013), and System 1 and System 2 processes (Evans, 2008; Kahneman, 2011). Despite differences in terminology across researchers, the descriptions of the processes are similar. Kahneman (2011) defines the two processes as follows:

> System 1 operates automatically and quickly, with little or no effort and no sense of voluntary control. System 2 allocates attention to the effortful mental activities that demand it, including complex computations. The operations of System 2 are often associated with the subjective experience of agency, choice, and concentration. (p. 20–21)

System 1 processes are rapid, nonconscious, and do not require measureable mental resources and processing capacity. System 2 processes are slower, conscious, effortful, and compete for finite mental resources used by other processes simultaneously employed in the cognitive system (Hasher & Zacks, 1979; Schneider & Shiffrin, 1977; Shiffrin & Schneider, 1977; Wickens, 1991). Research studies using brain imaging techniques reinforce the dual-processing idea, with default mode, central executive, and salience networks in the brain responsible for information processing related to different attentional modes (Raichle & Snyder, 2007; Seeley et al., 2007; Sridharan, Levitin, & Menon, 2008).

In terms of dual-mode processing and aesthetics, the idea that two modes of processing are involved has been incorporated into explanations of aesthetic experiences. One example comes from Hekkert, Snelders, and van Wieringen (2003). Hekkert et al. examined aesthetic preferences for consumer products (e.g., sanders, telephones, and tea kettles). Participants rated the products for degree of typicality and novelty. They found that both typicality and novelty affected preference. Hekkert et al. (2003) explained their findings as reflecting two separate processing mechanisms. The first mechanism processes familiar, typically encountered stimuli. They suggested that this mechanism is mediated by an automatic process that does not require awareness or intention. The second mechanism processes incongruous or novel items. This mechanism is characterized by a controlled, cognitively mediated mechanism. They suggested that the joint operation of both mechanisms determines the ultimate aesthetic judgment rendered by a viewer. The relative contribution of each mechanism is affected by the availability of processing time, context, and observer characteristics.

As discussed above, dual-mode processing is a primary feature of cognitive aesthetic processing models. In the PIA model from Graf and Landwehr (2015), automatic and controlled processes are a central concept. Graf and Landwehr suggest that when an aesthetic object is first encountered, it is immediately processed in an automatic fashion. This means that the processing is mandatory, occurs without the perceiver's intention, and proceeds without having to invest significant cognitive processing capacity. As they state, "This automatic processing is mainly stimulus driven and reactive, which is effectively expressed in the metaphor of the perceiver on autopilot" (pp. 398–399). They suggest that the output from this fast, short-duration, automatic level of processing is affective information that translates into an aesthetic evaluation of pleasure or displeasure. On the other hand, if sufficient attention is paid to the aesthetic object, then "perceiver driven" controlled processes are engaged. These are higher-order cognitive processes that involve detailed and deliberate stimulus analysis, assignment of meaning, and interpretation, with a requirement for substantial cognitive processing capacity. Controlled processing occurs over a relatively long duration of time. The output from controlled processes is an aesthetic evaluation related to boredom, interest, or confusion. Graf and Landwehr explain that aesthetic judgments can be produced by either processing mechanism, depending on whether a judgment is rendered quickly and spontaneously or whether a judgment is rendered only after much reflection and elaboration. Although their explanation is embedded within the paradigm of fluency-based aesthetics, the critical notion is that two qualitatively different modes of cognitive processing related to attention are involved in producing the aesthetic experience.

Other models of processing allude to dual-processing mechanisms but do not emphasize them as explicitly as Graf and Landwehr (2015). Leder et al. (2004), in their stage-processing scheme, labeled the lower-level perceptual analysis and implicit memory integration stages as "automatic" and labeled the higher-level explicit classification, cognitive mastering, and evaluation stages as "deliberate." In Pelowski et al.'s (2017) VIMAP model, they characterize stages of their model as bottom-up "artwork-derived" processes or top-down "viewer-centered" processes. More specifically, their perceptual analysis, implicit memory integration, and explicit classification stages are bottom-up and their cognitive mastery stage is top-down. Pelowski et al. also discuss automaticity and attention. For example, when describing perceptual analysis, implicit memory integration, and explicit classification, "First, we posit a series of stages (2–4) involving largely automatic, bottom-up processing of the formal features of the object" (p. 88). When describing implicit memory integration, "This involves a more focused period of attention, in which low-level features are segregated or grouped to form larger units" (p. 88). For the explicit classification stage, "In Stage 4's transition from automatic to more deliberate processing ... " (p. 110). For cognitive mastery, "The perceptual and contextual elements uncovered in the bottom-up processing above are met with a more top-down executive consideration ... " (p. 89).

The terminology used by Pelowski et al. (2017) illustrates an important point when considering dual-processing approaches. Generally speaking, there tends to be a correlation between bottom-up and top-down processes and automatic and controlled processes, respectively, when considering information flow in cognition. However, this is not always the case. There are situations where top-down processes can be invoked automatically without cognitive control. For example, in Pelowski et al.'s model, their pre-classification stage of processing where contextual information invokes art-related expectations or an art-related schema could be viewed by some as a "top-down" effect, albeit one invoked automatically and requiring little in the way of cognitive resources. Pelowski et al. also acknowledge that the processing checks built into their model could occur automatically. For example, when discussing congruency and self-relevancy checks, where a viewer assesses their feeling of mastery and the self-importance of the artwork, "It should also be specifically stated that these checks are most often not overtly conscious assessments. Rather, much like the broader art-processing outlined above, they are best thought of as another continuously-updated channel of information that can become more or less salient" (p. 91). The processing checks, in terms of information flow, could also be characterized as top-down, although not explicitly stated as such.

Another important point is that bottom-up processes are not always automatic. Pelowski et al. (2017) discussed focused attention as part of their bottom-up implicit memory integration stage, where low-level visual features are segregated or combined into larger units and perceptually organized. Past research has shown that focused attention used to combine visual features together in displays can consume measureable cognitive processing capacity (e.g., Treisman & Gelade, 1980), showing that it is a controlled process. Thus, Pelowski et al.'s implicit memory integration stage, although bottom-up in the sense of proceeding without cognitive control, may not be strictly automatic per se, at least when considering a definition of automaticity that posits no measureable use of processing capacity.

Thus, we need to be precise when we are applying a dual-process approach to a cognitive model of art appreciation. Processes can be characterized as bottom-up or top-down, but these processes also need to be described in terms of whether they are mandatory or not (i.e., under conscious control) and whether they utilize measureable cognitive processing capacity. If all these attributes are properly described, then the information-processing flow is clarified and the relationship of this flow to a dual-process perspective that posits two qualitatively different attentional processes during aesthetic processing can be properly delineated.

One way that dual-processing models are useful is that they provide a theoretical framework from which empirical studies examining art appreciation can be designed. In terms of the automaticity issue, a series of studies from my laboratory was performed to assess, in a global fashion, whether aesthetic judgments of visual art are performed using automatic or controlled processes. In one study, Mullennix et al. (2013) examined preference judgments for artistic photographs. Judgments were performed under varying conditions of cognitive load to assess whether automatic or controlled processes were utilized to process the photographs and to judge preference. The results showed that judgments were unaffected by the degree of cognitive load, suggesting that automatic processing was used. In a similar study, Mullennix, Varmecky, Chan, Mickey, and Polaski-Hoffman (2016) observed that the manipulation of color information (i.e., using false incongruent colors) and cognitive load did not affect aesthetic preference for photographs, providing further evidence for an automatic processing mode used to produce an aesthetic judgment. Together, the studies showed that when fairly quick and spontaneous aesthetic judgments are performed, capacity-free automatic processes are utilized.

However, the effects of cognitive load on aesthetic judgments may depend on the attributes of the artwork that viewers are told to judge. Brielmann and Pelli (2017) presented images to viewers that were pre-selected for level of beauty. Viewers indicated their rating of beauty for each image on a 4-point scale. When a secondary auditory two-track task was added to the rating task (the two-track task involves monitoring whether a currently presented auditory letter is the same as one presented two letters ago), the ratings for the beautiful images decreased. This suggested to the authors that the cognitive and attentional load of the secondary task interfered with the judgment of beauty, thus giving some credence to Kant's idea that the pleasure associated with perceiving beauty requires thought.

A dual-processing approach to appreciation of art would be strengthened by research in neuroaesthetics that identifies the brain processes and regions related to System 1 and System 2 processes used to produce an aesthetic experience. There is a growing corpus of research oriented toward identifying the brain regions activated when viewing artworks and making decisions about them (Chatterjee, 2011; Chatterjee & Vartanian, 2014; Cinzia & Vittorio, 2009; Leder, 2013; Nadal, 2013; Nadal, Munar, Capo, Rossello, & Cela-Conde, 2008; Vartanian & Skov, 2014). In terms of dual-processing research, Leder (2013) acknowledged that a neuroaesthetics approach would be useful for investigating levels of consciousness as represented by automatic and deliberate processes. In a study conducted by Cela-Conde et al. (2013), a magnetoencephalography (MEG) technique was used to examine activation of brain networks during aesthetic judgments. Participants viewed paintings and artistic photographs and were asked to make judgments of beauty for each of them. Their results showed that during this task two distinct brain networks were activated: an initial aesthetic network and a delayed aesthetic network. Cela-Conde et al. indicated that the activations of these networks were separated over time, with some suggestion that default mode brain network activity corresponded to the delayed aesthetic network. One interpretation of this study is that, generally speaking, earlier processes and later processes in stage models of aesthetic processing may have specific brain network correlates.

Researchers have also examined whether different brain areas are activated when the cognitive mode used to view artworks is manipulated. Cupchik, Vartanian, Crawley, and Mikulis (2009) performed a brain imaging study where participants viewed representational paintings under two conditions: pragmatic and aesthetic. In the pragmatic condition, participants were instructed to view artworks with a detached demeanor (to simply obtain information about the paintings). In the aesthetic condition, they were instructed to view the paintings in an engaged manner (focusing on the mood and feelings the paintings evoked). Cupchik et al. found more activation for the right fusiform gyrus in the pragmatic condition and more activation for the bilateral insula for the aesthetic condition. This suggested that the cognitive attentional mode the viewer used activated different areas of the brain when viewing representational paintings.

In summary, it would seem likely that neuroscience-based research will increasingly converge with behavioral research to elucidate dual-process theories of art appreciation. In the next section, specific attention is paid to the deliberative aspects of processing artworks and how cognitive control and executive function play into such deliberation.

COGNITIVE CONTROL AND
EXECUTIVE PROCESSES

Cognitive control is defined as the ability to adhere to rules, goals, or intentions in the face of competing reflexive demands (Rougier, Noelle, Braver, Cohen, & O'Reilly, 2005). Brain imaging research has shown that neural networks in the prefrontal cortex (Braver, Paxton, Locke, Barch, & Smith, 2009; Kerns et al., 2004; Miller & Cohen, 2001; Rougier et al., 2005), anterior cingulate cortex (Botvinick, Cohen, & Carter, 2004; van Veen & Carter, 2006), and posterior parietal cortex (Liston, Matalon, Hare, Davidson, & Casey, 2006) are involved in cognitive control. These areas have been combined into what is called the fronto-parietal control network (Harding, Yücel, Harrison, Pantelis, & Breakspear, 2015; Vincent, Kahn, Snyder, Raichle, & Buckner, 2008). This is a superordinate cognitive control network that supports numerous executive functions including cognitive flexibility, working memory, initiation, and inhibition (Niendam et al., 2012). The fronto-parietal network appears to be involved in mode switching between default and dorsal attention brain networks depending on moment-to-moment task demands (Spreng, Sepulcre, Turner, Stevens, & Schacter, 2013).

There is evidence that cognitive control is exerted via two modes of processing called "proactive control" and "reactive control" (Braver, 2012; Braver et al., 2009). As defined by Braver, "The proactive control mode can be conceptualized as a form of 'early selection' in which goal-relevant information is actively maintained in a sustained manner, before the occurrence of cognitively demanding events, to optimally bias attention, perception and action systems in a goal-driven manner. By contrast, in reactive control, attention is recruited as a 'late correction' mechanism that is mobilized only as needed, in a just-in-time manner, such as after a high interference event is detected" (Braver, 2012, p. 106). The prefrontal cortex is hypothesized as the locus for this aspect of control.

It appears that cognitive control can come into play in an anticipatory fashion, with a person adopting a top-down expectation based mode of processing for subsequent input. It also appears that cognitive control is exerted when a conflict occurs during information processing, with cognitive control mechanisms resolving the conflict by suppressing irrelevant information and selecting relevant information. The amount of conflict appears to determine how much control is invoked (van Veen & Carter, 2006).

It is obvious that deliberate cognitive control processes are involved in producing many aesthetic experiences. Viewers of art mull over the artistic style of the artwork, the content and meaning of the artwork, and memories of artworks encountered in the past that may come to mind while viewing an artwork. In terms of information-processing models, Leder et al. (2004) claimed that their explicit classification stage of processing involved the viewer's art knowledge and expertise, which is focused on the content of the artwork and identifying the artistic style. At that stage, processing is deliberate and can be verbally described. In the subsequent cognitive mastering and evaluation stage,

Leder et al. suggested that viewers derive meaning and understanding from the artwork, with conscious interpretation and evaluation of meaning occurring. This requires some measure of controlled processing and cognitive control.

In Pelowski et al.'s (2017) model, in their cognitive mastery stage a top-down executive process combines various sources of information together in order to "Form one coherent meaning, matching this to initial schema and expectations, and then attempt to formulate an appropriate evaluative or physical response, culminating in the creation of meaning, associations, evaluations, and the model's first outcomes" (p. 89). It would appear that this processing stage requires a conscious cognitive process under control of the viewer in order to arrive at an aesthetic judgment.

With regard to cognitive control, the overarching issue is how shifting one's attention to different aspects of an artwork or how shifting one's cognitive mode and approach to the artwork affects the aesthetic experience. There are a few studies that explicitly examine cognitive effort and control. As mentioned earlier, Cupchik et al. (2009) showed that top-down control of mode of processing and the intentional shifting of attention to different aspects of an artwork engaged different parts of the brain and altered the aesthetic experience of the viewer. This could be viewed as a form of "proactive control" (Braver, 2012). Gerger and Leder (2015), in a study examining the effects of titles on aesthetic appreciation for paintings, observed electromyography (EMG) recordings for facial muscles during judgments of liking and interest. One muscle of interest was the corrugator supercilli. Contraction of this facial muscle draws the eyebrows down (commonly known as the "frowning muscle"), with contraction correlated with increased mental effort to a task (Cacioppo, Petty, & Morris, 1985; Larsen, Kasimatis, & Frey, 1992; Stepper & Strack, 1993). Gerger and Leder found that for paintings with mismatched titles (random titles that did not match the painting's content), activation for the corrugator supercilli was higher. Gerger and Leder concluded that higher cognitive effort was expended in the mismatch condition, possibly incurred by a need for reducing the disfluency incurred by the mismatching titles. This situation appears to reflect a "reactive control" mechanism as discussed by Braver (2012).

To examine the role of cognitive control in the aesthetic experience, my colleagues and I conducted a study where cognitive effort was manipulated while viewers were making aesthetic judgments about artistic photographs (Mullennix et al., 2015). Participants made preference judgments about photographs under pragmatic or aesthetic instructions (similar to Cupchik et al., 2009) while their brow was relaxed or furrowed. When their brow was furrowed, this caused the corrugator supercilli muscle to be contracted. There is evidence suggesting that when this muscle is contracted, the proprioceptive feedback induces people to feel like they are expending more mental effort (Larsen et al., 1992). We found weak effects of mode of processing and muscle contraction on preference, with photographs preferred most under aesthetic instructions with the corrugator supercilli contracted. The results provided some suggestion that increasing cognitive effort in this way led to more positive aesthetic judgments.

When considering the role of controlled, effortful System 2 processes on the aesthetic experience, various avenues of research are potentially useful. One approach is to empirically test claims about conscious, effortful processing embedded into comprehensive models of cognitive processing and aesthetics (Graf & Landwehr, 2015; Leder et al., 2004; Pelowski et al., 2017; Silvia & Brown, 2007). For stage models where it is theorized that a stage of processing utilizes controlled, effortful processes, it is important to devise empirical tests that would support or rebut such a characterization. As part of this approach, it is important to disentangle top-down processes from controlled, effortful processes. As mentioned earlier, although often times a controlled process is also a top-down process, sometimes top-down processes proceed automatically without conscious control.

Another potentially useful approach to studying control processes lies with the distinction Braver (2012) made between proactive and reactive control processes. Some control processes appear to be proactive, such as Pelowski et al.'s (2017) pre-classification stage and the cognitive modes of processing examined by Cupchik et al. (2009). Other control processes appear to be reactive, such as the cognitive mastery and evaluation stages posited by Leder et al. (2004) and Pelowski et al. (2017). In these stages of processing, at times dissonant information encountered in artworks must be processed and interpreted. In such cases, reactive cognitive control may be required when unexpected difficulties in processing the elements of an artwork arise. Similarly, reactive control may arise when conflicts between the content of the artwork and contextual factors that surround the artwork, such as a title or the physical location of the artwork, arise.

Overall, dual-processing models provide a rich environment for furthering our knowledge about the cognition of aesthetics. In the next section, the role of memory in the aesthetic experience is examined.

MEMORY

Memory processes play a central role in the appreciation of art. Memory is an integral part of stage models of aesthetic processing, with memory processes involved in nearly every stage (Leder et al., 2004; Pelowski et al., 2017). Generally speaking, the role of memory in the aesthetic experience consists of: (1) holding information in working memory while viewing art, (2) contacting long-term memory representations of art during aesthetic processing, and (3) accessing knowledge about art from long-term memory in order to classify an artwork or to evaluate it. Research has also examined the degree to which artworks are retained in long-term memory after viewing them. These studies indicate that the depth of affective processing devoted to the artwork (Ishai, Fairhall, & Pepperell, 2007; Wang, Cant, & Cupchik, 2016) and contextual cues related to the physical location of the artwork (Brieber, Nadal, & Leder, 2015) affect how accurately artworks are remembered.

Working memory

Working memory is capacity-limited, with controlled processes throughout the cognitive system competing for the mental resources used to sustain information in working memory (Cowan, 2010; Wickens, 1991). Mental resources are often consumed during the perceptual analysis of an artwork. Resources are also consumed during retrieval of information from long-term memory during the viewing of art. The processing of art can involve a form of elaboration and problem solving (Muth & Carbon, 2013), which presumably requires intensive working memory processes. All of these disparate resource-consuming processes may impact the amount of information held in working memory about an artwork currently being viewed.

There is some evidence to suggest that the aesthetic experience derived from visual art depends on individuals' visual working memory capacity. Sherman, Grabowecky, and Suzuki (2015) presented fine art images to participants, who rated them for visual complexity and how "compelling" they were. They found evidence that visual-object working memory capacity was related to appreciation of visual complexity: people with higher visual working memory capacity preferred artworks that were more visually complex, and those with lower visual working memory capacity preferred artworks that were less complex. The implication is that individual visual working memory capacity affects the types of artworks that one prefers.

Long-term memory prototypes

In stage models of aesthetic processing, much emphasis is placed on how information in long-term memory shapes the aesthetic experience. Representations of art in long-term memory are contacted and utilized in different ways during aesthetic processing. One idea about how this occurs is the "preference for prototypes" model (Whitfield, 1983; Whitfield & Slatter, 1979). This model proposes that there are aesthetic categories stored in long-term memory organized around prototypes. During the viewing of art, aesthetic-related category representations of objects are contacted in memory. The degree to which an aesthetic object matches a stored prototype determines how much the aesthetic object is preferred (Whitfield, 1983). There is some evidence to support this idea (Farkas, 2002; Hekkert & Snelders, 1995; Hekkert & van Wieringen, 1990; Martindale, Moore, & Borkum, 1990; Whitfield, 1983; Whitfield & Slatter, 1979). However, others have pointed out that a prototype-based explanation of aesthetic processing cannot explain all the factors that affect aesthetic preference (Boselie, 1990; North & Hargreaves, 2000). Whitfield (2000) acknowledged some of the problems with the prototype idea (such as ill-formed aesthetic categories) and suggested that a hybrid model that included prototypes and arousal/motivational factors may be more appropriate.

Memory, art knowledge, and expertise

Empirical studies comparing naive viewers of art and art experts have shown that expertise affects many aspects of the aesthetic experience. As one would expect, liking, understanding, interest, cognitive appraisals, and emotional reactions to artworks differ across groups of participants varying in expertise (Leder, Carbon, & Ripsas, 2006; Leder et al., 2012; Leder, Gerger, Brieber, & Schwarz, 2014; Leder, Ring, & Dressler, 2013; Mullennix & Robinet, 2018; Silvia, 2006, 2007, 2013). Expertise also affects how pictorial elements in visual artworks are processed, with naive viewers focusing on individual objects in artworks while experts focus on the relationships between pictorial elements and compositional design (Nodine, Locher, & Krupinski, 1993).

The effects of expertise on the aesthetic experience indicate that the viewer's past experience and knowledge about art is retrieved from long-term memory and used during the processing of the artwork. This knowledge is used to identify artistic style, process the content and meaning of the artwork, and interpret the artwork via embedding it into a larger context in order to evaluate it. As suggested by various researchers, top-down processes access this information and make it available to the rest of the cognitive system for further processing (Graf & Landwehr, 2015; Leder et al., 2004; Pelowski et al., 2017). Leder et al. (2004) suggest that knowledge and expertise affect explicit classification and cognitive mastering/evaluation stages of processing. These stages of processing are deliberate, can be verbalized, and are devoted to processing the meaning of the artwork and producing an understanding of the artwork. Pelowski et al. (2017) also suggest that explicit classification and cognitive mastering are affected by expertise, as well as secondary control and metacognitive awareness processes.

Conclusion: Major Challenges, Goals, and Suggestions

In the years ahead, much empirical work is needed in order to elucidate the cognitive processes involved in producing an aesthetic experience. Aesthetic processing models such as those discussed above (Graf & Landwehr, 2015; Leder et al., 2004; Pelowski et al., 2017) have provided specific assertions that can be tested empirically. These assertions include the sequencing of processing stages, the time course of processing, the involvement of bottom-up and top-down processes at various stages, memory representations of aesthetic stimuli, and the retrieval of art-related information from memory. Converging data from both behavioral and neuroaesthetic approaches are integral to testing the viability of these models and will help to further refine these models and stimulate the development of alternative models of processing.

Specifically, there are several aspects of cognition and aesthetics that will require further investigation. One future area of research, as mentioned above, is to clarify the nature of bottom-up and top-down processes in art appreciation. Studies are needed which will show definitively whether bottom-up and top-down processes are automatic processes (System 1) or controlled (System 2) processes. It is important to determine whether bottom-up and top-down processes are mandatory, optional, and/or require measureable cognitive resources. Studies along these lines will expand our understanding of the cognitive demands placed on the person during the processing of art.

Another future area of research is to provide a more detailed examination of the effects of exerting and shifting cognitive control during the processing of art. The work of Cupchik et al. (2009) was an important initial step toward this goal. Future studies where the cognitive mode of the viewer is manipulated to focus on different aspects of the aesthetic experience will broaden our knowledge about how conscious control over what the viewer is attending to affects the aesthetic experience.

A third area of future research lies with studies that explicitly examine the connection between stored art expertise, knowledge about art, and the stages of processing theorized to utilize that knowledge. Pelowski et al. (2017) outlined a number of specific hypothesized connections between art experience and stages of processing with regard to meaning, appraisal, physiological responses, and emotion. Specific predictions such as these outlined by Pelowski et al. will prove useful is designing studies that test these specific claims and provide further information about how expertise and knowledge are accessed and used during cognitive processing.

Finally a fourth area of future research will address a significant limitation built into many processing models of art appreciation, which is the fact that these models are confined to visual art. Ultimately, these models need to be modified and expanded to address all aesthetic experiences. Numerous questions arise. Do the cognitive processes used to process visual art operate in similar fashion for music? Dance? Sculpture, architecture, consumer products? Is the dual-process approach applicable to all aesthetic experiences, with automatic and controlled processes engaged in the same manner? As the research on aesthetic processing continues, it is important to assess how the findings we observe for visual art generalize to other aesthetic domains. We need to assess whether there are there similarities in the cognitive processes used across aesthetic domains, or whether each aesthetic endeavor requires unique processes to produce an aesthetic experience.

When considering the research on aesthetics and cognition, it is important to step back and examine how this research impacts the average person. We live in a world where we surrounded by art, whether it be specific places we go to experience art, ubiquitous advertising and marketing designed to capture our attention, street art we see while walking around, architectural structures we see or interact with, or products designed to appeal to the aesthetic sense of the consumer. In this larger picture, understanding the cognitive processes underlying the aesthetic experience is potentially valuable for artists, designers, advertisers, and marketers of art. One example is Tinio's (2013) proposed "Mirror Model" of art. Tinio suggested that the creative art-making process and the aesthetic art-viewing process are mirror image temporal sequences of each other. If Tinio's suggestion has merit, one would believe that a better understanding of aesthetic processing would help our understanding of the artistic creative process. If creative artists have better insight into the cognitive processes they employ while creating art, in other words a "metacognitive" perspective on how they work, perhaps this would provide a new way of approaching the creative process and provide fertile ground for innovation in producing works of art.

Understanding the scientific basis of the cognitive/affective processing of art is useful for those who display and market art and for those who design architectural structures and consumer products that have an aesthetic appeal. One example of this is context. If one understands how context affects the cognitive/affective aesthetic experience (with context consisting of factors like one's art expertise, how an aesthetic object is labeled, or the physical environment where the aesthetic object is encountered), then one could target one's marketing strategy or design parameters for structures and products in a way that would produce maximum effect on the person who will see them or use them. Another example is dual processing. If one understands which aspects of the aesthetic experience are due to automatic, unconscious processes, and which aspects are due to controlled, conscious processes, one could tailor marketing and design toward the type of experience you wish to invoke in the consumer of art, the viewer of advertising, and the user of manufactured products. Although these are just two examples of how the basic scientific research addressed in this chapter could be channeled into practical applications, there is potential for many more. In this way, the research we are engaged in ultimately can have a real effect on the average person in terms of what they experience when they go about their day-to-day life.

In summary, we are engaged in an exciting period of research on aesthetics that is bit-by-bit revealing the underlying cognitive and physiological basis of the aesthetic experience. Future studies that examine areas of aesthetics outside of visual art will be illuminating. The key to this future work is research from behavioral and neuroscientific approaches that converge to provide comprehensive insights into the issues at hand. In addition, as advancements continue in general cognitive theory and neuroscience, these advancements will inform the theoretical and methodological approaches we take to empirical research on aesthetics. Understanding how aesthetic experiences are produced in people via their exposure to the works of creative artists is a weighty undertaking, but one that is fascinating to many. This endeavor is no doubt one that Gustav Fechner (1876) would heartily approve of and would encourage as our knowledge about aesthetics continues to grow.

References

Albrecht, S., & Carbon, C. C. (2014). The fluency amplification model: Fluent stimuli show more intense but not evidently more positive evaluations. *Acta Psychologica, 148*, 195–203. doi:10.1016/j.actpsy.2014.02.022

Belke, B., Leder, H., Strobach, T., & Carbon, C. (2010). Cognitive fluency: High-level processing dynamics in art appreciation. *Psychology of Aesthetics, Creativity, and the Arts, 4*(4), 214–222. doi:10.1037/a0019648

Boselie, F. (1990). Against prototypicality as a central concept in aesthetics. *Empirical Studies of the Arts, 9*, 65–73. doi:10.2190/ERDR-FN28-PUEE-EU7F

Botvinick, M. M., Cohen, J. D., & Carter, C. S. (2004). Conflict monitoring and anterior cingulate cortex: An update. *Trends in Cognitive Sciences, 18*(12), 539–546. doi:10.1016/j.tics.2004.10.003

Braver, T. S. (2012). The variable nature of cognitive control: A dual mechanisms framework. *Trends in Cognitive Sciences, 16*(2), 106–113. doi:10.1016/j.tics.2011.12.010

Braver, T. S., Paxton, J. L., Locke, H. S., Barch, D. M., & Smith, E. E. (2009). Flexible neural mechanisms of cognitive control within human prefrontal cortex. *Proceedings of the National Academy of Sciences of the United States of America, 106*(18), 7351–7356. doi:10.1073/pnas.0909197106

Brieber, D., Nadal, M., & Leder, H. (2015). In the white cube: Museum context enhances the valuation and memory of art. *Acta Psychologica, 154*, 36–42. doi:10.1016/j.actpsy.2014.11.004

Brielmann, A. A., & Pelli, D. G. (2017). Beauty requires thought. *Current Biology Report, 27*, 1506–1513. doi:10.1016/j.cub.2017.04.018

Broadbent, D. E. (1958). *Perception and communication*. London: Pergamon Press.

Cabeza, R., & Nyberg, L. (2000). Imaging cognition II: An empirical review of 275 PET and fMRI studies. *Journal of Cognitive Neuroscience, 12*(1), 1–47. doi:10.1162/08989290051137585

Cacioppo, J. T., Petty, R. E., & Morris, K. J. (1985). Semantic, evaluative, and self-referent processing: Memory, cognitive effort, and somatovisceral activity. *Psychophysiology, 22*(4), 371–384. doi:10.1111/j.1469-8986.1985.tb01618.x

Cela-Conde, C. J., Garcia-Prieto, J., Ramasco, J. J., Mirasso, J. R., Bajo, R., Munar, E., Flexas, A., del-Pozo, F., & Maestu, F. (2013). Dynamics of brain networks in the aesthetic appreciation. *Proceedings of the National Academy of the Sciences of the United States of America, 110*, 10454–10461. doi:10.1073/pnas.1302855110

Chatterjee, A. (2011). Neuroaesthetics: A coming of age story. *Journal of Cognitive Neuroscience, 23*(1), 53–62. doi:10.1162/jocn.2010.21457

Chatterjee, A., & Vartanian, O. (2014). Neuroaesthetics. *Trends in Cognitive Sciences, 18*(7), 370–375. doi:10.1016/j.tics.2014.03.003

Cherry, E. C. (1953). Some experiments on the recognition of speech, with one and with two ears. *Journal of the Acoustical Society of America, 25*, 975–979. doi:10.1121/1.1907229

Cinzia, D. D., & Vittorio, G. (2009). Neuroaesthetics: A review. *Current Opinion in Neurobiology, 19*, 682–687. doi:10.1016/j.conb.2009.09.001

Cowan, N. (2010). The magical mystery four: How is working memory capacity limited, and why? *Current Directions in Psychological Science, 19*(1), 51–57. doi:10.1177/0963721409359277

Cupchik, G. C., Vartanian, O., Crawley, A., & Mikulis, D. J. (2009). Viewing artworks: Contributions of cognitive control and perceptual facilitation to aesthetic experience. *Brain and Cognition, 70*, 84–91. doi:10.1016/j.bandc.2009.01.003

Evans, J. St. B. T. (2008). Dual-processing accounts of reasoning, judgment, and social cognition. *Annual Review of Psychology, 59*, 255–278. doi:10.1146/annurev.psych.59.103006.093629

Evans, J. St. B. T., & Stanovich, K. E. (2013). Dual-process theories of higher cognition: Advancing the debate. *Perspectives on Psychological Science, 8*(3), 223–241. doi:10.1177/1745691612460685

Farkas, A. (2002). Prototypicality-effect in surrealist paintings. *Empirical Studies of the Arts, 20*, 127–136. doi:10.2190/UD7Y-GN8P-Q0EV-Q13J

Fechner, G. (1876). *Vorschule der Aesthetik* [Preschool of Aesthetics]. Leipzig, Germany: Druck und Verlag von Breitkopf und Härtel.

Forster, M., Leder, H., & Ansorge, U. (2013). It felt fluent and I liked it: Subjective feeling of fluency rather than objective fluency determines liking. *Emotion, 13*, 280–289. doi:10.1037/a0030115

Gerger, G., Forster, M., & Leder, H. (2017). It felt fluent but I did not like it: Fluency effects in face versus patterns. *The Quarterly Journal of Experimental Psychology, 70*(4), 637–648. doi:10.1080/17470218.2016.1145705

Gerger, G., & Leder, H. (2015). Titles change the esthetic appreciation of paintings. *Frontiers in Human Neuroscience, 9*, 1–10. doi:10.3389/fnhum.2015.00464

Graf, L. K. M., & Landwehr, J. R. (2015). A dual-process perspective on fluency-based aesthetics: The pleasure-interest model of liking. *Personality and Social Psychology Review, 19*(4), 395–410. doi:10.1177/1088868315574978

Gray, J. A. (1990). Brain systems that mediate both emotion and cognition. *Cognition and Emotion, 4*(3), 269–288. doi:10.1080/02699939008410799

Harding, I. H., Yücel, M., Harrison, B. J., Pantelis, C., & Breakspear, M. (2015). Effective connectivity within the frontoparietal control network differentiates cognitive control and memory. *NeuroImage, 106*, 144–153. doi:10.1016/j.neuroimage.2014.11.039

Hasher, L., & Zacks, R. T. (1979). Automatic and effortful processes in memory. *Journal of Experimental Psychology: General, 108*, 356–388. doi:10.1037/0096-3445.108.3.356

Hekkert, P., & Snelders, D. (1995). Prototypicality as an explanatory concept in aesthetics: A reply to Boselie (1991). *Empirical Studies of the Arts, 13*, 149–160. doi:10.2190/KYRA-R5UR-ARA8-CXFN

Hekkert, P., Snelders, D., & van Wieringen, P. C. W. (2003). "Most advanced, yet acceptable": Typicality and novelty as joint predictors of aesthetic preference in industrial design. *British Journal of Psychology, 94*, 111–124. doi:10.1348/000712603762842147

Hekkert, P., & van Wieringen, P. C. W. (1990). Complexity and prototypicality as determinants of the appraisal of cubist paintings. *British Journal of Psychology, 81*(4), 483–495. doi:10.1111/j.2044-8295.1990.tb02374.x

Ishai, A., Fairhall, S. L., & Pepperell, R. (2007). Perception, memory and aesthetics of indeterminate art. *Brain Research Bulletin, 73*, 319–324. doi:10.1016/j.brainresbull.2007.04.009

Kahneman, D. (2011). *Thinking fast and slow*. New York: Farrar, Straus, and Giroux.

Kerns, J. G., Cohen, J. D., MacDonald III, A. W., Cho, R. Y., Stenger, V. A., & Carter, C. S. (2004). Anterior cingulate conflict monitoring and adjustments in control. *Science, 303*, 1023–1026. doi:10.1126/science.1089910

Larsen, R. J., Kasimatis, M., & Frey, K. (1992). Facilitating the furrowed brow: An unobtrusive test of the facial feedback hypothesis applied to unpleasant affect. *Cognition and Emotion, 6*(5), 321–338. doi:10.1080/02699939208409689

Leder, H. (2013). Next steps in neuroaesthetics: Which processes and processing stages to study? *Psychology of Aesthetics, Creativity, and the Arts, 17*(1), 27–37. doi:10.1037/a0031585

Leder, H., Belke, B., Oeberst, A., & Augustin, D. (2004). A model of aesthetic appreciation and aesthetic judgments. *British Journal of Psychology, 95*, 489–508. doi:10.1348/0007126042369811

Leder, H., Carbon, C., & Ripsas, A. (2006). Entitling art: Influence of title information on understanding and appreciation of paintings. *Acta Psychologica, 121*, 176–198. doi:10.1016/j.actpsy.2005.08.005

Leder, H., Gerger, G., Brieber, D., & Schwarz, N. (2014). What makes an art expert? Emotion and evaluation in art appreciation. *Cognition and Emotion, 28*(6), 1137–1147. doi:10.1080/02699931.2013.870132

Leder, H., Gerger, G., Dressler, S. G., & Schabmann, A. (2012). How art is appreciated. *Psychology of Aesthetics, Creativity, and the Arts, 6*(1), 2–10. doi:10.1037/a0026396

Leder, H., & Nadal, M. (2014). Ten years of a model of aesthetic appreciation and aesthetic judgments: The aesthetic episode – developments and challenges in empirical aesthetics. *British Journal of Psychology, 105,* 443–464. doi:10.1111/bjop.12084

Leder, H., Ring, A., & Dressler, S. G. (2013). See me, feel me! Aesthetic evaluations of art portraits. *Psychology of Aesthetics, Creativity, and the Arts, 7*(4), 358–369. doi:10.1037/a0033311

Ledoux, J. E. (1989). Cognitive-emotional interactions in the brain. *Cognition and Emotion, 3*(4), 267–289. doi:10.1080/02699938908412709

Liston, C., Matalon, S., Hare, T. A., Davidson, M. C., & Casey, B. J. (2006). Anterior cingulate and posterior parietal cortices are sensitive to dissociable forms of conflict in a task-switching paradigm. *Neuron, 50,* 643–653. doi:10.1016/j.neuron.2006.04.015

Martindale, C., Moore, K., & Borkum, J. (1990). Aesthetic preference: Anomalous findings for Berlyne's psychobiological theory. *Empirical Studies of the Arts, 6,* 79–96. doi:10.2307/1423259

Miller, E. K., & Cohen, J. D. (2001). An integrative theory of prefrontal cortex function. *Annual Review of Neuroscience, 24,* 167–202. doi:10.1146/annurev.neuro.24.1.167

Mullennix, J. W., Foytik, L. R., Chan, C. H., Dragun, B. R., Maloney, M., & Polaski, L. (2013). Automaticity and the processing of artistic photographs. *Empirical Studies of the Arts, 31*(2), 145–171. doi:10.2190/EM.31.2.c

Mullennix, J. W., & Robinet, J. (2018). Art expertise and the processing of titled abstract art. *Perception, 47*(4), 359–378. doi:10.1177/0301006617752314

Mullennix, J. W., Varmecky, A., Chan, C., Mickey, Z., & Polaski-Hoffman, L. (2016). The effect of color on automaticity of aesthetic judgments. *Empirical Studies of the Arts, 34,* 8–34. doi:10.1177/0276237415621183

Mullennix, J. W., Wagner, N., Hetrick, B., Malloy, N., Jerome, R., & Schminkey, M. (2015). Preference for visual art as a function of cognitive effort. *North American Journal of Psychology, 17*(3), 433–448.

Muth, C., & Carbon, C. C. (2013). The aesthetic aha: On the pleasure of having insights into Gestalt. *Acta Psychologica, 144,* 25–30. doi:10.1016/actpsy.2013.05.001

Nadal, M. (2013). Chapter 7: The experience of art: Insights from neuroimaging. *Progress in Brain Research, 204,* 135–158. doi:10.1016/B978-0-444-63287-6.00007-5

Nadal, M., Munar, E., Capo, M. A., Rossello, J., & Cela-Conde, C. J. (2008). Towards a framework for the study of the neural correlates of aesthetic preference. *Spatial Vision, 21,* 379–396. doi:10.1163/156856808784532653

Niendam, T. A., Laird, A. R., Ray, K. L., Dean, Y. M., Glahn, D. C., & Carter, C. S. (2012). Meta-analytic evidence for a superordinate cognitive control network subserving diverse cognitive functions. *Cognitive, Affective, and Behavioral Neuroscience, 12,* 241–268. doi:10.3758/s13415-011-0083-5

Nodine, C. F., Locher, P. J., & Krupinski, E. A. (1993). The role of formal art training on perception and aesthetic judgment of art compositions. *Leonardo, 26*(3), 219–227. doi:10.2307/1575815

North, A. C., & Hargreaves, D. J. (2000). Collative variables versus prototypicality. *Empirical Studies of the Arts, 8*(1), 13–17. doi:10.2190/K96D-085M-T07Y-61AB

Pelowski, M., Markey, P. S., Forster, M., Gerger, G., & Leder, H. (2017). Move me, astonish me ... delight my eyes and brain: The Vienna Integrated Model of Top-Down and Bottom-Up

Processes in art perception (VIMAP) and corresponding affective, evaluative, and neuro-physiological correlates. *Physics of Life Reviews, 21,* 80–125. doi:10.1016/j.plrev.2017.02.003

Phan, K. L., Wager, T., Taylor, S. F., & Liberzon, I. (2002). Functional neuroanatomy of emotion: M meta-analysis of emotion activation studies in PET and fMRI. *NeuroImage, 16,* 331–348. doi:10.1006/nimg.2002.1087

Raichle, M. E., & Snyder, A. Z. (2007). A default mode of brain function: A brief history of an evolving idea. *NeuroImage, 37,* 1083–1090. doi:10.1016/j.neuroimage.2007.02.041

Reber, R. (2012). Processing fluency, aesthetic pleasure, and culturally shared taste. In A. P. Shimamura, & S. E. Palmer (Eds.), *Aesthetic science* (pp. 223–249). New York: Oxford University Press.

Reber, R., Schwarz, N., & Winkielman, P. (2004). Processing fluency and aesthetic pleasure: Is beauty in the perceiver's processing experience? *Personality and Social Psychology Review, 8,* 364–382. doi:10.1207/s15327957pspr0804_3

Rougier, N. P., Noelle, D. C., Braver, T. S., Cohen, J. D., & O'Reilly, R. C. (2005). Prefrontal cortex and flexible cognitive control: Rules without symbols. *Proceedings of the National Academy of Sciences of the United States of America, 102*(20), 7338–7343. doi:10.1073/pnas.0502455102

Scherer, K. R. (2004). Which emotions can be induced by music? What are the underlying mechanisms? And how can we measure them? *Journal of New Music Research, 33*(3), 239–251. doi:10.1080/0929821042000317822

Scherer, K. R. (2005). What are emotions? And how can they be measured? *Social Science Information, 44*(4), 695–729. doi:10.1177/0539018405058216

Schneider, W., & Shiffrin, R. M. (1977). Controlled and automatic human information processing: I. Detection, search, and attention. *Psychological Review, 84*(1), 1–66. doi:10.1037/0033-295X.84.1.1

Schwarz, N. (2000). Emotion, cognition, and decision making. *Cognition and Emotion, 14*(4), 433–440. doi:10.1080/026999300402745

Seeley, W. W., Menon, V., Schatzberg, A. F., Keller, J., Glover, G. H., Kenna, H., ... Greicius, M. D. (2007). Dissociable intrinsic connectivity networks for salience processing and executive control. *The Journal of Neuroscience, 27*(9), 2349–2356. doi:10.1523/JNEUROSCI.5587-06.2007

Sherman, A., Grabowecky, M., & Suzuki, S. (2015). In the working memory of the beholder: art appreciation is enhanced when visual complexity is compatible with working memory. *Journal of Experimental Psychology: Human Perception and Performance, 41*(4), 898–903. doi:10.1037/a0039314

Shiffrin, R. M., & Schneider, W. (1977). Controlled and automatic human information processing: II. Perceptual learning, automatic attending, and a general theory. *Psychological Review, 84*(2), 127–190. doi:10.1037/0033-295X.84.2.127

Silvia, P. (2006). Artistic training and interest in visual art: Applying the appraisal model of aesthetic emotions. *Empirical Studies of the Arts, 24*(2), 139–161. doi:10.2190/DX8K-6WEA-6WPA-FM84

Silvia, P. (2007). Knowledge-based assessment of expertise in the arts: Exploring aesthetic fluency. *Psychology of Aesthetics, Creativity, and the Arts, 1,* 247–249. doi:10.1037/1931-3896.1.4.247

Silvia, P. (2009). Looking past pleasure: Anger, confusion, disgust, pride, surprise, and other unusual aesthetic emotions. *Psychology of Aesthetics, Creativity, and the Arts, 3*(1), 48–51. doi:10.1037/a0014632

Silvia, P. (2013). Interested experts, confused novices: Art expertise and the knowledge emotions. *Empirical Studies of the Arts*, 31(1), 107–115. doi:10.2190/EM.31.1.f

Silvia, P., & Brown, E. (2007). Anger, disgust, and the negative aesthetic emotions: Expanding an appraisal model of aesthetic experience. *Psychology of Aesthetics, Creativity, and the Arts*, 1(2), 100–106. doi:10.1037/1931-3896.1.2.100

Spreng, R. N., Sepulcre, J., Turner, G. R., Stevens, W. D., & Schacter, D. L. (2013). Intrinsic architecture underlying the relations among the default, dorsal attention, and frontoparietal control networks of the human brain. *Journal of Cognitive Neuroscience*, 25(1), 74–86. doi:10.1162/jocn_a_00281

Sridharan, D., Levitin, D. J., & Menon, V. (2008). A critical role for the right fronto-insular cortex in switching between central-executive and default-mode networks. *Proceedings of the National Academy of Sciences of the United States of America*, 105(34), 12569–12574. doi:10.1073/pnas.0800005105

Stepper, S., & Strack, F. (1993). Proprioceptive determinants of emotional and nonemotional feelings. *Journal of Personality and Social Psychology*, 64(2), 211–220. doi:10.1037/0022-3514.64.2.211

Tinio, P. P. L. (2013). From artistic creation to aesthetic reception: The mirror model of art. *Psychology of Creativity, Aesthetics, and the Arts*, 7(3), 265–275. doi:10.1037/a0030872

Treisman, A. M. (1964). Selective attention in man. *British Medical Bulletin*, 20, 12–16. doi:10.1093/oxfordjournals.bmb.a070274

Treisman, A. M., & Gelade, G. (1980). A feature-integration theory of attention. *Cognitive Psychology*, 12, 97–136. doi:10.1016/0010-0285(80)90005-5

van Veen, V., & Carter, C. S. (2006). Conflict and cognitive control in the brain. *Current Directions in Psychological Science*, 15(5), 237–240. doi:10.1111/j.1467-8721.2006.00443.x

Vartanian, O., & Skov, M. (2014). Neural correlates of viewing paintings: Evidence from a quantitative meta-analysis of functional magnetic resonance imaging data. *Brain and Cognition*, 87, 52–56. doi:10.1016/j.bandc.2014.03.004

Vincent, J. L., Kahn, I., Snyder, A. Z., Raichle, M. E., & Buckner, R. L. (2008). Evidence for a frontoparietal control system revealed by intrinsic functional connectivity. *Journal of Neurophysiology*, 100, 3328–3342. doi:10.1152/jn.90355.2008

Wang, T., Cant, J. S., & Cupchik, G. (2016). The impact of depth of aesthetic processing and visual-feature transformations on recognition memory for artworks and constructed design patterns. *Empirical Studies of the Arts*, 34(2), 193–220. doi:10.1177/0276237416637958

Whitfield, T. W. A. (1983). Predicting preference for familiar, everyday objects: An experimental confrontation between two theories of aesthetic behaviour. *Journal of Environmental Behavior*, 3, 221–237. doi:10.1016/S0272-4944(83)80002-4

Whitfield, T. W. A. (2000). Beyond prototypicality: Toward a categorical-motivation model of aesthetics. *Empirical Studies of the Arts*, 18, 1–11. doi:10.2190/KM3A-G1NV-Y5ER-MR2V

Whitfield, T. W. A., & Slatter, P. E. (1979). The effects of categorization and prototypicality on aesthetic choice in a furniture selection task. *British Journal of Psychology*, 70, 5–75. doi:10.1111/j.2044-8295.1979.tb02144.x

Wickens, C. D. (1991). Processing resources and attention. In D. L. Damos (Ed.), *Multiple-task performance* (pp. 3–34). London: Taylor and Francis.

CHAPTER 34

CHILDREN'S APPRECIATION OF ART

THALIA R. GOLDSTEIN

ALL children scribble, move their bodies, pretend play, and create rhythm and melody. But when do children become appreciative of such art, across art forms? When do they start to understand there is such a "thing" as art, and that elements of their own artistic creations contain elements of the works they see in public? Importantly, does this vary by art form? For example, is children's understanding of intention in the visual arts (where there has been substantial research) different from the understanding of intention in dance (where there are almost no published findings)?

In this chapter, I will explore research conducted on children's developing appreciation of art across art forms—theater, dance, visual arts, music, and literature. I'll focus on extant work, and gaps in the literature. I will not aim for a comprehensive review of all forms of aesthetic reasoning across all art forms, but instead focus on exemplary studies connected to child development as an organizing principle. As a note, this subject could be organized in three ways. First, by age. Perhaps in infancy, children understand art in one way, in toddlerhood another, then preschool, early childhood, middle childhood, and so on. Second, by art form. Perhaps children's general and specific understanding of theater varies from their understanding of visual arts, music, dance, etc. Finally, by aesthetic property. Perhaps the development of aesthetic appreciation is less about the target (i.e., the art), and more about the development of social (intention reading), emotional (personal response), or cognitive (understanding of ownership) abilities that underlie each type of engagement with the arts.

Questions in aesthetic reasoning guiding this chapter include: When do children understand the distinction and connection between their everyday artistic activities (i.e., pretend play, scribbling), and *art*? When do children understand authorship/creator intention? What about forgery and ownership? Copying versus originality? What are children's opinions about realism, impressionism, and abstraction? How and when do children understand emotionality within art, and separately, how and when do they experience aesthetic emotions?

Given the broad gaps in research that impede the development of a unified theory of children's understanding and appreciation of the arts (or even of an individual art form), much of a review by age or by art form would involve large sections where there is no research, and therefore difficulty developing coherence. While the same issue remains while reviewing the literature by aesthetic question or property, this chapter supposes that the reader is most interested in psychological constructs first (rather than age or art form first), and therefore the review of the literature proceeds in that order. Where there are gaps, I look to other findings in developmental psychology that may not have been applied to aesthetic reasoning but could be broadened to do so.

There have been some attempts previously to develop a comprehensive theory of children's aesthetic reasoning or appreciation. However, these tend to focus on individual art forms (e.g., the cognitive developmental experience of appreciating the visual arts; Parsons, 1976), or a specific focus on one aspect of development (e.g., neural development of aesthetic responses to music; Nieminen, Istók, Brattico, Tervaniemi, & Huotilainen, 2011), or an application of central developmental theories to art (e.g., Piagetian theory to understanding visual art; Machotka, 1966) rather than approaching aesthetics as a whole, across art forms.

Much like in creativity studies, there are elements of domain-generality and elements of specificity within each domain (Kaufman & Baer, 2004). With aesthetic responses, perhaps the development of aesthetic understanding has some elements that apply generally (that are developmentally universal), and some domain-specificity by art form. However, understanding of aesthetic response comparatively across art forms has not, to my knowledge, been conducted.

FROM CHILDHOOD ACTIVITY TO FORMALIZED ART

One basic developmental question is how early natural engagement in the arts is (or is not) related to later aesthetic appreciation. Children's engagement in what we would later identify as "art" forms begins early, and develops innately across many cultures (Gardner, 1990). I would argue that from birth through preschool, there is no distinction between the understanding of art and the appreciation of art. Children draw and look at others' drawings. They dance and watch others dance. They pretend and interact with theater, and they sing and listen to singing. Children are primarily sensorimotor at this age (Piaget & Inhelder, 1969), meaning they do not simply look at something for very long, but must instead engage in an embodied, physicalized experience to understand it. Formal artistic exhibitions or performances for this age group are rare (with Theatre for the Very Young and some musical performances being exceptions; Fletcher-Watson, 2016; Young, 2004, 2005; Young, Street, & Davies, 2007). Simply interacting with the world could be considered an aesthetic experience for the very young child. They are appreciating and focusing on all aspects of an object or experience—color, shape, weight, movement, light, etc.

When does this appreciation and broad focus (Gopnik, 2016) shift into more adult-like appreciation? And is this shift qualitative in nature (meaning fundamentally different) or quantitative (meaning a difference in scale)? One set of obvious, though mostly untested assumptions, is that there is a continuum of understanding and appreciation from childhood activities to adulthood art engagement—that pretend play leads to acting, scribbling with crayons to drawing, lullabies to music, and body movement to dance. Some retrospective studies of adult artists show a propensity toward the arts in childhood. For example, adult professional actors report being more emotionally sensitive and more drawn to fictional worlds than a comparison group of lawyers (Goldstein & Winner, 2009). Adult winners of the MacArthur Fellow status are significantly more likely to have created fully fledged imaginary worlds in childhood than college students (Root-Bernstein & Root-Bernstein, 2006). Artistic prodigies, however, are a mixed group (Winner, 1996). For example, historiometric studies of adult composers find some prodigy level abilities in childhood, but plenty of successful adult artists who were not prodigies (Simonton, 1994).

Similarly, there are studies of children's development within the arts showing true progress in drawing skill over the first 5 years of development (Milbrath, 1998) and a shift from literal to representational drawing from childhood to adolescence (Picard & Gauthier, 2012). Artistic activities that are often considered to discontinue after early childhood (i.e., the "U-shaped" curve of visual art creation; Davis, 1997; Gardner, 1990), although this work has focused entirely on visual arts creation, and may not necessarily discontinue (Kindler, 2000; Pariser & van den Berg, 1997), or may change dependent on which aspect of art production is being measured (Jolley, Barlow, Rotenberg, & Cox, 2016). There is a long-standing psychoanalytic theory that pretend play never really disappears (Colarusso, 1993), and some scientific research provides evidence for this claim (e.g. children and adults who report engaging in fantasy and imaginative play, often even with imaginary companions, through middle childhood and adolescence Sandberg, 2001; Smith & Lillard, 2012; Taylor, 2001; Taylor & Mannering, 2006). Yet direct evidence of connections from childhood drawing properties to adult aesthetic understanding, from pretend play to liking plays, from Mom's songs to symphony preferences is missing. The previously mentioned works are studies of artists and artistic creation, not art appreciation. Psychological studies of the trajectory nonartist children take from relatively universal activities such as scribbling and pretend play to adult appreciation of art are absent.

While these are not central questions in the study of adult aesthetic reasoning, they are critical for understanding where and how adult aesthetic reasoning develops and are open for inquiry. I now turn to a series of questions in aesthetic understanding more directly, looking at where there has been specific developmental research on the question itself, and where work on related questions may provide insight into the development of aesthetic understanding of reasoning. These questions include the understanding of intention, judgments of value, understanding emotion in art, and gaining aesthetic emotions. I then conclude with some remaining questions and challenges, as well as some practical application of these theories and findings to education.

INTENTION AND CREATION

Once children can understand that something can be considered "art," "music," "theater," "dance," etc., how do they begin to understand where it comes from? (Leaving aside the complex issues art historians continue to debate of what makes something "art"). A critical aspect of all arts performance and presentation is that it is original, and that the intention of the artist matters in both the presentation of the work and the audience's understanding of that work (Hick, 2010). A proven forgery can take the value of a work from millions of dollars down to practically nothing (Newman & Bloom, 2012). Work that is considered "derivative," rather than "inspired" is valued less than work that is wholly originally (Benhamou & Ginsburgh, 2006; Goldman, 2018; Landes, 2000). Unlike other areas of aesthetic understanding and appreciation, there has actually been a considerable amount of work in developmental psychology on children's understanding of intention and creation.

Representation and intention

Understanding of intention is the understanding that marks on a page (or movements on a stage) are meant to represent an object, concept, or idea. Without understanding a work of art is meant to mean something, children cannot understand the artist had an intention for meaning in its creation. Children begin to understand the representational nature of drawings (i.e., that a drawing is supposed to represent an object) as early as 18 months old, correctly labeling an object in the real world after having only seen it previously as a drawing (Preissler & Carey, 2004). Children are able to classify paintings based on representational content early in development (Martlew & Connolly, 1996). This is linked to children's understanding of symbolism (i.e., what is something supposed to represent, a foundational understanding for language; Deloache, 2004), and to their theory of mind (Callaghan & Rochat, 2003; Myers & Liben, 2012). Generally, understanding of symbols begins between 2 ½ and 3 years old (DeLoache, 1987), and understanding of intention in naming an object by 3 years old (Gelman & Bloom, 2000).

In a foundational and innovative study to measure children's understanding of artist intention in determining the content of a work of visual art, Bloom and Markson (1998) studied 3- and 4-year-old children's ability to label two perceptually identical drawings with different captions, depending on their intention when drawing. When drawn simply, a balloon and lollipop are perceptually identical. So, if the viewer has no knowledge of artist intention and is only focusing on pure representational similarity, the drawing they may accidentally mislabel the drawing. In their study, Bloom and Markson found that children take artist intention into account when labeling drawings by 4 years old, and children take metaphoric and representational elements of drawings into account when labeling them. When preschool-aged children are asked to consider other qualities about the artist's emotional state when judging an art product, they are able to do so beginning around 4 years old (Callaghan & Rochat, 2003). Between 4 and 8 years old, children's understanding of visual artists as agents, creating works, increases (Rodway, Kirkham, Schepman, Lambert, & Locke, 2016). Therefore, understanding artist intention in pictures seems to lag slightly behind understanding intention in other, nonartistic domains, perhaps because of the complex nature of defining art and artist intention, or perhaps because viewing art necessarily brings up not only thoughts of artist intention, but also a host of opinions, thoughts, beliefs, and responses in the viewer (Lange-Küttner & Thomas, 1995).

Forgery and copying

Once children understand that an artist has an intention in the creation of a work of art, they can begin to value intention as an essential quality in judgment of value and worth—such that works of art created with the intention of tricking the viewer or without original intention lose worth. For both development of intention understanding and development of judgments about forgery, research has focused mainly on visual arts and objects. An interesting open question is the domain-generality of reasoning about duplication, originality, forgery, and copying. Earlier editions of books are considered more valuable than later editions of books (Bloom, 2010). But are original Broadway cast recordings more valuable than revivals? In movies, remakes and sequels are often critically downgraded, and yet there is economic and popular value in remakes, otherwise they would not continue to be made. Certainly, there are millions of the exact same song sold/streamed every year, and tickets to the same production of the same theatrical performance continue to sell (*Phantom of the Opera* has played 13,589 performances as of May, 2022).[1] There may be more domain-specificity between art forms when it comes to the development of authenticity than in other questions of aesthetic judgment.

Generally, children can track the original versions of objects (Rhemtulla & Hall, 2009) and understand that the name of objects (and other identifying information) can be unique to a particular version of an object (Gutheil, Gelman, Klein, Michos, & Kelaita, 2008). In a study by Hood & Bloom (2008), preschool-aged children brought much loved objects into the lab, and through experimental psychology magic, were presented with a perfect replicant of their original object. Children happily accepted the new, replicant object if it was not an attachment object. However, they significantly preferred their own attachment object to a duplicate. Similarly, they preferred the original version of an object once owned by Queen Elizabeth II, but not other original objects when compared with their duplicates. This shows that by age 6, children have a cognitive understanding of originality, and a preference for originals over forgeries. Yet the more complicated question of how children understand multiple recordings of the same symphony, revivals of plays, shot-for-shot remakes of earlier movies, or even the fact that many people can watch the same television show over and over, is unknown.

PREFERENCES AND JUDGMENTS OF VALUE

Adults' understanding of whether a piece of art was made on purpose, or with intention beneath the physical appearance/performance of the art underlies their judgments of values and their preferences for the art (e.g., Hawley-Dolan & Winner, 2011; Nissel, Hawley-Dolan, & Winner, 2016). When do children start to understand and appreciate what is "good" and what is "talent"? How is that tied in with their understanding of author and artist intentionality? Across art forms, there are multiple developmental variables to consider. Abstract art, atonal music, contemporary dance, and experimental theater are nonrepresentational, and often require extensive cultural knowledge or an informed guide to place them in context for the viewer, to help them recognize the works' importance. Particularly as new formats and nontraditional works are created, there is a conversation at the highest academic levels of training of what constitutes art, and how it is interpreted through the lens of history and culture. Naïve adult judgments differ from expert judgments across a wide variety of artistic modes and genres (Augustin & Leder, 2006; Pihko et al., 2011; Winston & Cupchik, 1992). Certainly, therefore, naïve children without multiple graduate level courses in art history and criticism will not match cultural consensus on what constitutes "good" art.

Yet despite this reasonable claim, it may be preferences in naïve judgments of art change very little over development. Several exemplary research studies have found that even infants show similar preferences to adults in fundamental aspects of music and visual arts. When comparing original masterworks of nonrepresentational art to altered forms of the same paintings, infants at age 6 and 10 months and adults preferred original masterworks ((Krentz & Earl, 2013). This aligns with theories that processing fluency leads to preferences in art (Ramachandran & Hirstein, 1999). Original masterworks are likely to encourage processing fluency more than in their experimentally altered form. Earlier work on children's evaluation of paintings suggested that children first prefer work based on content they enjoy, then on realistic representation, and finally on culturally indicated markers such as style and composition (Machotka, 1966). Children prefer representational and realistic paintings (Kuscevic, Kardum, & Brajcic, 2014; Parsons, 1987); even children as young as 4 years old can distinguish work by artists from similar work by children or animals, and chose the work by artists as better (although it is not necessarily the work they like more) (Nissel et al., 2016).

Yet changes over development in appreciation and liking for art may not represent development per se, but rather general human instability in preferences for art. In a cross-sectional study, (Pugach, Leder, & Graham, 2017) compared young children, adolescents, undergraduates, younger adults, and elderly adults' preferences for painted and photographed landscapes and portraits. The participants ranked the pictures and paintings from least to most favorite twice, with a separation of two weeks. Across age groups, there was a rank change of at least one item, with young children showing slightly more than two rank changes. This shows more stability in young adults' aesthetic preference and liking compared with young children's, but still low test–retest reliability in aesthetic preferences.

In music, preferences for art music, jazz, and rock may not change significantly between even first grade and college, although there is a slight dip across genre in liking at grade 6 (LeBlanc, Sims, Siivola, & Obert, 1996). However, as young as 6 months of age, infants already show stable preferences, preferring consonance over dissonance, infant-directed music, and music accompanied by synchronous movement (Phillips-Silver & Trainor, 2005; Trainor, 1996; Trainor & Heinmiller, 1998), suggesting that these are core components to aesthetic liking. By 6 years old, children prefer tonal to atonal music, judging it as "prettier" (Zenatti, 1991), and prefer pieces in major mode to those in minor mode, rating them as more beautiful and happier (Nieminen, Istók, Brattico, & Tervaniemi, 2011). Similarly, in poetry, one of the few experimental studies shows that by 6 and 8 years old, at both age groups, children prefer poetry that uses devices such as alliteration, rhyming, and rhythm, over modified poems that do not, and this preference is stronger at 8 years old than at 6 years old (Jusczyk, 1977).

However, there does not seem to be much work in the development of judgments and liking for theater or dance. What is interesting is that while music and visual arts can be isolated and experienced in a lab space, at the time and place of the audience's choosing, theater and dance take place in a separated space, at a particular time. They are necessarily ephemeral experiences. While performances can be filmed and shown at a later time, this is not the primary way in which these art forms are experienced, while music can be experienced live or by recording, and high-quality/digital reproductions of artworks can be easily experienced outside of a museum. How this might affect judgment is unknown.

Understanding Emotion in Art

Apart from personal preferences and judgments of value, an important aspect of understanding and appreciating art is understanding its emotional content, and the artist's communicative intention. Children develop understanding of others' emotions, and the ability to read those emotions, slowly and in parallel with theory of mind and personal understanding of emotions' causes, consequences, and nonverbal cues (Denham, 1998; Denham, Zoller, & Couchoud, 1994; Rosnay & Harris, 2002). This development could predict the reading of emotions in art forms in which human cues are present—such as dance and theater, and perhaps the playing of live music. However, research in mainstream developmental psychology cannot provide evidence directly for the reading of emotions within recorded music or visual art—here, understanding of representational cues and ability to pull out artist intention and cultural norms is likely much more important.

Given many findings in this area are focused on processing fluency (which develops with age) and visual processing of stimuli (which is available early in development), it is surprising there are only a few developmental models of aesthetic emotion. In visual arts, preschool-aged children can recognize simple emotional content of both abstract and realistic visual art as early as 3 years old, and continue to improve through preschool (Pouliou, Bonoti, & Nikonanou, 2018). In music, some work has found children at 6 years old use rhythmic activity as well as meter to correctly determine emotion in music (Kratus, 1993). Other work has shown more developmental progression, where young children at 3–4 years old cannot distinguish happy from sad music, while 5-year-olds distinguish via tempo, and 6–8-year-old children use both tempo and mode to determine the positive or negative valence of music (Dalla Bella, Peretz, Rousseau, & Gosselin, 2001; Gregory, Worrall, & Sarge, 1996). When compared with adult reasoning about the emotional content of music, 6-year-old children agree with adults on positive and negative emotional categories, while four year olds only agree on happy segments (although girls also read fear in music better than boys) (Cunningham & Sterling, 1988), and the authors note that the patterns found in their study match broader emotion understanding in children outside of art forms. However, when children need to express emotions through music, they seem to focus on interpersonal communication expression, rather than musical expression, at least between the ages of 4 and 12 years old (Adachi & Trehub, 1998).

Lagerlöf & Djerf (2009) investigated how children between the ages of 4 and 8 years old understood the performance of emotions in dance movements by professional dancers. Four-year-old children were less able to label basic emotions correctly, but 5-year-olds performed at almost adult levels, as did 8-year-olds. This matches the understanding of emotions expressed generally (joy, anger, fear, and sadness) in everyday life. Basic research on children's understanding of emotions show that they use bodies and dynamic expression of emotion more than simple facial expressions, but these are with prototypical (i.e., not artistic) exemplars (Nelson & Russell, 2011b, 2011a). When investigating dance movements specifically, work by Boone & Cunningham (1998) showed that 4 year olds could correctly detect sadness; 5 year olds could detect sadness, fear, and happiness; and 8 year olds showed equivalent detection of emotion through dance as adults.

Key to remember is the large amount of cultural knowledge that children will have already processed by this age—given the universality of music (Dutton, 2009). It may not be that children have a maturational or inherent progression from less to more emotional understanding and comprehension from art, but rather they are simply learning the facts of their culture—which elements of which art forms are connected to which elements of which emotions.

Multiple questions remain in children's understanding of emotionality in artworks. Future work should focus on what cues children are using, across art forms, to understand emotion in various art forms. Similarly, whether development of emotion understanding in music is parallel, separate, or integrated with understanding in dance, visual arts, and theater is completely unknown. Finally, the relationship between understanding emotions in artworks and understanding emotions in daily life (i.e., theory of mind and empathy) is unstudied.

DEVELOPMENT OF AESTHETIC EMOTIONS

Separate from being able to read emotion in art is the experience of emotion in response to art—the so called "aesthetic emotions." This is distinguished too from simple liking or judgment of "goodness" or "value" in art. Aesthetic emotional development is a complex phenomenon, involving understanding of stimulus, context, and intraindividual components (Jacobsen, 2006). Aesthetic appreciation is thought to rely on cognitive understanding of a work (Heid, 2005; Parsons, 1987), and in the visual arts, at least, research has found that children's responses to art move from emotionally driven to cognitively driven (Schabmann et al., 2016). There is no reason why this should not be true generally across art forms. Outside of art appreciation, children gain in emotion regulation, emotional control, executive functions, and information-processing skills throughout developmental maturation (Denham, 1998; Zelazo, Carlson, & Kesek, 2008). These developments would and could also allow children to move from emotion to cognition in their processing of emotions in all forms of art (i.e., from simple emotional reaction to more complex, informed emotional understanding).

Previous theories of aesthetic appreciate have proposed children must move past egocentrism in liking, through preferences for veridical realism, into emotional realism, and then into cultural-based judgment in order to truly develop aesthetic emotions (although this was specific to visual arts, as discussion of realism in music or dance is harder to convey; Parsons, 1987). Given the continuing need to define, in adulthood, the range of emotions that occur in aesthetic contexts (Phillips-Silver & Trainor, 2005; Trainor, 1996; Trainor & Heinmiller, 1998), there is a similar need to understand not just *whether or not* children have aesthetic responses to art, dance, theater, and the like, but what is the range, type, intensity, and meta understanding of such aesthetic emotions. Children can obviously experience joy, disgust, terror, awe, empathy, in their daily lives, but it is unknown whether and when children experience these emotions in response to artistic stimuli. Perhaps children experience these emotions but do not know how to express them; perhaps they only have simple labels, linguistically, to express complex inner feelings; or perhaps it is only with the development of more complex language that children can begin to understand their more complex feelings, both generally and within the aesthetic realm (Pons, Lawson, Harris, & De Rosnay, 2003; Rosnay & Harris, 2002; Widen & Russell, 2008). For nonaesthetic emotions, development is relatively slow, with children gaining in understanding of the causes and consequences of emotions during preschool (Russell, 1990; Widen & Russell, 2010), and recognition and understanding of emotions continuing through adolescence (Crone & Dahl, 2012; Thomas, De Bellis, Graham, & LaBar, 2007).

One interesting paradox within aesthetic reasoning is that of benign masochism (Rozin, Guillot, Fincher, Rozin, & Tsukayama, 2013), or why individuals seek out art that will make them feel negative emotional states that they would otherwise want to avoid in real life (such as terror, or disgust). Children may or may not have the cognitive ability to distance themselves from emotional content through understanding it as fiction, and then embrace the qualities of the negative aspects of the art in order to enjoy it (Menninghaus et al., 2017). In fact, no research I know of has investigated whether children would ever seek out or enjoy art that makes them feel aversive emotions. Children's negative aesthetic emotions have been studied almost entirely in response to aggressive or violent media (e.g., Bushman, Gollwitzer, & Cruz, 2015; Christakis & Zimmerman, 2007; Coyne, 2016), but without a theory of whether children enjoy, seek out, or engage in metacognitive reflection about such aesthetic responses. Future research will have to determine when, how, and whether children understand, enjoy, and seek out negative media for the purposes of pleasure.

MAJOR CHALLENGES, GOALS, AND SUGGESTIONS

Remaining questions

The list of questions still to be investigated in this area is giant. To begin, there is no research investigating how aesthetic appreciation develops from the relatively universal childhood artistic activities of moving ones' body, singing lullabies, scribbling, and pretend play. How do individuals develop from a child engaging in or looking at art to an adult level of aesthetic appreciation when the child is not an artist? While there is some research on the development of artists in particular, how the nonartist (but art-appreciating) individual develops their sense of aesthetic reasoning is unknown. Similarly, the simple question of what children can appreciate about art, separately from their creation of it, is unknown. Questions of attention and pleasure, in particular, are understudied, while cognitive understanding of art and its creation (and uniqueness) is more understood. As is true with other questions in empirical research on the arts, the majority of work in this field has focused on music, with a strong showing by visual arts, while theater and dance are almost nonexistent.

Also needed are more focused theories of how aesthetic development is similar and different from other forms of development—cognitive processing, social knowledge, and emotional understanding—where there is extensive knowledge in the research literature. As such, studies where multiple forms of development, aesthetic, cognitive, social, are measured simultaneously, and over time, are necessary. For example, how does the development of theory of mind, particularly intentionality understanding, underlie, predict, or appear in parallel to understanding of intention in art specifically?

Finally, a large caveat to all of this review is this question: When are children *not* in appreciation of the artistic and aesthetic qualities of the world around them? Children live in a world of color, shape, movement, song, and play. Their lives are necessarily artistic, as might be defined by adults. While they may not be judging these experiences as artistic, they are engaging with them in a way that adults may engage with the arts. This global attention to the environment (what Gopnik, 2016 labels "lantern consciousness" rather than adult-like "spotlight consciousness") creates input to children that will necessarily shape their understand of the arts, albeit not formally.

Ties to emotional, social, and cognitive development

Aesthetic judgment is both cultural and personal; objective and subjective. It plays with basic perception and preferences along with complex inter- and intrapersonal understanding and reading of subtext and intention. Isolated theories of cognitive development are inappropriate for aesthetics, as the emotional experience of dance, theater, and art is central to engaging with it. Yet also theories of emotional development are incomplete, as engaging with a piece of music or visual arts requires a cognitive understanding, appreciation, and processing. Social theories, too, provide the situational and cultural context for development of aesthetic understanding, but are necessarily incomplete for the same emotional and cognitive reasons listed above. Therein lies the problem—there are necessarily gaps in the literature because it is impossible to cover all cognitive, social, and emotional development, across art forms, across age groups, at once. Aesthetics brings together these various subdisciplines of developmental psychology, perhaps, in a way that other areas of development do not. This may be its key— aesthetics and the arts cross areas of development and subdisciplines that falsely divide up child development.

Any understanding of aesthetic reasoning, preference, and judgment must take into the account the development of such processes outside of the arts. As is so often in developmental psychology, the question of whether preferences and aesthetic reasoning are separate developmental milestones from more underlying abilities such as executive functioning or social reasoning or awareness of emotions remains underexplored. The major challenge of any theory of the development of aesthetic reasoning is that it must determine whether there is a separation in the development of aesthetic reasoning per se, from general cognitive or social-emotional reasoning. Obviously, all aesthetic reasoning is based on cognitive and social abilities, skills, and reasoning. The question of whether such reasoning is separable and unique from well-established developmental skills is wide open (Parsons, 1987). Is the understanding of intention and forgery in art distinct from theory of mind understanding? Are preferences for beauty in aesthetics different from preferences for beauty in judgments of faces, or even from cultural understanding of products generally? And given the connections between artistic engagement in childhood and adult artistic understanding, is the pathway from scribbling to drawing, from pretend play to acting, from improvised to choreographed dance a qualitative one, or a quantitative one? Do children simply develop understanding and skills over time, through a typical course, or is there a distinct difference between a child scribbling a picture of Mommy in preschool and an adult artist painting in her studio (keeping in mind Picasso's famous quote that everyone is an artist). Is there a qualitative difference between pretend play and adult acting? There is of course evidence that childhood pretend play is related to adult creativity (Russ, Robins, & Christiano, 1999), but such measurement has been focused on more cognitive aspects of creativity in adulthood, rather than artistic product.

Children's aesthetic reasoning and appreciation is much bemoaned as having too little research (practically every article included in this review makes such a statement at some point). It is true that most textbooks in developmental psychology and most academic journals in developmental psychology never mention any art form (Goldstein, Lerner, & Winner, 2017; Lin & Thomas, 2002). "Real" art is thought of as too complex, and "children's" art, not actually art at all. Yet it is not true that there is *no* research, as the work reviewed here belies that claim. The question is how to create a coherent theory— one that goes beyond any individual art form or an overt reliance on cognitive development, ignoring emotional aspects. Comparative studies across art form, comparing by feature (e.g., realism, or emotional information, or artist intention for aesthetic response) within participant could begin to clarify such questions, and help the field progress to a unified theory of aesthetic development.

NOTE

1. https://www.ibdb.com/broadway-production/the-phantom-of-the-opera-4491.

REFERENCES

Adachi, M., & Trehub, S. E. (1998). Children's expression of emotion in song. *Psychology of Music, 26*(2), 133–153. https://doi.org/10.1177/0305735698262003

Augustin, D., & Leder, H. (2006). Art expertise: A study of concepts and conceptual spaces. *Psychology Science, 48*(2), 135.

Benhamou, F., & Ginsburgh, V. (2006). Copies of artworks: the case of paintings and prints. *Handbook of the Economics of Art and Culture, 1*, 253–283.

Bloom, P., & Markson, L. (1998). Intention and analogy in children's naming of pictorial representations. *Psychological Science, 9*(3), 200.

Bloom, Paul. (2010). *How pleasure works: The new science of why we like what we like.* London: Random House.

Boone, R. T., & Cunningham, J. G. (1998). Children's decoding of emotion in expressive body movement: The development of cue attunement. *Developmental Psychology, 34*(5), 1007.

Bushman, B. J., Gollwitzer, M., & Cruz, C. (2015). There is broad consensus: Media researchers agree that violent media increase aggression in children, and pediatricians and parents concur. *Psychology of Popular Media Culture*, 4(3), 200.

Callaghan, T. C., & Rochat, P. (2003). Traces of the artist: Sensitivity to the role of the artist in children's pictorial reasoning. *British Journal of Developmental Psychology*, 21(3), 415–445.

Christakis, D. A., & Zimmerman, F. J. (2007). Violent television viewing during preschool is associated with antisocial behavior during school age. *Pediatrics*, 120(5), 993–999.

Colarusso, C. A. (1993). Play in adulthood. *The Psychoanalytic Study of the Child*, 48(1), 225–245. https://doi.org/10.1080/00797308.1993.11822386

Coyne, S. M. (2016). Effects of viewing relational aggression on television on aggressive behavior in adolescents: A three-year longitudinal study. *Developmental Psychology*, 52(2), 284.

Crone, E. A., & Dahl, R. E. (2012). Understanding adolescence as a period of social–affective engagement and goal flexibility. *Nature Reviews Neuroscience*, 13(9), 636–650. https://doi.org/10.1038/nrn3313

Cunningham, J. G., & Sterling, R. S. (1988). Developmental change in the understanding of affective meaning in music. *Motivation and Emotion*, 12(4), 399–413. https://doi.org/10.1007/BF00992362

Dalla Bella, S., Peretz, I., Rousseau, L., & Gosselin, N. (2001). A developmental study of the affective value of tempo and mode in music. *Cognition*, 80(3), B1–B10. https://doi.org/10.1016/S0010-0277(00)00136-0

Davis, J. (1997). Drawing's demise: U-shaped development in graphic symbolization. *Studies in Art Education*, 38(3), 132–157.

DeLoache, J. S. (1987). Rapid change in the symbolic functioning of very young children. *Science*, 238(4833), 1556–1557.

Deloache, J. S. (2004). Becoming symbol-minded. *Trends in Cognitive Science*, 8(2), 66–70. https://doi.org/10.1016/j.tics.2003.12.004

Denham, S. A. (1998). *Emotional development in young children*. New York: Guilford Press.

Denham, S. A., Zoller, D., & Couchoud, E. A. (1994). Socialization of preschoolers' emotion understanding. *Developmental Psychology*, 30(6), 928.

Dutton, D. (2009). *The art instinct: Beauty, pleasure, and human evolution*. Oxford, England: Oxford University Press.

Fletcher-Watson, B. (2016). *"More like a poem than a play": towards a dramaturgy of performing arts for Early Years* (PhD Thesis). The University of St Andrews, St Andrews, Scotland.

Gardner, H. (1990). *Art education and human development* (Vol. 3). New York: Getty Publications.

Gelman, S. A., & Bloom, P. (2000). Young children are sensitive to how an object was created when deciding what to name it. *Cognition*, 76(2), 91–103. https://doi.org/10.1016/S0010-0277(00)00071-8

Goldman, A. (2018). *Aesthetic value*. London: Routledge.

Goldstein, T. R., & Winner, E. (2009). Living in alternative and inner worlds: Early signs of acting talent. *Creativity Research Journal*, 21(1), 117–124. https://doi.org/10.1080/10400410802633749

Goldstein, T. R., Lerner, M. D., & Winner, E. (2017). The arts as a venue for developmental science: Realizing a latent opportunity. *Child Development*, 88(5), 1505–1512. https://doi.org/10.1111/cdev.12884

Gopnik, A. (2016). *The gardener and the carpenter: What the new science of child development tells us about the relationship between parents and children*. London: Macmillan.

Gregory, A. H., Worrall, L., & Sarge, A. (1996). The development of emotional responses to music in young children. *Motivation and Emotion, 20*(4), 341–348. https://doi.org/10.1007/BF02856522

Gutheil, G., Gelman, S. A., Klein, E., Michos, K., & Kelaita, K. (2008). Preschoolers' use of spatiotemporal history, appearance, and proper name in determining individual identity. *Cognition, 107*(1), 366–380. https://doi.org/10.1016/j.cognition.2007.07.014

Hawley-Dolan, A., & Winner, E. (2011). Seeing the mind behind the art: People can distinguish abstract expressionist paintings from highly similar paintings by children, chimps, monkeys, and elephants. *Psychological Science, 22*(4), 435–441.

Heid, K. (2005). Aesthetic development: A cognitive experience. *Art Education, 58*(5), 48–53.

Hick, D. H. (2010). Forgery and appropriation in art. *Philosophy Compass, 5*(12), 1047–1056.

Hood, B. M., & Bloom, P. (2008). Children prefer certain individuals over perfect duplicates. *Cognition, 106*(1), 455–462. https://doi.org/10.1016/j.cognition.2007.01.012

Jacobsen, T. (2006). *Bridging the arts and sciences: A framework for the psychology of aesthetics.* Cambridge, MA: MIT Press.

Jolley, R. P., Barlow, C. M., Rotenberg, K. J., & Cox, M. V. (2016). Linear and U-shape trends in the development of expressive drawing from preschoolers to normative and artistic adults. *Psychology of Aesthetics, Creativity, and the Arts, 10*(3), 309.

Jusczyk, P. W. (1977). Rhymes and reasons: Some aspects of the child's appreciation of poetic form. *Developmental Psychology, 13*(6), 599.

Kaufman, J. C., & Baer, J. (2004). The amusement park theoretical (APT) model of creativity. *The International Journal of Creativity & Problem Solving, 14*(2), 15–25.

Kindler, A. M. (2000). From the U-Curve to dragons: Culture and understanding of artistic development. *Visual Arts Research, 26*(2), 15–28.

Kratus, J. (1993). A developmental study of children's interpretation of emotion in music. *Psychology of Music, 21*(1), 3–19. https://doi.org/10.1177/0305735693021001

Krentz, U. C., & Earl, R. K. (2013). The baby as beholder: Adults and infants have common preferences for original art. *Psychology of Aesthetics, Creativity, and the Arts, 7*(2), 181–190. https://doi.org/10.1037/a0030691

Kuscevic, D., Kardum, G., & Brajcic, M. (2014). Visual preferences of young school children for paintings from the 20th century. *Creativity Research Journal, 26*(3), 297–304. https://doi.org/10.1080/10400419.2014.929410

Landes, W. M. (2000). Copyright, borrowed images, and appropriation art: an economic approach. *George Mason Law Review, 9,* 1–24.

Lange-Küttner, C. E., & Thomas, G. V. (1995). *Drawing and looking: Theoretical approaches to pictorial representation in children.* London: Harvester Wheatsheaf.

Lagerlöf, I., & Djerf, M. (2009). Children's understanding of emotion in dance. *European Journal of Developmental Psychology, 6,* 409–431.

LeBlanc, A., Sims, W. L., Siivola, C., & Obert, M. (1996). Music style preferences of different age listeners. *Journal of Research in Music Education, 44*(1), 49–59. https://doi.org/10.2307/3345413

Lin, S. f., & Thomas, G. v. (2002). Development of understanding of popular graphic art: A study of everyday aesthetics in children, adolescents, and young adults. *International Journal of Behavioral Development, 26*(3), 278–287. https://doi.org/10.1080/01650250143000157

Machotka, P. (1966). Aesthetic criteria in childhood: Justifications of preference. *Child Development, 37,* 877–885.

Martlew, M., & Connolly, K. J. (1996). Human figure drawings by schooled and unschooled children in Papua New Guinea. *Child Development, 67*(6), 2743–2762. https://doi.org/10.2307/1131750

Menninghaus, W., Wagner, V., Hanich, J., Wassiliwizky, E., Jacobsen, T., & Koelsch, S. (2017). The distancing-embracing model of the enjoyment of negative emotions in art reception. *Behavioral and Brain Sciences, 40*, e347. https://doi.org/10.1017/S0140525X17000309

Milbrath, C. (1998). *Patterns of artistic development in children: Comparative studies of talent.* Cambridge, England: Cambridge University Press.

Myers, L. J., & Liben, L. S. (2012). Graphic symbols as "the mind on paper": Links between children's interpretive theory of mind and symbol understanding. *Child Development, 83*(1), 186–202.

Nelson, N. L., & Russell, J. A. (2011a). Preschoolers' use of dynamic facial, bodily, and vocal cues to emotion. *Journal of Experimental Child Psychology, 110*(1), 52–61.

Nelson, N. L., & Russell, J. A. (2011b). Putting motion in emotion: Do dynamic presentations increase preschooler's recognition of emotion? *Cognitive Development, 26*(3), 248–259.

Newman, G. E., & Bloom, P. (2012). Art and authenticity: The importance of originals in judgments of value. *Journal of Experimental Psychology: General, 141*(3), 558.

Nieminen, S., Istók, E., Brattico, E., Tervaniemi, M., & Huotilainen, M. (2011). The development of aesthetic responses to music and their underlying neural and psychological mechanisms. *Cortex, 47*(9), 1138–1146.

Nissel, J., Hawley-Dolan, A., & Winner, E. (2016). Can young children distinguish abstract expressionist art from superficially similar works by preschoolers and animals? *Journal of Cognition and Development, 17*(1), 18–29.

Pariser, D., & van den Berg, A. (1997). The mind of the beholder: Some provisional doubts about the U-curved aesthetic development thesis. *Studies in Art Education, 38*(3), 158. https://doi.org/10.2307/1320291

Parsons, M. J. (1976). A Suggestion concerning the development of aesthetic experience in children. *The Journal of Aesthetics and Art Criticism, 34*(3), 305–314. https://doi.org/10.2307/430012

Parsons, M. J. (1987). *How we understand art: A cognitive developmental account of aesthetic experience.* Cambridge, England: Cambridge University Press.

Phillips-Silver, J., & Trainor, L. J. (2005). Feeling the beat: Movement influences infant rhythm perception. *Science, 308*(5727), 1430.

Piaget, J., & Inhelder, B. (1969). *The psychology of the child* (Vol. 5001). New York: Basic Books.

Picard, D., & Gauthier, C. (2012). The development of expressive drawing abilities during childhood and into adolescence. *Child Development Research*, Article ID 925063, https://doi.org/10.1155/2012/925063

Pihko, E., Virtanen, A., Saarinen, V.-M., Pannasch, S., Hirvenkari, L., Tossavainen, T., ... Hari, R. (2011). Experiencing art: The influence of expertise and painting abstraction level. *Frontiers in Human Neuroscience, 5*, 94.

Pons, F., Lawson, J., Harris, P. L., & De Rosnay, M. (2003). Individual differences in children's emotion understanding: Effects of age and language. *Scandinavian Journal of Psychology, 44*(4), 347–353.

Pouliou, D., Bonoti, F., & Nikonanou, N. (2018). Do preschoolers recognize the emotional expressiveness of colors in realistic and abstract art paintings? *The Journal of Genetic Psychology, 179*(2), 53–61. https://doi.org/10.1080/00221325.2018.1424704

Preissler, M. A., & Carey, S. (2004). Do both pictures and words function as symbols for 18-and 24-month-old children? *Journal of Cognition and Development*, *5*, 185–212.

Pugach, C., Leder, H., & Graham, D. J. (2017). How stable are human aesthetic preferences across the lifespan? *Frontiers in Human Neuroscience*, *11*. https://doi.org/10.3389/fnhum.2017.00289

Ramachandran, V. S., & Hirstein, W. (1999). The science of art: A neurological theory of aesthetic experience. *Journal of Consciousness Studies*, *6*(6–7), 15–51.

Rhemtulla, M., & Hall, D. G. (2009). Monkey business: Children's use of character identity to infer shared properties. *Cognition*, *113*(2), 167–176. https://doi.org/10.1016/j.cognition.2009.07.012

Rodway, P., Kirkham, J., Schepman, A., Lambert, J., & Locke, A. (2016). The development of shared liking of representational but not abstract art in primary school children and their justifications for liking. *Frontiers in Human Neuroscience*, *10*, 21. https://doi.org/10.3389/fnhum.2016.00021

Root-Bernstein, M., & Root-Bernstein, R. (2006). Imaginary world play in childhood and maturity and its impact on adult creativity. *Creativity Research Journal*, *18*(4), 405–425.

Rosnay, M. D., & Harris, P. L. (2002). Individual differences in children's understanding of emotion: The roles of attachment and language. *Attachment & Human Development*, *4*(1), 39–54.

Rozin, P., Guillot, L., Fincher, K., Rozin, A., & Tsukayama, E. (2013). Glad to be sad, and other examples of benign masochism. *Judgment and Decision Making*, *8*(4), 439.

Russ, S. W., Robins, A. L., & Christiano, B. A. (1999). Pretend play: Longitudinal prediction of creativity and affect in fantasy in children. *Creativity Research Journal*, *12*(2), 129–139.

Russell, J. A. (1990). The preschooler's understanding of the causes and consequences of emotion. *Child Development*, *61*(6), 1872–1881.

Sandberg, A. (2001). Play memories from childhood to adulthood. *Early Child Development and Care*, *167*(1), 13–25. https://doi.org/10.1080/0300443011670102

Schabmann, A., Gerger, G., Schmidt, B. M., Wögerer, E., Osipov, I., & Leder, H. (2016). Where does it come from? Developmental aspects of art appreciation. *International Journal of Behavioral Development*, *40*(4), 313–323.

Simonton, D. K. (1994). *Greatness: Who makes history and why*. New York: Guilford Press.

Smith, E. D., & Lillard, A. S. (2012). Play on: Retrospective reports of the persistence of pretend play into middle childhood. *Journal of Cognition and Development*, *13*(4), 524–549.

Taylor, M. (2001). *Imaginary companions and the children who create them*. Oxford, England: Oxford University Press.

Taylor, M., & Mannering, A. M. (2006). Of Hobbes and Harvey: The imaginary companions created by children and adults. In A. Göncü & S. Gaskins (Eds.), *The Jean Piaget symposium series. Play and development: Evolutionary, sociocultural, and functional perspectives* (pp. 227–245). Mahaw, NJ: Lawrence Erlbaum Associates Publishers.

Thomas, L. A., De Bellis, M. D., Graham, R., & LaBar, K. S. (2007). Development of emotional facial recognition in late childhood and adolescence. *Developmental Science*, *10*(5), 547–558.

Trainor, L. J. (1996). Infant preferences for infant-directed versus noninfant-directed play songs and lullabies. *Infant Behavior and Development*, *19*(1), 83–92.

Trainor, L. J., & Heinmiller, B. M. (1998). The development of evaluative responses to music: Infants prefer to listen to consonance over dissonance. *Infant Behavior and Development*, *21*(1), 77–88.

Widen, S. C., & Russell, J. A. (2008). Children acquire emotion categories gradually. *Cognitive Development, 23*(2), 291–312.

Widen, S. C., & Russell, J. A. (2010). Children's scripts for social emotions: Causes and consequences are more central than are facial expressions. *British Journal of Developmental Psychology, 28*(3), 565–581.

Winner, E. (1996). *Gifted children* (Vol. 1). New York: Basic Books.

Winston, A. S., & Cupchik, G. C. (1992). The evaluation of high art and popular art by naive and experienced viewers. *Visual Arts Research, 18,* 1–14.

Young, S. (2004). "It's a bit like flying": developing participatory theatre with the under-twos: A case study of Oily Cart. *Research in Drama Education, 9*(1), 13–28.

Young, S. (2005). Changing tune: Reconceptualizing music with under three-year olds. *International Journal of Early Years Education, 13*(3), 289–303.

Young, S., Street, A., & Davies, E. (2007). The Music One-to-One project: Developing approaches to music with parents and under-two-year-olds. *European Early Childhood Education Research Journal, 15*(2), 253–267. https://doi.org/10.1080/13502930701321675

Zelazo, P. D., Carlson, S. M., & Kesek, A. (2008). The development of executive function in childhood. In C. A. Nelson & M. Luciana (Eds.), *Developmental cognitive neuroscience. Handbook of developmental cognitive neuroscience* (pp. 553–574). Cambridge, MA: MIT Press.

Zenatti, A. (1991). Aesthetic judgements and musical cognition: A comparative study in samples of French and British children and adults. *Psychology of Music, 19*(1), 65–73. https://doi.org/10.1177/0305735691191005

....

CHAPTER 35

THE INFLUENCE OF EXPERTISE ON AESTHETICS

....

AARON KOZBELT

OF the many ways of slicing individual differences in aesthetic cognition, the impact of expertise is surely one of the most powerful. Extensive research has revealed profound changes in ability resulting from accumulated experience and knowledge in domains as diverse as chess, mathematics, baseball, and physics (Ericsson, Hoffman, Kozbelt, & Williams, 2018). As this chapter will show, aesthetic domains are no exception, and there are many benefits to adopting an expertise approach toward them. Such a perspective highlights timely debate points on broad psychological issues like domain-generality versus domain-specificity, receptive versus productive processes, and evolutionary constraints on higher-order cognition. Further, moving beyond a predominant research emphasis on aesthetic response, expertise also impacts performance and creativity, since one's capacity to create culturally significant aesthetic artifacts invariably rests on a hard-won foundation of acquired skill and knowledge. Finally, while an expertise account provides a rich layer modulating descriptive models of aesthetic engagement, fully teasing out its implications informs the ultimate scope and prospects for how humans interact with and create aesthetic objects across different domains, modalities, and media, in an increasingly pluralistic aesthetic world (e.g., Danto, 1997).

In this chapter, I review how expertise impacts aesthetic experience and cognition. I shall first lay out some well-established methods and findings from the extensive research literature on expertise and expert performance and discuss how these relate to empirical aesthetics. Next, I describe general psychological mechanisms and models of aesthetic processing, emphasizing the potential role of expertise in modulating aesthetic cognition within such models. Since expertise is highly domain-specific, I then organize my exploration by proceeding sequentially through a range of aesthetic domains: visual art, design, architecture, photography, music, dance, writing, acting, and film. In each case, I consider behavioral measures (self-report and performance indices) and neuroscientific findings where available. When possible, I discuss not only aesthetic response but also performance and creativity as aspects vital for understanding expertise and its effects in aesthetic domains. After reviewing the aforementioned domains individually, I attempt to integrate these points by highlighting consistent patterns of results and by briefly considering a few unresolved conceptual issues.

Before proceeding, however, a few preliminaries cautioning against facile conclusions about expertise and aesthetic cognition are in order. First, while many domains have an easy claim on being broadly "aesthetic," they are not uniformly or purely so in the activities they encompass. Some, like architecture, are characterized by strong functional constraints that have little to do with specifically aesthetic choices; others, like photography or cinema, rely on modern technology and are of recent historical origin, in contrast to the long evolutionary backdrop for activities like painting, song, and storytelling. Second, "expertise" is not always carefully defined in the cognitive or aesthetics research literatures. While many studies discuss the differentiating effects of knowledge in aesthetic response, to make any headway, one must often consider finer distinctions—between transient and unstructured *exposure*, some degree of knowledge- or training-based *experience*, and full-blown *expertise*.[1] Such distinctions are often glossed over, and since true world-class experts are very rare, people with some domain-specific knowledge are often used as proxies for true experts in studies (Kaufman, Baer, Cropley, Reiter-Palmon, & Sinnett, 2013). Indeed, most novices have paltry knowledge of the arts anyway (Smith & Smith, 2006). Third, all aesthetic domains involve productions that vary enormously in quality and impact, to such a degree that some researchers might be loath to give bona fide "aesthetic" status to lower-echelon works. Similar distinctions apply in establishing continua of expertise in individuals' aesthetic production or reception—a point echoing Kaufman and Beghetto's (2009) demarcation of different levels of creative achievement, from "mini-c" and "little-c" to "pro-c" and "Big-C."

Such caveats highlight a longstanding failure of deep integration between the empirical aesthetics and expertise literatures. Expertise research has traditionally focused on advantages in sensory, motoric, memory, or problem-solving processes independent of aesthetics per se.[2] Despite fleeting points of contact and lip service to their mutual relevance, the unsystematic association between the two raises the possibility of more complex and refining interrelations, once these are more fully explored. A primary goal of this chapter is to lay the foundation for such a synthesis, both in summarizing research to date and in identifying promising paths for moving forward.

THE COGNITIVE PSYCHOLOGICAL LITERATURE ON EXPERTISE AND ITS IMPLICATIONS

Classic findings

Since the seminal research on chess grandmasters conducted by de Groot (1946/1965) and Chase and Simon (1973), expertise has been a major area of inquiry within cognitive psychology, and many of the methods and findings from this early work have remained staples of the literature. One common approach is to compare the performance of people who are experts in a domain (like chess) versus those who are nonexperts, on simple but domain-specific tasks. Ideally, these tasks are representative proxies for the main activity of a domain, yield on-demand superior performance from experts, and can be experimentally varied to inform the cognitive structures and mechanisms supporting that performance. For instance, in early studies of chess, a breakthrough finding was that besides playing excellent chess, grandmasters also have an astonishing ability to reconstruct the positions of twenty-some pieces on a mid-game chess board from memory, after having seen the board for just a few seconds. Memory performance was positively correlated with chess-playing skill, and the clustering of several pieces at a time as they were replaced reflected meaningful strategic (rather than just perceptual) patterns, or "chunks." Importantly, when pieces' positions did not reflect familiar mid-game patterns, experts' memory advantage essentially evaporated, and they performed on par with nonexperts.

This ensemble of results suggests that expert performance is attributable to a vast, highly organized domain-specific knowledge base of increasingly complex patterns in memory (Ericsson & Kintsch, 1995). In chess, this consists of tens of thousands of chess-related chunks that are acquired through intensive effort sustained over at least a decade—which is, not coincidentally, about the minimum time to achieve grandmaster status (for updated nuances and qualifications to these approximations, see Gobet & Charness, 2018). Like a large linguistic vocabulary, fluency with these patterns allows an expert to recognize, categorize, remember, understand, abstract, anticipate, and act appropriately when faced with familiar domain-specific situations. Unfamiliar situations do not engage this knowledge base, and experts typically forfeit their advantage. Reliance on pattern recognition reduces experts' cognitive load and obviates a need to search extensively for a next move. This conception of efficient expert performance as rooted in the recognition of familiar patterns, with its concomitant domain-specific fragility, was reinforced in other early studies (e.g., Chi, Feltovich, & Glaser, 1981; Ericsson, Chase, & Faloon, 1981), and it remains the dominant paradigm today.

Subsequent research has developed many details of this theoretical account. For instance, Ericsson and colleagues identified the mechanism of "deliberate practice"—effortful, purposive work to correct weaknesses and achieve mastery, typically under the supervision of a highly qualified teacher—as a primary determinant of high-level expert performance. In one classic study, Ericsson, Krampe, and Tesch-Römer (1993) found that cumulative levels of deliberate practice distinguished different levels of conservatory violinists, without resorting to innate talent as an explanatory factor. More recent research has also revealed how the effects of deliberate practice manifest themselves not only in cognitive changes, but also in physical ones, especially in athletic or other performative domains—as in the larger lung capacities found among singers and brass instrument players (Sundberg, 1987). Neuroimaging research has likewise shown robust changes in the structural and functional properties of the brain associated with the cognitive mechanisms arising from the demands of expertise acquisition (see Bilalić & Campitelli, 2018)—for instance, in the enlarged cortical representation of violinists' left-hand fingers compared with the left thumb, particularly for those violinists who had started training at younger ages (Elbert et al., 1998).

Links to psychological aesthetics, and complications therein

These core findings on expertise have significant implications for psychological aesthetics. For one, scholars in many aesthetic domains have incorporated expertise variables into their research program, at least in some form—indeed, a discussion of that literature will constitute the bulk of this chapter. Second, many provocative assertions about the nature of expertise have direct relevance to important questions about aesthetic cognition. For instance, Ericsson et al.'s (1993) claims about deliberate practice as the main source of high performance were challenged by Winner (1996), who argued that a decisive component of precocious artistic talent is a "rage to master," that is, a strong intrinsic motivation to engage in a preferred activity like music or drawing, which thus conflates talent and practice. Another issue concerns the artificiality of many domains of expertise and how this interacts with the presumed evolved naturalness of human aesthetic cognition. Along these lines, one may wonder about the potential scope of expert knowledge for reshaping aesthetic preferences, and whether extensive expertise is even necessary for full-fledged aesthetic experiences. Yet another point of contention is the prototypically fragile scope of expert advantages, normally taken to be confined to familiar patterns; recent evidence suggests that experts in some aesthetic domains (like drawing: see Kozbelt & Ostrofsky, 2018) may flexibly utilize more general aspects of perceptual processing rather than stereotypically relying on fixed chunks, as in chess.

This last point also speaks to a tension between routinized, efficient aspects of expertise and the creative demands of many aesthetic domains. Simonton (2000) criticized the traditional expertise view as overly rigid and inadequate for explaining cutting-edge creative productivity, with its inherent novelty, unfamiliarity, and uncertainty.[3] Relatedly, the subjectivity of aesthetic response and judgment sometimes makes it challenging to establish reliable expert–novice differences—though some tasks, like remembering musical patterns (Snyder, 2016) or rating paintings that are either modified or unmodified versions of an original (McManus, Cheema, & Stoker, 1993), involve objective criteria (see Kozbelt & Kaufman, 2014).

These and other issues will be taken up at the end of the chapter. For now, let's examine several general psychological mechanisms and models of aesthetic processing and how they situate the effects of expertise, before moving on to a domain-by-domain survey.

EXPERTISE EFFECTS IN GENERAL MECHANISMS AND MODELS OF AESTHETIC RESPONSE

Over the years, psychologists have proposed numerous mechanisms and models to account for patterns of human aesthetic response like preference, judgment, and emotion. Many of these explanations have been imported from other realms within psychology, where they may or may not have been proposed with expertise effects in mind. A longstanding thread in many of these explanations is that general-purpose mental mechanisms are easily adapted toward processing aesthetic stimuli. Emblematic of this viewpoint, Martindale (2007, p. 181) argued, "The laws of aesthetics and cognition are largely isomorphic. Fechner (1876) guessed this to be the case. In founding psychological aesthetics, he set forth a number of principles. He was explicit that most are principles of general psychology, rather than principles of aesthetics per se."

Psychobiological mechanisms

Several influential categories of explanations have been offered along these lines. In terms of sustained and cumulative impact, Berlyne's (1971, 1974) psychobiological model remains probably the best-known general framework, integrating a trove of hard-nosed experimental psychological research on reward, motivation, and action into a unified theory of human aesthetics. In his account, a statistically associated constellation of so-called collative variables (novelty, complexity, conflict, etc.) have strong, consistent effects on people's preferences for various categories of stimuli, frequently taking the form of an inverted U-shape or increasing linear relation, depending on the experiment (but see Nadal, Munar, Marty, & Cela-Conde, 2010). Berlyne and colleagues also explored the effect of expertise within the framework of his model and found, for instance, that experts tend to prefer more complex work (e.g., Hare, 1974; Walker, 1980; see also McWhinnie, 1966). The psychobiological foundations of aesthetics asserted by Berlyne have been echoed in later accounts, like Ramachandran and Hirstein's (1999) "laws of art," which include phenomena like peak shift, isolation, and contrast, some of which also informed Berlyne's model. Martindale's (2007) consolidation of several dozen aesthetic effects under the umbrella of basic neural network properties is another instance of a basic-mechanisms psychobiological approach.

Prototypicality

A second type of model is one emphasizing prototypicality; that is, preference for stimuli that are typical of their category. Prototypicality occurs in natural categories (a robin is a more typical bird than an ostrich), but also with aesthetic stimuli, such as paintings that exemplify an artistic style especially well. Many studies have found positive relations between prototypicality and liking (e.g., Farkas, 2002; Martindale & Moore, 1988; Smith & Melara, 1990; Whitfield, 1983). Expertise can impact assessments of prototypicality, as well as fluency (Bullot & Reber, 2013). However, such individual differences also imply a slippery subjectivity to the construct of aesthetic prototypicality in the first place (see Silvia, 2012): if individuals can differ substantially in their assessments of aesthetic prototypicality, this may call into question the usefulness of prototypicality as a generally applicable aesthetic construct.

Processing fluency

A more recent model is rooted in the construct of processing fluency (Reber, Schwarz, & Winkielman, 2004). This model asserts that stimuli (including aesthetic ones) that are familiar are easier to process, and that this thought process is itself hedonically marked. A key aspect of processing fluency involves differential exposure to artworks. In many cases, familiarity—even in passing—tends to be associated with increases in preference, in line with the classic mere exposure effect (Zajonc, 1968). For instance, in a large-scale ecologically valid study, Cutting (2003) found that long-term incidental exposure to certain Impressionist paintings (in books, advertisements, and so on) was associated with greater levels of liking. Other research likewise speaks to the impact on aesthetic response of frequency of occurrence in the environment, as well as prototypicality. For instance, color preferences reflect the statistics of how much people in general like objects that typically appear in those colors (Palmer, Schloss, & Sammartino, 2012). In such studies, participants are often unaware of the basis of their preferences; indeed, hedonic pleasure is thought to be higher if the source of fluency in processing is unknown and the experience comes as a surprise (Reber, 2012). As with language, developing fluency in aesthetic processing leads to significant changes in individuals' experience and ability when confronting aesthetic works. To the extent that people have a well-developed scheme for processing aesthetic information in a domain, they will prefer harder-to-process exemplars (Axelsson, 2007). Similarly, since experts feel more able to understand challenging artworks, they will tend to find them more interesting than novices do (Silvia, 2005). Even providing basic background information about artworks or artists can also increase liking (Leder, Carbon, & Ripsas, 2006; Millis, 2001; Russell, 2003; Swami, 2013), presumably by way of promoting greater processing fluency.

Leder et al.'s (2004) model of aesthetic processing

Besides such mechanisms, several other psychological models of aesthetic processing have been proposed, which likewise accommodate expertise factors. Of these, probably the best known is Leder, Belke, Oeberts, and Augustin's (2004) model of aesthetic appreciation and aesthetic judgment, and it will be our focus here. It is a stage model, whereby the response to an artwork (typically a work of visual art) is processed sequentially via the usual information-processing pathways of the mind. Specifically, once an artwork is classified as such, the viewer engages in perceptual analysis of its features, implicitly integrates the percept with information in memory (familiarity, prototypicality, etc.), explicitly classifies it in terms of style, interprets its meaning, and evaluates both the quality of the work and his or her emotional response, which is a by-product of the other processing stages. The resulting aesthetic responses then feed back into the viewer's knowledge, taste, and motivation, setting the stage for future encounters and, potentially, expertise development.

Later research has provided further support for the model's tenets, including those about expertise (Leder & Nadal, 2014). For instance, viewers with more experience in art respond in a more flexible and differentiated way across judgment criteria, compared with less experienced viewers (Leder, Gerger, Dressler, & Schabmann, 2012). More experienced viewers also show attenuated emotional responses to images, compared with novices (Leder, Gerger, Brieber, & Schwarz, 2013). Additionally, experts find complex artworks less confusing (Silvia, 2013) and more interesting (Axelsson, 2007).

Aspects of Leder et al.'s (2004) model echo Parsons's (1987) five-stage characterization of the development of aesthetic expertise, in terms of how people deal with artworks. Roughly, this sequence moves from responses based on the subject matter of artworks toward one based on autonomous stylistic characteristics of artworks. Style-based processing is often taken as a signature of aesthetic expertise (Winston & Cupchik, 1992; see also Augustin & Leder, 2006), in line with other factors like considering specifically aesthetic value, the ideas behind a work, and norms of good versus bad taste (Kirk, 2012).

OTHER MODELS OF AESTHETIC PROCESSING AND NEUROSCIENCE ASPECTS

Besides Leder et al.'s (2004) model, several other accounts have been proposed, with somewhat different parameters and emphases. These include Chatterjee's (2004) neurologically inspired model rooted in three basic stages of visual processing in the brain; Locher, Krupinski, Mello-Thoms, and Nodine's (2007) eye movement-inspired model describing three overlapping elements (the person context, artifact context, and interaction space); Silvia's (2005) appraisal theory focusing on emotional reactions to art; and Pelowski and Akiba's (2011) model emphasizing interactions with art that involve discrepancy and adjustment. Many aspects of these models overlap with that of Leder et al. (2004), and Pelowski, Markey, Lauring, and Leder (2016) reported a comprehensive comparison of processing stages, inputs, outputs, affective responses, perception, reaction, and longer-term impact across these models. Tellingly, even in Pelowski et al.'s very thorough analysis, expertise was not systematically addressed as a comparative item, and the mentioned effects of expertise were fleeting, as in Locher's (2015) suggestion that viewer expertise may be especially important in the initial gist impression of an artwork.

Finally, beyond this array of box-and-arrow models rooted in cognitive processes, a significant component of contemporary research is in the emerging domain of neuroaesthetics. A thorough review of neuroaesthetics is not possible here, but a few general points may be made, anticipating the domain-specific summaries that follow. First, as with cognitive processes, well-understood neural mechanisms support aesthetic cognition—for instance, sensorimotor, knowledge-meaning, and emotion-valuation systems in the brain (Chatterjee & Vartanian, 2014). Additionally, particular brain regions have been identified that seem to be involved in general aspects of aesthetic judgment, especially for visual artworks (for reviews see, e.g., Kirk, 2012; Kirk & Freedberg, 2015). For example, activation in the medial orbito-frontal cortex (or ventro-medial prefrontal cortex) has been associated with evaluating the hedonic and affective value of paintings (Kawabata & Zeki, 2004; Kirk, Skov, & Nygaard, & Christensen, 2009; Vartanian & Goel, 2004). Ishizu and Zeki (2011) found medial orbito-frontal cortex activation during the experience of both musical and visual beauty, with the strength of activation proportional to the strength of the declared intensity of the experience of beauty. Other studies have implicated the ventromedial prefrontal cortex in processing explicit contextual information in aesthetic judgment (de Araujo, Rolls, Velazco, Margot, & Cayeux, 2005; McClure et al., 2004; Plassmann, Doherty, Shiv, & Rangel, 2006), across various categories of stimuli. Yet additional brain areas have been implicated in other important studies of aesthetic judgment and experience (Jacobsen, Schubotz, Höfel, & Cramon, 2006; Vessel, Starr, & Rubin, 2012). Expertise effects, including identifying the dorsolateral prefrontal cortex as insulating experts from common processing biases, have also been studied (Kirk et al., 2009; Kirk, Harvey, & Montague, 2011). All told, neuroaesthetics studies have identified many promising avenues for future research on expertise and beyond (see also Liu, Lughofer, & Zeng, 2017), which complement and enrich traditional lab-based empirical aesthetics and expertise studies, including the domain-specific aspects described below.

Limitations of domain-general models

This brief overview of aesthetic processing may suggest an unwieldy theoretical proliferation. Perhaps this should not be surprising, given the variety of stimuli and experiences that any comprehensive theory of human aesthetics must explain. However, many of the perspectives reviewed above are compatible and mutually reinforcing, being grounded in general, well-established aspects of mental processing. Some include at least a nod to the importance of specialized artistic knowledge and characterizations of its basic effects, but finer intra-"expert" distinctions or truly high-level expertise are rarely examined directly.

From the standpoint of accounting for genuine expertise, the preceding models have other limitations. Besides a prototypical focus on visual art, they tend to rely on domain-general psychological mechanisms, rather than on the structure and deployment of highly specialized domain-specific knowledge. A related point is a strong emphasis on aesthetic reception, rather than on its more creative or performative aspects—as when one actually paints a picture or performs a piece of music, rather than merely looking or listening.[4] Overall, high levels of expertise—in reception, creation, or performance—likely engender even more radical changes in many aspects of aesthetic processing than are typically posited and directly studied by domain-general models. Along these lines, Silvia (2012, p. 253) noted:

> People vary greatly in their expertise in the arts, their knowledge about the arts, and the values they bring to an aesthetic encounter. These differences really matter. Experts in the arts are not merely faster, smarter or nerdier novices—their understanding of what art is, means and does is qualitatively different.

In this spirit, and since true expertise is invariably domain-specific, let's now consider research on how expertise can modulate aesthetic response, preference, judgment, performance, and creativity, within the context of some representative aesthetic domains. As with the preceding accounts, not all this research directly engages high levels of knowledge or skill. However, its domain-specific context better situates the details of expertise, even if its effects must be extrapolated somewhat. In the ensuing domain-by-domain discussion, I consider various aspects and levels of domain-specific experience (constrained by extant research foci) and examine receptive, performative, and creative aspects where relevant.

EXPERTISE IN VARIOUS AESTHETIC DOMAINS

Visual art

Visual art is the most paradigmatic domain of empirical aesthetics, and it is associated with a large and varied literature on the role of expertise on appreciation, judgment, and production. Many of the general findings on aesthetic preference described above involve visual stimuli (either artworks or other visual patterns), and the typical results—such as experts' preference for greater visual complexity and asymmetry, an expert focus on stylistic rather than subject matter cues, plus general neuroaesthetic findings—apply robustly to visual art. A similar distinction concerns aesthetic judgment criteria, particularly in assessments of the realism versus abstraction of paintings. Numerous studies have found that artists and other art experts value abstraction over realism, while novices show the opposite pattern (e.g., Hekkert & van Wieringen, 1996; Kozbelt, 2006).[5] Such patterns are consistent with experts' abilities to cognitively manipulate larger and more abstract knowledge structures in their domain.

Beyond aesthetic judgment criteria, expertise impacts other aspects of visual artistry, such as artists' perceptual abilities. Is the habitual experience of looking at the world with the intention of drawing it associated with changes in the functioning of the visual system? This research area (reviewed in detail by Kozbelt & Ostrofsky, 2018) has yielded several theoretical models and suggestive—if not conclusive—findings. Chief among artists' visual advantages are a more flexible top-down deployment of attention (Chamberlain & Wagemans, 2015), enhanced recognition of degraded visual stimuli (Kozbelt, 2001), better visual memory (Perdreau & Cavanagh, 2015), and a greater understanding of the structure of objects (Perdreau & Cavanagh, 2014). The evidence for purported advantages in lower-level aspects of visual perception and cognition—such as the ability to overcome perceptual constancies or the effects of visual illusions—is more mixed (Kozbelt & Ostrofsky, 2018). But a central claim, that artists must robustly solve the same problems as the visual system, suggests substantial flexibility in artists' perceptual processing. This may modulate classic claims about the scope and fragility of expertise, evident in the situationally narrow perceptual advantage of experts in domains like chess (e.g., Chase & Simon, 1973). Overall, this research area is a fruitful region of synergy between the expertise and empirical aesthetics literatures, with many issues tantalizingly unresolved—particularly developmental questions about the origin of artists' perceptual advantages.

Beyond raw perceptual abilities, behavioral measures also show expertise effects. Obviously, artists draw far better than nonartists, even when copying novel stimuli (Kozbelt, 2001) or using pared-down means of depiction (Kozbelt, Seidel, ElBassiouny, Mark, & Owen, 2010). Research on eye and hand movements in naturalistic drawing has found that artists can produce more motor output per unit of visually encoded material when drawing, relative to nonartists (Glazek, 2012). Artists also use a systematic eye–hand strategy while segmenting complex lines, while nonartists segment arbitrarily or not at all (Tchalenko, 2009; see also Solso, 2001). A venerable literature on eye movements while people look at art has also yielded notable results. For instance, experts engage in more specific and less diverse exploration, indicating they are more sensitive to compositions' structural designs, and focus less on pictorial detail (Locher et al., 2007).

Expertise differences continue in creative aspects of art-making. Expert artists show great willingness to revise their work (Getzels & Csikszentmihalyi, 1976; Kozbelt, 2008b), even when the revisions temporarily worsen an emerging depiction (Kozbelt, 2006)—indeed, more creative final outcomes are associated with significantly more jagged quality trajectories en route (Kozbelt & Serafin, 2009; Serafin, Kozbelt, Seidel, & Dolese, 2011). Think-aloud protocol analyses have also revealed that relative to nonartists, expert artists also make more goal statements, more positive evaluations, and fewer negative evaluations, as well as engaging in more metacognition having to do with monitoring the emerging progress of the drawing (Fayena-Tawil, Kozbelt, & Sitaras, 2011; see also Fava, 2014). All told, such results on behavioral and creative aspects of artistic expertise are largely consistent with general findings on experts' "big-picture" sensibilities on domain-relevant tasks.

Design

Like visual art, design is a natural human activity (Cross, 2018), with important aesthetic aspects (Hekkert, 2006) and progressive development of skill and expertise (Dreyfus & Dreyfus, 2005). Design activities are highly varied, encompassing physical objects like furniture or utensils and more rarefied productions like tax codes or computer software, and they directly involve creative problem-solving processes (Simon, 1996).

Given its versatile applications, design expertise encompasses both specific knowledge of content subdomains and more general design process principles. Process aspects of design include problem framing, solution conjecturing, and problem-solution co-evolution (Cross, 2018). Expert designers respond to challenges proactively, imposing an interpretation on the problem and engaging solution ideas from the start, especially if they are already experienced with that problem type; in contrast, novice designers tend to deductively analyze problems (Eastman, 1970; Lloyd & Scott, 1994). Experienced designers also co-evolve an understanding of the problem with partial solutions, oscillating attention between the two (Dorst & Cross, 2001; Suwa, Gero, & Purcell, 2000). In tandem with process differences, expert designers use recognition and knowledge of precedents and examples to productively plot their course through a design problem. Along these lines, Sio, Kotovsky, and Cagan (2015) meta-analyzed studies examining the use of examples to induce either design fixation (Jansson & Smith, 1991) or spark inspiration. They found that examples can negatively affect the variety of ideas generated but positively affect the novelty and quality of the ideas. Thus, experienced designers may modify their process to exploit and explore promising examples in more depth, improving solution quality. All told, design experts treat problems as "harder" than they need to be (Cross, 2018), which differs from mainstream, routinized domains, where efficiency is experts' trademark.

Aesthetic concerns can be relevant to any aspect of design (even software code; Kozbelt, Dexter, Dolese, & Seidel, 2012), but most often it is studied in the context of physical products. Hekkert and colleagues have performed extensive research on this topic, articulating several powerful and evolutionarily informed ideas about aesthetic pleasure in design. These include the four principles of maximum effect for minimum means, unity in variety, most advanced yet acceptable, and optimal match (Hekkert, 2006), as well as the notion that across domains and at the levels of perceptual, cognitive, and social processes, aesthetic choices are based on a trade-off between safety and accomplishment (Hekkert, 2014). Empirical tests of these premises (e.g., Berghman & Hekkert, 2017; Blijlevens et al., 2017; Da Silva, Crilly, & Hekkert, 2016) have yielded a rich emerging picture of design aesthetics. However, to date, studies of design expertise and design aesthetics have made relatively little overt contact with each other—a promising nexus, though, for future research.

Architecture

Like design, architecture involves inherently ill-defined problems and considerations of functionality. Many of the design process principles described above apply to architecture, with increased complexity. In handling such complexity, outstanding architects must maintain parallel processes of cognition simultaneously—for example, working on detail junctions of materials concurrently with general spatial concepts (Lawson, 1994). Expert architects impose order on ill-defined problems, developing starting points via the particulars of the work site or a personal set of guiding principles (Darke, 1979; see also Lloyd & Scott, 1995), and use those to generate a set of limited objectives to begin work. Such problem framing processes continue throughout design tasks (Goel & Pirolli, 1992). Such aspects of architectural design processes also apply to eminent architects like Frank Lloyd Wright, with the important addition of Wright's extraordinarily rich domain-specific knowledge base (Weisberg, 2011).

Neuroscience evidence (e.g., Gilbert, Zamenopoulos, Alexiou, & Johnson, 2009; Goel & Grafman, 2000) has underscored this complex dynamic of architectural design, specifically implicating the right dorsolateral and ventrolateral aspects of the prefrontal cortex, areas associated with the generation of solutions under reduced task constraints (Vartanian & Goel, 2004). Lesions to this region are associated with difficulties in the preliminary stages of design, suggesting problems in maintaining indeterminate representations during problem solving. In passing, I note that Vartanian (2017) has addressed additional important aspects of architectural creativity, including personality and divergent thinking factors.

Beyond considerations of the creative design process, other laboratory and neuroscience research on architectural aesthetics has yielded some notable findings, particularly on general preferences for curvilinear over rectilinear spaces, high over low ceilings, and open over closed spaces (Vartanian et al., 2013). While studies of expertise effects on architectural aesthetics are rare, one important study (Kirk et al., 2009) has directly addressed these issues. Kirk et al. used functional magnetic resonance imaging (fMRI) to study aesthetic judgments of architectural stimuli (and faces) among architects and nonarchitects. Despite null findings for the two groups' aesthetic ratings, bilateral activation in the medial orbito-frontal cortex was correlated with aesthetic ratings for both groups (and more strongly so among experts), while the subcallosal part of the anterior cingulate gyrus responded inversely to high and low ratings in the experts, compared with novices. Group differences were also evident in bilateral activation in the hippocampus and precuneus, though only for architecture stimuli. This suggests that experts integrate current input into a framework of prior knowledge and use this information to organize aesthetic judgments.

Photography

Photography differs from the previous domains in its historical recency and reliance on technology, and in raising new conceptual issues for aesthetics: it is mechanically reproduced, time-based, embodies metaphors of violence and capture, may or may not be said to capture reality, and is ultra-popular as an activity even among nonexperts (Serafin & Dollinger, 2017). While these factors could potentially complicate aesthetics and expertise in photography, the available evidence is mostly in line with findings in other domains.

First, numerous factors influence the aesthetic appeal of photographs. These include expressiveness and pleasantness (Axelsson, 2007), contrast, sharpness, and film grain (Tinio, Leder, & Strasser, 2011), and content and complexity (Tinio & Leder, 2009, 2013). Expert photographers have clear, coherent criteria in judging the photos' quality, including pleasantness, appeal, content, expressiveness, composition, and technical quality; novices' criteria are less well-defined and explain less variability, with overall quality mainly being associated with technical quality (Serafin, 2013). Professional photographers are better at processing photographic information (Axelsson, 2007), preferring photos that are more expressive and uncertain, while nonexperts prefer images that are familiar and pleasant—by this point in the chapter, an unsurprising result. Beyond aesthetic judgment criteria, more specific aspects of expert–novice differences have also been examined. Serafin (2013) compared expert and novice photographers' ability to correctly identify four categories of photographic flaws—lens, lighting, composition, and subject—an important skill in weeding out unsatisfactory images after a photo shoot. Expert photographers were more discriminating in judging quality and more likely to detect and define photographs' flaws, especially those involving lighting and lens issues. Serafin also found that, overall, experts are harsher judges of photographs than are novices.

Creative aspects of photography expertise have also been assessed, mainly through the activity of cropping images. For instance, McManus et al. (2011) explored photographic cropping as an aesthetic task in a series of six studies. Among other results, they found that experts crop pictures differently from nonexperts, take longer to do so, view a wider range of possible crops, pause longer to assess crops, and use more formal terminology when reflecting on their decisions. Notably, experts' crops were not rated higher than those of novices, either by expert or nonexpert judges. In a similar vein, but with different outcomes, Serafin (2013) also tested expert and novice photographers on image generation tasks that required them to simulate taking photographs either by cropping complex static images, pausing moving images, or cropping moving images in real time. Images were then rated by another sample of experts and nonexperts. In contrast to McManus et al.'s findings, Serafin found that in all three image generation tasks experts outperformed novices, especially according to the judgments of outside expert (but not novice) raters. Experts were also better than novices at identifying the best photos from among those they had taken, again validated by the judgments of independent experts.

Music

Like visual art, music is often regarded as a fundamental domain of mind (Feist, 2004; Gardner, 1983), with deep evolutionary roots in acoustic and phonetic analysis (Purves, 2017). Music's enormous popularity poses challenges for expertise research. For instance, experts and novices show few differences in emotional response to music (Pearce, 2015), despite characterizations of musical expertise along emotion lines (Sloboda, 1991). Claims about the transfer of music training benefits to other domains—like full-scale IQ (Schellenberg, 2004), compared with null effects for emotional intelligence (Schellenberg, 2011)—are also mixed. In navigating these issues, researchers must distinguish factors like raw musical experience versus more formal musical training (Pearce, 2015) and more domain-general receptive aspects from more domain-specific productive aspects (Kozbelt, 2017a).

A great deal is known about musical expertise (Lehmann, Gruber, & Kopiez, 2018), particularly the acquisition of musical skill and its psychological impact. Ericsson et al. (1993) famously argued that deliberate practice is the main determinant of skilled performance, based on retrospective data on conservatory violinists' cumulative practice (see also Sloboda, Davidson, Howe, & Moore, 1996; cf. Winner, 1996); one meta-analysis (Platz, Kopiez, Lehmann, & Wolff, 2014), reported a cumulative corrected correlation of .61 between task-relevant training and achievement.[6] Overall, the acquisition of world-class musical expertise takes about a decade, consistent with other domains (Ericsson & Crutcher, 1990), and likewise proceeds through several stages (Fitts & Posner, 1967; Sudnow, 1993). Acquired musical expertise produces numerous perceptual, cognitive, and physiological adaptations. Musicians show more refined auditory processing (Pantev et al., 2001) and finer discriminations in timing, pitch, and loudness than novices (Banai, Fisher, & Ganot, 2012; Houtsma, Durlach, & Horowitz, 1987; Micheyl et al., 2006; Rammsayer & Altenmüller, 2006). Expert musicians also have superior memory for musical material, especially when it follows tonal rules allowing anticipation (Chaffin, Demos, & Logan, 2016; Dowling, 1978; Dowling & Bartlett, 1981; Snyder, 2016), and represent deeper metrical hierarchies than novices (Palmer & Krumhansl, 1990). Experts likewise show physiological changes like increased lung capacity among singers or brass players (Sundberg 1987) or faster finger tapping among pianists (Keele, Pokorny, Corcos, & Ivry, 1985), as well as refined somatosensory perception and kinesthetic feedback (Elbert et al., 1998; Ragert, Schmidt, Altenmüller, & Dinse, 2004).

At the neural level, music training also has profound effects, due to brain plasticity (Altenmüller & Furuya, 2018). Effects are particularly strong among music performers (Brown, Penhune, & Zatorre, 2015; Elbert et al., 1998) and when training begins at early ages (Steele, Bailey, Zatorre, & Penhune, 2013), and they include early stages of auditory process (Skoe & Kraus, 2013). Even when just listening to music, more brain areas are involuntarily activated among experts than novices (Pantev et al., 2001; Bangert & Schlaug, 2006). Numerous other brain areas have been implicated in musical expertise (see Altenmüller & Furuya, 2018), but those details would take us too far afield presently.

In terms of aesthetics, expertise effects are evident in ways consistent with findings in other domains. For instance, experts prefer less prototypical chord progressions than novices (Smith & Melara, 1990), as well as more complex music (Burke & Gridley, 1990; Fung, 1996) and artificial tone sequences (Crozier, 1974; Simon & Wohlwill, 1968; Vitz, 1966). Consistent with this, some researchers have found rightward shifts in the prototypical inverted U-shaped relation between complexity and hedonic value (Berlyne, 1974) among expert musicians (Coggiola, 2004; North & Hargreaves, 1995), though not universally (Orr & Ohlsson, 2001, 2005). In a verbal association task on aesthetic value, musicians also use more adjectives related to originality and fewer adjectives related to mood, compared with novices (Istok et al., 2009). In making aesthetic judgments, experts also rely less on emotional reaction to music than do novices, as suggested by novices' enhanced emotion-related processing in an event-related potential (ERP) study of chord sequences (Müller, Höfel, Brattico, & Jacobsen, 2010). Finally, compared with novices, experts focus on different aspects of musical structure, like harmony (Conley, 1981), and show heightened responses to dissonant tone combinations (e.g., Bigand, Parncutt, & Lerdahl, 1996).

Dance

Of all the domains considered here, dance is the most kinesthetic: the dancer embodies both artist and artwork. Culturally valued and universal (Dils & Albright, 2001), dance partakes of neural systems concerned with action perception, simulation, and movement (e.g., Freedberg & Gallese, 2007; Rizzolatti, Fadiga, Gallese, & Fogassi, 1996; Prinz, 2006). Like music performance, expert-level dance training is intensive and highly structured (Chua, 2019), with concomitant cognitive and physical adaptations. For instance, motor expertise in affective body movement specifically modulates both behavioral and physiological sensitivity to others' affective body movements (Christensen, Gomila, Gaigg, Sivarajah, & Calvo-Merino, 2016). In passing, I note that studies of overt creativity in dance are less common and often occur in educational contexts (Thomson, 2017).

Aesthetic studies of dance are dominated by neuroscience approaches. Of special interest is the action observation network (AON; Cross, Kirsch, Ticini, & Schütz-Bosbach, 2011), a bilateral ensemble of brain areas—premotor cortex, inferior parietal lobule, occipito-temporal cortex, and supplementary motor area—involved in the observation of bodily movements. In a pioneering fMRI study, Calvo-Merino, Glaser, Grezes, Passingham, and Haggard (2005) found that when dancers trained either in classical ballet or capoeira watched their familiar type of dance style, they showed greater activity in the AON of the brain, versus watching a less familiar style. This suggests that years of practice in one style of dance fine-tune action resonance processes in sensory-motor areas for action perception and production. Likewise, fMRI research by Cross, Hamilton, and Grafton (2006) found that over six weeks, dancers rehearsing novel choreography became better at performing the movements, and more adept dancers showed increased activation in two AON regions. Recently, Burzynska, Finc, Taylor, Knecht, & Kramer (2017) examined long-term effects of dance training; compared with a matched novice sample, expert dancers showed no overall cognitive differences but were better at dance and balance tasks and showed stronger activation of the AON while observing dance as well as altered functional connectivity of the AON and the general motor learning network.

Aesthetic liking in dance has also been explored, in a variety of ways. For instance, automatic sensorimotor mechanisms concerned with positive appreciation of dance movements have been localized in early visual cortex and right premotor cortex of the brain (Calvo-Merino, Jola, Glaser, & Haggard, 2008). People viewing dance movements that they liked showed greater activation in AON areas such as bilateral medial visual cortices and right premotor areas (Calvo-Merino et al., 2008), and more preferred dance movements were also associated with higher activation in AON areas like the occipito-temporal cortex and the inferior parietal lobe—especially when those movements, like jumps, were more difficult to execute (Cross et al., 2011). Such results relate to findings on processing fluency and physical movements (Cross et al., 2011; Hayes et al., 2008), such that the perception or production of fluent grasping and dancing actions is associated with greater aesthetic liking. Finally, engaging in dance also affects aesthetic experience. For instance, Kirsch, Drommelschmidt, and Cross (2013) found that a week of practicing a dance sequence (i.e., not just watching it or listening to the accompanying music) led to increases in aesthetic ratings of dance movements across several preference dimensions. In an fMRI follow-up, Kirsch, Dawson, and Cross (2015) found a longitudinal shift in neural engagement from subcortical reward processing toward multisensory integration and higher-level emotion processing, as a result of dance practice.

Writing

Literary writing draws upon familiar expertise and aesthetics issues, with the added aspects of language, strong narrative content, and a healthy dose of theory of mind (Oatley, 2012). Writers themselves have often discussed aspects of their craft. For instance, Flaubert devised a five-stage process of creative writing: plan, draft scenarios, rough drafts, refined drafts, and final draft (see Oatley & Djikic, 2008). Authors like Annie Dillard (1989) have metacognitively documented optimal personal parameters enabling sustained writing (see also Kellogg, 2018), and eminent literary critics like Samuel Johnson (2008) and Harold Bloom (2002) have detailed their own expert-level introspection about the nature of literary aesthetics.

As in many other aesthetic domains, process issues in writing have received considerable attention. Graves and Frederiksen (1991) compared the protocols of students and experts describing a narrative conveyed by character dialogue. They found that while students closely paraphrased the text, experts used specific text information to make more inferential statements, commented more on the language used in the text, referred to narrative structure and functions of dialogue in the text, with reference to the author, reader, and the relationship between the two. Hayes and Flower (1980, 1986) likewise found substantial differences in the protocols of novices and experts while writing. Experts developed more elaborate goals while planning, including considering their readers; in generating sentences, experts manipulated sentence parts that were 50% longer than those of novices; in the rewriting phase, experts made three times as many alterations of meaning, using long-term working memory (Ericsson & Kintsch, 1995) to manipulate larger chunks of text. Other work suggests that revision is often minimal in inexperienced writers, with corrections focused primarily on word substitutions and surface-level changes (McCutchen, 1996; Sommers, 1980). As writers gain experience, there are systematic gains in vocabulary, sentence and clause length, grammatical complexity, and judged holistic quality, as in Haswell's (2000) longitudinal study of college students' essay writing. The ability to fluently combine high-level composition processes with low-level transcription and mechanics emerges only in advanced writers (Almargot, Plane, Lambert, & Chesnet, 2010). Overall, many perspectives have been offered on the nature of creativity in writing (see chapters in Kaufman & Kaufman, 2009), which occasionally connect with issues of aesthetics and expertise.

In general, the complex process of planning, translating, and revising during prewriting and drafting engages diverse cortical areas of the brain, including regions involved in language processing, semantic associations, cognitive control, and retrieval from long-term memory. Expertise modulates these basic effects (Shah, Erhard, Ortheil, Kaza, Kessler, & Lotze, 2013). For example, while writing, experienced creative writers show greater activation in Broca's language area and nearby areas subserving attention and cognitive control as well as an increase in resting state functional connectivity within the right hemisphere, compared with a control group (Erhard, Kessler, Neuomann, Ortheil, & Lotze, 2014). Compared with their less experienced peers, published poets show more deactivation of dorsolateral prefrontal cortex cognitive control regions while first generating the text; only later, during revision, do these areas come back online (Liu et al., 2015).

Acting

Acting combines performative and narrative aspects, presenting an imaginary reality to observers in a variety of collaborative settings and genres. In daily life, everyone engages in moments of pretense, complicating where to demarcate domain-specific acting expertise. A few studies have examined how actors memorize their lines, using cognitive principles and deep processing of emotion and characterization (e.g., Intons-Peterson & Smythe, 1987; Noice & Noice, 1993), and many practical methods of training actors exist (Goldstein & Levy, 2017; Noice & Noice, 2019).

The nature of acting expertise, independent of its relation to personal characteristics, has not been addressed as directly as in other domains, perhaps because these other factors are often regarded as essential for successful acting. For instance, Noice and Noice (2013, 2019) argued that individual differences in acting ability (i.e., spontaneously and truthfully functioning under imaginary circumstances) are enormous; motivation, training, and perseverance are insufficient to close that gap, and a strong technical skillset will rarely save a performance lacking spontaneity. Actors' personal qualities have been examined in numerous studies. They tend to have greater degrees of empathy, theory of mind, adaptive emotion regulation, absorption into imaginative worlds, extraversion, and openness to experience, compared with nonactors (e.g., Goldstein & Winner, 2010; Goldstein Tamir, & Winner, 2013; Goodman & Kaufman, 2014).

Creative aspects of acting have been discussed by Goldstein and Levy (2017). These researchers note that aspiring actors typically engage in many years of formal training in which they learn how to read a script, synthesize information from the script, follow a director's direction, and integrate self-knowledge into a character as part of a larger narrative. Acquiring the technical aspects of their craft allow them to engage in a meaningful creative process (Nemiro, 1997) using their expertise. Typically, this dynamic involves collaboration, trust in the director, and the ability to flexibly develop a personal interpretation.

Film

Film is a fittingly final aesthetic domain to consider, as it encompasses and potentially synthesizes virtually all of the other domains reviewed here (Brown & Dissanayake, 2018; Grodal, 2009). Despite its general popularity, and the vast logistical challenges and technical knowledge required to make quality films—involving issues like pacing, shot composition, camera movement, focus, editing, etc.—not much is known about expertise and the aesthetics of film. One of the few empirical studies to address this was conducted by Silvia and Berg (2011), who examined appraisals of film clips using a domain-specific measure of aesthetic fluency as a proxy for expertise. Consistent with other research, results showed that appraising a clip as complex and comprehensible predicted interest, while appraising it as complex and incomprehensible predicted confusion; experts found the films more interesting and less confusing, and their interest was more strongly predicted by complexity.

In passing, I note that other research has examined aesthetic experience of film (e.g., Goldstein, 2009) and predictors of films' critical success (e.g., Simonton, 2007). Overall, however, expertise and aesthetics in film remain woefully underresearched, as is also the case in aesthetic domains like environmental design (Kholina, 2015), interior decoration (Yildirim, Hidayetoglu, & Capanoglu, 2011), and emerging "new media" forms of digital art (Paul, 2008).

Evolutionary Integration, Looking Forward

The preceding domain-by-domain review—necessarily brisk—gives some sense of both the progress and challenges in understanding the impact of expertise on aesthetics. It may seem paradoxical to derive general conclusions from a line of research so emphatically domain-specific. But despite the diversity of domains reviewed, similar trends tend to emerge, and these are largely in line with the claims of the cognitive psycho-logical literature on expertise as well as general models of aesthetic processing. What are these overall conclusions? Aesthetic expertise or skill in any domain tends to be built on a foundation of thousands of domain-specific pieces of information acquired over the course of years. That knowledge base facilitates significant changes in task performance: in the ability to process increasingly large chunks of information, in aesthetic preference and aesthetic judgment criteria, and in the way the creative process unfolds. These psychological changes are often accompanied by transformations in physiology and in the structure and function of particular areas of the brain.

However, inter-domain commonalities are not the end of the story. Extant research on the nexus of expertise and aesthetics is, as noted above, haphazard. Even in the research reviewed here, there are many more lacunae, areas of vagueness, and occasional outright inconsistencies than definitively resolved issues. Consideration of larger-scale issues increases the scope of the unknown still further, but it also provides a basis for future research and eventual integration. To conclude, I now briefly discuss several related issues along these lines.

Probably the most important unanswered large-scale question on the nature of aesthetic expertise concerns the uneasy relation between the domain-specificity of expert knowledge and the domain-generality of the psychological and neural processes posited by many accounts of aesthetics. Consider how domain-specific expert knowledge plays out in creative or aesthetic domains, particularly when "artificial" expertise is contrasted with "natural" aesthetics. Most domains of expertise are human inventions, and detailed knowledge of them is incidental to our survival; one can lead a satisfying, meaningful life without ever playing chess. Typically, not only are the skills and the knowledge constituting expertise domain-specific, but the domains themselves have usually emerged recently and are often culture-specific. In contrast, humans have natural aesthetic responses to many evolutionarily important stimuli like faces, bodies, food, and habitats (Chatterjee, 2014; Orians, 2014). Aesthetic faculties of visual art and music have been regarded as fundamental modules of the mind (Feist, 2004; Gardner, 1983). And as we have seen, many researchers regard human aesthetics as rooted in biological, evolutionary, or neurological factors, with core domain-general tenets that transcend culture (e.g., Berlyne, 1971; Dutton, 2009; Martindale, 1990, 2007; Ramachandran & Hirstein, 1999).

How do these two fountainheads of aesthetic cognition interact? One first approximation may be that domain-general aspects of processing are more important in understanding aesthetic reception, while domain-specific aspects are more critical for performance and creativity (Kozbelt, 2017a). For high-level creativity, vast domain-specific knowledge is *de rigueur*; on the reception side, domain-specific knowledge is experience-enhancing along the lines of many aesthetic processing models, but one might conceivably get by on domain-general principles alone. Perkins (1981) noted that people's receptive abilities are typically more developed than their productive abilities: we can discern and appreciate works that we ourselves are powerless to create. Thus, a reasonable starting assumption is that domain-specific techniques and creativity are layered upon a domain-general foundation. But here, as usual, the devil is very much in the details. There is, moreover, no universal principle that represents a static recipe for creating aesthetic masterworks. While there have been few attempts to unpack how domain-specificity may grow out of domain-generality, a consilient evolutionary psychology approach (e.g., Pinker, 2002, 2007; Wilson, 1998) seems like the most promising path forward.

The dynamic evolution of artistic styles, propelled by the achievements of individual artists, is a related issue for understanding the nature of aesthetic expertise. Just as the arts each encompass substantial stylistic diversity, individual creators have idiosyncratic tastes and function in specific but ever-changing socio-cultural milieus (Csikszentmihalyi, 1988; Sawyer, 2006). Martindale (1990) amply documented the incessant pressure for novelty in any art form worthy of the name. For ambitious creators, this means devising ever-more unusual and artificial styles. In seeking to push or break the conventions of a domain, such creators may eventually run against the grain of evolutionarily canalized aesthetic preferences (Kozbelt, 2017b). Martindale (2009) argued that art is inherently defined in a way that guarantees it evolves in a certain way and dies in a certain way—viz., innovations become so radical that the works no longer communicate to audiences. The psychobiological principles identified by Berlyne (1971) are the presumed ineluctable basis of this trans-historical aesthetic death-spiral.

However, psychobiology may not be destiny when it comes to aesthetic domains, since not all thinkers are as pessimistic as Martindale (2009) about the endgame of art (Kozbelt, 2017b). What are the options for creators whose goals and impulses may drive them toward increasingly esoteric productions, and what does this tell us about the nature of human aesthetics and the role of expertise therein? One possibility is that the effect of culture swamps that of biology, along the lines of the blank-slate standard social sciences model (Tooby & Cosmides, 1992). While a strong version of this view seems unlikely given the abundant evidence on regularities in aesthetic cognition and preference, emphasizing the dynamic role of culture is a crucial but underemphasized component of aesthetic expertise (see Bullot & Reber, 2013). Conversely, perhaps domain-general aesthetic regularities are real, but they are highly malleable via individual or cultural experience (see Nadal & Chatterjee, 2018), leading over time to creator–audience co-evolution (see also Prum, 2013). Creators' blind stabs at innovation (Simonton, 2011) can result either in transient aesthetic fads or in genuine discoveries leading to enduring changes in how aesthetic works are produced and appreciated (see Gombrich, 1979). This process of canon formation—separating the aesthetic wheat from the chaff in a broader cultural context—is another vital dynamic involving aesthetic creativity and expertise (among other factors), which remains sadly underexamined.

The recent emergence of novel art forms is another useful test case for understanding the ultimate nature and limits of aesthetic expertise, which go well beyond the scope of extant research described in this chapter. Gopnik (2012) has argued that the emphases of empirical aesthetic researchers often seem trivial and outmoded to persons involved in contemporary art practice or theory. But are there *any* borders to the human aesthetic realm? Are human aesthetics truly an "anything goes" enterprise? Can we say that some modes of aesthetic production are so utterly unnatural (i.e., they run so squarely counter to domain-general principles of aesthetics and cognition) that we can be confident a priori that they will never catch on, either in the popular imagination or even among elite consumers of culture? For instance, many viewers find contemporary conceptual art baffling. Kranjec (2015), however, has explored how many aspects of conceptual art—such as an ontological and epistemological concern with time, language, meaning, and the nature of objects—are aesthetic in nature and complement prominent themes in the domain of cognitive neuroscience. Does conceptual art, or other novel aesthetic mode, show the same patterns in preference, expertise, and stylistic evolution as have been found in more traditional media?

As with so many issues in the nexus of expertise and aesthetics, these are empirical questions. Besides appreciating art's apparent diversity, it is salutary to marvel at the number of its regularities, which doggedly persist, and which suggest some psychobiological root to human aesthetic activity. In assessing the ultimate scope, nature, and flexibility of human aesthetic response and creativity—and their interaction with expertise—it would be wise to be led by the emerging constellation of findings from psychology and neuroscience. In just a few decades, we have learned much about how these constructs play out in established domains and established research questions. Against this backdrop, it is high time for the implications of aesthetic expertise to be intelligently extrapolated to bigger questions, and applied to new aesthetic horizons.

Notes

1. See also Bullot and Reber's (2013) distinction between three modes of aesthetic appreciation: basic exposure to an artwork, the artistic design stance, and artistic understanding.
2. For instance, the most recent edition of *The Cambridge Handbook of Expertise and Expert Performance* (Ericsson et al., 2018)—as definitive and comprehensive an encapsulation of the contemporary science of expertise as may be found anywhere—contains not a single page reference to "aesthetics" in its index, despite whole chapters on drawing, music, design, and other putatively aesthetic domains.
3. Both of these nomothetic characterizations of creativity—Simonton's (1999, 2011) blind variation and selective retention model and the classic expertise account espoused by Ericsson (1999) and Weisberg (1999)—have their own limitations (for a discussion, see Kozbelt, 2008a).
4. For arguments suggesting isomorphisms between creation and appreciation, see Martindale (2007) and Tinio (2013).
5. Though there are exceptions. Classically trained artists who reject abstraction sometimes show aesthetic judgment criteria more similar to those of novices (Serafin et al., 2011).
6. Some recent models (e.g., Gagné, 2009) have identified additional components beyond acquired expertise that impact musical achievement, including natural ability, intrapersonal factors, and environmental catalysts.

References

Almargot, D., Plane, S., Lambert, E., & Chesnet, D. (2010). Using eye and pen movements to trace the development of writing expertise: Case studies of a 7th, 9th, and 12th grader, graduate student, and professional writer. *Reading and Writing, 23*, 853–888.

Altenmüller, E., & Furuya, S. (2018). Brain changes associated with acquisition of musical expertise. In K. A. Ericsson, R. R. Hoffman, A. Kozbelt, & A. M. Williams (Eds.), *The Cambridge handbook of expertise and expert performance*, 2nd edition (pp. 550–575). Cambridge, England: Cambridge University Press.

Augustin, D., & Leder, H. (2006). Art expertise: A study of concepts and conceptual spaces. *Psychology Science, 48*, 135–156.

Axelsson, Ö. (2007). Individual differences in preference to photographs. *Psychology of Aesthetics, Creativity, and the Arts, 1*, 61–72.

Banai, K., Fisher, S., & Ganot, R. (2012). The effects of context and musical training on auditory temporal-interval discrimination. *Hearing Research, 284*, 59–66.

Bangert, M., & Schlaug, G. (2006). Specialization of the specialized in features of external brain morphology. *European Journal of Neuroscience, 24*, 1832–1834.

Berghman, M., & Hekkert, P. (2017). Towards a unified model of aesthetic pleasure in design. *New Ideas in Psychology, 47*, 136–144. doi:10.1016/j.newideapsych.2017.03.004

Berlyne, D. E. (1971). *Aesthetics and psychobiology*. New York: Appleton-Century-Crofts.

Berlyne, D. E. (Ed.). (1974). *Studies in the new experimental aesthetics: Steps toward an objective psychology of aesthetic appreciation*. New York: Hemisphere.

Bigand, E., Parncutt, R., & Lerdahl, F. (1996). Perception of musical tension in short chord sequences: The influence of harmonic function, sensory dissonance, horizontal motion, and musical training. *Perception & Psychophysics, 58*, 124–141.

Bilalić, M., & Campitelli, G. (2018). Studies of the activation and structural changes of the brain associated with expertise. In K. A. Ericsson, R. R. Hoffman, A. Kozbelt, & A. M. Williams (Eds.), *The Cambridge handbook of expertise and expert performance*, 2nd edition (pp. 233–253). Cambridge, England: Cambridge University Press.

Blijlevens, J., Thurgood, C., Hekkert, P., Chen, L. L., Leder, H., & Whitfield, T. W. (2017). The Aesthetic Pleasure in Design Scale: The development of a scale to measure aesthetic pleasure for designed artifacts. *Psychology of Aesthetics, Creativity, and the Arts, 11*, 86–98.

Bloom, H. (2002). *Genius*. New York: Warner Books.

Brown, R. M., Penhune, V. B., & Zatorre, R. (2015). Expert music performance: Cognitive, neural, and developmental bases. *Progress in Brain Research, 217*, 57–86.

Brown, S., & Dissanayake, E. (2018). The synthesis of the arts: From ceremonial ritual to "total work of art." *Frontiers in Sociology, 3*, 9. doi:10.3389/fsoc.2018.00009

Bullot, N. J., & Reber, R. (2013). The artful mind meets art history: Toward a psycho-historical framework for the science of art appreciation. *Behavioral and Brain Sciences, 36*, 123–137.

Burke, M. J., & Gridley, M. C. (1990). Musical preferences as a function of stimulus complexity and listeners' sophistication. *Perceptual and Motor Skills, 7*, 687–690.

Burzynska, A. Z., Finc, K., Taylor, B. K., Knecht, A. M., & Kramer, A. F. (2017). The dancing brain: Structural and functional signatures of expert dance training. *Frontiers in Human Neuroscience, 11*, 566. doi:10.3389/fnhum.2017.00566

Calvo-Merino, B., Glaser, D. E., Grezes, J., Passingham R. E., & Haggard, P. (2005). Action observation and acquired motor skills: An fMRI study with expert dancers. *Cerebral Cortex, 15*, 1243–1249.

Calvo-Merino, B., Jola, C., Glaser, D. E., & Haggard, P. (2008). Towards a sensorimotor aesthetic of performing art. *Consciousness and Cognition, 17,* 911–922.

Chaffin, R., Demos, A. P., & Logan, T. (2016). Performing from memory. In S. Hallam, I. Cross, & M. Thaut (Eds.), *The Oxford handbook of music psychology* (pp. 559–572). Oxford, England: Oxford University Press.

Chamberlain, R., & Wagemans, J. (2015). Visual arts training is linked to flexible attention to local and global levels of visual stimuli. *Acta Psychologica, 161,* 185–197.

Chase, W. G., & Simon, H. A. (1973). Perception in chess. *Cognitive Psychology, 19,* 151–165.

Chatterjee, A. (2004). Prospects for a cognitive neuroscience of visual aesthetics. *Bulletin of Psychology of the Arts, 4,* 55–60.

Chatterjee, A. (2014). *The aesthetic brain: How we evolved to desire beauty and enjoy art.* Oxford, England: Oxford University Press.

Chatterjee, A., & Vartanian, O. (2014). Neuroaesthetics. *Trends in Cognitive Sciences, 9,* e1444.

Chi, M. T. H., Feltovich, P. J., & Glaser, R. (1981). Categorization and representation of physics problems by experts and novices. *Cognitive Science, 5,* 121–152.

Christensen, J. F., Gomila, A., Gaigg, S. B., Sivarajah, N., & Calvo-Merino, B. (2016). Dance expertise modulates behavioral and psychophysiological responses to affective body movement. *Journal of Experimental Psychology: Human Perception and Performance, 42,* 1139–1147.

Chua, J. (2019). Talent development in dance: Perspectives from gatekeepers in Hong Kong and Finland. In R. Subotnik, P. Olszewski-Kubilius, & F. Worrell, F. (Eds.), *The handbook of high performance: Developing human potential into domain specific talent* (pp. 261–290). Washington, DC: American Psychological Association.

Coggiola, J. C. (2004). The effect of conceptual advancement in jazz music selections and jazz experience on musicians' aesthetic response. *Journal of Research in Music Education, 52,* 29–42.

Conley, J. K. (1981). Physiological correlates of the judged complexity of music by subjects differing in musical background. *British Journal of Psychology, 72,* 451–464.

Cross, E. S., Hamilton, A. F., & Grafton, S. T. (2006). Building a motor simulation de novo: Observation of dance by dancers. *Neuroimage, 31,* 1257–1267.

Cross, E. S., Kirsch, L., Ticini, L., & Schütz-Bosbach, S. (2011). The impact of aesthetic evaluation and physical ability on dance perception. *Frontiers in Human Neuroscience, 5,* 102. doi:10.3389/fnhum.2011.00102

Cross, N. (2018). Expertise in professional design. In K. A. Ericsson, R. R. Hoffman, A. Kozbelt, & A. M. Williams (Eds.), *The Cambridge handbook of expertise and expert performance,* 2nd edition (pp. 372–388). Cambridge, England: Cambridge University Press.

Crozier, J. B. (1974). Verbal and exploratory responses to sound sequences varying in uncertainty level. In D. E. Berlyne (Ed.), *Studies in the new experimental aesthetics* (pp. 27–90). New York: Hemisphere.

Csikszentmihalyi, M. (1988). Society, culture, and person: A systems view of creativity. In R. J. Sternberg (Ed.), *The nature of creativity: Contemporary psychological perspectives* (pp. 325–339). Cambridge, England: Cambridge University Press.

Cutting, J. E. (2003). Gustave Caillebotte, French Impressionism, and mere exposure. *Psychonomic Bulletin & Review, 10,* 319–343.

Da Silva, O., Crilly, N., & Hekkert, P. (2016). Maximum effect for minimum means: The aesthetics of efficiency. *Design Issues, 32,* 41–51.

Danto, A. (1997). *The Madonna of the future.* New York: Farrar, Straus and Giroux.

Darke, J. (1979). The primary generator and the design process. *Design Studies, 1*, 36–44.

de Araujo, I. E., Rolls, E. T., Velazco, M. I., Margot, C., & Cayeux, I. (2005). Cognitive modulation of olfactory processing. *Neuron, 46*, 671–679.

de Groot, A. (1946/1965). *Thought and choice in chess*. The Hague, the Netherlands: Mouton.

Dillard, A. (1989). *The writing life*. New York: Harper & Row.

Dils, A., & Albright, C. (2001). *Moving history/Dancing cultures: A dance history reader*. Middletown, CT: Wesleyan University Press.

Dorst, K., & Cross, N. (2001). Creativity in the design process: Co-evolution of problem- solution. *Design Studies, 22*, 425–437.

Dowling, W. J. (1978). Scale and contour: Two components of a theory of memory for melodies. *Psychological Review, 85*, 341–354.

Dowling, W. J., & Bartlett, J. C. (1981). The importance of interval information in long-term memory for melodies. *Psychomusicology, 1*, 30–49.

Dreyfus, H. L., & Dreyfus, S. E. (2005). Expertise in real world contexts. *Organization Studies, 26*, 779–792.

Dutton, D. (2009). *The art instinct*. New York: Basic Books.

Eastman, C. M. (1970). On the analysis of intuitive design processes. In G. T. Moore (ed.), *Emerging methods in environmental design and planning* (pp. 21–37). Cambridge, MA: MIT Press.

Elbert, T., Candia, A., Altenmüller, E., Rau, H., Sterr, A., Rockstroh, B., Pantev, C., & Taub, E. (1998). Alteration of digital representation in somatosensory cortex in focal hand dystonia. *NeuroReport, 9*, 3571–3575.

Erhard, K., Kessler, F., Neuomann, N., Ortheil, H.-J., & Lotze, M. (2014). Professional training in creative writing is associated with enhanced fronto-striatal activity in a literary text continuation task. *NeuroImage, 100*, 15–23.

Ericsson, K. A. (1999). Creative expertise as superior reproducible performance: Innovative and flexible aspects of expert performance. *Psychological Inquiry, 10*, 329–333.

Ericsson, K. A., Chase, W. G., & Faloon, S. (1981). Acquisition of a memory skill. *Science, 208*, 1181–1182.

Ericsson, K. A., & Crutcher, R. J. (1990). The nature of exceptional performance. In P. B. Baltes, D. L. Featherman, & R. M. Lerner (Eds.), *Lifespan development and behavior* (Vol. 10, pp. 187–217). Mahwah, NJ: Erlbaum.

Ericsson, K. A., Hoffman, R. R., Kozbelt, A., & Williams, A. M. (2018). *The Cambridge handbook of expertise and expert performance*, 2nd edition. Cambridge, England: Cambridge University Press.

Ericsson, K. A., & Kintsch, W. (1995). Long-term working memory. *Psychological Review, 102*, 211–245.

Ericsson, K. A., Krampe, R. T., & Tesch-Römer, C. (1993). The role of deliberate practice in the acquisition of expert performance. *Psychological Review, 100*, 363–406.

Farkas, A. (2002). Prototypicality-effect in surrealist paintings. *Empirical Studies of the Arts, 20*, 127–136.

Fava, M. (2014). *Understanding drawing: A cognitive account of observational process*. Unpublished doctoral dissertation. Loughborough University, Loughborough, England.

Fayena-Tawil, F., Kozbelt, A., & Sitaras, L. (2011). Think global, act local: A protocol analysis comparison of artists' and non-artists' cognitions, metacognitions, and evaluations while drawing. *Psychology of Aesthetics, Creativity, and the Arts, 5*, 135–145.

Fechner, G. T. (1876). *Vorschule der Aesthetik* (Vol. 1). Leipzig, Germany: Breitkopf & Härtel.

Feist, G. J. (2004). The evolved fluid specificity of human creative talent. In R. J. Sternberg, E. L. Grigorenko, & J. L. Singer (Eds.), *Creativity: From potential to realization* (pp. 57–82). Washington, DC: American Psychological Association.

Fitts, P. M., & Posner, M. I. (1967). *Human performance*. Belmont, CA: Brooks/Cole.

Freedberg, D., & Gallese, V. (2007). Motion, emotion and empathy in esthetic experience. *Trends in Cognitive Sciences, 11*, 197–203.

Fung, C. V. (1996). Musicians' and nonmusicians' preferences for world musics: Relation to musical characteristics and familiarity. *Journal of Research in Music Education, 44*, 60–83.

Gagné, F. (2009). Debating giftedness: Pronat vs. Antinat. In L. V. Shavinina (Ed.), *International handbook on giftedness* (pp. 155–98). Dordrecht: Springer.

Gardner, H. (1983). *Frames of mind*. New York: Basic Books.

Getzels, J. W., & Csikszentmihalyi, M. (1976). *The creative vision*. New York: Wiley.

Gilbert, S. J., Zamenopoulos, T., Alexiou, K., & Johnson, J. H. (2009). Involvement of right dorsolateral prefrontal cortex in ill-structured design cognition: An fMRI study. *Brain Research, 1312*, 79–88.

Glazek, K. (2012). Visual and motor processing in visual artists: Implications for cognitive and neural mechanisms. *Psychology of Aesthetics, Creativity, and the Arts, 6*, 155–167.

Gobet, F., & Charness, N. (2018). Expertise in chess. In K. A. Ericsson, R. R. Hoffman, A. Kozbelt, & A. M. Williams (Eds.), *The Cambridge handbook of expertise and expert performance*, 2nd edition (pp. 597–615). Cambridge, England: Cambridge University Press.

Goel, V., & Grafman, J. (2000). Role of the right prefrontal cortex in ill-structured planning. *Cognitive Neuropsychology, 17*, 415–436.

Goel, V., & Pirolli, P. (1992). The structure of design problem spaces. *Cognitive Science, 16*, 395–429.

Goldstein, T. R. (2009). The pleasure of unadulterated sadness: Experiencing sorrow in fiction, nonfiction, and "in person." *Psychology of Aesthetics, Creativity, and the Arts, 3*, 232–237.

Goldstein, T. R., & Levy, A. G. (2017). The constricted muse: Acting. In J. C. Kaufman, V. P. Glăveanu, & J. Baer (Eds.), *The Cambridge handbook of creativity across domains* (pp. 145–160). Cambridge, England: Cambridge University Press.

Goldstein, T. R., Tamir, M., & Winner, E. (2013). Expressive suppression and acting classes. *Psychology of Aesthetics, Creativity, and the Arts, 7*, 191–196.

Goldstein, T. R., & Winner, E. (2010). Engagement in role play, pretense, and acting classes predict advanced theory of mind skill in middle childhood. *Imagination, Cognition, and Personality, 20*, 249–258.

Gombrich, E. H. (1979). *The sense of order*. New York: Phaidon.

Goodman, G., & Kaufman, J. C. (2014). Gremlins in my head: Predicting stage fright in elite actors. *Empirical Studies of the Arts, 32*, 133–148.

Gopnik, B. (2012). Aesthetic science and artistic knowledge. In A. P. Shimamura, & S. E. Palmer (Eds.), *Aesthetic science: Connecting minds, brains, and experience* (pp. 129–159). Oxford, England: Oxford University Press.

Graves, B., & Frederiksen, C. H. (1991). Literary expertise in the description of a fictional narrative. *Poetics, 20*, 1–26.

Grodal, T. (2009). Film aesthetics and the embodied brain. In M. Skov & O. Vartanian (Eds.), *Neuroaesthetics* (pp. 249–260). Amityville, NY: Baywood.

Hare, F. G. (1974). Artistic training and responses to visual and auditory patterns varying in uncertainty. In D. E. Berlyne (Ed.), *Studies in the new experimental aesthetics* (pp. 159–168). New York: Hemisphere.

Haswell, R. H. (2000). Documenting improvement in college writing: A longitudinal approach. *Written Communication, 17*, 307–352.

Hayes, A. E., Paul, M. A., Beuger, B., & Tipper, S. P. (2008). Self produced and observed actions influence emotion: The roles of action fluency and eye gaze. *Psychological Research, 72*, 461–472.

Hayes, J. R., & Flower, L. S. (1980). Identifying the organization of writing processes. In L. W. Gregg, & E. R. Steinberg (Eds.), *Cognitive processes in writing* (pp. 3–30). Maywah, NJ: Erlbaum.

Hayes, J. R., & Flower, L. S. (1986). Writing research and the writer. *American Psychologist, 41*, 1106–1113.

Hekkert, P. (2006). Design aesthetics: Principles of pleasure in product design. *Psychology Science, 48*, 157–172.

Hekkert, P. (2014). Aesthetic responses to design: A battle of impulses. In J. K. Smith, & P. Tinio (Eds.), *The Cambridge handbook of the psychology of aesthetics and the arts* (pp. 277–299). Cambridge, England: Cambridge University Press.

Hekkert, P., & van Wieringen, P. C. W. (1996). Beauty in the eye of expert and nonexpert beholders: A study in the appraisal of art. *American Journal of Psychology, 109*, 389–407.

Houtsma, A. J., Durlach, N. I., & Horowitz, D. M. (1987). Comparative learning of pitch and loudness identification. *Journal of the Acoustical Society of America, 81*, 129–132.

Intons-Peterson, M. J., & Smythe, M. A. (1987). The anatomy of repertory memory. *Journal of Experimental Psychology Learning Memory and Cognition, 13*, 490–500.

Ishizu, T., & Zeki, S. (2011). Toward a brain-based theory of beauty. *PLoS ONE, 6*, e21852.

Istok, E., Brattico, E., Jacobsen, T, Krohn, K., Muller, M., & Tervaniemi, M. (2009). Aesthetic responses to music: A questionnaire study. *Musicae Scientiae, 13*, 183–206.

Jacobsen, T., Schubotz, R. I., Höfel, L., & Cramon, D. Y. v. (2006). Brain correlates of aesthetic judgment of beauty. *NeuroImage, 29*, 276–285.

Jansson, D. G., & Smith, S. M. (1991). Design fixation. *Design Studies, 12*, 3–11.

Johnson, S. (2008). *Johnson: The major works*. Oxford, England: Oxford University Press.

Kaufman, J. C., Baer, J., Cropley, D. H., Reiter-Palmon, R., & Sinnett, S. (2013). Furious activity vs. understanding: How much expertise is needed to evaluate creative work? *Psychology of Aesthetics, Creativity, and the Arts, 7*, 332–340.

Kaufman, J. C., & Beghetto, R. A. (2009). Beyond big and little: The four c model of creativity. *Review of General Psychology, 13*, 1–12.

Kaufman, S. B., & Kaufman, J. C. (Eds.). (2009). *The psychology of creative writing*. Cambridge, England: Cambridge University Press.

Kawabata, H., & Zeki, S. (2004). Neural correlates of beauty. *Journal of Neurophysiology, 91*, 1699–1705.

Keele, S., Pokorny, R., Corcos, D., & Ivry, R. (1985). Do perception and motor production share a common timing mechanism? *Acta Psychologica, 60*, 173–193.

Kellogg, R. T. (2018). Professional writing expertise. In K. A. Ericsson, R. R. Hoffman, A. Kozbelt, & A. M. Williams (Eds.), *The Cambridge handbook of expertise and expert performance*, 2nd edition (pp. 413–430). Cambridge, England: Cambridge University Press.

Kholina, A. (2015). Aesthetic responses made visible through voices of experts. *Journal of Research Practice, 11*, Article M7.

Kirk, U. (2012). The modularity of aesthetic processing and perception in the human brain: Functional neuroimaging studies of neuroaesthetics. In A. P. Shimamura, & S. E.

Palmer (Eds.), *Aesthetic science: Connecting minds, brains, and experience* (pp. 318–336). Oxford, England: Oxford University Press.

Kirk, U., & Freedberg, D. (2015). Contextual bias and insulation against bias during aesthetic rating: The roles of VMPFC and DLPFC in neural valuation. In J. P. Huston, M. Nadal, F. Mora, L. F. Agnati, & C. J. Cela-Conde (Eds.), *Art, aesthetics, and the brain* (pp. 158–173). Oxford, England: Oxford University Press.

Kirk, U., Harvey, A. H., & Montague, P. R. (2011). Domain expertise insulates against judgment bias by monetary favors through a modulation of ventromedial prefrontal cortex. *Proceedings of the National Academy of Sciences, 108,* 10332–10336.

Kirk, U., Skov, M., & Nygaard, N., & Christensen, M. S. (2009). Brain correlates of aesthetic expertise: A parametric fMRI study. *Brain & Cognition, 69,* 306–315.

Kirsch, L., Dawson, K., & Cross, E. S. (2015). Dance experience sculpts aesthetic perception and related brain circuits. *Annals of the New York Academy of Sciences, 1337,* 130–139.

Kirsch, L., Drommelschmidt, K., & Cross, E. S. (2013). The impact of sensorimotor experience on affective evaluation of dance. *Frontiers in Human Neuroscience, 7,* 521.

Kozbelt, A. (2001). Artists as experts in visual cognition. *Visual Cognition, 8,* 705–723.

Kozbelt, A. (2006). Dynamic evaluation of Matisse's 1935 "Large Reclining Nude." *Empirical Studies of the Arts, 24,* 119–137.

Kozbelt, A. (2008a). Longitudinal hit ratios of classical composers: Reconciling "Darwinian" and expertise acquisition perspectives on lifespan creativity. *Psychology of Aesthetics, Creativity, and the Arts, 2,* 221–235.

Kozbelt, A. (2008b). Hierarchical linear modeling of creative artists' problem solving behaviors. *Journal of Creative Behavior, 42,* 181–200.

Kozbelt, A. (2017a). Musical creativity. In J. C. Kaufman, J. Baer, & V. Glăveanu (Eds.), *The Cambridge handbook of creativity across domains* (pp. 161–180). Cambridge, England: Cambridge University Press.

Kozbelt, A. (2017b). Tensions in naturalistic, evolutionary explanations of aesthetic reception and production. *New Ideas in Psychology, 47,* 113–120.

Kozbelt, A., Dexter, S., Dolese, M., & Seidel, A. (2012). The aesthetics of software code: A quantitative exploration. *Psychology of Aesthetics, Creativity, and the Arts, 6,* 57–65.

Kozbelt, A., & Kaufman, J. C. (2014). Aesthetics assessment. In J. K. Smith & P. Tinio (Eds.), *The Cambridge handbook of aesthetics* (pp. 86–114). Cambridge, England: Cambridge University Press.

Kozbelt, A., & Ostrofsky, J. (2018). Expertise in drawing. In K. A. Ericsson, R. R. Hoffman, A. Kozbelt, & A. M. Williams, M. (Eds.). *The Cambridge handbook of expertise and expert performance,* 2nd edition (pp. 576–596). Cambridge, England: Cambridge University Press.

Kozbelt, A., Seidel, A., ElBassiouny, A., Mark, Y., & Owen, D. R. (2010). Visual selection contributes to artists' advantages in representational drawing. *Psychology of Aesthetics, Creativity, and the Arts, 4,* 93–102.

Kozbelt, A., & Serafin, J. (2009). Dynamic evaluation of high- and low-creativity drawings by artist and non-artist raters. *Creativity Research Journal, 21,* 349–360.

Kranjec, A. (2015). Conceptual art made simple for neuroaesthetics. *Frontiers in Human Neuroscience, 9,* Article 267, 1–5.

Lawson B. (1994). *Design in mind.* Oxford, England: Butterworth-Heinemann.

Leder, H., Belke, B., Oeberst, A., & Augustin, D. (2004). A model of aesthetic appreciation and aesthetic judgments. *British Journal of Psychology, 95,* 489–508.

Leder, H., Carbon, C. C., & Ripsas, A. (2006). Entitling art: Influence of different types of title information on understanding and appreciation of paintings. *Acta Psychologica, 121,* 176–198.

Leder, H., Gerger, G., Brieber, D., & Schwarz, N. (2013). What makes an art expert? Emotion and evaluation in art appreciation. *Cognition and Emotion, 28,* 1137–1147.

Leder, H. Gerger, G., Dressler, S. G., & Schabmann, A. (2012). How art is appreciated. *Psychology of Aesthetics, Creativity, and the Arts, 6,* 2–10.

Leder, H., & Nadal, M. (2014). Ten years of a model of aesthetic appreciation and aesthetic judgments: The aesthetic episode–developments and challenges in empirical aesthetics. *British Journal of Psychology, 105,* 443–464.

Lehmann, A. C., Gruber, H., & Kopiez, R. (2018). Expertise in music. In K. A. Ericsson, R. R. Hoffman, A. Kozbelt, & A. M. Williams (Eds.). *The Cambridge handbook of expertise and expert performance,* 2nd edition (pp. 535–549). Cambridge, England: Cambridge University Press.

Liu, J., Lughofer, E., & Zeng, X. (2017). Toward model building for visual aesthetic perception. *Computational Intelligence and Neuroscience,* Article ID 1292801. doi:10.1155/2017/1292801

Liu, S., Erkkinen, M. G., Healey, M. L., Xu, Y., Swett, K. E., Chow, H. M., & Braun, A. R. (2015). Brain activity and connectivity during poetry composition: Toward a multidimensional model of the creative process. *Human Brain Mapping, 36,* 3351–3372.

Lloyd, P., & Scott, P. (1994). Discovering the design problem. *Design Studies, 15,* 125–140.

Lloyd, P., & Scott, P. (1995). Difference in similarity: Interpreting the architectural design process. *Environment and Planning B: Planning and Design, 22,* 383–406.

Locher, P., Krupinski, E. A., Mello-Thoms, C., & Nodine, C. F. (2007). Visual interest in pictorial art during an aesthetic experience. *Spatial Vision, 21,* 55–77.

Locher, P. J. (2015). The aesthetic experience with visual art "at first glance." In P. F. Bundgaard, & F. Stjernfelt (Eds.), *Investigations into the phenomenology and the ontology of the work of art: What are artworks and how do we experience them?* (pp. 75–88). New York: Springer.

Martindale, C. (1990). *The clockwork muse: The predictability of artistic change.* New York: Basic Books.

Martindale, C. (2007). A neural-network theory of beauty. In C. Martindale, P. Locher, & V. M. Petrov (Eds.), *Evolutionary and neurocognitive approaches to aesthetics, creativity, and the arts* (pp. 181–194). Amityville, NY: Baywood.

Martindale, C. (2009). The evolution and end of art as Hegelian tragedy. *Empirical Studies of the Arts, 27,* 133–140.

Martindale, C., & Moore, K. (1988). Priming, prototypicality, and preference. *Journal of Experimental Psychology: Human Perception and Performance, 14,* 661–670.

McClure, S. M., Li, J., Tomlin, D., Cypert, K. S., Montague, L. M., & Montague, P. R. (2004). Neural correlates of behavioural preference for culturally familiar drinks. *Neuron, 44,* 379–387.

McCutchen, D. (1996). A capacity theory of writing: Working memory in composition. *Educational Psychology Review, 8,* 299–325.

McManus, I. C., Cheema, B., & Stoker, J. (1993). The aesthetics of composition: A study of Mondrian. *Empirical Studies of the Arts, 11,* 83–94.

McManus, I. C., Zhou, F. A., l'Anson, S., Waterfield, L., Stover, K., & Cook, R. (2011). The psychometrics of photographing cropping: The influence of colour, meaning, and expertise. *Perception, 40,* 332–357.

McWhinnie, H. J. (1966). Effects of a learning experience on preference for complexity and asymmetry. *Perceptual and Motor Skills*, *23*, 119–122.

Micheyl, C., Delhommeau, K., Perrot, X., & Oxenham, A. J. (2006). Influence of musical and psychoacoustical training on pitch discrimination. *Hearing Research*, *219*, 36–47.

Millis, K. (2001). Making meaning brings pleasure: The influence of titles on aesthetic experiences. *Emotion*, *1*, 320–329.

Müller, M., Höfel, L., Brattico, E., & Jacobsen, T. (2010). Aesthetic judgments of music in experts and laypersons—an ERP study. *International Journal of Psychophysiology*, *76*, 40–51.

Nadal, M., & Chatterjee, A. (2018). Neuroaesthetics and art's diversity and universality. *WIREs Cognitive Science*, e1487. doi:10.1002/wcs.1487

Nadal, M., Munar, E., Marty, G., & Cela-Conde, C. J. (2010). Visual complexity and beauty appreciation: explaining the divergence of results. *Empirical Studies of the Arts*, *28*, 173–191.

Nemiro, J. (1997). Interpretive artists: A qualitative exploration of the creative process of actors. *Creativity Research Journal*, *10*, 229–239.

Noice, H., & Noice, T. (1993). The effects of segmentation on the recall of theatrical material. *Poetics*, *22*, 51–67.

Noice, H., & Noice T. (2013). Extending the reach of an evidence-based theatrical intervention. *Experimental Aging Research*, *39*, 398–418.

Noice, T., & Noice, H. (2019). The development of acting talent: Possibilities and approaches. In R. Subotnik, P. Olszewski-Kubilius, & F. Worrell, F. (Eds.), *The handbook of high performance: Developing human potential into domain specific talent* (pp. 239–256). Washington, DC: American Psychological Association.

North, A. C., & Hargreaves, D. J. (1995). Subjective complexity, familiarity, and liking for popular music. *Psychomusicology*, *14*, 77–93.

Oatley, K. (2012). The cognitive science of fiction. *WIREs Cognitive Science*, *3*, 425–430.

Oatley, K., & Djikic, M. (2008). Writing as thinking. *Review of General Psychology*, *12*, 9–27.

Orians, G. (2014). *Snakes, sunrises, and Shakespeare*. Chicago, IL: University of Chicago Press.

Orr, M. G., & Ohlsson, S. (2001). The relationship between musical complexity and liking in jazz and bluegrass. *Psychology of Music*, *29*, 108–127.

Orr, M. G., & Ohlsson, S. (2005). Relationship between complexity as a function of expertise. *Music Perception*, *22*, 583–611.

Palmer, C., & Krumhansl, C. L. (1990). Mental representations for musical meter. *Journal of Experimental Psychology: Human Perception and Performance*, *16*, 728–741.

Palmer, S. E., Schloss, K. B., & Sammartino, J. (2012). Hidden knowledge in aesthetic judgments. In A. P. Shimamura & S. E. Palmer (Eds.), *Aesthetic science: Connecting minds, brains, and experience* (pp. 189–222). Oxford, England: Oxford University Press.

Pantev, C., Roberts, L. E., Schulz, M., Engelien, A., & Ross, B. (2001). Timbre-specific enhancements of auditory cortical representations in musicians. *Neuroreport*, *12*, 169–174.

Parsons, M. J. (1987). *How we understand art: A cognitive developmental account of aesthetic experience*. Cambridge, England: Cambridge University Press.

Paul, C. (2008). *New media in the white cube and beyond: Curatorial models for digital art*. Berkeley, CA: University of California Press.

Pearce, M. T. (2015). Effects of expertise on the cognitive and neural processes involved in musical appreciation. In J. P. Huston, M. Nadal, F. Mora, L. F. Agnati, & C. J. Cela-Conde (Eds.), *Art, aesthetics, and the brain* (pp. 319–338). Oxford, England: Oxford University Press.

Pelowski, M., & Akiba, F. (2011). A model of art perception, evaluation and emotion in transformative aesthetic experience. *New Ideas in Psychology*, *29*, 80–97.

Pelowski, M., Markey, P. S., Lauring, J. O., & Leder, H. (2016). Visualizing the impact of art: An update and comparison of current psychological models of art experience. *Frontiers in Human Neuroscience, 10*, 160.

Perdreau, F., & Cavanagh, P. (2014). Drawing skill is related to the efficiency of encoding object structure. *Iperception, 5*, 101–119.

Perdreau, F., & Cavanagh, P. (2015). Drawing experts have better visual memory while drawing. *Journal of Vision, 15*, 5.

Perkins, D. N. (1981). *The mind's best work*. Cambridge, MA: Harvard University Press.

Pinker, S. (2002). *The blank slate: The modern denial of human nature*. London: Penguin.

Pinker, S. (2007). Toward a consilient study of literature. *Philosophy and Literature, 31*, 161–177.

Plassmann, H. O., Doherty, J. Shiv, B., & Rangel, A. (2006). Marketing actions can modulate neural representations of experienced pleasantness. *Proceedings of the National Academy of Sciences, 105*, 1050–1054.

Platz, F., Kopiez, R., Lehmann, A. C., & Wolff, A. (2014). The influence of deliberate practice on musical achievement: A meta-analysis. *Frontiers in Psychology—Cognition, 5*, 646. doi:10.3389/fpsyg.2014.00646

Prinz, W. (2006). What re-enactment earns us. *Cortex, 42*, 515–517.

Prum, R. O. (2013). Coevolutionary aesthetics in human and biotic artworlds. *Biology and Philosophy, 28*, 811–832.

Purves, D. (2017). *Music as biology: The tones we like and why*. Cambridge, MA: Harvard University Press.

Ragert, P., Schmidt, A., Altenmüller, E. O., & Dinse, R. (2004). Superior tactile performance and learning in professional pianists: Evidence for metaplasticity in musicians. *European Journal of Neuroscience, 19*, 473–478.

Ramachandran, V. S., & Hirstein, W. (1999). The science of art: A neurological theory of aesthetic experience. *Journal of Consciousness Studies, 6*, 15–51.

Rammsayer, T., & Altenmüller, E. (2006). Temporal information processing in musicians and nonmusicians. *Music Perception, 24*, 37–48.

Reber, R. (2012). Processing fluency, aesthetic pleasure, and culturally shared taste. In A. P. Shimamura, & S. E. Palmer (Eds.), *Aesthetic science: Connecting minds, brains, and experience* (pp. 223–249). Oxford, England: Oxford University Press.

Reber, R., Schwarz, N., & Winkielman, P. (2004). Processing fluency and aesthetic pleasure: Is beauty in the perceiver's processing experience? *Personality and Social Psychology Review, 8*, 364–382.

Rizzolatti, G., Fadiga, L., Gallese, V., & Fogassi, L. (1996). Premotor cortex and the recognition of motor actions. *Brain Research and Cognitive Brain Research, 3*, 131–141.

Russell, P. A. (2003). Effort after meaning and the hedonic value of paintings. *British Journal of Psychology, 94*, 99–110.

Sawyer, R. K. (2006). *Explaining creativity: The science of human innovation*. Oxford, England: Oxford University Press.

Schellenberg, G. (2004). Music lessons enhance IQ. *Psychological Science, 15*, 511–514.

Schellenberg, G. (2011). Music lessons, emotional intelligence, and IQ. *Music Perception, 29*, 185–194.

Serafin, J. (2013). Expertise in artistic photography. Unpublished doctoral dissertation. The Graduate Center of the City University of New York, New York. *Dissertation Abstracts International: Section B: The Sciences and Engineering, 74*(6-B)(E). Accession number: 2013-99241-028.

Serafin, J., & Dollinger, S. J. (2017). Photography and creativity. In J. C. Kaufman, V. P. Glăveaunu, & J. Baer (Eds.), *The Cambridge handbook of creativity across domains* (pp. 123–144). Cambridge, England: Cambridge University Press.

Serafin, J., Kozbelt, A., Seidel, A., & Dolese, M. (2011). Dynamic evaluation of high- and low-creativity drawings by artist and non-artist raters: Replication and methodological extension. *Psychology of Aesthetics, Creativity, and the Arts, 5*, 350–359.

Shah, C., Erhard, K., Ortheil, H., Kaza, E., Kessler, C., & Lotze, M. (2013). Neural correlates of creative writing: An fMRI study. *Human Brain Mapping, 34*, 1088–1101.

Silvia, P. J. (2005). Cognitive appraisals and interest in visual art: Exploring an appraisal theory of aesthetic emotions. *Empirical Studies of the Arts, 23*, 119–133.

Silvia, P. J. (2012). Human emotions and aesthetic experience: An overview of empirical aesthetics. In A. P. Shimamura, & S. E. Palmer (Eds.), *Aesthetic science: Connecting minds, brains, and experience* (pp. 250–275). Oxford, England: Oxford University Press.

Silvia, P. J. (2013). Interested experts, confused novices: Art expertise and the knowledge emotions. *Empirical Studies of the Arts, 31*, 107–116.

Silvia, P. J., & Berg, C. (2011). Finding movies interesting: How appraisals and expertise influence the aesthetic experience of film. *Empirical Studies of the Arts, 29*, 73–88.

Simon, C. R., & Wohlwill, J. F. (1968). An experimental study of the role of expectation and variation in music. *Journal of Research in Music Education, 16*, 227–238.

Simon, H. A. (1996). *The sciences of the artificial*, 3rd edition. Cambridge, MA: MIT Press.

Simonton, D. K. (1999). *Origins of genius: Darwinian perspectives on creativity*. Oxford, England: Oxford University Press.

Simonton, D. K. (2000). Creative development as acquired expertise: Theoretical issues and an empirical test. *Developmental Review, 20*, 283–318.

Simonton, D. K. (2007). Is bad art the opposite of good art? Positive versus negative cinematic assessments of 877 feature films. *Empirical Studies of the Arts, 25*, 142–161.

Simonton, D. K. (2011). Creativity and discovery as blind variation: Campbell's (1960) BVSR model after the half-century mark. *Review of General Psychology, 15*, 158–174.

Sio, U. N., Kotovsky, K., & Cagan, J. (2015). Fixation or inspiration: A meta-analytic review of the role of examples on design processes. *Design Studies, 39*, 70–99.

Skoe, E., & Kraus, N. (2013). Musical training heightens auditory brainstem function during sensitive periods in development. *Frontiers in Psychology, 4*, 622.

Sloboda, J. A. (1991). Musical expertise. In K. A. Ericsson, & J. Smith (Eds.), *Toward a general theory of expertise: Prospects and limits* (pp. 153–171). Cambridge, England: Cambridge University Press.

Sloboda, J. A., Davidson, J. W., Howe, M. J. A., & Moore, D. G. (1996). The role of practice in the development of performing musicians. *British Journal of Psychology, 87*, 287–309.

Smith, J. D., & Melara, R. J. (1990). Aesthetic preference and syntactic prototypicality in music. *Cognition, 34*, 279–298.

Smith, L. F., & Smith, J. K. (2006). The nature and growth of aesthetic fluency. In P. Locher, C. Martindale, & L. Dorfman (Eds.), *Foundations and frontiers in aesthetics. New directions in aesthetics, creativity and the arts* (pp. 47–58). Amityville, NY: Baywood.

Snyder, B. (2016). Memory for music. In S. Hallam, I. Cross, & M. Thaut (Eds.), *The Oxford handbook of music psychology* (pp. 167–180). Oxford, England: Oxford University Press.

Solso, R. L. (2001). Brain activities in an expert versus a novice artist: An fMRI study. *Leonardo, 34*, 31–34.

Sommers, N. (1980). Revision strategies of student writers and experienced writers. *College Composition and Communication, 31*, 378–387.

Steele, C. J., Bailey, J. A., Zatorre, R. J., & Penhune, V. B. (2013). Early musical training and white matter plasticity in the corpus callosum: Evidence for a sensitive period. *Journal of Neuroscience, 33*, 1282–1290.

Sudnow, D. (1993). *Ways of the hand: The organization of improvised conduct.* London: Routledge & Kegan Paul.

Sundberg, J. (1987). *The science of the singing voice.* DeKalb, IL: Northern Illinois University Press.

Suwa, M., Gero, J., & Purcell, T. (2000). Unexpected discoveries and S-invention of design requirements: Important vehicles for a design process. *Design Studies, 21*, 539–567.

Swami, V. (2013). Context matters: Investigating the impact of contextual information on aesthetic appreciation of paintings by Max Ernst and Pablo Picasso. *Psychology of Aesthetics, Creativity, and the Arts, 7*, 285–295.

Tchalenko, J. (2009). Segmentation and accuracy in copying and drawing: Experts and beginners. *Vision Research, 49*, 791–800.

Thomson, P. (2017). Dance: The challenges of measuring embodied creativity. In J. C. Kaufman, J. Baer, & V. Glaveanu (Eds.), *Studying creativity across different domains* (pp. 181–195). Cambridge, England: Cambridge University Press.

Tinio, P. P. L. (2013). From artistic creation to aesthetic reception: The mirror model of art. *Psychology of Aesthetics, Creativity, and the Arts, 7*, 265–275.

Tinio, P. P. L., & Leder, H. (2009). Just how stable are stable aesthetic features? Symmetry, complexity, and the jaws of massive familiarization. *Acta Psychologica, 130*, 241–250.

Tinio, P. P. L., & Leder, H. (2013). The means to art's end: Styles, creative devices, and the challenge of art. In A. S. Bristol, J. C. Kaufman, & O. Vartanian (Eds.), *The Neuroscience of Creativity* (pp. 273–298). Cambridge, England: The MIT Press.

Tinio, P. P. L., Leder, H., & Strasser, M. (2011). Image quality and the aesthetics judgment of photographs: Contrast, sharpness, and grain teased apart and put together. *Psychology of Aesthetics, Creativity, and the Arts, 5*(2), 165–176.

Tooby, J. & Cosmides, L. (1992). The psychological foundations of culture. In J. Barkow, L. Cosmides, & J. Tooby (Eds.), *The adapted mind: Evolutionary psychology and the generation of culture* (pp. 19–136). Oxford, England: Oxford University Press.

Vartanian, O. (2017). The creation and aesthetic appreciation of architecture. In J. C. Kaufman, V. P. Glăveaunu, & J. Baer (Eds.), *The Cambridge handbook of creativity across domains* (pp. 110–122). Cambridge, England: Cambridge University Press.

Vartanian, O., & Goel, V. (2004). Neuroanatomical correlates of aesthetic preferences for paintings. *NeuroReport, 15*, 893–897.

Vartanian, O., Navarrete, G., Chatterjee, A., Fich, L. B., Leder, H., Modroño, C., … Skov, M. (2013). Impact of contour on aesthetic judgments and approach-avoidance decisions in architecture. *Proceedings of the National Academy of Sciences USA, 110*(Suppl. 2), 10446–10453.

Vessel, E. A., Starr, G. G., & Rubin, N. (2012). The brain on art: Intense aesthetic experience activates the default mode network. *Frontiers in Human Neuroscience, 6*, Article 66. doi:10.3389/fnhum.2012.00066

Vitz, P. C. (1966). Affect as a function of stimulus variation. *Journal of Experimental Psychology, 71*, 74–79.

Walker, E. L. (1980). *Psychological complexity and preference: A hedgehog theory of behavior.* Pacific Grove, CA: Brooks-Cole.

Weisberg, R. W. (1999). Creativity and knowledge: A challenge to theories. In R. J. Sternberg (Ed.), *Handbook of creativity* (pp. 226–250). Cambridge, England: Cambridge University Press.

Weisberg, R. W. (2011). Frank Lloyd Wright's Fallingwater: A case study of inside-the-box creativity. *Creativity Research Journal, 23,* 296–312.

Whitfield, T. W. A. (1983). Predicting preference for familiar, everyday objects: An experimental confrontation between two theories of aesthetic behavior. *Journal of Environmental Psychology, 3,* 221–237.

Wilson, E. O. (1998). *Consilience: The unity of knowledge.* New York.

Winner, E. (1996). *Gifted children: Myths and realities.* New York: Basic Books.

Winston, A. S., & Cupchik, G. C. (1992). The evaluation of high art and popular art by naïve and experienced viewers. *Visual Arts Research, 18,* 1–14.

Yildirim, K., Hidayetoglu, M. L., & Capanoglu, A. (2011). Effects of interior colors on mood and preference: Comparisons of two living rooms. *Perceptual and Motor Skills, 112,* 509–524.

Zajonc, R. B. (1968). Attitudinal effects of mere exposure. *Journal of Personality and Social Psychology Monograph Supplement, 9,* 1–27.

CHAPTER 36

THE INFLUENCE OF PERSONALITY ON AESTHETIC PREFERENCES

VIREN SWAMI AND ADRIAN FURNHAM

INTRODUCTION

DISCUSSIONS on the role of personality on aesthetic preferences can be traced back to Gustav Fechner's (1876) work on the aesthetics of rectangular figures. In these studies, he presented participants with rectangles that varied in height-to-width ratios and asked participants to indicate which they liked the most. In essence, Fechner (1876) had struck upon a method—what he called the "method of choice"—of examining aesthetic preferences at the level of the individual (see McManus, Cook, & Hunt, 2010). More than a century later, scholars agree that it is vital to better understand the role played by "the person," alongside stimulus and situational aspects, in shaping aesthetic preferences and experiences (Jacobsen, 2006, 2010; Jacobsen & Höfel, 2002). Although factors associated with "the person" are wide-ranging (see other chapters in Section 4), in this chapter we present an overview of the influence of personality on aesthetic preferences (see also Swami & Furnham, 2014). Although the focus of this chapter is primarily on visual arts, we also summarize the available literature on nonvisual art forms. To conclude, we assess the major challenges facing differential psychologists studying aesthetics and present some suggestions for future research directions.

PERSONALITY AND THE VISUAL ARTS

Eysenck and the "K" factor

A useful starting point for examining the impact personality on aesthetic preferences is the visual arts. Early work in this regard owes much to the work of Hans Eysenck.

Extending earlier work by Burt (1933), Eysenk (1940) presented participants with carefully selected visual stimuli and asked them to rank these according to their preferences. Based on factor analytic results, Eysenck (1940) discovered two factors related to aesthetic preferences. The first he called the "T" factor, which referred to an individual's ability to identify aesthetic quality (i.e., the extent to which participants had "good taste") and paved the way for later work on aesthetic sensitivity (e.g., Götz, Borisy, Lynn, & Eysenck, 1979). The second factor he identified was the "K" factor, a bipolar factor that distinguished between preferences for complex versus simple (or representative) art forms (Eysenck, 1941a). Eysenck (1941b, 1941c, 1942, 1968) would later replicate his factor analytic work concerning the T and K factors.

Eysenck's later work sought to clarify the relationship between personality and the K factor. To do so, he designed the "K test" (Eysenck, 1941d, p. 346), composed of visual stimuli constructed to differentiate between "modern" and "academic" art forms. Based on the K test, Eysenck (1941d) showed that a stronger preference for academic visual art was associated with a number of important individual differences, including greater introversion and conservativeness. His later work was likewise focused on the relationships between "K" and personality (Eysenck, 1988, 1992), with a particular focus on psychoticism (Eysenck & Furnham, 1993). In summarizing the Eysenck's contribution to the study of aesthetics, Myszkowski, Stormer, and Zenasni (2016, p. 158) concluded that "he connected the field of empirical aesthetics with individual differences psychology, showing, with innovative statistical methods and eloquence, that the focus of empirical aesthetics should not only be what is universally like, but also what differentiates individuals in their liking."

The Big Five

Eysenck's work on the K factor set the stage for later studies focused on individual differences and preferences for visual art forms (e.g., Barron, 1953; Child, 1965; Knapp & Wulff, 1963; Wilson, Ausman, & Matthews, 1973), but it was the emergence of the Big Five personality taxonomy that helped to consolidate and unify this body of work. The Big Five is a robust framework of traits that provides for an understanding of personality at the broadest level of abstraction (Costa & McCrae, 1992; Goldberg, 1993). The Big Five framework is a descriptive, hierarchical model consisting of five bipolar traits, namely agreeableness (a tendency to be helpful, cooperative, and sympathetic toward others), conscientiousness (a tendency to be disciplined, organized, and achievement oriented), neuroticism (a tendency to lack emotional stability and impulse control), extraversion (a tendency to be sociable and assertive), and openness to experience (a tendency to be intellectually curious and show a preference for novelty and variety).

The Big Five have been shown to have strong predictive validity in relation to a variety of real-world outcomes, including aesthetic preferences and judgments (Chamorro-Premuzic, 2007). In terms of the latter, one of the most consistent findings is a significant association between greater openness to experience and a stronger preference for visual arts in general (Chamorro-Premuzic, Burke, Hsu, & Swami, 2010; Chamorro-Premuzic & Furnham, 2004; Chamorro-Premuzic, Reimers, Hsu, & Ahmetoglu, 2009;

Feist & Brady, 2004; Furnham & Avison, 1997; Furnham & Bachtiar, 2008; Furnham & Chamorro-Premuzic, 2004; Furnham & Walker, 2001a, 2001b; Rawlings, 2000). It should be noted that the reported correlations have tended to be weak ($rs \approx .20–.30$), although the finding is robust and consistent across studies. In addition, openness to experience is also positively associated with aesthetic attitudes, including an appreciation of aesthetic quality (McManus & Furnham, 2006) and aesthetic emotions (e.g., pleasure; Fayn, MacCann, Tiliopoulos, & Silvia, 2015).

Beyond aesthetic preferences in general, greater openness to experience is also consistently associated with a stronger preference for nonconventional art forms (e.g., abstract and modern art; Chamorro-Premuzic, Reimers et al., 2009; Cleridou & Furnham, 2014; Furnham & Avison, 1997; Furnham & Rao, 2002). Some studies have demonstrated this association by asking participants to rate their liking of visual art by known abstract or modern artists; Swami and Furnham (2012), for example, reported that openness to experience was significantly associated with liking of Piet Mondrian's Neo-Plastic paintings. Other studies have asked participants to rate their preferences for visual art from different genres, and likewise report that openness to experience is positively associated with a preference for contemporary art forms (e.g., Cleridou & Furnham, 2014) and a lower preference for traditional (Chamorro-Premuzic, Reimer et al., 2009) and neutral visual art (Rawlings, Twomey, Burns, & Morris, 1998). One study has also classified visual art based on emotional valence (i.e., the ability of a composition to elicit arousal and positive or negative emotions on the part of the observer) and reported significant associations between openness to experience and emotionally positive art (Chamorro-Premuzic et al., 2010).

This is not to say that other Big Five traits are not associated with preferences for visual art forms, but rather that reported associations have tended to be weaker and more equivocal than that with openness to experience (Swami & Furnham, 2014). Take introversion, for example: whereas Eysenck (1941d) reported that introversion was positively associated with a preference for "academic" (or traditional) art forms, Cardinet (1958) later reported an association between introversion and preference for modern art. More recent studies have also reported equivocal findings, with some studies reporting positive associations and others reporting negative associations, depending on the methodology and specific stimuli used (Chamorro-Premuzic, Reimers et al., 2009; Furnham & Chamorro-Premuzic, 2004; Swami & Furnham, 2012). Beyond openness to experience and introversion, some studies have reported significant associations between preferences for visual art and conscientiousness, agreeableness, and neuroticism, respectively, although effects have been weak at best (and, in most cases, null; for a review, see Swami & Furnham, 2014).

Openness to experience or sensation-seeking?

Although it seems clear that openness to experience plays a role in aesthetic judgments, one difficulty with extant findings is that the association may be predicated on traits that share conceptual similarities with openness to experience, such as sensation-seeking. The latter refers to an individual's desire to seek out varied, complex, novel, and intense experiences, and the willingness to take risks for the sake of such experiences (Zuckerman, 1979). Indeed, openness to experience and sensation-seeking are typically moderately correlated (Zuckerman, 1994) and share many similar lower-order facets. Thus, it is sometimes unclear whether the findings reviewed above are truly reflective of an association with openness to experience, or whether they reflect common lower-order associations with sensation-seeking.

Certainly, the available research suggests that sensation-seeking is independently associated with a preference for complex designs (Rawlings et al., 1998; Zuckerman, 2006; Zuckerman, Bone, Neary, Mangelsdorff, & Brustman, 1972; Zuckerman, Neary, & Brustman, 1970), paintings that are higher in tension or that are emotionally charged (Rawlings, 2003; Zuckerman, Ulrich, & McLaughlin, 1993), and surrealist and abstract visual art (Furnham & Avison, 1997; Furnham & Bunyan, 1988). Importantly, where studies have measured both constructs concurrently, it has been reported that associations between aesthetic preferences and sensation-seeking tend to be weaker than those with openness to experience (Furnham & Avison, 1997; Furnham & Walker, 2001a; Rawlings et al., 1998). In addition, some studies have reported no significant associations between sensation-seeking and preferences for abstract art (Swami & Furnham, 2012). Swami and Furnham (2014) have suggested that these effects may be partly explained by the different ways in which sensation-seeking has been measured, which makes it difficult to draw firm conclusions about the role of this construct.

Other things to consider

The reliability of the association between openness to experience and visual art has led some scholars to conclude that it is a core component of an "artistic personality" (McCrae & Costa, 1997). For example, it has been suggested that open individuals have qualities that "are harmonious with the notions of abstract art being more modern, untraditional, and depicting subject matter through intrinsic qualities, rather than literal representational forms" (Chamorro-Premuzic, Reimers, et al., 2009, p. 503). In this view, it is argued that openness to experience includes lower-order personality facets associated with imagination, creativity, and nonconventionalism that translate into a preference for more complex and contemporary visual art forms, to enjoy aesthetic experiences, and to pursue and support the arts (Conner & Silvia, 2015; Kaufman, 2013; Swami & Furnham, 2014). Nevertheless, it should be noted that most studies have relied on measures of higher-order openness to experience (Swami & Furnham, 2014), which makes it difficult to draw conclusions about what specific facets may be driving reported associations. Of the few studies that have focused on lower-order facets of openness to experience, it appears to be an individual's sensitivity to, and interest in, art and beauty that are most strongly associated with artistic interests and preferences (Rawlings et al., 1998; Rawlings, Vidal, & Furnham, 2000).

In a similar vein, despite the reliability of the association, it should be noted that most studies have reported only weak-to-moderate associations between higher-order openness to experience and aesthetic preferences for visual art forms. Focusing on lower-order facets of openness to experience would seem to be the most straight-forward way of developing the above body of work, although there may also be utility in examining whether, and the extent to which, the relationship between openness to experience and aesthetic judgments is mediated by other variables. Prime mediating candidates include previous aesthetic experiences, familiarity with works of art, and aesthetic knowledge (Chamorro-Premuzic et al., 2010; Furnham & Walker, 2001a; Swami & Furnham, 2012). There may also be complex interrelationships between openness to experience and the ways in which visual art is presented. For example, there is some evidence that presenting context-relevant information about surrealist and abstract paintings improves aesthetic appreciation (Swami, 2013), and it may be useful to examine the extent to which openness to experience mediates such associations.

Personality and Other Aesthetic Media

Musical preferences

The empirical study of personality and aesthetic preferences for music has generally been framed in terms of the uses-and-gratification perspective (Rosengren, Wenner, & Palmgreen, 1985). This approach is focused on the motives for music consumption and, in broad outline, suggests that individuals prefer types of music that suit their personality profiles; more specifically, individuals show a preference for certain types of music over others because they have personalities that the music satisfies (Arnett, 1995; Arnett, Larson, & Offer, 1995). A classic example is provided by Berlyne (1960; see also Eysenck, 1990): because extraverts have low cortical arousal, they were expected to show a preference for upbeat or high-tempo music. Contemporary research has provided support for this broad perspective and it is now recognized that there are reliable associations between music preferences and personality traits (Juslin, Sakka, Barradas, & Liljeström, 2016; Pearson & Dollinger, 2002; Rentfrow & McDonald, 2009; Schwartz & Fouts, 2003).

The most comprehensive examination of the influence of personality on music preferences was conducted by Rentfrow and Gosling (2003). Based on factor analytic work, these authors first identified four dominant music preference dimensions, namely: (a) reflective and complex (defined by the blues, jazz, classical, and folk music); (b) intense and rebellious (rock, alternative, and heavy metal); (c) upbeat and conventional (country, soundtrack, religious, and pop music); and (d) energetic and rhythmic (rap, hip-hop, soul and funk, and electronica and dance music). Next, they examined relationships between these music dimensions and the Big Five personality traits. They reported that a preference for reflective and complex music and intense and rebellious music was positively associated with openness to experience. By contrast, a preference for upbeat and conventional music was positively related to extraversion, agreeableness and conscientiousness, but negatively related to openness. Finally, a preference for energetic and rhythmic music was positively correlated with extraversion and agreeableness.

These associations have also generally been confirmed in more recent studies (e.g., Delsing, ter Bogt, Engels, & Meeus, 2008; Vella & Mills, 2017). However, studies conducted in different cultural groups have not always returned consistent findings. For example, Brown (2012) examined associations between personality and music preferences in Japanese students. He reported that openness to experience was significantly associated with a preference for reflective music, whereas extraversion was significantly correlated with a stronger preference for popular music. In contrast, in Croatian adults, it was reported that agreeableness was significantly associated with a preference for all styles of music except classical music, whereas openness to experience was associated with a preference for all music styles excerpt jazz and world music (Reić Ercegovac, Dobrota, & Kuščević, 2015). In addition, in Croatian adults, extraversion was significantly associated with a preference for popular music (Reić Ercegovac et al., 2015). These finding suggest that there may some cross-cultural variation in specific relationships between personality and music preferences. One concern, however, is that personality traits do not strongly predict music preferences, which may explain why some studies with the same cultural population return different patterns of correlations (e.g., Reić Ercegovac & Dobrota, 2011; Reić Ercegovac et al., 2015).

Some studies have examined the influence of personality on specific musical genres. For example, Swami et al. (2013) presented participants with 10 tracks of contemporary heavy metal, which they were asked to rate for liking. Greater openness to experience was associated with greater composite liking across the tracks, possibly because they are more likely to be attracted to music that is nonmainstream and complex (e.g., the use of screamed and unpitched vocals). Indeed, the trait of openness to experience appears to be important in relation to other aspects of music preferences and experiences. For example, studies have found that openness to experience is positively associated with the intensity of emotions evoked by listening to music (Vuoskoski, Thompson, McIlwain, & Eerola, 2011), the experience of awe when listening to music (Silvia, Fayn, Nusbaum, & Beaty, 2015), and the experience of frisson (pleasurable aesthetic chills, such as goosebumps) when listening to music (Colver & el-Alayli, 2016; Silvia & Nusbaum, 2011).

Reading preferences

As with preferences for visual arts and music, openness to experience is also reliably associated with reading preferences. For example, Kraaykamp and van Eijck (2005) reported that openness to experience was positively associated with a preference for more complex and stimulating genres, particularly literary novels and literature in a foreign language. Other studies have similarly reported that openness to experience is more strongly associated with a preference for culture-related texts and science-related materials (e.g., Schutte & Malouff, 2004). Greater openness to experience has also been found to be associated with a stronger aesthetic liking of complex surrealist texts, even after controlling for familiarity with those texts (Swami, Pietschnig, Stieger, Nader, & Voracek, 2012). Taken together, these studies are generally consistent with the evidence reviewed above that open individuals show a preference for unconventional, intellectual, or difficult aesthetic experiences. More generally, openness to experience is also associated with greater time reading for pleasure (Finn, 1997).

Conversely, associations between reading preferences and the other Big Five traits are more equivocal. For example, where Finn (1997) reported that extraversion was negatively associated with time spent reading for pleasure, other studies have reported no significant correlation (Kraaykamp & van Eijck, 2005; Schutte & Malouff, 2004). In addition, significant negative associations have been reported between a preference for literary novels and agreeableness and conscientiousness (Kraaykamp & van Eijck, 2005). Finally, Schutte and Malouff (2004) also reported that conscientiousness was positively associated with a preference for science-related reading matter. In general, however, these associations have tended to be much weaker than those between reading preferences and openness to experience.

Film and television preferences

Very few studies have examined the associations between personality and aesthetic experiences related to film or television. The research that is available adopts the uses-and-gratification approach in suggesting that individuals prefer and select film or television programs based on needs that they fulfill. For example, there is some evidence to suggest that individuals who score highly on neuroticism are more likely to watch television for entertainment and companionship purposes than emotionally stable individuals (Weaver, 2003). To date, however, studies have generally not explicitly examined associations between personality and film or television preferences. Part of the problem may be that it has proved difficult to reduce the wide range of different film and television genres into coherent factor structures. For example, two studies that have attempted to do so have arrived at very different structures (Hirschman, 1985; North & Hargreaves, 2007).

An alternative approach would be to focus on preferences for film from specific genres. For example, some studies have examined associations between personality and a preference for violent or aggressive film content (for a review, see Chamorro-Premuzic, Kallias, & Hsu, 2014). These studies generally indicate that individuals who are low in the trait agreeableness tend to show a stronger preference for films with explicit violence (Weaver, 1991), possibly because they are less likely to empathize with victims of violence. Some studies have also reported that neuroticism is negatively associated with a preference for violent movie clips (Lee, Gibbons, & Short, 2010). Likewise, some studies have reported that neuroticism is negatively associated with a preference for scary films (Chamorro-Premuzic et al., 2014). Finally, one study asked participants to rate for aesthetic preference and familiarity a set of 10 clips of surrealist film (e.g., Luis Buñuel's *Un Chien Andalou*) (Swami et al., 2010). Results of the study indicated that preference for the film clips was associated with openness to experience.

Major challenges, goals, and suggestions

Overall, the evidence we have reviewed in this chapter points quite conclusively to the Big Five personality factor of openness to experience as a central component of what Chamorro-Premuzic et al. (2007) have termed the "artistic personality." It seems likely that the imagination, curiosity, and creativity associated with higher openness drive a greater proclivity for aesthetic experiences. Of course, this is not to deny the role played by other traits, such as sensation-seeking, in shaping aesthetic experiences. Nor does the perspective we have relied on in this chapter deny the importance of other person-related factors. Nevertheless, it does appear to be the case that personality generally, and openness more specifically, have an important role in determining aesthetic experiences. Even so, there are a number of ways in which this field could be moved forward in future research.

First, one of the main limitations of the above research is that studies have typically examined aesthetic preferences in only one medium. Thus, it remains unclear whether individuals who show a preference for, say, unconventional literature would also show a similar preference for unconventional music or film (Rentfrow, Goldberg, & Zilca, 2011). The difficulty in classifying aesthetic preferences across media is that such preferences can be measured at different levels of abstraction, from the superordinate to the low-order subordinate (Rentfrow & Gosling, 2003). Although there is some evidence that preferences for subordinate exemplars correlate highly with preferences for genre labels (Rentfrow & McDonald, 2009), very little research has examined preferences at the superordinate level. Verifying existing superordinate taxonomies (see Cleridou & Furnham, 2014; Ercegovac et al., 2015; Rentfrow et al., 2011) or creating new taxonomies would be one way in which the diverse areas of research could potentially be unified.

Second, there remains a need to broaden the scope of future research to examine in detail the associations between personality and media other than the visual arts. For instance, although there is now a growing body of research focused on music and reading, there remains a dearth of research focused specifically on film and television. In addition, there is still very little literature that specifically examines aesthetic preferences in relation to less mainstream art forms, such as dance and performance art as well as other aspects of aesthetics, such as architecture and design (Cook & Furnham, 2012). There is also scope to examine the reviewed associations and non-Western art (e.g., Swami, 2009). Although it might be expected that the associations with personality observed with other media will be replicated in future research, empirical data are still needed to ascertain the validity of such assumptions.

Third, there is a need to examine more fully the relationships between lower-order facets of openness to experience and aesthetic preferences. Doing so, however, may be more difficult that it seems, given that there is some debate as to the lower-order structure of openness to experience. For example, some models have proposed a lower-order structure consisting of two broad facets (openness and intellect; DeYoung, Grazioplene, & Peterson, 2012), whereas others have proposed four (Ashton & Lee, 2007; Kaufman, 2013) and six facets (McCrae & Costa, 2008; Woo et al., 2014). Even among the four- and six-facet models, there is no clear consistency in the specific facets that have been proposed. The aesthetics facet found in some models, which refers to an appreciation of beauty, and of less conventional domains and forms of art, appears to be the most important in terms of aesthetic preferences, but other facets may also be worthy of further investigation.

References

Arnett, J. J. (1995). Adolescents' uses of media for self-socialization. *Journal of Youth and Adolescence, 24*, 519–533.

Arnett, J. J., Larson, R., & Offer, D. (1995). Beyond effects: Adolescents as active media users. *Journal of Youth and Adolescence, 24*, 511–518.

Ashton, M. C., & Lee, K. (2007). Empirical, theoretical, and practical advantages of the HEXACO model of personality structure. *Personality and Social Psychology Review, 11*, 150–166.

Barron, F. (1953). Some personality correlates of independence of judgement. *Journal of Personality, 21*, 287–297.

Berlyne, D. E. (1960). *Conflict, arousal, and curiosity.* New York: McGraw Hill.

Brown, R. A. (2012). Music preferences and personality among Japanese university students. *International Journal of Psychology, 47*, 259–268.

Burt, C. (1933). *How the mind works.* London: Allen and Unwin.

Cardinet, J. (1958). Préférences esthétiques et personalité [Aesthetic preferences and personality]. *Année Psychologique, 58*, 45–69.

Chamorro-Premuzic, T. (2007). *Personality and individual differences.* Oxford, England: Wiley-Blackwell.

Chamorro-Premuzic, T., Burke, C., Hsu, A., & Swami, V. (2010). Personality predictors of artistic preferences as a function of the emotional valence and perceived complexity of paintings. *Psychology of Aesthetics, Creativity, and the Arts, 4*, 196–204.

Chamorro-Premuzic, T., & Furnham, A. (2004). Art judgment: A measure related to both personality and intelligence? *Imagination, Cognition, and Personality, 24*, 3–24.

Chamorro-Premuzic, T., Furnham, A., & Reimers, S. (2007). The artistic personality. *The Psychologist, 20*, 84–87.

Chamorro-Premuzic, T., Kallias, A., & Hsu, A. (2014). What type of movie person are you? Understanding individual differences in film preferences and uses: A psychographic approach. In J. C. Kaufman, & D. K. Simonton (Eds.), *The social science of cinema* (pp. 87–122). Oxford, England: Oxford University Press.

Chamorro-Premuzic, T., Reimers, S., Hsu, A., & Ahmetoglu, G. (2009). Who art thou? Personality predictors of artistic preferences in a large UK sample: The importance of openness. *British Journal of Psychology, 100,* 501–516.

Child, I. L. (1965). Personality correlates of esthetic judgment in college students. *Journal of Personality, 33,* 476–511.

Cleridou, K., & Furnham, A. (2014). Personality correlates of aesthetic preferences for art, architecture, and music. *Empirical Studies of the Arts, 32,* 231–255.

Colver, M. C., & el-Alayli, A. (2016). Getting aesthetic chills from music: The connection between Openness to Experience and frisson. *Psychology of Music, 44,* 413–427.

Conner, T. S., & Silvia, P. J. (2015). Creative days: A daily diary study of emotion, personality, and everyday creativity. *Psychology of Aesthetics, Creativity, and the Arts, 9,* 463–470.

Cook, R., & Furnham, A. (2012). Aesthetic preferences for architectural styles vary as a function of personality. *Imagination, Cognition and Personality, 32,* 103–114.

Costa, P. T., Jr., & McCrae, R. R. (1992). *Revised NEO Personality Inventory (NEO-PI-R) and NEO Five-Factor Inventory (NEO-FFI) manual.* Odessa, FL: Psychological Assessment Resources.

Delsing, M. J. M. H., ter Bogt, T. F. M., Engels, R. C. M. E., and Meeus, W. H. J. (2008). Adolescents' music preferences and personality characteristics. *European Journal of Personality, 22,* 109–130.

DeYoung, C. G., Grazioplene, R. G., & Peterson, J. B. (2012). From madness to genius: The openness/intellect trait domain as a paradoxical simplex. *Journal of Research in Personality, 46,* 63–78.

Eysenck, H. J. (1940). The general factor in aesthetic judgements. *British Journal of Psychology, 31,* 94–102.

Eysenck, H. J. (1941a). "Type"-factors in aesthetic judgements. *British Journal of Psychology, 31,* 262–270.

Eysenck, H. J. (1941b). A critical and experimental study of colour preferences. *The American Journal of Psychology, 54,* 385–394.

Eysenck, H. J. (1941c). The empirical determination of an aesthetic formula. *Psychological Review, 48,* 89–92.

Eysenck, H. J. (1941d). Personality factors and preference judgments. *Nature, 148,* 346.

Eysenck, H. J. (1942). The experimental study of the "Good Gestalt"-A new approach. *Psychological Review, 49,* 344–363.

Eysenck, H. J. (1968). An experimental study of aesthetic preference for polygonal figures. *The Journal of General Psychology, 79,* 3–17.

Eysenck, H. J. (1988). Personality and scientific aesthetics. In F. H. Farley, & R. W. Neperud (Eds.), *The foundations of aesthetics, art, and art education* (pp. 117–160). New York: Praeger Publishers.

Eysenck, H. J. (1990). Biological dimensions of personality. In L. A. Pervin (Ed.), *Handbook of personality: Theory and research* (pp. 244–276). New York: Guildford.

Eysenck, H. J. (1992). The psychology of personality and aesthetics. In S. Van, & G. H. Dodd (Eds.), *Fragrance: The psychology and biology of perfume* (pp. 7–26). New York: Elsevier Applied Science Publishers/Elsevier Science Publishers.

Eysenck, H. J., & Furnham, A. (1993). Personality and the Barron-Welsh art scale. *Perceptual and Motor Skills, 76,* 837–838.

Fayn, K., MacCann, C., Tiliopoulos, N., & Silvia, P. J. (2015). Aesthetic emotions and aesthetic people: Openness predicts sensitivity to novelty in the experiences of interest and pleasure. *Frontiers in Psychology, 6*, 1877.

Fechner, G. (1876). *Vorschule der ästhetik [Preschool of aesthetics]*. Leipzig, Germany: Druck und Verlag von Breitkopf Härtel.

Feist, G. J., & Brady, T. R. (2004). Openness to experience, non-conformity, and the preference for abstract art. *Empirical Studies of the Arts, 22*, 77–89.

Finn, S. (1997). Origins of media exposure: Linking personality traits to TV, radio, print, and film use. *Communication Research, 24*, 507–523.

Furnham, A., & Avison, M. (1997). Personality and preference for surreal paintings. *Personality and Individual Differences, 23*, 92–935.

Furnham, A., & Bachtiar, V. (2008). Personality and intelligence as predictors of creativity. *Personality and Individual Differences, 45*, 613–617.

Furnham, A., & Bunyan, M. (1988). Personality and art preferences. *European Journal of Personality, 2*, 67–74.

Furnham, A., & Chamorro-Premuzic, T. (2004). Personality, intelligence, and art. *Personality and Individual Differences, 36*, 705–715.

Furnham, A., & Rao, S. (2002). Personality and the aesthetics of composition: A study of Mondrian and Hirst. *North American Journal of Psychology, 4*, 23–242.

Furnham, A., & Walker, J. (2001a). The influence of personality traits, previous experience of art, and demographic variables on artistic preference. *Personality and Individual Differences, 31*, 997–1017.

Furnham, A., & Walker, J. (2001b). Personality and judgement of abstract, pop art, and representational paintings. *European Journal of Personality, 15*, 57–72.

Goldberg, L. R. (1993). The structure of phenotypic personality traits. *American Psychologist, 48*, 26–34.

Götz, K. O., Borisy, A. R., Lynn, R., & Eysenck, H. J. (1979). A new visual aesthetic sensitivity test: I. Construction and psychometric properties. *Perceptual and Motor Skills, 49*, 795–802.

Hirschman, E. C. (1985). A multidimensional analysis of content preferences for leisuretime media. *Journal of Leisure Research, 17*, 14–28.

Jacobsen, T. (2006). Bridging the arts and sciences: A framework for the psychology of aesthetics. *Leonardo, 39*, 155–162.

Jacobsen, T. (2010). Beauty and the brain: Culture, history, and individual differences in aesthetic appreciation. *Journal of Anatomy, 216*, 184–191.

Jacobsen, T., & Höfel, L. (2002). Aesthetic judgments of novel graphic patterns: Analyses of individual judgments. *Perceptual and Motor Skills, 95*, 755–766.

Juslin, P. N., Sakka, L. S., Barradas, G. T., & Liljeström, S. (2016). No accounting for taste? Idiographic models of aesthetic judgment in music. *Psychology of Aesthetics, Creativity, and the Arts, 10*, 157–170.

Kaufman, S. B. (2013). Opening up openness to experience: A four-factor model and relations to creative achievement in the arts and sciences. *The Journal of Creative Behavior, 47*, 233–255.

Knapp, R., & Wulff, A. (1963). Preferences for abstract and representational art. *Journal of Social Psychology, 60*, 255–262.

Kraaykamp, G., & van Eijck, K. (2005). Personality, media preferences, and cultural participation. *Personality and Individual Differences, 38*, 1675–1688.

Lee, S. A., Gibbons, J. A., & Short, S. D. (2010). Sympathetic reactions to the bait dog in a film of dog fighting: The influence of personality and gender. *Society and Animals, 18*, 107–125.

McCrae, R., & Costa, P. T., Jr. (1997). Conceptions and correlates of openness to experience. In S. R. Briggs, R. Hogan, & W. H. Jones (Eds.), *Handbook of personality psychology* (pp. 825–847). San Diego, CA: Academic Press.

McCrae, R. R., & Costa, P. T., Jr. (2008). The five-factor theory of personality. In O. P. John, R. W. Robins, & L. A. Pervin (Eds.), *Handbook of personality: Theory and research*, 3rd edition (pp. 159–181). New York: Guilford Press.

McManus, I. C., Cook, R., & Hunt, A. (2010). Beyond the golden section and normative aesthetics: Why do individuals differ so much in their aesthetic preferences for rectangles? *Psychology of Aesthetics, Creativity, and the Arts, 4*, 113–126.

McManus, I., & Furnham, A. (2006). Aesthetic activities and aesthetic attitudes: Influences of education, background and personality on interest and involvement in the arts. *British Journal of Psychology, 97*, 555–587.

Myszkowski, N., Stormer, M., & Zenasni, F. (2016). Order in complexity: How Hans Eysenck brought differential psychology and aesthetics together. *Personality and Individual Differences, 103*, 156–162.

North, A. C., & Hargreaves, D. J. (2007). Lifestyle correlates of musical preferences: 2. Media, leisure time, and music. *Psychology of Music, 35*, 179–200.

Pearson, J. L., & Dollinger, S. J. (2002). Music preference correlates of Jungian types. *Personality and Individual Differences, 36*, 1005–1008.

Rawlings, D. (2000). The interaction of openness to experience and schizotypy in predicting preference for abstract and violent paintings. *Empirical Studies of the Arts, 19*, 91–98.

Rawlings, D. (2003). Personality correlates of liking for "unpleasant" paintings and photographs. *Personality and Individual Differences, 34*, 395–410.

Rawlings, D., Twomey, F., Burns, E., & Morris, S. (1998). Personality, creativity, and aesthetic preference: Comparing psychoticism, sensation seeking, schizotypy, and openness to experience. *Empirical Studies of the Arts, 16*, 153–178.

Rawlings, D., Vidal, N. B., & Furnham, A. (2000). Personality and aesthetic preference in Spain and England: Two studies relating sensation seeking and openness to experience to liking for paintings and music. *European Journal of Personality, 14*, 553–576.

Reić Ercegovac, I., & Dobrota, S. (2011). Relationship between music preferences, sociodemographic characteristics, and Big Five personality traits. *Psychological Topics, 20*, 47–66.

Reić Ercegovac, I., Dobrota, S., & Kuščević, D. (2015). Relationship between music and visual art preferences and some personality traits. *Empirical Studies of the Arts, 33*, 207–227.

Rentfrow, P. J., Goldberg, L. R., & Zilca, R. (2011). Listening, watching, and reading: The structure and correlates of entertainment preferences. *Journal of Personality, 79*, 223–258.

Rentfrow, P. J., & Gosling, S. D. (2003). The do re mi's of everyday life: The structure and personality correlates of music preferences. *Journal of Personality and Social Psychology, 84*, 1236–1256.

Rentfrow, P. J., & McDonald, J. A. (2009). Music preferences and personality. In P. N. Juslin, & J. Sloboda (Eds.), *Handbook of music and emotion* (pp. 669–695). Oxford, England: Oxford University Press.

Rosengren, K. E., Wenner, L. A., & Palmgreen, P. (1985). *Media gratification research*. Beverly Hills, CA: Sage.

Schutte, N. S., & Malouff, J. M. (2004). University student reading preferences in relation to the Big Five personality dimensions. *Reading Psychology, 25*, 273–295.

Schwartz, K. D., & Fouts, G. T. (2003). Music preferences, personality style, and developmental issues of adolescents. *Journal of Youth and Adolescence, 32*, 202–213.

Silvia, P. J., Fayn, K., Nusbaum, E. C., & Beaty, R. E. (2015). Openness to experience and awe in response to nature and music: Personality and profound aesthetic experiences. *Psychology of Aesthetics, Creativity, and the Arts, 9*, 376–384.

Silvia, P. J., & Nusbaum, E. C. (2011). On personality and piloerection: Individual differences in aesthetic chills and other unusual aesthetic experiences. *Psychology of Aesthetics, Creativity, and the Arts, 5*, 208–214.

Swami, V. (2009). The effect of shape and colour symmetry on the aesthetic value of Dayak masks from Borneo. *Imagination, Cognition, and Personality, 28*, 283–294.

Swami, V. (2013). Context matters: Investigating the impact of contextual information on aesthetic appreciation of paintings by Max Ernst and Pablo Picasso. *Psychology of Aesthetics, Creativity, and the Arts, 7*, 285–295.

Swami, V., & Furnham, A. (2012). The effects of symmetry and personality on aesthetic preferences. *Imagination, Cognition, and Personality, 32*, 41–57.

Swami, V., & Furnham, A. (2014). Personality and aesthetics preferences. In J. Smith, & P. P. L. Tinio (Eds.), *The Cambridge Handbook of the psychology of aesthetics and the arts* (pp. 540–561). Cambridge, England: Cambridge University Press.

Swami, V., Malpass, F., Havard, D., Benford, K., Costescu, A., Sofitiki, A., & Taylor, D. (2013). Metalheads: The influence of personality and individual differences on preference for heavy metal. *Psychology of Aesthetics, Creativity, and the Arts, 7*, 377–383.

Swami, V., Pietschnig, J., Stieger, S., Nader, I. W., & Voracek, M. (2012). Beautiful as the chance meeting on a dissecting table of a sewing machine and an umbrella! Individual differences and preferences for surrealist literature. *Psychology of Aesthetics, Creativity, and the Arts, 6*, 35–42.

Swami, V., Stieger, S., Pietschnig, J., & Voracek, M. (2010). The disinterested play of thought: Individual differences and preferences for surrealist motion pictures. *Personality and Individual Differences, 48*, 855–859.

Vella, E. J., & Mills, G. (2017). Personality, uses of music, and music preferences: The influence of openness to experience and extraversion. *Psychology of Music, 45*, 338–354.

Vuoskoski, J. K., Thompson, W. F., McIlwain, D., & Eerola, T. (2011). Who enjoys listening to sad music and why? *Music Perception, 29*, 311–317.

Weaver, J. B., III. (1991). Exploring the links between personality and media preferences. *Personality and Individual Differences, 12*, 1293–1299.

Weaver, J. B., III (2003). Individual differences in television viewing motives. *Personality and Individual Differences, 35*, 1427–1437.

Wilson, G. D., Ausman, J., & Matthews, T. R. (1973). Conservatism and art preferences. *Journal of Personality and Social Psychology, 25*, 286–289.

Woo, S. E., Chernyshenko, O. S., Longley, A., Zhang, Z. X., Chiu, C. Y., & Stark, S. E. (2014). Openness to experience: Its lower level structure, measurement, and cross-cultural equivalence. *Journal of Personality Assessment, 96*, 29–45.

Zuckerman, M. (1979). *Sensation seeking: Beyond the optimal level of arousal.* Hillsdale, NJ: Erlbaum.

Zuckerman, M. (1994). *Behavioural expressions and biosocial bases of sensation seeking.* Cambridge, England: Cambridge University Press.

Zuckerman, M. (2006). Sensation seeking in entertainment. In J. Bryant, & P. Vorderer (Eds.), *Psychology of entertainment* (pp. 367–388). London: Routledge.

Zuckerman, M., Bone, R. N., Neary, R., Mangelsdorff, S., & Brustman, B. (1972). What is the sensation seeker? Personality trait and experience correlates of the sensation seeking scales. *Journal of Consulting and Clinical Psychology*, 65, 757–768.

Zuckerman, M., Neary, R. S., & Brustman, B. A. (1970). Sensation-seeking scale correlates in experience (smoking, drugs, alcohol, "hallucinations," and sex) and preference for complexity (designs). In *Proceedings of the 78th Annual Convention of the American Psychological Association* (pp. 317–318). Washington, DC: American Psychological Association.

Zuckerman, M., Ulrich, R. S., & McLaughlin, J. (1993). Sensation seeking and reactions to nature paintings. *Personality and Individual Differences*, 15, 563–576.

CHAPTER 37

AESTHETIC SENSITIVITY

NILS MYSZKOWSKI

DEFINITION

ALTHOUGH research in empirical aesthetics is largely focused on providing empirical definitions of beauty and on describing the processes underlying aesthetic appreciation (e.g., Leder, 2013; Leder, Belke, Oeberst, & Augustin, 2004; Tinio, 2013), the field of empirical aesthetics is also concerned with the individual differences that may explain aesthetic preferences and decisions—what is sometimes referred to as the *person* perspective (Jacobsen, 2006). While differences in aesthetic *preferences* are often explained through individual differences in personality traits (Feist & Brady, 2004; Furnham & Bunyan, 1988) and in expert skill or status (Chatterjee, Widick, Sternschein, Smith, & Bromberger, 2010; Plucker, Kaufman, Temple, & Qian, 2009), research also suggests that individuals also differ in how they are able to distinguish aesthetic quality: aesthetic sensitivity.

One could certainly combine multiple past and current definitions of aesthetic sensitivity by simply proposing that *aesthetic sensitivity corresponds to the ability to recognize aesthetic quality*. Beyond this simple definition, however, like many constructs, aesthetic sensitivity has several more or less precise definitions. Although controversial (Gear, 1986), a common shortcut for a definition is that aesthetic sensitivity is the scientific term for "good taste" (Bulley & Burt, 1933; Eysenck, 1983, 1940). In fact, the letter "T" (for Taste) was originally proposed by Hans Eysenck (1940) for the construct, and is still used to refer to aesthetic sensitivity (Myszkowski, Çelik, & Storme, 2018; Myszkowski & Storme, 2017)—after all, the general definition of good taste as making discerning aesthetic decisions quite closely corresponds to the definition of aesthetic sensitivity. Going in the opposite direction—meaning, in the direction of a more jargoning but also less controversial and more detailed definition—Irving Child's definition of aesthetic sensitivity as "the extent to which a person gives evidence of responding to relevant stimuli in some consistent and appropriate relation to the external standard" (Child, 1964, p. 49) is certainly one of the clearest, a probable reason for its regular referencing since then

(Myszkowski et al., 2018; Myszkowski & Storme, 2017; Myszkowski & Zenasni, 2016; Summerfeldt, Gilbert, & Reynolds, 2015).

Although Child's definition certainly clarifies that aesthetic sensitivity refers to forming aesthetic judgments that agree with standards, various aspects still remain up for discussion. First, "responding" is vague, in that a response here can refer to either the *tendency* or the *ability* to form standard judgments: is aesthetic sensitivity *preferring* stimuli that meet standards (without necessarily understanding that what is preferred may be of greater or lesser aesthetic value), or is it *evaluating the value* of stimuli in agreement with standards (without necessarily preferring the stimuli that were evaluated as of superior aesthetic quality)? Indeed, it appears obvious that, although related, one may *recognize* the aesthetic quality of a stimulus without necessarily *preferring* it. This ambiguity was pointed out as a methodological issue by Eysenck (1972), leading to current ways to operationalize of aesthetic sensitivity more clearly as an *ability* and not a set of preferences: currently used aesthetic sensitivity tests, like the Revised Visual Aesthetic Sensitivity Test in the visual domain (Myszkowski & Storme, 2017) and the Music Ear Test (Wallentin, Nielsen, Friis-Olivarius, Vuust, & Vuust, 2010) in the musical domain, evaluate *abilities* to recognize aesthetic quality, not preferences.

Finally, another important question that arises from Child's (1964) definition is how should we define *external standards* for aesthetic quality? Provided that it is possible and makes sense—which is certainly more of a philosophical question than an empirical one—the answer is essentially: anyway we can. In the section on the measure of aesthetic sensitivity, we will see that standards are typically defined by (1) controlling the construction of the stimulus, through the application of theoretical aesthetic rules (Graves, 1948; Wallentin et al., 2010) or the alteration of the aesthetic quality of stimuli (Götz, 1985; Meier, 1963, 1940), and/or (2) using content validity criteria, such as using laypeople consensus (Eysenck, 1940; Götz, 1985) and/or expert agreement (Child, 1964; Götz, 1985). In other words, the standards are defined through the construction of the task, and/or through gathering expert or consensual judgments first.

Given these theoretical considerations, in the following section, I will first depict the evolution of the study of aesthetic sensitivity, from its early measurement in various tests and batteries, to the search for evidence of its usefulness, the controversies around its measurability, and its place among various other individual differences.

History

Before the term *aesthetic sensitivity* was coined, the construct of good taste was of course already of interest for researchers. Although scientific interest in *perceptual* sensitivity already existed (Cattell & Galton, 1890; Galton, 1890), researchers' involvement in the understanding of *aesthetic* sensitivity can probably be dated back to the beginning of the 20th century, as prominent figures in individual differences research started studying individual differences in ability as it applies to arts domains.

As early as 1908, Binet remarks that, in his studies of giftedness in schools, some children tend to distinguish themselves with what he describes as "sensorial intelligence" (Binet, 1908, p. 334)—as opposed to verbal intelligence. Binet suggests that artists fall within the category of individuals with sensorial intelligence, and that the two forms of intelligence are not contradictory but may be relatively independent, which prompts his case study of the young Polish painter Tadeusz Styka, which he describes as demonstrating principally the former. In this case study, Binet observes that Styka's precocious painting mastery does not really mysteriously manifest itself in his artistic products: it appears as though the painter tends to "reason all the time" about art.

Shortly after this case study, first psychometric evaluations of aesthetic sensitivity start to appear, notably as Edward Thorndike first describes tests of "esthetic appreciation" (Thorndike, 1916), whose intended use is instruction and vocational guidance. These investigations, rooted in the psychometric tradition, may be considered as the start of the creation of valid aesthetic sensitivity tests, as they notably require examinees to rank stimuli of various aesthetic "merit" in the "correct" order—closeness with the correct order indicating higher abilities. Thorndike's test was quickly after notably used in Whipple's (1919) large scale examinations of giftedness in pupil classes. At this stage, Whipple already observes that, in spite of being conceptually connected, aesthetic sensitivity is actually empirically distinguishable from artistic skill—"Skill in drawing may coexist with poor esthetic taste" (Whipple, 1919, p. 144). In parallel, Seashore (1919) would conduct series of experimentations on musical abilities—which included the appreciation of rhythm, timbre, consonance, and volume—along with investigations on their relations with intelligence.

A little later on, the measurement of aesthetic sensitivity would attain a peak of interest in the visual field, as Karwoski and Christensen (1926) first, then Meier and Seashore (Meier, 1928; Meier & Seashore, 1929; Seashore, 1929), would publish tests dedicated to visual aesthetic judgment. Meier (1928) would here devise a central paradigm for item construction in the domain: the *controlled alteration* paradigm, which consists of altering the quality of an aesthetic stimulus in order to present examinees with pairs (altered/unaltered) to sort correctly. The McAdory Test would emerge concurrently (McAdory, 1929), triggering further psychometric investigations (Carroll, 1933; Siceloff, 1933). Further, Burt and Bulley would also experiment on their own test (Bulley & Burt, 1933; Dewar, 1938).

Later on, Hans Eysenck, under the direction of Burt, would write his PhD thesis—along with several articles—on the topic of aesthetic sensitivity. Eysenck would notably show, through the newly developed exploratory factor analysis methodologies, that a standard would emerge in the aesthetic preferences of various domains through consensus, and that individuals would differentiate themselves as a function of their closeness with the standard, consistently across domains (Eysenck, 1942, 1941, 1940). In other words, these findings indicate that our tendency to produce standard judgments, which Eysenck calls "T" for *taste*—quite explicitly mimicking the *g* letter used by other Spearmanians for intelligence (Myszkowski, Storme, & Zenasni, 2016)—is *consistent* across domains for a given individual, and explains our aesthetic preferences to an important extent.

After a number of publications on empirical aesthetics, Eysenck sought to build a test of T that would be as culture-free as possible, through notably removing cultural content—vases, landscapes, characters, etc.—found in other tests (Meier, 1940; Meier & Seashore, 1929). He directed his interests to other issues in psychology, but came back to the question of culture-free test development through very critical psychometric investigations (Eysenck, 1970; Eysenck & Castle, 1971, 1970) of Graves' Design Judgment Test (Graves, 1948, 1951). In the meantime, Irvin Child had made important advances in the field, by notably providing important terminology clarifications (Child, 1964), discussing relations between aesthetic sensitivity and other constructs, and studying relations among aesthetic sensitivity, mental ability, and personality (Child, 1965; Child & Iwao, 1968).

Eysenck's work later led to collaborations with the abstract painter Karl Otto ("KO") Götz—also critical of the Design Judgment Test (Götz & Götz, 1974)—who consequently painted abstract item pairs with the controlled alteration technique for the Visual Aesthetic Sensitivity Test (Eysenck, 1983; Götz, 1985). The Visual Aesthetic Sensitivity Test would later be the object of successful psychometric investigations (Chan, Eysenck, & Götz, 1980; Eysenck, Götz, Long, Nias, & Ross, 1984; Frois & Eysenck, 1995; Götz, Borisy, Lynn, & Eysenck, 1979; Iwawaki, Eysenck, & Götz, 1979), and of a revision (Myszkowski & Storme, 2017). Although not defining itself as research on aesthetic sensitivity, on the musical side a number of more and more comprehensive and psychometrically robust test batteries have started to emerge in the past few years (Kunert, Willems, & Hagoort, 2016; Law & Zentner, 2012; Ullén, Mosing, Holm, Eriksson, & Madison, 2014; Wallentin et al., 2010).

Since aesthetic sensitivity was introduced, it has been heavily studied as a psychometric challenge to face, as a form of cognitive ability, and as a personality-related individual characteristic. In the next sections, I will focus on the main findings on these aspects.

Measure

As I pointed out earlier, aesthetic sensitivity is often referred to as the more scientific—and perhaps less controversial—name used for "good taste." While advancing that individuals may be more or less equipped to understand art is already divisive, advancing that scientists can measure such ability is even more contentious (Gear, 1986). Nevertheless, in the purest psychometric tradition, this did not prevent a number of researchers from attempting to build such measures, to improve them, and to demonstrate their metrological qualities, often based on the promise that such measures could prove to be predictors of artistic and creative abilities (Carroll, 1933; Myszkowski & Zenasni, 2016; Seashore, 1919).

But, how can one (attempt to) measure aesthetic sensitivity? Essentially, at least in the visual domain, one central paradigm has been used (Myszkowski et al., 2018). This paradigm, called *controlled alteration* (Meier, 1928), starts with selecting a stimulus of aesthetic nature—for example, a painting or the photograph of a landscape. Then, an altered version of the stimulus is created. Typically—but not necessarily—this stage consists of a negative alteration, meaning that the aesthetic quality of the original stimulus is degraded to create the altered version (e.g., Götz, 1985; Meier, 1963, 1940). Regardless of the order of creation, this process results in two (or several) versions of a stimulus, which theoretically vary in aesthetic quality: these versions constitute the material for an item. During the testing process, examinees are presented items—with all the versions of a stimulus generally presented side by side. Their task consists of recognizing which of the versions is of better aesthetic quality—although, as I discuss later, some tests originally asked examinees which version they *prefer*. Such tests are largely employed in the visual domain—with the Meier Art Tests (Meier, 1963, 1940), the Graves Design Judgement Test (Graves, 1951, 1948), the Visual Aesthetic Sensitivity Test (Götz, 1985; Götz et al., 1979) (Figure 37.1), and the Revised Visual Aesthetic Sensitivity

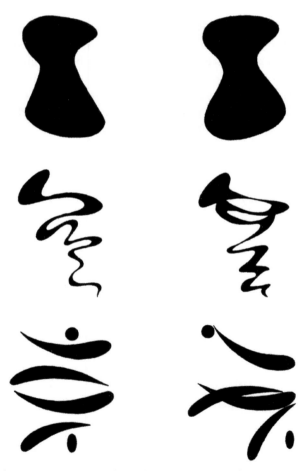

FIGURE 37.1. Three example items of a preliminary version of the Visual Aesthetic Sensitivity Test (Götz et al., 1979).

Test (Myszkowski & Storme, 2017)—and used to a more limited extent in the musical domain, with for example the Distorted Tunes Test (Drayna, Manichaikul, de Lange, Snieder, & Spector, 2001).

Although the reason for the centrality of such a paradigm is certainly that it appears to be a somewhat direct application of the very definition of aesthetic sensitivity as the ability to form judgments that correspond to standards, the process of construction should certainly not be the only piece of evidence for the validity of aesthetic sensitivity tests. Although it is not always the case that both aspects are verified (Myszkowski & Storme, 2017), Eysenck (1983) has laid out a clear summary of what is to be expected of a "correct" answer for such measures to ensure *content* validity: (1) the answer is agreed upon by a large majority—ideally, the unanimity—of experts; and (2) the answer is agreed upon by a majority of nonexperts. Regarding *predictive* validity, researchers typically investigate the extent to which scores of aesthetic sensitivity measures are related to artistic mastery in its many forms—being an art student, an art critic, professor, renowned artist, etc. However, in this regard, research tends to be unclear as to whether it is desirable that aesthetic sensitivity is predictive of artistic mastery or not: the former gives a measure evidence of practical usefulness (Myszkowski et al., 2016); the latter gives it evidence of singularity and distinctiveness from creativity and artistic training (Eysenck, 1983).

Also, although central and largely used in the visual domain (Götz, 1985; Graves, 1948; Meier, 1963, 1940), there are variations to the controlled alteration procedure. One of these variations, used especially in the musical domain, consists of creating alternative versions of an aesthetic stimulus, without one of the versions being necessarily of better aesthetic quality. This is frequently referred to as a *discrimination* test. The examinee is not asked to identify which stimulus is of better quality, but instead to identify the differences between them. For example, two melodies are played for the examinee, and the examinee's task is to identify the pairs of melodies that differ, and/or what differs in them (Law & Zentner, 2012; Ullén et al., 2014). In the visual field, discrimination tests are rarer, and they often consist of asking examinees to identify whether the presented stimuli are from the same author (Bamossy, Johnston, & Parsons, 1985; Bamossy, Scamoon, & Johnston, 1983; Smets & Knops, 1976).

In both the musical and the visual field, another source of variation that impacts the testing procedure and results is whether the aesthetic ability considered is conceptualized in an *atomistic* or a *Gestaltist* way. The *atomistic* conceptualization essentially considers the ability to be composed of several relatively separate abilities. In the musical domain, such abilities could be pitch recognition, rhythm recognition, tempo recognition, etc. (Kunert et al., 2016; Law & Zentner, 2012; Ullén et al., 2014; Wallentin et al., 2010), while in the visual domain, they could be symmetry recognition, balance recognition, style recognition, etc. The *Gestaltist* conceptualization would instead consider the aesthetic ability considered to be a global ability to recognize the aesthetic quality of an object, without necessarily possessing a detailed understanding of its features. This type of conceptualization is especially reflected in tests like the Visual Aesthetic Sensitivity Test (Götz et al., 1979) and its revised form (Myszkowski & Storme,

2017), which employs formal abstract art without necessarily specifically identifiable qualities or defaults.

Although perhaps a bit out of the scope of this chapter—since it could be argued that it concerns maybe more aesthetic preferences than aesthetic sensitivity— we should note that using aesthetic *preferences*—rather than discrimination/recognition tasks— was also explored as a way to measure aesthetic judgment ability. Originally, Eysenck's factor analyses (Eysenck, 1940) indicated that individuals differ not only in their tendency to form standard judgment ("T"), but also in their tendency to prefer complex stimuli ("K"). While "T" is often considered in relation to intelligence, "K" is often considered in relation to artistic personality and interests, and may not refer to the consensual definition of aesthetic sensitivity as forming standard judgments (Child, 1964). Nevertheless, because experts tend to differ from nonexperts in their preference for sophistication in art (Harsh, Beebe-Center, & Beebe-Center, 1939), it was advanced that preferences might also be used to assess aesthetic judgment ability (Bezruczko, 2002; Bezruczko, Manderscheid, & Schroeder, 2016; Bezruczko & Vimercati, 2004, 2002). Whether such procedures correspond to the definition of aesthetic sensitivity or not, they evidently consider sophisticated aesthetic preferences as indicators of the ability to judge art in an expert manner (Bezruczko & Vimercati, 2004), and thus, although methodologically different from traditional aesthetic quality recognition tasks (e.g., Götz, 1985), they may in a way still correspond to the definition of aesthetic sensitivity. Related to this question, the distinction between the preference aspect and the sensitivity aspect of aesthetic judgment probably in some aspect echoes questions around the distinction between intelligence and personality, which in some aspects is also blurred. Perhaps an intelligence-personality framework that may be relevant to consider and adapt to aesthetic ability here is the maximal-typical performance framework, which suggests that intelligence represents maximal performance, while personality represents typical performance (Goff & Ackerman, 1992). It might be similarly considered that aesthetic judgment ability has a maximal performance component, *aesthetic sensitivity*—which represents the maximum mobilization of aesthetic abilities to judge in the most exact way possible—and *aesthetic sophistication*—which represents the result of the typical mobilization of one's aesthetic ability abilities when judging art.

On a more statistical level, one could note that the sophistication and accuracy of the statistical methodologies used have considerably evolved over time. While the initial studies of aesthetic sensitivity employed very minimal methods (e.g., Meier, 1928), later on, methods permitting more accurate factor structure investigations would appear in aesthetic sensitivity research, with notably factor analysis (Eysenck, 1967) and later Item-Response Theory modeling (Bezruczko, 2002; Myszkowski & Storme, 2017). Although this probably reflects a variety of factors—individual researcher interests, field and subfield routines, availability of statistical methods, etc.—this has certainly generated a lot of heterogeneity in the investigations of aesthetic sensitivity measures. This heterogeneity in the methods is undoubtedly problematic, as it leads to a broad range of information quantity and quality among instruments, which subsequently prevents researchers and practitioners from selecting psychometric instruments in a well-informed way. Thus, there currently really is no scientific consensus over which in-strument to favor in any domain, and if there is one, it might simply be because it is the only instrument that was studied—which is still problematic.

Perhaps even more than other attempts to understand art scientifically, the study of aesthetic sensitivity through psychometric testing is controversial in the art world, where it has been heavily criticized. A famous example is Gear's (1986) exhaustive criticism of the Visual Aesthetic Sensitivity Test, which points out its multiple issues and restrictions of content validity—the fact that the stimuli are monochromatic, that they are two-dimensional, that they were created by a single painter, etc. This prob-ably summarizes the challenges of attempting to measure something that may be to some extent unmeasurable. It is also probably a backlash against—at the time—some researchers focusing mainly on the investigation of the predictors of aesthetic sensitivity and on the "ranking" of individuals—rather than on the potential *usefulness* of the con-struct and its measure (Myszkowski et al., 2016; Myszkowski & Zenasni, 2016). Perhaps one way to reconcile the two worlds is to instead put more effort into finding what aes-thetic sensitivity might help us understand. Indeed, just as intelligence research can help us make better informed educational and vocational decisions, aesthetic sensitivity re-search may help us better understand how to develop and identify artistic abilities and vocations—which, in fact, is its original purpose (Binet, 1908; Thorndike, 1916).

RELATIONS WITH MENTAL ABILITY

Are individuals with higher aesthetic sensitivity more intelligent? When observing intelligence research and aesthetic sensitivity research, one could instantly note an overlap in the author names: many of the researchers involved in aesthetic sensitivity research—Binet, Thorndike, Burt, Eysenck, Carroll—were also notorious for their re-search in the study of intelligence. It is thus not very surprising that a major point of interest in the study of aesthetic sensitivity is whether it is an aspect of, or oppositely, separable from, intelligence (Myszkowski et al., 2018). In fact, to some extent, one could point out that some intelligence test batteries include subtests that are very close to aes-thetic sensitivity measures—for example, the Binet–Simon Scale (Binet & Simon, 1916) included items that presented drawings of faces in pairs with the question "Which of the two faces is prettier (or uglier)?" (Wallin, 1911, pp. 222–223). Similarly, it can be argued that some spatial intelligence tasks—for example, Raven's Progressive Matrices Test (Raven, 1941)—involve strategies that may be of perceptual nature—rather than abstract reasoning.

As I explained earlier, historically, aesthetic sensitivity was introduced as a way to account for a form of intelligence that was not (enough) represented in typical cogni-tive ability testing (Binet, 1908; Thorndike, 1916; Whipple, 1919)—which is still the case. Later on, aesthetic sensitivity was more clearly discussed as "merely the manifestation of *g* when aesthetic material is used" (Eysenck, 1940, p. 101), and was coined "T" for *taste*

(Eysenck, 1983, 1940), which also evidently parallels the g used for genius/intelligence, and further indicates a conceptual overlap between the two.

It should be noted that, while most researchers have discussed aesthetic sensitivity and intelligence as related constructs (Chamorro-Premuzic & Furnham, 2004; Frois & Eysenck, 1995; Furnham & Chamorro-Premuzic, 2004; Myszkowski, Storme, Zenasni, & Lubart, 2014), it has also on some occasions been suggested that the relations between these two constructs are unimportant (Eysenck, 1983; Frois & Eysenck, 1995), or that they could be the result of methodological artifacts (Bezruczko & Frois, 2011), in that, for example, the instructions of aesthetic sensitivity tests are so thorny—the most aesthetically pleasing stimulus is not necessarily the one that one individually prefers—that intelligence could play an important role in their clear understanding.

Nevertheless, it seems that there is now sufficient evidence to indicate that there is a correlation between intelligence and aesthetic sensitivity in the visual domain. Indeed, Myszkowski, Çelik, and Storme (2018) conducted the first meta-analysis—which is a statistical procedure that consists of aggregating the results obtained in various studies, accounting for variability in methods and sample size—on the relations between intelligence measures and visual aesthetic sensitivity measures. They found that, over 23 samples and 1,531 participants—a relatively small amount, which reflects the scarcity of investigations compared with larger domains—there was a positive correlation estimated at .30 between the two constructs. Further, this relation did not appear to be significantly reduced or increased by age of the participants, gender of the participants, the aesthetic sensitivity measure used, or the intelligence measure used. In spite of the absence of a meta-analysis in the domain, regarding the relations between the intelligence and musical aesthetic sensitivity, a similar heterogeneity appears (Murphy, 1999), with both observed positive and null/negligible correlations.

These results suggest that there are cognitive processes that are involved in both aesthetic sensitivity measures and intelligence tests. It has been advanced that, for example, visual aesthetic sensitivity shares with general intelligence cognitive processes such as attention shifting, reflective processing, goal management, and emotional distance—the "aesthetic stance" (Leder, Gerger, Brieber, & Schwarz, 2014)—and abstraction. In the musical field, it has been suggested that processes of sensory discrimination—notably temporal discrimination—could be predictive of both musical aesthetic sensitivity and psychometric intelligence (Troche & Rammsayer, 2009; Ullén et al., 2014).

In general, research tends to suggest that high psychometric intelligence is related to high aesthetic sensitivity, but there is a substantial part of uniqueness to aesthetic sensitivity that cannot be explained by psychometric intelligence.

Relations with Personality

Looking at the type of measure used to capture it, it is quite clear that aesthetic sensitivity has been mainly studied as a cognitive ability, rather than as a personality trait

(Myszkowski & Storme, 2017). However, the tradition of research in empirical aesthetics, as well as in individual differences psychology, is also heavily focused on emotional and conative components. Thus, although research on the relations between aesthetic sensitivity and personality is certainly scarcer than that on the relations between aesthetic sensitivity and intelligence, a number of researchers have focused on how "good taste" may relate to personality: do individuals with higher aesthetic sensitivity share common personality traits?

When it comes to personality traits on the nonpathological spectrum, psychology researchers frequently refer to a few taxonomies, which often are based on or revolve around the Five Factor Model (Costa & McCrae, 1992), which is composed of the "Big Five" wide-ranging personality factors: Openness to experience, Conscientiousness, Extroversion, Agreeableness, and Neuroticism/Emotional Instability. Such general models of personality are a go-to when exploring relations between personality traits and other individual differences, but, in the study of the relations between aesthetic sensitivity and personality, they have been used with moderate success and lead to fluctuating conclusions. For example, some researchers (Frois & Eysenck, 1995; Götz et al., 1979) found no relations between aesthetic sensitivity and extraversion, while Chamorro-Premuzic and Furnham (2004) later found a negative relation between the two constructs—as well as a negative relation between aesthetic sensitivity and conscientiousness, and a positive relation between aesthetic sensitivity and neuroticism.

Nevertheless, confusing and heterogeneous results concerning the relations between wide-ranging personality dimensions and aesthetic sensitivity should not discourage researchers from investigating the role of personality in aesthetic sensitivity. Indeed, research also tends to suggest that, when individual specific personality traits are studied, stronger—and perhaps, more reproducible and interpretable—relations may be observed. High aesthetic sensitivity was for example found to be related to tolerance of complexity, unrealistic experience ambiguity, and ambivalence (Child & Iwao, 1968), as well as tolerance of complexity and independence of judgment (Child, 1965). Further, researchers have found that related traits, such as high sensation seeking, preference for order, openness to fantasy, openness to aesthetics, openness to feelings, and openness to ideas are positively correlated with visual aesthetic sensitivity (Myszkowski et al., 2014). Similarly, visual aesthetic sensitivity was found to be positively related to art interests (Summerfeldt et al., 2015). These more encouraging results tend to suggest that independent and open personalities—tolerant of new/complex/ambiguous ideas, sensation-seeking individuals—are indeed more likely to show higher aesthetic sensitivity.

Overall, one general conclusion that could be made here is that personality and vocational interests probably play a role in aesthetic sensitivity and its development—and certainly, traits that are known to be related to artistic abilities specifically need further investigation (Myszkowski et al., 2014). However, although personality may not be eliminated as a predictor of aesthetic sensitivity, it also appears that these relations remain not sufficiently investigated to form a clear picture here. In addition—and again, this is also in the psychometric tradition—personality traits of the normal spectrum have been primarily investigated (Chamorro-Premuzic & Furnham, 2004; Frois

& Eysenck, 1995; Furnham & Chamorro-Premuzic, 2004; Myszkowski et al., 2014), but some results—for example, the relation between preference for order and aesthetic sensitivity (Myszkowski et al., 2014)—might indicate that some pathological dispositions may be related to aesthetic sensitivity—the route of studying obsessive–compulsive disorder may for example be of interest here (Summerfeldt et al., 2015).

Development and Training

Unlike research on the relations between aesthetic sensitivity and intelligence, research on the natural development of aesthetic sensitivity is scarce. As was pointed out (Eysenck, 1972), advances in the topic have been slowed down by the challenges of accurately measuring aesthetic sensitivity, especially among children. More specifically, there is currently no measure in the visual field of aesthetic sensitivity dedicated to children of any age. It could be argued that most adult measures could be applicable to children, and, even though the few studies on aesthetic sensitivity in child populations have not been focused primarily on psychometric qualities—which is also related to the generally small sample sizes available—they seem to be encouraging. For example, Eysenck (1972) found acceptable internal consistencies for the Design Judgment Test among children of ages 9 and above. In the visual domain, it appears that research would suggest that aesthetic sensitivity increases until about the age of 14 (Frois & Eysenck, 1995). Again, however, the scarcity of research in the domain calls for more studies. Regarding the effects of training, it appears that art expertise—acquired, for example, through education—logically leads to increased levels of aesthetic sensitivity (Eysenck, 1972). However, it should be noted here that, since measures of aesthetic sensitivity are generally based on expert judgments as the main criterion for their content validity (Bamossy et al., 1983; Götz, 1985; Götz et al., 1979; Graves, 1948; Myszkowski & Storme, 2017), studying the effect of expertise could be considered tautological: experts perform better *because* aesthetic sensitivity is conceptualized and measured so as to reflect such differences.

In contrast with the visual domain, in the musical field, a more substantial amount of research focuses on the development of musical ear among children (e.g., Bamberger, 2003, 1995; Feierabend, 1990; Gruhn, 2002). It is interesting to note that, in the musical domain, in contrast with the visual domain (Frois & Eysenck, 1995), researchers are hardly interested in the "natural" development of musical aesthetic sensitivity, for the reason that musicality clearly does not develop in a vacuum: children are constantly exposed to and participate in a musical environment that develops certain aspects of their musicality. In other words, the development of musical ear in children occurs through a wide range of musical behaviors—singing, socialization into a dominant culture, participation in musical activities—and thus may be accelerated or slowed down by a variety of factors occurring through development (Welch, 2006). Even though, in the visual field, some researchers have suggested that aesthetic sensitivity might be genetic (Eysenck & Iwawaki, 1975; Frois & Eysenck, 1995; Götz et al., 1979)—and in some instance have attempted to build training-independent measures (Eysenck, 1983), the observed effects of training (albeit inconsistent), the observed benefits of art education on other aesthetic abilities, and the relations between personality traits and aesthetic sensitivity tend to indicate that, similar to the musical domain, visual aesthetic sensitivity certainly does not develop in a vacuum, and that a number of environmental factors—exposure to visual art, design of school and urban environments, etc.—may play an important role in the development of aesthetic sensitivity.

CONCLUSION AND FUTURE DIRECTIONS

The domain of aesthetic sensitivity is now more than a century old, but, in spite of its ever-growing body of research, it remains in many aspects largely unexplored and open to new tests and experimentations. I will here review some of the limitations of the existing literature, and propose ideas to overcome such limitations.

As I pointed out, aesthetic sensitivity is deeply rooted in the psychometric tradition. In spite of this, most recent investigations on aesthetic sensitivity have not closely followed the (r)evolutions of psychometric research. More specifically, psychometric research has been undergoing the silent revolution of Item-Response Theory (IRT) modeling— a framework that essentially models item response probabilities (e.g., choosing the correct drawing in a visual aesthetic sensitivity task) as a function of underlying latent variables. Although research in the field has started to take advantage of IRT (Bezruczko, 2002; Myszkowski & Storme, 2017), it remains, like in many other fields of psychology (Borsboom, 2006), underused. Indeed, more rudimentary methods such as linear correlations (Kunert et al., 2016) or Cronbach's α (Ullén et al., 2014)—and of course, sum scoring—are often preferred to more accurate and conceptually consistent methods. While these rudimentary methods are not always faulty, they do not permit the depth of analysis that IRT allows—for example, studying phenomena such as guessing may allow better understanding of the functioning of aesthetic sensitivity measures (Myszkowski & Storme, 2017)—and rely on assumptions that may not always be realistic. Further, models that jointly account for response accuracy and response time (e.g., Fox & Marianti, 2016) may bring new insight into the cognitive processes involved in aesthetic sensitivity measures (Myzkowski, 2019). Finally, even though aesthetic sensitivity is deeply rooted in "traditional" testing, the addition of new data collection technologies— especially eye-tracking in the visual domain—may prove useful in the better understanding and the improvement of aesthetic sensitivity measures.

Related to the statistical modeling of the psychometric data that result from aesthetic sensitivity tests, it appears that a large majority of models and conclusions on aesthetic sensitivity have mainly made the assumption that differences in aesthetic sensitivity are differences on a *continuum*, rather than differences in *kind*. The question of whether a construct represents differences in kind or on a continuum—or both—is largely explored in the domain of psychopathology (Borsboom et al., 2016), but it is completely unexplored in aesthetic sensitivity research. It is however a pertinent question, if we consider that, for example, aesthetic sensitivity could be composed of the availability of multiple skills or abilities—what I earlier referred to as the *atomistic* perspective. Indeed, research has so far either considered aesthetic sensitivity as a whole continuum—especially in the visual domain (Myszkowski & Storme, 2017)—or as a combination of distinct abilities that are evaluated separately—especially in the musical domain (Kunert et al., 2016; Law & Zentner, 2012; Ullén et al., 2014). A way to reconcile the two perspectives would be to define aesthetic sensitivity as a construct that may appear continuous, but that is in fact the result of a combination of distinct classes of individuals (possessing different sets of skills), which for some of them may allow for continuous variation (possessing varying degrees of the skill)—what is typically referred to as a *mixture* model. Indeed, if aesthetic sensitivity can be considered as a combination of distinct skills—for example, detection of pitch variations, rhythm variations, etc. for the musical domain—that constitute a general construct of aesthetic sensitivity, then this theoretical perspective should perhaps find a clearer echo in the psychometric models employed in the investigation of aesthetic sensitivity measures—for example, through the use of Cognitive Diagnosis Models (CDM; Rupp, Templin, & Henson, 2010).

Another important concern to address is that, even though efforts have been made to ensure that aesthetic sensitivity measures maintain some equivalence between cultures (e.g., Chan et al., 1980; Eysenck et al., 1984; Iwawaki et al., 1979), these investigations remain limited and may be outdated. More research is needed, both in the visual and in the musical domain, to better understand how such measures may or may not be culture-free. In addition, it is notable that the relations between aesthetic sensitivity and other talents in the aesthetic domain—for example, aesthetic fluency (Silvia, 2007; Smith & Smith, 2006) or aesthetic chills (McCrae, 2007; Silvia & Nusbaum, 2011)—are far from being extensively investigated. Consequently, it has been suggested that their relations should be studied further to explore the extent to which they may form a consistent set of aesthetic abilities (Myszkowski et al., 2016; Myszkowski & Storme, 2017; Myszkowski & Zenasni, 2016)—and why not, to envision the creation of test batteries similar to Intellectual Quotient test batteries (Myszkowski & Zenasni, 2016).

Related to this, an avenue that remains largely unexplored is the relations between emotional/social intelligence and aesthetic sensitivity. Indeed, if aesthetic sensitivity consists of the ability to judge in a standard way (Child, 1964), and if such standards are socially constructed—by experts or by laypersons (Eysenck, 1983), then aesthetic sensitivity essentially consists of the ability to grasp the response of others to artistic material. Thus, it may be, to some extent, a form of a social adaption or empathic response. Indeed, as research has found relations between aesthetic sensitivity and emotion-related personality traits (Chamorro-Premuzic & Furnham, 2004, 2004; Myszkowski et al., 2014), it might be interesting to investigate how it may also relate to social and emotional skills, such as perspective taking, social monitoring, emotion management—which relates to the aesthetic stance hypothesis (Leder et al., 2014), discussed earlier—or empathic concern.

Finally, one can note from the history of aesthetic sensitivity research that it has been from the start closely associated with research on psychometric intelligence (Binet, 1908; Binet & Simon, 1916; Whipple, 1919), which clearly demonstrates that it was considered as a form of giftedness. In contrast, nowadays, the domain of psychometric intelligence and the detection of giftedness is instead very centered on a condensed set of cognitive abilities that generally do not include any form of aesthetic—or creative (Kaufman, 2015)—ability. This may be regrettable. Indeed, aesthetic abilities have been found to give individuals an advantage in various domains, more specifically artistic domains (Kozbelt, Seidel, ElBassiouny, Mark, & Owen, 2010; Kozbelt & Seeley, 2007). Also, art reception has been found to play a role in mental health (e.g., Chatterjee & Noble, 2016), and aesthetic abilities could play a role in promoting and maintaining an individual's mental health as well. Aesthetic production and reception are often considered secondary, or less useful than perhaps verbal and mathematical abilities for the understanding of academic achievement, but aesthetic abilities constitute an important component of human potential, and their inclusion in such batteries may help understand and develop such potential in a more comprehensive way.

REFERENCES

Bamberger, J. (2003). The Development of intuitive musical understanding: A Natural experiment. *Psychology of Music, 31,* 7–36. doi:10.1177/0305735603031001321

Bamberger, J. S. (1995). *The mind behind the musical ear: How children develop musical intelligence.* Cambridge, MA: Harvard University Press.

Bamossy, G., Johnston, M., & Parsons, M. (1985). The assessment of aesthetic judgment ability. *Empirical Studies of the Arts, 3,* 63–79. doi:10.2190/1U13-U2DB-0BE3-A4FN

Bamossy, G., Scamoon, D. L., & Johnston, M. (1983). A preliminary investigation of the reliability and validity of an aesthetic judgment test. *Advances in Consumer Research, 10,* 685–690.

Bezruczko, N. (2002). A multi-factor Rasch scale for artistic judgment. *Journal of Applied Measurement, 3,* 360–399.

Bezruczko, N., & Frois, J. P. (2011). Comparison of several artistic judgment aptitude dimensions between children in Chicago and Lisbon. *Visual Arts Research, 37,* 1–15.

Bezruczko, N., Manderscheid, E., & Schroeder, D. H. (2016). MRI of an artistic judgment aptitude construct derived from Eysenck's K factor. *Psychology & Neuroscience 9,* 293–325. doi:10.1037/pne0000064

Bezruczko, N., & Vimercati, A. B. (2002) Rule-based aptitude measurement: Artistic judgment. *Popular Measurement, 24,* 24–30.

Bezruczko, N., & Vimercati, A. B. (2004). Advances in measuring artistic judgment aptitude. *Leonardo, 37,* 187–188. doi:10.1162/0024094041139472

Binet, A. (1908). La psychologie artistique de Tade Styka. *L'Année psychologique, 15,* 316–356. doi:10.3406/psy.1908.3760

Binet, A., & Simon, T. (1916). *The development of intelligence in children: The Binet–Simon scale.* Baltimore: Williams & Wilkins Company.

Borsboom, D. (2006). The attack of the psychometricians. *Psychometrika, 71,* 425–440. doi:10.1007/s11336-006-1447-6

Borsboom, D., Rhemtulla, M., Cramer, A. O. J., Maas, H. L. J. van der, Scheffer, M., & Dolan, C. V. (2016). Kinds versus continua: A review of psychometric approaches to uncover the structure of psychiatric constructs. *Psychological Medicine, 46,* 1567–1579. doi:10.1017/S0033291715001944

Bulley, M. H., & Burt, S. C. L. (1933). *Have you good taste?: A guide to the appreciation of the lesser arts.* London: Methuen & co., Ltd.

Carroll, H. A. (1933). What do the Meier-Seashore and the McAdory Art Tests measure? *The Journal of Educational Research, 26,* 661–665. doi:10.1080/00220671.1933.10880360

Cattell, J. M., & Galton, F. (1890). Mental tests and measurements. *Mind, 15,* 373–381.

Chamorro-Premuzic, T., & Furnham, A. (2004). Art judgment: A measure related to both personality and intelligence? *Imagination, Cognition and Personality, 24,* 3–24. doi:10.2190/U4LW-TH9X-80M3-NJ54

Chan, J., Eysenck, H. J., & Götz, K. O. (1980). A new visual aesthetic sensitivity test: III. Crosscultural comparison between Hong Kong children and adults, and English and Japanese samples. *Perceptual and Motor Skills, 50,* 1325–1326. doi:10.2466/pms.1980.50.3c.1325

Chatterjee, A., Widick, P., Sternschein, R., Smith, W. B., & Bromberger, B. (2010). The assessment of art attributes. *Empirical Studies of the Arts, 28,* 207–222. doi:10.2190/EM.28.2.f

Chatterjee, H., & Noble, G. (2016). *Museums, health and well-being.* New York, NY: Routledge.

Child, I. L. (1964). Observations on the meaning of some measures of esthetic sensitivity. *The Journal of Psychology, 57,* 49–64. doi:10.1080/00223980.1964.9916671

Child, I. L. (1965). Personality correlates of esthetic judgment in college students. *Journal of Personality, 33,* 476. doi:10.1111/1467-6494.ep8932870

Child, I. L., & Iwao, S. (1968). Personality and esthetic sensitivity: Extension of findings to younger age and to different culture. *Journal of Personality and Social Psychology, 8,* 308. doi:10.1037/h0025599

Costa, P. T., & McCrae, R. R. (1992). Four ways five factors are basic. *Personality and Individual Differences, 13,* 653–665. doi:10.1016/0191-8869(92)90236-I

Dewar, H. (1938). A comparison of tests of artistic appreciation. *British Journal of Educational Psychology, 8,* 29–49. doi:10.1111/j.2044-8279.1938.tb03181.x

Drayna, D., Manichaikul, A., de Lange, M., Snieder, H., & Spector, T. (2001). Genetic correlates of musical pitch recognition in humans. *Science, 291,* 1969–1972. doi:10.1126/science.291.5510.1969

Eysenck, H. J. (1940). The general factor in aesthetic judgements. *British Journal of Psychology, 31,* 94–102. doi:10.1111/j.2044-8295.1940.tb00977.x

Eysenck, H. J. (1941). The empirical determination of an aesthetic formula. *Psychological Review, 48,* 83–92. doi:10.1037/h0062483

Eysenck, H. J. (1942). Abnormal preference judgments as "complex" indicators. *American Journal of Orthopsychiatry, 12,* 338–345. doi:10.1111/j.1939-0025.1942.tb05913.x

Eysenck, H. J. (1967). Factor-analytic study of the Maitland Graves Design judgment test. *Perceptual and Motor Skills, 24,* 73–74. doi:10.2466/pms.1967.24.1.73

Eysenck, H. J. (1970). An application of the Maitland Graves Design Judgment Test to professional artists. *Perceptual and Motor Skills, 30,* 589–590. doi:10.2466/pms.1970.30.2.589

Eysenck, H. J. (1972). Personal preferences, aesthetic sensitivity and personality in trained and untrained subjects. *Journal of Personality, 40,* 544–557. doi:10.1111/j.1467-6494.1972.tb00079.x

Eysenck, H. J. (1983). A new measure of "good taste" in visual art. *Leonardo, 16*, 229. doi:10.2307/1574921

Eysenck, H. J., & Castle, M. (1970). A validation study of the Maitland Graves Design Judgment Test. *A Validation Study of Maitland Graves Design Judgment Test*, 1–8. doi:10.1037/e518002009-001

Eysenck, H. J., & Castle, M. (1971). Comparative study of artists and nonartists on the Maitland Graves Design Judgment Test. *Journal of Applied Psychology, 55*, 389–392. doi:10.1037/h0031469

Eysenck, H. J., Götz, K. O., Long, H. Y., Nias, D. K. B., & Ross, M. (1984). A new Visual Aesthetic Sensitivity Test: IV. Cross-cultural comparisons between a Chinese sample from Singapore and an English sample. *Personality and Individual Differences, 5*, 599–600. doi:10.1016/0191-8869(84)90036-9

Eysenck, H. J., & Iwawaki, S. (1975). The determination of aesthetic judgment by race and sex. *The Journal of Social Psychology, 96*, 11–20. doi:10.1080/00224545.1975.9923256

Feierabend, J. (1990). Music in early childhood. *Design For Arts in Education, 91*, 15–20. doi:10.1080/07320973.1990.9934833

Feist, G. J., & Brady, T. R. (2004). Openness to experience, non-conformity, and the preference for abstract art. *Empirical Studies of the Arts, 22*, 77–89. doi:10.2190/Y7CA-TBY6-V7LR-76GK

Fox, J.-P., & Marianti, S. (2016). Joint modeling of ability and differential speed using responses and response times. *Multivariate Behavioral Research, 51*, 540–553. doi:10.1080/00273171.2016.1171128

Frois, J. P., & Eysenck, H. J. (1995). The Visual Aesthetic Sensitivity Test applied to Portuguese children and fine arts students. *Creativity Research Journal, 8*, 277–284. doi:10.1207/s15326934crj0803_6

Furnham, A., & Bunyan, M. (1988). Personality and art preferences. *European Journal of Personality, 2*, 67–74. doi:10.1002/per.2410020106

Furnham, A., & Chamorro-Premuzic, T. (2004). Personality, intelligence, and art. *Personality and Individual Differences, 36*, 705–715. doi:10.1016/S0191-8869(03)00128-4

Galton, F. (1890). Exhibition of instruments (1) for testing perception of differences of tint, and (2) for determining reaction-time. *The Journal of the Anthropological Institute of Great Britain and Ireland, 19*, 27–29. doi:10.2307/2842529

Gear, J. (1986). Eysenck's Visual Aesthetic Sensitivity Test (VAST) as an example of the need for explicitness and awareness of context in empirical aesthetics. *Poetics, 15*, 555–564. doi:10.1016/0304-422X(86)90011-2

Goff, M., & Ackerman, P. L. (1992). Personality-intelligence relations: Assessment of typical intelligence engagement. *Journal of Educational Psychology, 84*, 537–552. doi:10.1037/0022-0663.84.4.537

Götz, K. O. (1985). *VAST: Visual aesthetic sensitivity test*, 4th ed. Dusseldorf, Germany: Concept Verlag.

Götz, K. O., Borisy, A. R., Lynn, R., & Eysenck, H. J. (1979). A new Visual Aesthetic Sensitivity Test: I. Construction and psychometric properties. *Perceptual and Motor Skills, 49*, 795–802. doi:10.2466/pms.1979.49.3.795

Götz, K.O., & Götz, K. (1974). The Maitland Graves Design Judgment Test judged by 22 experts. *Perceptual and Motor Skills, 39*, 261–262. doi:10.2466/pms.1974.39.1.261

Graves, M. E. (1948). *Design judgment test*. New York: Psychological Corporation.

Graves, M. E. (1951). *The art of color and design*, 1st edition. New York: McGraw Hill Book Company, Inc.

Gruhn, W. (2002). Phases and stages in early music learning. A longitudinal study on the development of young children's musical potential. *Music Education Research, 4*, 51–71. doi:10.1080/14613800220119778

Harsh, C. M., Beebe-Center, J. G., & Beebe-Center, R. (1939). Further evidence regarding preferential judgment of polygonal forms. *The Journal of Psychology, 7*, 343–350. doi:10.1080/00223980.1939.9917641

Iwawaki, S., Eysenck, H. J., & Götz, K. O. (1979). A new Visual Aesthetic Sensitivity Test: II. Cross-cultural comparison between England and Japan. *Perceptual and Motor Skills, 49*, 859–862. doi:10.2466/pms.1979.49.3.859

Jacobsen, T. (2006). Bridging the arts and sciences: A framework for the psychology of aesthetics. *Leonardo, 39*, 155–162.

Karwoski, T. F., & Christensen, E. O. (1926). A test for art appreciation. *Journal of Educational Psychology, 17*, 187–194.

Kaufman, J. C. (2015). Why creativity isn't in IQ tests, why it matters, and why it won't change anytime soon probably. *Journal of Intelligence, 3*, 59–72. doi:10.3390/jintelligence3030059

Kozbelt, A., & Seeley, W. P. (2007). Integrating art historical, psychological, and neuroscientific explanations of artists' advantages in drawing and perception. *Psychology of Aesthetics, Creativity, and the Arts, 1*, 80–90. doi:10.1037/1931-3896.1.2.80

Kozbelt, A., Seidel, A., ElBassiouny, A., Mark, Y., & Owen, D. R. (2010). Visual selection contributes to artists' advantages in realistic drawing. *Psychology of Aesthetics, Creativity, and the Arts, 4*, 93–102. doi:10.1037/a0017657

Kunert, R., Willems, R. M., & Hagoort, P. (2016). An independent psychometric evaluation of the PROMS measure of music perception skills. *PLoS ONE, 11*, e0159103. doi:10.1371/journal.pone.0159103

Law, L. N. C., & Zentner, M. (2012). Assessing musical abilities objectively: Construction and validation of the profile of music perception skills. *PLoS ONE, 7*, e52508. doi:10.1371/journal.pone.0052508

Leder, H. (2013). Next steps in neuroaesthetics: Which processes and processing stages to study? *Psychology of Aesthetics, Creativity, and the Arts, Neuroaesthetics: Cognition and Neurobiology of Aesthetic Experience, 7*, 27–37. doi:10.1037/a0031585

Leder, H., Belke, B., Oeberst, A., & Augustin, D. (2004). A model of aesthetic appreciation and aesthetic judgments. *British Journal of Psychology, 95*, 489–508. doi:10.1348/0007126042369811

Leder, H., Gerger, G., Brieber, D., & Schwarz, N. (2014). What makes an art expert? Emotion and evaluation in art appreciation. *Cognition & Emotion, 28*, 1137–1147. doi:10.1080/02699931.2013.870132

McAdory, M. (1929). The construction and validation of an art test. *Teachers College Contributions to Education, 383*, 35–35.

McCrae, R. R. (2007). Aesthetic chills as a universal marker of openness to experience. *Motivation & Emotion, 31*, 5–11.

Meier, N. C. (1928). A measure of art talent. *Psychological Monographs, 39*, 184–199. doi:10.1037/h0093346

Meier, N. C. (1940). *The Meier Art Tests: I, Art judgment*. Iowa City, IA: University of Iowa, Bureau of Educational Research and Service.

Meier, N. C. (1963). *The Meier Art Tests: II, Aesthetic perception. Bureau of Educational Research and Service, University of Iowa, IACity.*

Meier, N. C., & Seashore, C. E. (1929). The Meier-Seashore art judgment test, The Meier-Seashore art judgment test. Oxford, UK: University of Iowa, Bureau of Educational Research and Service.

Murphy, C. (1999). How far do tests of musical ability shed light on the nature of musical intelligence? *British Journal of Music Education, 16*, 39–50. doi:10.1017/S0265051799000133

Myszkowski, N. (2019). The first glance is the weakest: "Tasteful" individuals are slower to judge visual art. *Personality and Individual Differences, 141*, 188–195. https://doi.org/10.1016/j.paid.2019.01.010

Myszkowski, N., Çelik, P., & Storme, M. (2018). A meta-analysis of the relationship between intelligence and visual "taste" measures. *Psychology of Aesthetics, Creativity, and the Arts, 12*, 24–33. doi:10.1037/aca0000099

Myszkowski, N., & Storme, M. (2017). Measuring "good taste" with the Visual Aesthetic Sensitivity Test-Revised (VAST-R). *Personality and Individual Differences, 117*, 91–100. doi:10.1016/j.paid.2017.05.041

Myszkowski, N., Storme, M., & Zenasni, F. (2016). Order in complexity: How Hans Eysenck brought differential psychology and aesthetics together. *Personality and Individual Differences, Hans Eysenck: One Hundred Years of Psychology, 103*, 156–162. doi:10.1016/j.paid.2016.04.034

Myszkowski, N., Storme, M., Zenasni, F., & Lubart, T. (2014). Is visual aesthetic sensitivity independent from intelligence, personality and creativity? *Personality and Individual Differences, 59*, 16–20. doi:10.1016/j.paid.2013.10.021

Myszkowski, N., & Zenasni, F. (2016). Individual differences in aesthetic ability: The case for an Aesthetic Quotient. *Frontiers in Psychology, 7*, 750. doi:10.3389/fpsyg.2016.00750

Plucker, J. A., Kaufman, J. C., Temple, J. S., & Qian, M. (2009). Do experts and novices evaluate movies the same way? *Psychology & Marketing, 26*, 470–478. doi:10.1002/mar.20283

Raven, J. C. (1941). Standardization of progressive matrices, 1938. *British Journal of Medical Psychology, 19*, 137–150. doi:10.1111/j.2044-8341.1941.tb00316.x

Rupp, A. A., Templin, J., & Henson, R. A. (2010). Diagnostic measurement: Theory, methods, and applications. New York, NY: Guilford Press.

Seashore, C. E. (1919). *The psychology of musical talent.* New York, NY: Silver, Burdett and Company.

Seashore, C. E. (1929). Meier-Seashore Art Judgment Test. *Science, 69*, 380–380. doi:10.1126/science.69.1788.380

Siceloff, M. M. (1933). *Validity and standardization of the McAdory Art Test.* New York, Oxford, UK.

Silvia, P. J. (2007). Knowledge-based assessment of expertise in the arts: Exploring aesthetic fluency. *Psychology of Aesthetics, Creativity, and the Arts, 1*, 247–249. doi:10.1037/1931-3896.1.4.247

Silvia, P. J., & Nusbaum, E. C. (2011). On personality and piloerection: Individual differences in aesthetic chills and other unusual aesthetic experiences. *Psychology of Aesthetics, Creativity, and the Arts, 5*, 208–214. doi:10.1037/a0021914

Smets, G., & Knops, L. (1976). Measuring visual esthetic sensitivity: An alternative procedure. *Perceptual and Motor Skills, 42*, 867–874. doi:10.2466/pms.1976.42.3.867

Smith, L. F., & Smith, J. K. (2006). The nature and growth of aesthetic fluency. In P. Locher, C. Martindale, & L. Dorfman (Eds.), New directions in aesthetics, creativity and the arts, foundations and frontiers in aesthetics (pp. 47–58). Amityville, NY: Baywood Publishing Co.

Summerfeldt, L. J., Gilbert, S. J., & Reynolds, M. (2015). Incompleteness, aesthetic sensitivity, and the obsessive-compulsive need for symmetry. *Journal of Behavior Therapy and Experimental Psychiatry, Special Issue: Innovations in Understanding and Treating Obsessive-Compulsive Disorder, 49*(Part B), 141–149. doi:10.1016/j.jbtep.2015.03.006

Thorndike, E. L. (1916). Tests of esthetic appreciation. *Journal of Educational Psychology, 7,* 509–522.

Tinio, P. P. L. (2013). From artistic creation to aesthetic reception: The mirror model of art. *Psychology of Aesthetics, Creativity, and the Arts, 7,* 265–275. doi:10.1037/a0030872

Troche, S. J., & Rammsayer, T. H. (2009). Temporal and non-temporal sensory discrimination and their predictions of capacity- and speed-related aspects of psychometric intelligence. *Personality and Individual Differences, 47,* 52–57. doi:10.1016/j.paid.2009.02.001

Ullén, F., Mosing, M. A., Holm, L., Eriksson, H., & Madison, G. (2014). Psychometric properties and heritability of a new online test for musicality, the Swedish Musical Discrimination Test. *Personality and Individual Differences, 63,* 87–93. doi:10.1016/j.paid.2014.01.057

Wallentin, M., Nielsen, A. H., Friis-Olivarius, M., Vuust, C., & Vuust, P. (2010). The Musical Ear Test, a new reliable test for measuring musical competence. *Learning and Individual Differences, 20,* 188–196. doi:10.1016/j.lindif.2010.02.004

Wallin, J. E. W. (1911). A Practical guide for the administration of the Binet-Simon scale for measuring intelligence. *Journal of Clinical Psychology, 5,* 217–238.

Welch, G. F. (2006). The musical development and education of young children. In *Handbook of research on the education of young children*, 2nd edition (pp. 251–267). Mahwah, NJ: Lawrence Erlbaum Associates Publishers.

Whipple, G. M. (1919). *Classes for gifted children: An experimental study of methods of selection and instruction.* Bloomington, IL: Public School Publishing Company.

CHAPTER 38

CROSS-CULTURAL EMPIRICAL AESTHETICS

XIAOLEI SUN AND JIAJIA CHE

INTRODUCTION

PEOPLE across all cultures appreciate objects for their aesthetic qualities (Anderson, 2004). It is often assumed that because aesthetic appreciation is universal, the psychological processes involved in aesthetic appreciation, such as expectation, perception, memory, emotion, meaning, and judgment (Chatterjee & Vartanian, 2014; Leder & Nadal, 2014; Leder, Belke, Oeberst, & Augustin, 2004; Pearce et al., 2016) are common to humans in all cultures. However, the vast majority of studies on aesthetic appreciation have been conducted on participants from large-scale, Western, and industrialized countries. This raises the question of the generalizability of their results to other cultures, and of the universality of the cognitive and affective processes involved in aesthetic appreciation. Nevertheless, there are studies that have specifically addressed cross-cultural commonalities and differences in aesthetic appreciation. Here we review empirical evidence on both visual and music aesthetic appreciation in different cultures and provide an overview of the universal psychological processes involved in aesthetic appreciation.

Cross-cultural empirical aesthetics grew out of the early 20th-century fascination with ethnicity, inheritance, and social status. Some of the earliest comparisons of color preferences across cultures (Garth, 1922a, 1924; Garth & Collado, 1929), for instance, were part of the general study of the impact of ethnic background and education on mental abilities and academic performance (Garth, 1921a, 1921b, 1922b). The basic methods and theoretical scaffolding for cross-cultural empirical aesthetics originated in Cyril Burt's studies of children's artistic competence at schools administered by the London County Council during the 1920s and 1930s. At the time, British psychology was under the influence of Francis Galton's interest in individual differences, mental testing, correlations, and eugenics (Boring, 1950; Burt, 1962; MacKenzie, 1976). In line with this, Burt accepted as incontrovertible that intelligence and mental abilities were genetically based, that they were the main determinants of social position within the hierarchy of occupational classes, and that they could be measured objectively and accurately using mental tests (Norton, 1981). As part of his work for the London City Council, Burt introduced mental tests and psychometrics into the education system. He systematically studied the distribution of intelligence, mental abilities, and achievements of the London school population. The battery that Burt devised to measure children's abilities included several tasks of literary, musical, and visual appreciation and creation. These tasks required the children to rank fragments and images, paired and triple comparisons, composition, and drawing, and their answers were scored according to predefined correct solutions. He believed that there existed a unitary aesthetic ability, inherited and unalterable, that could be measured by means of responses to simple tests (Che, Sun, Gallardo, & Nadal, 2018). It was possible, thus, to determine the population's distribution of this hypothetical single factor of aesthetic appreciation. This suited administrative purposes well, because once the statistical norms were known, deviations could be easily detected, and individuals directed toward or away from careers in art (Burt, 1949). These early studies revealed a common factor explaining part of the variance in performance across tests. Burt referred to this as the general factor for artistic ability and believed it underlay the ability to appreciate relations among elements in art, combinations of lines and colors, sounds and words (Burt, 1933; 1949).

VISUAL AESTHETICS

When Burt's main research interest shifted to statistical theory, Eysenck (1940) continued the research on the general objective factor of aesthetic appreciation. He assembled 18 sets of pictures, including portraits, photographs of statues of Roman emperors, pencil drawings by Claude Lorrain, photographs of vases, Malayan masks, Japanese paintings, reproductions of colored embroidery, and curves of mathematical functions. He then asked 18 participants to rank the materials in each set in order of liking. Eysenck's (1940) factor analysis of participants' rankings revealed a factor accounting for 20.6% of the variance across sets, which he called the general objective factor of aesthetic appreciation. In Galton and Burt's line, he asserted that this factor was responsible for performance on virtually any conceivable test of aesthetic appreciation, that it was common to all humans, determined largely by biological factors, and innate (Eysenck, 1941a, 1941b, 1942, 1981).

Eysenck's (1940) assertion that the general objective factor of aesthetic appreciation was a universal factor, common to all humans regardless of culture, was empirically unfounded: he only had results from 18 British participants. So, it became important to actually test whether the general factor of aesthetic appreciation indeed cut across cultures. McElroy (1952) and Lawlor (1955) were the first to test Eysenck's (1940) universalist claims. McElroy (1952) presented 40 male Australian Aborigines and 20 white Australian males with 10 sets of images similar to those developed by Eysenck (colored reproductions of flowers, butterflies, fishes, birds, paintings of landscapes, polygons, and so on) and asked them to place the images in each set in order of liking. Lawlor (1955) asked 56 Ghanaian and 56 English participants to indicate the two most liked and the two least liked designs from a set of eight, taken from decorations on wooden carvings, metal figures, and woven material in common use in Ghana at the time. Both studies reported high within-culture agreement in ranking and preference, but negligible between-culture agreement. McElroy's (1952) cross-cultural rank correlations varied between −.18 and .11, depending on the set, and Lawlor's (1955) analysis produced a cross-cultural correlation value of −.17. Both studies agreed in their conclusions:

> Within each of the groups there is considerable agreement of choice and evidence of central tendency both in likes and dislikes; to this extent each group taken separately confirms the findings of previous workers (. . .) There is, however, no agreement at all between the preferences of the two cultural groups. The absence of correlations makes it clear that there is no general agreement which extends beyond the cultural boundaries.
>
> (Lawlor, 1955, p. 690)

Decades later, Eysenck turned to testing the universality of the general factor of aesthetic appreciation. In his studies, he used three different sets of materials in his studies: simple graphic designs, Birkhoff's (1932) polygons, and Götz, Borisy, Lynn, and Eysenck (1979) Visual Aesthetic Sensitivity Test (VAST). Eysenck and Iwawaki's (1971, 1975) studies revealed correlations in the liking ratings for simple designs and polygons awarded by British and Japanese participants that ranged from .60 to .82. Moreover, a factor analysis of the ratings revealed common preference types for rectangular, circular, interlaced, star-shaped designs. Soueif and Eysenck (1971, 1972) reported similar results comparing Egyptian and British pleasingness ratings for Birkhoff's (1932) polygons. The correlations in these studies ranged from .55 to .72, and a factor analysis again revealed common formal factors underlying participants' preferences: rectangularity, simplicity, symmetry, etc. Iwawaki, Eysenck, and Götz (1979) and Chan, Eysenck, and Götz (1980) concluded from these results that

> there appear to exist firm cross-cultural tendencies which predispose people to prefer certain polygonal forms to others; these predispositions not only govern overall preference judgments but extend to the finer detail into which the overall judgments can be split. Such a conclusion would seem to contradict a purely environmental, cultural interpretation of aesthetic judgments, and suggest the possibility of a more deeply based, biologically determined cause for aesthetic judgments.
>
> (Soueif & Eysenck, 1972, p. 152)

Eysenck's studies (Chan et al., 1980; Eysenck & Iwawaki, 1971, 1975; Iwawaki et al., 1979; Soueif & Eysenck, 1971, 1972) seem to show there is moderate agreement in the aesthetic preference of participants from different cultures. Still, the evidence for a general objective factor of aesthetic appreciation is limited in several ways. First, the samples were taken from only four countries (China, Egypt, Japan, and the United Kingdom), and in all studies the United Kingdom was always the point of reference. Second, cross-cultural agreement seems to have been moderated by the complexity of the stimuli and tasks. Eysenck's studies used simpler images than McElroy's (1952) and Lawlor's (1955): whereas Eysenck used geometric designs of one sort of another, McElroy (1952) and Lawlor (1955) used sets of artworks, following Eysenck's (1940) original approach. In addition, fewer stimuli were presented on each trial in Eysenck's tasks than in McElroy's (1952) and Lawlor's (1955): whereas Eysenck asked participants to rate individually presented stimuli or to choose one out of pairs of very similar designs, McElroy (1952) and Lawlor (1955) asked participants to rank order or choose among entire sets of between eight and 15 simultaneously presented images. Third, although participants seemed to generally agree in their responses to simple object features, it is not entirely clear what these features were. Birkhoff's (1932) polygons vary quantitatively in order and complexity, but Eysenck and Iwawaki's (1971, 1975) designs included qualitatively different classes of items, and although the VAST stimuli were designed to vary in harmony or "good Gestalt," the test itself is psychometrically weak (Myszkowski & Storme, 2017), and people's performance is related to their personality, intelligence, and creativity (Myszkowski, Çelik, & Storme, 2018; Myszkowski, Storme, Zenasni, & Lubart, 2014). The VAST, therefore, does not provide evidence for a specific ability for aesthetic appreciation. It actually proves that aesthetic preference arises from the interaction of many general cognitive, affective, and experiential factors (Leder et al., 2004).

Child (1962) was skeptical of Eysenck's notion of a biologically determined factor of aesthetic appreciation and of his assumption that the average ranking of images in a set represented their aesthetic value. Child (1962) believed that aesthetic sensitivity should be measured in relation to an external standard set by experts, not in relation to group averages. Moreover, individual differences in aesthetic sensitivity do not occur because of differences in biological constitution, but of differences in familiarity with, and acceptance of, traditions of aesthetic evaluation. In Child's (1962, 1965) view, aesthetic sensitivity is cultivated with practice and is the result not of a specific ability, but of general cognitive style and personality. High aesthetic sensitivity is the manifestation of an

actively inquiring mind, seeking out experience that may be challenging because of complexity or novelty, even alert to the potential experience offered by stimuli not already in the focus of attention, interested in understanding each experience thoroughly and for its own sake rather than contemplating it superficially and promptly filing it away in a category, and able to do all this with respect to the world inside himself as well as the world outside.

(Child, 1965, p. 508)

Child's (1965) views on aesthetic sensitivity led him to expect high agreement in aesthetic valuation among experts from different cultures, given the commonalities among the traditions of aesthetic assessment around the world, and the openness of art experts to the aesthetic features of other cultures. He compared the responses of African and North American participants to a set of 39 photographs of BaKwele tribal masks (Child & Siroto, 1965). Their sample included 16 male members of the African BaKwele tribe who had experience carving masks, participated in rituals involving masks, or showed a great interest in masks. Each of these participants chose the four he most preferred from the 39, then the next preferred four, and so on until all the masks had been selected. The second group of participants included 13 advanced art students from Connecticut. These participants were asked to rate the aesthetic value of the masks, or "how good they were as works of art." Child and Siroto's (1965) results revealed a reasonable agreement between both groups of participants: the images that had been judged as having greater aesthetic value by American experts were also those which BaKwele judges tended to prefer.

Child later compared the aesthetic response of Japanese and American experts in two studies (Iwao & Child, 1966; Iwao, Child, & García, 1969). American experts and Japanese potters were asked to judge the aesthetic value of pairs of black and white photographs of artworks and full-colored abstract paintings. Each pair represented artworks that had been judged as unequal in artistic quality by at least 12 out of 14 American experts. Iwao and Child (1966) asked traditional Japanese potters to choose the item in each pair that was better artistically. Iwao et al. (1969) presented the same materials and task to other Japanese participants related to the practice or teaching of at least one Japanese artistic tradition, including flower arranging, the tea ceremony, textiles dyeing, manufacture of dolls, woodcutting, painting, and calligraphy. Iwao and Child (1966) found that American and Japanese experts agreed on 61% of the pairs of black and white reproductions of artworks, and on 57.5% of the color artworks, and Iwao et al. (1969) found that they agreed on 58.5% of the pairs of black and white reproductions of artworks, and on 51.5% of the color artworks.

Child also paid attention to the issue of whether aesthetic sensitivity was related to other personal traits in a similar way in different cultures. Child and Iwao (1968) showed experts from North America, Pakistan, Greece, and Japan 80 pairs of artworks differing in artistic merit, and asked them to judge which of the artworks in each pair was generally considered to be better than the other by people with interests in art. They also asked participants to complete a 49-item questionnaire measuring personality traits. Results indicated that, in all four countries, aesthetic sensitivity was correlated with certain personality traits in different cultures: tolerance for complexity; independence of judgment; regression in the service of the ego; and preference for autonomy, variety, and intellectual and perceptual challenges (Anwar & Child, 1972; Child & Iwao, 1968; Haritos-Fatouros & Child, 1977). Child concluded that these results show that people from different countries who have an interest in art and aesthetic values judge artistic merit in very similar ways and that, despite all cultural differences, there is a great resemblance in the personal tendencies that lead people to develop an interest in art (Anwar & Child, 1972; Child & Iwao, 1968; Haritos-Fatouros & Child, 1977). In his view, thus, cross-cultural similarities in judgment were due to cross-cultural similarities in the way extensive experience with art, independent thinking, openness to new experiences, and attraction to challenges influence appraisals of art (Child, 1981).

Although Child's cross-cultural studies provide evidence for a moderate agreement in judgments of the artistic merit of visual artworks between North American art students, teachers, and artists, on the one hand, and West African, Greek, Pakistani, and Japanese craftsmen and artists, on the other, a number of issues question these results (Che et al., 2018). First, they are based on very few studies with sample sizes that were often small. It is uncertain whether the judgments obtained from such samples are representative of the populations they were selected from. Second, all his studies took North American experts as reference. This problem is exacerbated by what seems to be the repeated use of the same assessments by North American experts in several studies. Third, in some of his studies, Child asked all groups of participants to rate artistic merit, but in other studies he asked North Americans to rate artistic merit and non-North Americans to rate preference. Showing that two groups of experts agree in their assessment of artistic merit is different to showing that one group of experts prefer what another group of experts regards as artistically valuable.

During the 1960s and 1970s empirical aesthetics was transformed by Berlyne's (1971, 1974) program of psychobiological aesthetics, which set the trend for the field in the following decades. Berlyne conceived aesthetic creation and appreciation as intrinsically motivated stimuli-seeking behaviors that are reinforced by exposure to stimuli patterns. A stimulus' capacity to generate preference or pleasure depends on the amount of potential information transmitted to the organism through psychophysical, ecological, and collative features. Such features, including novelty, surprise, complexity, ambiguity, or asymmetry, are the prime constituents of the aesthetic aspect of objects. One of Berlyne's (1970, 1971) main predictions was that people, like all organisms, find the maximum of positive hedonic tone with intermediate levels of arousal, and that therefore they should prefer stimuli representing intermediate levels of collative properties, such as complexity. He created several sets of materials varying in different dimensions of visual complexity, and showed that people's preference is indeed influenced by variations in complexity (Berlyne, 1970, 1971). Berlyne's explanation of aesthetic appreciation relied on the basic functions of the brain's reward and aversion systems, common to all humans. It followed, therefore, that regardless of culture, people would respond in the same way to variations in complexity.

In the past three decades, a number of studies have set out to test this prediction. Farley and Ahn (1973) asked participants from Korea, India, Turkey, China, and the United States to look at polygons varying in complexity (defined as the number of sides, from four to 160) and select the four they liked the most. Results showed that regardless of country of origin, participants tended to choose the intermediately complex polygons. Berlyne, Robbins, and Thompson (1974) and Berlyne (1975) asked Ugandan, Canadian, and Indian participants to report how attractive or pleasing they found geometric designs varying in eight forms of complexity (irregularity of arrangement or shape, amount of material, heterogeneity of elements, amount of independent units, asymmetry, incongruity, and random redistribution). They found that Canadians, Ugandans, and Indians living in urban environments tended to prefer simple patterns, and Ugandans and Indians living in rural environments preferred complex patterns. Uduehi (1995) asked participants from the United States and Nigeria to take the Maitland Graves Design Judgment Test, which consists of 90 pairs or triplets of abstract geometric designs, asking participants to choose the one they preferred the most. Uduehi (1995)'s results showed that Americans preferred simple figures whereas Nigerians showed a preference for complex ones. A recent study by Bode, Helmy, and Bertamini (2017) compared the beauty ratings of 60 abstract patterns varying in complexity and symmetry by British and Egyptian participants. They found that although there was a large correlation in responses from both countries (.89), British participants' beauty ratings were uninfluenced by complexity, whereas Egyptians' ratings were inversely correlated with complexity. Makin, Helmy, and Bertamini (2018) asked 50 British and 50 Egyptian participants to rate how much they liked a series of regular and random patterns using a 0–100 scale. Their results show that participants in both samples rated symmetric patterns higher than random ones. Moreover, in both samples the relative preference for the patterns was linearly related to the amplitude of the sustained posterior negativity electroencephalogram (EEG) component, which is generated by the extrastriate visual cortex in response to symmetry.

Although most of these studies have focused on whether complexity has similar influences on aesthetic appreciation in different cultures, other studies have examined the role of symmetry, regularity, proportion, curvature, contrast, brightness, and abstraction (Uduehi, 1995; Bode et al., 2017; Makin et al., 2018; McManus & Wu, 2013; Gómez-Puerto et al., 2018; van Dongen & Zijlmans, 2017; Berlyne, 1976). In most of these studies, there was a considerable agreement across cultures: Americans and Nigerians showed a common preference for symmetric patterns (Uduehi, 1995); British and Egyptians gave higher beauty ratings for symmetric patterns (Bode et al., 2017); and British and Egyptians awarded higher liking scores for regular abstract patterns than random ones; and the EEG component generated by relative preference was similar in both ethnic groups. McManus and Wu (2013) asked people from China and the United Kingdom to respond to 23 rectangles varying in diverse height and width and found that both groups showed a preference for the golden section and for squares. Gómez-Puerto et al. (2018) examined cross-cultural preference for images varying in the dimension of curvature–sharpness and found that participants from Mexico, Ghana, and Spain commonly preferred curved contours to sharp-angled ones. van Dongen and Zijlmans (2017) studied the effect of contrast on artworks preference and found that participants from both the United States and India preferred high-contrast artworks.

Other cases, such as Berlyne's (1976) study on brightness and abstraction, showed cultural differences. Berlyne (1976) asked Canadian students, Indian students, and Indian villagers to express their preference for postcard-sized colored reproductions of Western paintings varying in brightness and abstraction. Results showed that Indian villagers preferred brighter paintings than the Canadian students, who preferred brighter paintings than the Indian students. Also, the preference of Canadian students for nonrepresentational artworks was significantly higher than that of Indian villagers, while the preference of Indian students for those images was intermediate between both other groups. Despite these differences, Berlyne (1976) argued that the preferences of the three groups of participants were influenced by how representational and how bright the paintings were.

In sum, the cross-cultural studies that followed Berlyne's (1971) approach provide convincing evidence that aesthetic preference across cultures is influenced by a common set of visual features: "Art all over the world, it appears, exhibits a common dependence on certain dimensions of variation related to collative stimulus properties, even if the preferred segments of these dimensions vary from society to society" (Berlyne, 1980, p. 354). Although there is cross-cultural agreement on the formal dimensions that people rely on when expressing liking or preference (complexity, symmetry, regularity, or curvature), there seems to be some cross-cultural disagreement on the preferred values of some of these dimensions: whereas preference for symmetry and regularity is highly consistent across cultures, preference for complexity seems to be inconsistent across cultures, with some expressing greater preference for complexity, others for simplicity, and others for intermediate levels of complexity/simplicity. Although these studies compared samples from countries in Africa, Asia, Europe, and North America, and have provided a broad coverage, sample sizes tended to be small, including fewer than 50 participants in most cases. Additionally, the amount and strength of the evidence for the role of the different collative variables in aesthetic preference are unequal. Complexity and symmetry/regularity have received most of the attention, while the remaining collative variables have received much less attention.

One of the key goals of empirical aesthetics is to clarify how the interactions of social and physical context, human beings, and objects affect aesthetic appreciation (Jacobsen, 2006; Pearce et al., 2016). A century and a half of research in empirical aesthetics has produced a complex picture of how such processes take place and are integrated. Empirical studies have shown, for instance, that art knowledge influences people's aesthetic appreciation by modulating psychological processes, from perception to affect (Leder, Gerger, Brieber, & Schwarz, 2014; Pang, Nadal, Müller-Paul, Rosenberg, & Klein, 2013; Wiesmann & Ishai, 2010); that framing changes the way people look at and value art and other people (Kirk, Skov, Hulme, Christensen, & Zeki, 2009; Leder, Tinio, Fuchs, & Bohrn, 2010; Locher, Krupinski, & Schaefer, 2015); and that context influences people's expectations and heightens or attenuates their enjoyment of art (Brieber, Nadal, & Leder, 2015; Pelowski, Forster, Tinio, Scholl, & Leder, 2017). However, such conclusions have been derived from studies conducted on European or North American samples. It is commonly assumed that knowledge, framing, and context have similar effects on the aesthetic appreciation of all humans—those living in large-scale industrialized and small-scale nonindustrialized societies alike. Although this is not an unreasonable assumption, actual evidence for this assumption is uneven, scarce, and weak.

Despite these limitations, the available evidence points to a moderate cross-cultural agreement in aesthetic appreciation for simple visual materials, owing to general perceptual, cognitive, and affective processes common to all humans. If there is anything universal about aesthetic appreciation, it is its reliance on certain formal dimensions, especially complexity and symmetry, but also proportion, contour, brightness, and contrast. These seem to be among the basic object features that contribute to aesthetic appreciation across cultures.

COLOR AESTHETICS

Color preferences are among the most intensely studied topics in empirical aesthetics. There is much evidence showing that age (Birren, 1950; Norman & Scott, 1952), gender (Eysenck, 1941a; Saito, 1996; Palmer & Schloss, 2010), personality traits (Eysenck, 1981; Birren, 1973), education (Garth, 1924; Garth, Ikeda, & Langdon, 1931), as well as such appearance parameters of colors as hue, saturation, and brightness (e.g., Palmer & Schloss, 2010), influence color preferences. People in different cultures use colors to convey meaning in different ways, which might also influence preference. For instance, on Chinese share price display screens, red means the share price is increasing and green means that it is decreasing, whereas in almost all other countries they operate the exact opposite way. The number and variety of factors influencing color preferences were so great that, initially, it seemed almost impossible to arrive at any systematic conclusions (Allesch, 1925; Chandler, 1934). However, Eysenck (1941a) showed that much of the early research relied on very different materials and inadequate statistical analysis, which contributed to the apparent unpredictability of color preferences. His own study showed that people preferred blue to red, red to green, green to violet, violet to yellow, and yellow to orange (or orange to yellow, in the case of men). Eysenck also realized that many studies had used similar colors to the ones he had used himself, and he averaged the rank for each of these colors in earlier studies. The average correlation for the preference order ranged from .82 for Caucasian samples to .72 for samples from other ethnic backgrounds. Eysenck (1941a) concluded that there was a universal order of color preference. How strong is the evidence for this conclusion?

The methods in these early studies of color preference involved mostly crude and simple surveys, rather than accurately controlled experiments. In the 1920s and 1930s, Garth and his colleagues conducted a series of studies that were one of the earliest and broadest attempts to test color preference empirically from a cross-cultural perspective. They compared the preferences of Caucasian American, Indian, Filipino, African American, Japanese, and Mexican children for seven colors: blue, green, red, violet, orange, yellow, and white (Garth, 1922a, 1924; Garth & Collado, 1929; Garth et al., 1931; Gesche, 1927; Mercer, 1925). The children were asked to arrange the seven Milton Bradley Company's color papers in the order of degree they preferred, from 1 (like very much) to 7 (do not like at all) (Garth, 1922a, 1924; Garth & Collado, 1929; Garth et al., 1931; Gesche, 1927; Mercer, 1925). The results revealed that children from all six samples preferred red and blue over the other colors. During the same period, the color preferences of Japanese children from 6–15 years old were also tested by Imada (1926) using six Zimmermann colors. The results of this study also showed a universal preference for red and blue regardless of the diverse materials.

Although earlier studies showed a cross-cultural agreement in preferring red and blue, Chou and Chen (1935) found that, as well as blue, Chinese students also preferred white, which was the least preferred in Garth's studies. One possible explanation is that the materials and methods were different. In their study, Chou and Chen (1935) used nine colored Chinese characters instead of the colored papers used in other studies. Each of these nine characters was paired with each of the other eight characters (36 pairings in all) and pairwise comparison was carried out. Chou and Chen (1935) concluded that Chinese students' preference for white was probably because white was the most frequently used color word in China, and white was the color of the national flag at that time. The preference for white in China was also found by Shen (1937), and he provided a different explanation associated with language use. Shen (1937) argued that the Chinese word "white" (白) represents not only pureness but also "everything open, clear and unselfish" (Chou & Chen, 1935, p. 311). Coincidentally, Saito also found a preference for white in other Asian regions, namely Japan, Indonesia, and Korea (e.g., Saito, 1981, 1996).

Cross-cultural similarities and differences in color preferences continued to turn up during the subsequent decades. A case in point is Adams and Osgood's (1973) and Choungourian's (1968) studies. Adams and Osgood (1973) asked male students from 23 culture groups to report affective meanings of colors in terms of different semantic dimensions, such as evaluation (good–bad), potency (strong–weak), and activity (excited–relaxed). Participants from different groups made more positive associations with blue, whereas black and gray were considered to be associated with bad feelings. In Choungourian's (1968) study, students from the United States, Lebanon, Iran, and Kuwait expressed their color preference for eight Ostwald colored papers in rank order through paired comparisons. As in other studies, the American participants ranked blue as their favorite color. However, participants from Lebanon, Iran, and Kuwait did not prefer blue but greenish colors, which may be due to the fact that the color green is used as a symbol in the Muslim world.

In sum, early studies on cross-cultural color preferences found both differences and commonalities. On the one hand, there was overwhelming evidence for a widespread preference for blue (e.g., Adams & Osgood, 1973; Birren, 1950; Eysenck, 1941a; Garth, 1922a, 1924; Garth & Collado, 1929; Garth et al., 1931; Gesche, 1927; Mercer, 1925). On the other hand, particular exceptions kept appearing: green was generally preferred to blue in some Islamic countries, such as Lebanon, Iran, and Kuwait (Choungourian, 1968), and white was the preferred color in some Asian countries, such as China (Chou & Chen, 1935; Saito, 1981, 1996; Shen, 1937). These conclusions, however, are qualified by certain methodological issues. First, those studies used different experimental materials. In a series of studies conducted by Garth and his colleagues, participants ranked the Milton Bradley Company's seven-color papers based on their preference (e.g., Garth, 1922a, 1924; Garth & Collado, 1929; Garth et al., 1931); Ostwald colored papers were ranked in Choungourian's studies (Choungourian, 1968, 1969, 1972); six Zimmermann colors were selected as stimuli in Japan (Imada, 1926); whereas in China, colored Chinese words were used, which might lead to a strong association with language, meanings, and symbols (e.g., Chou & Chen, 1935; Shen, 1937). Second, sample sizes in some of the studies showing cross-cultural differences were small. For instance, in Choungourian's (1968) study, there were only 40 subjects in each cultural group. In contrast, Garth (1931) recruited at least 1,000 participants for each racial group, while the sample sizes for color preference studies in East Asia were also over 500 (Chou & Chen, 1935; Imada, 1926; Shen, 1937). Third, fundamental color dimensions such as hue, saturation, and lightness, which have an effect on color preferences, were not well controlled in early studies (Palmer, Schloss, & Sammartino, 2013). Fourth, although studies reported both similarities and differences in color preferences across cultures, very few of them were able to explain why people preferred some colors, and why there were cross-cultural differences.

Explaining the causes of color preferences and cross-cultural agreements and disagreements has been an explicit goal of some of the studies conducted in the past two decades. Ou, Luo, Woodcock, and Wright (2004) developed a color–emotion model that explained how colors evoked various emotional feelings. In this model, four color–emotional dichotomies (warm–cool, heavy–light, active–passive, and hard–soft) were used to define color properties based on color activity, color weight, and color heat. Participants were asked to choose which word was more closely associated with the color presented, such as passive or active, like or dislike. Results showed that British participants preferred "cool" colors, whereas Chinese participants tended to prefer "clean," "modern," and "fresh" colors. In addition, both cultural groups showed a similar dislike for dark yellow, which is also reported by later studies for Caucasian (Palmer & Schloss, 2010) and Japanese participants (Yokosawa, Schloss, Asano, & Palmer, 2016). It seems, therefore, that people associate colors with certain value labels, which have more positive or more negative valence. People tend to prefer colors they learn to associate with positively valenced labels.

Hurlbert and Ling (2007) speculated that color preferences might originate in evolutionary/behavioral adaptations. They explained that color preferences arise from cone-opponent contrast components of stimuli relative to the background colors. In their experiment, eight colored rectangles varying only in hue (the saturation and lightness were precisely controlled) were presented as pairs. Participants were asked to choose the preferred color in each pair as fast as possible. Results showed that females preferred redder colors more than males, while the bluish colors were preferred by both genders. Hurlbert and Ling (2007) explained that the gender difference in redder color preference could be traced back to our Pleistocene hunter-gatherer ancestors. At that time, it was mostly females who engaged in fruit picking, and the ability to find red fruit would benefit them. These findings supported the speculation that the universal color preference patterns are the result of biological survival (Humphrey, 1971, 1976).

Hurlbert and Ling (2007) also found cross-cultural differences: Chinese participants preferred red significantly more than British participants. Hurlbert and Ling (2007) argued that such differences might be due to the fact that red means good luck in traditional Chinese society. The diverse color meanings were also noticed in a series of studies by Saito and her colleagues for participants from different Asian regions (Saito, 1981, 1996; Saito, Tomita, & Kogo, 1991). Results showed that, whereas vivid blue was preferred by most of the regions, white was preferred in Asian countries. Saito (1996) explained that this might be due to the special symbolic meaning of white. In Asia, white is always associated with the idea of being clean, pure, and refreshing, and is the symbol of sacredness in China.

In spite of the improvements in methodology and theory in the color preference studies, there were still wrinkles to iron out. For example, Palmer et al. (2013) argued that Hurlbert and Ling's (2007) model fit their own data well (explaining 70% variance), but that it did not explain much variance in others' data. For instance, it can only account for 37% of variance of color preference data collected by Palmer and Schloss (2010). The reason for this might be that the model could not account for some kinds of highly saturated colors because Hurlbert and Ling's (2007) data included only a narrow set of eight colors with the same saturation and similar luminance, whereas Palmer and Schloss's experiment included 32 chromatic colors consisting of four pairs of well-balanced hues and four saturation-lightness levels. Palmer and colleagues (2013) also questioned the color–emotion model by Ou et al. (2004) because it fails to explain how color preferences arise and why some kinds of color emotions predict preferences more accurately than others. Another obvious drawback is that an important emotional dimension, happy–sad, was not included in their model, perhaps because Ou et al. could not explain why happy was associated with a less preferred color (yellow) while sadness was associated with a more preferred color (blue). In addition, the above theories cannot provide a satisfactory explanation for the existence of numerous cross-cultural differences.

Palmer and Schloss (2010) put forward a new ecological valence theory (EVT) to attempt to overcome the shortcomings of previous theories. The EVT account of color preference draws on some of Humphrey (1976), Hurlbert and Ling (2007), and Ou and colleagues' color preference models. It is based on the idea that human color preferences are associated with evolutionary adaptations through emotional responses to colored objects in their physical and social environments. Palmer and Schloss (2010) suggested that people are inclined to like and approach the "good color" objects, which would be beneficial to their survival, and dislike and avoid the "bad color" objects, which may have potential risks to them. Palmer and Schloss (2010) also recognized the role of acquired learning in the fact that people tend to give a positive emotional response to the color associated with the colored objects in their physical and social environments. They tested EVT through the weighted affective valence estimates (WAVEs), which measure the extent to which color preferences are related to colored objects. In their experiments, WAVEs data can be calculated using a formula including four main parts: ratings of color preference, object description, ratings of object valence, and color–object matching. Palmer and Schloss (2010) tested their central assumptions of EVT by using the WAVEs procedure. A total of 48 American participants performed a color preference task including 32 chromatic colors of the Berkeley Color Project using a line-mark rating scale from −100 to +100, with a neutral zero-point. WAVEs data of 32 colors were collected by three different tasks: an object-association task, an object-valence rating task, and a color–object matching task. In the object-association task, 74 participants were required to give as many typical objects as they could that were specific to the colors they were presented. In the object-valence rating task, another 98 participants were asked to rate the valence of 222 black object descriptions on a white background on a line scale from negative to positive. An additional 31 participants were recruited for the color–object matching task. They were asked to rate the matching degree of the color of the described objects and the color presented on the screen using a line-mark scale from 0 to 1. The values of WAVEs were calculated by the following formula:

$$W_c = \frac{1}{n_c} \sum_{0=1}^{n_c} W_{co} v_0$$

where W_{co} is the average color–object match value for each pairing of a color (c) and an object description (o), V_0 is the average valence rating given to object o, and n_c is the number of object descriptions ascribed to color c. Schloss and Palmer (2009) also provided a possible explanation for the existence of cultural differences in color preference based on EVT: if there are cultural differences in perceiving and evaluating objects, then the color preference for these objects should differ correspondingly.

To verify the cross-cultural applicability of the EVT, Yokosawa, Yano, Schloss, Prado-Leòn, and Palmer (2010) measured the association between the WAVEs and color preference in Japan, Mexico, and the United States using a similar procedure to that of Schloss and Palmer (2009). Consistent with Schloss and Palmer (2009), the results showed that American WAVEs predicted American color preferences ($r = .89$) better than Japanese ($r = .77$) or Mexican preferences ($r = .54$), whereas Japanese WAVEs predicted their own color preference ($r = .66$), better than for Americans ($r = .55$) or Mexicans ($r = .29$). These findings indicated that the correlation between color preference and the WAVEs within cultures was stronger than those between cultures. More recently, Yokosawa et al. (2016) replicated the WAVEs procedure in Japan and analyzed the correlations of color preference and color–object associations within Japanese culture and between Japanese and American cultures. The results showed that Japanese WAVEs explained only 36% of the variance in Japanese color preferences. This level of explainable variation was far less than in previous American data reported by Schloss and Palmer (2009), where American WAVEs could explain 80% of the variance in American color preferences.

A possible reason was that in East Asia colors usually convey more symbolic meanings, rather than being associated with specific objects. This point of view was verified in the study investigating the correlations between both symbolic and object WAVEs and color preference in China (Palmer et al., 2014). The results reported that the Chinese WAVEs pattern increased to the same level as the American WAVEs pattern when both objective and symbolic associations were added to the WAVEs model. This viewpoint affirmed the idea that colors played different symbolic roles in diverse cultures (Saito, 1996). However, Taylor, Clifford, and Franklin (2013) tested British as well as nonindustrialized Himba participants using the same paradigm, and the result was quite different. Similar to Americans, the WAVEs correlated strongly with color preference in the British group (.81). For the Himba group, however, the negative correlation (−.41) meant that the more the Himba people liked the objects, the less they preferred the objects' colors. Taylor et al. (2013) concluded that not only the patterns of color preference, but also the underlying mechanisms of the cognitive processes might vary in different cultures. They further supposed that there was not just one universal explanation for color preference. Color preference might be influenced by object associations, basic psychophysical mechanisms, or biological components of color vision. Further research should pay more attention to people from nonindustrialized societies and provide a deeper, broader understanding of both differences and similarities in color preferences.

In addition to this complex picture of cultural influences on color preferences, many unresolved problems still remain. First, even though color preferences are closely related to specific objects and symbols, most of the empirical studies only used words or colored paper that represent these objects and symbols. Second, most of the cross-cultural studies on color preferences have sampled large-scale industrialized societies. The limited evidence from small-scale societies, such as the Himba, from Namibia, revealed a unique pattern of color preferences. The Himba generally like highly saturated colors, quite independently of hue (Taylor et al., 2013). Clearly, studies that sample more small-scale societies are required for a full cross-cultural understanding of color preferences.

Musical Aesthetics

Music is often said to be universal, but what does this mean exactly? Is there anything common to music in all cultures, besides the fact that it is produced (List, 1971)? The evidence suggests that music was present already in the early stages of our own species, and is part of a set of traits indicating behavioral and cognitive modernity (McBrearty & Brooks, 2000). The precise origin of music is hard to date, though it seems probable that by 60,000 to 30,000 years ago our ancestors were producing music (Cross & Morley, 2010; Shen, 1987). According to Morley (2009), there are over 120 Paleolithic sound-producing objects that have been considered to be musical instruments, of which 90 seem to have been flutes. Most of the archeological sites that have yielded these instruments were excavated before sophisticated stratigraphic and dating techniques were in use, so it is not possible now to determine whether some of these instruments were used as part of a group activity or whether they were played in isolation (Morley, 2009). The oldest objects broadly accepted as musical instruments are two pipes constructed from swan bones found at the site of Geissenklösterle, in Germany, and dated to 36,800 years ago, and more recently to 42,500 years ago (Higham et al., 2012).

The almost complete bone flute and fragmented ivory flutes discovered at the German sites of Hohle Fels and Vogelherd are also dated to more than 35,000 years ago (Conard, Malina, & Münzel, 2009). The site of Isturitz, in the Pyrenees, which seems to have been inhabited by large groups of people for several thousand years, has yielded—in addition to examples of parietal art and animal statuettes—17 flute-like artifacts, constituting the largest known concentration of sound-producing objects. Some of these instruments have been deliberately worked, showing truncated ends, drilled and smoothed holes, and incised lines (Morley, 2009). The sophistication in the manufacture of these musical instruments that are almost contemporary with the arrival of modern humans to Europe suggests, as noted by Conard et al. (2009), that *Homo sapiens* arrived in Europe with a well-established musical tradition, that instruments were probably in use much earlier, and that it is conceivable that musical behavior involving voice and body had a long history prior to the manufacture of instruments.

A growing body of cross-cultural research on music has produced evidence for the existence of commonalities and diversities on music aesthetics across cultures. Mehr et al. (2019) used the Natural History of Song (NHS) including an ethnographic corpus of 4,709 descriptions of song performances in 315 societies from 60 traditional cultural clusters, and a discography of 118 audio recordings from 30 geographic regions, to examine cross-cultural commonalities and differences. Through the analysis, they found that music is present in every society. Music is not, however, a fixed biological response with a single archetypal adaptive function. It varies more within than between societies in formality, arousal, and religiosity, and arises in different behavioral contexts around the world. In all societies, music is clearly associated with behaviors such as infant care, healing, dance, and love. Music with the same behavioral function tends to have similar musical features. For example, dance songs are usually more fast-paced than lullabies; religious healing songs have less melodic variation than dance songs; love songs have more accents and a wider range than lullabies; and healing songs use fewer but denser notes than love songs. Musical forms vary in melodic and rhythmic complexity, and the patterns of two dimensions follow power-law distributions. In addition, tonality exists widely, perhaps universally. The conclusion drawn from this study is that there are indeed common fundamentals in music, which can link musical styles to social functions and emotional responses across cultural differences around the world.

Following the reciprocal feedback model of Hargreaves, MacDonald, and Miell (2005), we discuss cross-cultural musical aesthetics through the "Music" (rhythms, familiarity, pitch level, musical scale), the "Listener" (an individual's emotional response and personality), and the "Situations and contexts" (social and cultural circumstances).

Musical expressivity is primarily linked to structural aspects of music (Meyer, 1956). Many authors have focused on the effects of enculturation on single features of music such as temporal and melodic structures. It is commonly agreed that most musical systems are isorhythmic, and such a rhythm tends to continue through the whole piece of music once it is established (Trehub, Becker, & Morley, 2015). There is another assumption that rhythmic perception is universal due to the reason that external temporal perception such as meters or rhythms is based on the mechanisms of neural oscillation entrainment (Drake, Jones, & Baruch, 2000; Large & Snyder, 2009). Savage, Brown, Sakai, and Currie (2015) analyzed a set of 304 pieces of world music recordings and found there to be statistical universality that most music recordings tend to have an isorhythmic beat and subdivide into two or three beats throughout the whole section. This finding supported the view of the existence of regular rhythms across the globe. In their empirical experiment, Toiviainen and Eerola (2003) also reported that Africans and Europeans showed no difference in tapping behavior in response to European melodies. Moreover, in a series of studies on the cognitive processing of musical phrase boundaries in a cross-cultural context, music closure positive shift (CPS) was observed in Chinese and German musicians and nonmusicians who were required to categorize Chinese and Western biphrasal melodies in both phrased and unphrased conditions (Nan, Knösche, & Friederici, 2006, 2009). The CPS is commonly used as a neural measure of phrase boundary perception in speech (Pannekamp, Toepel, Alter, Hahne, & Friederici, 2005; Steinhauer, Alter, & Friederici, 1999) and in music (Knösche et al., 2005; Neuhaus, Knösche, & Friederici, 2006). It was found that, in contrast to the unphrased condition, both groups of subjects with formal music training generated music CPS between 450 ms and 600 ms after the pause when listening to both types of phrased music (Nan et al., 2006), and a slightly right-lateralized music CPS was also observed in nonmusicians (Nan et al., 2009), indicating that the music CPS is not influenced by the relationship between the subjects' cultural background and the type of music. However, compared with Western music, German musicians and nonmusicians listening to unfamiliar Chinese music had an increased CPS amplitude, indicating that the increase in amplitude was influenced by the type of music (Nan et al., 2006, 2009). People usually process music through perceptual and cognitive networks built by experience. Throughout development, the particular musical structures acquired also shape individual cognitive networks. In the process, individuals' cognitive networks become increasingly mature and are in turn used to encode culture-specific musical structures. Hence, culture-specific brain structures are created when a human is exposed to a particular music system (Hannon & Trainor, 2007), so that musical structure organization is facilitated (Drake & El Heni, 2003). For example, through the analysis of functional magnetic resonance imaging (fMRI) data of cultural specificity of music memory, Morrison and Demorest (2009) found greater activation in the left cerebellar area, right angular gyrus, posterior preauricular, and right middle frontal areas when Americans and Turks listened to unfamiliar music from alien cultures compared with listening to familiar music from their own culture. So, it is not difficult to understand why it is so hard for Europeans to follow the rhythm of African melodies: it reflects the disadvantage of cultural unfamiliarity (Toivianinen & Eerola, 2003). Similarly, Soley and Hannon (2010) also found that American infants who were unfamiliar with Balkan music preferred Western rhythm to Balkan rhythm, whereas Turkish infants who were familiar with both types of music showed no such bias. For the reason that Balkan rhythm has more irregular metrical structures than Western rhythm, Soley and Hannon (2010) concluded that early temporal structure preference is affected by both universal simplicity and special cultural familiarity.

Enculturation processes for rhythm and pitch structures may develop in parallel (Hannon & Trainor, 2007). Melodic structures, especially in pitch level, have also been intensively investigated. Lynch, Eilers, Oller, Urbano, and Wilson (1991) investigated both the influences of enculturation and musical complexity on music perception through music mistuning tasks utilizing Western and Javanese musical patterns. Results showed that Western nonmusicians recorded a lower threshold for Western patterns than for Javanese patterns, whereas musicians showed less difference between the two patterns. This finding indicated that cultural familiarity could influence music perception, but acquired musical skills can be applied to music from other cultures. An event-related potential (ERP) investigation of musicians' processing of musical scale structures, comparing German, Turkish, and Indian participants, revealed that universal listening strategies were modified by culture (Neuhaus, 2003). Trehub, Schellenberg, and Nakata (2008) conducted an experiment to investigate the pitch memory of Japanese and Canadian children by shifting familiar music by one semitone. Despite less exposure to the target, Japanese children still showed better performance in identifying the original music.

In recent years, comparative studies of music and language have drawn more attention. It is generally considered that music and language share commonalities: they both have sounds with melodic and rhythmic patterns (Patel, 2003). The tonal characteristics of music in one culture must be related to the prosodic characteristics of language in the same culture for the following reasons: Both of them reflect emotions; speech is the source of pitch, which is the essential feature of music; melodic traits of music are closely related to vocal speech; and patterns of melody and rhythm are similar in language and music, at least in Western music (Han, Sundararajan, Bowling, Lake, & Purves, 2011; Thompson, Schellenberg, & Husain, 2004). Han et al. (2011) further analyzed the pitch interval of traditional music in tone (China, Thailand, and Vietnam) and nontone language countries (the United States, Germany, and France), and found that pitch direction changed more frequently and pitch intervals were larger in tone language countries, indicating the co-variation of tonality features of language and music across cultures. Similarly, Trehub et al. (2008) also attributed Japanese children's superior performance on pitch memory tasks to the use of tone language.

Some other studies concerned a unique cultural group, namely the "bimusical," who are exposed to two or more musical cultures. There is evidence that "bimusical" (Indian and Western) participants showed equal responses to musical tension and musical recognition tasks of music from both cultures, whereas participants with exposure to only one culture showed in-group bias (Wong, Roy, & Margulis, 2009). In future, this group must receive more attention from linguists as well as music psychologists.

In addition, music in daily life is strongly linked with emotions. Emotional responses are an essential component of the aesthetic response to music (Istók et al., 2009). Cross-cultural studies on music and emotion contain direct assessment of individuals' ability to understand the emotional meaning of music across cultures, and also indirect evidence for cross-cultural similarities in the relationship between music and emotion. There may be universal emotional cues that transcend enculturation (Mckay, 2002). Balkwill and Thompson (1999) revealed certain universal mood-targeted melodic cues in the comparisons of tonal characteristics between Western and Indian music. There is a strong relationship between the perception of tempo and melodic complexity and the interpretation of musically expressed emotion. For instance, joyful music is typically associated with fast tempo, major mode, wide pitch range, high loudness, regular rhythm, and low complexity (Gabrielsson & Juslin, 1996; Thompson & Robitaille, 1992). According to the cue redundancy model for representation and recognition of emotion in music (Balkwill & Thompson, 1999), composers and listeners were likely to express or recognize emotion in music through combining psychophysical cues and culture-specific cues.

The topic of most research on music and emotion has involved asking listeners to assess the emotions expressed in music from their own culture or other different cultures. Gregory and Varney (1996) compared British and Indian listeners' emotional judgment on commercially recorded excerpts of Hindustani ragas, Western classical music, and Western new age music, through indicating adjectives from a list of mood terms by Hevner (1936). Results showed that both British and Indian participants were sensitive to intended emotions in Western music, but not in Hindustani music, revealing that emotions expressed in unfamiliar music cannot always be recognized accurately. One possible cause is that the intended mood specified by the raga-rasa system could not be confirmed in those examples of commercially recorded music. By standardizing music stimuli in later research, the expression of basic emotions in different cultural music might be recognized to be universal, which is different from the cultural particularity found in the study of Gregory and Varney. Canadian and Japanese listeners were presented with excerpts from Japanese, Western, and Hindustani music that were appropriate for each emotion. The listeners were asked to judge the mood that best characterized the music. The results showed that both Japanese and Canadian listeners were sensitive to the emotions expressed in familiar or unfamiliar music, which was facilitated by psychophysical cues (Balkwill, Thompson, & Matsunaga, 2004). Therefore, listeners' understanding of the musically expressed emotion might be influenced not only by their familiarity with a culture-specific music system but also by their sensitivity to basic psychophysical cues. Those psychophysical cues for joy, sadness, and anger enable listeners to discard the influence of culture-specific unfamiliarity so as to make an accurate judgment of the emotions expressed in music (Balkwill & Thompson, 1999). Therefore, the similarity in regard to emotion was not only found in the musical structure, but also in the listeners' response to the music. For example, in the ethnomusicology study of Fritz and his colleagues (2009), 21 Mafa natives of Cameroon with no exposure to Western music and 20 Westerners were asked to link short, computer-generated music pieces to faces corresponding to Ekman's basic emotions (happy, sad, and scared). The results showed that Mafas could recognize the emotions of Western music with above-chance accuracy in the same way as Western listeners, indicating the universal ability to recognize the emotions expressed in music.

In the next experiment, Western and Mafa music were generated into four versions: original, reversed original, spectrally manipulated, and reversed spectrally manipulated. Westerners and Mafas were asked to evaluate their preference for those kinds of music. Results reported that both groups preferred the original Western and Mafa music to the spectrally manipulated version. Fritz et al. (2009) concluded that sensory consonance and dissonance might universally influence the processes of perceiving emotions in music.

McDermott, Schultz, Undurraga, and Godoy (2016) found that the Tsimane, a native Amazonian society, showed no differential preference for consonant and dissonant chords. In contrast, the rural and urban Bolivians showed significant preference for consonant music. Such findings call into question the generally accepted view of the innate biological basis of preferences for consonance. The results indicate that consonance preferences can be absent in cultures sufficiently isolated from Western music and are thus unlikely to reflect innate biases or exposure to harmonic natural sounds. The observed variation in preferences is presumably determined by exposure to musical harmony, suggesting that culture might have a dominant role in shaping aesthetic responses to music.

In addition to emotion, personality characteristics have been associated with music preferences in diverse studies (Dunn, de Ruyter, & Bouwhuis, 2012; Rentfrow & Gosling, 2006), including extraversion (Cattell & Saunders, 1954; Rentfrow & Gosling, 2003), neuroticism (Dunn et al., 2012), openness to experience (Rentfrow & Gosling, 2003; Zweigenhaft, 2008), and sensation seeking (Litle & Zuckerman, 1986). Music preference might uncover important aspects of personality (Cattell & Anderson, 1953).

A significant amount of research on the relationship between personality and music genre preference across different cultures has been compared, regarding both the similarities and differences. Several studies used self-reported assessments, mainly in the Short Test of Music Preference (STOMP) developed by Rentfrow and Gosling (2003) or other equivalent tests. A study of Dutch teenagers found a positive correlation between openness and preferring rock and classical music, and between extraversion and preference for hip-hop and pop music (Delsing, Ter Bogt, Engels, & Meeus, 2008). Likewise, young Germans with high openness to experience also prefer reflective (e.g., classical) and intense music (e.g., rock), but dislike upbeat music (e.g., pop); whereas extraverts showed a preference for upbeat and energetic music (e.g., hip-hop/rap) (Langmeyer, Rudan, & Tarnai, 2012). Moreover, studies of music preferences and personality among Brazilian students (Pimentel & Donnelly, 2008) and among Japanese students (Brown, 2012) reported similar results, but other personality traits were less associated with Japanese music preference. Similarly, those Canadian students who liked classical music were higher in openness to experience, while those who liked intense music were lower in conscientiousness and emotional stability (George, Stickle, Rachid, & Wopnford, 2007), and soul music was positively correlated with extraversion (Miranda & Claes, 2008).

However, self-report assessments require participants to have sufficient knowledge of musical styles to be able to differentiate them (Rentfrow, Goldberg, & Levitin, 2011).

On account of this limitation of self-reporting for music preference, participants were asked to listen to several music excerpts and indicate their degree of liking for each excerpt in other cross-cultural studies. Yoo, Kang, and Fung (2017) investigated which factors were related to world music preference of U.S. and South Korean participants, by use of Fung's (1996) World Music Preference Rating Scale (WMPRS), which includes 36 musical excerpts from Congo, Malawi, Nigeria, China, Japan, Korea, Cuba, Mexico, and Peru. Results indicated that, in both groups, familiarity was the strongest predictor of preferences for world music. Nevertheless, besides familiarity, for the Americans, openness to experience was mostly associated with world music preference, whereas for the South Koreans, a significant impact of openness to experience was only found on the preference for African music. In addition, sensation seeking was demonstrated to be linked with European music preference. A comparative study of Spanish and English showed that Spanish sensation seekers preferred hard rock music and disliked easy listening music, whereas English sensation seekers disliked soundtrack music (Rawlings, Barrantes i Vidal, & Furnham, 2000).

All of this evidence points to openness to experience, extraversion, and even sensation seeking as crucial personality characteristics underlying music aesthetic judgment across cultures. To some extent, the structure of music preference remains the same across cultures as well as the correlations with personality. Even so, current research on the association between personality and cultural musical preference has been short of breakthroughs, either owing to limited research techniques for personality or the musical task lacking diversification.

In this section, we have reviewed the studies on music perception and appreciation from a cross-cultural perspective. Through the exploration of different features in music (e.g., melody, rhythms, pitch), we have concluded that people perceive different music features in similar patterns and the way they perceive and evaluate these features is to some extent affected by the structure and rhythm of language and cultural familiarity. Next, the recognition of basic emotions expressed in music has been found across cultures, but familiarity with the culture-specific music system also plays an important role in listeners' understanding of the musically expressed emotion, which is facilitated by their sensitivity to basic psychophysical cues. Further, the influence of personality on music preference in different cultures is mostly embodied in individual differences in personality characteristics, such as openness to experience, extraversion, and sensation seeking. The correlation between music preference and personality is the same across cultures.

CONCLUSION

Looking back at the history of cross-cultural empirical aesthetics, in the early stages, researchers focused on general aesthetic abilities and factors, in the middle period, they explored the universal personality traits of art experts from different cultures, while today researchers are concerned with the topic of integrated characteristics underlying aesthetic preference. Due to universal human perceptual, cognitive, and emotional processes, there is a common set of visual features that influence aesthetic preferences across cultures, but individuals in different cultures diverge in their preferences for these formal dimensions (Berlyne, 1980). Research in experimental aesthetics has attempted to elucidate the aesthetic appreciation processes of objects by individuals in different social contexts. The interaction of knowledge, framing, and context may have similar effects on aesthetic appreciation across cultures for all humans, influencing the way people evaluate and appreciate aesthetics by modulating psychological processes.

As a particular visual dimension, color has attracted extensive attention. Early studies of color preference using simple pencil and paper materials found a cross-cultural consistency in the preference for blue and a cultural inconsistency in color preference influenced by religious factors and symbolism, as people use color in different ways to convey meaning in different cultures. In more recent studies, with more precise experimental materials and experimental controls, researchers have developed multiple hypotheses to investigate the mechanism of color preference theoretically and empirically. Ou et al. (2004) developed a color–emotion model, which found that people associate colors with certain value labels and prefer colors with positive value labels. Hurlbert and Ling (2007) hypothesized that color preference is influenced by evolutionary/behavioral adaptations and is a result of biological survival. Schloss and Palmer (2009) drew on and integrated previous theoretical models to propose the idea that human color preferences are related to evolutionary adaptations through emotional responses to colored objects in the physical and social environment. It is also crucial to note that the particular symbolic meaning of color in East Asian societies may be an important factor in the differences in color preferences between people in the East and the West. Color preferences may be influenced by object associations, underlying psychophysical mechanisms, or the biological components of color vision (Taylor et al., 2013).

In the final section, we explored the interaction of the individual, music, and the environment in cross-cultural musical aesthetics. There is a universality in the way individuals perceive different musical features. And it is clear that familiarity with culturally specific musical systems has a significant impact on an individual's recognition and understanding of music (Lynch et al., 1991). Universal listening strategies could be altered by culture (Neuhaus, 2003). Culture may play a dominant role in shaping aesthetic responses to music (McDermott et al., 2016). Across cultures, music carries the function of emotional expression as well as behavioral support. Emotional responses are an important part of the aesthetic response to music (Istók et al., 2009). Cross-cultural similarities between music and emotion suggest that there may be universal emotional cues that transcend cultural contexts (Mckay, 2002). What's more, the influence of personality on music preference in different cultures is primarily reflected in the individual differences in personality traits. Openness to experience, extroversion, and even sensation seeking are crucial personality traits in aesthetic judgments of music in different cultures. To some degree, the structure of musical preferences and their relevance to personality are the same across cultures.

REFERENCES

Adams, F. M., & Osgood, C. E. (1973). A cross-cultural study of the affective meanings of color. *Journal of Cross-Cultural Psychology, 4*(2), 135–156. https://doi.org/10.1177/002202217300400201

Allesch, G. J. v. (1925). Die ästhetische Erscheinungsweise der Farben. *Psychologische Forschung, 6*(1), 1–91. https://doi.org/10.1007/BF00444162

Anderson, R. L. (2004). *Calliope's sisters. A comparative study of philosophies of art* (2nd ed.). Upper Saddle River, NJ: Pearson Prentice Hall.

Anwar, M. P., & Child, I. L. (1972). Personality and esthetic sensitivity in an Islamic culture. *The Journal of Social Psychology, 87*(1), 21–28. https://doi.org/10.1080/00224545.1972.9918643

Balkwill, L. L., & Thompson, W. F. (1999). A cross-cultural investigation of the perception of emotion in music: Psychophysical and cultural cues. *Music Perception: An Interdisciplinary Journal, 17*(1), 43–64. https://doi.org/10.2307/40285811

Balkwill, L. L., Thompson, W. F., & Matsunaga, R. (2004). Recognition of emotion in Japanese, North Indian and Western music by Japanese listeners. *Japanese Journal of Psychological Research, 46*, 337–349. https://doi.org/10.1111/j.1468-5584.2004.00265.x

Berlyne, D. E. (1970). Novelty, complexity, and hedonic value. *Perception & Psychophysics, 8*(5), 279–286. https://doi.org/10.3758/bf03212593

Berlyne, D. E. (1971). *Aesthetics and psychobiology*. New York, NY: Appleton-Century-Crofts.

Berlyne, D. E. (1974). The new experimental aesthetics. In D. E. Berlyne (Ed.), *Studies in the new experimental aesthetics: Steps toward an objective psychology of aesthetic appreciation* (pp. 1–26). Washington, DC: Hemisphere Publishing Corporation.

Berlyne, D. E. (1975). Extension to Indian subjects of a study of exploratory and verbal responses to visual patterns. *Journal of Cross-Cultural Psychology, 6*(3), 316–330. https://doi.org/10.1177/002202217563004

Berlyne, D. E. (1976). Similarity and preference judgments of Indian and Canadian subjects exposed to Western paintings. *International Journal of Psychology, 11*(1), 43–55. https://doi.org/10.1080/00207597608247346

Berlyne, D. E. (1980). Psychological aesthetics. In H. C. Triandis & W. J. Lonner (Eds.), *Handbook of cross-cultural psychology* (Vol. III, pp. 323–361). Boston, MA: Allyn & Bacon.

Berlyne, D. E., Robbins, M. C., & Thompson, R. (1974). A cross-cultural study of exploratory and verbal responses to visual patterns varying in complexity. In D. E. Berlyne (Ed.), *Studies in the new experimental aesthetics: Steps toward an objective psychology of aesthetic appreciation* (pp. 259–278). Washington, DC: Hemisphere Publishing Corporation.

Birkhoff, G. D. (1932). *Aesthetic measure*. Cambridge, MA: Harvard University Press. https://doi.org/10.4159/harvard.9780674734470

Birren, F. (1950). Color psychology and color therapy: A factual study of the influence of color on human life. *Academic Medicine, 25*(4), 303. https://doi.org/10.1001/jama.1950.02920030068033

Birren, F. (1973). Color preference as a clue to personality. *Art Psychotherapy, 1*(1), 13–16. https://doi.org/10.1016/0090-9092(73)90005-7

Bode, C., Helmy, M., & Bertamini, M. (2017). A cross-cultural comparison for preference for symmetry: Comparing British and Egyptian non-experts. *Psihologija, 50*(3), 383–402. https://doi.org/10.2298/psi1703383b

Boring, E. G. (1950). *A history of experimental psychology* (2nd ed.). New York, NY: Appleton-Century-Crofts. https://bit.ly/3ixz2oo

Brieber, D., Nadal, M., & Leder, H. (2015). In the white cube: Museum context enhances the valuation and memory of art. *Acta Psychologica, 154*, 36–42. https://doi.org/10.1016/j.actpsy.2014.11.004

Brown, R. A. (2012). Music preferences and personality among Japanese university students. *International Journal of Psychology, 47*(4), 259–268. https://doi.org/10.1080/00207594.2011.631544

Burt, C. (1933). *How the mind works*. London: Allen & Unwin. https://bit.ly/3bT3nW9

Burt, C. (1949). The structure of the mind: A review of the results of factor analysis. *British Journal of Educational Psychology, 19*, 176–199. https://doi.org/10.1111/j.2044-8279.1949.tb01621.x

Burt, C. (1962). Francis Galton and his contributions to psychology. *The British Journal of Statistical Psychology, 15*(1), 1–49. https://doi.org/10.1111/j.2044-8317.1962.tb00081.x

Cattell, R. B., & Anderson, J. C. (1953). The measurement of personality and behavior disorders by the I. P. A. T. Music Preference Test. *Journal of Applied Psychology, 37*(6), 446. https://doi.org/10.1037/h0056224

Cattell, R. B., & Saunders, D. R. (1954). Musical preferences and personality diagnosis: I. A factorization of one hundred and twenty themes. *The Journal of Social Psychology, 39*(1), 3–24. https://doi.org/10.1080/00224545.1954.9919099

Chan, J., Eysenck, H. J., & Götz, K. O. (1980). A new visual aesthetic sensitivity test: III. Cross-cultural comparison between Hong Kong children and adults, and English and Japanese samples. *Perceptual and Motor Skills, 50*(3_suppl), 1325–1326. https://doi.org/10.2466/pms.1980.50.3c.1325

Chandler, A. R. (1934). *Beauty and human nature. Elements of psychological aesthetics.* New York, NY: Appelton-Century.

Chatterjee, A., & Vartanian, O. (2014). Neuroaesthetics. *Trends in Cognitive Sciences, 18*(7), 370–375. https://doi.org/10.1016/j.tics.2014.03.003

Che, J., Sun, X., Gallardo, V., & Nadal, M. (2018). *Cross-cultural empirical aesthetics. Progress in Brain Research, 237*, 77–103. https://doi.org/10.1016/bs.pbr.2018.03.002

Child, I. L. (1962). Personal preferences as an expression of aesthetic sensitivity. *Journal of Personality, 30*(3), 496–512. https://doi.org/10.1111/j.1467-6494.1962.tb02319.x

Child, I. L. (1965). Personality correlates of esthetic judgment in college students. *Journal of Personality, 33*(3), 476–511. https://doi.org/10.1111/j.1467-6494.1965.tb01399.x

Child, I. L. (1981). Bases of transcultural agreement in response to art. In H. I. Day (Ed.), *Advances in intrinsic motivation and aesthetics* (pp. 415–432). New York, NY: Plenum Press. https://doi.org/10.1007/978-1-4613-3195-7_17

Child, I. L., & Iwao, S. (1968). Personality and esthetic sensitivity: Extension of findings to younger age and to different culture. *Journal of Personality and Social Psychology, 8*(3p1), 308–312. https://doi.org/10.1037/h0025599

Child, I. L., & Siroto, L. (1965). BaKwele and American esthetic evaluations compared. *Ethnology, 4*(4), 349–360. https://doi.org/10.2307/3772785

Chou, S. K., & Chen, H. P. (1935). General versus specific color preferences of Chinese students. *The Journal of Social Psychology, 6*(3), 290–314. https://doi.org/10.1080/00224545.1935.9919740

Choungourian, A. (1968). Color preferences and cultural variation. *Perceptual and Motor Skills, 26*(3_suppl), 1203–1206. https://doi.org/10.2466/pms.1968.26.3c.1203

Choungourian, A. (1969). Color preferences: A cross-cultural and cross-sectional study. *Perceptual and Motor Skills, 28*(3), 801–802. https://doi.org/10.2466/pms.1969.28.3.801

Choungourian, A. (1972). Extraversion, neuroticism, and color preferences. *Perceptual and Motor Skills, 34*(3), 724–726. https://doi.org/10.2466/pms.1972.34.3.724

Conard, N. J., Malina, M., & Münzel, S. C. (2009). New flutes document the earliest musical tradition in southwestern Germany. *Nature, 460*, 737–740. https://doi.org/10.1038/nature08169

Cross, I., & Morley, I. (2010). The evolution of music: Theories, definitions and the nature of the evidence. In S. Malloch & C. Trevarthen (Eds.), *Communicative musicality* (pp. 61–82). Oxford: Oxford University Press. https://bit.ly/2LHujox

Delsing, M. J. M. H., Ter Bogt, T. F. M., Engels, R. C. M. E., & Meeus, W. H. J. (2008). Adolescents' music preferences and personality characteristics. *European Journal of Personality, 22*(2), 109–130. https://doi.org/10.1002/per.665

Drake, C., & El Heni, J. B. (2003). Synchronizing with music: Intercultural differences. *Annals of the New York Academy of Sciences, 999*(1), 429–437. https://doi.org/10.1196/annals.1284.053

Drake, C., Jones, M. R., & Baruch, C. (2000). The development of rhythmic attending in auditory sequences: Attunement, referent period, focal attending. *Cognition, 77*(3), 251–288. https://doi.org/10.1016/s0010-0277(00)00106-2

Dunn, P. G., de Ruyter, B., & Bouwhuis, D. G. (2012). Toward a better understanding of the relation between music preference, listening behavior, and personality. *Psychology of Music, 40*(4), 411–428. https://doi.org/10.1177/0305735610388897

Eysenck, H. J. (1940). The general factor in aesthetic judgments. *British Journal of Psychology. General Section, 31*(1), 94–102. https://doi.org/10.1111/j.2044-8295.1940.tb00977.x

Eysenck, H. J. (1941a). A critical and experimental study of colour preferences. *American Journal of Psychology, 54*(3), 385–394. https://doi.org/10.2307/1417683

Eysenck, H. J. (1941b). The empirical determination of an aesthetic formula. *Psychological Review, 48*(1), 83–92. https://doi.org/10.1037/h0062483

Eysenck, H. J. (1942). The experimental study of the 'good Gestalt'—a new approach. *Psychological Review, 49*(4), 344–364. https://doi.org/10.1037/h0057013

Eysenck, H. J. (1981). Aesthetic preferences and individual differences. In D. O'Hare (Ed.), *Psychology and the arts* (pp. 76–101). Brighton: The Harvester Press.

Eysenck, H. J., & Iwawaki, S. (1971). Cultural relativity in aesthetic judgments: An empirical study. *Perceptual and Motor Skills, 32*(3), 817–818. https://doi.org/10.2466/pms.1971.32.3.817

Eysenck, H. J., & Iwawaki, S. (1975). The determination of aesthetic judgment by race and sex. *The Journal of Social Psychology, 96*(1), 11–20. https://doi.org/10.1080/00224545.1975.9923256

Farley, F., & Ahn, S.-H. (1973). Experimental aesthetics: Visual aesthetic preference in five cultures. *Studies in Art Education, 15*(1), 44–48. https://doi.org/10.2307/1320057

Fritz, T., Jentschke, S., Gosselin, N., Sammler, D., Peretz, I., Turner, R., . . . Koelsch, S. (2009). Universal recognition of three basic emotions in music. *Current Biology, 19*(7), 573–576. https://doi.org/10.1016/j.cub.2009.02.058

Fung, C. V. (1996). Musicians' and nonmusicians' preferences for world musics: Relation to musical characteristics and familiarity. *Journal of Research in Music Education, 44*(1), 60–83. https://doi.org/10.2307/3345414

Gabrielsson, A., & Juslin, P. N. (1996). Emotional expression in music performance: Between the performer's intention and the listener's experience. *Psychology of Music*, 24(1), 68–91. https://doi.org/10.1177/0305735696241007

Garth, T. R. (1921a). The results of some tests on full and mixed blood Indians. *Journal of Applied Psychology*, 5(4), 359. https://doi.org/10.1037/h0071643

Garth, T. R. (1921b). White, Indian and Negro work curves. *Journal of Applied Psychology*, 5(1), 14–25. https://doi.org/10.1037/h0071540

Garth, T. R. (1922a). The color preferences of five hundred and fifty-nine full-blood Indians. *Journal of Experimental Psychology*, 5(6), 392–418. https://doi.org/10.1037/h0072088

Garth, T. R. (1922b). A comparison of mental abilities of mixed and full blood Indians on a basis of education. *Psychological Review*, 29(3), 221–236. https://doi.org/10.1037/h0073260

Garth, T. R. (1924). A color preference scale for one thousand white children. *Journal of Experimental Psychology*, 7(3), 233–241. https://doi.org/10.1037/h0071899

Garth, T. R. (1931). *Race psychology*. New York, NY: Whittlesey House (McGraw-Hill). https://bit.ly/2M3JmkO

Garth, T. R., & Collado, I. R. (1929). The color preferences of Filipino children. *Journal of Comparative Psychology*, 9(6), 397–404. https://doi.org/10.1037/h0075071

Garth, T. R., Ikeda, K., & Langdon, R. M. (1931). The color preferences of Japanese children. *The Journal of Social Psychology*, 2(3), 397–408. https://doi.org/10.1080/00224545.1931.9918981

George, D., Stickle, K., Rachid, F., & Wopnford, A. (2007). The association between types of music enjoyed and cognitive, behavioral, and personality factors of those who listen. *Psychomusicology*, 19(2), 32–56. https://doi.org/10.1037/h0094035

Gesche, I. (1927). The color preferences of one thousand one hundred and fifty-two Mexican children. *Journal of Comparative Psychology*, 7(4), 297–311. https://doi.org/10.1037/h0072520

Gómez-Puerto, G., Rosselló, J., Corradi, G., Acedo-Carmona, C., Munar, E., & Nadal, M. (2018). Preference for curved contours across cultures. *Psychology of Aesthetics, Creativity, and the Arts*, 12(4), 432–439. https://doi.org/10.1037/aca0000135

Götz, K. O., Borisy, A. R., Lynn, R., & Eysenck, H. J. (1979). A new visual aesthetic sensitivity test: I Construction and psychometric properties. *Perceptual and Motor Skills*, 49(3), 795–802. https://doi.org/10.2466/pms.1979.49.3.795

Gregory, A. H., & Varney, N. (1996). Cross-cultural comparisons in the affective response to music. *Psychology of Music*, 24(1), 47–52. https://doi.org/10.1177/0305735696241005

Han, S. E., Sundararajan, J., Bowling, D. L., Lake, J., & Purves, D. (2011). Co-variation of tonality in the music and speech of different cultures. *PLoS ONE*, 6(5), e20160. https://doi.org/10.1371/journal.pone.0020160

Hannon, E. E., & Trainor, L. J. (2007). Music acquisition: Effects of enculturation and formal training on development. *Trends in Cognitive Sciences*, 11(11), 466–472. https://doi.org/10.1016/j.tics.2007.08.008

Hargreaves, D. J., MacDonald, R., & Miell, D. (2005). How do people communicate using music? In D. Miell, R. MacDonald, & D. J. Hargreaves (Eds.), *Musical communication* (pp. 1–26). Oxford: Oxford University Press. https://doi.org/10.1093/acprof:oso/9780198529361.003.0001

Haritos-Fatouros, M., & Child, I. (1977). Transcultural similarity in personal significance of esthetic interests. *Journal of Cross-Cultural Psychology*, 8(3), 285–298. https://doi.org/10.1177/002202217783003

Hevner, K. (1936). Experimental studies of the elements of expression in music. *The American Journal of Psychology*, 48(2), 246–268. https://doi.org/10.2307/1415746

Higham, T., Basell, B., Jacobi, R., Wood, R., Ramsey, C. B., & Conard, N. J. (2012). Testing models for the beginnings of the Aurignacian and the advent of figurative art and music: The radiocarbon chronology of Geißenklösterle. *Journal of Human Evolution, 6,* 664–676. https://doi.org/10.1016/j.jhevol.2012.03.003

Humphrey, N. (1971). Colour and brightness preferences in monkeys. *Nature, 229*(5287), 615–617. https://doi.org/10.1038/229615a0

Humphrey, N. (1976). The colour currency of nature. *Colour for Architecture, 5,* 95–98. https://doi.org/10.4324/9781315881379-3

Hurlbert, A. C., & Ling, Y. (2007). Biological components of sex differences in color preference. *Current Biology, 17*(16), 623–625. https://doi.org/10.1016/j.cub.2007.06.022

Imada, M. (1926). Color preference of school children. *Japanese Journal of Psychology, 1,* 1–21. https://doi.org/10.4992/jjpsy.1.373

Istók, E., Brattico, E., Jacobsen, T., Krohn, K., Müller, M., & Tervaniemi, M. (2009). Aesthetic responses to music: A questionnaire study. *Musicae Scientiae, 13*(2), 183–206. https://doi.org/10.1177/102986490901300201

Iwao, S., & Child, I. L. (1966). Comparison of esthetic judgments by American experts and by Japanese potters. *The Journal of Social Psychology, 68*(1), 27–33. https://doi.org/10.1080/00224545.1966.9919662

Iwao, S., Child, I. L., & García, M. (1969). Further evidence of agreement between Japanese and American esthetic evaluations. *The Journal of Social Psychology, 78*(1), 11–15. https://doi.org/10.1080/00224545.1969.9922334

Iwawaki, S., Eysenck, H. J., & Götz, K. O. (1979). A new visual aesthetic sensitivity test (VAST): II. Cross-cultural comparison between England and Japan. *Perceptual and Motor Skills, 49*(3), 859–862. https://doi.org/10.2466/pms.1979.49.3.859

Jacobsen, T. (2006). Bridging the arts and sciences: A framework for the psychology of aesthetics. *Leonardo, 39*(2), 155–162. https://doi.org/10.1162/leon.2006.39.2.155

Kirk, U., Skov, M., Hulme, O., Christensen, M. S., & Zeki, S. (2009). Modulation of aesthetic value by semantic context: An fMRI study. *Neuroimage, 44*(3), 1125–1132. https://doi.org/10.1016/j.neuroimage.2008.10.009

Knösche, T. R., Neuhaus, C., Haueisen, J., Alter, K., Maess, B., Witte, O. W., & Friederici, A. D. (2005). Perception of phrase structure in music. *Human Brain Mapping, 24*(4), 259–273. https://doi.org/10.1002/hbm.20088

Langmeyer, A., Rudan, A. G., & Tarnai, C. (2012). What do music preferences reveal about personality? A cross-cultural replication using self-ratings and ratings of music samples. *Journal of Individual Differences, 33*(2), 119–130. https://doi.org/10.1027/1614-0001/a000082

Large, E. W., & Snyder, J. S. (2009). Pulse and meter as neural resonance. *Annals of the New York Academy of Sciences, 1169*(1), 46–57. https://doi.org/10.1111/j.1749-6632.2009.04550.x

Lawlor, M. (1955). Cultural influences on preference for designs. *The Journal of Abnormal and Social Psychology, 51*(3), 690–692. https://doi.org/10.1037/h0047219

Leder, H., Belke, B., Oeberst, A., & Augustin, D. (2004). A model of aesthetic appreciation and aesthetic judgments. *British Journal of Psychology, 95*(4), 489–508. https://doi.org/10.1348/0007126042369811

Leder, H., Gerger, G., Brieber, D., & Schwarz, N. (2014). What makes an art expert? Emotion and evaluation in art appreciation. *Cognition & Emotion, 28*(6), 1137–1147. https://doi.org/10.1080/02699931.2013.870132

Leder, H., & Nadal, M. (2014). Ten years of a model of aesthetic appreciation and aesthetic judgments: The aesthetic episode—developments and challenges in empirical aesthetics. *British Journal of Psychology, 105*(4), 443–464. https://doi.org/10.1111/bjop.12084

Leder, H., Tinio, P. P. L., Fuchs, I. M., & Bohrn, I. (2010). When attractiveness demands longer looks: The effects of situation and gender. *The Quarterly Journal of Experimental Psychology, 63*(9), 1858–1871. https://doi.org/10.1080/17470211003605142

List, G. (1971). On the non-universality of musical perspectives. *Ethnomusicology, 15*, 399–402. https://doi.org/10.2307/850640

Litle, P., & Zuckerman, M. (1986). Sensation seeking and music preferences. *Personality and Individual Differences, 7*(4), 575–578. https://doi.org/10.1016/0191-8869(86)90136-4

Locher, P., Krupinski, E., & Schaefer, A. (2015). Art and authenticity: Behavioral and eye-movement analyses. *Psychology of Aesthetics, Creativity, and the Arts, 9*(4), 356–367. https://doi.org/10.1037/aca0000026

Lynch, M. P., Eilers, R. E., Oller, D. K., Urbano, R. C., & Wilson, P. (1991). Influences of acculturation and musical sophistication on perception of musical interval patterns. *Journal of Experimental Psychology: Human Perception and Performance, 17*(4), 967–975. https://doi.org/10.1037/0096-1523.17.4.967

MacKenzie, D. (1976). Eugenics in Britain. *Social Studies of Science, 6*(3–4), 499–532. https://doi.org/10.1177/030631277600600310

Makin, A. D., Helmy, M., & Bertamini, M. (2018). Visual cortex activation predicts visual preference: Evidence from Britain and Egypt. *Quarterly Journal of Experimental Psychology, 71*(8), 1771–1780. https://doi.org/10.1080/17470218.2017.1350870

McBrearty, S., & Brooks, A. (2000). The revolution that wasn't: A new interpretation of the origins of modern human behavior. *Journal of Human Evolution, 39*, 453–563. https://doi.org/10.1006/jhev.2000.0435

McDermott, J. H., Schultz, A. F., Undurraga, E. A., & Godoy, R. A. (2016). Indifference to dissonance in native Amazonians reveals cultural variation in music perception. *Nature, 535*(7613), 547–550. https://doi.org/10.1038/nature18635

McElroy, W. A. (1952). Aesthetic appreciation in aborigines of Arnhem land: A comparative experimental study. *Oceania, 23*(2), 81–94. https://doi.org/10.1002/j.1834-4461.1952.tb00190.x

McKay, C. (2002). Emotion and music: Inherent responses and the importance of empirical cross-cultural research. Course Paper. McGill University. https://bit.ly/3sHXlor

McManus, I. C., & Wu, W. (2013). "The square is ... bulky, heavy, contented, plain, good-natured, stupid. . .": A cross-cultural study of the aesthetics and meanings of rectangles. *Psychology of Aesthetics, Creativity, and the Arts, 7*(2), 130–139. https://doi.org/10.1037/a0030469

Mehr, S. A., Singh, M., Knox, D., Ketter, D. M., Pickens-Jones, D., Atwood, S., ... Glowacki, L. (2019). Universality and diversity in human song. *Science, 366*, eaax0868. https://doi.org/10.1126/science.aax0868

Mercer, F. M. (1925). Color preferences of one thousand and six negroes. *Journal of Comparative Psychology, 5*(2), 109–146. https://doi.org/10.1037/h0072192

Meyer, L. B. (1956). *Emotion and meaning in music.* Chicago, IL: University of Chicago Press. https://bit.ly/3ixvpaM

Miranda, D., & Claes, M. (2008). Personality traits, music preferences and depression in adolescence. *International Journal of Adolescence and Youth, 14*(3), 277–298. https://doi.org/10.1080/02673843.2008.9748008

Morley, I. (2009). Ritual and music: parallels and practice, and the Palaeolithic. In C. Renfrew & I. Morley (Eds.), *Becoming human. Innovation in prehistoric material and spiritual culture* (pp. 159–175). Cambridge: Cambridge University Press. https://bit.ly/35YjE8k

Morrison, S. J., & Demorest, S. M. (2009). Cultural constraints on music perception and cognition. *Progress in Brain Research, 178*, 67–77. https://doi.org/10.1016/s0079-6123(09)17805-6

Myszkowski, N., Çelik, P., & Storme, M. (2018). A meta-analysis of the relationship between intelligence and visual "taste" measures. *Psychology of Aesthetics, Creativity, and the Arts, 12*(1), 24–33. https://doi.org/10.1037/aca0000099

Myszkowski, N., & Storme, M. (2017). Measuring "good taste" with the visual aesthetic sensitivity test-revised (VAST-R). *Personality and Individual Differences, 117*, 91–100. https://doi.org/10.1016/j.paid.2017.05.041

Myszkowski, N., Storme, M., Zenasni, F., & Lubart, T. (2014). Is visual aesthetic sensitivity independent from intelligence, personality and creativity? *Personality and Individual Differences, 59*, 16–20. https://doi.org/10.1016/j.paid.2013.10.021

Nan, Y., Knösche, T. R., & Friederici, A. D. (2006). The perception of musical phrase structure: A cross-cultural ERP study. *Brain Research, 1094*(1), 179–191. https://doi.org/10.1016/j.brainres.2006.03.115

Nan, Y., Knösche, T. R., & Friederici, A. D. (2009). Non-musicians' perception of phrase boundaries in music: A cross-cultural ERP study. *Biological Psychology, 82*(1), 70–81. https://doi.org/10.1016/j.biopsycho.2009.06.002

Neuhaus, C. (2003). Perceiving musical scale structures. *Annals of the New York Academy of Sciences, 999*(1), 184–188. https://doi.org/10.1196/annals.1284.026

Neuhaus, C., Knösche, T. R., & Friederici, A. D. (2006). Effects of musical expertise and boundary markers on phrase perception in music. *Journal of Cognitive Neuroscience, 18*(3), 472–493. https://doi.org/10.1162/jocn.2006.18.3.472

Norman, R. D., & Scott, W. A. (1952). Color and affect: A review and semantic evaluation. *The Journal of General Psychology, 46*(2), 185–223. https://doi.org/10.1080/00221309.1952.9710652

Norton, B. (1981). Psychologists and class. In C. Webster (Ed.), *Biology, medicine and society 1840–1940* (pp. 289–314). Cambridge: Cambridge University Press. https://doi.org/10.1017/CBO9780511562822.010

Ou, L. C., Luo, M. R., Woodcock, A., & Wright, A. (2004). A study of colour emotion and colour preference. Part I: Colour emotions for single colours. *Color Research & Application, 29*(3), 232–240. https://doi.org/10.1002/col.20010

Palmer, S. E., Schloss, K. B. (2010). An ecological valence theory of human color preference. *Proceedings of the National Academy of Sciences, 107*, 8877–8882. DOI: 10.1073/pnas.0906172107

Palmer, S. E., Schloss, K. B., & Sammartino, J. (2013). Visual aesthetics and human preference. *Annual Review of Psychology, 64*(1), 77–107. https://doi.org/10.1146/annurev-psych-120710-100504

Palmer, S. E., Schloss, K. B., Yokosawa, K., Asano, M., Kanazawa, N., Guo, T., … Peng, K. (2014). Ecological influences on color preferences in Japan, China, and the US. Paper presented at the 2nd Annual Visual Science and Art Conference, Belgrade, Serbia.

Pang, C. Y., Nadal, M., Müller-Paul, J. S., Rosenberg, R., & Klein, C. (2013). Electrophysiological correlates of looking at paintings and its association with art expertise. *Biological Psychology, 93*(1), 246–254. https://doi.org/10.1016/j.biopsycho.2012.10.013

Pannekamp, A., Toepel, U., Alter, K., Hahne, A., & Friederici, A. D. (2005). Prosody-driven sentence processing: An event-related brain potential study. *Journal of Cognitive Neuroscience*, *17*(3), 407–421. https://doi.org/10.1162/0898929053279450

Patel, A. D. (2003). Language, music, syntax and the brain. *Nature Neuroscience*, *6*(7), 674–681. https://bit.ly/3qBmrMx

Pearce, M. T., Zaidel, D. W., Vartanian, O., Skov, M., Leder, H., Chatterjee, A., & Nadal, M. (2016). Neuroaesthetics: The cognitive neuroscience of aesthetic experience. *Perspectives on Psychological Science*, *11*(2), 265–279. https://doi.org/10.1177/1745691615621274

Pelowski, M., Forster, M., Tinio, P. P. L., Scholl, M., & Leder, H. (2017). Beyond the lab: An examination of key factors influencing interaction with "real" and museum-based art. *Psychology of Aesthetics, Creativity, and Arts*, *11*(3), 245–264. https://doi.org/10.1037/aca0000141

Pimentel, C. E., & Donnelly, E. D. O. P. (2008). The relation between music preference and the big five personality traits. *Psicologia: Ciência e Profissão*, *28*(4), 696–713. https://doi.org/10.1590/S1414-98932008000400004

Rawlings, D., Barrantes i Vidal, N., & Furnham, A. (2000). Personality and aesthetic preference in Spain and England: Two studies relating sensation seeking and openness to experience to liking for paintings and music. *European Journal of Personality*, *14*(6), 553–576. https://doi.org/10.1002/1099-0984(200011/12)14:6<553::aid-per384>3.3.co;2-8

Rentfrow, P. J., Goldberg, L. R., & Levitin, D. J. (2011). The structure of musical preferences: A five-factor model. *Journal of Personality and Social Psychology*, *100*(6), 1139–1157. https://doi.org/10.1037/a0022406

Rentfrow, P. J., & Gosling, S. D. (2003). The do re mi's of everyday life: The structure and personality correlates of music preferences. *Journal of Personality and Social Psychology*, *84*(6), 1236–1256. https://doi.org/10.1037/0022-3514.84.6.1236

Rentfrow, P. J., & Gosling, S. D. (2006). Message in a ballad: The role of music preferences in interpersonal perception. *Psychological Science*, *17*(3), 236–242. https://doi.org/10.1111/j.1467-9280.2006.01691.x

Saito, M. (1981). A cross-cultural research on color preference. *Bulletin of the Graduate Division of Literature of Wasada University*, *27*, 211–216.

Saito, M. (1996). A comparative study of color preferences in Japan, China and Indonesia, with emphasis on the preference for white. *Perceptual and Motor Skills*, *83*(1), 115–128. https://doi.org/10.2466/pms.1996.83.1.115

Saito, M., Tomita, M., & Kogo, C. (1991). Color preference at four different districts in Japan: 1. Factor analytical study. *Journal of the Color Science Association of Japan*, *15*(1), 1–12. https://bit.ly/39Vtqtk

Savage, P. E., Brown, S., Sakai, E., & Currie, T. E. (2015). Statistical universals reveal the structures and functions of human music. *Proceedings of the National Academy of Sciences*, *112*(29), 8987–8992. https://doi.org/10.1073/pnas.1414495112

Schloss, K. B., & Palmer, S. E. (2009). An ecological valence theory of human color preferences. *Journal of Vision*, *9*(8), 358–358. https://doi.org/10.1167/9.8.358

Shen, N. C. (1937). The color preference of 1368 Chinese students, with special reference to the most preferred color. *The Journal of Social Psychology*, *8*(2), 185–204. https://doi.org/10.1080/00224545.1937.9919999

Shen, S. (1987). Acoustics of ancient Chinese bells. *Scientific American*, *256*(4), 104–110. https://doi.org/10.1038/scientificamerican0487-104

Soley, G., & Hannon, E. E. (2010). Infants prefer the musical meter of their own culture: A cross-cultural comparison. *Developmental Psychology, 46*(1), 286–292. https://doi.org/10.1037/a0017555

Soueif, M. I., & Eysenck, H. J. (1971). Cultural differences in aesthetic preferences. *International Journal of Psychology, 6*(4), 293–298. https://doi.org/10.1080/00207597108246695

Soueif, M. I., & Eysenck, H. J. (1972). Factors in the determination of preference judgments for polygonal figures: A comparative study. *International Journal of Psychology, 7*(3), 145–153. https://doi.org/10.1080/00207597208247048

Steinhauer, K., Alter, K., & Friederici, A. D. (1999). Brain potentials indicate immediate use of prosodic cues in natural speech processing. *Nature Neuroscience, 2*(2), 191–196. https://doi.org/10.1038/5757

Taylor, C., Clifford, A., & Franklin, A. (2013). Color preferences are not universal. *Journal of Experimental Psychology: General, 142*(4), 1015–1027. https://doi.org/10.1037/a0030273

Thompson, W. F., & Robitaille, B. (1992). Can composers express emotions through music? *Empirical Studies of the Arts, 10*(1), 79–89. https://doi.org/10.2190/nbny-akdk-gw58-mtel

Thompson, W. F., Schellenberg, E. G., & Husain, G. (2004). Decoding speech prosody: Do music lessons help?. *Emotion, 4*(1), 46–64. https://doi.org/10.1037/1528-3542.4.1.46

Trehub, S. E., Becker, J., & Morley, I. (2015). Cross-cultural perspectives on music and musicality. *Philosophical Transactions of the Royal Society B: Biological Sciences, 370*(1664), 20140096. https://doi.org/10.1098/rstb.2014.0096

Trehub, S. E., Schellenberg, E. G., & Nakata, T. (2008). Cross-cultural perspectives on pitch memory. *Journal of Experimental Child Psychology, 100*(1), 40–52. https://doi.org/10.1016/j.jecp.2008.01.007

Toiviainen, P., & Eerola, T. (2003). Where is the beat? Comparison of Finnish and South African listeners. In R. Kopiez, A. C. Lehmann, I. Wolther, & C. Wolf (Eds.), *Proceedings of the 5th triennial ESCOM conference* (pp. 501–504). Hanover: Hanover University of Music and Drama. https://bit.ly/2Nmt5rU

Uduehi, J. (1995). A cross-cultural assessment of the Maitland Graves Design Judgment Test using U.S. and Nigerian subjects. *Visual Arts Research, 21*, 63–70. https://bit.ly/3qDPuiF

van Dongen, N. N., & Zijlmans, J. (2017). The science of art: The universality of the law of contrast. *American Journal of Psychology, 130*(3), 283–294. https://doi.org/10.5406/amerjpsyc.130.3.0283

Wiesmann, M., & Ishai, A. (2010). Training facilitates object recognition in cubist paintings. *Frontiers in Human Neuroscience, 4*, 11. https://doi.org/10.3389/neuro.09.011.2010

Wong, P. C., Roy, A. K., & Margulis, E. H. (2009). Bimusicalism: The implicit dual enculturation of cognitive and affective systems. *Music Perception: An Interdisciplinary Journal, 27*(2), 81–88. https://doi.org/10.1525/mp.2009.27.2.81

Yokosawa, K., Schloss, K. B., Asano, M., & Palmer, S. E. (2016). Ecological effects in cross-cultural differences between US and Japanese color preferences. *Cognitive Science, 40*(7), 1590–1616. https://doi.org/10.1111/cogs.12291

Yokosawa, K., Yano, N., Schloss, K. B., Prado-Leòn, L. R., & Palmer, S. E. (2010). Cross-cultural studies of color preferences: US, Japan, and Mexico. *Journal of Vision, 10*(7), 408–408. https://doi.org/10.1167/10.7.408

Yoo, H., Kang, S., & Fung, V. (2017). Personality and world music preference of undergraduate non-music majors in South Korea and the United States. *Psychology of Music, 46*(5), 611–625. https://doi.org/10.1177/0305735617716757

Zweigenhaft, R. L. (2008). A do re mi encore: A closer look at the personality correlates of music preferences. *Journal of Individual Differences, 29*(1), 45–55. https://doi.org/10.1027/1614-0001.29.1.45

SECTION 6

THE CONTEXT

CHAPTER 39

....

THE GENERAL IMPACT OF CONTEXT ON AESTHETIC EXPERIENCE

....

MATTHEW PELOWSKI AND EVA SPECKER

Context and approach, antecedent moment and goal, are part of the aesthetic experience...

–Robert Ginsberg (1986, p. 77)

A minute in the world's life passes! ... To become that minute, to be the sensitive plate. What we make of that ... moment when it is before our eyes depends upon what we expect ... and that in turn depends today upon what we have already experienced...

–Paul Cezanne (in Berger, 1972)

CONTEXT is the ever-present counterpoint to the person and the stimuli discussed in the previous chapters, mediating how these come into relation to create an aesthetic experience.

Researchers are becoming increasingly aware that our preferences, our tastes, our emotions and decisions are not stable but are constructed during an interaction and from a complex interplay of factors (for reviews, see Pelowski, Forster, Tinio, Scholl, & Leder, 2017; Reber, Schwarz, & Winkielman, 2004). Notable context effects—which will be tackled in this and in the forthcoming chapters—include, but are definitely not limited to: participant mood, labels or contextual information, suggested cost or authenticity, the social environment or knowledge of peer ratings, museums and theaters vs. laboratory settings, personality, previous training and interactions; not to mention the outside weather, odors; even doing jumping jacks or walking instead of sitting. All may change what we think is beautiful, important, or how we classify and engage with a stimulus.

This suggests an almost endless supply of potential research directions. Indeed, in composing an introductory chapter on context, it is tempting to write "context is potentially everything, have a nice day!" and leave it at that. However, there is much to be said about the interaction of context. First and foremost, this involves moving beyond certain studies or identified effects to how these might be fit together into present knowledge of the processing and sequences in aesthetic experience. This can also help us to anticipate new context issues and consider how and where they might play a role and be investigated. At the same time, aesthetics is also itself rather unique in its relationship to context and its analysis. Built from a philosophy that argues against context effects, much aesthetic writing suggests, on the one hand, a highly personal or, on the other, a *universal*, context-free basis for our judgments (for a review, see Leder & Nadal, 2014). To borrow a few famous clichés, either there is "no accounting for taste"—and therefore not much to really talk about using typical empirical methods—or our aesthetic reactions are made to qualities inherent in objects and thus "objective," "unprejudiced" (Hume, 1757), "unchanged by circumstance" (Bell, 1914, p. 37). This attitude can be traced into the present day in the design of highly controlled, reductive studies. Thus, one might rightly ask not only how do we approach context, but are their certain features that are immutable? How do we design empirical and consider studies in this domain?

In this chapter we offer an introduction to this complex topic. This will serve as a gateway to the next several chapters. As many of context's specific areas—the social, the physical or institutional, background or personality-related features—have been considered or will be tackled later, we will offer a more general consideration. Beginning with the interest in context throughout the history of aesthetics, we build to present empirical approaches and especially theory, focusing on context's main layers and points of influence. We then discuss how key context issues might be considered in theories or models of aesthetic processing, with the goal of providing a framework for better approaching context aspects in this book and in your own future studies. This is interspersed with what we consider to be some of the more intriguing books and papers—spanning literature on empirical and psychological aesthetics, as well as the humanities, art criticism, and sociology—in order to spur your thinking about the potential for studying context. We conclude with major issues, candidates for future consideration, and suggestions for further reading and education.

A Brief History of Context in Aesthetics

Context—at least philosophically within the field of aesthetics—is marked as much by its ambivalence as it is by its ever-present acknowledged importance. It is therefore useful to briefly consider history as this does inform our approach and understanding of context studies. This is by no means an exhaustive review but is designed to give a taste of the prevalent discussion and, one might say *the context*, for present issues in empirical study.

Where did we come from? Empiricist perspectives … but only for the right people

The beginning of aesthetics, again, stems from an essentially empiricist or formalist perspective. This claims that the aesthetically relevant properties of an object—such as its beauty—are innate; "they are directly exhibited and can be registered with the senses at any time, anywhere, by any observer" (Deines, 2013, p. 24). For example, Cicero (roughly 100–50 BCE; paraphrased by Summers, 1987, p. 50) suggests that aesthetic experience begins in "seeing, hearing, and understanding hidden and wonderful things." These "are seen at once" without modulation by outside factors. Similar arguments can be traced through Plato (e.g., 1987) and Aristotle, and a long line of philosophers suggesting immutable but perhaps intangible qualia that exist at the basis of the world and our sense perceptions (Dennett, 1988; Summers, 1987). Aesthetics, in turn, was essentially being the pursuit of such qualities or their perception and appreciation.

Yet, if one looks through the same history of writings with a contemporary perspective, we do find a continuous if implicit argumentation for context—mixed with a dollop of classicism. To continue the quote of Cicero, formal qualities may be argued to be immutable, but "nature and reason" are required to " 'transfer' … what we gain from sense from a lower to a higher sphere, 'from the eyes to the mind' " (Summers, 1987, p. 50). That is, by having the necessary knowledge, life experiences, or interest, or perhaps even by being born with the correct abilities, one could properly tune to and then appreciate the qualities of the world and in a sense get at their underlying importance or "truth." This is explicit with Plato, whose iconoclastic idea of the danger of images, art, or poetry—expressed via his allegory of the cave (Plato, 1987)—explicitly suggested that one might develop enough knowledge to "see past" the artifice. "The intelligence," notes Murdoch (1977, p. 2), "moves from uncritical acceptance of sense experience … to a more sophisticated and morally enlightened understanding." In turn, artists were not banned—another famous suggestion—because they made objects that were deficient, but because they were so convincing that they could easily seduce the novice masses— "simple-minded fellow[s]" taken in by a "charlatan" (Plato, 1987, p. 340).

Similar arguments can be traced through the Middle Ages, to the Renaissance (see Summers, 1987), to Descartes (e.g., Descartes, 1965), and Leibniz (1902). Context also played an implicit role in Baumgarten's (1750) introduction of aesthetics as a unique field (for a review, see Osborne, 1979). His argument for aesthetic experience, what Baumgarten called the "perfection of sensate cognition" (Baumgarten, 1954), although focused again on low-level features or immutable sensual perceptions, implied an element of training or other interpersonal difference. Although formal properties (e.g., shape and color) can be perceived by anyone, "the use of taste, perceptiveness, and sensitivity is necessary" (Sibley, 1959, p. 421) for aesthetic perception or discerning what made the properties special. These were acquired through learning or education. In fact, according to Poppe (1907, p. 47) Baumgarten may have been specifically motivated by a pamphlet from the late 17th century (Pierre Bonhours') that Germans, including Baumgarten, were "incapable" of appreciating art and beauty. One might therefore say that our entire field is based on a key context element—nationalism. (Incidentally, as an American and Dutch author, happily working under a German boss, it should be noted that whether Germans can actually appreciate art has still, to our knowledge, not been systematically considered.)

Early empirical study to 1980—differences in taste, aesthetic sensitivity, art training, culture

As empirical aesthetics slowly emerged as a practice, we find a similar context focus. Fechner (1876) with the introduction of empirical aesthetics as a science, talks of both lower relationships involving sensual materials but also of the formation and development of higher relationships—manifest in top-down associations that can create differing meanings or appreciations. These involve the cultivated understanding of differences—"In short, not only width but height," that is, experience and education (for similar discussion of Hume, etc., see also Deines, 2013; Harris, 2013).

In the early to mid-20th century, the early assessments on aesthetic sensitivity or ability (Barron & Welsh, 1952; Child, 1962; Iwawaki, Eysenck, & Gotz, 1979), which might be said to mark some of the first artwork rating studies, and which asked individuals to choose a "superior" (more pleasing, more artistic, more satisfying) image, also typically used previous ratings by experts (those trained, or at least those studying art history, art making, etc.) as the point of reference for "correct" judgments. Child (1970) went even further, positing what he called the "t" factor, which was argued to be separate from intelligence or creativity. He explicitly connected to context in crafting his empirical studies. "Some people feel that a scientific approach requires giving equal status to everyone. I would argue on the contrary that people greatly interested and ... knowledgeable in the fine arts are likely to respond to a painting or sculpture in especially illuminating ways" (p. 47). Interestingly, he also raised the possibility that aesthetic ability was not necessarily the product of training, but came about naturally through personality—involving a liking for challenge, novelty, independent judgment, emotional awareness (Child, 1970, p. 48; see also Eysenck, 1972)—which would drive individuals to obtain more art exposure or to seek out careers in aesthetics.

With the 1970s, and the wave of researchers at the cusp of contemporary empirical aesthetics study, we find an even more overt focus. Parsons (1987) suggested a cognitive developmental model of art appreciation becoming more nuanced as one had more and more exposure, especially in adult stages. Berlyne (1974) introduced the importance of background in his discussion of aesthetic enjoyment. His four channels of information by which we attend to stimuli, for example, listed a semantic source consisting of the meaning of things in "reality," an expressive and a cultural aspect requiting awareness of art and social norms, and a syntactic source that gives significance to formal elements. In his empirical studies, such as with assessment of paintings (Berlyne, Ogilvie, & Parham, 1968), he also specifically excluded individuals who did show art interest or recruited art-interested individuals. See also Martindale (1988), who explicitly suggested the role of background and expertise in major processing stages.

Moving back through the 20th century, context also became a factor in studies of cultural differences, which might be said to mark some of the first explicit context-focused empirical investigations (incidentally, this area is still extremely underinvestigated). In an early study, Abel and Hsu (1949) showed that Chinese-born participants perceived ink blots as a whole pattern more frequently than did American-born participants. Chiu (1972) showed that Chinese children tended to group two objects on the basis of the relational-contextual information; American children tended to group objects based on shared analytic features or categories. Berlyne (1976) found that judgments of similarity for art works (colored postcard reproductions of Western paintings) differed between Indian villagers and Canadian participants. The villagers also showed higher preference for brightness. Osgood and colleagues (e.g., Tanaka, Oyama, & Osgood, 1963) considered cultural influence on topics such as color perception and assessment of art. He reported a more universal consistent way of making evaluations—although not necessarily similar evaluations themselves—suggesting that our ratings might divide into hedonic/evaluative, potency, and activity clusters. He also reported a shared preference for blue (Adams & Osgood, 1973). See Komar and Melamid (1997) for a particularly compelling modern parallel in cross-country preferences in painting.

Other notable studies include McArthur and Berry (1987), who considered facial attractiveness and report a shared response to baby faces in Koreans and Westerners, or the ecological approach to vision by Gibson (1979), which dispelled notions that the eye could be reduced to a camera and highlighted context aspects of mobility or expectations to guide perception.

1990—expertise, labels, museums

This path continued into the burgeoning of psychological aesthetics in the 1990s. Early context-related studies looked at the importance of art expertise as modulating expectations and visual artwork ratings (Cupchik, 1995; Hekkert & Van Wieringen, 1996; Winston & Cupchik, 1992; for a very early study, see also Getzels & Csikszentmihalyi, 1969). Another main early empirical focus considered the impact of accompanying labels or titles, which were shown to increase an artwork's felt importance, encourage meaning making (Cupchik, Shereck, & Spiegel, 1994), and can also boost a work's ratings (Russell & Milne, 1997). Branching afield to general museum studies, art education, and sociology, researchers assessed the role of museum or gallery spaces (discussed further in a forthcoming chapter and below). Notably, Bitgood (1992; Bitgood & Patterson, 1993; see also Falk, 1993) offered a number of studies looking at display conditions, noting that, for example different lighting, placing an object on a higher plane as compared with other objects, changing wall colors, etc., could increase the object's importance and viewer attention or even enjoyment. Studies also have considered "museum fatigue" (e.g., Melton, 1972) or the effect from repeated art viewing. Moving back a bit, in what must be one of the earliest context studies, Robinson (1928) showed that, upon showing participants a succession of art prints and asking them to look as long as they wished, they showed a progressive decrease in attention.

This brings us, essentially, to the present day. Building on past history, there is an awareness that context is important, and especially that it may manifest in aspects of training, experience, and even personality. There is also an awareness that certain modes of perception, setting, or culture may be important. Of course, some researchers did and perhaps still do also argue against the importance of especially background in appreciation of art. For example, the gestalt psychologist Arnheim (see Funch, 1997) considered the perception of visual forces to be direct and without the influence of knowledge (for a few such arguments regarding the brain, see also Ramachandran & Hirstein, 1999).

How is context assessed in empirical studies?

It is also useful to give a brief note about how context is empirically studied. There are several main methods that have emerged throughout the above review. These include the use of two or more conditions, varied between- or within-participants, and whereby one or more factors are changed (say abstract vs. representational art; 5- vs. 10-s presentations; museum vs. lab setting; Japanese vs. Western viewers). Another way is to simply manipulate the prompting or supporting information that is given to participants. This is often done with cues or labels, for example, showing art in tandem with elaborative or descriptive titles (as reviewed above). Similar studies may involve social or setting information (telling participants that "this came from a museum" vs. "this is computer generated" (Kirk, Skov, Hulme, Christensen, & Zeki, 2009). Researchers can also manipulate presentation. Gartus and Leder (2014), for example, showed art images with either a street background or with white walls of a typical museum. Causative studies (e.g., transcranial direct current stimulation (tDCS), transcranial magnetic stimulation (TMS), pharmacology) might use repeated designs with a sham vs. experimental condition, or single- or double-blind procedures so as to eliminate other, unwanted aspects of context and priming.

So, context is important and has always been—how is this presently considered?

Context is (probably most often) important, but this also raises the important question of how can this be more carefully considered? Where do these different aspects fit and how can they be understood within present understanding of aesthetic experience? It is this question—asking us to move beyond an intuited idea of certain factors' modulation, or an empirical study's identification of certain effects, to a more cohesive approach of theoretical and empirical studies that, we would argue, marks the next step for context study, and the primary topic for today.

This can be answered by walking through several emerging discussions regarding context importance, models of aesthetic processing, and notable aspects, all of which we will consider below.

What are the general categories for context studies?

To begin a discussion of present approaches, we might first consider the present arguments for main context areas. A review of literature, does suggest that context arguments have been grouped into a few main clusters. Many of these are noted above. Note also that comprehensive discussions of general context layers, or early review papers, are also mostly found outside the explicit area of empirical aesthetics. Rather, they begin in general considerations of museums, sociology, or other reviews of human interactions with the environment, and which have gradually been incorporated into explicit discussion of media experience.

Among notable examples, Falk and Dierking (1992), in their review for general interactions in museums, suggested three overlapping sectors: once again, following the above past studies, first an individual's interests and motivations, as well as social context, and the physical context/space. They argue that it is primarily the interplay of these factors that can shape our enjoyment, behavior, and understanding. Bitgood (1992), in a similar review for museums and public spaces, suggested both the setting/architecture, object, display configuration, social/cultural factors, and "extra-exhibit" aspects—including labels, catalog copy, maps, audio guides, text information (see also Griswold et al., 2013). Moving into the focus on visual aesthetics, Gartus and Leder (2014) note that current psychological models divide factors "roughly into three groups": basic visual characteristics of the processed art, characteristics of the viewer, and other surrounding social or physical aspects of the environment. Recently, we (Pelowski, Forster, Tinio, Scholl, & Leder, 2017) reviewed these and other studies, highlighting five areas (shown in Figure 39.1): (a) once again the *viewer context*—personality, demographics, etc.; (b) the *object context*, including the formal or physical features of a stimulus, whether art, music, or other media; (c) the *presentation context*, physical aspects of the setting, other stimuli, or objects; (d) the *social context* or interactions between individuals; and (e) the *cultural context*, including learned attitudes toward the stimulus and aspects of the interaction, as well as, for example, stimulus history.

Looking to Figure 39.1, with just these general layers one can of course think of multiple questions or potential effects of context. Whether it be a work of music or art, a football match or a ballet, experienced in a theater or gallery or alone in our homes, in person or on TV, our interactions are always embedded within such a rich, multilayered experience. Where and how is a stimulus presented? Are we alone or with other people?

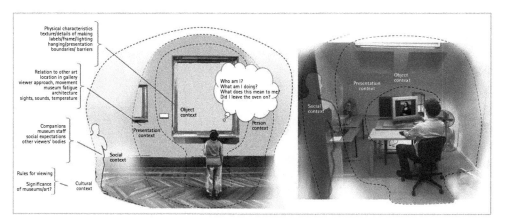

FIGURE 39.1. An example of main layers of context in aesthetic experience.

What is the size, color, texture, or resolution if on a screen? What are your mood and your expectations?

Moving beyond a collection of effects—embedding context within aesthetic experience

To better consider the actual psychological or processing implications, the above layers can be combined with present models of aesthetic experience. Models were reviewed in an earlier chapter (see also Pelowski, Markey, Lauring, & Leder, 2016), therefore we will not delve deeply into their nuance here. Suffice it to say, for the purpose of beginning to think about the multiple impacts of context, models are useful because they give at least a theoretical frame for the multiple points and processes that might be modulated. A few examples of main models can be seen in Figure 39.2, with their explicit mention of context layers circled so that the reader can have a taste of what we mean.

For the purpose of a more detailed review, we have created a hybrid model, shown in Figure 39.3. This is based on the work of Leder, Belke, Oeberst, & Augustin (2004), Chatterjee (2004), Locher, Overbeeke, and Wensveen (2010), etc. (for a similar model to the one used in this paper in the context of museum context studies, see also Pelowski, Forster et al., 2017). Thus, it is especially geared, in early stages, to visual stimuli and to the processing of art. However, when considering its general progression and inputs/outputs, it can apply to other nonvisual or everyday stimuli. It also explicitly lays out outputs and inputs at each stage of experience, again based on a review of empirical literature and present models. Obviously, this discussion cannot hope to be exhaustive, nor do we suggest that this is necessarily the best or only way to explain specific aspects. Rather, treat this as a thought experiment, with suggestions that we hope will be teased out further in later chapters or within your own future research!

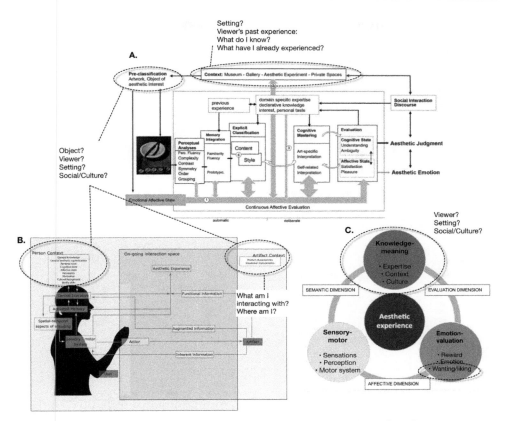

FIGURE 39.2. Examples of context layers and key aspects in models of aesthetic experience. (A) The model of aesthetic appreciation and aesthetic judgment of Leder et al. (2004; updated by Leder & Nadal, 2014) explicitly integrates an *object context* in a stage of preclassification, as well as *setting context* ("museum, gallery, aesthetic experiment, private spaces"), and a *social context* (in this case framed as person–person or person–artist interaction). The authors also add key features of *person context*, domain-specific expertise or training, especially in mid-stages. (B) More geared to design and general object usage, Locher et al. (2010, p. 77) also note "two driving forces," the "artifact itself"—modulated by aspects such as quality impression, assumed function, novelty, etc.—and a "person context" (p. 72), which might be modulated by previous cultural, social, and personal expectations. Similarly, use of an object is argued to activate featural and semantic information in the user's knowledge base, influenced by the person context including level of aesthetic sophistication, experience, personal tastes, cultural background, personality, and emotional and cognitive state during the aesthetic experience, which influence how viewers "perceive," and "evaluate" (p. 73). (C) Similar considerations can also be found in models of neural processes and key correlates of aesthetic processing in the brain. Chatterjee and Vartanian's (2014) "aesthetic triad" highlights the role of several features. They suggest that aesthetic experiences arise from the interaction among sensory–motor, emotion–valuation, and meaning–knowledge neural systems, with especially the latter tied to context, but where all may be modulated by person, stimulus, and environment.

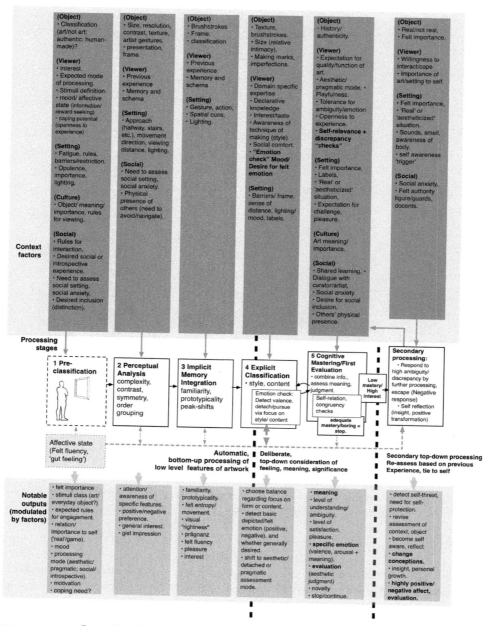

FIGURE 39.3. General model of aesthetic processing experience (main focus on visual stimuli), with posited context inputs and implications (outputs) for each stage. Model adapted from Pelowski, Forster et al.'s (2017) review of museum context factors and based originally on visual processing model by Leder et al. (2004).

This model proposes six stages, beginning with an initial preclassification or set of conditions and expectations, moving to an initial processing stage of *perceptual analysis*, where we first become aware of and attend to the low-level features of a stimulus (e.g., shape, contrast, lines colors, etc.). This is followed by a stage of *memory integration*, during which features might be grouped into more complex aspects based on previous experiences, expertise, and the particular schema held by the viewer, leading then to an *explicit classification*, which involves attention to conceptual or formal aspects (style/content) and where we also may become aware of higher level supporting features such as history, artist, and even begin to identify evoked emotions. These aspects then feed into a stage of *cognitive mastering*, in which individuals combine elements and create meaning, and culminating in the outputs of understanding, aesthetic judgment, and affective response.

Depending on the outcome of an initial cycle through such processing, which itself may be accomplished in a matter of seconds (see Pelowski, Markey, Forster, Gerger, & Leder, 2017), individuals may stop, disengaging or moving onto a new stimulus, or may again cycle through various stages, as might occur if individual factors draw specific interest, or if one finds these interactions particularly discrepant. Such an outcome may lead one to feel negative emotion and attempt to disengage or escape, often leading to negative emotion or appraisals, or may also engender more overt top-down, viewer-centered outputs in which one may undergo periods of reflection, adjustment of schema, and even highly pleasurable or transformative experience (e.g., Pelowski & Akiba, 2011). As can be seen in the top part of Figure 39.3, at each stage we can talk of impact from most if not all context layers. Below we discuss a few main aspects, walking in general through each stage.

Pre-state—What is it? Who am I? What should happen? How do I respond?

First, in the pre-state, before even meeting a stimulus, context (noted as inputs) may play a major role in shaping our forthcoming engagement. This state might be thought of as defining the conditions whereby we engage with a stimulus (noted as outputs at the bottom of the model). Aspects may include our level of interest, our expectations, the expected stimuli type, which can direct our behavior, drive what we look for or our attention, how we respond, or influence the nature of processing itself. The results may then themselves feed into the next stages.

Viewer, object, setting context—motivations and expectations

One of the most basic aspects here pertains to our expectations for what we will be doing or experiencing. If we expect a stimulus to be important, novel, boring, mundane, or challenging we might look for differing features or respond differently. For example, Hendon, Costa, & Rosenberg (1989) found that galleries containing art that participants were most interested in before a visit were rated as most interesting at the end of their visit as well. These can be modulated by, say, the *Setting*, *Person*, or the *Object* (as in the box above the pre-state in Figure 39.3). Visiting a museum or concert hall vs. a laboratory, or engaging within one's home, might engender very differing expectations, as would the level of opulence, cultural importance, or even size of an object.

The very decision to visit aesthetic media may set the basis for the entire experience. For example, a good deal of studies have explored visitors' motivations and expectations for going to museums or other cultural events (Pelowski, Forster et al., 2017; Tinio, Smith, & Smith, 2014). For example (see more in chapter *Studying Empirical Aesthetics in Museum Contexts*), Falk (2009) identified five motivations: intention to explore, have new experiences, recharge/rejuvenate, facilitate art experience for friends or children, and see specific artworks or exhibits. Pekarik and Schreiber (2012) suggested that visitors may expect to learn new information, make an emotional connection, find beauty, reflect, feel specific reactions such as awe, imagine exotic events or locations, or have interactions with rare, real objects.

The above expectations may provide a particular cognitive frame of reference through which information is processed (see e.g., Darley, Fleming, Hilton, & Swann, 1988). Individuals who expect learning or exploration may be more likely to deeply engage, cognitively process, and seek out and respond positively to challenge or confusion. Those seeking pleasure may respond more positively to positively valenced stimuli, seek out emotion, or consider only style and visual aspects (see the discussion of emotion below). The level of enjoyment that individuals report may also directly tie to whether or not their specific expectations are met (e.g., Tinio et al., 2014). Aspects may certainly be modulated by *culture* or *social* context as well: think of expectations for what reactions *should* occur, or rules for engaging—be quiet, heed other people, do or do not show emotion (see Figure 39.4).

Personality and background

Of course, multiple studies have also looked at personality determinants of aesthetic processing (for reviews, see Hekkert & Van Wieringen, 1996; Myszkowski, Storme, Zenasni, & Lubart, 2014). Particularly relevant might be the Big Five factor of "openness to experience" (McCrae, 2007). This involves a willingness to seek out novel encounters and has shown correlation with deeper appreciation for and engagement with the arts (Fayn, MacCann, Tiliopoulos, & Silvia, 2015; Myszkowski et al., 2014), higher general art preference (Chamorro-Premuzic, Reimers, Hsu, & Ahmetoglu, 2009). It also significantly predicts physiological reactions when viewing art (chills, feeling touched, absorption; Silvia & Nusbaum, 2011). Similar results may be found for "sensation seeking" (Swami, Stieger, Pietschnig, & Voracek, 2010). Conversely, the need for cognitive closure—suggesting a disliking of ambiguity or desire for clear classifications—might show negative correlation with the above aspects (Roets & Van Hiel, 2011). Another difference may involve, say, personal independence (Markus & Kitayama, 1991), which may interact with social setting to increase anxiety or context impact. Once again, just about any personality construct might be a worthy candidate!

Differences may also be found in demographics. In general, as noted by Hanquinet (2013), in an assessment of engagement with museums or other types of aesthetic media, visitors fit a general pattern of likely white-collar professionals, Euro-American with generally higher levels of income and education, which may be the best predictor of attendance (Chang, 2006). These can be further broken into subpatterns (Hanquinet, 2013, p. 809)—for example, "omnivorous," educated, younger visitors who frequently visit and seek both high- and low-brow culture; individuals with classical, conservative art tastes, who do or do not seek out other cultural experiences. The demographic profile of a typical visitor is presumably quite different from the typical laboratory participant, who is most probably an undergraduate student, while the profiles again may help to direct our engagement. As one example, Hanquinet notes that younger or omnivore viewers may be more likely to be active rather than passive cultural consumers, actively questioning or being critical of aesthetic media (see also Bitgood, 1992).

Object classification

Another important aspect in regards to expectations involves the classification of what an individual will experience. For example, a main topic might be classification of something as an "aesthetic event" or a work of "art." In most cultures, art often demands a certain reverence and implicit ties to luxury, beauty, or importance (Hagtvedt & Patrick, 2008). Becker (1982, p. 133) notes that many may "believe art is better, more beautiful, and more expressive" than other objects. Art viewing, when contrasted to viewing other objects thought not to be art, has been empirically related to higher ratings of beauty, pleasure, and liking (Locher, Smith, & Smith, 2001). Furthermore, telling someone— via contextual information—that an object is "art" can lead to a higher positive aesthetic rating than when the exact same image is presented with other priming (Arai & Kawabata, 2016).

Returning to the model and the preclassification stage, this may tie to certain expectations of reward or engagement—an argument supported both behaviorally where an art context may lead to expectations for having pleasurable and positive emotional experience (Leder et al., 2004), and by recent imaging findings that show that viewing objects expected to be art correlates to higher activation of reward and vision areas in the brain (Kirk et al., 2009; Kühn and Gallinat, 2012; Lacey et al., 2011).

An art context can also change processing on a cognitive level, which would manifest throughout the subsequent stages. Perceivers attend more to stylistic and formal properties of stimuli (Cupchik, Vartanian, Crawley, & Mikulis, 2009; Jacobsen, Schubotz, Höfel, & Cramon, 2006; Kirk et al., 2009) and show a more elaborative processing style that goes beyond simple object recognition (Nadal, Munar, Capo, Rossello, & Cela-Conde, 2008). Art or aesthetic contexts may also involve a "transfiguration" or suffusing of ordinary objects and events with deeper meaning (Danto, 1974). This might cause viewers to look harder for significance, beyond an initial visual impression, or give more attention and veneration (Bailey, 2000). This may also allow them to enjoy even ambiguous, challenging, or negative images (for a laboratory study example, see Gerger, Leder, & Kremer, 2014, Wagner, Menninghaus, Hanich, & Jacobsen, 2014). Arthood can encourage a search for intention or prime an expectation of communication. Boas (1943, p. 116) notes, for many viewers, "the fundamental distinction" of art/not-art is between controlled and random behavior. This "faith in the artist" (Parsons, 1987, p. 74) may motivate individuals to "persist in looking … when otherwise [they] would be tempted to pass onto something more meaningful" (see Zeglin Brand, 2000 for this aspect and *cultural* context).

Artistic expression, often from a real human, may also be important in prompting empathic responses. The anthropologist Gell (1998) believing that a stimulus is in some way a product of or signal from another may be key for engaging our artistic interest or for looking for meaning. An interesting study by Umilta, Berchio, Sestito, Freedberg, and Gallese (2012), which showed individuals photographs of artworks by Lucio Fontana, composed of slashes cut into a canvas, as well as black-and-white line representations of the same slashes, showed higher Mu suppression over bilateral premotor and motor regions in the original case. The authors suggest this showed so-called mirroring of the artist actions. The authors also report that the participants viewed the photographs as more "real art."

The determination of object classification itself could then be modulated by context. Often empirical studies may explicitly provide supporting information as in a label or cue that a stimulus is art, or may do so more implicitly through an instruction, say, that a participant "will be shown some works of art" or explicitly asked to "rate how much you like the artwork." Arthood may also be evoked via setting, or modulated by interpersonal differences. The individual probably carries an understanding of what constitutes art—to them, personally (for a recent study of art/not-art classifications and tie to both liking and interpersonal differences see, for example, Pelowski, Gerger, Chetouani, Markey, & Leder, 2017).

Authenticity; gallery/theater vs. lab

A related issue involves authenticity. Much as individuals may respond in certain ways to art, seeing objects as "real"—one-of-a-kind objects from artists with a historical provenance—may also feed into perceived importance or aesthetic merit. Kirk et al. (2009) found that paintings (shown in digital reproductions), which were thought to be created by esteemed artists and borrowed from museums, as opposed to images made by a researcher, were evaluated as more appealing. Similarly, Wolz and Carbon (2014) found that paintings presented as veridical artworks as opposed to forgeries received significantly lowered estimations of quality. A functional magnetic resonance imaging (fMRI) study by Huang et al. (2011) found that images of Rembrandt portraits, when viewers were told that they were going to be originals vs. forgeries, resulted in higher activation of orbitofrontal areas connected to reward (see also Noguchi and Murota, 2013).

This may also be found in comparison between "real" (i.e., corporeal) art and reproductions in the lab. As will likely be explored more in the forthcoming chapter on museums, researchers often find that museum vs. lab art presentations, while not changing assessment of pictorial content or composition, may lead to higher felt interest, pleasantness, surprise, or novelty (Locher et al., 1999; Locher and Dolese, 2004), to longer viewing durations (Brieber, Nadal, Leder, & Rosenberg, 2014), and to better recall for what one had seen (Brieber, Nadal, & Leder, 2015). It is also interesting to consider the discussion of a "transferability thesis" (Currie, 1985), which questions whether viewers are willing to treat an underlying digital reproduction as an artwork. Several studies, which simplified artworks or contrasted physical objects against images, have found that these are considered less "real" by viewers (e.g., Lacey et al., 2011; Umilta et al., 2012).

Processing mode—aesthetic or pragmatic approach

A related aspect to framing also involves the processing mode. It has often been argued that individuals may adopt two general approaches (e.g., Cupchik, 2013; Gerger et al., 2014): (a) a "pragmatic" mode where we tend to perceive and respond to a stimulus based on its utility, meaning, and importance or relation to the self, and often argued to align to our typical or "everyday" way of engaging the environment—"Can I use it?" "What does it mean?" "Will it hurt or help me?". And (b) a more "aesthetic" focus, wherein we may pay less attention to meaning or use and instead focus on an object's sensory or emotive aspects. This latter approach is also often suggested to coincide with a certain "psychological distance" (e.g., Bullough, 1912) or detached perspective in which one can process without consideration of personal threat or relevance, or even to approach engaging in fiction or play without "real-life" consequence.

This may modulate all the following stages, impacting what features individuals attend to—style or formal aspects vs. meaning or content (Cupchik et al., 2009; Jacobsen et al., 2006). Individuals may be less goal oriented and may be more tolerant of surprise, ambiguity (e.g., Wagner et al., 2014), and especially negative emotions or content. Psychological distance from emotionally negative events reduces signs of arousal and increases relative pleasantness (Lazarus & Alfert, 1964; Speisman, Lazarus, Davison, & Mordkoff, 1964). Such a mode may coincide with classification of objects as art (Cupchik, 2002; Dissanayake, 2007; Tan, 2000), engendered by explicit contextual information or, for example, with entering a museum or other media space.

General importance of framing and pre-expectations

Of course, the above discussion does not have to be specific to art or any other media. Rather classifications and contextual framing might be thought of as one way of assigning a particular level of importance. This can of course be done with any object, and in myriad ways—hanging something high on a wall, placing on a pedestal, using expensive looking materials (for discussion with design, see e.g., Locher et al., 2010). Think also of the importance we might give to the football pitch—a field of grass with some white chalk lines marked upon it. Consider also how someone classifies "music" and how they might respond differently to the dissonant compositions of Charles Ives or 4'33" by John Cage (for an extended discussion, see e.g., Becker, 1982).

The social setting can also do the same. Lauring et al. (2016) showed that telling participants that a painting they are about to see was expensive or liked by an expert or peer group led to higher ratings of the same art. Interestingly, when telling individuals that art was disliked by an undesirable group, participants again gave the art higher ratings (for philosophical discussion of social context and framing, see also Pinney & Thomas, 2001). Similarly, following the work of Bourdieu (1984), we might talk of "distinction," or seeking out media as a means of joining a desired group or distancing oneself from others, which may also dictate how we behave or look for. Returning to the model, note that while these factors may play a role especially in the first stage, they can also interject at points later in the experience—in relation to how we respond to emotion or certain content (e.g., in cognitive mastery); in whether we keep interacting or disengage if faced with a negative stimulus (secondary processing); see further discussion in the sections "Mood, desired emotion" and "Self-importance, perceived detachment/threat—specific emotions or aesthetic outcomes" below.

Perceptual analysis/implicit memory integration—low-level features and framing

When we then engage and begin to process, we encounter several more aspects of context. As suggested by the boxes regarding outputs, we might first process low-level features, group them together, and generate a gist impression (involving basic identification or negative/positive valence). Interestingly, occasionally it might be thought that these early features are less impacted by context—indeed, it is these aspects that might align with historical discussion of immutable, context-free formal aspects of a stimulus. However, research does suggest many modulating effects.

Here, we might attend to aspects such as complexity, contrast, order, and grouping, all of which might be impacted stimulus size, resolution, presentation, as well as the ambient environment. Visual surroundings are important in perception and object recognition (Bar, 2004; Todorović, 2010). Think, for example, of the Ebbinghaus illusion (Figure 39.4A), which has shown that perception of size can be modulated by surrounding visual information. A similar impact might be had from a picture frame, which may "tell the eye" where to look or potentially "complete" a painting (Ensor & Hamilton, 2014, p. 121), or, in one of the only empirical studies, might reduce recall of an artwork (Koutstaal, 1998).

Features may also once again tie to aspects of classification or felt importance, which can be further modulated within a processing experience. Texture, size, or felt authenticity may give a sense that something is special or made by a human (see Figure 39.4). These latter aspects may then impact early processing experience (see Hagtvedt & Patrick, 2008) or may be recalled in stages involving memory integration and knowledge of the participant. We may even talk of social context. In perception of faces, there is the so-called "cheerleader effect," where we tend to rate others as more attractive when surrounded by others in a peer situation (see e.g., Walker & Vul, 2014). Framing can also occur via external information such as with packaging and marketing programs, which

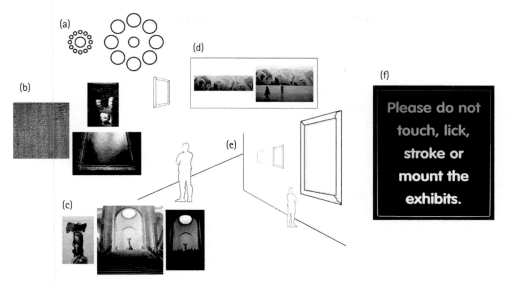

FIGURE 39.4. Examples of physical context and impact on classification, expectations, framing, perceived importance, even visual recognition and attention to objects. (A) The Ebbinghaus illusion, which can change the perceived size of the middle circle, although both left and right are the same actual size. (B) Texture or lighting. (C) Approach and physical or social/cultural context (Nike of Samothrace in the Louvre, Paris). (D) Image size (*The Unfinished Dance* (1931) by Matisse: left image might be how this appears in a typical laboratory study; right side shows its actual appearance in the Palais de Tokyo, Paris). (E) Hanging and impact on importance. (F) Museum rules, posted at the Museum of Sex, New York City. (All photos by the first author.)

can influence value and even meaning or symbolic associations (Locher et al., 2010), or even the approach, whereby we come into a first impression of a work or where it may be slowly revealed. Think, for example, of the staircase in the Louvre and the Nike of Samothrace (Figure 39.4C). Here, we may also attend to aspects such as brushstrokes or other features that tell us we are engaging with the work of another human, or cues regarding gestures.

Explicit classification—memory, expertise, training

Intermediary stages of vision should involve processing that recruits access to memory and or involve higher-order cognitions such as the perceiver's knowledge and background experiences. For example, certain features may lead to felt familiarity or prototypicality/novelty of media or contribute to assessed meaning in the final model stages (see also Tinio, 2013). We may also consider style of an aesthetic piece.

A particularly well-traveled though still very fruitful area of study involves expertise or particular knowledge about a topic. Numerous studies have shown that art expertise—especially involving past training in the arts or aesthetic contexts, as well as working artists—influences our perception, understanding, and evaluation of art (Augustin & Leder, 2006; Brieber, Nadal, & Leder, 2015; Chamberlain & Wagemans, 2015; Leder, Gerger, Brieber, & Schwarz, 2014). For example, experts may have an emphasis on formal, stylistic, and relational properties rather than content, craftsmanship, or mimesis (Hekkert & Van Wieringen, 1996). Cupchik and Gebotys (1988) showed that art-naïve viewers may take an approach to art that is essentially an extension of everyday perception. Thus, they mainly search for recognizable elements that can elicit pleasurable associations.

Becker (1982, p. 48) notes that specialized audience members may also use "the history of attempts to make similar works in that medium or genre; characteristic features of different styles and periods in the history of the art; ... an acquaintance with various versions of the same work; and an ability to respond emotionally and cognitively to the manipulation of standard elements in the vocabulary of the medium." Deines (2013, p. 29) calls such contextual factors "relational properties": "If I dislike a work because I think it deals with important [issues] in too simple a manner, if I find it boring because the artist repeats him or herself ... if I find it witty ... all these properties ... depend on my knowledge of its context, of the time of production, of the artist and her or his previous work." Fenner (2003, p. 48), similarly speaking from the purview of art criticism, also suggests numerous other "contexts under which we consider aesthetic objects" including ethnic, racial, class, gender ("Do I see Milos Forman's One Flew Over the Cuckoo's Nest as essentially misogynist?"), national or political (think back to Baumgarden). We might also connect knowledge to specific *objects*. Certain pieces or styles may require certain backgrounds or can lead to very different reactions for different *persons* (for more on this aspect, focusing on art history, see Bullot & Reber, 2013; for a discussion tied to design, see Locher et al., 2010).

The role of expertise is also far from settled. Locher (2015) suggests that experts may give more importance to the initial impression and resulting affective reaction when appraising value or authenticity of artworks. Experienced viewers may also be more likely to see an artwork as an autonomous entity, and to perceive artworks "for their own sake" (Hekkert & Van Wieringen, 1996).

Expertise and knowledge throughout stages of experience

Interestingly, like many factors, previous knowledge may also play a role throughout several model stages. For example, expertise can impact initial framing. Winston and Cupchik (1992) suggest novices hold beliefs that art should please, evoke peaceful feelings, positive memories, and appeal to many people. Experienced people often expect that art will challenge the viewer's conception, express the artist's deep feelings, and require some effort. This then again may determine what we look for, what we perceive, and how we respond to perceived aspects.

Differences as a function of expertise can even manifest in low-level visual processing. Experts tend to look more at a painting's periphery, evaluate the entirety of the canvas, and use a global or visual "gist" perspective, whereas art-naïve viewers focus more on the center of a work (Pihko et al., 2011). Experts have even been shown to be less swayed by context or priming—i.e., as in labels or added social information (Kirk, Harvey, & Montague, 2011).

Mood, desired emotion

One factor that presumably plays a role in all stages, but may be especially important in explicit classification, involves mood or emotional experience. As can be seen in the processing model, as well as that of Leder et al. (2004), mood/emotion might be thought of as its own channel of important information, continuously updated through our interactions. Before beginning an encounter, mood or emotion carried over from prior interactions may influence experience. Cognition can be mediated through mechanisms of arousal or general valence tied to how one is feeling (Derryberry, 1988; Gendolla, 2000). Mood may also modulate processing via "directive impact" (Gendolla, 2000) by influencing behavioral preferences in "compliance with a hedonic motives"—i.e., avoiding displeasure, seeking pleasure. Individuals who are in a bad mood may seek out happy or positive experiences so as to regulate their feelings. We may then use this information to modify our engagement—i.e., continuing to interact with or leaving alone an artwork. Derryberry (1988, p. 26), for example, notes a "mood congruity effect," a phenomenon in which individuals tend to recall information consistent with their on-going mood.

We may also modify our processing mode so as to diminish the emotion-arousing potential. Such a "selective attention" (Derryberry, 1988) may essentially align with taking a more detached aesthetic approach, focusing on formal aspects instead of emotion-related content. For example, Cupchik and Wroblewski-Raya (1998; for a review, see Cupchik, 2013) considered participants who were assessed on a measure of loneliness, and who were asked to assess paintings of solitary (presumably lonely) figures. Already lonely subjects preferred stylistic qualities, such as color or composition, over the subject matter. This may influence selection of media in the pre-state, but may be particularly important in the explicit classification stage, where Pelowski, Forster, and colleagues (2017) suggest that there may be an "emotion check" wherein individuals first become aware of more complex emotional content or evoking potential—beyond basic valence (see also Cupchik, 2013)—and then modulate their mode of engagement to maximize or minimize their resulting feelings. Individuals may also not always seek out pleasure or avoid negative affect. They may do the opposite if this fits the particular personality and context—think of an individual listening to sad music after a break up (for empirical evidence, see e.g., Kemp & Cupchik, 2007). Moods may also change depending on weather, odors, lighting (for a review, see Gendolla, 2000).

Cognitive mastery and secondary processing— judgments, specific emotions

Moving onto the later model stages, it is argued that the individual will essentially build up a collection of information from the earlier processing (low-level sensory aspects, identified objects, felt familiarity/novelty, arousal and valence, meaning and associations) and combine these to create final meaning or understanding, to define specific judgments, or to further engage or to process particularly compelling or difficult aspects. Here, we can also talk of some key aspects of context.

Processing success, congruency, fluency/discrepancy

First, the felt ease or difficulty one has had in their interaction up until this stage may be key, especially in formulating a judgment. This can be used in a declarative fashion, as in many studies—answering if something is beautiful, pleasing, interesting—or more organically can guide future behavior—do I purchase it, do I want to see it again?—or to drive further engagement. Empirical and theoretical work has suggested that evaluations—i.e., whether we like or find something pleasing—might often be shaped by our own felt difficulty within the processing experience. This is often connected to "fluency" (Forster, Leder, & Ansorge, 2016; see also the chapter on *Processing Fluency*). As noted by Graf and Landwehr (2015, p. 6), fluency might occur on two or more levels—perceptual fluency is concerned primarily with identifying the physical identity of a stimulus; conceptual fluency is concerned primarily with stimulus meaning or associations. Especially in cases of quick responses—such as a typical 1–5-s lab rating task—or where one does not have much vested interest, we may default to our fluency to make an assessment (i.e., easy = good; see Schwarz, 2011). Fluency may also fit into more general discussions of a "gut" response. Gendlin (1995; also Schwarz, 2011) explicitly connects this to aesthetic acts such as finding the "right" word for a poem. This may also be a source for aesthetic sensitivity wherein we choose a superior piece, perhaps without being able to truly articulate why (think back to mid-20th-century empirical studies—perhaps a nice future target).

Disfluency or discrepancy can also be important. This may serve as a cue that leads us to engage further or adopt a systematic approach—carefully perceiving and thinking about a stimulus or renewing processing through subsequent cycles—whereas fluency leads to more superficial processing (Bullot & Reber, 2013). Silvia (2009) also suggests that felt ease or perhaps more often difficulty are a basis of appraising relative novelty, familiarity, challenge, as well as general positive or negative affective valence.

While acting as a component of context in its own right, fluency can also of course be impacted by other context. As noted by Graf and Landwehr (2015, p. 6), this might occur on two or more levels—perceptual fluency is concerned primarily with identifying the physical identity of a stimulus, and may be impacted by aspects such as high contrast, color saturation, symmetry. Conceptual fluency is concerned primarily with stimulus meaning and modulated by one's training and previous exposure (see also Reber, Schwarz, & Winkielman, 2004). Fluency can also be manipulated by other ambient factors. In one intriguing study, Lee, Kim, and Schwarz (2015) suggested that the environment might be changed to make something feel a bit "off." By putting fish oil under a desk—creating the ambient feeling of something fishy or strange, even though this occurred below the level of overt awareness—they increased participants' likelihood of detecting a semantic distortion or to engage in negative hypothesis testing (falsifying their own initial hunch).

Self-importance, perceived detachment/threat—specific emotions or aesthetic outcomes

At the same time, especially when interaction is disfluent or discrepant, felt ease may also be complemented by another component involving whether or not they really care about the outcome of their viewing, or whether or not they really have an interest in or need to process. If one is only minimally engaging, or finds their interaction particularly fluent, they may have a generally positive appraisal and move on. However, one may also find that the event is deeply important, or they may have a vested interest in the outcome; it may also be dangerous.

Notably, Silvia (2009) in his discussion of "appraisal theories" suggests two checks—for "congruency" and "self-relevance"—which may guide the actual types of emotions we may experience and report (determined in the cognitive mastery stage) beyond basic arousal and valence. For example, in the case of interest, Silvia (2005) suggests that our appraisal structure would consist of: (a) a judgment of high novelty/complexity (low congruence), combined with (b) low self-relevance or little importance for one's goals, expectations, or low threat. In contrast, anger (Cooper and Silvia, 2009) would combine appraising an event as (a) inconsistent with one's schema (low schema congruence), but also with (b) close ties to one's goals/self, and thus leading to a vested interest. He also adds the third element of "coping potential" (Silvia, 2005) or the need to stick out an engagement or take responsibility; low in the anger case (i.e., an experience is someone else's fault). Because of this structure, Silvia concludes that in any situation, different people will have different responses to these processing checks, and thus different emotions to the same stimulus, or the same person may even have different emotions depending on context.

This role of self-relation, and resulting adjustment, may also tie to the topic of aesthetic processing mode, which would essentially be a detached low self-relation event, or may be sought out to create such conditions by switching attention to formal aspects. This may also relate to felt vs. perceived (or so-called "aesthetic") emotions. Several theories propose that emotions in the arts can be distinctively different from emotions occurring in everyday life (Frijda, 1988; Scherer, 2005; for a review, see Gerger et al., 2014). Presumably this is because the aesthetic or art setting is disengaged from personal importance or implications, or one can perceive what emotion a work is "trying" to communicate without actually feeling it (for a nice art critical discussion, see Barwell, 1986). However, this could probably be duplicated in other contexts.

Pelowski and Akiba (2011; refined in Pelowski, Forster et al., 2017) go further and argue that self-schema matching and relation to the environment may be used to differentiate broad varieties of experience—from mundane to profound. Following previous researchers such as Carver (1996), they suggest that, in addition to general personality characteristics or differences in background and motivation, individuals hold this set of postulates—an "ideal self-image." This can be thought of as a hierarchical set of postulates, headed by core goals (who am I and who do I want to be?) branching down into goals for general actions (what should I do to protect and advance my core aspirations and beliefs?) and then further branching down into lower and more specific beliefs and schema. Interacting would then always entail the matching of the self, via specific schema, to the "reality" of the environment, and thus itself a core aspect of context from the pre-state onward.

They suggest the same essential congruency and self-relevance checks, situated between memory integration and cognitive mastery, and divide outcomes of experience into five varieties—(a) cases where individuals have a low self-relevance and low discrepancy, leading to rather facile or surface engagement with little emotion; (b) discrepancy but also low self-relevance, which may allow individuals to find and enjoy novelty or small insights (discovering a new way to depict something or an unexpected word use, but which is not terribly upsetting to one's entire worldview); (c) cases with high self-relevance but also low discrepancy, which, especially where one can process with ease or finds a resonant emotion, may lead to felt harmony or even "flow" type experiences; and cases where one has both discrepancy and high self-relevance which lead to a felt threat, potentially leading either to (d) negative emotion and evaluations as one tries to extricate themselves and protect the self; or (e) a potential for self-revision and transformative experience. As can be seen in Figure 39.5, at all stages, the way that feelings and reactions are assessed can be explicitly tied to context, as well as several levels of information that all may be assessed to determine an outcome or guide response.

The determinant of whether or not one feels self-relevance or how they cope with threat may in turn be modulated by factors. This could vary greatly between laboratory and in situ engagements. Individuals may not feel personal involvement or threat (see also Mandel, 2003). How we respond to particularly strong emotions or reactions could also tie to context. On one hand they may resonate or create particularly pleasurable experience. At the same time, if one feels such a response in cases where they are inappropriate due to social norms or other factors, they may cause individuals to disengage or negatively respond (Gendolla, 2000). The sociologist Goffman (1974, p. 353) talks of "flooding out," which "occurs when an individual must accept restraints on bodily behavior over an appreciable portion of his body" and may thus lead to negative response. When facing particularly challenging and self-important situations, contextual sensations (hearing one's own footsteps, sensation of blown air conditioning) may also help to shift attention from coping or avoiding issues to one's current actions, encouraging self-reflection or insight (for discussion with art, see e.g., Pelowski et al., 2012). These physical "triggers" maybe important for future research (for discussion outside art, see also Rothbaum, Weisz, & Snyder, 1982).

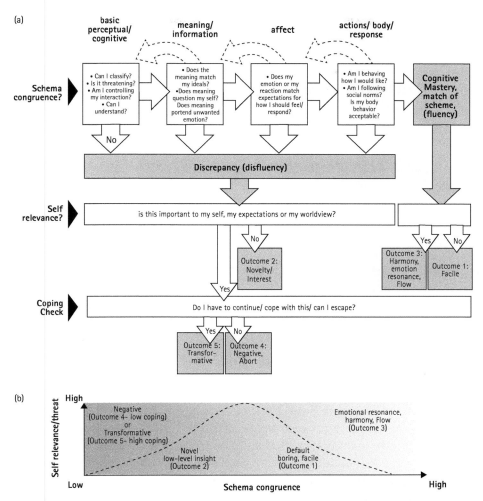

FIGURE 39.5. Proposed tie between self-relevance, schema congruency, and need for coping "checks" and outcomes of aesthetic experience as well as examples of processing levels.

Adapted from Pelowski, Forster et al. (2017).

Time; general movement through stages

Finally, by placing the above myriad context features into a general framework, we can of course also consider context aspects that might provide important tools to unlocking or assessing the above progressions or processing sequences. For example, time may be a key factor that is only beginning to be fully understood (see e.g., Locher et al., 2010). Truncating time for viewing (e.g., below about 5 s) may lead to higher variance in appraisals due to inability to conduct all processes or integrate all information that individuals may normally use (Augustin, Leder, Hutzler, & Carbon, 2008; Bachmann

& Vipper, 1983). This also nicely fits the above processes to the topic of the underlying functional neurobiology (Cela-Conde et al., 2013).

MAJOR CHALLENGES, GOALS, AND SUGGESTIONS

This was again but a small taste of the context discussion, but hopefully can be useful in making clear how prevalent and important context is in aesthetic or basic perceptual and psychological experience. By tying this discussion to several models and theoretical frameworks, it is hoped that the reader might go further and have a sense of how and where context might play specific roles in modulating processes or outputs. This is not to say that the above models and discussion are necessarily perfect or could not benefit from other explanations. To conclude this chapter, we consider some other questions and avenues for future research:

Other aspects of context—brains, bodies, an endless list of possibilities

First, there are of course innumerable other areas deserving of research that could not be mentioned in this chapter. Emerging evidence suggests that individuals who develop brain damage or disease (e.g., fronto-temporal dementia, Parkinson's disease) can show marked changes in the way they produce or appreciate art (Gretton & Ffytche, 2014; Lauring et al., 2019). Studies also document changes that can occur, temporarily, via causative manipulation of brain activity (Cattaneo, Lega, Flexas et al., 2014, Cattaneo, Lega, Gardelli et al., 2014, Cattaneo et al., 2015)—for example, modulating assessed beauty or liking. Neuropsychopharmacology or modulating the levels of hormones (e.g., testosterone) or other neurotransmitters such as dopamine or serotonin may also greatly impact experience (for an aesthetic-related review, see Spee, Ishizu, Leder, & Pelowski, 2018), but have so far not been applied empirically. Other causative interventions such as drugs or alcohol may play important roles—for example, drinking a glass of wine may increase our likelihood of rating others as attractive (Van Den Abbeele, Penton-Voak, Attwood, Stephen, & Munafò, 2015).

Other intriguing areas involve the role of and awareness of the body and how this may tie to felt valence, difficulty, or drive perception (e.g., Gibson, 1979; Turner & Penn, 2002). For example, Kapoula, Adenis, Lê, Yang, and Lipede (2011) showed that postural sway and stability when individuals stand before paintings can be modulated depending on local depth information and that individuals unconsciously adopt the leaning or upright postures of tall sculptures by Richard Serra. Moving one's body in accordance with the brushstrokes of a painting (pointillism or postimpressionism) positively affected liking of art in a style corresponding to the movement (Leder, Bär, & Topolinski, 2012). Walking as opposed to sitting may also modulate engagement. This leads to increased activation in the prefrontal cortex; even mentally preparing to walk to a target, as might occur upon seeing a painting across a gallery, leads to increased activation (Suzuki, Miyai, Ono, & Kubota, 2008).

We might also look at specific physiological responses, such as tears, which could be a signal to the individual that something profound is happening and they should withdraw or introspect (Cotter, Silvia, & Fayn, 2017; Pelowski, 2015). Other feelings such as chills may also signal a harmony or peak emotional or resonant experience (in a song, movie, or art; McCrae, 2007; Pelowski, Markey, & Leder, 2018). There may also be specific ties between emotions—for example, Eskine, Kacinik, and Prinz (2012) showed that priming individuals with fearful movies increased their liklihood of rating images as sublime, as did exercise (jumping jacks) before viewing.

It is also important to consider how we assess context. Carefully weigh the costs and benefits of certain designs. A researcher might in fact try to weigh multiple possible context features to decide which can and cannot be manipulated. At the same time, researchers, in study planning, should also spend time brainstorming context effects that they had not considered but which might have influence or confound findings. Since context can by definition be almost everything an experimenter has to select specific properties out of numerous possibilities to make context into an experimental factor that can be investigated. At least for the first author, the failure to catch a conflating explanation is a common reason for rejecting journal paper submissions! Context studies are also impacted by what we don't know about aesthetic processing. For conducting experimental laboratory research, it is necessary to know in advance what the key variables are, but it is not clear if empirical aesthetics has already figured out all of these variables. Therefore, it still remains a great challenge to investigate the effect of context on aesthetic processing.

On-site aesthetics, what can be done in the lab?

The experimental setting also needs consideration. As asked by Leder and Nadal (2014, pp. 453–454) "To what extent does the laboratory distort or attenuate aesthetic episodes?" This question also contains within it the same ambivalence as found throughout aesthetics' history. " ... Given how much ... work has been performed in laboratory settings, it is also clear that the psychology of art and aesthetics has traditionally accepted the formalist argument that aesthetic experience is, to a large extent, contextually impermeable." This may not be true.

It is also important to stress that these layers and issues are *not* only present in so-called ecologically valid interactions or with a "real" stimulus. They can and do manifest in the laboratory (see the left side of Figure 39.1). It may also be that there are certain reactions—intense emotion, feelings of self-threat, change, transformation—that are very difficult to evoke in a lab, precisely because the context is not of the right type (Cela-Conde, Agnati, Huston, Mora, & Nadal, 2011; Tallis, 2008). The next decade plus of study must go out into the field to capture and understand such rich experiences. This is already beginning with mobile measures of eye-tracking, brain imaging (electroencephalogram (EEG), near-infrared spectroscopy (NIRS)), and physiology that can bring complex data from the "real world."

Predictive coding and top-down/bottom-up processing

Another important area for considering context involves the topic of "predictive coding" or the possibility that, especially when considered at the neural level, many of our interactions or perceptions—at least in the initial stages—are driven largely by prior schema or internal models that guide and adjust perception (Clark, 2013). This at once offers the theoretical promise of fitting aesthetic models or processes to mathematical functions, which may provide a much higher level of nuance. It also raises the questions of what can truly be thought of as bottom-up, environment-derived perceptions vs. top-down aspects of the perceiver.

What is not impacted by context—a search for immutable aesthetic factors

Another important question involves the topic of what factors are or are not ultimately modulated by context differences. As made clear in the above introduction, the field of aesthetics derives from a history of, at least intuited if not often empirically verified, ideas that some reactions are innate or immutable. It would be fascinating to find out what factors might be more or less stable across differing conditions, and which may not. Some intriguing directions include evidence in aesthetic ratings of paintings by dementia or Alzheimer's patients, who, despite no longer remembering past trials tend to show both consistency in their judgments and also with healthy control groups (Graham, Stockinger, & Leder, 2013; Halpern, Ly, Elkin-Franklin, & O'Connor, 2008). There is also a need for more cross-cultural study. For example, curves as opposed to sharp edges may be universally preferred (Gómez-Puerto et al., 2017). A similar point of general agreement might involve color. For example, following the early shared taste (for blue) found by Osgood, similar more recent studies have shown a general dislike of dark yellow/olive (Palmer & Schloss, 2010; however, see Saito, 1996 for differences in appreciation of white). Intriguingly, it may be that which remains when context is accounted for that can be a window into our shared aesthetic response. As put by Jerry Fodor (in Rollins, 2001, p. 177) "The universality of an artwork consists precisely in its independence from its historical [and, presumably other] context." We might also ask if is ever meaningful to assess reactions to stimuli divorced from context. Why and what could this tell us about psychology or empirical aesthetics?

APPLICATION TO THE CLASSROOM OR THE APPLIED SETTING

Last, many of the above topics can also make their way into the classroom for discussing context. Once one considers the scope whereby context impacts our aesthetic interpretations, the potential for application in the classroom or in the world is, of course, endless. However, to provide a few more examples, it may be interesting as a learning device to take well-grounded studies or ideas from aesthetics (preconceptions, mood, expectations) and discuss how these would translate to the reactions and evaluations we make every day. How does what we know about the effect of social priming on our evaluations of others' beauty impact our shopping or job-hiring decisions? How does mood or our response to others impact how we "see" and respond to the world. Not only at the level of our hedonic appraisals or emotions, but also at the cognitive level regarding what we pay attention to or how we respond to cognitive processes?

We would also advise students to look outside empirical aesthetic books and journals to a number of other sources. Some of the best descriptions of context importance, and research ideas, in the first author's own training have come from sociology, anthropology, etc. For particularly interesting reads, try *The Meaning of Things; Domestic Symbols and the Self* (Csikszentmihalyi & Rochenberg-Halton, 1981); *Frame Analysis; An Essay on the Organization of Experience* (Goffman, 1974); see also Alexander (1977) for great consideration of the built environment; Gell (1998) for an anthropological perspective of the co-relationship with art; *Art Worlds* (Becker, 1982); *Nudge: Improving Decisions about Health, Wealth, and Happiness* (Thaler & Sunstein, 2008); and *The Transfiguration of the Commonplace* (Danto, 1981). Those interested in context might also consider the discussions of cultural literacy (Hirsch, 1987), visual literacy, techno literacy (Dakers, 2006), etc., and how what "we all know" or more likely what we "should know" in order to "properly respond" in aesthetics may reveal what is going on under the surface.

REFERENCES

Abel, T., & Hsu, F. L. K. (1949). Some aspects of personality of Chinese as revealed by the Rorschach test. *Rorschach Research Exchange and Journal of Projective Techniques, 12,* 285–301.

Adams, F. M., & Osgood, C. E. (1973). A cross-cultural study of the affective meanings of color. *Journal of Cross-cultural Osychology, 4*(2), 135–156.

Alexander, C. (1977). *A pattern language; towns, buildings, construction.* Oxford, England: Oxford University Press.

Arai, S., & Kawabata, H. (2016). Appreciation contexts modulate aesthetic evaluation and perceived duration of pictures. *Art & Perception, 4*(3), 225–239.

Augustin, M. D., & Leder, H. (2006). Art expertise: A study of concepts and conceptual spaces. *Psychological Science, 48,* 135–156.

Augustin, M. D., Leder, H., Hutzler, F., & Carbon, C. C. (2008). Style follows content: On the microgenesis of art perception. *Acta Psychologica, 128*(1), 127–138.

Bachmann, T., & Vipper, K. (1983). Perceptual rating of paintings from different artistic styles as a function of semantic differential scales and exposure time. *Archiv fur Psychologie, 135,* 149–161.

Bailey, G. W. S. (2000). Art: Life after death? In N. Carroll (Ed.), *Theories of art today* (pp. 160–174). Madison, WI: The University of Wisconsin Press.

Bar, M. (2004). Visual objects in context. *Nature Reviews Neuroscience, 5*(8), 617–629.

Barron, F., & Welsh, G. S. (1952). Artistic perception as a possible factor in personality style: Its measurement by a figure preference test. *The Journal of Psychology, 33*(2), 199–203.

Barwell, I. (1986). How does art express emotion? *The Journal of Aesthetics and Art Criticism, 45*(2), 175–181

Baumgarten, A. G. (1750). *Aesthetica*. Hildesheim, Germany: Olms.

Baumgarten, A. G. (1954). *Reflections on poetry: Meditationes philosophicae de nonnullis ad poema pertinentibus*, K. Aschenbrenner and W.B. Holther (Eds.). Berkeley, CA: University of California Press.

Becker, H. S. (1982). Art worlds. Berkeley, CA: University of California Press.

Bell, C. (1914). *Art*. London: Chatto and Windus.

Berger, J. (1972). *Ways of seeing*. London: BBC.

Berlyne, D. E. (1974). *Studies in the new experimental aesthetics: Steps toward an objective psychology of aesthetic appreciation*. Washington, DC: Hemisphere.

Berlyne, D. E. (1976). Similarity and preference judgments of Indian and Canadian subjects exposed to Western paintings. *International Journal of Psychology, 11*(1), 43–55.

Berlyne, D. E., Ogilvie, J. C., & Parham, L. C. C. (1968). The dimensionality of visual complexity, interestingness, and pleasingness. *Canadian Journal of Psychology, 22*, 376–387.

Bitgood, S. (1992). The anatomy of an exhibit. *Visitor Behavior, 7*, 4–15.

Bitgood, S., & Patterson, D. D. (1993). The effects of gallery changes on visitor reading and object viewing time. *Environment and Behavior, 25*, 761–781.

Boas, G. (1943). Art and reality. *College Art Journal, 2*, 115.

Brieber, D., Nadal, M., & Leder, H. (2015). In the white cube: Museum context enhances the valuation and memory of art. *Acta Psychologica, 154*, 36–42.

Brieber, D., Nadal, M., Leder, H., & Rosenberg, R. (2014). Art in time and space: Context modulates the relation between art experience and viewing time. *PLoS One, 9*, e99019.

Bourdieu, P. (1984). *Distinction: A social critique of the judgment of taste* (R. Nice, Trans.). Cambridge, MA: Harvard University Press.

Bullot, N. J., & Reber, R. (2013). The artful mind meets art history: Toward a psycho-historical framework for the science of art appreciation. *Behavioral and Brain Sciences, 36*(2), 123–137.

Bullough, E. (1912). "Psychical distance" as a factor in art and an aesthetic principle. *British Journal of Psychology, 2*, 87–118.

Carver, C. S. (1996). Cognitive interference and the structure of behavior. In I. G. Sarason, G. R. Pierce, & B. R. Sarason (Eds.), *Cognitive interference; theories, methods, and findings* (pp. 25–46). Mahwah, NJ: Lawrence Erlbaum Associates.

Cattaneo, Z., Lega, C., Flexas, A., Nadal, M., Munar, E., & Cela-Conde, C. J. (2014). The world can look better: Enhancing beauty experience with brain stimulation. *SCAN, 9*, 1713–1721.

Cattaneo, Z., Lega, C., Ferrari, C., Vecchi, T., Cela-Conde, C.J., Sivanto, J., & Nadal, M. (2015). The role of the lateral occipital cortex in aesthetic appreciation of representational and abstract paintings: A TMS study. *Brain and Cognition, 96*, 44–53.

Cattaneo, Z., Lega, C., Gardelli, C., Merabet, L. B., Cela-Conde, C.J., & Nadal, M. (2014). The role of prefrontal and parietal cortices in esthetic appreciation of representational and abstract art: A TMS study. *Neuroimage, 99*, 443–450.

Cela-Conde, C. J., Agnati, L., Huston, J. P., Mora, F., & Nadal, M. (2011). The neural foundations of aesthetic appreciation. *Progress in Neurobiology, 94*, 39–48.

Cela-Conde, C. J., García-Prieto, J., Ramasco, J. J., Mirasso, C. R., Bajo, R., Munar E., ... Maestú, F. (2013). Dynamics of brain networks in the aesthetic appreciation. *Proceedings of the National Academy of Sciences USA, 110*, 10454–10461.

Chamberlain, R., & Wagemans, J. (2015). Visual arts training is linked to flexible attention to local and global levels of visual stimuli. *Acta Psychologica, 161*, 185–197

Chamorro-Premuzic, T., Reimers, S., Hsu, A., & Ahmetoglu, G. (2009). Who art thou? Personality predictors of artistic preferences in a large UK sample: The importance of openness. *British Journal of Psychology, 100*(3), 501–516.

Chang, E. (2006). Interactive experiences and contextual learning in museums. *Studies in Art Education, 47*, 170–186.

Chatterjee, A. (2004). Prospects for a cognitive neuroscience of visual aesthetics. *Bulletin of Psychology and the Arts, 4*, 55–60.

Chatterjee, A., & Vartanian, O. (2014). Neuroaesthetics. *Trends in Cognitive Sciences, 18*(7), 370–375.

Child, I. L. (1962). Personal preferences as an expression of aesthetic sensitivity 1. *Journal of Personality, 30*(3), 496–512.

Child, I. L. (1970). Aesthetic judgment in children. *Trans-action, 7*(7), 47–51.

Chiu, L. H. (1972). A cross-cultural comparison of cognitive styles in Chinese and American children. *International Journal of Psychology, 7*(4), 235–242.

Clark, A. (2013). Whatever next? Predictive brains, situated agents, and the future of cognitive science. *Behavior and Brain Science, 36*(03), 181–204.

Cotter, K. N., Silvia, P. J., & Fayn, K. (2017). What does feeling like crying when listening to music feel like? *Psychology of Aesthetics, Creativity, and the Arts, 12*, 216–227.

Csikszentmihalyi, M., & Rochenberg-Halton, E. (1981). *The meaning of things: Domestic symbols and the self*. Cambridge, England: Cambridge University Press.

Cupchik, G. C. (1995). Emotion in aesthetics: Reactive and reflective models. *Poetics, 23*(1–2), 177–188.

Cupchik, G. C. (2002). The evolution of psychical distance as an aesthetic concept. *Culture & Psychology, 8*(2), 155–187.

Cupchik G. C. (2013). I am, therefore I think, act, and express both in life and in art. In T. Roald, & J. Lang (Eds.), *Art and identity: Essays on the aesthetic creation of mind: Consciousness, literature the arts* (pp. 67–92). Amsterdam: Rodopi.

Cupchik, G. C., & Gebotys, R. J. (1988). The search for meaning in art: Interpretive styles and judgments of quality. *Visual Arts Research, 14*, 38–50.

Cupchik, G. C., Shereck, L., & Spiegel, S. (1994). The effects of textual information on artistic communication. *Visual Arts Research, 20*, 62–78.

Cupchik, G. C., Vartanian, O., Crawley, A., & Mikulis, D. J. (2009). Viewing artworks: Contributions of cognitive control and perceptual facilitation to aesthetic experience. *Brain and cognition, 70*(1), 84–91.

Cupchik, G. C., & Wroblewski-Raya, V. (1998). Loneliness as a theme in painting. *Visual Arts Research, 24*, 65–71.

Currie, G. (1985). The authentic and the aesthetic. *American Philosophical Quarterly, 22*, 153–160.

Dakers, J. R. (Ed.). (2006). *Defining technological literacy: Towards an epistemological framework*. London: Palgrave.

Danto, A. C. (1974). The transfiguration of the commonplace. *The Journal of Aesthetics and Art Criticism, 33*, 139–148.

Danto, A. C. (1981). *The transfiguration of the commonplace: A philosophy of art*. Cambridge, MA: Harvard University Press.

Darley, J. M., Fleming, J. H., Hilton, J. L., & Swann Jr., W. B. (1988). Dispelling negative expectancies: The impact of interaction goals and target characteristics on the expectancy confirmation process. *Journal of Experimental Social Psychology, 24,* 19–36.

Deines, S. (2013). Art in context: On cultural limits to the understanding, experience and evaluation of works of art. In J. deMul, & R. van de Vall (Eds.), *Gimme shelter: Global discourses in aesthetics, international yearbook of aesthetics* (Vol.15; pp. 23–40). Amsterdam: Amsterdam University Press.

Derryberry, D. (1988). Emotional influences on evaluative judgments: Roles of arousal, attention, and spreading activation. *Motivation and Emotion, 12*(1), 23–55.

Descartes, R. (1965). *Discourse on method, optics, geometry and meteorology,* P. J. Olscamp (Trans.). New York: Hackett.

Dissanayake, E. (2007). What art is and what art does: An overview of contemporary evolutionary hypotheses. In C. Martindale, P. Locher, & V. Petrov (Eds.), *Evolutionary and neurocognitive approaches to aesthetics, creativity, and the arts* (pp. 1–14). Amityville, NY: Baywood.

Ensor, K., & Hamilton, M. (2014). Effect of distinctive frames on memory for pictures. *Empirical Studies of the Arts, 32,* 121–131.

Eskine, K. J., Kacinik, N. A., & Prinz, J. J. (2012). Stirring images: Fear, not happiness or arousal, makes art more sublime. *Emotion, 12*(5), 1071.

Eysenck, H. J. (1972). Personal preferences, aesthetic sensitivity and personality in trained and untrained subjects. *Journal of Personality, 40*(4), 544–557.

Falk, J. H. (1993). Assessing the impact of exhibit arrangement on visitor behavior and learning. *Curator, 36,* 133–146.

Falk, J. H. (2009). *Identity and the museum visitor experience.* Walnut Creek, CA: Left Coast Press.

Falk, J., & Dierking, L. (1992). *The museum experience.* Washington, DC: Whalesback Books.

Fayn, K., MacCann, C., Tiliopoulos, N., & Silvia, P. J. (2015). Aesthetic emotions and aesthetic people: Openness predicts sensitivity to novelty in the experiences of interest and pleasure. *Frontiers in Psychology, 6,* 1877.

Fechner, G. T. (1876). *Vorschule der aesthetik.* Leipzig, Germany: Breitkopf und Härtel.

Fenner, D. E. (2003). Aesthetic experience and aesthetic analysis. *Journal of Aesthetic Education, 37*(1), 40–53.

Forster, M., Leder, H., & Ansorge, U. (2016). Exploring the subjective feeling of fluency. *Experimental Psychology, 63*(1), 45.

Frijda, N. H. (1988). The laws of emotion. *American Osychologist, 43*(5), 349.

Funch, B. S. (1997). *The psychology of art appreciation.* Copenhagen: Museum Tusculanum Press, University of Copenhagen.

Gartus, A., & Leder, H. (2014). The white cube of the museum versus the gray cube of the street: The role of context in aesthetic evaluations. *Psychology of Aesthetics, Creativity, and the Arts, 8,* 311–320.

Gell, A. (1998). *Art and agency, an anthropological theory.* Oxford, England: Oxford University Press.

Gendlin, E. T. (1995). Crossing and dipping: Some terms for approaching the interface between natural understanding and logical formulation. *Minds and Machines, 5,* 547–560.

Gendolla, G. H. E. (2000). On the impact of mood on behavior: An integrative theory and a review. *Review of General Psychology, 4,* 378–408.

Gerger, G., Leder, H., & Kremer, A. (2014). Context effects on emotional and aesthetic evaluations of artworks and IAPS pictures. *Acta Psychologica*, *151*, 174–183.

Getzels, J. W., & Csikszentmihalyi, M. (1969). Aesthetic opinion: An empirical study. *Public Opinion Quarterly*, *33*(1), 34–45.

Gibson, J. J. (1979). *The ecological approach to visual perception*. Boston, MA: Houghton Mifflin.

Ginsberg, R. (1986). Experiencing Aesthetically, Aesthetic Experience, and Experience in Aesthetics. In: M. H. Mitias (Ed.), Possibility of the Aesthetic Experience (pp. 61-78). Martinus Nijhoff Philosophy Library, vol 14. Springer, Dordrecht. https://doi.org/10.1007/978-94-009-4372-8_5

Goffman, E. (1974). *Frame analysis: An essay on the organization of experience*. Cambridge, MA: Harvard University Press

Gómez-Puerto, G., Rosselló, J., Corradi, G., Acedo-Carmona, C., Munar, E., & Nadal, M. (2017). Preference for curved contours across cultures. *Psychology of Aesthetics, Creativity, and the Arts*, *12*, 432–439.

Graf, L. K, & Landwehr, J. R. (2015). A dual-process perspective on fluency-based aesthetics: The pleasure-interest model of aesthetic liking. *Personality and Social Psychology Review*, *19*, 395–410.

Graham, D. J., Stockinger, S., & Leder, H. (2013). An island of stability: Art images and natural scenes–but not natural faces–show consistent esthetic response in Alzheimer's-related dementia. *Frontiers in Psychology*, *4*, 107.

Gretton, C., & Ffytche, D. H. (2014). Art and the brain: A view from dementia. *International Journal of Geriatric Psychiatry*, *29*(2), 111–126. doi:10.1002/gps.3975

Griswold, W., Mangione, G., & McDonnell, T. E. (2013). Objects, words, and bodies in space: Bringing materiality into cultural analysis. *Qualitative Sociology*, *36*, 343–364. doi:10.1007/s11133-013-9264-6

Hagtvedt, H., & Patrick, V. M. (2008). Art infusion: The influence of visual art on the perception and evaluation of consumer products. *Journal of Marketing Research*, *45*, 379–389.

Halpern, A. R., Ly, J., Elkin-Franklin, S., & O'Connor, M. G. (2008). I know what I like: Stability of aesthetic preference in Alzheimer's disease. *Brain and Cognition*, *66*, 65–72.

Hanquinet, L. (2013). Visitors to modern and contemporary art museums: Towards a new sociology of "cultural profiles." *The Sociological Review*, *61*, 790–813.

Harris, J. A. (Ed.). (2013). *The Oxford handbook of British philosophy in the eighteenth century*. Oxford, England: Oxford University Press.

Hekkert, P., & Van Wieringen, P. C. (1996). Beauty in the eye of expert and nonexpert beholders: A study in the appraisal of art. *The American Journal of Psychology*, *109*, 389–407.

Hendon, W. S., Costa, F., & Rosenberg, R. A. (1989). The general public and the art museum: Case studies of visitors to several institutions identify characteristics of weir publics. *American Journal of Economics and Sociology*, *48*, 230–243.

Hirsch, Jr., E. D. (1987). *Cultural literacy: What every American needs to know*. Boston, MA: Houghton Mifflin Company.

Huang, M., Bridge, H., Kemp, M. J., & Parker, A. J. (2011). Human cortical activity evoked by the assignment of authenticity when viewing works of art. *Frontiers in Human Neuroscience*, *5*, 134.

Hume, D. (1757). *Four dissertations*. London: A. Millar.

Iwawaki, S., Eysenck, H. J., & Götz, K. O. (1979). A new visual aesthetic sensitivity test (VAST): II. Cross-cultural comparison between England and Japan. *Perceptual and Motor Skills*, *49*(3), 859–862.

Jacobsen, T., Schubotz, R. I., Höfel, L., & Cramon, D. Y. V. (2006). Brain correlates of aesthetic judgment of beauty. *Neuroimage, 29*(1), 276–285.

Kapoula, Z., Adenis, M.-S., Lê, T.-T., Yang, Q., & Lipede, G. (2011). Pictorial depth increases body sway. *Psychology of Aesthetics, Creativity, and the Arts, 5*, 186–193.

Kemp, S. W. P., & Cupchik, G. C. (2007). The emotionally evocative effects of paintings. *Visual Arts Research, 33*, 72–82.

Kirk, U., Skov, M., Hulme, O., Christensen, M. S., & Zeki, S. (2009). Modulation of aesthetic value by semantic context: An fMRI study. *NeuroImage, 44*, 1125–1132.

Kirk, U., Harvey, A., & Montague, P. R. (2011). Domain expertise insulates against judgment bias by monetary favors through a modulation of ventromedial prefrontal cortex. *Proceedings of the National Academy of Sciences of the USA, 108*, 10332–10336.

Komar, V., & Melamid, A. (1997). *Painting by numbers: Komar and Melamid's scientific guide to art*. Berkeley, CA: University of California Press.

Koutstaal, W.. (1998). Memory for picture frames. *Empirical Studies of the Arts, 16*, 47–57.

Kühn, S., & Gallinat, J. (2012). The neural correlates of subjective pleasantness. *Neuroimage, 61*(1), 289–294.

Lacey, S., Hagtvedt, H., Patrick, V. M., Anderson, A., Stilla, R., Desh- pande, G., ... Sathian, K. (2011). Art for reward's sake: Visual art recruits the ventral striatum. *NeuroImage, 55*, 420–433.

Lauring, J. O., Ishizu, T., Kutlikova, H. H., Dörflinger, F., Haugbøl, S., Leder, H., Kupers, R., Pelowski, M. (2019). Why would Parkinson's disease lead to sudden changes in creativity, motivation, or style with visual art?: Case evidence and neurobiological, contextual, and genetic hypotheses. *Neuroscience and Biobehavioral Reviews, 100*, 129–165.

Lauring, J. O., Pelowski, M., Forster, M., Gondan, M., Ptito, M., & Kupers, R. (2016). Well, if they like it ... Effects of social groups' ratings and price information on the appreciation of art. *Psychology of Aesthetics, Creativity, and the Arts, 10*(3), 344.

Lazarus, R. S., & Alfert, E. (1964). Short-circuiting of threat by experimentally altering cognitive appraisal. *The Journal of Abnormal and Social Psychology, 69*(2), 195.

Leder, H., Bär, S., & Topolinski, S. (2012). Covert painting simulations influence aesthetic appreciation of artworks. *Psychological Science, 23*, 1479–1481.

Leder, H., Belke, B., Oeberst, A., & Augustin, D. (2004). A model of aesthetic appreciation and aesthetic judgments. *British Journal of Psychology, 95*, 489–508.

Leder, H., Gerger, G., Brieber, D., & Schwarz, N. (2014). What makes an art expert? Emotion and evaluation in art appreciation. *Cognition and Emotion, 28*(6), 1137–1147.

Leder, H., & Nadal, M. (2014). Ten years of a model of aesthetic appreciation and aesthetic judgments: The aesthetic episode–Developments and challenges in empirical aesthetics. *British Journal of Psychology, 105*(4), 443–464.

Lee, D. S., Kim, E., & Schwarz, N. (2015). Something smells fishy: Olfactory suspicion cues improve performance on the Moses illusion and Wason rule discovery task. *Journal of Experimental Social Psychology, 59*, 47–50.

Leibniz, G. W. (1902). *Discourse on metaphysics: Correspondences with Arnauld, and monadology*, G. Montgomery (Trans.), P. Janet (Ed.), Chicago, IL: Kessinger.

Locher, P., & Dolese, M. (2004). A comparison of the perceived pictorial and aesthetic qualities of original paintings and their postcard images. *Empirical Studies of the Arts, 22*, 129–142.

Locher, P., Overbeeke, K., & Wensveen, S. (2010). Aesthetic interaction: A framework. *Design Issues, 26*(2), 70–79.

Locher, P., Smith, L. F., & Smith, J. K. (1999). Original paintings versus slide and computer reproductions: A comparison of viewer responses. *Empirical Studies of the Arts, 17*, 121–129.

Locher, P. J. (2015). The aesthetic experience with visual art "at first glance." In P. F. Bundgaard, & F. Stjernfelt (Eds.), *Investigations into the phenomenology and the ontology of the work of art: What are artworks and how do we experience them?* (pp. 75–88). New York: Springer.

Locher, P. J., Smith, J. K., & Smith, L. F. (2001). The influence of presentation format and viewer training in the visual arts on the perception of pictorial and aesthetic qualities of paintings. *Perception, 30*, 449–465.

Mandel, D. (2003). Counterfactuals, emotions, and context. *Cognition & Emotion, 17*, 139–159.

Markus, H. R., & Kitayama, S. (1991). Culture and the self: Implications for cognition, emotion, and motivation. *Psychological Review, 98*(2), 224.

Martindale, C. (1988). Aesthetics, psychobiology, and cognition. In F. H. Farley, & R. W. Neperud (Eds.), *The foundations of aesthetics, art, and art education* (pp. 117–160). New York: Praeger.

McArthur, L. Z., & Berry, D. S. (1987). Cross-cultural agreement in perceptions of babyfaced adults. *Journal of Cross-cultural Psychology, 18*(2), 165–192.

McCrae, R. R. (2007). Aesthetic chills as a universal marker of openness to experience. *Motivation and Emotion, 31*(1), 5–11.

Melton, A. W. (1972). Visitor behavior in museums: Some early research in environmental design. *Human Factors, 14*, 393–403.

Murdoch, I. (1977). *The fire and the sun; why Plato banished the artists*. Oxford, England: Oxford University Press.

Myszkowski, N., Storme, M., Zenasni, F., & Lubart, T. (2014). Is visual aesthetic sensitivity independent from intelligence, personality and creativity? *Personality and Individual Differences, 59*, 16–20.

Nadal, M., Munar, E., Capó, M. À., Rosselló, J., & Cela-Conde, C. J. (2008). Towards a framework for the study of the neural correlates of aesthetic preference. *Spatial vision, 21*(3), 379–396.

Noguchi, Y., & Murota, M. (2013). Temporal dynamics of neural activity in an integration of visual and contextual information in an esthetic preference task. *Neuropsychologia, 51*, 1077–1084.

Osborne, H. (1979). Some theories of aesthetic judgment. *The Journal of Aesthetics and Art Criticism, 38*(2), 135–144.

Palmer, S. E., & Schloss, K. B. (2010). An ecological valence theory of human color preference. *Proceedings of the National Academy of Sciences, 107*, 8877–8882.

Parsons, M. J. (1987). *How we understand art; a cognitive developmental account of aesthetic experience*. Cambridge, England: Cambridge University Press.

Plato. (1987). *The republic*, 2nd edition, D. Lee (Trans.). London: Penguin.

Pekarik, A. J., & Schreiber, J. B. (2012). The power of expectation. *Curator, 55*, 487–496.

Pelowski, M. J. (2015). Tears and transformation: Feeling like crying as an indicator of insightful or "aesthetic" experience with art. *Frontiers in Psychology, 6*, 1006

Pelowski, M., & Akiba, F. (2011). A model of art perception, evaluation and emotion in transformative aesthetic experience. *New Ideas in Psychology, 29*(2), 80–97.

Pelowski, M., Akiba, F., & Palacios, V. (2012). Satori, Koan and aesthetic experience: Exploring the "realization of emptiness" in Buddhist enlightenment via an empirical study of modern art. *Psyke & Logos, 33*(2), 33.

Pelowski, M., Forster, M., Tinio, P. P., Scholl, M., & Leder, H. (2017). Beyond the lab: An examination of key factors influencing interaction with "real" and museum-based art. *Psychology of Aesthetics, Creativity, and the Arts, 11*(3), 245.

Pelowski, M., Gerger, G., Chetouani, Y., Markey, P. S., & Leder, H. (2017). But is it really art? The classification of images as "art"/"not art" and correlation with appraisal and viewer interpersonal differences. *Frontiers in Psychology, 8,* 1729.

Pelowski, M., Markey, P. S., Forster, M., Gerger, G., & Leder, H. (2017). Move me, astonish me ... delight my eyes and brain: The Vienna integrated model of top-down and bottom-up processes in art perception (VIMAP) and corresponding affective, evaluative, and neurophysiological correlates. *Physics of Life Reviews, 21,* 80–125.

Pelowski, M., Markey, P. S., Lauring, J. O., & Leder, H. (2016). Visualizing the impact of art: An update and comparison of current psychological models of art experience. *Frontiers in Human Neuroscience, 10,* 160.

Pelowski, M., Markey, P., & Leder, H. (2018). Chills, aesthetic experience, and new versus old knowledge—What do chills actually portend?: Comment on "Physics of mind: Experimental confirmations of theoretical predictions" by Schoeller et al. *Physics of Life Reviews, 25,* 83–87.

Pihko, E., Virtanen, A., Saarinen, V. M., Pannasch, S., Hirvenkari, L., Tossavainen, T., ... Hari, R. (2011). Experiencing art: The influence of expertise and painting abstraction level. *Frontiers in Human Neuroscience, 5,* 94.

Pinney, C., & Thomas, N. (Eds.). (2001). *Beyond Aesthetics.* Oxford, England: Berg.

Poppe, A. (1907). *Alexander Gottlieb Baumgarten: Seine bedeutung und stellung in der Leibniz-wolffischen philosophie und seine beziehungen zu Kant.* Leipzig, Germany: Buchdruckerei Robert Noske.

Ramachandran, V. S., & Hirstein, W. (1999). The science of art: A neurological theory of aesthetic experience. *Journal of consciousness Studies, 6*(6–7), 15–51.

Reber, R., Schwarz, N., & Winkielman, P. (2004). Processing fluency and aesthetic pleasure: Is beauty in the perceiver's processing experience? *Personality and Social Psychology Review, 8*(4), 364–382.

Robinson, E. (1928). *The behavior of the museum visitor.* Washington, DC: American Association of Museums.

Roets, A., & Van Hiel, A. (2011). Item selection and validation of a brief, 15-item version of the Need for Closure Scale. *Personality and Individual Differences, 50*(1), 90–94.

Rollins, M. (2001). The invisible content of visual art. *Journal of Aesthetics and Art Criticism, 59,* 19–27.

Rothbaum, F., Weisz, J. R., & Snyder, S. S. (1982). Changing the world and changing the self: A two-process model of perceived control. *Journal of personality and Social Psychology, 42*(1), 5.

Russell, P. A., & Milne, S. (1997). Meaningfulness and hedonic value of paintings: Effects of titles. *Empirical Studies of the Arts, 15*(1), 61–73.

Saito, M. (1996). Comparative studies on color preference in Japan and other Asian regions, with special emphasis on the preference for white. *Color Research & Application, 21*(1), 35–49.

Scherer, K. R. (2005). What are emotions? And how can they be measured? *Social Science Information, 44*(4), 695–729.

Schwarz, N. (2011). Feelings-as-information theory. In P. Van Lange, A. Kruglanski, & E. T. Higgins (Eds.), *Handbook of theories of social psychology* (pp. 289–308). London: Sage.

Sibley, F. (1959). Aesthetic concepts. *The Philosophical Review, 68*(4), 421–450.

Silvia, P. J. (2005). Emotional responses to art: From collation and arousal to cognition and emotion. *Review of General Psychology, 9*(4), 342.

Silvia, P. J. (2009). Looking past pleasure: Anger, confusion, disgust, pride, surprise, and other unusual aesthetic emotions. *Psychology of Aesthetics, Creativity, and the Arts, 3*, 48–51.

Silvia, P. J., & Nusbaum, E. C. (2011). On personality and piloerection: Individual differences in aesthetic chills and other unusual aesthetic experiences. *Psychology of Aesthetics, Creativity, and the Arts, 5*(3), 208

Spee, B., Ishizu, T., Leder, H., & Pelowski, M. (2018). Neuropsychopharmacological aesthetics: A theoretical consideration of pharmacological approaches to causative brain study in aesthetics and art. *Progress in Brain Research, 237*, 343–372.

Speisman, J. C., Lazarus, R. S., Davison, L., & Mordkoff, A. M. (1964). Experimental analysis of a film used as a threatening stimulus. *Journal of Consulting Psychology, 28*(1), 23

Summers, D. (1987). *The judgment of sense: Renaissance naturalism and the rise of aesthetics.* Cambridge, England: Cambridge University Press.

Suzuki, M., Miyai, I., Ono, T., & Kubota, K. (2008). Activities in the frontal cortex and gait performance are modulated by preparation. An fNIRS study. *NeuroImage, 39*, 600–607.

Swami, V., Stieger, S., Pietschnig, J., & Voracek, M. (2010). The disinterested play of thought: Individual differences and preference for surrealist motion pictures. *Personality and individual differences, 48*(7), 855–859.

Tallis, R. (2008). The limitations of a neurological approach to art. *Lancet, 372*, 19–20.

Tan, E. S. (2000). Emotion, art, and the humanities. *Handbook of Emotions, 2*, 116–135.

Tanaka, Y., Oyama, T., & Osgood, C. E. (1963). A cross-culture and cross-concept study of the generality of semantic spaces. *Journal of Memory and Language, 2*(5), 392.

Thaler, R. H., & Sunstein, C. R. (2008). *Nudge: Improving decisions about health, wealth, and happiness.* Yale: Yale University Press.

Tinio, P. P. L. (2013). From artistic creation to aesthetic reception: The mirror model of art. *Psychology of Aesthetics, Creativity, and the Arts, 7*, 265–275.

Tinio, P. P. L., Smith, J. K., & Smith, L. F. (2014). The walls do speak: Psychological aesthetics and the museum experience. In P. L. Tinio, J. K. Smith, & L. F. Smith (Eds.), *The Cambridge handbook of the psychology of aesthetics and the arts* (pp. 195–218). Cambridge, England: Cambridge University Press.

Todorović, D. (2010). Context effects in visual perception and their explanations. *Review of Psychology, 17*(1), 17–32.

Turner, A., & Penn, A. (2002). Encoding natural movement as an agent-based system: An investigation into human pedestrian behaviour in the built environment. *Environment and planning B: Planning and Design, 29*(4), 473–490.

Umilta, M. A., Berchio, C., Sestito, M., Freedberg, D., & Gallese, V. (2012). Abstract art and cortical motor activation: An EEG study. *Frontiers in Human Neuroscience, 6*, 311.

Van Den Abbeele, J., Penton-Voak, I. S., Attwood, A. S., Stephen, I. D., & Munafò, M. R. (2015). Increased facial attractiveness following moderate, but not high, alcohol consumption. *Alcohol and Alcoholism, 50*(3), 296–301.

Wagner, V., Menninghaus, W., Hanich, J., & Jacobsen, T. (2014). Art schema effects on affective experience: The case of disgusting images. *Psychology of Aesthetics, Creativity, and the Arts, 8*(2), 120–129.

Walker, D., & Vul, E. (2014). Hierarchical encoding makes individuals in a group seem more attractive. *Psychological Science, 25*, 230–235.

Winston, A. S., & Cupchik, G. C. (1992). The evaluation of high art and popular art by naive and experienced viewers. *Visual Arts Research, 18,* 1–14.

Wolz, S. H., & Carbon, C. C. (2014). What's wrong with an art fake? Cognitive and emotional variables influenced by authenticity status of artworks. *Leonardo, 47,* 467–473.

Zeglin Brand, P. (2000). Glaring omissions in traditional theories of art. In N. Carroll (Ed.), *Theories of art today* (p. 186). Madison, WI: University of Wisconsin Press.

CHAPTER 40

EMPIRICAL AESTHETICS
Context, Extra Information, and Framing

HELMUT LEDER AND MATTHEW PELOWSKI

INTRODUCTION—AESTHETIC EXPERIENCES—SPECIAL BUT EMBEDDED?

AESTHETIC experiences, in most people's lives, are probably frequent and can be had in multiple situations. Imagine the last time that you had an encounter that one or all of the writers in this book might label "aesthetic"—you might have enjoyed a work of art, listened to a piece of music; experienced the beauty of a face or a sunset (or, when you are older and wake up far too early, even the dawn). You might even have found yourself saddened or moved to tears by a theatrical tragedy or uniquely compelled by something that would otherwise be troubling or disgusting. While we often tend to organize our memories of such events around the most central objects—the painting, the musical piece, the sun, or clouds—if you reflect on the experiences carefully, of course these "objects" are only part of the remembered encounter. Usually, aesthetic experience involves an episode with the experiencing person in a specific situation, stretched out over time, in which certain objects, their environment, and various constituting elements are brought together (Leder & Nadal, 2014).

Although this can of course involve multiple aspects—many of which will be considered throughout this book—one particularly important factor involves the extra information that might be provided together with a target object, or even brought as prior experiences and knowledge into the encounter by an individual. Labels, signs, and titles may serve to inform, to frame, and perhaps even to determine what happens. What if you were told, before seeing or interacting with the abovementioned objects or scenes, that rather than a sunset you were perceiving an orange glow from nuclear bomb testing, a painting composed immediately before the death of its creator, a musical piece composed for a funeral or a wedding, or an artistic forgery; not "art" at all, but a computer-generated pattern generated by an algorithm with no thought or feeling? Would this information change your reaction, your evaluations, or even the feelings and responses of your body? The same could be asked regarding social or other implicit and explicit information; for example, the reactions of your peers—whether others find this important or bad, sad, or funny.

In this chapter we provide a general introduction on the importance of such contextual factors in aesthetic experiences. We first give a brief overview of the nature of aesthetic experiences as a topic beyond aesthetic objects, with regard to how aesthetic experiences emerge as interactions between person, objects, and environment, and thus how they are embedded in informational contexts. We then discuss in particular the importance of information context: how we frame, anticipate, explain, and understand the factors of our experiences as we live them. We also examine how, in psychological studies, extra information or titles presented with pictures and artworks, or instructions regarding the context—so-called framing effects—have been shown to affect aesthetic experiences. We end this chapter with an outlook on major challenges, goals, and future directions.

Throughout this chapter, we also want to promote the idea that the way we tend to categorize our world into separable objects is often part of an illusion. Specifically, the assumption that the environment is composed of clearly separable entities, which are in turn all perceived, recognized, and evaluated individually in isolated ways, might in itself be an illusion. Think of alternative answers to the starting question, which might have been different had the question been phrased in slightly different ways. What if you had been asked in which kind of situation have you recently had an aesthetic experience? The answer might have been "in a museum," "at home this morning," "in the car," or "looking into a mirror," etc. Different questions activate different ways of looking at the same events and objects.

Isolated objects versus flows of experience

For a very long time, psychology in general, and empirical aesthetics in particular, had a strong focus on the study of rather singular, isolated objects. This was for two main reasons: first, a belief in the experimental laboratory approach that, step-by-step, demanded higher control of the studied object, often reducing it to specific, well-controlled features (well-describable, measurable, and controllable by the experimenter). This reductionist approach was based on the assumption that such a method was needed to ensure effects that later, eventually, could be tested in increasingly complex "ecologically valid" settings. As put by Berlyne and Ogilvie (1974, p. 182) in their work relaunching the empirical study of aesthetics as a psychological topic, a "synthetic approach" involving controlled studies in a laboratory was vital to being taken seriously as a "real" science; however, this "must sooner or later be supplemented with 'analytic' studies in which reaction to genuine works [and settings]" are investigated "with a view to unravelling their determinants."

A positive example of the above empirical progression is the relationship between facial beauty and viewing time. An early study by Shimoyo, Simion, Shimojo, and Scheier (2003) presented pairs of faces in isolation, and found that when perceivers were asked to decide which of the two they considered more attractive, the face chosen was also looked at for longer (and toward the moment when the decision was made, even longer still). In order to study whether faces of people in real scenes also show such a positive relation between facial beauty and presentation time, Leder, Tinio, Fuchs, and Bohrn (2010) studied these effects with scenes in which the faces of two photographed people had been systematically replaced by either attractive or less attractive faces. As a next step into a more realistic context, Leder, Mitrovic, and Goller (2016) then used colored photographs of real scenes in which faces naturally (and, importantly, quite subtly) differed in terms of beauty. Again, they replicated the positive relation between looking times and beauty. However, in many areas of empirical aesthetics, the expectation—that effects found for isolated objects or even their features can be translated into more complex real-world contexts—still awaits testing.

The second reason why cognitive psychology has often focused on single object classes is the understanding of the human mind as modular. Since the emergence of cognitive psychology in the late 1960s, slowly replacing behaviorist approaches, there has been a strong interest in a rediscovered inner mind, and in specialized areas of the brain and mind (i.e., modules) that are occupied with the processing of specific objects rather than concerned with general principles (Fodor, 1983). Typical cognitive psychology questions were concerned with how we identify and recognize objects in the world, whether processes in the cognitive mind differ for different kinds of objects, and how these relate to theories of human memory, often linking perception and memory retrieval. As a consequence, since the cognitive turn, psychological research has tended to look at single objects, often treating them as the relevant instances of perception and memory.

Why was the above the case? Since Eleanor Rosch's seminal paper on basic objects (Rosch, Mervis, Gray, Johnson, & Boyes-Bream, 1976) it seemed plausible that the so-called "basic level" would be the most efficient level for assessing the environment. According to this theory, human minds organize the world as consisting of "chairs," "paintings," "dogs," "cups," and "computers," rather than the more abstract level of furniture, artwork, animal, etc., and also not on the more specific and idiosyncratic level of, let's say, an Eames chair, a Picasso, or a dachshund. However, the general claim that our world consists of basic-level objects has, unsurprisingly, been questioned. For example, Tanaka and Taylor (1991) demonstrated in the special case of faces that the initial level of object access could shift with experience, from "face" to a specific person (e.g., Bill Clinton). A similar shift had been shown away from basic object levels to specific levels in perception of art where the artist's name (if known) seemed the first level of conscious encounter (e.g., this is a Picasso), rather than a "portrait" or even a "painting" (Belke, Leder, Harsanyi, & Carbon, 2010). Thus, in the domain of aesthetic objects, especially when it comes to art, the idiosyncratic nature of single artworks might be questioned.

The necessary assumption that objects can be studied independently of their surrounding context has also been used for the argument that artworks or other aesthetic stimuli can be studied independently of their context, as their inherent structure determines their aesthetic value. In the domain of art an argument for neglected context is based on the nature of art, and the origin of the aesthetic effects it elicits. The British art critic Clive Bell (1914), when stating his theory of significant shape, argued that if form is the source of aesthetic experience, and form is unchanged by the circumstances, it follows that "Great art remains stable and unobscure because the feelings that it awakens are independent of time and place … " (p. 37). This statement undermines the idea that context might often be relevant, as it cannot affect the aesthetic effects of the artworks.

The (early) opposite view is found in Ernst H. Gombrich's *Art and Illusion* (1960). When he thought about the role that contrast effects in light and color vision might play, he suggested that what he called "relationships" (p. 46), external to the physical object and as studied by psychologists, must have effects on the local aesthetic effects of artworks for the perceiver, and even beyond. However, this truism is still only emerging in empirical study. As Leder and Nadal (2014, p. 453) summarized, "given how much of this work has been performed in laboratory settings, it is also clear that the psychology of art and aesthetics has traditionally accepted the formalist argument that aesthetic experience is, to a large extent, contextually impermeable, that is to say, that aesthetic episodes in the laboratory differ little from those that occur in other contexts."

Today's Psychology—Widening the Scope Toward a Broader Study of Object–Context Interactions

The isolated object view grew out of more than a century of tradition in which sensory sensations (Wundt, 1908)—a flash of light, a single tone (Helmholtz, 1867)—finally had developed into more meaningful entities such as letters, words, and images of faces. Not only did all these domains have successful research programs, they often arrived at the argument that different classes of objects are marked by specific, even encapsulated cognitive processes (Fodor, 1983). For example, reading is based on neighborhood effects (Grainger, O'Regan, Jacobs, & Segui, 1989); attention to letters is guided by singletons (i.e., the gist of an image can be guessed after very brief presentation times; Oliva & Torralba, 2006); and in faces, configurations have been postulated as a special class of information (Leder & Bruce, 2000) and recently have also been challenged (Burton, Schweinberger, Jenkins, & Kaufmann, 2015). Consequently, the cognitive psychology of perception is still often divided into these different objects by different specialist areas, each of which has its own societies and scientific meetings and is represented often rather independently from others in psychological textbooks.

Today, psychology is on an interesting edge, with more and more doubt that the way we conducted studies in the past finally leads to a comprehensive theory of human life. Thus, there is increasing awareness that this division in psychological research needs to be overcome. In part, this is due to a shift in the dominant paradigms.

In light of our phenomenological experiences, the psychological approach to focus research on specific object classes seems surprising. When you look around there are no single objects that are isolated. Rather, our visual experience is a complete ensemble of visual structures, with no end and no beginning, which moves when we move our head or eyes. This comprehensive, dynamic, and holistic experience has been studied by Gibson (1979), who called it our visual or optical array. The currently most comprehensive approach toward a holistic, more complete way of studying the human mind developed as the predictive coding approach. This describes the main purpose of the human mind an9d brain as predicting sensory input from one moment to the next, through multilayer brain activities that adapt whenever an unpredicted "error" is detected requiring adaptation on several levels to correct for the next prediction. Such an understanding of how the brain works dates back to Helmholtz, and Andy Clark in his (2013) theoretical paper clearly draws a line to these historical sources and beautifully describes the mind's challenge:

> From Helmholtz comes the key idea that sensory systems are in the tricky business of inferring sensory causes from their bodily effects. This in turn involves computing multiple probability distributions, since a single such effect will be consistent with many different sets of causes distinguished only by their relative (and context dependent) probability of occurrence.
>
> (Clark, 2013, p. 182)

Predictive coding, therefore, suggests that only in an interactive combination of bottom-up and top-down processes, with continuous learning (adapting) and updates can the system optimize its main purpose: to reveal efficient predictions about the outside world. Interestingly, Clark in this quote also refers to the contextual dependence of our mental states. This directly guides us to the topic of our chapter: the context dependence of aesthetic processing, especially concerning external, supporting information, as one class of human experiences.

Aesthetic experiences—their nature and information context dependence

Over the past decade, the psychology of aesthetics and the arts has witnessed a growth in theoretically grounded interest in aesthetics in general (Chatterjee & Vartanian, 2014; Leder, Belke, Oeberst & Augustin, 2004), and, in tandem, an increasing awareness of context. Chatterjee and Vartanian (2014) describe aesthetic experiences as emerging from a complex "interaction between sensory–motor, emotion–valuation, and meaning–knowledge neural systems" (p. 370). They identify three major systems that contribute in various amounts and in as yet largely unspecified ways to create the variety and diversity of aesthetic experiences. Leder et al. (2004) describe the processing stages and components involved in aesthetic experience of artworks. Their model contains a succession of five processing stages, from early perceptual, via memory-related stages in which implicit and explicit resonances, as well as representations of style and content guide the processing; toward later stages of interpretation, finding meaning, and reducing ambiguity. The interplay of processing stages covers the full set of determinants that constitute a holistic experience over time.

In Leder et al. (2004) the components of information processing that constitute an aesthetic experience are described as being determined by a specific context, in which they happen. "As artworks are no longer obvious as such, their initial classification requires adequate context variables" (p. 491). Since 2004, most theoretical accounts of aesthetic experiences have considered such context as a relevant variable. Indeed, Leder and Nadal (2014) provided an updated discussion of context, especially framing information, as one of the "hot topics" in empirical aesthetics. In turn, Pelowski, Markey, et al. (2017) extended the original Leder et al. (2004) model and explicitly discussed the role of context to enable emotional, and even transformative, experiences: "Even more, beyond basic vision and judgment, art viewing is notable for its unique blending of bottom-up processing of artwork features (form, attractiveness) with top-down contributions of memory, personality, and context" (p. 81). Especially the latter can be driven by how an object is framed or understood—regarding external information.

Various approaches have been developed to study empirically the effects of contextual information, from art–title combinations, or instructed framing effects in experiments, to field studies that demonstrate how art and beauty interact with environmental variables in the real world. All the approaches discussed in this chapter therefore somehow challenge the general idea that artworks are autonomous, independently effective entities. Therefore, in this chapter we present typical approaches that together illustrate how researchers have employed paradigms that implement the various concepts of context in empirical studies of the arts (and aesthetics more generally). In the following paragraphs, we discuss a number of approaches by describing examples of typical studies and their corresponding findings.

Aesthetic experiences—art and information in priming paradigms

Some typical approaches have emerged in the tradition of cognitive psychology, in which context can be understood as related information that affects the way an object of interest is cognitively processed. The typical paradigm to test the overlap of simultaneously or sequentially presented information is a priming study. This involves explicitly or implicitly providing information before or in tandem with a target stimulus that is meant to modulate or frame how a stimulus is encountered. Priming studies differ in design depending on the underlying research question and the objects under consideration—faces, artworks, etc.

Priming and processing time and sequences

Early priming studies were conducted to study the nature of concepts in the mind by testing the relative overlap between processing sequences. Logically, the extent to which the processing of an object is facilitated or hindered by another stimulus is interpreted as evidence of the closeness of the involvement of other associated processing networks— and how much two concepts share processing. For example, Warren and Morton (1982) found that the presentation of a picture facilitated the recognition of that same picture in a tachistoscope up to 45 min later. Even a picture of an object with the same name could produce such a priming effect, but not reading the word alone. The authors discussed that this would be evidence for a distinction between categorization systems for words or pictures. In another example, regarding the role of priming context in face recognition, Bruce, Carson, Burton, and Kelly (1998) found that images of faces that had been seen on posters which were used to search for participants in experiments showed priming effects in the form of facilitating recognition when later tested in the laboratory, even 1 month after the first exposure to the posters. Interestingly for face recognition, these effects were stronger when the same image was used in subsequent testing, but modulation could even be shown when different views of a face were used. This indicates that the appearance of the person, and not the mere image, produced the effect.

While, in principle, combining different kinds of information and presentation in priming paradigms became a standard procedure in experimental psychology, the way this kind of research paradigm was used in empirical aesthetics needed some adaptation to the specific research topics. In faces the components proposed in the cognitive processing model by Bruce and Young (1986) guided many research questions regarding representations. In art, the priming with information derived from theories and models of aesthetic experiences was used to see which extra information would change the quality of an aesthetic experience, or often, the liking for it.

Context Implemented Through Jointly Presented Artwork–Title Information

In the consideration of art, most initial priming studies considered labels and titles. It might be argued that the most direct way of combining art and information is taken from the naturally occurring pairing of artworks with titles as practiced in galleries, museums, and art books. This familiar pairing allows the researcher to control systematically for the quality or quantity of information provided for the art processing, mainly through the selection of the kind of title. Millis (2001) studied the effects of different kinds of titles on aesthetic experiences (note, not of artworks). His participants viewed and rated illustrations and photographs based on how much they understood, and aesthetically appraised them while title presence (title vs. no title) and kind (literal vs. metaphorical) were manipulated across conditions and experiments. Analyses revealed that metaphorical titles produced higher ratings in terms of aesthetic experiences compared with either no title or descriptive titles. Millis called this an "elaboration effect." The effect was found for participants with art experience, but only for representational and not abstract stimuli (again, not art!). Similarly, providing titles has been shown to increase ratings of meaningfulness and decreased abstractness, but had no effect on liking of the tested artworks (Russell & Milne, 1997).

Regarding the stage model of aesthetic experiences (Leder et al., 2004), Leder, Carbon, and Ripsas (2006) aimed to disentangle descriptive from elaborate information and the corresponding processes. They combined abstract and representational (classical modernism, early 20th century) paintings with two kinds of fabricated titles, again descriptive titles that described the content of the artwork, or elaborate titles, which suggested a possible interpretation. For example, a painting of a winter scene by Cuno Amiet could be paired with either the title "Houses in snow" or with the more elaborate version "Hibernation." In a first experiment, they found that elaborative titles increased the understanding of abstract paintings but not their appreciation. In a second experiment, they compared the effects of versions of titles under different presentation times, only for abstract paintings. For short presentation times (1 s), descriptive titles increased understanding more than elaborative titles, whereas for medium presentation times (10 s) elaborative titles increased understanding more than descriptive titles. These findings were interpreted as a first indication that the different processing stages indeed have different time courses, a finding that later was considered in the updated version of the model by Leder and Nadal (2014).

Mastandrea and Umiltà (2016) studied a more specific, rather art-historically relevant, effect of artwork–title interplay. They wanted to explore how words in real titles given to futuristic artworks and regarding movement affect perceived dynamism, a feature often deemed essential for this style of art. For 10 futurist artworks they tested four title conditions: the original tile, containing a movement term, one in which that term was enhanced through insertion of a reinforcing adjective, one in which the term was eliminated, and a fourth (control) condition with no title at all. The original and the enhanced movement condition increased the evaluated level of movement assigned to the artworks. Moreover, the more that movement was highlighted through the labels, the higher the liking. This is not only a good example of a careful, specific manipulation of titles to test the interplay of perception and appreciation, but also an example of how empirical aesthetics can test hypotheses relevant for art history.

Belke, Leder, Strobach, and Carbon (2010) systematically combined titles and artworks to produce and test effects of fluency and disfluency. They employed a cross-modal conceptual priming paradigm, in which semantically related or unrelated titles, as well as a "no title" condition, preceded the presentation of artworks (paintings of different degrees of visual abstraction). Results supported a fluency-affect-liking hypothesis. Related titles produced the highest appreciation, followed by the no title and unrelated title conditions. Interestingly, the effect was moderated by the degree of abstraction of the paintings, such that fluency effects were particularly strong for representational paintings, and weaker for abstract paintings. However, this again supports the special role of abstract art, which can deal better with ambiguous, nonmatching titles.

Gerger and Leder (2015) examined how the combination of fluency and effortful elaborate processing influences aesthetic experiences. They employed three different title types—semantically matching titles (fluent), semantically nonmatching titles (nonfluent), and an "untitled" condition (control)—and considered their effect on ratings and physiological correlates of positive and negative affect, using facial electromyography (fEMG) responses to abstract, semiabstract, and representational art. Matching titles and the more effortful untitled condition were liked more compared with the nonmatching title condition. These results were also reflected in fEMG, with stronger M. corrugator (frowning muscle) activations in the nonmatching condition followed by the untitled condition. Only in the matching condition were there indicators of positive emotions (smiling) due to fluency. Interestingly, these results support the idea that high levels of disfluency and cognitive effort reduce liking, and that fluency as well as moderate levels of effort contribute to more positive aesthetic experiences.

Regarding more natural interactions between titles and artworks, Smith, Smith, and Tinio (2017) studied how long people look at art in a real museum, and also included measurements of the time people spent reading titles. They found considerable variation, and that about 15% of participants in this study "engaged in an interesting viewing pattern (. . .) first they looked at the art briefly, then read the label, and then glanced back at the art before moving along. In other words, they spent most of their time with the label, not the work" (p. 81). This study relates the findings of title–artwork interactions to the more applied field of museum research. Equally interesting, as will be considered further in the sections on museum context or physical aspects, in the context of an art museum study Tröndle and Tschacher (2012) mentioned, albeit quite anecdotally, that individuals tend to stand to the side of a painting that has a corresponding title—with the label essentially acting as an anchor for the viewer and thus changing even the angle of their perception (for a review, see Pelowski, Forster, et al., 2017).

Related to the above suggestion, there are also some studies that have tested directly whether titles affect the way we physically perceive artworks. In an early study, employing interesting methods, Franklin, Becklen, and Doyle (1993) studied how perceivers of artworks responded to a painting under different titling conditions. Their participants looked at an artwork and, after listening to a spoken title, not only reported their "visual experience" introspectively but also used a light pointer to indicate where they believed they were looking. Different titles affected what people reported but did not affect their indicated "looking spots." Referring to this study, Kapoula, Daunys, Herbez, and Yang (2009) measured real eye movements with three Cubist paintings (by Leger) and compared an original title condition with a task in which no title was present but where participants were asked to produce a title. In this comparison the original titles revealed longer fixation durations. Bubić, Sušac, and Palmović (2017) demonstrated another effect of titles on art perception. When titles contained elements that were themes of the artworks, similar to descriptive titles (as in Leder et al., 2006), analyses of eye movements revealed that participants looked longer at those parts of the artworks, and often returned their gaze to these areas. This was more pronounced for representational artworks, compared with abstract artworks. Thus, presenting short titles affects aesthetic experiences already at the early level of visual exploration.

Hristova, Georgieva, and Grinberg (2011) also reported an interesting interaction between art style, task, and title condition (title vs. no title). They studied eye movement patterns while participants were looking at famous Surrealist or Baroque paintings. Participants were asked to rate their aesthetic appreciation or provide a description. Interestingly, when the titles were presented for Baroque paintings, effects on eye movements were small but the aesthetic ratings increased. For Surrealist paintings, in contrast, titles changed eye movement patterns but did not affect the aesthetic ratings.

To summarize these approaches: adding and varying titles of artworks is an efficient way of changing the way artworks are perceived, and sometimes how they are appreciated. A careful, theoretically driven variation of titles and artworks can be quite informative regarding theories of aesthetic experiences. In more applied fields of research, titles have also been considered in art exhibitions to learn more about the relevant dimensions for adult learning (Samanian, Nedaeifar, & Karinimi, 2016) as well as studies that examine the effects of titles in nontypical art contexts (Smith, Smith, Arcand, Smith, & Bookbinder, 2015).

Context as Joint Presentation of Art and Extra Information Beyond Titles

Another way to show that artworks are processed depending on flanking conditions is the combination of artworks with extra information, beyond mere titles, such as words or text that is more or less associated with the artwork. In nonart contexts such paradigms often were developed to show automatic effects of simultaneously or temporarily associated information. Such priming paradigms were used to show that information regarding one object could not be processed independently of another object. In empirical aesthetics the kind of information presented and the mode of presentation are again often inspired by the way art is experienced in real-world contexts: information as in the museum consists of background information given as text, or information beyond the title or the artist are also provided.

First regarding what might occur when a label is added to a display, according to Bitgood and Patterson (1993, p. 762), "two alternative and seemingly incompatible visitor reactions have been postulated." The need to read a label may "distract attention or compete with other components," or may disrupt aesthetic or spontaneous reactions by shifting focus to didactic information (for similar discussion, see Funch, Kroyer, Roald, & Wildt, 2012). On the other hand, labels may positively direct attention and stimulate interest. This so-called "attention-directing hypothesis" would fit the art-related laboratory findings above, and perhaps connect labels to fluency and resulting hedonic assessment (Leder et al., 2006). This difference has not been tested systematically.

Nevertheless, added extra contextual information has been a target for empirical assessment, especially in laboratory studies of appraisal. Cupchik, Sherek, and Spiegel (1994) conducted a study in which they presented images of 24 sculptures by two artists to their participants twice. During the first presentation they asked for ratings, and in a second phase in which the artworks were now accompanied by short texts that were introduced as "information supplied by the artists," participants were asked to read that information and evaluate the artworks again, in light of this information (while exposed to image of sculpture plus text). They were also asked to indicate how helpful the texts had been. Results of a number of analyses were rather ambiguous, and the observed pattern quite complex, with many unplanned comparisons. However, there were some effects of the text information, which was rated as more informative and helpful by participants with higher art expertise. Also, information classified as descriptive in this study reduced affective and cognitive evaluations of the artworks. Formalistic (stylistic) information had mixed effects, and the authors argued that during the required task it might have directed attention to some visual aspects of the art, which likewise reduced its holistic potency.

Jakesch and Leder (2009) conducted an experiment with artworks and statements to address specifically the role of ambiguity in aesthetic experiences. They combined matching and nonmatching statements regarding specific contemporary abstract artworks with different proportions, in order to test effects of experienced ambiguity. They implemented "three levels of matching," individually asking each participant to evaluate how much they thought each artwork and information would match, thus creating conditions of no-, full-, and mixed match. They found that, as expected, neither fully matching nor completely unmatching art–statement combinations were liked most: people liked, and found it most interesting when some information matched, and was combined with nonmatching statements. These findings were interpreted as support for an ambiguity preference in art appreciation, and, interestingly, in conflict with predictions of a fluency account, that people prefer what is easy to process (Reber, Schwarz, & Winkielman, 2004).

Jucker, Barrett, and Wlodarski (2014) were interested in the role of an artist's intention, which often is deemed important to find meaning and an aesthetically pleasing level of understanding (Leder et al., 2004). They argued that artworks might automatically trigger speculation "about the artist's intention, and that it is intuitively assessed as an act of symbolic communication" (p. 149). They tested this hypothesis by presenting participants with various artifacts and works of art, together with differing levels of information regarding the artist's intentions. It was found that participants used the artist's intentions to decide whether certain artifacts were instances of "art" and that titles, which were interpreted as representing artist's intentions, not only increased participants' understanding but also liking. In accordance with the general effects of context, the authors concluded that art experience apparently not only is "about beauty or hedonistic pleasure, but involves assessment of the artist's intention and of the history behind the work of art" (p. 149).

Swami (2013) studied how different kinds of information have effects on two artists and art styles: Surrealist paintings by Max Ernst and blue-period representational style paintings by Pablo Picasso. In a first experiment he combined one of four kinds of information with 12 paintings by Max Ernst. This involved a control condition in which participants were told just to look at artworks, a condition in which they were similarly instructed but also saw the titles of the paintings, and two levels of contextualizing information, one in which background information about the painter was given, and one in which information about the specific style was also presented. The latter regarded a description of the principle of grattage (scraping fresh paint off the canvas), which Max Ernst used. A between-subjects design was employed. For each painting participants indicated how much they liked each artwork and how interesting they found it, how familiar each artwork was, and, using four additional scales, how well they thought they would understand each artwork. Different types of information influenced the ratings of understanding of the paintings. The provision of a title, the broad genre, and content-specific (stylistic and artist background) information all resulted in higher ratings of understanding of the paintings than in the control group. Swami (p. 291) noted "broadly speaking, these results are consistent with previous work showing that elaborate or brief titular information results in improved understanding and appraised meaningfulness of abstract stimuli." Interestingly and different from Leder et al. (2006), higher understanding was associated with higher aesthetic appreciation of the artworks. And again, although any type of contextualizing information heightened understanding, only content-specific information resulted in higher aesthetic appreciation.

In a second study, similar contextualized information was compared with stylistic information, the former information about Picasso's blue period, and the latter about the Cubist style that Picasso helped to invent. Again, contextualizing information led to higher understanding of Cubist style art by Picasso. Consistent with earlier findings (Leder et al., 2006), title information did not positively affect understanding of representational art. Finally, in a third study, Swami (2013) also demonstrated that information effectively changes the processing of artworks only when it is relevant. This very informative set of studies confirms that elaborate, "relevant, and content-specific information about artworks has the greatest impact on understanding, which in turn affects aesthetic appreciation" (p. 293), and that these effects were strongest for abstract art, which often requires a specific impact of knowledge and information. As a consequence, abstract art seems best suited to produce effects of context through joint presentation with extra information.

The argument that the kind of artwork seems critical was also supported by the work of Stojilovic and Markovic (2014), who studied effects of lectures on abstract or renaissance art, compared with a control group with no lecture, on the evaluation of different kinds of artworks. They report that aesthetic experience was mainly enhanced for abstract art, after the abstract art lecture.

Park, Yun, and Jeong (2015) studied how presentation of background information affects the appreciation of artworks. They found that extra information in the form of commentaries by the artist and an art critic significantly increased subjective aesthetic ratings. They also tested whether knowledge causes experts to attend to certain visual features in a painting and to link them to the evaluative conventions. To that end, Park et al. also recorded eye movements of subjects while viewing a painting with a commentary by the artist and with a commentary by a critic, and found "that critics' commentaries directed the viewers' attention to the visual components that were highly relevant to the presented commentary" (p. 1).

What is known about effects of labels with artworks within in a museum? Over the years, studies have revealed some interesting effects of information. Peart (1984) (for a review, see Bitgood & Patterson, 1993) demonstrated that an object with a label (not confined only to artworks but also considering other exhibits) generally produces a higher percentage of stopping and longer viewing times. Novitz (2001, p. 158) suggests that contemporary art installations typically involve overt qualities that either artist, or more often curator, "wish to have taken seriously," and thus use of labels may lead viewers to pay more attention or look for deeper meaning. This may be particularly relevant for certain (postmodern, conceptual) works. Viewing museum art with labels has also been shown to make visitors evaluate works more within the supporting context (Higgs, Polonsky, & Hollick, 2005). At the same time, studies have also shown that removal of labels may enhance enjoyment. Pekarik's (2004) study of a MoMA (Museum of Modern Art) modern sculpture exhibition, which included only basic identifications, revealed that "none" (p. 14) of the interviewed visitors pointed out the lack of extra information as a problem. A similar argument was made in the same study for more classical or mimetic art. Baber et al. (2001) showed that the inclusion of didactic content led to less careful observation and recall of a painting's physical elements, perhaps because viewers did not feel a need to search the art carefully (see the above-described elaboration, and effort effects). Thus, the use of labels within the museum is also a ripe target for psychological research.

The studies summarized here show the possible strengths of information presented with artworks. The advantage of these paradigms is the flexibility of information in the presented texts, its quality, and quantity. If necessary for the research question, participants can also be confronted with fabricated, theoretically relevant, but actually unnecessary authentic extra information.

Context as an Explicitly Instructed—Framed—Context

A different, though related way of testing the effects of context on aesthetic experience consists of an experimental manipulation known as framing. It has a strong anchoring in prospect theory, and is an example of a cognitive bias in which people react to a particular choice differently depending on how it is presented. The way material is presented usually is implemented by the way in which the task is introduced to the participants by the experimenter. In empirical aesthetics, one of the most basic, and perhaps most strongly impactful, aspects of contextual framing involves when an object is seen as "art" or not. This is not trivial. Recently, Pelowski, Gerger, Chetouani, Markey, and Leder (2017) showed how strongly this classification affects aesthetic processing, but also that, even with apparently painted artworks, perceivers do not automatically agree that they are seeing artworks.

A second, also very relevant, distinction related to the art vs. nonart classification is concerned with the origin of the stimulus. Whether something is designated as art, or nonart, as art or fake, or possibly a copy (Leder, 2003), or as made by man or machine, makes a huge difference. One of the most influential papers employing a systematic variation of designated origin through instructional framing was by Kirk, Skov, Hulme, Christensen, and Zeki (2009). They showed their participants the same images in one of two different, randomly assigned conditions, either as designated as artworks from an art gallery, or as a computer-generated pattern. Each participant saw half of the images with the word "computer," and the other half with the word "gallery." Images assigned to the gallery condition were appreciated significantly more. Moreover, the contextual variation showed clear effects in differences in activity in the medial orbitofrontal and the prefrontal cortex. Both contexts also had a main effect as they correlated with bilateral activations of the temporal pole and bilateral entorhinal cortex. The authors interpreted their findings as evidence for biases in aesthetic processing due to top-down induced expectations.

In a similar study, with only a few participants, Silveira, Fehse, Vedder, Elvers, and Henning-Fast (2015) framed a set of pictures of paintings that had been chosen from MoMA, preselected as not clearly being recognizable as high art, under two different framing instructions. Stimuli were designated as either artworks (from MoMA) or coming from an adult education center. Artworks seen under the museum art label condition elicited higher activity in the right precuneus, the bilateral anterior cingulate cortex, and the temporoparietal junction. Surprisingly, artworks were not rated higher when presented under the art frame, which raises the question of whether the main manipulation regarding induced value through framing was at all successful.

A slightly different approach was taken by Cupchik, Vartanian, Crawley, and Mikulis (2009). They also wanted to test what is different when images are seen as artworks.

However, they focused more on a special mode of processing, which they deemed aesthetic. In this case they instructed individuals to look at art, but to focus either on their subjective feelings and emotions elicited by the work (what they called the aesthetic context) or merely to identify what they saw (pragmatic). They found that in an aesthetic mode, bilateral insula activation was found, which Cupchik et al. (2009) attributed to the experience of emotion. "Moreover, while adopting the aesthetic orientation activated the left lateral prefrontal cortex, paintings that facilitated visuospatial exploration activated the left superior parietal lobule. The results suggest that aesthetic experience is a function of the interaction between top-down orienting of attention and bottom-up perceptual facilitation" (p. 84). Note, however, that some of the terminology in this study (focus on personal emotions and subjective feelings as "aesthetic") is rather out of line with other classical philosophical (e.g., Kantian) arguments of an aesthetic mode as a detached or personally distanced state of appreciation.

Gerger, Leder, and Kremer (2014), on the other hand, tested the idea that an aesthetic/art mode is marked by an emotional distancing effect in which emotions are experienced as weaker. They measured emotional responses (via fEMG face muscle activations) as well as emotion and aesthetic evaluations for photographic pictures of contemporary art as well as International Affective Picture System (IAPS) photos of positive or negative valence. Presented under two different framing instructions, as artworks or press photographs, it was found that positive emotional reactions indeed were attenuated (M. zygomaticus activation) in an art compared with a nonart context. Context had little influence on any measure of negative emotional reactions (ratings of anger, disgust, fear, sadness, shame; as well as M. corrugator activation). Most interestingly, only artworks with emotionally negative content were judged more positively in an art context. The authors concluded that the "study, in accordance with the assumption of a distanced aesthetic mode, shows that an art context fosters appraisal processes that influence emotional experiences, allowing to judge negative stimuli aesthetically more positively thus suppressing the immediacy of emotional stimulus content" (p. 174).

Wagner et al. (2016) conducted a very elaborate study to demonstrate differences in aesthetic emotions due to framing. They measured responses to anger in a real theater performance in a real theater space in Berlin that was systematically framed as either an aptitude test of a recruitment firm or as a theater performance. As predicted, self-reported emotions and measures of blood pressure were different between the scenarios, and supported the idea of an art-schema that elicits more positive feelings.

Another variation of framing a set of stimuli as art or nonart was used by Arai and Kawabata (2016) to study indirectly the subjective feeling of passed time or duration when looking at emotional images. Beyond the effects of context on aesthetic qualities, they measured context-dependent time perception with a temporal reproduction task (similar to Belke, Leder, & Augustin, 2006). Upon arrival at the laboratory, participants were assigned, covertly, either to a realistic photograph context condition or an artistic context condition. IAPS pictures were presented for one of three durations (2,500 ms, 4,500 ms, or 6,500 ms), and the participants were asked to reproduce their perceived (experienced) viewing time. An art context enhanced the judged pleasantness of the images. Context also affected the duration estimations, with longer time estimates in the realistic photographic context. The authors argued that "it can be deduced that the difference in time perception between *realistic* and *art contexts* is based on the different emotions and cognitive systems that people have for *art* and *realistic contexts*. Consequently, the question arises as to why perceived durations of the IAPS pictures were longer in the *realistic* compared to the *art context*" (p. 236).

Instructed framing—art, nonart, or fake

Whether a perceiver is made to believe that what he or she is going to see is a fake or a copy can also easily be manipulated through instruction, and affects other heuristic processes involved in aesthetic experiences. Leder (2001) presented the results of five studies in which the relationship between familiarity and liking for 54 reproductions of van Gogh paintings (presented in small scale on a computer screen) was investigated under different conditions of evaluation and information given about the paintings. The first two studies found positive correlations between liking and familiarity ratings even when it was possible that some of the stimuli seen were not original paintings. Such correlations were significantly reduced in a third and fourth study when the beholder was told that all stimuli were fakes of van Gogh paintings. In a fifth study the correlation was reduced when inspection time was increased. From these findings it was concluded that familiarity–liking relations are weakened by knowledge in a systematic way, and also that they are more pronounced in spontaneous judgments. Locher, Krupinski, and Schaefer (2015) also studied variations in beholders' belief about the authenticity of artworks. They labeled images of artworks shown to art experts and nonexperts as originals, copies, or fakes. For each artwork the authors measured eye movements and other parameters of perception and interpretation, and used scales for pleasantness, artistic merit, and potential monetary value. Analyses revealed that viewers' beliefs about the authenticity status of a painting were used as a contextual cue, directly and indirectly, for the various evaluations. However, findings regarding lengths and distribution of fixations showed mainly effects of expertise: art-educated people who saw differences focused on fewer areas of the overall paintings than those who did not see differences. Similar differences were not found for the different groups of naive viewers. Employing electroencephalogram (EEG), Noguchi and Murota (2013) showed that positive activation components measured over the parietal cortex 200–300 ms after stimulus onset were sensitive to art-fake title manipulation, artworks denoted as fakes or genuine, as well as visual deformation of images of sculptures.

Finally, an interesting functional magnetic resonance imaging (fMRI) study was conducted by Huang, Bridge, Kemp, and Parker (2011), in which Rembrandt paintings suggested to be originals and also works that had been determined to be copies, such as by other members of his workshop, were shown to participants. These were preceded by a cue that they were "an original" or "a copy." Those cued as authentic (vs. copies) resulted in higher activation of orbitofrontal areas of the brain that are associated with reward. Interestingly, this activation was found even before the actual painting was shown to a viewer—suggesting a priming of reward areas themselves ("this is going to be a positive experience"). Perhaps unsurprisingly, the actual historical status of the works did not have an effect on reactions. In the copy conditions on the other hand, higher activation was seen in visual areas, perhaps related to a participant's attempts to find the cues for the work's inauthenticity.

OTHER CONTEXT EFFECTS

Different from framing contexts through instruction, Gartus and Leder (2014) compared the appropriateness of a virtual context for two different kinds of art. They compared abstract paintings and graffiti or street art (carefully matched for complexity in prestudies), when images of these were either embedded in a museum context or in an urban street setting. Moreover, they measured individual variation in interest in art and graffiti art with a questionnaire. A positive attitude toward either kind of art had strong effects on evaluations of the stimuli. Those participants with high interest in graffiti art showed stronger positive emotional responses to art presented in a street context as compared with museums. This study is a demonstration that the visual representation of a context produces clear effects on aesthetic evaluations; however, these effects are modulated by individual attitudes. In a follow-up study, Gartus and Leder (2015) again found an interaction of context and individual interest in graffiti for beauty ratings and interest ratings. They also found a main effect of context on exploration (eye movements), with generally longer viewing times in museum than in urban street contexts.

Many more versions of context could be discussed: for example, context effects in terms of assimilation or contrast, as in Tousignant and Bodner (2014); or for abstract patterns as in Tinio and Leder (2009); interactions between artworks, paintings, images, and music (see Marin & Leder, 2013, 2018); or the effects of contexts on the perception and (aesthetic) appreciation of consumer products (Bliijlevens, Gemser, & Mugge, 2012; da Silva, Crilly, & Hekkert, 2015); as well as the many studies that have shown how internal, acquired knowledge, such as expertise, affects aesthetic experiences.

MAJOR CHALLENGES, GOALS, AND SUGGESTIONS

In this chapter, we put a strong focus on context as information available or framing suggested by instructions, as well as participants' knowledge. The systematic use of these manipulations produced interesting results and revealed that an aesthetic context changes how people process emotions (Gerger et al., 2014), experience duration of episodes (Arai & Kawabata, 2016), or show different brain activities when being exposed to artworks (Kirk et al., 2009). However, in art-related sciences, context very typically is understood as the museum space or any other physical environment. In the museum context art is often accompanied by supporting "extra-exhibit media" (Bitgood, 1992; Griswold, Mangione, & McDonnell, 2013), including texts and labels, but also catalog copy, maps, and audio guides. Increasingly, viewing is augmented with digital technology (interactive apps, social media sharing, guides linked to geolocation; see Baber et al., 2001). These of course provide interesting topics for future research.

When we return to our introduction, then, the strong role that context has in aesthetic experiences challenges the formalist statements provided by Clive Bell (1914) when he asked "What quality is shared by all objects that provoke our aesthetic emotions?" and answered "In each, lines and colours combined in a particular way, certain forms and relations of forms, stir our aesthetic emotions" (Bell, 1914, p. 8), and that "Great art remains stable and unobscure because the feelings that it awakens are independent of time and place … " (Bell, 1914, p. 37).[1] In light of the studies discussed above, we illustrate that such a formalist view can rightfully be rejected. We might instead refer to John Dewey's statement that "experience is a matter of the interaction of organism with its environment, an environment that is human as well as physical, that includes the materials of tradition and institutions as well as local surroundings" (Dewey, 1934, p. 256). One of the main challenges—and positive adventures—for empirical aesthetics remains the transition from the laboratory into the field. Toward that end, the future will see many more ways of exploring art and aesthetic experiences in increasingly natural and complex environments.

ACKNOWLEDGMENTS

We thank Eva Specker and Michael Forster for their feedback and support in writing this chapter. The writing of this chapter was supported by a grant WWTF CS18-021 FusLed and EU Horizon 2020 TRANSFORMATIONS-17-2019, Societal Challenges and the Arts (870827 — ARTIS, Art and Research on Transformations of Individuals of Society) to MP.

NOTE

1. Cited in Leder and Nadal (2014) in their section "Out into the real world: The challenging role of context."

REFERENCES

Arai, S. & Kawabata, H. (2016). Appreciation contexts modulate aesthetic evaluation and perceived duration of pictures. *Art & Perception, 4*(3), 225–239.
Baber, C., Bristow, H., Cheng, S.-L., Hedley, A., Kuriyama, Y., Lien, M., … Sorrell, P. (2001). *Augmenting museums and art galleries.* Paper presented at the 13rd Conference on Human-Computer Interaction—Interact. Lisbon, Portugal.

Belke, B., Leder, H., & Augustin, D. (2006). Mastering style – Effects of explicit style-related information, art knowledge and affective state on appreciation of abstract paintings. *Psychology Science, 48*, 115–134.

Belke, B., Leder, H., Harsanyi, G., & Carbon, C. C. (2010). When a Picasso is a "Picasso": The entry point in the identification of visual art. *Acta Psychologica, 133*(2), 191–202.

Belke, B., Leder, H., Strobach, T., & Carbon, C. C. (2010). Cognitive fluency: High-level processing dynamics in art appreciation. *Psychology of Aesthetics, Creativity, and the Arts, 4*(4), 214–222.

Bell, C. (1914). *Art*. New York: Frederick A. Stokes Company.

Berlyne, D. E., & Ogilvie, J. C. (1974). Dimensions of perception of paintings. In D. E. Berlyne (Ed.), *Studies in the new experimental aesthetics: Steps toward an objective psychology of aesthetic appreciation* (pp. 181–226). Washington, D. C.: Hemisphere Publishing Corporation.

Blijlevens, J., Gemser, G., & Mugge, R. (2012). The importance of being "well-placed": The influence of context on perceived typicality and esthetic appraisal of product appearance. *Acta Psychologica, 139*(1), 178–186. https://doi.org/10.1016/j.actpsy.2011.11.004

Bitgood, S. (1992). The anatomy of an exhibit. *Visitor Behavior, 7*, 4–15.

Bitgood, S., & Patterson, D. D. (1993). The effects of gallery changes on visitor reading and object viewing time. *Environment and Behavior, 25*, 761–781.

Bruce, V., Carson, D., Burton, A. M., & Kelly, S. (1998). Prime time advertisements: Repetition priming from faces seen on subject recruitment posters. *Memory & Cognition, 26*(3), 502–515.

Bruce, V., & Young, A. W. (1986). Understanding face recognition. *British Journal of Psychology, 77*, 305–327.

Bubić, A., Sušac, A., & Palmović, M. (2017). Observing individuals viewing art: The effects of titles on viewers' eye-movement profiles. *Empirical Studies of the Arts, 35*(2), 194–213. https://doi.org/10.1177/0276237416683499

Burton, A. M., Schweinberger, S. R., Jenkins, R., & Kaufmann, J. M. (2015). Arguments against a configural processing account of familiar face recognition. *Perspectives on Psychological Science, 10*(4), 482–496.

Chatterjee, A., & Vartanian, O. (2014). Neuroaesthetics. *Trends in Cognitive Psychology, 18*(7), 370–375. https://doi.org/10.1016/j.tics.2014.03.003

Clark, A. (2013). Whatever next? Predictive brains, situated agents, and the future of cognitive science. *Behavioral and Brain Sciences, 36*, 181–204.

Cupchik, G., Sherek, L., & Spiegel, S. (1994). The effects of textual information on artistic communication. *Visual Arts Research, 20*, 62–78.

Cupchik, G. C., Vartanian, O., Crawley, A., & Mikulis, D. J. (2009). Viewing artworks: Contributions of cognitive control and perceptual facilitation to aesthetic experience. *Brain and Cognition, 70*(1), 84–91. http://doi.org/10.1016/j.bandc.2009.01.003

Da Silva, O., Crilly, N., & Hekkert, P. (2015). How people's appreciation of products is affected by their knowledge of the designers' intentions. *International Journal of Design, 9*(2), 21–33.

Dewey, J. (1934). *Art as experience*. New York: Minton, Balch & Company.

Fodor, J. A. (1983). *Modularity of mind: An essay on faculty psychology*. Cambridge, MA: MIT Press.

Franklin, M. B., Becklen, R. C., & Doyle, C. L. (1993). The influence of titles on how paintings are seen. *Leonardo, 26*, 103–108.

Funch, B. S., Krøyer, L. L., Roald, T., & Wildt, E. (2012). Long-term effect of aesthetic education on visual awareness. *Journal of Aesthetic Education, 46*(4), 96–108.

Gartus, A., & Leder, H. (2014). The white cube of the museum versus the grey cubes of the street: The role of context in aesthetic judgments. *Psychology of Aesthetics, Creativity, and the Arts, 8*(3), 311–320. doi:10.1037/a0036847

Gartus, A., & Leder, H. (2015). The effects of visual context and individual differences on perception and evaluation of modern art and graffiti art. *Acta Psychologica, 156*, 64–76. http://dx.doi.org/10.1016/j.actpsy.2015.01.005

Gerger, G., & Leder, H. (2015). Titles change the aesthetic appreciations of paintings. *Frontiers in Human Neuroscience, 9*, 464. doi: 10.3389/fnhum.2015.00464

Gerger, G., Leder, H., & Kremer, A. (2014). Context effects on emotional and aesthetic evaluations of artworks and IAPS pictures. *Acta Psychologica, 151*, 174–183. doi:10.1016/j.actpsy.2014.06.008

Gibson, J. J. (1979). *The ecological approach to visual perception.* Boston, MA: Houghton Mifflin.

Gombrich, E. H. (1960). *Art and illusion.* Princeton, NJ: Princeton University Press.

Grainger, J., O'Regan, J. K., Jacobs, A. M., & Segui, J. (1989). On the role of competing word units in visual word recognition: The neighborhood frequency effect. *Perception & Psychophysics, 45*(3), 189–195.

Griswold, W., Mangione, G., & McDonnell, T. E. (2013). Objects, words, and bodies in space: Bringing materiality into cultural analysis. *Qualitative Sociology, 36*, 343–364.

Helmholtz, H. (1867). *Handbuch der physiologischen Optik.* Leipzig, Germany: Leo Voss.

Higgs, B., Polonsky, M. J., & Hollick, M. (2005). Measuring expectations: Forecast vs. ideal expectations. Does it really matter? *Journal of Retailing and Consumer Services, 12*, 49–64.

Hristova, E., Georgieva, S., & Grinberg, M. (2011). Top-down influences on eye-movements during painting perception: The effect of task and titles. In A. Esposito et al. (Eds.), *COST 2102 International Training School 2010 (Toward autonomous, adaptive, and context-aware multimodal interfaces: Theoretical and practical issues)*, LNCS 6456 (pp. 104–115). Heidelberg: Springer.

Huang, M., Bridge, H., Kemp, M. J., & Parker, A. J. (2011). Human cortical activity evoked by the assignment of authenticity when viewing works of art. *Frontiers in Human Neuroscience, 5*, 134.

Jakesch, M., & Leder, H. (2009). Finding meaning in art: Preferred levels of ambiguity in art appreciation. *The Quarterly Journal of Experimental Psychology, 62*(11), 2105–2112.

Jucker, J. L., Barrett, J. L., & Wlodarski, R. (2014). "I just don't get it": Perceived artists' intentions affect art evaluations. *Empirical Studies of the Arts, 32*(2), 149–182.

Kapoula, Z., Daunys, G., Herbez, O., & Yang, Q. (2009). Effect of title on eye-movement exploration of cubist paintings by Fernand Léger. *Perception, 38*, 479–491.

Kirk, U., Skov, M., Hulme, O., Christensen, M. S., & Zeki, S. (2009). Modulation of aesthetic value by semantic context: An fMRI study. *NeuroImage, 44*, 1125–1132.

Leder, H. (2001). Determinants of preference. When do we like what we know? *Empirical Studies of the Arts, 19*(2), 201–212.

Leder, H. (2003). Familiar and fluent! Style-related processing hypotheses in aesthetic appreciation. *Empirical Studies of the Arts, 21*(2), 165–175.

Leder, H., Belke, B., Oeberst, A., & Augustin, D. (2004). A model of aesthetic appreciation and aesthetic judgements. *British Journal of Psychology, 95*(4), 489–508.

Leder, H., & Bruce, V. (2000). When inverted faces are recognized: The role of configural information in face recognition. *The Quarterly Journal of Experimental Psychology Section A, 53*(2), 513–536.

Leder, H., Carbon, C. C., & Ripsas, A. (2006). Entitling art: Influence of different types of title information on understanding and appreciation of paintings. *Acta Psychologica*, *121*(2), 176–198.

Leder, H., Mitrovic, A., & Goller, J. (2016). How beauty determines gaze! Facial attractiveness and gaze duration in images of real world scenes. *i-Perception*, *7*(4). doi:10.1177/2041669516664355

Leder, H., & Nadal, M. (2014). Ten years of a model of aesthetic appreciation and aesthetic judgments: The aesthetic episode—Developments and challenges in empirical aesthetics. *British Journal of Psychology*, *105*(4), 443–464. doi:10.1111/bjop.12084

Leder, H., Tinio, P. T., Fuchs, I., & Bohrn, I. (2010). When attractiveness demands longer looks: The effects of situation and gender. *Quarterly Journal of Experimental Psychology*, *63*(9), 1858–1871.

Locher, P., Krupinski, E., & Schaefer, A. (2015). Art and authenticity: Behavioral and eye-movement analyses. *Psychology of Aesthetics, Creativity, and the Arts*, *9*(4), 356–367.

Marin, M., & Leder, H. (2013). Examining complexity across domains: Relating subjective and objective measures of affective environmental scenes, paintings and music. *PLoS ONE*, *8*(8), e72412.

Marin, M., & Leder H. (2018). Exploring aesthetic experiences of females: Affect-related traits predict complexity and arousal responses to music and affective pictures. *Personality and Individual Differences*, *125*, 80–90. https://doi.org/10.1016/j.paid.2017.12.027

Mastandrea, S., & Umiltà, M. A. (2016). Futurist art: Motion and aesthetics as a function of title. *Frontiers in Human Neuroscience*, *10*, Article 201. https://doi.org/10.3389/fnhum.2016.00201

Millis, K. (2001). Making meaning brings pleasure: The influence of titles on aesthetic experiences. *Emotion*, *1*, 320–329.

Noguchi, Y., & Murota, M. (2013). Temporal dynamics of neural activity in an integration of visual and contextual information in an esthetic preference task. *Neuropsychologia*, *51*(6), 1077–1084. doi:10.1016/j.neuropsychologia.2013.03.003.

Novitz, D. (2001). Participatory art and appreciative practice. *The Journal of Aesthetics and Art Criticism*, *59*, 153–165.

Oliva, A., & Torralba, A. (2006). Building the gist of a scene: The role of global image features in recognition. *Progress in Brain Research*, *155*, 23–36.

Park, S. A., Yun, K., & Jeong, J. (2015). Reappraising abstract paintings after exposure to background information. *PLoS ONE*, *10*(5), e0124159. https://doi.org/10.1371/journal.pone.0124159

Peart, B. O. B. (1984). Impact of exhibit type on knowledge gain, attitudes, and behavior. *Curator*, *27*, 220–237.

Pekarik, A. J. (2004). To explain or not to explain. *Curator*, *47*, 12–18.

Pelowski, M., Forster, M., Tinio, P., Scholl, M., & Leder, H. (2017). Beyond the lab: An examination of key factors influencing interaction with "real" and museum-based art. *Psychology of Aesthetics, Creativity, and the Arts*, *11*(3), 245–264. doi:10.1037/aca0000141

Pelowski, M., Gerger, G., Chetouani, Y., Markey, P., & Leder, H. (2017). But is it really art? The classification of images as "art"/"not art" and correlation with appraisal and viewer interpersonal differences. *Frontiers in Psychology*, *8*, 1729. https://doi.org/10.3389/fpsyg.2017.01729

Pelowski, M., Markey, P., Forster, M., Gerger, G., & Leder, H. (2017). Move me, astonish me … delight my eyes and brain: The Vienna Integrated Model of top-down and bottom-up processes in Art Perception (VIMAP) and corresponding affective, evaluative and neurophysiological correlates. *Physics of Life Reviews*, *21*, 80–125. https://doi.org/10.1016/j.plrev.2017.02.003

Reber, R., Schwarz, N., & Winkielman, P. (2004). Processing fluency and aesthetic pleasure: Is beauty in the perceiver's processing experience? *Personality and Social Psychology Review, 8,* 364–382. https://doi.org/10.1207/s15327957pspr0804_3

Rosch, E. H., Mervis, C. B., Gray, W. D., Johnson, D. M., & Boyes-Braem, P. (1976). Basic objects in natural categories. *Cognitive Psychology, 8*(3), 382–439. doi:10.1016/0010-0285(76)90013-X

Russell, P. A., & Milne, S. (1997). Meaningfulness and hedonic value of paintings: Effects of titles. *Empirical Studies of the Arts, 15*(1), 61–73. https://doi.org/10.2190/EHT3-HWVM-52CB-8QHJ

Samanian, K., Nedaeifar, H., & Karinimi, M. (2016). A survey on the influence of titles on the visitor's interpretation and learning in art galleries: An Iranian context. *Australian Journal of Adult Learning, 56*(1), 29.

Shimojo, S., Simion, C., Shimojo, E., & Scheier, C. (2003). Gaze bias both reflects and influences preference. *Nature Neuroscience, 6,* 1317–1322.

Silveira, S., Fehse, K., Vedder, A., Elvers, K., & Hennig-Fast, K. (2015). Is it the picture or is it the frame? An fMRI study on the neurobiology of framing effects. *Frontiers in Human Neuroscience, 9,* 528. https://doi.org/10.3389/fnhum.2015.00528

Smith, L. F., Smith, J. K., Arcand, K. K., Smith, R. K., & Bookbinder, J. A. (2015). Aesthetics and astronomy: How museum labels affect the understanding and appreciation of deep-space images. *Curator: The Museum Journal, 58*(3), 282–297.

Smith, L. F., Smith, J. K., & Tinio, P. P. L. (2017) Time spent viewing art and reading labels. *Psychology of Aesthetics, Creativity, and the Art, 11*(1), 77–85. https://doi.org/10.1037/aca0000049

Stojilovic, I., & Markovic, S. (2014). Evaluation of paintings: Effects of lectures. *Psihologija, 47*(4), 415–432.

Swami, V. (2013). Context matters: Investigating the impact of contextual information on aesthetic appreciation of paintings by Max Ernst and Pablo Picasso. *Psychology of Aesthetics, Creativity, and the Art, 7*(3), 285–296.

Tanaka, J. W., & Taylor, M. (1991). Object categories and expertise: Is the basic level in the eye of the beholder? *Cognitive Psychology, 23*(3), 457–482.

Tinio, P. P. T., & Leder, H. (2009). Just how stable are aesthetic features? Symmetry, Complexity and the jaws of massive familiarization. *Acta Psychologica, 130*(3), 241–250.

Tousignant, C., & Bodner, G. E. (2014). Context effects on beauty ratings of photos: Building contrast effects that erode but cannot be knocked down. *Psychology of Aesthetics, Creativity, and the Arts, 8*(1), 81–86. https://doi.org/10.1037/a0034942

Tröndle, M., & Tschacher, W. (2012). The physiology of phenomenology: The effects of artworks. *Empirical Studies of the Arts, 30,* 75–113.

Wagner, V., Klein, J., Hanich, J., Shah, M., Menninghaus, W., & Jacobsen, T. (2016). Anger framed: A field study on emotion, pleasure, and art. *Psychology of Aesthetics, Creativity, and the Arts, 10*(2), 134–146. doi:10.1037/aca0000029

Warren, C., & Morton, J. (1982). The effects of priming on picture recognition. *British Journal of Psychology, 73,* 117–129.

Wundt, W. (1908). *Völkerpsychologie: Eine Untersuchung der Entwicklungsgesetze von Sprache, Mythus und Sitte. Dritter Band: Die Kunst.* Neu bearbeitete Auflage. Leipzig, Germany: Wilhelm Engelmann.

CHAPTER 41

STUDYING EMPIRICAL AESTHETICS IN MUSEUM CONTEXTS

JEFFREY K. SMITH AND LISA F. SMITH

NOBODY goes to an art museum to participate in a research study.

And yet, if we are to study aesthetics as aesthetic experience actually happens, we must go to the art museum, because that is where the vast majority of what we traditionally think of as aesthetic experience takes place. That being said, we agree with Dewey (1958) that art occurs throughout life as we use objects with decorations or admire the design of our automobile. The buildings and parks we encounter as we commute into work in the morning provide more aesthetic encounters (Livi Smith, 2014), but fundamentally people seek out aesthetic experience in art museums. They do so deliberately, and for a variety of reasons (Falk, 2009; Pekarik, Doering, & Karns, 1999; Pekarik & Schreiber, 2012; Smith & Wolf, 1996; Tinio, Smith, & Smith, 2014). They do not stumble into an art museum; their visit was almost always planned and often greatly anticipated. And so, as ornithologists of the elusive speckled aesthete, to study our prey we must travel to the natural habitat of the lover of paintings and sculptures—the art museum. It is where the psychology of aesthetics takes place.

THE ART MUSEUM AND THE PSYCHOLOGY LABORATORY

It would be hard to imagine two institutions less similar than an art museum and a psychological research laboratory. The director of the Metropolitan Museum of Art once described aesthetics as "the delectation of the eye" (de Montebello, 1988, personal communication). The purpose of an art museum is to provide objects of beauty, provocation, and stimulation, and to allow for contemplation (Carr, 2006, 2011), and restoration (Kaplan, Bardwell, & Slakter, 1993; Packer & Bond, 2010). The purpose of a psychological research laboratory is to provide the environment and equipment required to study the nature of the mind, human behavior, cognition, emotion, etc. They both have their place in society, but no one would confuse one for the other. And so, it can be difficult to see how one might substitute one for the other. Can we really study what happens in an art museum with people who are in a psychological laboratory? A corollary question is: Do we have to? Can we study the psychology of aesthetics in a museum setting instead of a laboratory setting? For us, the answer is a firm: "somewhat and sometimes." The remainder of this chapter is devoted to looking at what can (and to a lesser degree, what cannot) be studied with regard to the psychology of aesthetics in an art museum, and how one would go about doing it. We explore the fundamental nature of the differences between the museum and the laboratory in terms of what they allow and prohibit, and then walk through the aspects of a research study, looking at what can and cannot be done in art museum research and how one would go about conducting such research where it is possible.

How Art Museums and Research Laboratories Differ

Perhaps the two biggest differences between art museums and psychological laboratories are that art museums have art and psychological laboratories have equipment. To a degree, we can overcome such limitations, but only to a degree. Locher, Smith, and Smith (1999) demonstrated that participants saw real artworks in a museum in a roughly similar fashion to seeing the same works on a computer or on slides in a lecture room, although their clear preference was for the real thing. They coined the term *facsimile accommodation* to describe the fact that when discussing works, participants focused on the art rather than the medium through which they were seeing the art. Although all their participants were actually *in* an art museum, their findings indicated that, to a degree, reproductions of works of art can be used effectively in aesthetics research, depending on what is being studied.

Conversely, Tröndle and his colleagues, in a highly innovative series of studies, have shown that one can bring technology into the museum in an effective fashion (Tröndle & Tschacher, 2012; Tröndle, Greenwood, Kirchberg, & Tschacher, 2014). Their equipment was unobtrusive and did not appear to affect the nature of the visit, but it was limited to recording location, heart rate, and skin response.

There are other differences as well, and important ones. Art museums are designed to be places of contemplation and inspiration. Psychological laboratories are designed to be stimulus-neutral. Consider a psych lab in comparison with Musée D'Orsay or the Guggenheim Museum. Even without the art, the buildings are awe-inspiring; whereas, the lab is likely to be four white walls, possibly without windows. Next, populate the different institutions with their natural objects and inhabitants. In one you have machinery of various sorts, people—possibly in lab coats (the staff)—and university students (participants). In the other you have great works of art, guides and guards (the staff), and people from all walks of life who share a common love of art (participants). In making these comparisons, we note that we are great fans of aesthetic research carried out in laboratory settings. We are learning a tremendous amount about psychological reactions to art via groundbreaking laboratory research into aesthetics (see e.g., Cela-Conde, Agnati, Huston, Mora, & Nadal, 2011 or Chatterjee & Vartanian, 2014, for excellent summaries of research on neuroaesthetics). It's just that they are not as appealing an environment as an art museum.

We have painted a picture that would seem to deliberately favor conducting research in an art museum, but as we shall see, it is fraught with difficulties and limitations, only some of which can be overcome. We now examine the conduct of aesthetic research in art museums, occasionally contrasting it with what can and cannot be done in more controlled (laboratory) settings.

Conducting Aesthetic Research in Art Museums

As mentioned above, we structure the main component of this chapter using the headings one would expect to find in a typical journal article: Questions and Hypotheses, Participants, Designs, and Interpretation.

Questions and Hypotheses

The first stop in this journey through the conduct of research on aesthetics in art museums has to do with questions asked and/or hypotheses posed. There is an incredibly wide variety of research questions that can be asked within the confines of an art museum (or any museum for that matter). They are rich with possibilities; in fact, there is a field called *museology*, a Visitor Studies Association dedicated to research in museums and similar institutions,[1] scholarly volumes published on the topic (see e.g., Macdonald, 2006), and at least three journals devoted to the topic, *Journal of Museum Studies*, *Visitor Studies*, and *Curator*. To get an idea of the kinds of issues that might be studied in art museums, it would be useful to look at Silvia (2009), or L. F. Smith (2014).

However, many of the questions one finds addressed in such venues are only tangentially related to the topic of interest here: the empirical study of aesthetics. We can learn who visits museums and why, how long they stay, what kinds of museums they prefer, how they learn about museums, how their experiences online affect what they see and do in a subsequent museum visit, who they are with, and how they construct their visits. But are these questions really about aesthetics, about how people look at art, how they react to it, and how they process and make sense of it? Those are the underlying questions of empirical aesthetics research, and only some of them can be studied with any rigor in an art museum setting.

Empirical research on aesthetics in recent years has seen some important work in terms of presenting conceptual and theoretical models of how the fundamental notion of aesthetics works. Housen (1983) and Parsons (1987) presented some early offerings in this regard, taking a Piagetian perspective on how individuals develop the ability to appreciate art. Their models were based on interviews with visitors to art museums, and their findings and theories provided the basis for some of the more recent efforts. But most of the models in this area today focus on what happens when an individual encounters a work of art. Chatterjee (2014), Locher, Overbeeke, and Wensveen (2010), Leder, Belke, Oeberst, and Augustin, (2004), Tinio (2013), and J. K. Smith (2014b) all have provided theoretical models on how individuals understand, perceive, and react to works of art and other artistic endeavors (such as functional objects built with an artistic perspective). On a somewhat different tack, Camic and Chatterjee (2013) examined how art museums can be beneficial to individuals suffering from mental health issues. Each provides insight into how we might inquire about aesthetics, what we might ask, and how we should interpret results. But as we ask those questions, we start to come to grips with very fundamental issues in conducting empirical research in art museums, as well as outside of art museums. Those are best explored by examining the nature of the conduct of such research.

Participants

The opening sentence in this chapter lays out one of the basic issues in empirical aesthetics: whom do we study? If we recruit volunteers for a study to be conducted in a research laboratory, we may or may not get participants who are interested in art. To be sure, we can screen art lovers in (or out) through preliminary assessments. But as our participants enter the laboratory, we know one thing for certain: they are not visitors who have chosen to enter an art museum. They did not arrive at their current destination to partake of artistic genius. They came because the potential reward (financial or course credit) was sufficiently of value to them, or, absent reward, because they are good citizens willing to help out by volunteering to participate. But, and this is critical, they are not seeking out an aesthetic experience. And that makes them fundamentally, and importantly, different from another person who is walking into an art museum at the same time. On the other hand, the person walking into the art museum is not seeking out participation in an empirical study. That person *is* seeking an aesthetic experience (in the vast majority of cases).

Is there a "proper" participant for empirical research in aesthetics? Is it the person who is eager for an aesthetic experience (Dewey, 1958; Jackson, 1998), or the person meeting a course requirement by participating in an experiment? We know that art experts and novices differ on a number of dimensions in looking at art (Hekkert & van Wieringen, 1996). We know that visitors to different kinds of museums have different goals, and often different personality characteristics (Mastandrea, Bartoli, & Bove, 2009; Smith, Wolf, & Staradoubtsev, 1994). We also know that viewing works in an art museum versus a lab setting will produce different reactions to those works (Brieber, Nadal, & Leder, 2015; Brieber, Nadal, Leder, & Rosenberg, 2014). This research, in conjunction with the earlier work of Locher, Smith, and Smith (1999, 2001) affirms our speculation that there "is nothing like the real thing." Interestingly, the Brieber et al. (2014) study was conducted with psychology students, and the Locher et al. (1999) study was conducted with visitors to the Metropolitan Museum of Art. The findings of the two veins of research suggest at least some level of similarity between art museum visitors who are recruited to participate in a study, and nonvisitors who go to an art museum as part of a study.

But the question remains: Whose aesthetic experience? What are we trying to explain? Are we interested in studying people as they are seeking out an aesthetic experience? Or, do we want to look at research participants whom we try to assign to an aesthetic experience? It seems that the very fact that we identify something as art causes a very different set of reactions in our brain than if we perceive it as an everyday object (Cupchik, Vartanian, Crawley, & Mikulis, 2009).

The question of whose aesthetic experience is not only a challenge, it is also an opportunity. When conducting research in museums (or anywhere, for that matter), one always has to ask: who is likely to be able to provide an answer to this question? The authors of this chapter spent over 30 years conducting empirical research at the Metropolitan Museum of Art and other major cultural institutions. The questions that arose in working with those institutions often required hard thinking about who might be able to provide an answer. For example, if we wanted to know how we could increase the attendance at a given museum, then interviewing the people *in the museum* could not really provide all the information we wanted. We could certainly find out why the people who came to the museum did so, but in essence, the museum already had them! We wanted to talk to people who thought about coming to the museum, but didn't. Those were the people on the cusp of a visit. We came to call them "cuspers," after a suggestion from our Met colleague, Harold Holzer. What could the museum do to entice them to step over the line and make a visit? Going out into the public to find cuspers would be next to impossible, so how could we get useful information that would speak to the museum's interest in increasing attendance? Well, perhaps the next best group would be first-time visitors to the museum. Until they made that first visit, they were exactly the group that we wanted. So, we interviewed a large sample of people "coming in the door" and segmented out the responses of first-time visitors for special attention and analysis. They were as close as we could get to the people who had the information we were seeking.

Can undergraduate university students tell us what we want to know about aesthetic experience? In some cases yes, in others, we simply have to go to a museum. And then we are faced with the challenge of recruiting participants for our study. But to a degree, that is not quite as hard as it seems. People who come to visit a museum have a positive affinity toward the museum as they enter. They chose this place. They might even be members. If approached properly, they are often willing to help out. Another key issue in recruiting participants in museum research is who is doing the asking. We have found that some individuals who have worked for us as "research volunteers" have an incredible ability to get people to participate, while others are much less successful. We even differ between the two of us in our ability to do so!

Designs

Once one has a question to ask and has determined whom the participants for the study will be, there is the question of how to design the study. Very broadly, this can be conceptualized as an issue of how to organize a set of circumstances that will allow the researcher to observe the phenomenon of interest and to control for as many extraneous variables as possible (Schauble, Leinhardt, & Martin, 1997; Yalowitz & Bronnenkant, 2009). For example, if one is interested in how families interact in an art museum, one could simply carefully observe a number of family groups as they make their visits. Alternatively, one could interview families after they have visited the museum, or could connect family visitors with recording devices and record their conversations in front of objects (Knutson & Crowley, 2010). Another approach would be to offer some families the opportunity to use a program designed to enhance adult–child interactions in the museum (Tolmie, Benford, Greenhalgh, Rodden, & Reeves, 2014). This could be part of a randomized design to compare the efficacy of the program with what occurs without the program. Each is a valid approach; each has strengths and weaknesses. There have been a variety of ways to classify research approaches over the years; it might be useful to think about studying aesthetics in art museums using the following approaches: observation, questionnaire/interview/focus group, and experimental/quasi-experimental.

Observation

As the sagacious Yogi Berra once said, "You can observe a lot by just watching" (Gorman, 2015). And you can. Much, perhaps most research done in art museums is observational in nature. But that does not mean just wandering around seeing what people are up to, although that can, at times, be productive. Most observational studies are carefully conceptualized and designed, and executed in a rigorous fashion in order to answer a specific research question. Such research can be very straightforward and unobtrusive, or it can be highly complex, and, well, substantially intrusive. On the unobtrusive side, Smith and Smith (2001), and Smith, Smith, and Tinio (2017) asked the relatively straightforward question, "How long do people look at a work of art?" They observed a sample of people looking at masterpieces in the Metropolitan Museum of

Art in 2001 and then replicated that study at the Art Institute of Chicago in 2017. Their studies consisted of positioning themselves near works of art and timing the visitors as they came to look at the works. By the way, the mean in the first study was roughly 27s and in the second study 25s. The longest anyone looked in either study (total $n = 600$) was 3min, 48s.

On the other end of the spectrum, researchers have fitted participants with light-weight eye movement cameras and observed how they view works of art in a museum setting (Heidenreich & Turano, 2011). And in a series of studies, Tröndle and his colleagues have tracked large samples of visitors throughout their museum visit via a glove that was wired to record location, heart rate, and skin response as they looked at works of art. They also had the participants respond to measures before and after their visits (Tröndle et al., 2014; Tröndle & Tschacher, 2012). The more the ability to bring sophisticated equipment into the museum setting without creating a disturbance for the general audience increases, the more we will see a blending of techniques that were formerly limited to the research laboratory.

Questionnaire/Interview/Focus Group/Comment Books

One of the most common approaches to empirical aesthetic research in museums utilizes questionnaires or interviews. Focus groups are also popular, but questionnaires and interviews dominate. Classic examples of interviews are Housen's (1983) work on creating a developmental theory of how individuals look at art, and Csikszentmihalyi and Robinson's (1990) extensive interview study with museum professionals on how they look at art. Smith and Carr (2001) took a somewhat novel approach to an interview study by having six researchers independently interview samples of visitors to an exhibition of Byzantine art at the Metropolitan Museum of Art. They also analyzed their interviews independently, and then shared their findings to come up with an overall set of results.

Although we have included questionnaires under the heading of Design, it is important to note that they are measures as well as approaches, and could just as easily have been listed under "Measures and data-gathering techniques." The general approach with questionnaires is to sample a number of people who fit the category of participants one wants to study, and then administer a series of questions in written form. Although we don't have the space here to go into a detailed discussion of how to construct questionnaires, several pieces of advice particular to using questionnaires in museums might be useful, as we have done literally hundreds of such questionnaires in our careers:

- Don't make the questionnaire too long. People will give you some time, but not a whole lot of time. We always tried to make our questionnaires one page front and back, at most.
- People don't mind ticking boxes, but they don't like to write a lot.

- People don't like to take tests. Be very careful not to make your questionnaire into a test. Better to ask people if they know something rather than pose it as a question to be answered.
- Be cautious with using questions about future behavior. People are much better at telling you what they've done than what they will do.
- Don't write too much. People will give you about 30% of their attention while answering a questionnaire. If you have an explanation of how to respond that is four sentences long, people are likely to just skim through it. Be as brief as possible while still being clear.

Some people think of interviews as oral versions of questionnaires; we do not. Interviews have some real advantages and disadvantages with respect to questionnaires. Interviews allow for in-depth exploration of ideas, for the thrust of the interview to change to new and interesting directions, and for follow-up explorations and examination of ideas—none of which is possible with the use of questionnaires. Also, one is far less likely to have an interviewee misinterpret a question in an interview as such behavior can be identified and corrected quickly. On the other hand, interviews typically mean that far fewer individuals can be sampled in a study, and that there is more potential for bias in the sample, as most potential participants are less amenable to agreeing to an interview than to filling out a questionnaire.

Focus groups have become a popular research approach in the past 20 years, and are popular within the museum community, as well. We have used focus groups to examine the difference in how astrophysicists look at art and at astrophysical images (deep space pictures) as compared with members of the lay public (Smith et al., 2011). But generally, looking at empirical research in *aesthetics* (as opposed to general research about visitation in art museums), the focus group approach might not the best alternative, as it is better geared toward the attitudes of a group than of individuals.

Finally in this category, we include "comment book" as an approach. Although there are a number of problems with comment books (only people who choose to do so fill them in, many comments are just silliness, and the researcher has no idea who the respondent is), there is a reason for using them. Why? Because they can be a source of insight for future investigation. Comment books are simply books of blank pages that are left at the end of an exhibition or at some other prominent place in the museum, where people can write in what they wish. Sometimes we would prompt the visitor with a question at the top of the blank page such as, "If the curator for this exhibition were here, what question would you have for him/her?" Among comments about lighting, crowding, and cost of the art (very popular), we once received this question in an exhibition of dress during the time of Napoleon: "What did twelve-year old girls wear in the age of Napoleon?" We found that question incredibly moving (J. K. Smith, 2014b), as did the curator. It was one that got right at the heart of what we believe to be an important question of aesthetics: What does this mean to me? Where do I fit in here? It is a question that we have pursued in a host of fashions over the years, and it came from a comment book. There is a lot of what researchers call "dross" (useless material) in comment books, but then there is the occasional gem. It doesn't matter how many people say it, a single utterance can be truly insightful.

Measures and Data-Gathering Techniques

How people react to works of art is a fundamentally difficult issue to address. Those reactions are not on open display, although Pelowski (2015) has argued that crying is a reasonable response to art, even to painting. More typically, however, to assess someone's reaction to a work of art, we need to ask the person about it. We need to have people tell us what their reactions are, as we cannot assess those reactions directly, as we can for such variables as time spent in front of a painting, how their eyes traverse a painting, or even which works of art they choose to look at.

As mentioned, questionnaires, interviews, focus groups, etc. can be considered to be an approach, or a design, for conducting aesthetic research; they are also measures, so we will not address them again here. Instead, we will look at some novel and promising approaches, along with some classical work. Tröndle and Tschacher (2012) combined physiological measurements (heart rate and skin conductance) with time spent in front of various works of art and evaluations of those works (see also, Tröndle et al., 2014). Serrell (1997) argued that the holding power of a display in a general museum or a work of art in terms of the time people spent in front of the work was useful as a measure of the interest the visitor has in that work, a concept with powerful intuitive appeal. Carbon (2017) presented a variety of intriguing approaches to try to capture the richness of the art experience, including posturography and facial expression.

But it is probably the case that paper-and-pencil measures (and their computer-based equivalents) dominate the measures that are used in aesthetic research in art museums. Locher (1995) pioneered the use of Mehrabian and Russell's (1974) Information Rate Scale with the addition of items for "interestingness" and "pleasantness" to assess aesthetic reactions to paintings. Smith and Smith (2006) developed the Aesthetic Fluency Scale, a 10-item measure that asks respondents whether specific artists (e.g., Mary Cassatt, Isamu Noguchi) or concepts in art (e.g., Fauvism, Abstract Expressionism) are part of their regular vocabulary, using a 5-point response scale ranging from "I have never heard of this artist or term" (1 point) to "I can talk intelligently about this artist or idea in art" (5 points). Silvia (2007) has adapted that format for a variety of areas within the arts.

There are a number of issues to take into consideration in the measures used in a study. Using an existing measure has many positives; the most salient among these is that there should be evidence of the validity of the measure available. However, it may be the case that there is no extant measure that really fits the demands of a particular research endeavor. Many studies develop a measure for use in the research. In doing so, one should take a number of factors into consideration. First and foremost, the measure must be "fit for purpose"; that is, it must capture the construct one is wishing to measure. In the field of aesthetics, this can be a difficult task. Second, for use in a museum context, measures always need to pass a practicality test. Can the measure actually be administered within the confines of the museum setting and the research design? Third, it is important not to try to validate a new instrument and use it to address a research hypothesis or question within the same study, unless separate components have been executed for the validity concerns and the examination of the research hypothesis/question.

Procedures

As stated at the outset of this chapter, people do not go to art museums to be participants in aesthetics research studies. That is, unless you have recruited a group of participants and sent them to the museum (e.g., Camic & Chatterjee, 2013; Knutson & Crowley, 2010; Wolf & Smith, 1993). Thus, the procedures that one engages in when conducting such research should not occupy too much of the participants' time or be too intrusive on their experience. This does not mean that one cannot conduct experimental research in museum settings, nor does it mean that one cannot attempt to capture behavior over an extended period of time. As mentioned earlier, Tröndle and his colleagues have developed an approach through the development of highly innovative technology, to recording the visiting patterns, viewing times, physiological responses, and reactions via questionnaire all within the framework of a single study (Tröndle et al., 2014).

We have used an approach to randomization of subjects that solves a number of problems in conducting research on visitors without being excessively intrusive. In a study examining how and how much visitors learned in the exhibition, *The Origins of Impressionism*, at the Metropolitan Museum of Art (Smith & Smith, 2003), we randomly assigned participants to one of two questionnaires to be completed at the entry to the exhibition. After viewing the exhibition, participants then completed the other questionnaire at the end of the exhibition. On one of the questionnaires, we asked participants how much they knew about the origins of Impressionism, and how much they knew about particular Impressionists. Thus, at the completion of data collection, we had a sample of people who responded to the questionnaire before viewing the exhibition, and a second sample who completed it after viewing the exhibition. Because participants were randomly assigned to pre or post conditions, we had a comparison free of confounding measurement reactivity (no participant was "cued" into paying attention to aspects of the exhibition). Additionally, we added two artists who were *not* Impressionists (and thus not in the exhibition) to the list of artists. We found that the post group was higher on all questions with the exception of the two artists who were not Impressionists. We were also able to relate visiting behaviors to the magnitude of pre/post differences.

In general, designing empirical research on aesthetics in museums takes care, respect for the visitors, and a fair degree of ingenuity. Advances in what can be done in museum settings are being made on a regular basis, but reliance on traditional approaches such as observation, interviews, and questionnaires still dominate the field.

Interpretation

What do we make of findings? This is a challenging aspect of research in most fields, especially those that do not have exceptionally strong theoretical bases. Although empirical research on aesthetics has a long history, theoretical models of aesthetic interactions have seen a recent rise, and as yet are not thoroughly tested (see e.g., Chatterjee, 2014; Leder et al., 2004; Locher et al., 2010; J. K. Smith, 2014b; Tinio, 2013). With a strong theoretical base, it is easier to tie findings back to the theory; in the absence of such a base, one is left to speculate among alternatives. That is not necessarily a bad thing, but it leaves interpretation of results open to alternative hypotheses.

Consider an example of flawed interpretation of results from our own research. We were asked by the director of the Metropolitan to investigate whether visitors would prefer to have to wait on line to enter a very popular exhibition, or if they would prefer to secure tickets with a guaranteed admission at a fixed time. There was a major exhibition on at the time that was drawing large crowds, and the museum had decided to put up a rope line (like at a Disney theme park) to control entry into the exhibition. We decided to interview people waiting on that line to see what their preferences were. We found that about three quarters of the people preferred to "take their chances" and wait on line. New Yorkers and people from overseas were highly in favor of the "take their chances" model, while people from the tri-state area outside of New York were split almost evenly. We reasoned that New Yorkers felt they could always come back at a later time if the lines were too long, and international visitors would not have known to get advance tickets, and so were happy with a wait. Although we never published the study, we presented it at museum workshops several times. At one of those presentations, in mid-sentence, we had an experience that our fellow New Zealanders refer to as "when the penny dropped." *Of course* those individuals would mostly prefer waiting on line to buying advance, timed tickets. That is exactly what they were doing when we interviewed them! If they really disliked waiting on line, they wouldn't have been on that line.

In general, we are advocates of Occam's razor in interpreting results. Simpler explanations, as long as they are not simplistic, are usually the strongest. In working with museums for over 30 years now, we have developed the following rule of thumb. As far as museum professionals are concerned, there are two kinds of findings: ones they already knew, and ones they don't believe. Our goal has always been to find the "sweet spot" in between those two extremes. One other recommendation on interpreting results before leaving this section: If the data don't make sense, don't trust them. Sometimes findings can be confusing, but rarely do findings in any of the social sciences reach the level of mystical.

Occasionally an insight will help resolve seemingly contradictory findings. For example, we have always found that people are extremely positive in their reactions to museum visits (J. K. Smith, 2014a). At the same time, we see that they only spend somewhere between 10 and 30s looking at any particular work of art, and almost never as much as 4 min (Smith & Smith, 2001; Smith et al., 2017). Furthermore, when asked which artwork in an exhibition was the most impressive to them, they have difficulty answering, saying instead that it was the whole exhibition that overwhelmed them. How can that be? How can visitors have experiences that they use the strongest of superlatives to describe when they seemingly flit from one piece of art to another, not even spending as much as a single minute on even the masterpieces? For us, the answer is that the work of art is not the proper unit of analysis. Visitors don't think of an individual work as "the thing" of a museum visit any more than they consider a passage in a musical piece, or a scene in a movie, or an event in a book as "the thing." It is *the visit* that is "the thing." The proper unit of analysis (we contend) is not an individual work of art, but the entire exhibition, or even the museum visit as a whole. That is what we should be studying. This sets what we call the *museum effect* approach to aesthetic appreciation (J. K. Smith, 2014b) apart from other models (all of which we cherish as outstanding contributions in their own right).

Major Challenges, Goals, and Suggestions

We exist at a particularly exciting time in the field of empirical aesthetics. Interest is high; great journals are publishing the research; strong professional organizations are available; and, perhaps most importantly, real breakthroughs exist in our ability to observe and assess aesthetic experiences. These breakthroughs, particularly things like functional magnetic resonance imaging (fMRI) research, have greatly increased our understanding of the mental processes that underlie how we look at art (Cupchik et al., 2009; Chatterjee, 2014; Chatterjee & Vartanian, 2014). Research using fMRI is conducted in laboratories, and is unlikely to find its way to museum settings. Nor are we likely to find original works of art in an fMRI lab any time soon. However, the findings from such research can inform what we do when studying individuals viewing art in museum settings. And conversely, what we are finding in museum-based empirical aesthetic research can inform the questions that are asked in lab settings. The two approaches are complementary, if contrasting.

From our perspective as long-time museum-based aesthetic researchers, the challenge lies in how we can conduct even more rigorous investigations in museum settings without posing an undue burden on museums. Museum professionals rightly pose the question to aesthetic researchers: what is in this for us? We have typically responded to that question by blending the issues that are of importance to the museum with questions that are of more purely academic/aesthetic interest. We have found that the museums are usually interested in those issues once we have results!

Another challenge lies in the nexus between psychological and philosophical issues in aesthetics. If we look at the models described above about aesthetic interactions, they always involve people who are encountering a work of art. They really are not about undergraduates fulfilling a course requirement in an introductory psychology course. And yet, much research in the field is conducted with university students. But is it really possible to conduct research in aesthetics with people who do not, at the time of the study, have the affective disposition to look at and appreciate great art? Can an aesthetic experience (Dewey, 1958) take place with a person not disposed to having such an experience? We leave that question open.

In terms of suggestions and recommendations for a way forward, we encourage stronger interaction between those who conduct research on empirical aesthetics, and those responsible for presenting art to the public; that is, museum professionals. We have found something of a reluctance that is similar to what we call "the seventh grade dance problem." The girls are on one side of the gym and the boys are on the other, with neither comfortable in making a foray out to engage the other side. We need people from both the research and the museum community to reach out to one another, engage in serious discussion, and look at the possibilities for meaningful collaboration.

Classroom and Practical Aspects

For many laypeople, psychological research has the aura of hooking people up to electrodes, and indeed, it does that from time to time. But empirical work in aesthetics can be much simpler and more straightforward to conduct, and can be done by relative novices if the study is well designed. Note that no research should be conducted in a museum without the explicit permission of the museum, and all research should meet ethical standards and have the approval of an ethics committee where appropriate. Perhaps the most interesting museum research that could be done by students in a course studying aesthetics is simple observation of museum behavior by visitors. With class members engaged in the same observation protocol, very interesting data could be generated. For example, it is not difficult to time people in front of works of art (Smith & Smith, 2001; Smith et al., 2017). One of the findings from the Smith et al. (2017) study was that about a third of the visitors took "selfies" of themselves in front of the works, which we called "arties." That finding leads to additional questions that can be investigated. It would be easy to design a study to determine whether the artie phenomenon is more prevalent among millennials and younger visitors than it is with older visitors. Similarly, is it more prevalent among males or females, single visitors or visitors in groups? How often do people mimic or interact with the work in doing so? How often do they then use social media to share their arties? What is their motivation behind doing so (note that this would require permission to interview visitors)?

Now to some, this might not seem to be a set of the most pressing issues in empirical aesthetics, but we might differ with that assessment. Why? Because this is currently how people are interacting with art. These are the aesthetic experiences of one third of the museum audience, at least in some museums. Another question that could be studied by members of a class would be one that we have frequently used in our own work: if the curator for this exhibition were here, what question would you have for him/her? The same question could be posed substituting "artist for this work" for "curator for this exhibition." What is it that is on people's minds when they encounter and view a work of art? There is obviously a host of other questions that could be asked, and question finding (sometimes called "problem finding") is as important an intellectual task as answering those questions, maybe more so (Getzels & Csikszentmihalyi, 1976; J. K. Smith, 2014a).

Summary and Discussion

So where to from here? There are many recommendations and exhortations that we might make. We anxiously await the next studies based on fMRI and eye movement cameras, and the next study based on interviews of large samples of museum visitors. More research, more light.

But we also make a suggestion that might not at first be obvious: let's take some time to read what has already been accomplished and what we have found out in just the past 5–10 years. Let's have more communication and build more on the bases we have established. We can also productively wander into philosophical discussions of aesthetics, or even look at what artists have to say about themselves. Research in aesthetics is incredibly wide-ranging, and there is no doubt more that is being discovered than any of us individually can process. But we might soon be reaching a time when some level of consolidation and integration of what we know would be beneficial to the field as a whole. This volume alone provides an incredibly rich source of information to scholars in the field of empirical aesthetics, one that might allow us to say, "This is where we stand today."

Note

1. https://www.visitorstudies.org/

References

Brieber, D., Nadal, M., & Leder, H. (2015). In the white cube: Museum context enhances the valuation and memory of art. *Acta Psychologica*, *154*, 36–42.

Brieber, D., Nadal, M., Leder, H., & Rosenberg, R. (2014). Art in time and space: Context modulates the relation between art experience and viewing time. *PLoS One*, *9*(6), e99019.

Camic, P. M., & Chatterjee, H. J. (2013). Museums and art galleries as partners for public health interventions. *Perspectives in Public Health*, *133*(1), 66–71.

Carbon, C. C. (2017). Measurement problems and measurement strategies for capturing the rich experience of art. *Electronic Imaging*, *2017*(14), 242–247.

Carr, D. W. (2006). *A Place not a place: Reflection and possibility in museums and libraries.* Oxford, UK: Alta Mira Press.

Carr, D. W. (2011). *Open conversations: Public learning in libraries and museums.* Santa Barbara, CA: Libraries Unlimited.

Cela-Conde, C. J., Agnati, L., Huston, J. P., Mora, F., & Nadal, M. (2011). The neural foundations of aesthetic appreciation. *Progress in Neurobiology, 94*(1), 39–48.

Chatterjee, A. (2014). *The aesthetic brain: How we evolved to desire beauty and enjoy art.* Oxford, UK: Oxford University Press.

Chatterjee, A., & Vartanian, O. (2014). Neuroaesthetics. *Trends in Cognitive Sciences, 18*(7), 370–375.

Csikszentmihalyi, M., & Robinson, R. E. (1990). *The art of seeing: An interpretation of the aesthetic encounter.* Los Angeles, CA: Getty Publications.

Cupchik, G. C., Vartanian, O., Crawley, A., & Mikulis, D. J. (2009). Viewing artworks: Contributions of cognitive control and perceptual facilitation to aesthetic experience. *Brain and Cognition, 70*(1), 84–91.

Dewey, J. (1958). *Art as experience.* New York: Capricorn Books, G. P. Putnam's Sons.

Falk, J. H. (2009). *Identity and the museum visitor experience.* Walnut Creek, CA: Left Coast Press.

Getzels, J. W., & Csikszentmihalyi, M. (1976). *The creative vision: A longitudinal study of problem finding in art.* New York: John Wiley & Sons.

Gorman, M. (2015). Yogi Berra's most memorable sayings. *Newsweek*, September 23, 2015. http://www.newsweek.com/most-memorable-yogi-isms-375661. Accessed July 8, 2015.

Heidenreich S. M., & Turano, K. A. (2011). Where does one look when viewing artwork in a museum? *Empirical Studies in the Arts, 29*(1), 51–72.

Hekkert, P., & van Wieringen, P. C. W. (1996). Beauty in the eye of expert and nonexpert beholders: A study in the appraisal of art. *The American Journal of Psychology, 109*, 389–407.

Housen, A. (1983). *The eye of the beholder: Measuring aesthetic development.* Unpublished doctoral dissertation, Harvard Graduate School of Education, Cambridge, MA.

Jackson, P. W. (1998). *John Dewey and the lessons of art.* New Haven, CT: Yale University Press.

Kaplan, S., Bardwell, L. V., & Slakter, D. B. (1993). The museum as a restorative environment. *Environment and Behavior, 25*, 725–742.

Knutson, K., & Crowley, K. (2010). Connecting with art: How families talk about art in a museum setting. In M. K. Stein & L. Kucan (Eds.), *Instructional explanations in the disciplines* (pp. 189–206). Boston, MA: Springer.

Leder, H., Belke, B., Oeberst, A., & Augustin, D. (2004). A model of aesthetic appreciation and aesthetic judgments. *British Journal of Psychology, 95*, 489–508.

Livi Smith, A. (2014). Aesthetics and the built environment: No painting or musical piece can compete. In P. P. L. Tinio, & J. K. Smith (Eds.), *The handbook of the psychology of aesthetics and the arts* (pp. 385–419). Cambridge, UK: Cambridge University Press.

Locher, P. (1995). A measure of the information content of visual art stimuli for studies in experimental aesthetics. *Empirical Studies of the Arts, (13)*, 183–191.

Locher, P., Overbeeke, K., & Wensveen, S. (2010). Aesthetic interaction: A framework. *Design Issues, 26*, 70–79.

Locher, P., Smith, J. K., & Smith, L. F. (2001). The influence of presentation format and viewer training in the visual arts on the perception of pictorial and aesthetic qualities of paintings. *Perception, 30*, 449–465.

Locher, P., Smith, L. F., & Smith, J. K. (1999). Original paintings versus slide and computer reproductions: A comparison of viewer responses. *Empirical Studies in Arts, 17*, 121–129.

Macdonald, S. (Ed.) (2006). *A companion to museum studies*. Oxford, UK: Blackwell Publishing.

Mastandrea, S., Bartoli, G., & Bove, G. (2009). Preferences for ancient and modern art museums: Visitor experiences and personality characteristics. *Psychology of Aesthetics, Creativity, and the Arts, 3*(3), 164.

Mehrabian, A., & Russell, J. (1974). *An approach to environmental psychology*. Cambridge, MA: MIT Press.

Packer, J., & Bond, N. (2010). Museums as restorative environments. *Curator, 53*, 421–436.

Parsons, M. J. (1987). *How we understand art: A cognitive developmental account of aesthetic experience*. Cambridge, UK: Cambridge University Press.

Pekarik, A. J., Doering, Z. D., & Karns, D. A. (1999). Exploring satisfying experiences in museums. *Curator, 42*, 152–173.

Pekarik, A. J., & Schreiber, J. B. (2012). The power of expectation. *Curator, 55*, 487–496.

Pelowski, M. J. (2015). Tears and transformation: Feeling like crying as an indicator of insightful or "aesthetic" experience with art. *Frontiers in Psychology, 6*, 1006.

Schauble, L., Leinhardt, G., & Martin, L. (1997). A framework for organizing a cumulative research agenda in informal learning contexts. *Journal of Museum Education, 22*(2–3), 3–8.

Serrell, B. (1997). Paying attention: The duration and allocation of visitors' time in museum exhibitions. *Curator, 40*(2), 108–125.

Silvia, P. J. (2007). Knowledge-based assessment of expertise in the arts: Exploring aesthetic fluency. *Psychology of Aesthetics, Creativity, and the Arts, 1*(4), 247.

Silvia, P. J. (2009). Looking past pleasure: Anger, confusion, disgust, pride, surprise, and other unusual aesthetic emotions. *Psychology of Aesthetics, Creativity, and the Arts, 3*(1), 48.

Smith, J. K. (2014a). Art as mirror: Creativity and communication in aesthetics. *Psychology of Aesthetics, Creativity, and the Arts, 8*(1), 110–118.

Smith, J. K. (2014b). *The museum effect: How museums, libraries, and cultural institutions civilize society*. Lanham, MD: Rowman & Littlefield.

Smith, J. K., & Carr, D. W. (2001). In Byzantium. *Curator, 44*, 335–354.

Smith, J. K., & Smith, L. F. (2001). Spending time on art. *Empirical Studies of the Arts, 19*(2), 229–236.

Smith, J. K., & Smith, L. F. (2003). "Origins of Impressionism" relating behavior to perceived learning. *Bulletin of Psychology and the Arts, 4*(2), 80–85.

Smith, L. F. (2014). Trials, tribulations, and triumphs of applied research in museum settings. *Psychology of Aesthetics, Creativity, and the Arts, 8*(2), 253–259.

Smith, L. F., & Smith, J. K. (2006). The nature and growth of aesthetic fluency. In P. Locher, C. Martindale, L. Dorfman, V. Petrov, & D. Leontiev (Eds.), *New directions in aesthetics, creativity, and the psychology of art* (pp. 47–58). Amityville, NY: Baywood.

Smith, L. F., Smith, J. K., Arcand, K. K., Smith, R. K., Bookbinder, J., & Keach, K. (2011). Aesthetics and astronomy: Studying the public's perception and understanding of imagery from space. *Science Communication, 33*(2), 201–238.

Smith, L. F., Smith, J. K., & Tinio, P. P. L. (2017) Time spent viewing art and reading labels. *Psychology of Aesthetics, Creativity, and the Arts, 11*(1), 77–85.

Smith, J. K., & Wolf, L. F. (1996). Museum visitor preferences and intentions in constructing aesthetic experience. *Poetics: Journal for Empirical Research in Literature, Media and the Arts, 24*, 219–238.

Smith, J. K., L. F. Wolf, & Staradoubtsev, S. (1994). Visitor characteristics in two art museums: The Poushkin and the Metropolitan. Paper presented at the annual meeting of the American Educational Research Association, New Orleans, LA.

Tinio, P. L., Smith, J. K., & Smith L. F. (2014). The walls do speak: Psychological aesthetics and the museum experience. In P. P. L. Tinio & J. K. Smith (Eds.), *The handbook of the psychology of aesthetics and the arts* (pp. 195–218). Cambridge, UK: Cambridge University Press.

Tinio, P. P. L. (2013). From artistic creation to aesthetic reception: The mirror model of art. *Psychology of Aesthetics, Creativity, and the Arts, 7*(3), 265–275. doi:10.1037/a0030872

Tolmie, P., Benford, S., Greenhalgh, C., Rodden, T., & Reeves, S. (2014, February). Supporting group interactions in museum visiting. In *Proceedings of the 17th ACM conference on Computer supported cooperative work & social computing* (pp. 1049–1059). New York, NY: ACM.

Tröndle, M., Greenwood, S., Kirchberg, V., & Tschacher, W. (2014). An integrative and comprehensive methodology for studying aesthetic experience in the field: Merging movement tracking, physiology, and psychological data. *Environment and Behavior, 46*(1), 102–135.

Tröndle, M., & Tschacher, W. (2012). The physiology of phenomenology: The effects of artworks. *Empirical Studies of the Arts, 30,* 75–113.

Wolf, L. F., & Smith, J. K. (1993). What makes museum labels legible? *Curator, 36,* 95–110.

Yalowitz, S. S., & Bronnenkant, K. (2009). Timing and tracking: Unlocking visitor behavior. *Visitor Studies, 12*(1), 47–64.

CHAPTER 42

AESTHETIC EXPERIENCE IN EVERYDAY ENVIRONMENTS

PAUL J. SILVIA AND KATHERINE N. COTTER

WHERE are you right now? Most readers, we suspect, are in ordinary places: at work or home, perhaps on a train, possibly outdoors with a cold drink and a furry dog. Few of you, if any, are reading this in the elegant Long Room at Trinity College Library or the Main Reading Room at the United States Library of Congress. To stretch and simplify an old dichotomy (Durkheim, 1915/2008), some aesthetic spaces are sacred and others are profane. Some environments for encountering art are marked as special, as art with a capital *A*. These are the grand museums and concert halls, to be sure, but also other sanctified places that people uphold as special and sublime, such as the Cave of Altamira and California's Sequoia groves. As Smith (2014) notes in *The Museum Effect*, it isn't the place per se but the receptive and contemplative mindset people bring to culturally marked aesthetic places.

Other spaces are profane. We mean this in the older sense of *ordinary*, *humble*, and *mundane*, although there probably is more cursing in your car than in the New York Met. Most of the aesthetic encounters people have are in ordinary places that are not culturally marked as special sites for art. We listen to music in cars and bars, stores and gyms; we see great paintings reproduced on tablet screens, postcards, and posters; and we see and touch things in the world that were intended to be aesthetically appealing.

Aesthetic experience in everyday environments isn't yet a discrete research tradition in empirical aesthetics. Nevertheless, a large body of work has built up—much of it in other areas of psychology and in kindred fields—that illuminates the daily context of the arts. In this chapter, we adopt a collage approach by bringing together a diverse collection of ideas and research. Our hope is that a broad survey of an intriguing problem might stretch how readers think about the environmental context of aesthetic experience and nudge a few researchers to try collecting data outside of their profane research lab.

WHERE AESTHETICS AND CREATIVITY MEET

The field of empirical aesthetics cohabitates with a few kindred fields. In journals and conferences, empirical aesthetics usually appears with the psychology of the arts, its closest cousin, and with the psychology of creativity. These categories, like all scholarly categories, are fuzzy, but they are especially hairy in regions like aesthetic experience in everyday environments. This is a place where the concerns of aesthetics and creativity come together.

In everyday life, people are both creator and audience, curator and visitor. Gordon Allport (1937, 1958), the influential personality theorist, argued that people shape their environments in ways both powerful and subtle. To start, people choose which environments to avoid and to enter. Once there, they tinker with the environment according to their personality traits, goals, and interests (Gosling, 2009). When people have a great deal of control over their environments, they tend to mold and craft those places to suit their tastes. In some cases, people act as curators: they select and arrange objects that they didn't make to attain an aesthetic goal. This includes picking physical objects—lamps and posters and rugs that really tie the room together—and sensory elements, such as lighting, scents, and sounds. In other cases, people act as creators: they apply make-up, make jewelry, and compose music that appeals to them. In both cases, we see that people's aesthetic experiences in everyday environments are often brought about by their own choices and decisions.

THE AESTHETICS OF PEOPLE

It seems fatuous to say that people are obsessed with people, but they are. For most people, the most salient elements of the environment are other people. The aesthetic appeal of people has received the most attention in the fields of evolutionary aesthetics and cultural anthropology, both of which explore how humans adorn and modify their bodies—and how others, in turn, react.

People are complex and sensual aesthetic beings. They can be appealing and intriguing in their scents; in the textures of their bodies and the objects that cover it; in the sounds of their voices, movements, and possessions; and, of course, in how they look. Human visual appeal is a topic that would fill a bookshelf at this point. In all cultures, people modify how they look (Brain, 1983). Many of the changes modify the body itself: decorating the skin; shaping, adorning, and removing the hair and nails; and trying to change, with varying success, where the fat beneath the skin goes. Other changes cover the body: shoes and shirts, pants and purses, gold earrings and shell necklaces, and stainless-steel watches.

The field of evolutionary aesthetics tends to emphasize how sexuality, youth, and fertility are linked to human forms that other people find beautiful and appealing. For human faces—the body part that has attracted the most research attention—many aspects of facial morphology make it more appealing. Some of these features are well known to psychologists, such as how a face's symmetry, averageness, and typicality affect visual appeal (Rhodes et al., 2001; Thornhill & Gangestad, 1999). Other features are less well known, such as how the perceptual contrast of a face—how much the eyes and mouth, for example, stand out from the surrounding skin—affect perceptions of a face's femininity, youth, health, and attractiveness (Russell, 2003, 2009; Russell et al., 2016).

People's intuitive understanding of the aesthetics of faces seems savvy. Many studies of how make-up affects the appeal of faces have found that people are accurately targeting the factors that increase visual preference. When applying make-up, for example, women do so in ways that change the apparent size of facial features, such as making noses seem smaller and eyes seem bigger (Jones, Porcheron, & Russell, 2018). Likewise, common make-up techniques increase facial contrast (e.g., darkening the lips and eyes relative to the surrounding skin). Faces with higher contrast, in turn, appear more feminine, youthful, and attractive (Porcheron et al., 2017; Russell, 2009).

The biological emphasis of evolutionary aesthetics is complemented by cultural anthropology, which explores how cultural practices of body modification and adornment acquire value and appear beautiful to the culture's members (Brain, 1983). There's no single, simple answer to culturally unique notions of beauty, but a common theme is that features associated with social status and cultural power often diffuse through the culture and become appealing and beautiful.

One of the most interesting examples comes from the history of deliberate skull modification. As Tubbs, Salter, and Oakes (2006, p. 372) note:

> The practice of intentional alteration of the head shape in accordance with certain preconceived ideas of beauty has been found from almost every geographical area of the world and is only possible during infancy when the cranium or more specifically the calvaria is malleable.

Changing head shape is interesting not only because it is widespread and permanent, but also because it's something that adults do to infants to improve their visual appeal and social value. Some cultures would flatten and elongate the forehead, presumably to make the body appear taller and more formidable to opponents (e.g., via a broader, flatter forehead; Carré, McCormick, & Mondloch, 2009). Others would seek conical shapes, often because they were associated with aristocracy or royalty. And in modern Western cultures, parents use baby helmets to correct for flat spots that arise when back-sleeping infants favor one head direction.

We can only scratch the surface of the aesthetics of human bodies here, but we hope to highlight an underappreciated point for future research: in everyday environments in everyday life, people are usually the aesthetic objects that other people are most curious about.

NATURE AND THE BUILT ENVIRONMENT

People are always somewhere. The aesthetics of natural and built environments have not received much attention in empirical aesthetics, but other fields—particularly environmental psychology—have developed intriguing bodies of work on how people experience natural and urban spaces. A hot topic in modern work is the notion of a widespread aesthetic preference for natural scenes over human-made scenes (Chatterjee, 2013; Orians & Heerwagen, 1992). People do seem to prefer images of nature, especially images containing "green space" (plants, trees, and other vegetation) and "blue space" (bodies of water), over images of buildings and human artifacts (e.g., Kaplan, Kaplan, & Wendt, 1972; White et al., 2010), and these preferences for natural scenes are relatively homogeneous compared with preferences for human artifacts (Vessel, Maurer, Denker, & Starr, 2018).

One of the quirkier facts of people's aesthetic experience of nature is that they think about nature in artistic terms. People bring a conceptual vocabulary of the fine arts to their aesthetic experiences of the natural world (Carlson, 2009, chapter 2). This seems particularly true of landscape paintings and actual landscapes. Many tourist sites, for example, have elevated scenic vistas for people to view natural scenes in ways much like a landscape painting, with enough elevation and distance to see major elements as figures against the background. At these places, people can remark how much like a postcard or painting the scene looks while they frame their snapshot.

The aesthetics of urban environments have primarily been taken up in architecture, particularly the design of structures, landscapes, and interiors. Structures are difficult to study using the traditional lab-based methods of empirical aesthetics because much of the aesthetic effect comes from a person's spatial relationship to a building. As Carlson (2000, chapter 13) notes, people first see a building's exterior from a distance, move toward it, and ultimately enter it and interact with the interior. The experience of the building at different times and scales is central to its aesthetic purpose and success.

Nevertheless, photographs of exteriors and interiors are good places to start for lab-based work. Most work has revealed continuity between built spaces and other domains of the arts. In some of Berlyne's last published work, Oostendorp and Berlyne (1978a, 1978b) applied popular methods for studying visual art to images of building exteriors that reflected a range of architectural styles. The dimensions underlying people's judgments and the patterns of outcomes paralleled the findings from Berlyne's (1971) classic experimental aesthetics work, such as underlying dimensions related to complexity and their relationships with self-reported and behavioral measures of preference and exploration. More recently, Vartanian et al. (2013, 2015) examined self-reported and magnetic resonance imaging (MRI)-based brain responses to images of architectural interiors. Imaging markers of approach and avoidance responses were associated with many features of interiors. Relatively expansive spaces with higher ceilings, for example, and curved versus angular spaces were more appealing.

Their own aesthetic appeal aside, urban spaces can be sites for art. A growing subfield of aesthetics research explores how people experience and think about public art, graffiti, and street art. In a striking recent study, participants walked through the Danube Canal in Vienna, a site known for its street art, while wearing a mobile eye-tracker that recorded what people viewed as they traversed it (Mitschke, Goller, & Leder, 2017). Later, participants visited the lab to provide descriptions and self-report ratings of what they viewed. People spent around half of the walk viewing art objects, and their viewing behavior correlated with their later ratings of liking and interest.

ARTIFACTS AND CONSUMER PRODUCTS

Within the built environment, we have what designers call the *near environment* and neuroscientists call *peripersonal space*: the objects and surfaces around the body that people can touch. The aesthetics of artifacts has traditionally been the concern of design theorists. In the school of thought known as *emotional design* (Jordan, 2000; Norman, 2004), designers seek to understand people's emotional interactions with objects and how to design products to achieve emotional aims.

Pleasure is an obvious aesthetic response to objects (Jordan, 2000). Some pleasures of objects are sensory and kinesthetic, such as a comfy leather lounge chair or a stereo knob that turns with a precise and silky feel. Other pleasures come from how objects relate to one's goals, such as a small purse that magically holds all your stuff or a shampoo bottle that easily opens with a single slippery hand. But designers often hope to evoke other emotions, such as surprise and interest, and to avoid others, such as anger and frustration.

To expand the scope of emotional design, Demir, Desmet, and Hekkert (2009) applied appraisal models of emotion (Lazarus, 1991) to people's emotional encounters with everyday consumer products. In an intriguing experience-sampling study, they had people keep diaries of their emotional interactions with consumer products. Emotions sparked by product interactions were common and diverse. Negative emotions were widespread, especially anger and irritation, but the sample reported a wide range of feelings. The participants were interviewed after the diary phase to unpack their appraisals of the objects, such as whether an object advanced or thwarted a goal, matched their expectations, and met norms and standards, among others. People's emotions from consumer products reflected general appraisal–emotion relationships, suggesting some unity between the study of consumer products and aesthetic emotions in other domains (Silvia, 2005, 2012) and the promise of an appraisal approach for emotional design.

Music

Music is so ubiquitous in everyday life that it is hard to imagine a time when hearing it was rare. Before the advent of recorded music, the only way to hear music was to make it yourself or attend a live performance. In the modern era, when storing, transporting, and playing music is inexpensive, music plays a complex role in everyday environments. In their analysis of music in everyday life, Clarke, Dibben, and Pitts (2010, pp. 2–7) propose that music serves four broad psychological functions:

1. *Ordering and organizing time and space.* Music is used to mark transitions between events and to signify boundaries between places. In sporting events, for example, music is often played before a match starts and during pauses in play. Likewise, turning off music can signal a natural hinge, such as the start of a meeting or ceremony. Music can also mark boundaries in a space. The blandly upbeat songs in the main halls of a shopping mall, for example, are replaced by the intense, rebellious pop music when you enter a clothing store that caters to teens.

2. *Representing and expressing values.* Music in an environment conveys information about social identities and cultural values. The mall clothing store playing loud, rebellious music, for example, could be next door to a fancy menswear store playing serene, "high culture" classical music.

3. *Coordinating a group's behavior.* Music can organize and coordinate large groups of people, whether is it prompting people to rise and sing a national anthem before a soccer game, promoting informal chatting before a meeting, or capturing and directing a group's attention.

4. *Manipulating emotional states.* Finally, and most directly related to aesthetics, music is used to manipulate subjective energy levels and emotional states.

Because environments often impose music on people, it's easy to think of examples in which music is used to manipulate emotions: the soft, calming music in a dentist's waiting room; the slow, contemplative music in a church service; the upbeat, energetic music during a cardio spin class. But people often manipulate themselves with music. Research on emotion regulation shows that music ranks among the top few strategies people use to manage their energy and affect, up there with eating food, interacting with other people, and resting or exercising (Parkinson, Totterdell, Briner, & Reynolds, 1996). Whether people want to focus or to distract themselves, to crank up their energy or to calm down after a hectic day, they commonly use music to sculpt the valence and intensity of their feelings (Sachs, Damasio, & Habibi, 2015; Thayer, Newman, & McClain, 1994).

So far, we have emphasized the experience of music as a behavioral technology for controlling actions and emotions, but music in everyday life is much more than this. Music listening in daily life can produce intense and memorable aesthetic experiences, sometimes called simply "strong experiences with music" (Gabrielsson, 2002, 2006, 2011). These strong experiences are often accompanied by getting goosebumps or chills (Laeng, Eidet, Sulutvedt, & Panksepp, 2016; Nusbaum & Silvia, 2011; Nusbaum et al., 2014), and feeling moved, touched, or awe-inspired by the music (Menninghaus et al., 2015; Silvia, Fayn, Nusbaum, & Beaty, 2015). Markers of strong experiences with music are associated with both positive and negative experiences (Kuehnast, Wagner, Wassiliwizky, Jacobsen, & Menninghaus, 2014; Maruskin, Thrash, & Elliot, 2012).

One interesting marker of strong musical experiences is crying. Because the behavior of crying is controlled by powerful social norms, researchers who study aesthetic crying usually define crying broadly to include not only actual crying but also feeling like crying, such as tearing up and feeling a lump in the throat (Pelowski, 2015). Many of the narratives in Gabrielsson's research mention crying, which seems to have at least two major kinds. The first is a positive, transcendent, euphoric experience (Braud, 2001; Miceli & Castelfranchi, 2003; Pelowski, 2015). In these cases, crying might come from trying to understand an experience that is overwhelmingly beautiful or wondrous but ultimately failing, resulting in feelings of hopelessness that are released through crying (Miceli & Castelfranchi, 2003; Pelowski & Akiba, 2011). But this positive, transcendent sense of aesthetic crying might also occur directly from intense positive feelings of joy, awe, or wonder (Braud, 2001).

The second sense of aesthetic crying is the more intuitive sense—crying accompanied by feelings of sadness and distress. In addition to the many compositional and lyrical devices that can evoke a sense of sadness (Sloboda, 1991; Vuoskoski & Eerola, 2011), people can have associations with a song that produce negative emotions (e.g., a song played at their father's funeral, or music associated with an ex-boyfriend). In this case, it isn't the content of the song that causes the crying but past associations and the broader context surrounding the music.

Studies that have asked large samples of adults to remember and describe an experience of crying from music find support for euphoric and distressed kinds of events. Instances of awe-inspired crying are marked by awe, euphoria, happiness, inspiration, being touched, chills, amazement, and pleasantness; instances of sad crying are marked by anger, anxiety, upset, overwhelm, sadness, depression, and feeling out of control (Cotter, Silvia, & Fayn, 2018). During "awe" experiences, people described music as being more complex and beautiful, were more likely to report listening to religious or classical music, and tended to be with others and at a live performance. During "sad" experiences, people frequently were listening to popular music genres (e.g., pop, R&B, country), described the music as cold and unpleasant, and reported that the music reminded them of someone or that they already felt like crying prior to listening to the music (Cotter, Prince, Christensen, & Silvia, 2019).

"Inner Aesthetics" and the Mental Environment

People's everyday environments are wide-ranging, diverse, and idiosyncratic. We probably see this point most clearly when looking at the environment that psychologists study the most but understand the least—people's own minds. Through mental imagery, people generate visual images, sounds, and narratives. In turn, people can respond emotionally to their own mind's creations. For internally generated aesthetic imagery, people are the creator, audience, and performance venue.

Creativity researchers see mental imagery as fundamental to the artistic process (Finke, 1996), but not much is known about people's aesthetic responses to the images, sounds, and stories in their minds. An exception is mental music, which is the topic of an increasingly large body of work. People commonly hear music playing in their minds that isn't also playing in the environment, a phenomenon known as *musical imagery* or *inner music*. Hearing music in your mind seems common. When experience-sampling studies repeatedly signal people at quasi-random times during normal days, they find a big range of how often people hear inner music, including 17% (Beaty et al., 2013), 25% (Bailes, 2006; Cotter & Silvia, 2017), 31–32% (Bailes, 2007, 2015), and 52%(Cotter & Silvia, 2020). People are more likely to hear musical imagery when they have more musical expertise and when they are higher in openness to experience, a trait related to vivid imagery experience more generally (Cotter, 2017; Cotter, Christensen, & Silvia, 2016).

From the standpoint of aesthetics, it is interesting to consider what people are hearing and how they experience it. In most cases, people's musical imagery is music that is familiar (Bailes, 2007, 2015; Liikkanen, 2008, 2011), such as pop songs, commercial jingles, television themes, or children's songs (Beaman & Williams, 2010; Jakubowski, Finkel, Stewart, & Müllensiefen, 2017). The content of inner music is usually music that people recently heard somewhere (Bailes, 2007, 2015; Williamson et al., 2011), but sometimes people will deliberately initiate inner music (Bailes, 2015; Cotter, Christensen, & Silvia, 2019; Cotter & Silvia, 2020). Jakubowski et al. (2017) found that songs with fast tempos and relatively common melodic contours (i.e., the pattern of rising and falling melodic lines) were more likely to be imagined than slower songs or music with uncommon melodic features. Interestingly, inner music is not limited to only pre-existing music—people occasionally report imagining original compositions and developing new musical ideas in their minds (Bailes, 2015), and composers do so routinely (e.g., Bailes, 2009; Bailes & Bishop, 2012; Cowell, 1926; Mountain, 2001).

As for the emotional experience of imagined music, contrary to the stereotype of the painfully irritating earworm that people can't get out their head, people generally find their inner music to be a pleasant experience (Beaman & Williams, 2010; Beaty et al., 2013; Cotter, Christensen, & Silvia, 2019). There are times when people are ambivalent toward these imagery experiences or dislike their inner music (Liikkanen, 2011; Williamson & Jilka, 2014), but most of the time people report enjoying the music that their minds are playing (Cotter, Christensen, & Silvia, 2019). These judgments of valence experiences are complex and metacognitive. For example, someone may just enjoy having music run through her mind, regardless of what music is being imagined. In other cases, these experiences may be enjoyable only if the imagined song is one of her favorites. Williamson and Jilka (2014) found that positive experiences tended to be caused by imagining liked songs or by not finding the experience intrusive or disruptive, whereas negative experiences were driven by finding the music annoying or feeling a lack of control over the experience.

If the notion of aesthetic responses to imagined music seems off-beat, there's a small but growing literature on the experience of music during sleeping dreams. The mind is a concert venue that rarely closes. Theories of mental imagery have long proposed a continuity between waking and sleeping imagery (Klinger, 1971). Although sleeping dreams are more distorted and bizarre than daydreams, waking and sleeping imagery are more similar than different.

Hearing music in sleeping dreams seems less common than in waking imagery (Vogelsang, Anold, Schormann, Wübbelmann, & Schredl, 2016), but just as musicians hear much more inner music during the day, they are much more likely to report music in their dreams. Nocturnal musical imagery, like waking imagery, is usually well-known music, but some people report hearing something novel that the mind is composing or improvising during the imagery experience (Uga, Lemut, Zampi, Zilli, & Salzarulo, 2006). Musicians describe their musical dreams as fun, fascinating, and inspiring (Schädlich & Erlacher, 2018), so they are apparently enthusiastic audiences for their mind's own creations.

Conclusion

Aesthetic experience in everyday environments is not a body of work in its own right but rather a way of looking at how people think about and experience the arts in the places they typically inhabit. As our brief overview of many different areas illustrates, studying aesthetics in daily life constructively expands the scope of empirical aesthetics research. Debates over whether aesthetic experience is a special kind of experience—such as a sublime or disinterested state—won't soon end. Nevertheless, when you explore how people appreciate the people, objects, and scenes around them, a focus on intense and ostensibly "pure" reactions in culturally marked places for art seems needlessly narrow and restrictive. It's regrettable that people do not attend museums and concert halls more often, but it's telling that they aesthetically sculpt their daily experience through their many small decisions about where to go, what to do, and what to adorn themselves with and bring along for the day's journey.

REFERENCES

Allport, G. W. (1937). *Personality: A psychological interpretation*. New York: Holt, Rinehart, & Winston.

Allport, G. W. (1958). What units shall we employ? In G. Lindzey (Ed.), *Assessment of human motives* (pp. 239–260). New York: Holt, Rinehart, & Winston.

Bailes, F. (2006). The use of experience-sampling methods to monitor musical imagery in everyday life. *Musicae Scientae, 10*, 173–190.

Bailes, F. (2007). The prevalence and nature of imagined music in the everyday lives of music students. *Psychology of Music, 35*, 555–570.

Bailes, F. (2009). Translating the musical image: Case studies of expert musicians. In A. Chan, & A. Noble (Eds.), *Sounds in translation: Intersections of music, technology and society* (pp. 41–59). Canberra: ANU Press.

Bailes, F. (2015). Music in mind? An experience sampling study of what and when, towards and understanding of why. *Psychomusicology: Music, Mind, and Brain, 25*, 58–68.

Bailes, F., & Bishop, L. (2012). Musical imagery in the creative process. In D. Collins (Ed.), *The act of musical composition: Studies in the creative process* (pp. 53–78). Abingdon, England: Routledge.

Beaman, C. P., & Williams, T. I. (2010). Earworms ("stuck song syndrome"): Towards a natural history of intrusive thoughts. *British Journal of Psychology, 101*, 637–653.

Beaty, R. E., Burgin, C. J., Nusbaum, E. C., Kwapil, T. R., Hodges, D. A., & Silvia, P. J. (2013). Music to the inner ears: Exploring individual differences in musical imagery. *Consciousness and Cognition, 22*, 1163–1173.

Berlyne, D. E. (1971). *Aesthetics and psychobiology*. New York: Appleton-Century-Crofts.

Brain, R. (1983). *The decorated body*. London: Harper Collins.

Braud, W. (2001). Experiencing tears of wonder-joy: Seeing with the heart's eye. *Journal of Transpersonal Psychology, 33*(2), 99–111.

Carlson, A. (2000). *Aesthetics and the environment: The appreciation of nature, art, and architecture*. Abingdon, England: Routledge.

Carlson, A. (2009). *Nature and landscape: An introduction to environmental aesthetics*. New York: Columbia University Press.

Carré, J. M., McCormick, C. M., & Mondloch, C. J. (2009). Facial structure is a reliable cue of aggressive behavior. *Psychological Science, 20*, 1194–1198.

Chatterjee, A. (2013). *The aesthetic brain: How we evolved to desire beauty and enjoy art*. Oxford, England: Oxford University Press.

Clarke, E., Dibben, N., & Pitts, S. (2010). *Music and mind in everyday life*. Oxford, England: Oxford University Press.

Cotter, K. N. (2017). *Understanding inner music: A dimensional approach to musical imagery*. Master's Thesis. Retrieved from ProQuest Dissertations and Theses database. UMI No. 10259933.

Cotter, K. N., Christensen, A. P., & Silvia, P. J. (2016). Musical minds: Personality, schizotypy, and involuntary musical imagery. *Psychomusicology: Music, Mind, and Brain, 26*(3), 220–225.

Cotter, K. N., Christensen, A. P., & Silvia, P. J. (2019). Understanding inner music: A dimensional approach to musical imagery. *Psychology of Aesthetics, Creativity, and the Arts, 13*, 489–503.

Cotter, K. N., Prince, A. N., Christensen, A. P., & Silvia, P. J. (2019). Feeling like crying when listening to music: Exploring musical and contextual features. *Empirical Studies of the Arts*, 37, 119–137.

Cotter, K. N., & Silvia, P. J. (2017). Measuring mental music: Comparing retrospective and experience sampling methods for assessing musical imagery. *Psychology of Aesthetics, Creativity, and the Arts*, 11, 335–343.

Cotter, K. N., & Silvia, P. J. (2020). Tuning the inner radio: The mental control of musical imagery in everyday environments. *Psychology of Music*, 48, 876–888

Cotter, K. N., Silvia, P. J., & Fayn, K. (2018). What does feeling like crying when listening to music feel like? *Psychology of Aesthetics, Creativity, and the Arts*, 12(2), 216–227.

Cowell, H. (1926). The process of musical creation. *American Journal of Psychology*, 37(2), 233–236.

Demir, E., Desmet, P. M. A., & Hekkert, P. (2009). Appraisal patterns of emotions in human–product interaction. *International Journal of Design*, 3, 41–51.

Durkheim, E. (1915/2008). *The elementary forms of the religious life* (J. W. Swain, Trans.). Mineola, New York: Dover.

Finke, R. A. (1996). Imagery, creativity, and emergent structure. *Consciousness and Cognition*, 5, 381–393.

Gabrielsson, A. (2002). Old people's remembrance of strong experiences related to music. *Psychomusicology*, 18, 103–122.

Gabrielsson, A. (2006). Strong experiences elicited by music—What music? In P. Locher, C. Martindale, & L. Dorfman (Eds.), *New directions in aesthetics, creativity, and the arts* (pp. 251–267). Amityville, NY: Baywood.

Gabrielsson, A. (2011). *Strong experiences with music: Music is much more than just music* (R. Bradbury, Trans.). Oxford, England: Oxford University Press.

Gosling, S. (2009). *Snoop: What your stuff says about you.* New York: Basic Books.

Jakubowski, K., Finkel, S., Stewart, L., & Müllensiefen, D. (2017). Dissecting an earworm: Melodic features and song popularity predict involuntary musical imagery. *Psychology of Aesthetics, Creativity, and the Arts*, 11(2), 122–135.

Jones, A. L., Porcheron, A., & Russell, R. (2018). Makeup changes the apparent size of facial features. *Psychology of Aesthetics, Creativity, and the Arts*, 12(3), 359–368.

Jordan, P. (2000). *Designing pleasurable products: An introduction to the new human factors.* Abingdon, England: Taylor & Francis.

Kaplan, S., Kaplan, R., & Wendt, J. S. (1972). Rated preference and complexity for natural and urban visual material. *Perception and Psychophysics*, 12, 354–356.

Klinger, E. (1971). *Structure and functions of fantasy.* Chichester, England: Wiley.

Kuehnast, M., Wagner, V., Wassiliwizky, E., Jacobsen, T., & Menninghaus, W. (2014). Being moved: Linguistic representation and conceptual structure. *Frontiers in Psychology*, 5(1242), 1–11.

Laeng, B., Eidet, L. M., Sulutvedt, U., & Panksepp, J. (2016). Music chills: The eye pupil as a mirror to music's soul. *Consciousness and Cognition*, 44, 161–178.

Lazarus, R. S. (1991). *Emotion and adaptation.* Oxford, England: Oxford University Press.

Liikkanen, L. A. (2008). Music in every mind: Commonality of involuntary musical imagery. Paper presented at the 10th International Conference on Music Perception and Cognition, Sapporo, Japan.

Liikkanen, L. A. (2011). Musical activities predispose to involuntary musical imagery. *Psychology of Music*, 40(2), 236–256.

Maruskin, L. A., Thrash, T. M., & Elliot, A. J. (2012). The chills as a psychological construct: Content universe, factor structure, affective composition, elicitors, trait antecedents, and consequences. *Journal of Personality and Social Psychology, 103*, 135.

Menninghaus, W., Wagner, V., Hanich, J. Wassillwizky, E., Kuehnast, M., & Jacobsen, T. (2015). Toward a psychological construct of being moved. *PLoS ONE, 10*(6), 1–33.

Miceli, M., & Castelfranchi, C. (2003). Crying: Discussing its basic reasons and uses. *New Ideas in Psychology, 21*, 247–273.

Mitschke, V., Goller, J., & Leder, H. (2017). Exploring everyday encounters with street art using a multimethod design. *Psychology of Aesthetics, Creativity, and the Arts, 11*(3), 276–283.

Mountain, R. (2001). Composers and imagery: Myths and realities. In R. I. Godøy, and H. Jørgensen (Eds.), *Musical imagery* (pp. 271–288). Abingdon, England: Routledge.

Norman, D. (2004). *Emotional design: Why we love (or hate) everyday things.* New York: Basic Books.

Nusbaum, E. C., & Silvia, P. J. (2011). Shivers and timbres: Personality and the experience of chills from music. *Social Psychological and Personality Science, 2*, 199–204.

Nusbaum, E. C., Silvia, P. J., Beaty, R. E., Burgin, C. J., Hodges, D. A., & Kwapil, T. R. (2014). Listening between the notes: Aesthetic chills in everyday music listening. *Psychology of Aesthetics, Creativity, and the Arts, 8*, 104–109.

Oostendorp, A., & Berlyne, D. E. (1978a). Dimensions in the perception of architecture: I. Identification and interpretation of dimensions of similarity. *Scandinavian Journal of Psychology, 19*, 73–82.

Oostendorp, A., & Berlyne, D. E. (1978b). Dimensions in the perception of architecture: II. Measures of exploratory behavior. *Scandinavian Journal of Psychology, 19*, 83–89.

Orians, G. H., & Heerwagen, J. H. (1992). Evolved responses to landscapes. In J. H. Barkow, L. Cosmides, & J. Tooby (Eds.), *The adapted mind: Evolutionary psychology and the generation of culture* (pp. 555–579). Oxford, England: Oxford University Press.

Parkinson, B., Totterdell, P., Briner, R. B., & Reynolds, S. (1996). *Changing moods: The psychology of mood and mood regulation.* London: Longman.

Pelowski, M. (2015). Tears and transformation: Feeling like crying as an indicator of insightful or "aesthetic" experience with art. *Frontiers in Psychology, 8*(1006), 1–23.

Pelowski, M., & Akiba, F. (2011). A model of art perception, evaluation and emotion in transformative aesthetic experience. *New Ideas in Psychology, 29*, 80–97.

Porcheron, A., Mauger, E., Soppelsa, F., Liu, Y., Ge, L., Pascalis, O., Russell, R., & Morizot, F. (2017). Facial contrast is a cross-cultural cue for perceiving age. *Frontiers in Psychology, 8*, 1208. doi:10.3389/fpsyg.2017.01208

Rhodes, G., Yoshikawa, S., Clark, A., Lee, K., McKay, R., & Akamatsu, S. (2001). Attractiveness of facial averageness and symmetry in non-Western cultures: In search of biologically based standards of beauty. *Perception, 30*(5), 611–625.

Russell, R. (2003). Sex, beauty, and the relative luminance of facial features. *Perception, 32*, 1093–1107.

Russell, R. (2009). A sex difference in facial contrast and its exaggeration by cosmetics. *Perception, 38*, 1211–1219.

Russell, R., Porcheron, A., Sweda, J. R., Jones, A. L., Mauger, E., & Morizot, F. (2016). Facial contrast is a cue for perceiving health from the face. *Journal of Experimental Psychology: Human Perception and Performance, 42*(9), 1354–1362.

Sachs, M. E., Damasio, A., & Habibi, A. (2015). The pleasures of sad music: A systematic review. *Frontiers in Human Neuroscience, 9*(404). doi:10.3389/fnhum.2015.00404

Schädlich, M., & Erlacher, D. (2018). Lucid music—A pilot study exploring the experiences and potential of music-making in lucid dreams. *Dreaming, 28*(3), 278–286.

Silvia, P. J. (2005). Emotional responses to art: From collation and arousal to cognition and emotion. *Review of General Psychology, 9*, 342–357.

Silvia, P. J. (2012). Human emotions and aesthetic experience: An overview of empirical aesthetics. In A. P. Shimamura & S. E. Palmer (Eds.), *Aesthetic science: Connecting minds, brains, and experience* (pp. 250–275). Oxford, England: Oxford University Press.

Silvia, P. J., Fayn, K., Nusbaum, E. C., & Beaty, R. E. (2015). Openness to experience and awe in response to nature and music: Personality and profound and aesthetic experiences. *Psychology of Aesthetics, Creativity, and the Arts, 9*(4), 376–384.

Sloboda, J. A. (1991). Music structure and emotional response: Some empirical findings. *Psychology of Music, 19*, 110–120.

Smith, J. K. (2014). *The museum effect: How museums, libraries, and cultural institutions educate and civilize society.* Lanham, MD: Rowman & Littlefield.

Thayer, R. E., Newman, J. R., & McClain, T. M. (1994). Self-regulation of mood: Strategies for changing a bad mood, raising energy, and reducing tension. *Journal of Personality and Social Psychology, 67*, 910–925.

Thornhill, R., & Gangestad, S. W. (1999). Facial attractiveness. *Trends in Cognitive Sciences, 3*(12), 452–460.

Tubbs, R. S., Salter, E. G., & Oakes, W. J. (2006). Artificial deformation of the human skull: A review. *Clinical Anatomy, 19*, 372–377.

Uga, V., Lemut, M. C., Zampi, C., Zilli, I., & Salzarulo, P. (2006). Music in dreams. *Consciousness and Cognition, 15*, 351–357.

Vartanian, O., Navarrete, G., Chatterjee, A., Fich, L. B., Gonzalez-Mora, J. L., Leder, H., … & Skov, M. (2015). Architectural design and the brain: Effects of ceiling height and perceived enclosure on beauty judgments and approach-avoidance decisions. *Journal of Environmental Psychology, 41*, 10–18.

Vartanian, O., Navarrete, G., Chatterjee, A., Fich, L. B., Leder, H., Modroño, C., … & Skov, M. (2013). Impact of contour on aesthetic judgments and approach-avoidance decisions in architecture. *Proceedings of the National Academy of Sciences, 110*(Suppl. 2), 10446–10453.

Vessel, E. A., Maurer, N., Denker, A. H., & Starr, G. G. (2018). Stronger shared taste for natural aesthetics domains than for artifacts of human culture. *Cognition, 179*, 121–131.

Vogelsang, L., Anold, S., Schormann, J., Wübbelmann, S., & Schredl, M. (2016). The continuity between waking-life musical activities and music dreams. *Dreaming, 26*(2), 132–141.

Vuoskoski, J. K., & Eerola, T. (2011). Measuring music-induced emotion: A comparison of emotion models, personality biases, and intensity of experiences. *Musicae Scientae, 15*, 159–173.

White, M., Smith, A., Humphryes, K., Pahl, S., Snelling, D., & Depledge, M. (2010). Blue space: The importance of water for preference, affect, and restorativeness ratings of natural and built scenes. *Journal of Environmental Psychology, 30*(4), 482–493.

Williamson, V. J., & Jilka, S. R. (2014). Experiencing earworms: An interview study of involuntary musical imagery. *Psychology of Music, 42*(5), 653–670.

Williamson, V. J., Jilka, S. R., Fry, J., Finkel, S., Müllensiefen, D., & Stewart, L. (2011). How do "earworms" start? Classifying the everyday circumstances of involuntary musical imagery. *Psychology of Music, 40*(3), 259–284.

CHAPTER 43

THE IMPACT OF THE SOCIAL CONTEXT ON AESTHETIC EXPERIENCE

STEFANO MASTANDREA

INTRODUCTION

AN aesthetic experience can be defined as the outcome of cognitive and affective processes leading the perceiver to apprehend objects as belonging to a particular class of items, called art. From a psychological perspective, many studies and discussions have concluded that the aesthetic experience is the outcome of the coordinated action of mental processes involving perception, attention, memory, imagination, thought, and emotion (Cupchik, 1993, Leder, Belke, Oeberst, & Augustin, 2004; Locher, Krupinski, Mello-Thoms, & Nodine, 2007; Mastandrea, 2014). The aesthetic experience triggered by artworks exhibited in museums and galleries, but also encountered in churches, urban spaces, or natural environments, can give rise to a contemplative form of behavior that at high levels of intensity can lead to an authentic aesthetic emotion, reflecting fascination, admiration, and wonder.

Both the artwork and the observer are fundamental and necessary components of the aesthetic response. Most of the research on experimental aesthetics has focused on features of the artworks (starting from Fechner, 1876), comprehending structural (lines, shapes, colors, textures, material), and compositional characteristics (balance, symmetry, depth, dynamism) (Arnheim 1974; Mastandrea & Umiltà, 2016).

However, aesthetic enjoyment can be due to features of both the object and the perceiver. People usually like a piece of art if it is *typical*, *familiar*, and moderately *complex*. These three categories take into account on one hand the qualities of the object itself, and on the other hand the characteristics of the perceiver (e.g., level of education, training in the art, museum visit frequencies, etc.). An artwork is typical when it is representative of a more general class of objects. Several studies have shown that prototypical forms are preferred over nonprototypical ones (Winkielman, Halberstadt, Fazendeiro, & Catty, 2006). Preference for prototypical examples has been found in several areas: design objects, facial attractiveness, architectural facades, and in the visual arts. A number of studies, for example, reveal a positive link between prototypicality and aesthetic appraisals in colored forms (Martindale & Moore, 1988), furniture (Mastandrea & Maricchiolo, 2014; Whitfield & Slatter, 1979), and paintings (Hekkert & van Wieringen, 1996). Moreover, studies from the field of cognitive psychology have shown that prototypical stimuli are processed faster and more easily than nonprototypical stimuli (Curci, Lanciano, Maddalena, Mastandrea, & Sartori 2015; Posner & Keele, 1968). As suggested by Winkielman and colleagues (2006), prototypical items are evaluated more positively because they are easier to process. Prototypical stimuli have also appeared to elicit stronger electromyography responses from the zygomaticus region, indicating positive affect (Winkielman & Cacioppo, 2001).

Familiarity refers to how recognizable, well-known, or common an object is. Another characteristic of the aesthetic evaluation is related to the mere exposure effect (Zajonc, 1968). Several studies have found that repeated exposure to a stimulus increases the affective preference for it (Cutting, 2003; Kunst-Wilson & Zajonc, 1980; Lanciano, Curci, Mastandrea, & Sartori, 2013; Zajonc, 1968). Familiar stimuli are processed faster and preferred over novel stimuli. The association between familiarity and positive affect may be grounded in a biological predisposition to exercise caution in encounters with potentially harmful novel objects (Zajonc, 1968).

Complexity refers to the number and the perceptual organization of the elements in a composition. In general, a moderate level of complexity seems to be most preferred in artworks, in architecture, and also in environmental scenes (Berlyne, 1971; Kaplan & Kaplan, 1989; Nadal, Munar, Marty, & Cela-Conde, 2010; Purcell, Peron, & Berto, 2001). In general, people without art training prefer simple and symmetric visual elements, whereas people with art training prefer complex and asymmetric visual elements (Locher & Nodine, 1989; McWhinnie, 1968; Silvia, 2005). These three plausible explanations of aesthetic preference (i.e., protypicality, familiarity, and complexity) can be incorporated into a more general model of aesthetic preference called *processing fluency* (Reber, Schwarz, & Winkielman, 2004). According to this model, there is a strong relationship between the characteristics of the objects in terms of typicality, familiarity, complexity, and the individual who is processing the objects: the more fluent the object processing (i.e., perception of the identity and the meaning of the work), the more positive will be the aesthetic response (Mastandrea, Bartoli, & Carrus, 2011).

The Perceiver's Context

An important aspect that has received less attention compared with the objective features of the object involves the characteristics of the perceiver. Several aspects of the perceiver—cognitive, behavioral, and personality traits—are deeply related to the aesthetic preference. There is a long tradition of research on art preference and personality. In several studies, Eysenck (1941) explored people's aesthetic preferences by asking participants to rank different art style pictures and typology (e.g., portraits, landscapes) on aesthetic value. Analyses of these choices revealed a two-factor model of aesthetic preference, which included a general aesthetic appreciation factor, called T (taste), constant for people across domains, and a second factor (called K) that distinguished colorful, complex, impressionistic, and expressionistic art styles normally preferred by extraverted people, and simpler, symmetric, less colored, realistic art styles positively rated by introverted people. Eysenck (1941) also found that the personality trait of psychoticism correlated with the preference for complex visual stimuli. Related to that early research, Cardinet (1958) found that aesthetic preference mirrored internal personality characteristics: independent and creative people tend to prefer abstract art; convergent and dependent individuals are more likely to appreciate realistic art.

More recently, two constructs of personality, "openness to experience" (Costa & McCrae, 1992) and "sensation seeking" (Zuckerman, 1979), have been extensively used to investigate preferences for different art styles. There have been wider examinations of these personality characteristics as they relate to abstract and modern art as compared with representational and traditional art. Furnham and Avison (1997) found that sensation seekers were more likely to appreciate surreal art than traditional or representational art. Furnham and Walker (2001) found that openness to experience was associated with positive ratings of abstract, pop, and representational art. Rawlings, Vidal, and Furnham (2000) confirmed the link between sensation seeking and preference for abstract art, whereas regarding openness to experience, results showed a preference only for one group of the sample investigated. Feist and Brady (2004) demonstrated that participants with high levels of openness to experience and sensation seeking gave higher preferential evaluations to abstract rather than representative art images, compared with people with lower levels in these traits. The openness to experience personality trait has consistently correlated with an appreciation for visual arts in general (Chamorro-Premuzic & Furnham, 2004). This factor constitutes a central component of what can be called the artistic personality (Chamorro-Premuzic, Burke, Hsu, & Swami, 2010).

Another personality constructs such as the need for closure (the desire for stable and solid knowledge in order to avoid uncertainty, and the need to have a clear answer to a question to avoid ambiguity; Kruglanski & Webster, 1996) contribute to a stronger appreciation of representational art compared with abstract art. Findings of two studies showed that either at an explicit or at an implicit level, the evaluation and hence the appreciation of an artwork strongly depends not only on the characteristics of the object, but also on personality traits. These findings held across representational and abstract styles. Need for closure, as a dispositional trait or experimentally induced with a cognitive task, was positively associated with the preference for representational but not for abstract art (Chirumbolo, Brizi, Mastandrea, & Mannetti, 2014; Wiersema, Van Der Schalk, & van Kleef, 2012).

All of these studies have dealt with this particular topic by the means of laboratory research. In most cases, participants were asked to express their preferences for different types of art (realistic vs. abstract, cubist vs. modern, etc.) presented through the use of slides, computer screens, or sheets of paper, and were assessed along various personality dimensions. While the importance of these laboratory studies is largely recognized, we have to consider that participants in these studies are in most cases students who may have no knowledge of or interest in art, and in different cases some of them may not have even set foot in an art museum. We believe it is important also to report some research that has been conducted with real museum visitors with an authentic interest in art.

Considering Both the Social Context and Art Styles: Differences Between Ancient and Modern Art Museum Visitors

In several investigations conducted in different art museums according to the art styles of the collection hosted (modern/contemporary art and ancient/realistic art), it was found that there were two distinguishable groups of visitors in terms of education, profession, and frequency of museum visitations (Mastandrea, Bartoli, & Bove, 2007, 2009; Smith, 2014). Visitors who appreciated museums displaying ancient art had a somewhat lower educational level, were mainly clerks and employees, and went to museums less frequently than those who attended modern/contemporary art museums. People who visited modern art museums were of higher social status compared with people who visited ancient art museums. These findings are in line with those concerning art style preferences (Chamorro-Premuzic & Furnham, 2004; Chamorro-Premuzic et al., 2010; Feist & Brady 2004; Rawlings, Vidal, & Furnham, 2000), which demonstrate that people who prefer abstract and modern art, and we can add those who go to contemporary art museums, have a higher socioeconomic status than those who prefer representational art and attend ancient art museums.

People who favor visiting ancient art museums are attracted by the museum as a famous place where they can see artworks created by famous artists; they are not very motivated by a strong interest in the arts (Mastandrea & Crano, 2019). They are not strong museum-goers compared with modern art visitors. On the contrary, modern art visitors are familiar with museums and art galleries, especially those housing modern and contemporary art. They make frequent visits to art museums. Also, the way they conduct their visits is different. In most cases, modern art devotees like to make the visit alone and frequently consult art history books in preparation for their museum visit.

The overall approach is also different: visitors to ancient art museum put into action behaviors dictated by motivations, expectations, and interests, and are intent on the acquisition of understanding and knowledge. They adopted a kind of cognitive approach to the aesthetic experience. The visitors to modern art museums, on the other hand, seem to have adopted an emotional, pleasure seeking approach. Their answers provided to various questions (i.e., visitors' expectations, motivations, and satisfactions regarding the visit) describe the experience of visitors in terms of pleasure, of having seen fascinating works, of having been moved emotionally; indicators of a desire to learn about art were present, but remained secondary (Mastandrea et al., 2007, 2009).

It can be said that visitors who appreciate museums displaying ancient art saw the visit as an opportunity to fill a perceived "cultural gap" in their knowledge of art (perhaps because many have a lower social and educational level than modern art visitors). So for them, the primary reason for their visit was to learn and to enrich their knowledge about art. Second, the content of a representational artwork has a clear and definite meaning, at least superficially. It is possible that ancient art itself requires a more cognitive approach to the aesthetic experience due to the historical significance and cultural weight that these artworks from the distant past bring with them.

Visitors to modern art museums are somewhat more educated and likely have more knowledge about art (cf. aesthetic fluency, Smith & Smith, 2006) compared with the visitors to the Borghese Gallery and Museum. They can, therefore, immediately take an emotional approach to the experience, not having the primary need to fill a perceived cultural gap. Second, abstract art, being composed of colors, form, and materials that have no direct meaning or representation of real objects, invites viewers to assume a more emotional, hedonistic, and perhaps a more playful and lighter attitude and disposition during an aesthetic experience. In research that compared visitors to two different art style museums such as the Guggenheim Museum in Venice (modern art) and the Borghese Gallery and Museum in Rome (ancient art), it was found that the average enjoyment level for both groups increased as the educational level of visitors increased (Mastandrea et al., 2007). Regardless of the art style under consideration, a higher level of education likely provides the possibility to better understand the artworks exhibited, and thereby obtain greater aesthetic pleasure.

Concerning personality traits (openness to experience and sensation seeking), in a study Mastandrea et al. (2009) conducted in two different museums (Braschi and the National Gallery of Modern Art, both in Rome), no difference between the two groups on the openness to experience dimension was found (both groups reported high scores). It seems reasonable that people who go to museums do so with an open mind, an interest in culture, and a desire to acquire new experiences, no matter the type of museum. The difference, on this topic, is probably more between people that go and those who do not go to museums, instead of the difference between people who choose museums with different kinds of artistic expressions (DiMaggio, 1996). Differences in the two typologies of visitors taken into consideration were rather found in the sensation seeking characteristic. People who go to modern art museums are willing to go in search of sensation more than people who go to ancient art museums. This finding can be related to that found between preference for abstract vs. representative art in laboratory studies (Feist & Brady, 2004; Furnham & Walker, 2001); we also can apply it to visitors to art museums of the two types considered. As confirmation of this result, emotions aroused by modern art visitors reached higher scores than those visiting ancient art museums (Mastandrea, 2011). More generally, the level of perceived congruence between the characteristics of the setting and one's specific needs and inclinations, which can be called compatibility, can drive people to visit specific art style museums: if we are not interested in modern art, we will visit other types of museums that we consider more congruent with our personal interest, values, and beliefs. People with higher scores in sensation seeking preferred to visit contemporary art museums, while low sensation seekers favored visiting ancient art museums (Mastandrea et al., 2009). In other words, people make their aesthetic choice according also to personal interests and knowledge, and the compatibility with the museum setting they opt to explore.

THE SOCIAL CONTEXT 1: PIERRE BOURDIEU AND THE USER'S SOCIAL CONTEXT

As we know already, it is not only cognitive and affective processes that determine an aesthetic experience; another important issue to consider has to do with the social context while experiencing the arts. Several studies have shown that the aesthetic impact of a work of art depends on, to an important extent, the different socio-demographic factors including age, class, social status, health, wealth, and so on.

The most influential scholar who deeply investigated the world of the arts from the social context point of view of the users was the French sociologist Pierre Bourdieu. His approach to the arts focused on social factors rather than the artwork itself, which on the contrary is the core of the empirical aesthetics research. Bourdieu distinguishes two kinds of capital: "economic capital" (in simple terms how much money an individual possesses) and "cultural capital" (knowledge and culture). Starting from a Marxian point of view, Bourdieu (1984) stated that the upper middle class had not only economic power but also cultural capital. He affirmed that the enjoyment for the arts has a strong social component: only people with cultural capital can appreciate places like museums that he defines "temples of culture" (Bourdieu, 1984). People who visit museums have been shown to have a higher socioeconomic status (in education and by profession) than those who do not visit them. He maintained that the museum had the potential to emphasize the feeling of belonging for this group, and for people without cultural capital, the feeling of exclusion (Bourdieu & Darbel, 1969). People belonging to the cultural upper middle class feel comfortable in such places. Since their childhood, their parents would have taken them to museums; the education they possess allows them the capacity to understand and enjoy the artworks displayed in such temples of culture.

Bourdieu and Darbel (1969) affirmed that access to the art museum culture was characterized by strong social differences, and that the approach to art was strongly influenced by social conditions. In the analysis carried out in the work *L'amour pour l'art*, Bourdieu and Darbel (1969) stressed the fundamental role of the familiar influence and the possession of symbolic goods such as education, knowledge, and culture for the middle upper class family. Inglis (2005) states that people feel comfortable in places like museums because since their childhood they have absorbed a familiarity with these places; they have built up the capacity to understand and decode what is offered in such contexts—a feeling of confidence with the arts that is lacking in people from other classes. Bourdieu developed this concept from his early studies in the books *L'amour pour l'art* (Bourdieu & Darbel, 1969) and the *Distinction* (Bourdieu, 1984). Social belonging therefore has an influence not only on earnings and money, but also in term of taste, symbolic goods, and cultural disposition. Bourdieu affirms that a work of art "only exists as such for a person who has the means to appropriate it, or in other words, to decipher it" (Bourdieu, 1984, p. 22). People who had the advantage to be born into an educated family have a great advantage. DiMaggio (1982) affirms that cultural possibilities are most strongly cultivated within upper socioeconomic status, those of the professional and intellectual class. Art experience and consumption are normal and facile activities in the world of the elite.

Bourdieu employed quantitative, qualitative, and ethnographic methods to try to demonstrate how taste can be considered a form of capital that constitutes possible inequalities based on an economic/social gap. In a famous study, Bourdieu (1984) demonstrated a difference between manual workers and upper class people in terms of different art style preferences (music and visual arts). At the extreme upper class taste level, he found a preference for the *Well-Tempered Clavier* by Bach in music, and Bruegel and Goya in painting, whereas at the popular taste extreme, the preference was found for the *Blue Danube* by Strauss in music and Utrillo and Renoir in paintings. Bourdieu (1984) attributed this distinction in terms of taste and preferences to the cultural education and social class of the two groups.

DiMaggio and Mukhtar (2004), in an analysis regarding the preference for fine and popular arts, showed a difference among social classes: people from the upper middle class participated more in high culture events (exhibition galleries, museum, etc.), while people from lower classes took part mainly in popular culture events (cinema, pop music concerts, etc.). Peterson (1992, 2005), made an interesting distinction between so-called "omnivores," people from the social elite who participate in high culture events but also hold varied aesthetic interests in popular culture, versus "univores," people who usually belong to the lower class and are oriented only to popular art forms of culture.

In line with the findings that Bourdieu achieved in the *Distinction* (Bourdieu, 1984), Chan and Goldthorpe (2007) showed in a sample of British citizens that education and occupational status were good predictors of broad consumption of different kinds of arts, such as the so-called "fine" (theater, dance) and "popular" (cinema) arts. Moreover, Chan and Goldthorpe (2007) found that wide participation in visual fine arts was highest among groups with higher levels of education.

Bourdieu's studies were influential by showing how the social context and the cultural capital can have a consequence on the kinds of cultural objects and consumption that people belonging to different social class enjoy and prefer.

The criticisms addressed to Bourdieu's social theory of art is that it possibly overestimated the class factors and that it represents a reductionist view of the art experience, as it envisioned the aesthetic response as a socioeconomic formula in which appreciation of art and aesthetics was a byproduct of other social processes (Inglis, 2005). According to Upright (2004), Bourdieu did not consider the continuing education process that can develop from an individual's social experiences, social relationships, and other forms of social participation in society.

Not only the family but also an individual's scholastic curriculum is an important factor in the development of cultural capital. Aschaffenburg and Maas (1997) argued that Bourdieu might have underestimated the possibility for people to acquire cultural capital through the education received at school; this so-called scholastic route could provide the cultural tools and the necessary learning to reach aesthetic enjoyment of the arts later in life. Even without a highly educated family background, a person can acquire through great efforts the training via other opportunities to enjoy the aesthetic experience, in addition to facilitation provided by education. As education is a relevant predictor of art consumption, the school experience can foster the opportunity to comprehend and enjoy different kinds of arts. In a recent study conducted with a sample of Italian undergraduate students on museum attendance, Mastandrea et al. (2016) showed a positive correlation between art education training received in high school and the number of students' museum visitations in the past 12 months. Art education classes in high school could provide useful sources of knowledge about art that can lead students to enjoy museum visits in the future, contradicting or supplementing Bourdieu's conception of cultural capital being transmitted by the family from one generation to the other, thereby providing grounds for more hope for museum attendance and the art experience.

THE SOCIAL CONTEXT 2: HOWARD BECKER AND THE ARTIST'S SOCIAL CONTEXT

Another aspect regarding the social context refers to the artist. The most influential author who discussed this topic, from a sociological point of view, was Howard Becker. Becker's sociological approach to the arts does not engage with aesthetic judgments; rather, it was concerned primarily with the production and consumption of artworks. Becker looked at art as a collective activity. His most famous work, *Art Worlds* (Becker, 1982), describes art and the artist as parts of a complex system: the interaction network of the artist and the broader context where the artist operates in his or her art world. Becker stressed the importance of the relationships that artists have with the different kinds of people that surround them. It is not sufficient to possess a special gift to be considered an artist; in their careers, artists usually need teaching, school, and education. To express their talent and creativity, artists need to be involved in the art market and to establish contacts with the distributors of art, such as galleries or museums (Cluley, 2012). To become established as an artist, the individual artist needs to be appreciated by consumers and visitors.

Becker's view is contrary to the romantic myth of the artist who possesses a special gift and is talented and creates his or her work based on introspection and inspiration obtained from himself and his inner world. According to Becker, "all artistic work, like all human activity, involves the joint activity of a number, often a large number, of people" (Becker, 1982, p. 1). The artist can compose music or paint only if there are other people that help and surround him or her during the artistic process. The teaching, for instance, that artists receive during their career is part of their social world. Becker calls the group of persons that surround the artist "support personnel," and sees these persons as important as the artist in the production of cultural goods. Becker says that "it is not unreasonable to say that it is the art world, rather than the individual artist, which makes the work" (Becker, 1982, p. 194).

We already know that some significant input to art creation also comes from technologies and new materials. Chemistry made amazing progress with the production of new pigments in the 19th century. The French chemist Michel-Eugéne Chevreul (1839) made an important contribution to the industrialization of chemical pigmented colors and wrote extensively on the nature and effect of these new colors. In the same period we find the invention of the paint tube, which is attributed to the American painter John Goffe Rand. The tube closed with a screw-on cap, allowing the use of oil paint without the risk of drying it. This invention could have contributed to the French Impressionism style, allowing the artists to leave their studios and take their work to the outdoors, enabling them to perceive and take inspiration from the real natural landscape while directly painting it, "*en plein air*," and conveying on the canvas the direct effect of natural light, the main poetics of their new style.

All this means that is not the artist alone, but also technological inventions (which are to be considered social because they are made by people in a specific historical context) as well as the social relationships that support the artistic creation. As Becker insists, the artist is a part of the social and cooperative network that backs and surrounds his or her creations.

If we think of some contemporary artists, we can directly perceive how art creation comes from the joint efforts of social network collaboration. For example, the British artist Damien Hirst creates his pieces of art (objects and installations) with the fundamental contribution of a team composed of people with different specializations—biologists, historians, marketing dealers, etc. Many artists work now as art entrepreneurs. The American artist Jeff Koons has a particular reputation for his sculptures, and is very active in art marketing with a particular attention to reaching his audience through different media communications. The artist as entrepreneur it is not entirely new. Andy Warhol is probably the most famous example in modern times. In fact, Warhol called his studio a "factory"; the factory has a sort of working class connotation where manual workers contribute to the assemblage of different pieces to produce a utilitarian object. This was at the basis of the idea of Warhol's art as popular art; he was in fact the pioneer of Pop Art, which has in his terms a popular connotation of being an art that takes inspiration from the popular culture, from ordinary everyday goods, and from the media (e.g., advertisements, television, cinema).

The criticism addressed to Becker's social theory holds that it is impossible to think that every choice the artist makes is determined by the social conditions that surround him (Sullivan, 2002). Artist cannot be equated with the people he collaborates with, because the artist has the ideas and the creative spirit, while the others are very often material executors, with some skill of course, but their contribution is to realize the project that the artist-in-chief designs and creates. For example, we know that the famous sculpture *Pauline Bonaparte as Venus Victrix* by Antonio Canova (created between 1805 and 1808) was realized in his studio, perfectly organized as an industrious workshop, with the help of numerous collaborators (skilled sculpture executors) who tried to avoid for Canova any type of secondary or repetitive mechanical operations, allowing him to concentrate on exquisitely creative tasks and on executive refinements works. The choices, independent of social conditions, are left up to the artist's aesthetic sense (Zangwill, 2014).

The Early Social Context of the Art Experience

Elementary school children make up a significant proportion of museum visitors; for numerous museums, family groups are the biggest category of visitors (Chang, 2006). In the United States, Australia, and the United Kingdom ~60–70% of visitors are families; adult group or school groups make up ~25–30%, and only 5% of museum attendees visit on their own (Ellenbogen, Luke, & Dierking, 2007). These numbers tell us that the social dimension is a fundamental aspect of the museum visit. Dierking (2013) states that the process of learning through informal conversation and interaction needs the contribution of others. Social sharing of the experience focused on the objects exhibited in a museum can enrich the sociocultural meanings of the experience. Families are the first learning group a person belongs to (Dierking, 2013), and probably the first recall of a museum visit is with parents. Usually the child's visit to a museum comes from a family decision to spend their leisure time in a cultural place. Parents decide to visit museums because they think these are good places where children can learn about a wide range of topics with the social mediation of the parents themselves or of the museum educators (Piscitelli, 2001). Different reasons are at the basis of the decision, including entertainment, learning, and social sharing of the experience.

Falk and Dierking (2016) conducted several studies where they demonstrated that adults' museum visit frequencies and participation was influenced by their early childhood experience with the family. There is a relationship between the cultural activities conducted in childhood and future museum visitations. Whether or not an adult goes to museums is rooted in previous experience with their parents. A good predictor of future museum visitations is therefore the parents' frequency of visiting museums with their child.

Piscitelli and Anderson (2000), reviewing the literature on young children's museum's experience, have observed that there are not many studies of young children and the museum experience. This lack of information might be due to the fact that children have a limited possibility to communicate and reflect on their experiences. Interesting to note is that from conversations with children and from self-produced graphic representations, the memories of their museum experiences were mainly coming from natural, ethnological, and science museums.

There are several typologies of museums, not only art museums, where children are accompanied. Children generally find art museums not very interesting and a bit diffi-cult to understand compared with science museums (Chang, 2012). In science museums they can probably enjoy and experience curiosity, interest, fun, and, often, hands-on exhibits.

School visits can provide a good opportunity for children to experience museums, mainly in those cases where children have few opportunities to visit museums with their parents. A recent study conducted in Austria, France, Hungary, Italy, New Zealand, Portugal, Taiwan, and the United States, found that about 20% of undergraduate uni-versity students had never visited a single museum with their parents (Mastandrea & Maricchiolo, 2016). It was quite a surprising finding that a good number of these students had never had this experience with their families.

Museum visits with school teachers in children's early years do not substitute for family interest in museums and culture, but can partially fill this gap. In many elemen-tary schools all over the world, strong attention is paid to art and visual education, and this might be a starting point to facilitate future museum behaviors for children, espe-cially for those who did not have the opportunity to visit museums with their parents.

Bamford (2006) makes an interesting distinction between education in the arts and education through the arts. Education in the arts refers to systematic teaching and learning, theory, and skills, in different art typologies such as music, drama, and dance, not only the visual arts. Education through the arts means the use of arts as a sort of pedagogical cultural system useful for many topics, such as literacy, history, etc. Education in and through the arts both improve knowledge and culture of course, but reinforce also group cohesion and social identity (Mastandrea, Wagoner, & Hogg, 2021). Social identity refers to how the self is constructed, sustained, and expressed by the social groups that people belong to and identify with (Abrams & Hogg, 2010; Tajfel & Turner, 1986). The artworks exhibited in a museum are the expression of the iden-tity of a community at different levels: local, regional, national, international. Among several positive benefits, artwork, galleries, and museums play an important role in the construction and communication of a society's identity, and thus of the identity of the members of that society. Many school and out-of-school art programs also have the goal of improving intercultural and social inter-ethnic relationships among pupils. To teach other people's cultures through the arts can be seen as a good introduction to understanding other people. These programs use art education to encourage more democratic competencies and promote intercultural dialogue.

Art education practice is based on the idea that the opportunity to view artworks in museums stimulates interest and curiosity, and enriches the learning process (Henry, 2004). It is important to encourage children's interaction with artworks in different and meaningful ways within the museum environmental context (Chang, 2012). For example, they should be stimulated to look at art, talk about artworks, and ask question from adults and educators. This approach promotes the increase of the vocabulary, the visual capacity of observation, and other personal skills (Danko-McGhee, 2004). Moreover, art education is not only valuable by itself; some studies have reported a positive correlation between education in the arts and through the arts with the increase of positive feelings, wellbeing, and social relationships (Eyestone-Finnegan, 2001; Mastandrea et al., 2018). A 3-year study conducted in Singapore focusing on education through the arts produced an enhancement of literacy in language and speech; moreover, the outside-school art education, through museum and gallery visits and public art events and performance participation, promoted positive attitudes and confidence in the children. In China, arts education promoted children's enjoyment of learning and social communication with their friends (Bamford, 2006).

Regarding adolescents and their participation in museum visits, several surveys have shown that adolescents are not strongly attracted to visits to these temples of culture. In the United States in 2008, a large-scale survey of public participation in different cultural events reported that only 12.9% of Americans between the ages of 18 and 24 years had visited at least one museum during the previous year (Williams & Keen, 2009). In Germany, ~23% of young people between 15 and 25 years reported visiting at least one museum of art, science, or history during the 12 months before the survey (Kirchberg, 1996). These findings have been confirmed by other data around the world: in France, people between 15 and 24 years represented only ~15% of museum visitors (Lemerise, 1999). In Australia and New Zealand, art museum visitors between 20 and 29 years of age formed 26% of the visitor population (Mason & McCarthy, 2006). The findings from these surveys show that young people do not find visits to a gallery attractive, even though the museum may be in close proximity. These results suggest that in many different parts of the world, museums do not attract many young people.

There are a number of reasons that may explain this lack of interest. From a psychological point of view, Mason and McCarthy (2006) reported two main reasons that prevent people from attending museums: threshold fear (Fleming, 1999; Prince & Schadla-Hall, 1985), which consists of a "psychological barrier which dissuades people from entering spaces where they feel uncomfortable" (Mason & McCarthy, 2006, p. 22), and personal and social identity related to a sort of dissonance between the cultural meaning represented by the museum and the individual and cultural identity of young people (Bartlett & Kelly, 2000; Kelly, 2009).

Adolescents often see museums as a place for old people, more focused on the past, while their interests and needs are more oriented to the present and the future (Shrapnel, 2012). What often leads this group to attend a museum is not real interest, but a mere curiosity or duty that forces them to take part in an experience. Without being accompanied by a genuine desire, attendance is related to attitudes of indifference (Bartlett & Kelly, 2000).

Many young people make the equation that museum = school: both are places to acquire knowledge regarding a great number of subjects (art, science, history, anthropology, etc.). Regarding the learning process, it might be difficult for them to distinguish museums from school; the risk is that museums are seen as an addition to their learning workload and therefore look very unattractive and boring. Moreover, adolescents have limited budgets for entertainment and leisure activities; they probably prefer to spend their money engaging in other cultural activities, like going to the cinema or concerts.

Final Considerations

The experience of positive feelings should be one of the most important goals of museum visits in early childhood. Having a satisfactory experience of amusement, fun, and enjoyment can create positive dispositions and attitudes for future visitations. As in many domains of education, starting with an easy and enjoyable experience can encouraging engagement in more difficult and challenging tasks later on. At the beginning children need to have an easy feedback to their actions consisting of surprise, curiosity, joy, and fun. This creates an interest in the repetition of similar experiences in the future. As in the flow model by Csikszentmihalyi (1990), if the challenge is too difficult people get frustrated and do not want to repeat the experience. If it is too easy they get bored. The optimal experience occurs when there is a good balance between abilities, skills, and task requirements. In such cases people are in a state where they can understand what is going on. If they can reach a positive mood, then they probably will prove willing to repeat the experience. If, on the contrary, the experience is too difficult, boring, and frustrating because they do not understand the "rules" or do not experience positive feelings, then this would lead to an unsatisfying condition that reduces the chance of repeating the activity in the future.

As shown in several cross-cultural studies on education in the arts (learning how to dance, to perform, to draw, etc.) and through the arts (the use of the arts to understand art itself and as a pedagogical tool in other subjects), the art experience is characterized by important goals and benefits such as, among others, improvement of understanding sociocultural meanings and social relationships (Bamford, 2006; Falk & Dierking, 2016).

Children's direct involvement in the arts experience is an important requisite. It is not enough to take children or adolescents to a museum to aim at a positive relationship and satisfaction with the arts; sometimes, without the right preparation, it can have the opposite effect and become a boring and/or dissatisfying experience. And this concept can be extended also to adults. It is important first to plan the museum experience, before, during, and after the visit, in order to follow and complete the different stages of the process that will lead to a satisfactory art experience and aesthetic enjoyment.

REFERENCES

Abrams, D., & Hogg, M. A. (2010). Social identity and self-categorization. In J. F. Dovidio, M. Hewstone, P. Glick, & V. M. Esses (Eds.), *The SAGE handbook of prejudice, stereotyping and discrimination* (pp. 179–193). London: Sage.

Arnheim, R. (1974). *Art and visual perception*. Berkeley, CA: University of California Press.

Aschaffenburg, K., & Maas, I. (1997). Cultural and educational careers: The dynamics of social reproduction. *American Sociological Review, 62*, 573–587.

Bamford, A. (2006). *The wow factor: Global research compendium on the impact of the arts in education*. Munich, Germany: Waxmann Verlag.

Bartlett, A., & Kelly, L. (2000). *Youth audiences: Research summary*. Sydney, Australia: Australian Museum Audience Research Centre.

Becker, H. S. (1982). *Art Worlds*. University of California Press.

Berlyne, D. E. (1971). *Aesthetics and psychobiology*. New York: Appleton-Century-Crofts.

Bourdieu, P. (1984). *Distinction: A social critique of the judgment of taste*. Cambridge, MA: Harvard University Press. (First published 1979.)

Bourdieu, P., & Darbel, A. (1969). *The love of art*. Stanford, CA: Stanford University Press [1990].

Cardinet, J. (1958). Préférences esthétiques et personnalité. *L'année psychologique, 58*, 45–69.

Chamorro-Premuzic, T., & Furnham, A. (2004). Art judgment: A measure related to both personality and intelligence? *Imagination, Cognition and Personality, 24*(1), 3–24.

Chamorro-Premuzic, T., Burke, C., Hsu, A., & Swami, V. (2010). Personality predictors of artistic preferences as a function of the emotional valence and perceived complexity of paintings. *Psychology of Aesthetics, Creativity, and the Arts, 4*(4), 196–204.

Chan, T. W., & Goldthorpe J. H. (2007). Social stratification and cultural consumption: The visual arts in England. *Poetics, 35*, 168–90.

Chang, E. (2006). Interactive experiences and contextual learning in museums. *Studies in Art Education, 47*(2), 170–186.

Chang, E. (2012). Art trek: Looking at art with young children. *International Journal of Education through Art, 8*(2), 151–167.

Chevreul, M. E. (1839). *De la loi du contraste simultané des couleurs et de l'assortiment des objects colorés*. Paris: Pitois-Levrault.

Chirumbolo, A., Brizi, A., Mastandrea, S., & Mannetti, L. (2014). Beauty is no quality in things themselves: Epistemic motivation affects implicit preferences for art. *PLoS ONE, 9*(10), e110323. doi:10.1371/journal.pone.0110323

Cluley, R. (2012). Art words and art worlds: The methodological importance of language use in Howard S. Becker's sociology of art and cultural production. *Cultural Sociology, 6*(2), 201–216.

Costa, P. T., & McCrae, R. R. (1992). *Revised NEO personality inventory and NEO five-factor inventory*. Lutz, FL: Psychological Assessment Resources.

Csikszentmihalyi, M. (1990). *Flow*. New York: Harper and Row.

Cupchik, G. C. (1993). Component and relational processing in aesthetics. *Poetics, 22*, 171–183.

Curci, A., Lanciano, T., Maddalena, C., Mastandrea, S., & Sartori, G. (2015). Flashbulb memories of the Pope's resignation: Explicit and implicit measures across differing religious groups. *Memory, 23*(4), 529–544.

Cutting, J. E. (2003). Gustave Caillebotte, French impressionism, and mere exposure. *Psychonomic Bulletin & Review, 10*, 319–343.

Danko-McGhee, K. (2004). The museum-university connection: Partners in early childhood education art experiences. *Art Education, 57* (6), 35–40.

Dierking, L. D. (2013). Museum as social learning spaces. In I Brændholt Lundgaard, & J. T. Jensen (Eds.), *Museums: Social learning spaces and knowledge producing processes* (pp. 198–215). Copenhagen: Styrelsen Danish Agency for Culture.

DiMaggio, P. (1982). Cultural entrepreneurship in nineteenth-century Boston: The creation of an organizational base for high culture. *Media, Culture & Society, 4*(1), 33–50.

DiMaggio, P. (1996). Are art-museum visitors different from other people? The relationship between attendance and social and political attitudes in the United States. *Poetics, 24,* 161–180.

DiMaggio, P., & Mukhtar, T., 2004. Arts participation as cultural capital in the United States, 1982–2002: Signs of decline? *Poetics, 32*(2), 169–194.

Ellenbogen, K., Luke, J. J., & Dierking, L. D. (2007). Family learning in museums: Perspectives on a decade of research. In J. Falk, L. Dierking, & S. Foutz (Eds.), *In principle, in practice: Museums as learning institutions* (pp. 17–30). Lanham, MD: AltaMira Press.

Eyestone-Finnegan, J. (2001). Looking at art with toddlers. *Art Education, 54,* 40–45.

Eysenck, H. J. (1941). "Type"-factors in aesthetic judgements. *British Journal of Psychology, 31*(3), 262–270.

Falk, J. H., & Dierking, L. D. (2016). *The museum experience revisited.* Abingdon, England: Routledge.

Fechner (1876). Various attempts to establish a basic form of beauty: Experimental aesthetics, golden section, and square. *Empirical Studies of the Arts, 15,* 115–130 [1997].

Feist, G. J., & Brady, T. R. (2004). Openness to experience, nonconformity, and the preference for abstract art. *Empirical Studies of the Arts, 22,* 77–89.

Fleming, D. (1999). A question of perception. *Museums Journal, 4,* 29–31.

Furnham, A., & Avison, M. (1997). Personality and preference for surreal paintings. *Personality and Individual Differences, 23,* 923–935.

Furnham, A., & Walker, J. (2001). Personality and judgments of abstract, pop art, and representational paintings. *European Journal of Personality, 15,* 57–72.

Hekkert, P., & van Wieringen, P. C. W. (1996). Beauty in the eye of expert and nonexpert beholders: A study in the appraisal of art. *American Journal of Psychology, 109,* 389–407.

Henry, C. (2004). The art museums and the university in preservice education. *Art Education, 57*(1), 35–40

Inglis, D. (2005). Thinking art sociologically. In D. Inglis & J. Hughson (Eds.), *The sociology of art, ways of seeing* (pp. 11–29). London: Palgrave Macmillan.

Kaplan, R., & Kaplan, S. (1989). *The experience of nature: A psychological perspective.* Cambridge, England: Cambridge University Press.

Kelly, L. (2009). *Young people and museums.* The Australian museum audience research department. Retrieved July 5, 2016 from http://australianmuseum.net.au/Young-People-and-Museums

Kirchberg, V. (1996). Museum visitors and non-visitors in Germany: A representative survey. *Poetics, 24*(2), 239–258.

Kruglanski A. W., & Webster, D. M. (1996). Motivated closing of the mind: Seizing and freezing. *Psychological Review, 103,* 263–283.

Kunst-Wilson, W. R., & Zajonc, R. B. (1980). Affective discrimination of stimuli that cannot be recognized. *Science, 207,* 557–558.

Lanciano, T., Curci, A., Mastandrea, S., & Sartori, G. (2013). Do automatic mental associations detect a flashbulb memory? *Memory, 21*(4), 482–493.

Leder, H., Belke, B., Oeberst, A., and Augustin, D. (2004). A model of aesthetic appreciation and aesthetic judgments. *British Journal of Psychology, 95*, 489–508.

Lemerise, T. (1999). Les adolescents au musée: Enfin des chiffres! *Publics et Musées, 15*, 9–29.

Locher, P., & Nodine, C. F. (1989). The perceptual value of symmetry. *Computers and Math Applications, 17*, 475–484.

Locher, P., Krupinski, E. A., Mello-Thoms, C., & Nodine, C. F. (2007). Visual interest in pictorial art during an aesthetic experience. *Spatial Vision, 21*(1–2), 55–77.

Martindale, C., & Moore, K. (1988). Priming, prototypicality, and preference. *Journal of Experimental Psychology: Human Perception and Performance, 14*, 661–670.

Mason, D., & McCarthy, C. (2006). The feeling of exclusion: Young people's perceptions of art galleries. *Museum Management and Curatorship, 21*, 20–31.

Mastandrea, S. (2011). Il ruolo delle emozioni nell'esperienza estetica. *Rivista di estetica, 48*(3), 95–111.

Mastandrea, S. (2014). How emotions shape aesthetic experiences. In P. Tinio, & J. Smith (Eds.), *The Cambridge handbook of the psychology of aesthetics and the arts* (pp. 500–518). Cambridge, England: Cambridge University Press.

Mastandrea, S., Bartoli, G., & Bove, G. (2007). Learning through ancient art and experiencing emotions with contemporary art: Comparing visits in two different museums. *Empirical Studies of the Arts, 25*(2), 173–191.

Mastandrea, S., Bartoli, G., & Bove, G. (2009). Preferences for ancient and modern art museums: Visitor experiences and personality characteristics. *Psychology of Aesthetic, Creativity, and the Arts, 3*(3), 164–173.

Mastandrea, S., Bartoli, G., & Carrus, G. (2011). The automatic aesthetic evaluation of different art and architectural styles. *Psychology of Aesthetic, Creativity, and the Arts, 5*(2), 126–134.

Mastandrea, S., & Crano, W. (2019). Peripheral factors affecting the evaluation of artworks. *Empirical Studies of the Arts, 37*(1), 82–91.

Mastandrea, S., & Maricchiolo, F. (2014). Implicit and explicit aesthetic evaluation of design objects. *Art & Perception, 1–2*(2), 141–162.

Mastandrea, S., & Maricchiolo, F. (2016). International perspective on museum research: A comparison among countries. In S. Mastandrea, & F. Maricchiolo (Eds.), *The role of the museum in the education of young adults: Motivation, emotion and learning* (pp. 203–210). Rome: Roma Tre Press.

Mastandrea, S., Maricchiolo, F., Bove, G., Carrus, G., Marella, D., & Perucchini P. (2016). Psychological aspects of museum visits for undergraduate Italian students. In S. Mastandrea, & F. Maricchiolo (Eds.), *The role of the museum in the education of young adults: Motivation, emotion, and learning* (pp. 141–164). Rome: Roma Tre Press.

Mastandrea, S., Maricchiolo, F., Carrus, G., Giovannelli, I., Giuliani, V., & Berardi, D. (2018). Visits to figurative art museums may lower blood pressure and stress. *Arts & Health, 11*, 123–132. doi:10.1080/17533015.2018.1443953

Mastandrea, S., & Umiltà, M. A. (2016). Futurist art: Motion and aesthetics as a function of title. *Frontiers in Human Neuroscience, 10*, 201. doi:10.3389/fnhum.2016.00201

Mastandrea, S., Wagoner, J. A., & Hogg, M. A. (2021). Liking for abstract and representational art: National identity as an art appreciation heuristic. *Psychology of Aesthetics, Creativity, and the Arts, 15*(2), 241–249. https://doi.org/10.1037/aca0000272

McWhinnie, H. J. (1968). A review of research on aesthetic measure. *Acta Psychologica, 28*, 363–375.

Nadal, M., Munar, E., Marty, G., & Cela-Conde, C. J. (2010). Visual complexity and beauty appreciation: Explaining the divergence of results. *Empirical Studies of the Arts, 28*, 173–191.

Peterson, R. A. (1992). Understanding audience segmentation: From elite and popular to omnivore and univore. *Poetics, 21*(4), 243–258.

Peterson, R. A. (2005). Problems in comparative research: The example of omnivorousness. *Poetics, 33*, 257–282.

Piscitelli, B. (2001). Young children's interactive experiences in museums: Engaged, embodies, and empowered learners. *The Museum Journal, 44*(3), 224–229.

Piscitelli, B., & Anderson, D. (2000). Young children's learning in museum settings. *Visitor Studies Today, 3*, 3–10.

Posner, M. I., & Keele, S. W. (1968). On the genesis of abstract ideas. *Journal of Experimental Psychology, 77*, 353–363.

Prince, D., & Schadla-Hall, R. T. (1985). The image of the museum: A case study of Kingston upon Hull. *Museums Journal, 85*, 39–45.

Purcell, T., Peron, E., & Berto, R. (2001). Why do preferences differ between scene types? *Environment and Behavior, 33*(1), 93–106.

Rawlings, D., Vidal, N., & Furnham, A. (2000). Personality and aesthetic preference in Spain and England: Two studies relating sensation seeking and openness to experience liking for painting and music. *European Journal of Personality, 14*, 553–576.

Reber, R., Schwarz, N., & Winkielman, P. (2004). Processing fluency and aesthetic pleasure: Is beauty in the perceiver's processing experience? *Personality and Social Psychology Review, 8*, 364–382.

Shrapnel, E. (2012). *Engaging young adults in museums: An audience research study.* The Australian Museum Audience Research Department. Retrieved May 7, 2016, from http://australianmuseum.net.au/document/Engaging-Young-Adults-in-Museums.

Silvia, P. J. (2005). Emotional response to art: From collation and arousal to cognition and emotion. *Review of General Psychology, 9*, 342–357.

Smith, J. K. (2014). *The museum effect: How museums, libraries, and cultural institutions educate and civilize society.* Lanham, MD: Rowman & Littlefield Publishers.

Smith, L. F., & Smith, J. K. (2006). The nature and growth of aesthetic fluency. In P. Locher, C. Martindale, & L. Dorfman (Eds.), *New directions in aesthetics, creativity, and the arts* (pp. 47–58). Amityville, NY: Baywood.

Sullivan, A. (2002). Bourdieu and education: How useful is Bourdieu's theory for researchers? *Netherlands Journal of Social Sciences, 38*(2), 144–166.

Tajfel, H., & Turner, J. C. (1986). The social identity theory of intergroup behavior. In S. Worchel, & W. G. Austin (Eds.), *Psychology of intergroup relations* (pp.7–24). Chicago, IL: Nelson-Hall.

Upright, C. B. (2004). Social capital and cultural participation: Spousal influences on attendance at arts events. *Poetics, 32*(2), 129–143.

Whitfield, T. W. A., & Slatter, P. E. (1979). The effects of categorization and prototypicality on aesthetic choice in a furniture selection task. *British Journal of Psychology, 70*, 65–75.

Wiersema, D. V., Van Der Schalk, J., & van Kleef, G. A. (2012). Who's afraid of red, yellow, and blue? Need for cognitive closure predicts aesthetic preferences. *Psychology of Aesthetic, Creativity and the Arts, 6*, 168–174.

Williams, K., & Keen, D. (2009). *2008 survey of public participation in the arts* (Research Report 49). National Endowment for the Arts. Retrieved May 11, 2020 from https://www.arts.gov/sites/default/files/2008-SPPA.pdf.

Winkielman, P., & Cacioppo, J. T. (2001). Mind at ease puts a smile on the face: Psychophysiological evidence that processing facilitation leads to positive affect. *Journal of Personality and Social Psychology, 81*, 989–1000.

Winkielman, P., Halberstadt, J., Fazendeiro, T., & Catty, S. (2006). Prototypes are attractive because they are easy on the mind. *Psychological Science, 17*(9), 799–806.

Zajonc, R. B. (1968). Attitudinal effects of mere exposure. *Journal of Personality and Social Psychology, 9*(2), 1–27.

Zangwill, N. (2014). Music, metaphor, and aesthetic concepts. *The Journal of Aesthetics and Art Criticism, 72*(1), 1–11.

Zuckerman, M. (1979). *Sensation seeking: Beyond the optimal level of arousal.* Mahwah, NJ: Erlbaum.

SECTION 7

APPLICATIONS

CHAPTER 44

DESIGN AND AESTHETICS

PAUL HEKKERT

Introduction

In June of 2019, Apple's chief design officer Jonathan Ive announced his departure from the company after more than 20 years of service. Newspaper articles around the world reminded us of some of his greatest achievements, among them the Apple iMac, iPod, and iPhone. These products were not just incredibly innovative and intuitive, they were also stunningly beautiful. Designed objects, such as Apple devices, may not be primarily designed for an aesthetic purpose—after all, they must perform a function—but they also need to bring aesthetic pleasure in order to succeed and survive. For works of art, the subject of most studies in the field of aesthetics, considerations of beauty have become increasingly less important over the past century.[1] Designed artifacts cannot afford to discard beauty since attractive products appear, for example, more usable and valuable (Tractinsky, Katz, & Ikar, 2000; see Hekkert, 2014 for an overview). The field of product design thus demands and conveniently allows for studying beauty or aesthetic pleasure in the "pure" sense.

Aesthetic Pleasure

Whenever scholars, and lay people alike, talk about "aesthetics" or "aesthetic pleasure," they are notoriously vague in specifying what they are actually looking at or talking about. This is troublesome, because the concept of "aesthetics" can refer to different things, both in everyday language and in academic contexts. As Koren (2010, p. 11) notes in his lovely booklet on the 10 different definitions of "aesthetic" and "aesthetics," "because these terms confusingly refer to so many disparate but often connected things, the exact meaning of the speaker or writer, unless qualified, is sometimes unclear. . ." This really is an understatement. For the record, there are essentially three different ways that the word "aesthetic" is used as an adjective:

1. To describe or express "the way things look" or "the care that has been given to a thing's appearance," often in contrast to an object's functioning. Think for example of expressions such as "aesthetic properties," "Japanese aesthetics," or "the aesthetics of automobiles." Here aesthetic(s) is almost used as similar to careful design or "form giving."

2. To refer to works of art or artistic material. This is the most common use of the term and can be found in phrases such as "philosophical aesthetics," "the aesthetic process," or "the aesthetic experience offered by a Van Gogh." In these instances, the word aesthetic can refer to properties of artworks, and also to any type of response—not just a pleasurable one—one might have toward a work of art.

3. To indicate a special type of response that people might have to man-made objects and natural scenes. It is the kind of response that is often contrasted to a more utilitarian response and regarded as purposeless (Kant, 1952) and distanced (Bullough, 1912). We tend to articulate this response in terms of "direct pleasure" (Dutton, 2009), liking, appreciation, or beauty, as in "I aesthetically prefer this chair," "an aesthetic landscape," or "a beautiful idea."

The beauty of this third connotation is that it allows us to speak of aesthetic responses to any stimulus, man-made or natural, physical or mental, morally laudable or loathsome. It allows us to talk about beautiful watches and nail clippers, a beautiful goal in a football match, a beautiful girl or gesture, a beautiful science experiment (e.g., Crease, 2003), and even a beautiful robbery[2] or a beautiful death. This third connotation therefore makes most sense in the context of "everyday aesthetics" (Saito, 2007) or "design aesthetics" (Hekkert, 2006).

This notion of aesthetics as a descriptor for a particular response or experience is best captured by the concept of "aesthetic pleasure." Elsewhere, we have defined aesthetic pleasure as "the pleasure people derive from processing the object for its own sake, as a source of immediate experiential pleasure in itself, and not essentially for its utility in producing something else that is either useful or pleasurable" (Dutton, 2009, p. 52; Hekkert, 2014). Following this definition, we recently developed a scale to measure this aesthetic experience (Blijlevens et al., 2017). To measure the known determinants of aesthetic pleasure for discriminant validity purposes, our study included scales tapping into the concepts of typicality, novelty, unity, and variety. We identified reliable items representative of aesthetic pleasure and confirmed these findings across three countries: Australia, the Netherlands, and Taiwan. The final scale consists of five items, "beautiful," "attractive," "pleasing to see," "nice to see," and "like to look at," which together reliably capture the construct of aesthetic pleasure. Although these items are phrased for visual inspection, they could easily be adapted to measure aesthetic pleasure in other sensory domains (e.g., "This product is pleasing to touch" and "I like touching this product," for tactile aesthetic appreciation; see Post, Blijlevens, & Hekkert, 2014).

The scale can be applied to any domain, from designed artifacts to people, nature, and art, and also to more abstract categories, such as concepts, organizations, and ideas. We humans have acquired an aesthetic sensibility that we can apply to any phenomenon in the world and we can thus derive aesthetic pleasure from seeing, touching, or contemplating any object or idea. The most interesting question therefore is not "What do we like?" but "*Why* do we like?"

Why Do We Have an Aesthetic Sense?

The fact that we can aesthetically appreciate anything does not mean that aesthetic laws or principles apply equally across domains. To understand the mechanisms underlying aesthetic pleasure, each domain has its own inherent logic (Thornhill, 2003), and one could not simply transfer principles from one domain to the other. In other words, what makes female faces beautiful to look at, i.e., features that signal health and fertility, is grounded in different laws than those that govern our aesthetic preferences for things such as landscapes or designed artifacts (see Hekkert, 2014). In this chapter, we will confine ourselves to this latter category: what makes human artifacts pleasurable to perceive and comprehend? This is the type of aesthetic pleasure that is most intensively studied in empirical aesthetics.

The logic underlying our aesthetic appreciation of human-made artifacts has been explained elsewhere at length as the by-product of the cognitive and sensorial faculties that help us to make sense of our surroundings. These faculties support the major drivers of our existence. The two most fundamental drivers of human motivation and behavior are, however, opposing ones: our "need for safety" and our "need for accomplishment."

> On the one hand, humans seek that which is safe to approach, offers security, and makes little demand on their limited processing capacity. On the other hand, humans are motivated to take risks, engage in exploratory behaviour, extend their capabilities, and promote their learning.
>
> (Hekkert, 2014, p. 281)

Whereas uncomplicated sensory information facilitates the rapid, economical, and safe operation of our senses, discordant input stretches our existing capacities and invites them to identify prospects for accomplishment. After all, the primary task for any organism is the preservation of life and the furtherance of conditions for growth (Damasio, 1999). Wouldn't it be beautiful if we could do this simultaneously? Indeed, the pleasure elicited by a stimulus potentially depends on the perceived balance it strikes in satisfying these conflicting urges: we like things that simultaneously make us feel safe (because they look familiar and organized, for example) and *also* nurture our need for fresh challenges (because they are new and different). In the next section, we will discuss a number of aesthetic principles that are based on this reconciliation of apparent contradictions.

Human-made artifacts can take many forms: products, buildings, works of art, gardens, meals, organizations, and ideas. What these all have in common is that they are *designed*—they are purposively constructed to serve a particular instrumental (e.g., shelter, nutrition) or experiential (e.g., admiration, fun) goal. Based on the evolutionary balancing act outlined above, we further argue that an artifact's aesthetic value resides in how well this purpose has been fulfilled. It is important to note here that even though people can aesthetically appreciate *the way* an artifact fulfills its purpose, this does not mean that an aesthetic response is "interested"; we can appreciate an elegantly functioning motorcycle engine without needing a motorcycle, or even aiming to ride one.

Three Sources of Pleasure in Design

The basic tenet of our framework of aesthetics is that our aesthetic pleasure or sense of beauty arises from the successful co-existence or reconciliation between experiences of *safety* (e.g., neophobia, familiarity, smoothness) and *accomplishment* (e.g., neophilia, novelty, naturalness). This reconciliation applies to all levels of processing an artifact. These two poles or opposing forces, at each level of processing, are all concerned with the way something is done, i.e., with the *how*. Artifact aesthetics therefore deals with organization, with seeing relationships; with *how* the maker's intention has been translated into a solution; *how* the result relates to other (previous) results of a similar kind; and, most apparent, with *how* the object properties are organized. These three types of assessment not only apply to the artifact as such, but also to *how we interact* with the artifact—and how the artifact interacts with us.

Formal aesthetics

Artifacts have various properties: the materials and colors in a painting, the formal and functional elements of a car dashboard or web page, the parameters of a mathematical or scientific formula. Inconsistency in an artifact's materials or variety in its elements is a given. Designers and makers must smooth out this roughness—they must bring order to this inherent complexity. Aesthetic pleasure is generated when the designer allows for maximum variety or naturalness while establishing an optimum of unity, regularity, smoothness, or organization. Hence, we tend to like unity-in-variety, a smooth finish on natural materials, good proportions, and harmonious organizations (Figure 44.1).

The most famous and widely studied of these formal aesthetic laws is the principle of unity-in-variety. In three studies, we investigated how unity and variety combine to predict the aesthetic appreciation across a range of product designs, from lamps to espresso

FIGURE 44.1. The funeral of the hippopotamus. A harmonious organization exhibiting unity-in-variety (design Bodhi Vrdoljak).

machines, motorcycles, and USB flash drives (Post, Blijlevens, & Hekkert, 2016). Results revealed that, as predicted, both unity and variety, while suppressing each other's effects, positively affect aesthetic appreciation. This means that product designs exhibiting an optimum balance between unity and variety are aesthetically preferred. One of the studies looked into the effect of an observer's motivational state on the preferred levels of unity and variety. People may differ in their chronic regulatory focus (Higgins, 1997) in that promotion seekers are generally more concerned with growth, advancement, and accomplishment, whereas prevention seekers have as a main goal to protect and seek safety. Following our framework, it was predicted that promotion seekers will appreciate variety more than safety seekers, and safety seekers will appreciate unity more than accomplishment seekers. For the category of motorcycles, it was indeed found that prevention seekers prefer unity to a larger extent than promotion seekers. The three studies further showed that this trade-off is asymmetric: people like to perceive as much variety as possible, but to enjoy it they need to see the unity in it. And while unity is universally liked, the appreciation of variety greatly depends on the presence of (sufficient) unity. This asymmetry between unity and variety in predicting aesthetic preference is in fact perfectly captured by the wording of the principle: it is "unity-*in*-variety" after all.

FIGURE 44.2. Unity-in-variety in website design.

In two follow-up studies, we found further evidence supporting the validity of the unity-in-variety principle by systematically varying the levels of unity and variety presented by different websites (Post, Nguyen, & Hekkert, 2017; Figure 44.2), and, in a study with car keys, empirically demonstrated that the principle also holds in the tactile domain (Post et al., 2014). This latter finding lends weight to the idea that Gestalt laws of proximity, similarity, good continuation, and closure may also influence tactile perception and its aesthetic appreciation (Gallace & Spence, 2011), also known as the phenomenon of cross-sensory consistency.

Relative aesthetics

In 2017, *Atlantic* editor Derek Thompson published a book on popular culture, examining the success of 20th-century blockbuster films, pop songs, fashion, and product designs (Thompson, 2017). His main conclusion was that people like a familiar surprise, products that are bold yet sneakily recognizable. One of his main sources of inspiration was the famous American designer Raymond Loewy.

> Loewy understood that attention doesn't just pull in one direction. Instead, it is a
> tug-of-war between the opposing forces of neophilia versus neophobia, the love of

the new versus the preference for the old; people's need for stimulation versus their preference for what is understandable. A hit is new wine in old oak, or a stranger who somehow feels like a friend—a familiar surprise.

(Thompson, 2017, p. 56)

Loewy coined this balancing act MAYA—Most Advanced Yet Acceptable.

From songs to product designs, artifacts are never perceived in isolation. As soon as we see or hear something, we compare it to other instances of the (assumed) same family or category. Artists and designers always strive for novelty or innovation so as to overcome repetition or habituation and also outdo their predecessors—albeit to a limited extent. Too much divergence or too much novelty prevents assimilation and comprehension. For that reason, artists and designers ought to strike a balance between novelty and familiarity. Whereas familiarity leads to safe choices, novelty challenges us to try something new. When a designer manages to bring these two drivers into unison, aesthetic pleasure is maximized. This we demonstrated in an empirical investigation of the MAYA principle (Hekkert, Snelders, & van Wieringen, 2003), a principle that has since that publication been shown to explain the aesthetic appreciation of such diverse phenomena as tourist destinations (Kirillova, Fu, Lehto, & Cai, 2014), wine labels (Celhay & Passebois, 2011), and advertising (van Enschot-van Dijk & van Mulken, 2014).

Artifacts also play an important part in the social world and are often associated with specific use contexts (e.g., office, beach) and particular users (e.g., hipsters, academics). Here we assume a similar trade-off between safety (as inclusion or conformity) and accomplishment (as uniqueness or autonomy). In a recent series of four studies (Blijlevens & Hekkert, 2019), we demonstrated that products that offer maximum autonomy, yet preserve connectedness (to a group of significant others) are aesthetically preferred. To show that conditions of safety and risk moderate the effects of the principle—as predicted by our framework—we looked into different classes of products, including socially safe ones (such as staplers) and risky ones (such as sneakers/trainers), and systematically manipulated the social context in which the evaluation took place. In line with our predictions, in risky conditions people favored the safe sense of connectedness over autonomy, and vice versa, in safe social conditions, people preferred products that strengthened their autonomy. Regardless of the conditions, people's aesthetic preferences always strike a balance between these two factors of autonomy and connectedness. We have dubbed this aesthetic principle *Autonomous, yet Connected*.

Intentional aesthetics

Finally, human-made artifacts are typically a means to an end. Whenever we are confronted with an artifact, we take a "design stance" and assume an underlying idea or intention (Da Silva, Crilly, & Hekkert, 2015). We may have foreknowledge of this intention, or grasp it after reading an instruction manual or display card next to an artwork, or even infer it from what we see. Whatever the source, the intention allows us to appraise the object in this light: to what extent did the maker realize what was intended? We may disapprove of the intention as such (e.g., a bank robbery), but we can still appreciate *the way* the intention was enacted. Was it achieved properly, efficiently, elegantly, or economically?

The most plausible candidate for capturing the aesthetic quality of this relationship is the principle of *Maximum Effect for Minimal Means* (Boselie & Leeuwenberg, 1985; Da Silva, Crilly & Hekkert, 2016; Hekkert, 2006). People aesthetically prefer those works of art, designed objects, mathematical proofs, and chess moves that require lesser means (i.e., energy, parameters, elements, steps) to attain a greater effect (i.e., goal, explanation, performance, result), a trade-off that breathes the same balance of safety (i.e., efficiency) and accomplishment (i.e., wide impact) as the principles discussed before.

In two studies, we tested the hypothesis that the aesthetic appreciation of a product would be positively affected by the perception of the product as providing the minimum means necessary to achieve the maximum effect (Da Silva, Crilly, & Hekkert, 2017). In the first study, we used products that naturally varied in the effects they were intended to create, while in the second study we systematically varied the means–effect relationship that the product represented. Both studies provided empirical proof for the Maximum Effect for Minimal Means (MEMM) principle: the perception of a product as the minimum means achieving the maximum effect has a positive influence on the aesthetic appreciation of that product (Figure 44.3). The beauty of the MEMM principle—yes, principles in themselves can also be considered beautiful, especially if they apply to

FIGURE 44.3. Product used in our 2017 MEMM study: Gauge vase by Jim Rokos (2012). Permission to reproduce by Jim Rokos.

the MEMM rule—is that all kinds of things can be aesthetically appreciated even if they do not exhibit a conventional form or their form is not regarded as beautiful in itself. For example, there are beautiful literary metaphors (Ramachandran & Hirstein, 1999) and beautiful logical arguments (Walsh, 1979), scientific theories (Orrell, 2012), science experiments (Crease, 2003), chess moves (Margulies, 1977), mathematical demonstrations (Hardy, 1967), and even criminal acts (Black, 1991). These very different things can all be regarded as artifacts because they achieve certain intended effects (Dipert, 1993), and they can all be aesthetically appreciated for *how* they achieve those effects.

Aesthetics in/of interaction

The three types of aesthetic processing proposed here do not only apply to artifacts as objects of passive admiration and contemplation. Some artifacts, such as consumer products, need to be touched and used, and such interactions can be pleasing for reasons along similar lines to the ones we outlined above. First, the interaction can be aesthetically pleasing in terms of its interaction properties or attributes (Diefenbach, Lenz, & Hassenzahl, 2013). For example, some people like the smooth, steady, and elegant way a cork sometimes slides from a wine bottle. Lenz, Diefenbach, and Hassenzahl (2014) reviewed 19 studies reporting on such interaction attributes that were purported to enhance the aesthetics of an interaction. They found no less than 151 of them! Most of these attributes fell into two groups: spatio-temporal attributes describing physical aspects of the interaction (e.g., speed, duration, pressure), and attributes describing feelings and meaning emerging from the interaction (e.g., surprise, magic, playfulness). Attributes in this second group only shift the attention to other, sometimes metaphorical, descriptions of the experience. Also, they often describe emotional experiences beyond what would normally be labeled as aesthetic.

Considering the first group of spatio-temporal attributes, one may wonder whether looking for single dimensions is a fruitful endeavor when aiming to explain aesthetics in interaction. In line with our argumentation for formal aesthetics earlier, we should look for candidate pairs that capture the trade-off between safety and accomplishment. An interaction can be considered "safe" when we are in control and can predict the consequences of our actions, and this is especially true when it comes to electronic appliances or smart products, such as intelligent thermostats. At the same time we like to give up (part of our) control and be challenged by the smartness or agency of the machine: we like the machine to make our work easier. The balance between user control and product agency seems a suitable candidate for explaining our aesthetic appreciation of the interaction at the more formal level.

Second, and following our reasoning for *relative aesthetics*, a comparison with other products can also be made at the interaction level. A product might perform its task in a novel yet familiar fashion and thus be aesthetically appreciated. We tested this hypothesis with a variety of corkscrews, and, in line with the MAYA principle, showed that the ones that simultaneously maximized novelty and familiarity in their interactions were appreciated most (Cila, Rozendaal, Berghman, & Hekkert, 2015).

Finally, the way in which a corkscrew allows you to open a bottle can be appropriate for the need that was intentionally embodied in the device itself (e.g., quick, professional, showing off). This idea was tested in another study with two exemplars from the same set of corkscrews (Lenz, Hassenzahl, & Diefenbach, 2017). The authors reasoned that in a particular context, people aim for an experience that then determines whether an interaction "feels right." "An interaction that is private and a little secretive (i.e. autonomy-related) feels better, i.e. is more 'aesthetic', in our terms, if it is slow, fluent, delayed, and gentle" (Lenz et al., 2017, p. 82). Lenz and colleagues found evidence for such a relationship for two types of corkscrews that are more "fit" for competence or relatedness purposes, respectively. Although this result seems in line with the proposal for *intentional aesthetics*, it is problematic that the "why" is not based on the intention of the designer ("what interaction is appropriate to foster a certain need?"), but rather on the experiential needs ascribed to the user, and as awakened by two different use scenarios. As a result, the assessment is no longer disinterested, and the "fit" response indicated probably refers more to usefulness for the particular context than aesthetic pleasure per se. Nevertheless, the study is a good first attempt to capture the relationship between intentions (the "why") and the experiential quality of the interaction (the "how").

Conclusion and competition

Looking at all the studies presented to support our aesthetic framework, we can arrive at some preliminary conclusions about aesthetic appreciation in relation to designed artifacts and artifacts in general.

Aesthetic pleasure—in terms of liking and beauty—is greatest when products simultaneously maximize the perceived and opposing qualities (e.g., unity vs. variety, connectedness vs. autonomy) grounded in the two major drivers of human behavior and motivation: the need for safety and the need for accomplishment. Furthermore, the effect of the two opposing forces is asymmetric: we aesthetically appreciate the challenging factor in each pair (i.e., variety, or autonomy), as long as it is accompanied by the safe counterpart (i.e., unity, or connectedness).

This balance between opposing forces predictably depends on (a) product category, (b) expertise/background, and (c) regulatory focus: promotion vs. prevention seekers/seeking. For "safe" products or when a product is used under safe conditions, the balance tends toward a preference for risky alternatives. Conversely, under riskier conditions we aim for safer alternatives. All this makes perfect sense from the perspective of our evolutionary framework. When it comes to expertise/background, it is important to note that all aesthetic principles, based on a balance between safety and accomplishment, do not (necessarily) lead to uniform choices or inter-individual agreement. The balance is based on two opposing attributes that can be perceived and rated differently according to each individual's background, culture, or level of expertise. So, where people may highly differ as to which designs exhibit unity or variety, or enable autonomy or connectedness, they always aesthetically prefer those items that maximize both opposing qualities at the same time. There may be a lot of individual variation in what we like, but these differences are not the less lawful.

All of these principles operate simultaneously when we are confronted with a designed artifact, and together they shape our aesthetic experience. In a recent study combining some of the above principles, we showed that not only do they correlate—which is predictable, given their joint source—but also that each *independently* explains part of the variance in our aesthetic pleasure ratings (Berghman & Hekkert, 2017). Although in that study, the unity-in-variety principle turned out to be a stronger predictor of aesthetic preference than the principles of MAYA or "autonomous, yet connected," their relative contribution to artifact aesthetics remains an interesting issue for further studies. Finally, these aesthetic principles not only apply to physical products, but they also seem to explain our aesthetic appreciation of nontangible services and product–service systems (Post, Da Silva, & Hekkert, 2015). In addition, there are many theoretical reasons to believe that they also apply to other nontangible prestages in the design process, such as visioning, framing, idea generation, and concepting.

Beautiful Consequences

Designers do not merely solve the problems people face today, they also create new meanings, a process also known as design-driven innovation (e.g., Hekkert & van Dijk, 2011; Verganti, 2009). Innovative value creation is based on more fundamental insights about people and society, and is often enabled by advancements in technology. Consider, for example, the mobile phone. In a classic Dutch television program, people on the street were asked whether they would like to have a device that would allow them to make phone calls 24/7 from wherever they were. The typical response was that such a device would not offer any added value and that its use would be totally superfluous. That program was made in 1999 and now, 20 years later, we can simply not imagine a world without handheld communication devices. Design-driven innovation is about translating user insights into propositions—new meanings—that people love, but never knew they wanted or needed.

Designing is, therefore, a future-shaping endeavor. Policymakers and other stakeholders in the public domain are increasingly turning to design to inform, shape, and direct their efforts. As a result, a wave of approaches has emerged that seek to channel the positive and considerable impact design can have on improving individuals' quality of life, and that of society more generally, including design for health (e.g., Tsekleves & Cooper, 2016), design for behavior change (e.g., Niederer, Clune, & Ludden, 2018), social design (e.g., Tromp & Hekkert, 2019), and design for wellbeing (e.g., Desmet & Pohlmeyer, 2014). For example, the famous traffic light countdown timers found across the globe were designed to reduce stress; compel cyclists, pedestrians, and motorists to obey the law; and generally increase safety in inner cities (see Tromp & Hekkert, 2019; Figure 44.4). All of these approaches shift the designer's focus away from fulfilling immediate user needs—the traditional role of design in a consumption society—toward addressing the less immediate and longer-term social implications of design. If we cannot wait for these consequences to actually happen, what then can we rely on for assessing the quality of a design process?

In this speculative, final section we argue that aesthetic principles can also guide this process of prediction. Designers need to foresee/predict how their products and services will be perceived, experienced, and adopted in a future context. Decision makers need to assess whether new propositions are appropriate and viable.

In a typical top-down design process, future propositions can take a variety of shapes. Often designers will start by creating a new frame through which to perceive the world. This new worldview, frame, or vision will imply or even directly express the kind of impact the designer is aiming to create—a particular experience, behavior, or attitude they want to foster. For example, in his book *Designing With and Within Public Organizations* (2018), social designer André Schaminée describes a project in Amsterdam where bike tunnels had to be temporarily closed for road construction purposes, much to the frustration of the local inhabitants. To solve this problem, a detour was needed. No agreement could be reached, however, on how long the detour for cyclists should be. At that time, and based on the insight that for most people detour time is not their biggest

FIGURE 44.4. The countdown at traffic lights, an example of design for impact.

concern, André and his team came up with the idea to reframe the problem of "detour time" into "The Best Detour of the Netherlands" (in terms of social and physical safety). The client was very enthusiastic and recognized the (aesthetic) appeal of this new frame.

After the framing stage, the value proposition/intended effect is embodied into a design concept for a product, service, or system. Remember, concepts are aesthetically pleasing when they realize that intention in an effective, minimal way. But at all previous stages, designers need to feel that they are on the right track and clients need to be convinced that the direction chosen will bring a desired outcome. At every stage, aesthetic principles can be a reliable guide.

A prime candidate for explaining the aesthetic appreciation of frames, intentions, or propositions comes from our work on the aesthetic appreciation of product metaphors (Cila, Borsboom, & Hekkert, 2014). We demonstrated that metaphorical associations—the references underlying a product metaphor—are aesthetically most attractive when they strike a balance between understandability and novelty. Designing a pencil sharpener in the shape of a beaver is an original, but understandable way of establishing a metaphorical reference between a target (the sharpener) and a source (the beaver; Figure 44.5). This parallels with how a product's creative dimension is typically

FIGURE 44.5. Kastor pencil sharpener by Rodrigo Torres (for Alessi). Permission to reproduce by Alessi.

assessed: as a function of both the design's novelty and its appropriateness (Runco & Charles, 1993). It can thus be hypothesized that early deliverables in a design process (e.g., ideas, propositions, frames) are considered attractive (and therefore worthy of agreement) when they maximize novelty/originality *and* understandability (a certain logic) at the same time. This balance between understandability and novelty fits perfectly into the now familiar safety-accomplishment framework.

A second candidate for capturing the beauty of design ideas resides in the beauty of the anticipated outcome—the beautiful consequence. The question here is, "What makes a particular experience, behavior or attitude 'beautiful'?" One could be tempted to bring in moral considerations for this assessment: beautiful behaviors or attitudes are those that make people "do the right thing." However, the notion of aesthetic pleasure we put forth here clearly separates it from ethical concerns, as we have argued earlier (recall the beautiful robbery or death). Following the logic of our evolutionary framework, new behaviors or beliefs are aesthetically pleasing when they require little effort to accommodate them in the context of people's everyday lives, yet also promise some major impact on their wellbeing or on the quality of our society at large. Note this would be a contextual variant of the MEMM principle. A final aesthetic consideration that may drive a design process and offer a direction that enables actors to assess its quality relates to the internal consistency between all phases of the process. Within all its inherent complexity, processes are aesthetically apt when they are harmonious, fluent, and consistent.

Admittedly, many of the aesthetic laws proposed in this last section are mere assumptions. However, these assumptions are firmly rooted in the aesthetic framework discussed in this chapter, the framework that predicts that any aesthetic judgment involves a careful balancing between manifestations of our inner drives toward safety and accomplishment. These assumptions therefore demonstrate the richness and predictive power of our framework. It also shows that aesthetic principles operate well beyond the design outcome itself and inform the quality of the process as much as the quality of the product, thereby extending the capacity of our aesthetic sense—that useful and beautiful sense.

NOTES

1. We will however argue in this chapter that considerations of beauty or aesthetic pleasure also apply to all forms of modern or conceptual art in that such artworks can be effective responses to the intention of the artist (see the section on "Intentional Aesthetics").

2. At the time of this writing, many are excited about the Spanish Netflix series *El casa de papel*, a series depicting a sophisticated execution of a robbery at the Spanish Central Bank.

REFERENCES

Berghman, M., & Hekkert, P. (2017). Towards a unified model of aesthetic pleasure in design. *New Ideas in Psychology, 47*, 136–144.

Black, J. (1991). *The aesthetics of murder: A study in romantic literature and contemporary culture*. Baltimore, MD: John Hopkins University Press.

Blijlevens, J. & Hekkert, P. (2019). "Autonomous, yet connected": An esthetic principle explaining our appreciation of product designs. *Psychology & Marketing, 36,* 530–546.

Blijlevens, J., Hekkert, P., Leder, H., Thurgood, C., Chen, L-L., & Whitfield, T. W. A. (2017). The Aesthetic Pleasure in Design Scale: The development of a scale to measure aesthetic pleasure for designed artifacts. *Psychology of Aesthetics, Creativity, and the Arts, 11,* 86–98.

Boselie, F., & Leeuwenberg, E. (1985). Birkhoff revisited: Beauty as a function of effect and means. *American Journal of Psychology, 98,* 1–39.

Bullough, E. (1912). "Psychical distance" as a factor in art and an aesthetic principle. *British Journal of Psychology, 5,* 87–118.

Celhay, F., & Passebois, J. (2011). Wine labelling: Is it time to break with tradition? A study of the moderating role of perceived risk. *International Journal of Wine Business Research, 23,* 318–337.

Cila, N., Borsboom, F., & Hekkert, P. (2014). Determinants of aesthetic preference for product metaphors. *Empirical Studies of the Arts, 32,* 183–203.

Cila, N., Rozendaal, M., Berghman, M., & Hekkert, P. (2015). Searching for balance in aesthetic pleasure in interaction. In L.-L. Chen, T. Djajadiningrat, L. Feijs, J. Hu, S. Kyffin, L. Rampino, E. Rodriguez, & D. Steffen (Eds.), *DeSForM 2015, Aesthetics of interaction: dynamic, multisensory, wise* (pp. 19–27). Milan: Italy.

Crease, R. P. (2003). *The prism and the pendulum: The ten most beautiful experiments in science.* New York, NY: Random House.

Da Silva, O., Crilly, N., & Hekkert, P. (2015). How people's appreciation of products is affected by their knowledge of the designers' intentions. *International Journal of Design, 9,* 21–33.

Da Silva, O., Crilly, N., & Hekkert, P. (2016). Maximum effect for minimum means: The aesthetics of efficiency. *Design Issues, 32,* 41–51.

Da Silva, O., Crilly, N., & Hekkert, P. (2017). Beauty in efficiency: An experimental enquiry into the principle of maximum effect for minimum means. *Empirical Studies of the Arts, 35,* 93–120.

Damasio, A. R. (1999). *The feeling of what happens: Body and emotion in the making of consciousness.* New York, NY: Harcourt Brace & Company.

Desmet, P. M. A., & Pohlmeyer, A. E. (2014). Positive design: An introduction to design for subjective well-being. *International Journal of Design, 7,* 5–19.

Diefenbach, S., Lenz, E., & Hassenzahl, M. (2013). An interaction vocabulary. Describing the *how* of interaction. *CHI 2013 Extended Abstracts,* April 27–May 2, 2013, Paris, France.

Dipert, R. R. (1993). *Artifacts, art works, and agency.* Philadelphia, PA: Temple University Press.

Dutton, D. (2009). *The art instinct.* New York, NY: Oxford University Press.

Enschot-van Dijk, R. van, & Mulken, M. J. P., van (2014). Visual aesthetics in advertising. In A. Kozbelt (Ed.), *Proceedings of the 23rd Biennial Congress of the International Association of Empirical Aesthetics* (pp. 192–196). New York: IAEA.

Gallace, A., & Spence, C. (2011). To what extent do Gestalt grouping principles influence tactile perception? *Psychological Bulletin, 137,* 538–561.

Hardy, G. H. (1967). *A mathematician's apology.* Cambridge: Cambridge University Press.

Hekkert, P. (2006). Design aesthetics: Principles of pleasure in product design. *Psychology Science, 48,* 157–172.

Hekkert, P. (2014). Aesthetic responses to design: A battle of impulses. In T. Smith & P. Tinio (Eds.), *The Cambridge handbook of the psychology of aesthetics and the arts* (pp. 277–299). Cambridge: Cambridge University Press.

Hekkert, P., Snelders, D., & van Wieringen, P. C. W. (2003). "Most advanced, yet acceptable": Typicality and novelty as joint predictors of aesthetic preference in industrial design. *British Journal of Psychology, 94*, 111–124.

Hekkert, P., & van Dijk, M. B. (2011). *Vision in design: A guidebook for innovators*. Amsterdam: BIS Publishers.

Higgins, E. T. (1997). Beyond pleasure and pain. *American Psychologist, 52*, 1.280–1.300.

Kant, I. (1952). *The critique of judgement* (J. C. Meredith, Trans.). Oxford: Clarendon Press. (Original work published 1790).

Kirillova, K., Fu, X., Lehto, X., & Cai, L. (2014). What makes a destination beautiful? Dimensions of tourist aesthetic judgment. *Tourism Management, 42*, 282–293.

Koren, L. (2010). *Which "aesthetics" do you mean? Ten definitions*. Point Reyes, CA: Imperfect Publishing.

Lenz, E., Diefenbach, S., & Hassenzahl, M. (2014). Aesthetics of interaction—A literature synthesis. In *Proceedings of NordiCHI'14* (pp. 628–637). New York, NY: Association for Computing Machinery.

Lenz, E., Hassenzahl, M., & Diefenbach, S. (2017). Aesthetic interaction as fit between interaction attributes and experiential qualities. *New Ideas in Psychology, 47*, 80–90.

Margulies, S. (1977). Principles of beauty. *Psychological Reports, 41*, 3–11.

Niederer, K., Clune, S., & Ludden, G. (2018). *Design for behaviour change: Theories and practices of designing for change*. London: Taylor & Francis.

Orrell, D. (2012). *Truth or beauty: Science and the quest for order*. New Haven, CT: Yale University Press.

Post, R. A. G., Blijlevens, J., & Hekkert, P. (2014). Aesthetic appreciation of tactile unity-in-variety in product designs. In A. Kozbelt (Ed.), *Proceedings of the 23rd Biennial Congress of the International Association of Empirical Aesthetics*. New York: IAEA.

Post, R. A. G., Blijlevens, J., & Hekkert, P. (2016). "To preserve unity while almost allowing for chaos": Testing the aesthetic principle of unity-in-variety in product design. *Acta Psychologica, 163*, 142–152.

Post, R. A. G., Da Silva, O., & Hekkert, P. (2015). The beauty in product-service systems. In V. Popovic, A. Blackler, B.-B. Luh, N. Nimkulrat, B. Kraal, & Y. Nagai (Eds.). *Proceedings of IASDR 2015 Interplay* (pp. 1717–1730) Brisbane: Queensland University of Technology.

Post, R., Nguyen, T., & Hekkert, P. (2017). Unity in variety in website aesthetics: A systematic inquiry. *International Journal of Human-Computer Studies, 103*, 48–62.

Ramachandran, V. S., & Hirstein, W. (1999). The science of art. *Journal of Consciousness Studies, 6*(6–7), 15–51.

Runco, M. A., & Charles, R. E. (1993). Judgments of originality and appropriateness as predictors of creativity. *Journal of Personality and Individual Differences, 15*, 537–546.

Saito, Y. (2007). *Everyday aesthetics*. New York, NY: Oxford University Press.

Schaminée, A. (2018). *Designing with and within public organizations*. Amsterdam: BIS Publishers.

Thompson, D. (2017). *Hit makers: The science of popularity in an age of distraction*. New York, NY: Penguin Press.

Thornhill, R. (2003). Darwinian aesthetics informs traditional aesthetics. In E. Voland and K. Grammar (Eds.), *Evolutionary aesthetics* (pp. 9–35). Berlin: Springer.

Tractinsky, N., Katz, A. S., & Ikar, D. (2000). What is beautiful is usable. *Interacting with Computers, 13*, 127–145.

Tromp, N., & Hekkert, P. (2019). *Designing for Society: Products and services for a better world.* London: Bloomsbury.

Tsekleves, E., & Cooper, R. (2016). *Design for health.* London: Routledge.

Verganti, R. (2009). *Design-driven innovation: changing the rules of competition by radically innovating what things mean.* Boston, MA: Harvard Business Press.

Walsh, D. (1979). Occam's razor. *American Philosophical Quarterly, 16,* 1–4.

CHAPTER 45

THE ROLE OF EMPIRICAL AESTHETICS IN CONSUMER BEHAVIOR

VANESSA M. PATRICK AND HENRIK HAGTVEDT

Only one company can be the cheapest. All others must use design.
Rodney Fitch, Fitch & Co. (from Insights, the Design Council [U.K.])

In the modern marketplace, it is difficult to differentiate products based on price, functionality, or quality. Consequently, firms have found other ways to do so, and aesthetics is increasingly becoming a decisive differentiating factor (Simonson & Schmitt, 1997). Reflecting these marketplace developments, a growing stream of research is focused on investigating the influence of aesthetics on consumer behavior within a plethora of realms (Hoegg & Alba, 2008; Patrick, 2016), including product design (Bloch, 1995; Homburg, Schwemmle, & Kuehnl, 2015; Liu, Li, Chen, & Balachander, 2017), packaging (Raghubir & Greenleaf, 2006; Reimann, Zaichkowsky, Neuhaus, Bender, & Weber, 2010), retail displays and interiors (Argo & Dahl, 2018; Dion & Arnould, 2011; Sevilla & Townsend, 2016), websites (Gorn, Chattopadhyay, Sengupta, & Tripathi, 2004; Jiang, Wang, Tan, & Yu, 2016; Wang, Minor, & Wei, 2011), advertising and promotion (Gorn, Chattopadhyay, Yi, & Dahl, 1997; Townsend, 2017), logos (Henderson, Giese, & Cote, 2004; Janiszewski & Meyvis, 2001; van der Lans et al., 2009), and financial instruments (Townsend & Shu, 2010).

According to Patrick (2016, p. 60), everyday consumer aesthetics entails "non-art, non-nature aesthetic experiences that are diverse and dynamic and result in specific consumer actions (e.g. purchasing) and consumption behaviors (e.g. recycling)." Much of the current chapter's focus on visual aesthetics within consumer-relevant contexts aligns with this conceptualization; the focus is generally restricted to the aesthetics of products, product outlets, organizations, and promotional materials, and does not include natural aesthetics such as faces or landscapes. This focus comprises consumer responses to specific visual features such as shape and color, as well as general aesthetic appeal. Some of the former topics may overlap with the broader realm of sensory marketing (Krishna, 2012), whereas aesthetic appeal generally pertains to sensory experience that the perceiver considers to be special, beautiful, emotionally stirring, or cognitively engaging, often in a way that provides insight and meaning.

The structure of the chapter is as follows. We begin by discussing the cognitive and emotional responses to visual features. In this context, we delve into a few key visual features that have been examined more than others, namely color, shape, and surface appeal, and introduce visual concepts such as cuteness and anthropomorphism. We then move on to a discussion of the outcomes of aesthetic appeal and a broad categorization of aesthetic products. We conclude with challenges and future directions for the study of consumer aesthetics.

Consumer Responses to Visual Features

From cognition and emotion to downstream consumption behavior

A limited amount of research in marketing focuses on basic cognitive responses (e.g., size estimates) to the visual features (e.g., shape or color) that one might term formal qualities or basic building blocks of aesthetics. For example, the taller of two objects with equivalent volume tends to appear larger when consumers rely on their visual impressions, but not when they only rely on touch (Krishna, 2006; Raghubir & Krishna, 1999). Relatedly, Ordabayeva and Chandon (2013) find that people mentally add changes in an object's height, width, and length to compute its volume. Completely shaped products appear larger than incompletely shaped ones of equal size and weight (Sevilla & Kahn, 2014), and packages appear to have higher volume when their shape attracts greater attention (Folkes & Matta, 2004). In the realm of color, Hagtvedt and Brasel (2017) demonstrate that increased saturation leads to increased perceived product size, and color contrast can similarly affect size perceptions (Van Ittersum & Wansink, 2012). Related work documents the effect of color on consumer responses such as attention (Labrecque, Patrick, & Milne, 2013), arousal (Bagchi & Cheema, 2013; Gorn et al., 1997; Labrecque & Milne, 2012), regulatory focus (Mehta & Zhu, 2009), and construal level (Lee, Deng, Unnava, & Fujita, 2014). Recent research on crossmodal correspondence, which investigates combined influences of sensory input from different sensory modalities, has uncovered consumer-relevant effects at the intersection of visual aesthetics and other sensory experience (Spence, 2012). For instance, Hagtvedt and Brasel (2016) show that high-frequency (vs. low-frequency) sounds guide visual attention toward light-colored (vs. dark-colored) objects.

Consumers also have an emotional response to visual cues in their consumption environments (Bloch, 1995; Coates, 2003; Norman, 2004). Thomas Hine, author of the book *The Total Package*, poignantly describes how marketing stimuli like promotions and packaging go beyond mere functionality to fulfill human needs from relationships to power: "Packages . . . are about containing and labeling and informing and celebrating. They are about power and flattery and trying to win people's trust. They are about beauty and craftsmanship and comfort. They are about color, protection, survival" (Hine, 1995, p. 25). A great deal of research in consumer behavior is grounded in the idea that products and brands have symbolic value and confer emotional benefits on consumers that go beyond functionality (Belk, 1988; Levy, 1959). Desmet (2002) found that a product design can evoke 14 different types of emotions in consumers: desire, inspiration, admiration, amusement, satisfaction, fascination, pleasant surprise, disgust, indignation, contempt, unpleasant surprise, dissatisfaction, disappointment, and boredom. Recent research has investigated behaviors that arise from such aesthetics-related emotions. For example, Patrick and Hagtvedt (2011a) show that an aesthetic mismatch among consumers' possessions elicits frustration and prompts them to buy more products to resolve this incongruity, thereby reestablishing harmony in the consumption space. Wang, Mukhopadhyay, and Patrick (2017) demonstrate that cute images elicit tenderness, which explains why they are more effective in nudging consumers to recycle compared with noncute images.

From a practical perspective, part of the reason why cognitive and emotional responses of these kinds are important is that they in turn affect outcomes such as product evaluation, choice, and purchase. The following are some examples of visual features that researchers have investigated to gauge their influence on consumer response. These examples are not exhaustive, for at least two reasons. First, there tends not to be a clear cut-off point that separates aesthetics research from the broader realm of sensory perception. Second, we have focused on a few, relatively salient areas of current consumer aesthetics research. In particular, we have chosen to highlight shape, color, and surface characteristics; these visual features are pertinent to most consumption-related contexts—for instance, it is difficult to envision any physical product without a shape, color, or surface characteristics. Conceptually, color could be considered a surface characteristic, but given its central role in visual perception—a role that is increasingly reflected in current consumer aesthetics research as well—we treat it as a separate visual feature. Conversely, a characteristic such as symmetry could be considered a separate feature pertaining to composition or configuration of visual elements—as would generally be the case in art theory—but here we discuss it as part of the broader category of shape; a shape can be symmetrical or asymmetrical.

Shape

In research on shape, the focus ranges from general influences of clear, unchanging shapes to contextual influences and mutable shapes. As an example of the former, Orth and Malkewitz (2008) identified five holistic types of package shapes and demonstrated their effects on perceptions of brand personality. As an intermediate example, revisiting a question posed by the ancient Greeks, namely whether people prefer shapes with certain ratios, Raghubir and Greenleaf (2006) demonstrate that purchase intentions for rectangular products are affected by the ratio of the rectangle. However, people appear to prefer a range of ratios rather than one specific ratio, especially in relatively serious contexts. As an example of mutable shapes, Trudel and Argo (2013) show that the consumer's decision to recycle versus throw a product in the trash may be determined by how distorted the product has become during the consumption process.

The influence of ambiguous shape also appears to depend on the context; ambiguously cropped objects in ads encourage favorable product evaluations when viewers have adequate motivation and ability to mentally complete the object and verify the ad claims (Peracchio & Meyers-Levy, 1994). Relatedly, ambiguously incomplete logos increase perceptions of a firm's innovativeness but decrease perceptions of its trustworthiness, potentially contributing negatively to attitude toward the firm, but only for individuals with a prevention, rather than promotion, focus (Hagtvedt, 2011). Logo shapes have been a focus area for consumer research for some time (Henderson & Cote, 1998), with recent research uncovering a number of effects in this domain. Jiang et al. (2016) demonstrate that circular versus angular shapes activate associations of softness and hardness, respectively, which in turn influences perceptions of products and firms. Bajaj and Bond (2017) examine the effect of symmetry in logos on perceived brand personality, finding that asymmetry increases excitement. Rahinel and Nelson (2016), on the other hand, show that unstable-looking logos tied to safety-oriented products can cause consumers to infer that the environment (rather than the brand) is unsafe, thereby boosting demand for the product. Relatedly, the influence of logo frames depends on the level of risk associated with a purchase; a perception of high (low) risk highlights a logo frame's association with protection (confinement), thereby increasing (decreasing) purchase intent (Fajardo, Zhang, & Tsiros, 2016).

Color

Along with shape, color is arguably a particularly obvious contributor to an object's aesthetics, and a growing stream of research is uncovering color-related effects in consumer behavior, from website design (Labrecque & Milne, 2012) to advertising (Wedel & Pieters, 2014; for a review on the role of color, see Labrecque, Patrick, & Milne, 2013). Recent research shows that the attention and arousal stimulated by products with saturated color causes consumers to evaluate those products more (less) favorably and exhibit higher (lower) willingness to pay when usage goals call for large (small) size (Hagtvedt & Brasel, 2017). Bagchi and Cheema (2013) demonstrate that red (vs. blue) hue encourages aggression, which in turn influences price negotiations and auction bidding behavior. Relatedly, male consumers perceive savings to be greater when prices are shown in red rather than black (Puccinelli, Chandrashekaran, Grewal, & Suri,

2013). Whereas color with high chroma increases liking toward an ad by stimulating excitement, light color does by eliciting feelings of relaxation (Gorn et al., 1997). In the context of computers, perceived download speeds are greater when the background screen color is blue rather than red or yellow, light rather than dark, and with low rather than high chroma; all of these effects are tied to feelings of relaxation. Crossmodal correspondences involving color also have practical consumption outcomes: the aforementioned match between light (dark) color and high-frequency (low-frequency) not only guides attention, but it also aids recall of marketing messages and increases purchasing behavior (Hagtvedt & Brasel, 2016).

Surface characteristics

Surfaces can be smooth or rough, soft or hard, glossy or matte, and recent research has investigated the impact of such design choices on consumer response. Zhu and Meyers-Levy (2009) demonstrate that the surface (glass vs. wood) on which a product is placed influences product perceptions (modern vs. natural/traditional, respectively). In a similar vein, Meyers-Levy, Zhu, and Jiang (2010) argue that the ground underfoot (carpet vs. hard tile) can prompt bodily sensations that influence product evaluation. In research on packaging, Deng and Srinivasan (2013) find that when food is bite-sized and visually attractive, transparency increases consumption, but transparent packaging decreases consumption for larger, less visually appealing foods. Relatedly, the surface appeal of currency notes, whether crisp or dirty, can influence spending (Di Muro & Noseworthy, 2012). Grubby, well-used currency is more likely to be spent than crisp clean bills. Along with the various effects of surface appeal, other research has sought to understand the mechanism underlying long-standing consumer preferences for specific surface characteristics. For instance, Meert, Pandelaere, and Patrick (2014) explore different explanations for the preference for glossy surfaces, including socialization and visual appeal, and link it to the need for water as a resource.

Other visual features

A number of other design features can contribute to aesthetic impact and influence consumer behavior. A lot of this work suggests that consumers form grounded embodied associations with certain aesthetic elements. For example, consumer perceptions of product and brand characteristics are affected by motion in logos, whether real (Brasel & Hagtvedt, 2016; see also Roggeveen, Grewal, Townsend, Krishnan, 2015) or implied (Cian, Krishna, & Elder, 2014), or by the placement of logos, images, or product information high or low on a package (Cian, Krishna, & Schwarz, 2015; Deng & Kahn, 2009; Sundar & Noseworthy, 2014). Specifically, since power may be associated with height (Schubert, 2005), Sundar and Noseworthy (2014) argue that consumers are more likely to prefer powerful brands when the logo is placed high rather than low on the package design. Cian, Krishna, and Schwarz (2015) propose that since rational elements of a package (e.g., health information) are associated with the head, they work better when placed higher on a package, whereas emotional elements, which are associated with the heart (e.g., taste information), work better when placed lower. Evaluations of products and brands also depend on aspects of presentation, ranging from camera angle in ads (Meyers-Levy and Peracchio 1992) to interstitial spaces in retail outlets (Sevilla & Townsend, 2016) to packaging that displays or reveals products in a flattering manner (Patrick, Atefi, & Hagtvedt, 2017). As discussed, the above is not an exhaustive treatment of all research on visual features in consumer aesthetics, but it provides a brief overview of some central streams of work.

Concepts based on visual features

We now turn to some examples of concepts that arise from the assessment of visual features. Several concepts of this kind have been touched on in the preceding sections, but there are a few others, such as cuteness, anthropomorphism, and novelty, that appear to constitute focus areas in their own right.

The classic criterion for cuteness is known as Kindchenschema, which refers to the degree to which an object is baby-like in appearance (Lorenz, 1943). Building on this concept of cuteness, Wang et al. (2017) show that consumers are more likely to recycle when exposed to cute versus noncute message appeals. Another dimension of the cuteness schema is playfulness and whimsical fun. Focusing on this dimension, Nenkov and Scott (2014) find that consumers exhibit indulgent behavior after exposure to whimsically cute products. Although cuteness ultimately arises from specific visual features such as shapes and colors, an assessment of cuteness may arise from a number of different constellations of formal qualities. In this manner, the concept of cuteness differs from, for instance, angularity, which specifically arises from angles and nothing else, or color hue, which results from the dominant wavelength of electromagnetic radiation. In an example from a service context, Pounders, Babin, and Close (2015) find that consumers respond favorably to similar appearance among providers when such similarity drives perceptions of belonging. We would classify similarity as a general assessment that is not restricted to a specific basis such as color hue or degree of angularity.

Anthropomorphism is the concept of "attributing humanlike properties, characteristics, or mental states to real or imagined nonhuman agents and objects" (Epley, Waytz, & Cacioppo 2007, p. 865). In the context of consumer behavior, brand anthropomorphism can be elicited by giving a brand human-like features such as a face (Kim, Chen, & Zhang, 2016), a body (Kim & McGill, 2011), or personality characteristics (Aaker, 1997). The concept of anthropomorphism is linked to the idea that the salience, or addition, of human-like physical features to products can potentially enhance product value (Aggarwal & McGill, 2007; Landwehr, McGill, & Herrmann, 2011; MacInnis & Folkes, 2017).

Novelty and typicality are among the consumer assessments that have received a considerable amount of attention from consumer researchers. For instance, Goode, Dahl, and Moreau (2013) show that product evaluations can suffer if consumers have trouble categorizing innovative aesthetics. Various investigations in the context of automobile design have produced related insights. Atypical versus typical designs tend to be better liked after more versus less exposure, suggesting that atypical (typical) car designs may be more successful in the long (short) run (Landwehr, Wentzel, & Herrmann, 2013). Providing added nuance to these findings, Talke, Müller, and Wieringa (2017) show that products may perform well when their design is highly novel compared with the competitive set but only moderately novel compared with the brand's product portfolio and with the preceding model. According to Stanton, Townsend, and Kang (2016), consumers prefer unique designs within specific market segments, although they prefer prototypical design across the whole passenger car market, whereas Liu et al. (2017) find that consumers prefer moderate levels of both segment prototypicality and brand consistency.

AESTHETIC APPEAL AND AESTHETIC PRODUCTS

Like novelty and typicality, overall aesthetic appeal is a consumer assessment that may arise from various constellations of specific features. Although some research highlights effects of visual preference that are not associated with prettiness, consumer aesthetics research typically affords beauty a central role.

Building on early work in psychology (Berlyne, 1974), a limited amount of consumer research has focused on determinants of aesthetic appeal, such as unity, prototypicality (Veryzer & Hutchinson, 1998), complexity (Cox & Cox, 2002), optimal arousal, and visual coherence (Deng, Hui, & Hutchinson 2010). Other research has shed light on circumstances under which aesthetic appeal becomes particularly important. For instance, anthropomorphism (i.e., the attribution of human characteristics to nonhuman objects) increases the importance that people place on the appearance of products (Wan, Chen, & Jin, 2017). As another example, strong brands appear to increase the impact of attractive product designs, albeit only when perceived risk is high (Landwehr, Wentzel, & Herrmann, 2012).

Outcomes of aesthetic appeal

Marketers appear to be increasingly aware of the importance of aesthetic appeal in areas such as product design, retail interiors, and promotional and branding materials. For example, neuroimaging findings reveal that an aesthetically pleasing package design activates the brain's reward circuitry (Reimann et al., 2010; see also Lacey et al., 2011). Whereas firms can satisfy their customers with the functional and ergonomic dimensions of product design, the aesthetic dimension of design tends to be more effective in stimulating delight, which in turn affects market performance (Chitturi, Raghunathan, & Mahajan, 2008; Jindal, Sarangee, Echambadi, & Lee, 2016). For example, Jindal et al. find that older-generation vehicles with aesthetically pleasing designs achieve larger market shares than corresponding vehicles with superior design in terms of function or ergonomics. Aesthetically pleasing product design has a favorable influence on a number of consumer responses, such as purchase intent, willingness to pay, and word of mouth (Homburg, Schwemmle, & Kuehnl, 2015). Additionally, aesthetically pleasing products provide psychological benefits to consumers. Townsend and Sood (2012), for example, show that choosing a product with good design affirms the consumer's sense of self, while this effect does not occur for the choice of products that are superior on attributes such as function, brand, or hedonics. Whereas some researchers have treated aesthetic pleasure as largely cognitive in nature (Reber, Schwarz, & Winkielman, 2004), others have tied it to emotions (Armstrong & Detweiler-Bedell, 2008; Silvia, 2005; see also Kumar & Garg, 2010).

In general, a favorable impact of aesthetic appeal on consumption behaviors is perhaps to be expected, but consumer research has uncovered limitations of this influence and even unfavorable outcomes as well. For example, aesthetic design can compensate for minor flaws in functionality, but not for major ones (Hagtvedt & Patrick, 2014). When aesthetics and functionality conflict, consumers may in fact be biased toward unattractive rather than attractive products (Hoegg, Alba, & Dahl, 2010). In connection with nondurable products, aesthetic appeal can inhibit both consumption and enjoyment, because the act of consumption entails destroying something that the consumer appreciates (Wu, Samper, Morales, & Fitzsimons, 2017). In the context of nonprofit donor solicitations, Townsend (2017) finds that although highly aesthetic elements can signal professionalism and therefore encourage donations, such enhancements can backfire when the cost implications signal organizational wastefulness.

Categories of aesthetic products

At this stage, we should note that there are different categories of aesthetic products, based on the role played by aesthetics. Levy and Czepiel (1999, p. 88) argue that the "amount of aesthetics" in products might be thought of as a continuum, ranging from a product design "dictated by its function" to one that "becomes (or claims to be) a work of art." Whereas most of the literature discussed so far deals with what may be termed everyday consumer aesthetics (Patrick, 2016), consumer researchers have also focused on categories in which aesthetics is particularly central (Charters, 2006; Lee, Andrade, & Palmer, 2013). Visual art, which has aesthetic concerns at its core, arguably lies at the extreme end of this continuum (Hagtvedt & Patrick, 2011a; Joy & Sherry, 2003b). Indeed, some scholars have argued that it is difficult to reconcile art with a traditional marketing concept (Hirschman, 1983; Joy & Sherry, 2003a). However, not only is arts marketing growing as a field of inquiry, with topics such as arts sponsorship (Martorella, 1990; Schwaiger, Sarstedt, & Taylor, 2010) and the branding of artists (Baumgarth & O'Reilly, 2014; Preece & Kerrigan, 2015; Rodner & Kerrigan, 2014; Schroeder, 2005; see also Newman & Bloom, 2012), but research has also focused on the use of artworks in the context of consumer products and brands.

Investigating the role of fine art in marketing, Hagtvedt and Patrick (2008a) demonstrate the phenomenon of art infusion, in which consumers tend to evaluate consumer products more favorably when they are associated with artworks via, for instance, advertising or product design. One reason for this effect is the spillover of luxury perceptions from the artwork to the consumer product. Relatedly, an association with visual art also enhances a brand's ability to introduce new and distant brand extensions (Hagtvedt & Patrick, 2008b). This effect of art on the brand is explained by an enhancement of the brand image as well as an increase in the viewer's cognitive flexibility; the latter enables people to see similarities between the brand and diverse extension categories. In research that nonetheless reveals tensions between art and marketing, Hagtvedt and Patrick (2011b) show that highlighting the content of artworks diminishes their specialness; when art images used in advertising or product design become mere illustrations, their influence on consumers becomes dependent on the fit between the art image and the advertised product. In contrast, artworks that are left to communicate via aesthetics, that is, via the manner of depiction, have a favorable influence regardless of context or fit with consumer products with which they are associated (Hagtvedt & Patrick, 2008a; see also Lacey et al., 2011).

MAJOR CHALLENGES, GOALS, AND SUGGESTIONS

Related to the latter observations, some of the challenges associated with aesthetics research in the realm of consumer behavior pertain to ongoing tensions between marketing and business on one side and art and aesthetics on the other (Hirschman, 1983; Joy and Sherry, 2003a; Patrick and Hagtvedt, 2011b). In the domain of financial documents, for example, Townsend and Shu (2010) find that a favorable influence of aesthetic design diminishes for investments that involve entities for which aesthetics is intrinsically valuable. On the other hand, consumers appear to respond favorably when some luxury stores take on elements of art galleries and museums (Joy, Wang, Chan, Sherry, & Cui, 2014). As a particularly striking example, the very definition of art seems mutable, depending on developments in the art world determined largely by market forces. Exacerbating this situation, philosophers of art may contribute insights that are interesting but not applicable in a given context of scientific research, whereas some social scientists might tailor definitions to the specific populations or contexts they are studying. In the general context of consumer behavior, Hagtvedt and Patrick (2008a) suggest that the consumers' perceptions and assessments should serve as the basis for the construct of art, therefore defining art as that which viewers categorize as such. They further argue that such works tend to be characterized by the creativity and skill that their creators bring to bear on the manner with which they express themselves, regardless of the specific content of those communications (Hagtvedt & Patrick, 2008a, 2011a).

Along with the tensions between art and market, it can sometimes be unclear whether researchers are measuring responses to innate, general aesthetic principles or to more ephemeral tastes and fashions. Additionally, research has documented differences between individuals (Bloch, Brunel, & Arnold, 2003; Holbrook, 1986), genders (Meyers-Levy & Zhu, 2010), and countries (van der Lans et al., 2009), as well as differences in variables such as expertise (Holbrook & Addis, 2007), age, or attitudes (Holbrook & Schindler, 1994), in terms of how people respond to aesthetics. In addition to complicating research questions in general, these differences and similarities have practical implications in a modern marketplace that combines globalism with increasingly efficient narrowcasting.

The relationship between form and function further complicates aesthetics research in the realm of consumer behavior. Aside from certain products (e.g., paintings or music) that are consumed first and foremost for their aesthetic properties, most consumer products are expected to perform other functions of various kinds: cars should facilitate driving and pens should facilitate writing. A product's form may be incidental to that function, it may be designed to facilitate that function, or it may even impede that function, and either way the resulting consumer assessments can interact with varying levels of appreciation for the aesthetics of that form (Hagtvedt & Patrick, 2014; Hoegg, Alba, & Dahl, 2010; Homburg, Schwemmle, & Kuehnl, 2015).

Related to these types of challenges are the general goals that consumer research should not only develop and extend theory but also provide insights of practical relevance to consumers and other consumer-relevant entities such as firms. Managers appear to make many design decisions based on intuition and personal experience, and aesthetics research can improve this process by providing general insights and guidelines.

One path that future research can take to provide such insights is to continue investigations into features such as shape and color, which are central to most design solutions, whether in product development, promotional materials, or elsewhere. Although much research focuses on one specific feature at a time, given that this approach facilitates experimental design, consumers rarely encounter features in an isolated state in the marketplace. It would therefore behoove researchers to investigate combined effects as well, including crossmodal ones (Hagtvedt & Brasel, 2016; Krishna, Elder, & Caldara, 2010; Spence, 2012), or ones stemming from juxtaposed visual and verbal information (Schnurr & Stokburger-Sauer, 2016).

Another potentially fruitful avenue for future research is aesthetics-based symbolism, which can pertain to products and brands (e.g., product gender; van Tilburg, Lieven, Herrmann, & Townsend, 2015) or to the consumers themselves. Domains such as luxury and fashion may be particularly fertile for research in this vein, given the role of both self-presentation and self-signaling in those contexts. Generally speaking, there is much scope for cross-pollination between aesthetics and related fields such as art, luxury, and sensory marketing (Berthon, Pitt, Parent, & Berthon, 2009; Hagtvedt & Patrick, 2008a; Kapferer, 2014; Krishna, 2012; Venkatesh, Joy, Sherry, & Deschenes, 2010). Future research can continue to explore the influence of aesthetics in a variety of other domains as well, ranging from politics to prosocial behavior and from self-identity to self-control.

The transformative potential of aesthetics is of particular relevance for public policy. For example, aesthetics can serve as a nudge in contemporary consumer behaviors such as recycling, energy conservation, donation, online action, personal hygiene practices, safe driving, organ donation, online practices, and retirement savings (Patrick & Sundar, 2017). Patrick (2016, p. 63) defines an aesthetic nudge as a visual or design feature "of choice architecture that has the potential to alter people's behavior in predictable, positive ways without constraining autonomy or significantly altering economic consequences." This notion highlights how consumer researchers, rather than maintaining a restrictive focus on aesthetics as beauty, are considering aesthetics as a potentially transformative tool to move consumers to positive action.

REFERENCES

Aaker, J. L. (1997). Dimensions of brand personality. *Journal of Marketing Research, 34*, 347–356.

Aggarwal, P., & McGill, A. L. (2007). Is that car smiling at me? Schema congruity as a basis for evaluating anthropomorphized products. *Journal of Consumer Research, 34*(4), 468–479.

Argo, J. J., & Dahl, D. W. (2018). Standards of beauty: The impact of mannequins in the retail context. *Journal of Consumer Research, 44*(5), 974–990.

Armstrong, T., & Detweiler-Bedell, B. (2008). Beauty as an emotion: The exhilarating prospect of mastering a challenging world. *Review of General Psychology, 12*(4), 305–329.

Bagchi, R., & Cheema, A. (2013). The effect of red background color on willingness-to-pay: The moderating role of selling mechanism. *Journal of Consumer Research, 39*(5), 947–960.

Bajaj, A, & Bond, S. D. (2017). Beyond beauty: Design symmetry and brand personality. *Journal of Consumer Psychology, 28*(1), 77–98.

Baumgarth, C., & O'Reilly, D. (2014). Brands in the arts and culture sector. *Arts Marketing: An International Journal, 4*(1/2), 2–9.

Belk, R. W. (1988). Possessions and the Extended Self. *Journal of Consumer Research, 15*, 139–168.

Berlyne, D. E. (Ed.). (1974). *Studies in the new experimental aesthetics: Steps toward an objective psychology of aesthetic appreciation.* Washington, DC: Hemisphere Publishing Corporation.

Berthon, P., Pitt, L., Parent, M., & Berthon, J.-P. (2009). Aesthetics and ephemerality: Observing and preserving the luxury brand. *California Management Review, 52*(1), 45–66.

Bloch, P. H. (1995). Seeking the ideal form: Product design and consumer response. *Journal of Marketing, 59*(3), 16–29.

Bloch, P. H., Brunel, F. F., & Arnold, T. J. (2003). Individual differences in the centrality of visual product aesthetics: Concept and measurement. *Journal of Consumer Research, 29*(4), 551–565.

Brasel, S. A., & Hagtvedt, H. (2016). Living brands: Consumer responses to animated brand logos. *Journal of the Academy of Marketing Science, 44*(5), 639–653.

Charters, S. (2006). Aesthetic products and aesthetic consumption: A review. *Consumption, Markets, and Culture, 9*(3), 235–255.

Chitturi, R., Raghunathan, R., & Mahajan, V. (2008). Delight by design: The role of hedonic versus utilitarian benefits. *Journal of Marketing, 72*(3), 48–63.

Cian, L., Krishna, A., & Elder, R. S. (2014). This logo moves me: Dynamic imagery from static images. *Journal of Marketing Research, 51*(2), 184–197.

Cian, L., Krishna, A., & Schwarz, N. (2015). Positioning rationality and emotion: rationality is up and emotion is down, *Journal of Consumer Research, 42*(4), 632–651.

Coates, D. (2003). *Watches tell more than time: Product design, information, and the quest for elegance.* London: McGraw-Hill.

Cox, D., & Cox, A. D. (2002). Beyond first impressions: The effects of repeated exposure on consumer liking of visually complex and simple product designs. *Journal of the Academy of Marketing Science, 30*(2), 119–130.

Deng, X., Hui, S. K., & Hutchinson, J. W. (2010). Consumer preferences for color combinations: An empirical analysis of similarity-based color relationships. *Journal of Consumer Psychology, 20*(4), 476–484.

Deng, X., & Kahn, B. E. (2009). Is your product on the right side? The "location effect" on perceived product heaviness and package evaluation. *Journal of Marketing Research, 46*(6), 725–738.

Deng, X., & Srinivasan, R. (2013). When do transparent packages increase (or decrease) food consumption? *Journal of Marketing, 77*(4), 104–117.

Desmet, P. M. A. (2002). *Designing emotions.* Delft, the Netherlands: Delft University of Technology.

Di Muro, F., & Noseworthy, T. J. (2012). Money isn't everything, but it helps if it doesn't look used: How the physical appearance of money influences spending. *Journal of Consumer Research, 39*(6), 1330–1342.

Dion, D., & Arnould, E. (2011). Retail luxury strategy: Assembling charisma through art and magic. *Journal of Retailing, 87*(4), 502–520.

Epley, N., Waytz, A., & Cacioppo, J. T. (2007). On seeing human: A three-factor theory of anthropomorphism. *Psychological Review, 114*(4), 864–886.

Fajardo, T. M., Zhang, J., & Tsiros, M. (2016). The contingent nature of the symbolic associations of visual design elements: The case of brand logo frames. *Journal of Consumer Research, 43*(4), 549–566.

Folkes, V., & Matta, S. (2004). The effect of package shape on consumers' judgments of product volume: Attention as a mental contaminant. *Journal of Consumer Research, 31*(2), 390–401.

Goode, M. R., Dahl, D. W., & Moreau, C. P. (2013). Innovation aesthetics: The relationship between category cues, categorization certainty, and newness perceptions. *Journal of Product Innovation Management, 30*(2), 192–208.

Gorn, G. J., Chattopadhyay, A., Sengupta, J., & Tripathi, S. (2004). Waiting for the web: How screen color affects time perception. *Journal of Marketing Research, 41*(2), 215–225.

Gorn, G. J., Chattopadhyay, A., Yi, T., & Dahl, D. W. (1997). Effects of color as an executional cue in advertising: They're in the shade. *Management Science, 43*(10), 1387–1400.

Hagtvedt, H. (2011). The impact of incomplete typeface logos on perceptions of the firm. *Journal of Marketing, 75*(4), 86–93.

Hagtvedt, H., & Brasel, S. A. (2016). Cross-modal communication: Sound frequency influences consumer responses to color lightness. *Journal of Marketing Research, 53*(4), 551–562.

Hagtvedt, H., & Brasel, S. A. (2017). Color saturation increases perceived product size. *Journal of Consumer Research, 44*(2), 396–413.

Hagtvedt, H., & Patrick, V. M. (2008a). Art infusion: The influence of visual art on the perception and evaluation of consumer products. *Journal of Marketing Research, 45*(3), 379–389.

Hagtvedt, H., & Patrick, V. M. (2008b). Art and the brand: The role of visual art in enhancing brand extendibility. *Journal of Consumer Psychology, 18*(3), 212–222.

Hagtvedt, H., & Patrick, V. M. (2011a). Fine arts. In D. Southerton (Ed.), *Encyclopedia of consumer culture* (pp. 605–606). London: Sage Publications.

Hagtvedt, H., & Patrick, V. M. (2011b). Turning art into mere illustration: Concretizing art renders its influence context dependent. *Personality and Social Psychology Bulletin, 37*(12), 1624–1632.

Hagtvedt, H., & Patrick, V. M. (2014). Consumer response to overstyling: Balancing aesthetics and functionality in product design. *Psychology & Marketing, 31*, 518–525.

Henderson, P. W., & Cote, J. A. (1998). Guidelines for selecting or modifying logos. *Journal of Marketing, 62*(April), 14–30.

Henderson, P. W., Giese, J. L., & Cote, J. A. (2004). Impression management using typeface design. *Journal of Marketing, 68*(October), 60–72.

Hine, T. (1995). *The total package: The evolution and secret meanings of boxes, bottles, cans and tubes.* Boston, MA: Little, Brown and Company.

Hirschman, E. C. (1983). Aesthetics, ideologies and the limits of the marketing concept. *Journal of Marketing, 47*(Summer), 45–55.

Hoegg, J., & Alba, J. W. (2008). A role for aesthetics in consumer psychology. In C. P. Haugtvedt, P. M. Herr, & F. R. Kardes (Eds.), *Handbook of consumer psychology* (pp. 733–754). New York: Taylor & Francis Group.

Hoegg, J., Alba, J. W., & Dahl, D. W. (2010). The good, the bad, and the ugly: Influence of aesthetics on product feature judgments. *Journal of Consumer Psychology, 20*(4), 419–430.

Holbrook, M. B. (1986). Aims, concepts, and methods for the representation of individual differences in esthetic responses to design features. *Journal of Consumer Research, 13*(3), 337–347.

Holbrook, M. B., & Addis, M. (2007). Taste versus the market: An extension of research on the consumption of popular culture. *Journal of Consumer Research, 34*(3), 415–424.

Holbrook, M. B., & Schindler, R. M. (1994). Age, sex, and attitude toward the past as predictors of consumers' aesthetic tastes for cultural products. *Journal of Marketing Research, 31*(3), 412–422.

Homburg, C., Schwemmle, M., & Kuehnl, C. (2015). New product design: Concept, measurement, and consequences. *Journal of Marketing, 79*(3), 41–56.

Janiszewski, C., & Meyvis, T. (2001). Effects of brand logo complexity, repetition, and spacing on processing fluency and judgment. *Journal of Consumer Research, 28*(1), 18–32.

Jiang, Z., Wang, W., Tan, B. C. Y., & Yu, J. (2016). The determinants and impacts of aesthetics in users' first interaction with websites. *Journal of Management Information Systems, 33*(1), 229–259.

Jindal, R. P., Sarangee, K. R., Echambadi, R., & Lee, S. (2016). Designed to succeed: dimensions of product design and their impact on market share. *Journal of Marketing, 80*(4), 72–89.

Joy, A., & Sherry, J. F. (2003a). Disentangling the paradoxical alliances between art market and art world. *Consumption, Markets and Culture, 6*(3), 155–181.

Joy, A., & Sherry, J. F. (2003b). Speaking of art as embodied imagination: A multisensory approach to understanding aesthetic experience. *Journal of Consumer Research,* *30*(September), 259–282.

Joy, A., Wang, J. J., Chan, T.-S., Sherry, J. F., & Cui, G. (2014). M(Art)Worlds: Consumer perception of how luxury brand stores become art institutions. *Journal of Retailing, 90*(3), 347–364.

Kapferer, J.-N. (2014). The artification of luxury: From artisans to artists. *Business Horizons, 57,* 371–380.

Kim, S., Chen, R. P., & Zhang, K. (2016). Anthropomorphized helpers undermine autonomy and enjoyment in computer games. *Journal of Consumer Research, 43,* 282–302.

Kim, S., & McGill, A. L. (2011). Gaming with Mr. Slot or gaming the slot machine? Power, anthropomorphism, and risk perception. *Journal of Consumer Research, 38,* 94–107.

Krishna, A. (2006). Interaction of senses: The effect of vision versus touch on the elongation bias. *Journal of Consumer Research, 32*(4), 557–566.

Krishna, A. (2012). An integrative review of sensory marketing: Engaging the senses to affect perception, judgment, and behavior. *Journal of Consumer Psychology, 22*(3), 332–351.

Krishna, A., Elder, R. S., & Caldara, C. (2010). Feminine to smell but masculine to touch: multisensory congruence and its effect on the aesthetic experience. *Journal of Consumer Psychology, 20,* 410–418.

Kumar, M., & Garg, N. (2010). Aesthetic principles and cognitive emotion appraisals: How much of the beauty lies in the eye of the beholder? *Journal of Consumer Psychology, 20*(4), 485–494.

Labrecque, L. I., & Milne, G. R. (2012). Exciting red and competent blue: The importance of color in marketing. *Journal of the Academy of Marketing Science, 40*(5), 711–727.

Labrecque, L. I., Patrick, V. M., & Milne, G. R. (2013). The marketer's prismatic palette: A review of color research and future directions. *Psychology and Marketing, 30*(2), 187–202.

Lacey, S., Hagtvedt, H., Patrick, V., Anderson, A., Stilla, R., Deshpande, G. . . . Sathian, K. (2011). Art for reward's sake: Visual art recruits the ventral striatum. *NeuroImage, 55*(1), 420–433.

Landwehr, J. R., McGill, A. L., & Herrmann, A. (2011). It's got the look: The effect of friendly and aggressive facial expressions on product liking and sales. *Journal of Marketing, 75*(3), 132–146.

Landwehr, J. R., Wentzel, D., & Herrmann, A. (2012). The tipping point of design: How product design and brands interact to affect consumers' preferences. *Psychology & Marketing, 29,* 422–433.

Landwehr, J. R., Wentzel, D., & Herrmann, A. (2013). Product design for the long run: Consumer responses to typical and atypical designs at different stages of exposure. *Journal of Marketing, 77*(5), 92–107.

Lee, C. J., Andrade, E. B., & Palmer, S. E. (2013). Interpersonal relationships and preferences for mood-congruency in aesthetic experiences. *Journal of Consumer Research, 40*(2), 382–391.

Lee, H., Deng, X., Unnava, H. R., & Fujita, K. (2014). Monochrome forests and colorful trees: The effect of black-and-white versus color imagery on construal level. *Journal of Consumer Research, 41*(4), 1015–1032.

Levy, S. (1959). Symbols for sale. *Harvard Business Review, 37*(4), 117–124.

Levy, S. J., & Czepiel, J. (1999). Marketing and aesthetics. In S. J. Levy & D. W. Rook (Eds.), *Brands, consumers, symbols, and research* (pp. 84–102).

Liu, Y., Li, K. J., Chen, H., & Balachander, S. (2017). The effects of products' aesthetic design on demand and marketing-mix effectiveness: The role of segment prototypicality and brand consistency. *Journal of Marketing, 81*(1), 83–102.

Lorenz, K. (1943). Die Angeborenen Formen Möglicher Erfahrung [The innate forms of potential experience]. *Zeitschrift für Tierpsychologie, 5,* 233–519.

MacInnis, D. J., & Folkes, V. S. (2017). Humanizing brands: When brands seem to be like me, part of me, and in a relationship with me. *Journal of Consumer Psychology, 27*(3), 355–374.

Martorella, R. (1990). *Corporate art.* New Brunswick, NJ: Rutgers University Press.

Meert, K., Pandelaere, M., & Patrick, V. M. (2014). Taking a shine to it: How the preference for glossy stems from an innate need for water. *Journal of Consumer Psychology, 24*(2), 195–206.

Mehta, R., & Zhu, R. (2009). Blue or red? Exploring the effect of color on cognitive task performances. *Science, 323*(5918), 1226–1229.

Meyers-Levy, J., & Peracchio, L. A. (1992). Getting an angle in advertising: The effect of camera angle on product evaluations. *Journal of Marketing Research, 29*(4), 454–461.

Meyers-Levy, J., Zhu, R., & Jiang, L. (2010). Context effects from bodily sensations: Examining bodily sensations induced by flooring and the moderating role of product viewing distance. *Journal of Consumer Research, 37*(1), 1–14.

Meyers-Levy, J., & Zhu, R. (2010). Gender differences in the meanings consumers infer from music and other aesthetic stimuli. *Journal of Consumer Psychology, 20,* 495–507.

Nenkov, G. Y., & Scott, M. L. (2014). "So cute i could eat it up": Priming effects of cute products on indulgent consumption. *Journal of Consumer Research, 41*(2), 326–341.

Newman, G. E., & Bloom, P. (2012). Art and authenticity: The importance of originals in judgments of value. *Journal of Experimental Psychology: General, 141*(3), 558–569.

Norman, D. A. (2004). *Emotional design: Why we love (or hate) everyday things.* New York: Basic Books.

Ordabayeva, N., & Chandon, P. (2013). Predicting and managing consumers' package size impressions. *Journal of Marketing, 77*(5), 123–137.

Orth, U. R., & Malkewitz, K. (2008). Holistic package design and consumer brand impressions. *Journal of Marketing, 72*(3), 64–81.

Patrick, V. M. (2016). Everyday consumer aesthetics. *Current Opinion in Psychology, 10,* 60–64.

Patrick, V. M., Atefi, Y., & Hagtvedt, H. (2017). The allure of the hidden: The act of unveiling confers value. *International Journal of Research in Marketing, 34*(2), 430–441.

Patrick, V. M, & Hagtvedt, H. (2011a). Aesthetic incongruity resolution. *Journal of Marketing Research, 48*(2), 393–402.

Patrick, V. M, & Hagtvedt, H. (2011b). Advertising with art: Creative visuals. In M. Runco, & S. Pritzker (Ed.), *Encyclopedia of creativity* (2nd ed.). San Diego, CA: Elsevier.

Patrick, V. M., & Sundar, A. (2017). Everyday consumer aesthetics. In A. Gneezy, V. Griskevicius, & P. Williams (Eds.), *Advances in Consumer Research* (vol. 45, pp. 1006–1006). Duluth, MN: Association for Consumer Research.

Peracchio, L. A., & Meyers-Levy, J. (1994). How ambiguous cropped objects in ad photos can affect product evaluations. *Journal of Consumer Research, 21*(June), 190–204.

Pounders, K., Babin, B., & Close, A. (2015). All the same to me: Outcomes of aesthetic labor performed by frontline service providers. *Journal of the Academy of Marketing Science, 43*(6), 670–693.

Preece, C., & Kerrigan, F. (2015). Multi-stakeholder brand narratives: An analysis of the construction of artistic brands. *Journal of Marketing Management, 31*(11/12), 1207–1230.

Puccinelli, N. M., Chandrashekaran, R., Grewal, D., & Suri, R. (2013). Are men seduced by red? The effect of red versus black prices on price perceptions. *Journal of Retailing, 89*(2), 115–125.

Raghubir, P. & Greenleaf, E. A. (2006). Ratios in proportion: What should the shape of the package be? *Journal of Marketing, 70*(2), 95–107.

Raghubir, P., & Krishna, A. (1999). Vital dimensions in volume perception: Can the eye fool the stomach? *Journal of Marketing Research, 36*(3), 313–326.

Rahinel, R., & Nelson, N. M. (2016). When brand logos describe the environment: Design instability and the utility of safety-oriented products. *Journal of Consumer Research, 43*(3), 478–496.

Reber, R., Schwarz, N., & Winkielman, P. (2004). Processing fluency and aesthetic pleasure: Is beauty in the perceiver's processing experience? *Personality and Social Psychology Review, 8*(4), 364–382.

Reimann, M., Zaichkowsky, J., Neuhaus, C., Bender, T., & Weber, B. (2010). Aesthetic package design: A behavioral, neural, and psychological investigation. *Journal of Consumer Psychology, 20*(4), 431–441.

Rodner, V. L., & Kerrigan, F. (2014). The art of branding—Lessons from visual artists. *Arts Marketing: An International Journal, 4*(1/2), 101–118.

Roggeveen, A. L., Grewal, D., Townsend, C., & Krishnan, R. (2015). The impact of dynamic presentation format on consumer preferences for hedonic products and services, *Journal of Marketing, 79*(6), 34–49.

Schnurr, B., & Stokburger-Sauer, N. E. (2016). The effect of stylistic product information on consumers' aesthetic responses. *Psychology & Marketing, 33*(3), 165–176.

Schroeder, J. E. (2005). The artist and the brand. *European Journal of Marketing, 39*(11/12), 1291–1305.

Schubert, T. W. (2005). Your highness: vertical positions as perceptual symbols of power. *Journal of Personality and Social Psychology, 89*, 1–21.

Schwaiger, M., Sarstedt, M., & Taylor, C. R. (2010). Art for the sake of the corporation: Audi, BMW Group, DaimlerChrysler, Montblanc, Siemens, and Volkswagen help explore the effect of sponsorship on corporate reputations. *Journal of Advertising Research, 50*(1), 77–90.

Sevilla, J., & Kahn, B. E. (2014). The completeness heuristic: product shape completeness influences size perceptions, preference, and consumption. *Journal of Marketing Research, 51*(1), 57–68.

Sevilla, J., & Townsend, C. (2016). The space-to-product ratio effect: How interstitial space influences product aesthetic appeal, store perceptions, and product preference. *Journal of Marketing Research, 53*(5), 665–681.

Silvia, P. J. (2005). Emotional responses to art: From collation and arousal to cognition and emotion. *Review of General Psychology, 9*(4), 342–357.

Simonson, A., & Schmitt, B. H. (1997). *Marketing aesthetics: The strategic management of brands, identity, and image.* London: Simon and Schuster.

Spence, C. (2012). Managing sensory expectations concerning products and brands: Capitalizing on the potential of sound and shape symbolism. *Journal of Consumer Psychology, 22*(1), 37–54.

Stanton, S. J., Townsend, J. D., & Kang, W. (2016). Aesthetic responses to prototypicality and uniqueness of product design. *Marketing Letters, 27*(2), 235–246.

Sundar, A., & Noseworthy, T. J. (2014). Place the logo high or low? Using conceptual metaphors of power in packaging design. *Journal of Marketing, 78*(5), 138–151.

Talke, K., Müller, S., & Wieringa, J. E. (2017). A matter of perspective: Design newness and its performance effects. *International Journal of Research in Marketing, 34*(2), 399–413.

Townsend, C. (2017). The price of beauty: Differential effects of design elements with and without cost implications in nonprofit donor solicitations. *Journal of Consumer Research, 44*(4), 794–815.

Townsend, C., & Shu, S. B. (2010). When and how aesthetics influences financial decisions. *Journal of Consumer Psychology, 20*(4), 452–458.

Townsend, C., & Sood, S. (2012). Self-affirmation through the choice of highly aesthetic products. *Journal of Consumer Research, 39*(2), 415–428.

Trudel, R., & Argo, J. J. (2013). The effect of product size and form distortion on consumer recycling behavior. *Journal of Consumer Research, 40*(4), 632–643.

van der Lans, R., Cote, J. A., Cole, C. A., Leong, S. M., Smidts, A., Henderson, P. W., . . . Schmitt, B. H. (2009). Cross-national logo evaluation analysis: An individual-level approach. *Marketing Science, 28*(5), 968–985.

Van Ittersum, K., & Wansink, B. (2012). Plate size and color suggestibility: The Delboeuf illusion's bias on serving and eating behavior. *Journal of Consumer Research, 39*(2), 215–228.

van Tilburg, M., Lieven, T., Herrmann, A., & Townsend, C. (2015). Beyond "Pink It and Shrink It" perceived product gender, aesthetics, and product evaluation. *Psychology & Marketing, 32*(4), 422–437.

Venkatesh, A., Joy, A., Sherry, J. F., & Deschenes, J. (2010). The aesthetics of luxury fashion, body, and identity formation. *Journal of Consumer Psychology, 20*(4), 459–470.

Veryzer, R. W., & Hutchinson, J. W. (1998). The influence of unity and prototypicality on aesthetic responses to new product designs. *Journal of Consumer Research, 24*(4), 374–394.

Wan, E. W., Chen, R. P., & Jin, L. (2017). Judging a book by its cover? The effect of anthropomorphism on product attribute processing and consumer preference. *Journal of Consumer Research, 43*(6), 1008–1030.

Wang, T., Mukhopadhyay, A., & Patrick, V. M. (2017). Getting consumers to recycle NOW! When and why cuteness appeals influence prosocial and sustainable behavior. *Journal of Public Policy & Marketing, 36*(2), 269–283.

Wang, Y. J., Minor, M. S., & Wei, J. (2011). Aesthetics and the online shopping environment: Understanding consumer responses. *Journal of Retailing, 87*(1), 46–58.

Wedel, M., & Pieters, R. (2014). The buffer effect: The role of color when advertising exposures are brief and blurred. *Marketing Science, 34*(1), 134–143.

Wu, F., Samper, A., Morales, A. C., & Fitzsimons, G. J. (2017). It's too pretty to use! When and how enhanced product aesthetics discourage usage and lower consumption enjoyment. *Journal of Consumer Research, 44*(3), 651–672.

Zhu, R., & Meyers-Levy, J. (2009). The influence of self-view on context effects: How display fixtures can affect product evaluations. *Journal of Marketing Research, 46*(1), 37–45.

CHAPTER 46

ON THE EMPIRICAL AESTHETICS OF PLATING

CHARLES SPENCE

INTRODUCTION

IT was Apicius, the Roman gourmand who, long ago, purportedly coined the phrase "We eat first with our eyes" (see Apicius, 1936). The latest evidence from the emerging field of gastrophysics—that is, the study of gastronomy combined with psychophysics (the measurement arm of psychology's perception science; see Spence, 2017a)—is increasingly supporting his assertion. For instance, neuroimaging evidence shows that there is nothing that gets our brains quite as excited as the sight of our favorite meal (possibly augmented by the aroma and, in this study, the taste/flavor of the dish being rubbed across the participant's lips with a Q-tip) when we are hungry, leading to a 24% increase in cerebral blood flow in one study (Wang et al., 2004). No wonder they call all those beautiful plates of food on Instagram "food porn"/"gastroporn" (McBride, 2010; Poole, 2012, p. 59; see also the Instagram feed, "The art of plating"; http://theartofplating.com/). A growing body of evidence suggests that the brain rapidly computes the energetic value in food images and decides where to pay attention accordingly (e.g., Toepel, Knebel, Hudry, Lecoutre, & Murray, 2009). It turns out that our attentional resources are almost immediately preferentially allocated to the energy-dense objects (i.e., foodstuffs) on the plate (see Harrar, Toepel, Murray, & Spence, 2011; Sawada, Sato, Toichi, & Fushiki, 2017). No wonder then that food porn is so attractive/attention capturing for us (Spence, Okajima, Cheok, Petit, & Michel, 2016, for a review).

Much of the research interest in the science of plating in recent years has been focused on trying to make the food look as attractive (or aesthetically pleasing) and/or plentiful as possible. As an example of the former, Franco-Colombian chef (and recent contestant on Netflix's *The Final Table* cooking show) Charles Michel created a salad based on Kandinsky's "Painting number 201" hanging in the Museum of Modern Art in New York (see Michel, Velasco, Gatti, & Spence, 2014; see also Figure 46.1). We conducted a series of experiments here in the Crossmodal Research Laboratory in Oxford, but also in the dining room of Somerville College, Oxford in order to assess how diners would respond to food that has been beautifully/artistically plated. No prize for guessing that people (the participants served this dish in the laboratory) reported being willing to pay significantly more for the aesthetically appealing plating than for the tossed version of exactly the same ingredients. When we followed up with a study conducted with 160 actual diners at Somerville College, Oxford University, half of whom ate the Kandinsky-inspired presentation and the remainder received a tossed salad version, the results showed that the diners were willing to pay more than double for exactly the same food (Michel, Velasco, Fraemohs, & Spence, 2015a). The art infusion effect (Hagtvedt & Patrick, 2008) may have something to do with this.

But can the diner's eyes, or rather their brain, really be tricked into thinking (and more importantly feeling) that there is more food on the plate than is actually the case. This was the aim behind a study by Rowley and Spence (2018) in which the arrangement of food on the plate (stacked vs. spread out) was found to exert a profound influence over how much food there appeared to be (and, more importantly, how much people reported being willing to pay for the dish).[1] As is often the way these days, we first conducted an internet-based study in order to assess the impact of plating (either spreading the various elements out on the plate, or stacking them up vertically; see Figure 46.2) on people's rating of how much food they thought there was. In this case, our participants ($N = 122$) did not get to taste anything, only look at a picture and rate

FIGURE 46.1. Kandinsky Salad (left, courtesy of chef Charles Michel), and the painting on which it was based (Kandinsky's painting number "201") (figure courtesy of Michel et al., 2014).

what they saw. Nevertheless, the results demonstrated that people estimated there to be 64% more food when the elements were spread out across the plate than when exactly the same components were stacked up instead. What is more, when asked to estimate how much they would be willing to pay for the dish, price estimates for the spread arrangement were more than 60% higher than when the same elements were stacked up instead. Participants' liking of the visual appearance of the dish was also higher for the spread arrangement of the elements, but there was no significant effect of plating arrangement on ratings of how artistic the dish looked.

Having demonstrated the basic idea that visual appearance matters, we then conducted a follow-up study in a dining room of one of the Oxford colleges (Rowley & Spence, 2018, Experiment 2). In this case, 124 diners attending one of the regular college guest nights were either served a stacked or spread arrangement of the same ingredients. The dish (the starter in a three-course meal) consisted of meat pâté or mixed vege-table pâté for vegetarians. The diners were required to rate the dish that they had been served, both prior to tasting and after having finished the dish. Once again, the results clearly demonstrated that spreading the food elements out led to people judging there to be more food than with the stacked arrangement. The diners reported that they would have been willing to pay significantly more for the dish (almost twice as much in fact). Intriguingly, however, in this case, the diners rated the vertical arrangement of the starter as looking significantly more artistic than the horizontal arrangement. What is also of interest is that both of the studies reported a strong correlation between perceived portion size and liking and/or willingness to pay.

These results are consistent with those from another series of studies in which we tested the kitchen folklore suggesting that chefs should plate odd rather than even numbers of elements on the plate (see Woods, Michel, & Spence, 2016).[2] At the Science

FIGURE 46.2. Which plate looks like it has more food? The same ingredients (comprising a warm salad with three slices of grilled aubergine, two slices of tomato, and two slices of moz-zarella) shown either vertically stacked (left) or horizontally arrayed (right) to participants in Rowley and Spence's (2018; Experiment 1) online study. Participants preferred the horizontally arrayed plating and were willing to pay significant more for the dish (figure courtesy of Rowley & Spence, 2018).

FIGURE 46.3. Which plate of seared scallops would you prefer to be served/to eat? Example of the kind of preference judgment presented to the participants in Woods et al.'s (2016) odd vs. even plating study.

Museum in London (as part of the Cravings Exhibition; https://blog.sciencemuseum.org.uk/cravings-can-your-food-control-you/), and in a series of follow-up online experiments, we showed people two white plates of seared scallops side by side (see Figure 46.3). The simple question that people had to respond to is which plate they preferred (i.e., to be served/to eat). All that we varied was whether the plates (round or square) had an odd or even number of scallops on them. The results of seven related experiments, in which the preferences of several thousand individuals were assessed, revealed that people do not actually seem to care whether there is an odd or even numbers of items on the plate. At the same time, however, our participants did not choose randomly either. Instead, the data suggested that people systematically tended to prefer the plate that happened to display the slightly larger number of food items (even when controlling for the total amount of food).

Interim summary

Taken together, therefore, the latest research clearly shows why we should all care about the fact that we eat first with our eyes. The results that have been discussed so far add weight to claims that food is not an aesthetic object, because people seem unable to make disinterested judgments (i.e., lacking any connection to desire) about what they are looking at. Indeed, one of the theoretically challenging issues in this area relates to traditional notions of what counts as an object of aesthetic appreciation. A beautifully presented plate of food would not seem to fit within Kant's (1892/1951) influential framework outlined in his book *Critique of Judgment*. There the eminent philosopher stated that aesthetic judgments are characterized by three key features: (a) their subjectivity, (b) their disinterested nature, and (c) their claim of universality. Along similar lines, in their review of the scientific literature on visual aesthetics, Palmer, Schloss, and Sammartino (2013, p. 81) have argued that aesthetic judgments are: "'disinterested' in the sense that they do not involve desire. Preferring a larger to a smaller piece of cake would not count as an aesthetic judgment in Kant's framework, because such a judgment is (presumably) about one's desire to consume the larger one."[3] However, while it may well be true that when the options that people are given to choose between contain (or appear to contain) different amounts of food, their preference judgments tend to be biased toward the plate or dish containing more food (e.g., Petit, Velasco, & Spence, 2018; Woods et al., 2016), it is important to stress that a number of studies have also demonstrated reliable preferences under those conditions in which the options that people are given to choose between do not vary in terms of their calorie content. It is to that research that we turn next.

THE SCIENCE OF AESTHETIC PLATING

At the outset, here, it is worth noting that the idea that food should be plated beautifully has not always been a pressing concern among chefs (see Deroy, Michel, Piqueras-Fiszman, & Spence, 2014, for a review). Indeed, some culinary experts (writing nearly a quarter of a century ago, note) have deliberately chosen to avoid the topic for fear of encouraging "the increasingly popular, and in some cases misguided, emphasis that some chefs have placed on the visual presentation of food" (Dornenburg & Page, 1996, p. 3). However, in the past, when the topic of beautiful plating has been mentioned it has normally been treated as an art, rather than a science (Yang, 2011). This view is captured in the titles of Styler and Lazarus's (2006) volume, *Working the Plate: The Art of Food Presentation*, or Siple and Sax's (1982) earlier publication entitled *Foodstyle: The Art of Presenting Food Beautifully*).

The intense focus on beautiful plating has been linked by some to the arrival of nouvelle cuisine,[4] though it is relevant here to note that the Japanese cuisine by which nouvelle cuisine was inspired has a long history of emphasizing the importance of aesthetic plating (and plateware). As Halligan (1990, p. 121) puts it:

> Really, the concern with how the food looked can be traced back to the emergence of nouvelle cuisine. The pictures of these dishes have set themselves in the mind of the public. Nouvelle cuisine was essentially photogenic ... Think of the glorious coloured photographs of these dishes, which have become eponymous with the purveying of recipes.

A few psychologists, but admittedly until recently it has been a very few, have also expressed an interest in the impact of attractive visual appearance on people's responses to food (e.g., see Lyman, 1989).

Importantly, however, a number of empirical studies of people's plating preferences have been published over the past decade or so where the results cannot simply be accounted for in terms of a desire for the plate displaying more food (see Spence, Piqueras-Fiszman, Michel, & Deroy, 2014, for a review; and see also Shimamura & Palmer, 2012, on the growing interest in empirical aesthetics more generally). That said, it should be kept in mind here that one of the challenges associated with working in this area is that fashions in plating come and go on a regular basis. Hence, just because asymmetrically plated dishes, say, were rated highly a couple of years ago, that really provides no convincing grounds to believe that the same preference will be documented today. Zellner, Loss, Zearfoss, and Remolina (2014) conducted a study with diners in a restaurant looking at the attractiveness of the visual presentation of a plate of food and its impact on liking. The diners were presented with a sautéed chicken breast with a *fines herbs* sauce, sautéed green beans with toasted almonds, and brown rice pilaf. The dish was prepared and arranged in one of two ways by a professional chef from the Culinary Institute of America (based in Upstate New York). For the "standard," or traditional, presentation, a chicken breast and sauce were placed at the bottom of the round white china plate (i.e., closest to the diner) and the rice and beans were placed in the two upper quadrants of the circular plate. The alternative, more creative or contemporary presentation, involved the rice being placed in the center of the plate, with the chicken breast and sauce spiraling outward, and with the beans situated around the edges of the plate. The latter presentation was judged as significantly more attractive and was liked more by the diners ($N = 91$) in this between-participants study. What is more, they also thought that the latter presentation had been prepared with more care. That said, the diners who took part in this study were not willing to pay any more for the more attractive (creative) plating, with the suggestion here being that since they had been to the campus restaurant before, they perhaps had a clear notion of what the dishes in the restaurant ought to cost.

Balanced plating

Many studies have highlighted the fact that viewers appear to exhibit a preference for balance, no matter whether they happen to be viewing paintings or simple geometric patterns (e.g., Banich, Heller, & Levy, 1989; Gordon & Gardner, 1974; Levy, 1988; Locher, 1996; McManus, Cheema, & Stoker, 1993; Wilson & Chatterjee, 2005). So, for example, people tend to prefer dot patterns that are symmetrical over those arranged asymmetrically (Garner & Clement, 1963). Meanwhile, viewers also tend to prefer those shapes that are more symmetrical (e.g., Jacobson & Höfel, 2002; Palmer & Griscom, 2013). As Zellner (2015, p. 165) puts it:

> Balance is a visual feature that has been found to be important in the aesthetic evaluation of a painting (see Locher 1996 for a review). A painting canvas, or in the case of food, a plate, is considered to be balanced when the elements are arranged around the

center of the painting or plate in such a manner that they appear anchored or stable. The more balanced an artwork, the greater the aesthetic appeal (Lega et al., 2003).

Note here also that the round white plate, so popular in the West,[5] serves to emphasize centric composition. Indeed, as Arnheim (1988, p. 72) notes when talking about the visual arts: "The most radical promoters of centric composition are the round enclosures—circular frames, disks, spherical volumes. Such fully symmetrical structures are entirely determined by their focus in the middle." No wonder then, that during their training, chefs are normally taught the fundamental importance of balance, and centralized layout (though see below for the recent rise in asymmetrical plating) to beautiful plating.

But what does the empirical aesthetics literature actually show concerning the importance of balance to plating? In one early study, Zellner, Lankford, Ambrose, and Locher (2010) had their participants (68 undergraduates) evaluate the visual attractiveness of a disposable white plate on which were arranged several slices of water chestnut (off-white) and various spots and dribbles of tahini (served either white or green and red). Next, the participants had to rate the taste of the food. In this between-participants study, the food elements were either presented in a balanced or unbalanced arrangement, and were either served monochrome white or with the tahini colored (i.e., there were four groups of participants in total). Numerically speaking, the balanced presentation of the dish was rated as looking somewhat more visually attractive than the unbalanced version, and the participants also reported being a little more willing to try the food from the balanced plate. Importantly, however, neither of these main effects quite reached statistical significance (perhaps because of the relatively small number of participants in each group in this between-participants experimental design). At the same time, no effect of visual presentation was documented on participants' hedonic taste ratings either. It is, however, worth noting that the visual presentation used in Zellner et al.'s study was very simple, much simpler, in fact, than one would likely find in any restaurant setting. One certainly would not really want to describe any of the presentations that were given to the participants as being especially aesthetically appealing,[6] and hence the results should perhaps be interpreted accordingly.

In order to try and address such concerns, Zellner and her colleagues worked with a somewhat more complex visual presentation subsequently (Zellner et al., 2011). In this case, the plating consisted of a balanced or unbalanced mound of hummus placed on a romaine leaf with three baby carrots, three cherry tomatoes, and four pita chips. Somewhat surprisingly, however, the balanced presentation was not judged to be any more attractive than the unbalanced presentation, nor was there any difference between the groups in terms of their willingness to try the dish. Once again, though, this between-participants study was quite small ($N = 41$). That said, the hummus was liked more when sampled from the balanced plate.

So does balanced presentation really make the food look/taste better? Zellner et al. (2011; Experiment 2) went on to demonstrate that it might have been messiness, rather than balance, that affected their participants' rating of the taste of food. (Indeed, the unbalanced presentation served in their first study looked rather as if the food had simply slid to the bottom of the plate!) In Zellner et al.'s second experiment, therefore, a chicken salad was served, with the balance held constant, but the neatness/messiness varied. The participants ($N = 31$) now had to judge how attractive the chicken salad looked, and their liking for the dish on tasting it. The salad was either presented on a romaine leaf in a neat mound in the center of the leaf/plate or spread out across the lettuce leaf in a messy but nevertheless balanced manner. The neat presentation was not judged as any more attractive than the messy presentation, though the taste of the food in the neat presentation was rated a little higher (cf. Hurling & Shepherd, 2003).

In a final experiment, Zellner et al.'s (2011) participants looked at pictures from the first two experiments and rated the amount of care taken by whoever had prepared the dish. This was judged to be higher in the neat than in the messy presentation. People also said that they would have been willing to pay more for the neat than for the messy presentation, and thought any restaurant preparing such food would be of higher quality. Thus perhaps the most appropriate conclusion to draw on the basis of Zellner et al.'s research on balanced plating is that neat food suggests higher quality, and a better taste. And given such an ambivalent set of results concerning the importance of balance to aesthetically pleasing plating, it is easy to see why Zellner (2015, p. 166) was led to the conclusion that "although balance might be an important visual contributor to the attractiveness of visual art, it is less important than neatness when it comes to food presentation." Elsewhere, though, as we saw earlier, Michel et al. (2014) attempted to discriminate between the perceived effort in plating a dish and the aesthetic impact of the final result. Importantly, they found little evidence to suggest that neat and effortful plating was valued except when the end result was itself also aesthetically pleasing.

That said, my colleagues and I take issue with Zellner's (2015) claim that balance doesn't matter to plating, given a number of our own results showing that neat and balanced presentations are clearly preferred over neat but unbalanced presentations (e.g., Velasco, Michel, Woods, & Spence, 2016a). We have shown a clear preference for centered plating over asymmetric plating in a number of studies conducted in both the restaurant and online setting (Michel et al., 2015a; Velasco et al., 2016a; see also Rowley & Spence, 2018). In what is perhaps the clearest demonstration of the importance of balance, Velasco et al. conducted a number of computer-based studies in which almost 7,500 individuals were asked to choose between a pair of plates containing four seared scallops, one plate with a balanced presentation and the other not; the results clearly showed a preference for the former.

Similarly, a study by Roque, Guastavino, Lafrairec, and Fernandeza (2018) also highlighted the importance of balanced plating to people's ratings of the creativity of the chef. In their study, participants were shown 16 different platings of the same dish created by two chefs on a monitor in a fine-dining setting. Balance of overall composition on the plate, position of the main item in the composition, and color were manipulated systematically in order to investigate the effect of these plating-related variables on diners' ratings of culinary creativity. Finally, here, the diners in Rowley and

Spence's (2018; Experiment 2) study (mentioned earlier) were served a dessert that was either centered or offset. The dessert consisted of a cylindrical vanilla, white chocolate, and raspberry cheesecake served with a quenelle of milk chocolate mousse, raspberry coulis, and topped with fresh raspberries, fresh mint, and a sprinkling of icing sugar. The 62 diners in this between-participants study served the centered dessert preferred it and were willing to pay significantly more for it too than the equal number of diners offered the offset (or unbalanced) plating. Intriguingly, however, the latter group actually rated the offset plating as looking significantly more artistic than did those served the balanced plating.

Taken together, therefore, while messiness undoubtedly can detract from the aesthetic appeal of a dish (Zellner et al., 2010, 2011), when people are asked to choose between balanced and unbalanced presentations of "restaurant-quality" dishes, they prefer the balanced presentation and are often willing to pay more for it (see Velasco et al., 2016a). However, as to whether they judge the balanced or unbalanced presentations as more artistic/creative appears to depend on the study in question (Roque et al., 2018; Rowley & Spence, 2018; though see also Michel, Velasco, & Spence, 2015c). One final point to note here concerns the influence of the context in which the plating is observed. Research from the visual arts has demonstrated that works of art tend to be valued more if seen in the context of the art gallery (Brieber, Nadal, & Leder, 2015). Something similar is likely to occur in the case of unusual plating, or surprising combinations of ingredients/flavors (see Piqueras-Fiszman & Spence, 2012; Velasco et al., 2016b; cf. Edwards, Meiselman, Edwards, & Lesher, 2003; Spence, 2017a).

The aesthetic oblique effect

Research by Youssef, Juravle, Youssef, Woods, and Spence (2015; Experiment 3) recently revealed that people prefer those plates with a dominant linear food component to be arranged so that the linear element ascends to the right. In their study, the chef prepared two versions of a dish (consisting of smoked cox apple crème, cobnuts, homemade curd, apple caviar, and beetroot reduction). One hundred participants were then invited to rotate the plates into their preferred orientation in this within-participants online study. The results (see Figure 46.4) revealed no significantly preferred orientation for the round version of the food, but a clear preference for the ascending-to-the-right orientation in the plate displaying a linear element. Now, quite why this particular orientation should have been preferred is as yet unclear. That said, it is interesting to note that oblique lines ascending to the right are also a distinctive feature of a number of Kandinsky's paintings presented, most unusually, in a round form (i.e., just like a white plate; see Spence, 2017b). What is more, we have obtained essentially the same pattern of results with a number of other dishes containing a linear element that we have had people rotate online. Elsewhere, research by Schlosser, Rikhi, and Dagogo-Jack (2016) has demonstrated that product logos that ascend to the right convey notions of activity. But, that said, activity doesn't seem like such a relevant concept here.

FIGURE 46.4. Circular data plot and pink rose diagrams of the 100 plate orientations for each dish selected by participants in Youssef et al. (2015; Experiment 3). The surrounding line shows a kernel density estimate (bandwidth of 40); this is a nonparametric estimate of the underlying density of the data (each data point is in effect "blurred" and so contributes to a range of points that make up the line; the more data points at a given orientation, the greater the bulge of the line). For clarity and ease of interpretation, the food has been added to the figure and oriented by the mean orientation in which the food was placed by participants (figure courtesy of Youssef et al., 2015).

However, according to an alternative account of the ascending-to-the-right effect, it may be related to the fact that people simulate the act of interacting with/consuming a dish (even when only viewing a picture of the dish on the internet). Hence, anything that makes it look like it would be easier to consume the food (i.e., items that ascend to the right may simply be easier to cut for right-handed diners) will likely result in increased liking. Relevant here, it has been shown previously that mugs are preferred if oriented so as to afford grasping (cf. Tipper, Paul, & Hayes, 2006). Meanwhile, placing a spoon on the right of a bowl of soup displayed on product packaging, say, also appears to increase liking as compared with when the spoon is shown on the nondominant left side instead (i.e., given that the vast majority of people are right-handed; Elder & Krishna, 2012). One of the interesting questions for future research in this area (i.e., in order to try to discriminate between alternative accounts) would be to investigate whether a viewer/diner's handedness affects their preferred orientation for dishes that ascend to the right vs. left. And if this preference should really be reducible to an ease-of-consumption effect, then one might not expect to see it, or at least to see it less strongly for inedible food items (Shibuya, Kasuga, Sato, Santa, Homma, & Miyamoto, 2022). Of course, all this talk of embodied mental simulation seems a long way removed from the disinterested assessment originally suggested by Kant (1892/1951) as being necessary for a judgment to be aesthetic.

Contour curvature and the inverted triangle effect

Both humans and great apes have been shown to exhibit a general preference for round over angular forms (e.g., Bar & Neta, 2006; Ghoshal, Boatwright, & Malika, 2016; Gómez-Puerto, Munar, & Nadal, 2016; Leder, Tinio, & Bar, 2011; Munar, Gómez-Puerto, Call, & Nadal, 2015; Silvia & Barona, 2009).[7] Round forms also tend to be associated with sweetness, whereas all of the other basic tastes are associated with angularity instead (see Spence & Deroy, 2012, for a review; see also Fairhurst, Pritchard, Ospina, & Deroy, 2015). Meanwhile, a separate body of empirical research has also shown that people do not like it when angular shapes point toward them. The suggestion from a number of researchers is that it may trigger an involuntary fear response associated with the presence of something dangerous (e.g., Larson, Aronoff, Sarinopoulos, & Zhu, 2009; Larson, Aronoff, & Stearns, 2007). It is in this context that one of the dishes served by Brazilian chef Alberto Landgraf at his restaurant Epice, in Sao Paulo is so interesting. This dish ("red onions, tapioca, sugar cane vinegar, peanut, fermented cream"; see Figure 46.5) consists of three small onions that can be grouped (in a Gestalt manner) into a triangle. This beautiful bit of food porn is all over the internet. There are, in fact, grounds for considering it the chef's signature dish. Given our interest in people's dislike for angular shapes that point toward them (e.g., see Velasco, Woods, & Spence, 2015), we were interested to understand the motivation behind, and relevance of, the chef's decision to arrange the elements so that the "triangle" points away from the diner. On talking to the chef, the latter clearly articulated that he had indeed thought carefully about the orientation/presentation of the elements on the plate, and had eventually relied on his intuition about which arrangement looked best (undoubtedly honed by years of practice). However, given how popular this dish has become online etc., one might obviously hope for a more robust empirical assessment of the aesthetic appeal of the dish.

Michel, Woods, Neuhäuser, Landgraf, and Spence (2015b) therefore decided to conduct a series of large-scale online (and museum) studies of this particular dish in order to determine whether this design decision mattered materially to people's aesthetic appreciation of the food. In the largest study, 1,667 people were invited to rotate the plate online into the orientation that they would have preferred to have been served. The results revealed clear preferences for specific orientations of the plate. Overall, the average preferred orientation was with the triangle pointing 3.4° past 12 o'clock (shown by the arrow in Figure 46.5). What is more, the participants reported that they would have been willing to pay significantly more for the dish when the elements were arranged in one of the preferred orientations, than for exactly the same plate of food when presented in a different orientation instead. Such results would therefore seem to provide clear evidence that people can make an aesthetic judgment concerning the best orientation of a given portion of food (and that a significant majority concur in the same judgment). And while in this case the chef intuitively chose more-or-less the most aesthetically

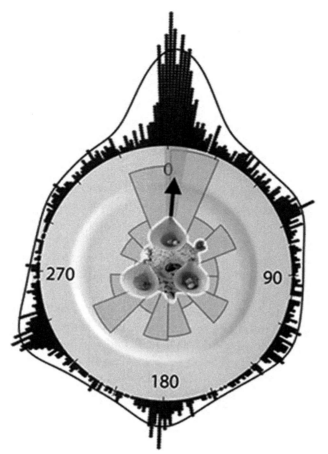

FIGURE 46.5. Circular data plot and rose diagram showing the 1,667 plate orientations selected by participants. The surrounding line provides an estimate of the preferred orientation (indicated by the bulge of the line). The food has been added to the figure and oriented by 3.20° clockwise (the bias-corrected, mean orientation in which the food was placed by participants). An arrow indicates the mean angle that participants placed the food in (beneath which is a blue wedge indicating the lines 95% confidence intervals). In this case, then, the chef's decision to place the dish pointing at 12 o'clock was pretty much in line with the preferences demonstrated by the group (figure from Michel et al., 2015b, with permission).

appealing orientation for the dish (12 o'clock), it is important to note that intuition does not always provide the answer (from a population preference perspective).

The Golden Section/Ratio

Another aesthetic rule that has been mentioned in the context of plating is the Golden Section/Ratio (see Deroy & Spence, 2014, for a review), obtained by dividing a line into two sections, such that the ratio of the longer part to the shorter is roughly 1.61:1. The suggestion in the literature is that those images/forms that incorporate the Golden Section/Ratio will, all other things being equal, tend to be judged as more aesthetically appealing (e.g., see Fechner, 1997; Green, 1995). The physicist Mark Hadley (2013), in an unpublished industry-sponsored report (sponsored by Tilda Rice if you must know), put forth the suggestion that diners would be likely to judge a circular central portion of curry sitting atop a circular bed of rice as looking most attractive if the ratio of rice to curry happened to obey the Golden Section/Ratio. That said, it should be noted that Hadley provided no empirical evidence whatsoever in support of his suggestion. Hence, while the idea is intriguing, and is no doubt worth testing empirically (by someone), the fundamental visual perception literature underpinning the aesthetic appeal of the Golden Section/Ratio is weak at best (e.g., Angier, 1903; Boselie, 1992; Godkewitsch, 1974). Indeed, the ambivalence of the research findings in this area has led some to suggest that any such preference for those stimuli incorporating the Golden Section/Ratio, should it exist, likely varies as a function of both the individual and situation (see McManus, 1980; Raghubir & Greenleaf, 2006; Thorndike, 1917).

Perceptual Uncertainty/Ambiguity on the Plate

In a couple of more recent papers, I have been working with London-based chef Jozef Youssef on the concept of the "aesthetic aha" (see Muth & Carbon, 2013). This is the name given to the positive feeling/response that people typically experience when they resolve a perceptual problem/puzzle. Muth and Carbon have demonstrated this kind of positive carry-over effect in those exposed to challenging examples from the visual arts, including cubist paintings by the likes of Picasso, Braque, and Gris. We have been working on an edible version of a bistable perceptual stimulus as well as with the Gestalt principle of emergence. The basic idea here is that the diners are confronted with an aesthetically appealing, yet challenging visual dish presentation. In such cases, the full meaning (or interpretation) of what the diners happen to be looking at is not immediately obvious. However, after some period of cogitation (together possibly with a hint from the service staff and/or other diners sitting at the table) the meaning is revealed (or reveals itself). It is this sudden resolution that triggers the "aesthetic aha," a normally positively valenced experience. It is our hope that the emergence of the Gestalt will likely also exert a positive influence over the diner's liking for the food (not to mention their enjoyment of the dining experience)—that is, over and above any gustatory pleasure they may have.

In one of our recent dishes, known as "Every act of creation" (see Spence & Youssef, 2016), a plate is brought to the table showing what initially looks like nothing more than merely a random series of red shapes (red beetroot) set against the white background of the plate (see Figure 46.6). When we tested this dish on 100 diners in a series of four meals served at a central London restaurant, only four of the guests were immediately able to see the face "hidden" in the plate. However, eventually, all but four saw Picasso's silhouetted face (or at least the half of it stenciled on the plate).[8] Indeed, informal observation of the diners as they struggled to interpret this dish suggests that when the latter finally "saw" Picasso's half-portrait stenciled in beetroot on the surface of the plate it was a rewarding and enjoyable experience. What is perhaps also worth noting here is how the chef's introduction to the dish, before it is even served, also primes thoughts of Picasso. As such, it is somewhat surprising how difficult it is for diners to see the great artist's silhouette in the plate. Who knows, perhaps this is because of a set effect, namely that we are not used to seeing faces in our food (Giuseppe Arcimboldo's famous portraits of heads made out of fruit and vegetables excepted).

FIGURE 46.6. "The Picasso Dish" (otherwise known as "Every Act of Creation" after Picasso's famous claim that "Every act of creation first begins with an act of destruction"; see Spence & Youssef, 2016) as served by chef Jozef Youssef. Picasso's half-silhouette can be seen stenciled in red beetroot on the right of the plate (picture courtesy of Kitchen Theory).

Elsewhere, we have been working to make a bistable visual image edible in the context of the Gastrophysics Chef's Table (Youssef, Sanchez, Woods, & Spence, 2018). As it so happens, there are few visual illusions that are more chef-friendly than Jastrow's famous duck–rabbit. This image, first popularized more than a century ago (e.g., see Jastrow, 1899), works from a chef's perspective, as duck and rabbit are often found together in, for example, recipes for terrines.[9] After several iterations (and almost 1,000 online participants), the final version of the bistable visual illusion that is currently being served in the restaurant is shown in Figure 46.7. Preliminary testing with this version of the dish (in the restaurant setting) shows that, while some people initially see the duck, others see the rabbit (as intended; see Youssef et al., 2018). It is this very difference of opinion that generates some enthusiastic discussion at the dining table (which appears to constitute a pleasurable interaction). We are currently waiting to see whether the predominant meat taste of the dish is affected by, or changes as a result of, the visual interpretation (or change in visual interpretation) of the dish (cf. Spence, Wang, & Youssef, 2017). However it turns out, though, both of the just-mentioned dishes involve surprise and possibly also the aesthetic aha. They are, in a sense, playful, and can be seen as

FIGURE 46.7. "Jastrow's Bistable Bite" dish as served at the Gastrophysic's Chef's Table at Kitchen Theory (picture courtesy of Kitchen Theory).

adding to a growing sense among practitioners that play and food may be legitimately (and joyfully) combined (despite all those suggestions to the contrary from our parents; Goldstein, 2005; Murer, Aslan, & Tscheligi, 2013).

The aesthetics of size

One final aspect of the aesthetics of plating that deserves to be mentioned before closing this piece relates to the size of the presentation itself. While traditionally the layout of the food has normally been restricted to the surface area of the plate on which it was served, it is interesting to see how a number of chefs have, in recent years, started to go beyond the confines of the crockery in order to plate the entirety of the table instead. The most famous example here probably being the dessert course served by Grant Achatz at his restaurant Alinea in Chicago (see Spence & Piqueras-Fiszman, 2014), where the star chef and his associates plate the entire table. And where Achatz has been credited with leading, a number of other young chefs have followed. Charles Michel, the Franco-Colombian chef we came across earlier has, for instance, been experimenting with plating his Kandinsky-inspired salad not on a plate or small canvas, but on the entirety of the table surface, with the size of the presentation (or should that be performance) then being determined by the size and shape of the latter.

Similarly, chef Jozef Youssef of Kitchen Theory in London also serves several of the dishes on his current Gastrophysics Chef's Table menu (https://gastrophysics.co.uk/) by plating the table. In this case, projection mapping is used so that the diner not only sees the plating of the table by the chefs but also interleaved images projected onto the tabletop itself. In one memorable case, a black squid ink risotto is plated on the table while a dramatic black calligraphy work from artist Aerosyn-Lex Mestrovic "Works of Ink and Pressure" is projected onto the tabletop (see https://vimeo.com/76401889). While I am not aware of any empirical assessment of the aesthetic impact of such large-scale food presentations having been carried out, my own impression, having attended a number of such theatrical large-scale platings, is that a single large plating of the table is treated very differently by the diner than if the same amount of food were to be individually plated (no matter how many diners there happen to be at the table). Having been lucky enough to attend a number of such plating performances over the years, what is noticeable is how part of the aesthetic appeal in such cases relates to the theatricality (and scale) of the plating itself (and for a historical take, see El-Khoury, 2004; see also Kirshenblatt-Gimblett, 1999). Oftentimes, the sheer amount of food, not to mention the surface area that needs to be plated, means than two or more chefs may be involved (often with their respective movements carefully choreographed). I would also like to argue that the scale of some of these presentations, which typically involve sharing and/ or eating with one's hands (the latter sometimes being necessary to preserve the structural integrity of the table/table-covering) can sometimes induce a feeling of awe in the mind of the diners, both at the sheer amount of food being laid out before them, and at the awe-inspiring scale of the presentation itself.[10] Potentially relevant here, of course, are findings from the world of art appreciation where the (large) size of a work, or its re-production, has also been shown to influence the way in which viewers respond aesthetically (Silvera, Josephs, & Giesler, 2002).

CONCLUSION

In summary, the literature that has been reviewed in this chapter has hopefully given a sense of how the art of plating food beautifully is increasingly being studied scientifically within the emerging field of empirical aesthetics. And while a number of the same rules that modulate the aesthetic appeal of paintings also seem to apply to the plating of food, it is important here to stress that the research has also revealed some intriguing differences (such as, for example, in terms of preferred colors/color palate in paintings versus on the plate). Note here only how the preference for blue and green on the canvas is rarely replicated in the world of food,[11] with blue being about the least desirable color as far as food is concerned (Spence, 2018a). Meanwhile, most people tend to associate the color green with bitter-tasting vegetables and sour-tasting foods (e.g., Saluja & Stevenson, 2018; Spence et al., 2015). Rather the preferred colors on the plate tend to be those that are associated with sweet foods (see also Lyman, 1989), while the nutritionists are keen to suggest that what we should be appreciating on the plate is rather a wide variety of color—and hence, potentially, food groups (e.g., see König & Renner, 2018).

What the studies reviewed here highlight is the fact that while people's preferences as far as plating are concerned can undoubtedly be swayed by the amount of food that is presented, not all of our aesthetic preferences/responses as far as plating are concerned are reducible to such "primitive" or "interested" judgments. Ultimately, therefore, Kant's influential suggestion that food cannot be considered an object of aesthetic appreciation, because people are unable to make disinterested judgments about it, would appear incorrect, at least some of the time (see also Carey, 2005).

Looking to the future, while the majority of the dishes that have been studied in the present review (and in the underpinning empirical aesthetics literature) have involved only static elements (even if the perceptual interpretation of the dish itself has sometimes changed; see Spence & Youssef, 2016; Youssef et al., 2018, for a couple of recent examples), there does appear to be something aesthetically intriguing (in either a good or a bad way) about those dishes/foods that are in some sense animate and/or where the food transforms before the diner's eyes (see Spence, 2018b, for a review). On the aesthetically positive side, one might think only of the ancient Roman fascination with the surmullet, a fish that was brought from the kitchen in order to be paraded before the lucky diners as its skin shimmered through a dazzling rainbow of colors (see Andrews, 1949). In this case, the changing color of the dish would seem to deliver an aesthetic pleasure/delight that is independent of any nutritional content that the dish provides. And while the surmullet, or goat fish as it is also known, is today nothing more than a historical curiosity, nowadays those foods that change color also seen to capture the public's attention, as well as that of the media (e.g., see Blake, 2017, on the sell-out success of color-changing tea); Others, meanwhile, have been working on ice-creams that change color when they are licked—that is, on contact with saliva (e.g., see Moon, 2014).[12]

While such color-changing food and drink would appear to be positively valenced, it should be noted that elsewhere there has been (an often horrified) interest in those dishes where the animal on the plate (typically seafood it should be said) seems to come back to life, as in the case of the dancing squid (see Spence, 2018b; see also Vanhamert, 2013; and Soranzo, Petrelli, Ciolfi, & Reidy, 2018, on the aesthetics of interactivity). In this case, the strong aversive response that such dishes evoke in many diners may relate to the choking/asphyxiation hazard that such foods represent (Allen, 2012) and/or the "meat paradox" (this the name given to the observation that while many of us like to eat meat, few of us necessarily feel happy being reminded of the life that was lost in order to provide it; see Bastian & Loughnan, 2017; Loughnan, Bastian, & Haslam, 2014).

One of the other areas of interest for the future concerns the extent to which aesthetic preferences for specific styles of plating are shared cross-culturally (see Zampollo, Wansink, Kniffin, Shimuzu, & Omori, 2012; see also Zhao, An, Spence, & Wang, 2018; Zhou, Wan, Mu, Du, & Spence, 2015) and/or in different groups of consumers (e.g., Reisfelt, Gabrielsen, Aaslyng, Bjerre, & Møller, 2009). While it is certainly true to say that our own plating studies have been conducted on relatively diverse populations in the lab, online (see Woods, Velasco, Levitan, Wan, & Spence, 2015), in the restaurant, and museum setting (e.g. see Velasco et al., 2016b), what we have yet to do is a systematic comparison of the "rules" of aesthetic plating cross-culturally. Here, of course, one should perhaps also consider the impact of individual differences in terms of the viewer's level of expertise (cf. Hekkert & van Wieringen, 1996).

A final intriguing future research question here concerns how realistic the representation of food needs to be in order for it to induce embodied mental simulation (Elder & Krishna, 2012). Are such processes also engaged when looking at still life paintings in an art gallery, say (see Bendiner, 2004)? Potentially relevant here, such simulations do appear to be triggered by the images of food that one sees on product packaging (see Petit et al., 2018). In fact, it is striking to see just how often mere visual images of food appear to generate exactly the same neural responses as the actual presentation of the food itself (though see Spence, 2011, for a few intriguing exceptions to this generalization from the world of salivation research). It is easy to foresee how future neuroaesthetics research may be helpful in resolving such issues (see also Chatterjee, 2010; Leder, 2013).

NOTES

1. Note here that altering the arrangement of the food on the plate, either stacking the food vertically or else spreading it out horizontally, was also shown to influence the perception of portion size and the quantity of food consumed in another study (Szocs & Lefebvre, 2015, 2017). According to the latter research, the participants also reported that there was less food and so (perhaps unsurprisingly) ate more when the elements were

stacked vertically on the plate as compared with when they were laid flat (i.e., horizontally) against the surface of the plate (see also Nelson, Atkinson, & Darbyshire, 1994).

2. Here, it is interesting to note that the aesthetic preference for odd over even numbers of elements has also been reported in the case of German flower sellers and Japanese ornamental stone garden design (see Shimoyama, 1976; Van Tonder & Lyons, 2005).

3. I do not have space to delve here into the fraught question of whether food is, or can be considered as art (e.g., see Deresiewicz, 2012; Gonsoulin, 2013; Neill & Ridley, 2002; Tefler, 2002).

4. The rise of nouvelle cuisine also seemingly being accompanied by the introduction of the large white American plate, often monogrammed with the chef's initials, or else the name of the chef or their restaurant (see Halligan, 1990).

5. According to Hultén, Broweus, and van Dijk (2009), half of all plates sold in the West are both round and white.

6. Indeed, one might be tempted to question whether the title of the paper "Art on the plate" was really justified.

7. Anecdotally, Gopnik (2012) notes that a disproportionate number of the foods that people might be expected to struggle to eat (black pudding etc.) also typically seem to be presented in round form, as if to make them easier to swallow.

8. One of the intriguing things about such examples of emergence is that once you have seen them, it becomes next to impossible to unsee them.

9. And, important to an increasing number of chefs, rabbit is also currently a sustainable food source.

10. Not to mention awe/trepidation that one feels in terms of the sheer amount of food that one is being asked to eat. This is definitely the response to British chef Jesse Dunford-Woods' marvellously Willy-Wonka-esque tableful of desserts, as served exclusively at his chef's table by the kitchen at Parlour, North London (see https://parlourkensal.com/chefs-table/#contact).

11. Those studies that have assessed people's preferences for different colors (hues) typically reveal a general preference for cool colors such as blue, cyan, and green, over warm colors such as red, orange, and yellow (e.g., see Palmer & Schloss, 2010). In fact, when evaluating abstract color patches, blue tends to be most preferred color and yellow to yellow-green the least preferred (Palmer et al., 2013). That people's color preferences should vary as a function of context certainly fits with Palmer and Schloss's (2010) ecological valence theory. Their suggestion is that people like/dislike a particular color to the degree that they like/dislike those environmental objects that they happen to associate with that color. As such, people's liking for the colors of foods on the plate then likely depends on their liking for all of the foods that they have eaten that are associated with that color (cf. Saluja & Stevenson, 2018).

12. Perhaps relevant here note how it is chocolate's transformation from solid to liquid form at body temperature that has been suggested to be a part of what makes such a food so pleasurable.

References

Allen, J. S. (2012). *The omnivorous mind: Our evolving relationship with food.* London: Harvard University Press.

Andrews, A. C. (1949). The Roman craze for surmullets. *The Classical Weekly, 42*(12), 186–188.

Angier, R. P. (1903). The aesthetics of unequal division. *Psychological Review Monograph Supplement, 4,* 541–561.

Apicius (1936). *Cooking and dining in Imperial Rome* (c. 1st century; translated by J. D. Vehling). Chicago, IL: University of Chicago Press.

Arnheim, R. (1988). *The power of the center: A study of composition in the visual arts.* Berkeley, CA: University of California Press.

Banich, M., Heller, W., & Levy, J. (1989). Aesthetic preference and picture asymmetries. *Cortex, 25,* 187–195.

Bar, M., & Neta, M. (2006). Humans prefer curved visual objects. *Psychological Science, 17,* 645–648.

Bastian, B., & Loughnan, S. (2017). Resolving the meat-paradox: A motivational account of morally troublesome behavior and its maintenance. *Personality and Social Psychology Review, 21,* 278–299.

Bendiner, K. (2004). *Food in painting: From the Renaissance to the present.* London: Reaction Books.

Blake, I. (2017). Too pretty to drink? Sell-out colour-changing tea turns from blue to purple before your eyes (and it's flying off shelves faster than classic Earl Grey). *Daily Mail Online,* September 25. Retrieved from http://www.dailymail.co.uk/femail/food/article-4910522/The-viral-colour-changing-tea-s-selling-fast.html

Boselie, F. (1992). The golden section has no special aesthetic attractivity! *Empirical Studies of the Arts, 10,* 1–18.

Brieber, D., Nadal, M., & Leder, H. (2015). In the white cube: Museum context enhances the valuation and memory of art. *Acta Psychologica, 154,* 36–42.

Carey, J. (2005). *What good are the arts?* London: Faber & Faber.

Chatterjee, A. (2010). Neuroaesthetics: A coming of age story. *Journal of Cognitive Neuroscience, 23,* 53–62.

Deresiewicz, W. (2012). A matter of taste? *The New York Times,* October 26. Retrieved from https://www.nytimes.com/2012/10/28/opinion/sunday/how-food-replaced-art-as-high-culture.html

Deroy, O., Michel, C., Piqueras-Fiszman, B., & Spence, C. (2014). The plating manifesto (I): From decoration to creation. *Flavour, 3,* 6.

Deroy, O., & Spence, C. (2014). Can you find the golden ratio in your plate? *Flavour, 3,* 5.

Dornenburg, A., & Page, K. (1996). *Culinary artistry.* New York: John Wiley & Sons.

Edwards, J. S. A., Meiselman, H. L., Edwards, A., & Lesher, L. (2003). The influence of eating location on the acceptability of identically prepared foods. *Food Quality and Preference, 14,* 647–652.

Elder, R. S., & Krishna, A. (2012). The "visual depiction effect" in advertising: Facilitating embodied mental simulation through product orientation. *Journal of Consumer Research, 38,* 988–1003.

El-Khoury, R. (2004). Delectable decoration: Taste and spectacle in Jean-François de Bastide's *La Petite Maison.* In J. Horwitz & P. Singley (Eds.), *Eating architecture* (pp. 301–311). Cambridge, MA: MIT Press.

Fairhurst, M., Pritchard, D., Ospina, D., & Deroy, O. (2015). Bouba-Kiki in the plate: Combining crossmodal correspondences to change flavour experience. *Flavour, 4,* 22.

Fechner, G. T. (1997). Various attempts to establish a basic form of beauty: Experimental, aesthetics, golden section, and square. *Empirical Studies of the Arts, 15,* 115–130. (Translation of chapter XIV of Fechner, 1876).

Garner, W. R., & Clement, D. E. (1963). Goodness of pattern and pattern uncertainty. *Journal of Verbal Learning & Verbal Behavior, 2,* 446–452.

Ghoshal, T., Boatwright, P., & Malika, M. (2016). Curvature from all angles: An integrative review and implications for product design. In R. Batra, C. Seifert, & D. Brei (Eds.), *The psychology of design: Creating consumer appeal* (pp. 91–105). New York: Routledge.

Godkewitsch, M. (1974). The golden section: An artefact of stimulus range and measure of preference. *American Journal of Psychology, 87,* 269–277.

Goldstein, D. (2005). The play's the thing: Dining out in the new Russia. In C. Korsmeyer (Ed.), *The taste culture reader: Experiencing food and drink* (pp. 359–371). Oxford, UK: Berg.

Gómez-Puerto, G., Munar, E., & Nadal, M. (2016). Preference for curvature: A historical and conceptual framework. *Frontiers in Human Neuroscience, 9,* 712.

Gonsoulin B. (2013). The art of food. Retrieved from http://gapersblock.com/drivethru/2013/03/14/food_the_new_art/#more

Gopnik, A. (2012). *The table comes first: Family, France, and the meaning of food.* London: Quercus.

Gordon, I. E., & Gardner, C. (1974). Responses to altered pictures. *British Journal of Psychology, 65,* 243–251.

Green, C. D. (1995). All that glitters: A review of psychological research on the aesthetics of the golden section. *Perception, 24,* 937–968.

Hadley, M. (2013). A perfect curry. Unpublished manuscript commissioned by Tilda Rice.

Hagtvedt, H., & Patrick, V. (2008). Art infusion: The influence of visual art on the perception and evaluation of consumer products. *Journal of Marketing Research, 40,* 379–389.

Halligan, M. (1990). *Eat my words.* London: Angus & Robertson.

Harrar, V., Toepel, U., Murray, M., & Spence, C. (2011). Food's visually-perceived fat content affects discrimination speed in an orthogonal spatial task. *Experimental Brain Research, 214,* 351–356.

Hekkert, P., & van Wieringen, P. C. W. (1996). Aesthetic preference for paintings as a function of expertise level and various stimulus proerties. *Acta Psychologica, 94,* 117–131.

Hultén, B., Broweus, N., & van Dijk, M. (2009). *Sensory marketing.* Basingstoke, UK: Palgrave Macmillan.

Hurling, R., & Shepherd, R. (2003). Eating with your eyes: Effect of appearance on expectations of liking. *Appetite, 41,* 167–174.

Jacobson, T., & Höfel, L. A. (2002). Aesthetic judgments of novel graphic patterns: Analyses of individual judgments. *Perceptual & Motor Skills, 95,* 755–766.

Jastrow, J. (1899). The mind's eye. *Popular Science Monthly, 54,* 299–312.

Kant, I. (1892/1951). *Critique of judgment.* New York, NY: Haffner.

Kirshenblatt-Gimblett, B. (1999). Playing to the senses: Food as a performance medium. *Performance Research, 4*(1), 1–30.

König, L. M. & Renner, B. (2018). Colourful = healthy? Exploring meal colour variety and its relation to food consumption. *Food Quality and Preference, 64,* 66–71.

Larson, C. L., Aronoff, J., Sarinopoulos, I. C., & Zhu, D. C. (2009). Recognizing threat: A simple geometric shape activates neural circuitry for threat detection. *Journal of Cognitive Neuroscience, 21,* 1523–1535.

Larson, C. L., Aronoff, J., & Stearns, J. J. (2007). The shape of threat: Simple geometric forms evoke rapid and sustained capture of attention. *Emotion, 7*, 526–534.

Leder, H., (2013). Next steps in neuroaesthetics: Which processes and processing stages to study? *Psychology of Aesthetics, Creativity, and the Arts, 7*(1), 27–37.

Leder, H., Tinio, P. P. L., & Bar, M. (2011). Emotional valence modulates the preference for curved objects. *Perception, 40*, 649–655.

Lega, L., Paula-Pereira, L., Giron, D., Pastor, D., Locher, P., & Hoyos, G. (2003). A cross-cultural analysis of the visual rightness theory of picture perception. *Bulletin of Psychology and the Arts, 4*, 86–89.

Levy, J. (1988). Cerebral asymmetry and aesthetic experience. In I. Rentschler, B. Herzberger, & D. Epstein (Eds.), *Beauty and the brain: Biological aspects of aesthetics* (pp. 219–242). Basel, Switzerland: Birkhäuser.

Locher, P. (1996). The contribution of eye-movement research to an understanding of the nature of pictorial balance perception: A review of the literature. *Empirical Studies of the Arts, 14*, 143–163.

Loughnan, S., Bastian, B., & Haslam, N. (2014). The psychology of eating animals. *Current Directions in Psychological Science, 23*, 104–108.

Lyman, B. (1989). *A psychology of food, more than a matter of taste.* New York: Avi, van Nostrand Reinhold.

McBride, A. (2010). Food porn. *Gastronomica, 10*, 38–46.

McManus, I. C. (1980). The aesthetics of simple figures. *British Journal of Psychology, 71*, 502–524.

McManus, I. C., Cheema, B., & Stoker, J. (1993). The aesthetics of composition: A study of Mondrian. *Empirical Studies of the Arts, 11*, 83–94.

Michel, C., Velasco, C., Fraemohs, P., & Spence, C. (2015a). Studying the impact of plating on ratings of the food served in a naturalistic dining context. *Appetite, 90*, 45–50.

Michel, C., Velasco, C., Gatti, E., & Spence, C. (2014). A taste of Kandinsky: Assessing the influence of the artistic visual presentation of food on the dining experience. *Flavour, 3*, 7.

Michel, C., Velasco, C., & Spence, C. (2015c). Cutlery influences the perceived value of the food served in a realistic dining environment. *Flavour, 4*, 26.

Michel, C., Woods, A. T., Neuhäuser, M., Landgraf, A., & Spence, C. (2015b). Rotating plates: Online study demonstrates the importance of orientation in the plating of food. *Food Quality & Preference, 44*, 194–202.

Moon, M. (2014). Physicist concocts ice cream that changes color when you lick it. Retrieved from http://www.engadget.com/2014/07/29/ice-cream-changes-colors/

Munar, E., Gómez-Puerto, G., Call, J., & Nadal, M. (2015). Common visual preference for curved contours in humans and great apes. *PLoS ONE, 10*(11), e0141106.

Murer, M., Aslan, I., & Tscheligi, M. (2013). LOLLio—Exploring taste as playful modality. *TEI 2013*, February 10–13. Barcelona.

Muth, C., & Carbon, C. C. (2013). The aesthetic aha: On the pleasure of having insights into Gestalt. *Acta Psychologica, 144*(1), 25–30.

Neill, A., & Ridley, A. (2002). The art of food. In A. Neill & A. Ridley (Eds.), *Arguing about art: Contemporary philosophical debates* (2nd Ed.; pp. 5–8). London: Routledge.

Nelson, M., Atkinson, M., & Darbyshire, S. (1994). Food photography 1: The perception of food portion size from photographs. *British Journal of Nutrition, 7*(5), 649–663.

Palmer, S. E., & Griscom, W. (2013). Accounting for taste: Individual differences in preference for harmony. *Psychonomic Bulletin & Review, 20*, 453–461.

Palmer, S. E., & Schloss, K. B. (2010). An ecological valence theory of human color preference. *Proceedings of the National Academy of Sciences of the USA, 107*, 8877–8882.

Palmer, S. E., Schloss, K. B., & Sammartino, J. (2013). Visual aesthetics and human preference. *Annual Review of Psychology, 64*, 77–107.

Petit, O., Velasco, C, & Spence, C. (2018). Are large portions always bad? Using the Delboeuf illusion on food packaging to nudge consumer behaviour. *Marketing Letters, 29*, 435–449.

Piqueras-Fiszman, B., & Spence, C. (2012). Sensory incongruity in the food and beverage sector: Art, science, and commercialization. *Petits Propos Culinaires, 95*, 74–118.

Poole, S. (2012). *You aren't what you eat: Fed up with gastroculture.* London: Union Books.

Raghubir, P., & Greenleaf, E. A. (2006). Ratios in proportion: What should the shape of the package be? *Journal of Marketing, 70*, 95–107.

Reisfelt, H. H., Gabrielsen, G., Aaslyng, M. D., Bjerre, M. S., & Møller, P. (2009). Consumer preferences for visually presented meals. *Journal of Sensory Studies, 24*, 182–203.

Roque, J., Guastavino, C., Lafrairec, J., & Fernandeza, P. (2018). Plating influences diners' perception of culinary creativity. *International Journal of Gastronomy & Food Science, 11*, 55–62.

Rowley, J., & Spence, C. (2018). Does the visual composition of a dish influence the perception of portion size and hedonic preference? *Appetite, 128*, 79–86.

Saluja, S., & Stevenson, R. J. (2018). Cross-modal associations between real tastes and colors. *Chemical Senses, 43*, 475–480.

Sawada, R., Sato, W., Toichi, M., & Fushiki, T. (2017). Fat content modulates rapid detection of food: A visual search study using fast food and Japanese diet. *Frontiers in Psychology, 8*, 1033.

Schlosser, A. E., Rikhi, R. R., & Dagogo-Jack, S. W. (2016). The ups and downs of visual orientation: The effects of diagonal orientation on product judgment. *Journal of Consumer Psychology, 26*, 496–509.

Shibuya, K., Kasuga, R. Sato, N., Santa, R., Homma, C., & Miyamoto, M. (2022). Preliminary findings: Preferences of right-handed people for food images oriented to the left vs. right side. *Food Quality and Preference,* **97**:104502. https://doi.org/10.1016/j.foodqual.2021.104502.

Shimamura, A. P., & Palmer, S. E. (Eds.). (2012). *Aesthetic science: Connecting minds, brains, and experience.* Oxford, UK: Oxford University Press.

Shimoyama, S. (1976). Translation of *Sakuteiki: The Book of the Garden* (Tokyo: Town and City Planners). Attributed to Toshitsuna Tachibana, late 11th/early 12th century.

Silvera, D. H., Josephs, R. A., & Giesler, R. B. (2002). Bigger is better: The influence of physical size on aesthetic preference judgments. *Journal of Behavioral Decision Making, 15*, 189–202.

Silvia, P. J., & Barona, C. M. (2009). Do people prefer curved objects? Angularity, expertise, and aesthetic preference. *Empirical Studies of the Arts, 27*, 25–42.

Siple, M., & Sax, I. (1982). *Foodstyle: The art of presenting food beautifully.* New York: Crown Publishers.

Soranzo, A., Petrelli, D., Ciolfi, L., & Reidy, J. (2018). On the perceptual aesthetics of interactive objects. *Quarterly Journal of Experimental Psychology, 71*, 2586–2602.

Spence, C. (2011). Mouth-watering: The influence of environmental and cognitive factors on salivation and gustatory/flavour perception. *Journal of Texture Studies, 42*, 157–171.

Spence, C. (2017a). *Gastrophysics: The new science of eating.* London: Viking Penguin.

Spence, C. (2017b). The art and science of plating. In N. Levent & I. D. Mihalache (Eds.), *Food and museums* (pp. 237–253). London: Bloomsbury Academic.

Spence, C. (2018a). What is so unappealing about blue food and drink? *International Journal of Gastronomy & Food Science, 14*, 1–8.

Spence, C. (2018b). Why are animate dishes so unappealing? *International Journal of Gastronomy & Food Science, 13,* 73–77.

Spence, C., & Deroy, O. (2012). On the shapes of tastes and flavours. *Petits Propos Culinaires, 97,* 75–108.

Spence, C., Okajima, K., Cheok, A. D., Petit, O., & Michel, C. (2016). Eating with our eyes: From visual hunger to digital satiation. *Brain & Cognition, 110,* 53–63.

Spence, C., & Piqueras-Fiszman, B. (2014). *The perfect meal: The multisensory science of food and dining.* Oxford, UK: Wiley-Blackwell.

Spence, C., Piqueras-Fiszman, B., Michel, C., & Deroy, O. (2014). Plating manifesto (II): The art and science of plating. *Flavour, 3,* 4.

Spence, C., Wan, X., Woods, A., Velasco, C., Deng, J., Youssef, J., & Deroy, O. (2015). On tasty colours and colourful tastes? Assessing, explaining, and utilizing crossmodal correspondences between colours and basic tastes. *Flavour, 4,* 23.

Spence, C., Wang, Q. J., & Youssef, J. (2017). Pairing flavours and the temporal order of tasting. *Flavour, 6,* 4. doi:10.1186/s13411-017-0053-0

Spence, C., & Youssef, J. (2016). Constructing flavour perception: From destruction to creation and back again. *Flavour, 5,* 3.

Styler, C., & Lazarus, D. (2006). *Working the plate: The art of food presentation.* New York: John Wiley.

Szocs, C., & Lefebvre, S. (2015). Stack it up or spread it out? The effects of vertical versus horizontal plating on calorie estimates and consumption decisions. *Advances in Consumer Research, 43,* 707–708.

Szocs, C., & Lefebvre, S. (2017). Spread or stacked? Vertical versus horizontal food presentation, portion size perceptions, and consumption. *Journal of Business Research, 75,* 249–257.

Tefler, E. (2002). Food as art. In A. Neill & A. Ridley (Eds.), *Arguing about art: Contemporary philosophical debates* (2nd Ed.; pp. 9–27). London: Routledge.

Thorndike, E. L. (1917). Individual differences in judgments of the beauty of simple forms. *Psychological Review, 24,* 147–153.

Tipper, S. P., Paul, M. A., & Hayes, A. E. (2006). Vision-for-action: The effects of object property discrimination and action state on affordance compatibility effects. *Psychonomic Bulletin & Review, 13,* 493–498.

Toepel, U., Knebel, J., Hudry, J., Lecoutre, J., & Murray, M. (2009). The brain tracks the energetic value in food images. *Neuroimage, 44,* 967–974.

Vanhamert, K. (2013). Yikes! Three skin-crawling dishes that combine fine dining and synthetic biology. *Wired,* July 24. Retrieved from https://www.wired.com/2013/07/ahhhh-three-skin-crawling-dishes-that-combine-fine-dining-and-synthetic-biology/

Van Tonder, G. J., & Lyons, M. J. (2005). Visual perception in Japanese rock garden design. *Axiomathes, 15,* 353–371.

Velasco, C., Michel, C., Woods, A., & Spence, C. (2016a). On the importance of balance to aesthetic plating. *International Journal of Gastronomy and Food Science, 5–6,* 10–16.

Velasco, C., Michel, C., Youssef, J., Gamez, X., Cheok, A. D., & Spence, C. (2016b). Colour-taste correspondences: Designing food experiences to meet expectations or to surprise. *International Journal of Food Design, 1,* 83–102.

Velasco, C., Woods, A. T., & Spence, C. (2015). Evaluating the orientation of design elements in product packaging using an online orientation task. *Food Quality & Preference, 46,* 151–159.

Wang, G.-J., Volkow, N. D., Telang, F., Jayne, M., Ma, J., Rao, M., … Fowler, J. S. (2004). Exposure to appetitive food stimuli markedly activates the human brain. *NeuroImage, 212*, 1790–1797.

Wilson, A., & Chatterjee, A. (2005). The assessment of preference for balance: Introducing a new test. *Empirical Study of the Arts, 23*, 165–180.

Woods, A. T., Michel, C., & Spence, C. (2016). Odd versus even: A scientific study of the "rules" of plating. *PeerJ, 4*, e1526. doi:10.7717/peerj.1526

Woods, A. T., Velasco, C., Levitan, C. A., Wan, X., & Spence, C. (2015). Conducting perception research over the internet: A tutorial review. *PeerJ, 3*, e1058.

Yang, J. (2011). The art of food presentation. *Crave (Hong Kong)*. Retrieved from http://www.cravemag.com/features/the-art-of-food-presentation/

Youssef, J., Juravle, G., Youssef, L., Woods, A., & Spence, C. (2015). On the art and science of naming and plating food. *Flavour, 4*, 27.

Youssef, J., Sanchez, C. C., Woods, A., & Spence, C. (2018). "Jastrow's Bistable Bite": What happens when visual bistable illusion meets the culinary arts? *International Journal of Gastronomy & Food Science, 13*, 16–24.

Zampollo, F., Wansink, B., Kniffin, K. M., Shimuzu, M., & Omori, A. (2012). Looks good enough to eat: How food plating preferences differ across cultures and continents. *Cross Cultural Research, 46*, 31–49.

Zellner, D. A. (2015). Effect of visual cues on sensory and hedonic evaluation of food. In A. Hirsch (Ed.), *Nutrition and chemosensation* (pp. 159–174). Boca Raton, FL: CRC Press.

Zellner, D. A., Lankford, M., Ambrose, L., & Locher, P. (2010). Art on the plate: Effect of balance and color on attractiveness of, willingness to try and liking for food. *Food Quality and Preference, 21*, 575–578.

Zellner, D. A., Loss, C. R., Zearfoss J., & Remolina S. (2014). It tastes as good as it looks! The effect of food presentation on liking for the flavor of food. *Appetite, 77C*, 31–35.

Zellner, D. A., Siemers, E., Teran, V., Conroy, R., Lankford, M., Agrafiotis, A., … Locher, P. (2011). Neatness counts. How plating affects liking for the taste of food. *Appetite, 57*, 642–648.

Zhao, H., An, J., Spence, C., & Wang, X. (2018). Influence of the color and size of the plate on the subjective ratings of, taste expectations concerning, and willingness-to-pay for, Asian noodles. *Journal of Sensory Studies, 33*, e12443.

Zhou, X., Wan, X., Mu, B., Du, D., & Spence, C. (2015). Crossmodal associations and subjective ratings of Asian noodles and the impact of the receptacle. *Food Quality & Preference, 41*, 141–150.

INDEX

Tables and figures are indicated by *t* and *f* following the page number

A

abstract art preference 264, 348–9, 975–6
Academy of Motion Picture Arts and Sciences
  (AMPAS) 687, 692
ACC *see* anterior cingulate cortex (ACC)
Acconci, Vito 108
Achatz, Grant 1042
acting 803–4
action and movement appreciation *see also*
  body movements
  aesthetics of 605–6, 616–19
  and neuroscience insights into 611–16
  and perception 606
  and psychological studies into 608–11
  theoretical considerations 606–7
action observation network (AON) 611–13,
  626, 801–2
action programs 156–8, 157*f*
action research 616–17
Adams, F.M. 862
adaptive acts 56
"aesthetic aha" 410, 436, 1039, 1041
aesthetic appreciation
  and cognitive electrophysiology 294–7
  contemporary accounts of 12–19
  definition 256–7
  model 127, 127*f*
  notion 156, 168–9
aesthetic emotions *see also* emotions
  in the 19th/20th centuries 137–40
  in the 21st century 140–3
  complex model of 122–5
  definition 136–7, 146–7
  negative and positive 123–5, 124*f*
  and the prefrontal cortex 344–7
  and the Romantic Movement 143–6

aesthetic experience
  concept 45, 57
  description 925–6
  overview of 256–7
Aesthetic Fluency Scale 951
aesthetic pleasure *see also* pleasure; Pleasure-
  Interest Model of Aesthetic Liking (PIA
  Model); processing fluency
  and design 993–6, 1002–3
  as mode of art appreciation 117–22, 142–3
  principles 8, 41, 46
aesthetic sensitivity *see also* personality
  definition 834–5
  development and training for 844–5
  future directions of 845–7
  history of 835–7
  measurement 59–62, 837–41
  and relations with mental ability 841–2
  and relations with personality 842–4,
    856–8, 888
  and sensory valuation 164–5
aesthetic stability 466–7
"aesthetic triad" model 265, 662–70, 673,
  893*f*
Aesthetics and Psychobiology (Berlyne) 68–9
aesthetics-based symbolism 1019–20
affective priming 258–9, 497
affective processing 111, 345, 439–40, 760, 764
affective sensitiveness 48
age 537, 546–7, 586–8 *see also* children
agreeableness
  as Big Five trait 821
  and film and television preference 826
  and music preference 590, 825
  as pure sensuous pleasure 49–50
  and reading preference 826

agreement
  and facial attractiveness 542–3
  measures of 47
Akiba, F. 905–6
alcohol consumption 545
Alhambra, Granada, Spain 489, 489f
ambiguity 409–11, 931
American functional empirical
  aesthetics 47–50
American psychology 47
amygdala 323–5, 341, 518
anatomical labels 313–14
ancient art museums 976–8
Angell, James Rowland 47, 52
Angier, Roswell Parker 44
angles 262, 511, 512–13, 516–20, 524–6, 527
animals 47, 168–70, 184–7, 190–1, 494–5, 497
anterior cingulate cortex (ACC) 314, 320–1,
  517, 525, 669, 758
anterior insula cortex 314, 321, 440
antero-posterior movement 286
anthropometric measures for drawing 247–8
anthropomorphism 1015, 1016
antlers 186–7
AOIs see areas of interest (AOIs)
appetitive phase 154, 155f, 393
Apple products 993
Appleton, J. 666
approach-avoidance 156f, 260, 515, 525
appropriateness 229–30
Arai, S. 935–6
Archer, J. 728, 730
architectura, De (Vitruvius Pollio) 490, 490f
architecture
  aesthetic responses to 660–2, 673, 963–4
  aesthetic triad of 662–70, 673
  and the brain 670
  and curvature effect 525
  and emotion-valuation systems 662,
    669–70
  and empirical aesthetics 26
  and expectations 668
  expertise 797–8
  historical context of 660–2
  and implicit associations 263
  and knowledge-meaning systems 667–70
  and mental health and wellbeing 672–3

neuroscience of 662–3, 671–3, 798
psychology of 671
and sensorimotor systems 663–7
and vision 663–6
areas of interest (AOIs) 274, 276
Aristotle 108, 144, 727–8
ARMUIAC model (acquire, represent,
  manipulate, and use information in
  artistic communication) 104–6
Arnheim, Rudolf 10–11, 66–7, 139, 1033
Aronoff, J. 513
arousal levels
  and aesthetic emotions 142–3
  arousal-boost mechanism 387
  arousal-jag mechanism 387
  and the brain 391–5
  measurement 390–1
  motivational 391–2
  and music and dance 642
  and novelty 395
  objective measures 107
  theory 3–4, 6–7, 11, 68–9, 386–7, 387f, 576
art see also visual art
  and aesthetic appeal 1018
  aesthetic judgements of 48–9
  appreciation of 116–26, 126–31, 128f, 142–3,
    770–1
  and art-making process 200–21, 225–6
  biological foundation of 184
  categories of 105–6, 108–12
  and cognitive science 101–2, 103–6
  and color preference 468
  and color regularities 463–4, 464f
  and communication 101–5, 109–10, 112
  criticism of 105
  education 277–8, 983–4
  expertise 125–6, 238–40, 244, 276–7, 521–2,
    795–6
  and handicap principle 186–7
  history of 26, 100–2, 105
  locating 109–12
  and male selection 188
  and marketing 1018–19
  and normative conventions 109–10
  ontology of 99, 101, 102, 105–6
  perceptual systems of 104
  philosophy of 99–106, 112

"presence of" 366, 371
production 286–8
theory of 26, 101–3, 109
Art as Experience (Dewey) 19, 44
art exhibitions 221
art images 450, 451*t*
art museums *see* museums
Art Worlds (Becker) 980
artifacts
    aesthetic pleasure in 995–6
    aesthetics of 964, 996–1003
    and aesthetics of interaction 1001–2
artistic aptitude 59
artistic beauty 285, 329, 490
artistic images 456–9
artistic research 372–3
artists
    creative 205–8
    expertise 125–6, 238–40, 244, 276–7, 521–2,
        795–6
    health 187
    and historiometric methods 208
    social context of 980–2
    strategies of 104
    and symmetry 490–1, 490*f*, 494
ascending reticular activating system
        (ARAS) 391–2, 576
Aschaffenburg, K. 980
associative factors of liking and disliking 41,
        85–6
asymmetry 492*f*, 493, 495–8, 502
atomistic conceptualization 839, 846
attachment styles 725
attention restoration theory (ART) 665–6
attention-attraction 188–9
Attneave, F. 451
audience 363–5, 647–8
audition 667
augmented observation 228–9
authenticity 898–9, 936
authorship 375–6
automatic embodied simulation
        mechanisms 266
automatic processing 13–14, 258, 261–5, 436,
        753–7
autonomous, yet connected 999, 1003
averageness 538

B
Bamford, A. 983–4
Barlow, Philip 453–4, 454*f*
Barrett, J.L. 931–2
Barron, Frank (Francis Zavier) 62–4
Barron-Welsh Art Scale 63, 64
Barsics, C. 240
Bartoli, G. 263
baseball game 110–11
Bauer, D. 276–7
Baumgarten, Alexander Gottlieb 84, 116,
        887–8
beat perception 407–8, 649
beauty
    in abstraction 326
    and aesthetic emotion 138–9, 141
    approaches to defining 118–19
    in architectural design 660
    and attention-attraction 188–9
    biological foundation of 184, 187–8, 192
    and design 993, 994, 1003–6
    and electrophysiology 295, 296*f*, 297–8,
        300
    evolution of 183–4
    and facial attractiveness 533–4, 540–3, 923
    and halo effect 540–1
    and mate selection 184–6
    and neuroaesthetics 309–13, 315, 317–19,
        326–7, 329–30
    and neuroscience 170–1, 498–500
    and pleasure 317–19
    in sensory perception 310–11
    and symmetry 295, 296*f*, 490, 495–6
    types of 490
Becker, Howard 902, 980–2
Becklen, R.C. 929–30
Beebe-Center, John Gilbert 55–6
"beer goggles" effect 545
behavioral genetics 591–2
behavioral sciences 25–6
behaviorism 9, 50–7, 57–65, 140
behaviors 21–2, 153–8, 500–2
Beilock, S.L. 608
Being-I 145–6
Belke, B. 929
Bell, Clive 924, 938
Bennett, S. 243–4

Berlyne, Daniel E.
  and aesthetic appreciation 7, 13, 858
  and aesthetic emotions 142
  and ambiguity and clarity 409
  and arousal theory 6–7, 107, 386–7, 391–2,
    576
  and brightness and abstraction 859–60
  and collative variables 386–8
  and complexity 120, 402–3, 576–7
  conception of empirical aesthetics 3–4, 11
  and curiosity 389
  and current perspectives on
    theories 388–91
  and expertise 791
  and hedonic value 389–90
  and impact of work 67–9
  and music appreciation 576
  and new experimental aesthetics 385–8
  and novelty and familiarity 395–6
  and object features 17
  and psychobiological aesthetics 858
  and *psychobiological theory* 221
  and surprise and expectedness 398–9
Berridge, K.C, 156, 162–3, 393
Bertamini, M. 261–2, 492*f*, 494, 497–8, 518–19
Beudt, S. 298
Biederman, I. 251
Big Five Framework 821–2, 827, 843
Binet, A. 836
Bingham, Walter V. 52
Binnie, J. 279
biological aesthetics 183–4, 186–90, 192
biophilia hypothesis (BH) 665–6
bipolar factors 10, 60–1, 63, 821
birds 185–7, 190
Birkhoff, G.D. 403, 491, 492*f*
birth order 65
Bitgood, S. 931
blood oxygenation level-dependent (BOLD)
    signals 308, 312, 328, 516
Bloom, P. 773–4
blue color preference 462, 464, 476–8, 482,
    483, 861–2, 864, 1043
Bluetooth proximity sensor 227
blur 453–4, 454*f*, 455
body movements 286, 363–4, 520, 615–16,
    624–6, 649

body perspective 293, 294*f*
BOLD signals *see* blood oxygenation level-
    dependent (BOLD) signals
Boring, Edwin G. 71
Bosanquet, B. 137–8, 139, 144
bottom-up processes 257, 280–1, 284, 438–9,
    752, 755–6, 910
Bouissac, Paul 137
Bourdieu, Pierre 978–80
brain imaging 15, 308–9, 325, 328, 392, 615–16,
    754, 758
brain processes 119, 394, 757
brain systems 669
Brattico, E. 299–300
BRECVEM model 579
Brieber, D. 279–80
brightness 479–80, 481, 860–1
Brock, T.C. 733–4
Brown, S. 321–2, 669
brown color preference 462
Bubić A. 930
Buchanan, J.A. 480
Bullot, N.J. 128–30, 128*f*
Bullough, E. 139–40, 144
Burger-Pianko, Z. 204
Burt, Cyril 59–60, 853–4

C

Cabeza, R. 441–2
Cage, John 588
calligraphy 325
Calvo-Merino, B. 350, 613–14, 615–16, 628, 629–30
Cambridge Face Memory Test 240
Canova, Antonio 982
car designs 514, 1016
Carbon, C.C. 224, 225, 514, 928, 929, 1039
Carr, Harvey A. 52, 56
Carrus, G. 263
categories of art 108–12
catharsis 108, 144
Cattaneo, Z. 344–5, 347–8, 349*f*, 350
Cattell, James McKeen 47–9, 70
Cela-Conde, C.J. 329, 757
Çelik, P. 842
Chamberlain, R. 248–9
Chandler, A.R. 54, 57–8
characters 722–7, 730

Chatterjee, Anjan 16, 170, 171, 265, 893*f*, 925–6
Chen, H.P, 862–3
chess 789
Chevreul, Michel-Eugéne 981
Child, Irvin Long 61–2, 834–5, 837, 856–8, 888
children
   and aesthetic emotions 776–9
   and aesthetic sensitivity 844
   and art appreciation 770–1, 779–81
   and artworks 125–6, 280–1
   and characters 723–4, 730
   and engagement with art 771–3
   and facial attractiveness 546–7
   and intention and creation of art 773–5
   mental tests on 59–60
   and music appreciation 46, 119, 584, 844
   preferences and value judgements of 775–6
   and social context of art experience 982–5
Child's Test of Esthetic Judgement 64
chill responses 393–4, 400, 580–1, 586, 592–3
Chinese pictograms 325
Chinese typefaces 302
choice, method of 8, 41, 87, 90–1, 94, 95
choreography 643–4
Chou, S.K. 862–3
Christensen, J.F, 171, 642–3
Chumbley, J.R. 170
Cicero 887
cinema *see* movies
clarity 100, 409–11, 706
Clay, F. 138–9
clinical psychology 42
closure, need for 975
coarse emotions 136–7, 147
cognition
   and aesthetics 751–3, 762–4, 787–8
   and cognitive control 758–60
   and context 764, 903–7, 907*f*
   and context features 18–19
   and dual-mode processing
     frameworks 753–7
   embodied 371–2
   and memory 760–2
   and prototypicality 11–12
cognitive electrophysiology
   of aesthetic appreciation 294–7
   background to 292–4

challenges, goals, and suggestions 303–4
   and everyday objects appreciation 302–3
   and facial attractiveness 301–2
   and music appreciation 299–301
   and poetry appreciation 299–301
   and visual art appreciation 297–9
cognitive mastering 14–15, 589, 594, 762, 895
cognitive models 167–8
cognitive neuroscience 291, 309–10, 340*f*,
   611–16, 626
   as properties of stimuli 339
cognitive psychology 18, 291, 923
cognitive science 103–6, 109–10, 112
Cohen, D. 287–8
Cohen, D.J. 243–4
collative motivation 386, 388–91
collative variables
   in ambiguity and clarity 409–11
   in complexity and simplicity 402–8
   and music 390
   in novelty and familiarity 395–8
   as properties of stimuli 68, 69
   role of 385–8, 411–13
   in surprise and unexpectedness 398–402
color effects in movies 690–1
color preference
   and brightness 479–80, 481
   and color combinations 482–3
   and color patches 462, 480, 481
   and color statistics 462–4, 468
   consumer responses to 1013–14
   cross-cultural 861–6, 873
   empirical aesthetics on 49, 50*f*
   and hue 476–9, 477*f*, 480–1
   reasons for 481–2
   and saturation 48, 479, 481
   and single colors 476–81
   studies in 9, 54, 475–6
   summary of 483
   when plating food 1043
color-changing food 1043–4
comment books 950–1
common currency hypothesis 161
communication
   and art 101–5, 109–10, 112
   biological 190
   of music 191–2

complexity
    and aesthetic pleasure 120
    in architecture 664–5
    and art preference 403, 974
    in music appreciation 576–7
    and simplicity 62–5, 402–8
    and symmetry 491–2
compression algorithms 404, 406
compulsive behaviors 500–2
computational aesthetics 24
computer-graphic imagery (CGI) 327, 694, 696
conceptual art 807
conceptual fluency 432–3, 435, 753, 904
concert research 362–72, 362t, 365f, 366f, 376–7,
    593–4
conflict 68, 729, 731, 758
Conflict, Arousal and Curiosity (Berlyne) 68,
    386
congruency
    and context in aesthetics 905–6, 907f
    between music and dance 647–8
connectionist prototype model 11–12
conscientiousness 821, 824–5
consciousness 9, 47
consumer behavior
    and aesthetic products 1016–18
    and responses to virtual features 1011–16
    role of empirical aesthetics in 1010–11,
        1018–20
content analysis 200, 203–4, 210
context see also social context
    and aesthetic experience 885–6, 925–6
    and application to the setting 910–11
    and architecture 668
    assessment of 890–1
    and authenticity 898–9
    categories for 891–2, 892f
    challenges and suggestions 908–10, 937–8
    and cognition 18–19, 764, 903–7, 907f
    and cross-cultural differences 889
    effects of for color preference 480–1
    and emotions 903
    and empirical aesthetics 888–9
    empiricist perspectives of 887–8
    and expertise 901–3
    and explicit classification 901–3
    and extra information 930–3

and features 18–19, 907, 907f
and framing 899–900, 901f, 934–7
history of 886–90
importance of 921–2
and models of aesthetic experience 892–5,
    893f, 894f
and mood 903
and music appreciation 578
and object classification 897–8, 901f
and object interactions 924–7
other aspects of 908–9
other effects of 937
and perceptual analyses 900–1, 901f
and personality 896–7
and predictive coding 910
pre-state 895–900
and processing mode 899
and psychological aesthetics 889–90
and single objects 922–4
and time 907–8
and titles of artworks 927–30
Continuous Evaluation Procedure (CEP) 410
contour see curvature effect
contrast
    in architecture 663
    in faces 551, 962
    in movies 684–5, 695, 696
    in theaters 684–5
controlled alteration 836, 837–9
controlled processing 13–14, 436–7, 753–6, 760
copies of artworks 936–7
copying in children's art 774–5
corrugator supercilli muscle 266, 298, 759
creative artists 205–8
creative art-making process 220–1, 225–6
creativity 62–5, 961
Cross, E.S. 609, 615–16, 629–30
cross-cultural
    aesthetic sensitivity 62
    aspects in neuroaesthetics 324–5
    color preference 861–6, 873
    curvature effect 521
    empirical aesthetics 853–4, 872–4, 889
    facial attractiveness 285–6
    hue preferences 479
    music preference 589–90, 825, 866–72, 873–4
    visual preference 854–61, 873

crying 966
cultural capital 978–80
Cupchik, G. 757, 759, 931, 934–5
curiosity 68, 389
curvature effect
    in aesthetic judgements 262–3
    and applied science 523–6
    concept 527
    and evolved or learned preference 514–15
    and individual and contextual
        differences 520–2
    and non-visual processing 519–20
    preference for 510–11
    and sensorimotor systems 516–17
    studies in the 20th century 511–13
    studies in the 21st century 514–26
    and threat hypothesis 517–19
    type of stimuli and presentation time 522–3
curved buildings 669
cuteness 1015
Cutting, J.E. 465–6

D

dance see also music and dance
    aesthetic perception of 645–7
    aesthetics of 623–4, 628–9
    and attractiveness 638–9
    challenges and suggestions 632–3
    and children's preference 776
    cognitive neuroscience insights into 612–16
    concept 623–4
    embodied perception of 630–1
    expertise 631–2, 644, 801–2
    explicit aesthetic appreciation of 629–30
    and expression 627–8
    and groove 650–1
    implicit aesthetic appreciation of 629
    influence of music on perception of 641–8
    influence on music perception 649–51
    and mate selection 638–9
    and nonexpertise 612–15
    and the observer 631–2
    and parietal cortex 350
    physiological studies of 609–11
    and triad of body, movement and
        expression 624–31, 625f
    universal 624

danger 262, 517
Danto, Arthur 101–2
Danziger, Kurt 137, 142
Darbel, A. 978–9
darkness 684–5
Darwin, Charles 183, 186
data gloves see electronic gloves
data integration 373–5
data-gathering techniques 951–2
Davies, A. 282
Davies, David 107
Dawson, K. 616
De Tommaso, M. 297
decision-making processes 157
deep learning 405, 469
default mode network (DMN) 323
deliberate practice 789–90, 800
delirium 130–1
demographics 897
Derrick, J.L. 725, 735
descriptive knowledge 5
design
    and aesthetic pleasure 993–4, 1002–3
    and aesthetic sense 995–6
    and aesthetics 993
    and artifact aesthetics 996–1003
    and beautiful consequences 1003–6
    and empirical aesthetics 26
    and expertise 797
    and implicit associations 263–4
    and innovation 1003–6, 1004f
    in museum contexts 948
    structural skeleton of 10–11, 66–7
Design Judgement Test 837, 844
"design stance" 128, 999
developmental model of art appreciation 126,
    127f, 129
Devue, C. 240
Dew, I.T.Z. 441–2
Dewey, John 19, 44, 47, 116, 139, 140, 938
Di Dio, C. 321, 606–7
diachronia perspective 293, 294f
Dickie, George 107
Diefenbach, S. 1001
Dierking, L.D. 891, 982–3
digital morphing 538
Dilthey, Wilhelm 359

DiMaggio, P. 979
dimensionality 671–2
Ding, Y. 303
direct factors of liking and disliking 41, 85–6
direct observation 223–6
directed tension or *expression* 66–7
discrimination test 839
disinterested interest 394
dissonance 583
distancing 123–5, 124*f*, 139–40, 144, 317
diversive exploration 389
Djerf, M. 777
dlPFC *see* dorsolateral prefrontal cortex (dlPFC)
Dollard, John 61, 67
domain-general processing 804–6
domain-specific processing 804–6
dopamine 393–4, 581, 591
dorsal stream 347–51
dorsal subdivision (dACC) 321
dorsolateral prefrontal cortex (dlPFC) 319–20, 327, 329, 344–6
Doyle, C.L. 929–30
drawing *see also* observational drawing research
  accuracy 287–8
  expertise 796
Dreher, J.-C. 318
dual-mode processing frameworks 753–7, 764
dual-processing model *see* Pleasure-Interest Model of Aesthetic Liking (PIA Model)
Dudley, S. 279
Dunbar, R.I.M. 639

E
Eastman Kodak 691
Ebbinghaus illusion 900, 901*f*
ecological valence theory (EVT) 482, 864
ecological validity 365–8, 376–7, 594
economic capital 978
ECR-Experimental Concert Research project 362–5, 362*t*, 365*f*, 366*f*, 367, 368–76
edge orientation entropy 457, 458
Edison, Thomas 52, 683, 688
EEG *see* electroencephalogram (EEG)
Eerola, T. 411, 577

Eisenman, Russell 65, 492–3
"elaboration effect" 928
electroencephalogram (EEG) 264, 292, 300, 328, 441–2, 594, 672
electromyography (EMG) 266, 298, 500, 610, 759
electronic gloves 226–7, 299, 360–2, 361*f*, 362*f*, 368
electrophysiology
  and action and movement 613
  of aesthetic appreciation 294–7
  cognitive 292
  and everyday objects 302–3
  and faces 301–2
  methods 291, 303–4
  and music and poetry 299–301
  and symmetry 500
  and visual art 297–9
Ellamil, M. 320
embodiment 606, 609–11, 615–16, 627, 630–1
embracing 123–5, 124*f*, 317
EMG *see* electromyography (EMG)
eMotion: mapping museum experience project 360–2, 361*f*, 362*f*, 365–76, 374*f*
emotional action programmes 156–8, 157*f*
emotional valence 155–6
emotions *see also* aesthetic emotions
  children's development of aesthetic 778–9
  children's understanding of 776–8
  coarse 136–7, 147
  and context 903
  and emotion processing 390–1
  and emotional ambiguities 411
  and expression as part of dance triad 627–8
  and framing 935
  interrelation with sensation 265–6
  in music 191–2
  and music and dance 642–3
  and music appreciation 579–80, 869–70
  and music influences on dance perception 642–3
  in poetry 711–12
  in stories 729–30
  subtler 136–7, 147
  to visual features 1012
emotion-value systems 662, 669–70

empirical aesthetics
  and aesthetics 7–8
  and aesthetics from above and below 3, 8,
    40, 84–5, 293
  American functional 47–50
  and behaviorism 9, 50–7
  brief history of 8–12
  conceptions of 3–8, 11, 17
  and contemporary accounts 12–19
  development of 41–2
  and empirical methods 6–7
  factors of 16–19
  first 100 years of 69–71
  foundation of 8–9, 39–41, 69–71
  history of 8–12
  incremental 6
  and knowledge 5–6
  measurement methods 19–22
  and neighboring fields 25–7
  and philosophical skepticism 106–9
  pioneers of 41–7, 43f
  psychometric 57–65
  as a scientific field 5–6
  and sociocultural context 208–10
  subdomains of 22–5, 23f
endogenous factors 165–7, 166f
environmental aesthetics 24
environments see also everyday
    environments
  in architecture 664
  and emotion-valuation systems 669–70
  mental 967–8
  and music appreciation 592–3
  physical 592
  and spatiotemporal statistics 468–9
Ericsson, K.A 789, 790, 800
Ernst, Max 932
ERP studies see event-related potentials (ERP)
    studies
Escher, M.C. 489
estrus 166–7
Euclidean plane 488, 489f
event-related potentials (ERP) studies 292,
    294–7, 299, 405, 407, 410, 498–500
everyday environments
  aesthetic experience in 960, 968
  and aesthetics of people 961–2

artifacts and consumer products in 964
  and "inner aesthetics" 967–8
  and meeting of aesthetics and
    creativity 961
  and music 965–6
  and nature and the built
    environment 963–4
everyday objects 257, 302–3
evolutionary aesthetics 23–4
exaptation 187–8
executive factors 165, 166f, 167–8
exercise principle 47
expectedness 398–402
experience sampling method (ESM) 592
experimental aesthetics 67–9, 199
expertise
  in acting 803–4
  and aesthetic responses 791–2
  and aesthetic sensitivity 844
  in architecture 668, 797–8
  in art 125–6, 244, 276–7, 521–2, 796
  cognitive psychological literature
    on 788–90
  compared with nonexperts 789
  and context 901–3
  in dance 612–15, 631–2, 644, 801–2
  in design 797
  in drawing 238–40, 251–2, 796
  and evolutionary integration 804–7
  influence of on aesthetics 787–8
  and memory 762
  in movies 804
  in music 299–300, 799–801
  in neuroscience 798
  and nonartists 238–40, 251–2
  in other models of aesthetic
    processing 793–5
  in photographs 798–9
  and processing fluency 792
  and prototypicality 791–2
  in various aesthetic domains 795–804
  in writing 802–3
explanatory knowledge 5
explicit classification 14, 901–3
extrastriate body area (EBA) 322, 350, 625
extraversion 590, 821, 824–5, 826, 871
extreme pessimism 107–9, 111–12

eye movements
  and art education intervention 277–8
  and art expertise 276–7
  and cultural differences in art
    portraits 285–6
  and future research 288
  and interplay with body movements 286
  as measurement of empirical aesthetics 21–
    2, 273–4
  and mobile tracking investigations 274–6
  and museum versus laboratory
    studies 278–81
  of a painter 286–8
  pioneering studies of 42–3
  and pleasing or displeasing effects of
    proportion 42
  and social context 283–4
  and symmetry 494
  and time course of an aesthetic
    experience 282–3
  and titles and wall texts 281–2
  and tracking analysis methods 274
eyes
  convergence 684
  and facial attractiveness 535–6
Eysenck, Hans J.
  and aesthetic appreciation 10, 60–1, 854–6
  and aesthetic sensitivity 836–7
  and color preferences 54, 861
  and the "K" factor 820–1, 840, 975
  and symmetry 493

F
face recognition 240, 457
face-drawing studies 240, 241–2, 246–7, 250
facial attractiveness
  and aesthetic appreciation 301–2
  aesthetics of 962
  and age 546–7
  and agreement 542–3
  and brain regions 314–15, 350–1
  and children 546–7
  and Chinese females 285–6
  and cognitive electrophysiology 301–2
  in empirical aesthetics 533–4
  and evolution 539–40
  and the eyes 535–6

  and the face bearer 539–42
  and face inversion 550
  and facial features 534–5
  and familiarity 541–2
  and global characteristics 537–8
  and halo effect 540–1
  and head hair 536–7
  and infants 547
  and mating 545–6
  measurement of 552
  and the observer 542–50
  and observer variables 544–5
  and own attractiveness 547–8
  within-person variation 539
  and physiology 548–9
  and research limitations 550–2
  and reward 548–9
  and serial dependency 551
  and sexual factors 543
  and the skin 536
  and symmetry 494, 495, 497
  and tracking of eye movements 283–5
  and viewing time 923
  and visual attention 549–50
facial expressions 265–6, 364–5
facial hair 535
facial muscles 610, 759
facsimile accommodation 944
fakes 936–7
Falk, J.H. 891, 982–3
familiarity
  and art preference 974
  and artifacts 999
  and facial attractiveness 541–2
  and first impression formation 263
  and novelty 395–8
  and processing ease 430–1, 494
families 982–5
Farnsworth, Paul Randolph 51–2
fatigue 48
fear 138, 517, 669
feature counting measures 249
Fechner, Gustav T.
  and aesthetics from above and below 84–6,
    95–6
  conception of empirical aesthetics 3, 8–9,
    17, 84–5

and experimental aesthetics 310
as founder of empirical aesthetics 39–40,
  83–4, 84*f*
as founder of psychophysics 39–40, 69, 293
and golden ratio 93–4
methods of 8, 40–1, 86–91, 94–5
and personality 820
and principles of aesthetic pleasure 8, 41,
  46, 385
and selection of participants 91–2, 117
and symmetry 492
Fehr, E. 170
females
  and facial attractiveness 285, 302, 534–5, 543
  and mate selection 183, 186
Féré, Charles 475
Ferrari, C. 350
Festinger, L. 142
fiction 108, 123–5, 727, 729, 736
fictional characters *see* characters
films *see* movies
first impression formation 263
Fisherian runaway principle 183
Fitzpatrick scale 536
Flexas, A. 265
"Flextiles" 89
flicker 688, 696
fluency *see* processing fluency
fMRI *see* functional magnetic resonance
  imaging (fMRI)
focus groups 950
Following Piece (Acconci) 108
Fontana. Lucio 607
food porn 1027, 1037
foregrounding 737–9
forgery 774–5
formalist approach to aesthetic
  engagement 143, 144–7
fractul dimension 455–6, 665
framing 899–900, 901*f*, 934–7
Francuz, P. 277
Franklin, M.B. 929–30
freckles 542–3
Frederiksen, C.H. 802
Freedberg, D. 266, 606, 607
free-hand drawing tasks 240–2
Freytag, G. 728

Friedman, L. 288
Friedrich, Caspar David 122
Fritz, T. 870–1
Fuller, Samuel 123
functional magnetic resonance imaging
  (fMRI) 158, 308, 312–14, 321, 328, 347,
  441–2, 626, 954
functional psychology 52–3, 56
functionalism 660–1
fusiform body area (FBA) 625–6

G
Gabriel, S. 725
Gallese, V. 266, 606, 607
Galton, Francis 59–60
Gardner, H. 126
Gardner, W.L. 722
Garth, T.R. 861–3
Gartus, A. 937
gastrophysics 1027
gender 65, 262, 588
general objective factor of aesthetic
  appreciation 10, 60, 854
genetics 25, 60, 64
Geneva Musical Emotion Scale 316
genres 203–4, 735–6
geometric patterns 89, 90, 91, 297
Georgieva, S. 930
Gerger, G. 266, 298, 759, 929, 935
Gerrig, R.J. 733
Gestalt school of psychology 10–11, 45, 46, 55,
  65–7, 576, 839–40
glide reflections 488
glossiness 460–2, 460*f*, 468
gloves *see* electronic gloves
Goel, V. 308
golden ratio/section 44, 87, 93, 93–4, 118, 118*f*,
  1038–9
Goller, J. 275
Gombrich, E.H. 104, 491, 924
"good taste" *see* aesthetic sensitivity
Gordon, Kate 49
Gosling, S.D. 824–5, 871
Götz, Karl Otto 61, 837
Gould, Elliot 187–8
Graf, L.K.M. 13, 120–2, 436–8, 753, 754–5
graffiti art 201, 275

Graham, D.J. 461
Graves, B. 802
Green, M.C. 733–4
green color preference 476, 861, 862, 1043
Greenwald, A.G. 259
Gregory, A.H. 870
Grice, Paul 109
Grinberg, M. 930
groove 650–1
Grosbras, M.H. 350
Guan, Z. 301
Gumbrecht, H. 366
Guo, F. 303

H
habitat theory 666
Hadley, Mark 1039
Hagtvedt, H. 1018, 1019
hair 535–7
halo effect of beauty 540–1
handicap principle 186–7
handmade obects 129–30
Harvard Psychological Clinic 62–3
Hassenzahl, M. 1001
"Hawthorne effect" 368
Hayes, A.E. 608–9
Hayn-Leichsenring, G. 285
head hair 536–7
heart rate 226, 367–8, 373, 374f, 732
hedonic coldspots 162–3
hedonic hotspots 162–3, 315
hedonic valuation
    and action programs 156–8, 157f
    and the aesthetic 168–71
    and arousal potential 387f
    and the brain 152–4, 156, 157f, 158–64, 159f
    current perspectives of 389–90
    explained 151–2, 152f, 155–6
    and factors modulating 164–8
    and integration with diverse
        disciplines 153f
    intervention studies in 161–2
    key functional purpose of 156f
    and neural systems 158–64
    neurobiology of 150–3, 171–2
    regulating behavior 153–8
    and reward processing 155f

hedonic-based beauty 319
Hekkert, P. 754, 797
Helmholtz, Hermann von 575
heterogeneity 202
Hevner, Kate 52–3
high dynamic range (HDR) 696–7
higher frame rates (HFRs) 697
higher-order fluency *see* conceptual fluency
high-order beauty 319
Hirst, Damien 981
historiometric methods
    aesthetic products 201–5
    creative artists 205–8
    development of 211–12
    explained 199–200
    future of 211–12
    as measurement of empirical
        aesthetics 19–20
Hobbit: An Unexpected Journey, The (film) 697
Höfel, L. 294–7, 299–300, 301–2, 492f, 498–9
Hogarth, W. 510
Holmes, C.B. 480
Holt, L.E. 608
homo sapiens 191–2
Hood, B.M. 774
hormone levels 166–7
Hosoya, G. 141
Hovland, Carl I. 67
Hristova, E. 930
Huang, M. 936–7
hue in color preference 476–9, 477f, 480–1
Hugenberg, K. 725
Hull, Clark 61
human body 283–5, 490, 512, 605–6, 961–2
humanities 26
Hurlbert, A.C. 863–4
Huron, D.B. 578
hypotheses 221

I
IAPS *see* International Affective Picture
    System (IAPS)
IAT *see* Implicit Association Test (IAT)
Igartua, J.J. 727
immersive technologies 618–19
Implicit Association Test (IAT) 259, 261–2,
    263–4, 497, 517

implicit memory integration 14
implicit processes in aesthetic appreciation
    definition 257–8
    measurement of 257–60
    role of 260–5
    studies in 267–8
Impressionism 110
inclusivity 369–70
indirect observation 226–8
individuals 520–2, 590–2
infants 478–9, 547, 649, 775–6, 962
Information Rate Scale 951
information-processing models 14–15, 261,
        751–3, 758–9, 792–3, 926
"inner aesthetics" 967–8
installation art 228
integrated methods 359–60, 365–76, 376–7
intelligence 841–2
intensity 66
intention
    and artifacts 999–1001
    in children's art 773–5
    and forgery and copying 774–5
    and music appreciation 588–9
interaction 119, 652–3, 724–5, 924–7, 1001–2
interior settings 525
International Affective Picture System
        (IAPS) 298, 935–6
internet 211–12
Interpersonal Reactivity Index 284
interpretation
    and conducting research in a
        museum 953–4
    difference with statistical approach 359–60
    theory of 109
interviews 949–50
*Introduction to the Experimental Psychology of
    Beauty* (Valentine) 46–7
introspection 20, 46
introversion 822
ipsichronia perspective 293, 294*f*
Ishiguro, C. 277–8
Ishizu, T. 170–1
Istók, E. 300
Item-Response Theory (IRT) framework 845
Ive, Jonathan 993
Iwao, S. 857

J
Jacobsen, T. 293–9, 301–2, 492*f*, 498–9
Jakesch, M. 931
James, William 136–7, 147
Japanese paintings 324–5
Jaśkiewicz, M. 300
Jastrow, J. 1041, 1041*f*
"Jastrow's Bistable Bite" dish 1041, 1041*f*
Jazz Singer, The (film) 689
Jeong, J. 933
Jockers, M.L. 728, 730
Johnston, V.S. 301
jokes 109
Jola, C. 646
joystick test 260
Jucker, J.L. 931–2
Jurafsky, D. 712

K
"K" factor 821, 840, 975
Kahneman, D. 754
Kandinsky, Wassily 1027–8, 1028*f*, 1035
Kandinsky Salad 1028, 1028*f*
Kant, I. 1030–1
Kao, J. 712
Kaplan, S. 665–6
Kapoula, Z. 281–2, 286, 930
Kawabata, H. 308, 346, 935–6
Ke, Y. 453
Kim, J.G. 251
Kindchenschema 1015
kinetoscope movies 683
Kirk, U. 315, 327, 798, 934
Kirsch, L.P. 610–11, 613, 616
knowledge-meaning systems 662,
        667–70
Knowles, M.L. 722
Koffka, K. 65–6
Köhler, Wolfgang 65–6
Komogortsev, O. 288
Konečni, Vladimir 578–9
Koons, Jeff 981
Kozbelt, A. 204
Kremer, A. 298, 935
Kreuzbauer, R. 129
Kringelbach, M.L. 170
Krumhansl, C.L. 641–2

Krupinski, E. 282–3, 936
Külpe, Oswald 7, 9, 45, 46, 49, 70

L
labels of works 281–2, 889–90, 930–3
laboratories 222, 278–81, 909, 922–4, 943–5
Lacey, S. 347
Lagerlöf, I. 777
Lai, R. 645
Landgraf, Alberto 1037
landscape painting 104–5, 110
Landwehr, J.R. 13, 120–2, 435–8, 753, 754–5
Lang, A. 286
language 869
Lanska, M. 432–3
Lappi, O. 275
late positive potential (LPP) 295, 300, 301–2
Launay, J. 639
Lawlorm, M. 854–6
learning
    animals 494–5
    choreography 643–4
    deep 405, 469
    and early social context 982–5
    and hedonic value 389
    and pleasure and reward 393
    spatial 668
Leder, H.
    and contextual setting 298
    and emotional component 265–6, 935–7
    and eye-tracking methods 275, 279–80
    and information-processing model 14–15,
        261, 751–3, 755, 758–9, 792–3, 893f, 894f,
        926, 928–9
    and model of aesthetic appreciation 126–7,
        127f, 129
    and the role of ambiguity 931
left primary motor cortex (lPMC) 346–7
Lenz, E. 1001–2
Lewin, K. 137
Li R. 302
liking and disliking
    and the brain 393
    factors of 41, 85–6
    and processing fluency 431
    Representation Matching Model 395
    and symmetry 44

and wanting 394–5
"limited-line tracing task" 244
Ling Y. 863–4
linguistic correctness 705
literary narratives 140–1, 399, 732–6, 737–9,
    802–3 *see also* stories
Locher, P. 282–3, 286, 893f, 936, 944
locomotion 224–5
Loewy, Raymond 998–9
logos 1013, 1014–15
Loui, P. 162
Louvre Museum 227
LPP *see* late positive potential (LPP)
luminance 459–62, 468, 696

M
Maas, I. 980
Machotka, P. 125–6
MacKinnon, Donald W. 62–3
Madison, G. 397
magnetic fields 308
magnetoecephalography (MEG) 308, 323,
    324, 328–9, 594, 757
Magritte, Rene 435
Makin, A.D.J. 261–2, 492f, 494
Maksimainen, J.P. 411
male dancing 638–9
male faces 535
Manikin task 260, 262–3
Maricchiolo, F 263–4
marketing 617–18, 1018–19
Marković S. 140–1, 264
Markson, L. 773–4
Martin, Lillien Jane 45–6, 70
Martindale, Colin 11–12, 20, 200, 209, 577
Martinez-Molina, N. 162
Marzi, T. 302–3
Mas-Herrero, E. 346
mass contrast 55
Massaro, D 284–5
Mastandrea, S. 263–4, 928, 977–8, 980
mate selection 184–6, 545–6, 638–9
mathematical beauty 318
maximal-typical performance
    framework 840
Maximum Effect for Minimal Means
    (MEMM) 1000–1, 1000f

MAYA (Most Advanced Yet Acceptable) 120,
    999, 1001–2, 1003
McDermott, J.H. 871
McElroy, W.A. 854–6
McManus, I.C. 248–9, 476, 478, 799
meaning-making 125
measurement methods
    of aesthetic sensitivity 59–62, 837–41
    of agreement 47
    of arousal levels 107, 390–1
    of artistic aptitude 59
    of artists 206–8
    of empirical aesthetics 19–22, 85–6
    of eye movements 273–4
    of facial attractiveness 552
    implicit processes in 257–60
    in a museum 951–2
    of musical talent 58–9
    for observational drawing research 247–9,
        250–1
    operationalization and stimuli 552
    of products 203–4
    psychophysiological 367–8
    of sociocultural mileu 209–10
medial orbitofrontal cortex (mOFC) 308,
    312–19, 322, 326
medial prefrontal cortex (mPFC) 346–7
medical aesthetics 24–5
Meegeren, Han van 127–9
MEG see magnetoecephalography (MEG)
Mehr, S.A. 867
Meier, Norman C. 58–9
Meier Art Tests: I. Art Judgement (Meier) 59
Meier Art Tests: II. Aesthetic Perception
    (Meir) 59
Meier-Seashore Judgement Test 58, 59
melancholy 317
melody 406–7, 583, 708–9
memory
    and architecture 668
    and art knowledge and expertise 762
    and cognition 760–2
    and long-term prototypes 761
    and performance in chess 789
    and pleasantness and
        unpleasantness 49–50
    working 761

Menninghaus, W. 123–5, 124f, 138, 141–3, 317
menstrual cycle 544
mental ability 841–2
mental chronometry of aesthetic
    processing 293–4
mental environment 967–8
mental health 65, 672–3
mental perspective 298
mental processes 256–60 see also implicit
    processes in aesthetic appreciation
mental tests 47, 60
mere-exposure effect 395
mesocorticolimbic reward system 162–3, 169
Mestrovic, Aerosyn-Lex 1042
metabolic regulation 154, 155f
meter in poetry 707–8
methods see also measurement methods
    choice 8, 41, 87, 90–1, 94, 95
    combining 90–1
    electrophysiology 291, 303–4
    empirical 6–7
    of Fechner 8, 40–1
    historiometric 199–212
    integrated 359–60, 365–77
    multiple 86–91, 95–6
    observation 219–32
    of production 94–5
    production 8, 41, 88–9, 90–1, 95
    use 8, 41, 89–90, 95
Metropolitan Museum of Art (New York) 223,
    947, 948, 952, 953
Meumann, Ernst 44, 70
Meyer, Max Friedrich 51
Miall, R. 287
Michel, Charles 1037, 1038f, 1042
Miller, Neal E. 61
Millis, K. 928
mind perspective 293, 294f
"Mirror Model" of art 763–4
mirror neurons 606, 611, 626
mirror symmetry 538
mismatch-negativity (MMN) paradigm 398
Mitschke, V. 275
mixed emotions 123–5, 124f
models of art appreciation 892–5
modern art museums 976–8
modern music 594

modulatory neurotransmitter network *see*
    ascending reticular activating system
    (ARAS)
mOFC *see* medial orbitofrontal cortex
    (mOFC)
Moll, J. 318
Montagner, C. 463
mood 712, 903
moral beauty 319
Morellet, François 451–2, 453f
morphing 538
morphometric methods 248–9
motion energy analysis (MEA) 363–4
motivational theory 45, 67–9
motor cortex 323–5
motor representations 626–8
motor simulatation 631
movement 667 *see also* action and movement
    appreciation
    as part of dance triad 626
movies
    aesthetics of 682
    challenges and suggestions 698–9
    in the digital era 687, 695–8
    effects of 3D 693–5
    effects of added sound 689–90
    effects of color 690–1
    and expertise 804
    foregrounding in 739
    and horror 123
    and measurement 203
    personal vs public viewing 683–5
    and personality 826–7
    and projection in theaters 683–5
    reasons for being called flicks 688
    reasons for transitions and shots 685–7
    reasons for wider images 692–3
    and spatiotemporal regularities 465, 468
Mowrer, O. Hobart 61
Mukhtar, T. 979
Mullennix, J.W. 756, 759
Müller, Georg Elias 42, 45, 299–300
multilevel modeling 205
multiple methods 86–91, 95–6
multivariate approach 328
multi-voxel pattern analysis (MVPA) 328
Munsell color system 476

Münsterberg, Hugo 43–4, 70
Murota, M. 298
Murray, C. 207
Murray, Henry A. 63
museum visitors 976–8, 982–5
museums
    and augmented observation 228–9
    challenges and suggestions 954–5
    classroom and practical aspects 955–6
    conducting aesthetic research in 945–54
    context of 889–90, 943, 956
    difference to laboratories 278–81, 943–5
    eMotion: mapping museum experience
        project 360–2, 361f, 362f, 365–76, 374f
    observation methods in 219–20, 226–8
    and physical movement and
        locomotion 224–5
    and practical applications of methods 94–5
    and time spent on art 223–4
music and dance
    aesthetic perception of 645–7
    and attractiveness 638–9
    audio-visual aesthetics of 641
    and the brain 640–1
    and congruency 647–8
    and dance influences on music
        perception 649–51
    and emotional responses 642–3
    and groove and danceability 650–1
    and interactions in 652–3
    and mate selection 638–9
    and music influences on dance
        perception 641–8
    relationship between 653
    rhythm in 640–1
    and shared evolutionary origins 638–40
    and social bonding 639–40
    and understanding and learning
        choreography 643–4
    and visual attention 645
music appreciation *see also* music and dance
    and aesthetic sensitivity 844
    aesthetics of 299–301, 965–8
    biological aesthetics of 189–90
    and the brain 398, 580–1, 583, 585
    challenges and suggestions 593–5
    and children's preference 119, 776

and cognitive electrophysiology 299–301
cognitivist theories 577–8
collative variables of 390
and complexity and simplicity 405–7
contextual theories 577–8
cross-cultural 866–72, 873–4
and *ECR-Experimental Concert Research*
    project 362–5, 362*t*
emotional pleasure and communication
    of 191–2
emotional responses to 869–70
emotivist theories 579–80
empirical aesthetics of 51–4, 573–4, 593–5
expertise 299–300, 799–801
and expressiveness 53–4
and external context 592–3
and focus 588–9
historical beginnings of aesthetic
    responses 575–7
and historiometric methods 201
major theories 575–81
and musical mode 583–4
and neuroaesthetics 315–16
and neuroscientific models 580–1
and novelty/familiarity effects 397–8
and personality 824–5, 871–2
and predictive coding theory 401
and reward cycle 393–4
sad 316–17
and stimulus features 346, 582–6, 582*t*
and surprise and unexpectedness 399, 400
of tones and intervals 46
and top-down factors 586–92, 587*t*
music closure positive shift (CPS) 868
Music Ear Test 835
music information retrieval (MIR) 585
musical instruments 866–7
musical talent 58–9
musical testing 57–8
musicians 589–90
Myszkowski, N. 842

N

Nadal, M. 127, 261, 265, 279–80, 893*f*
Nakamura, K. 346
narrative worlds, genres 732–6
Nascimento, S.M.C. 463–4, 464*f*

Natural History of Song (NHS) 867
natural scene 460*f*, 461, 963
natural science 5
naturalness 665
nature 186–7
navigation 667, 668
neatness 1034
negative and positive emotions 123–5, 124*f*
negatively valenced aesthetic
    experiences 316–17
neural systems 158–64, 160*t*
neuroaesthetics
    and amygdala and motor cortex with
        ugliness 323–4
    and anterior cingulate cortex (ACC) 320–1
    and beauty 309–13, 315, 317–19, 326–7,
        329–30
    and brain regions 309–10, 311*f*
    cross-cultural aspects in 324–5
    default mode network (DMN) 323
    and dorsolateral prefrontal cortex
        (dlPFC) 319–20
    and dual-mode processing frameworks 757
    and empirical aesthetics 15–16, 23, 309–10
    and expertise 794
    field of 662–3
    and inconsistent use of anatomical
        labels 313–14
    and insula cortex 321–2
    and music 315–16
    and negatively valenced aesthetic
        experiences 316–17
    and noninvasive brain stimulation studies
        in 344–51
    and orbitofrontal cortex (OFC) 312–13
    and other techniques 327–9
    and potential of noninvasive brain
        stimulation 351–2
    processes in 394–5
    and sensory and motor cortices 322
    as subdomain of empirical aesthetics 23
    and ventral striatum 314–15
    and ventromedial prefrontal cortex 313
neurobiology 150–3, 171–2
Neurocognitive Poetics Model (NCPM) 714
neurocognitive psychology 293–4
neuroethics 26

neurogenomics 26
neuroimaging 308–9, 594, 611
neurophysiology 498–500, 606
neuroscience
    of architecture 662–3, 671–2
    cognitive 291, 309–10, 339, 611–16, 626
    and dance 628–9
    and empirical aesthetics 25–6
    and expertise in architecture 798
    and hedonic valuation 168–71
    and implicit associations 264
    models 580–1
    and statistical features 447
neuroticism 821, 826–7
new experimental aesthetics 67–9
Noë, Alva 109, 110
Noguchi, Y. 298
nomothetic hypothesis 199–200
nonconventional art forms 822
noninvasive brain stimulation 339–44, 340*f*,
    344–51, 351–2
nonverbal behavior 21–2
non-visual processing 519–20
normative conventions 109–10
nouvelle cuisine 1031
novel art forms 806–7
novelty 395–8, 999, 1016
nucleus accumbens (NAcc) 161–2, 315–16, 317

O

objective complexity 403–4
objective measurement methods 247–9,
    250–1
objectivist approaches to beauty 118
objects
    aesthetics of 964
    classification 897–8, 901*f*
    features 17
    focus on single 922–4
    interactions with context 924–7
    properties 387–8
observation methods
    augmented 228–9
    conducting 229–32
    direct 223–6
    in empirical aesthetics 219–32
    and empirical aesthetics research 222–3

indirect 226–8
    as most fundamental research method 232
    in museums 948–9
    uses of 220–2
observational drawing research
    and correlation in drawing and nondrawing
        tasks 237–8, 251–2
    directions for future 249–52
    and expertise studies between artists and
        nonartists 238–40, 251–2
    factors that influence drawing
        performance 240–2, 251
    and free-hand drawing tasks 240–2
    and measures of drawing performance 249
    and objective measurement methods 247–
        9, 250–1
    overview of 235–7, 252
    and product-oriented approach 236–7
    and subjective rating methods 245–7, 250–1
    and tracing tasks 243–4
observer
    and dance 631–2
    and facial attractiveness 542–50
obsessive compulsive disorder (OCD) 501
obtrusiveness of data acquisition 368–9
occipital place area (OPA) 663
Ocean, Humphrey 287
odor 49–50
Ogden, Robert Morris 46, 65
oil painting 100
Okada, T. 277–8
Olds, J.M. 432
olfaction 667
Oliver- Rodríguez, J.C. 301
One Love Manchester concert 573
ontological trap 137
ontology of art 99, 101, 102, 105–6
Op Art (Optical Art) 286
openness to experience
    and aesthetic preference 827
    as Big Five trait 821–2
    and context 896
    and museum visitors 977
    and music preference 824–5
    and other considerations 823–4
    and personality 975
    and reading preference 825–6

and sensation-seeking 822–3
optical errors 454
orbitofrontal cortex (OFC) 312–13, 315, 318, 319–20, 393, 669
order in architecture 664
orienting response 395, 732
Orlandi, A. 614
Orlando, V. 302–3
Osaka, N. 324–5
Osgood, C.E. 862
Ou, L.C. 863
own attractiveness 547–8

P

packages 524, 1012, 1014–15
painting
    and implicit associations 264
    Japanese 324–5
    landscape 103–5, 110
    oil 100
    and plating food 1027–8, 1028f
    realism in 104–5
    and tracking of eye movements 277, 279–84
painting gist 281, 284
Palmer, Stephen 462, 476–9, 480–1, 482–3, 864–5
Palmović M. 930
Palumbo, L. 262, 518–19
paradox of fiction 123
parahippocampal place area (PPA) 663
parallelism in poetry 706–10
parasocial interactions and relationships 724–5
parietal cortex 349–50
Park, S.A. 933
Parsons, M.L. 126
participants 91–2, 117, 946–8
Patrick, V.M. 1018, 1019
pattern recognition 789
Patterson, D.D. 931
Pavlović M. 264
peacocks and peahens 185–7
peak experiences 573
"peak shift" 494–5
Pecchinenda, A. 261–2, 492f, 497
peep shows 683–4

Pelowski, M. 225, 228, 752–3, 755–6, 759, 763, 894f
people aesthetics 961–2
perceiver 974–6
perception
    and action 606
    analyses 14, 900–1, 901f
    and curiosity 389
    models 400–1
    and perceptibility hypothesis 454–5
    promoted by hedonic values 158
perceptual fluency 119, 432, 435, 752–3
perceptual qualia 261–5
performative artwork 618
person perspective 293, 294f
personality see also aesthetic sensitivity
    and aesthetic sensitivity 45, 842–4
    challenges and suggestions 827–8
    and context 896–7
    and empirical aesthetics 17–18
    influence of on aesthetic preference 820
    and music appreciation 590–1, 871–2
    and other aesthetic media 824–8
    and predispositions 256–7
    and the visual arts 820–4
Pfaff, Judy 105–6
philosophical aesthetics 26, 84, 222
philosophical skepticism 106–10
philosophy of art
    and cognitive science 103–6
    and empirical aesthetics 99–100, 112
    history of 100–2
    and psychology 101–3
    starting points 102–3
phonological parallelism 706–10
photographs 279–80, 697–8, 798–9
physiology
    and empirical aesthetics 26
    and facial attractiveness 548–9
    and music appreciation 586
    to plot in stories 731–2
    promoted by hedonic values 157–8
Picasso, Pablo 287, 932, 1040, 1040f
"Picasso Dish" 1040f
pictograms 325
Pierce, Edgar 44
pioneers of empirical aesthetics 41–7, 43f

pitch in music 583
plating food
    and aesthetic oblique effect 1035–6, 1036f
    and aesthetics of size 1042–3
    balanced 1032–5
    and color changing food 1043–4
    and contour curvature 1037–8, 1038f
    empirical aesthetics of 1027–32, 1029f,
        1043–4
    and Golden Section/Ratio 1038–9
    and perceptual uncertainty/
        ambiguity 1039–43
    science of aesthetic 1031–9
    of the whole table 1042
Plato 108, 887
Platonic solids 488
pleasantness and unpleasantness
    and memory 49–50
    psychology of 54–7
pleasingness see also liking and disliking
    and arousal 107
    current perspectives 390
    importance of 85–6
pleasure see also aesthetic pleasure
    versus attention-attraction 189
    and beauty 317–19
    current perspectives 391
    and principles of aesthetic 8, 41, 46
    and reward 393
    threshold of 8, 41
Pleasure-Interest Model of Aesthetic Liking
    (PIA Model) 13–14, 120–2, 121f, 435–8,
        753, 764
plot
    cognitive reactions to 730–1
    emotional reactions to 729–30
    physiological responses to 731–2
    in stories 727–32
    structures 728–9
    twists 732
poetry
    aesthetic appreciation of 299–301
    aesthetic virtues associated with 704–5
    and the brain 394
    and children's preference 776
    and cognitive electrophysiology 299–301
    correctness of 705–6

digital analysis of 712–13
empirical aesthetics of 704, 713–14
expectations 709–10
future directions 713–14
and implicit associations 264
and mood representation 712
and parallelistic diction 706–10
and poetic diction 705
and poetic license 705
preference for 713
semantic figures in 710–11
and sound-iconic expressions of
    emotions 711–12
using EEG techniques 300–1
who likes which kind of 713
portraits 276–7, 285–6, 350–1
positive and negative emotions 123–5, 124f
positive hedonic value 389
posterior parietal cortex 349, 758
power spectra 447–9, 449f, 450–6
"pre-aesthetic" factors 45
predictive coding 400–2, 407, 438–42, 910
prefrontal cortex 313, 319–20, 344–7, 393, 670,
    758, 794
Preschool of Aesthetics (Fechner) 40
presence 692–3
"presence of art" 366, 371
priming, affective 258–9, 497
priming studies 926–30
Prince, Morton 63
principles of aesthetic pleasure 8, 41, 46
probabilists 578
processing, affective 430–40, 760, 764
processing fluency
    of aesthetic pleasure 119
    and aesthetic responses 433–6
    and affective processing 111, 345, 439–40,
        760, 764
    in architecture 664
    and brain structures 441–2
    challenges and suggestions 441–2
    concept 430–1
    and conceptual fluency 432–3, 435, 753, 904
    criticism of 119–20
    definition 752–3
    expertise 792
    and familiarity 430–1

hypotheses 261–2, 263
and liking 431
malleability of 432–3
model 12–13, 752–3
and music appreciation 576
and object features 17
overview of 430
and perceptual fluency 119, 432, 435, 752–3
and the PIA 435–8
and predictive coding 438–42
reduction in 121–2
relative 433
and repitition of stimulus 431–2
and symmetry 496
theory 45
types of 432
production, method of 8, 41, 88–91, 94–5
products
aesthetic 199, 201–5
and aesthetic appeal 1016–18
analyses 204–5
consumer 764, 964
design 1012
fragmentation of 202
metaphors 1005–6, 1005f
sociocultural context of 208–9
Propaedeutics of Aesthetics (Fechner) 40
prototypicality
and art preference 973–4
and connectionist prototype model 11–12
and expertise 791–2
and first impression formation 263
in music appreciation 577
Proverbio, A.M. 614
psychiatry 63
psychical distance 123–5, 124f, 139–40, 144
psychobiology
aesthetics 11
mechanisms 791
model 386, 388–9, 393
theory 221
psycho-historical framework for the research
    on art appreciation 128–9, 128f
psychological aesthetics
and context 889–90
and expertise 790
as subdomain of empirical aesthetics 22

psychological disorders 63
psychological studies 608–11
psychology
of aesthetics 292–3, 294f
American 47
applied 43–4, 52
of architecture 671
clinical 42
cognitive 18, 291, 923
and consciousness 9
and empirical aesthetics 25–6
functional 52–3, 56
and philosophy of art 101–3
of pleasantness and unpleasantness 54–7
Psychology of Art (Ogden) 46
Psychology of Meaning, The (Gordon) 49
psychometric aesthetics 9–10, 24, 57–65,
    845–7
psychopathology 63
psychophysics
and curvature effect 527
development of 41–2
and experimental psychology 8
foundation of 39–40
as measurement of empirical aesthetics 22
and methods of empirical aesthetics 6
public policy 1020
Pythagoras 575

Q

qualitative research 359–60
quantitative research 359–60
questionnaires 949–50, 952
questions and hypotheses 945–6
Quételet, Adolphe 211
quilts 90
Quiroga, R.Q. 279

R

Rand, John Goffe 981
random samples 201–2, 205–6
Rappaport, J. 492–3
reading preference 825–6
realism 104–5
Reason, M. 646–7
Reber, R. 13, 128–30, 128f, 261, 430, 752–3
recognition memory 432

recycling 1015
red color preference 478–9, 863–4
Redies, C. 458
Redouté, J. 318
reflections 488
Regressive Imagery Dictionary 200
regulatory concerns 165–8, 166f
reliability 229, 230–1, 466–7
Rembrandt 898, 936–7
Rentfrow, P. J. 824–5, 871
replicability 5–6, 201–2
Representation Matching Model 395
Revised Visual Aesthetic Sensitivity Test 835
revision 6, 796
reward
    and the brain 315
    and dopamine 393–4
    and facial attractiveness 548–9
    and hedonic valuation 155f, 163–4
    and music 393–4
    and pleasure 393
    promoted by hedonic values 158
Rhodes, Gillan 492f
rhyme 707–8
rhythm 407–8, 584–5, 640–1, 649, 867–8
Rigas, I. 288
Righi, S. 302–3
Riley, H. 248–9
Ripsas, A. 928
Rizzolati, Giacomo 606–7, 626
Rokos, Jim 1000f
Romantic Movement model 143–6, 147
rotations 488
Rothko artworks 225
round and roundness *see* curvature effect
Rowley, J. 1028–30, 1029f, 1030f, 1034–5
Roye, A. 301–2
Ruta, N. 262

S
Saarikallio, S.H. 411
sad music 316–17
Saito, T. 480
satiation 161, 166
satiety phase 154, 155f
saturation 48, 479, 481
scanpath representations 274, 283

Schacht, A. 301
Schaefer, A. 282–3, 936
Schaminée, André 1004–5
Scherer, K.R. 138, 140, 143
Schiavi, S. 350
Schindler, I. 141
Schiolde, G. 397
Schlegel, August 144
Schloss, Karen 462, 476–9, 480–1, 482–3,
    864–5
schools 983, 985
Schwan, S. 276–7
Schwarz, N. 13, 261, 430
Scripture, Edward Wheeler 58
sculptures 275, 321
Seashore, Carl Emil 10, 58–9, 836
Seashore Measures of Musical Talents
    (Seashore) 10, 58
Segal, Jakub 17–18, 44–5
selection bias 90
"selfies" 955
self-modifying feelings 730–1
self-relevance 905–6, 907f
semantic figures 710–11
sensation 40, 45, 265–6, 822–3, 975, 978
sensitiveness *see* affective sensitiveness
sensorimotor systems
    and architecture 662
    and curvature effect 516–17
    and dance 631
sensory objects 164–8, 166f
sensory organs 56
sensory valuation
    and the "aesthetic" 168–71
    and beauty 310–11
    and the brain 152–4, 156, 158–64, 159f, 160t
    explained 151–2
    factors modulating 164–8, 166f
    neural systems involved in 158–64, 160t
    neurobiology of 150–3, 172–3
    and reward processing 155f
Serafin, J. 799
Sescousse, G. 318
sexual orientation 544–5
sexual selection 27
shapes 526, 1012–13
sharpness 527

sheep 186, 187
Sherek, L. 931
Shimoyo, S. 923
Shklovsky, V. 146
Short Test of Music Preference (STOMP) 871
Silveira, S. 934
Silvia, P.J. 905
Simonton, D.K. 19–20, 206, 208
simplicity, and complexity 62–5, 402–8
situation perspective 293, 294f
size 1042–3
skepticism 106–9
skewness 459–62, 460f, 468
skin 367–8, 374f, 536
smartphone 303
Smith, J.K. 223–4, 929, 944
Smith, L.F. 223–4, 929, 944
Snow, C.P. 359
social bonding 639–40
social context
    of artists 980–2
    and early art experience 982–5
    of the human figure 283–5
    impact on aesthetic experience 973–4, 985
    of museum visitors 976–8
    of perceivers 974–6
    of users 978–80
social function 266–7
sociocultural context 208–10, 210
somatosensation 350–1, 667
Sommer, W. 301
sound 688–9, 711–12
sound-making 191–2
space-cells 227
spaces 525
spatial learning 668
spatial regularities 450–3, 452f, 454–5, 455
spatial statistics 447–59, 449f, 456–9, 467–8
spatiotemporal statistics 465–6, 468–9
species survival 183–5
specific exploration 389
specific musical anhedonia (SMA) 162
Specker, E. 228–9
speculative aesthetics 107
Spehar, B. 454–5
Spence, C. 1028–30, 1029f, 1030f, 1034–5
Spiegel, S. 931

statistical approach 359–60
statistical features
    comparative approaches 468
    deep learning 469
    definition 447
    questions for future research 468–9
    regularities in color 462–4
    regularities in luminance 459–62
    regularities in spatial 447–59
    regularities in spatiotemporal 465–6
    and reliability of aesthetic responses 466–7
    summary of preference 467–8
statistics 204–5
stimuli types 522–3
stimulus features 6, 55–6, 385–8, 582–6, 582t
stories
    aesthetic response to 721–2, 739–40
    characters in 722–5
    future goals and challenges 739–40
    identification with characters in 726–7
    in movies 685–7, 690
    narrative worlds in 732–6
    plot in 727–32
    style of 736–9
Storme, M. 842
Stratton, George Malcolm 42–3, 511
Strauss, E.D. 480–1
structural skeleton of design 10–11, 66–7
Studies in the New Experimental Aesthetics
    (Berlyne) 68
Stumpf, Carl 51, 576
Styka, Tadeusz 836
style in stories 736–9
subjective rating methods 245–7, 250–1
subjectivist approach to beauty 118–19
subtler emotions 136–7, 147
superior temporal sulcus (STS) 350–1
surface characteristics 1014
surprise 398–402
Surprise Symphony (Haydn) 399
Sušac, A. 930
Swami, V. 932–3
symbolism 1019–20
symmetry
    in architecture 664
    and artists 490f
    and attractiveness 496–8

symmetry (*cont.*)
  and balance 491, 664
  clinical evidence 500–2
  and complexity 491–2
  contrasted with judgements of beauty 295,
    296*f*
  and early experimental work 492–3
  and evolution 496
  and facial attractiveness 538
  in the human body 490
  hypotheses about why linked to
    beauty 495–6
  interest in 488–9, 502–3
  and liking 44
  and neurophysiological evidence 498–500
  not always preferred to asymmetry 496–8
  positive response to 261–2
  preference for 502–3
  recent studies and models 492*f*, 493–5
  transformations in 489*f*
  in visual arts 490–1
synchrony 639–40
syncopations 650–1
synthetic research approach 388

T
"T" factor 821, 834, 836–7, 840, 888, 975
Tarr, B. 639
Taylor, C. 866
Tchalenko, J. 239, 287
technologies 226–8, 231, 682, 981
television 683–4, 826–7
tempo 584
theaters 683–5, 776
think-aloud procedure 228–9
Thinking-eye 145–6
Thompson, Derek 998
Thorndike, Edward Lee 47, 70, 836
threat hypothesis 517–19
3D 693–5
threshold of pleasure 8, 41
Thurstone, Louis Leon 52, 70–1
time 223–4, 282–3, 672, 907–8
Tinio, P.P.L. 223, 266, 763–4, 929
Titanic (film) 722
Titchener, E.B. 46, 48, 70
titles of works 281–2, 435, 927–30

Tobler, P.N. 170
tonal features 583
top-down processes
  and aesthetic experience 586–92
  and cognitive control 759–60
  and dual-mode processing
    frameworks 755–6
  and gaze behavior 280–1
  and information-processing model 14–15,
    752
  and predictive coding 438–9, 910
Topolinski, S. 608
tracing tasks 243–4
traffic lights countdown 1004, 1004*f*
transcranial alternating current stimulation
    (tACS) 343
transcranial direct current stimulation
    (tDCS) 342–3, 344–7, 353
transcranial electrical stimulation (tES) 339–
    44, 340*f*
transcranial magnetic stimulation
    (TMS) 340*f*, 344–52, 349*f*
transcranial random noise stimulation
    (tRNS) 343–4
transformations in symmetry 488, 489*f*
transitions in movies 685–7
translations in symmetry 488
transportation 733–4
Tree, J.J. 240
triad models
  "aesthetic" 265, 662–70, 673, 893*f*
  architecture 662–70, 673
  dance 624–31, 625*f*
Tröndle, M. 226–7, 952
Trost, W. 315–16, 317
Tschacher, W. 226, 299
two-factor theory 386
typefaces 302
typicality 1016

U
Uduehi, J. 859
Uemura, A. 209
ugliness 323–4
Ulrich's psychoevolutionary
    framework 669–70
Umiltà, M.A. 322, 607, 928

understanding mode of art appreciation 118, 125–6
union of diverse elements 41
unity-in-variety 996–8, 997f, 998f, 1003
unpleasantness and pleasantness 49–50, 54–7
urban spaces 963–4
use, method of 8, 41, 89–90, 95

V
V5 347–8
Valentine, Charles Wilfred 46, 512
validity 229, 231–2
value expectations 158
Van Geert, E. 402–3
van Peer, WIllie 737
Varney, N. 870
Vartanian, O. 16, 265, 308, 893f
VAST see Visual Aesthetic Sensitivity Test (VAST)
Vaughan-Evans, A. 264
ventral anterior cingulate cortex (vACC) 308
ventral stream 318–19, 347–51
ventral striatum and nucleus accumbens (NAcc) 314–15
ventromedial prefrontal cortex (vmPFC) 308, 313–14
verbal ratings and judgements 20–1
Vessel, E.A. 16
Vicary, S. 639, 640
video recordings 369
Vienna Integrated Model of Top-Down and Bottom-Up Processes in Art Perception (VIMAP) 127, 752, 755
viewer 895–7
Villani, D. 284
virtual reality (VR) 618–19
virtues of artistic representation 123–4, 124f
Vischer, Robert 144
vision 663–6
visual accuracy 236
Visual Aesthetic Sensitivity Test (VAST) 10, 61, 838f, 839–41, 856
visual aesthetics 57, 854–61, 873
visual art
    and aesthetic appeal 1017–18
    aesthetic appreciation of 297–9
    and aesthetic sensitivity 844

and ambiguity 409–10
and cognitive electrophysiology 297–9
and complexity and simplicity 403
expertise 795–6
and personality 820–4
and surprise and unexpectedness 399
symmetry in 490–1
use of predictive coding theory 401
visual attention 227–8, 549–50, 645
visual cortex 322, 663
visual domain 9, 402–4
visual features 1011–16
visual forms 54
visual perception 261
Visual Thinking (Arnheim) 66
Vitruvian Man (da Vinci) 490, 490f
Vitruvian Triad 660, 661f
Vitruvius Pollio, Marcus 490, 490f, 660
Vonnegut, Kurt 728
Vorschule der Aesthetik (Fechner) 40–1, 69, 95, 385
voxel-based morphometry (VRM) 327–9
Vreba, Elisabeth 187–8

W
Wabi-Sabi (Japanese school of aesthetics) 189
Wagemans, J. 402–3
Wagner, V. 935
Walker, F. 280
walking 649
wall texts 281–2
Wallace, Alfred 183
Walt Disney 691
Wang, J. 285–6
Wang, T. 315
Wang, X. 285–6, 298
wanting 163, 393, 394–5
Warhol, Andy 981–2
Washburn, Margaret Floy 47–8, 70
Watson, John Broadus 50–1, 52
website design 998f
weighted affective valence estimates (WAVEs) 864–6
Weisberg, R. 287
Weiss, Albert P. 51
wellbeing 672–3
Welsh, G.S. 63

Welsh Figure Preference Test 63
Werheid, K. 301
Wertheimer, Max 65–6
Westerman, D.L. 432
Whipple, G.M. 836
white color preference 862, 864
white noise 450–3, 452*f*, 455
Whiting, John W.M. 61
wider images 692–3
William James lectures 44
Wilson, E.O. 665–6
Winkielman, P. 13, 261, 431
Winner, E. 790
wishful identification 723–4
Witek, M.A. 651
within-person variation 539
Witmer, Lightner 9, 42, 70
Wlodarski, R. 931–2
Woods, A.T. 1030*f*
Woolhouse, M.H. 645
working memory 761

writing 802–3 *see also* literary narratives; stories
Wundt, Wilhelm 42, 47, 70

Y

yellow color preference 476–7
Yokosawa, K. 277–8
Yoshimura, Y. 227
Youssef, Jozef 1035–6, 1036*f*, 1039–42
Yun, K. 933

Z

Zabielska- Mendyk, E. 300
Zahavi, Amotz 183, 184, 186–7
Zajonc, R.B. 396, 577
Zaniewski, I. 277
Zeitgeist 514
Zeki, Semir 170–1, 308, 347
Zhang. Y. 285–6, 302
Zillmann, D. 123
Zimmerman, J. 639
Zur experimentalen Ästhetik (Fechner) 95